AF822546

THE INTERNATIONAL HANDBOOK OF PARENTAL ALIENATION SYNDROME

Publication Number 1108

AMERICAN SERIES
IN
BEHAVIORAL SCIENCE AND LAW

Edited by

RALPH SLOVENKO, B.E., LL.B., M.A., Ph.D.

Professor of Law and Psychiatry
Wayne State University Law School
Detroit Michigan

THE INTERNATIONAL HANDBOOK OF PARENTAL ALIENATION SYNDROME

Conceptual, Clinical and Legal Considerations

Edited by

RICHARD A. GARDNER, M.D.

S. RICHARD SAUBER, Ph.D.

DEMOSTHENES LORANDOS, Ph.D., J.D.

CHARLES C THOMAS • PUBLISHER, LTD.

Springfield • Illinois • U.S.A.

Published and Distributed Throughout the World by

CHARLES C THOMAS • PUBLISHER, LTD.
2600 South First Street
Springfield, Illinois 62704

ISBN 978-0-398-09450-8 (paper)
ISBN 978-0-398-08460-8 (ebook)

Library of Congress Catalog Card Number: 2006040449

With THOMAS BOOKS *careful attention is given to all details of manufacturing and design. It is the Publisher's desire to present books that are satisfactory as to their physical qualities and artistic possibilities and appropriate for their particular use.* THOMAS BOOKS *will be true to those laws of quality that assure a good name and good will.*

Printed in the United States of America
UB-R-3

The Library of Congress originally cataloged the hardcover version of this book as the following:

Library of Congress Cataloging-in-Publication Data

The international handbook of parental alienation syndrome / edited by Richard A. Gardner, S. Richard Sauber, Demosthenes Lorandos.
p. cm. -- (American series in behavioral science and law)
Includes bibliographical references and index.
ISBN 0-398-07647-2
1. Parental alienation syndrome--Handbooks, manuals, etc. I. Gardner, Richard A. II. Sauber, S. Richard. III. Lorandos, Demosthenes, 1946-IV. Series.

RJ506.P27I58 2006
618.92'89--dc22 2006040449

DEDICATED TO RICHARD A. GARDNER, M.D.

Sir Isaac Newton said, "If I have seen further, it is by standing upon the shoulders of giants." In the study of alienated children there is one man upon whose shoulders everyone stands. Anyone who studies, writes about, or seeks to understand the phenomenon of alienated children cannot do so without paying homage to Dr. Richard A. Gardner.

Dr. Gardner passed away on May 25, 2003. To say that he was a man of great achievements is an understatement. Most psychiatrists would be content to have a thriving clinical practice. Some have one or two published articles to their credit. The more ambitious have written more articles, perhaps even a book or two. The highest achievers have an impressive output of five or ten books at most.

Dr. Gardner wrote more than 130 articles that were judged by panels of expert reviewers to be worthy of publication in scholarly journals. He wrote 40 books. His contributions to the field of general psychotherapy with children, psychotherapy with children of divorce, and custody evaluations, are considered classic works in the field and are cited often in the professional literature and in psychotherapy textbooks. One indication of Gardner's stature among his colleagues is that he was invited to contribute several chapters to the standard reference work in his field, the *Basic Handbook of Child Psychiatry*, whose Board of Editors includes many of the world's leading experts in child psychiatry. Most authors are flattered to be invited to contribute only one chapter.

Gardner wrote the first self-help book for children of divorce. It was lauded by *Time* magazine, excerpted in the *Sunday New York Times Magazine*, and is currently in its 28th printing. He devised a therapeutic technique, mutual storytelling, that is included in child psychiatry curriculums and listed as one of 35 significant events in the history of play therapy, along with contributions from luminaries such as Sigmund Freud, Anna Freud, Melanie Klein, and Jean Piaget. In addition, he originated an entire therapeutic modality with his introduction of the first therapeutic board game for use in psychotherapy with children. The use of such games has since become standard in child psychotherapy with many games following Gardner's lead. One noted expert in psychotherapy called Gardner's creation "one of the most popular therapeutic games available" and a Website for therapeutic resources claimed that, "Most child therapists consider it an indispensable part of their playroom equipment." Gardner's books and therapeutic games have been translated into nine languages. The American Psychological Association, in addition to citing three of Gardner's books in a highly selective list of references pertinent to child custody evaluations, honored him by selecting him as one among only a few professionals included in a series of training videotapes by "distinguished psychotherapists."

For most of his professional career, Dr. Gardner enjoyed the reputation and stature appropriate to a man of his achievements and innovations. Then he wrote about Parental Alienation Syndrome and about sex abuse allegations. He was one of the first to say publicly that sometimes children do lie and that we should not automatically accept all allegations of abuse as true. As a result of this work, Dr. Gardner was attacked, smeared, and vilified. In their attempt to alienate audiences from Dr. Gardner's work, his critics used the same tactics as do parents who demonize a parent or grandparent in an effort to poison children's affection and respect.

None of this stopped Dr. Gardner. He set an inspiring example of a talented and courageous man willing to walk new and difficult paths and defend unpopular stands with conviction, strength, and integrity. I am reminded of the words of Theodore Roosevelt:

> It is not the critic who counts, not the man who points out how the strong man stumbled, or where the doer of deeds could have done them better. The credit belongs to the man who is actually in the arena; . . . who strives valiantly, who errs and comes short again and again; who knows the great enthusiasms, the great devotions, and spends himself in a worthy cause; who, at the best, knows in the end the triumph of high achievement; and who, at the worst, at least fails while daring greatly, so that his place shall never be with those cold and timid souls who know neither victory nor defeat.

No one ever accused Richard Gardner of being timid. He was in the arena his entire professional life, to the very end passionately, eagerly, and tirelessly sharing his knowledge and insights. I spoke to him two nights before his death. His terrible pain did not keep him from expressing great enthusiasm and excitement about his latest project. For those of us who remain in the arena, Dr. Gardner's legacy will be an inspiration for years to come.

For all these reasons, we dedicate this volume to Dr. Gardner's memory in recognition of his unparalleled contributions to the welfare of children throughout the world.

Richard A. Warshak, Ph.D.

CONTRIBUTORS

Walter Andritzky, Dr. Phil. Dipl.-Psychologist, Dipl.-Sociologist, is a former faculty member of the University of Düsseldorf, Institute of Medical Psychology and of the University of Cologne, Department of Sociology of the Handicapped. Currently, he is a practicing clinical and forensic psychologist in Germany.

Richard B. Austin, Jr., Ph.D., clinical and forensic psychologist, has presented on parental alienation syndrome issues at national meetings, and testified in PAS cases in Texas, Washington D.C., North Carolina, Oregon, and Paris, France. He consulted as an expert to the Texas Legislature Committee providing standards for sexual abuse evaluation.

Eduard Bakalář, Ph.D., earned a degree in psychology from Charles University, Prague and worked for the psychiatric department for children and adults. Since1967, he has been a court expert in child custody disputes, and since1992 he has been the head of Consultancy for Fathers. He publishes articles and books on divorce/custody/fathers.

R. Christopher Barden, Ph.D., J.D., LP, has been introduced as "the only licensed psychologist and attorney in America to receive two national research awards in psychology and a law degree with honors from Harvard Law School." He is President of the National Association for Consumer Protection in Mental Health Practices.

William Bernet, M.D., is a professor in the Department of Psychiatry at Vanderbilt University School of Medicine, and Director of the Division of Forensic Psychiatry. A graduate of Harvard Medical School, Dr. Bernet is a distinguished fellow of the American Psychiatric Association and a fellow of the American Academy of Child and Adolescent Psychiatry.

Sandra S. Berns, Ph.D., is a professor of law at Griffith University in Brisbane, Queensland. She holds a B.A. from the University of California at Berkeley and an LL.B. and Ph.D. from the University of Tasmania. She is the author of four books (one co-authored) and numerous academic articles.

Barry Bricklin, Ph.D., served on the faculties of Jefferson Medical College, Hahnemann University and Widener University. Author of dozens of books, book chapters, and articles on custody, two of his tests are the most widely used in the nation. He was recently invited to teach in China, Australia and Canada.

Barry Brody, Ph.D., is a marriage and family therapist with more than 30 years' clinical experience. Dr. Brody maintains a private practice in Florida, and is the director of Forensic Family Services, Inc. Dr. Brody has testified as an expert witness regarding child custody issues and parental alienation syndrome in particular.

Janelle Burrill, Ph.D., J.D, B.C.D., is an appointed child custody mediator and evaluator for numerous courts in northern California. She received a Ph.D. in clinical psychology, having written her dissertation on parental alienation syndrome. She serves as a special master and is an expert in child psychotherapy, custody evaluation, and mediation.

Glenn F. Cartwright, Ph.D., is a psychologist and professor in the Department of Educational Psychology and Counseling and Associate Dean of the Faculty of Education at McGill University in Montreal. He is a fellow of both the American and the World Associations for Social Psychiatry.

Gail Elliot, Ph.D., conducts research in child development and family systems. She is Vice Chair of the *Professional Academy of Custody Evaluators.* With Dr. Barry Bricklin, she has published several journal articles, book chapters and child custody tests, as well as many of her own assessment tools.

Craig A. Everett, Ph.D., is the director of the Arizona Institute for Family Therapy and Editor of the *Journal of Divorce and Remarriage.* He is a past president of the American Association for Marriage and Family Therapy and a former professor and director of graduate programs at Florida State University and Auburn University.

Richard A. Gardner, M.D. (1931–2003) coined the term and developed the theory, practice, the diagnosis and treatment for *the parental alienation syndrome.* He was Clinical Professor of Child Psychiatry at Columbia University. Recognized for his innovative contributions to child psychiatry, he wrote more than 40 books and 250 articles.

Daniel J. Gottlieb, Psy.D., a clinical psychologist and family therapist, is Associate Director of the Israeli Institute for Systemic Studies, Family and Personal Change, Herzliya, Israel. He serves as a court-appointed expert in child custody and adoption cases. He has published several papers on forensic psychology in the Hebrew literature.

Tony Hobbs, J.P., L.L.M., is a researcher in family law and teaches at Keele University, England. He is a chartered clinical and counseling psychologist, associate fellow of the British Psychological Society, and a lay magistrate. His favorite pastime is playing with his own family, and he is eternally grateful that they are not afflicted by PAS.

Ursula Kodjoe, M.A., is a psychologist, family therapist and mediator in Germany. She serves as a court-appointed representative for children in parental alienation cases. She has authored and delivered seminars [regarding conflict resolution, visitation models and reorganization of post-divorce families] for members of child care institutions, lawyers, therapists, and teachers.

Leona M. Kopetski, M.S.S.W., founded a private clinic for divorced families in Colorado and utilized a team model for custody evaluations, which became the standard for the state. The early alienation cases, encountered in the 1970s, prompted her to develop a paradigm for helping children maintain relationships with both parents.

Annelie Künneth, M.A., earned her magistra artium at Hagen University for her scientific work concerning the social-psychological aspects of parental alienation syndrome. She earned an honorary judgeship at the law court in Hof, Germany, and has worked at the Franconia Rehabilitation Clinic in Bad Steben, Germany since 1982.

Werner Leitner, Ph.D., is an expert in family court and a psychotherapist in Küps-Theisenort, Germany. He teaches developmental psychology at Leipzig University and has taught at Dresden University in the Institute of Pedagogical and Developmental Psychology. For ten years he served as an educational scientist at Bamberg University and Giessen University.

Jeffery M. Leving, J.D., received his Juris Doctor from IIT Chicago-Kent College of Law. He concentrates on matrimonial law and fathers rights. He is co-author of the Illinois Joint Custody law, author of the book *Fathers' Rights*, and serves as an expert on government panels and local and network television and radio programs.

David L. Levy, J.D., is President of the Children's Rights Council, a national child advocacy organization based in the Washington, D.C. area. CRC has existed since 1985, and has chapters in 32 U.S. states, Canada, Great Britain, Japan, and Sierra Leone. Levy has contributed as an editor in this area as well.

Demosthenes Lorandos, Ph.D., J.D., is a clinical psychologist and attorney. He is a member of the State Bar of Michigan, California, New York, and the United States Supreme Court. He has written two law and science books with psychologist Terence Campbell. Currently, he is completing his third training text for lawyers and judges.

Ludwig F. Lowenstein, M.A., Ph.D., obtained his M.A. and Doctorate in Psychology and Education at University of London. His background includes work in mental hospitals, child guidance clinics, and residential care centers for maladjusted adolescents. He has been an examiner for more than 40 years. His appointments include being a chief psychologist for the county of Hampshire.

Jayne A. Major, Ph.D., is the author of *Breakthrough Parenting: A Revolutionary New Way to Raise Children.* She specializes in educational programs for high-risk, in-crisis families. She teaches, consults, and appears as an expert witness in child custody disputes. Dr. Major is the founder of Breakthrough Parenting, Inc.

Deirdre Rand, Ph.D., is a forensic psychologist who specializes in Munchausen syndrome by proxy and other complex forms of child abuse. She is known for her two part review, "The Spectrum of Parental Alienation Syndrome." Dr. Rand and Dr. Randy Rand collaborated with Leona Kopetski on a follow-up study on interventions.

Randy Rand, Ed.D., is the clinical director for The Rachel Foundation, providing reintegration services for parent abducted and severely alienated children and their families. He is also the developer of Behavioral Personnel Assessment Devices (B-PAD), which is used by police and public safety departments throughout the United States and Canada.

S. Richard Sauber, Ph.D., holds Diplomates in Clinical and Family Psychology, ABPP. He was professor of psychology in the departments of psychiatry at the medical schools of Brown, Penn and Columbia. Trained at Harvard, he has written/edited 16 books and is the Editor of *The American Journal of Family Therapy.*

Lena Hellblom Sjögren, Ph.D., is a licensed psychologist and practices as an investigative psychologist in family and criminal courts. She has investigated PAS cases and worked to educate legal professionals since her first published work about PAS in 1997 and investigation of reliability in sexual criminal cases.

Barbara Sobal, J.D., is a graduate of N.Y.U. Law School and fellow of the International Academy of Matrimonial Lawyers. She has experience in more than 350 Hague Convention cases, and is a frequent lecturer, author, and television speaker. She has consultative status with the National Center for Missing and Exploited Children.

Wilfried von Boch-Galhau, M.D., specializes in psychiatry, neurology and psychotherapy. Practicing in Germany, he is a member of the interdisciplinary working group, "Counselling for Parents of Divorce and Separation." He was one of the organizing members of the international Parental Alienation Syndrome Conference in Frankfurt, Germany, in 2002.

Richard A. Warshak, Ph.D., is a clinical and research psychologist, Clinical Professor at the University of Texas Southwestern Medical Center, and author of a text on custody. He serves on the Editorial Board of Family Court Review, has published extensively on divorce, and consults with attorneys throughout the world.

FOREWORD

This is an important book and I am honored to write its Foreword. Richard A. Gardner, M.D. first described *parental alienation syndrome* (PAS) in his text, *The Parental Alienation Syndrome and the Differentiation Between Fabricated and Genuine Child Sex Abuse*, in 1987. Previously, he had used the terminology "the brainwashed child" as the "active program of vociferous condemnation" in his book, *Family Evaluation in Child Custody Litigation* (1982). He made reference to J.W. Duncan's discussion of the "brainwashing parent" in 1978. Dr. Gardner was the founder and tireless articulator and advocate of the concept as well as of its diagnosis and treatment. I say "was" because of Dr. Gardner's untimely death in May of 2003. Although most psychological concepts evoke little response, PAS has struck a cord in the professional and lay community, with most holding rather strong opinions about it.

Regardless of one's position on PAS, it is hard to deny the far-reaching implications it has had in the five basic human service delivery systems (Cf. Sauber, 1983). Most notable and obvious has been its impact on family law and in family mental health. Besides these, PAS has had considerable impact on the criminal justice system in terms of petitions for domestic violence, restraining orders, false police reports filed, etc. Its impact on the social welfare system is commonly exemplified in state agencies or departments of child and family services which are called upon to differentiate child abuse and neglect from fabricated complaints, as well as to file reports to the civil court. It should be noted that such state agencies typically have their own mental health evaluators and anger managers who are called upon to fulfill these agencies' legal mandate of "impartiality" and "protection." Furthermore, the mental health system is directly involved in the evaluation and treatment aspects before, during, or after the discovery and identification of the PAS phenomenon. Other human service delivery systems described by the contributors to this book include health care and education. It should not be surprising that symptoms related to PAS are reported by health care providers such as pediatricians, gynecologists, internists and family practitioners. In addition, children's and adolescent's grades decline as family conflicts intensify and the minors internalize and act out their parents' own power struggles. The point is that the impact and implications of PAS are immense.

Because of its far-reaching effects, it has now become incumbent on the mental health community to learn about PAS and how to diagnose and treat it. Despite its widespread harm to children and family members, confusion about PAS remains. For example, the terms "parental alienation" and "parental alienation syndrome" are mistakenly used synonymously. Similarly, controversy remains about PAS as mental health experts and family law attorneys debate its existence and the harmful effects that alienation has on the entire family. Accordingly, Dr. Gardner endeavored to further clarify and operationalize the terminology both in a seminal publication in the *American Journal of Family Therapy* (2002) as well as in this book. Without a doubt, this book represents the definitive statement of PAS to date and should be of inestimable value to the professional reader, particularly those in the mental health field.

It should be noted that the contributors to this remarkable handbook are distinguished leaders in this cutting edge, interdisciplinary field. Many of them have offered expert testimony in court. Many have lectured to the professional community at association meetings and conventions. All of these distinguished contributors have collaborated in producing this definitive text. This group of international experts has worked to provide important perspectives on several different clinical and forensic challenges regarding PAS. Needless to say, these challenges are inevitable in legal family systems because of the inherent adversarial and conflictual nature–regardless of one's entry point or one's view. No other single source that provides the depth and breadth of coverage of the topic than the clinically and forensically valuable chapters in this book.

Although Dr. Gardner's name is typically associated with, and has even become synonymous with PAS, it is important to note that his life's work and commitment were much broader. Indeed, Dr. Gardner's primary passion was, above all else, to the health and well-being of all children. He was a giant among his peers in advocating for the humane care, treatment, and basic rights of children. With the great loss and unexpected passing of Dr. Gardner, the torch is now passed to others to continue to write, research, teach, testify and advocate for children in complex divorce situations. Although this book was not initially intended to be Dr. Gardner's final contribution to the professional community, it serves as a fitting tribute and memorial to a courageous pioneer. It also serves to acknowledge the contributions of some of the many colleagues whom he mentored and collaborated with over the years.

Len Sperry, M.D., Ph.D.
Clinical Professor of Psychiatry and Behavioral Medicine
Medical College of Wisconsin

REFERENCES

Duncan, J.W. (1978). Medical, psychological, and legal aspects of the child custody disputes. *Mayo Clinic Proceedings, 53*, 463–468.

Gardner, R.A. (1982). *Family evaluation in child custody litigation.* Cresskill: New Jersey: Creative Therapeutics.

Gardner, R.A. (1985). Recent trends in divorce and litigation. *Academy Forum, 29*(2), 3–7.

Gardner, R.A. (1987). *The parental alienation syndrome and the differentiation between fabricated and genuine child sex abuse.* Cresskill, New Jersey: Creative Therapeutics.

Gardner, R.A. (2002). Parental alienation syndrome vs. parental alienation: Which diagnosis should be used in child custody litigation? *The American Journal of Family Therapy, 30*(2), 101–123.

Sauber, S. R. (1983). *The human services delivery system: Mental health, criminal justice, social welfare, education, and health services.* New York: Columbia University Press.

CONTENTS

THE INTERNATIONAL HANDBOOK OF PARENTAL ALIENATION SYNDROME

Section I

CONCEPTS

Chapter 1

INTRODUCTION

Richard A. Gardner
May, 2003

Since the 1970s, we have witnessed a burgeoning of child-custody disputes unparalleled in history. This increase has primarily been the result of two recent developments in the realm of child-custody litigation: the replacement of the tender-years presumption with the best-interests-of-the-child presumption and the increasing popularity of the joint-custodial concept. The assumption was made that mothers, by virtue of the fact that they are female, are intrinsically superior to men as child-rearers. Accordingly, the father had to provide to the court compelling evidence of serious maternal deficiencies before the court would even consider assigning primary custodial status to the father. Under its replacement, the best-interests-of-the-child presumption, the courts were instructed to ignore gender in custodial considerations and evaluate only parenting capacity, especially factors that related to the best interests of the child. This change resulted in a burgeoning of custody litigation as fathers now found themselves with a greater opportunity to gain primary custodial status. Soon thereafter the joint-custodial concept became popular, eroding even further the time that custodial mothers were given with their children. Again, this change also brought about an increase and intensification of child-custody litigation.

PARENTAL ALIENATION SYNDROME

Definition of Parental Alienation Syndrome

In association with this burgeoning of child-custody litigation, we have witnessed a dramatic increase in the frequency of a disorder rarely seen previously, which I refer to as the parental alienation syndrome (PAS). In this disorder we see not only programming ("brainwashing") of the child by one parent to denigrate the other parent, but self-created contributions by the child in support of the alienating parent's campaign of denigration against the alienated parent. Because of the child's contribution I did not consider the terms *brainwashing, programming,* or other equivalent words to be applicable. Accordingly, in 1985, I introduced the term *parental alienation syndrome* to cover the *combination* of these two contributing factors (Gardner, 1985, 1986, 1987). In accordance with this use of the term I suggest this definition of the parental alienation syndrome:

> The *parental alienation syndrome* (PAS) is a disorder that arises primarily in the context of child-custody disputes. Although the dispute is most often between the parents, it can arise in other types of conflicts over child custody, e.g., parent vs. stepparent, parent vs. grandparent, parent vs. relative, etc. Its primary manifestation is the child's campaign of denigration against a parent, a campaign that has no justification against a good, loving parent. It results from the *combination* of a programming (brainwashing) parent's indoctrinations and the child's own contributions to the vilification of the target parent. When true parental abuse and/or neglect is present, the child's animosity may be justified, and so the parental alienation syndrome explanation for the child's hostility is not applicable. Inducing a parental alienation syndrome into a child is a form of emotional abuse because it can result in the attenuation and even destruction of the child's bond with a good, loving parent. (Gardner, 1998)

Although PAS certainly existed prior to the 1980s, it was relatively uncommon, especially because, as mentioned, its ubiquity is primarily the result of the aforementioned recent developments regarding how the courts determine primary custodial parental status.

In the past 20 years, although we have had the opportunity to learn much about the etiology, pathogenesis, clinical manifestations, management, and treatment of PAS, we have not had enough time and experience to be able to know with certainty what the consequences of PAS are in adulthood.

Definition of the Word "Syndrome"

A syndrome, by definition, is a cluster of symptoms, appearing together, that characterizes a specific disease. The symptoms, although seemingly disparate, warrant being grouped together because of a common etiology or basic underlying cause. Furthermore, a consistency with regard to such a cluster, in that most (if not all), of the symptoms usually appear together. A well-known example would be Down syndrome: which includes mental retardation, mongoloid-type facial expression, drooping lips, slanting eyes, short fifth finger, and atypical creases in the palms of the hands. People who suffer from Down syndrome often look very much alike, and most typically exhibit all these symptoms. The common etiology of these disparate symptoms relates to a specific chromosomal abnormality. It is this genetic factor that is responsible for linking together these seemingly disparate symptoms.

The Progression for the Recognition of a Syndrome

There are three levels of progression for the recognition of a syndrome. At the first level are isolated signs or symptoms without reference to other particular symptoms; these are of little predictive value. Examples would be headache or stuttering or constipation. They are isolated symptoms with many possible causes and many possible forms of treatment.

At the second level is a clinical picture formed by the grouping of specific signs and symptoms into a distinctive syndrome. Down syndrome would be an example. The fact that the symptoms occur together is one of the hallmarks of the syndrome, even though all may not be present in the milder forms.

At the third level is the identification of a particular pathological process or causative agent that brings about that particular constellation of symptoms that are referred to as that specific syndrome.

The Current Level of Recognition of PAS

PAS has reached the third level of recognition. We are not dealing with level one, where there is an isolated symptom that can have many different causes. Nor are we dealing with isolated and seemingly random symptoms that do not necessarily appear together. When I first began to see this cluster in the early 1980s, it was at level two. At that point, I saw a cluster that repeatedly appeared together. These were the eight primary symptoms of the PAS that I described in my first article on this disorder (Gardner, 1985). When I identified the cause as programming by an alienating parent, I had reached level three. This link between the programming parent and the presence of these symptoms in the child were described in my publications during the next two years (Gardner, 1986, 1987a, 2001). The vast majority of the peer-reviewed articles that have been published on PAS identify the alienator as the causative agent. Some claim that the victim parent's behavior has brought about the symptoms. If that is the case, then we are not dealing with PAS, but bona fide abuse or neglect. This principle is stated in the definition of PAS, wherein I state "when true parental abuse and/or neglect is present, the child's animosity may be justified, and so the parental alienation syndrome explanation for the child's hostility is not applicable." All the articles that have been described and referenced in this text on PAS agree that the alienating parent is the causative agent. The DSM IV has equivalents for the PAS diagnosis if this reference is necessary to provide a substantive diagnosis until the next meeting of the committees for the DSM V can consider the relatively new term "PAS" (Gardner, 2003).

PARENTAL ALIENATION VS. PARENTAL ALIENATION SYNDROME

Parental alienation (PA) is a *general* term that covers any situation in which a child can be alienated from a parent. It can be caused by parental physical abuse, verbal abuse, emotional abuse, mental abuse, sexual abuse, abandonment, and neglect. Adolescents, as an act of rebellion, may become alienated from a parent. Young people seduced into cults may be programmed to become alienated from a parent. A child can also be programmed by one parent to be alienated from another. That particular category of parental alienation is generally referred to as parental alienation syndrome.

Parental alienation syndrome is one subtype of parental alienation. It is the subtype that is caused by a parent systematically programming the children against the other parent who has been a good, loving parent.

Can PA and PAS be Used Synonymously?

Using the terms PA and PAS synonymously cause much confusion, as general term is being used to refer to a specific disorder. It is the equivalent of saying that a person who has colon cancer just has cancer. There are many different kinds of cancer and each one requires a specific kind of treatment. When one says "colon cancer," one is referring to a specific type of cancer that gives specific information about a particular form of the disease. With this information the doctor can provide a specific course of treatment, different from the treatment of other types of cancer. To refer to colon cancer as simply cancer "muddies the waters," confuses the diagnosis, and does not provide much specificity for proper treatment. Doctors today do not treat "cancer"; they do treat a wide variety of specific types of cancer.

Reasons for the PA vs. PAS Controversy

Many reasons for the PA vs. PAS controversy – One relates to the fact that the PAS diagnosis requires identification of a *specific* programmer. There is no getting around it. In contrast, the PA diagnosis is *not* specific and opens the door to either parent being responsible for the alienation. Accordingly, an attorney representing an alienating parent would much prefer to use the PA term. For example, an attorney who represents an alienating father may say to the court, "Your Honor, no one denies that these children are alienated from their mother. We don't deny that. We believe that she has brought on the children's alienation by her own behavior rather than their being programmed by my client." Using the term *PAS* lessens the likelihood that this argument can be used. In PA, either parent can be responsible; with PAS one parent is focused upon and is likely to be quickly identified.

Attorneys who represent alienating parents are likely to seek the services of an expert who eschews the PAS term. If *all* mental health experts were to agree that PAS exists and recognize that the use of the term PA "muddies the waters" and can serve to help alienators deny that they are alienators, then attorneys would be unlikely to use this argument in courts of law because they would not be able to find a competent expert who would deny the existence of PAS.

This controversy contains numerous other factors, many of which have been described elsewhere (Gardner, 2002; Warshak, 2003). Several articles in this volume also address this controversy, especially Barry Brody's, "The Misdiagnosis of PAS." In addition, articles in this book are dedicated to rebuttals that focus not only on the PAS vs. PA debate, but on other PAS-related controversies as well.

RECOGNITION OF PAS IN COURTS OF LAW

Courts of law throughout the United States and many foreign countries recognize PAS. At the time of this writing, it has been recognized in the following countries: United States (22 states), Canada (7 provinces), Australia, Germany, Great Britain, Israel, and Switzerland. With respect to the cases in the United States, see *Parental Alienation Syndrome in American Law* in this handbook.

The Frye Test

In the United States, most states subscribe to the *Frye* test to assess the admissibility of a new theory into a court of law (*Frye v. United States* 293 F. 1013 [D.C. Cir. 1923]). For the theory to be admitted in a court of law it must have been generally accepted in the relevant scientific community. The judge makes *no* decision regarding its scientific validity. In 1600, astrology would have passed Frye. In 1800, bloodletting for the treatment of fever would have passed Frye (incidentally, that's how George Washington died).

The Mohan Test

The *Mohan* test for admissibility is used in Canada. It is more stringent than *Frye*, but less stringent than *Daubert* (see next section). The following criteria are necessary for admission under *Mohan* criteria:

1. The theory must be relevant
2. The theory must be necessary to assist the court
3. The theory must be admissible in court pursuant to the rules of evidence
4. A qualified expert must be available to testify about the theory. (*Her Majesty the Queen v. Mohan* [1994] 2 S.C.R.9)

PAS has passed *Mohan* in Ontario, Canada.

The Daubert Test

Some states in the US subscribe to the *Daubert* test. Daubert is much more stringent than *Frye*, and even more stringent than *Mohan.* Under Daubert, the judge must determine whether the theory is scientifically valid (Lorandos and Campbell, *in press*). Requiring a judge to ascertain whether a theory is scientifically valid presents a problem, because most judges do not have scientific training. The judge must determine that the theory:

1. is testable and falsifiable
2. has many peer-reviewed publications in reputable scientific journals
3. can provide an error rate determined by scientific studies
4. can demonstrate existence and maintenance of standards controlling its operation
5. has obtained general acceptance in the relevant scientific community. (*Daubert v. Merrell Dow Pharmaceuticals, Inc.* [1993] 509 U.S. 579, 113 S.Ct. 2786, 125. L. Ed. 2d 469)

At this point, PAS satisfies only numbers 2 and 5. However, most diagnoses in the *Diagnostic and Statistical Manual of Mental Disorders – Fourth Edition* (1994) (DSM-IV) do *not* satisfy the 1, 2 and 4 criteria; nor do most psychological tests, e.g., the Rorschach. Therefore, they should not be admissible in *Daubert* states, but they are because strict adherence to *Daubert* would preclude the testimony of most mental health professionals, especially with regard to the standard instruments they use in their evaluations. My sex abuse protocols have passed the *Daubert* test in Saint Thomas, in the U.S. Virgin Islands. This recognition has relevance for the admissibility of PAS cases in which there has been a derivative sex abuse accusation.

THE PAS GUIDELINE TABLES

Differential Diagnosis of the Three Levels of PAS Children

Table 1.1. presents the criteria that I have found useful for differentiating among the three levels of PAS

TABLE 1.1. Differential Diagnosis of the Three Levels of Parental Alienation Syndrome (PAS) – Children

	The Child's Symptom Level		
Factors	**Mild**	**Moderate**	**Severe**
Primary Symptomatic Manifestations			
The campaign of denigration (May or may not include a false sex-abuse accusation)	Minimal	Moderate	Formidable
Weak, frivolous, or absurd rationalizations for the deprecation	Minimal	Moderate	Multiple absurd rationalizations
Lack of ambivalence	Normal ambivalence	No ambivalence	No ambivalence
The independent-thinker phenomenon	Usually absent	Present	Present
Reflexive support of the alienating parent in the parental conflict	Minimal	Present	Present
Absence of guilt	Normal guilt	Minimal to no guilt	No guilt
Borrowed scenarios	Minimal	Present	Present
Spread of the animosity to the extended family and friends of the alienated parent	Minimal	Present	Formidable, often fanatic
Additional Differential Diagnostic Considerations			
Transitional difficulties at the time of	Usually absent	Moderate	Formidable, or visit not possible
Behavior during visitation	Good	Intermittently antagonistic and provocative	No visit, or destructive and continually provocative behavior throughout visit
Bonding with the alienator	Strong, healthy	Strong, mildly to moderately pathological	Severely pathological, often paranoid bonding
Bonding with the alienated parent prior to the alienation	Strong, healthy, or minimally pathological	Strong, healthy, or minimally pathological	Strong, healthy, or minimally pathological

Note: The *diagnosis* of PAS is based on the level of symptoms in the child, not on the symptom level of the alienator.

children. It is important to emphasize that the diagnosis of PAS is based upon the level of symptoms in *the child* (Table 1.1.), *not* on the symptom level of the alienator (Table 1.2.). Table 1.1. provides guidelines for ascertaining whether the child's symptoms are at the mild, moderate, or severe level. This can be accomplished by referring to the eight primary symptomatic manifestations listed at the top of the extreme left column of the table. The additional differential diagnostic considerations listed at the bottom of the extreme left column of the table are also useful for differentiating among the levels. Especially valuable within this section are the criteria "transitional difficulties at the time of visitation" and the child's "behavior during visitation." It is essential that the examiner determine the child's level of alienation in order to provide proper recommendations for both court-ordered and therapeutic interventions.

Differential Diagnosis of the Three Levels of PAS Alienators

Whereas the *diagnosis* of PAS is based on the assessed level of the *child's* symptoms (Table 1.1.), the court's decision for *custodial transfer* should be based primarily on the *alienator's* symptom level (Table 1.2.). It is only when these two levels have been ascertained that the evaluator can make proper recommendations to the court as well as to other mental health professionals subsequently involved in the children's treatment (Table 1.3.).

Differential Management and Treatment of the Three Levels of PAS Alienators for Each of the Child's Symptom Levels

It is important for the evaluator to appreciate that the

TABLE 1.2. Differential Diagnosis of the Three Levels of Parental Alienation Syndrome (PAS) – Alienators

	The Alienator's Symptom Level		
Factors	**Mild**	**Moderate**	**Severe**
Presence of severe psychopathology prior to the separation[1]	Most often absent	May or may not have been present	Most often present
Frequency of programming thoughts	Occasional	Frequent	Persistent
Frequency of programming verbalizations	Occasional	Frequent	Persistent
Frequency of exclusionary maneuvers[2]	Occasional	Frequent	Whenever possible
Frequency of complaints to the police and child protection services	Occasional	Frequent	Repeated
Litigiousness	Occasional	Frequent	Repeated
Episodes of hysteria[3]	Occasional	Frequent	Very frequent
Frequency of violation of court orders[4]	Occasional	Frequent	Repeated
Success in manipulating the legal system to enhance the programming	Minimal attempts	Occasional to moderate	Repeatedly successful
Risk of intensification of programming if granted primary custody	Very low	Mild to moderate	Extremely high to the point of being almost inevitable

Note: Whereas the *diagnosis* of PAS is based upon the level of symptoms in the child, the court's decision for custodial transfer should be based primarily on the *alienator's symptom level* and only secondarily on the child's level of PAS symptoms.

[1] For example, shared psychotic disorder, delusional disorder, paranoid personality disorder, borderline personality disorder, narcissistic personality disorder, and antisocial personality disorder.

[2] For example, visitation obstruction, blocking of telephone access, failure to provide information regarding school, medical care, and psychological treatment.

[3] These are the primary characteristics of hysteria: emotional outbursts, overreaction, assumption of danger when it does not exist, dramatization, attention-getting behavior, impairment of judgment, release of anger with scapegoatism, capacity for spread, and instensification of symptoms in the context of lawsuits.

4 The alienator can rely on court delays and court reluctance and even refusal to penalize the alienator with such measures as posting a bond, fines, community service, probation, house arrest, incarceration, and custodial change.

TABLE 1.3. Differential Management and Treatment of the Three Levels of Parental Alienation Syndrome (PAS) Alienators for Each of the Child's Symptom Levels

		The Child's Symptom Level	
Approach	**Mild-level Alienators**	**Moderate-level Alienators**	**Severe-level Alienators**
Legal approaches	Court ruling that primary custody shall remain with the alienating parent	Plan A (most common) 1. Court ruling that primary custody shall remain with the alienating parent 2. Court appoint of PAS therapist's 3. Sanctions: a. Post a bond b. Fines c. Community service d. Probation e. House arrest f. Incarceration Plan B (occasionally necessary) 1. Court ruling that primary custody shall be transferred to the alienated parent 2. Court appointment of PAS therapists 3. Extremely restricted visitation by the alienating parent, monitored to prevent indoctrinations	1. Court ruling that primary custory shall be transferred to the alienated parent 2. Court-ordered transitional-site program
Psychotherapeutic approaches	None usually necessary	Plans A and B, Treatment by a court-appointed PAS therapist	Transitional-site program monitored by court-appointed PAS therapists[1,2]

Note: Whereas the *diagnosis* of PAS is based upon the level of symptoms in the child, the court's decision for custodial transfer should be based primarily on the *alienator's symptom level* and only secondarily on the child's level of PAS symptoms.

[1] Gardner, R.A. (1996). *The Parental Alienation Syndrome*, Second Edition, Cresskil, NJ: Creative Therapeutics, Inc.

[2] Gardner, R.A. (2001). *Therapeutic Interventions for Children with Parental Alienation Syndrome*, Cresskill, NJ: Creative Therapeutics, Inc.

guidelines presented here are only general, and require modification for a specific case. First, the evaluator should ascertain the child's symptom level, indicated at the top of Table 1.3. Next, the evaluator must determine the category in which the alienator in that particular case falls. When the child is in the moderate level of PAS, the two possible symptom levels for the alienator are most often moderate and severe. If the alienator is at the moderate level, then Plan A (in the moderate column under the child's symptom level) is applicable. In contrast, if the alienator is at the severe level, then Plan B is applicable. If the child is at the severe level and the alienator is at the severe level, then the recommendations in the extreme right column of the table are applicable. In accordance with what I have stated about these guidelines not being hard and fast, situations might arise in which the alienator is at the severe level, and yet the child is only at the mild level. These would be the situations in which the alienated parent has had the opportunity to have significant contact with the child, thereby counterbalancing the efforts of the alienating parent. In these cases, the evaluator might still recommend custodial transfer in order to prevent the progression of the PAS symptomatology in the child.

It is my hope that this handbook and the materials from the contributors will encourage mental health professionals all over the world to come to the aid of families dealing with parental alienation syndrome. The recognition of this syndrome by colleagues from Australia, Sweden, Germany, Czechoslovakia, Canada, Israel, the U.K. and the United States illustrates a growing awareness of the need for good diagnosis and timely intervention. This is the hope and the promise of this international handbook.

REFERENCES

_______ American Psychiatric Association (1994). *Diagnostic and statistical manual of mental disorders* (4th ed.). Washington, D.C.: American Psychiatric Press.

Gardner, R. A. (1985). Recent trends in divorce and custody litigation. *Academy Forum* (a publication of the American Academy of Psychoanalysis), *29*(2), 3–7.

_______ (1986). *Child custody litigation: A guide for parents and mental health professionals.* Cresskill, New Jersey: Creative Therapeutics, Inc.

_______ (1987). *The Parental Alienation Syndrome and the differentiation between fabricated and genuine child sex abuse.* Cresskill, New Jersey: Creative Therapeutics, Inc.

_______ (1987). Child custody. In *Basic handbook of child psychiatry*, ed. J. D. Noshpitz, vol. V, pp. 637–646. New York: Basic Books, Inc.

Gardner, R. A. (1998). *The Parental Alienation Syndrome* (2nd ed.). Creskill, New Jersey: Creative Therapeutics, Inc.

Gardner, R. A. (2001). *Therapeutic interventions for children with Parental Alienation Syndrome.* Creskill, New Jersey: Creative Therapeutics, Inc.

_______ (2002). Parental alienation syndrome vs. parental alienation: Which diagnosis should evaluators use in child-custody litigation? *The American Journal of Family Therapy, 30*(2), 93–115.

Gardner, R. A. (2003). Does DSM IV have equivalents for the Parental Alienation Syndrome (PAS) diagnosis? *The American Journal of Family Therapy, 31*(1), 1–21.

Lorandos, D. and Campbell, T. (in press) *Benchbook in the behavioral sciences: Psychiatry, psychology, social work.* Durham, North Carolina: Academic Press.

Warshak, R. (2003). Current controversies regarding the parental alienation syndrome. In *The Parental Alienation Syndrome: An interdisciplinary challenge for professionals involved in divorce.* Eds. W. von Boch-Galhau, U. Kodjoe, W. Andritzky, and P. Koeppel, pp. 207–234. Berlin, Germany: VWB-Verlag für Wissenshaft and Bildung.

Chapter 2

PAS AS A FAMILY TRAGEDY: ROLES OF FAMILY MEMBERS, PROFESSIONALS, AND THE JUSTICE SYSTEM

S. RICHARD SAUBER

OVERVIEW

The phenomenon of PAS is understood to take place as a result of well-defined psychological forces that occur in divorce litigation; thus, a study of systemic dynamics is necessary to evaluate, treat, and intervene in the human services intersystems and family subsystems. Mental health professionals, attorneys, judges, and the lay public frequently attempt to read the minds of other people. This chapter provides a look at the ideas and thoughts that these individuals – i.e., the judge, the attorneys, the mental health professionals and the custody evaluator, the alienated parent, the parent, the significant others – intimate partner or remarried spouse of each parent, the alienated child, the maternal and paternal grandparents of the alienated child, and the friends of each of the parents. What are they considering with respect to the roles they are performing as the family litigation process moves forward to obtain a divorce that results in favorable terms according to their respective positions in the final "agreement"?

THE JUDGE

When the judge first hears the term *PAS* presented, the first major fact is whether he or she is familiar or unfamiliar with the concept. The function of the judge is to interpret the laws by which the contestants are operating and to address the rules of procedure during the trial according to the enforcement requirements set forth by the family court system. Judges are impartial, offering a neutral posture and a passive fact-finding mission to consider all of the evidence presented. If the judge is familiar with the concept, then the next question is how knowledgeable and acquainted he or she is with determining the implications of PAS, its case implications, and his or her willingness to utilize his or her judicial powers. If the judge is unfamiliar with the concept, then what recourse does he or she have in order to obtain a better understanding and knowledge of a term that will be addressed during the trial? Going beyond the concept of PAS, the role of the judge, of course, is to understand each variable or factor in reference to the law. Some states have recognized that the term *PAS* has met the criteria of scientific evidence for satisfying the Frye Test, the criteria for admissibility in a court of law. For example, such as in the trial of *Kilgore v. Boyd* (2000), see Gardner's testimony concerning parental alienation syndrome which has been admitted in courts of law in many states and countries.

Generally, reference to the concept of PAS is in the allegation or it is used as a basis for a motion to schedule a hearing, sometimes an emergency hearing. Parental alienation syndrome is defined as a disorder primarily in children who have been involved in protracted custody litigation. The term refers only to the situation in which the parental programming or "brainwashing" is combined with the child's own scenarios of disparagement of the vilified parent. The reasons for the indoctrination are unjustified or exaggerated but disrupt the alienated parent's bond and role in the child's upbringing. (Sauber et al., 1993; Gardner, 1998). After all, this form of child abuse is, in fact, a product of the adversary system and that the degree to which the PAS symptoms are pronounced may be directly proportionate to the intensity of the divorce litigation. It also may be pointed out that it is the court that has the power and influence, even more so than the mental health professional, e.g., psychologist, psychiatrist, mental health counselor, social worker, or family therapist, to moderate or alleviate this mental disorder. When the judge first reads the initial complaint or motion or receives the response by opposing counsel regarding various complaints that include PAS, it may well be that the judge has confused the term "parental alienation" with "PAS." It is beyond the scope of this chapter to address this distinction but the clarification as to which term or diagnosis should be used by the evaluators in litigation or child custody disputes may be explained in the article "Parental Alienation Syndrome vs. Parental Alienation: which diagnosis should be used in child custody litigation?" (Gardner, 2002b).

Judges certainly recognize their judicial power; however, in most cases, they are unaware that they also possess the only real power to exert extreme measures for corrective action when PAS is identified within a family system. It is the role of the attorney to advise his or her client with regard to appropriate behavior and manage the distraught nature of their emotions as to being a victim of PAS, while, at the same time, present to the judge examples, facts, and detailed descriptions of the particulars that are taking place. The attorney has the responsibility to carefully select an expert either by mutual agreement with the opposing counsel, submitting the name of the expert to the judge for court appointment, or retaining the expert to assist in his or her client's presentation to the court. Thus, the attorney is responsible for educating the judge and bringing to the forefront his or her awareness of this systemic term, its emotional consequences and the potential damages over time that it may create for not only the child but for the other members of that family. The attorney, through motions, client testimony, and direct examination with his or her witnesses, is responsible for highlighting for the judge the deliberate nature of the actions of the other party. The attorney must demonstrate how the behavior is contributing and causing the symptoms of PAS, whether in its early stages of "mild symptoms" or in the progressed stage of "moderate symptoms," when the campaign of denigration, emotional poisoning, and brainwashing is accelerated because of what is happening in the family in accord with the pace of the litigation. The end result of what might be called "severe alienation" will be observed in the manifestation of the extreme symptoms. The damage already has taken place and it is the attorney's challenge to carefully explain to the judge how this came about, assign appropriate responsibility and blame, and to offer suggestions to ameliorate this condition.

The attorneys and mental health professionals working with the alienated parent or family system have no power other than to recommend, suggest, and help others gain insight. It is only through the threat of reporting to the judge that others gain power and assume the ability to influence and intervene. Judges who refer or order those into treatment without access to judicial power and orders are impotent and ineffective. The judge must realize that the court has to impose proper restraints and restrictions on the PAS inducer. The PAS-trained therapist knows that the alienating parent has been warned and that the court may, should, or will impose sanctions if he or she violates any of the court orders regarding conduct and interference with the children. For examples, the alienated child goes to a PAS-trained therapist and soon reports to the alienating parent that the child does not feel comfortable with this psychologist or simply does not like the therapist and refuses to attend or participate. The PAS therapist must compromise confrontation and other techniques in questioning the frivolousness of the child's complaints while trying to establish a relationship or at least rapport with the child in order to prevent premature termination. We know the child will enter therapy already with the alienator's influence and react with hostility when questioned about any positive features, characteristics, or events associated with the targeted parent.

It is likely that the opposing counsel will blame the child's alienation and desire for his or her avoidance and emotional detachment on the alienated parent, claiming that the parent's disinterest, inadequate parenting, and/or abuse or neglect of the child or children is the real cause. The credibility of the parties and presentation of information as compelling evidence is the basis for which the judge must rely upon in making his or her decision and sorting out the truth and the objective reality in the conduct of each of the parties. It is the "best interest of the children" that guides him or her through this maze. It is the legal approach or the particulars of the judge's order that serves as the foundation for establishing and evaluating effectiveness of family therapy.

Parent coordination is a form of dispute resolution for high conflict that goes beyond mediation, psychotherapy, and a multitude of other family services. Parent coordination is a nonconfidential, child-centered process for parents "for whom mediation is inappropriate due to high levels of conflict or domestic abuse in the relationship." Parent coordinators (PC) are usually trained psychotherapists who are designated to work with select families.

Parent coordination is a response to the significant number of children caught in the middle of custody battles and postdivorce litigation. "Perhaps the most rapidly growing interventions for high-conflict cases are parental coordinators and special masters." According to the Association of Family and Conciliation Courts Task Force on Parent Coordination (2002), "Parent coordination is an innovative approach which has been repeatedly recommended in the professional literature as a means to deal with high conflict and alienating families in domestic relations proceedings before the court." In the broadest sense, a parent coordinator can be viewed as a high-conflict manager for the family in which the power assigned to the PC is defined by the court system to authorize court orders (Boyan and Termini, 2005, p. 28b). The PAS-trained parent coordinator does not need to tiptoe in his or her treatment of the child, and his or her requests of the parents. His or her court appointment, access to the judge, and credibility to the court provides the power necessary to recommend and follow-up with changes that need to be implemented within the family system.

One may suspect that at least one of the attorneys is attempting to confuse, distort, and/or divert the judge's attention away from the real issues. The attorney's mission is to protect the children from the PAS inducer or from being persuaded that the alienated parent has, in fact, abused them. Opposing counsel will attempt to assign blame to the alienated parent for the children's suffering and defend his or her client as the loving one, even relying at times on "Solomon's wisdom." Thus, one might consider the analogy of the classroom in contrast to a courtroom in which the former consists of a professor explaining to students, some interested and others disinterested, a variety of concepts and definitions. The basis of learning is offering a clear presentation while attempting to motivate the students to grasp the new information. In the latter milieu, however, one attorney is attempting to educate the judge through complex examples with built-in defensive coverage while the other attorney is attempting to protect his or her client by disrupting the focus of the judge, changing and redefining the meaning of the term and altering the context of the examples. Further, he or she is likely to question the criteria for asserting the PAS diagnosis, which is not yet listed in the DSM. Thus, in the courtroom, continual interference in the educational endeavor exists, while the judge attempts to participate in the disrupted and disjointed learning process. The judge is exposed to greater distraction and impaired comprehension than a graduate student would experience with a clown or hyperactive student disturbing the learning environment of the classroom. The judge certainly understands the attorney's tactics but it does not make it any easier for him or her to figure out what is going on, who is lying and distorting the truth, and how to follow the laws which are supposed to protect children and support their best interests.

The role of the expert becomes crucial as the direct examination unfolds and the attorney opens the door and provides the time and direction for the judge to appreciate the theory, understand the causes, and grasp the brainwashing methods of the alienator. He or she begins to appreciate the development of the child's emotional symptoms and the estranged parent-child relationship. At a minimum during this format, the judge has an opportunity to absorb the material in spite of the cross-examination of opposing counsel's attempt to refute the theory, discredit the expert, and put a different spin on the examples as he or she attacks the alienated parent as the abuser. He or she asserts that the other party is responsible for the child's anger and hostility for that parent.

If the expert is weak and inexperienced in the courtroom or lacks sufficient understanding of and knowledge about PAS, the opposing counsel may succeed in confusing the judge, and diminishing the scientific and clinical basis for the findings and the identification of PAS symptoms. The attorney may be effective in interrupting the course of action in the expert's explanation, which needs a continuous momentum to describe the child's perspective and the parent's behavior as the direct cause of the symptoms of alienation. The attorney defends his or her client by referring to the large support system which echoes "the truth." Thus, it is difficult for the judge to decide and to offer his or her wisdom when two competing attorneys are trying to convince the judge of two extreme and very different points of view and seemingly contradictory causes and findings.

Is it true that the parent has been alienated by the other parent through a deliberate campaign of denigration, or has the alienated parent committed child abuse? Each explanation would elucidate why the child wants nothing to do with that parent or any of that parent's family or friends. So, what is on the judge's mind and what should his or her role be? Generally, he or she would describe his or her frustration and confusion in carefully trying to focus on the issues and circumstances in order to ascertain the truth of the matter of which parent is responsible for the distressing display of the emotional deterioration of the child. The judge also is faced with the challenge of which order and intervention would be constructive and therapeutic for the child. The orders required, such as psychiatric hospitalization or removal of the child from the home of the alienator, are likely to exceed the comfort level of the judge. Thus, the judge often will refer the case to an evaluator, who may or may not be knowledgeable about PAS. The evaluation generally takes months to complete, and then depositions must be heard before a hearing is scheduled. As time proceeds, the symptoms become more pronounced as the children become even more intensely entrenched in the alienation programming. Often, judicial intervention required in PAS cases requires extreme measures, such as reversing custodial arrangements, imposing supervised contact, or suspending visitations with the indoctrinating parent. However, it takes "guts" for a judge to order this reversal even if the evidence is compelling, knowing how much the children will "hate" and protest living with the "despised" parent.

In addition, it is not always that the attorneys are presenting the PAS terminology and requesting judicial intervention to aid the identified child. It may well be an entirely staged event to gain his or her sympathy for one parent and outrage toward the other in order to influence and distract the judge. The subterfuge may be directed toward gaining the financial advantage by receiving a greater or lesser proportion of the marital assets and altering the amount of alimony and child support. For example, a mother who is doing everything within her capability to malign and destroy her child's relationship with the kind and caring father may be seen by the judge as a woman who needs to spend her time working to provide a financial contribution to the family, with less time available to continue her campaign of deprecation in interfering with the father's now increased visitation after school and during weekends. Another example is a father who unjustly blames the mother for alienating him from the children in his effort to increase the time-sharing, which will alter the formula of child support. Equal visitation schedules or rotational custody in sharing the responsibilities in raising the children will decrease his financial contribution, according to the child support tables. The judge may reprimand one party and order that parent to cease their harmful psychological manipulations and behaviors that exhibits emotional child abuse while outlining the consequences. Failure to respect "the best interests of the child" may carry over to the judge's discretion in other areas of the divorce.

THE ALIENATED PARENT'S ATTORNEY

A parent retains an attorney and presents to that attorney how distraught he or she may feel because his or her children no longer wish to have contact with him/her as the alienated parent. He or she loves his or her children and describes how for years he or she has been a close and devoted father or mother. The child has become so disruptive and resistant to the visitation that the new client is overwhelmed as to how to approach or even attempt to change the situation or solve the problem. The parent shares how depressed they feel; not about the separation from their spouse, but what has happened to his or her children and their relationship. He or she cannot believe that his or her spouse would be so "stupid" to hurt the children and so angry to place the children in this divided loyalty position. The other parent knows how loving and responsive he or she has been to the children, but others continuously begin to question his or her parenting and his or her prior description of his or her positive family relationships.

The attorney certainly appreciates the pain and suffering of his or her new client, as he or she is accustomed to the emotional disturbance that occurs during the process of divorce. It causes most individuals – whether it is the husband or the wife – to feel devastated by the loss, the failure, the hostility and accusations of blame, and the changes that their lives now must undergo as a result of the marital separation.

Is it the responsibility of the rejected parent to determine if the child's symptoms appear to be PAS related? The attorney must decide what strategy to plan and how to incorporate this information. Generally, the parent is unfamiliar with the concept and has not figured out how this process came about other than describing how his or her spouse would use words to bash him or her, calculate storytelling and name-calling in front of the children, or identifies the motivation of his or her spouse in trying to deliberately undermine and destroy his or her relationship with the children. He or she simply wants him/her out of their lives. Although recognition of the terms *alienation* and *parental alienation syndrome* has become more widespread in recent years, it is generally found that many matrimonial attorneys still have minimal knowledge and awareness of the concept's definition and a limited understanding of its causes and how to treat it. This statement is not intended to shed a criticism upon family law attorneys; the same remark also applies to mental health professionals and, to some extent, even child and family therapists. However, it is more difficult for members of the legal community to appreciate and learn about the concept because their training and attempts at comprehension are impaired by opposing forces to discredit the existence of this diagnosis and the validity of its findings in order to defend their clients. When the attorney then represents the party of the opposite position, he or she merely uses similar selective arguments in support of his or her client who now is faced with the counteraccusations. Thus, continuous interruption and false information is disseminated to disrupt the academic process of becoming educated about this fundamental mental disturbance.

The Mental Health Professional

Similarly to family law attorneys, mental health professionals and many family therapists are not exposed to PAS as part of their formal education and training because little of their curriculum is devoted to courtroom expert preparation, forensic roles, and the legal implications of their work with children and families. The term *PAS* originates as a result of the adversarial legal system rather than as a part of the natural growth and development of children. Unfortunately, the term also is excluded in the teachings of the dynamics of the family life cycle and the dysfunctions of family systems and communication. Mental health students have their attention directed, for example, toward the influence of substance abuse in the family on children and various rehabilitative and clinical treatments to assist children, adolescents and their family members. Many mental health professionals have never heard of the concept nor have they read the writings of its originator, Psychiatrist Richard Gardner. Until an attorney presents the term in reference to the very family for which they are providing the child counseling, the therapist may not fully be aware of the process of indoctrination and poisoned chalice. They are, however, aware of the general difficulties of the children living through their parents' divorce.

The attorney then asks the mental health professional, "Are you familiar with the diagnosis PAS?" The mental health professional, often too embarrassed to say "no," begins to search through his or her reference books for definitions or asks colleagues so that he or she may present himself or herself in a more knowledgeable and respectful way to his or her client's attorney. Often attorneys command both the respect and the intimidation of the mental health community. The therapist wants to be helpful in assisting the parent who has brought the child to him or her because of the divorce or other child-related problems occurring during the divorce. The therapist hears what is going on and wishes to become the advocate for the child and support the parent in coping with the terrible circumstances and behaviors that they have been told about. Some mental health counselors also may become zealous in their desire to be a "hero to save the children." The attorney representing the alienated parent listens carefully to the symptomatology presented. He or she must prepare his or her argument for either increased or maintaining visitation, a strategy to approach the custody dispute, or now to put the other spouse in a more unfavorable light given that this conduct will certainly be objectionable when examples are presented to the judge. It is a common fact, as we would hope, that judges detest any type of abusive parental conduct, especially that which would be deliberate for the purpose of exploiting or hurting a child or injuring a child's need for a bond and attachment with one or both of the parents.

The attorney will quickly realize that he or she may need to depend upon an expert to help the client feel empowered and understood and to assist him or her in the presentation of findings to the court. Or, the attorney may wish to rely upon the child, adult, or family therapist already working with one or more members of the family to explain how the parental alienation syndrome has developed and how it has manifested in this particular family. Attorneys find it easier to rely on the treating doctors because they already are involved with the family and they are likely to assume an advocacy position, which would be assuredly consistent with that of the attorney's representation. Also, it would be a reasonable assumption for the attorney to think that the mental health professional or especially the family therapist would have knowledge of PAS and be able to effectively address this concern.

Why would an attorney not think that the child, adult, or family therapist that is dealing with the PAS symptoms, which may be severe in nature and highly disruptive to the family, would not understand its origin, the dynamics of the subsystem interplay, and how to treat the condition? We now understand that what occurs with many mental health professionals, including family therapists, is a professional insecurity based upon lacking a sophisticated familiarity with the PAS concept, especially because it is gaining acceptance in the legal community. Furthermore, when submitting names of custody evaluators or relying on county-or state-employed or subcontracted independent custody evaluators, an assumption that these individuals are familiar with the concept of PAS as well as capable of assessing the validity of the symptoms exists. It is regretful that this assumption has more often than not been false. Frequently, mental health professionals would prefer to avoid accepting responsibility for the PAS diagnosis and prefer to limit their comments to the typical concerns identified, such as "one parent is making negative comments or discouraging the children from spending time and shared activities with the other parent." Once a custody evaluator is willing to accept responsibility for making this determination, he or she puts himself or herself in a contentious position of one attorney trying to exploit his or her findings for the benefit of the client while knowing that the other attorney will challenge the findings, attack him or her and try to discredit his or her qualifications, observations, and recommendations. Thus, it is safer for the custody evaluator to point out in his or her report to the judge that conflicts and difficulties are taking place within a family and leave it to the judge to decide how he or she wishes to pursue the matter. The custody evaluator may take the easy way out because of his or her underlying fears of showing their professional inadequacy, incompetence, or unwillingness to be put in a confrontational format in a cross-examination. Unfortunately, too many custody evaluators and mental health professionals provide little assistance to the judge other than organizing the background of family information in order for the judge to have a better acquaintance with the family members and be able to scrutinize the outline of the problems that have been described in the case file. The lack of sophistication and commitment of some mental health professionals causes the attorney more frustration and uncertainty as to how to proceed and advise his or her client.

Preferably, the attorney will recognize that the influence of a treating mental health professional may be compromised by his therapeutic role and that it would better serve his or her client to secure the evaluative services of a highly trained expert in PAS. One might think that this would be an obvious and straightforward task, but when it comes to the state of affairs in the mental health community, it is not simple for the attorney to find such a professional. Managed care has had a devastating impact on the quality of care in the health system and it has likewise contributed to the disarray among the mental health community. The clinicians' attempt to avoid dependence upon the managed care insurance delivery system has caused extreme competition for self-paid patients. The way in which many mental health professionals obtain new self-pay clients in a declining free marketplace is to advertise and present themselves as an expert in "everything." The public, and naturally the attorney, will have difficulty sorting out who is really a specialist in what, and how to adequately screen and make a determination for case retention. The attorney may have his or her own expert to whom he or she regularly refers or retains as an expert on the basis of mutual referrals. Thus, the expert may not be a PAS expert but rather someone with whom the attorney feels comfortable working, perhaps on a referral basis for financial client-building purposes.

Once the attorney selects an expert, it is possible that the expert may find evidence that is contrary to support the position of his or her client. Then the attorney runs the risk of a bar complaint and termination of his or her services by the client. Understandably, it would be disappointing for a client after paying large sums of money to an attorney as well as the financial investment in retaining an expert to later discover that the expert becomes his or her "enemy" who might testify on behalf of the opposing party. Even if the client admits that he or she has falsified the data and claims and knows that the expert is correct and properly doing his or her job, the client does not want the presentation of the truth. It is the job of the attorney to explain to the client that an expert is paid as an impartial professional to ascertain the truth, relying as much as possible on scientific methods and objective data, and that the results may not be in keeping with what the client would want to hear. Simply paying for the expert service does not ensure the client of the results that they would like to see, as is expected when one retains an attorney as a champion for his or her cause.

The attorney representing the alienated parent is likely to suggest to his or her client a number of ways of documenting past events, recording details of occurrences, and identifying potential witnesses. People who have been involved in observing the parenting process and the alienation phenomenon assist in preparing his or her defense and questions for deposition and, eventually, testimony of the client. The attorney will explain that it is merely insufficient to list a date and description of the occurrence. Cases of PAS require documentation, witnesses, exact quotations of what was said, and actual detailed descriptions of behavior (e.g. facial grimaces that were expressed must be accounted for with precision). An expert in PAS also will assist in collecting the data and organizing it in such a way that what has occurred becomes compelling evidence to meet the criteria of PAS, which should convince the judge of the planned manipulation of the alienation and the poisoning injections taking place into the mind of the vulnerable child. The expert will need to interview all parties separately and observe various family subsystems interact, conduct home visits, psychological testing, review records, and interview collateral contacts. These are all essential in preparing his or her findings.

Opposing Counsel

The position of opposing counsel is somewhat different from that of the attorney representing the alienated parent. Certainly, that attorney is concerned when he or she hears about the child's emotional problems, poor school grades, mood swings, and resistance to spending time with the other parent, but he or she gently slips into the posture of supporting the explanation of his or her client. The PAS inducer asserts the terrible and insensitive ways in which the other parent interacts with the child and offers justification as to why that parent should have little or no contact with the children. These stories expressed are quite emotionally convincing, even for an experienced family law attorney. The attorney wants to side with his or her client, not only because being on the same wavelength makes it easier in the "representation" but also because it makes common sense that an "irresponsible, neglectful parent" who treated the child in such a disheartening way would likely push that child in the direction of wanting to resist and avoid contact with that parent. Generally, the programming parent also would include in his or her story how horrible the in-laws and friends have been (for example, how inlaws have contributed to harming their own grandchildren). The attorney begins to believe the lies of the child and the distortions of the abusing parent that they are representing.

The parent who is heavily involved in the campaign of denigration of the other parent becomes a well-rehearsed actor or actress in the drama of this presentation. Thus, it is natural for the opposing counsel to accept and not question or recognize what is actually taking place. The attorney becomes part of the drama and an enabler of the alienation process. Now, the parent has a legal member on his or her team who has the influence, power, and access to the legal system to help promote the picture of the other parent as being such a disgraceful human being that he or she should not be allowed to have anything to do with his or her victimized child, e.g., "the child who still is being unmercifully tortured without adequate protection." One can only imagine how many times these stories have been retold with all its richness of emotional detail to attract the sympathy and attention of the listener and convince others of the veracity and validity of the remarks. The attorney whose position now is to represent this client must, in fact, offer a course of action in which he or she will be a legal hero to his or her client in helping to protect the innocent child from being continuously abused and, of course, to justify their fee.

Well-meaning family lawyers do warn their clients not to engage in the process of inserting disparaging comments about the other parent to their children and express their instructions to exercise caution in making these negative statements when the children are present. This, in part, is done because of the humane interest of the attorneys not wanting to further obstruct the other parent's opportunity to have a relationship with the children; it also is done with the intention of not giving the opposing party the opportunity to document these statements that their client is making, which may be injurious to his or her client's legal position. The opposing counsel will know that the other party has been instructed to record these statements, which will come back at the time of trial to undermine his or her client's allegations. Once opposing counsel sees or hears that he or she will be confronted with the fact that the other party has engaged a PAS expert against their client, he/she will begin to prepare the usual defense and legal arguments that "PAS does not exist. It does not have a diagnostic code nor is it presented in the most recent DSM of the American Psychiatric Association," etc. (For an explanation and trial defense see the journal article "Misinformation Versus Facts – About the contributions of Richard A. Gardner, M.D.," 2002) and "Does DSM IV have the equivalence for the Parental Alienation Syndrome (PAS) diagnosis?" (2003a).

The attorney will become a protector of his or her client much like the parent will assume the various roles of "protecting the children" from the parent that is actually being alienated. The protective attorney then carefully examines the cast of characters that either has been selected or are likely to be selected to be certain that the custody evaluator, treating therapist, or any potential evaluators that may be asked to participate in the case are not specialists in PAS and are not sufficiently well-trained to address or undermine the accusations of him or her client. On the other hand, the attorney himself or herself may be sufficiently indoctrinated such that he or she, in fact, believes the client and that the alienated parent truly is the abusing parent. Then he or she may wish to hire the PAS expert to argue the absence of PAS as the other side asserts its presence. This intention is to co-opt the PAS expert as well as protect and establish posture for his or her client. The attorney recognizes that he or she runs the risk that the expert may not agree with what his or her client purports to be true. However, he or she would not agree to such an expert if not "certain" about the "facts" presented by the distressed client.

THE ALIENATED PARENT

The alienated parent often describes his or her experience as one of feeling powerlessness and devastation as he or she sees what is happening before his or her very eyes and there is nothing that he/she can do to stop the nightmares, stories, and ongoing actions. This deterioration in the relationship with the child or children obviously is harmful, and he or she is unable in any way to directly or indirectly influence the process to alter or reverse the course of the foreseen destiny. The parent begins to obsess as to what he or she can do differently to end the attacks of the other parent's campaign to brainwash his or her children. He or she expresses bewilderment and surprise. Why would the other parent actually be willing to hurt the children by setting them up and exploiting them as pawns as a way to seek revenge and retaliation for the problems of the marriage or the financial gain in the divorce?

The alienated parent initially presents the position of the universally known fact and accepted axiom that "parents never should put their children in the middle of the conflicts of the separating spouses at the expense of injuring the children." The alienated parent repeatedly will espouse how we all know it is not good to say disparaging remarks about the other parent because it is common sense that what is best for the child always is to have a loving and respectful relationship with each parent. The alienated parent may wonder why in the past the bashing parent would make excuses, and try to support or even defend them to the children. Now more than ever, because they are getting separated, the children need unity and cooperation with the parents. It is very difficult to accept that the PAS inducer now would take an oppositional position of trying to destroy what may have been a good parent-child relationship that has existed for many years.

However, soon enough, the alienated parent realizes that it is not an accidental remark or spontaneous name-calling or even that the child overheard that parent talking on the phone to one of his or her friends. Instead, the alienated parent comes to the realization that this kind of successive denigration does not occur by whim, as he or she begins to put together the pieces of all of the remarks that the child has expressed against him or her. These remarks often have an adult-like quality that is characteristic of the other parent and mirrors what this programming parent would say directly to the alienated parent if he or she did not use the children as the messenger. The alienated parent becomes disgusted at how cruel the other parent is in using these tactics as they become aware of the internalization process of victimization. He or she looks to his or her attorney and the court as a way of providing justice, pleading innocence to the accusations against him or her, and proving how the conduct of the PAS inducer is alienating him or her from the child. He or she hopes to both punish that parent and correct the distressing situation between him or her and the children. An immediacy of need exists, because the alienated parent sees daily experiences or occurrences becoming worse. He or she is disgusted by what he or she hears and sees the other parent doing. He or she demands a sudden cessation to this wrongful and damaging behavior. However, the alienated parent soon discovers that his or her attorney does not have immediate access to the courtroom or the ability for a hero-like solution. The attorney instead begins to pacify and tries to calm him or her down during their emergency telephone conversations, during which the alienated parent calls for help, and so on thereafter demands help.

The alienated parent becomes fearful: *What if* the judge believes the children's programming and accepts the performance of the convincing actor or actress (e.g., his or her assertions as representing the truth)? He or she will be at the mercy of the court and lose the children and his or her pocketbook. Initially, the alienated parent has confidence in the legal system and wants his or her day in court. As time progresses, he or she begins to clearly see the well-planned and executed effort that the other parent has put together, supported by an increasingly large number of fans waving the banner in behalf of these poor children exposed to such an "abusive, terrible parent." The alienated parent becomes hopeless, feeling depressed with the constant observation of his or her children's anger and hatred against the parents as they pull away emotionally and physically. Their argument and justification for not wanting to see the alienated parent is completely illogical, but yet their screams gain the attention of others, who want to relieve the children's pain and offer them comfort, security, and, ultimately, protection against this alleged "cruel, irresponsible, insensitive, and abusive parent." Then the alienated parent becomes more dependent on others for support and sympathy, especially his or her attorney (now being the only one that can help save him or her and the relationship with his or her children as well as his or her reputation in the community).

The alienated parent cannot help but obsess day and night, worrying about the next step in the brainwashing parent's formulation of where and how to dissuade the children from any of his or her efforts, gifts, cards, trips, or other expressions of caring, love, or desire to share time with them. The alienated parent clearly observes that the children are suffering and becoming psychologically damaged. He or she expresses helpless feelings in not knowing what to do and how to react. Often, alienated parents will take desperate actions to convince their children of the unfair statements and to question the tactics of the other parent. Unfortunately, this action backfires and they find themselves further distanced from their children and very much criticized for these "disloyal" actions. Alienated parents feel that no matter what they do, they are doomed. Finally, they begin the internal debate of whether it is worth it to fight for the truth, to try to hold onto their diminishing relationship with their children, or to withdraw and escape the onslaught of lies that have been targeted at his or her heart and soul in trying to continue a meaningful relationship with their children.

The alienated parent attempts a number of countermeasures against the campaign of alienation and the successful internalization of the child's own beliefs and statements against that parent. The typical and common attempts include the following:

1. He or she denies the child's accusations and what really is occurring to himself or herself and to the children and others.
2. The alienated parent tries to convince the children that the statements that the alienating parent is making are false, incorrect, and simply not true. Attempts are made at refuting these remarks, replacing them with the truth. The parent tries to tell the child to be cautious against future comments as exemplified by the past brainwashing behaviors.
3. The alienated parent begins to loosen his or her hold on disciplinary methods and actions to avoid further engagement of power struggles with the already resistant, distant, and angry children. In the past, that parent may have adopted a firm set of rules and disciplinary requirements to which the children had to adhere. Now, the parent begins to allow the children to assume more power and dictate what they want in his or her attempts to avoid conflict, please, and win over the children.
4. The alienated parent tries to indulge the child's request, or even offers nonrequested indulgence, to gain the child's affection and establish an alliance with the child. The child knows only too well how to exploit that parent for gifts and favors. Once the child's exploitation has become complete and the child gets desired material items, the child demands more, which sets a pattern that becomes more unmanageable for the alienated parent.
5. The alienated parent may choose to withdraw, either temporarily or for a longer duration of time, because the other parent's attacks are either too emotionally draining or the experience with the children leads to such emotional pain that the alienated parent can no longer tolerate this level of discomfort and conflict with the unresolved, ongoing tension. The parent may decide to wait until after the divorce in hopes of reinstituting visitation or time-sharing. He or she might even believe or hope that the other parent will experience such victory in controlling the children that they will no longer need or desire to continue this effort of brainwashing.

Sitting on the sidelines and taking this position is extremely hurtful for the alienated parent as statements expressed about his or her parenting and basic integrity as a person are diminished in the eyes of the court, friends, family, and community at large. The reality of his or her no longer having contact with the children or not being seen with them in any of their activities is now being interpreted as a reflection of his or her abandonment, disinvolvement, and uncaring disinterest in the well-being and welfare of the children. His or her lack of contact is explained to the children as a justification of their feelings and to honor their preference in not having contact with that parent. The alienated parent may well be the financially providing parent. Writing out the child support check becomes insult to his or her injury of suffering the loss of the children while at the same time paying for the other parent's manipulation and use of his/her money with the children. It is one thing for the alienated parent to feel pushed out of the lives of the children and another to feel as if he or she has to pay for rewarding the other parent's efforts in this "disgusting" power play. As the alienated parent withdraws, he or she must convey to his or her attorney his or her position of acceptance of giving up. This has implications on how the attorney will represent him or her, and to what extent the attorney is now willing to enter into the battlefield without the client offering personal energy, financial incentives, and time investment in his or her own case. The attorney may respond by referring the client to a therapist to help alleviate his or her mixed symptoms of depression and anxiety.

This referral is often made with reluctance. The attorney knows that the opposing counsel will wish to subpoena these records and use them to show how emotionally unfit the client is to parent and to manipulate his or her mental status. The alienated parent may feel that the therapist does not believe that he or she has been set up and that he or she has in fact disappointed the children in the way that he or she has acted in the past and presently is portrayed. Again, a critical need for a PAS-trained therapist exists.

The alienated parent's friends, and maybe even family, may begin to question him or her, "If only he or she could have done some things differently." Others may impart to him or her some level of responsibility and blame for what has happened to the child. When family and friends become involved and hear about the children's pleas and complaints, it is only natural for them to wonder if there is some truth or merit to such extreme reactions by and refusal of the children to speak or see the alienated parent. They might believe to some extent that the hostile spouse is angry about the divorce, episodes, or wrongdoings that have taken place during the marriage, or even financial considerations in dispute at the time of the divorce. Most individuals, however, do not think of the children as the perpetrators of this continued alienation in terms of "unjustified" or "fabricated accusations." They see the "innocent" children caught up in their parents' battle now stepping forward to identify those things they did not like about that parent for quite some time.

The children assume a new power that they have never experienced in dethroning the alienated parent. The withering comfort of the prior support system of the alienated parent begins to affect his or her original courage for his or her convictions to the point of causing self-doubt and insecurity or withdrawal and depression. He or she no longer seeks out family or friends to discuss these happenings. The alienated parent not only feels his or her weakened position but experiences feelings of hopelessness and powerlessness. He or she finds himself or herself alone in a state of devastation. The alienated parent feels as if he or she has lost sense of self-respect and position of membership in the residential community, suffers from the lost and failed marriage, and feels sadness from lack of contact with the children and extended family. He or she also feels despair due to financial ruination caused by distributing the assets, the high cost of litigation and obtaining separate residences, and their likely impaired productivity in the day-to-day work. A depressed individual, especially an alienated parent going through the kind of litigation process in which PAS has taken place, experiences excess rumination day and night, which naturally interferes with anyone's ability to concentrate, intensifies the irritability and lack of patience, and often heightens the probability for carelessness and mistakes in work performance. The alienated parent does not gain much sympathy nor empathy from anyone because these feelings are misdirected toward these manipulated children who also are emotionally suffering.

THE ALIENATING PARENT

The PAS inducer feels justified in what he or she is doing; after all, stopping the other parent from having contact with "their" children is best for the children and the alienator. A divorce is a marital divorce; it should not be a family divorce. However, the alienating parent wishes to think in terms of divorce as terminating the other parent from seeing the children such that there should be no reason for having contact with the other "undeserving" parent. Parents of divorce soon realize that they are still required to maintain ongoing communication with the other parent because of the activity level of children today: school functions, after-school plans, playdates, etc. Thus, divorced parents complain that they now have to spend more time talking with each other about the kids and jointly planning activities then they did during their married life. The reason for this is that during the marriage, often one parent is designated as the primary caretaker and chauffeur of the children while the other is the primary wage earner. This is not to say it has been an exclusive arrangement; certainly, the other parent may participate in child-rearing as well as the other parent may participate in wage earning. The contrast often is such that one parent has a career, the primary responsibility for earning money, whereas the other parent has assumed the career of motherhood or fatherhood as the primary responsibility toward caretaking. The alienating parent often possesses a residue of long-standing hostility against his or her spouse and the strong desire to enjoy his or her newfound power through the courts; asserting his or her rights provides a sense of freedom that marriage never afforded them. The alienating parent no longer believes that he or she has to confer with the other parent about financial and child-related matters as in the past. He or she wishes to conduct his or her life as he or she selfishly wishes, no longer having to compromise with someone else's needs or perceived demands.

Another consideration and understanding in what goes on in the thought process of the alienating parent may be a history in which they were exposed to a similar scenario. It may be that this parent was a child of a divorce and was raised by the mother or the father who similarly "bad-mouthed" or alienated one of his or her parents. One of the parents may have either abandoned them or displayed little interest or desire for contact, and particularly for shared child rearing. For example, a father may have had to work two jobs in order to support his children and those children in his new remarriage. The child of that parent may have been told by the other parent, "Your father does not care to spend time with you and he only cares about his new baby." The explanation presented to the child is that the father has deserted him or her. When the father, in his rare free time, attempts to contact his children from his former marriage, he meets with reluctance and finds their schedule too busy to have time to meet with him. It is often a matter of the spin or interpretation that the parent provides to the child that helps formulate the opinion and perception of the alienated child. Once the alienated child has been exposed to this kind of propaganda and prejudice, it is likely that this child soon will begin to experience the same prejudice. The child will start to echo the words of the parent who initially brainwashed or indoctrinated him or her: "My father has abandoned me and his interest is only with his new family."

Studies of cults and prejudice offer formation models for simple duplication and replication to be applied to the alienating parent. Alienating parents adopt a method of ritual abuse, a phenomenon reported with increasing frequency throughout the world. For many, the notion that innocent people are deliberately ritually traumatized is unthinkable, the stuff of science-fiction novels or fantasy films. For others, it is an unspeakable but distinct reality of an experience that they have actually endured and continue to relive indirectly through nightmares and flashbacks. Similarly, these claims are made by people who allege to be victims, perpetrators, and witnesses of parental alienation syndrome. The public's reactions to these assertions, not surprisingly, have been mixed. In many cases, emotional and polarized responses have resulted. Alienating parents are creative in their use of bizarre and varied mind-controlling techniques, unlike anything taught in the course of a traditional university curriculum. Significant controversy has arisen, resulting in bitter disputes among professionals and between and within families in which allegations have been made. The alienating parent has gathered an audience using these assertions among friends and family, which now serves as the choir to further reinforce those within the network and, in particular, to convince the children of the veracity of the remarks. The ecological environment creates a well-supported case to convince the judge of the "best interests of the children."

The alienating parent now has found a way to displace anger through the medium of the children as the messenger to express feelings of revenge and desire for retaliation toward the other parent. The basis for the anger may be rational or irrational. Certainly, putting the child at risk determines that the anger is explosive, uncontrollable, and unreasonable. Whether the anger is justified is another consideration. Its expression, displacement toward, and manipulation of the children is never justified or acceptable. However, the alienating parent does not care and will adopt any method or means of getting the other parent out of his or her life and the lives of the children. Often, an underlying financial incentive is suspected, and quickly denied. This parent will assert and believes as the issue that the other parent is incapable of parenting and certainly undeserving of any benefit of contact with the children. He or she now has the opportunity to convince the court, which has the power to make these enforcing decisions to minimize contact or exclude the other parent. The alienating parent wishes the other parent to be fully excluded except to the extent of stopping him or her from paying child support and alimony. The alienating parent typically will simply instruct the other parent to put the check in the mail, by sending it through the court system or garnishing his or her salary. "Don't call us; we never want to see or hear from you" is the warning. The basis for the financial determination also may be exploited in the time-sharing or custody realm, according to the guidelines of child support formulation.

Thus, these parents may use a number of different tactics. First, expression of anger is accompanied by methods of revenge and retaliation. Second is the belief that they are the primary and sole caregivers to the children and that it is not necessary to have another parent's involvement, particularly when it leads to dissention and conflict. They are convinced that the other parent is incapable of and/or not necessary to the developmental process of the children. Third, the alienating parent has chosen the method of parental alienation as the syndrome of choice in order to gain a financial edge in exploiting the other parent for money. If that parent has less time and involvement with the child, then the alienating parent deserves a larger sum of money for his or her full-time parenting role, plus alimony for reduced time to work and pursue a career. For example, a rotating custody or 50 percent time-sharing arrangement in many states will reduce the financial child support obligation because of the mutual and shared parental responsibility and expense. Thus, the parent engaging in a PAS battle is ultimately likely to remove that parent from a meaningful position of time-sharing and thereby increase the financial support and benefit from other considerations. Furthermore, regarding marital distribution and alimony, by pointing out to the judge what a terrible individual and targeted parent this party is, the alienating parent's hope is that the other parent will be penalized financially by offering the alienated parent a disproportionate amount of the assets. Fourth, the alienating parent may be diagnosed as having a narcissistic personality disorder or similar predisposition. He or she believes that he or she knows what is best for the child's needs and they should determine how the children will show their loyalty and preferences, even at the expense of hurting the children. They are intent upon removing the opportunity of having an independent relationship with the children's other parent as they invite the introduction of a same-sex, competing stepparent, or new role model into their new family. This person believes that he or she can meet all of the children's emotional and child-rearing requirements, believing the other parent is unnecessary to their well-being and development. This parent insists on total control, to dominate the parenting and the children's activities. He or she refuses to allow, negotiate, or share in any kind of parenting arrangement. The narcissist acts out his or her own self-centered needs by ascribing them to the children as "beneficial," and it is the children's responsibility to fulfill these narcissist-like wishes and desires.

The phenomenon that exists in the mind of the alienating parent generally is characterized by the feeling that he or she has a mission or cause to accomplish as his or her priority and reason for being to help the children regardless of the cruelty and injury to other parties. As the campaign against the other parent continues to grow with their friends' and families' support in hearing horror stories about how terrible and awful the other parent is, it is relatively easy to convince the children to carry the banner as well. Then these parents recede and allow their kids to take the lead in echoing and mimicking the remarks and behaviors of the alienating parent, as if they had nothing to do with the internalization of the feelings by their children.

Then the children begin to express that they do not like the way the other parent dresses, or the kind or color of the car they drive. They no longer like the parent's attitude in any respect. They are repulsed by the way that parent looks at them. They dislike everything about that parent, which includes their friends and family. The children refuse to eat with that parent; they no longer like their cooking or choice of foods. They resist engaging in activities with that parent because they describe the experience as extremely unpleasant and distasteful to them. The alienating parent defends and protects the children from being so upset and objects to them having any contact with that parent. This vicious circle feeds into the children's statements and further supports them against the other parent. Both a conscious and unconscious satisfaction in the new alliance are strengthened by the alienating parent and the children. They have a common bond and common shared objective and purpose against the opposing that wishes to "intrude" into their lives. They plot together both spontaneously and deliberately in creating plans and ways to sabotage the interest and efforts of the other parent in continuing in a relationship and spending time with his or her children. The children are grateful to the alienating parent for being sensitive to how they feel and to helping them avoid the obligation of spending time with the "disliked" parent.

It may be that upon returning from a pleasant and enjoyable visit with the alienated parent, the children know as soon as they enter the alienating parent's house that they must say their scripted lines as expected. These lines in their rehearsed play include "I had a miserable time; I was bored and I hated every minute of spending time with my father or mother." Whatever the activity or the people involved, the children then describe their experience in a negative, terrible way. They often say that the parent "forced them" to eat or to see a movie or to do an activity that they did not want to do. Positive encounters depicted on videotape and pictures as feedback for confrontation are minimized with excuses.

Unfortunately, what is described in these above statements is the early stage of alienation. During the latter stage of alienation, the experience actually taking place is one in which the children *do*, in fact, feel unhappy and malcontent regardless of how pleasant the experience with the alienated parent is, because they have been programmed to feel this way. Alienating parents become experts as to how to communicate subtle psychological cues in various disguises, or it may simply be overt parent bashing against the targeted parent, such as that described in *Divorce Poison* (Warshak, 2001). Warshak writes about the range of techniques, from occasional bad-mouthing to bashing that no longer contains occasional blaming but has now reached the stage of continuous brainwashing. Bashing becomes more destructive when it is not challenged and it is conducted on a repetitive basis during which the children are programmed to join in the vilification of the targeted parent. The result of bad-mouthing, bashing, or brainwashing is the fostering of the condition of parental alienation syndrome. The repetitive support of this condition with the children is not always related to the prealienation relationship or whether the children are even predisposed for PAS indoctrination. It is the crisis created by the divorce and the marital separation that opens the door for the alienating parent to choose to exploit the children during this process of change, heightened sensitivity and insecurity, and disruption in the homeostasis in every aspect of their lives.

THE SIGNIFICANT OTHER

Whether the involvement is a dating partner, live-in boyfriend or girlfriend, or new, remarried spouse, the significant other has no choice but to support the parent, their partner, as this person is fully emotionally involved in either the injury of the painful loss of the relationship with the child or involved in the perpetuation of the successful alienation. Alienation is a full-time activity, neither passive nor part-time in nature, that requires ongoing planning and execution. Being the target of alienation affects the alienated parent constantly; effects include depression and preoccupation with the process. Thus, the new partner experiences distraction from intimacy and lack of the attention that he or she previously enjoyed. For that partner to continue in a romantic and/or shared relationship having any meaning to the alienated parent or the alienating parent, they must join in the mission and eventually become part of it. The parent either conducting or receiving the alienation will know if his or her intimate partner is sincere and that they have his or her support versus only providing lip service without commitment. When the partner depicts any insincerity or lack of devotion, the parent going through the divorce litigation will likely interpret this reaction as one of incompatibility between the two of them or lack of real love for each other. No neutral bystanders in an intimate relationship or among friends and family can be found when one is in the midst of casting the divorce poison or being its recipient. The central focus of daily activities will be upon the process of alienation; the intimate partner will be unable to convince the parent to escape this experience. There is no relief or vacation during the litigation.

The development of PAS and exacerbation of the symptoms generally continue for a fairly lengthy period of time; little opportunity for intimacy exists, other than the support that one lends (e.g., both partners are thinking of strategies and implementing further steps, in which the intimate partner now plays an essential role). If the partner continues in the relationship with the alienator, then the intimate partner will want to come up with ideas and suggestions to further the cause to gain the appreciation, attention, and affection of the alienator. If the intimate partner is involved with the alienated parent, he or she will share in the sorrow and sadness of the loss. The intimate partner will share in the most personal disclosures of the alienated parent, which will bind and bond the partners in a sharing unprecedented by any other experience in their relationship, bringing them even closer together than their sexual union. The intimate partner will have the opportunity to comfort the alienated parent as others draw away from him or her, and he or she becomes the primary support system. The partner sees what the children are doing to their loving parent and they begin to feel anger for the children's disrespectful and disruptive behavior. However, he or she quickly will find himself or herself in a similar circumstance to the alienated parent; sooner or later the children will express hatred toward him or her as well, by the nature of his or her association.

The alienated parent may begin to question, as others will inevitably do, that perhaps the intimate partner is contributing to the alienation that is taking place. Perhaps the children are angry with him or her because they do not approve of his or her intimate partner and that is playing a role in why they do not want to see the parent. He or she may attribute their avoidance to the visitation because the intimate partner is present. Soon, we can expect that the alienated parent will offer time to the children during which the partner is not present, and he or she will discover that the children will react in the same way, with the same vehemence and volatility that they expressed when the intimate partner was present. The consideration for the alienated parent would be to terminate or temporarily discontinue his or her relationship with the intimate partner in hopes that the children would reconsider if he or she was 100 percent available to give them full attention without diversion or association with the scapegoat, the intimate partner. Unfortunately, by choosing this course of action, the alienated parent would lose the little support that he or she has left in having a friend who is compassionate to his or her needs and empathetic to his or her suffering.

Whether the intimate partner is involved in the dating relationship, being the live-in boyfriend or girlfriend, or becomes a remarried spouse, becomes part of the process, part of the experience, and part of the pain. The only exception might be the dating partner that decides to exit the relationship because of the lack of attention they are receiving, disliking the high level of conflict that exists, and being incapable of coping with the depression or anger that the alienated parent is exhibiting. The dating partner may feel that this process will continue beyond their level of patience and they would rather re-enter the singles marketplace than remain in the unsettling disturbance in which their needs for companionship, attention, and romantic shared activities are no longer being fulfilled. On many occasions, the live-in partner will become discontent and disillusioned with the intensity of the alienation and express ambivalence to exit rather than remain over the forecasted lengthy duration of the litigation. On the other hand, it is the remarried spouse that may affect the alienating or alienated parent in a different way. The remarried spouse may object to the conduct of the alienating parent, especially if they have their children residing in the same household. He or she might not wish to submit his or her children to this example of parent-child relationship feelings, as it will have a harmful effect on their children. In addition, he or she may feel selfish enough that he or she may not want to alter his or her life to the extent of joining in with the alienating parent, which is required. For the parent that is alienated, the remarried spouse may require this parent to withdraw and give up the struggle and battle to maintain the relationship with his or her ungrateful, unappreciative, and hostile children. This demand may either force the alienated parent to separate from this source of support or forgo the mission of trying to win back or win over his children in order to refocus on his current marriage, which has been compromised because of the attention and expense caused by the postdivorce litigation. However, these latter possibilities are less likely in cases of true intimacy.

THE CHILD

The thoughts and behavior of a child experiencing the symptoms of parental alienation syndrome are easy to observe and distinguish from other kinds of symptomatology with different etiologies. The clinical manifestations in this child are well-described in the books written by Dr. Richard Gardner, such as the second edition of *The Parental Alienation Syndrome* (1998). His fourth chapter describes the preoccupation of the child's thoughts with deprecation and criticisms of the parent such that the denigration often is very exaggerated in most cases without any justification. The term "brainwashing" implies that one parent is systematically and consciously programming the child to denigrate the other. Certainly, the concept of brainwashing is another way of inquiring as to "what is on the child's mind." However, PAS goes beyond this terminology to include subconscious and unconscious factors within the alienating parent that contribute to the child's alienation from the targeted parent. The child begins to develop his or her own internal thought processes and analysis, which Gardner refers to as the "thoughts that require independence of parental contributions" that play a role in this syndrome (Gardner, 1998). Thus, "the independent-thinker" phenomenon is such that the child creates his or her own agenda supported by his or her emotional determination to add substance to the already existent feelings of despising and hating the identified parent. What becomes of the role of the child is very much comprised of the PAS inducer that promulgates, brainwashes, and programs the child to develop an internalized set of constructs that further the cause or mission of the parent with which the child is identifying. This parent then reinforces the child's negative responses by subtle verbal messages as well as direct nonverbal methods of encouragement. For example, a mother might say to her daughter, "Since you are thinking about not going with your father this afternoon as scheduled, let's go shopping."

Gardner identifies eight cardinal symptoms of parental alienation syndrome:

1. the campaign of denigration one or the other plays,
2. weak, frivolous, and absurd rationalizations for the deprecation,
3. lack of ambivalence,
4. the "independent-thinker" phenomenon,
5. reflective support of the alienating parent in the parental conflict,

6. absence of guilt over cruelty to and/or exploitation of the alienated parent,
7. presence of borrowed scenarios, and
8. spread of the animosity to the extended family of the alienated parent.

Examples would be the hostility expressed toward the grandmother, or a child forced in a visitation with the denigrated parent who observes his father wearing a new workout outfit. The child expresses his or her alarm that the father would spend money on himself rather than on financial support for his children and their mother as he has been told to do by his mother's attorney or the court. The child throughout the day expresses his or her hatred for the "ugly" workout clothes and how he or she hates to look at the father while he is wearing such a "disgusting outfit." Whatever the vilified parent says or does, it only adds fuel to the fire; the initial stimuli of the money spent for a new clothing item is generalized to a variety of other behaviors to which the child directly attributes to the repulsed and estranged parent. Dr. Richard Warshak, in his book *Divorce Poison* (2001), also elaborates on the thoughts contained in the alienated child's mind. He gives, for example, the trivial explanations by which the child expresses the hatred he or she feels, as "I don't love you anymore." Shortly thereafter, the child will express, "I don't want to see you anymore," obsessing over all the reasons to justify the cessation of contact with the victimized parent.

The two major themes that are constantly expressed in the child's behavior mark all of the reasons why that child hates the rejected parent and all of the reasons to justify why that child should no longer have contact with the now poisoned parent. Certainly, the former thoughts initially lead to feelings of avoidance and irritation and then to anger and rage. Finally, the goal of revenge and retaliation for what they feel is "bad, unfair" treatment by the repulsed parent is observed. The latter situation causes the child to engage in a variety of maneuvers to avoid contact and reduce time with the targeted parent in any way that they can. This may be manifested in the form of psychosomatic symptoms, unwillingness to go to certain restaurants or see certain movies, or to have any contact with a individuals associated with this parent, whether it be intimate partners, friends, or family members. Warshak (2001) highlights this in his book by writing about a father who received a letter from his thirteen-year-old daughter. "I do not wish to visit you at all this summer. The more you demand and force me, the stronger I will resist you. Every time you force me to go with you, I lose more respect for you so now I wish to end my relationship or what is left of my relationship with you" (p. 42).

Warshak also discusses a child stating "I don't want you to have any part in my life because everything in my life has been good except when you have forced me to go with you" (page 51). The disparaged parent needs to be particularly careful of the false accusations that are spread by the alienated child. Children can be easily manipulated to tell false stories about fictitious events in their lives, particularly embellished with details that surround their intense emotions toward the hated parent. The thoughts are extreme and the emotions are intense for the alienated child. This phenomenon is the polarization that occurs between the parents, or as they have been referred to as the "saints and sinners."

Appreciating the complexity of the child's thinking process and roles enacted involves not only attending to the continual references made by the programming parent but also recognizing elements of the child's own constructs of alienation as a result of the child's thought patterns, motivations, and behaviors. The momentum of the child's feelings or repulsion against the deprecated parent takes on a life of itself. If the child's thinking and adopted roles are so easy to read and to identify the manifestations of alienation, why are so many misdiagnoses made and many assume that the child's statements are a consequence of parental abuse of that child or of turbulence from the disintegration of a marriage and the interactive effects of the parental conflict. The child's thoughts, expressions of emotions, and behavior can be distinguished and rightly clarified from these other questionable sources, and the criteria is available elsewhere, with many references in Gardner's writings. Because considerable information is available on this subject in other chapters of this book as well as in other publications, comments here have been limited to the essential themes.

The role and thought-processes of the child become centered on one track, focused on the prejudice of their perception of the past, present, and future as representing selfish, cruel, evil, and terrible actions that justify the child's hostility and refusal to look at, speak to, and share time and activities with the alienated parent. It simply does not matter what the alienated parent says or does – that parent is wrong and horrible, now and in their historical recollections. The child has no willingness for compromise or alternative beliefs or even an attempt at having a pleasant limited experience of any kind with that parent. The degree of unwillingness, of course, can be classified according to the criteria of mild, moderate, or severe PAS.

Given the atmosphere of litigation and the support of the "audience" to reinforce this perception on a daily basis, it is relatively impossible to improve or certainly reverse the adverse reactions without sophisticated intervention of both the PAS expert and the judge. The assistance of a mental health professional is generally ineffective and often may be an enabling factor in the continuation of alienation. The enforcement of judicial orders and threats of custodial reversal and/or removal of the child from the home of the alienator, although it rarely takes place, is the most effective deterrent to the maintenance of the brainwashing. The child's anger begins to interfere with his or her school performance and cause symptoms of emotional disturbance. Physical complaints begin to appear. The assignment of blame, of course, is attributed to the alienated parent. The child is convinced that the alienated parent is "making me sick" and that the parent is responsible for his or her declining grades and any other misfortunes that may occur along the way. The child is truly suffering, but this is masked by his or her energetic internalization of the alienating parent's campaign. The child begins to incorporate new agendas to substantiate what have become his or her beliefs, which originated only as the alienating parent's beliefs. Without the appropriate specialized PAS psychotherapy, the child expectantly will exhibit an emotional disorder and experience impairment in future adult relationships (see Gardner, 1998, 2001, 2003a).

THE GRANDPARENTS

Grandparents, as blood relatives, typically support their child, the alienating parent – whether or not they fully agree with their actions during their marriage as well as during the time of the divorce. However, consider how grandparents feel about and love grandchildren and the kinds of information that is being transmitted by the alienating parent to the grandparents about the targeted parent. One can only imagine that if the grandparent has ambivalence for that parent in the past, they would become very angry. Without question, the intergenerational united front forms, and they join in the campaign of bad mouthing, bashing, and brainwashing against the "other" parent. The influence of grandparents should not be underestimated or minimized. Grandchildren are highly susceptible to the influence of grandparents, who generally unconditionally love them, accept them, and indulge them. Unfortunately, the grandparents often play a role in confirming the past and adding to the justification of the current illustrations of alienation. They also are likely to support false accusations because of their own entanglement in the fictitious reality that soon becomes their subjective reality.

Grandparents as well begin to attribute malignant motives, which may be expressed in forms of paranoia, statements of hostility toward the denigrated parent, or suggestions for revenge. Grandparents, in many cases, offer financial support, particularly because of the litigation cost, to "save" their grandchild from either "the big bad wolf" or "the witch." When grandparents observe the hurt of the alienated child, they become devastatingly concerned about the child's welfare and want to protect that child from the targeted parent. Typically, they cannot remain in a neutral stance or they will lose contact with the PAS inducer, even if that parent is their own son or daughter. That is, when the grandparents are in the company of the promulgating parent, the grandparents must join the chorus. However, when the grandparents are in the presence of the alienated child without the brainwashing parents, it is possible, although not likely, for them to remain uninvolved in any remarks that the child may make regarding the other parent by merely not responding and changing the subject. However, should they offer a defensive statement on behalf of the estranged parent, the child is likely to report the grandparents' disloyalty to the PAS inducer, and repercussions from the alienating parent surely will follow.

Parents of the Alienated Parent

The parents of the victimized parent are likely to be confused about what to do. On the one hand, they do not believe that their child would act in such a way to justify the grandchild's rejection of his or her as the alienated parent. On the other hand, they experience the intensity of feelings that the grandchild expresses in despising that parent. The grandchildren offer numerous scenarios to support their contentions; the grandparents often begin to wonder if, in fact, some basis for the child's complaints and desire to minimize contact with that parent exists. Typically, grandparents will assert contradictory statements based upon their own degree of certainty as to how to act as supportive grandparents. They realize that if they encourage their child, the parent, to withdraw from the battle and "let go," it means that they, too, are highly likely to no longer have contact with their grandchild. On the other hand, if they assist in arming the alienated parent with financial resources and emotional support, they become embittered with no relationship and become further estranged from their grandchild. Often, they will try to speak to the children about the truth and provide support of the rejected parent. They quickly find themselves alienated grandparents; the children begin to depict negative attitudes and feelings toward them as well. Their well-meaning advice to the maligned parent causes them frustration because of the impossibility of the rejected parent implementing any of their suggestions. Grandparents become frustrated, often as a reflection of their own sense of powerlessness and the failure of their adult child in taking effective, corrective action. The alienated grandparents now become included in the process of denigration and deprecation by their grandchildren, which is reinforced by the indoctrinating parent. Grandparents put pressure on the alienated parent to "get their attorney to do something" or to change attorneys to get "a good one."

The parents of the rejected parent express confusion as to what to do and what advice to offer their suffering adult child who has been rejected and estranged by his or her children. They want to believe that their child has been a good parent and done all the right things in raising and loving their grandchildren so that they can provide support and financial resources to their adult child. On the other hand, they are likely to have doubts in their own minds when they observe the grandchildren and see the intensity of their emotions and listen to their scenarios of the cruelty espoused by the rejected parent. These children often portray a very convincing drama. The grandparents may find it difficult to question that the child may be fabricating and/or misrepresenting the story. In their own inquiry to the now rejected parent, they convey subtle reference to blaming of that parent for why the children despise them to the extent that they do. They also may ask "How could you?" after hearing the children's account of the variety of occurrences.

Parents of the estranged parent feel helpless and confused in that they can do little to support their adult child. Should they try to challenge their grandchildren's negative statements, they, too, will be rejected and the children will no longer want to see them. If they support or do not defend the targeted parent, then the alienated parent will feel a sense of betrayal and lack of support by one's own parents. In some instances, these grandparents have aligned themselves with the PAS inducer in order to sustain contact with their grandchildren. They realize that if they support the rejected parent or even remain neutral to their own adult child, then they will lose their relationship with their grandchildren. The alienated child is not naive and sees that the rejected parent's parents, their grandparents, are now siding against the alienating parent. The children react and become even more convinced of the validity of their feelings and thoughts. On the other hand, if the grandparents offer a pledge of allegiance to the other side and demonstrate to their grandchild that the brainwasher is indeed correct and their own adult child is wrong and worthy of their rejection and hatred, then the PAS inducer will encourage the children to bond with the in-law grandparents. One can understand why the denigrated parent may experience feelings of devastation and further depression and loneliness as a result of the potential or actual rejection by his or her own parents.

THE FRIENDS

The friends of the alienated parent begin to dissipate. Many question if some of the accusations are not true, because why else would the other parent go to such lengths to prove their point, especially when they see a child acting-out in such an extremely hostile manner? Friends accept that some of these accusations must be truthful. We are all aware and admit that we never really know what goes on behind closed doors. As the private becomes public record during a divorce, what is reported has a way of reifying its existence as if it really did occur and the "facts," in fact, become facts. Also, friends do not like to choose or to be on the side of the loser, the person accused of such terrible misdeeds and maltreatment of their children. Friends clearly say that they do not want to become involved or choose sides, they do not want to become court witnesses, and they begin to doubt the sincerity and integrity of their onetime friend, the alienated parent.

Generally, the public is not familiar with PAS and, therefore, its widespread existence has not been accepted or even understood. During divorce litigation, the public only has become accustomed to traditional mudslinging between the parties, not the well-planned and executed indoctrination of the child followed by the child's own campaign against the target parent. Unfortunately, friends of the alienating parent join forces in the mission as they hear how terrible the other parent is and witness the child's hatred and avoidance of contact with the targeted parent. They become sympathetic to the alienating parent and want to help the child victim who they see as angry, pained, and suffering. These friends join the club and find that power in the number of sympathetic supporters. Thus, the alienated parent's circle of support becomes smaller as his or her friends tire of the process and become suspicious of what is "really happening." The number of people against the alienated parent increases, as school personnel, the parents of friends of the alienated child, and other children and adults as well as acquaintances made through community involvement. No one wants to be on the side of an underdog, especially a parent accused of acting so nasty, inappropriately, and abusively toward his or her own children.

Friends of the PAS inducer may tend to disengage from their friendship because of the emotional turmoil surrounding that household and the acting-out of the alienated child. These friends simply do not wish to get entrenched and dragged into the time-consuming emotional bleeding that takes place. However, a few well-meaning, long-term friends will join with the badmouthing, bashing parent; they feel terrible sympathy for the alienated child having to suffer from such cruel behavior of the other parent. They will do everything they can to help their friend protect the innocent child. Of course, this supportive friendship causes contagion, and they will add to the corruption of reality of the alienated child. Friends simply cannot remain two steps removed. The programming parent generally will have a number of close friends that will become involved on a day-to-day basis in the intricacies of their PAS campaign. Their children may be friends of the alienated child; these children also play a supportive and reinforcing role with the alienated child.

In contrast, it is more difficult for the rejected parent to maintain friendships because of the frustration of these friends in feeling the powerlessness of the alienated parent and not knowing what to do to avoid aiding in the alienated child's hatred. Their children no longer see the children of the alienated parent because of his or her diminished contact or the hostility and tension that arises when his or her children are present. They, too, are likely to question the truth of the child's assertions because this child is so well-rehearsed and convincing in his or her statements and convictions. Most people do not think that a child would lie, intentionally distort, and falsify such accounts toward his or her own parent. These friends, not being family members, have less energy and commitment to sustain their friendship over the course of time as the PAS battle continues. Also, the rejected parent is injured and no longer able to be a friend to them, to participate in activities, and show interest in their lives because of their full-time preoccupation with the injustice that is being done to them. The alienated parent once again feels further rejection as he or she slowly loses his or her cherished relationships and sources of emotional and social support.

CUSTODY EVALUATORS AND MENTAL HEALTH EXPERTS

Most mental health professionals have heard of the term *PAS* but confuse it with "parental alienation" and simply do not understand the symptoms, criteria, and scope of PAS as a form of child abuse (see Gardner, 2002). Psychotherapists are reluctant to admit limited grasp of this concept as a reflection of their professional egos and competence to complete the task to which they are professionally involved. Custody evaluators and mental health professionals feel an obligation to address the accusations when confronted with a complaint about the other parent and listen to the alienated child's resistance towards continuing the relationship with the alienated parent. The common response to the identification of this phenomenon is the example of requesting that the alienating parent stop making disparaging statements in front of the child, and asking that they encourage the child to make an effort to spend time with and give the alienated parent another opportunity to be a "good parent." They almost always recommend that the alienated parent take a parenting course to learn how to better or more effectively parent. Unless the custody evaluator or mental health professional goes beyond this rudimentary role, the alienation process will continue. Custody evaluators and mental health professional counselors generally do not wish to make this concern an issue for fear that they may become dragged into the litigation process. Each attorney respectively will challenge them unless they support the parent's position for whom they represent. Advocacy for one parent will lead the opposing counsel to attempt to discredit them professionally, disregard their evaluation, or present their treatment as inadequate in an effort to remove them from the case.

Mental health professionals often are considered tender-minded, softhearted, handholding professionals whose responsibility it is to offer comfort and nurturance to those children and adults in pain and in need. They are not considered gladiators (as attorneys often are portrayed). Therapists are not prepared and willing to be taken out of the comfort zone of their secure private treatment office and placed in an unfamiliar courtroom environment playing by unfamiliar rules as they become the target of examination. Many mental health professionals would acknowledge their preference to resist a higher fee for deposition and courtroom testimony in favor of the safety afforded in their private offices. Custody evaluators and mental health professionals may assume the role of providing the data that they have collected, offer a report to the court, and carefully avoid determining and asserting their professional opinions. They argue that it is the judge's role to offer an opinion, and that their position is to provide the information as reported by the different sources in their information-gathering process. However, making a PAS diagnosis and recommendation to the court is the professional responsibility as a result of the collection, analysis and synthesis of the data; or, it may be that the results indicate that the data are insufficient to support a finding of PAS because of its inherent complexity. This can be a legitimate finding commanding further evaluation. It is the formulation of the opinion based upon the evidence that will be essential to assist the judge in conducting his or her inquiry and his or her ultimate decision.

Custody evaluators vary in terms of credentials, training, and experience – whether they are employed by the county or state governments, agencies, or in general clinical or child-related independent practice. Many custody evaluators still remain misinformed and lack a depth of understanding and knowledge about PAS. These professionals have a layman's appreciation that divorced parents will say unkind or nasty words about the other parent and deliberately denigrate them either directly or indirectly in front of their children or within hearing distance of their children when they speak to friends when visiting or talking on the telephone.

The custody evaluation certainly takes into account which parent is more likely to support access to the other parent and shared decision-making and children's activities. However, custody evaluators' role is historical description and current assessment in a broad sense. They may suggest a diagnosis of PAS, but mental health professionals often are reluctant to indicate substantiated child abuse by documenting the criteria of a PAS diagnosis that has been met by analysis of the child and parent's behavior in this regard.

Without PAS expertise, it may be difficult or too time-consuming to determine this diagnosis and focus, which distracts from the case overview. Children's accounting may be too subjective, distorted, and confusing for them to make a differential diagnosis. Fortunately, as the contributions of Dr. Richard Gardner and his academicians and clinical practitioners become part of the general literature and lingo of mental health and legal professionals, the court system and its custody evaluators will routinely indicate or address the presence or absence of PAS accusations in each of their reports. For example, it is a routine function for a mental health professional in examining a patient to inquire about and report in his or her findings specific data regarding substance abuse. Hopefully, custody evaluators will similarly include reference to PAS as a standard part of their process of investigation and the statutes will itemize this variable, as they do with other parental considerations of cooperation in their checklist for judicial decisions and court orders.

Some custody evaluators perceive their role as descriptive and others see it as prescriptive; that is, legitimately offering recommendations to the judge as to custody and the factors involved. It seems that some judges will not incorporate suggestions of the custody evaluators in formulating their overall opinions and other judges will rely almost exclusively upon the recommendations of the custody evaluator. After all, they have put in excessive hours of data collection and they are trained to make this determination. Most often, judges will read the report and evaluate the custody evaluator's methods and findings. Well-done documentation and a convincing presentation will have significance. PAS-trained or experienced custody evaluators may not hesitate in making strong recommendations to combat the further development of PAS; on the other hand, they are aware of the resistance that they will encounter, particularly from the more powerful side of the PAS inducer and his or her attorney.

The alienated parent will feel great relief that someone finally understands and recognizes what the programmers are doing. They will hope and rely upon the custody evaluator's report. The promulgator will depend upon their legal armor to bash the custody evaluators' remarks and critically attempt to invalidate their findings. One should not be surprised at how many custody evaluators attempt to remain neutral and limit their role to describing their observations, relying on quotations as to what they have learned during their interviews. No one enjoys being attacked during the deposition phase or made to look incompetent in trial. Suggestive comments are more comfortable to offer than conclusive ones. Who wants to claim that the "child is lying" and question the integrity of the "concerned" alienating parent and unfavorable point of view contrary to the large number of supporters of the injured child's presentation? Should they feel that sufficient evidence for a PAS diagnosis exists, the thrust of the report then shifts in distinct favor of one party against the other parent. The preponderance of evidence dominates the report to substantiate PAS while including an overall description and purview of the family. The immediate criticism of opposing counsel is "bias," and then efforts are made toward the exclusion of the custody evaluator as an expert witness. Going with the flow of recommending mothers in their traditional role as the primary residential parent is often presented in custody evaluators' reports. In this way, they can successfully complete their job without having to fear repercussions, such as an attorney attacking them or the family's political-social influence compromising them in the community or jeopardizing their employment position within the county courthouse. Ethics or malpractice complaints are filed to the state board of Professional Regulation. Thus, a PAS expert might need to be retained to either supplement the custody evaluator's findings or to challenge results of the custody evaluator. Additional information may be provided to the custody evaluator to be incorporated into his or her report or the expert might be asked to supply to the court an independent supplemental report and could potentially be called upon for testimony at a hearing.

Obviously, in cases involving PAS – a distinct form of child abuse – the mental health professionals employed on both sides need to have some degree of expertise in understanding the litigious phenomenon of PAS. Their position either may be to argue the support of the presence of PAS or negate the misinformation and false diagnosis of the PAS presented.

It may well be the case that PAS does not exist or certain behaviors should not be attributed to the innocent parent accused of programming. In some cases these factors are difficult to disentangle. An example is a case in which one parent is upset with the other parent's behavior with the children and that parent is likely to offer negative comments and hostile nonverbal expressions against the other. However, this behavior is not done in the format of a campaign. The children may exemplify behavior characteristic of alienation because that parent exhibits poor judgment or places demands on the child or forces them to say or do things that they may not ordinarily wish to do. These children will adversely react to the other parent and align themselves with the favored parent, and hence we have a division of the "good" and "bad" parent in the eyes of the child. The "good" and "bad" may soon turn into the "saint and sinner" or the "wonderful and cruel." In these cases, one must be careful not to jump to conclusions about PAS and realize that the favored parent is the parent with the power of influence, emotional connections, or financial control with the children, which causes the angry attitudes of the child against the other parent. The parent now finds himself or herself in a rather powerless position in which he or she now must exert even more effort to win over and manipulate the children to take his or her side in their power struggle. The more he or she tries to indulge or maneuver the children to prefer or choose him or her as the ideal or favored parent the more he or she only manages to erode the relationship between themselves and their children. In these instances, the family and friends also participate as the chorus and tend to reinforce this drama. The custody evaluator or mental health professional providing counseling obtains child preferences that have been contaminated; their feelings are essentially based upon misleading information.

The PAS expert upon retention must explain to the party and their attorney who financially renumerates the expert that his or her findings may be contrary to their desired position. Thus, it is possible that the expert is retained by one party, but ends up testifying and finally being paid by the opposing party. Clients have trouble understanding this role because they are "purchasing" an attorney to represent them. Whether or not the attorney likes or believes in their position, they are being paid as the hired guns to defend their clients. PAS experts, like any other forensic experts, are hired as independent professionals. The role of the expert, such as the custody evaluator, is to provide a professional opinion based on sufficient scientific evidence or medical certainty. The role of the expert is not to gather biased information to support the client that retains him or her against the other party. It may be tempting for some experts, similar to what is often referred to as the phenomenon of "the treating doctor becoming the advocate for the patient" because of their involved relationship of caring and helping. However, an experienced and well-trained forensic expert will not be easily persuaded by a psychotherapist or the first party that provides him or her the emotionally charged information. He or she will be able to remain objective as the cast of characters input data into his or her final analysis, which is substantiated by a variety of sources and procedures, to present the truth within the degree of certainty that may be expected of them in their testimony to the court system.

It is important to note that some forensic experts take on cases involving PAS because of their forensic background. However, a number of forensic experts lack sufficient training and knowledge in child psychology and child development, family dynamics, and family systems theory. Thus, the best qualified PAS expert is a well-trained specialist in child and family mental health or a family psychologist who has acquired in graduate school or through postgraduate training expertise in the field of forensic examinations, forensic psychology, or forensic psychiatry. Child therapists often do a poor job in the evaluation of PAS cases if lacking sophistication of the forensic techniques and skills needed. When entering a foreign territory such as the legal system and the litigation process, traditional mental health education and practice offers no preparation for performance in this specialized area. When one plays chess, he or she needs to clearly understand the specific rules or the game abruptly ends in checkmate. The legal system has its well-formulated laws and procedures for operating; it is risky for an unfamiliar practitioner to assume they can apply their clinical confidence in the courtroom. A forensic consultant or supervisor would be most helpful to the mental health professional to better understand, identify, describe, and recommend appropriate steps and interventions to help the subtle and direct forces that are operating in this often unpredictable and turbulent system of justice.

REFERENCES

Association of Family and Conciliation Courts Task Force on Parenting Coordination (2002). Parenting Coordination: Implementation issues. Available at http://www.afccnet.org/catalog/.

Boyan, S.M. & Termini, A.M. (2005). *The psychotherapist as parent coordinator in high conflict divorce.* New York: Haworth Press.

Gardner, R. A. (1998). *The Parental Alienation Syndrome* (2nd ed.). Cresskill, NJ: Creative Therapeutics, Inc.

Gardner, R. A. (2001). *Therapeutic interventions for children with Parental Alienation Syndrome.* Cresskill, NJ: Creative Therapeutics, Inc.

Gardner, R. A. (2002a). Misinformation vs. facts about the contribution of Richard A. Gardner, M.D. T*he American Journal of Family Therapy, 30*(5), 395–416.

Gardner, R. A. (2002). Parental Alienation Syndrome vs. Parental Alienation: Which diagnosis should be used in child custody litigation? *The American Journal of Family Therapy, 30*(2), 101–123.

Gardner, R. A. (2003a). Does DSM-IV have the equivalence for the Parental Alienation Syndrome (PAS) diagnosis? *The American Journal of Family Therapy, 30*(1), 1–21.

Sauber, S.R., L'Abate, L. Weeks, E.R. and Buchanan, W.L. (1993). *The dictionary of family psychology and family therapy* (2nd ed.). Newbury Park, CA: Sage Publications.

Warshak, R. A. (2001). *Divorce poison.* NY: Harper Collins Publishers Inc.

Chapter 3

THE PARENTAL ALIENATION SYNDROME AND THE CORRUPTIVE POWER OF ANGER

RICHARD A. GARDNER

Heaven has no rage, like love to hatred turned.
Nor hell a fury, like a woman scorn'd.
William Congreve

Heaven has no rage, like love to hatred turned.
Nor hell a fury, like a man scorn'd.
R. Gardner modification

I have found the missing link between the higher ape and civilized man: It is we.
Konrad Lorenz

The opposite of love is not hate, but indifference.
Source unknown

Love and hate are two sides of the same coin.
Source unknown

OVERVIEW

PAS indoctrinators are very angry people, and PAS children are either mildly angry, moderately angry, or severely angry – depending upon their level of symptomatology. Alienated parents, by virtue of the fact that they are being scapegoated by their former spouse and alienated children, are also angry – but they are usually fearful of expressing it, lest they invoke even more rage from their persecutors. The purpose of this article is to delineate specifically the way in which anger plays a role in the etiology, symptom development, and treatment of the PAS family.

DEFINITION OF TERMS

Anger

An emotion resulting from injury, mistreatment, opposition, etc., usually associated with a desire to fight back at the supposed cause of this feeling. It is usually associated with the injection of Adrenaline to the bloodstream. The supposed cause may be real or imagined. Anger has survival value. It enhances the individual's capacity to remove those forces that have provoked the anger. Individuals who suppress or repress too much of the anger response are likely to be exploited. In contrast, those who too freely express it may find themselves severely punished by outside authorities (e.g., social isolation, incarceration, and even execution). Accordingly, all individuals must find some middle road, some balance between inappropriate expression and inappropriate and even dangerous free expression. The proper use of anger, especially anger directed toward removal of the noxious stimuli, is normal and healthy.

Rage

Rage is high intensity of anger that may be associated with irrational acts that are in the nonpsychotic ("neurotic") range. The individual usually has insight into the fact that the behavior was irrational and may subsequently experience embarrassment over the fury, an even higher level of anger associated with psychotic behavior. The individual may have no insight into the degree of irrationality and may deny the unjustifiability of the behavior. Anger, rage, and fury are on a continuum.

Romantic Love

This is a psychological state in which the individual experiences euphoric feelings about and strong sexual desires for another individual, who is viewed as somehow being different from everyone else in the world of that gender. It is associated with massive denials of obvious deficiencies that the individual may possess and significant drawbacks and problems that may result if the relationship is continued. It is usually associated with the injection of sexual hormones into the bloodstream, which simultaneously create in the individuals strong desires for sexual encounters. Although these hormones appear to be operating mainly on the genitals, they also operate simultaneously on the frontal lobes of the brain, thereby impairing good judgment.

Romantic love satisfies all the hallmarks of a transient psychopathological state, even though it is not in the DSM-IV. It is well-viewed as "nature's trick" that serves to fulfill God's dictum to Adam and Eve: "Be fruitful, and multiply, and fill the earth." The problem with the romantic love phenomenon is that it is usually of short duration because the body cannot continually keep pumping sexual hormones into the bloodstream. Accordingly, the denial mechanisms are also reduced, and when the individuals return to reality, they may regret what has occurred to them. (In a small percentage of cases, the individuals do go on to form a more stable relationship with occasional hormonal injections and romantic feelings, but this is probably enjoyed by only a small percentage of the population.)

Shame

Shame is a feeling of low self-worth that an individual experiences after significant others have learned that the individual has entertained thoughts, experienced feelings, or perpetrated acts that the individual and observers all agree are reprehensible, unacceptable, and criticizable. Shame is an interpersonal process in which the individual is actually observed to be perpetrating unacceptable acts or envisions their observation. It is a powerful deterrent for getting people to behave "properly" and is especially focused on in Eastern societies, e.g., Japan and China. It is necessary for the survival of a civilized society. Without shame, anarchy and chaos would likely result.

Guilt

In guilt the individual experiences a feeling of low self-worth after having entertained thoughts, experienced emotions, and/or perpetrated acts that he or she has learned in childhood are reprehensible, bad, and "wrong." The rules that have been broken have become internalized so that the individual ends up criticizing himself or herself. This is in contrast to shame, by which self-esteem is lowered in association with the criticism of others (real or fantasized). Similar to shame, guilt is necessary for the survival of a civilized society. The Judeo-Christian ethic relies heavily on guilt evocation as a method for discouraging individuals from exhibiting unacceptable behavior.

ANGER AND THE PAS ALIENATOR

Mothers as Alienators

The Fury of the Scorned Woman

Although Congreve may not have defined fury as I did (with the indication of psychotic mechanisms being operative), he certainly chose to use the word rather than some milder form on the anger continuum. Here I will focus on the fury of the scorned women; in the section below, I will focus on the fury of the scorned man. Mr. Congreve well-recognized the formidable anger resulting from a rejection by someone with whom one is in love. The anger so engendered is likely to result in irrational behavior. The PAS is one vehicle for the expression of such anger. Its purpose is to rob the rejecting spouse of his or her most treasured possessions: the children. The campaign of denigration may help the alienating parent gain leverage in court and is used in the service of attaining the goal of removing the children entirely from the hated ex-spouse. In order to gain the vengeful gratifications of this pathological maneuver, the alienating woman must blind herself to the fact that she is depriving the children of the only biological father they will ever have, a father who is more likely to be devoted to their care than any other person on Earth. This is the central element in the irrationality of this pathological use of the anger response. Because PAS-inducing mothers are usually living separately from their husbands and cannot retaliate directly against them, they may use the children to wreak their vengeance.

One of the reasons why such brainwashing is less common in fathers is that they, more often than mothers, have the opportunity to find new partners. Less frustrated, they are less angry and less in need of wreaking vengeance. If the ex-husband has become involved with a new woman friend – either before or soon after the separation – the rage so engendered in the rejected woman may be even greater. This is especially the case if the abandoned woman has not been provided or perceived as having been provided with the compensatory gratifications attendant to a new involvement herself.

Turkat (1994, 1995) considers the malice element in PAS to be so paramount that he has used the term *malicious mother syndrome* to describe indoctrinating mothers. Such a mother tends to team up with a similarly malicious partner; they then join forces to cause grief to the targeted parent. Turkat emphasizes that the punishment-for-abandonment factor is a central issue in bringing about this syndrome. These mothers are always on the attack with an array of tactics, including relentless litigation. Programming the children against the father, and thereby getting the children to join forces with her against him, is yet another weapon. Lying and deception are also routine.

The rage that fuels PAS will generally exhibit itself elsewhere, so formidable is it. It is almost as if PAS is not enough to drain out the fury. One mother, whose former husband was court-ordered to pay for all the mother's household expenses, kept lights on in the house 24 hours a day in most rooms and only put out those in her own and the children's bedrooms when they went to sleep. It was not uncommon for her to simultaneously turn on the heating system and all the window air conditioners. Water bills were astronomical, as she purposely left water running continuously for weeks. The legal system, for reasons that are presented repeatedly throughout this book, predictably serves as a useful tool for enabling such women to vent their rage on their estranged husbands.

It is common for victimized fathers to report that when they first broached the subject of separation to their wives, they received replies such as "If you leave me, you'll never see the children again" or "Let God be my witness, if you leave this marriage, you'll be leaving the children also. I'll never let you see them again." Typically, PAS mothers deny ever having made such a statement, but all their actions lend support to the husband's claim that it was made. It is at that moment that the PAS process has generally begun.

Economic Disparity

The indoctrinating mother's fury may be fueled by the economic disparity between the two spouses following the separation. With rare exception, divorce causes economic privation for both spouses. Only the wealthy avoid this consequence of the separation. Also with rare exception, the woman suffers more economic privation than the man. These frustrations and the attendant anger may fuel PAS. Furthermore, the woman may be less capable of affording more competent lawyers and may therefore find herself in a more vulnerable position in the courtroom. As a result of this legal disadvantage, she may resort to programming the children against the father as a way of prevailing in the courtroom. Moreover, the inevitable frustrations that most litigating parents suffer in their experiences with their lawyers may generate even more anger. In such cases, the anger cannot be directed at its source, the mother's own lawyer, because of her obvious dependence on him or her. It then becomes displaced onto the husband, the alleged source of her grief in the first place, and enhances thereby the PAS maneuvers designed to deprive him of his children.

Power

Anger release provides an individual with a sense of power. When expressing anger, and especially when venting rage, adrenaline is being pumped into the bloodstream. Under such circumstances one can fight harder and more effectively. Women traditionally have been relatively at a societal disadvantage when compared to men, and it has only been in the past hundred years or so that they have begun to achieve a certain amount of egalitarianism in this realm. Yet, the facts are that women rarely have more money than their ex-husbands and are less likely to engage the services of more powerful counsel. Inducing PAS in a child is a way of putting power into one's own hands. It is a way of influencing the legal system, which is still viewed by most women as male-dominated and male-biased. The fantasy of many mothers who induce PAS in their children is that the court will interview their children directly, put the children on the witness stand, or, at worst, learn of the children's professions of hatred through the lawyers and mental health evaluators. The PAS children, then, provide them with some kind of compensatory power in a situation in which they feel powerless.

Inducing PAS in children is very simple to do, considering their cognitive immaturity and suggestibility. Court delays and the predictability of nonaction by the courts increase the likelihood of a lack of untoward consequences to the parent for making use of this powerful weapon. Relevant here is the wisdom attributed to Lord Acton: "Power corrupts, and absolute power corrupts absolutely." Parents inducing PAS are corrupt. They have to be corrupt because they corrupt their children. Moral and ethical parents do not corrupt their children by the induction of PAS. Courts, by their delays and ultimate inaction, corrupt PAS-indoctrinating parents and contribute thereby to the corruption of their children.

In the history of civilized society, corruption of children has generally been considered to be one of the most heinous crimes. The Draconian punishment we mete out to pedophiles is an example of this in our society today. Murderers have a better chance of getting out on parole than pedophiles. After release from prison, murderers are not required to notify the community in which they live of the nature of the crime(s) for which they have been convicted. Under Megan's Law, pedophiles must do just that. It is relevant that Socrates' crime was not so much that he said things that irritated people, but that his teachings, according to the ancient Greeks, corrupted youth. This was the crime for which he was convicted, and this was the crime that led him to drink hemlock – executing himself rather than providing his accusers with that gratification. When a sex-abuse element is spun off a basic foundation of PAS, the PAS-inducing parent has even greater power. Then she will have at her disposal a multimillion-dollar industry that will be quick to take action and destroy her despised ex-spouse's life, sometimes within a few hours.

Many women, I am certain, would love to murder the husbands who abandoned them. But they refrain from doing so from the awareness of the social consequences. Now, the legal process and the sex-abuse industry enable them to accomplish just this goal without suffering any repercussions at all. In fact, in certain quarters she would be considered a heroine. Murdering someone generally only takes a few seconds or a few minutes and might not be as gratifying to the murderer as someone who brings about the slow death of one's victim. Inducing PAS in children, alienating them from their father – one of the two most important people in their lives – can bring about a slow death to a loving father. When the false sex-abuse accusation is added, he may die in prison. If most had a choice between the quick death and the slow death for their hated victims, they would probably choose the slow death. In a sense, then, inducing PAS in a man's children is better than murdering him. It provides more power than murder with no consequences (at least to the indoctrinator).

Clawar and Rivlin (1991) consider the child-custody dispute to be a forum in which a woman can prevail over a man in a conflict in which she has some chance of winning. This is in contrast to her sense of unfairness in most other areas in life, especially career, financial earnings, social status, and physical strength. This is her domain: the home and the children. This is the battlefield on which she is comfortable, and her stronger bonding with the children increases the likelihood that she can engage their services as her allies. The children, then, are used as pawns in this power struggle, which is what the custody dispute degenerates into.

Reaction Formation

"Heaven hath no rage like love to hatred turned." Congreve's statement here is related to the psychological mechanism of reaction formation. Basically, reaction formation is a mechanism by which an individual professes just the opposite of what are one's real, deep-seated, true beliefs. A good example of this is to be seen in courts of law when a lawyer introduces a comment to the judge with the words: "With all due respect, Your Honor. . . ." The proceedings may have gone on for weeks without the use of this introductory clause. At the moment when it is used, it is likely that the lawyer is very angry, and his "blood may be boiling." One would think that this would be the most unlikely point in the proceedings when such a statement would be made. It is clearly a cover-up for the disrespect and even revulsion that the lawyer may feel toward the judge at that point. Another common example of reaction formation would be the person who says: "The last thing in the world I would want to do would be. . . ." If one gives serious thought to this comment, one may find out that the act is something that the individual might very well want to do, so much so that it might be considered the "first thing in the world" that the individual would like to do.

The mechanism of reaction formation is very much applicable to an understanding of the psychodynamics of PAS-inducing parents. As mentioned, the opposite of love is not hate but indifference. Love and hate are better viewed as opposite sides of the same coin. One boy breaks up with his girlfriend and has no subsequent thoughts about her and goes his way. Another boy breaks up with his girlfriend and writes her a 30-page letter detailing all the reasons why he no longer wants to date her. The girl in the first situation has far less hope for rapprochement than the girl in the second. At some level, the latter may appreciate that the letter writer is still "hooked" and "hanging in there" and therefore is a better candidate for reconciliation. Just as romantic, loving feelings can serve to suppress anger – and this can be especially useful during the courting period, when it may be necessary to call into play denial mechanisms if one is to overcome the tensions and anxieties attendant to getting married – angry feelings at the time of divorce can be used to suppress residual loving feelings. Moreover, the exaggerated angry feelings energize the steps necessary to bring about the severance of the relationship (Gardner, 1991b).

As a psychiatrist, I have access to information about people that is not readily available to others (including lawyers). My experience has been that about 10 percent of people who are involved in vicious divorce and custody litigation still occasionally have sexual relations. They might not reveal this to their attorneys because of the potential compromise of their legal position, and they might not even reveal this to their friends, because of embarrassment. I do not believe that my sample is atypical and, when one considers the reaction-formation factor, such manifestations of residual affection are not surprising. With these people it is almost as if they are saying, "Well, now that we've gotten the orgasms out of the way, let's get back to the battlefield." Henry Kissinger said it well: "The war between the sexes will never be won. There's too much fraternization with the enemy."

In one case in which I was involved, the mother was a severe PAS inducer 95 percent of the time. She was continually on a campaign of denigration against the father and was programming their two sons against him. The parents were involved in a vicious child-custody dispute in which the father was trying to prove to the court that the mother was inducing moderately severe PAS in the two boys. Periodically, for no known reasons, she would suddenly switch, invite her estranged husband back to the marital home, have him join her and the two boys for dinner, and even go to bed with him. Then, as suddenly as it disappeared, the campaign of denigration reappeared. When I spoke to her about this, she stated, "I only did it to get more money from him. It was pure seduction." I do not believe this was the case. I believe the mother was using the seduction/bribe explanation as a rationalization for the deep affection that she still felt for this man, affection and attraction that she could not allow herself to consciously admit, even during those short-lived periods of rapprochement. We see here also a good example of the phenomenon that is often referred to as the "return of the repressed." Because of guilt and embarrassment, the mother had to repress (i.e., relegate out of conscious awareness) basic loving feelings for her estranged husband. Occasionally, such feelings erupt into conscious awareness. This is what we see in this case.

The aforementioned examples of reaction formation refer to the mother's feelings about her husband and the need to use anger as a mechanism to cover up affection. I focus now on the role of the reaction-formation element in the relationship of PAS mothers to their children. It is important for the reader to appreciate that many PAS mothers are far less loving toward their children than their actions would suggest to the naive observer. Ostensibly, all their attempts to protect the children from harm perpetrated by the victimized parent are made in the service of their love for their children. Actually, the truly loving parent appreciates the importance of the noncustodial parent in the lives of the children and, with the exception of the genuinely abusing parent, facilitates meaningful contact between the children and the estranged spouse. The campaigns of denigration that PAS mothers embark upon are not in the children's best interests and are per se manifestations of parental deficiency. The PAS mothers' obsessive love of their children is often a cover-up for their underlying hostility. It is an example of reaction formation. People who need to prove to themselves continuously that they love are often fighting underlying feelings of hate. On a few occasions, I have observed dramatic examples of this in my custody evaluations. In the midst of what could only be considered to be violent custodial conflicts – in which both parties were swept up in all-consuming anger – the mother would suddenly state that she was giving up the custody conflict and handing the child over to the father.

In short, we see another motivation for the obsessive affection that PAS mothers exhibit toward their children, namely, the need to suppress and repress continually their unacceptable, unconscious impulses to reject, abandon, and otherwise harm their children. This is consistent with my view that inducing PAS in a child is a form of emotional abuse. When PAS mothers "win" in the courtroom they not only win custody, but they win total alienation of their children from the hated spouse. The victory here results in psychological destruction of the children that, I believe, is what

PAS-inducing mothers may basically want anyway, their professions of undying love notwithstanding. Perhaps some of them are dimly aware, at some level, that their unrelenting litigation, indoctrination, and alienation will be destructive to their children.

Pathological Maintenance of the Marital Bond

Inducing PAS in a child will predictably keep a relationship going between the PAS-inducing parent and the estranged spouse. One might think that two people who divorce would want to remove themselves entirely from each other and do everything possible to cut their ties. It would be nice if this were indeed the case. Many separated people, although ostensibly working toward the goal of divorce, are actually doing the opposite. Hostile interaction is contact nonetheless and the induction of PAS in children will predictably bring about more hostile interaction. It may be the "glue" that keeps the relationship together, professions of the desire to remove themselves from each other notwithstanding. We see operative here, once again, the principles that "the opposite of love is not hate, but indifference" and "Love and hate are two sides of the same coin." Litigation can predictably strengthen this morbid attraction. If people see themselves as only having a choice between abandonment (with its attendant loneliness) and hostile interaction (with its attendant grief), most often they choose hostile interaction. For such people, loving and benevolent interaction may not be in their scheme of things or not something they can reasonably hope for. Their position is that it is better to be fighting with someone than to be totally isolated. At least fighting fills the vacuum. They may not feel they are worthy of any other kind of involvement. This, of course, is a central element in masochism (Thompson, 1959). Inducing PAS is a predictable way in which a malevolent relationship can be maintained with a former spouse. Such a programming parent appears to be operating on the principle that it is better to be hated than to be ignored. Again, this is related to the old wisdom that the opposite of love is not hate, but indifference.

Furthermore, if any mechanism was ever devised that will predictably ensure the perpetuation of hostile interaction, it is our legal system. If any acrimony existed at the outset of the child-custody dispute (the usual situation), it is likely to be multiplied many times over in the course of such litigation, especially when it is protracted (again, the usual situation). With lawyers who are ethically bound to zealously support their client's position, it is even more likely that the parent who craves such pathological involvement will find satisfaction here. Under these circumstances, nothing ever gets solved, agreements are ignored, the courts do nothing, and the victimization of the estranged parent goes on and on, seemingly forever. Matters never get settled, and the children ultimately become too old to be under the jurisdiction of a court. Again, we see the principle that time is on the side of the alienating parent.

Diversionary Maneuver

PAS can serve as a diversionary maneuver, a "smoke screen." This is especially seen in situations in which the behavior of the alienating parent has been the primary cause of the marital problems that ultimately resulted in the separation. At the time that the decision is made, even though the parents may try to hide from the children the reasons for the separation, they are likely to learn about them anyway. This is especially the case if they have been exposed to ongoing hostilities, screaming, and shouting matches. At this point, the children, with some justification, are likely to blame the parent whose reprehensible behavior was primarily responsible for the separation and ultimately the divorce.

One way of redirecting the children's attention away from these issues is to create in the children a campaign of denigration against the other spouse. A mother, for example, whose affair resulted in the breakup of the marriage may not only deny this to the children – obviously evidence of it notwithstanding – but will then engender in the children a program of denigration that distracts them from any anger being directed at her. The anger is then displaced onto the father and she is "free and clear." In this way, the children's rage is vented on the father, adding significantly to the grief he has suffered over his wife's affair. Generally, such a mother will program the children to believe that the father is a liar whenever he brings up the subject of the mother's infidelity. We see here how the reflexive support of the alienating parent serves to strengthen this diversionary maneuver.

Overprotection

Significant overlap exists between maternal overprotection and the development of PAS. Although the two phenomena can certainly exist independently, there is no question that mothers who are overprotective during the course of the marriage may incorporate the same mechanisms into the programming of their children in the course of producing PAS. Most often, it serves as a foundation for superimposed PAS indoctrinations. It is almost as if the overprotection has served to give the mother "practice" for the next step of PAS indoctrinations.

The overprotective mother is essentially communicating to her child the following message: "The world is a dangerous place and calamity may befall you at any time. Stick ever by my side and I will protect you from these catastrophes. Separate from me and venture forth and you may die at any time, before you even appreciate what has happened to you." It is not my purpose here to discuss in detail the complex psychodynamic patterns that are operative in maternal overprotection and the separation anxiety disorder that often results from it. I have discussed these in greater detail elsewhere (Gardner, 1986, 1998). I will, however, focus here on those psychodynamic factors that relate to anger and PAS.

One factor operative in maternal overprotection is anger. The mother is always anticipating violent catastrophes befalling the child. These images, which go above and beyond reality, relate to her own hostile thoughts and feelings, expressed in primitive fashion and dealt with by the mechanisms of projection and reaction formation. For some readers this statement may warrant some elaboration. One does well to think of memories as similar to a movie with both pictures and soundtrack. The soundtrack is superimposed on the picture. The picture reveals the true intentions of a person, and the soundtrack can serve to confirm, elaborate, deny, excuse, or rationalize what is happening in the picture. The visual imagery represents the real wishes, intentions, or views of the individual. The soundtrack can be consistent with the true wish or serve more complex purposes. For example, friend B tells friend A that he has been having frequent dreams that friend A has been killed, each dream depicting a somewhat different form of violent death. Although friend A may be a little flattered at first, after a series of such dreams friend A cannot but feel a little queasy about friend B's concerns here. Something about them just does not sit well with friend A. Friend A will probably recognize, at some level, that these are basically hostile dreams converted into worries and concerns. He may come to realize the proverbial: "With a friend like this, I don't need enemies." This is basically what the mechanism of reaction formation is all about. Generally, it serves to reduce guilt and anxiety over true recognition of one's basic wishes.

The overprotective mother's excessive concerns about harm befalling her children basically reveal that deep within her there exist wishes that such harm will befall them. I am not claiming that the mother wants the children to be hit by cars, drowned in swimming pools, etc. I am only claiming that she also harbors primitive impulses that are generally exaggerated forms of some hostility. She may basically resent the child-rearing role and feel very guilty over such resentment, believing that good mothers enjoy every moment of it. She cannot allow herself to accept as her own the frustrations and inevitable resentments that are part of the child-rearing process. By converting angry thoughts and wishes into fears, she can feel guiltless. When such mothers act out on their overprotectiveness, they are expressing their hostility without realizing it. The children of overprotective mothers become trapped and suffer significant frustrations and humiliations. They are not permitted to venture forth into streets where their peers are free to play. They cannot swim in depths in which their peers are swimming. They are not permitted to go away to sleepaway camp when their peers are doing so. Under the guise of love, hate is being expressed. This is a good example of the "return-of-the-repressed mechanism." It is hostility that is being repressed here, and it is being expressed in a more comfortable way for the mother, namely, by overprotection.

Scapegoatism

In scapegoatism, the scapegoat is generally believed to be the source of all the problems suffered by those who abuse the scapegoat. The word derives from biblical times when communities selected a goat whom they decided was the cause of all their grief. By driving that goat out of the community (allowing the goat to escape), they believed that they would free themselves from all the suffering that they attributed to the goat. Obviously, this very primitive, magical mechanism for solving a problem did not really work, but the psychological forces operative to attract people to it are powerful.

PAS target parents are generally scapegoated. What may begin narrowly as an attempt to wreak vengeance on a despised husband by depriving him of his most precious possessions, the children, can become expanded into scapegoatism. The victim parent becomes the whipping boy of both the alienating mother and children. All are brought to believe that all the problems they suffer are the result of his depravities. Some of the complaints can easily be linked to the target parent, e.g., the financial privations attendant to the divorce, transfer from private to public schools, moving to a less spacious home, and the general commotion associated with the divorce, especially in cases of litigation. All this grief and suffering is believed to have been started by the target parent and somehow would be reduced by continually flagellating him.

The Mother's New Partner

It is not uncommon for the mother's new partner to quickly join her coterie of enablers and supporters. He may then support, and even actively join in, the mother's maneuvers designed to indoctrinate the children's alienation from their father. Generally, he believes every criticism, every distortion, every lie that the mother tells him, with the result that he can quickly view the former spouse as the incarnation of evil. Under the circumstances, he can easily view himself as the knight in shining armor who has come to protect and even rescue the damsel in distress. They then involve themselves in a cause célèbre, the noble goal of which is to destroy the woman's ex-husband. This common cause may bind them together and may become the "glue" upon which the relationship is maintained and perpetuated. The arrangement, then, can also serve as an outlet for anger generating within the new partner, anger having other sources that is now released through joining in with the mother in indoctrinating PAS into the children.

The Father's New Partner

One situation that is likely to increase a rejected mother's anger is the father's involvement in a new amorous relationship. I have seen many women who began their campaign to indoctrinate the children into PAS against the father soon after learning about the new relationship. Clearly, these women have residual affection for their former spouses, affection that they do not wish to admit. The rage so engendered in her by the new relationship quickly can fuel a PAS campaign of denigration in the children. We see here a good example of the fusion of love and hate (opposite sides of the same coin), a love that the woman would not admit to others and even not admit to herself. If the new woman has no children of her own, then the PAS indoctrinations may be even more formidable because of the fear that this woman would try to take over her maternal role with the children.

Other Sources of Anger That May Fuel PAS

Significant anger might have antedated the marriage, anger that found release in marital squabbles and conflicts and is now fueling PAS. A wide variety of factors may have been operative in producing such anger, e.g., deprivations in her own childhood, death of a parent, substance abuse or physical illness. Separation and divorce, in themselves, produce significant anger. In addition, if the parents are litigating, especially over custody of their children, the anger generated is likely to be formidable. Inducing PAS in one's children can serve as a predictable vehicle for releasing such rage. One does not simply induce the disorder and then sit back; rather, it requires constant attention and monitoring. Accordingly, the fires need continual fueling if the program of denigration is to prove successful. I have discussed this mechanism elsewhere (Gardner, 1976, 1977, 1982a, 1982b, 1991b).

Fathers As Alienators

Fury of the Scorned Man

Although we do not say, "Hell hath no fury like that of a man scorned," many men who have been spurned by their wives are angry. Although it is probably true that women are more likely to be enraged following a marital abandonment than a man, this still does not preclude men reacting with intense anger when they are rejected. A woman's lot is generally worse than that of a man's following a separation, especially if she has children. The financial disparity is still prevalent, attempts at rectification of this inegalitarianism notwithstanding. Accordingly, the frustrations for women are greater and rage is more likely. However, sources of anger other than financial privation exist, and loss of self-esteem is one of them. A man in such a situation may wish to wreak vengeance upon a woman who has rejected him; taking away her children will predictably be the most effective way of achieving this goal. Accordingly, the vengeance motivation may very well operate in men who program their children against their mothers – in a manner similar to rejected women who program their children to be alienated from their fathers. Just as a woman is likely to be angry if her husband has a new involvement, a man is likely to be angry if his wife has a new involvement, especially if the new involvement antedated and was the cause of the separation.

Economic Disparity

The economic disparity following a separation works differently for men and women with regard to the induction of PAS in their children. Divorced women will generally argue that the divorce makes them more vulnerable economically than the man. In contrast, men will generally argue that the divorce has caused them to suffer more than the woman in the economic realm. Most will agree on one thing: Divorce causes economic deprivation for both parents, with the exception of those who are very wealthy. Courts generally take the position that the woman should remain in the marital home with the children. In this way they have continuity in their lives: same neighborhood, same friends, same school. At that point the father has to assume the added burden of a second domicile. If he wishes to form a relationship with a new woman, whether it is to live with her or get married, he faces additional expenses. If he is to express his anger by withholding money (which he may or may not have), he will be quickly be labeled "a deadbeat dad" by the courts and treated quite punitively. This, too, produces an enormous sense of impotent rage, which might be expressed via PAS indoctrinations. Furthermore, a fringe benefit for inducing PAS indoctrination exists in that situation. Specifically, if the father is successful, he may ultimately convince the court that the children should be living with him. Then, he can justifiably ask for a reduction in his support payments.

Reaction Formation

Just as the mother's residual love of her husband may be dealt with by reaction formation – resulting in hatred as the main manifestation of her affection – the husband may react similarly. This hatred may manifest itself by programming the children against her. Inducing PAS is a way of maintaining a relationship with a hated spouse in that it will predictably result in ongoing involvement of a hostile kind. As is true for the mother, programming PAS in the children may be the "glue" that keeps the relationship going, professions of desire for the divorce notwithstanding. Furthermore, just as the mother's obsessive love of the children may serve as reaction formation to underlying deficiencies in maternal capacity, the father is not immune to these mechanisms as well. In both cases, the reaction-formation element may contribute to the father's need to program PAS in the children. Under the guise of love and affection, the induction of PAS is basically a form of emotional abuse of the children and is not engaged in by truly loving parents.

I have seen many fathers who were uninvolved with their families prior to the separation. Some were workaholics and were minimally involved with their families. Then, at the time of the separation, a dramatic transformation of their personalities occurs. Suddenly, they become "fathers of the year"! The children and the mother all recognize this. Astute evaluators, as well, appreciate this phenomenon and are not going to give great weight to it. The campaign proving to the world that they are "super fathers" serves to compensate for the feelings of paternal inadequacy from which they basically suffer. It may also serve to assuage the guilt they have over their past neglect of their children. Inducing PAS in their children, then, can serve these mechanisms by enabling them to convince themselves that they are superior to the mothers with regard to parenting capacity. As is true of PAS-inducing mothers, such fathers do not seem to appreciate that alienating the children from a parent is in no way a manifestation of affection for them.

Power

Few would doubt that men have much more power than women in our society, and this has been the case throughout the history of humanity. Even though women may subtly wield power over men in certain circumscribed situations, there is no question that the balance is tipped in favor of men. Men not only have more power, but serve as a symbol for it. Children especially are likely to view the father as the more powerful figure, their stronger bonding with their mothers notwithstanding. When I attended grade school, unruly children often would be threatened that if they continued misbehaving, their mothers would be called to school. If, however, things really got bad, then their father might be brought in as well. If the school authorities had to resort to calling in one's father, it meant that the situation had indeed deteriorated to a very low level. It was then time for the "big guns" to be rolled in. Heavyweight action then had to be taken, action that involved the father – the symbol of power and strength.

Although not as clear-cut today, I believe the situation still prevails. The father in most cases earns more money, has the power to purchase more material items, has the greater power to decide whether he wants to remarry, and is more likely to employ and/or supervise people than the mother. From a young age, children appreciate this. This may play a role in the children's gravitating toward the father in the parental conflict and contribute to their being willing subjects to his PAS-inducing manipulations. This power is used to release the anger that enables them to wreak vengeance on wives who may have rejected them. The father may be able to win the children over with the lure of his superior financial position. This is especially the case if he has material evidence for his economic superiority. A larger house (especially one with a pool), a better neighborhood, roomier quarters, more toys, a bigger backyard, play equipment, etc., can all contribute to the children's viewing the father's home as a more desirable place to live. Bribing in such situations is common, e.g., "If you come to live at my house, I'll buy you a dog" and "Why do you want to live in a place where you have to share a room with your brother? In my house, you'll have your own room." "Why do you want to live in a house with only one television set? In my house you can have a whole entertainment center."

Pathological Maintenance of the Marital Bond

Father alienators, like mother alienators, may also create PAS in the service of maintaining the marital tie. They do so for the same reason as described for alienating mothers. Because they are living apart, the only contact may be transition times when the children are dropped off and picked up. Exclusionary maneuvers typically create problems around transfer and the anger so generated is likely to result in ongoing altercations. These prolong contacts and provide a morbid opportunity for further involvement. As mentioned for the mothers, these fathers would prefer to be fighting with someone than to be totally isolated and alone. Fighting for them fills the vacuum and, once the legal system is brought in, one can predict with 100 percent certainty that even more anger and fighting will be generated to fill up the emptiness of his life.

Scapegoatism

Alienating fathers may also vent their rage by scapegoating the mother. By viewing her to be the cause of all the grief that he has ever suffered, he finds a simple explanation for his psychological pain. He operates under the fantasy that if he could destroy her entirely, then all would be well in his life. PAS-engendering maneuvers may be particularly attractive in this situation because they involve the father deluding himself into believing that if the mother were to evaporate off the face of the earth, the children would suffer no loss. He therefore marshals their aid in the service of this noble cause.

Diversionary Maneuver

Fathers, too, can also use PAS as a diversionary maneuver to protect themselves from criticism that would otherwise be directed toward them. This is especially true if the criticisms involve behavior that was responsible for the breakup of the marriage. As is true for the mother, an extramarital affair as the cause of the marriage or breakdown is commonly covered up with PAS programming. Basically the father can then say to the children: "It is not I who did anything that brought about the breakup of the marriage; it is your mother who did so because of XYZ behaviors. Again, if he can be successful in creating PAS, he can rely upon the reflexive support of the children to support this smoke screen. I have seen fathers, very powerful individuals, who are persuasive enough to be successful with this maneuver, even though it has been very obvious that their abusive behavior was the primary cause of the separation. The children are so intimidated by this man, and so fearful of confronting him with their knowledge of him as the cause of the separation, that they submit to his programming and ultimately believe his smoke-screen propaganda.

The Father's Involvement with a New Woman

My experience has been that the jealous rage that women exhibit when an estranged husband involves himself with a new woman is far greater than jealous rage that men may experience when their estranged wives become involved with a new man. One factor operative here is the financial one. The father may welcome his former wife's new involvement because the newcomer may have the resources to offset his former wife's financial demands upon him. In addition, if his former wife meets a rich man, he may actually be joyful. A parallel situation generally does not exist for the woman. Actually, the reverse is more often true. If her former husband meets a woman of limited financial means, she may drain the man's resources even more, thereby creating an additional economic threat for the estranged wife. If, however, he marries a rich woman, this is not likely to enhance her financial position in that a court of law is not likely to require him to give more money because of his new wife's wealth. Furthermore, his involvement with such a woman is likely to engender even more jealous rage in his ex-wife. Invoking PAS against the father is one way the rejected woman can vent the jealous rage she feels over the appearance of the father's new woman friend – regardless of whether she is rich, poor, or somewhere in between. This element, more than the economic, is usually the major factor in PAS mothers enhancing their PAS-inducing efforts after the appearance of the new woman.

It has been my experience that a mother's new male involvement is not as likely to play as formidable a role in the development of the children's PAS as a father's involvement with a new woman. A father's new woman friend is more likely to try to win the children over to the father's side, in order to entrench her relationship with the father, than a mother's new man friend will try to lure the children to him. I am not claiming that the mother's new man friend never involves himself in PAS manipulations, only that he is less likely to do so than a father's new woman friend. I believe that this phenomenon is related to the greater vulnerability of women in the marital situation. A father's encouraging the children to join forces with him against his former wife will enhance the likelihood of the new woman's establishing a more solid family in the father's home and increase, thereby, the likelihood of this new arrangement becoming permanent. As described elsewhere (Gardner, 1977, 1991b), stepmothers are more likely to be rivalrous with biological mothers than stepfathers with biological fathers. This rivalry stems, in part, from women's vulnerabilities and insecurities in their relationships with men. In some cases, the new woman's contribution to the PAS begins with her attempts to ingratiate herself with the children when first meeting them. This may be one of the maneuvers designed to attract their father to her. The PAS, then, develops as an outgrowth of this early seductive stratagem. Then, if her new husband has a need to program the children against their mother (for one or more of the variety of reasons described here), she becomes his willing cohort – now in the attempt to strengthen her relationship with him. I am not claiming that all these maneuvers are conscious designs; many are unconscious. In either case, they have the effect of enhancing the likelihood that the children will become alienated from their mother.

A particularly dangerous situation that is likely to result in the development of PAS is when the new woman partner who has never had children herself sees little prospect of having them, considering her age, and views the acquisition of the father's children as a "last chance" to have children and a "regular" family. Such women may then create a PAS situation that did not exist prior to their arrival on the scene. Such women may actively invade the "territory" of the biological mother and go on a campaign, the goal of which is to take over the children from her. In the process of this campaign, she may actually program the father to be her assistant programmer and the biological mother may know that this woman is "pulling the strings."

New partners, almost predictably, become embroiled in the PAS power struggle. Typically, each parent can rely upon the support of the new partner in fueling the PAS conflagration. The mother's new partner may jump into the fray, in macho-like fashion, in order to protect her and enhance her power in the conflict. We see then a male-male rivalry between the mother's new partner and the father. The father's new woman friend is also likely to join forces with him. Here, it is more likely related to female-female jealous rivalry over the man's affections. It is for these considerations that evaluators should interview new partners when conducting a PAS assessment. My experience has been that they invariably provide useful information when trying to understand the causes and development of PAS in a particular case. Examiners who fail to conduct such inquiries with these "third parties" (often the case) compromise their evaluations. This is especially the case when such third parties testify in court. Examiners who have not interviewed these parties are obviously compromised in their ability to make statements about them on the witness stand and provide, hence weaker testimonies.

ANGER AND PAS CHILDREN

Absence of Guilt over Cruelty to and/or Exploitation of the Alienated Parent

The child may exhibit a guiltless disregard for the feelings of the victimized parent. There will be a complete absence of gratitude for gifts, support payments, and other manifestations of the vilified parent's continued involvement and affection. Often PAS children will want to be certain the alienated parent continues to provide support payments, but at the same time adamantly refuse to visit. Commonly they will say that they never want to see the targeted parent again, or not until their late teens or early twenties. To such a child I might say, "So you want your father to continue paying for all your food, clothing, rent, and education – even private high school and college – and yet you still don't want to see him at all, ever again. Is that right?" Such a child might respond, "That's right. He doesn't deserve to see me. He's mean, and paying all that money is a good punishment for him." Many PAS fathers find themselves in this situation. They are asked to make the sacrifices necessary to finance an education, but the mother and children see absolutely nothing reprehensible in making these demands, even though the children will have no contact at all with their father. PAS children exhibit absolutely no guilt over such cruelty and exploitation. This is not surprising when one considers the fact that the alienating parent is supporting completely such psychopathic attitudes and behavior.

Two boys, ages 13 and 15, went to a restaurant with their father. They literally threw their food in his face, and one turned over a bowl of soup on his head. Not surprisingly, the manager asked them to leave the restaurant immediately. As they walked out they mocked him loudly with vile profanities, loud enough for all around to hear. The boys had absolutely no appreciation for the father's mortification. Probably the only person on Earth who would put up with such sadistic treatment is a loving parent, and it is testament to this man's deep affection for his sons that he still "hung in there" after his humiliation in the restaurant, which, not surprisingly, was not an isolated example of their cruelty. These boys also had no shame and no sense of lowered self-worth when they were making public spectacles of themselves to the point where they were asked to leave the restaurant.

In one family session with a PAS family, the father was crying bitterly and begging the children to be sympathetic to him. Soon after he began crying, the older boy began laughing at him, and his younger sister immediately followed suit. The older one said, "There's nothing I like more than to see you cry." The mother sat by and said absolutely nothing. When I asked her what thoughts she had about what had just occurred, she replied, "Doctor, I've said it many times. I want to be left out of it. It's between them and him." Again, the programmer's sanction of the PAS child's psychopathy comes with "neutrality." I have seen many PAS children who consider it a wonderful form of entertainment to scapegoat the victim parent. One child said to me, "It's fun to see him cry." I've seen situations where the children together are laughing, mocking, and denigrating the victim parent in escalating fashion. I was reminded of people who are jeering at an opposing team at a sports event. They prod one another and they all get swept up in the fray.

Probably one of the best examples of the cruelty that PAS inducers can engender in their children is the conscious and deliberate creation of a false sex-abuse accusation in the child. In such situations, victimized parents' lives have literally been destroyed and many have been sent to jail, in some cases for years. The lack of guilt in PAS children is not simply explained by cognitive immaturity (often the case, especially for very young children); rather, it is a statement of the extent to which children can be programmed. Specifically, they can be programmed to such levels of cruelty that they are totally oblivious to the effects of their sadism on innocent victims. Elsewhere, in my discussion of the accusing children in the Salem witch trials (Gardner, 1991a), I have elaborated on this point.

Anger Related to the Separation/Divorce

The development of PAS can serve as a vehicle for the release of anger, which may have a variety of sources. It is as if the PAS involves a "sucking in" of a wide variety of anger-evoking experiences and allows for a sanctioned release of the accumulated rage. If not for the presence of the PAS, such anger might have been suppressed, repressed, or channeled into other modes of release, both healthy and pathological. The PAS, then, rests on a foundation of rumbling resentment that is looking for a safe and acceptable vehicle for release, and the divorce situation involves many frustrations and resentments that can be pulled into and fuel PAS.

Generally, the children view the parent who leaves the home (more often the father than the mother) as an abandoner. No matter how much the departing parent professes to still love the children – and that it is the other parent who is not loved – the children still continue to hold the view that the departing parent is an abandoner. Their basic position is: "If you really loved us you would suffer whatever indignities and pains you are experiencing in your relationship with your spouse in order to stay with us. Because you haven't done this, you obviously don't love us, and you are abandoning us" (Gardner, 1976, 1991b). This expression of resentment can fuel PAS. It is supported by the alienating parent, both overtly and covertly. It is part of a maneuver by which the children become willing weapons in the programming parent's hands, weapons that enable the alienator to discharge his or her hostility through them. PAS children are basically being used as the puppets of the angry alienating parent. To refer to them as pawns is an understatement. A better analogy is that they are attacking queens, bishops, and rooks – so powerful are they as weapons in the parental conflict.

Children may be angry at the father for the financial compromises that are most often attendant to divorce – especially a litigated divorce. When parents are swept up in their divorce and custody-dispute hostilities, they pay less attention to their children, and this produces frustration and anger in them. Not only are the children deprived of attention, but even when they are focused on, the parents have little remaining emotion for their children, so drained have they been by the divorce hostilities. The children may be angry over the presence of new partners in their parents' lives. These strangers are generally viewed as unwelcome intruders. However, the children have no power over their presence and are most often resentful of them. Such resentment is particularly powerful in situations in which an adolescent girl learns that her father has left her mother for another woman. She, especially via identification with her mother, may exhibit the proverbial fury of the woman scorned. A teenage son may react similarly if his mother develops an intimate relationship with a new man friend. Children may be angry over the thwarting of reconciliation preoccupations that, as time goes on, become ever more futile – especially if new partners appear on the scene. Elsewhere (Gardner, 1976, 1978, 1982a, b, 1986, 1991b), I have discussed in detail these and other sources of anger for children of divorce, especially those involved in custody disputes. All of these sources of anger find release very effectively via PAS.

Identification with the Aggressor

The identification-with-the-aggressor phenomenon may be operative in the development of PAS. This phenomenon manifests itself when a person is in a weak or impotent position in relation to a more overpowering, threatening individual. The weaker party may deal with the situation by taking on the characteristics of the stronger person. In this way the impotent individual compensates for the feelings of insecurity and the sense of impotency attendant to being weak and vulnerable. The child whose raging mother is incessantly denigrating his father may join forces with her in an attempt to protect himself from being the target of her enormous hostility. He does this from the fear that if he were to join with his father, he, too, would be the target of such violent outbursts. The mechanism is operative in the old principle, "If you can't beat 'em, join 'em." Also operative here is the "There-but-for-the-grace-of-God-go-I" mechanism. By joining the mother, the child can say to himself or herself, "If I don't join with my mother, I might find myself in my father's position." Also operative here is the mechanism of jumping on the bandwagon of the stronger party in order to share in the joys of victory.

The same process may be operative when a child joins forces with a father against the mother. In situations in which the mother has been the primary caretaker (more often the case), the father's indoctrinations may have to override the child's preference to join the mother's side in the parental conflict. Often the money/power factor is operative here, in that the child may recognize that the father is superior to the mother in financial capacity. These factors may be especially operative when the child switches over and belatedly supports the father in the denigration of the mother.

A paranoid alienator may be so successful in programming the child against the victimized parent that the child will take on the programmer's paranoid delusions. In such cases, the child may exhibit morbid fear at the prospect of the vilified parent's coming to the home – lest the terrible consequences predicted by the alienator be realized. Such children may even hide in closets and under beds when the alienated parent comes to the home, and visitation under such circumstances may be extremely difficult, if not impossible. In this case the bonding with the paranoid parent is unhealthy, and is a situation that should lead the examiner to strongly consider recommending that primary custody be transferred to the victimized parent.

A common situation in which a child will develop a campaign of denigration against the targeted parent is one in which the child has observed a sibling being treated harshly, and even being rejected by the programming parent for expressing affection for the victimized parent. One PAS boy, Fred, repeatedly observed his mother castigating his sister, Wendy, for her expressions of affection for their father. Wendy was older and could better withstand and recognize as absurd the mother's vociferous denigration of her because of her loyalty to her father. Fred, however, was frightened by his mother's outbursts of rage toward Wendy and was adamant in his refusal to see his father, claiming that he hated him, but only giving inconsequential reasons for his hostility. In this way Fred protected himself from his mother's turning her rage toward him. Fred was utilizing the identification-with-the-aggressor mechanism. Fred chose to identify with his mother rather than become the target of her hostility. He could not fight his mother, so he chose to join her. We see here clearly how Fred's rejection of his father was not a response to alienating qualities within his father, but from fear of the loss of his mother's affection.

One girl observed her mother making terrible threats to her older brother: "If you go to court and tell the judge that you want to live with your father, I'll have you put away as a psychotic. I'll have the child authorities put you away. You're crazy if you want to live with him." In this case, the father was an unusually good parent, and the mother suffered with a moderately severe psychiatric disturbance. The older brother was strong enough to overtly express his preference for living with the father and appreciated that the mother had no power to unilaterally and perfunctorily have him committed to a mental hospital. The younger sister, however, believed that such placement was a possibility (if not a high probability), and so told the judge that she wanted to live with her mother. Again it was fear, not love, of the mother that brought about the child's professions of preference for her.

Dave repeatedly observed his father sadistically and mercilessly beating his mother. In order to protect himself from similar maltreatment, Dave professed deep affection for his father and hatred of his mother. The professions of love here stemmed from fear rather than from genuine feelings of affection. Dave was operating on the identification-with-the-aggressor principle. Those who were knowledgeable about the father's brutal treatment of the mother expressed amazement that Dave was obsessed with hatred of his mother and love of his father, and they were unable to understand why he kept pleading for the opportunity to live with his father. Another factor that may be operative in such situations is the child's model of what a loving relationship should be like. Love is viewed as manifesting itself by hostile interaction. The father demonstrates his "affection" for the mother by beating her. In order to be sure of obtaining this "love," the child opts to live with the father, the allegedly "loving" parent. This mechanism, of course, is central to *masochism.*

It is important for the reader to appreciate that PAS is a separate entity from physical, emotional, and sexual abuse. This does not mean that PAS may not coexist with bona fide abuse, abuse that may even affect or become incorporated into PAS. Cancer and pneumonia are two separate diseases, but this does not mean that a person with cancer cannot also get pneumonia. Nor does it mean that the presence of one cannot affect the other. I have already mentioned the incorporation of a false sex-abuse allegation into PAS. They are still separate entities and each can certainly exist without the other. In Dave's case, his father physically abused his mother. If Dave developed animosity toward his father (the expected response), then I would not consider the PAS explanation to be applicable. Genuine abuse warranted the father's rejection as an abuser. In this case, Dave reacted in an entirely unexpected way; namely, he joined with his abusing father against his mother. Primary here was the identification-with-the-aggressor mechanism, which, as mentioned, is one of the factors operative in bringing about PAS. In this case, if any label of emotional abuse was to be utilized, it would be the father's inducing PAS in his son. In general, the parent who is inducing PAS is perpetrating a kind of emotional abuse. However, with PAS the child's anger at the targeted parent is not the result of the vilified parent's abuse of the child, but of the programmer's abuse – the induction of PAS.

Reaction Formation

A common factor that contributes to the PAS child's obsessive hatred of the victimized parent is the utilization of the reaction formation mechanism. Obsessive hatred is often a thin disguise for deep love. This is especially the case when there is absolutely no reason to justify the preoccupation with the despised person's defects. True rejection is neutrality, which includes little, if any, thought of the person. "The opposite of love is not hate, but indifference." Each time these children think about how much they hate their vilified parents, they are still thinking about them. Although the visual imagery may involve hostile fantasies, the targeted parent is still very much on their minds. The love, however, is expressed as hate in order to assuage the guilt and fear they would feel over overt expressions of affection for the denigrated parent, especially in the indoctrinating parent's presence. One child said to me, "I hate him because he loves his girlfriend more than me." This statement indicates that the child is still craving affection from his father, his professions of hatred notwithstanding.

It is normal for teenage girls to have "crushes" on their fathers, especially if he is a young father. Occasional sexual fantasies may even occur. However, in the normal youngster these are transient, weak, and quickly dismissed. They do not create a problem. The same is true for teenage boys with their mothers, especially if they are young and attractive mothers. One way of dealing with this is exaggerated disgust and revulsion via the mechanism of reaction formation. This serves to protect the youngster from emergence of the amorous and even sexual fantasy. This normal phenomenon can piggyback on PAS. In the normal family, the youngster's mother may view such revulsion as normal or one of the idiosyncrasies of adolescent girls and not give it any further thought. A PAS-indoctrinating mother will exploit this phenomenon and entrench it. Although the normal teenage girl, in spite of her alleged revulsion, will still take reasonable opportunities to be with her father (some adolescent separation and individualization notwithstanding), when this revulsion is combined with PAS, total rejection quickly ensues.

A teenage girl in that situation may write her father a lengthy letter (15 to 30 pages is not unusual) delineating all the reasons for which she hates him. She will then describe all the problems in her life as the result of his maltreatment of her. She blames him for all her insecurities, feelings of self-doubt, disappointments, and disillusionments in life. Of course, the fact that she spends all this time writing him provides her with an opportunity for contact. An analogy to this phenomenon is the previously mentioned comparison between two young men who decide to sever an amorous relationship. One writes a two-to-three-page letter and the other writes a 20 to 30-page letter in which he delineates in great detail all the reasons why he has decided to part ways with her. Question: "Which girl has the better chance of reconciliation with the boyfriend?" Answer: The second. Question: Why? Answer: Because the second is still deeply involved with her, far more than the first. Little activity exists in the brain circuitry of the first boy. In contrast, there is an enormous amount of activity in the brain circuitry existing in the second. This will not be obliterated so quickly and it is the main reason why the second relationship may still go forward. Using the important dictum that the *opposite of love is not hate, but indifference, the first boy is close to indifferent.* The second boy is now exhibiting the hatred that is the other side of the love-hate coin.

The adolescent girl, whose "crush" on her father feeds into the PAS, is likely to exhibit further manifestations of the reaction formation phenomenon if her father becomes involved with a new woman, especially a younger woman. Furthermore, it would be a worse situation if he involves himself with a woman who is her age. If he has a series of amorous relationships to which she is exposed, this, too, can intensify her jealous rage that might be exploited by her PAS-indoctrinating mother. The greater the love here, the greater the hatred. I am not claiming that all of this is conscious. The child may be only peripherally aware of the phenomenon of what is happening (subconscious), or it may be unconscious. Those who deny the existence of the unconscious deprive themselves of an important explanation for some (I did not say all) forms of human behavior, both normal and pathological. Such a girl's anger is a good example of the "nor hell a fury like a woman scorned" phenomenon.

Power

When PAS is present, the child is being sanctioned by the programming parent to vent rage against the targeted parent, thereby increasing the likelihood that the child will feel more powerful. Venting rage provides an individual with a sense of power, even though it may be specious power. One is attacking, rather than being attacked. Accordingly, a youngster may spit in the victimized parent's face, curse at him or her vociferously, and know that the alienating parent will provide protection from significant repercussions by the alienated parent. The PAS child is thereby provided with a power over a parent not generally enjoyed by other children in other situations. At the home of the vilified parent the child may arrogantly say, "We don't have to listen to you" or "My mother (father) says you have no authority over me." In such situations the alienated parent's sense of impotence may be increased by the fact that if he or she tries to use any kind of physical coercion whatsoever, this would be reported immediately to child abuse authorities. In such situations the PAS child may repeatedly threaten the targeted parent: "My mommy (daddy) said to me that if you ever touch me I should call 911 immediately." If the PAS child does make the call, no matter how unjustified, the victimized parent is likely to be "hit" with a restraining order, which results in immediate cessation or formidable curtailment of visitation. In some cases a visitation may only be provided under conditions in which it is monitored and/or supervised. Children with PAS (especially the older ones) know this, and this enhances even more their sense of morbid power. The children may have been told that any form of imposition of normal childhood restrictions and disciplinary measures is "abuse" and "harassment," and they may frequently threaten, "We're going to call CPS [Child Protection Services] if you don't stop abusing us. Mommy (Daddy) gave us the number just in case."

The child protection industry, especially the sex abuse division, is ever at hand to impose the most Draconian restrictions on any parent suspected, even remotely, of any kind of abuse. The industry thereby places in the hands of child-abuse accusers – both adult and children – a very powerful weapon. I am not claiming that the industry will automatically and gullibly accept as valid any accusation; I am only claiming that their evaluators are likely to be overzealous and err on the side of seeing abuse when it does not exist. Such is the climate in which we have lived in recent years. I have discussed this elsewhere (Gardner, 1991a, 1995).

Protection of the Alienator

Alienators, when successful, convince the children that it is they who are the victims rather than the target parent. The alienating parent will convince the children that they are indeed in a dangerous situation whenever the target parent is in the vicinity. Sometimes they will huddle together in fear. At other times the children are encouraged to become the protectors of the alienator from the viciousness of the target parent. This role is especially attractive to boys – the traditional hunters, warriors, and protectors – even if they are four or five years old. PAS encourages their taking a macho role, in the context of which they can vent rage at the victim parent without any fears of discipline or punishment. These young "heroes" know that the alienator is encouraging the scapegoatism of the victim parent and the victim parent is afraid to fight back lest the children become even more enraged and rejecting. In the context of the development of this mechanism, the children are taught to believe that the alienator is weak, vulnerable, and needs their protection. Defending the alienator then becomes a cause célèbre and becomes a source of morbid ego enhancement for the PAS child.

PAS and Teen Rebellion

The anger of teen-age rebellion can often get "sucked in" to PAS; the two then complement one another. This element may present differential diagnostic difficulties for the evaluator. One difference is that the antisocial behavior of the rebellious teenager is usually seen in group settings where the youngster involves himself with other rebellious youths. In contrast, with PAS, the anger is focused on the victim parent. Another difference is that rebellious teenagers usually are vile and disrespect, and denigrate both of their parents. In contrast, PAS children confine the rage to the target parent. Rebellious teenagers are likely to be rebellious outside the home and even get into difficulty with external authorities. PAS children, in contrast, although they may spread their animosity to the friends and relatives of the alienated parent, do not go beyond that and usually recognize that it is important to be civilized human beings in society in general. The anger, however, that fuels teens' rebellion is still present, and PAS will often provide a vehicle for release that is sanctioned by one of the parents. From the teenager's point of view, this may be preferable to traditional release, which brings down the hostility of both parents on him or her.

CONCLUDING COMMENTS

The grandmother of PAS children wrote this to me in a letter: "I am the mom of six children and the grandmother of 24 grandchildren. In my whole life I have never seen young people in my family act with such disrespect and cruelty as Bobbie and Anne have been these last few months. They become different children. I hate to use the word, but I often think to myself, 'They've turned into monsters.'" Grandma is describing typical PAS children. They have been programmed to become psychopaths by the alienating parent. They are often viewed as "monsters" by those who observe them, and especially those who are victimized by them. They have no shame or guilt over the grief they visit upon the victim parent and subsequently the extended network of friends and family who also become victims of their rage.

REFERENCES

Clawar, S. S. and Rivlin, B.V. (1991). *Children held hostage: Dealing with programmed and brainwashed children.* Chicago, IL.: American Bar Association.

Gardner, R. A. (1976). *Psychotherapy with children of divorce.* New York: Jason Aronson, Inc.

______ (1977). Children's guilt reactions to parental death: psychodynamics and therapeutic management. *Hiroshima Journal of Psychology,* (4), 45–57.

______ (1978). *The boys and girls book about one-parent families.* New York: G.P. Putnam's Sons.

______ (1982a). *Family evaluation in child custody litigation.* Cresskill, New Jersey: Creative Therapeutics, Inc.

______ (1982b). *The boys and girls book about stepfamilies.* New York: Bantam Books.

______ (1986). *Child custody litigation: A guide for parents and mental health professionals.* Cresskill, New Jersey: Creative Therapeutics, Inc.

______ (1991a). *Sex abuse hysteria: Salem Witch Trials revisited.* Cresskill, New Jersey: Creative Therapeutics, Inc.

______ (1991b). *The parents book about divorce* (2nd ed.) (Hard Cover). Cresskill, New Jersey: Creative Therapeutics, Inc.

______ (1995). *Protocols for the sex abuse evaluation.* Cresskill, New Jersey: Creative Therapeutics, Inc.

______ (1998). *Parental Alienation Syndrome* (2nd ed.). Cresskill, New Jersey: Creative Therapeutics, Inc.

Thompson, C. (1959). The interpersonal approach to the clinical problems of masochism. In *Individual and family dynamics,* ed. J. Masserman. New York: Grune & Stratton.

Turkat, I.D. (1994). Child visitation interference in divorce. *Clinical Psychology Review, 14*(8), 737–742.

______ (1995). Divorce related malicious mother syndrome. *Journal of Family Violence, 10*(3), 253–264.

Chapter 4

DESCRIPTIVE STATISTICS OF THE MILD, MODERATE, AND SEVERE CHARACTERISTICS OF PARENTAL ALIENATION SYNDROME

JANELLE BURRILL

OVERVIEW

This chapter presents descriptive statistics on 30 cases of parental alienation syndrome (PAS), compiled by the author in 2000–2001. The data on the incidence of PAS among Gardner's three group types mild, moderate, and severe summarize the research of 30 court referred custody dispute cases assessing the behaviors of the parents and their children to determine the presence or absence of PAS. The data obtained from the case sample describe the parents using Gardner's parental criteria for PAS: mild, moderate and severe. Data from Gardner's criteria for the children's symptoms for PAS: mild, moderate and severe are reviewed for each case. Nonparametric statistics and demographic data analyze the difference between the children's group as well as the demographic data. The data from this study appear to support Dr. Gardner's observations of PAS. In its severe form, PAS is more distinctive than the mild form. The criteria to determine the parent and their children's behaviors are Gardner's definition of PAS and categories. The parents were placed in one of three categories (mild, moderate, or severe) based on their symptoms and behaviors. Their children (59) were then categorized into three groups (mild, moderate, or severe) depending on their symptoms and behaviors. This study's purpose was to determine additional information regarding PAS, including whether Gardner's PAS could be considered a valid and identifiable syndrome. Reluctance by the courts and mental health community to accept the validity of PAS contributes to the perpetuation of the disruption of parent-child relations in custody disputes. This study addressed only parents and their children involved in custody disputes and only used cases in which physical abuse was not substantiated. The data and observations and definitions of PAS indicate that the parents in the mild PAS category have children who exhibit fewer negative behaviors toward alienated parents, whereas children whose parents are in the severe category exhibit more negative behaviors toward to alienated parents. This study found that the more negative behaviors a child exhibit toward an alienated parent, the more severe their parent's symptoms and behaviors. PAS is a distinctive form of child abuse generally found only in intractable custody disputes. The purpose of this study was to determine whether support for Gardner's criteria for PAS exists. As mentioned, additional behaviors and symptoms manifested by this study's participants (data collected) were defined using the Diagnostic and Statistical Manual of Mental Disorders, Fourth Edition *(APA, 1994), 685–729.*

STATISTICAL ANALYSIS TO SUPPORT PAS

Legal, psychological, and psychiatric communities still "cringe" when PAS is suggested outright or is included in a court report. The psychology community denounces PAS because it is not listed as a valid syndrome. Some psychological researchers and clinicians believe a "syndrome" belongs in the medical community (Sullivan, M., 2000). A syndrome is defined as a grouping of signs and symptoms, based upon their frequent occurrence, which may suggest a common underlying pathogenesis, course, familial pattern, or treatment selection (DSM 4th Edition, 1994). The syndrome identified by Gardner seeks to describe the process of a child aligning with one parent against the other parent in a legal context. This study's purpose was to support PAS, as first presented in 1985, within the legal context of custody and/or divorce. Secondarily, its goal was to determine if a difference between the three groups of children in this study exists.

Thirty court-referred cases involving 59 children were reviewed to determine the "presence" or "absence" of PAS. The present study reviewed the case data to determine if the existence of PAS in custody cases could be verified.

Descriptive statistics were used to answer the question as to the presence or absence of PAS. One-way analysis of variance "ANOVA" was used here. Next, the difference in the demographics including race, gender and, age was examined. Nonparametric statistics were used here. The assumption was that if the data of the children supports Gardner's findings, then Gardner's observations and findings are valid.

Discussion of Data Processing

The thirty court cases (each parent and each child) in this study were categorized based on the PAS *parental* and the PAS *child* behaviors. Each parent and each child was placed in the appropriate category: mild, moderate or severe based on their behaviors and the criteria met. Each parent and each child had data, including gender, age, race, behaviors (and symptoms) collected prior to the study. Each child and each parent was then placed in the appropriate category depending on their symptoms and behaviors.

Descriptive statistics described potential differences in the number of symptoms observed in the children and parents. Demographics from each group were compared. These data were examined using nonparametric one-way statistical analysis. The data were compiled, and then compared and described whether these thirty court-referred, custody cases support the existence of PAS.

Selection of Data

Thirty court referred custody cases were randomly selected for this study. The cases were referred by the court because of continuing conflict between the parents. The cases had been in the court system previously (two or more times) and were referred by the court to this investigator because of intractable conflict between the parents for mediation, investigation or evaluation. All cases are highly contested custody disputes. The cases reviewed were referred from January 1, 1998 and the following twenty-four months.

Description of Research Design

The thirty cases were assigned to either the mild, moderate or severe category based on the PAS criteria of the parents and of their children. Each parent and each child was placed in the appropriate category mild, moderate, or severe, based on their behaviors and the criteria met. The children's data for each group was reviewed using the PAS criteria for mild, moderate, or severe to determine the children's responses. Demographic data were compared in each group.

Once the cases were categorized based upon the parental PAS criteria, each child from each case was then categorized into the children's criteria for mild, moderate, or severe PAS. Each case was examined to determine the level of PAS associated behaviors exhibited by the parents and their children. Then the three groups of children were compared to confirm the existence and severity of PAS within and between the three groups.

Each child's history was reviewed to determine the progression of the children's symptoms. Children whose parents have mild PAS were compared to children whose parents have moderate and severe PAS. The severity of the symptoms of the children in each category was examined to determine whether these research data support the presence or absence of PAS.

Importance of this Research

Little empirical evidence supports the efficacy of methods typically used by professionals in sorting out facts as they relate to PAS. Diagnosis of and acceptance of PAS is very important in the field of custody and divorce. Detection of PAS and an understanding of appropriate remedial interventions to restore the child's relationship with an alienated parent is in the best interest of children. This research may provide support for the concept of PAS. The professionals who now shy away from diagnosing PAS may find greater support for their findings of PAS in the legal and mental health communities.

Methodological Assumptions and Limitations

This study has limitations. More specifically, to assume a small sample (n=30) can be generalized necessitates assumption that the sample is representative of PAS in intractable custody disputes. The cases reviewed are court referred only. Examination of intractable custody dispute cases only creates a restriction of the range of the cases analyzed. Therefore, generalization may be limited.

This study also addressed the degree of alienation on the part of the alienating parent and related it to the degree of negative behaviors expressed by his or her child. Dr. Gardner believed that the amount of alienation experienced by a child is directly related to the amount of hostility expressed by the custodial parent towards the noncustodial parent. The purpose of this study was to determine whether support for PAS exists. A second focus of this study was on the relationship between the findings of this study and the PAS criteria based on the children's symptoms. One might anticipate that a mildly alienated child should come from a mildly alienating parent with mild symptoms. This relationship would be expected to apply to moderate and severe PAS.

The data from the study indicate that parents in the mild PAS category have children who exhibit fewer negative behaviors towards the alienated parent. For example, there were 22 children in the "mild anger" group and they expressed no anger toward the alienated parent. Contrarily, in the "severe anger" group, 18 out of 20 children expressed anger towards the alienated parent, and more of their parents were angry. This is significant. In the moderate group, 10 children expressed anger, and 7 children did not express anger toward the alienated parent.

In addition, one out of 22 children in the mild group refused visitation, whereas 17 out of 20 children in the severe group refused visitation with the alienated parent. The parents in this category also exhibited more negative behaviors. This indicates that the more negative the parent's behaviors, the more disruption to the alienated parent's relationship with the child. These data support the research questions. The data from this study do appear to support PAS, using the parents' PAS criteria and their respective children's PAS criteria to identify the existence, degree, and category of PAS.

The data also support the differences between the three groups of children using the PAS criteria of mild, moderate, and severe symptoms in both the children and the parents. The milder group of children had fewer negative behaviors and a relationship with the alienated parent. However, the severe group of children had more negative behaviors and greater resistance to a parent-child relation with the alienated parent. The more negative symptoms the parents had, the more negative the behaviors of the child.

This study focused on the relationship between the findings of this study and the criteria for PAS based on the children's symptoms. The data indicate that there is a relationship between the alienating parent's behaviors and their child's negative behaviors towards the alienated parent exists. One might anticipate that a mildly alienated child should come from a mildly alienating parent with mild symptoms, a moderately alienated child should come from a moderately alienating parent, and a severely alienated child should come from a severely alienating parent with severe symptoms and negative behaviors.

The differences in the number of negative behaviors towards the alienated parent were compared between the three groups of children. The children's symptoms and behaviors, based upon the PAS children's criteria for mild, moderate or severe symptoms and behaviors, which determined which group each child was placed in. ANOVA was used to compare these three groups.

More specifically, this was used to assess the variance between and within the three groups of the children to determine the number of symptoms in each child in each group, and the presence or absence of PAS. The data found that the more negative behaviors the child expressed, the more likely it was that severe PAS was present. Contrarily, children with fewer negative behaviors were in the mild group. A relationship between the negative behaviors in the parents and the negative behaviors in the child exists.

The data indicate that more children in the mild category than expected had visitation with the alienated parent, and there were fewer children in the severe group than expected did not have visitation with the alienated parent. The data support a significant difference between the mild group and severe group of children.

The difference in the demographics, including race, gender, and age, was compared between the groups of children. The third question was whether demographics impacted PAS. The study found no significant difference between the demographic characteristics of children and their PAS category. Descriptive statistics were used to compare the demographics, which included race, gender and age. There were 30 families and 59 children. No child under age five years was in the severe group.

Visitation with the Alienated Parent

In Table 4.1, chi-square = 28.39 ($df = 2$ $p < .05$). This is significant because the three groups were statistically different with regard to visitation. Therefore, the null hypothesis of no difference between the three groups is rejected. As the degree of severity increased (refusal to visit), the percent of children visiting the alienated parent decreased. More children (21 with an expected count of 13.1) in the mild group had visitation with the alienated parent than in the severe group (3 with an expected count of 11.9). In the moderate group, 11 children with an expected count of 10.1 had visitation with the alienated parent.

TABLE 4.1. Mild PAS vs. Moderate PAS vs. Severe PAS/ *Visitation* with AP[1]

Mild PAS vs. Moderate PAS vs. Severe PAS		Visitation with AP[1]		
		0=No	1=Yes	Total
1 Mild PAS	Count	1.0	21.0	22.0
	Expected count	8.9	13.1	22.0
2 Moderate PAS	Count	6.0	11.0	17.0
	Expected count	6.9	10.1	17.0
3 Severe PAS	Count	17.0	3.0	20.0
	Expected count	8.1	11.9	20.0
Total	Count	24.0	35.0	59.0
	Expected count	24.0	35.0	59.0

[1] AP = alienated parent.

Express Affection with the Alienated Parent

In Table 4.2, chi-square = 6.49 (df = 2 $p < .05$). The three groups were statistically different with regard to expression of affection. The null hypothesis of no difference between the three groups is rejected. As the degree of severity increased, the percent of children-expressing affection to the alienated parent decreased. More children (18 with an expected count of 14.2) in the mild group had expressed affection for the alienated parent than in the severe group (9 with an expected count of 12.9). In the moderate group, 11 children with an expected count of 10.1 had visitation with the alienated parent. The moderate group did not exhibit any statistical differences.

TABLE 4.2. Mild PAS vs. Moderate PAS vs. Severe PAS/*Express Affection* with AP[1]

Mild PAS vs. Moderate PAS vs. Severe PAS		Express Affection with AP[1]		
		0=No	1=Yes	Total
1 Mild PAS	Count	4.0	18.0	22.0
	Expected count	7.8	14.2	22.0
2 Moderate PAS	Count	6.0	11.0	17.0
	Expected count	6.1	10.9	17.0
3 Severe PAS	Count	11.0	9.0	20.0
	Expected count	7.1	12.9	20.0
Total	Count	21.0	38.0	59.0
	Expected count	21.0	38.0	59.0

[1] AP = alienated parent.

Anger at Alienated Parent

In Table 4.3, chi-square = 35.27 (df = 2 $p < .05$). The three groups were statistically different with respect to the level of anger expressed towards the alienated parent. No children in the mild group expressed anger.

TABLE 4.3. Mild PAS vs. Moderate PAS vs. Severe PAS/Anger at AP[1]

Mild PAS vs. Moderate PAS vs. Severe PAS		Anger at AP[1]		
		0=No	1=Yes	Total
1 Mild PAS	Count	22.0	0	22.0
	Expected count	11.6	10.4	22.0
2 Moderate PAS	Count	7.0	10.0	17.0
	Expected count	8.9	8.1	17.0
3 Severe PAS	Count	2.0	18.0	20.0
	Expected count	10.5	9.5	20.0
Total	Count	31.0	28.0	59.0
	Expected count	31.0	28.0	59.0

Chi-square Tests

	Value	df	Asymptotic Significance (2-sided)
Pearson Chi-square	35.268[a]	2	.000
Likelihood ratio	45.601	2	.000
Linear-by-linear association	33.759	1	.000
n of valid cases	59.00		

[1] AP = alienated parent.
[a] 0 cells (.0%) have expected count less than 5. The minimum expected count is 8.07.

However, in the severe group 18 out of 20 children expressed anger at the alienated parent. It is significant that no children in the mild group expressed anger at the alienated parent. Examination of the results reveals no children in the mild group expressed anger whereas more children in the severe group expressed anger. Therefore, the difference in the three groups is between the mild and severe groups. The null hypothesis of no difference between the three groups is rejected. In the moderate group, out of 17 children, 7 were angry with the alienated parent.

Denigration of Alienated Parent

In Table 4.4, chi-square = 20.86 ($df = 2$ $p < .05$). Fewer children in the mild group exhibited behaviors of denigration towards the alienated parent. However, in the severe group, more children than the expected count exhibited symptoms of denigration toward the alienated parent. This is statistically significant. The null hypothesis is rejected. In this case, the three groups were statistically different with regard to denigration. As the degree of severity of negative behaviors increased, the number of children denigrating the alienated parent increased. The moderate group had 10 children who exhibited behaviors of denigration as opposed to the expected 6.3.

TABLE 4.4. Mild PAS vs. Moderate PAS vs. Severe PAS/*Denigration* of AP[1]

Mild PAS vs. Moderate PAS vs. Severe PAS		Denigration of AP[1]		
		0=No	1=Yes	Total
1 Mild PAS	Count	22.0	0	22.0
	Expected count	13.8	8.2	22.0
2 Moderate PAS	Count	7.0	10.0	17.0
	Expected count	10.7	6.3	17.0
3 Severe PAS	Count	8.0	12.0	20.0
	Expected count	12.5	7.5	20.0
Total	Count	37.0	22.0	59.0
	Expected count	37.0	22.0	59.0

Chi-square Tests

	Value	df	Asymptotic Significance (2-sided)
Pearson Chi-square	20.86[a]	2	.000
Likelihood ratio	27.98	2	.000
Linear-by-linear association	16.28	1	.000
n of valid cases	59		

[1] AP = alienated parent.
[a] 0 cells (.0%) have expected count less than 5. The minimum expected count is 6.34.

The Sum of Children's Behaviors

Table 4.5 is the last analysis of the number of behaviors expressing PAS (refusal of visitation, affection, anger, negative feelings, and denigration), which were summed to obtain a total number of symptoms observed for each child. The groups were then compared to determine any differences with regard to the total number of behaviors. To accomplish this, anger and denigration were recoded. Therefore, a 1 = positive or presence of behaviors and a 0 = negative or absence of behaviors, so the sum of all behaviors is a higher value. A negative number is representative of fewer behaviors. One-way analysis of variance was used for this comparison.

TABLE 4.5. Sum of Visitation, Affection, Positive Feelings, Anger, Denigration

	N	Mean	Std. Deviation
1 Mild PAS	22	4.5455	0.7385
2 Moderate PAS	17	2.8235	1.9441
3 Severe PAS	20	1.3000	1.3018
Total	59	2.9492	1.9246

Analysis and evaluation of findings.

In Table 4.5, the children in the mild PAS group expressed fewer negative behaviors than the moderate or severe PAS groups. The mild PAS children expressed more positive behaviors toward the alienated parent or less negative behaviors toward the alienated parent shown by $F = 2.977$ $(2, 56)$, $p < .05$. The more severe the child's behaviors toward the alienated parent, the fewer positive behaviors on the part of the children. The null hypothesis of no difference between the three groups is rejected. In this study, the three groups were statistically different for each category (anger, refusal to visit, denigration, affection, and positive feelings). As the degree of severity increased, so did the child's behavior, and the percent of the children visiting the alienating parent decreased.

Little empirical evidence support the methods typically used by professionals in sorting out facts as they relate to PAS and their cases. Dr. Gardner recognized the symptoms of PAS and categorized them into three groups: mild, moderate, and severe.

This study's research findings appear to support the existence of PAS. A statistical relationship between the "anger" of the parent and its effect upon the child exists. As the alienating parent became more hostile towards the alienated parent, the children exhibited greater alienation toward the alienated parent.

The three groups of children were statistically different regarding the behaviors reviewed. Children in the mild group typically had fewer negative behaviors and more visitations with the alienated parent. Conversely, children in the severe group had more negative behaviors and fewer visitations with the alienated parent. A clear distinction between the mild and severe groups exists. PAS is such a serious disruption of the parent-child relationship that earlier intervention can now be recognized and accepted.

Demographics were not significant as a predictor of the severity of PAS in this study. The children's ages range from two years to 17 years with an average age of 9.6 years (SD = 3.5). The severe PAS group contained 20 children. However it is significant to note that the minimum age in the severe category for children is five years; in the mild and moderate categories, the minimum age drops to two years old. More females were in the moderate (11) and severe (12) categories than males (8). In sum, 83.1 percent Caucasian, 0.2 percent African American and 8.2 percent Asian. No statistically significant differences appeared in this category. The large number of noncontrolled variables in this study makes it impossible to significantly determine whether one culture is more prone to PAS than another culture.

It is significant that very young children "those under age five years" were not found in the severe group. Children under age five years may lack the psychological and emotional maturity to be programmed.

The phenomenon of PAS occurs in the context of a highly conflicted family system which is composed of a child, an alienating parent, and an alienated parent who is victimized by this process. Actually, the child is the real victim in the end. This study indicates that the child becomes estranged from the alienated parent by the alienating parent. This family system has a number of identifiable signs, symptoms, and behaviors. The characteristics and behaviors of the alienating parent, the alienated parent, and the children, as well as the techniques used in this study, appear to support the existence of PAS.

CONCLUDING COMMENTS

The data support PAS. The courts, attorneys, evaluators, and mental health providers are best served when the more specific term parental alienation syndrome rather than the more general term parental alienation. A cluster of symptoms that typically appear together was observed in custody cases by Dr. Gardner in 1985 (Gardner, 2000). A "syndrome" is defined in the DSM IV™, 4th Ed. as "A grouping of signs and symptoms, based on their frequent co-occurrence, which may suggest a common underlying pathogenesis, course, familial pattern, or treatment selection." PAS encompasses the requisite criteria to meet this definition. PA does not. PA is not well defined in the literature nor is it specific to any particular cause.

Gardner (2000) stated that the term "syndrome has a purity because most (if not all) of the symptoms in the cluster predictably manifest themselves together as a group (p. 3)." PAS fits this description in that it involves a cluster of symptoms that appear together resulting in the reliability of the diagnosis. PA is general and cannot be specific to a recognized cause. The consistency and reliability of PAS results in the children of moderate and severe PAS resembling one another. In contrast, PA is not a syndrome with any specific underlying cause. Typically, children who suffer from PAS will exhibit most of the symptoms found in the children's criteria. When mild PAS cases progress to moderate or severe, it is very likely that most of the symptoms will be present. Children under the PA diagnosis are not likely to be good research candidates because of the vague and wide variety of disorders that can be subsumed into PA; examples include physical abuse, sexual abuse, neglect, defective parenting, and mental illness of the child or parent. PAS could even be subsumed into the broad definition of PA. PA is a broad, vague, and insufficiently defined term. It leaves the court, counsel, clients, and mental health professionals without understanding or remedies.

The number of PAS cases in the family law courts has not decreased. The most important diagnostic tool for serious disturbance between alienated parents and their children continues to be ignored in courtrooms and by the mental health community. In the courts, there continues to be fear of retaliation by parents, the mental health community, family law litigators and judges. An astute evaluator easily recognizes PAS. Very distinct criteria for identifying and diagnosing PAS exist, particularly for the moderate and severe types. Only by using discrete identifying criteria such as that found in PAS can families and children in the legal context be protected.

Once the cause of the child's alienation from a parent is identified, then expert mental health professionals can provide the appropriate treatment for the family. This can only occur within the context of an identifiable syndrome (cluster of specific symptoms), which manifest together as a group. This study lends credibility to Dr. Gardner's finding that PAS exists within the context of identifiable behaviors and symptoms.

However, this is simply not the case with PA, which does not rely on valid or discrete criteria. Also, PA does not specify the cause of the alienation between the parent and the child. PA does not appear to have a common etiology. Therefore, an evaluator cannot provide the court or mental health providers information about the cause of the children's alienation.

Moreover, improper conclusions from a custody evaluation cannot assist the court with the proper data with which to make its order. PAS (and its cause) is specific and identifiable; therefore, its treatments and remedies can be recommended by an evaluator. Consequently, the court can use the evaluation to make and enforce recommendations to protect the children and their parental relations. This is in the best interests of children.

REFERENCES

American Psychiatric Association. (1994; 2000). *Diagnostic and statistical manual of mental disorders,* (4th ed.) Washington, D.C.: Author.

Gardner. R. (2002). Parental alienation syndrome vs. parental alienation: Which diagnosis should evaluators use in child-custody disputes? *The American Journal of Family Therapy, vol. 30 (2):* 93–115.

Gardner, R. (1986). *Child custody litigation.* Creskill, NJ: Creative Therapeutics.

Gardner, R. (1986). *Family evaluation and child custody mediation, arbitration, and litigation.* Cresskill, NJ: Creative Therapeutics.

Gardner, R. (1986). *The psychotherapeutic techniques of Richard A. Gardner.* Rev. ed., Cresskill, NJ: Creative Therapeutics.

Gardner, R. (1985, 1992, 1998). *The parental alienation syndrome: A guide for mental health and legal professional* :Cresskill, NJ: Creative Therapeutics.

Sullivan, M. (2000). *The alienated child.* Unpublished (presented at UCD at the Sacramento Valley Psychological Seminar.)

Sullivan, M.J. & Kelly, J.B. (2001). Legal and psychological management of cases with an alienated child. *Family Court Review,* 39(3), 299–315.

Kelly, J.B. & Johnston, J.R. (2001). The alienated child: A reformulation of parental alienation syndrome. *Family Court Review, (39),* 249–266.

Chapter 5

PAS AS A CHILD AGAINST SELF

Richard B. Austin, Jr.

OVERVIEW

The Parental Alienation Syndrome child is both victim and victimizer. The importance of a Parent Alienation Syndrome diagnosis is to steer the courts in the right direction and to establish a realistic, effective treatment plan. . . . In this chapter a treatment model (Case One) for long-term therapy with a PAS patient is suggested. For a successful outcome, conditions almost have to be ideal. Patience, perseverance, and measuring improvement in small increments are important factors for getting results. Case Two presents an adult long-term PAS victim who, after three decades, reconciled with an estranged parent. What courts and experts can do to help these victims based on research and forensic experience is also reviewed.

PAS has the ability to turn a child against the inner self. PAS is a cluster of symptoms with clearly recognizable behaviors that usually surfaces in the context of divorce and/or custody litigation. Richard Gardner, M.D., child psychiatrist and psychoanalyst, first introduced the components of this syndrome in the 1980s via multiple publications in peer-reviewed literature and books (see the Parental Alienation Syndrome, 1987).

Although PAS is not officially in the DSM-IV, it is moving toward that inclusion. Much like any syndrome that is based on behaviors, such as attention deficit disorder, which was covered under "minimal brain disorders" in the early years of my practice, or posttraumatic stress disorder that was designated as an anxiety disorder before evolving to PTSD, PAS may be included in the DSM-IV under "Parent-Child Relational Problem" or "Disintegrative Childhood Disorder." It is critically important to use PAS as a primary diagnosis, if it applies, to keep the integrity of the syndrome to communicate a clear message to the courts for the sake of the children involved, and to educate the courts and attorneys (Gardner, 2003b). As Gardner points out in his definition of the syndrome (1998), PAS results from a combination of the parent's indoctrination and the child's own contribution to a denigration and rejection of the target parent. PAS creates a major problem in the child's relationship with the target parent, and in severe cases the child is often disturbed enough to warrant a separate DSM-IV diagnosis (oppositional defiant disorder, etc.).

Because child custody cases involve the highest level of combatant legal representation in the family law courts, attorneys defending their clients in custody proceedings involving issues of PAS have attacked the syndrome to defend and win cases for their client. Forensic psychologists who factor PAS into custody recommendations, often are challenged by a ferocity rarely seen in family law to protect their clients from the loss of custody. The child's interests are rarely a priority for an attorney protecting a client from a custody loss, and guardians ad litem appointed to represent the child's interests are often undereducated about PAS.

There is hope, however, that the legal community is becoming progressively more aware of this syndrome. "Parental Alienation: How to deal with it in your family law case" by attorney Stewart W. Gagnon (Fulbright & Jaworski) with Tiffany Bingham of The Harvard Law School was presented in a State Bar of Texas course in 1998 to educate family law attorneys. The author concludes that attorneys must investigate to discover if the PAS exists before beginning any type of litigation, and then, if applicable, instruct their clients to terminate the destructive PAS behavior immediately. The author is aware that enforcement of court orders to ensure visitation with the target parent is essential. In spite of the fact that many courts, both in the United States and abroad, use the PAS term in their final decrees, many are often reluctant to do so; however, the impact of their ruling is clear.

I was once appointed to a custody case outside of Houston, and I, along with another psychologist, clearly found PAS. The judge accepted my custody recommendation but did not use PAS in his findings. He simply said that in his 30-plus years as a judge, he had seen this alienation pattern before, and that the children have the best chance for a positive relationship with both parents if the nonalienating parent gets custody. As a senior judge, he got the message. In the context of family law custody litigation, I have been an advisor to the court and for depositions, and have often testified to the growing number of court cases that include PAS as a factor in custody or visitation decisions.

The American Psychological Association's "Guidelines for Child Custody Evaluations in Divorce Proceedings" include as authoritative references Gardner's books on PAS. An entire issue of T*he Custody Newsletter* was devoted to PAS (Ward, 1993).

Independent from the PAS literature, the long-term 20-year follow-up studies by psychologist Judith Wallerstein, Ph.D. of children during and after divorce show that although over half of her sample suffers significantly from the divorce, the children embroiled in a loyalty conflict – a pressure to form an alliance with one parent over the other – end up more impaired as measured by school difficulties or self-esteem problems. Wallerstein states that this "loyalty problem" from which a child perceives he or she must ally with one parent and push the other parent away, unfortunately is very widespread today. This is especially true in the context of custody litigation, where we have established that PAS is more likely to emerge. If one parent does not actively support a positive relationship with the other parent, that parent is giving passive support to a child who may perceive a need to take sides in a divorce. This process begins the good/bad split within the child, leading to a child divided within himself or herself; in essence, "a child turned against self."

CASE ONE – BJ

As the following case shows, the rejected parent, his mother, was the primary nurturer, mentor, and teacher of the child during early developmental years. A serious PAS rejection of her in sync with the hostile rejection of her by the "loved parent" is a rejection of himself at all levels of his personality development. The all-good versus all-bad parental expressions by BJ signaled a good/bad split within his personality with devastating consequences to his personal life and overall functioning. Developmentally, each child bonds with both birth parents except in rare cases of prolonged absence, and identification with both parents takes place at unconscious levels. This attachment/identification dynamic is necessary for learning which is only partially verbal. Parental characteristics are internalized as part of the child's personality.

BJ acted out the "bad" part of himself, made "bad" by PAS behaviors such as lying, running away, stealing, and family violence. At one time he physically attacked his mother. Another time he destroyed family property. He was hospitalized after displaying out- of-control behaviors at his mom's house. Even more devastating to his mental health was the programming by the "loved parent," the father, to feel guilty, either liking or loving his mother, or simply being around her. This PAS programming extended to his grandfather and to every other member of his mother's family. Taken over by PAS, and no longer in control of his thought processes and actions regarding his mother and her family, BJ could find nothing good to say about her, and would not, for example, eat her cooking. The extent of this child's disturbance from PAS is well-documented by records from mental health professionals and hospital personnel.

Data from these hospital records alone support a serious level of PAS and demonstrate the abusive damage PAS does to a child. It is essential to first make a correct diagnosis of PAS, as Gardner so aptly points out; this is basic to the medical model of correct diagnosis before any treatment is implemented. It is important to not just rely on what parents tell you, or even what the child tells you.

What the child tells you in regard to which parent is preferred and which parent is rejected is usually the opposite of the dynamic below the surface; the parent who gives more unconditional acceptance and who creates a secure atmosphere for the child is the truly "loved parent," and the preferred parent is the one who creates insecurity and fear within the child by requiring a total allegiance that demands a rejection of the other parent to obtain the alienating parent's acceptance.

BJ is a classic case in that regard, as medical records show that when BJ was five his father told him to take sides with him, or he would never again go to basketball games or take him fishing. The child admitted that his dad got angry with him if he was nice to his mother or said anything nice about her. BJ told his therapist,

"You know how mad Dad gets when we are nice to my mother, and I'm afraid of Dad's anger." Here we have the fear component as part of the dad's preferred parent PAS indoctrination, as well as the threatened abandonment of special activities. The alienating parent is actually the feared parent, while the target parent who does not generate fears of rejection in the child is loved.

Just prior to this psychologist's first meeting with the patient, a crisis occurred, leading to a psychiatric hospitalization of the child. Some of the symptoms stated in the psychiatrist's record clearly show the violent nature of severe PAS. These included the serious alienation of the child from his true self and how he had turned dramatically against himself as he attacked, physically and verbally, the parent he loved and was most attached to in his early years

For example, BJ illustrated oppositional behavior illustrated by using phrases such as "You have no control over me." BJ had to be restrained from hitting his mom. The behavior also had spread to his grandparents. Parallel to this home behavior, BJ had increasingly "oppositional, defiant behavior" in the classroom, although before that time he had had only minor problems in school, and received above-average grades. Despite all the detailed clinical information from psychological assessments, psychological/psychiatric interviews of various people, progress reports from the hospital, no professional diagnosed PAS. The evidence showed all eight symptom manifestations of PAS. Unfortunately, without a correct diagnosis, effective court action or psychotherapy will rarely take place.

The Breakdown of Boundaries

Consensus is that PAS is abuse of a child. One form of that abuse is a breakdown of boundary issues. PAS tears down personal boundaries – healthy boundaries – that are created as a child differentiates who he or she is from who he or she is not. A boundary protects the child's self, truth, experience, personal empowerment, freedom to decide, and ownership of his own life. PAS causes destruction of the child's boundaries, opening the child to an indoctrination of rejection or hate for a parent; this affects the child at every level: emotional, mental, physical, and spiritual. It is an invasion of the child's very being.

Before the onset of PAS, a consensus description of BJ (through age five years) is of an engaging, endearing, warm-hearted, empathetic child who smiled often and treated everyone with sensitivity and compassion, with no exceptions. BJ's relationship with his mother was extremely close, and they were very attached. As BJ identified with his dad's anger and denunciation of his mother, the child she knew gradually disappeared from view until his behavior reached a crisis stage. His treating psychologist recommended hospitalization. I have a letter written by BJ written when he was away at camp before the major PAS programming saying how much he loved and missed his mother.

So, the differential diagnosis was clearly established for BJ at a severe level as follows: There was no guilt or ambivalence in the multiple frivolous rationalizations the patient gave to put his mother down, often using "borrowed scenarios" in which the child would repeat some of the exact derogatory words of the father, or a story about the mother concocted by the alienating parent. BJ's absolute, reflexive support of the "good dad" had no exceptions, and he not only claimed to be doing his own thinking, independently of anyone, but also embellished the denigration campaign with his own contributions, such as "I can't remember any good times with my mom." This process is the "amnesia" that Gardner describes as the alienation syndrome takes control of a child's thoughts and behaviors. This complete campaign of denigration of the target parent spread to her entire family.

A thorough investigation of a case (records, interviews outside of the parent-child loop), is necessary to explore the alternative that PAS is not taking place, and to verify that the child's complaints are not based on abusive behavior by the targeted parent, or that the child is simply forming an allegiance with one parent, which is typical during divorce proceedings. A scientific approach is to not look for PAS, but to gather information in a neutral, unbiased manner. This unbiased method, which gathers the data systematically, uses a convergent validity approach to determine if the aggregate of the behavioral information falls within or out of a PAS diagnosis to confirm or reject existence of the syndrome. The PAS criteria are readily observable. The data, not a professional's expectations, assumptions, or beliefs, lead the way toward a scientifically sound diagnostic conclusion. A preliminary investigation of PAS by attorneys and mental health professionals is possible if a "campaign of denigration" shows up early in the case – as it almost always does with PAS.

Preliminary Investigation

A campaign of denigration by one parent and a child toward the target parent rests on a foundation that is trivial, lacking in credibility, often absurd, and without confirming fact, which shows up in preliminary investigations. Also, it is my clinical experience that children who are mistreated or abused by a parent will still want to see that parent, and the abused child can always find, with few exceptions, something positive to say about that parent. Victim guilt and ambivalence is usually expressed by children who have valid reasons to reject a parent.

Another primary clue for a preliminary investigation of PAS is to what extent a parent appreciates a relationship between the child and the other parent. In BJ's case, the mother was aware of a need for her son to have a positive relationship with both parents, and she did not depreciate the father's value to the child or show negative feelings toward him.

However, a target parent at times looks like someone in the numbed stage of a posttraumatic disorder. It is one thing to have a former spouse belittle and attack you, but it is even more traumatic to have a loved child reject you as "all bad," to seemingly forget about all the years of positive family life and to only remember events that are negative, and to show hatred and rejection toward you. At times, a target parent feels and looks upset, unsure, and overwhelmed. The famous psychiatrist Carl Menninger of Menninger Clinic once said, "The fish with a hook in its mouth looks crazy to the other fish who don't have that hook in their mouth." Any parent with a PAS "hook in their mouth" knows what this means. When a professional correctly diagnoses PAS, the target parent is immediately relieved that someone understands his or her dilemma.

A Treatment Model for PAS

In general, PAS, especially the severe type, is not readily treatable; it operates like a paranoid delusion. The perceptual lenses that a PAS child uses to understand the targeted parent distorts the personality, character, and behavior of that parent so that only a caricature of that person remains. The symptoms of PAS operate as a "closed system" not open to outside facts, especially those contrary to the PAS belief of a "bad parent." Therapeutic intervention consistently fails, as it often has in my practice. I am proposing a therapeutic model, based on two cases, to help children recapture the true selves, past positive experiences, and the power of free choice.

My therapeutic model, which was modified over time, used a cognitive-interpretive approach in the context of a constant strengthening of the therapeutic alliance with the child by connecting with the current issues presented by BJ and using his personally charged issues to bring him back to reality and the ownership of his life. The strength of the therapeutic rapport and alliance was continually assessed to determine what level of interpretation was possible without undue risk to the alliance. All therapeutic influence was mediated through the relationship. The child, as a result of the relationship, gave some power to the therapist to influence or teach him.

At the onset I examined why he was in the session. One goal was to have a regard and respect for both of his parents, and another was to truly make his own choices free from the conflict between his parents, and free from the personal agenda or point of view of either parent, when it might not be his own point of view. I allied myself with his need for independence and personal growth. I explained that during and after divorce, especially with strong parental feelings, it is difficult to disengage oneself from the divorce turmoil and conflict and be your own person. I told him I would like to help him with that goal. This framework gave me working room to deal with PAS symptoms and behaviors, and later a more direct reeducative approach to his PAS experience and the use of re-decision therapy to undue some of the PAS damage.

Sometime later BJ said to me, "You'll never let me go live with my father – until I'm 18 years old." However, this statement showed that deep down BJ knew that he needed protection from the alienation process. If an attorney ad litem had mistakenly understood the child's verbalization as a desire to live with his father (and I have observed many do just that) this child would have been irretrievably lost. He would have lost meaningful contact with a parent, and the chance to recapture his identity and resolve an inner good/bad conflict that would follow him the rest of his life.

I cannot stress enough the need for family attorneys, psychiatrists, psychologists, and licensed psychotherapists to become familiar with PAS. It is the only way to avoid making decisions that could result in lasting damage to children. A continued denial by attorneys, judges, and professionals that "PAS doesn't exist" is almost, without exception, based on little or no knowledge and postdivorce experience with custody matters or children.

Brief History of BJ: Let's first look at BJ's psychological history beginning at the first stages of PAS. The onset of these problems started shortly after parental separation. BJ, an only child, was described as a bright, engaging, endearing child whose behaviors increasingly changed as ordinary discipline did not work.

BJ's father had anger problems during the marriage, which became increasingly worse after separation and then divorce. His anger progressed to rage. Over time,

BJ became involved with, enmeshed with, his father's rageful attitude and actions toward his mother.

Treatment Plan

The original treatment plan for BJ included 6 points:

1. Stay out of all adult conflict and fights.
2. Respect, by your actions, both parents.
3. Find something positive in what you say about and do with your mother.
4. Let yourself be a child. Don't worry about your parents; stick to *your* business.
5. Stay away from taking sides with either parent.
6. Learn to do your own independent thinking.

Early on, my treatment plan embraced a reeducative therapy approach to understand the concept of parental alienation. I used drawings and graphs to illustrate my points, as I learned that BJ liked to think in visual imagery terms. Following are 10 "lessons" discussed with BJ, that offer ways to avoid being taken over by parental issues. I placed myself on his side, suggesting a plan to help him have breathing room so he could be true to himself, independent, and have personal power. Power would be taken back from the power of PAS, and would help him accept the part of himself that was internalized from the alienated parent.

Lesson #1 shows how BJ has no middle ground, no safe place, to relate harmoniously to both parents, as he must accept one parent and reject the other. You align with the "loved parent" or you are rejected by that parent; there is no ambiguity. One parent is all good and one is all bad.

Lesson #1

Parental Alienation

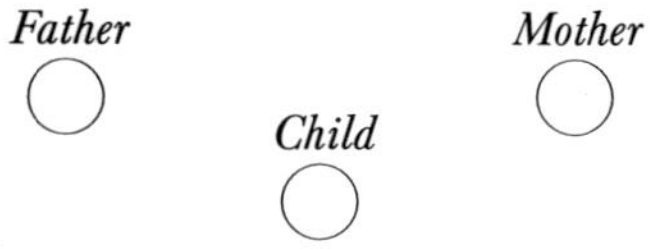

Child Is in the Middle

Messages:
- You can only like one parent
- You have to take sides
- One parent is *all* good; one parent is *all* bad

Solution: Do not take sides – create a positive connection with all persons.

Lesson #2 shows how PAS affects the child at a subconscious level. Rejection of a parent equals rejection of part of self. Blocking out positive memories of the rejected parent, the child disassociates from part of his or her life experience associated with that parent. Hence the child is "cut off" from part of himself.

Lesson #2

Half of Self Is Bad; Half Is Good

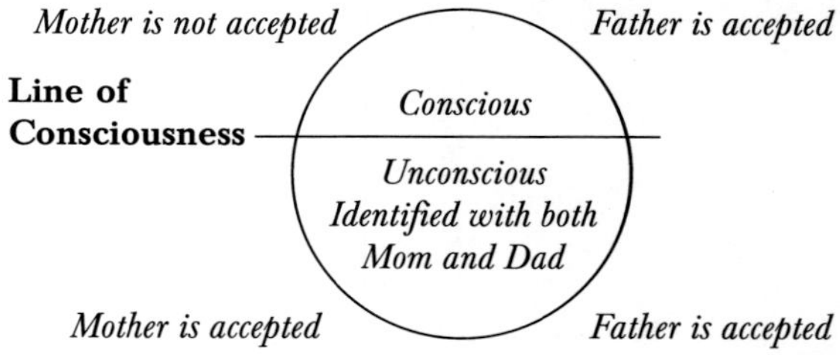

His Unconscious Message: "Part of me is bad."

Solution: Recognizing his history of a good mom.

Lesson #3

Acceptance of Yourself

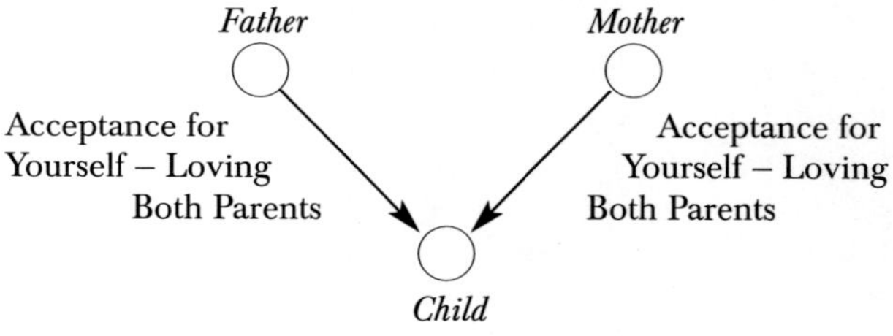

New messages conveyed:
- It's acceptable to like (love) your father and your mother.
- I'm responsible for not taking sides, or forming alliances.
- Loving (or giving) to one parent doesn't take away from the other.

Lesson #4

Getting Power Back to the Self

Problem: Pressure, however subtle, to conform to one parent's agenda.

Solution: Take a position against any parental condition or pressure that isn't the result of your actual choice.

Take a position on parental alienation.

1. Stop fighting the battle for or against a parent. (Truth: Parents fight each other through their children.)
2. Your position may be a silent one, but decide in your mind to not form an alliance.

Lesson #5

Look at Both Bad and Good

Look at the good and bad characteristics of both parents. They exist in reality. It is necessary to anchor your perceptions to reality. The examples illustrate an early stage of awareness.

Mother: Good and bad characteristics by BJ

Good	*Bad*
Doesn't nag about brushing his teeth She won't enforce bedtime Never carries out threats	Works too hard and long Grabbed him Treats me like a child Doesn't pay attention to me Threatens and doesn't carry through "Hospital thing" His housekeeper is gone

The hospital incident still loomed large for BJ although it had taken place 3 years earlier. He still didn't see a cause and effect relationship between his out- of-control behavior and his hospitalization. His blind spots about his mother's good attributes remain securely intact here.

Dad: Good and bad characteristics by BJ

Good	*Bad*
Gives him attention Discusses choices Always fair A good sense of humor When he rides (horses), he helps me If a problem, finds a way to help me He likes playing games	He eats junk food, etc. He leaves things undone – like the horse (buckle and later for horse) Sometimes he plans for us to do stuff and can't get it done Forgets groceries or to run some errands Falls asleep on the couch – and snores too loud Driving overnight he stays out too long and gets really sick (carsick).

BJ at this time made some effort to see negatives in his Dad. Interestingly, although he has seen his Dad get violent with his mother, he overlooks this fact. However, he remembers anything physical that is associated with his mother.

Lesson #6

PAS Dynamics

Conscious and Unconscious Levels

Unconscious Mind

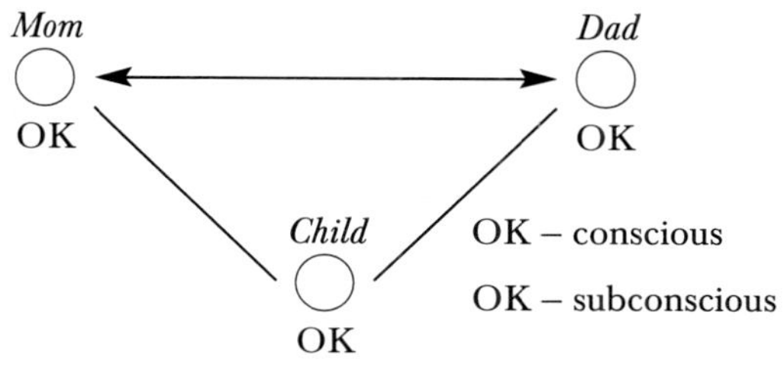

Conscieous Mind

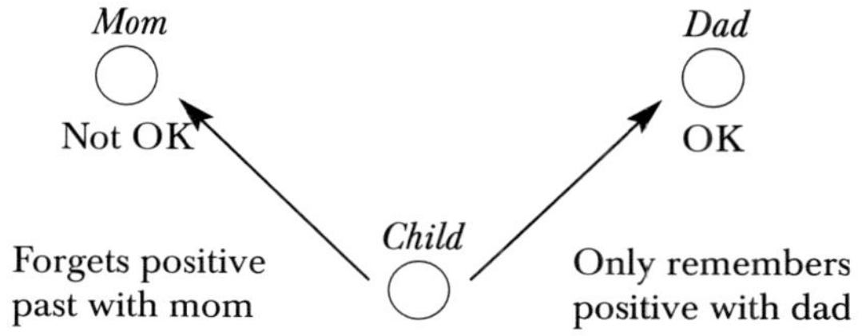

One-half of himself judged "not ok."

This is one of the illustrations used in therapy to develop an awareness of how one's mind works in the grip of PAS control. The solution is a return to reality, reconnecting the present with the past, restoring a major part of his life experiences. Close and attached with his mom as a child, identified with her, he rejects part of himself to resolve his conflict, and to anchor change to one of BJ's beliefs.

Lesson #7

Alliance Making

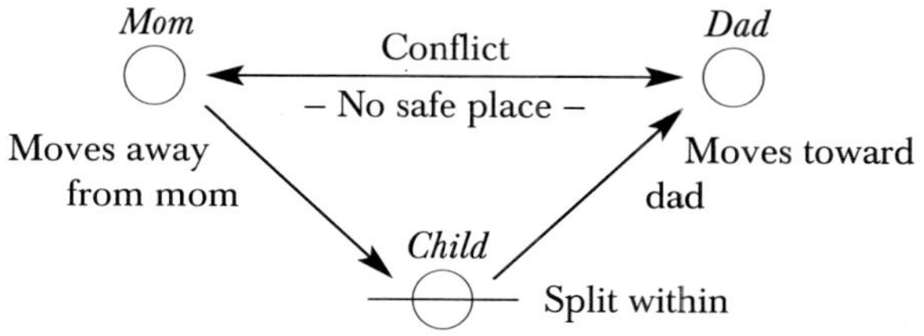

1. Mom/Dad in conflict
2. No space for child
3. Child moves over to Dad's side – embraces his attitude to get out of conflict
4. Seeming to avoid external conflict, child creates internal conflict
5. The child makes new decisions about conflict (alliance not needed)

The child's solution for dealing with conflict, or finding the least dangerous situation for himself, is to ally with Dad, who requires a total allegiance. He knows Mom will not reject him, or retaliate, so it seems safer. However, the price he pays is not worth it, as he pays with part of his reality, part of who he is, and gives up part of his history.

The child is given a way out of his situation, as illustrated in the following figure, where positive feelings are generated toward all parts of the family, as he withdraws from alliances. By making the decision to relate positively to his maternal family he takes back his own power. Change is also tied to values he accepts, such as the Ten Commandments, which gives him extra incentive to change, e.g., "Honor your father and mother." This method was tried to avoid feelings of guilt on his part.

Lesson #8

The Power of the Positive

Generating positive feelings and actions to all parts of the family helps him to be himself.

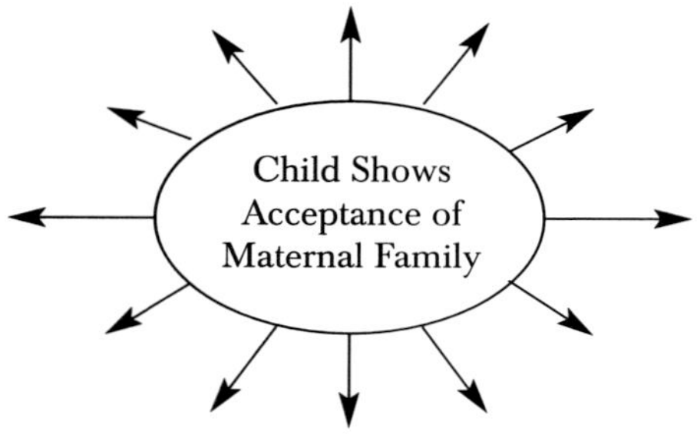

Learning the power of the positive – out of alliances – helps him take a position that he chooses.

Lesson #9

Child Empowerment

The child detaches from paternal enmeshment and parental issues in background.

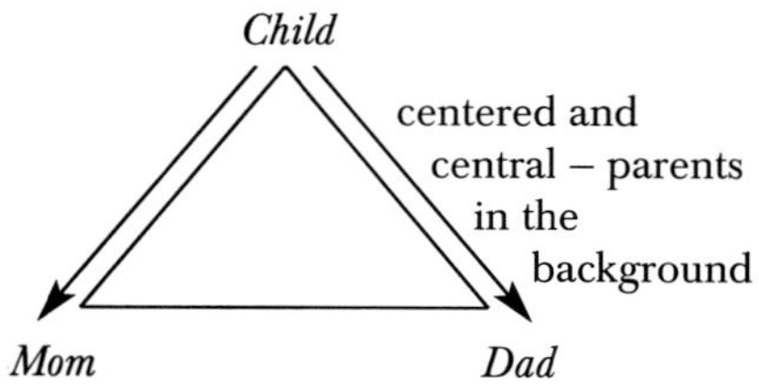

BJ changed over time, gradually, as his gifted intellectual capabilities were enlisted to reach our goals. However, his natural empathy was an even more important resource for change. Gradually, his grades went up, peer relationships improved, and respect, even affection, for his mother, was restored. Generating positive feelings and actions toward all parts of the family helps him to be himself.

Parental Support: A key part of the therapeutic impact on BJ was the role of his mother. Not only did she not react to his provocations at home, but she gave him firm and loving discipline and reality checkpoints to counter his distortions. She also participated in a regular (about every 4–6 weeks) family group session with BJ for a checkpoint to assess progress.

BJ knew that the session was the place for feedback on his progress, and his chance to air complaints in the family. As a group psychotherapist I have often observed the power of the group process to rapidly alter maladaptive behaviors. In this case, the power of the group was more than the sum of its parts. The group process moved BJ farther along the road of recovery by:

1. Dealing with specific PAS behaviors with special attention to improvement and gains, therefore reinforcing a change toward reality and better treatment of family members.
2. Utilizing a family group identity to support his underlying identification with his mother, and a positive attachment to her.
3. Affirming his power of individual choice so he could understand that he could be safe without an alliance with his dad.
4. His mother was authentic, empathetic, and positive toward BJ, qualities that psychologist Carl Rogers found, after 50 years of research, are highly correlated with positive therapeutic outcome.

CASE TWO – JOE

Joe, a 35-year-old male, highly successful in business, had been prevented from seeing his father following the divorce of his parents, when Joe was 12. His dad had been presented to him as violent, irresponsible, and undesirable to be around. This reputation, spread by his mother, was accepted by Joe and his siblings. No effort for contact had been made when Joe started therapy for his chronic dissatisfaction and self-esteem issues.

After it became apparent that he was shut off from remembering much about his father, the diagnostic data suggested long-standing PAS.

After the use of light hypnosis to recapture early experiences and guided imagery that made reality more vivid, Joe recaptured lost experiences and remembered positive aspects about his relationship with his father. He questioned the information he had accepted about his father, and diligently searched until he found him. They restored the father-son relationship, which flourishes to this day. At first, his mother rejected him due to the contact with his dad, and pressured his siblings to do the same. Failing to persuade his siblings, Joe's mother has reluctantly allowed some renewed mother-son contact.

Well read, Joe understands that he was a victim of PAS, and he is grateful that the diagnosis, and the resulting insight helped free him from being cut off from his dad. In my opinion, PAS did considerable damage to his image of himself as a male, impaired intimate relationships, and gave him a distorted view of himself as a parent. Although the ending in his case is an optimistic one, the devastation of having PAS in his life will not be repaired. He still mourns the losses that resulted from the perceptual distortions of PAS.

Family Court Actions

Often, a remedy for a PAS case is not possible without specific actions by the family court that has jurisdiction over the case. These actions are summarized in the sequence that they occur.

1. The court limits telephone contact with the alienating parent.
2. The court rejects a child's affidavit in support of a PAS parent in the context of diagnosed PAS.
3. The court disciplines a parent for violations of the court orders concerning visitation.
4. The court appoints an ad litem to adjust visitation or recommend custody changes if alienation continues.
5. The court changes custody to the rejected parent after a time of transition.

I recently testified in a court case and I traced PAS in which a father's visitation with his sons had been disrupted over the years. Although not court appointed, I gave overwhelming data consistent with a PAS diagnosis. When the judge asked my advice, I testified that therapy was tried and did not help, and that only court intervention could make a difference. The judge appointed an attorney ad litem that is experienced in PAS. She has vigorously reestablished visitation and was ready to change custody if necessary. When the mother in this case questioned whether she could make her teenage sons visit, the judge assured the sons that their mother would be incarcerated if they did not visit. Visitation has been progressing very well to the present, and the father-son relationship improved.

Although it helps to be court appointed in PAS cases, it is not necessary, as effective testimony can be given even if the scope of the evaluation is less than a full custody assessment. Consistent with American Psychological Association (APA) ethics, it is only necessary to testify within the scope of the evaluation. Specific custody recommendations are needed only when requested.

As with a sexual abuse assessment, an assessment for PAS includes content (specific evaluation information) and context (all relevant background data and fact). It is also important to be armed with research facts, and information about PAS found in peer-reviewed articles and court custody conclusions. Do not expect the behavior of parents who alienate to change from the presentation of facts in court. Their beliefs are too entrenched.

CONCLUSIONS

I have observed that the PAS extracts a heavy price for unresolved anger and rage toward the ex-spouse by using the children for revenge. Many cases in my clinical practice have shown that the alienating parent often changes for the worst and becomes more unhappy, obsessed with the situation, and apparently unaware of the cause and effect of their actions, (e.g., turning a child against himself or herself).

The emotional abuse that results from this process is usually irreversible. Court intervention can help decrease the continuing impact of PAS on the child, perhaps giving therapy a chance for improvement over time.

In BJ's case, the courts had given custody to the alienated mother and supported therapy by actions that restricted communication between the father and child. The psychotherapy was slow, painstaking, and long-term. The results in changed behavior were significant and readily observable in all areas of life. A treatment model was suggested.

Joe, a 35-year-old man separated from his father at age 12, reestablished a relationship with the dad after 23 years. This was accomplished through two years of therapy. Interestingly, Joe's mother rejected him for reuniting with his father but due to sibling pressure has reestablished some contact with him.

It is essential that a PAS diagnosis be formulated so that the court can be properly informed and take corrective action. It is also important for a PAS diagnosis to be established for the facilitation of an effective treatment plan in clinical practice. Without correct diagnosis, therapeutic solutions are, at best, partial.

REFERENCES

Bone, J. M. & Walsh, M. R. (1999). Parental alienation syndrome: How to detect it and what to do about it. *The Florida Bar Journal, 73*(3), 44–48.

Borris, E. B. (1997). Interference with parental rights of noncustodial parent as grounds for modification of child custody, *Divorce Litigation*, January 1997, pp. 1–13.

Cartwright, G. F. (1993). Expanding the parameters of parental alienation syndrome. *The American Journal of Family Therapy, 21*(3), 205–215.

Clawar, W. S. & Rivlin, B. V. (1991). *Children held hostage: Dealing with programmed and brainwashed children.* Chicago: American Bar Association.

Dunn, J. & Hedrick (1994). The parental alienation syndrome: An analysis of sixteen selected cases. *Journal of Divorce and Remarriage, 21*(3/4), 21–38.

Gagnon, S. & Bingham, T. (1998). *Parental alienation: How to deal with it in your family law case.* State Bar of Texas, Family Law Section.

Gardner, R. A. (1987). *The parental alienation syndromne and the differentiation between fabricated and genuine child sex abuse.* Cresskill, New Jersey: Creative Therapeutics, Inc.

Gardner, R. A. (1991a). Legal and psychotherapeutic approaches to the three types of parental alienation syndrome families: When psychiatry and the law join forces. *Court Review, 28*(1), 14–21.

Gardner, R. A. (1991). *Sex abuse hysteria: Salem Witch Trials revisited.* Cresskill, New Jersey: Creative Therapeutics, Inc.

Gardner, R. A. (1997). Recommendations for dealing with parents who induce a parental alienation syndrome in their children. *Journal of Divorce & Remarriage, 8*(3), 174–178.

Gardner, R. A. (1998). Recommendations for dealing with parents who induce a parental alienation syndrome in their children. *Journal of Divorce & Remarriage, 28*(3/4), 1–23.

Gardner, R. A. (2001a). *Therapeutic interventions for children with parental alienation syndrome.* Cresskill, New Jersey: Creative Therapeutics, Inc.

Gardner, R. A. (2001b). The parental alienation syndrome: Sixteen years later. The Academy Forum. New York: *The American Academy of Psychoanalysis, 45*(1), 10–12.

Gardner, R. A. (2001c). Should courts order PAS children to visit/reside with the alienated parent? A follow-up study. *The American Journal of Forensic Psychology, 19*(3), 60–106.

Gardner, R. A. (2002a). Parental alienation syndrome vs. parental alienation: Which diagnosis should evaluators use in child-custody litigation? *The American Journal of Family Therapy, 30*(2), 101–123.

Gardner, R. A. (2003a). Does DSM-IV have equivalents for the parental alienation syndrome (PAS) diagnosis? *The American Journal of Family Therapy, 31*(1), 1–21.

Gardner, R. A. (2003b). The judiciary's role in the etiology, symptom development, and treatment of the parent alienation syndrome. *The American Journal of Family Therapy, 21*(1), 39–64.

Lowenstein, L. F. (1998). Parent alienation syndrome: A two-step approach toward a solution. *Contemporary Family Therapy, 20*(4), 505–520.

Lowenstein, L. F. (1999). Parental alienation syndrome. *Justice of the Peace (UK), 163*(3), 446–450.

Major, J. A. (2002). Parents who have successfully fought parent alienation syndrome. http://www.breakthrough-parenting.com/PAS.htm.

Palmer, N. R. (1988). Legal recognition of the parental alienation syndrome. *The American Journal of Family Therapy, 16*(4), 361–363.

Rand, D. C. (1997a). The spectrum of parental alienation syndrome (part 1). *American Journal of Forensic Psychology, 15*(3), 23–51.

Rand, D.C. (1997b). The spectrum of parental alienation syndrome (part 2). *American Journal of Forensic Psychology, 15*(4), 39–92.

Waldron, K. H. and Joanis, D. E. (1996). Understanding and collaboratively treating parental alienation syndrome. *Journal of Family Law, 10*, 121-133.

Warshak, R. A. (1999). *Psychological syndromes: Parental alienation syndrome.* Expert Witness Manual, Chapters 3–32. Dallas, TX: State Bar of Texas, Family Law Section.

Warshak, R. A. (2000). Remarriage as a trigger of parental alienation syndrome. *American Journal of Family Therapy, 28*, 229-241.

Warshak, R. A. (2001). Current controversies regarding parental alienation syndrome. *American Journal of Forensic Psychology, 19*(3), 29–59.

Willbourne, C. & Cull, L. (1997). The emerging problem of parental alienation. *Family Law* (British Publication) December, 1997, pp. 807–808.

Chapter 6

INCIDENCE, GENDER, AND FALSE ALLEGATIONS OF CHILD ABUSE: DATA ON 84 PARENTAL ALIENATION SYNDROME CASES

LEONA M. KOPETSKI, DEIRDRE CONWAY RAND, AND RANDY RAND

OVERVIEW

This chapter presents descriptive statistics on 84 cases of parental alienation syndrome (PAS), compiled by a custody evaluator in Colorado. Kopetski's work on alienation began in the 1970s and was fully developed by the time she learned of Richard Gardner's work. In 1991, Kopetski presented her work on PAS at the Fifteenth Annual Child Custody Conference in Keystone, Colorado (Kopetski, 1991). She recognized Gardner's contribution in the introduction, and described her astonishment upon learning of his work in 1987. Simultaneously, while unaware of Gardner's work, she had arrived at observations and conclusions that were remarkably similar in many respects. The paper included descriptive statistics on 84 cases, which Kopetski used to test some of Gardner's findings and hypotheses, such as those relating to the disproportionate number of alienating mothers. Kopetski's clinical observations of PAS families were eventually published in The Colorado Lawyer (Kopetski, 1998a,b). Her descriptive statistics on 84 cases are published here for the first time. They document a significant increase in PAS cases from 1976 to 1990. The ratio of mothers to fathers alienating was 2 to 1. False allegations of child abuse, defined as physical or sexual abuse, or child neglect, appeared in 54 percent of cases, with child neglect alleged primarily by alienating fathers and sex abuse alleged primarily by alienating mothers.

For more than 20 years, Kopetski and a psychologist colleague conducted evaluations as a team, developing a team model for custody evaluations which became the standard for their state (Metropolitan Denver Interdisciplinary Committee on Child Custody, 1992). When Kopetski encountered the early alienation cases in the 1970s, terms such as "parental alienation" were not yet in common use. Initially, she thought of these families simply as "disturbed." It would be another decade before Gardner (1985) introduced the name parental alienation syndrome.

As Kopetski encountered more cases, a pattern emerged in which some children had developed a kind of phobic reaction to one parent. The problem was not ameliorated by the traditional recommendations for gradually increased visits with the target parent and therapy for the child. Kopetski noted that children in these scenarios usually lost one parent in the divorce. She found this outcome unacceptable and began searching for new ideas. In the late 1970s, Kopetski began utilizing John Bowlby's treatment for school phobia as a model for custody and visitation recommendations in the alienation cases she evaluated. She found that orders for enforced visitation, or placement of the child in the primary custody of the target parent, were often effective in interrupting alienation, while therapy as the primary intervention was not (Kopetski, 1991; Rand, Rand and Kopetski, 2005).

Kopetski hoped to get the 1991 paper published and to continue her PAS research, but these plans were put on hold when she developed health problems that forced her to retire. The unpublished manuscript circulated informally and eventually found its way into the hands of Deirdre Rand, who referenced it in her comprehensive literature review titled "The Spectrum of Parental Alienation Syndrome" (Rand, 1997a,b). The articles by Kopetski which were featured in *The Colorado Lawyer* the following year described her clinical observations of PAS families, but not her descriptive statistics on 84 cases. Kopetski was too ill by then to write up this important data, and no longer motivated. The professional community had shown little interest in the facts and figures she had compiled on the frequency of PAS, sex of the alienating parent, and justifications given for alienation.

In August 2000, Deirdre and Randy Rand traveled to Kopetski's home in Montana, where the three of them met for the first time. The purpose of the visit was to begin work on a PAS follow-up study, utilizing Kopetski's cases. Kopetski passed away several weeks before the preliminary findings of the project were presented in 2003 at the Nineteenth Annual Symposium of the American College of Forensic Psychology (Kopetski, Rand and Rand, 2003). The study was subsequently published in the *American Journal of Forensic Psychology* (Rand, Rand and Kopetski, 2005). As part of this collaborative effort, Deirdre and Randy Rand obtained Kopetski's permission to develop her descriptive statistics on 84 PAS cases into a chapter for this book.

METHODOLOGY

Sample

The present study of incidence, gender, and false allegations of child abuse in PAS is based on a sample of 84 alienation cases, drawn from Kopetski's practice as a custody evaluator in Colorado. The cases comprised 20 percent of 413 families she evaluated from 1976 to 1990. The families were from diverse social economic backgrounds. The sample contained 49 alienating mothers, 31 alienating fathers, and four cases in which a relative or stepparent appeared to be the primary alienator. The diagnosis of PAS was based on Kopetski's criteria (Kopetski, 1991, 1998a,b).

Of the 84 cases, Kopetski reported that there were 49 in which alienation appeared to be interrupted, 15 in which alienation was completed, 8 in which there was ongoing litigation and risk of completed alienation, and 12 with outcome unknown (Kopetski, 1991). Taken together, there were 28 cases which involved repeated litigation, continuing for a period of two to ten years. The longest litigation was in cases where the alienating parent had custody, but refused to stop litigating until the target parent's access was completely terminated. Kopetski's interpretation of this finding was that the alienating parent's behavior was motivated by a desire to prevent or sever the child's existing attachment to the other parent, rather than an effort to protect a normal attachment between the child and alienating parent, as Gardner had suggested. Of the 49 cases in which alienation seemed to be interrupted, 31 settled by stipulated agreement and 18 were settled by court order.

Incidence of PAS and Gender of the Alienating Parent

Kopetski's 1991 paper included data on the frequency of PAS for each year from 1976 to 1990, and the gender of the alienating parent or relative in each case. For the handbook, this data was clustered into three five-year time frames. A bar graph for each time frame provides a breakdown for the number of mothers and fathers found to be alienating (*see* Fig. 6.1 on p. 67).

False Allegations of Child Abuse

In the 1991 paper, Kopetski listed the primary justification for alienation in each case. She identified 19 different justifications, including separation anxiety, child fearful of the other parent, child doesn't need father, child abuse, spousal abuse, and child is older and has a right to refuse visits. Some cases involved allegations of child abuse, along with other kinds of justifications, such as mother alleged separation anxiety and sex abuse, or father alleged mother was emotionally unstable and neglected the children. There were several cases in which more than one type of child abuse was alleged. Kopetski noted a significant shift in the kinds of justifications given over the years, as different social causes became the focus of attention. The data presented in Table 6.1 (p. 68) are for the three main types of child abuse, including sex abuse, physical abuse, and child neglect.

Type of Abuse Alleged and Gender of the Alienating Parent

For each case, Kopetski noted the justification given for alienation and gender of the alienating parent. This made it possible to examine the relationship between gender of the alienating parent and type of child abuse alleged, as shown in Table 6.1 (p. 68). The majority of false allegations were for sex abuse or child neglect. False allegations of sex abuse were made primarily by alienating mothers (*see* Fig. 6.2 on p. 69). False allegations of child neglect were made primarily by alienating fathers (*see* Fig. 6.3 on p. 69).

Limitations of the Study

Kopetski's sample was comprised of divorced families in Colorado, evaluated during the time period

1976 to 1990. Her cases may not be representative of other geographic locations, or of PAS developments since 1990. Kopetski's team model for evaluations became the standard for Colorado, but may not be the norm in other states. Her team approach involved a series of steps designed to control for bias. Potentially, this could make her findings more reliable and valid than those of a single evaluator, whose protocol may be less demanding.

By the late 1970s, Kopetski had rejected primary parent theory as the basis for her custody recommendations. In her view, evaluators who continued to rely on primary parent theory, especially feminist evaluators, usually recommended custody to the mother, which may have made them more popular with women. Kopetski's services may have been more sought after by fathers, because of her emphasis on children's need for relationships with both parents, and on making custody recommendations based on which parent was more likely to support the child's relationship with the other parent.

The descriptive statistics Kopetski compiled on false allegations of child abuse were for her PAS cases only. She did not collect this information for the other 329 cases (80%) she evaluated, in which PAS was not a significant issue. The data for the incidence study presented here is on parents and adult issues. Little information about the children is provided, such as children's age, gender, and adjustment, and how many children the 84 families had between them. The follow-up study by Rand, Rand and Kopetski, 2005, focuses more on the children.

RESULTS

Incidence of PAS

Kopetski documented a significant increase in PAS from 1976 to 1990, as shown in Figure 6.1. The rate at which PAS increased seems to have accelerated during the time frame from 1986 to 1990, with the number of cases in that five-year period equaling the number of cases during the ten years from 1976 to 1985. In the 1991 paper, Kopetski reported that the proportion of alienation families in her practice also increased, going from 16 percent in the 1970s to 50 percent in 1990. Her data provide empirical support for Gardner's assertion that the frequency of children becoming obsessed with denigration of one parent had been increasing for six or seven years, such that a special name was warranted (Gardner, 1985).

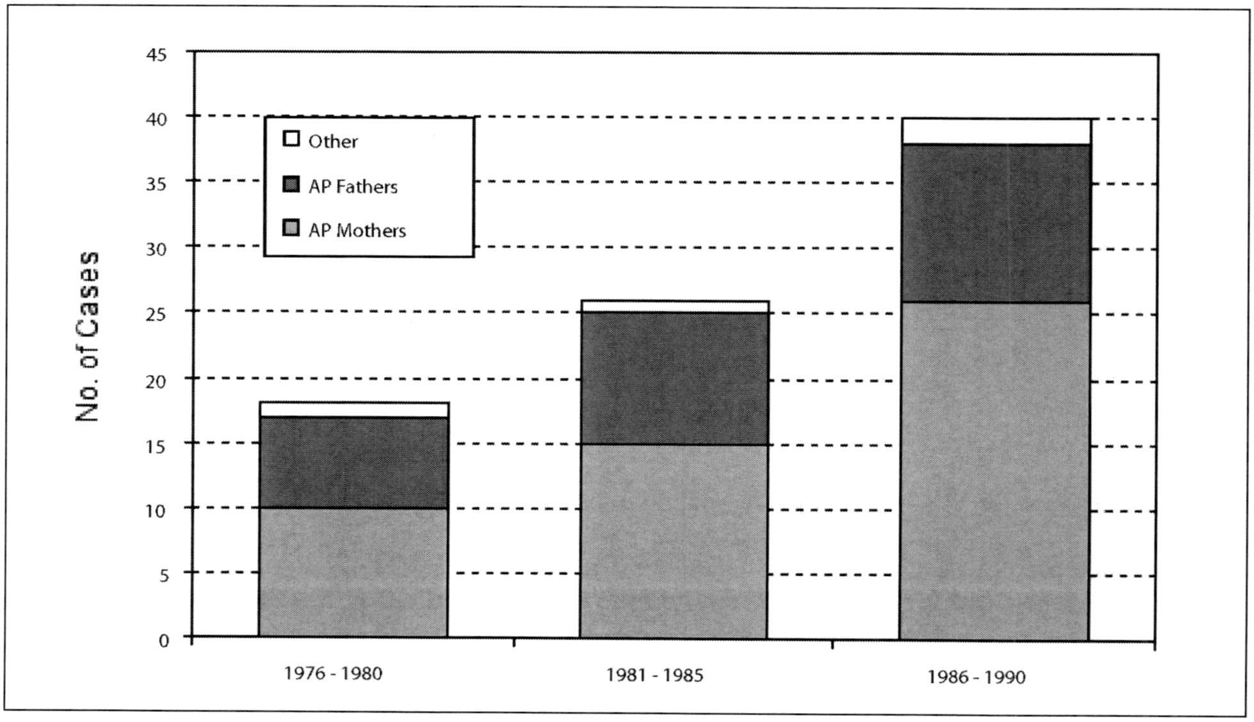

Figure 6.1. Incidence of PAS and gender of the alienating parent (AP).

Kopetski's findings with respect to the incidence of PAS are comparable to those of other researchers, despite differences in geographic location and time frame. Kopetski found significant PAS in 84 of the 413 families she evaluated between 1976 and 1990 (20%). A survey of 21 custody evaluators by a psychologist in California estimated that PAS was found in 33 percent of the families evaluated (Nicholas, 1997). A study of divorce judgments from 1995 to 2000 in Brisbane, Australia, found PAS was present in 29 percent (Berns, 2001).

Proportion of Alienating Mothers to Alienating Fathers

As shown in Figure 6.1, the proportion of alienating mothers to alienating fathers was 2 to 1, not just in the early years, but in all three time frames. However, the number of alienating fathers did increase, as Gardner and others have observed in recent years. It has been generally assumed that the increase in alienating fathers means that fathers are now as likely to alienate as mothers, but according to Kopetski's data, alienating mothers continued to outnumber alienating fathers by a ratio of 2 to 1. As the number of alienating fathers increased, so did the number of alienating mothers, paralleling the increase in PAS cases.

Kopetski's findings regarding the higher proportion of alienating mothers are similar to those of other researchers (Wallerstein and Kelly, 1980; Clawar and Rivlin, 1991; Dunne and Hedrick, 1994; Gardner, 2001; Burrill, 2001). Given the consistency of these studies, it unlikely that her findings are due to gender bias. Kopetski (1991) concluded that PAS is not a gender-determined disorder, and that the personality characteristics and the behavior of alienating parents are the same, regardless of whether the parent is male or female.

Kopetski believed that cultural attitudes and social climate were responsible for most of the gender differences found in PAS. The focus on the plight of women and children in recent years means that more social causes have been available for exploitation by alienating mothers. Several fathers in Kopetski's sample had been physically attacked by their ex-wives and had documented injuries, but allegations of domestic violence were made only by mothers. Alienating fathers sought to capitalize on the moral outrage engendered by the idea of a mother who neglects her children for the sake of her own self-centered interests. In the past, when cultural mores dictated that the wife and children were the property of the father, alienating fathers were more common. In Leo Tolstoy's novel *Anna Karenina* (1965), Anna lost the right to see her children when she left her husband for another man, reflecting the culture of the day.

False Allegations of Child Abuse

Prior to the evaluation, child abuse allegations had typically been investigated one or more times, with findings of "unsubstantiated." Kopetski did an investigation of her own, as part of the evaluation, in all cases with allegations of child abuse or domestic violence. Whether bona fide abuse was involved, or an allegation was unfounded, understanding the history surrounding the allegations had important clinical ramifications for her findings and recommendations.

Kopetski found false allegations of child abuse in 45 of the 84 cases. Due to multiple allegations in two cases, the total number of false allegations came to 48, as shown in Table 6.1. The breakdown for type of abuse alleged was 29 percent sex abuse, 15 percent physical abuse, and 56 percent child neglect. False allegations of sex abuse were made primarily by alienating mothers. False allegations of neglect were frequently made by alienating fathers.

TABLE 6.1. False allegations of child abuse and gender of the alienating parent

	Mother	Father	Other
Sex Abuse	11	2	1
Physical	5	1	1
Neglect	3	21	3

Type of Abuse Alleged and Gender of the Alienating Parent

In cases involving false allegations of sex abuse, the mother was the accusing parent in 79 percent. In cases with false allegations of child neglect, the father was the accusing parent in 76 percent (*see* Figures 6.2 and 6.3, next page).

Many of the unfounded claims of sexual abuse involved young children whose mothers inferred sexual meaning to affectionate behavior and the child's normal attempts to engage and get close to the father after an abnormally exclusive relationship with the mother. An accusation of sex abuse by the mother was more likely to be taken seriously by child protection authorities, resulting in restrictions on the father's

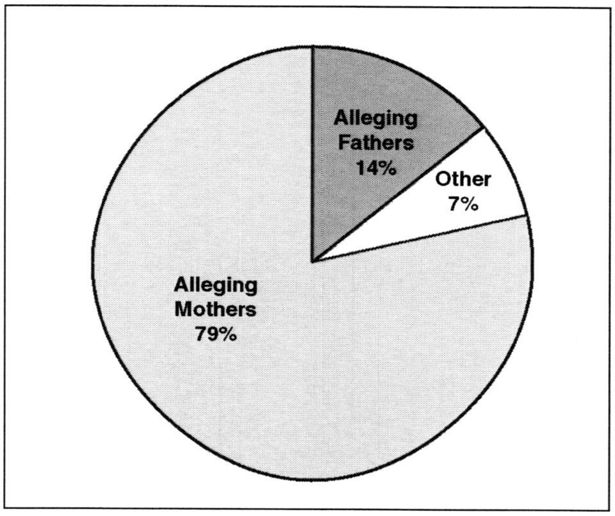

Figure 6.2. False allegations of sex abuse and gender of the alienating parent.

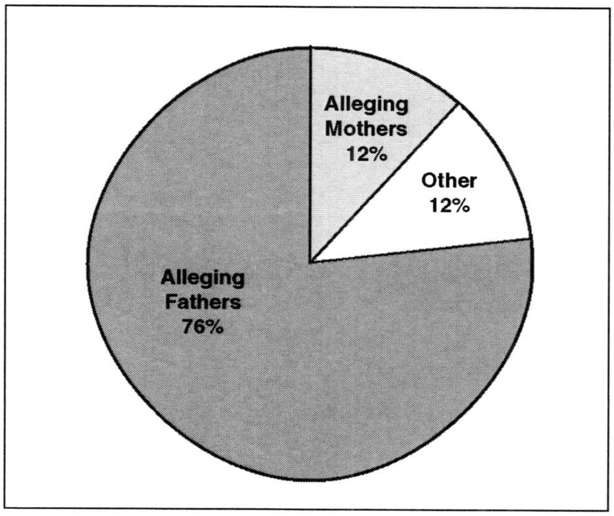

Figure 6.3. False allegations of child neglect and gender of the alienating parent.

access. A father could be on supervised visitation for two years, or have no contact with the child for months, before it was determined that abuse was not substantiated. In some cases, allegations of sex abuse were added on, when other justifications for alienation were not enough to eliminate contact with the target parent.

False allegations of child neglect played out differently. For example, both parents may have neglected the child, due to problems with substance abuse during the marriage. At evaluation, mother may have been deemed the healthier of the two parents, having made significant changes after the divorce. However, the father continued to amplify and exploit the allegation of neglect, which had been true at one time. Another example is that of a mother who developed a serious illness that affected her mental state and made it difficult for her to care for the children. In a normal, intact family, the father and other family members would have offered to help until the mother recovered. In an alienation scenario, however, the father would exploit the fact that there was a period of time when mother was incapacitated, portraying her as a neglectful, unfit mother. Some alienating fathers were so relentless that the mother gave up, exhausted.

CONCLUSION

Reflecting on what she had learned from working with PAS families, Kopetski wrote:

> No human being, adult or child, male or female, accuser or accused, victim or perpetrator, convict or free individual, should be allowed the entitlement of being believed without question. And, no human being, adult or child, male or female, accuser or accused, victim or perpetrator, convict or free individual, should ever be deprived of the right to be heard by a mind open to the possibility that the individual speaking is telling the truth. Important to life as they are, emotions, beliefs and convictions, cannot be substituted for truth or reality. Reality is not a reflection of the internal contents of human beings; the internal mirrors formed by our neurological structures are supposed to *reflect* reality (italics added) so that we can become aware of it. Sometimes, those mirrors introduce a distortion. We, in the legal and mental health professions must assiduously guard our right to question and evaluate and to base our conclusions about the people we serve on truth and fact considered in context. Distortions must be accounted for if we are to achieve and help children achieve descriptions which approximate reality. (Kopetski, 1991, p. 29)

Leona Kopetski, M.S.S.W.
1938–2003

REFERENCES

Berns, S. (2001). Parental alienation syndrome in the family court – magic bullet or poisoned chalice? *Australian Journal of Family Law, 15*(3), 191-214.

Burrill, J. (2001). *Parental alienation syndrome in court referred custody cases.* Unpublished doctoral dissertation, North Central University, California.

Clawar, S. and Rivlin, B. (1991). *Children held hostage: Dealing with programmed and brainwashed children.* Chicago: American Bar Association.

Dunne, J. and Hedrick, M. (1994). The parental alienation syndrome: an analysis of sixteen selected cases. *Journal of Divorce and Remarriage, 21*(3/4), 21–38.

Gardner, R.A. (1985). Recent Trends in Divorce and Custody Litigation. *Academy Forum, 29*(2), 3–7.

Gardner, R. A. (2001). Should courts order PAS children to visit/reside with the alienated parent? A follow-up study. *American Journal of Forensic Psychology, 19*(3), 61–106.

Kopetski, L. (1991). *Parental alienation syndrome: Recent research.* Paper presented at the Fifteenth Annual Child Custody Conference, Keystone, Colorado.

Kopetski, L. (1998a). Identifying cases of parent alienation syndrome – Part I. *The Colorado Lawyer, 27*(2), 65–68.

Kopetski, L. (1998b). Identifying cases of parent alienation syndrome – Part II. *The Colorado Lawyer, 27*(3), 61–64.

Kopetski, L., Rand, D.C. and Rand, R. (2003). "Helping children in alienation scenarios maintain relationships with both parents: A follow-up study on 45 PAS children." Paper presented at the Nineteenth Annual Symposium of the American College of Forensic Psychology, Palm Springs, CA.

Metropolitan Denver Interdisciplinary Committee on Child Custody. (1992). *Child Custody Guidelines.* Denver: Author.

Nicholas, L. (1997). "Does parental alienation syndrome exist? Preliminary empirical study of the phenomenon in custody and visitation disputes." Paper presented at the Thirteenth Annual Symposium of the American College of Forensic Psychology, Vancouver, British Columbia, Canada.

Rand, D.C. (1997a). The spectrum of parental alienation syndrome – Part I. *American Journal of Forensic Psychology, 15*(3), 23–52.

Rand, D.C. (1997b). The spectrum of parental alienation syndrome – Part II. *American Journal of Forensic Psychology, 15*(4), 39–92.

Rand, D.C., Rand, R. and Kopetski, L. (2005). The spectrum of parental alienation syndrome – Part III. *American Journal of Forensic Psychology, 23*(1), 15–43.

Tolstoy, L. (1965). *Anna Karenina.* New York: Random House, Inc.

Wallerstein, J., & Kelly, J. (1980). *Surviving the breakup: How children and parents cope with divorce.* New York: Basic Books, Inc.

Chapter 7

PAS IN THE UNITED KINGDOM: PROBLEMS IN RECOGNITION AND MANAGEMENT

TONY HOBBS

OVERVIEW

This chapter traces the principles that underlie the ability of parents and children to maintain their relationships after parental separation, as revealed through UK case law. The effects of the existence of PAS having been denied in a flawed report by court-appointed experts are considered. The beneficial effect of European supremacy over UK courts is demonstrated, with specific regard to the effect of European case law management of PAS and the passing into law across the UK of the 1989 Human Rights Act. Current developments and obstacles are reviewed.

CURRENT POSITION

Within the various UK jurisdictions, the current position with regard to PAS is at best one of confusion and at worst one of straightforward denial that PAS exists at all as a valid entity. In our family courts even our most senior and respected family judiciary acknowledge that they are regularly faced with the apparently intransigent dynamics that are involved in parental alienation (e.g., *see* comments by: Lord Justice Thorpe at para 25 and Lady Justice Arden at para 57 in *Re T (A Child) (Contact: Alienation: Permission to Appeal)* [2003] 1 FLR 531; Family Division President Butler-Sloss in Re L, V, M, H [2000] 2 FLR 334 at pp. 351F-352A; and Ward LJ in *Re M (A Minor) (Contempt of Court: Committal of Court's Own Motion)* [1999] Fam 263 at para 41.i). Crucially, however, the unified nature of these dynamics when they present in a child showing PAS is not recognized, and the existence of PAS is not accepted. Therefore, the condition is not appropriately addressed, and the harsh consequence is that the child often loses contact with the target parent as the court unwittingly colludes with the alienator. The component parental hostility is often referred to by the insufficiently precise term "implacable hostility," with infrequent reference to "parental alienation." There is a strong judicial reluctance to use the term "syndrome" at all in this context, as to do so would suggest judicial support for the existence of PAS, which the judiciary have been advised by court appointed "experts" is a condition that does not exist.

Confusion has become apparent since the President of the Family Division of the High Court gave judgment in February 2002 in the case of *Re C (Prohibition on Further Applications)* [2002] 1 FLR 1136. This Appeal had been presented with an enormous amount of information, some of it on PAS. In giving her judgment, the then Family Division President, Dame Elizabeth Butler-Sloss, is on public record as having given leave for the "C" family situation to be assessed by a psychiatrist or psychologist: "to see whether there is any way out of the problems and not to concentrate upon the issue of parental alienation syndrome. *That will, of course, take its place in any consideration* but not to obscure the other matters that may need to be looked at" (para 13, emphasis added). Thus, for the first time ever, the Court of Appeal acknowledged that a family before it should be reviewed (significantly, but necessarily not solely) with regard to the possible role of PAS in its specific situation.

This Court of Appeal pronouncement by the country's most senior family judge was accurately noted by Hobbs to set a significant precedent in UK family law practice (2002b, p. 381). Official reaction was swift, as

Charles Prest, Director of Legal Services, Children and Family Court Advisory and Support Service, strongly denied this development in a memorandum sent in June 2002 to all CAFCASS officers nationally. Prest stated that Hobbs' claim was incorrect. Although Prest correctly added that the Court of Appeal had not acknowledged the existence of PAS in any case before it, he then did not properly inform his officers that the Family Division President's published judgment in *Re C* was that assessment for PAS had "its place in any consideration." Furthermore, CAFCASS Legal never sought the assessment for PAS within the children of family C, for which the Court had specifically given it permission.

Although the current judicial position with regard to PAS remains to be further clarified in the courts, such denials may mean that the judicial position has effectively reverted to that held by the Court of Appeal in the conjoined cases of *Re L (Contact: Domestic Violence); Re V (Contact: Domestic Violence); Re M (Contact: Domestic Violence); Re H (Contact: Domestic Violence)* [2000] 2 FLR 334. For this case the Official Solicitor, appointed by the court to act on behalf of the children involved, commissioned a report from two consultant child psychiatrists, as expert witnesses, to address and help resolve the court's dilemma regarding how best to manage child-parent contact in situations involving domestic violence. It is much to the court's credit that such a report was sought (see Sturge, C. & Glaser, D. "Contact and Domestic Violence – The Experts' Court Report" [2000] *Family Law*, 615–629). In the course of their report, which, it must be stressed, was of impeccable quality as far as their specific remit regarding situations where domestic violence had actually occurred, the two experts denied that PAS existed. However, the quality of their research on PAS for this comprehensive review for the court was uncharacteristically negligent. It remains extremely unfortunate that the high professional standards so evident in the rest of their report were not applied to either their research on PAS or on their reporting in a professional manner on PAS to the court. It seems almost incredible that in a review of such import to be presented to the President of the Family Division of the High Court, sitting in the Court of Appeal, which would obviously be of massive influence for children and families nationwide, their dismissal of PAS appears to have crucially relied on just one journal article alone, which had itself already been discredited.

Case law both before and subsequent to *Re L, V, M, H* [2000] and *Re C* [2002] has continued to grapple with intransigent dynamics that on proper assessment may have been shown to be PAS related, but it has steadfastly made minimal reference to PAS. Such a state of confusion as exists currently should not necessarily cause defeatism, however. The achievement of most case law-derived legal milestones has inevitably been preceded by apparently contradictory judgments as the judiciary struggle with balancing the highly complex nuances of individual cases with new information and concepts.

Before examining in greater detail the report made to the Court of Appeal by Sturge and Glaser, the significance of the commissioning of their report and of its consequent likely impact on UK family law practice needs to be placed into appropriate perspective via a brief review of the case law-derived principles of child-parent contact following parental separation.

RELEVANT CASE LAW PRECEDENTS

Within the United Kingdom three different jurisdictions exist – England and Wales, Scotland, and Northern Ireland. However, at the time of writing this, Northern Ireland is currently administered from the London-based parliament at Westminster. This review is limited to case law from within the jurisdiction of England and Wales. It demonstrates some of the developments in the family judiciary's constant struggle to disentangle and address the uncompromising dynamics that they so often face – dynamics similar to those that occur in PAS. Court judgments frequently reiterate the basic principle that a child benefits from contact with both parents and that this should be the norm unless exceptional circumstances exist. However, this appears sometimes in practice to be little more than lip service, as the courts seem unable to manage a resident parent's unrelenting hostility toward the other parent. When this hostility causes or may cause distress to the child during contact with the nonresident parent, this can amount to a sufficient "exceptional circumstance" for parental contact to be stopped. This review shows that when PAS may exist but is unrecognized, the courts have left themselves extremely vulnerable to unwitting collusion with the alienating process.

These issues were comprehensively considered in *M v. M (Child: Access)* [1973] 2 All ER 81, in which an adoptive father refused the adoptive mother access. Wrangham J said: "the companionship of a parent is in any ordinary circumstances of such immense value to the child that there is a basic right in him to such companionship. . . . [N]o court should deprive a child of access to either parent unless it is wholly satisfied that it is in the interests of that child that access should cease, and that is a conclusion at which a court should be extremely slow to arrive" (p. 85e-f). Wrangham supported his judgment by quoting Edmund Davies LJ in *B v B* [1971] 3 All ER (p. 688), in which the mother had refused access to the father: "For a court to deprive a good parent completely of access to his child is to make a dreadful order. . . . Very seldom can the court bring itself to make so Draconian an order, and rarely is it necessary" (p. 85g).

In *B v B* [1971], the Official Solicitor (the child's representative in court) reported that the mother had honestly believed access to his father was not in the child's best interest, and so had simply done nothing to urge him to visit his father. No suggestion of any malicious alienation was apparent, even though alienation of the child from his father had occurred. Edmund Davies LJ commented: "In general, one parent who takes that attitude in relation to the other parent is undertaking a tremendous responsibility and discharging it thoroughly badly. Again, speaking generally, it is the duty of parents, whatever their personal differences may be, to seek to inculcate in the child a proper attitude of respect for the other parent" (p. 86b). Also giving judgement in *M v. M (Child: Access)*, Latey J observed:

> So what is this basic right in a parent to access to his or her child? It is I believe no more and no less than a fact of human experience and of common sense. . . . If one goes back in history there was a time when an adulterous mother not only had no chance at all of keeping or of having the care of her child but she had little chance of having access to it and so of keeping contact with it and giving it some companionship. . . . That has all changed. Why has it all changed? *Because medical and other expert discovery has shown that that approach, believed right at the time, was in fact wholly wrong.* Wrong not necessarily if one looked at the pros and cons between the parents themselves, but wrong from the point of view of what was best for the children. . . . When a court has to consider whether the parent not having the care of the child should have access to the child, should there be any difference in principle? I cannot for the life of me see any reason at all why there should be any such difference, and I do not believe that there is. . . . [W]here the parents have separated and one has the care of the child, access by the other often results in some upset in the child. *Those upsets are usually minor and superficial. They are heavily outweighed by the long term advantages to the child* of keeping in touch with the parent concerned so that they do not become strangers, so that the child later in life does not resent the deprivation and turn against the parent who the child thinks, rightly or wrongly, has deprived him, and so that the deprived parent loses interest in the child and therefore does not make the material and emotional contribution to the child's development which that parent by its companionship and otherwise would make.
>
> So viewed, the cases which speak of the basic right to access of the non-custodian parent are to my mind . . . reconcilable and make sense. . . . They mean and are meant to mean not that a parent has any proprietorial right to access but that save in exceptional circumstances to deprive a parent of access is to deprive a child of an important contribution to his emotional and material growing up in the long term. (p. 88a-h, emphasis added)

Subsequent case law has developed the notion of "exceptional" circumstances. The appeal in *Re BC (A Minor) (Access)* [1985] Fam Law 223 held that if the effect of the conduct of a noncustodial parent was such as to cause *genuine and justified* anxiety in the mind of the custodial parent sufficient as to possibly affect his or her care of the child, then, although that conduct had no direct effect on the child in the sense that he or she was not ill-treated, the effect on the mother was a factor that the court would take into account.

Significantly, in *Re SM (A Minor) (Natural Father: Access)* [1991] 2 FLR 333, p. 339, a warning was issued to courts "not to apply too rigidly something described as the theoretical general principle of access being maintained between a child and [natural father]" without considering the practical consequences of such access. In *Re H (Minors) (Access)* [1992] 1 FLR 148, it was held that a court should be extremely slow to conclude that access to a parent should cease, and that (applying Latey's judgment in *M v. M* [1973]) the long-term advantage, in emotional and material terms, to a child in knowing his or her parents far outweighed the initial upset that separation often caused a child at access times.

If the possibility of undiagnosed PAS is held in mind, the judgment in *Re D (A Minor) (Contact: Mother's Hostility)* [1993] 2 FLR 1 is alarming. It was held that the mother's implacable hostility towards the father put the child at serious risk of emotional harm and consequently was sufficient reason for denying contact to the father. Waite LJ said: "I see no reason to think that the judge fell into any error of principle in deciding . . . that the mother's present attitude towards contact puts D at serious risk of major emotional harm if she were to be compelled to accept a degree of contact to the natural father against her will" (p. 7g).

In *Re H (Contact: Principles)* [1994] 2 FLR 969, it was again upheld that a child living with her mother should have contact with her father, unless cogent reasons for the child to be denied such contact existed. In this case, it was also noted that the mother intended to disobey any order for contact made or upheld by the court and "that was not a very attractive argument against contact and M's attitude was a very irresponsible one." In *Re M (Minors) (Contact: Welfare Test)* [1995] 1 FLR 274, it was held that the court must consider whether the fundamental emotional need of a child to have an enduring relationship with both parents was outweighed by the depth of harm that a child might suffer by virtue of a contact order, and that the judge had been entitled to form the view that the risk of distress to the children outweighed the strong presumption in favor of contact. Indirect contact with the mother over a period of some years had not been successful, and her application for renewal of direct contact was dismissed.

The general principles governing contact with nonresident parents were laid out in *Re O (A Minor) (Contact: Imposition of Conditions)* [1995] 2 FLR 124. Among these was that the welfare of the child was of paramount consideration but it was almost always in the best interest of the child that he or she have contact with both parents. Courts were reminded that they should not readily accept that the child's welfare would be injured by direct contact, and it was stressed that neither parent should be permitted to think that they were more likely to get their own way if they behaved more stubbornly. In *Re P (Contact: Supervision)* [1996] 2 FLR 314, the father of two children appealed against an order that he should have only indirect contact with them, due to the implacable hostility of the mother. He argued that the judge had given undue weight to the feelings of the mother in holding that the risk to her health caused by anxiety would put the children at serious risk of emotional harm. Justice Wall found (as per the rules in *G v. G* [1985] 1 WLR 647) that the judge had wrongly balanced the evidence and agreed with the father, whose behavior had been found to be exemplary. In *Re D (Contact: Reasons for Refusal)* [1997] 2 FLR 48, "implacable hostility" was defined as a situation in which *no* good reason for the parent's opposition to contact existed. It was held that the courts should be slow to conclude contact as harmful in such situations. *Re DG (A Minor: Evidence to Support Need for Supervised Contact)* [1997] (Lawtel, Document No. AC9100003, unreported elsewhere), held that the implacable hostility of the mother should in most cases not obstruct an order for unsupervised contact. The father had claimed that continued supervision of contact was greatly reducing the value of the contact, and the court ordered unsupervised contact. The mother had expressed a broad range of fears (from sexual abuse of the children to fears that the father was incapable of controlling them), which the court held to be wholly misplaced. The mother refused to allow unsupervised contact, and appealed. Ward LJ stated: "All orders of the Court are there to be obeyed; and even if it is a mother with young children who sets her face persistently and without reason against the enforcement of the order, then in the most extreme circumstances and in the face of persistent contumely, the Court will enforce the order by a sentence of imprisonment for contempt. It is of course the resort of last degree. But it should not be thought by anyone and it should not be thought by this mother that the armory of the Court is bare. I say again it is *not* – and the "not" can be underlined to give emphasis to it" (p. 4).

Re S (A Minor) (Contact: Justices Reasons) [1998] 2 FCR 446, held that the wishes and feelings of the child, or the objections of the mother, could outweigh the principle that it was a fundamental right of every child to have an enduring relationship with both parents.

PAS, although not assessed, seems likely to have been a key factor in the "implacable hostility" case of *Re M (A Minor) (Contempt of Court: Committal of Court's Own Motion)* [1999] Fam 263. It is relevant to note that in this case the father represented himself in court, reflecting the growing trend in the UK family courts of self-representation rather than parents placing their trust or any reliance on the services of a professional legal team. So many have felt seriously betrayed by family lawyers and by the judgments made by the family justice system, whereby all contact with their children was unnecessarily lost for years if not permanently, seemingly at the capricious whim of their ex-partner, that an increasing number of parents are electing to take the conduct of the law into their own hands in an attempt to achieve a just outcome for their families. Training courses on how to represent oneself in court, devised and run by already experienced in the practice, are now offered by some groups that are dedicated to achieving change in family law practice (e.g., *see* http://www.equalparenting.org/services_and_products.htm).

Ward LJ, at the beginning of his detailed judgment in this case, stated:

> One of the thorniest of the problems which face the judges exercising the "private law" jurisdiction of the Children Act 1989 is how to cope with the irrational, unjustifiable hostility shown by one parent towards the other which has the effect of alienating the children from the other parent and thus obstructing their contact with that parent. The courts have become sadly familiar with the troublesome question of whether or not a contact order should be made. Then the problem arises as to how the court should react when a party openly defies

> that contact order and the judges are being constrained on rare occasions to commit a parent to prison for breach of such orders. . . . [Coningsby J] summarised the findings he had made in his main judgment and emphatically rejected the mother's case that the father had been violent to the mother . . . and, importantly, that he had been violent to the children. He held that there was no justification for those allegations. He found that the mother had influenced or manipulated the children to make allegations against their father, that the mother was not an honest person whose word could be trusted, that her protestations that she really did wish to see face-to-face contact taking place between the father and the children was false. . . . The mother is determined to put an end to direct contact and has imposed those views on the children. (paras 1–4)

Ward LJ acknowledged that resident parents frequently ignore court orders for their children's contact with the nonresident parent, saying: "Turning now to the facts and circumstances of this case . . . the factors which appear to me to be important are these: (1) It is a sorry fact of life in the family courts that there was nothing exceptional about this case" (para 41). It is a sorry fact of life that UK family courts patently failed to address the problem of resident parents breaching contact orders when it first emerged. So often have resident parents been allowed freely to exercise such contempt that modern folklore holds that courts will allow them to "get away with it" as a foregone conclusion. Judges remain extremely reluctant to take sanctions against parents, particularly mothers, who flout court orders. By failing to act appropriately they undermine the credibility of the entire justice system. Yet the positive effects of the imprisonment in May 2002 of one mother who had persistently failed to send her children to school were felt nationwide, as previously truant schoolchildren suddenly appeared in school. Former Education Minister Estelle Morris said that education chiefs heard "dozens" of anecdotal tales of parents of truants arriving at school with their children – as a direct result of hearing about Patricia Amos's case. Amos told the BBC Radio 4 "Today" news program that prison had been "horrible," and that she would from then on ensure she was everywhere that she was meant to be. Interestingly, Amos noted that maybe she had to go to prison to "wake her up" and to make her recognize the responsibilities she carried as a parent (report online at http://news.bbc.co.uk/1/hi/education/2011268.stm)

If Amos's being sent to prison made her realize she was a parent with responsibilities and influenced the behavior of recalcitrant parents nationwide, it is probable that similar media coverage of the imprisoning of a parent for flouting court contact orders would have a similar effect. It is also, of course, a sorry fact of life that Lord Justice Ward in *Re M* [1999] could recognize such potential PAS cases as being "unexceptional" in our courts, but be unable to recognize or address PAS. This moves us on to a critical examination of "The Experts' Court Report" by Sturge and Glaser (2000).

"THE EXPERTS' COURT REPORT"

In their report to the court, Sturge and Glaser (2000) made reference to only one article written about PAS and they supported their denial of PAS's existence with this sole publication. These specially commissioned experts gave the court no indication whatsoever of the existence either of a large PAS theoretical and research literature, or of the many judicial decisions in other countries successfully based on it. Most unfortunately, although they also failed to mention this crucial fact, the sole article on which they relied had itself already been significantly discredited just a short time later in the very same journal in which it had been published (*see* Faller, 1998, and Gardner, 1998).

The national significance of this report should not be underestimated. That Sturge and Glaser's review of issues in contact and domestic violence is accepted as a fundamental and definitive statement of basic principle is demonstrated by its most grateful acceptance by the Court of Appeal in the case of *Re L, V, M, H* [2000]; by its similarly grateful acceptance in its entirety into the Children Act Subcommittee of the Lord Chancellor's Advisory Board on Family Law 2001 consultation paper "*Making Contact Work: The Facilitation of Arrangements for Contact between Children and their Non-Residential Parents and the Enforcement of Court Orders for Contact*" (e.g., *see* para 2.5); by its acceptance in its entirety in the resultant February 2002 "*Making Contact Work*" Report to the Lord Chancellor from the same subcommittee (see the report's Recommendation 1, page 113); and by the Government's own subsequent acceptance of that Recommendation ("*The Government's Response to the Report of the Children Act Sub-Committee of the Lord Chancellor's Advisory Board on Family Law Report 'Making Contact Work',*" Family Policy Division 2, August 2002, p. 4). This means that the entire Family Division of the Court of Appeal, the Lord Chancellor's Children Act Subcommittee of his Advisory Board on Family Law, and the Government itself via the Lord Chancellor were not made aware of the increasing global scientific and judicial recognition and acceptance of PAS. This was a direct result of their bona fide trusted experts' serious failure to provide the relevant comprehensive and impartial review required with regard to PAS. The wide-ranging acceptance and influence of this report is certainly excellent news for improving family law practice with regard to the management of situations in which actual domestic violence has occurred. However, at the same time, it elevates the seriousness of the same "experts'" gross failure to provide those bodies with an impartial review of the substantial PAS theoretical and research literature and case law, perhaps immeasurably. For two senior professionals appointed to provide an experts' report at such a level, this extremely partial treatment of PAS is simply inexcusable.

The limitations of Sturge and Glaser's Report with regard to PAS were addressed by Hobbs [2002a], and were submitted along with other materials about PAS to the Court of Appeal in *Re C (Prohibition on Further Applications)* [2002], and the total lack of reference to their report in the judgment in *Re C* was in itself a remarkable fact. A subsequent and comprehensive rebuttal of the report has been published online by Gardner (at http://www.rgardner.com/refs/ar19.html).

It has long been recognized in the PAS literature that acrimony, due to which PAS may develop in a child, is frequently associated with the alienating parent making *false* allegations of abuse against the target parent (e.g., *see* Gardner 1985, 1992). Almost every article written on PAS stresses the fact that a diagnosis can only be made where there exists *no* justified reason (such as actual violence or other abuse) for the child to develop such alienation. Nevertheless, it was entirely relevant and appropriate that one of the questions the Official Solicitor posed to Sturge and Glaser was "(3) what weight is to be placed upon the following factors in children contact cases? . . . (iv) where there is a case of parental alienation syndrome?" (Sturge and Glaser, 2000, pp. 619–622). The experts replied: Parental Alienation Syndrome does not exist in the sense that it is "[i] not recognised in either the American classification of mental disorders (DSM-IV) or the international classification of disorders (ICD-10); [ii] not generally recognised in our or allied child mental health specialities. We do not consider it to be a helpful concept and consider that the sort of problems that the title of this disorder is trying to address is better thought of as implacable hostility" (p. 622).

As PAS was an emerging and inadequately researched body of knowledge when the DSM and ICD committees were meeting in the early 1990s prior to publication of their respective diagnostic manuals, PAS most certainly should not have been included in either diagnostic manual; but as a direct result of the burgeoning research literature and case law on PAS, which these "experts" totally failed to bring to the courts' attention, it will be appropriate for those committees to consider seriously its inclusion in the next editions. In general clinical practice, most child and adolescent psychiatrists do recognize and assess the relevant factors on all sides of a PAS-conflicted family and, when providing comment in court, they will appropriately discuss these factors. However, they are reluctant to use the term PAS even if they are aware of the work done on it elsewhere in the world, and they generally will not refer to PAS voluntarily in court. This probably occurs for two main reasons. First, there exists a natural and commendable wish to avoid psychiatric labeling of children wherever possible. Second, when professionals know of the judicial nonacceptance of PAS, they may also hold the potentially valid belief that the court would be less likely to respect their expert testimony if the family's difficulties were overtly referred to in PAS terminology. The expert testimony of Dr. Ludwig Lowenstein in the *Re M* appeal in *Re L, V, M, H* [2000], for which the Sturge and Glaser report was commissioned, was a clear demonstration of this (p. 351g–h). Sturge and Glaser's suggestion that PAS equates to "implacable hostility" suggests that they hold minimal comprehension of what constitutes PAS. PAS could indeed be said to be a specific form of implacable hostility, but in PAS it is the child who is centrally involved in enacting the alienation. It is quite inappropriate to fail to distinguish PAS from other forms of implacable hostility that present in courts.

The assertion that PAS does not exist on the basis that it does not appear in the two relevant psychiatric diagnostic manuals must in any case now be an entirely fruitless line of reasoning within UK case law. In recent years in the UK criminal courts a series of cases have occurred, where women who have killed their partners have then successfully claimed they suffered from "battered woman syndrome" (BWS) as a defense of provocation to no less than the ultimate human crime of murder: *R v. Ahluwalia* [1992] 4 All ER 889; *R v. Thornton (Sarah Elizabeth)* [1992] 1 All ER 306; *R v. Thornton (Sarah Elizabeth) (No 2)* [1996] 1 WLR 1174; *R v. Grainger (Dawn Tracey)* [1997] 1 Cr App R 369; *R v. Hobson (Kathleen)* [1998] 1 Cr App R 31; *R v. Fell (Tara Mary)* [2000] 2 Cr App R 46; *R v. Jacob (Brenda)* [2000] CA. (Crim) No: 99/6066/Y4 (3-5-00); *R v. Anderson (Deborah Margaret)* [2000] CA. (Crim) No. 200002064/X5

(27-11-00); *R v. Muscroft (Anita)* [2001] EWCA Crim 604; *R v. Smith (Josephine)* [2002] EWCA Crim 2671.

BWS arguably occurs when a person has been subjected over a long period of time to sustained brutality. The theory is that deep resentment slowly builds up within the affected person to a degree where, akin to the sudden release of steam from a pressure cooker, the person suddenly loses control and strikes back at their attacker, with potentially fatal results. Recognized features of BWS include: chronic depressive illness, feelings of hopelessness, helplessness, and despair, inability to act effectively, inability to see any escape from the situation or any hope for the future, self-blame for the violence inflicted upon her by her male partner, a failure to see that what was happening was abnormal because she was isolated from reality, shame and a poor sense of self-worth, and submission as a form of self-protection. As with PAS, those in the psychiatry and psychology fields disagree as to whether this condition exists. Also similar to PAS, clinically the characteristic constellation of factors appearing together are recognized by many senior practitioners as predictive, unified, and as comprising a syndrome. Crucially, however, also similar to PAS, BWS is not contained in either DSM-IV or ICD-10; nor could it have been, as it also has only recently been recognized by the scientific community.

Section 3 of the 1957 Homicide Act provides for the defense of provocation: "Where on a charge of murder there is evidence on which the jury can find that the person charged was provoked (whether by things done or by things said or by both together) to lose his self-control, the question whether the provocation was enough to make a reasonable man do as he did shall be left to be determined by the jury; and in determining that question the jury shall take into account everything both done and said according to the effect which, in their opinion, it would have on a reasonable man." British case law has long held that for provocation to be proven there had to be "some act, or series of acts, done by the dead man to the accused which would cause in any reasonable person, and actually causes in the accused, a sudden and temporary loss of self- control, rendering the accused so subject to passion as to make him or her for the moment not master of his mind" (*Duffy* [1949] 1 All ER 932). Exactly this same principle was applied in the case of Sarah Elizabeth Thornton (*R v. Thornton* [1992] 1 All ER 306): ". . . for the question of provocation to be shown, there had to be conduct that suddenly and temporarily deprived the accused of the power of self-control. Provocative acts in the course of domestic violence that did not cause a sudden loss of control did not amount to provocation in law." She was convicted in 1989 of murdering her partner. However, in 1995, subsequent to the admission of newly available medical information about BWS in particular its "slow-burn" nature (that results in a possible delay between the provocation and subsequent violent retaliation), combined with legal argument to the effect that she may have been suffering from a personality disorder in addition to BWS at the time of the killing. Thornton's murder conviction was duly quashed *(R v. Thornton (No 2)* [1996] 1 WLR 1174). It is maybe intriguing to note that the requisite British legal comparative "reasonable man" in this case, effectively took on the attributes of a personality disordered (and therefore inherently *un*reasonable) woman.

In other cases where this defense has been successful on Appeal, often the result of the new medical evidence having been made available, the previous conviction for murder has been reduced to one of manslaughter and the prison sentence reduced accordingly. There has also been a series of cases in which women convicted of manslaughter subsequent to repeated domestic violence have had probation substituted for the sentences passed, albeit after some of the prison term was served *(R v. Gardner (Janet Susan)* [1993] 14 Cr. App. R.(S.) 364; *R v. Grainger (Dawn Tracey)* [1997] 1 Cr. App. R.(S.) 369 and *R v. Higgins (Leslie Susan)* [1996] 1 Crim. App. R. (S.) 271. It is entirely anomalous that in British courts a clinically accepted syndrome that is unrecognized in the relevant diagnostic manuals (DSM-IV and ICD-10) can repeatedly be justifiably used in British courts in a provocation defense of a person charged with murder, whereas the occurrence of PAS can be disregarded in family courts largely on the basis that it is not recognized in the same relevant diagnostic manuals, with the consequent destructive, trans-generational effects on both child and target parent.

In partial defense of Sturge and Glaser, they do acknowledge that they were not "asked to address the issue of the mother's part in any domestic violence" (p. 621). By current definition, domestic violence ranges enormously in degree, from an angry shout after immense provocation, to its most extreme example, when one partner murders the other. Usually, it is the man who murders the woman, but this is by no means exclusively so, as the several cases depending on BWS as a defense to a charge of murder so clearly demonstrate. In *Re L, V, M, H* [2000], Lord Justice Thorpe wisely rejected a part of Sturge and Glaser's recommendations that related to this issue:

The danger of elevating any one factor in what will always be an extremely complex evaluation is to move the pendulum too far and thus to create an excessive concentration on past history and an over-reflection of physical abuse within the determination of individual cases. I would not adopt the suggestion in the expert psychiatric report [2000] Fam Law 615, 623: "From all that is written above, it will be clear that we consider that there should be no automatic assumption that contact to a previously or currently violent parent is in the child's interests; if anything the assumption should be in the opposite direction and the case of the non-residential parent one of proving why he can offer something of such benefit not only to the child but to the child's situation . . . that contact should be considered."

As the quotation itself suggests, there is a spectrum within the broad categorisation of domestic violence from the slap that may have been provoked to premeditated murder. There is the equally obvious distinction between past abuse which has been acknowledged and addressed and a continuing risk of future violence if any opportunity is created. In my opinion the only direction that can be given to the trial judge is to apply the welfare principle and the welfare check list, section 1(1)(3) of the Children Act 1989, to the facts of the particular case. It follows that I am doubtful as to whether specific guidelines are now required but my preference would be for brevity and simplicity always bearing in mind the risk of creating satellite litigation as to how the guidelines should be construed and applied. (p. 370d-h)

As noted, it has long been recognized that PAS frequently occurs along with repeated false allegations of sexual and/or other forms of physical or emotional abuse, neglect, or a fabricated history of spousal abuse. Although it needs to be borne in mind that in PAS parents of either gender can be the alienator, just as parents of either gender may be violent, such terrible allegations as these comprise severe provocation to the recipient partner. Those allegations are intended to hurt the target parent and to manipulate key others to effect their removal from their children, and these allegations *will* precipitate anger in response. In fact, they may be expressly designed in order to precipitate an angry response so that the alienating parent can present that successfully provoked anger as further evidence against the target parent. Currently in the United Kingdom, if the target parent even verbally expresses this natural response, it may be deemed criminal domestic violence and thereby used as a further weapon in the fight for alienation. Sturge and Glaser twice further address this issue, albeit indirectly. Indeed, it is almost uncanny how, despite their rejection of PAS, they nevertheless frequently describe PAS dynamics yet entirely fail to appreciate their significance. First, in relation to the impact of psychiatric disorder, they state:

The context of the overall situation is highly relevant to decision making. The contribution of psychiatric disorders to situations of domestic violence and emotional abuse must be considered. Such disorders will have put enormous pressures not only on the child but on the other parent. Depression and delusional disorders are obvious examples but personality disorders may be most relevant in this context. Where such a personality disorder affects interpersonal relationships both the relationship with the partner and with the child are likely to have been marked by unstable and intense relations on an inter-personal level with extremes of feelings, anger problems and other behavioural problems – for example, jealousy and irrational ideas, threats or acts of self-harm and marked impulsivity. (p. 620, emphasis added)

Second, in a list of reasons for a resident parent taking a position of "implacable hostility (by implication to the ex-partner as much as to contact)" (p. 622), they included:

(e) *Wholly biased hostility which is not based on real events or experience.* This may be conscious and malign or perceived to be true. The latter encompass the full continuum from misperceptions and misunderstandings through overvalued ideas to delusional states. The former may result from a simple wish to wipe the slate clean and start again and can be seen after relationships that were initially highly romantic or idealised and for the breakdown of which the woman can only account for by vilifying the partner in order to avoid facing the possibility that the breakdown in the relationship was her failure and amounts to rejection.

It is in this . . . situation (e), in which there are often sexual abuse allegations emanating mainly from the resident carer, which particularly exercise experts and the courts as the fathers may be well-functioning, well-meaning and represent a real potential for a good relationship with the child. (p. 623, emphasis added)

In his powerful rebuttal, Gardner [2002] several times points out how the descriptions of the violently abusive parent given by Sturge and Glaser may be equally applied to the alienating parent in PAS. He repeatedly demonstrates how Sturge and Glaser

are blind to the fact that a parent who induces a PAS in a child is, per se, an abusive parent – specifically, an emotionally abusive parent. The indoctrination of a PAS into a child is a form of emotional abuse because it can bring about the attenuation, and even destruction, of the bond between the child and a good, loving parent. PAS indoctrination is also a form of abuse of the alienated spouse because that parent, although a good and loving parent, has become the focus of the child's campaign of denigration,

> aided and abetted by the alienating parent. In essence, a PAS indoctrinator is both an abusing parent and an abusing ex-partner. The authors' denial of the PAS is consistent with their denial of the existence of this form of abuser.

Gardner [2002] develops this in reference to Sturge and Glaser's comments on the risks of direct and indirect contact. Sturge and Glaser had referred to the risk of "emotional abuse through the denigration of the child directly or the child's resident carer, through using the contact as a means of continuing or escalating the 'war' with the resident parent, for example, seeking derogatory information, engendering secrets, making derogatory remarks in an attempt to undermine the resident parent. This can also be seen as increasing distortions in the child's perceptions and understanding of reality" (p. 618).

Gardner [2002] comments:

> Sturge and Glaser are describing here, quite precisely and accurately, exactly what PAS indoctrinators do. And this is especially the case when the PAS indoctrinator is the residential parent. If one were to believe these two, there is no such thing as a residential parent who would be a PAS indoctrinator. They only attribute such behaviors to a non-residential parent, and just label them as a form of emotional abuse of the child and the resident caretaker. However, if one follows Sturge and Glaser's own guidelines here, then one should reduce the child's access to such a parent – and even transfer custody away from the parent – who engages in this activity. This is exactly what I myself recommend regarding the alienating parent (which the authors here describe as the abusing parent).

Another risk the authors describe follows, p. 618 (ii)(c):

> Continuation of unhealthy relationships, for example, inappropriately dominant or bullying relationships, controlling relationships through subtly or blatantly maintaining (or initiating) fear or through other means (for example bribes, emotional blackmail).
>
> Of course, there are abusive parents who are not PAS indoctrinators who behave this way. However, this is also exactly what PAS indoctrinators do. They have an unhealthy relationship with the child because they are controlling, bribing, and they use emotional blackmail in order to get the child to profess antagonism toward the good, loving target parent. Once again, I am in agreement with the authors that the child's access to such bullies should be reduced if not cut off entirely. I am in agreement also with the authors that such parents are also justifiably referred to as emotional abusers. The only difference I have with the authors here– and it is a formidable one – is that they have not selected out from this group of abusers the subgroup of abusers properly recognized as PAS indoctrinators. Rather, because of their failure to have researched PAS competently prior to dismissing it outright, they let them blend in – unidentified – with the rest of the bullies of the world. There are different categories of bullies, and each category must be dealt with differently.

Gardner [2002] concludes his rebuttal with the observation that:

> Although they attempt to discredit and ultimately to deny the existence of PAS, they instead unwittingly provide strong support for its existence by delineating the measures that must be taken to protect children from abusing parents. Similarly, they also unwittingly provide confirmation for my own recommendations regarding the measures that should be utilized for protecting children from PAS indoctrinators.
>
> Those who follow Sturge and Glaser's recommendations, and who as a result do not properly differentiate between PAS indoctrinators and other forms of emotional abusers, will fail to discriminate between these two groups and they will consequently fail to be able to deal effectively with them. . . . Those who follow this "Expert's" report, and consequently fail to make these vital differentiations, will contribute to the entrenchment of the PAS in these children and the ongoing grief of PAS victim spouses – both male and female.

In practice, one of the crucially important factors for children after their parents' separation is that the parents attempt to confine their anger to within the parent-parent relationship, and subsequently to minimize its ability to impose and have a destructive effect on either of the parent-child relationships. This applies equally to the parent venting their hurt and anger through violence or to attempts via repeated forceful denigration to alienate the child from the target parent. At such a traumatic time children will greatly need the stability of maintaining, and even increasing, their physical and emotional closeness with both of their parents. This will help them survive this tremendous upheaval in their own lives. This will particularly apply to those children who have previously enjoyed close, loving relationships with both of their parents. Children need to know, and to feel, that it is their parents' relationship that has broken down and not their own with either parent. Courts also need to protect children's knowledge of this. Sturge and Glaser, most appropriately, observed "If there is a strong relationship, bond or attachment, that is a good reason to continue and promote contact as failure to do so will be an emotional loss for the child and much more likely to be experienced as an abandonment or rejection" (p. 622).

Children quickly pick up on their parents' emotional states; the manner in which they do this differs according to age and other factors. Children sense each parent's feelings for them when they are with them and, therefore, they need the significant personal validation and reassurance from time spent with each parent, particularly if they have enjoyed a good relationship previously. In addition, when the alienation process has already begun to affect the child, he or she will benefit from frequent opportunities to reality-test the other parent's imparted negative views, and this will need to be sensitively handled by the nonresident parent. The alienating parent, if moved to undo the damage, will need to provide therapeutic counter statements for the "increasing distortions in the child's perceptions and understanding of reality" (Sturge and Glaser, p. 618) that they have caused. A degree of support and education may be beneficial for both of the parents and the children. In the United States and elsewhere, a body of knowledge on the successful management of PAS is accruing. This success is assisted, in many cases, by appropriate parent education, although it remains fundamentally dependent on effective judicial action, combined with necessary training of all relevant professionals. The aim should be to enable the child to once again enjoy and benefit from the best possible relationship with both his or her parents, rather than with only one.

Intriguingly, a potentially helpful aid for courts in assessing an alienating parent's motivation to overcome his or her previous destructive behavior might be to apply an appropriately paraphrased version of Sturge and Glaser's own checklist for balancing the advantages and disadvantages of contact (p. 624a-g). Their checklist can be paraphrased as follows:

> Inculcation of PAS involves a very serious and significant failure in parenting – failure to protect the child emotionally and failure to protect the child's other parent. If the following characteristics are not present in the alienating parent, contact with that parent should be limited or discontinued, unless or until that parent achieves such characteristics (possibly through engaging in appropriate therapy):
>
> (a) a reasonable (preferably full) acknowledgment of the alienation precipitated;
>
> (b) some acceptance (preferably full, if appropriate i.e., if the sole instigator of alienation), of responsibility for that alienation;
>
> (c) full acceptance of the inappropriateness of the denigration contributing to the resultant alienation, particularly in respect to the target parent's parenting ability and love for the child, and of the ill effects on the child;
>
> (d) a genuine interest in the child's welfare and full commitment to the child (i.e., a wish for contact for which he or she is not making the conditions);
>
> (e) a wish to make reparation to the child and work toward helping the child recognize the inappropriateness of the alienation and the attitude toward and treatment of the target parent, and helping the child to develop appropriate values and attitudes;
>
> (f) an expression of regret and the showing of some understanding of the impact of the behavior on the ex-partner in the past and currently;
>
> (g) indications that the previously alienating parent can reliably sustain a realistic nondenigrating stance regarding the previously targeted parent in their ongoing relationship with their mutual child.

Both parents then need to be able to forgive (but not necessarily forget) past misdeeds, and to find a way to move on psychologically, for the considerable benefit of their child.

Finally, in deliberating on PAS in the future, it may be helpful for courts to bear in mind that the Sturge and Glaser review is not a formal statement from the Royal College of Psychiatrists, nor do the authors make such a claim. Although some colleagues read and supported their work, their report was not presented to, debated or adopted by the executive of the child and adolescent faculty of the Royal College. Its status is, therefore, that of a personal statement by two properly respected and senior members of their profession, which, although generally of impeccable quality, I believe is of no value whatsoever in relation to PAS. It is appropriate to observe that Sturge and Glaser's dismissal of PAS could appropriately be put to the test for professional negligence applied in *Bolam v. Friern Hospital Management Committee* [1957] 1 WLR 582 (*see also Bolitho v. City and Hackney Health Authority* [1998] AC 232; *Sidaway v. Board of Governors of the Bethlem Royal Hospital and The Maudsley Hospital and Others* [1985] AC 871; and *Maynard v. West Midlands Regional Health Authority* [1984] 1 WLR 634). Would a court take the view that these two expert psychiatrists, in a report of this predictable level of significance, omitting even to mention let alone impartially review the large body of research and case law on PAS was unreasonable?

THE EUROPEAN COURT OF HUMAN RIGHTS AND PRACTICE OF UK FAMILY LAW

Subsequent to the UK's entry into the European Economic Community in 1957 via the Treaty of Rome (retitled the Treaty of the European Communities by the Maastricht 1992 Treaty of European Union), the European Court of Justice has had judicial supremacy over the UK courts, however grudgingly our domestic courts may initially have acquiesced to this (*see*, e.g., Lord Denning in *MacCarthys Ltd v. Smith* (129/79) [1980] ECR 1275 and Lord Bridge in *Factortame Ltd v. Secretary of State for Transport (No 1)* [1989] 2 All ER 692).

What is of particularly crucial relevance to the UK's recognition and management of PAS subsequent to Sturge and Glaser's findings on PAS, is that the 1998 Human Rights Act came into force throughout the UK in October 2000. Since that time, all domestic legislation and previous precedent case law must be construed in accordance with the enacted portions of the 1950 European Convention on Human Rights, and, of course, in accordance with the judgments of the European Court of Human Rights.

The first case referring to PAS in the Strasbourg-based European Court of Human Rights (ECHR) occurred in July, 2000. In the carefully reasoned judgment in *Elsholz v Germany* [2000] 2 FLR 486, the ECHR held (p. 501, para 70) that the German judiciary had interfered with "one of the most fundamental rights, namely, that of respect for family life". This contravened Article 8 of the 1950 European Convention for the Protection of Human Rights and Fundamental Freedoms, the relevant part of which provides: "(1) Everyone has the right to respect for his . . . family life. (2) There shall be no interference by a public authority with the exercise of this right except such as is in accordance with the law and is necessary in a democratic society . . . for the protection of health or morals, or for the protection of the rights and freedom of others." In addition, the ECHR held that the German judiciary had breached Elsholz's right to a fair and public hearing. The relevant part of Article 6.1., the right to a fair trial, provides: "In the determination of his civil rights and obligations . . . everyone is entitled to a fair and public hearing within a reasonable time by an independent and impartial tribunal established by law."

Although this case did not contain an assessment for PAS, the facts contain hallmark similarities to so many other cases in which PAS has gone unrecognized. From early on, identifiable signs of potential PAS were not acknowledged as such and the power of the courts, and the very substantial delays inherent in the court process, were collusively enlisted to support the alienating parent's resistance to any reasonable contact. Crucially for future European and UK family court practice, serious allegations were not tested for accuracy and expert evidence on PAS was refused. Effectively, the alienated parent was not allowed a fair hearing and became perceived as a troublemaker because he would not accept his District, Regional, or Federal courts' decision.

The child enjoyed a relationship with both parents until July 1991 (when the child was four-and-a-half). This successful period included 3 years following the parents' separation. Suddenly, he began to refuse contact with his father. From early on evidence showed that he was strongly influenced by the mother's negative perception of his father. In 1992, when the child was 6 years old, the district court observed:

> that the child had been heard and had stated that he no longer wished to see his father who, *according to the child*, was bad and had beaten his mother repeatedly. The mother likewise had strong objections to the applicant which *she had imparted on the child, so that the child had no possibility of building an unbiased relationship with his father.* The District Court concluded that contacts with the father would not enhance the child's well being. (p. 489, para 13, emphasis added)

The German judiciary, in giving the mother sole custody of the child, thereby unwittingly colluded with the alienation process. The mother then needed to do little to maintain the child's self-perpetuating alienation. Further challenges from the father, who clearly wanted to maintain his relationship with his son, were seen as his challenging the considered decision of the German judiciary. In 1993, the father's new request to be granted access was dismissed. His son was now seven. The ECHR judgment acknowledges that the district court had noted:

> that the applicant's relationship with the child's mother was so strained that the enforcement of access rights could not be envisaged as this would not be in the interests of the child's well being. *The child knew about his mother's objections to the applicant and had adopted them.* . . . After two long interviews with the child, the District Court reached the conclusion that his development would be endangered if the child had to take up contacts with his father *contrary to his mother's will.* The District Court . . . found it unnecessary to obtain an expert opinion. (p. 489, para 16, emphasis added)

At the supra national judicial level of Europe, the father argued that U.S. research and case law on PAS should be considered, and the ECHR agreed. This parent had had to choose between walking away from his own child and taking on his country at a constitutional level. Although such refusal to acknowledge and take proper account of PAS continues in domestic courts, it cannot be surprising that so many alienated parents eventually give up, losing all contact with their children.

In October 2001, the ECHR gave judgment in the conjoined *Sahin v. Germany; Sommerfeld v. Germany; Hoffmann v Germany* [2002] 1 FLR 119. Once again the authorities were held to have violated families' Human Rights under Article 8. Exceptionally for this court, Sahin appeared as a litigant in person. Sahin and his partner were unmarried and their child was born in 1988. The parents separated in 1989/1990 and the mother had refused Sahin all contact with their child since November 1990. No reason other than the mother's dislike of the father was ever offered for this refusal of contact; however, the resultant courts' failure even to challenge the mother's attitude and behavior ensured that, as desired by the mother, no access continued. The local District Court rejected Sahin's application for access one day per week and in its judgment the ECHR noted that:

> The [District] court considered that the applicant's wish to see his daughter resulted from his sincere bonds and true affection. Nevertheless, the court reached the conclusion that access was not in the child's interest as Ms D had taken such a strong dislike to the applicant and opposed any contacts so firmly that the child would be put into a situation of antipathy and tension which would probably considerably affect her well-being.
>
> The court saw no special circumstances which, nevertheless, could render such contacts beneficial for the child. The relations which had developed between the applicant and his child during the period of cohabitation could not possibly be of such importance as to take the risk that the child be irritated on account of the mother's feelings of dislike. (para 12)

The court's words are cause for considerable concern when seen from a potential PAS viewpoint. The court and its power were clearly targeted by the potentially alienating parent, as happens so often in PAS cases, and because of the court's inability to perceive accurately what it was faced with, it unwittingly colluded with this child being deprived of the benefit of one of her parents simply at the whim of the other parent. A psychologist, appointed by the Regional Court to provide expert opinion, failed to assist or alert the court in this regard. At first meeting the father objected to this supposedly independent and objective expert's overtly apparent bias. Astonishingly, having already made her recommendations to the court, (that there should be no contact between father and child), this expert later "indicated that she had not directly asked the child about her father" at any time (para 18). Based on the insufficiently competent "expert's" report, which provided the court with its crucial information, when considering the general issue of contact between unmarried fathers and their children:

> The Regional Court considered that such contacts could be ordered only if this was advantageous and beneficial for the child's well-being. It could be assumed that, as a rule, such contacts were ordered as regular contacts between a father and his child offered the possibility of a normal development and facilitated the forming of the child's own personality. In applying these principles in the applicant's case, the court found that the applicant applied for access on the ground of true love for his daughter. However, such responsible motives could not result in granting a right of access which would have to be enforced. The child would suffer from the existing tensions between the parents on the occasion of every contact and her further development would be disturbed. (para 21)

In contrast, the ECHR pointed out that, according to its 1996 judgment in *Johansen v. Norway* [1997] 23 EHRR 33, "the mutual enjoyment by parent and child of each other's company constitutes a fundamental element of family life, even if the relationship between the parents has broken down, and domestic measures hindering such enjoyment amount to an interference with the right protected by Article 8 of the Convention" (para 34). Finding in Sahin's favor, the ECHR awarded pecuniary compensation and considered its finding that the applicant's human rights had been violated as itself comprising some degree of compensation. One wonders whether Sahin or Elsholz have as yet successfully met with their own children, let alone had the advantage of any relevant professional expertise to enable resolution of residual emotional disturbance within the child, or themselves, arising from the enforced separation and alienation of their children from them.

In a recent case comment on *Sahin* (EHRLR, 2002, 3, pp. 403–406), attention was drawn to the judgment in *Soderback v. Sweden* (2000) 29 EHRR 95, in which it was noted that:

> the concept of family life on which Article 8 is based embraces, even where there is no cohabitation, the tie between a parent and his or her child, regardless of whether or not the latter was born in wedlock. . . . Article 8 cannot be interpreted as only protecting family life which has already been established but, where the circumstances warrant it, must be extended to the potential relationship which may develop between a natural father and a child born out of wedlock. Relevant factors in this regard include the nature of the relationship between the natural parents and the demonstrable interest in and commitment by the natural father to the child both before and after birth.

The commentary observed that where such a tie has been established the fact that only limited contacts have subsequently occurred will not be sufficient to break that tie. This judgment could surely be used in support of reinstatement of the targeted parent-child contact in PAS cases, although any person intending using this case should, as always, carefully check the original source, as it contained cogent arguments that could be used alternatively.

England and Wales

The apparent recognition of PAS by the President of the High Court Family Division, sitting in the Court of Appeal with senior colleagues, in the landmark case of *Re C (Prohibition on Further Applications)* [2002] was highlighted at the beginning of this chapter. In giving her judgment Butler-Sloss P gave leave for the "C" family situation to be assessed by a psychiatrist or psychologist "to see whether there is any way out of the problems and not to concentrate upon the issue of parental alienation syndrome. *That will of course take its place in any consideration* but not to obscure the other matters that may need to be looked at" (para 13, emphasis added).

It is relevant to question whether Hobbs' bold statement that "the Court of Appeal in *Re C* has now acknowledged the existence of PAS. This is a significant development in UK family law practice" (2002b, p. 381), was indeed valid. Consideration of the exact words used by the president in her judgment and comparison with relevant previously published judgments described in this chapter support as incontrovertible fact that this was indeed an unprecedented acknowledgement of PAS. However, a simple confusion of necessarily pedantic semantics may provide helpful explanation. It has become obvious that more than one level of judicial recognition of PAS exists. One level is the courts' recognition of the necessity of assessing for PAS as part of any comprehensive assessment, as indisputably given in *Elsholz* [2000], *Sahin* [2002], and *Re C* [2002]. This level of recognition, however, can by no means equate to the comprehensive acknowledgment or *confirmation* of PAS as a distinct syndrome that occurs once it is necessarily subjected to the *Frye*, *Daubert* or *Mohan* tests. These are the judicially required tests applied in other jurisdictions to test the acceptability of new scientific knowledge, as a direct result of which PAS has been accepted as a viable scientific entity in several jurisdictions.

Perhaps it is therefore appropriate to observe that although the fundamental principles underlying the dynamics involved in PAS now appear to be acknowledged by the Court of Appeal as being at least relevant for assessment in any conflicted contact cases, the formal acceptance in this country of PAS as an acknowledged scientific entity remains at some point in the future. This is despite its scientific credentials having already successfully passed the stringent tests applied in several other jurisdictions. PAS successfully passed the *Frye* test in Florida, within six months of Sturge and Glaser's denial of its existence in the UK Court of Appeal (*Kilgore v. Boyd*, Circuit Court of the 13th Judicial Circuit of the State of Florida, Hillsborough County, Family Law Division. Case no. 94-7573, Div. D. Nov 22, 2000). It is widely, though only informally, acknowledged that part of this difficulty in the UK is the application of the term "syndrome" in this context. Two recent cases, both of which studiously manage to avoid a direct reference to PAS, confirm this judicial position.

Lord Justice Thorpe gave judgment in October 2002 in *Re T (A Child) (Contact: Alienation: Permission to Appeal)* [2003] 1 FLR 531. The case involved complex family relationships, with the child himself suddenly refusing the American father all contact several months after the father's brother (who violently assaulted the father and was charged with a criminal offence) had contacted the British mother (with whom in Britain the son resided) and alleged the father was not a safe parent. Thorpe LJ notes that the father's relationship with his son had previously been a good one. The father stated, "when I tried to speak to JW in the car park he told me I was a liar, was drunk all the time and that nobody liked me. He told me never to call him again" (para 6). Thorpe LJ's detailed judgment gives several examples of JW's behavior that, if given in context in a proper assessment, could be deemed as symptomatic of PAS. He observed that the father's case emphasized:

> the chronology of the emergence and growth of JW's antagonism. It is clearly established that (a) supervised contact ended happily on July 4th; (b) angry accusations of drink, drugs and guns were leveled on July 27th and August 6th; (c) despite another period of successful supervised staying contact in August they revived with the new dimension of homosexuality on October 23rd. The father's failings could not provide the explanation. The chronology could only be explained by the mother's deliberate indoctrination. (para 19)

In response, Thorpe LJ observed, the mother's advocate gave "a comprehensive review of the evidence of the father's failings during U.S. contact visits and generally, particularly from the evidence of his brother, niece, and two former family retainers. She submitted that the alienation issue was essentially settled by the judge's findings as to the father's conduct. Finally, she submitted that the European decisions cited by [father's attorney] added nothing to our own jurisprudence" (para 20). Thorpe LJ found that:

the judge failed to address the issue of alienation sufficiently and to make sufficient findings on that issue. [The mother's attorney's] survey of the long history of the father's failings during contact in America simply does not meet the emphatic point that all JW's aggression and rejection emerge for the first time on July 27th, and then escalate significantly between August 10th and October 23rd. Her reliance on the case of *Re H* is inapt where the child's alienation is self-evident and the judge has the quasi-inquisitorial task to assess its origins. *I reject her dismissive submission that the Strasbourg cases add nothing to the domestic jurisprudence. Those cases as they stand suggest that the methods and levels of investigation that our courts have conventionally adopted when trying out issues of alienation may not meet the standards that Articles 6 and 8 require.* There are policy issues here that the government and the judiciary may need to consider collaboratively. Should judges see children to ascertain their wishes and feelings? If that is to become the norm, what training should judges receive? To what extent should separate representation be made available to the child at the heart of the case in private law proceedings? What services can CAFCASS [Children and Family Court Advisory and Support Service] be expected to provide in order to assist the forensic process to satisfy Convention standards? (para 25, emphasis added)

However, Thorpe LJ apparently distances himself from any potential inference being made regarding PAS (it having been directly referred to in those European judgments) as he continues: "These European cases were not cited to the judge below. I do not in the present appeal found my conclusion upon them. The obligation to investigate the origins of alienation, rather than an allegation of malign alienation, in my judgement stems from our conventional domestic standards and not from higher standards arguably required by the cases cited" (para 25). Also giving detailed judgment in this case, Lady Justice Arden stated:

In all the circumstances, I do not think that it would be right for this court to conclude that there was no conclusion that the judge could reasonably have reached other than that the mother had deliberately caused the alienation.

However, as I have concluded that the judge failed to make a finding or sufficiently reasoned finding on alienation by the mother or to make it clear that he was not making such a finding, I consider that this appeal should be allowed.

I should like to add this postscript. JW's alienation from his father is worrying. As the judge recognised, it is important that it should be addressed as soon as possible. Obviously the matter will have to be considered by the judge to whom this matter is now remitted but it is to be hoped that conditions can be devised so that contact can be restored between JW and his father as soon as possible. There will be an opportunity at that hearing to address a separate point, which has not been raised on this appeal, as to the representation of JW in these proceedings. The interests of JW are paramount (Children Act 1989, section 1). These proceedings have now become a dispute between JW's parents, and in that dispute many allegations and cross-allegations have been made of a very personal nature, which must inevitably cause great hurt and emotion. I have no doubt that the judges of the Family Division have great experience of this situation, but it may be that in these special circumstances and given the evident ability of the parents to pay for that representation, consideration should be given for JW to be separately represented. This may be a way, in the particular circumstances of this case, in which the wishes of JW can be ascertained in accordance with the recent jurisprudence of the European Court of Human Rights on article 8 of the Convention. (paras 55–57)

This passage contains the worrying but nevertheless harshly realistic prospect that in this country it may be the financial ability of the parents of a PAS child that determines whether that child's own wishes, and the underlying reason for those wishes, will be adequately represented to the court "in accordance with the recent jurisprudence of the European Court of Human Rights on article 8 of the Convention." To set a new case precedent, those wishes would require an extensive assessment for PAS by an expert. Currently, it is likely that this assessment and subsequent court appearance would involve the massive expense of flying in a PAS expert, probably from America. Few parents could afford this.

Finally, the February 2003 case of *IP v. NP* [2003] EWHC 151 (Family) has directed that the case papers should be seen by a child psychiatrist, though if the psychiatrist's recommendations include an interview with the children, the mother should have a right to make further recommendations to the court. The court was influenced by the harm apparently being done to the children by the mother's sustained antipathy towards the father, which, it was noted, she "was plainly sharing with the children. She was depriving them of any knowledge or even contact with their father whose health was significantly deteriorating. Secondly, the children themselves had no adverse recollection of the father nor did they know whether they liked seeing him in the past or not. Thirdly, the parents and children were members of unusually close families." It was also held that "the history was of a mother who had successfully imbued the children with a negative attitude even when it was seen that their distress was at times artificial. The balance between the harm that was doing and the potential harm of actual contact required further consideration in the children's best interest."

Sadly, mention must be made of the grossly inadequate role played by CAFCASS Legal (the still relatively new term for the old "Official Solicitor" appointed by courts to represent children) in this case, considering the current European and domestic case law, and the long-standing knowledge of PAS in other jurisdictions. Had not the CAFCASS director denied PAS existence, this CAFCASS report may have been able to help the family towards resolution of its difficulties. A report was requested from a CAFCASS legal officer to consider, among other things, the reason why contact had not taken place and what recommendations could be made for future involvement of experts or other disciplines. The officer reported that the father and children had not had direct contact for three years, but failed to recommend an investigation into the background allegations between the parties as "he did not believe it would have any significant outcome." His view was that the children had been brought up with a clear belief of the truth of the mother's account, with consequent antipathy towards the father. He believed there would be no improvement in the mother's position with or without any expert intervention. Even though he found no overwhelming reason why the father should not have a relationship with the children, he believed that such contact could not come about without a significant change in the mother, which he stated would not occur. He reported that to continue the proceedings would be abusive of the children and in their interests he recommended that the proceedings should be dealt with summarily on the basis of indirect contact. Perhaps it should again be noted here that despite the strong direction given to CAFCASS by the Family Division President in *Re C* [2002] that the "C" family be assessed for possible PAS effects, CAFCASS Legal made no attempt for any such assessment to be done.

Family courts rely heavily on the professional opinions of their main advisers. These dedicated personnel, drawn from a combination of probation and social work backgrounds, were regrouped in the United Kingdom as the Children and Family Court Advisory and Support Service (CAFCASS), under the Criminal Justice and Court Services Act 2000, Chapter II. This still relatively new service struggles with considerable difficulties (*see* Gerlis, 2002; http://www.cafcass.gov.uk/; www.nagalro.com/cafcass_page.htm); its problems have been so serious that, in December 2003, the then Minister for Children, Maragaret Hodge, backed by the then constitutional affairs secretary, Lord Falconer, demanded the resignation of the entire CAFCASS board (*see* news report at http://society.guardian.co.uk/children/story/0,1074,1100877,00.html).

No disrespect is intended to these officers, who *must* be helped to perform their crucial work effectively and efficiently, but without the benefit of carefully designed and appropriately implemented intensive training – including about the management of PAS – along with essential professional supervision and regulation of practice, no one could be expected to be able to properly perform such an immensely challenging task as the one they face. Their senior managers need to concentrate urgently on tackling the very real ongoing training needs that their officers have in order for them to perform competently. Indeed, some CAFCASS reporters are currently working beyond their level of competence, which could easily damage, rather than ameliorate what are extremely complex child and family situations, as is demonstrated in the case of *IP v. NP* [2003]. An accredited training scheme urgently needs to be devised and implemented to support these officers in their vital work.

Scotland

No relevant case law on PAS in Scotland currently exists. The Children (Scotland) Act 1995 states that in relation to their child *a parent has the responsibility* "(c) *if the child is not living with the parent, to maintain personal relations and direct contact* with the child on a regular basis" (Section 1.1c). This provision is to be balanced by section 11.7a, which states that the court "shall regard the welfare of the child concerned as its paramount consideration." The father in the case of *White v. White* [2001] SLT 485 put his parental responsibilities under this Act to judicial test after he had been refused contact with his children by the mother, with both children subsequently refusing to see him. In his argument to the court he drew on the ECHR case of *Elsholz v. Germany* [2000]. In judgment the court made no reference to PAS, but strongly confirmed both parents' right to maintain their relationships with their children.

However, in Scotland citizens may directly petition their parliament on matters of concern. George McAulay, Chairman of the pressure group UK Men's Movement (UKMM), has now raised PAS on three occasions through such petitions. Petition 413 called for the Scottish Parliament to

> (a) recognise Parental Alienation Syndrome as a cruel and serious form of child and domestic abuse and to develop intervention strategies to prevent it; (b) ensure that agencies coming into contact with children are given

> training in early diagnosis and prevention and in true gender neutrality; and (c) request that the Scottish Executive commission a study by a respected and neutral academic of PAS. (online at http://www.scottish.parliament.uk/business/petitions/docs/PE413.htm)

This original Petition 413 was linked with a further Petition 438, also from UKMM, which called for the Scottish Parliament:

> to take the necessary steps to establish procedures in order for a minor child to be able to access the resources necessary to establish a right of contact with his or her sibling(s) where such sibling(s) have been willfully alienated by a parent having custody of those sibling(s). (online at http://www.scottish.parliament.uk/business/petitions/docs/PE438.htm)

Evidence was given in person to the Public Petitions Committee by the petitioner, by an alienated father, and most effectively by Hayley Forrest, a 13-year-old girl who had lost contact with her siblings after she refused to collude with her mother's attempted alienation of her father through making false allegations of abuse. The transcript is available online at http://www.scottish.parliament.uk/business/committees/historic/petitions/or-02/pu02-0102.htm#Col 1522, (Cols. 1522-1534).

Both petitions were referred to the Scottish Executive for further information, and the views of the Scottish Child Law Centre were also sought. In June 2002 the following was noted:

> The Executive's response is that parental alienation syndrome is not a medically recognised condition nor is it a term that is used in legislation in Scotland. The response mentions that the term is not used in the definition of child abuse or domestic abuse. . . . The Executive does not agree that parental alienation syndrome is a medical term that is sufficiently well defined to make its diagnosis certain. The Executive also does not agree that the use of the term would be appropriate in legislation. It takes the view that Scots law already deals with the issues that may arise and which may be attributed to parental alienation syndrome. (http://www.scottish.parliament.uk/business/committees/historic/petitions/or-02/pu02-1102.htm)

In January 2003, with elections looming, after having noted that only anecdotal evidence had been given in support of the petitions and that PAS was not recognized by either the Scottish Executive or the Scottish Child Law Centre, the Justice 2 Committee agreed to take no further action at this stage but to flag the petition up for a future committee's consideration once the Children (Scotland) Act 1995 had been in force for sufficient time to merit a review.

However, a further petition (589) on behalf of the UK Men's Movement now calls for the Scottish Parliament "to take the necessary steps to recognise Parental Alienation Syndrome and to develop early intervention strategies to prevent parental alienation." The Petitions Committee has agreed to seek details of any European Court of Human Rights rulings as to whether a failure to both recognize PAS and to provide appropriate training to the relevant bodies in relation to the condition may constitute a contravention of Article 8 of the Convention.

Non-United Kingdom – the Channel Islands' State of Jersey

The Island of Jersey is situated 14 miles off the northwest coast of France and 85 miles from the English coast. Jersey is the largest of the Channel Islands. The Island has its own parliament, called the States of Jersey. Jersey also has its own system of local administration, fiscal and legal systems, and courts of law. Jersey is neither part of the United Kingdom nor a colony. It is not represented in the United Kingdom Parliament, whose Acts extend to Jersey only if the Island expressly agrees that they should do so. The Island owes allegiance to the British crown and the United Kingdom is responsible for the Island's defense and international relations.

The relevance of expert assessment for PAS was acknowledged by the President of the State of Jersey's Court of Appeal in the case of *B v. N* [2002] JLR 2002/135. It is relevant to track the judicial rationale of *B v. N* in some detail, as this was the first case in the independent jurisdiction of Jersey to acknowledge the debate over PAS in the British law literature and to apply the recognition of PAS on the British mainland in the case of *Re C (Children: Prohibition on Further Applications)* [2002] 1 FLR 1136. The case arose directly from the father's advocate having recently learned about PAS (*see B v. N* [2002], at para 6; and *B v. N* [2001] JLR 2001/142).

The Jersey Court of Appeal, having acquainted itself with relevant authorities (including on PAS), was decisive in its determination to bring to a conclusion the lengthy delays and obstructions that meant that this matter had remained unresolved and the father had had no real contact with his children for more than five years. It was a matter of express concern for the Court of Appeal:

> . . . first, that a matter critical to the welfare of those children remains unresolved; secondly that the very efflux of time has worked to the disadvantage of the father; thirdly that the court's orders appear, without adequate

reason or response, not to have been heeded either in the letter or in the spirit. It is quite clear on the evidence before the Royal Court and this court that the children are adamantly opposed to contact with their father. It is less clear what has caused this state of mind. The father attributes this to the mother (aided and abetted by her parents), having a desire to sabotage access because of hostility to the father; the mother, for her part, denies any such desire. (para 11)

The court deliberated on the necessary protection of the children's rights and welfare, noting that a psychiatrist in 1997 had said: "I do feel the children might suffer long term emotional harm if they do not see their father; even absent parents play significant roles to their children's development and if the children do not have knowledge of a parent they will still have fantasies" (para 19). The court balanced this against the guardian ad litem's (the court-appointed children's legal representative) opinion that examination of the children by psychologists as now applied for by the father would be unacceptable to the children, noting in particular her conclusion that "Such examination would be harmful" (para 16), and quoted Waite LJ's summary in *Re F (Contact: Restraint Order)* [1995] 1 FLR 956:

> The starting point, as always, is that every child has a right to be brought up in knowledge of his noncustodial parent. That is a right which the courts are determined to preserve, and they will not – save in the most exceptional circumstances – allow a custodial parent to deprive the child of a benefit of it through his or her own obduracy – or (I would add) by adopting an attitude which results in the child becoming averse to contact with the noncustodial parent.

The court acknowledged potential and avoidable delays. At the same time it was crucially alert to any risk of potential harm being caused to the children through precipitate action, and highlighted the essential collaborative approach necessary to ensure best practice in management of any such potential PAS cases:

> The difficulty with the mother's proposal is, firstly, that it merely postpones resolution of this issue further, in as much as it invites the Royal Court rather than the Court of Appeal to order a review by a psychiatrist of the relevant material. The difficulty with the father's proposal is that it exposes the children to what might be a traumatic, or at any rate, an unwelcome experience, without any confidence that it is justified on the state of the evidence at present, or that it would have any beneficial result. Counsel for the father invited us to infer the presence in this case of PAS from the material presently before the Court: but in our view, in the absence of an expert's analysis of it, the Court could not conscientiously do so.
>
> Given that the Royal Court had recognised in 1997 the value of a psychiatrist's report; that it had been five years since such a report had been commissioned; that the Court itself claimed unawareness of the source of the children's alienation; and that Parental Alienation Syndrome was conceded to exist as a phenomenon by the mother and had been raised as a possibility in this case by the father, in our judgment it would have been logical for the Court itself to have specifically requisitioned such a report. . . . (paras 22–24)

The court then ordered:

> That an appropriate psychiatrist . . . be appointed to examine all the relevant papers in this matter (a bundle of such papers to be produced forthwith for such purposes by the Advocates of both parties) and to report to the Royal Court, on the basis of such papers, whether there is evidence of any parental alienation syndrome or other matter relevant to the issue of access by the father to the children which needs to be considered, and to make such recommendations as are appropriate, in particular whether examination of the children or any other persons is necessary or desirable to enable the Royal Court to make a decision in this matter. Such Report is to be produced to the Royal Court as soon as practicable. (para 30.iii)

Prior to giving its considered order, the court had concluded:

> This sequential approach appears to us to be in entire harmony with the approach of the English Court of Appeal in the case of [*Re C (Children: Prohibition on Further Applications)* [2002] 1 FLR 1136] (where the issue of PAS was raised) per the President at para 12. It accelerates the proceedings in a way that neither the Royal Court's nor even the mother's proposal achieve – and I have already commented on the depressing delays that have bedevilled them so far. It ensures that any order for psychiatric examination of the children (which remains a possibility) is not prematurely made on the basis of inadequate evidence. It preserves the interests of both the mother and the father, but most vitally, those of the children themselves. (para 27)

It may also be worth noting that this case demonstrates one of the real problems of inter-disciplinary collaboration in which the associated disciplines are not part of the same administrative system. Cases become delayed by the pressure from sheer weight of demands made on each of the separate systems, and further delays occur at the interface between these systems. The desire and intention to make swift progress with regard to successful management of PAS may genuinely exist in Jersey, unlike in England and Wales, but the infrastructure and resources to enable this to be achieved in practice apparently do not yet exist in either jurisdiction.

THE DILEMMA NOW FACING THE UK FAMILY COURTS

It is rarely possible to deal with any problem effectively until it and its key components are adequately recognized for what they are. The acceptance of Sturge and Glaser's dismissal of PAS by the Court of Appeal will stand until a future Court of Appeal, House of Lords, or European court judgment overturns it. At the same time it needs to be recognized that several aspects of the current mode of practice within the UK legal system leave it particularly vulnerable to the dynamics through which PAS has its effect. For example, even when PAS is finally accepted by UK family courts, much education and training will be needed in order to enable our courts, their related services and associated professions to recognize and address PAS effectively. The author's own clinical experience in the training and management of trauma and crisis psychology suggests that effective PAS training may need to address some personal challenges inherent in such work. Some of the psychological factors involved in PAS are based in the vulnerability, dependence and interpersonal rivalry known to each of us during our own childhoods, and carried onward, in differing forms, throughout life. These serve to construct strong personal attitudes that operate at both conscious and subconscious levels. Those engaging in this work will require a reasonable degree of understanding of the effects of these psychological processes both within themselves and on their own professional work if they are to be able to detach these personal biases from their necessarily objective assessments of the dynamics of other families. Professionals of all disciplines should, in every case, be required to adhere to strict codes of professional practice. Effective action should be taken where these codes are transgressed. It should go without saying that when experts are asked to provide information regarding PAS that this should be given fully and impartially.

Despite Lord Woolf's (1996). attempts to achieve reforms to the contrary, the UK family courts still operate within an adversarial system in which lawyers vie to present their clients in the best light possible, and to portray their opponents as negatively as possible. This provides a worrying incentive to exaggerate and effectively to misrepresent the family reality. Such adversarial practice can act as a potent fuel where PAS is involved, despite the ethical codes of practice of the Family Law Bar Association and "Resolution: First for Family Law," which represents family law solicitors. The common public experience of this adversarial system is that it serves to enhance the anger already prevalent in the situation. Some court users are cynically convinced that this is intentional, as it operates to the pecuniary advantage of legal practitioners. Recent media articles have reported that a growing number of affected parents, including many from professional backgrounds, and even some grandparents, are taking to the streets and picketing outside the houses of some family court judges in direct protest at what they are now claiming to be a corrupt and unacceptable system.

While the potentially dangerous antics of the militant Fathers4Justice group have attracted global attention by purple flour-bombing the Prime Minister as he spoke in Parliament, by attempting to climb onto the Queen's balcony at Buckingham Palace, and by harassing senior family judiciary in their homes, other political pressure groups representing parents have chosen more responsible and constructive forms of action. The increasing tendency for litigants to represent themselves in person, supported by "*McKenzie* Friends," (people who assist litigants in person in court), has already been mentioned. Herr Sahin represented himself at the European level; in the Court of Appeal in *Re C*, Mr. C presented his own appeal and was assisted by *McKenzie* Friends. In March 2002, the Equal Parenting Council (website at www.equalparenting.org) announced a new national telephone help-line designed to offer lay support at minimal cost from parents who are already experienced in the *McKenzie* role to other separated parents who are still struggling through the courts to be able to properly maintain their parent-child relationships. Obviously, an extremely serious crisis of confidence in the UK family court system exists.

The problem facing the UK family courts is, in part, a consequence of the structure of family law in the UK. In particular, as soon as couples separate, the nonresident parent has no right of access to his or her children, with whom he or she may have enjoyed many years of close, loving relationships. Nonresident parents may be forced to engage in legal dispute for months, or in many cases for years, simply in order to be able to continue their parent-child relationships. The basic societal presupposition of shared parenting that now exists in many other jurisdictions, is lacking.

The family justice system is not a system existing in isolation. What is also required is the necessary recognition by parents that their responsibilities as parents are lifelong and not just for as long as they get along well with the other parent. It could be argued that, to an extent, both parents also retain a duty of responsibility – if not of care – to each other, specifically in order that the welfare of their offspring may be adequately protected and enhanced.

On a personal note, as provider of clinical psychological services to a community mental health team in years gone by, I regularly worked in our local Women's Aid Refuge. Many of these women had been truly appallingly treated by their partners; a few of these had been psychologically and physically tortured (no other word could describe it), along with being raped by their partners over a substantial period of time. No one can go through this without being hurt to their core. Unless you've had this happen to you or to someone who you are close to or worked closely with, the effects are incomprehensible. I met it through my work as a psychologist, and I still meet it in my work as a magistrate; now I see the gruesome pictures of the physical wounds inflicted. Many pressure groups that criticize domestic violence legislation only see it from their own necessarily limited perspectives. The same seems to be true, but in reverse, with regard to recognition of PAS. Many people feel strongly opposed to it without an adequate comprehension of what PAS actually is. Sturge and Glaser described much of the abuse that occurs in PAS perfectly, but somehow they remained blind to what faced them.

A CAVEAT

As PAS becomes more widely accepted, undoubtedly instances will arise in which false and/or malicious claims of children being inculcated into PAS are made. This may be regrettable but it should not be surprising, as it will only represent the converse of the many false claims of abuse that have become prevalent against PAS target parents. Although the false abuse claims were leveled predominantly against fathers, now that it is known that PAS equally affects both mothers and fathers, it is unlikely that any gender split in false PAS allegations will occur. Professionals assessing for PAS will need to be alert to this likelihood, and courts must be swift to robustly address such a maneuver.

In a recent ECHR case it was suggested that PAS against *both* parents may apparently be "inevitably" inculcated in children by the State via their judicially ordered separation from both parents! (*See Kutzner v. Germany* [2003] 1 FCR 249, [2002] 35 EHRR 25, paras 54–55). Although this case appropriately addresses the national system's failures with this family, the erroneous claim made in this case with regard to the PAS "from which the children would suffer," albeit with no necessary diagnostic preconditions having been fulfilled, demonstrates the propensity of some lawyers to hijack and attempt to exploit any new scientific knowledge as it percolates into judicial recognition. This case gives strong support to the argument that only appropriately trained and carefully regulated professionals must make assessments and diagnoses of PAS.

REFERENCES

Faller, K. (1998). The Parental Alienation Syndrome: What Is It and What Data Support It? *Child Maltreatment, 3*(2), 100–115.

Gardner, R. A. (1985). Recent trends in divorce and custody litigation. *Academy Forum, 29*(3).

Gardner R. A. (1992). *The Parental Alienation Syndrome: A guide for mental health and legal professionals.* Cresskill, New Jersey: Creative Therapeutics, Inc.

Gardner, R. A. (1998). Rebuttal to K. Faller's Article. *Child Maltreatment, 3*(4), 309–312.

Gardner, R. A. (2002). Rebuttal to C. Sturge and D. Glaser's Article: "Contact and Domestic Violence: The Experts' Court Report." *Family Law,* [2000], pp. 615–629. Published online at http://www.rgardner.com/refs/ar19.html.

Gerlis, S. (2002). CAFCASS: Twisted Knickers. *Family Law,* p. 144.

Hobbs, T. (2002a). Parental Alienation Syndrome and UK Family Courts, Part 1. *Family Law, 32,* 182–189

Hobbs, T. (2002b). Parental Alienation Syndrome and UK Family Courts: The Dilemma. *Family Law, 32,* 381–387.

Lord Chancellor's Advisory Board on Family Law: Children Act Sub-committee. "Making Contact Work: the Facilitation of Arrangements for Contact between Children and their Non-Residential Parents and the Enforcement of Court Orders for Contact. Consultation Paper." March 2001.

Lord Chancellor's Advisory Board on Family Law: Children Act Sub-committee. "Making Contact Work: A Report to the Lord Chancellor on the Facilitation of Arrangements for Contact between Children and their Non-Residential Parents and the Enforcement of Court Orders for Contact." February 2002.

Sturge, C. & Glaser, D. (2000). Contact and Domestic Violence: The Experts' Court Report. *Family Law,* 615–629.

Woolf, H. K. (1996). *Access to justice draft civil proceedings rules 1–39,* London HMSO.

Chapter 8

PARENTAL ALIENATATION SYNDROME – AN ISRAELI PERSPECTIVE: REFLECTIONS AND RECOMMENDATIONS

DANIEL S. GOTTLIEB

OVERVIEW

The phenomenon of parental alienation syndrome (PAS) has not passed over Israel and, in fact, figures prominently in many divorce and custody cases, particularly in those with high conflict. No PAS legislation exists in Israel, the case law is rich with examples of the dim view of PAS situations taken by Israeli courts. PAS is not without its critics in Israel, both among parents' groups and members of the professional community, but it has been widely accepted by the court system. This chapter briefly reviews relevant Israeli family law and recent PAS decisions in custody, move-away, and Hague Convention cases. Treatment and ethical issues and dilemmas are examined, as well as future directions for systemic prevention and treatment of PAS.

INTRODUCTION

And he shall turn the heart of the fathers to the children and
the heart of the children to their fathers;
Lest I come and smite the land with utter destruction.
(Malachi, 3:24)

Israeli folk wisdom has it that it takes about 15 years for most good things from America to work their way to Israel while the bad things come almost immediately. The case PAS (Gardner, 1998b). would seem to prove at least the second part of the adage.

Although no official statistics describe the incidence of PAS, my experience as a clinical psychologist and family therapist with an extremely active divorce-related practice reflects the high frequency of PAS cases, particularly among the high-conflict and contested-divorce families.

In the Hebrew literature, PAS is referred to by different names: syndrome *nikur hori* (Parental Alienation Syndrome), *hitnakrut he-horeh* (alienation from a parent) or *sarvanut kesher* (contact refusal). The differences in terminology do not reflect different theoretical approaches, nor are they indicative of the different positions espoused in the PAS debate in the United States (*see* for example Gardner, 2002a and Kelly and Johnston, 2001) but rather all point to the same constellation of symptoms and dynamics that comprise PAS as described by Gardner (1998b).

PAS IN THE ISRAELI PROFESSIONAL LITERATURE

Generally speaking, the Israeli professional psychological literature is quite limited; most Israelis who publish do so in the American journals. Nonetheless, the past few years have seen two journal articles, one completed master's thesis, and another in preparation all relating to PAS.

Habusha (2000). in her Master's thesis attempted to describe the frequency of refusal of children to maintain contact with noncustodial fathers. In addition, she attempted to describe the relationship between father-refusal and family, parental, and individual variables in order to explore treatment ramifications. She surveyed all 443-child welfare officers in the country and received a response rate of about 30 percent. These child welfare officers had at that time 2,161 families in their treatment, in 220 of them father-refusal was evident. As the group of children in the caseload of the welfare officers responding was found to be representative of the population as a whole, it was concluded that the frequency of father-refusal was about 9 percent. The author noted that this figure is considerably lower than the 30 percent previously reported in Israel (Levita et al. 1997) and the 90 percent reported by Gardner (1992). Habusha posits that this discrepancy is due to the fact that she focused exclusively on refusal of children to see their fathers, while the other studies focused on refusal to see fathers *or* mothers. In addition, she hypothesized that the difference may be attributed to lack of sufficient awareness on the part of child welfare officers of the phenomenon of PAS. Habusha notes that in those families in which father-refusal appeared, 70 percent of the children refused contact, thus suggesting that some family dynamic may be contributing to the refusal behavior of the child. Moreover, she postulates that the refusal behavior may serve as a focal point for identification around which the new, postdivorce family system develops itself.

The author concludes that father-refusal is multidetermined. She sees it as a systemic or familial "syndrome" rather than one individual's solution. Secondly, she sees father refusal as a functional reaction of the system in dealing with the divorce crisis. She sees a greater likelihood of father refusal in families with difficulty in regulating interpersonal relationships in terms of closeness-distance causing difficulties in differentiation of each parent and as such impaired parenting and blurred boundaries between the parental and child subsystems. She seems to suggest that families with father-refusal are different from other families and that predivorce family dynamics contribute to this particular postdivorce expression.

Bergman and Weitztum (1995) discussed PAS in the context of parental abduction of children, noting the different degrees of PAS discussed by Gardner (1992). They note that PAS is a form of psychological kidnapping and emphatically state the separation of the child from the alienating parent is a sine qua non for successful treatment. Levita *and colleagues* (1997) reviewed the PAS literature and discussed different treatment approaches that they considered to be helpful. Gottlieb (2000), in an article on the concept of time as a factor in judicial decision making regarding children, discussed the necessity of swift and decisive intervention in PAS cases.

PAS AND ISRAELI LAW

As compared with the massive and at times convoluted corpus of American family law, the volume of Israeli family law is quite slim and straightforward. A small handful of laws govern the treatment of children in cases of custody, child welfare, and adoption. Unquestionably, the "best-interest" standard as promulgated by Goldstein, Freud and Solnit (1973). has served as the guidepost for all legislation regarding children as well as for the body of case law that has evolved over the years.

The evolution of children's rights has had its effect on Israeli family law as well. In 1991, Israel adopted the United Nations charter on children's rights (developed in 1989). Since then, matters of children's rights have been addressed in numerous court decisions, particularly with regard to the right of children to be heard and to have their wishes taken into consideration. The landmark children's rights case (Supreme Court Docket 2263/93) focused on the right of a custodial parent to inculcate a child with religious training opposed by the noncustodial parent. This decision brought the issue of children's rights to the forefront and gave it an equivalent standing with the best-interest standard.

It should be noted that the recent attention and primacy accorded to children's rights has proven to be something of a double-edged sword. On the one hand, it has compelled the courts to pay even closer attention to *children's* rights and needs and has added weight to *children's* rights in the ever-delicate balance between *children's* and *parents'* rights. On the other hand, many parents now vigorously wave the banner of children's rights when, in fact, they are using it as a fig leaf to cover up their own misdeeds. Thus, in PAS cases, particularly those involving late-latency and adolescent children, there will often be heard the claim that the child's voice must not only be *heard* but also heeded. Alienating parents clearly enlist this charter, or at least a misguided interpretation of it, to bolster their argument in favor of disrupting the contact between the child the other parent. Such selective use of the charter, allows the alienating parent to cleanse himself of any culpability or responsibility, thus shifting the focus for far-reaching decisions to a young child who allegedly has the backing of the law. Moreover, alienating parents tend to provide their children with early civic training and inform them that the law accords them the "right" to do what they want in these matters. This false empowering of children, in addition to being contrary to the spirit and intention of the law, is also insidious in that it puts the child at risk for generalizing this "I-have-the-right-to-do-what-I-want" attitude to other areas that may well be unacceptable to the same parent (Gardner, 2002a). A somewhat paradoxical situation may be created in which, within the context of contact, the parent is very understanding and supportive of the child's right to decide, but in other areas fights the child tooth and nail to maintain his or her parental authority.

Israel currently has no specific laws relating to PAS. Nevertheless, between 2002–2004 the Knesset (Israeli Parliament) Committee for the Advancement of the Status of the Child held hearings on difficulties in implementing court-ordered visitation. Although the committee has yet to issue its conclusions and recommendations, those appearing before the committee emphasized the difficulties in implementing court orders and suggested ways of enhancing parental compliance. The possibility of broader use of contempt of court and/or brief incarceration was raised, as well as the need for better and perhaps mandatory education for divorcing parents. All those speaking before the committee, including parents whose visitation rights were not adequately enforced, spoke of the terrible price children pay in these situations as well as to the affront to their best interest and the violation of their rights.

Knesset Committee hearings of this sort have relatively little effect on what occurs in the "trenches" and, in fact, generally remain obscured from the general public. Nonetheless, the willingness of the Committee to address the issue reflects a growing legislative sensitivity to the needs of children of divorce in general and PAS children in particular. Perhaps these hearings are a harbinger of a more clearly articulated policy regarding the welfare of children of divorced parents.

The Structure of the Israeli Legal System

In dealing with PAS, as with other matters regarding children and families, it is imperative to have a working understanding of the legal system under which you are operating, particularly when taking a systemic approach to the problem. Mental health professionals alone are often not sufficiently equipped to independently affect change in what are frequently recalcitrant family systems. Viewing the problem from a systems perspective compels us to view the courts as an integral and essential part of the system. Two primary reasons for this exist.

First, the degree to which they have a comprehensive appreciation of PAS will without doubt affect their response to various treatment recommendations proposed by the mental health professional. A responsive court can be of paramount assistance to the treating professional. As such, it is the duty of the mental health professional to, on the one hand, learn the law and, on the other hand, to educate and inform the judiciary so that the eventually both parties or partners can "speak the same language."

Second, each legal system has its limitations; these include those that are inherent to it by dint of the laws and sanctions available to the courts and those that may be related to personal world views and temperaments of particular judges. To the extent that the mental health professional is familiar with these factors, he can more precisely tailor his recommendations to fit into the legal and personal framework of the court, thus increasing the chances that the recommendations will be accepted, implemented, and adhered to.

Family Courts and Rabbinical Courts

When dealing with matters of personal status such as marriage, divorce, and child custody, Israel has two somewhat parallel legal systems, the Civil Family Court (functioning by power of the Family Court Law (1995).) and the Rabbinical Court (governed by the Rabbinical Court Law (1953)). An individual initiating divorce and custody proceedings may do so in either court system and by doing so hitherto grants that court system exclusive jurisdiction in the matter, forcing the respondent to argue his case in that particular system. The exception to this are all matters relating to the "get," the religious divorce, which are, by law, adjudicated exclusively in the Rabbinical Courts. In the Rabbinical court all cases are heard by a panel of three Rabbinical judges, whereas in the Family Court cases are heard by one judge who is not perforce of any particular religious persuasion or affiliation.

Conventional wisdom has it that men fare better in the Religious Courts, particularly in monetary matters, whereas women fare better in the Civil Courts. As with most conventional wisdom, this too is not necessarily true, but as with other truisms, this one also dies hard. Nonetheless, certain significant differences in the world views of the two court systems exist. The Family Court relies on common law whereas the Rabbinical Court relies on Jewish Law as set forth in the Talmud and developed in the rabbinical responsa over the last 2,000 years. Although the two systems are not per se in conflict with each other, each may evidence different nuances in determining what the child's best interest is, as well as somewhat disparate *a priori* assumptions. Thus, for example, the Rabbinical Courts tend to assign greater weight to religious considerations in determining custody and visitation and may tend to favor paternal custody for older boys and maternal custody for older girls. Nonetheless, these are only *a priori* assumptions that must be tested on a case-by-case basis. Both Family Court and Rabbinical Court decisions can be appealed to two higher courts. Although the Rabbinical Courts rely, as stated, on Jewish Law, their decisions are ultimately subject to review and appeal by the state Supreme Court.

Integration of Mental Health Professionals in the Legal Process

Generally speaking, when a legal conflict develops between parents, the court refers them to the municipal social service office where a special child welfare officer prepares a report on the family's situation, complete with recommendations. In the more complex and difficult cases, such as when dealing with PAS, the court will usually appoint a mental health professional to conduct an in-depth evaluation into the family dynamics and the personality traits of the parent and the children. The appointed expert submits his findings to the court complete with operative recommendations and may be cross-examined by either side on his or her findings. Nonetheless, because the court – with the consent of both parties – appoints the expert, the chances of a serious debate regarding the qualifications of the expert are highly unlikely. As such, court time is spent debating the expert's findings and their implications rather than trying to discredit or defend the expert.

In addition to the municipal child welfare officer, all the Family Courts now have adjunct to them special assistance units staffed by social workers, a consulting psychologist and a consulting psychiatrist, as per the Family Court Law (1995). As part of their mandate, these units attempt to assist divorcing parents reach negotiated agreements, make referrals for psychological treatment, and provide psychoeducational services for families. All too often, however, the power of the pathology thwarts even the most ardent efforts of these workers.

In certain extreme cases in which the court feels that the conflict between the parent has reached preposterous proportions, the court may elect to appoint a guardian ad litem (GAL). The GAL will assume the legal representation of the child, thus essentially neutralizing lawyers who both claim to represent the child's best interest but in practice are not doing so. Although this notion is widely accepted in theory, in practice the limited availability of GALs – owing to funding problems – makes their appointment a somewhat rare occurrence.

RELEVANT LAWS

While there are as of yet no laws relating specifically to PAS, several laws that may have considerable bearing on such cases do exist. The following is a brief review of these laws.

Legal Capacity and Guardianship Law of 1962

This is the primary law that governs almost all custody and visitation proceedings. The law does not contain any sections that deal directly with PAS, but does include some that can be interpreted as relating to PAS-type situations. Thus, although divorcing parents retain the guardianship of their children, the courts may intervene under "special circumstances," if convinced that the child's well-being has been or may in the future be compromised. In such situations, the court may empower someone – a child welfare worker, a psychologist, or a GAL to determine the precise nature of visitation arrangements.

Section 25 stipulates that the court may, under "special circumstances" transfer the child to the custody of someone other than the parents. Thus, for example, in Haifa Family Court Docket 462/84, the court considered removing a child from the custody of an alienating mother and transferring the child to a foster care setting.

Youth Law: Treatment and Supervision (1960)

This law is rarely invoked in child custody cases although Family Court judges are authorized to apply this law. According to Section 3 of the law, if it can be demonstrated that the child's welfare is in danger or about to be endangered, the court may remove him or her from the custody of the endangering parent and place him or her in a residential facility or with a foster family. In addition, the court may order an evaluation of the child. The law recognizes psychological distress as a factor that may endanger a child's welfare.

The Jerusalem Family Court (Docket 10401/99) transferred to foster care two young children who were subjected to PAS by the father and who were physically and verbally abusive to their mother during the supervised visits. In this case, the judge actually went to the local social welfare office to witness the visit with the father and, having been convinced that the children were being brainwashed against their mother ordered their transfer to an emergency shelter. After a few weeks the children were returned to the mother and the visitation arrangement was promptly and properly implemented.

More recently, in 2001, the Tel Aviv Family Court (Docket 71681/96) ruled that two brothers age 10 and 14, one living with the mother and the other living with the father, were minors in need of supervision and that they should be removed from the custody of each respective parent and be placed in a residential setting. This was due to the father's severe alienating behavior, the mother's weakness as a parent, and the older child's refusal to have contact with his mother. The father appealed the decision to the Tel Aviv District Court (Docket 1034/01). In her decision, Judge S. Rotlevi ruled that the children not be removed from their parents' custody owing to their age, their expressed opposition, and the need to give more weight to their right to be heard. Although it did not remove the children from parental custody, the court did recognize the children as being in need of supervision and ordered the local child welfare officer to maintain his involvement with the family, supervise the visitation, and provide the court with periodic reports. Despite the court's final position, the judge did clearly indicate that the children were victims of PAS by the father. The judge, citing Gardner, (1998b), asserted that in severe cases such as the one at hand, it is necessary to act with alacrity and assertiveness to restore the connection between the child and the alienated parent. She also stated that it even be necessary to remove a child from the custody of the alienating parent. According to the court's decision, had the lower court acted sooner as per the recommendations of numerous psychologists, it would have been more feasible to remove these boys from their parents' custody.

Family Courts Law (1995)

This law revolutionized the courts' approach to family law by centralizing all matters relating to families – divorce, custody, property distribution, guardianship, surrogacy, etc. – under one roof and by the appointment of family court judges who sit in court houses in the different regions of the country. The law provides for child welfare officers to initiate or become party to proceedings regarding minors in which there exists a possibility of a substantive encroachment of a child's rights. The law provides for the court to assume the power and the authority ordinarily reserved for the Juvenile Court. In addition, the law stipulates that the court may elect to hear the testimony of a child without the presence of anyone else. The court may also prevent or stop the testimony of a child if it is deemed harmful to him or her.

Hague Convention Law (Return of Abducted Children) (1991)

This law, which is essentially a word-for-word adoption of the United Nations convention, provides for the immediate return of abducted children to the country from which they were illegally removed. Although it does not relate specifically to PAS, this law encompasses those not-infrequent situations in which a child who has been abducted by one parent and then is "brainwashed" against the other.

PAS IN ISRAELI COURT DECISIONS

As previously mentioned, the volume of Israeli family law is quite slim and as such, it is the constantly evolving body of case law that serves as the legal basis for most court decisions. In the absence of an intricate system of statutes, the overwhelming majority of these cases are decided based on considerations that are more psychological rather than legal in their nature. Only, perhaps, in cases involving the Hague Convention on the Civil Aspects of International Child Abduction or cases pitting biological parents against nonparents (such as grandparents) are matters of "best interest" assigned a backseat to considerations that are primarily *legal* and not *psychological.*

In Israel, and most likely everywhere else, no clearly delineated definition of who is the best parent to raise a particular child at any given point in time exists. Nonetheless, the court tries to guide its experts by providing them with guidelines for conducting the evaluation as well as a list of issues that they are to relate in their report to the court. The clearest guidelines in Israel are those of the former Vice President of the Tel Aviv District Court, the Honorable Chaim Porat, which have been adopted by most Family Court judges. In his instructions to the court-appointed expert, he stipulates that the ability of each parent to foster a healthy relationship with the other parent needs be evaluated. In practice, despite this being only one of about 20 variables examined, it proves to be seminal if not at times decisive.

In Family Docket 12870/97, the father/respondent asked the Haifa Family Court to reject the appeal of the mother appellant for increased child support payments claiming, among other things, that he had no contact with his 13-year-old child as a result of the alienating behavior of the custodial mother. The Honorable A.

Globinsky rejected the request stating that a 13-year-old child could not be blamed for the behavior of the parent and citing Gardner (1998b). As PAS was not at the focal point of this particular debate but rather a claim that arose as a defense in a monetary claim, the court did not delve into the PAS issue. Nonetheless, and despite the court's refusal to link child support to visitation, the court did make it clear that the parent and not the child should be held accountable for failure of visitation.

In a highly emotional and widely publicized case of two girls abducted by their Orthodox Jewish mother from their Catholic father in Italy, the Tel Aviv Family Court (Docket 5062/97) ruled that the girls were, in fact, kidnapped as per the Hague Convention and as such were to be returned to the father. The mother appealed to the Tel Aviv District Court (Docket 28/97), whose panel of three judges ruled unanimously to reject the appeal and return the girls to Italy. In doing so the court stated:

> It is known from the literature in Israel and abroad, as well as from the case law, that a case of kidnapping begets by the very act of the abduction a situation of brainwashing as small children cannot survive without an adult at their side and they are unable to critically and morally evaluate others and to adequately exercise mature judgement regarding the adult in whose presence he is. The literature commonly equates kidnapping to captivity and just as the captive forms a dependency *vis à vis* his captor, so too children become dependant on the parent abductor.

In Supreme Court Docket 245/87 the High Court heard an appeal on a District Court ruling allowing a mother to retain custody of her daughter despite the fact that she had repeatedly defied court orders instructing her to allow the girl to meet with the non-custodial father. Although the lower court had considered the possibility of removing the child from the mother's custody and transferring her either to the father's custody or to a foster care arrangement, the opinion of a court-appointed expert stating that removal from the mother's custody would be detrimental to the child prevailed.

In this decision, the court gave full credence to viewing alienating parents as endangering the welfare of the child and the concomitant possibility of removing a child from the custody of an alienating parent. Nonetheless, and despite the refusal of the mother to cooperate not only with the visitation order but also with the court-ordered evaluation, the court ruled to accept the lower court's determination that removing the child from the mother's custody would be detrimental to her wellbeing. The decision notwithstanding, the Court did open the way for the father to bring contempt of court charges against the mother and for the lower court to resort to imprisonment of the mother as a way of enforcing the visitation arrangement.

In Tel Aviv District Court Docket 1008/99 the father/appellant challenged a Family Court decision ordering him to vacate the apartment in which the couple had lived together. Among his claims was that the children, who despite being in the mother's custody, were living with him and were alienated from the mother and would suffer if he were to have to vacate the apartment. This claim was deemed reprehensible by the District Court, that stated:

> . . . it is clear that alienation is extremely negative and opens the way for emotional disturbances in children and a parent who is oblivious to this, is not worthy of any support or praise.

In another case (Supreme Rabbinical Court Docket 057531410-64-1) involving the divorced parents of eight children, the mother from the very outset confounded the father's visitation with the children. Years of wrangling in rabbinical court and family court did not bring about any real resolution to the problem and left the mother resolute in her claims that the children were at the risk of sexual abuse by the father. The mother has consistently ignored all court decisions regarding visitation. Currently, the rabbinical court is considering a recommendation that some of the children be transferred to the father's custody. Concurrently, the mother is on trial in the Civil Court for defying a court order.

A lawyer whose client had not seen his children for several months who claimed that his ex-wife was inciting the children against him (thus creating a PAS situation) recently consulted me. The consulting lawyer was considering bringing a civil suit against the mother for damages from mental strain caused to the father as a result of the unsuccessful battle he had to wage in order to be able to see the children as stipulated in the divorce agreement. As I was unable to conduct a full evaluation of the family, it was quite unreasonable to think that the mother would consent to participate. I agreed to write a brief on PAS, its potential damages to children and possible treatment approaches.

PAS and the Hague Convention

In Family Docket 41/97, the Tel Aviv District Court denied the appeal of a mother who had abducted her six-year-old daughter from Illinois. She was instructed by the Family Court to return the child to the father who had been awarded custody by an Illinois court.

During the course of the appeal, the mother/appellant raised several defenses offered by the Hague Convention, one of them being that the child would be placed in "grave danger" (Article 13), were if she returned to the father's custody. According to the mother, the father had sexually abused the child when she was about three years old. This claim was repeated by the child during the course of psychological evaluations conducted in the U.S. and Israel. When asked during the Israeli evaluation why she was meeting with the psychologist, the girl launched into a emotionless diatribe, saying; "I have a bad father who tells me dirty things. I remember that he taught me 'your lips are my lips, your nose is my nose, your legs are my legs.' I want to be with my mother . . . I am sitting and he says 'come here and close my buttons' . . . I love my mother. I don't love my father; he left my mother when she was pregnant . . . He taught me dirty things, he was crazy." The girl's statement was an almost verbatim rendition of the mother's claims against the father, and she was unable to provide any specific details of the events that purportedly took place three years prior, when she was three years old.

In its decision, the Court – relying on expert opinions – determined that ". . . the mother was thwarting any possibility of contact between the father and the girl and as such was alienating the child from the father (parental alienation), however, the moment the mother is out of the child's field of vision, warmth exudes from both sides and the girl is comfortable with and enjoys the father's company." The court further stated that "Parental alienation is a common feature in most abduction cases and that the child's mimicking what she thinks the mother is thinking is one of the hallmarks of the process of parental alimentation."

Claims emanating from article 13 were not accepted. The Court stated:

> All the expert opinions regarding the parents and the relationship of the child with the parents indicate that the mother frustrates all possibilities for a relationship between the father and the girl and as such creates a situation of alienation from the father (parental alienation). However, the moment that the other is not within the child's view and the child is with the father, warmth flows from both sides and the child is relaxed and enjoys being in the presence of her father.

This situation is recognized in the literature and is related to almost every abduction case.

The American court so indicated this in their decision and this was borne out by the mother's behavior in this country. Most of the hearings in the lower court revolved around the mother's refusal to allow the father to meet with the child and her manipulations to prevent the meetings and the great efforts that had to be made to enable the visits to take place despite that the father presented no danger to his daughter and she was not afraid of him but rather mimicked the fear from the mouth of the mother. The experts noted that the girl mimicked what she thinks the mother wants her to say and this is one of the more typical manifestations of parental alienation.

The judge then continued to consider the possibility of immediately assigning the girl to the temporary custody of the father and stated:

> An immediate transfer under such circumstances, has proven successful in previous cases brought before me (for example, *In re: Foxman,* where the brainwashing of the child was extreme and the assistance of the police and social services were required to get the children on the plane but, as was reported to me, the moment the plane door was shut, all the protestations were silenced and the girls cuddled with their father). Situations of this sort are familiar to me from custody cases as well where the moment the child is transferred (to the custody of the alienated parent, d.g.), following false allegations of sexual abuse, etc., the child's situation completely changed, he was freed from the pathological dependence on the mother and developed nicely with the father. Drastic and immediate transfer combined with a temporary distancing of the "brainwashed" child from the parent that caused such brainwashing, may sound a bit extreme but is efficient, doable and solves problems. There is no doubt that the child is being harmed in her current situation both as a result of the kidnapping as well as a result of the alienation from the father (alienation which from the child's perspective is external but not internal, d.g.)

This case was brought before the Supreme Court (Docket 6181/97) however, the court elected not to hear a further appeal on the district court's decision.

In District Court Dockets 1167/99 and 1168/99, the court heard the appeals of two parents on a Family Court decision. The Family Court had allowed the abducting mother to remain in Israel with the abducted child and not return the child to the father in the United States despite the fact of the kidnapping and despite the father having legal custody. The District Court upheld the lower court ruling, opining that the circumstances of the case justified the application of the defenses put forth in Sections 12, 13, and 20 of the Hague Convention. Nonetheless, in its analysis of the case, the Court dwelled on the detrimental effects of PAS and the need for psychological intervention so that the child may eventually have a relationship with the father and so that the court may in the future consider returning the child to the United States.

PAS and Relocation Cases

An analysis of Israeli case law reveals that the Israeli courts have adopted a fairly liberal approach to move-away cases. Although there has yet to be a landmark decision such as in the cases of Burgess or Tropea, the courts have generally adopted an approach that sanctions relocation if it can be demonstrated that the move will not be detrimental to the child and that it will considerably improve the lot of the relocating parent. In assessing what may or not be detrimental for the child, the question of continued contact with the noncustodial parent assumes paramount proportions. One of the central points to be evaluated is the motivation of the parent for requesting the move as well as his or her ability to foster a long-distance relationship between the child and the other parent. By its very nature, a move to a foreign country or even a move from one state to another will effect the frequency of face-to-face contact. Although studies seem to indicate that frequency of contact is not the only determinant – and perhaps not even the main determinant – of the quality of the parent-child relationship (*see*, for example Wallerstein and Tanke, 1998, and Gardner 1998a, it is a major contributor, particularly for younger children).

Given the technical and psychological difficulties associated with move-away cases, one must always assess the presence of or the potential for PAS. When a determination of PAS or a PAS process is determined, it may become imperative to opt for denying a relocation request. Two recent cases illustrate this point.

In the first, two children of non-Israeli born parents were living in Israel after a foreign court granted the mother's relocation request in 2001. The father, who was living in a different foreign country, was granted visitation with the children in Israel as well as rights to telephone contact. The visitation proved very difficult to implement and needed to be closely supervised by the court. The mother opposed unsupervised visits, claiming that the children were afraid of the father and that he could potentially harm them. In fact, the children were initially quite hesitant with the father, however, as time passed the visits were quite pleasant and relaxed and the children were effusive in the expression of love for their father. Nonetheless, upon his return to his country, an almost complete breakdown in the communication between the children and their father occurred. Despite a commitment of the mother to enable telephone and videophone conferences, these never seemed to work out. This situation notwithstanding, the mother once again requested the court to approve yet another relocation – to a third country – a little more than a year after the first request was granted. The psychological evaluation of the family indicated that the mother was thwarting the contact between the children and their father and that there existed a very real danger that a move to a different country, particularly one where the enforcement of visitation arrangements is dubious, could lead to a total termination of the father's relationship with his children. As such, the recommendation was to deny at this time the mother's request (Tel Aviv Family Court Docket 89790/00). As the deliberations proceeded, a compromise solution was proposed in which the mother would be allowed to relocate against a significant monetary guarantee. The Israeli court would retain jurisdiction over the case and the visitation would continue in Israel twice a year.

In the second case, the Israeli mother of a six-year-old girl petitioned the court in 2001 to allow her to relocate to a foreign country where she planned on marrying a man whom she had known for a few months. The father, who lived in the same city as the mother and who was awarded visitation rights by the court, opposed the move on the grounds that the mother's plans were poorly delineated and that it was in no way clear that her relationship with this man would be healthy or that the girl, who did not know the man, would be able to acclimate to the new home, surroundings, culture and country. In the course of the evaluation, it became clear that the mother has a thinly veiled hate for the father, that she sees him in excessively and unrealistically negative terms and that today, when the father lives about 10 minutes from the girl, the visitation does not go smoothly and the girl often "refuses" to see the father. Moreover, the girl spoke about hating her father and being afraid of him without being able to give any concrete age-appropriate examples and in way that was diametrically opposed to her observed behavior with the father.

As in the previous case, here, too, the recommendation was to deny the mother's request until such time that a healthier relationship between the child and the father could be demonstrated (Ashdod Family Court Docket 47/96).

PAS AND RELIGIOUS ISSUES

U.S. courts tend to shy away from focussing on religious issues that arise within the context of custody cases in order to protect the integrity of separation of church and state. Nonetheless, religious issues often legitimately lie at the heart of custody disputes, and the courts are compelled to determine what type of religious practice or education will be in the child's best interest. Religious issues often provide fertile ground in which PAS can take root. They often provide a seemingly socially acceptable rationale for a child to distance himself from a parent. Many divorce processes are accompanied by changes that parents make in different areas of their lives, one of them being that of religious practice. A parent who is in the process of reevaluating his life may opt to become more committed religiously or, conversely, to abandon religious practice. These changes often create a considerable chasm between parent and child and may be used or misused by the other parent as a rationale for restricting visitation. As religion tends to be a very sensitive and emotional issue, particularly in Israel where there are also considerable political undertones, custody disputes with a religious component tend to be quite intense and emotionally laden. For many parents religion is a matter of "do or die." Thus, a child who grew up in an orthodox home where all the laws and restrictions of Sabbath and kashruth (kosher dietary laws) were meticulously observed may have trouble visiting the parent who elected to abandon these practices. Similarly, a child who grew up in a secular home may have considerable trouble accepting the practices of the newly religious parent, particularly when these practices are forced on the child. When parents are determined to resolve the divorce amicably, hurdles of this sort are easily cleared through negotiation, consideration and conciliation. By the same token, these issues may become the focal point of PAS, with the alienating parent claming that he or she is interested in the contact but that it is contrary to the child's best interest given the change in the other parent. Although in some cases such an argument has merit, it is often a disguise for alienation.

PAS and Children's Rights

Since ratifying the UN Convention on the Rights of the Child in 1991, the Israeli courts have become more acutely aware of children's rights issues. Children's rights figured prominently in a 1992 case involving a Jewish-turned-Jehovah's Witness custodial parent who wanted to rear the child according to her. The Jewish father opposed this move and the case reached the Supreme Court. The Court ruled that it was not only in the child's best interest but also consistent with his rights that he be raised in the Jewish faith and not by the principles of the Jehovah's witnesses.

Two sections of the Convention are of particular relevance when dealing with PAS cases. Although I have never seen specific reference to these sections, they certainly warrant noting. Article 9 states: "You should not be separated from your parents unless it is for your own good. For instance, your parents may be hurting you or not taking care of you. Also if your parents decide to live apart, you will have to live with one or the other of them, but you have the right to contact both parents easily."

The implications of the section for PAS cases are eminently obvious. Divorce by its very nature infringes upon the child's right to grow up with the support of both parents; in this conflict between the parents' rights and those of the child, the parents win out and the child must bear the consequences. Nonetheless, Article 9 articulates very clearly the child's right to "easy" contact with both parents. As such, indoctrinating parents or those who simply are unable to promote the child's contact with the other parent may be seen as violating the Convention. A similar, although more broadly stated, principle is put forth in Article 18: "Both of your parents should be involved in bringing you up and they should do what is best for you."

The major thrust of the literature on the adjustment of children to divorce demonstrates that the child's favorable adjustment is closely associated with his or her ability to maintain ongoing contact with both parents and their involvement in child-rearing. All of this should be in an environment that is as conflict-free as possible. A parent who is unable to allow his counterpart to be involved in child-rearing is not acting in the best interest of the child. Although not every noncustodial parent is willing or able to take an active role in the day-to-day nitty-gritty of child-rearing, this in no way negates the importance of ongoing contact and the maintenance of a positive relationship.

Although no legal teeth are associated with acceptance of the UN Convention, the above mentioned articles can serve as a further moral-social justification in dealing with PAS cases.

PAS in the Israeli Press

To date, only two articles in the general press have related directly to the topic of PAS. An article that appeared in the *Jerusalem Post*, portrayed the distress of several fathers who have been unable to maintain regular contact with their children because of PAS (Siegel-Itzkovich, 2000). It also takes note of an organization called Equal Parenting (www.equalparenting.org) which is devoted to asserting the rights of parents after divorce.

A second article that appeared in the *Haaretz* focused on the controversy around PAS as a meaningful diagnostic category as well as on the some of the criticisms and personal attacks on Gardner himself (Traubmann, 2003). This article also notes the opposition of some women's groups to the adoption of PAS by Israeli mental health professional and courts.

TREATMENT

This section describes several treatment techniques that have proven somewhat helpful in mitigating the effects of PAS. I use the term "mitigating" because I am not sure that any true "cure" for PAS exists, particularly, the more severe cases. Even in those cases in which it is possible to affect a rapprochement between the alienated parent and the child, it is a far more formidable task to ignite that tiny change in perspective in the alienating parent that may help him or her realize that the other parent is not really that demonic.

Treating PAS is much easier said than done. The level of pathos aroused in all involved is tremendous. The ability of parents and children to apply rational thought processes is generally severely compromised. Reason usually does not work, but then neither is coercion always a viable solution. Often, a truly recalcitrant parent is more powerful than the presiding judge. The Talmud has a somewhat paradoxical principle – "He is coerced until he assents" – that may have some relevance in PAS cases. In some cases PAS is about power, control, and punishment. Courts that are able to creatively utilize the power vested in them may turn recalcitrant rebels into willing subjects.

The Team Approach

The team approach is often helpful in PAS cases. First, because of the emotional strain of these cases, it is helpful to have a colleague with whom to discuss the case. Second, because of the need to be empathetic toward parents espousing diametrically opposed positions as well as a child with a position of his own, it is often helpful to have more than one therapist. Third, because of the possibility of manipulation by the family members, it is advisable to have a team that is less vulnerable to manipulations and that can implement its own strategic moves.

The One-Way Mirror

The use of a one-way mirror has proven helpful when a child has developed a phobic like reaction towards the alienated parent. In cases in which a child refuses to even sit in the same room as a parent, it may be helpful to allow the child to view the parent through the one-way mirror as a way of creating a degree of desensitization to the parent. This can be best accomplished when the parent sits in the room with a therapist and the two discuss things such as what the child may be feeling, why the child may be angry and what the parent would like the child to know abut how he or she is feeling. This is also a good opportunity for the parent to discuss with the therapist "the good old days" before the alienation as a way of arousing in the child repressed or suppressed positive memories. The child, who is viewing this interaction from the adjacent room – where he or she is also sitting with a therapist – has the opportunity to hear the parent and to see a side of the parent that is different from the one to which he is generally exposed, either via the alienating parent or via his own imagination. This experience of seeing the parent through the one-way mirror can create a degree of cognitive dissonance within the child, who must now find a way of integrating diametrically opposed perceptions of the same parent.

Children often make the preposterous claim that the alienated parent never had any good traits. For example, they might say, "My mother starved me; she hit me every day and never took me any place." The use of old photographs depicting the alienated parent and the child at birthday parties, on outings and engaged in other activities, may compel the child to revise his or her assessment of the parent and frame it in more realistic terms that will then allow the therapy to focus on the real issues and problems.

Letter Writing

Children who at first are unwilling to meet with the alienated parent may be willing to have a letter written by the parent read to them. This, too, is a desensitization technique. It is, however, important to coach the parent with regard to the content of the letter. In one case in which I did not adequately coach the parent, his letter was replete with invective against the custodial parent. These segments were obviously censored when the letter was read to the children.

Extrication

Removal of the child from the custody or guardianship of the alienating parent is perhaps the most difficult of the treatments to apply for several reasons. First, in most cases the custodial parent has already been determined to be the best suited to raise the child, whether by agreement between the parents or decree by the court. As such there may be considerable doubt whether ample justification for removing the child from that parent's care and transferring him or her to the care of the other parent (who was previously considered less suitable for the task) exists. Furthermore, if the custodial parent is deemed to be adequately raising the child in all other domains, one must carefully weigh the risks of custodial transfer versus maintenance of the status quo, problematic as it may be. In many cases interim placement in an out-of-home setting may be helpful until a final determination can be made or until parents come to their senses. Israel courts have been quite cautious – or perhaps, reticent – in implementing such far-reaching remedies. Nonetheless, in a 2002 decision handed down by the Supreme Court (C.A.3009/02) the court, in a 2–1 decision, upheld a District Court ruling removing two children from the custody of both parents and placing them in an emergency diagnostic and treatment shelter for one month. The children had been assigned to the custody of their father by the rabbinical court that heard the custody case however, the decision was stayed pending appeal. In the interim, the child welfare officer petitioned the juvenile court to remove the children to an emergency shelter for evaluation claiming that they were suffering from emotional abuse. The request was denied but on appeal the District Court concurred with the child welfare officer's position and ruled that the children be temporarily removed. This decision was subsequently appealed. In its decision, the Supreme Court briefly reviewed the PAS literature and recalled that several years prior the mother had made unsubstantiated claims of sexual abuse against the father. The court appointed an expert psychologist who concluded that the children were suffering from severe PAS and as such, in absence of any more effective alternative, recommended that the children be removed to a neutral setting where they could receive appropriate treatment. In its summary, the court stated that "the family system . . . is suffering, apparently, from parental alienation syndrome, the precise degree of severity need not be determined at this point. The current situation points, unfortunately, to the fact that the children's well-being is in jeopardy. As such, the child welfare officer's petition was justified. . . ."

Nonetheless, in 2004, the court, in an expanded five-justice panel, reversed itself (C.R.6041/02). The majority decision held that the child welfare officer had not adequately exhausted all other treatment options prior to opting for removal of the children and had not adequately considered factors relating to the children's wishes and the effect on the children of such a drastic step. Thus, the Israeli Supreme Court set a very high standard for removal of children in general and in PAS cases in particular. The court did not, however, reverse its previously stated position on PAS.

Therapy as an Ordeal

The ordeal of court-ordered therapy may prove helpful in treating PAS cases. There is no question that court mandated treatment and follow-up can prove to be a significant financial and time burden on parents. Many PAS families display tremendous resistance to pain and suffering and are willing to sacrifice any semblance of a normal life for the sake of the hallowed cause. Nonetheless, they may reach the point at which the burden of visitation between the child and the parent in the therapist's office may outweigh the benefits of continuing the battle.

Non-PAS Contact-Refusal

Sometimes a cigar is just a cigar. Some PAS-like cases are, in fact, simply about a kid who does not want to see his father because his father behaves in an abusive manner towards him. As the PAS literature becomes more widely spread and known to the general public one risk is that parents may incorrectly diagnose and claim PAS. Although a father may see the child's behavior as being driven by the mother and her family in a grand plan of revenge against him, the therapist must nevertheless consider the possibility that the child's behavior is reasonable and even justified given the father's relationship with him. This is not to say that treatment is not indicated in such cases, but rather that the focus of such treatment needs to be different. Any child who does not want to see a parent is in distress, regardless of whether he admits it, but not every child has been brainwashed.

When signs of contact refusal are present, it is important to conduct a careful evaluation of the entire family in order to ascertain the root of the refusal. In many cases, the custodial parent may be quite ambivalent about the contact with the noncustodial parent; this in turn, may engender some hesitation or even resistance in the child. However, this alone may not be sufficient to cause PAS. Often, ironic as it may seem, it is actually the behavior of the alienated parent that enhances or at times even induces the alienation behavior in the child. In these cases, the alienated parent must be helped to examine and change his behavior and to allow the child to express his legitimate anger.

Treatment Dilemmas

When is the prescribed treatment worse than the presenting ailment? This is a question that frequently arises in PAS cases. At times, the resistance of the children is so strong that it extends to the therapy as well, making positive results most impossible. Parents often present the therapist with their problem in bringing the child to therapy and say, "I tell him that he needs to go but he says that he doesn't want to. He's thirteen years old; what can I do?" The parent may then also suggest that the child be given a few months of "peace and quiet" and then, perhaps he will be more amenable to therapy and to contact with the alienated parent.

Therapists do not like to give up or admit failure. They want to believe in rescue fantasies and that all matters are treatable. Nonetheless, they are often faced with situations in which they lock horns with children in a way that alienates them from us as therapists and perhaps from future therapists as well. As such, as difficult as it may be to admit, for some situations the most prudent course is to suspend attempts at reunification. This may be particularly necessary with older children or when the legal system is unwilling or unable to take decisive steps.

Dealing with Countertransference

Countertransference is a concept that is based in psychoanalytic theory. Transference is the unconscious projection onto the therapist of feelings and thoughts from previous significant relationships. The transferential relationship becomes a significant aspect of the therapeutic relationship. The other side of the patient-therapist relationship is *countertranference*, the displacement onto the patient of attitudes and feelings of the therapist from previous life experiences. Although the proper use of countertransference may be very helpful in the therapeutic process, if the therapist is not adequately aware of his countertransferential reactions, he may not act in the best interest of the patient. Transference and countertranference exist in all human relationships. As PAS cases by their very nature arouse intense visceral emotional reactions in parents, it is only to be expected that the professionals involved in these cases will also have strong emotional responses.

PAS cases are characterized by tremendous free-floating anger. The alienating parent is angry with the alienated parent. He or she is hurt, often having been coerced into accepting an unwanted divorce or separation. The winds of revenge may often be blowing or even howling. This anger is often times denied and is displaced or takes the form of passive aggressive behaviors. This anger often has an obsessive-compulsive quality, with the parent insisting that he or she is not angry and stating that he or she no longer has feelings toward the other parent and wants nothing to do with him or her. However, he or she is unable to desist from talking about that parent. The alienated parent is no less angry. He or she feels a tremendous sense of helplessness against the extraordinary force of the child who refuses contact. This parent is often angry at the whole system – judges, psychologists, and social workers – which has proven unable to enforce visitation schedules. This anger also is often displaced and may be used as an excuse for the parent not adequately looking at his or her own behavior and evaluating his or her contribution the PAS logjam. Unfortunately, the anger of the alienated parent is all-too-often vented at the child, providing him or her with a pseudo-legitimate excuse to persist in his or her anger towards the alienated parent. In younger children, the alienating parent often helps out by fanning the fire. Adolescents are usually capable of being angry and hostile without much assistance.

The therapist is not immune from PAS anger. He or she is a very convenient lightning rod for the parents' anger. The alienated parent expects the therapist to perform wonders in a flash. This can only lead to disappointment and anger. The alienating parent does not feel that he has or she any problem. He or she does not understand what the courts and the psychologists want from him or her. He or she has no insight and is not interested in change, yet is being forced into a therapeutic relationship. This engenders anger and the therapist is the object. This is one example of countertransference. The way the therapist reacts to the parents being angry with him may well inform the treatment process. Moreover, the therapist is likely to have personal feelings about PAS. It is very easy to be angry at alienating parents and children who confabulate all kind of excuses not to have contact with a parent.

The therapist who has a lot of experience in PAS cases also has his or her share of failures. Although ideally we would have that the therapist be able to apply the lessons from previous treatment failures to future cases, one must consider the possibility that the therapist's reaction to a particular case is a function of his or her own personal frustration or feelings of inadequacy. Let there be no doubt, nice theories notwithstanding, that dealing with PAS can be quite treacherous and anxiety provoking even for the experienced therapist.

Parents, in PAS cases function under considerable stress. They are mired in a legal process in which they are, to a certain extent, at the mercy of others. They feel that they are not understood and that the world is sharply divided between those who are with them and those who are against them. Each sees in the evaluator or therapist a savior and vindicator. Tremendous pressure is exerted to draw the therapist or evaluator into the conflict and have him take the same one-sided monolithic view that each parent has. The therapist who resists getting drawn into thus also risks the ire of one or both of the sides. Although as a therapist it is usually easier to work with people who are not angry at you, the PAS therapist needs to carefully consider if his actions are designed to help the family or simply to avoid or deflect parents' anger.

Court-ordered treatment might be difficult for some mental health professionals. The old joke goes, "How many psychologists does it take to change a lightbulb?" The answer is, "None; the light bulb has to want to change." Most people in court-ordered treatment do not want to change. At the very most, they want to comply with the order. A mental health professional is not comfortable with court-ordered treatment and who should not be involved in PAS cases for which court involvement is a sine qua non.

Although in many cases the only option is to use strong-arm methods for renewing parent-child contact, more traditional therapeutic approaches are always preferable. This may, however, be difficult because of the feelings of antagonism that may be aroused in the therapist by the alienating parent. Nonetheless, the therapist must keep in mind that this parent too is in distress and is looking to have his needs recognized and met. A hostile relationship with this parent only diminishes the chance of successful treatment. On the other hand, the natural tendency to identify with the alienated parent and to view him or her as he or she views himself or herself as an innocent victim may also be detrimental to the treatment process. Even where clear alienation on the part of one parent is evident, the other parent may exhibit behaviors that provide the substrate upon which the alienation occurs.

The Systemic Approach

The dynamics of PAS notwithstanding, therapists must always ask themselves, "What is a parent trying to gain from PAS?" Alienating a child requires a tremendous investment and untold energies. To do it properly, one must be of single mind and purpose, never missing an opportunity to devalue the other parent and never allowing something that may be perceived as positive to slip through without being distorted.

Even alienating parents have needs. They need to be identified with, even though they often arouse considerable anger in therapist and judges. The therapist must help the parent seek alternative ways of meeting needs such as feeling comfortable when the child is with the other parent, a sense of personal security from the other parent, financial security and the ability to live one's life free of harassment. The therapist should explore the possibilities of enlisting other subsystems, such as extended family, social services and the courts, that may be able to meet some of the unanswered needs of the parent.

Selective PAS – Divide and Conquer

Alienation between siblings is often the tragic and perverse result or spin-off of PAS. Situations in which custody is divided, either by dint of court order or as a result of a partisan maneuver by a parent or child, are particularly vulnerable to alienation between siblings. This may prove difficult as each parent will cling to "his" children both as a way of bludgeoning the other and from fear that that child will "defect" to the other side. In these situations children develop a system of attributions regarding their siblings that endows them with all of the negative qualities of the alienated parent. It is essential to move with the greatest alacrity to restore the sibling subsystem to normal functioning. This is accomplished by holding meetings between the children in the therapist's office, in some other neutral settings or even in the house of one of the parents.

PARTICULAR EXPRESSION PAS IN ISRAELI CLINICAL PRACTICE

The Bar Mitzvah

A bar mitzvah is always a happy time. Well, almost always. It can also be Hell on earth. Parents often devote much time and attention to compiling the guest list, paying careful attention not to inadvertently omit any friends, relatives, or business associates. Although the police are never included on the official guest list, on occasion they may find themselves invited as well but usually on such short notice they are unable to bring a gift. I have told clients, "you can have two Bar Mitzvahs, but not two weddings." On second thought, I add, "at this rate you will be able to have weddings also; one parent will make the first wedding and the other will make the second." Those parents who are only up to their noses in conflict – when it has not yet reached the level of the eyes – are able to guffaw at my crack; however, I don't think that this would-be sobering reality has ever convinced an alienating parent to cease and desist.

REFLECTIONS

Court Attitudes to PAS

PAS as a phenomenon or even as a diagnosis *per se* has never been challenged in an Israeli court and as such the Israeli Supreme Court has not been required to delve into the issue. Therefore no decisions that can be considered landmark in their nature exist. Nonetheless, the thrust of the case law clearly reveals that Israeli courts recognize the phenomenon of PAS and take a dim view of parents who alienate their children. The courts do not get bogged down in legalistic debates over whether PAS is a syndrome, but clearly recognize it as a pattern of behavior. Still they are at times somewhat reticent in fully utilizing the legal means at their disposal to effectively and decisively intervene. Although it is hard to say for certain, but the courts' approach may be informed by a tendency to believe that most people will do the reasonable thing, particularly when a little bit of pressure is applied. This is generally true. Most people respect, or are at least in awe of, the court system and as a result abide – more or less – by its decisions. However, this assumption about human nature may need to be suspended or at least amended in PAS cases. Alienating parents often flirt with faulty reality testing (circumscribed as it may be) and as such are unable to assume a reflective and insightful position on their behavior. For them, the rest of the world tends to be sharply divided into those people who are with them and those who are against them. Divorced of the ability to rationally view the child's true needs, these parents tend to assume a distorted view of their position and that of the child vis a' vis the courts and court officers. These false and harmful perceptions - e.g., that a child of eight knows better than adults what is ultimately in his best interest - tend to be reinforced by a sometimes wishy-washy approach of courts that, on one hand, decry PAS but, on the other hand, are at times somewhat anemic in the measures that they apply.

Early Identification of PAS

The value of early identification in PAS cases cannot be overstated. Experience has taught that as with other conditions or situations, PAS has its early warning signs and when detected early can be controlled, treated, and eliminated. Although one can never say with absolute certitude that a particular constellation of factors will eventually lead to PAS, clinical experience has taught that most PAS cases are characterized by a certain constellation of discrete and discernable dynamics that can be identified proactively.

Denigration

People get divorced because they do not like each other. It therefore follows that divorcing parents will be very critical of each other. This is normal and to be expected, and it would be Pollyannaish to assume otherwise. However, the need for concern arises when a parent is unable to present a somewhat balanced picture of his counterpart. A saying in the Talmud states: "There is no evil that does not have in it some good." In most cases, even bad parents have some good qualities. A parent who has adopted a monolithically negative view of the other parent will be unable to convey to his or her child any positive – or at least neutral – messages about the other parent. Even if a parent is not yet actively conveying any negative message to the child about the other parent, the inability to see anything positive may well be a precursor to later PAS if other conditions are present. This dynamic of black and white thinking is particularly perplexing in those parents who had the divorce forced upon them and who still hold hope for rapprochement. They find themselves in the paradoxical position of idealizing a relationship with a demonized person.

Obsessive-Compulsive Features

Although many custody battles prove to be all encompassing and all consuming, PAS cases are particularly so. Alienating parents become obsessed with the parent whom they claim to want to have nothing to do with. They say they do not want to talk about the other parent but that is all they seem to do. They are willing to devote untold amounts of time, energy, and even money to their crusade. Not every parent who tends to be obsessive-compulsive in a custody battle will necessarily develop into an alienating parent, but the potential does exist.

Intractable Divorce Conflict

High conflict divorces may present a greater risk for PAS symptoms. When one parent is unable to speak to the other, a not-so-subtle message is transmitted to the child. The parent does not need to say "Your mother is bad" or "Don't go to your father's house, he is dangerous." The child observes the parent's behavior and derives the appropriate conclusion. Often parents will present to the children confusing messages, such as, "If you want to see your mother, that is fine. But as far as I am concerned she doesn't exist." This message can be conveyed implicitly or explicitly but either way children then find themselves in a bind that they can resolve only by choosing one parent over the other. Cognitive Dissonance theory informs us that it is very difficult to love two people who hate each other, particularly when one of them presents an implicit expectation that his or her enemy will be yours as well.

Blaming

Divorce is a failure. As such, the people involved have a natural tendency to find someone to blame. Most parents having not been trained in systems theory and the dynamics of marital relationships, will quite naturally simplistically seek to blame each other for the marital breakdown. It is not only the parent who has had an extra-marital affair, but also the one who has initiated divorce proceedings or who picks up and leaves the house who is usually perceived as the home wrecker. Blaming, to a certain extent, is inevitable, but when a parent places the entire onus on his counterpart, one needs to be concerned.

When the parent who is opposed to divorce is the "chief blamer," this may significantly influence the children. The parent's blaming position may well dovetail with children's natural tendency to perceive the parent who wants the divorce as the one who is at fault. Parents who enhance such dichotic thinking in children may be sowing the seeds of the PAS position that idealizes one parent while demonizing the other.

Developmentally Inappropriate Attributions, Statements and Behaviors

Children evidencing developmentally inappropriate behaviors and statements should always arouse suspicion. It is always wise to consider the possibility that the child in question may be precocious, but a five-year-old child who talks about "custody" or a nine-year-old child who talks about his parents' lawyers is probably being exposed to inappropriate stimulation from at least one of the parents. When parents are unable to see the inappropriateness of such behaviors or statements in their children or when they support and justify them, one needs to consider that a PAS situation may be developing, even if overt behaviors indicating that the child is resistant to contact with one of the parents are apparent.

Distorted View of the Child

One test of a parent's understanding of his or her child is the ability to provide a balanced and realistic description of the child. Often the parent's description of the child's behavior with the other parent differs from actual behavior observed in the office when the child is actually with that parent. Thus, for example, a parent may describe the child as being apprehensive and withdrawing when in the presence of the other parent, while, in fact, the therapist observes a child who is relaxed, in good cheer, and even initiates physical contact with the other parent. Although this distortion may be inadvertent, or, in fact, may be what the parent observes when the child is put in a conflictual situation in which both parents are simultaneously present, one must consider the potential for such a distortion to trickle down to the child, thus creating what may ultimately be a self-fulfilling prophecy.

Ethical Considerations

Ethics is a subject that generally draws little attention or interest until, of course, one gets into trouble. Given the slippery slope on which many PAS cases take place and the established litigious inclination of the parents, a few comments regarding ethical considerations and PAS are in order.

Perhaps the most difficult ethical problem associated with the treatment of PAS families relates to conflicting loyalties and the possibility that an action that may be beneficial towards one member of the family may be perceived as detrimental by another. The therapist's primary objective is to help the family attain a healthier level of functioning. Nonetheless, polar positions of different members can place the therapist in a position whereby not only does he or she not meet the needs – stated or unstated – of a particular family member, but actually acts in a way that causes greater distress to someone or to the system as a whole. As opposed to a regular therapeutic situation in which pain is often the path to gain, in most PAS cases the treatment is court ordered and as such the informed consent that we ordinarily seek is less than complete and volitional. One parent may perceive the reinstitution of the parent-child connection as detrimental to the child, as in a case of purported but unsubstantiated sexual abuse.

As with any other therapy involving more than one person, the limits of the confidentiality are, perforce, more restricted than in individual therapy. It is therefore recommended to adhere to the ethical guidelines of the American Psychological Association and inform family members of these restrictions at the outset of the treatment. Beyond the fact that several family members participate in the treatment, the confidentiality is also compromised by the fact that what transpires in the treatment can and will ultimately find its way into the court record. This is obviously an impediment to treatment, as it may result in people being less than candid and self-revealing, but given the nature of PAS, it seems to be a necessary evil.

As with other divorce-related evaluation and treatment procedures, therapists dealing with PAS may be particularly vulnerable to malpractice suits and ethics complaints. It is very important to keep in mind that both parents involved in PAS disputes are extremely stressed and angry, and are fighting what they consider do-or-die battles. By the very nature of PAS, one parent is displacing his anger and aggression and "using" an innocent bystander in a war against someone whom he or she once loved. Under such circumstances, it is not difficult for the evaluator or therapist to find himself in the crosshairs of one of the parents, particularly if one of them has a tendency towards a borderline or narcissistic personality disorder.

Although there can be no easy recipe for avoiding ethical conundrums other than the normal caution that therapists should practice on a daily basis, an awareness of the particular pitfalls of PAS cases should help us exercise particular caution in clearly articulating the limits of confidentiality, maintaining proper documentation, attaining appropriate releases, or securing proper stipulations from the court about release of information. Moreover, because of the strong countertransference that may arise, it is necessary for the therapist to constantly monitor his actions and reactions so as to avert any responses that are rooted in his or her personal feelings rather than his or her professional repertoire.

CONCLUSIONS AND RECOMMENDATIONS

Clinical practice and a review of the Israeli legal and psychological literature on PAS lead to several conclusions:

1. PAS is a very common feature of high-conflict divorces and commands considerable time, energy and resources of the courts and mental health professionals.
2. At times, a truly recalcitrant parent may prove to be more powerful than the court, especially if the courts are reticent and apprehensive about using their powers, or if they are unable to exercise creativity in employing the sanctions available tothem. PAS is often about power and control; the courts need to understand and speak the language of these parents.
3. Although PAS is a psychological problem, most cases cannot be resolved without a joint effort of the courts and a mental health professional. As a psychologist, I would like to think that I can affect change based on my clinical skills alone, but in cases of PAS, I usually require the strong and constant backing of the court system.
4. PAS situations are usually quite complex. At first glance, the solution always seems easier than it is in practice. The hate and antipathy that are often ingrained in PAS children knows no companion in the realm of clinical work with children. Even the children of abusive parents often show more willingness for contact. As such, there can be no hocus-pocus approach to the treatment. All those involved need to know that they are in for a long and sometimes expensive haul.
5. As with other forms of illness, early identification and treatment is often of paramount importance. I have discussed what I consider to be some of the early warning signs of PAS in formation. Given that problems of this sort tend to get worse with time – unlike some fears, for example, that children "grow out of" – early intervention is essential in order to avoid what with time may develop into an intractable problem. As with any diagnostic procedure, some false positive and false negatives occur, but given the severity of PAS, one needs to err on the side of investigating the possibility of PAS even where it may turn out not to be rather than letting any bona fide cases go undiagnosed.
6. The psychological treatment is best done by a team that can provide the child and the parents each with a therapist of their own with one of the therapists serving as the team coordinator. PAS parents and children are very powerful. The children in particular usually have a distorted view of their power and influence. The therapists need to walk the delicate tightrope between empathy and acceptance at one end and firmness and conviction at the other.

7. Consider different subtypes of PAS and the particular dynamics of the case. Treatment and intervention need to be differential and tailored to the particular family. The risk associated with the various treatment approaches may vary in different subtypes of PAS. For example, the use of a more authoritative approach may be more effective with younger children who are in a development stage during which they respond to authority. The treatment approach to an actively alienating parent may need to be different from that used with a parent who alienates more passively. Further research and thought is required to identify more specific types of family dynamics that result in PAS behavior.
8. A more systemic approach should be adopted in order to more fully understand the contribution of *both* parents *and* the child to the maintenance of the problem. For many alienated parents, PAS has become an excuse for not adequately examining their own behaviors and for not properly investing in the relationship with their children.
9. The courts need to carefully reconsider the ways in which their given powers are implemented. Courts need to work collaboratively and systemically with mental health professionals. They need to be intensely involved in these cases, even at the expense of having to convene frequent court sessions. Compelling parents to appear in court every two weeks may serve as a potent stimulus for otherwise recalcitrant parents.
10. The tendency to adopt a wait-and-see approach to PAS cases is understandable given the levels of hostility generated and the desire of courts and mental health professionals to mitigate conflict wherever possible. Nonetheless, time often works to the disadvantage of children who are cut off from their parents. The longer one waits to mend severed ties, the more difficult it becomes. PAS requires definitive intervention. Alienating parents do not "see the light" on their own.
11. Attention needs to be paid to new ways of preventing PAS. In addition to early identification, it is necessary to examine the structure of the entire divorce legal process to see if changes can be made that will contribute to faster and more amicable resolution of divorce conflicts, thus reducing, perhaps, the risk of PAS.
12. Collaboration between legal and mental health professionals must be enhanced. The better each is able to understand the tools and limitations of the other, the better they will be able to form a cooperative unit that will provide a systemic response to a complex problem.

PAS cases represent a significant and seemingly growing proportion of Israeli divorce cases, particularly of the high-conflict variety. As such, there needs to be a greater awareness of the clinical features of PAS as well as the early warning signs. Israel has not become preoccupied with the debate over whether PAS is a discrete syndrome. Although the particular constellation of behaviors and dynamics are recognized by many mental health professionals, attorneys, and judges, treatment approaches for PAS still are not always clearly understood. The particular nature of PAS renders it different and distinct from other forms of psychological distress that mental health professionals are called upon to evaluate and treat. Treatment of PAS is easier said than done. Proper treatment requires the long-term cooperation of antagonistic parties (e.g., the parents) as well as parties who may not share the same therapeutic-conceptual framework (e.g., the court and the therapist). Effective treatment of PAS requires a systemic approach that will recognize the needs and capabilities of all involved in a particular case. Ultimately, PAS presents a formidable challenge for cooperation between mental health professionals and the judiciary.

BIBLIOGRAPHY

Bergman, Z.B. & Wietztum, E. (1995). Parental kidnapping and parental alienation syndrome. *Sichot, 9*(2), 115–130.

Gardner, R.A. (1992). T*he Parental Alienation Syndrome* (1st ed.). Cresskill, NJ: Creative Therapeutics, Inc.

Gardner, R.A. (1998a). The Burgess decision and the Wallerstein brief. *J. American Academy of Psychiatry and Law, 26*(3), 425–31.

Gardner, R.A. (1998b). *The Parental Alienation Syndrome* (2nd ed.). Cresskill, NJ: Creative Therapeutics, Inc.

Gardner, R.A (2001). *Therapeutic interventions for children with Parental Alienation Syndrome.* Cresskill, NJ: Creative Therapeutics, Inc.

Gardner, R.A (2002a). The empowerment of children in the development of parental alienation syndrome. *American Journal of Forensic Psychology, 20*(2), 5–29.

Gardner, R.A (2002b). Denial of the parental alienation syndrome also harms women: What's good for the goose is good for the gander. *American Journal of Family Therapy, 30*(3), 191–202.

Goldstein, A., Freud, A. & Solnit, A. (1973). *Beyond the best interests of the child.* New York: Free Press.

Gottlieb, D. (2000). The concept of time as a factor in decision making regarding children: Implications for the psycho-legal system. S. Ben Natan (Ed.) In: *Borrowed time.* Tel Aviv: Prague Press.

Habusha, R. (2000). *Contact resistance to the non-custodial father.* Master's thesis, Bar Ilan University, Ramat Gan, Israel.

Kelly, J.B. & Johnston, J.B. (2001). The alienated child: A reformulation of parental alienation syndrome. *Family Court Review, 39*(3), 249–266.

Levita, Z., Etzion, N., Vitali, P., Abramovitch, O., Kotler, P. & Nir, M. (1997). Contact refusal: Parent-child conflict in separation and divorce. *Sichot, 11*(2).

Siegel-Itzkovich, J. When parents knock each other, kids get brainwashed. *Jerusalem Post*, September 3, 2000.

Traubmann, T. Junk science has its way in court. *Haaretz,* Friday, August 15, 2003.

Wallerstein, J.S. & Tanke, T.J. (1996). To move or not to move: Psychological and legal considerations in the relocation of children following divorce. *Family Law Quarterly ,30*(2), 305–331.

Chapter 9

PARENTAL ALIENATION SYNDROME: THEORY AND PRACTICE IN GERMANY

WERNER LEITNER AND ANNELIE KÜNNETH
(TRANSLATED FROM GERMAN BY ELIZABETH ELLIS)

OVERVIEW

The first German-language publications on parental alienation syndrome appeared in 1998 (among them that of Leitner and Schoeler, 1998). These publications may be divided into three groups: (1) contributions that adapt and develop Richard Gardner's views in a German context, (2) articles concerning PAS that have little in common with Gardner's views, and (3) contributions that question and criticize Gardner.

The results of an empirical study by Leitner (1998, 2000a,b,c,d) showed that in many cases expert assessments formulated for family courts in Germany failed to meet the basic requirements needed for a well-founded PAS diagnosis. In a survey of youth welfare workers and child advocates, Künneth (2002) came to the conclusion, however, that PAS is known to many of these professionals in Germany. On the basis of existing knowledge of Gardner's theory of psychodynamics in children and Lewin's field theory, she outlines in her study socio-psychological influences that can affect PAS.

INTRODUCTION

In Germany, as elsewhere, PAS frequently plays an important role in disputes concerning visitation and custody. In this chapter, we first review German-language specialty literature on PAS. Three groups can be distinguished: (1) publications based on Gardner's contributions that have been modified in order to better adapt to the situation in Germany, especially the family reform and child custody legislation dated July 1, 1998, and innovations such as the appointment of a child advocate. This group of publications includes the first German-language articles on PAS, such as those of Leitner and Schoeler (1998), Leitner (1999a,b,c,d; 2000a,b,c,d; 2001a,b) and von Boch-Galhau (2000, 2002), (2) studies concerned with PAS that have only a loose connection with Gardner's contributions (e.g., Jopt, 1999, Jopt and Behrend 2000a,b), and (3) contributions that question or criticize PAS (e.g., Fegert, 2001a,b). Then, on the basis of an empirical study (Leitner, 1998, 1999c, 2000b,d) we discuss the question of the extent to which expert assessments commissioned by the courts in Germany meet the requirements of a well-substantiated PAS diagnosis. Finally, we explore current practice in Germany and present the results of a survey among employees of youth welfare offices and child advocates carried out in 2002 (Künneth, 2002), which indicate the extent to which PAS is known to professional helpers and plays a role in their work.

PAS PUBLICATIONS IN GERMANY

Adaptation and Further Development of Gardner's PAS Contribution

The first German-language publications on the subject of PAS appeared in 1998 from, among others, Leitner and Schoeler (1998). Their description of PAS is closely related to that of Gardner (1992, 1997). This medically-based approach was supplemented at some points by utilization of a flexible and intervention-guided procedure in which diagnosis and intervention influence each other mutually. When utilizing a procedure involving both diagnosis and intervention, it is sometimes necessary to return from intervention to the diagnosis in order to use the insights obtained through intervention for a more detailed diagnosis. This method allows us to make more precise hypotheses and find more specific intervention possibilities (Leitner, 1994, 1995, 1999b). Leitner and Schoeler adapted their contribution to the situation in Germany, in particular to the new legislation on families valid in Germany since July 1, 1998. This legislation makes special provision for the involvement of a child advocate in problematic visitation and custody cases (Leitner and Schoeler, 1998, p. 849). The authors emphasize that PAS cannot be equated with "brainwashing"; the child's own PAS contribution complements the alienator's programming. Nor is the PAS diagnosis applicable when the hated parent is actually guilty of abuse. Leitner and Schoeler describe the varying degrees of PAS and their main manifestations (p. 850ff). They also describe degrees of severity with reference to legal interventions, therapeutic efforts, and the efforts of the child advocate (p. 853ff).

PAS can affect programmed children in a variety of ways. They may develop behavioral problems or have difficulties at school (Leitner, 2002). One common problem is that teachers will gullibly concur with the wish of the alienating parent that the alienated parent should not be informed about the child's school activities. Geiss (1997) conducted a survey among primary school teachers to find out whether they were familiar with the family situations of their pupils. He came to the conclusion that approximately one-third of teachers had very little knowledge of the family situations of their students (Geiss, 1997, p. 23ff in Leitner, 1999a, p. 143f). In such situations, the teacher may unwittingly join in with the programming of the PAS indoctrination process. This is of particular significance in view of the fact that, despite the availability of American publications in specialist circles, PAS was for a long time a relatively unknown phenomenon in Germany. As Hübner (2001) states "the public (should) learn of the existence of this syndrome and be sensitized to the problems connected with PAS" (p. 92). Because the problems associated with PAS manifest themselves in the family, the neighborhood, and the schools, adequate knowledge of PAS is important for parents and teachers if they are to properly deal with such children.

von Boch-Galhau (2000, 2002) is also a close follower of the views of Gardner and of Leitner and Schoeler. He emphasizes the consequences of PAS for the personality development of these children. According to him, PAS can produce a sense of deep self-alienation in the child. In time, PAS children reach the point at which they are no longer able to trust their own feelings and perceptions about themselves. Their personal identities become deeply insecure. Ultimately, they find it difficult to become independent of both the idealized and the alienated parent. This can give rise to long-term developmental problems in these children (von Boch-Galhau, 2000, p. 8f).

Programming parents may suffer from unresolved psychological problems from childhood as well as pathological reactions to the divorce. As a result of these unresolved problems, the ex-partner is seen as the main cause of the alienating parent's suffering; the alienating parent has no awareness of his or her own contributions to the family grief. Alienating parents are motivated by a deep fear of losing the child. They form a coalition with the child and this results in a pathogenic fear-based bond in which the child is trapped. It is important to remember that up to about the age of ten, children cannot distinguish between their own perception and their own imagination and stories they have heard (cf. von Boch-Galhau, 2000, p. 9f).

von Boch-Galhau suggests the following therapeutic and legal measures: Early recognition of PAS is important so that appropriate help can be provided at the earliest possible time. The child needs the love and care of both parents, even after separation and divorce. He suggests preventive programs, advisory sessions, therapeutic intervention for deeply divided families, psychological intervention by order of the court, and ongoing support. The author also makes reference to Gardner's proposals (cf. Leitner and Schoeler, 1998) for mild, moderate and severe PAS cases (von Boch-Galhau, 2000, p. 11f). Finally, he comments in his foreword to the German edition of Gardner's follow-up study that French legislation on divorce (Article 357, Code Pénal) and some American states (such as Pennsylvania and California) have already legislated legal action to be taken against parents who prevent visitation (von Boch-Galhau, 2002, p. 8 [the author refers here to Gardner, 1998, p. 445]; cf. also Gardner, 2002b). Similar legislation has yet to be created in Germany.

Publications That View PAS Independently of Gardner's Contributions

There also have been German-language publications that in many ways view PAS independently of Gardner's concepts, although the perspectives have certain parallels and points in common (some only implicit). Jopt (1999), for example, divided PAS into two phases. The first phase relates to factors in the child's development during his or her earlier life with the caring parent (before the separation) that led to the rejection of the other parent. In the second phase, the alienation is intensified by the child himself or herself and by the caring parent. As the child believes that contact with the alienated parent would amount to a betrayal of the alienating parent, he or she avoids such involvements. The child's attitude towards the alienated parent then changes (cf. Jopt, 1999). Jopt and Behrend (2000a, p. 225) describe the consequences of Gardner's eight main PAS manifestations (Gardner, 1998, p. 76f) through which, in their opinion, PAS can be diagnosed. The symptom of the "campaign of denigration" leads to the exclusion of the alienated parent. This gives rise to a feeling of cognitive dissonance. The phenomenon of "absurd rationalizations" emerges to reduce the dissonance. "A lack of ambivalence" leads to exclusion and "emphasis on independent thought" is used as dissonance reduction. "Reflexive support of the alienating parent" leads to exclusion. The "absence of feelings of guilt" is used as dissonance reduction, "borrowed scenarios" lead to exclusion, "an extension of hostilities" is used as dissonance reduction. By avoiding all empathy, the child succeeds in rejecting a once loved parent (cf. Breunig, 2001, p. 66).

The mental tension experienced by a PAS child when meeting the rejected parent subsides after parting from this parent. (The authors call this tension cognitive dissonance and refer in this context to Frey and Gaska [1993]). In this way, the child learns that it is good for him or her to avoid that parent. Finally the alienating parent extremely strengthens this feeling. Jopt and Behrend view this aspect of PAS somewhat differently from Gardner. They do not share "Gardner's view that the child does not want to lose the caring parent as well" (Jopt and Behrend, 2000a, p. 228). Jopt and Behrend see a need for developing a new PAS model, based (among other factors) on the fact that, unlike Gardner, they believe that programming by the alienating parent is often subconscious (Jopt and Behrend, 2000a, p. 229). They (2000a, p. 229) state that their theory of subconscious influence does not exclude intention. "But there is no evidence that this is what usually happens and the adults themselves vigorously deny any intention." Jopt and Behrend comment that all conclusions as to the motives of adults drawn from observation of PAS must remain hypothetical as long as "we have no valid theory into which the known symptoms can plausibly be incorporated" (2000a, p. 229). They go on to say that although the drawing up of hypotheses is a basic principle of scientific research their value is measured by "how accurately and comprehensively they not only depict, but also explain the phenomenon in question."

Bortz and Döring (2002, p. 17) comment, however, that "it is the function of theories . . . to describe, explain and forecast matters. . . . Social theories (are made up of) a network of proven hypotheses or recognized empirical 'laws.'" According to Bortz and Döring (2002, p. 12) a scientific hypothesis can be used to indicate "a more or less precise relationship between two or more variables which apply to a certain population of comparable objects or events." Jopt and Behrend nevertheless overinterpret the term "hypothesis" in the context quoted. Jopt and Behrend (2000a, p. 229) aim to "show that nonuse of the motive of intentionality allows us to develop for the first time a theory on PAS which goes well beyond the taxonomy known to date." The authors make it clear, however, that "intentionality cannot be basically excluded from their theory" (p. 229). It would not be easy, in our opinion, to definitively reject "a motive of intentionality" under these circumstances. This is especially the case because Gardner holds that the alienating parents' denial of culpability for indoctrinating PAS in the children is a conscious and deliberate lie – a lie designed to exonerate them – and should not be believed (Gardner, 1998).

Critical Views of PAS

The main critic of PAS among German-language authors is Fegert (2001a). He fears that the "debate on so-called PAS" (p. 3f) will lead to polarization among experts and supports critics of the concept. "This is why many experienced psychological experts have described . . . PAS and its associated vocabulary 'programming parent,' 'brainwashing', etc. as an inadmissible simplification and unproven assumption, even as a 'panacea' or 'psychological cudgel' (Salzgeber and Stadler, 1998, p. 168) or 'super-criterion' (p. 179)." In fact, PAS – as can be seen from Gardner's publications – may on no account be equated with the terms "brainwashing" or "programming" (Gardner, 1998, p. xix). Fegert (2001a, p. 4), also complains that PAS is not mentioned in DSM-IV. Gardner (2002a) comments on this: "It is important to note that DSM-IV does not frivolously accept every new proposal. Their requirements are very stringent with regard to the inclusion of newly described clinical entities. The committees require many years of research and numerous publications in peer-review scientific journals before considering the inclusion of a disorder, and justifiably so." Gardner (2002a) also states that in the early 1990s, when DSM-IV committees were meeting, there were too few peer-review publications to warrant a submission. DSM-V committees will begin meeting in 2006, at which time a submission is planned. A frequently updated list of peer-reviewed articles on PAS may be found on the Internet at: http://www.rgardner.com/refs.

Fegert (2001a) is critical of the fact that Gardner has been using the term "PAS," not just since 1992, but since the mid-1980s. This is certainly true, because Gardner's first article on PAS appeared in 1985 (Gardner, 1985). However, Fegert does not state why this fact is justification for criticism. He concludes his article with these words: "This view of the long-term course of events raises very definite questions as to the mechanical 'gung ho pragmatism' boldly practiced in recent jurisdictions and the apparently unproblematic use of accompanied visitation as the solution to many conflicts" (Fegert, 2001a, p. 6). Fegert bases his statements mainly on long-term studies by Wallerstein and Lewis (1998), who state, "children, especially young children, sometimes side with one parent, usually the parent whom they are most concerned about or whom they are most sorry for" (quoted in Fegert, 2001a, p. 3). He continues that most children then revise their opinion of their parents on the basis of their own observations (cf. Wallerstein and Lewis [1998]).

In the second part of his article, Fegert (2001b, p. 41f.) writes that child advocates, with their opportunity to form a relationship with the child, can make an important contribution if the child talks to them about his or her parental loyalty conflicts. He raises the criticism, however, that "the emotional cost to the child and his/her severe mental strain have not yet been sufficiently considered in decision-making" (Fegert, 2001b, p. 42). Supervised visitation is certainly justified as a transitional phase, but must be rejected as a permanent solution (Fegert, 2001b, p. 42). The author believes that the wishes of the child should not be neglected: "If the declared wishes of the child are at odds with the visitation wishes of adults it appears problematic to generally assume that the rights of the child may be disregarded by subjecting his will to the wishes of adults or the continuation of the relationship" (Fegert, 2001b, p. 42). Fegert concludes that:

> the suspicion cannot but arise that it is exactly the imprecise, generally descriptive nature of PAS as a term which makes it unfit for clinical use but extremely well-suited as a tactical weapon in visitation disputes. A critical examination of the actual situation should therefore always be made when the side desiring visitation raises the accusation of PAS. Without this reference to questions which can actually be answered, it must always be feared that what we have is in fact a 'Parental Accusation Syndrome,' a syndrome of accusation and incrimination. (p. 42)

Although Fegert is not convinced of the existence of PAS as "a syndrome of clinical value" (Fegert, 2001a, p. 5), he nevertheless recommends "in the case of presumed denial of visitation" (Fegert, 2001b, p. 40f) that certain areas should be investigated. He would like the question of whether indications of "so-called brainwashing" exist clarified. Fegert comments that these indications may not be deduced from the behavior of the child "as the authors of PAS assume," rather, they must be deduced from the "statements of the child" (Fegert, 2001b, p. 40f). Fegert points out that when the parents are being evaluated, any indications of "mutual defamation and an increased loyalty conflict in the child" should be noted. In his question as to whether "indications of influencing or loyalty conflicts can be detected in empirically proven and projective procedures," Fegert provides no specific definition of what he understands to be "empirically proven . . . procedures." Does he mean tests that meet the main criteria of objectivity, reliability, and validity (cf. Brickenkamp, 1997 on this)? All in all, Fegert's criticisms appear dubious on many points and cannot ultimately call into question the well-founded basis of the PAS concept and its usefulness in family arbitration in Germany.

TO WHAT EXTENT IS PAS KNOWN IN GERMANY AND HOW IS IT USED IN FAMILY ARBITRATION PRACTICE?

Having described existing views on PAS using examples from our three categories, we will now proceed to the questions of how well-known PAS is in Germany and to what extent it is used in family arbitration and psychological expert assessments of families.

Basic Legal Aspects

Relevant legal texts in Germany such as the Palandt commentary on the German Civil Code, Edition 2000 (Art. 1626 – Parental Custody – Marginal No. 29, p. 1686) now include references to PAS. Under the heading "Visitation denial in the relationship of the parents to each other," the Palandt Civil Code states the following:

> Withdrawal of parental custody on the grounds of inability to care for a child may be the ultima ratio if the parent who has custody makes it impossible for the other parent to have contact with the child . . . or places considerable or repeated unacceptable difficulties in the way and by transferring his own motives exposes the child to considerable strain in processing the conflict between the two parents. (p. 1686)

With reference to earlier decisions in which this behavior was largely tolerated, the comment is made that:

> according to the new legislation this will seldom be the case. . . . A comparison may be made with the modern discussion on reactive parental rejection as a result of alienation of the child by one parent (Parental Alienation Syndrome – PAS): Bakalar ZfJ 98, 268; Rummel ZfJ 97, 202; Leitner/Schoeler DAV 98, 849; Koedjoe/Koeppel KiPrax 98, 138; Salzgeber and others and Rexilius KiPrax 99, 107 and 149. (p. 1686)

Büte (2001), a judge at the Higher Regional Court in Celle, describes PAS from the legal point of view. He discusses PAS in detail and concludes that "in all cases of PAS the intensive cooperation of youth welfare workers, the court, and experts is necessary" (p. 104f). An expert assessment may be required if – after the parents, the child, and the youth welfare office have been heard – questions in the areas of psychology or child psychiatry that are important to the court's decision remain to be clarified. The questions must be answered by an expert who has the necessary expertise to draw up an assessment in this realm (p. 27f). The expert assessment must be reviewed critically by the family court. "The guidelines for the preparation of psychological expert assessments (Leitner FuR 2000, 57ff) provide standards for deciding whether the expert assessment satisfies basic scientific requirements" (p. 28).

The Limitations of Traditional Psychological Assessment Instruments for the Diagnosis of PAS

Leitner (1998, 1999a,b,c,d; 2000a,b,c,d) investigated the diagnostic strategies and interventions that had been used to help children and young people whose parents had separated or divorced and many of them were PAS cases. The evaluators determined which parent offered the best child-rearing conditions. On the basis of the assessment, one parent was given custody and the other was given rights of visitation. As a decision aid, in addition to the reports of the youth welfare offices, the family court may order psychological expert assessments of the family, especially in disputed PAS cases.

Many of the psychological expert assessments proved to be problematic, however. In his study (cf. Leitner, 1998, p. 152ff; 2000d, p. 57ff), the methods used in 52 psychological expert assessments in various regions of Germany were examined. Most of the expert assessments in the sample had been drawn up in the mid-1990s. Attention focused on whether the tests used, the observation of behavior, and the exploration and the proper use of theories and findings (especially in the field of bonding research) met basic scientific requirements. In many PAS cases, the court's questions referred to the rejection of one parent by the child and the court often specifically requested that the bonds with the parents should be examined. In spite of this very clear request, virtually no sufficiently valid, reliable, and objective bonding-specific procedures were to be found among the total of 117 tests administered in the 52 family assessments. The Family as Animals Test (Brem-Gräser, 1995) and the Family Relations Test (Bene and Anthony, 1957, 1985) were the two most frequently used tests; each was used 16 times. The following listed shows 85 of the 117 tests used, in order of frequency. Not listed are the less frequently used tests.

1. **Family As Animals (Brem-Gräser), used 16 times.**
   Value criteria according to Brickenkamp (1997, pp. 964, 968ff):
   Objectivity – no; reliability – no; validity – no; standardization – partial.
2. **Family Relations Test (Bene and Anthony), used 16 times.**
   Value criteria according to Brickenkamp – not recorded.
3. **Fable Method (Düss), used 13 times.**
   Value criteria according to Brickenkamp (1975, p. 520ff):
   Objectivity – no; reliability – no; validity – no; standardization – yes.
4. **Incomplete Sentences, used 11 times.**
   Value criteria according to Brickenkamp – not recorded.
5. **Children Apperception Test (Bellak and Bellak), used 8 times.**
   Value criteria according to Brickenkamp (1997, pp. 942, 949f):
   Objectivity – no; reliability – no; validity – no; standardization – no.
6. **Draw a Person (Ziler), used 7 times.**
   Value criteria according to Brickenkamp (1997, pp. 964, 973ff):

Objectivity – yes; reliability – partial; validity – yes; standardization – yes.

7. **Draw a Castle, used 7 times.**
Value criteria according to Brickenkamp – not recorded.
8. **Scenotest (von Staabs), used 7 times.**
Value criteria according to Brickenkamp (1997, pp. 964, 981):
Objectivity – partial; reliability – partial; validity – partial; standardization – no.

The test "Family as Animals" is considered by Hermann (2001) to be suitable at best for the generation of hypotheses, but certainly not as a basic for actual decisions. Hermann (2001, p. 258) argues that the information provided by this test should be used only as a source of various hypotheses, each to be tested via further exploration and psychometric procedures. The expert assessments surveyed contained little evidence that the test findings had been treated in this way. With regard to the Family Relations Test, according to the evidence provided by Beelmann and Schmidt-Denter (2001, p. 71ff), the validity of this test in decision-related contexts has still not been adequately proved. Beelmann (1995, p. 38) spoke in Leipzig on "Recent studies with the Family Relations Test." In his talk and in the discussion that followed, Beelmann described the use of this test in diagnostic practice as "hair-raising." He pointed out that, for reasons of cost, inadmissible modifications are often made when the test is administered. It is important to note that the most frequently used tests did not satisfactorily meet test validation criteria. Severe deficits also occurred on other levels (e.g., a lack of systematic observation of behavior, insufficient exploration, and a lack of reference to research on bonding). PAS was not explicitly taken into consideration as a specific diagnosis in any of the expert assessments in the survey.

The Familiarity of Professional Helpers with PAS (Youth Welfare Workers and Child Advocates)

Künneth (2002) conducted an empirical study at the Hagen University in which 63 youth welfare officers and child advocates (23 men and 40 women) were asked about their knowledge of PAS (Künneth, 2002, p. 67). One of the aims of Künneth's survey was to assess, using Lewin's field theory, the effect of social/psychological aspects on Gardner's PAS concept (Lewin, 1951). Lück (2001, p. 46ff) provides an introduction to Lewin's work, in which he describes the field theory viewpoint on the emergence and continuance of conflicts, of rewards or punishment (Lewin, 1975). Of the 63 respondents, 40 were familiar with the term PAS, 13 were not, and 1 only vaguely so.

Participants rated the importance of the knowledge of PAS for professional practice as shown here.

Can't say	4
Virtually no importance	6
Some importance	25
Very important	28

With regard to familiarity with the Leitner/Schoeler (1998) diagnostic scheme based on that of Gardner, 23 of the respondents replied that they were familiar with it and 40 responded that they were not.

According to Lewin, a force induced by a person (P) in a child (C) may be regarded as a force field of this person over the child. A person who has power over the child is able to induce through commands to the child positive and negative behaviors. Through restrictive instructions P changes the nature of the region, which could result in an impassible barrier if C tries to resist P's influences. A conflict between the child's own desires and the external inducing forces may result in the child's trying to undermine the power of P, at least in the area of conflict (Lewin, 1946, 1982b; Künneth, 2002, p. 39f). Using Lewin's theory as a reference, we now address specific elements in Gardner's PAS contribution.

The first element we will review is "maintenance of the primary psychological bond":

> The most important contributing factor relates to the fact that the child's basic psychological bond with the alienating parent is stronger than that with the alienated parent. Actually, the child is psychologically bonded to both parents, but there is generally a stronger bonding with the parent who was the primary caretaker in the earliest years of the child's life. (Gardner, 1998, p. 110)

If the child's bond with the alienating parent is initially stronger than the bond the child had with the alienated parent, the alienating parent attempts to exploit this (by inducing a force) in order to draw the child fully over to his or her side. This initially causes a conflict situation in the child, as he or she does not wish to lose the other parent as well (an expression of his own force) (Lewin, 1946). The child may, however, wish to avoid conflict with the alienating parent and thereby submit to the PAS indoctrinating forces. Such submission results in the development of PAS.

Respondents in Künneth's (2002) study (p. 81) were asked the following questions. Their answers are listed after each question.

Do PAS children identify primarily with the alienating parent?

Largely	28
Partially	24
Scarcely	5
No response	6

Are conflicts avoided by identification with the alienating parent?

Largely	27
Partially	16
Scarcely	11
No response	9

Are conflicts avoided through identification with persons from the social environment of the alienating parent?

Largely	18
Partially	19
Scarcely	12
No response	14

Lewin's views on induced needs, group aims, and individual aims are that an individual's needs are determined to a great extent by social factors. The needs of a growing child change and new needs emerge as the result of the many small and large social groups to which the child belongs. Three kinds of situations in which needs arise from social relationships can be distinguished: (1) an individual's behavior can be motivated by the desire to benefit someone else (an altruistic act), (2) the individual's needs can be induced by the force field of another person or group (such as the obedience of a weaker person in compliance with the coercive pressures of a stronger one), and (3) the individual's needs arise as the result of belonging to a group and the pursuit of its aims. Lewin sees these three types as closely interrelated (Lewin, 1982b, p. 436f). What is significant in this context is that induced needs which are opposed to the individual's own needs may lead to a permanent state of conflict, which may be concealed. If a conflict of this kind cannot be resolved by breaking the dominant sphere of influence then it is possible that the child will become aggressive towards less powerful persons (Lewin, 1982b, p. 442). This leads ultimately to an "absorption of alien aims." An induced need can gradually change to become one's own need. In other words, the person not only obeys orders, but he or she "absorbs" them internally (makes them his or her own) (Lewin, 1982b, p. 442; Lewin, 1946; Künneth, 2002, p. 41f). This phenomenon is often referred to as "identification with the aggressor."

This aspect of Lewin's theory is reminiscent of Gardner's description of PAS children's "identification with an idealized person." Gardner states:

> Related to the identification-with-the-aggressor phenomenon is the process of identification with an idealized person. In the course of the alienator's deprecation, the victimized parent becomes viewed as loathsome, worthless, and an individual with few, if any, admirable qualities. Identification with and emulation of such a person become compromised. Deprived of one admirable parent to identification, the child may then switch to the alienator as the only parent worthy of emulation. At the same time that the programming parent vilifies the targeted parent, she (he) is likely to whitewash and even idealize herself (himself). (Gardner, 1998, p. 115)

The child idealizes the alienating parent and possibly that parent's social environment as well. Under the influence of this person or this group (which Gardner refers to as the coterie of enablers and supporters) the PAS child grows ever closer to him or her and increasingly rejects the alienated parent. One of the child's motives could be to act in an altruistic way (cf. Lewin, 1982b, p. 436f) with the intention of supporting the parent with whom he or she lives after the separation. The influence of the idealized parent can be so great that the child takes over his or her aims or needs (cf. Lewin, 1982b, p. 442). This issue raised the following questions (cf. Künneth, 2002, p. 82):

In cases of PAS, are children influenced by the parent with whom they live?

Largely	52
Partially	6
Scarcely	–
No response	5

Is this influence also exercised by the social environment of this adult?

Largely	25
Partially	30
Scarcely	1
No response	7

Do the children give in to the will of these persons?

Largely	25
Partially	28
Scarcely	1
No response	9

According to Lewin, it is possible for the same personality to manifest itself in virtually opposing behavioral manifestations. In other words, a particular personality pattern in a person corresponds to a variety of forms of behavior and can only be deduced by simultaneous assessment both of visible behavior and of the situation. This is another way of saying that behavior (B) is determined by the person (P) and the environment (E) (B=F [P, E]) and not by the person or the environment alone (Lewin, 1982b, p. 379; cf. Lewin, 1946; cf. Künneth, 2002, p. 43). In PAS, this means that the child's actions are influenced initially less by his or her own personal wishes or emotions than by the emotions of the parent causing PAS, which Lewin would describe in this regard as influences from the child's psychological environment. Initially, therefore, spheres of influence on the child's behavior shift towards forces from his or her environment and away from his or her own forces.

Gardner describes this situation as an example of "infectiousness of emotions." He states: "Then there is what I refer to as the vibrating-tuning-fork principle. This relates to the infectiousness of emotions. Emotions have a way of transmitting themselves from one individual to another, often in very rapid fashion" (Gardner, 1998, p. 117f). This principle prompted the following question (Künneth, 2002, p. 83):

Do PAS children fulfill the wishes of the alienating parent?

Largely	39
Partially	18
Scarcely	–
No response	6

Lewin states that a conflict may be characterized in psychological terms as a situation in which opposing forces of approximately equal magnitude bear upon an individual simultaneously. It is possible that one of the two opposing field vectors is of a positive nature and the other is of a negative nature. In such situations, a conflict only arises if the individual does not find himself or herself between the two, but if the positive and negative vectors bear upon the child from the same side. The child would like to stroke a dog, for example, but is also afraid of it; or, he or she would like to eat the cake that has been forbidden (Lewin, 1982b, p.120f, cf. Lewin, 1935). These conflict situations usually develop quite quickly. The child first sees a difficult barrier (B) between himself or herself and his or her aim (A), which prevents the completion of his or her actions in the direction of the field forces. However, when the child has approached the barrier a number of times, the barrier itself takes on a negative character. A negative vector emerges in addition to the positive one. The negative vector usually grows gradually stronger until it is stronger than the positive vector. The child then leaves the field. Leaving the field can be a physical occurrence, in which the child withdraws, turns away, or leaves the room, or it can be an inwardly directed leaving of the field, (e.g., the child begins to play with or turns his or her attention to something else). In these situations the leaving of the field is usually temporary. The child turns away, but after a while makes another attempt at the barrier (Fajans, 1933). A last and final leaving of the field usually occurs only after several temporary withdrawals, which grow longer in duration until finally the child does not return (Lewin, 1982b, p. 188f; cf. Lewin, 1931; Künneth, 2002, p. 44f.). In terms of Gardner's PAS concepts this means that the child would like to approach the alienated parent again, but is not allowed to do so. What Lewin calls an acceptance/aversion conflict arises. This situation can go so far as to drive the child "off the field": he or she apparently rejects the alienated, but actually still-loved parent, in order to not jeopardize the affection of the other parent and to avoid a difficult conflictual situation.

Gardner refers to this phenomenon as the "fear of disruption of the primary psychological bond." He states: "Related to the aforementioned desire of the child to maintain the psychological bond with the alienating parent . . . is the fear of disruption of that bond. And there is also the fear of alienating the indoctrinating parent. The victimized parent is only ostensibly hated; there is still much love" (Gardner, 1998, p. 111f).

The following study questions explored this issue (cf. Künneth, 2002, p. 83f):

Does the child say that he or she wishes to approach the rejected parent again?

Largely	6
Partially	28
Scarcely	23
No response	6

Does the alienating parent prevent an approach?

Largely	33
Partially	18
Scarcely	3
No response	9

Is an approach prevented by persons in the social environment of the alienating parent?

Largely	12
Partially	31
Scarcely	9
No response	11

What Lewin refers to as a barrier-free punishment situation may also be seen in PAS. In certain PAS cases, no particular barrier seems evident despite the threat of punishment. The child is faced with an unpleasant task of a distinctly negative nature – namely, rejecting a loved parent. The child carries out the wishes of the alienating parent without any particular barrier being visible – a barrier that prevents the child from leaving the field, even, it almost seems, without the threat of punishment. The alienating parent's instruction to perform the task seems sufficient to cause the child to perform the unpleasant task obediently. Especially in situations in which the child's attitude toward the adult is hostile and alienated, the child's behavior can often look as if he or she was "voluntarily" taking on the unpleasant task at the adult's instruction without the need for particularly rigid punitive barriers. In these circumstances, the alienating parent often points out with pride that the child is not being set "rigid limits," but is being given a good deal of freedom. The power of the alienating adult's threats of punishment have permeated the child's life space to such an extent that the child has virtually no areas in which he or she can move freely and independently. It is not necessary to prevent the child from leaving the field through external barriers because the function of these barriers has spread throughout the entire field. This child is situated in a field that is completely dominated at every point by the power of the alienating adult. This is a situation in which the alienating adult, either by particularly severe punishments or by certain ideologies, has gained such control over the child that he or she "does not dare to rebel" but carries out unpleasant duties without complaint. This is because his or her life space is inwardly dominated by the wishes of the adult. This dependence is so strong that the threat of a particular punishment becomes unnecessary. In extreme cases, it is hardly necessary for the adult to verbalize his or her wish that the child reject the alienated parent.

The programming ultimately becomes so internalized that the influence of the alienating parent may not at all be recognized. However, the less it appears outwardly, the stronger it may be (Lewin, 1982b, p. 127ff; cf. Lewin, 1935; cf. Künneth, 2002, p. 46ff). Gardner considers the "identification with the aggressor" factor to be operative here. He states:

> The identification-with-the-aggressor phenomenon may be operative in the development of the PAS. This phenomenon manifests itself when a person is in a weak or impotent position in relation to a more overpowering, threatening individual. The weaker party may deal with the situation by taking on the characteristics of the stronger person. In this way, the impotent individual compensates for the feelings of insecurity and the sense of impotency attendant to being weak and vulnerable. The child whose raging mother is incessantly denigrating his father may join forces with her in an attempt to protect himself/herself from being the target of her enormous hostility. Children do this from the fear that if they were to join with the father, they, too, would become the target of such violent outbursts. . . . The same process may be operative when a child joins forces with a father against the mother. . . . A paranoid alienator may be so successful in programming the child against the victimized parent that the child will take on the programmer's paranoid delusions. (Gardner, 1998, p. 112f)

It is probable that the barrier-free punishment situation as described by Lewin is present in severe cases of PAS in particular. In these cases the alienating parent can be relatively certain that the child will act as the parent wishes; the inner domination over the child is so well established that the child usually acquiesces parents' wishes. It must be borne in mind that "power" is not actually mentioned in the following findings. Yet the unconditional, unhesitating support of one parent may be interpreted as that parent's power over the child. The adult's power over the child in the barrier-free punishment situation as described by Lewin is so great that the child complies apparently "voluntarily" with this adult's wishes and supports him or her "spontaneously." This element of PAS was assessed with these questions (Künneth, 2002, p. 85).

Does the child unhesitatingly support the alienating parent?

Largely	20
Partially	24
Scarcely	12
No response	7

Does the child use words which are not typical of his or her age?

Largely	27
Partially	24
Scarcely	5
No response	13

The life space of PAS children in relation to adults is more severely limited than that of children who are not in a PAS situation, as they have little or no contact with the alienated parent. According to Lewin, behavior = the function of the person and the environment = the function of the life space ($B = F [P, E] = F [L]$).

This means that the instability of the psychological environment leads in some respects to an instability of the person. In a new, not yet established situation the field is not particularly strongly divided up; whatever differentiation may have occurred is not firmly established. In a less divided field, an individual's move from one region to another may be only one step. For a more strongly divided field it must be seen as a major change (the equivalent of several steps) (Lewin, 1982a, p. 196f; cf. Lewin, 1939; Künneth, 2002, p. 49f). This is especially true of children and young people. Lewin therefore believes that children and young people can quickly adopt radical attitudes. As the life space of a PAS child shows disproportionately low differentiation, Lewin argues that originally positive feelings towards the alienated parent can quite easily turn into negative feelings, such as rejection or even hate. The step from a positive feeling to a negative feeling is a relatively small one for a child. This is particularly true of children affected by PAS, as their life space may be more restricted than that of other children because of the lack of contact with the alienated parent.

In his discussion of the underlying psychodynamics of the PAS child, Gardner emphasizes the important psychological mechanism "reaction formation." He states:

> A common factor that contributes to the PAS child's obsessive hatred of the victimized parent is the utilization of the reaction formation mechanism. Obsessive hatred is often a thin disguise for deep love. . . . Each time these children think about how much they hate their vilified parents, they are still thinking about them. Although the visual imagery may involve hostile fantasies, the targeted parent is still very much on their minds. The love, however, is expressed as hate in order to assuage the guilt and fear they would feel over overt expressions of affection for the denigrated parent, especially in the indoctrinating parent's presence. (Gardner, 1998, p. 112)

It must be remembered that the life space of PAS children is less differentiated than non-PAS children because it is primarily limited to the alienating parent. Lewin believes that extreme reactions are more common among children and young people than among adults because their life space is less differentiated ("established") than that of adults. Thus, a child finds the change from one region of life space to another much easier than an adult, who must pass through several regions. Lewin therefore perceives a certain instability among children, which is enhanced in PAS children. To further expplore this issue, the following question was posed (Künneth, 2002, p. 86):

Are PAS children more prone to *extreme* reactions?

Largely	18
Partially	30
Scarcely	7
No response	8

In Lewin's terms, PAS may be described as a conflict that does not relate to one force field, but to the overlapping of at least two force fields. A system of possible conflicts was therefore set up to examine how force fields can mutually overlap in such a way that, at certain points of the field, equal but opposing forces emerge. This procedure would allow the systematic treatment of the conditions and consequences of conflicts (Lewin, 1982a, p. 82f, cf. Lewin, 1944; cf. Künneth, 2002, p. 51).

The parents' separation or divorce can expose the child to many possible force fields. The parent with whom the child lives, his or her social environment, and the noncustodial parent all exercise varying influences on the child. Each of these fields can potentially serve as a vehicle for "release of hostility." Gardner states:

> The development of a PAS can serve as a vehicle for the release of anger, which may have a variety of sources. It is as if the PAS involves a 'sucking in' of a wide variety of anger-evoking experiences and allows for a sanctioned release of the accumulated rage. If not for the presence of the PAS, such anger might have been suppressed, repressed, or channeled into other modes of release, both healthy and pathological. The PAS, then, rests on a foundation of rumbling resentment that is looking for a safe and acceptable vehicle of release. And the divorce situation involves many frustrations and resentments that can be pulled into and fuel the PAS. (Gardner, 1998a, p. 115f)

With regard to this issue, these questions were formulated (cf. Künneth, 2002, p. 86f):

Are PAS children exposed to different reactions from their two parents?

Largely	39
Partially	14
Scarcely	3
No response	7

Does the social environment of the parents also exert an influence?

Largely	17
Partially	29
Scarcely	7
No response	10

Do these influences lead to irritation or hostility in the child?

Largely	21
Partially	27
Scarcely	5
No response	10

THE FUTURE

As part of the integration and further development of theories, and making use of Lewin's field theory, it is possible to draw up some hypotheses on the emergence and persistence of PAS. The results of the survey by Künneth (2002) favor explanations based on field theory (i.e., social-psychological explanations). Further research into PAS should seek to integrate existing concepts. However, the suffering of the children concerned should not be forgotten in the course of this theoretical work. An intervention-guided procedure can be helpful here (cf. Leitner, 1994, 1998, 1999b). Professional helpers should integrate existing, scientifically evaluated theories on PAS into their day-to-day practice. Experience and skills based on well-founded interventional diagnoses can be of great value in interdisciplinary teamwork. Such knowledge should be made widely available to those professionals in Germany who are often required to work without this important information, much to the detriment of children affected by separation, divorce, and alienation. It is therefore very important to look to the future and, without vilifying or glossing over the mistakes of the past, make the very useful contribution of PAS theory extensively available to professional helpers, experts, and family courts.

REFERENCES

Beelmann, W. (1995). Neuere Untersuchungen mit dem Family Relations Test – Normierungen und Anwendung in Scheidungsfamilien. (Recent studies with the Family Relations Test – its standardization and use for families in conflict.) In K. U. Ettrich, G. Friedrich, M. Fries, E. Witruk (Hrsg.) *Volume of abstracts for the conferences of the specialist groups: Developmental psychology and the psychology of education.* Leipzig, 1995, p. 8.

Beelmann, W. and Schmidt-Denter, U. (2001). Der Family Relations Test (FRT). In Sturzbecher, D. (Hrsg.): *Spielbasierte Befragungstechniken.* Göttingen: Hogrefe, pp. 64–73.

Bene, E. and Anthony, E.J. (1957/1985). *Family Relations Test* (FRT). Göttingen: Hogrefe.

Bortz, J. and Döring, N. (2002). *Forschungsmethoden und Evaluation für Human- und Sozialwissenschaftler* (3., überarbeitete Auflage). (*Research methods and evaluation for the social sciences* [3rd, revised edition]) Berlin u.a.: Springer.

Brem-Gräser, L. (1995). *Familie in tieren. (Family as animals)* München: Reinhardt.

Breunig, Y. (2001). *Das Parental Alienation Syndrome (PAS). Psychodynamik von Kindern, Eltern, Folgen, Therapie/Intervention und Kritik. Im Zusammenhang mit spezifischen Lern- und Verhaltensschwierigkeiten. (PAS. The psychodynamics of children, parents, consequences, therapy/intervention and criticism)* Unpublished thesis for the 1st state examination for primary school teachers. Bamberg: Otto-Friedrich University. Chair for Primary School Education and Didactics.

Brickenkamp, R. (1975/1997). *Handbuch psychologischer und pädagogischer tests. (Manual of psychological and pedagogical tests)* Göttingen: Hogrefe.

Büte, D. (2001). *Das Umgangsrecht bei Kindern geschiedener oder getrennt lebender Eltern. Ausgestaltung – Verfahren – Vollstreckung. (Visitation rights for children of divorced or separated parents. Development – Procedures – Execution)* Berlin: Erich Schmidt-Verlag.

Fajans, S. (1933). Erfolg, Ausdauer und Aktivität beim Säugling und Kleinkind. (Success, perseverance and activity among babies and young children.) *Psychologische Forschung 17,* 268–305.

Fegert, J. M. (2001a). Parental Alienation oder Parental Accusation Syndrome? (Teil 1). Die Frage der Suggestibilität, Beeinflussung und Induktion in Umgangsrechtsgutachten. (Parental Alienation or Parental Accusation Syndrome? (Part 1). The question of suggestibility, influence and induction in legal evaluations on visitation) *Kind-Prax, 1,* 3–7.

Fegert, J. M. (2001b). Parental Alienation oder Parental Accusation Syndrome? (Teil 2). Die Frage der Suggestibilität, Beeinflussung und Induktion in Umgangsrechtsgutachten. (Parental Alienation or Parental Accusation Syndrome? (Part 2). The question of suggestibility, influence and induction in legal evaluations on visitation) *Kind-Prax, 2,* 39–42.

Frey, D. and Gaska, A. (1993). Theorie der kognitiven Dissonanz. (The theory of cognitive dissonance) In: D. Frey and M. Irle (Hrsg.), *Theorien der Sozialpsychologie. Bd. 1: Kognitive Theorien* (p. 275ff.). Bern: Huber.

Gardner, R.A. (1985). Recent trends in divorce and custody litigation. *The Academy Forum* (a publication of the American Academy of Psychoanalysis) 29(2), 3–7.

Gardner, R.A. (1998). *The Parental Alienation Syndrome. A guide for mental health and legal professionals.* (2nd Ed.). Cresskill, New Jersey: Creative Therapeutics.

Gardner, R. A. (1997). *Recommendations for dealing with parents who induce a Parental Alienation Syndrome in their children.* Cresskill, New Jersey: Creative Therapeutics.

Gardner, R.A. (2002a). *Does DSM-IV have equivalents for the Parental Alienation Syndrome (PAS) diagnosis?* Unpublished manuscript. Accepted for Publication. Available at http://www.rgardner.com/refs.

Gardner, R.A. (2002b). Das elterliche Entfremdungssyndrom. Anregungen für gerichtliche Sorge- und Umgangsregelungen, hg. von W. v. Boch-Galhau. Berlin: VWB. (PAS. Proposals for court decisions on custody and visitation, ed. W. v. Boch-Galhau). An article presenting the results of the study on which this book was based appeared as: Gardner, R. A. (2002b). Should courts order PAS children to visit/reside with the alienated parent? A follow-up study. http://www.rgardner.com/refs. (This article also appeared in 2001 in the *American Journal of Forensic Psychology, 19*(3), 61–106, available at http://www.forensicpsychology.org.)

Geiss, W. (1997). *Scheidung als kritisches Lebensereignis und Eingriff in kindliche Lebenswelten des Grundschulkindes. (Divorce as a critical event impacting the life of the primary school child)* Unpublished thesis for the 1st state examination for primary school teachers. Bamberg: Otto-Friedrich University. Chair for Primary School Education and Didactics.

Hermann, U. (2001). Das Verfahren "Familie in Tieren." ("The family as animals" procedure) In: Sturzbecher, D. (Hrsg.) *Spielbasierte Befragungstechniken.* Göttingen: Hogrefe, pp. 242–259.

Hübner, R. (2001). *Das Parental Alienation Syndrome (PAS). Definition, Ausprägung, Indizien und Induktionen in Zusammenhang mit spezifischen Lern- und Verhaltensschwierigkeiten. (PAS, its Definition, Manifestation, Indices and Induction in connection with Specific Learning and Behavioral Difficulties)* Unpublished thesis for the 1st state examination for primary school teachers. Bamberg: Otto-Friedrich University. Chair for Primary School Education and Didactics.

Jopt, U. (1999). *Ein Zwei-Phasen-Modell zu PAS. (A two-phase model for PAS)* Manuscript of a lecture given at the conference "The Will of the Child and Parental Separation" from April 23–24, 1999 at the Catholic Academy of Trier.

Jopt, U. and Behrend, K. (2000a). Das Parental Alienation Syndrome (PAS) – Ein Zwei-Phasen-Modell (Teil 1). (PAS, a two-phase model [Part 1]) *Zentralblatt für Jugendrecht, 6,* 223–231.

Jopt, U. and Behrend, K. (2000b). Das Parental Alienation Syndrome (PAS) – Ein Zwei-Phasen-Modell (Teil 2). (PAS, a two-phase model, [Part 2]) *Zentralblatt für Jugendrecht, 7,* 258–271.

Künneth, A. (2002). *Das Parental Alienation Syndrome. Einflussfaktoren der zwischenmenschlichen Beziehungen unter sozialpsychologischen Aspekten. (PAS: The socio-psychological aspects influencing interpersonal relationships)* Hagen University: Master's thesis in the field of the psychology of social processes.

Leitner, W. G. (1994). *Interventionsgeleitete Einzelfallhilfe im Rahmen einer Beratung im Schulbereich. Bezugsrahmen und theoretische Grundlegung. (Intervention-guided case studies within a school advisory service. Scope and theoretical basis).* Regensburg: Roderer.

Leitner, W. G. (1995). *Pädagogisch-Psychologische Diagnostik. Interventionsgeleitete Befunderstellung im exemplarischen Einzelfall. (Pedagogical/psychological diagnosis. Examples of intervention-guided diagnosis).* Bamberg: WVB, Wissenschaftlicher Verlag Bamberg.

Leitner, W.G. (1998). Evaluation psychologischer Entscheidungshilfen für Familiengerichte. (An evaluation of psychological decision aids for family courts) In Evangelische Akademie Bad Boll (Hrsg.) *Psychologie im Familienrecht. Bilanz und Neuorientierung,* pp. 152–165.

Leitner, W.G. (1999a). Kindliche Lebenswelten unter besonderer Berücksichtigung der Situation von Scheidungswaisen im familiären und schulischen Kontext. (The child and his world, with particular reference to children of divorced parents in the context of family and school.) In N. Seibert (Hrsg.) *Perspektive Schulpädagogik. Kindliche Lebenswelten. Eine mehrperspektivische Annäherung.* Bad Heilbrunn: Klinkhardt, pp.127–156.

Leitner, W.G. (1999b). Intervention-guided single case-help and Parental Alienation Syndrome (PAS). Differential diagnosis and treatment approaches. In S. Sebre, M. Rascevska, S. Miezite (Hrsg.) *Identity and self-esteem. Interactions of students, teachers, family and society.* Riga: SIA, pp. 253–260.

Leitner, W.G. (1999c). Psychological expert assessments for family court decisions in Germany. In S. Sebre, M. Rascevska, S. Miezite (Hrsg.) *Identity and self-esteem. Interactions of students, teachers, family and society.* Riga: SIA, pp. 261–273.

Leitner, W.G. (1999d). School Psychologists As Mediators in Conflicts caused by Separation and Divorce. Abstract. XXII. International School Psychology Colloquium 30. July – 03. August 1999. Global thinking – individual acting, Kreuzlingen/Konstanz (Switzerland/Germany): ISPA.

Leitner, W.G. (2000a). Diagnose und Intervention bei PAS (Parental Alienation Syndrom). (Diagnosis and intervention in cases of PAS) In *Forschungsschwerpunkt Familienforschung 1999/2000.* Universität Bamberg, pp. 12–14.

Leitner, W.G. (2000b). Gutachten für Familiengerichte – häufigste Mängel. (Expert evaluations for family courts – the most common shortcomings) In *Forschungsschwerpunkt Familienforschung 1999/2000.* Universität Bamberg, pp. 14–17.

Leitner, W.G. (2000c). Lern - und Verhaltensstörungen bei Kindern im Trennungs - und Scheidungskonflikt bei "Parental Alienation Syndrom (PAS)" (Learning and Behavioral Problems in Children affected by Divorce Conflicts or Separation with PAS) In S. Rolus-Borgward, U. Tänzer and M. Wittrock (Hrsg.) *Beeinträchtigung des Lernens und/oder des Verhaltens - Unterschiedliche Ausdrucksformen für eine gemeinsames problem.* Oldenburg: DiZ, pp. 107–116.

Leitner, W.G. (2000d). Zur Mängelerkennung in familienpsychologischen Gutachten. (Recognizing shortcomings in Psychological Family Expert Evaluations) *Familie und Recht. Zeitschrift für die anwaltliche und gerichtliche Praxis, 2,* pp. 57–63.

Leitner, W.G. (2001a). *Lernstörungen bei Parental Alienation Syndrome (PAS). (Learning Difficulties Caused by PAS)* 2nd conference of the Commission "Primary School Research and Primary Level Education" of the DGfE (Section on School Education) held from September 27–29, 2001 at the Martin-Luther University in Halle.

Leitner, W.G. (2001b). Differentialdiagnostische Ansätze, Befunde und Forschungsperspektiven zum Parental Alienation Syndrome (PAS). (Attempts at Differential Diagnosis, Findings and Research Possibilities for PAS) In H. Rauh and L. Krappmann (Hrsg.) *Abstract-Band 15.* Conference of the specialist group for developmental psychology of the German Association for Psychology in Potsdam in 2002, p. 99.

Leitner, W.G. (2002). Learning and behavior problems in separation and divorce conflicts. Abstracts. XXV. School Psychology Colloquium 25 July – 29. July 2002. Education for All - How Inclusive Can You Get. Nyborg (Denmark): ISPA, p. 71.

Leitner, W.G. and Schoeler, R. (1998). Maßnahmen und Empfehlungen für das Umgangsverfahren im Blickfeld einer Differentialdiagnose bei Parental Alienation Syndrom (PAS) unterschiedlicher Ausprägung in Anlehnung an Gardner (1992/1997). (Measures and Recommendations for Visitation Procedures in View of a Differential Diagnosis in cases of PAS) In Der Amtsvormund (DAVorm). *Monatsschrift des Deutschen Instituts für Vormundschaftswesen, 71*, 11/12, pp. 849–868.

Lewin, K. (1931). Environmental forces in child behavior and development. In C. Murchison (Ed.), *A handbook of child psychology* (pp. 94–127). Worcester, MA: Clark University Press.

Lewin, K. (1935). The psychological situations of reward and punishment. In K. Lewin (ed.), *Dynamic theory of personality* (pp. 114–170). Translated by: D. K. Adams and K. E. Zener. New York: McGraw-Hill.

Lewin, K. (1939). Field theory and experiment in social psychology: Concepts and methods. *American Journal of Sociology, 44*, 868–897.

Lewin, K. (1944). Constructs in psychology and psychological ecology. *University of Iowa Studies in Child Welfare, 20.*

Lewin, K. (1946). Behavior and development as a function of the total situation. In L. Carmichael (Ed.), *Manual of child psychology.* New York: Wiley, pp. 791–844.

Lewin, K. (1951). *Field theory in social sciences.* New York: Harper & Brothers.

Lewin, K. (1975). *Die Lösung sozialer Konflikte. Ausgewählte Abhandlungen über Gruppendynamik (4. Auflage)* (Solving Social Conflicts: Selected Essays on Group Dynamics [4th Edition]), Ed. Gertrud Weiß Lewin). Bad Nauheim: Christian-Verlag. (Title of original publication: Lewin, K. [1948]. Resolving social conflicts. New York: Harper.)

Lewin, K. (1982a). *Kurt Lewin Werkausgabe, (The Works of Kurt Lewin)* Ed. C.-F. Graumann. Band 4. Feldtheorie, hg. von Carl-Friedrich Graumann. (Vol. 4, *Field Theory*, ed. C.-F. Graumann) Bern: Huber, Stuttgart: Klett-Cotta.

Lewin, K. (1982b). *Kurt Lewin Werkausgabe,* hg. von C.-F. Graumann. *Band 6. Psychologie der Entwicklung und Erziehung,* hg. von Franz E. Weinert und Horst Gundlach. (The Works of Kurt Lewin, ed. C.F. Graumann. Vol. 6. *The psychology of development and education,* ed. by Franz E. Weinert and Horst Gundlach) Bern: Huber, Stuttgart: Klett-Cotta.

Lück, H. E. (2001). *Kurt Lewin. Eine Einführung in sein Werk. (Kurt Lewin. An introduction to his works)* Weinheim und Basel: Beltz.

Palandt Bürgerliches Gesetzbuch (2000). *Beck'sche Kurz-Kommentare, Band 7, (Palandt Civil Code [2000]. Beck's Short Commentary, Vol. 7),* 59th revised edition; revised by P. Bassenge, U. Dietrichsen, H. Heinrichs, H. Putzo, G. Brudermüller, W. Edenhofer, A. Heldrich, H. Sprau, H. Thomas). München: C.H. Beck.

Salzgeber, J. and Stadler, M. (1998). Beziehung kontra Erziehung. Kritische Anmerkungen zur aktuellen Rezeption von PAS. Ein Plädoyer für Komplexität. (Relationship vs. education. Some critical notes on the current reception of PAS. A plea for complexity) *Kind-Prax 6,* pp. 167–171.

Saß, H., Wittchen, U., Zaudig, M. (2000). *DSM-IV and ICD-10 Fallbuch. Fallübungen zur Differentialdiagnose nach DSM-IV und ICD-10. (Case studies on differential diagnosis according to DSM-IV and ICD-10)* Göttingen, Bern, Toronto & Seattle: Hogrefe. (Title of American original: Frances, A. and Ross, R. [1996]. DSM-IV Case Studies: A Clinical Guide to Differential Diagnosis. Washington, D.C.: American Psychiatric Press.)

von Boch-Galhau, W. (2000). Das Parental Alienation Syndrome (PAS). *ISUV/VDU – Merkblatt. MB 82 / 02,* pp. 3–17.

von Boch-Galhau, W. (Hrsg.) (2002). Einführung zum Buch: Gardner, R. A. Das elterliche Entfremdungssyndrom. Anregungen für gerichtliche Sorge – und Umgangsregelungen. (Introduction to Gardner, R. A., The Parental Alienation Syndrome. Proposals for Court Decisions on Custody and Visitation) Berlin: VWB.

Wallerstein, J. P. and Lewis, J. (1998). The long-term impact of divorce on children – A first report from a 25-year study. *Family and Conciliation Courts Review, 36*(3), 368–383.

Chapter 10

RECOGNITION OF PAS IN AUSTRALIA

SANDRA S. BERNS

OVERVIEW

After introducing the statutory provisions applicable to disputes over children, this chapter addresses the difficulties posed by the current approach in PAS cases. It identifies the particular features of PAS that make it difficult to argue in the family court, including the intense controversy surrounding the syndrome, the weaknesses of much of the expert evidence tendered to date, the statutory focus upon the rights of the child rather than upon the needs or rights of the parent and the financial barriers including the limited access to legal aid and the increasing prevalence of self-represented litigants. It concludes with some suggestions regarding the presentation of expert evidence where PAS is alleged.

INTRODUCTION

PAS in Australia, as in the United States and elsewhere, has generated much controversy, with both its advocates and its opponents making injudicious statements (that is, statements largely directed at establishing legitimacy for their respective positions) rather than directly examining the "stage" on which such allegations are played out and its unique dynamics. Coming from the perspective of a legal academic with a substantial research interest in family law, and a particular interest in what are often termed intractable disputes involving children, the perspectives that will be advanced in this paper are very different from those advanced by psychiatric professionals, forensic psychologists, and litigators. They are also very different from those advanced by the spokespersons for various interest groups.

As stated in earlier publications (Berns, 2001, p. 198), I take no position in the clinical debate regarding PAS. That debate can only be settled by scientific research conducted following rigorous principles and using generally accepted scientific protocols such as double-blind studies. To my knowledge no research fully meeting these criteria has been published to date. My interest lies in the role played by PAS allegations in litigation and in the problems such allegations cause for the family court and for other agencies dealing with parents and children in high conflict families, such as contact centers. In what follows, I will outline basic relevant facts about the structure of Australian family law and the approach taken by the Australian family court in cases where PAS has been alleged, discuss some of the difficulties posed by the legislative framework in dealing with such allegations, and, finally, outline the main barriers to the reception of arguments regarding PAS by the Australian courts.

THE LEGAL FRAMEWORK

Although Australia, like the United States, is a federation, unlike the United States the commonwealth government has constitutional power to legislate concerning marriage and divorce. The Family Law Act 1975 sets out the powers of the Family Court of Australia, which, together with the recently created Federal Magistrate's Court, hears all applications for principal relief (nullity and divorce) and children's matters incidental to applications for principal relief. While in contrast to the multiple jurisdictions of the United States, this arrangement is appealingly simple, jurisdictional difficulties frequently arise because the states have exclusive power concerning other children's matters (including allegations of physical or sexual abuse) and because the Family Court's power over children's matters is limited to those children who may be termed "children of the marriage." This term has been interpreted to include children who are the biological children of both husband and wife, children who have been adopted by both husband and wife, and children born to the couple through the use of advanced reproductive technology (including in vitro fertilization and artificial insemination by donor) procedures. The states have referred power to the commonwealth to legislate regarding the ex-nuptial children of either the husband or the wife, bringing them within the jurisdiction of the Family Court. The stepchildren of either party are, however, excluded. Family Law Act 1975 section 60F sets out the criteria used to determine whether a child is a child of the marriage. Section 60H deals specifically with children conceived through ART procedures.

The states also have exclusive power over criminal matters, including domestic violence and stalking. As a consequence, in seriously conflicted families, there often are concurrent proceedings in the Family Court and in State Magistrates or Supreme Courts.

Several sections in the Family Law Act 1975 are directly relevant to the approach the court must take to allegations of PAS. Section 43 directs the court to have regard to "the need to protect the rights of children and to promote their welfare" and "the need to ensure safety from family violence." It also directs the court to have regard to "the means available for assisting parties to a marriage to consider reconciliation or the improvement of their relationship to each other and to their children" (Family Law Act 1975 sections 43(c) & (ca)). While section 43 is little more than what used to be termed a "motherhood statement," it forms an essential part of the interpretive background for children's matters.

Part VII of the Family Law Act 1975 deals exclusively with children's matters. The philosophy of the legislation is set out in section 60B. It provides that:

> (1) The object of this Part is to ensure that children receive adequate and proper parenting to help them achieve their full potential, and to ensure that parents fulfil their duties, and meet their responsibilities, concerning the care, welfare and development of their children.
> (2) The principles underlying these objects are that, except when it is or would be contrary to a child's best interests:
>
> (a) children have the right to know and be cared for by both their parents, regardless of whether their parents are married, separated, have never married or have never lived together; and
> (b) children have a right of contact, on a regular basis, with both their parents and with other people significant to their care, welfare and development; and
> (c) parents share duties and responsibilities concerning the care, welfare and development of their children; and
> (d) parents should agree about the future parenting of their children.

Part VII of the act represents a significant change in the overall thrust of the legislation and was enacted in 1996 following active lobbying by, inter alia, fathers' rights groups. It sought to break down the perception of divorcing parents that some people are "winners" and some people are "losers" in children's matters. To this end, the traditional property-based discourse of "custody" and "access" was replaced with the ostensibly neutral language now in use; "joint parental responsibility" replacing "guardianship" and "custody," "residence" replacing "physical custody" and "contact" replacing "access." Research into the impact of the 1995 reforms suggests a small but apparently measurable trend towards "symbolic" joint residence orders has occurred. These are orders couched in residence/residence terms that are, in terms of the time actually spent with each parent, actually indistinguishable from residence/contact orders (Dewar and Parker, 1999, pp. 21–22). The current model is premised upon an ideal of ongoing cooperative postdivorce parenting, with consultative joint decision making regarding children.

Although these ideals are worthy, the reforms have proved problematical in practice. The presumption of joint parental responsibility (particularly against the background of a statutory child support formula administered through the taxation system) encouraged a belief among many contact parents that joint residence would become the norm, thus eliminating the obligation to pay child support. In families with a history of deeply entrenched conflict both during the marriage and after separation, cooperative postdivorce parenting has not proved viable and some evidence suggests that the provision for parenting plans and specific issues orders has provided warring parents with further ammunition rather than defusing conflict, as was intended. Research on the impact of the legislation suggests that the concept of shared parental responsibility has proved harmful in high-conflict families and encouraged acrimony rather than reducing it (Dewar and Parker, 1999, p. 80, Rhodes, Graycar, and Harrison, 2000, pp. 1–2).

Division 2 of the Family Law Act 1975 introduces the legislative framework in children's matters and deals specifically with "parental responsibility," defining it in section 61B as "all the duties, powers, responsibilities, and authority which, by law, parents have in relation to children," thus encompassing guardianship. Section 61C provides that each of the parents of a minor child (child under 18) has parental responsibility for that child and that parental responsibility is not affected by separation or divorce unless explicitly declared in a court order. For practical purposes following divorce, parental responsibility is shared by both parents and is equivalent to what is, in the United States and Canada, termed joint legal custody.

Section 61D deals with the effect of "parenting orders." It provides that a parenting order confers parental responsibility upon a person to the extent provided for in that order but does not disturb the parental responsibility of any other person unless explicitly provided for in the order. Section 63C deals with parenting plans, specifying that such plans may deal with the person or persons with whom the child is to live, contact between the child and any other person or persons, the maintenance of the child, and any other aspect of parental responsibility for the child. The object of Section 63 is to encourage the parents of a child to reach consensual agreement on all matters concerning the child's welfare and to avoid litigation and the need for court orders. The legislation directs the parents to make the interests of the child the primary consideration in negotiating a parenting plan. Parenting plans have not been widely used, and discussions concerning the possibility of abandoning them are currently ongoing. If the parents are unable to reach an agreement, the Family Court will make a parenting order (Family Law Act 1975 Section 64B). Such an order may deal with residence (where the child is to live), contact (with the other parent), or maintenance. Early research into the reforms suggest that relatively few couples opt for the parenting plan route, preferring to pursue the "tried and true" option of a consent order registered with the court (Dewar and Parker, 1999, p. 54). A specific issues order (Family Law Act 1975 Section 64B[6]) – that is, a parenting order dealing with an aspect of parental responsibility other than residence, contact, or maintenance, may also be made if required, and the available empirical research into the impact of the changes suggests that specific issues orders are often used to reinstate the previous distinction between guardianship and custody, i.e., between responsibility for long-term welfare as opposed to day-to-day care and control (Dewar and Parker, 1999, p. 54).

The factors to be considered by the Court in determining what the child's best interests require are set out by Section 68F(2) and are reproduced here:

(2) The court must consider:
- (a) any wishes expressed by the child and any factors (such as the child's maturity or level of understanding) that the court thinks are relevant to the weight it should give to the child's wishes;
- (b) the nature of the relationship of the child with each of the child's parents and with other persons;
- (c) the likely effect of any changes in the child's circumstances, including the likely effect on the child of any separation from:
  - (i) either of his or her parents; or
  - (ii) any other child, or other person, with whom he or she has been living;
- (d) the practical difficulty and expense of a child having contact with a parent and whether that difficulty or expense will substantially affect the child's right to maintain personal relations and direct contact with both parents on a regular basis;
- (e) the capacity of each parent, or of any other person, to provide for the needs of the child, including emotional and intellectual needs;
- (f) the child's maturity, sex and background (including any need to maintain a connection with the lifestyle, culture and traditions of Aboriginal peoples or Torres Strait Islanders) and any other characteristics of the child that the court thinks are relevant;
- (g) the need to protect the child from physical or psychological harm caused, or that may be caused, by:
  - (i) being subjected or exposed to abuse, ill-treatment, violence or other behaviour; or
  - (ii) being directly or indirectly exposed to abuse, ill-treatment, violence or other behaviour that is directed towards, or may affect, another person;
- (h) the attitude to the child, and to the responsibilities of parenthood, demonstrated by each of the child's parents;
- (i) any family violence involving the child or a member of the child's family;
- (j) any family violence order that applies to the child or a member of the child's family;
- (k) whether it would be preferable to make the order that would be least likely to lead to the institution of further proceedings in relation to the child;
- (l) any other fact or circumstance that the court thinks is relevant.

Unlike some American jurisdictions in which the courts make use of broad principles in determining where the child's best interests lie (for example, the "friendly parent rule"), the Family Court is invested with a broadly-based discretion. The sole statutory presumption is that the child's interests are best served by joint parental responsibility, although in practice considerable weight is given to the desirability of stability and continuity in the child's life and the court has historically been reluctant to disturb settled living arrangements, most particularly at interim hearings. This has occasionally been the case even in child abduction matters (Secretary, Attorney-General's Department and TS [2000] FCA 1692; In the Marriage of Schenk [1981] 7 Fam LR 170).

Although the foregoing is not an exhaustive statement of the law, it highlights a series of relevant issues. Because family law in Australia has recently been through an extensive period of reform and research suggests that the reforms to the parenting provisions of the legislation have produced a number of "unintended consequences" this section will summarize some of those consequences. We will then turn to an exploration of their implications in the context of PAS.

Research suggests that preserving contact with the nonresident parent recently has assumed a much higher priority in the minds of those involved with the administration of family law and this, together with increased assertiveness on the part of contact parents, has fueled a very significant increase in the number of applications for residence and contact. In 1995/1996 (immediately prior to the implementation of the new provisions) there were 13,814 applications for access; in 1996/1997 (immediately after) there were 21,897 applications for contact (Dewar and Parker, 1999, pp. 68–69). Contact is now more likely to be ordered even in cases with a history of family violence, and it has been suggested that the need to protect the child from psychological harm as a consequence of violence or abuse (including psychological abuse) has been conceptually subordinated to the child's "right" to contact (Dewar and Parker, 1999, p. 71). Whether this focus is desirable remains doubtful. Some researchers (Amato and Gilbreth, 1999, p. 559) suggest that contact itself is not beneficial, but that a close relationship with an authoritative father can be. As noted earlier, the courts have shown a slight but measurable tendency to make what have been termed "symbolic" residence/residence orders, even where the amount of time spent with each parent is very different and often approximates a "standard" residence/contact order. Finally, specific issues orders (that is, orders covering specific aspects of parental responsibility other than residence, contact, and maintenance) have had mixed effects. Although they have made negotiations more flexible when the parents are genuinely seeking to cooperate, they have also fueled disagreement between "warring" parents and proved an effective weapon for contact parents who seek to maintain ongoing control over a former partner (Dewar and Parker, 1999, pp. 72–73). Overall, it has been suggested that the reforms have intensified the pre-existing dispositions of parents; that is, those parents who were in any case inclined to agree now have a much richer range of resources with which to frame the agreement, while those parents who were inclined to disagree now have a much more powerful armoury with which to do so (Dewar and Parker, 1999, p. 76).

The overall legal framework in Australia, similar to that in the United States, is adversarial and increasing court lists often result in significant delays in attaining a full hearing. However, in practice family court judges have significantly greater latitude than do judges in other Australian jurisdictions. Family court publications emphasize that its jurisdiction in children's matters ought not be seen as an adversarial jurisdiction and that the sole concern of the court is to determine which orders are most likely to serve the best interests of the child rather than to decide which parent "deserves" to have the child live with him or her. Particularly where litigants in person are involved, family court judges can be substantially more interventionist than is normal in adversarial proceedings; the judge may assist in examining witnesses and by explaining the potential impact of various requests by counsel. Guidelines for the conduct of judges in cases involving a litigant in person were most recently set out by the Full Court in Re F: Litigants in Person Guidelines [2001] Fam CA 248.

Finally, it is important to recognize that the Family Court is only one player in negotiations and arrangements for postdivorce parenting. The vast majority of parenting arrangements are resolved outside the courtroom and formalized by the filing of consent orders (ostensibly, though not always actually) embodying an agreement between the parents. Dewar and Parker suggest that the expectations and attitudes of the parties and their strategic behaviour will depend upon how they entered the overall system – that is, whether through lawyers, through counselors or mediators, or with the assistance of support groups (Dewar and Parker, 1999, p. 81). They stress the role of the lawyer in producing the "rational client," attuning client's expectations and strategies to prevailing interpretations of legal texts and attempting to defuse unrealistic or fanciful expectations (Dewar and Parker, 1999, p. 70).

Only about five percent of matters proceed to fully defended litigation. Of this five percent, an increasing proportion involves one or more litigants without legal representation. Litigants in person pose a significant challenge for the Family Court. Many have unrealistic expectations regarding possible outcomes and little or no familiarity with court processes and rules of evidence. Litigants in person frequently pursue unconventional or counterproductive strategies, either because they are relying on their own perceptions of what the law is or ought to be – in many cases filtered through mass media reports – or because they have been advised to pursue such strategies by support or self-help groups. Some are unrepresented as a strategic choice; they are either hoping to exhaust the legal aid available to their former partner, thus prompting agreement to disadvantageous consent orders, or they feel that they will not be able to communicate their personal views and arguments to the court if they work through lawyers. A significant minority of litigants in person are serial litigants, making multiple applications over a period of many years.

Perhaps the most significant finding of the research to date is the appearance of a shift in the balance of bargaining power between parties in favor of the contact or nonresident parent (Dewar and Parker, 1999, p. 70). This shift in the balance of bargaining power seems likely to further destabilize the behavior of both parents in high conflict families, upping the stakes for the resident parent and perhaps encouraging this parent to seek sole residence and no contact with the other parent, whilst predisposing the contact parent to push for substantially greater contact or for joint residence.

IMPLICATIONS WHERE PAS IS ALLEGED

Impact of the 1995 Reforms

The legal affirmation of the child's right to contact, the centerpiece of the 1995 reforms, is a double-edged sword in cases in which either party alleges PAS. Although this principle makes it more likely that the Court will view the conduct of a parent who willfully frustrates contact or attempts to turn the child against parent with whom child lives as a weighty matter warranting intervention, it also makes it much more difficult for the Court to deny contact in any circumstances, including those in which the court has concluded that the children have been alienated from either parent. The level of difficulty is clear in T and F and the Commissioner of the Australian Federal Police and the Children's Representative [1999] Fam CA 738 where the court ordered contact despite the fact that the mother and child were in a witness protection program and the Commissioner argued strenuously that allowing contact would jeopardize the safety of both mother and child. In earlier research done by the author, PAS was apparently substantiated in four cases, and in two of these a change of residence was ordered. However, contact orders were made in all four cases (Berns, 2001, p. 213). Conversations with other researchers in family law suggest that very often in such cases supervised contact through a contact center is ordered. However, contact centers are reluctant to take on such cases and fear that in many of these families supervised contact is not in the child's best interests. Research shows that adults who, as children, had supervised contact with their nonresident parent, are more likely to require contact services for their own children following relationship breakdown. It has clearly become more difficult to obtain orders for no contact when domestic violence has been established (at least at interim hearings) and it seems likely that the same will be true in the case of other serious allegations, including PAS. At interim hearings, which are characteristically brief and which canvass the evidence only where essential to make what are, in effect, emergency orders, the court will typically seek to maintain the status quo where residence is concerned and confine itself to putting such contact arrangements in place as may be necessary. These include orders for supervised contact in cases of serious allegations to be explored at a full hearing.

A significant concern emerges from the suggestion previously noted, that the cumulative effect of the reforms has shifted the bargaining power from the resident parent to the contact parent. In the author's research into the incidence of allegations of PAS in the Brisbane registry of the Family Court, the allegedly alienating parent was the resident parent in 21 of the 31 cases. In the remaining 10 cases, the allegedly alienating parent was the contact parent (Berns, 2001, pp. 205–206). Eleven of the 31 cases had at least one litigant in person, and in several cases only the children had legal representation. The cases examined provided evidence that "litigants in person were more likely to advance tactical or poorly founded allegations of PAS . . . and that the allegations made by LIPs were the most extreme in the sample" (Berns, 2001, p. 214).

The number of allegations made without appropriate attention to evidentiary requirements has had a significant impact on the receptiveness of the court to PAS allegations. In the unreported judgments reviewed by the author, the court normally relied on family reports prepared by court counselors and on reports from consultant psychologists in making its assessment of the facts, including any allegations of PAS. Particular difficulties arose when the party alleging PAS was self-represented. In two such instances, the allegations appeared to be tactical. In one, following an extensively documented history of serious violence during the marriage and ongoing violence following separation that was under police investigation and that the mother believed to have been perpetrated by the father, the litigant in person (father) alleged PAS, relying upon a report from a clinical psychologist based entirely upon a 45-minute interview with the father only (Berns, 2001, p. 207). This evidence was given no credence by the court. In the second, the counsel for the father alleged PAS without providing any supporting evidence, arguing that the contact mother was a "malignant personality" who could not see the father in a positive light. This case was noteworthy because the father's behavior suggested, in fact, that he was attempting to alienate the children and that the PAS allegations were a preemptive strike because he feared that the mother might succeed in her bid to secure a change of residence. Given that research into the impact of the reforms suggests both that the bargaining power of the resident parent has been weakened and that a substantial (indeed almost overwhelming) increase in the number of applications for contact has occurred, it seems likely that the reforms have exacerbated the conditions predisposing vulnerable resident and contact parents towards PAS-inducing behaviors.

As noted earlier, Australian law does not contain a statutory formula for determining residence and although the presumption of joint parental responsibility and the presumption that the child has a right to contact have circumscribed the discretion available to the judge in determining the best interests of the child, a substantial area of discretion remains, including the weight to be given the various matters in section 68F(2). This means, inter alia, that, if a parent is predisposed to see an application as a threat, he or she cannot argue on the basis of any established legal presumptions, but must provide the court with convincing reasons that the other parent is somehow unfit (Berns, 2000, pp. 1–4). This has the potential to create an environment in which a parent consciously or unconsciously seeks to denigrate a former partner, and the heightened tension and the threat of loss predispose the child to form an alliance with one parent. Together with the increasing prevalence of unrepresented litigants, many of whom have irrational expectations and a lack of understanding of court processes and requirements, it seems likely that, despite the increasing emphasis upon primary dispute resolution (i.e., counseling, mediation, and arbitration services designed to enable the parties to resolve their dispute consensually), these background conditions will continue to provide fertile soil for alienating behaviors.

FACTORS PREDISPOSING THE COURT TO ADOPT A CONSERVATIVE APPROACH TOWARD PAS ALLEGATIONS

The Controversy Surrounding PAS

Although the Australian Family Court will admit evidence of PAS in appropriate cases (M v H [1996] FLC 92-695; N Johnson v ML Johnson [1997] FLC 92-764; Renshaw v Reschke [1997] FLC 92-777) and has given that evidence weight in decision making, the intense politicization of PAS remains a significant problem for the court. Injudicious statements both by those advocating full legal recognition of PAS and by those opposing such recognition have created a climate in which the courts and the legal profession are skeptical and reluctant to move too far in advance of settled legal and psychiatric opinion. Some early statements by those advocating recognition of PAS suggest (at least to some readers) that PAS is a factor in almost every contested parenting case (Gardner, 2002) and fathers' rights advocates have enthusiastically adopted these statements and argued that all contact difficulties stem from PAS. Earlier research by the author into parenting disputes in the Family Court of Australia suggested that PAS was a factor in slightly less than one-third of the cases examined and that no evidence was found either of alienation or attempts to alienate the children in the balance of the cases reviewed, most of which revolved around other difficult factual issues, such as substance abuse, criminal activities or the desirability of a new partner being involved with the children (Berns, 2001, p. 199).

The extreme behavior of some interest groups, for example, the Blackshirts, has further clouded the water. The Blackshirts are a right-wing group based in Melbourne, Australia and are similar in stance to some of the neo-Nazi militia groups in some of America's states. They have adopted attire that mixes black paramilitary garb with face masks akin to those of Klansmen and came to public prominence because their activities include stalking, picketing, and otherwise harassing the former partners of their members and other female single parents (www.blackshirts.info/index2.html).

The Conduct of Expert Witnesses

As in other jurisdictions, substantial difficulties have arisen with respect to expert evidence. In W and W: Abuse allegations; expert evidence [2001] FLC 93-085 the Full Court of the Family Court explored at some length the role of the expert witness and potential difficulties with expert evidence. Two matters emerged that were of particular concern to the Court. First, the Court expressed extreme disquiet about the tendency of expert witnesses, particularly those hired by one of the parties, to step outside the appropriate role and effectively act as advocates for the position of the party hiring the expert. In W and W, which dealt primarily with the credence to be given to the testimony of a child psychiatrist in a case allegedly involving child sexual abuse, the Full Court was highly critical of the testimony of the expert, who recommended that the children be removed from the mother's care and only be allowed limited supervised contact. The expert's evidence presented three major problems. First, the expert (hired by the husband) had never seen the husband, the wife, or the child (age 12). Second, the expert made categorical statements about the likely behavior of the wife and the child without the benefit of any contact with either of them. His statements differed markedly from the views expressed by other experts, all of whom had had contact with one or more of the parties. Third, at several points during evidence in chief and cross-examination, the expert strayed into direct advocacy for the husband's position. The Full Court made very clear its view that limited credence could be given to expert testimony of this kind and that, in exercise of its discretion, the Court was required to discount it. The Court expressed the view that in parenting disputes it was essential that the expert see the parents and the children separately and observe the children interacting with each parent. According to the majority of the Full Court:

> This case is a classic example of the misuse of expert evidence. . . . We think that the trial Judge should have harboured significant reservations about the evidence and opinions of Dr. W because Dr. W was more than prepared to express views favourable to [the husband] and contrary to the position of [the wife] about her suitability as residential parent without the opportunity to properly assess the issues. (W and W: Abuse allegations; expert evidence, 2001 FLC 93-285 at § 167)

A Family Court Discussion Paper notes that a recent Australian Institute of Judicial Administration (AIJA) report indicated that "17 percent of judges surveyed considered that experts were 'often biased' and 67 percent considered experts to be occasionally biased" (www.familycourt.gov.au/papers/pdf/expertwitness.pdf).

In R and R: (Children's Wishes) [2002] Fam CA 383, a case in which evidence of PAS was directly relevant, the Full Court relied upon W and W in finding that the evidence given by the child's treating psychiatrist was unreliable and discounting it accordingly, noting that the psychiatrist had interviewed the child only in the presence of her mother and had not only failed to interview the child alone, but had failed to interview the father or the child and the father jointly. After rejecting the evidence of the treating child psychiatrist and noting that the tenor of his evidence suggested that he was an advocate for the mother's position, the Full Court referred to the guidance obtained from an article on PAS and the dilemma faced by the Court in such cases, before suggesting that the remedy lay in a change of attitude on the part of the mother. The Court made it clear that if the mother did not change her attitude towards contact it might become necessary in the future to place the two younger children with the father.

My research has not uncovered a single Australian case involving allegations of PAS, reported or unreported, in which expert evidence fully meeting the tests previously outlined was put before the Family Court. This would undoubtedly account for part of the somewhat reserved attitude of the Court. In the unreported judgments examined in previous research, a significant number of expert witnesses advanced their opinions as to the likelihood of PAS without the benefit of contact with one of the parents or with the child. These difficulties are quite well-known in the legal community, and one survey of Family Court judges (discussed at length in W and W [2001]) indicated that about 90 percent of judges had encountered cases in which the testimony of the expert witness transgressed acceptable bounds and strayed into open advocacy for the position of the party hiring the witness. Such advocacy is prohibited by procedural rules specifying that an expert witness has a duty to the court that overrides any duty he or she may have to the party who hired the witness.

In Australia, as in the United States, PAS remains the subject of substantial controversy in the psychiatric community, both with respect to its recognition as a discrete pathology and in respect to the appropriate treatment where one or more children are significantly alienated from either parent. As long as this remains the case, although the Family Court will hear expert evidence suggesting the presence of PAS, it cannot properly give the recommendations of such experts (even when the evidence itself is presented in an exemplary manner and does not stray into advocacy) any greater credence than is given to countervailing recommendations made by other expert witnesses of equivalent expertise who are skeptical of PAS. Any judge who did otherwise would almost certainly have his or her decision reversed on appeal on the basis that the judge's discretion had been exercised unreasonably. This should not be understood as a problem with the adversary system but rather as a reflection of a properly judicial approach to recommendations in circumstances where experts disagree on the most appropriate approach. A cautious approach is essential, the primary obligation of the judge is to act in what appears to him or her to be the best interests of a particular child (based on all of the available evidence). The legislation mandates that the judge turn his or her mind to a statutorily prescribed list of relevant considerations in exercising that discretion. Justice Richard Chisholm, in a very useful paper on the role of expert evidence in children's matters, noted that:

> where the expert is drawing on a particular body of theory, particularly where there is a dispute within the field, it is only fair to indicate the extent to which he or she has an idiosyncratic or particular view of the area in question . . . [t]he importance of identifying the reasoning and, where appropriate indicating that the theoretical base is fragile or controversial, is all the greater in the case of court experts. . . . It is important that the Court does not get the false impression that the particular theoretical approach of the expert is the only available approach. (Chisholm, 2002)

Statutory Emphasis upon the Child's Rights and Interests Rather than the Needs of the Parents: A final, and perhaps obvious, caution warrants particular attention. The structure of the legislation, including the child's right to contact and the focus upon the best interests of the child, is intended to emphasize that, in children's matters, the primary focus is the child and the arrangements that best serve the interests of that child. While the Australian legal system, like that in the United States, is adversarial, the Family Court has emphasized that proceedings involving children's matters ought not be seen as adversarial but rather as a judicial inquiry as to the residential and contact arrangements that are most likely to be in the best interests of a particular child. The parents' interests and the question of justice between the parents are relevant only to the extent that they have an impact upon the best interests of the child (for example in circumstances in which only one parent is realistically capable of providing appropriate care for the child and where proposed contact arrangements might have a seriously detrimental effect upon the ability of that parent to care for the child). The focus of the legislation is upon the rights of the child, not upon the rights or needs of either parent. It follows that an emphasis upon a "vengeful" alienating parent and a "virtuous" or innocent target parent is not helpful to the Court, whether as part of expert evidence or in PAS literature. Such an emphasis removes the focus from the child's interests and directs it to the parents and the need to do justice between them.

The author's previous research suggests that this picture of high conflict families is, in any case, largely fallacious. In the majority of cases examined during her study, both parties had serious limitations as parents, and, in many, both parents had engaged in alienating behaviors. Rather than a clear-cut choice between an excellent or at least adequate parent and one whose relationship with the children is seriously disordered, the Court was, in effect, compelled to identify the "least damaging" arrangements for the children. A counselor in the Sydney registry of the Family Court, who believes that evaluation of PAS is useful in some high conflict cases, has commented that:

> While one could gain the impression from some of the literature that the alienated parent is a passive victim, our experience has been that this is an oversimplification. The scenario in which a "toxic" parent turns a child against an unambiguously "good" parent is comparatively rare. In my view, more often than is recorded, there is usually some mutuality in the alienating process. (Lodge, 1998)

LOOKING FORWARD

The Standards Expected of Expert Witnesses

Australia does not appear to have any equivalent to the *Frye* test, often cited in American literature dealing with PAS, and thus no "formal bar" to the admission of relevant expert testimony exists. However, the admission of expert evidence and the weight to be given that evidence is a matter within the discretion of the presiding judge. If evidence of PAS is to be credible, it is essential that expert witnesses adhere scrupulously to the guidelines set down in the relevant case law, even where this may initially appear to run counter to their basic arguments. In most cases in the Family Court of Australia, expert evidence will be received by way of formal written submission and the expert will not necessarily be called to give oral testimony subject to cross-examination. When the particular theory advanced by the expert is controversial, it is essential that the expert witness flag the controversial nature of PAS at the outset of the report and acknowledge that within the relevant scientific community opinions differ as to whether the behavior patterns described are a response to the pressures of a high conflict divorce or the outward manifestations of a discrete pathology. It is also essential that the expert acknowledge differences of opinion as to the most appropriate treatment for the children, even in cases where alienation is severe. This will significantly enhance the credibility of the evidence presented as would the ability to introduce evidence drawn from studies of PAS families conducted according to generally accepted scientific protocols, particularly with respect to the outcomes of treatment.

Second, and equally important, the expert witness must not stray, or give the appearance of straying, into open advocacy for either party. The role of the expert is to provide accurate, dispassionate, factual, and opinion evidence to the Court. As all family law matters are heard by a single judge acting both as trier of law and trier of fact, rhetorical or forensic flourishes are far more likely to antagonize the judge than to give additional force to the arguments being put forth. Wherever possible, it is essential that the expert have had an opportunity to interview all of the parties in the dispute individually and, in the case of each parent and the child or children, to observe each parent interact individually with the child or children. It follows that where this is not possible, as when the expert is hired by one parent and the other parent declines to be interviewed and refuses to permit the children to be interviewed, the expert witness must not make comments about the conduct of those parties or their future likely behavior and should clearly state to the Court the circumstances in which permission to interview was sought and the reasons, if any, given for the refusal. It is not, however, proper for the expert to draw any inferences from these circumstances for the benefit of the Court. Such inferences are for the judge, as trier of fact and law, to make.

It is equally important that all professionals working with parents and children who may be affected by PAS encourage their clients to have realistic expectations and to recognize that it is essential to obtain legal advice, even if it may be difficult for them to raise the necessary resources to do so. The author's previous research, as previously noted, suggested that self-represented litigants were unlikely to successfully argue PAS and that this was often due to their failure to understand the evidence required and the arguments that will be accepted by the Court.

CONCLUSION

Although the Family Court has not embraced PAS enthusiastically, and although there remains substantial debate both in the legal community and in the psychiatric community as to its validity and as to the appropriateness of the treatment protocols recommended by Gardner, it is clear that in appropriate cases there are no institutional barriers to the acceptance of PAS. Rather, the barriers largely stem from factors outside the direct control of the Family Court. These barriers include the intense controversy surrounding PAS, the willingness of some experts who have provided testimony to stray well outside the legally appropriate role of the expert witness and to put forward diagnoses without actually having an opportunity to interview all those involved, and the cost factors that make it difficult for the parties to obtain legal advice and the services of expert witnesses.

Acceptance is more likely to be forthcoming if the controversy abates or is resolved through appropriate evidence and if experts prepared to make a PAS diagnosis are mindful of their overriding duty to the Court when framing their evidence. The necessary protocols were outlined earlier. If adhered to, it is much more likely that the Court would be receptive to appointing Court-appointed experts, thus guaranteeing appropriate access to all parties and removing the allegations that experts appointed by one parent are partisan, or indeed, "hired guns."

REFERENCES

Amato, P.R. & J.G. Gilbreth, (1999). "Nonresident fathers and children's well-being: A meta-analysis" *Journal of Marriage and the Family, 61*, 557–375.

Berns, S. (2000). "Folktales of Legality: Family Law in the Procedural Republic." (2000). *Law & Critique 11*, 1–4.

Berns, S. (2001). "Parents behaving badly: Parental alienation syndrome in the Family Court – magic bullet or poisoned chalice." *Australian Journal of Family Law, 15*, 191–213.

Chisholm, Richard, "The role of experts assisting courts in children's cases: A judicial view. http://www.family-court.gov.au/papers/pdf/chisholm2002.pdf.

Dewar, J. and S. Parker. 'Parenting, planning and partnership: The impact of the new Part VII of the Family Law

Act 1975, Family Law Research Unit Working Paper 3, March 1999 available on line at: http://www.gu.edu.au/centre.flru.wp3.pdf p 68.

Gardner, Richard A. (2002). 'The Empowerment of Children in the Development of Parental Alienation Syndrome.' *The American Journal of Forensic Psychology, 20,* 5.

Lodge, Paul. "Alienation Revisited" accessed on 21 March, 2003 at http://www.familycourt.gov.au/papers/fca3/lodge.pdf and presented at the Third National Family Court Conference, Sofitel Hotel, Melbourne, 1998.

Rhodes, H. R. Graycar & M. Harrison 'The Family Law Reform Act 1995: The first three years' accessed 24 March 2003 at: www.familycourt.gov.au/papers/html/fla1.html.

Chapter 11

PAS IN COMPULSORY PUBLIC CUSTODY CONFLICTS

Lena Hellblom Sjögren

INTRODUCTION

Programming of children by parent substitutes in public custody disputes can cause Parental Alienation Syndrome. Such programming involving public authority is designed to strengthen the position of the programming parent substitute in courts of law. The purpose of this article is to describe the alienation process in five Swedish cases where children have developed PAS after having been influenced to reject their mothers by local social welfare agencies. It is concluded that children and their parents are best served if PAS can be recognised, and efforts made to educate professionals about how harmful it can be.

As described by Richard Gardner and according to his widely accepted definition of PAS four main points can be stressed:[1]

1. A child-parent relationship is transformed to rejection of a formerly loved parent.
2. The transformation is due to programming by the other parent or, as in the following cases, by a parent substitute.
3. The child contributes in the campaign of denigration of the alienated parent seemingly out of his or her own will.[2]
4. The child develops a cluster of symptoms related to a twofold cause: continuous negative influence about the targeted parent from the parent or parent substitute on whom the child is dependent and who is fighting to obtain or keep custody, and from the child him/herself, who has incorporated a negative picture of the formerly loved parent whom the child is kept separated from.

The incorporation of a negative picture is due to what is said about the targeted parent and, perhaps more important, what is done. The children in an ongoing custody conflict are vulnerable. In particular, small children are totally dependent on the parent or parent substitute for their daily care. It is impossible for them not to notice and be influenced by the rejection of the parent they are separated from.

If a child has been abused, severely neglected, or maltreated by a parent and therefore rejects that parent, then, of course, the child's rejection is justified, as are the local authorities' endeavors to protect the child. It is beneficial to have laws to safeguard children under such conditions. If the child's rejection of a parent is due to severe maltreatment, mental illness, drug problems, or abuse, PAS is not applicable.

PAS can be identified in custody conflicts when the parent substitute programs a child to denigrate a parent without justification, and acts to alienate the child from the parent, resulting in the child's own denigration of a formerly loved parent. The five cases presented here all involve rejection of the mother.[3]

When children's well-being and rights are at stake, even those whose mothers or fathers are severe criminals need to have contact with their parents.[4] All children have human rights to be with their family.[5] These rights are violated for many children who are taken into public care. Although some social workers and child psychiatrists claim that a foster family is as much a family as the child's biological family.[6] This disregards the fact that the foster parents are being paid to take care of someone else's child, with one to three months notice of withdrawal. In November, 2001, 10,200 Swedish children were in foster homes, two-thirds on a voluntary or semi-voluntary basis and one-third in accordance with the Act containing Special

Provisions on the Care of Young Persons (LVU-Law 1980:621). This law gives the social authorities power to take children from their parents when an official believes that a young person's health or development is at risk.[7]

In Sweden, nearly every second marriage ends with divorce and about 70 percent of the "common law" relations end with separation. In comparison with the many cases of divorces or separations where children can become involved in custody conflicts between two parents, the compulsory public custody conflict cases can be seen as a minor problem. However, for the children involved, who without justification are programmed to perceive their mothers or fathers as negatively as the officials, the parent substitutes from the social welfare agencies, in these cases do, it is not a minor problem.

The purpose of this chapter is to contribute to our understanding of the unjustified alienating processes resulting in PAS when the identified alienator is a parent substitute in compulsory public custody conflicts and the mother is the alienated parent. The targeted mothers described here, whose cases I have investigated thoroughly as an investigative psychologist, have given their permission for me to write about their cases. All names are fictitious, but all the details and excerpts from documents and other quotations are authentic[8] (translation from Swedish to English by myself).

As has been pointed out, unanimously[9] breaking off the relationship, and contact between a child and a parent, subsequent to a separation, is traumatic for both the child and the parent.

In the case studies presented here this is evident. The cases are as follows:

- *Case one.* Emma was separated from her mother when she was one-year old.
- *Case two.* Erika was two-and-a-half years old when her mother was said to be no good for her.
- *Case three.* Jenny was separated from her mother as a newborn, her one-year-old younger sister was separated when she came back with her mother from eight years of exile.
- *Case four.* Four children were separated from their mother, the youngest was later allowed to go home.
- *Case five.* Dan was separated from his mother just before age 12 and died when he was almost 15.

After a presentation of the cases I discuss some issues: Are there any common traits in the way the alienator acts? Do the alienated mothers have something in common? How severely have the children been harmed? What can be said about intervention and nonintervention by the authority officials, who are obligated to make decisions in the best interest of the child?

CASE ONE: EMMA

Baby Emma, a British citizen, was separated from her mother, Susan, when she was one year old. She is a teenager now, and lives in her second foster home, where she was placed when she was one-and-a-half years old.

Susan came from Britain to Sweden and married a Swede. After ten years, the marriage broke up and Susan was upset and began to occasionally drink too much. She was treated for this, but was not diagnosed as an alcoholic by any medical doctor. Five years later when Susan had been in a stable relationship for some time, she and her boyfriend longed for children. It turned out to be impossible for Susan's boyfriend to make her pregnant, they decided that Susan would try to become pregnant by a man who agreed to donate sperm. Susan and her boyfriend welcomed the baby girl and named her Emma. (According to Swedish law, Emma is a British citizen because her mother was unwed. Emma's British citizenship was confirmed before she was six months old.)

From all contemporary witnesses it is documented that there was a loving, close mother-child relation, and nothing to worry about concerning Emma's well-being in her mother's care. For example, in a report from the pediatrician who had investigated Emma it is written: "In summary Emma is judged to be a healthy, normally developed and in every aspect a functioning 9 months old girl."

The social agency had been informed from a social counselor at the hospital that perhaps this was a mother in need of some help, as she had five years earlier had some drinking problems in reaction to a stressful situation. A social worker came to the birth clinic and said that she wanted to arrange professional help for the mother in her home, something the mother rejected. When, in spite of Susan's refusal, the same social worker some weeks later came to her home with a therapist, Susan felt that her integrity had been violated, and expressed that frankly. In the journals kept by the social agency, it is documented that this rejection was taken personally. A later statement from the social workers said that they remembered unpacked boxes and an untidy apartment, and pointed out that this reflected Susan's "inner chaos." According to them, it proved that she was mentally ill.

Several months later, Susan was visited by an old pupil (from a time when she taught English courses). At the time of the visiting Susan did not feel well because of a stomachache and an infection, and she had not tidied up her apartment. This woman thought Susan needed some help and contacted the social agency. This information, and information from Susan's former mother-in-law plus comments from another person stating that Susan had been drunk gave reason for the same social worker to make a second home visit. She was again criticized by Susan, who had had some alcohol, but was not so drunk that she could not take care of her baby.

The social worker had the local social council decide about immediate compulsory public custody, called the police and took Emma to a children's home. Susan was desperate; she cried for her child and was aggressive towards the officials. According to the social agency, Susan's behavior towards the officials from the social agency justified their opinion about Susan being unfit to take care of her child. They argued that Susan was mentally ill and would again start drinking. Their opinion could not be altered although professionals argued strongly against a separation of mother and child.

At first, Susan was allowed to come and visit Emma and occasionally to breastfeed her as she had done as long as Emma lived with her. When Susan was allowed to stay in an institution with Emma, she tried to hide with Emma from the social agency. She was caught by the police, who took Emma from her at the request of the social agency. After that incident the social agency decided to not tell Susan where her daughter was. The social record stated that: "the mother has 'kidnapped' the daughter several times."

The social agency decided for the second time to take Emma into forced custody. Emma, then eleven months old, had been moved between three different institutions. She was placed in a temporary foster home while the social agency looked for a more permanent foster home. Emma became attached to the temporary foster mother with whom she was placed for as long as six months. Emma was kept at a secret address away from her mother. The reason for this was explained by the social agency: "Susan has not known the address because she has been very emotionally unstable and unpredictable."

In the social record, it is written after a meeting between the temporary foster mother and two social workers: "We speak generally about Emma's needs and the responsible social worker doesn't think it will be difficult to find a suitable home for the child. On the other hand it is important that the family home[10] can tackle Susan."

After six months the social agency had found a home that could, in their opinion, "tackle Susan," who was then not allowed to see her daughter at all. Emma was to be accomplished adjustment to her new foster mother, with the help of the temporary foster mother, according to a plan made up by the social agency.

Susan had been cut off from her daughter by the social agency. The parent substitute demonstrated by their actions, which were impossible for Susan to stop, that they did not think that she, as Emma's mother, was an important or necessary person for Emma to have in her life.

During the past 15 years, Emma has never been allowed to see her mother at the foster home. The address of Emma's new home was also kept secret from Susan, whom the social agency described as an alcoholic and mentally disturbed. This was, in spite of the fact, according to all the medical expertise that Susan had been in contact with, she was not regarded as an alcoholic. The officials from the social welfare agency later labeled Susan psychotic. However, this is not a diagnosis from any medical or psychiatric report, which have repeatedly diagnosed Susan's drinking and loss of control as a reaction to the forced loss of her child and the continuous lack of normal contact with her child.

The social agency had decided that Emma should be rooted in the foster home. The goal was that Emma should perceive the foster parents and the other children placed in the same foster home as her family. Nevertheless, Emma's foster home is a "family home" on duty, with a contract, according to which it can give notice of termination of a child it gets paid to take care of[11] three months in advance, after which the home is obliged to take another child.

The social agency had regular contact and supervision of the foster home. Every contact is documented in a social record. The following notes were made by a social worker when Emma had been placed for about six months: "The foster mother says that her head gets empty – Susan unceasingly speaks her stuff, ('is harping on the same string')." Six months later, when Emma had been in the foster home for one year, still without any normal contact with her mother Susan, the following notes were written: "Susan has been worse than ever – she calls often – keeps talking about all the old stuff, ('like a record-player')."

The fact that Susan cannot think or talk about anything else than the loss of her child is used against her. She is, in the opinion of the social agency, " nagging."

This is a word Emma picks up and also uses against her mother, as an explanation for not wanting to see her.

Susan was not allowed to phone Emma at the foster home until Emma was three years old. At that time, the social agency suggested for the first time a transfer also of the legal guardianship from Susan to the foster parents with a continued payment from the social agency. This issue is not yet settled.

Susan kept sending cards to Emma, sometimes nearly every day. In the social journal we can read: "The family sorts the cards – and prevents contacts between Emma and Susan." And from another day: "The family chooses when Emma can have a card."

Emma was allowed by the social agency to meet her mother once a month outside the foster home under supervision of her foster parents. Emma called her mother mummy during the first years, then by her first name as the social agency has always done. Emma's mother wanted Emma to learn her own language, English, but this was not supported by the social agency or the foster home. Emma has been told that her mother is ill and unable to take care of herself or Emma, neither of which is a proven fact.

Emma has never during her years in public custody been allowed to meet with her mother in an everyday situation, or without supervision. All meetings took place – and still take place – under the supervision of the foster parents, outside the foster home.

When Emma was six years old the social agency reported that Emma did not want to see her mother any more. Before a meeting they claimed that Emma had said about her mother: "If she insults and yells, I want to go home."

This is a borrowed adult expression. Year by year, as Emma grows older, she has gradually taken more and more part in the denigration campaign of her mother. She has expressed a hatred of English and a total rejection of Susan. The social agency, responsible for the programming, argues that this proves that Emma doesn't *want* to see her mother, and that their decision to transfer the legal guardianship to the foster parents is the right thing to do.

The powerlessness Susan experiences because of the removal of her daughter by the social agency has made her do desperate things. She has set fire to papers from the social agency and has twice been sentenced to forced psychiatric care with special court review. The professor who made the forensic psychiatric evaluation on Susan wrote in 1996, and then again in 2001: "The most crime-preventive measure is more contact between mother and daughter." A British psychiatrist who examined Susan stated: "To make fires gives her a useful tool of communication and expresses her frustration, resentment and despair."

The social agency has suggested a transfer of the legal guardianship of the British citizen Emma to the Swedish foster parents a total of nine times. One expert, who was requested by the social agency to give an opinion, wrote:

> Emma seems to be an easy-going, merry and confident girl. She lives and has her life with mum and dad, her family home parents. She is well aware that she has a biological mother, Susan, but she doesn't feel anything particular for her, or has thoughts about what a life with her would be like. Emma seems to live a good life in her family home and ought not to be worried through a constant tug-of-war between those she regards as her family and Susan. My suggestion is that the custody is transferred to the family home parents.

In another statement from the social agency, it was concluded that "For Emma to be able to maintain a realistic picture and not to lose contact with her biological mother we suggest that the existing contact is reduced to let's say two occasions a year."

In 2002, when Emma was 12 years old and had been in the same foster home since she was one-and-a-half, the social agency had asked another agency to investigate Emma. That investigator met Emma with the foster mother in the foster home. The requested investigator found that:

1. "Emma has not one positive thing to say about Susan."
2. "Emma doesn't think it is amusing, it is boring and not exciting to see Susan."
3. "To the question if she would like and dare to say to Susan that she is always nagging Emma answers – Yes, but I don't anyway, but I can tell the foster mother."
4. "Emma doesn't feel any kinship or connection with Susan."
5. "Susan has sometimes been sad and has argued with the foster parents. Emma doesn't listen then."
6. "During our talk Emma clearly demonstrates irritation about Susan. She cannot describe Susan for me, she says she doesn't remember what she looks like."
7. "She thinks she is always nagging and that she asks Emma a lot of questions. She compares the situation with the one when I, in my capacity as investigator, come and ask her questions."

If we add that Emma has rejected any contact with her mother's family in England, we have an illustration of all eight criteria described by Richard Gardner for diagnosing the child's behavior as a result of alienation with an identified alienator: PAS.

In the Administrative Court of Appeal, Susan had appealed the social board's decision not to grant her and Emma at the time 13 years old, more extensive visiting rights. In my capacity as a private expert witness, I argued that Emma had developed PAS and that she was unable to express her own will because of the heavy programming she has been exposed to since she was a baby.

In the verdict from April, 2003 PAS was mentioned twice, when my statement was referred as the court had understood it[12]:

> When Emma was to attach to the family home mother the social welfare board decided about restrictions for Susan so that she was not allowed to see her child. The social welfare board thus acted as an alienator between mother and child. Emma's contact with her mother is today seriously damaged as a consequence of all restrictions decided about their access. Such damage is called PAS – Parental Alienation Syndrome – and can be read off in a child's behavior. The only way of breaking the PAS condition is to remove Emma from the family home. It can take longer or shorter time for Emma to attach to her mother.

The court decided, in spite of PAS as the cause for Emma not wanting to see her mother, not to judge otherwise than according to what had been recommended by the social agency and formally by the social welfare board.

Susan's attorney has made three applications to the European court without success.[13] The total number of trials about Susan and her right to be with her child, in the courts over the years is according to her attorney 158.[14]

CASE TWO: ERIKA

Erika was three-and-a-half years old when her mother Ann was said to be no good for her. Ann and Åke were married and longing for children. When Ann at last got pregnant marital problems arose. When their daughter Erika was born she had colic for three months, something Åke could not stand. When Erika screamed, he would start screaming. This was something Ann said she wanted to protect Erika from. Åke moved out. After their separation, Ann wanted Erika to meet with her father but in Ann's presence. The problems grew. Åke phoned during the nights and had problems accepting that he could not come whenever he wanted. The parents started to fight about custody and contact. Ann and Erika moved. When Erika was two-and-a-half years old, Ann, who was tired from calls and visits at night from Åke – and from her fibromyalgia – asked the social authorities for some help. She requested that Erika could stay with another family for one weekend per month so she could have some rest. This is a social service called "having a contact family" that can be approved by the social agency for single parents who need some personal time or assistance.

Ann did not get that help. Instead, her ability as a mother was questioned. At the same time it was to be decided in court where Erika should live, with her mother as she did, or with her father. The social authorities decided that Ann, Erika, and Åke should all be observed together in a child psychiatric clinic, where they had to stay day and night for four weeks. This was a difficult situation for all of them, but especially for Ann, who did not have the sympathy from the staff in the clinic or from anyone in the social agency, as Åke had. Ann's behavior was questioned by Åke and by the staff.

The observations in the clinic clearly demonstrated that Erika, then two years and seven months old, was attached to her mother. No disturbances other than those that could be attributed to the unnatural situation of being in a clinic were reported in the journals. Here is one example: "Erika is often worried and goes crying to stand close to Ann. When Ann at last leaves, Erika's worry and crying grow and she runs around looking for her mother. Once she went to a corner thumb-sucking."

The report includes observations from diaper changes where it was said that the mother didn't realize that these were like "abuse" for Erika. However, Erika had a reason for not liking diaper changes; she had had several severe constipations and one month before the intake for psychiatric observations had been operated on (extirpation of two anal polyps). These natural explanations for Erika's pains in her private parts were not considered by the staff in the clinic or by the social agency. They thought that Ann was somehow sexually abusing Erika. This was something Ann had thought that Åke might have done, after having been questioned by the doctor who operated on Erika if she had any such suspicions.

When the observations after the four-week stay at the psychiatric clinic ended, Erika was described by the psychiatrist in charge as having a disturbed behavior. Ann was found to be an unfit mother. Evaluators said she denied her problems and did not seek help enough. Here is what the psychiatrist wrote:

> Ann has, although she cares very much for the girl, no empathy in function for the girl's autonomous needs, and she seems to experience herself and the girl as a mental unit. Ann has a manifest consciousness about the girl's behavior disturbances, but shows no need to accept help from her surroundings. Ann always has rationalized explanations to her own and the girl's behavior.

On the other hand, the psychiatrist wrote that Åke had not "demonstrated any signs of unfitness as a parent." The observations regarding the girl and the father, according to the psychiatrist cooperating with the social agency "show adequate quality and we have in this context seen nothing of the behavior described by Ann."

The father was not discussed in terms of any mental disturbance (according to Ann he had medicine for being psychotic, a reason for early retirement later). On the other hand the mother was seen as mentally disturbed by the staff. They had observed her at the clinic with Åke, from whom she had escaped, and who slandered her as an unfit mother for their child. One doctor wrote in a daily note in the record: "Still perceive this mother as evidently mentally disturbed which all here in the hospital have. But cannot see that I in any way can report her of neglect of the child. There are no signs of trauma or damage on the child."

The social agency some weeks later decided, although there was no proof of neglect in Ann's care, that Erika, then three years old ought to be moved to a "qualified family home" for a "longer stay." Erika, three-and-a-half years old, was taken by force from her mother. The preconditions for Erika to be allowed to return home to Ann were formulated by the social agency:

> *that* Erika has reached a stability, maturity and trust to her surroundings and that it is judged to be lasting,
> *that* Ann has reached a lasting stability and maturity and insight about Erika's needs,
> *that* Ann lastingly has gained insight and learnt to control situations where she easily gets into mental insufficiency,
> *that* Ann has gained lasting stability and maturity in her relationship with other people.

The social agency has the power to decide when these preconditions, which it had formulated, are met.

Erika was placed by the social agency in a foster home. She was allowed to see her mother shortly once in January, once in February, once in May and once in August. In September, Erika was suddenly allowed to see her mother a whole day – under supervision of a psychologist, a psychiatrist and the social workers in yet another clinic. This was part of the second child psychiatry investigation, requested by the social agency. The mother was this time observed to have "used words that are abstract and doesn't show any ability to empathy with Erika, she is not sensitive for the wishes and the needs of the child. The mother also violates Erika's integrity in the play but however we cannot observe any physical violations. Some warmth between mother and daughter can be observed."

The father was also observed with Erika in the clinic. He was praised for his ability to meet the child's needs and for his opinion shared by the social agency and the expertise, that the mother was unfit as a mother for Erika: "The father also expresses his relief that Erika has been placed in a family home as he has been very worried about her situation due to the mother's lacking ability as a parent."

The experts recommended placement during the years Erika was growing up, this was something they called "placement during childhood and adolescence," a concept not mentioned in the Swedish law. The following is a quotation from the conclusions written by the chief physician, the psychologist and the social workers:

> Erika has been greatly damaged concerning the development of her personality. She has now in a safe and stable setting developed in a positive direction but we judge that she has a fragile and easily damaged personality at great risk for future mental problems and also for a negative development of her personality.
>
> We judge it as totally out of question that her biological parents would be able to take the parental responsibility. We therefore recommend a placement during childhood and adolescence and also a transfer of custody to the family home parents.
>
> We judge that the contact with the biological mother is so trying for Erika that it must be restricted more than before to let's say one hour per occasion at most once a month.

It was also said that it would be best to let Erika meet her mother outside the foster home, in a "neutral setting," and under strict supervision: "The mother and Erika must not under any conditions be left alone which is why a third person must be present the whole time." Erika's contact with her mother was restricted to only a few short supervised contacts and a few telephone calls during the next year.

The social agency then for the third time requested that Erika and her parents be investigated by a child psychiatry team. Erika, then five years old, was moved to a clinic where she had to stay for four weeks. One of these weeks the mother was demanded to come, and another week the father. Six new experts were now judging Erika and her parents, after a separation of two-and-a-half years, again in a totally unnatural setting.[15] The following is an excerpt from the summary after four weeks in the clinic:

> The biological mother's relation to Erika is obviously destructive. The biomother is not capable to protect Erika against dangers. What is worse, the biomother has a theoretical idea of her own that Erika is not to be protected, that Erika is worse off when protected. The biomother lacks ability to see Erika as an individual of her own. She sees herself and Erika as one unit, describes 'not visible bonds' between them.

Ann, when asked, told me about the reason for the accusations of no protection. In company with several observers, she had been allowed to go for a walk with her daughter. She had then encouraged Erika to balance where she judged no danger existed for Erika if she fell. She had also told the observers that she thought it important for a child to learn by doing and to try things. Here is another quotation from the summary after the third child psychiatry investigation:

> The family home must be given the authority to totally keep up Erika's boundaries. It is necessary that the family home are psychological parents also in reality. The biomother must be stopped from psychologically invading the family home. One example of such invasion was that she did not approve of the shoes bought for Erika by the family home. The biomother's telephone calls with Erika must end totally. Since every such telephone call means a trespass on Erika's boundaries, where she has to protect herself against her mother's trespassing.

The substitute parents, that is, the social agency, the experts they asked to investigate, and the foster parents they had chosen all said that it was no good for Erika to be with her mother, or her father. The opinion expressed by the foster mother was quoted in the third investigation made: "She has a hope that Erika with time will have an inner ability to keep her personal boundaries. She thinks that the visits by the parents have disturbed Erika's development in that respect."

The social agency and the politicians responsible decided, on the recommendation from the child psychiatry team, that Erika should be allowed to meet her mother twice a year under supervision of a staff member outside the family home, and that the mother and Erika should not be allowed to speak on the phone.

Ann appealed and argued that she wanted to see her daughter at least three hours every fourth week and to be allowed to phone her daughter once a week. She argued that the restrictions were against the intentions of the law related to forced custody and against the European Union convention on human rights and against the United Nation convention on children's rights. The court argued against her appeal: "The restrictions in contact, according to the appealed decision, is in accordance with the latest child psychiatric statement. What the mother has argued in support for her appeal and what has emerged otherwise do not constitute reasons enough to abandon that thus by child psychiatric expertise has been judged to be necessary for the best of Erika."

Erika was six then. The contact with her mother was totally broken for one year, because the social agency reported Ann to have crossed sexual boundaries with Erika, under supervised access. This report was found to be not substantiated by the police. Gradually, the social agency has allowed Erika to see her mother more often than twice a year – at most once a month for three hours under supervision of a social worker. The time amount was after five years altered to five hours a month. Ann then asked the social agency if she could be allowed to see her daughter without supervision. She was supported in her request by the foster parents.

Erika had rejected Ann. For a long time Erika did not even know that Ann was her mother. When Erika was 12 years old she started calling Ann mother. Ann says she had to adjust to the violations of her child's and her own human rights to family life. She states "The violations turn pale, now when it has changed to the better."

CASE THREE: JENNY AND JESSICA

Jenny was separated from her mother Jean when she was a newborn. Her sister Jessica, one year younger than Jenny, was separated from her mother when she came back with her mother from their eight years' exile in her father's home country, at the time she was eight years old.

Jenny's parents had longed for a child. The delivery was traumatic and involved the use of the vacuum extractor and fundal pressure. Jenny had frequent regurgitations and could not properly use her right arm. (The cause was damage to the brachial plexus, and a small degree of injury to the brain could not be excluded.) The parents took Jenny to the baby clinic weekly, where she was weighed naked and treated by a physiotherapist for her damaged arm. No reports of fractures or bruises surfaced. When Jenny was two months old her parents took her to the hospital to be examined after they had discovered that her damaged right arm was swollen. The admitting doctor in the course of his examination did not find any bruises on the arm. He also did not see any evidence of injury on the legs, according to the medical record. Swelling of the lower part of the left thigh was not seen by anyone until the afternoon of the same day the parents had brought Jenny to the hospital. Some bruises were discovered later during that same day in hospital. After x-ray examination three fractures also were found. This caused the chief physician to report the parents to the social agency for child abuse. Two days later, the social agency decided to take Jenny into public care.

The chief physician did not consider brittle bone disease, as did another physician from Scotland, who has been concerned with research and patient care in the field of bone disease since 1964. In 1991, this physician investigated Jenny on Jenny's parents' request. He wrote a thorough report after the examination of Jenny, her medical records, her radiographs, family history of diseases and the clinical information. He stated: "While there can be little doubt that some form of brittle bone disease played a significant part in the causation of Jenny's fractures, it is not clear which form is most likely to be present."

Jenny had at that point already been taken into forced custody, and had not been allowed to see her parents. Jean became pregnant when the parents had good reason to hope to have Jenny back. The background for their belief was the statement about brittle bone disease, and the report by a psychologist, who had found nothing in support of child abuse or anything that made Jenny's parents unfit.

The parent's good hope turned to despair. They did not get Jenny back. The social agency decided to take the awaited child into forced custody as well – to protect her – as they, in their view, had protected Jenny from her parents. The parents fled to Jenny's father's home country in Central Europe.

For two years, Jean and her husband wrote to all the authorities they could, and fought every day to have Jenny back. After this, Jean says, that the children's father has no energy left to fight against the social agency. He studies a lot, his parents are fighting for their grandchildren.

Their second daughter Jessica was born. While in Central Europe Jessica learned the language from her father and his parents, who were very close. She also, of course, learned Swedish from her mother. Jessica knew she had a sister, but she never went to visit Jenny in Sweden. The parents called Jenny in her foster home, wrote cards and visited her once. At that time the police ordered visitation of their home. The police came with two officials from the social agency.

The marriage broke up. Jean went back to Sweden, her mother had died and she had to have an operation. Jessica stayed with her father and her grandparents. Jean resumed the fight to get Jenny back. This was not easy as the social agency had told Jenny that her parents had abused her and broken her bones when she was a baby. Jenny did not want to see or talk to her mother. She had been moved from her first foster home to another one, and the social agency considered that couple as Jenny's parents.

The children's father – who found it very hard to stand the humiliation of not being able to get Jenny back – wanted to get away by working on a ship. Jean therefore took Jessica with her to Sweden. Jessica was then seven years old and was supposed to start school in the autumn. Jean thought it a good idea for Jessica to meet future classmates and practice Swedish by attending the church's preschool. Jessica was appreciated by the teachers and the other children there, and later at school. She was, according to her teacher, curious to learn, and did well.

Suddenly Jessica was taken from school! Two policemen and two social workers came and took Jessica from school to a secret address. Why? The day before, the same social workers had come to see Jessica and her mother. They said that they had begun an investigation after having received a report from the social agency where Jessica's sister Jenny lived. That agency had gotten a report from the father's home country saying that Jenny's and Jessica's father had been reported to the police for suspected abuse. When the social workers had visited they said they were coming back the next week. However, as mentioned, they came back the next day – with the police. They claimed that the mother had not protected Jessica and now they had decided to protect Jessica by taking her into forced custody.

Jessica was placed 100 kilometers from home in an institution with many other children who came from broken and problematic homes. Jessica, who really had enjoyed school and liked her teacher, was cut off from school and her friends, as well as from her mother and her grandparents. One female on the staff, Sheila, in close collaboration with the social agency, acted as a substitute mother. After one month of total isolation from her former network Jessica was reported to have sexual contacts with the boys in the institution. Sheila talked to Jessica and asked her questions about sexual details. After one more week of questioning and talking, Sheila reported to the social agency that Jessica had told her that she had been sexually abused by the man her mother had lived with after the return to Sweden.

The focus was not on the disconcerting conditions for Jessica in the institution, but on Jessica's mother. She really was a bad person not capable of protecting her child, stated the social agency.

However, Sheila was a good person, according to the social agency. She was close to Jessica and could comfort her, it was argued. This, in fact, was to help in the intensified denigration of Jessica's mother.

Sheila was the one reporting to the social agency about Jessica's behavior in the institution. After three months' stay, when the ban on visitation by the mother had been lifted, it was reported: "Jean visited Jessica in the institution twice a week accompanied by the staff, to prevent a negative influence on Jessica. The time of access was prolonged from one to two hours per occasion."

After nine months in the institution, when Jessica had stopped talking her native language and learnt a lot of things a little girl ought not to know about sexuality, stealing and so forth, she was placed in a second foster home. (The first one the social agency took her to was not considered qualified enough.) This foster home was situated 300 kilometers away from Jessica's mother. The social agency allowed Sheila to visit Jessica whenever she wished, but Jessica's mother was not allowed to visit at all.

When Jessica had been transferred her mother wrote to the local politicians responsible:

> My daughter needs peace and quiet, after having been placed in a children's home for nine months and after what she has endured during her time in forced custody. Now it has come to my knowledge that her foster home is also a foster home on call. I wonder if it has been considered what is best for Jessica. I only want what is best for my daughter, and am persistent if something is wrong, and am then considered to be a troublesome person. But the social agency only stresses negative things about me in order to win.

The father's parents, who had been very important in Jessica's first seven years of life, were not allowed to visit or call her. When they wrote to the social agency and complained that Jessica had been placed with strangers, and criticized the fact that Sheila was allowed to visit Jessica in the foster home, they got a letter saying: "That Sheila visits Jessica is due to her having become an important person for Jessica, a person Jessica herself wants to meet. The family home has our full confidence, they are kind and caring towards Jessica, which is their task."

After six months in the "family home," Jessica was taken by the social agency to a psychologist specializing in sexual trauma. She evaluated Jessica and recommended therapy (by herself) for at least one year – twice a week the first half year. This expert conducted her investigation and her therapy at the request of the social agency, who also informed her, as it had informed the family where they had placed Jessica.

The psychologist had thus been informed that Jessica had not been protected by her mother when Jessica had been traumatized by her father's physical abuse and by sexual abuse perpetrated by the man living with Jessica's mother. These were two alleged crimes but no decision to prosecute was taken. The alleged crimes were taken for granted as the foundation for the therapy given to Jessica. A child who is not a victim of sexual abuse but is treated as if she is can be severely damaged by such treatment. Of course, it serves as a powerful tool in alienating the mother and everything connected to her.

The social agency wrote in their report about Jessica's rejection of the mother and the grandparents as if it was the child's own will, not realizing that it was a foreseen result of their alienation:

> In the end of October Jean phoned Jessica and said /my remark: how can the social agency know what the mother said on the phone before they had started bugging? that if she didn't talk to her grandparents they would come and fetch her. Jessica had then answered her mother that if she kept threatening her, Jessica would report her mother to the police. The mother had answered that the father, she herself and the grandparents would come for her. Jessica went out to the family home father so that he could hear the mother's threats. Jean denied that she had threatened her daughter. Jessica commented that the mother lies very much. To her instructor from the social agency Jessica said that she wanted the phone calls to be bugged, as was done in the institution she lived before, that was much better.

In November, 2000 the instructor from the social agency (a person Jessica's mother had tried to have replaced via a letter) instructed Jean:

> Hello!
> The foster mother informed me this morning that Jessica refuses to talk to you until the calls can be bugged.
> Kind regards,
> Social Secretary.

After this Jessica called her mother once, and then did not want to phone her mother any more, reports the social agency. The programming proved to have been efficient. When Jessica had said she did not want to speak to her grandparents, the social agency reported: "The son in the family repeated that the grandparents had to respect Jessica's will, or otherwise it must be seen as molestation and be reported to the police. After this the telephone calls ended for a while."

When the grandfather called again after some months the social agency wrote:

> The grandfather argued that he had a right to his grandchild. He wanted to speak to Jessica. The family home mother then asked Jessica to tell her grandfather what she wanted. Jessica looked afraid, but came to the phone and said that she didn't want to speak with them. The grand father doubted this. He also said that he would come and see for himself and hung up. Jessica said afterwards 'Imagine if they come and fetch me.'

That Jessica could have been afraid (it must have been the foster mother who had reported to the social agency that Jessica looked afraid) because she knew that she must reject her grandfather in the presence of the foster mother, is not something that came into the mind of anyone in the social agency.

The grandparents called again, and the foster home changed its phone number. The social agency in their report stated:

> On a political social agency meeting, in which Jean chose not to participate, prohibition of access for Jean was decided, and it was decided that she would only be allowed to speak to Jessica every second week and that the calls should be bugged.
>
> The same social secretary wrote another letter to Jean a month after the last one:
>
> Hello!
> Now the family home has a new phone number you can call,/the number/. It will be installed /date/. We decided that they shall have the line open every second Sunday 19.30-20.00 starting now Sunday. Sundays, because we think it suits you as this is the only day you are free during the week and in the evening so that the family home is free to do other things during the day. Jessica doesn't want you to give this number to her grandfather or grandmother.

The social agency reported constantly that Jessica did not want to see her mother and that Jessica did not want to talk to her grandparents. They were satisfied that Jessica was afraid and preferred them, they wrote in the report cited earlier:[16]

> The mother phoned on Christmas Eve, the first possible time for her to phone, after the family home had opened a special phone for the mother's calls. She told Jessica that it is illegal to bug and that she has presents at home that Jessica can have when they meet. She also said that she didn't intend to call more, which she hasn't. Jessica has said that was a relief. When the instructor from the social agency talked to Jessica about seeing her mother during the spring, Jessica could agree to see her mother in /name of the town/ together with the family home father and the social agency.

The social agency then wrote to Jessica's mother and told her that she could see Jessica on the railway station in the town chosen (200 kilometers from Jean) for one hour under the supervision of them and the foster father.

The mother refused to see her daughter under these humiliating circumstances, she argued contact between them would be impossible.

The trauma Jessica, eight years old, suffered when she was cut off from her mother from one day to another, was not investigated or even considered by the social agency or the psychologist contracted by the social agency. The continued traumatization caused by the cutting off not only of Jessica's mother, but of her whole family, her native language, school and network with neighbors and friends was not considered either.

All actions have been motivated by the social agency using the argument that they are responsible for the protection of Jessica. The feedback that they have harmed Jessica, instead of helped her, never comes through, as Jessica is kept isolated from her mother, seemingly of her own will preferring to stay in her "family home."

Jessica's mother wrote to the social agency:

> I request that the forced custody of my daughter Jessica Svensson ends. Your care of her is destructive and harmful. As you know, and according to witnesses Jessica was a very caring girl until you took her in September /year/. The latest reports about her are very worrying and I know my daughter better than anyone of you. As the contact between me and Jessica has been minimal because of you I see a very dangerous development in her. First you place her in the institution where abuse takes place. Then in a foster home where the foster mother is not cooperative and is about to break down my daughter mentally.
>
> Kind regards,
> Jean Svensson

The social agency claimed that the problems, arising while in forced custody, were caused by the mother's neglect. After Jessica had spent six months in the foster home which was instructed by the therapy institution specialized in sexual abuse, where Jessica's psychologist works, the social agency stated in their report: "According to the therapy institution specialized in sexual abuse where the psychologist works it is important that Jessica is made as safe as possible and that contacts with relatives who make her worry are minimized so that Jessica can profit from the therapy given."

The social agency, ignorant of how it had abused Jessica, reported:

> In a telephone call with Jessica /date/ she said that she had listed some things she wanted to read aloud:
> 'She /Jessica's mother/ doesn't need to send me anything. I manage without.'
> 'I do not want to see her, because she does foolish things.'
> 'I do not like her when she lies.'
> 'I do not want to talk to her.'

Jessica was thus reported to have totally rejected her mother of her own free will, with absurd explanations and borrowed adult expressions and words.

At the end of the report the social agency listed all the attempts made by the mother and the grandparents to report them to supervising authorities. The social agency was content to have won in every instance.

The conclusive judgment from the social agency presented in the report to the court was:

> The investigation implies that Jean still has no insight into her daughter's need for care and that she cannot see her own participation in the traumas Jessica has endured. Jean lacks ability to understand that the different symptoms Jessica now presents emanate from Jean's lack of caring skills. In contrast, Jean claims that Jessica has been mentally damaged while in forced custody. There is a considerable risk that Jessica's health and development will be damaged and that she will suffer more traumatic experiences if the mother's wish that forced custody should be ended is met.

The wish expressed by the social agency to keep Jessica in their care was met by the court. Jessica has no contact at all with her mother.

Jessica's elder sister Jenny has some contact with her mother. Jean thinks Jenny was abused in her first foster home. The official explanation given by the social agency for moving Jenny to a new foster home in 1994 was economic. (The foster mother had requested a very high monthly payment to care for Jenny.) The social agency has long wanted to transfer the legal guardianship to the new foster home, but the foster parents do not think that is the right thing to do. The mother, who has a good relationship with Jenny's new foster parents, agreed to Jenny staying with them, but on a voluntary basis. This agreement included regular monthly visits between Jenny and her mother. The social agency decided to transfer the legal guardianship to an elderly woman, a lawyer who has only met Jenny twice. The court has decided according to this.

When I talked to Jean on the phone she told about a meeting with the social agency and the psychologist, at that time still giving Jessica therapy for the abuse that was found unsubstantiated by the police. Jean had asked critical questions. The instructor from the social agency had pointed out to Jean that she was an official. This is a fact. The mother, who has full-time work as an assistant nurse within psychiatry said regarding her 15-year fight to have her children back: I know that they are in power and that our children never will be allowed to come home. But I "want to help others if I can, and prevent others from the suffering we have had and have."

CASE FOUR: EVE, EILEEN, ELLEN AND OLLE

This is about four children who were separated from their mother Eliza. Eve and Eileen born in the eighties, and Ellen born in the middle of the nineties, were taken into compulsory public custody in December, 1996. After a court decision in October, 1997 that all three were to live with their mother, the two oldest were allowed to return, but not Ellen. Eve and Eileen were placed in the same foster home again in March 1999. Eliza's youngest child, Olle, born in 2001, was separated from her as a newborn, but was allowed to go home when he was one-and-a-half years old.

Eliza moved from the north of Sweden to have a less physically demanding job than the one she had had in a slaughterhouse. She had had an accident: the corpse of a cow had fallen on her back, giving her bad back pains. She met Paul in the bakery where she found work. They got married and had two daughters. The eldest, Eve, had difficulty in getting to sleep and learning to talk, and they sought help. In the following years she was diagnosed by three doctors as having developmental damage with autistic traits. She was given special education. The next daughter, Eileen, had allergic and asthmatic problems. The parents decided to move to the country to have better living conditions for the children. The father kept his work in the city and was not often home. Eliza had two halftime jobs that could be combined with her taking part in Eve's special education. It was a difficult situation, and the marriage broke down after ten years. The girls stayed with their mother, who moved to a flat in Paul's neighborhood so that the girls could go and see their father.

Eliza longed for another child and when she got pregnant by a friend of her former husband she decided to marry for the second time. Towards the end of this pregnancy, the man started threatening and beating her. (He was not sentenced for these crimes until three years later, when Eliza was safe with another man in her third marriage.)

Eliza had early contractions and had to spend four weeks in hospital before her third daughter, Ellen, was born. During that period the abusive man was, for the first time, alone with Eve and Eileen in the apartment. Eliza was worried about them. She was very disturbed by the man's behaviors towards them and towards her. The staff at the hospital found Eliza's behaviors and statements odd. The medical records suggest that they did not understand her and that they disliked her. When she complained that her right knee was hurting and asked for an examination she was not taken seriously. (The knee was operated on four months later.) When she said she had bad pains in her back, and that she threw up, they thought she was making this up, or she was said to exaggerate her medical problems. (Oesophagitis was diagnosed shortly after Ellen's birth, and a year later Eliza was twice operated on for a slipped disc.) The doctor at the child clinic reported the staff's concern to the social agency in the community where Eliza lived. He also suggested that Eliza could have been suffering from Munchausen syndrome, and might also have been inventing illnesses for her two elder daughters i.e., he indicated that Eliza was a suspected Munchausen syndrome by proxy case.

Ellen, a healthy child of 4000 grams, was kept against Eliza's will for ten days at the maternity clinic. When they got home, two social workers arrived and told Ellen's parents to come to their office the next day. They were then given a choice: If they did not agree to live in an institution where the whole family could be investigated, Ellen would be taken into forced custody for protective reasons.

The man who threatened and abused Eliza, Ellen's father, had a sister who had the same boss as the social worker in charge. He was ordered to protect Ellen from Eliza. At the institution Eliza was able to move around in the wheelchair she needed when her back and knee pains were too bad, so that she could take care of her daughters. The staff at this first institution had no complaints regarding the parenting. They reported a healthy normal contact between mother and child. Nevertheless, the social agency decided to move the family to another institution, which they said employed an expert on Munchausen syndrome by proxy. No protests from the two older girls, from the person in charge of the first institution, or from Eliza helped. At the new institution it was impossible for Eliza to move in her wheelchair because of many staircases.

The older girls were at that point not allowed to go to their ordinary schools. The social agency decided to take all three children into forced custody, after just a few days in the new institution. After four weeks at this new institution with new staff the social agency suddenly one day decided that Ellen, then two months old, must be moved to a temporary foster mother 140 kilometers away. They decided this would protect her from her mother's dangerous influence. Breastfeeding and daily physical contact were ended. Ellen was allowed to see her mother once a week under supervision by the social agency. The older girls and their mother were kept in this second institution against their will for three more months.

Ellen's father started work when Ellen had been moved to the temporary foster home. His mother, Ellen's grandmother, regularly reported negative statements about Eliza to the social agency. According to her, Eliza was unfit to be a mother, all the daughters would be better off in foster homes. A psychologist came to the institution to test and to observe the girls and to talk about the girls with the staff, at the request of the social agency. The psychologist concluded that Eve was not developmentally damaged with autistic traits, as she had been repeatedly diagnosed by medical doctors. The psychologist talked about disturbed emotional relations between Eliza and her daughters, and concluded that Eliza was unfit to take proper care of her children. The older girls were moved to a free religious foster home 2000 kilometers away. Ellen was placed in another foster home, also far away. The protests formulated by the temporary foster mother that this was not in the best interest of the child, did not help. The temporary foster mother, who had gradually become acquainted with Eliza, and thought of her as a good and caring mother, could not understand why Ellen was not allowed to stay with Eliza. In a written statement given to Eliza's lawyer, she also wrote about the picture of Eliza that had been painted: "From the staff at /the second institution/ I was informed that Eliza was mentally ill and dangerous to her child and in general. When I went to the foster mother together with a social worker she said that the child was to stay there forever. 'Here Ellen is to grow up.'"

The transfer of Ellen from the temporary foster home to the foster home when Ellen was six months old was made by the social agency before the court had decided if Ellen and her sisters should be in forced custody. When Ellen was ten months old, the court decided that all three girls should come home and stay with their mother. The older two were brought home and resumed schools, and former activities. Ellen was not allowed to go home, because the social agency decided to forbid the move. They said that it was not good for small children to be moved.

When it was obvious that the social agency acted against the law, they decided that Ellen should be taken to an institution for three weeks. She was to meet her parents while the foster mother stayed there. But the foster mother left after two days. Eliza, more so than Ellen's father, took care of Ellen, who, now 13 months old, started calling her "Mummy," and according to a psychologist's report became very attached to her mother. After three weeks, Eliza brought Ellen to a house in the countryside to have some peace and quiet. The social worker in charge and the police came and took Ellen by force from her mother. It was winter and Ellen got pneumonia. In the social worker's and the third institution's opinion, Ellen had not gotten attached to her mother and had to be taken into forced custody and be brought back to the foster home.

The social agency decided that Eliza should not be allowed to see Ellen, so as not to disturb Ellen when she was to accept her foster mother. The contact was broken.

The mother appealed every decision possible to appeal. Once more a court decided that Ellen was to be brought home immediately. The social agency considered the mother's appeals and protests as proof of Munchausen syndrome by proxy. They asked a child psychiatrist, considered to be an expert in Munchausen syndrome by proxy, to make a statement. He never met Eliza or any of her children, but he diagnosed Eliza with Munchausen syndrome and stated that she abused her children, a Munchausen syndrome by proxy case (MSBP). Since then the courts have decided against the return of Ellen to her mother.

In the social records it is documented that Ellen had been traumatized by the loss of her mother when she had suddenly been separated from her for the second time in her short life, after three weeks of intense contact and rebonding. Notes in the social records, based on phone calls with the foster mother, indicate that Ellen cannot sleep, is depressed, is aggressive towards her foster mother, has nightmares, and at times cries constantly. The social agency chose to consider the problems they describe to have been caused by Ellen's contact with her mother. They decided to protect Ellen from her mother more than before. The child psychiatrist who had diagnosed Eliza as a Munchausen syndrome by proxy case was phoned and asked for advice after a description of Ellen's behavior, following this second separation from her mother. Here is the social agency's comment on the matter:

> The behavior Ellen is described to have is a destructive behavior independent of what the cause is, says the child psychiatrist. It is more than Ellen can take and the signal is to protect her from this strain. The situation is too difficult for Ellen. Ellen's state can be compared to a brain-damaged child, although Ellen has no injury. The child psychiatrist says that it is important to be observant of the signals from Ellen during contact. He suggests for example that the contacts become more rare, that the contacts become shorter, and that a photo of the parents is put in the family home for Ellen to keep an image of them. Through the contact the child is to keep the image of the parents alive for future needs, even if the child is not going home to the parents today or understands who they are.

The MSBP diagnosis was also used in court when the social agency decided to take the two older daughters back to the former foster home in forced custody and had support for that decision in court. Eliza had reason to believe that Eve had been sexually abused in her foster home, where she stayed in a little cottage of her own (there was not enough room in the house for the four children the elderly foster parents had in forced custody). During her first stay in the foster home, Eve had developed a venereal disease, according to the medical documentation. The police did not conduct any investigation regarding the mother's report of suspected sexual abuse in the foster home. Eliza's report was sent to the social agency, who answered that they fully trusted the foster home, and that Eliza had mental problems.

The MSBP-diagnosis made on request by the social agency was used when Eliza gave birth to her fourth child, Olle. He was taken into forced custody when he was 20 days old, after the social agency in Eliza's new community had been informed the same morning by the social agency in her old community that she was very dangerous to her children. The baby was taken by the police and social workers on duty while being breastfed by Eliza in the evening. Eliza and her husband decided that he should stay by their son's side. The next day, Eliza, who was not allowed to know where her husband and child were, said she wanted the social officials to give her son her breast milk, as he was born three weeks too early and needed it for his immune defense. They replied that it was not possible, as it could be poisoned.

Son and father were kept at different institutions a year and a half. After two weeks, Eliza was allowed to visit for one hour a week under the supervision of different social workers. She was not allowed to breastfeed or to give her son anything to eat, as the social agency kept saying she could poison him. Eliza's husband was given reports on Munchausen syndrome by proxy and was informed that Eliza was dangerous to her children. The social agency encouraged him repeatedly to make a choice between his child and his wife. He refused. He and Eliza kept calling each other and supported each other.

When Eliza developed life-threatening cancer and was operated on, her husband could not be by her side. They were both afraid that the social agency would then take the baby away also from his father. When Eliza informed the social agency about her cancer and asked if she could see her two oldest daughters to tell them about the diagnosis herself, the social workers said (according to Eliza's lawyer, who was present) to her that she was lying or exaggerating to be able to see her daughters. Eliza was not allowed to inform her daughters. The social agency did that. On condition that Eliza's husband was not present in the hospital, the daughters were allowed to visit their mother there once under supervision. The social agency had prepared the girls to ask the doctor questions, as they said Eliza invented illnesses for herself and her children. They wrote in a report after the visit that Eliza had lied about her stomach pains to her daughters. They wrote that this was a lie, as the girls, when talking to the doctor in their presence and on their recommendation had learned that "the cancer doesn't bring about stomach pains." Eliza was fortunate and recovered from her cancer.

In 2002, Eliza's fourth child was allowed to be in forced custody in his home – but only if Eliza moved out. This caused great problems. After many months (and many meetings with the officials from the social agency), Eliza was allowed to reunite with her husband and their son.

A psychiatrist, requested by the National Board of Health and Welfare to examine and diagnose Eliza, stated, that the MSBP-diagnosis was not correct.

The right to at least practice the human right to family life with her youngest child has strengthened Eliza to continue her fight for the three daughters who are still in forced custody. The social agency responsible for them argues that even if the old diagnosis was wrong, Eliza is mentally ill and dangerous to her children, and that she is definitely unfit to be a mother.

The denigration campaign has been intensified since Eliza has requested sole custody in order to be able to fight for Eve's and Eileen's right to be with their mother and father. Eliza and Paul decided in 1999 that the only chance to have their girls back home, because of Eliza's MSBP diagnosis, was for Paul to have sole custody. Paul moved to a bigger flat and waited for their daughters to return home. The social agency did not take any notice of the fact that he would have sole custody and wanted to have the girls to live with him. In the very long fight to have the children back, Paul has lost his energy. The social agency now tells Eliza that Paul wants the girls to stay in the foster home.

The older daughters were, against their parents' will, placed in a free religious foster home. Since the statement from the National Board of Health and Welfare about their mother having been wrongly diagnosed, they have been programmed that the devil lives in their mother. It is because of the devil in their mother the girls told her on the phone that the diagnosis was altered. They say they *know* that she has Munchausen syndrome by proxy, and that they *know* that she is dangerous.

Since that conversation, they have not been available to answer the phone during their telephone times as decided by the social agency (a quarter of an hour each every second Monday from 6:00 to 6:30), and they have refused to see their mother on the rare possible occasions decided by the social agency (outside the foster home, six times a year for two hours under supervision of one or two social workers). They have only met their mother once in 2003, and since then until summer 2005 not at all. On that occasion they told her, as did the social workers, that she must withdraw her request to have sole custody of them and to take them home, or she will lose contact with them forever.

The two older girls have not been allowed by the social agency to have any contact with their mother's family. When they were younger they usually stayed with Eliza's parents for part of their summer holidays. Their grandmother died in their home when they stayed with their mother. It happened when Ellen was not allowed, like them, to return home in 1997, although their grandma had tried to explain to the social workers that the social agency had to obey the court's decision. Their grandpa has not been allowed to visit them in the foster home or meet them somewhere else. Neither their aunt nor their cousin on the mother's side can visit. It is a case of massive alienation.

Ellen does not know that Eliza is her mother. However, when they are allowed to meet (every second month for two hours, under supervision of the foster mother and a social worker at a café or going shopping as Eliza is not allowed to visit the foster home) they try to play and talk. Eliza is worried because, according to her, Ellen is not respected or loved by her foster mother. (Ellen was placed there shortly after one of the foster mother's own children had died.) She is also worried because Ellen's clothes are bad, and she has not had her eyes examined regularly although she has a squint.

In 2002, Eliza again requested in court that the forced custody of Ellen should be ended, since it was proved that she was not a MSBP case, and she and her new husband lived a normal family life with their son, Olle. None of the sisters have been allowed by the social agency to see their brother.

The custody conflict is manifest. The social agency acts to keep Eliza's daughters in its forced custody. In response to Eliza's request regarding having Ellen back home, it stated that Ellen, then six-and-a-half years old, was well in her foster home, referring to a medical examination from the time when Ellen was two years old. The social agency argues that it is best for Ellen to stay in the foster home chosen by them, as her mother Eliza "has no insight into her problems."

When this is stated by the social agency and repeated or quoted in court it is regarded as a fact, because this is the way the system works. In 2005, the mother wanted Ellen, then eight years old, to visit her home for the first time in her life and also to meet with her little brother for the first time. The social workers stated in their so-called investigation: "Ellen is asked if she is curious to see Olle. Ellen says no. Ellen is asked to describe what she thinks that a visitation at Eliza's would be like. Ellen says that when she arrives to Eliza's she would run back to the car. She would sit there and refuse to step out." Notice the consequent use of the mother's first name and the consequent avoidance of the word mother, effective in the ongoing programming of Ellen to reject her mother.

The social agency's lawyer in her petition to the court[17] stated (with often-used formulations): "It is necessary, taken into consideration the aim of the care, that the visitation restrictions, according to the decision made by the social agency, are kept. Nothing has evolved, not in the investigation of the case, and not in the appeal, indicating that Ellen has a need of increased contact with Eliza Anderson or that it would be in accordance with her best interest."

According to the statutes, the social agency is a neutral authority in charge of helping children and families, always acting in the best interest of the children. However, in this case, as in the other cases, the social agency is a parent substitute in a complicated custody conflict, defending partial interests and sadly not the children.

CASE FIVE: DAN

Dan was separated by force from his mother, Marion, when he was nearly twelve. He was moved from a child psychiatric clinic, to a children's home, to a foster home, and then sent to live with a former alcoholic. He died from his epilepsy nearly fifteen years old.

Dan, Marion's third child, was born after she had been divorced for a long time and her oldest children were adults. Dan's father never lived with Marion. He has been absent in Dan's life. Marion had several medical problems involving her heart and her lungs, and early retired because of those difficulties.

In the medical records it is documented that Dan was only six months old when he was taken to a child's medical clinic because of his many infections. When he was one-year-old he was examined for a heart problem (later found not to have any functional importance). When Dan was five years old he started treatment for epilepsy. He matured physically and reached manhood at 11 years old, which was probably caused by a tumor found in the hypothalamus.

Marion was worried when Dan was in day care and the other children coughed or had a cold. She did not want Dan to be infected because of his medical problems, but Dan's medical problems were not an issue for the staff at the day care institution who thought Marion exaggerated Dan's problems. As she, herself, was not very healthy, she asked the social agency for some support to help her to better take care of Dan. Her concern for Dan was interpreted as overprotection. In the social record it is written that Marion had a symbiotic relationship with her son, and that she was unable to set up boundaries for her son. The social agency in cooperation with the child psychiatry department where Dan was investigated, decided that it was best for Dan to move from his mother to an anthroposophy boarding school. It had very strict rules and was far away from home. Marion objected. She wanted Dan to stay with her and to have extra help from a teacher in his ordinary school. This idea of getting help to help yourself was not appreciated by the social agency.

Marion criticized the care given to Dan and the other children in the institution where Dan was placed by the social agency. She contacted other parents who were also critical, and requested that the National Board of Health and Welfare inspect the facility. The staff at the boarding school found Marion impossible to cooperate with. The social worker, responsible for Dan, from the social agency, wrote in her journal that Dan had an "ongoing conflict of loyalties between his mother and the school. Dan has difficulties to attach and to profit by the treatment, he must all the time be loyal to his mother and they have some contacts that the school not fully appreciates."

The social agency saw Dan's mother as a threat to a healthy development for Dan. He was taken to the child psychiatry department and after several months was placed in a children's home by the social agency. The social worker explained that the purpose was to keep Dan there until they had found a qualified "family home" or another special home. Dan's studies were stopped and he only got five hours' schooling per week in the children's home. The social worker visited Dan and talked to the staff. After ten days' placement and a meeting she had had with the director for the children's home, three of the employees there, and the director for the social agency, she wrote in her journal:

> The children's home has reacted with force to Marion's and Dan's relation and their contact. They think that it is a curious relationship between mother and son. Dan is very demanding, he is 'climbing' – having a lot of body contact with Marion, provokes her and pushes her. Marion tries to defend herself but has difficulty handling the contact with her son by herself. It is noticed that she kisses him on his cheek a little too much, considering Dan's age. I describe Dan's and Marion's relation, and inform about Dan's person whom I do not consider adequate for his age, he is on a much lower level but starts signalling that he wishes to be emancipated from Marion out of the 'symbiotic' relation that Marion and Dan have had earlier during Dan's whole life.

Dan's home was lost when his mother was evicted, instead of getting temporary economic help to pay the rent for one month she had missed. The social worker wrote in her record that the monthly child benefit from the state for Dan "goes to the social agency to help Marion buy clothes for Dan." Marion was consequently marginalized and humiliated, as was Dan when he, physically a man, was forced to stay in a children's home, not allowed to go to school, or to go home.

The social agency found a foster home they thought qualified. The foster parents were a newly married couple. The man had not quite ended his third treatment for his drug addiction and the mother had a son Dan's age with an unknown father, and a child on its way. They were invited by the social agency to the children's home to meet Dan.

The social agency had decided to take Dan into forced custody, as they found Marion uncooperative and without insight into Dan's needs. Dan was transported by the social agency to his foster home 400 kilometers away later in the summer, when the foster mother had given birth. The couple had also taken two young juvenile criminals as foster children. Dan's mother decided that she would move to another part in the neighborhood and start studying at a folk high-school there, so that she could see Dan regularly. The first time she visited Dan's "family home," was when he had been there a few weeks. She came on a notified visit together with the social worker. The next day, when she had stayed to arrange for her studies, she made an unannounced visit to the foster home. Dan was the only one awake at 11:00 A.M. and was watching a video, according to the mother. The foster father came down and told Marion she was not welcome that day, or any other day. This was supported by the social agency.

Dan had been separated from his mother by the social agency and placed first in an institution/boarding school far away from home, then in a psychiatric clinic, then in a children's home without schooling, and then in a foster home far away from his home. The social agency did not comment on the insecurity and lack of love and also medical care Dan had experienced when he had been separated from his mother. The social worker wrote in her investigation presented to the court that the forced custody and transfer of Dan to the chosen foster home should be confirmed legally:

> Dan has his special difficulties and handicaps which have been exaggerated and reinforced by his mother's overprotection and constant worry. He has little insight or ability to handle his situation and his motoric perceptual handicap. . . .
>
> He must have harmony and peace in his living so that he can begin a personality development. . . . Dan must have help to grow up in another home setting, where one lives a more regular and connected life. A setting of adequate size for Dan to understand, catch up with and grasp every day. A setting that both activates him and stimulates him, but is at the same time restricted and understandable.

A child psychiatrist who was a former colleague to the social worker, who had helped her to find the foster home for Dan, wrote at the request of the social agency a statement to the court:

> The problems, which have evolved from early infant years, must therefore be related to the obvious difficulties, that the biological mother has in giving her son such care and setting such boundaries as children need. Therefore a placement in a family home seems to be the only credible alternative. In such a future family home

> placement of Dan, it is of great importance that the mother's contact with him is restricted, so that the placement enables the boy, not only to root in his new setting, but also to be relieved from unnecessary loyalty conflicts in accordance with earlier patterns that would considerably obstruct the placement.

When the social worker had written earlier to the medical doctor responsible for Dan she had asked if it was not enough regarding Dan's special needs that a former colleague, of the child psychiatrist was on the case: "The official in charge of handling Dan's family home is /name/ and she has worked 17 years in the rehabilitation of disabled children in /X-town/. Can that not be seen as satisfying enough?"

Dan was not disabled. Dan's doctor answered, when the foster home had already been chosen, that he took it for granted that they would demonstrate great care picking a foster home with experiences with children with behavioral impairments as Dan had, and knowledge about how to take care of children with seizures.

The social worker must have known that the foster home they had picked did not fulfill the criteria set up by Dan's doctor. But the documented fact that the social worker was personally provoked and frustrated by Marion was more important. In her position, the social worker in charge, she had the power to judge Dan's mother as unfit to raise Dan for the rest of his youth. She concluded in her plea to the court (she is referring to herself when she mentions "the investigator"):

> As implied by the investigation, Dan's home setting has a pattern of upbringing with wrongful demands and inadequate boundaries. This together with mental stress exposes Dan to such situations that his mental health and his social development is threatened. . . . The investigator's understanding is that: the most serious aspect of Dan's development is his lack of fundamental identity, caused by the fact that Dan never gets physical and mental peace to develop his ability and his person. The investigator suggests placement in a family home according to the LVU-law all the time ahead until adult life and living of his own.

Dan's seizures came more and more often while he was in the foster home. He was not regularly checked for his epilepsy as he should have been, or otherwise medically examined. The responsibility for his medical care was not transferred to a new doctor in the area where he had been placed until two years had passed. The social worker thought the most important thing was for Dan to lose weight. Dan wrote during the early stages of placement to his mother, that he was not allowed to eat as much as he wanted. Dan's mother was very sad and extremely worried about the well-being of her son, but when she called doctors and teachers she was told that they had nothing to say to her. The social worker was the one who received information and who informed everyone else about Dan – and about his mother's harmful influence on him. She visited Dan in the foster home regularly, and at the same time supported the view that the mother should not be allowed to visit her son at all. The social agency paid a good deal of money for Dan in the foster home, and they also paid for an extra teacher for him – something they had not wanted to do when Dan lived with his mother.

The foster mother claimed, and the social agency supported her claim, that it was Dan's mother who was responsible for the gradual escalation of Dan's seizures. They said that it was when he had talked to his mother that he had the attacks. The solution for that was for the social agency to restrict Dan's contact with his mother even more than they had already done. They decided to allow no contact at all.

The social workers who have both the task to investigate, decide, execute the decisions, and evaluate their own activities, wrote before the decision: "Dan is often feeling very bad after talking on the phone with his mother. He sweats a lot, develops anxiety and seizures for days after." The social agency explained to the higher authority the mother had forwarded her complaints and worries so that the contact prohibition was decided "as an effort to help Dan in the conflict of loyalties he experienced regarding his mother and which was considered to influence his epilepsy." When Dan called his mother, others in the foster home had listened. He was called his mother's spy by the foster parents. The authority investigator declared in her report: "The opinion of the family home is that Dan was commissioned by his mother to check up on the family and report their activities and that he was also rewarded by her." Dan was told by his parent substitutes that his mother did not want to see him and that she was bad for him. He stopped writing letters, stopped asking her for money, as he had previously done. He also stopped calling her.

If there had been any truth in the claim that Dan's mother was the cause of his seizures, they would have stopped when Dan's contacts with his mother were totally broken, but they did not. They escalated. Dan died from a series of major seizures. That was after he had suffered proven sexual abuse by an older boy in the foster home, and had been moved to the home of a former alcoholic (a friend of his foster parents who separated).

It has been decided in two court procedures that the social agency did nothing wrong.[18] The message is: Social agencies as parent substitutes are allowed to alienate children from their parents. That is, they are allowed to psychologically abuse children, as this, in accordance with the way the system works, can be considered as protection of the child.

DISCUSSION

Swedish politicians and professionals have much confidence in the compensatory powers of foster care, which is reflected both in legislation and practice. In the five cases investigated, the mothers have provided normal, loving parenting.[19] The fathers have been absent from the beginning, or have disappeared during the separation and struggled to have the children back. This fact has probably contributed to the severe alienation of the mothers by the father substitutes, who have the power to decide that the children cannot be taken care of by their mothers.

Is there something in common regarding the parent substitutes as alienators?

In these five cases, the social agency has acted as the alienator. In comparison with an alienating parent in a custody conflict, the social agency as alienator has an incomparably strong power position. The social agency has, in the cases described here, been embodied in a social worker – a female social worker in all the investigated cases – who has from the very start taken a personal interest in the case and acted out her antipathy towards the children's mothers, not only for some time but over a period of many years. This personal and prestigious involvement has, of course, not been acknowledged, but it is very obvious in a close reading of the social documents. As a public authority figure, she has received support from the rest of the social agency, the experts involved by the social agency, the politicians formally responsible for the decisions to cut off the children from their mothers, the courts, and the supervising authorities, including the Swedish Parliamentary Commissioner for the Judiciary and Civil Administration.

In June 2002, a competition between law students from all the Nordic countries (the so-called Sporrong Lönnroth Competition) was about a case similar to the ones presented here. The competition is a yearly event initiated in 1984 by the now retired professor in law Jacob Sundberg.[20] The students are processing from the point of view of the European Convention of Human Rights, the judges are judges from the European Court of Human Rights.

It has formerly been possible to have complaints in forced custody cases accepted in the European Court of Human Rights.[21] The fact that the state, as a part in these cases from Sweden and Finland, has been criticized has not resulted in a reunion between the alienated children and their parents.[22] Nor have the verdicts of guilty from the European Court of Human Rights made the state curtail the power delegated to the social agencies.

Similar to parents in a custody conflict in which one of them gains advantages by accusing the other of abusing the child, sexually or physically, this can also be seen in the cases of alienation of children resulting in PAS in forced custody conflicts.

More attention has been paid to the experts referred to by the accusing/alienating party than to the experts referred to by the accused/alienated party. This is the case even if the alienated party in the conflict has statements from well-known medical experts stating that the parent cannot be blamed for the symptoms in their children because they are genetic or caused by well-documented illness, congenital injuries, or traumatization after separation from their parents.

The parent substitute being the authorities' responsible for the protection of children, can argue that their actions of separating the child from a parent, is in the best interest of the child or protection of the child.[23] A mother believed to be dangerous to her child by an official from a social agency cannot argue against the official and claim her child needs her. That can be used against her by the authorities in the social welfare state, as they tend to see the child as an individual who stands by himself or herself, independent of his or her family and family roots.[24]

Do the alienated mothers have something in common?

The mothers in the five cases have one thing in common: they have not been helpless, but strong and stubborn. They have fought for their children's lawful rights and have challenged the social agency by opposing the actions and restrictions. They have told the social officials that they were acting against the law or against the intention of the law.

The officials from the social agency are not comparable with a parent in a parental conflict, as the social agency, the substitute parent, has a power position by being a public authority. The other party, the mother, has no power at all. The mothers had, at the time of forced separation, provided normal, loving parenting, but the fathers had been absent or weak, a fact that has probably contributed in different ways to deepen the alienation of the mothers by the father substitute, the female social workers in the social agency.

The mothers, as individuals with unique personalities, have had less importance than the descriptions of them as unfit or dangerous mothers. Negative, but no positive characteristics and actions, have been attributed to them. The constructed pictures[25] of the mothers as having "inner chaos," as "unfit," as "not protective enough," as a "MSBP case," or as "over-protective," have proven to be very effective and not possible for the mothers to conquer. The social agency has the preferential right of interpretation. When questioned or criticized by the mothers knowledgeable about their own and their children's rights, the social agency has acted to defend itself and the officials' prestige by denigrating the mothers. They use the children in their denigration campaign, and this is something the mothers have not been able to successfully fight against.

How severely have the children been harmed?

The ten children involved have all been severely harmed through the long-term alienation process resulting in PAS, with one exception (the baby brother in case four who was reunited with his mother after a year and a half of separation starting when he was 20 days old). One child died. The eight remaining children involved are afraid to have contact with their mothers, or reject their mothers. All of them had a loving relationship before the forced separation and forced custody.

The children removed by the substitute parent seem to have developed problems similar to the ones described by other abducted children: loss of identity, loss of love, insecurity, and instability.[26] The children's relations to their fathers have not been systematically investigated, but from what is known in these cases the biological fathers have been absent physically or emotionally for their children. They have not fought against the alienators to keep contact with their children as have the mothers.

Research is lacking about the long-term effects of mother deprivation and of forced separation.[27] The research on foster children indicates that children who are separated from their parents are at risk of developing severe problems.[28] What can be foreseen is that many of these children – when they survive[29] and do not become criminals, drug addicts, or psychiatric patients – will be lonely and have identity problems. They will suffer from stress.[30] The substitute parent has no obligations when these children have reached legal maturity.

What can be said about intervention and nonintervention by authorities in charge of making decisions in the best interest of the child?

From what is known about foster children from studies and from experiences in war time, placing children in a foster home ought to be used only as a last resort. However, systematic follow-up studies of children in foster homes are lacking.

A dilemma exists between the intentions of the law – a rapid reunion between parents and children – and the practice – children in compulsory public custody who are kept for a long time in "family homes." Attempts have been made to take the intention of the law regulating compulsory public custody seriously, that is, to work for a reunion of the child with his or her parents. This has been called "inclusive fostering"[31] but no evaluations have been made. On the other hand, Sweden decided in 1983 that children, who have been rooted in their "family homes" could stay there under the legal guardianship of their "family home parents." Not until it was decided that they could have a continuous payment was there a breakthrough for this transfer of legal guardianship from the biological parents to the foster parents for the placed children.

In order to make the conditions, as it is expressed, more safe for the children who have been placed in foster care it was suggested in an official report from the Swedish government (SOU 2000:77) that not only the custody but also the legal guardianship regularly should be transferred to the foster parents. According to the governmental report placed children will be more safe in the sense that the children's parents cannot legally request to have their children back.

A new Swedish law making it mandatory for social agencies to consider transfer of custody after a child has spent three years in a foster home was considered and passed in June 2003.[32] Protests were formulated about the disadvantages for the child,[33] but in vain. Foster homes, officially called "family homes," can nowadays also be organized by commercial private companies including consultants and experts with former officials from the social agencies included. This kind of semi-official network[34] which might have an economic interest in forced custody can influence the placed children to reject their parents. This violates the individual and human rights of the children.

What can be done to improve the conditions for children who have been alienated in compulsory public custody conflicts?

Parental alienation syndrome has not been recognized as a form of psychological abuse. The harm that is done to the alienated children is not yet well known. Therefore, it is of vital importance that PAS is written and talked about and that social workers, psychologists, and psychiatrists learn about it in their professional education. If PAS is recognized I do hope that in the future it will not be possible for social agency officials as parent substitutes (who, compared to parents in custody conflicts, can be neutral) to defame a parent and to integrate the children in their campaign of denigration, thereby alienating the children from a formerly loved parent, and possibly doing them irreparable harm.

ENDNOTES

1. PAS is more specific than Parental Alienation, PA, as has been pointed out by Richard Gardner (2001). Parental Alienation Syndrome vs. Parental Alienation: Which Diagnosis Should Evaluators Use in Child Custody Disputes? *30*(2) *The American Journal of Family Therapy* 93–115. This can be seen as a rebuttal to Carol Bruch (2001): Parental Alienation Syndrome and Parental Alienation: Getting it wrong in Child Custody Cases? *35 Family Law Quarterly* 527. PAS in comparison with other similar problems or syndromes that children in custody conflicts can develop, see Deirdre Conway Rand (1997). The Spectrum of Parental Alienation Syndrome (Part I), *The American Journal of Psychology 3.*
2. Compare identification with and defense of the one you become totally dependent on, seen in cases of kidnapping as, for example, Patricia Hearst, and in cases of hostages, the so-called Stockholm syndrome.
3. Two of them are shortly introduced in my article: Making a Parent Dangerous – PAS in Sweden and Norway in (2003). *The Parental Alienation Syndrome (PAS). An Interdisciplinary Challenge for Professionals Involved in Divorce.* International Conference, Frankfurt (Main), 18–19. October, 2002. Berlin, Verlag fur Wissenschaft und Bildung.
4. K. Ebert, Die Rechtssituation bei Kindesentfremdung im Europäischen Vergleich, dargestellt vornehmlich an Fallbeispielen der Strassburger Menschenrechte-Judikatur in (2003). *PAS. An interdisciplinary challenge for professionals involved in divorce.* He quotes the summary of three judges in the case *Olsson v. Sweden* (No. 2): "to allow access, a right which is not even refused to criminal parents in other countries."
5. Eugen Verhellen. Children's rights in Europe – An overview and a framework for understanding in Peter Koeppel (1996) Hrsgb. *Kindschaftsrecht und Völkerrecht im Europäischen Kontext.* Luchterhand.
6. See the judgment 12 July, 2001 from ECHR, Case of *K. and T. v. Finland Child* where child psychiatrist Dr J.P. is quoted, p. 15: "From the children's point of view, especially, but naturally also from that of the foster parents, the foster family is a family to which the principles concerning family life enshrined in the United Nations Convention on the Rights of the Child and in the European Convention for the Protection of Human Rights and Fundamental Freedoms can be applied in the same way as to biological families. This point of view is especially important when, through the force of circumstances, the biological family has not lived together."
7. Statistics from The National Board of Health and Welfare. The voluntary placements are often in reality not consensual, as the choice is to agree to a placement or having your child placed anyway. In Denmark, 12, 733 children and juveniles under the age of 18, almost 1% of the population in the relevant age groups, were placed outside their home, the vast majority of these placements being consensual, see summary from a project under the auspices of the Ministry of Social Affairs entitled Quality in the Placement of Children and Juveniles. Report 03:04 by Tine Egelund & Anne-Dorthe Hestbaek.
8. The exact references and date of journals and other documents are available from me if requested for scientific purposes.
9. See Wilfrid von Boch-Galhau. Folgen der PAS-indoktrinierung fur betroffene erwachsene Scheidungskinder and other writers in (2003). *The Parental Alienation Syndrome (PAS). An interdisciplinary challenge for professionals involved in divorce*, Berlin, Verlag fur Wissenschaft und Bildung.
10. As has been pointed out by the sociologist Stefan Carlsson, foster home has, ironically enough, in the Swedish social welfare state changed name to "family home." Stefan Carlsson (1995): *Socialtjänstens kompetens och funktion, Socialstatsprojektet* 1995: 1, Stockholm City University Press.
11. The monthly payment from the social agency (tax money) for the foster parents to have Emma is not an information the social agency has wanted to give, but in 1995 Susan's attorney at law found out that at that time it was about 1700 USD.
12. Quotation from p. 3(5). Verdict/Dom 2003–04–16 Case No./Mål Nr xx, Kammarrätten i /name/.
13. Application no. 44259/98, Application no. 67814/01, Application no. 67931/01.
14. The attorney at law representing the social officials (a woman without children of her own who in the last trial in April 2003 where I was present said that the mother should not think that the daughter was there for her) has been the same over all the years. She is paid by the local social welfare board. Susan's attorney at law has estimated

that this case has cost the Swedish taxpayers over a million USD. She is not paid as the mother has no assurance, no public money for legal help and doesn't have any money of her own.

15. Relevant observations are difficult to make when you place child and parents in a clinic, breaking their daily routines, their networks and influencing their relations. Preferable, as I see it, is to observe the child relating to his or her parent in everyday life situations at home.
16. Utredning/Investigation jml 50 § SoL concerning Jessica Svensson (birth number), 2001-06-07, NN kommun, Socialförvaltningen, Familjegruppen.
17. The 29th of March, 2005. Case No.XX, The social authority in /name of the community/. Eliza Anderson, regarding visitation according to the LVU-law /Lagen om Vård av Unga/The Law of Care of the Young/
18. Dom/Verdict No. T 4989-00, Svea hovrätt 2001.
19. Five cases can only indicate some common traits of the severe alienation of mothers resulting in PAS in forced custody conflicts. Further research is needed. I have in several cases of alleged, but not substantiated, sexual abuse studied how children have been alienated from their fathers and have developed PAS as a result of the denigration campaigns they themselves have taken part in after having been separated from their fathers who also had provided normal loving parenting.
20. The competition is part of the special course in law "Practical European Process" at Stockholm University. Ten Nordic universities have the same course. Responsible is Jacob Sundberg. He was installed as an honourable member in the American Academy of Arts & Sciences in October, 2002 for his pioneering work within the domain of human rights. He is also the founder of the Institute for Public and International Law in Stockholm. A report is published yearly by the institute to document the competition.
21. Siv Westerberg, medical doctor and attorney at law, has appealed ten times and won seven of her appeals, six of them concerning compulsory public custody, listed below:
    Paulsen-Medalen & Svensson v. Sweden
    Gärdh & Kjell Persson v. Sweden
    Cecelia & Lisa Eriksson v. Sweden
    Margareta & Roger Andersson v. Sweden
    Gun & Stig Olsson v. Sweden
    Gun & Stig Olsson 2 v. Sweden
22. Case of *K. and T. v. Finland*, Judgment from the European Court of Human Rights Strasbourg 12 July, 2001. The application (no.25702/94) was registered in November, 1994. A sad fact about these approved cases is that the children have not, in spite of the acknowledgement in the European Court of Human Rights, been reunited with their parents.
23. The now retired judge Brita Sundberg-Weitman opposed to the arbitrariness in the new starting in the seventies, the so-called frame laws, she claimed Sweden ought to be a state governed by law, see her book (1981). Matter-of-factness and arbitrariness in adminstration of justice and public adminstration/*Saklighet och godtycke i rättskipning och förvaltning.* Norstedts, Stockholm. (The writer is planning a new edition.)
24. In the partly dissenting opinion of judge Bonello in the Case of *K. and T. v. Finland*, Judgment from the European Court of Human Rights Strasbourg 12 July, 2001, he says: "Had I, like the Finnish authorities been faced with choosing whether to be cruel to the mother or to the child, I know which way I would have looked."
25. How devastating and extremely difficult it is to defeat a constructed picture is well documented in an exceptional verdict by the Honourable Mr Justice Eady, the 30th of July, 2002 in the High Court of Justice, Queen's Bench Division, Royal Courts of Justice, Strand, London, WC2A 2LL. Case No. :HQ9903605, HQ9903606, *Christopher Lillie & Dawn Reed v. Newcastle City Council* and other defendants.
26. Cecile, Finkelstein. The Heart of an Abducted and Alienated Child, and, Sarah or Cecilie: The Identity Issue (2003) in *PAS. An interdisciplinary challenge for professionals involved in divorce.* Berlin, Verlag fur Wissenschaft und Bildung.
27. An overview of research has recently been made by a Norwegian psychologist, Tore Andreassen. (2003) *Treatment of adolescents in institutions. What does the research tell us?* Behandling av ungdom i institusjoner, Hva sier forskningen? No Nordic studies on the effects of placing children outside their home passed the scientific standards, so in fact there is no standardized knowledge about the treatment and what happens afterward. One Swedish descriptive study (Vinnerljung et al. 2001) concludes that 30–37% of the placements were broken within five years, and most of the placements broke down the first year. In April 2003, a report was published by the Danish Institute for Social Research. It is about the 14,000 Danish children in public care costing 6.5 billion Danish crowns (2001) and about the lack of knowledge about the consequences for the children taken into public care.
28. In an old Swedish study (1980) by Bohman & Sigvardsson, boys placed in stable foster homes were compared with boys who had been left in their risk homes although they were meant to be placed in foster homes, and with a group of boys who were adopted. All these three groups were compared with control groups and were followed up at the ages of 11, 15 and 18. It was found that the boys in foster homes were registered more frequently as criminals and for drinking too much alcohol. The boys left at home were doing just as well as the boys in the control groups.
29. Bo Vinnerljung & Martin Ribe (2001). Mortality after care among young adult foster children in Sweden, *10*(3) *Journal of Social Welfare* 164–173.

30 See for example: Mark V. Flinn & Barry G. England (1995). Childhood Stress and Family Environment, *36*(6) *Current Anthropology* 854–866. Bo Vinnerljung (1996).

Foster children as adults/Fosterbarn som unga. Dissertation (with summary in English).

31. SOU 1979/80:44, p. 79.
32. Proposition 2002/03:53 called "Reinforced protection for children." It was decided in the Swedish Parliament in June, 2003. The title is referring to the child's rights not be moved to his or her parents when the child has been what is called rooted in the family home. That the significance of de facto custody ought to be increased was proposed by Johanna Schiratzki (1997) in her dissertation *Custody and custody disputes*, Stockholm University. When the social agency is responsible to limit or obstruct the parent's possibilities of de facto custody without justification it must be questioned whether it is the right thing to do to transfer the legal guardianship to the foster home chosen by the social agency. Of course, this new law can be questioned for many other reasons, one being that biological bonds and loving bonds between children and parents are not replaceable. But the importance of these family and love bonds seem not to be appreciated in the modern social welfare state, where the child is seen as an individual released from the parents.
33. Siv Westerberg, 2001, *see* www.nkmr.org
34. One such network organization that started already in 1993 in northern Sweden, has now an office in Stockholm. The name is Nåjden treatmentconsultant, *see* www.najden.se.

Chapter 12

THE NEED FOR PUBLIC AWARENESS AND POLICY MAKERS TO RESPOND TO PAS: A NEGLECTED FORM OF CHILD ABUSE

DAVID L. LEVY

OVERVIEW

The Children's Rights Council (CRC), an international child advocacy organization, has received thousands of complaints about alienation of children since its formation in 1985.[1] *Both fathers and mothers are capable of alienating children. CRC advises alienated parents to join a support group as soon as possible, from among the 950 organizations listed on the organization's website, www.info4parents.com, so they do not go through this alone, and can get good advice. On the broader front, America recognizes that hitting a spouse, or leaving a child alone in an overheated car, are forms of abuse. Social workers, courts, and legislators need more education on how to identify PAS as a form of child abuse, and how to distinguish it from other forms of alienation and abuse. They also need to be able to prescribe proper treatment, prevention, and legal remedies to punish perpetrators and educate the public as to the social unacceptability of this conduct.*

First, it is important to define the subject that this chapter discusses – parental alienation syndrome is defined as:

> a disorder that arises in child custody disputes in which a child will view one parent as all good and another as all bad. More often the mother, who has been the primary child-rearer, is viewed as perfect or close to it, and the father, who is disputing for custody, is viewed as a despicable individual. Such children guiltlessly vilify the father and create a variety of malevolent delusions about him especially with regard to how despicable and heinous he is. For example, these children have been programmed by their mothers to hate their father and to subject him to a campaign of denigration, but the children themselves often contribute their own scenarios of hostility. It is this combination of both the parent's and the child's contribution that warrant the term *parental alienation syndrome.* (*See* Gardner, 1985, 1987, 1989, 1992a.)

CRC AND PAS

The Children's Rights Council is an international organization that advocates for joint custody (shared parenting), because children deserve ongoing emotional support from their parents and extended family, regardless of the parent's commitment to each other. Currently, in many places children often are still seen as property of a marriage to be divided and "given" to one parent following a marital dissolution. As part of its mission, CRC maintains one of the largest collections of research materials in the nation on parenting and divorce. We also maintain a "Parenting Directory" that lists 950 organizations around the country that offer information and resources to never-married, separated, divorced parents, and the professionals who work with them.

This chapter of the book deals with the experiences of the Children's Rights Council since 1985 in handling complaints from parents about lack of access to their children after divorce. Many of those complaints involve alienation of children from one parent or the other. CRC has received thousands of such complaints, from mothers as well as from fathers – and from other family members, including grandparents – who feel alienated from their children and grandchildren. We know that in some instances, the alienation may be induced by a parent in the form of poor parenting skills, abuse, or neglect, that has caused the child to withdraw from the offending parent. In these cases, the child may have good reasons for withdrawal, and this problem must be dealt with. The child must be protected. This chapter, however, focuses on a very different situation – what it takes for social and political institutions to be able to readily identify the characteristics of PAS and its treatment and then to apply this information to family law and the broader sociopolitical system.

Most bad acts are readily defined. For example, we can easily recognize when someone hits someone else. DNA is often a way to determine if a rape has occurred, and when a child is kidnapped, evidence is usually found. But how can we recognize that a parent has been able to induce a child to join in an unjustified verbal attack on the other parent? How can we differentiate such an attack from legitimate reasons why a child is uncomfortable about the prospects of being with the other parent? Furthermore, once we recognize the symptoms of PAS, how can we induce social and political institutions to understand that PAS is not only bad behavior, but also a serious form of child abuse? Lastly, what will it take for judges and those who work with the courts, including custody evaluators and mediators, state departments of child and family services in the states, and legislatures, to recognize PAS as abuse of children?

Other questions that need to be addressed include: How can the various government and social service institutions intervene to assist PAS victims and thereby to curb its practice? Ultimately, what will it take for the public to understand that PAS is, like child sexual abuse, domestic violence, neglect, and child kidnapping, unacceptable behavior? PAS is unacceptable regardless of the parent who causes it because, as with other forms of abuse, it is the damage to the child that is perfidious. To quote from Richard Gardner, M.D., a pioneer in the identification and treatment of this disorder:

> Inducing a PAS in a child is a form of emotional abuse. As is true for physical and sexual abuse, PAS symptomatology may be lifelong. The attenuation and even destruction of what was previously a good parent-child bonding may be permanent. They may not be able to resume a relationship after a hiatus of a few years. (*Therapeutic intervention for children with parental alienation syndrome*, p. xxi)

NATONAL ADVOCACY GROUP HELPS FULFILL NEEDS OF CHILDREN AFFECTED BY PAS

My understanding of alienation of children arises in the context of the Children's Rights Council (CRC). As previously noted, CRC is an international child advocacy organization, which I co-founded in 1985, and have been president of since CRC was founded in 1985. CRC has chapters in 32 states, Washington, D.C. and four foreign countries – Canada, Great Britain, Japan, and Sierra Leone.

CRC and its chapters work to change laws and attitudes to bring about more two-parent involvement, regardless of the parents' marital situation. We also operate community-based programs – including 30 Neutral Drop-Off and Pick-Up Sites for Children in 9 states and Washington, D.C. – for which we do not charge parents.

Individual parents and extended family members look to CRC for resources and referrals on how they can maintain contact with their children despite separation and divorce. CRC has counseled thousands of parents over the years, and made innumerable referrals from our database of organizations. Much of this information is available on CRC's websites, www.gocrc.com and www.info4parents.com. Many of the parents who call us feel "locked out" of their children's lives. Some have undoubtedly, through poor parenting skills, or neglect or abuse, contributed to this. However, many are what women's advocates tell us are "good enough parents" to parent their children. Most parents do not abandon their responsibilities because of divorce. Many people do not realize, because the media has not reported it, most divorced parents do, in fact, pay their child support. This is distinguishable from the often young, poorer, never-married parents, who have a much more difficult time earning enough money to pay child support. In addition to paying support (as they should), some divorced parents spend thousands of additional dollars on lawyers. They also pay expert witnesses, lose time from work, and suffer mental and emotional anguish, all for the purpose of gaining something else – the joy of once again being a meaningful part of their own children's lives. They wish to regain the part they played, or believe they played, and had the legal right to play, during the marriage. These parents have generally "lost" custody, and are reduced to seeing their children every other weekend from Friday to Sunday (the "normal" visitation in most courts). Even that occasional court-ordered contact is sometimes not adhered to by the parent with custody, who, by virtue of having custody, can block the child from having even limited visitation.

Once it was primarily fathers who contacted CRC requesting help, but now, that number of fathers receiving sole custody has risen from five percent to more than 15 percent. CRC receives an increasing number of calls from mothers who do not have primary custody of their children and need help maintaining contact. We also get calls from grandparents and other family members seeking access to the children. Whether the call comes from a father or a mother or a grandparent, the complaint is invariably the same: "the parent with custody is blocking me from being a part of the child's life."

In perhaps 10 percent of cases, the interference with access is accompanied by an allegation in the context of a custody battle that the noncustodial parent has physically or sexually abused the child. In 90 percent of the cases, however, the reason alleged for the interference by a parent is attributed to lack of appreciation of the value of both parents to the child, or to hatred of one parent for the other.

Certainly it is possible that abuse has in fact occurred, in which case the child must be protected. These situations should be handled, however imperfectly, by authorities charged with their resolution, not by one parent acting as accuser, judge, and jury. We must work to improve our legal system, not supplant it with one parent's omniscient power over the child.

PUBLIC EDUCATION AND RESOURCES TO ASSIST THOSE PAS VICTIMS

Children's Rights Council, which is a nonprofit organization, has no way of determining the truth of an allegation, but we do have to try to figure out from the parent seeking help the type of problem involved so we can refer the parent to appropriate resources. We do not represent the parent in court, or determine which parent is right, but we do have chapters around the country and a list of 950 organizations that can help a parent on a local level move their issues forward.

If a person seems to be having a problem with parenting issues, we will refer the parent to a parent education group. We must also spread the message of PAS to the general public, through the media – radio, print, and television. This coverage should include the need for new policies, regulations, and resources to assist PAS victims, primarily the children. We must educate the public on the need for resource allocation, including training of family workers in state agencies.

"Child welfare, juvenile justice, childcare, youth services, and others who work with children across the country are nearing a state of crisis," said a report from the Annie E. Casey Foundation and the Brookings Institution in March, 2003 (*see* Casey Foundation, 2003). They noted that child and family service agencies are plagued by low pay, high workloads, and an average annual turnover rate of 40 percent for child welfare staff in private agencies. Brooking and the Casey Foundation announced an initiative to strengthen America's human services work force. Douglas W. Nelson, president of the Foundation, said that everyone who works with children knows the importance of low turnover and small caseloads to keep kids straight, but almost no one who reads the newspapers knows it. "That knowledge needs to be part of every citizen," Nelson said. So does an awareness of PAS. Frontline child care workers need to be as knowledgeable about PAS as they are about other forms of child abuse and neglect. Distinguishing between the various types of abuse is the job of the frontline worker, the social workers, the courts, the legislature, and all others who work with children.

In some cases, parents complain that not only are they being unfairly blocked from seeing their child, but also that the child is being turned against them. Sometimes, the parents who contact CRC use the term "parental alienation" to describe what is happening to them and their child, and sometimes they use the term "parental alienation syndrome." Whether they are aware of such terminology or not, they are in emotional pain and are capable of speaking at great length (which we encourage), about the anguish they are experiencing. However, our main focus is on helping them find a solution.

The conditions they describe all have a familiar pattern: contact with the child is denied and this is accompanied by a slammed door, shouts and accusations, or excuses that the child is too busy, is sick, does not want to see the parent, or is afraid of the parent. Sometimes, the message is delivered silently or by unanswered phone calls, or an empty house at the time of court-ordered access. Invariably, the excuse is relayed by the blocking parent, rather than by the child. However, given the effects of PAS, the child may well reiterate the excuse.

We try to explain to parents that denying access of a child to a parent is wrong, but this alone does not mean that we are witnessing parental alienation syndrome. We may be witnessing poor parenting skills, abuse, or neglect. The PAS, we explain, occurs when a variety of symptoms are present and which are described in books written by Richard Gardner and others.

One typical example involved a 15-year-old girl whose mother had blocked her from seeing her father for 5 years. When the father phoned, during one of his intermittent attempts to establish contact with his daughter, the daughter said, "I hate you. I have always hated you, and my mother hates you. Don't ever call here again." This father had helped raise the child from birth to age 10, when he and the mother divorced. I explained to him that the child was exhibiting the typical symptoms of PAS, to wit; making outrageous claims, seeing things in black and white, forgetting happy times the child and father had spent together, and quoting others in her expression of hatred for him. Of course, we all know that from time to time, teenagers hate their parents and reject them, but PAS symptomatology is quite different, such as in consistency and duration of hostility and that these parents need to be recognized and need assistance. It is my experience that children simply do not reject a parent in such absolutist terms, as did this 15-year-old who had not seen her father in five years.

In a *New York Times* column on June 21, 1998, noted writer Gail Sheehy coined a phrase "deadbolted Dad." She said: "The newest reality is the Deadbolted Dad – locked out of his children's hearts after divorce . . . with little attention paid to enforcing or honoring their visitation rights." Some of these parents walk away from their children, Sheehy acknowledged, but many are deadbolted out. True, not all dads who are deadbolted out of their children's lives are the victims of PAS. But many are, it is not just fathers.

I recall attending a conference in 1999 in New York City at which Dr. Gardner spoke to the OnStep Institute at Mt. Sinai Hospital about PAS. He said that although it was mainly mothers who had been alienating their children from their fathers in the 1980s, he had seen an increase in the number of mothers who were victims. He wondered why. During a conference refreshment break, I approached Dr. Gardner and said that I thought the reason for the increase in alienation against mothers was due to an increasing number of fathers obtaining custody. At that point, Dr. Gardner walked back to the meeting, resumed his presentation, and said he had just been provided with a perfectly valid reason for the increase in fathers causing PAS: The parent who has greater access to a child has greater ability to alienate the child against the less involved parent. See Gardner's article about PAS regarding gender vs. custodial power (Gardner, 2002).

PAS is not a gender-specific phenomenon; either parent can perpetrate it, and for a variety of reasons. These reasons include the need for control and power, fear of the parent, or the wish to truly "x" your "ex" out of your life. This is done in spite of the presence of children and the need to consult about their well-being if as they presumably would have the benefit of two involved parents, as they would have had during the marriage.

It should be noted that CRC almost never receives complaints of alienation in the context of shared parenting (joint custody). That is, rarely does a parent who calls CRC say that they have difficulty getting to see their child when they have an agreement or a court order for meaningful contact with their child. Virtually all the battles we at CRC witness are in the context of sole or primary custody – one battling the other for custody while the latter is doing everything to remain a part of their children's lives. The struggling parent wants to avoid what noted California Doctor Frank Williams, M.D., described in the 1980s as a "parentectomy" – the removal of a parent from a child's life.[2]

Dr. Williams said that the way to avoid high conflict custody battles, which often result from the fear of a parentectomy, was to give those warring parents joint custody with highly structured access (visitation). Joint custody means that each parent would have frequent and continuing contact with the child, and highly structured access (visitation) would avoid disagreements over where and when each parent was to have his or her time with the child. This approach would decrease the high likelihood of conflict divorces, said Williams. CRC believes it would also decrease the occurrence of other PAS, and high conflict divorce.

Views on how many divorces result in custody battles, how many cases of interference with access exist, and how many of these high-conflict divorces with children vary. Research reveals "approximately five percent of divorcing couples with minor-aged children for whom access is particularly problematic. Mistrustful of one another, these parents exhibit high levels of conflict both inside and outside the court" (Pearson, 1996). About one million couples in the United States divorce each year, and about one million children are affected. Five percent of one million means that about 50,000 *divorces* are high-conflict each year. This suggests an indeterminate number of high conflict situations involving *never-married* parents.

One parent who contacted CRC has been denied access to his children for four years. The mother had alleged he abused one of the children, yet he was never charged or arrested, let alone convicted of any crime. A psychologist and a custody evaluator who made separate investigations three years apart each concluded that the mother had alienated the children against their father. A Connecticut court once tried to give him supervised visitation, but the children had been so poisoned against their dad that they rejected him at the one meeting that was allowed. After that incident, he could never again convince a judge to allow him access (visitation) to his own children. Still, he pays $1,000 a month in child support and alimony. He goes to public events – graduations, sports events – where he hopes to catch a glimpse of the children. His mother and father are afraid they will die without ever seeing their grandchildren again. This is the very kind of parent that Congress has urged upon the country as desirable – the involved, caring, paying, responsible parent. Still, the courts seem uncertain as to how to intervene to help him have a normal relationship with his own children.

In another example, a father had cut a New York City mother out of her four children's lives. She spent five years in court fighting for access, and was finally reunited with her children. During the time she was denied access, she bravely continued to participate in the PTA at the school her children attended so that she would not become completely isolated and seem like a stranger to the principal, teachers, and other parents in the community. She now gets to see them on a regular basis. This story has a relatively happy ending – happier than the parents who contact the CRC who never get to see their children once a charge is levied.

Many parents tell CRC that they allowed the other parent to move out of state, based on his or her promise to provide for generous access (visitation) to the children. Once the move took place, access stopped, and the long distance and huge expense involved in pursuing access rights proved access impossible to obtain. Other parents did not know of the impending cross-country move, and thus had no opportunity to negotiate a different parenting schedule. They wound up with no parenting time at all, and this further facilitated the alienation.

Many of these parents say it is difficult to get anyone to believe them. The typical response is "You must have done something wrong," or "Things like that don't happen in America." Sometimes, it is not until months or years later, when these same skeptics are served with their own divorce papers, lose custody, and are themselves victims of PAS. This results in many a "these people understand" moment, when the newcomer to alienation realizes the truth of what his or her friend had told him or her about severe interference in the access to one's child.

I recently met a high school teacher in Virginia who is in his 60s. I asked him if he knew about PAS. He said he was a living example of it. I was momentarily taken aback, not knowing what he meant. He explained that he had been alienated from his daughter many years before, but that a reconciliation was just now beginning. The daughter was now in her mid-40s. I was dumbfounded. A reconciliation beginning only now? How did this come about? I asked him. He said that he recently learned that the girl's mother (the teacher's former wife) had died. He obtained his daughter's phone number from a relative and called her to offer condolences. That call prompted a door to open. He and his daughter are now starting to communicate. They are communicating about an alienation that occurred more than a quarter century ago. The communication is in the tentative stage, and the teacher said that a lot of understanding and working through issues would probably be necessary to effectuate a complete, loving reunion. The death of the alienator – the mother – may be the catalyst that is bringing about this reconciliation. One of the problems is that the daughter is going to have to accept the possibility that the mother was lying to her for years – meaning that she may have to now reject her (or at least her lying), whereas she previously was obligated to reject her father – on the basis that the father was evil. I hope that not all children have to wait 30 years to be reconciled with a victim parent.

Instead of the win-win situation that all mediation seeks to accomplish, PAS is a lose-lose situation for the child – even if the child is now in his mid-50s, and still has to deal with this affront to his personality. He "lost" one parent (the accused), and now, in a sense, he may "lose" the other parent (respect for the one who lied to him). In either event, the child has to face some horrible facts. I believe that PAS bears a resemblance to rape; the child has been violated in the most intimate way possible. Again, I am not talking about situations in which a court finds credible evidence that justifies legal restrictions placed on access of a child to a parent. I am talking about alienation of a child by one parent against the other parent. A significant difference exists between these two situations.

The children, of course, are the main victims. They suffer not only from the divorce, but also from the acrimony, and the alienation. Generally, some alienation is associated with most divorce situations, as a parent will bad-mouth the other parent to the child, or try to make the child believe that he or she is the better parent and the other parent is not necessary. Some will go so far as to try to totally obliterate the other parent from the child's life, and also get the child to join in the obliteration. Sometimes the attempt will fail, because the child is resistant to the attempt, for one reason or another. In most cases, the acrimony will not reach the level of alienation.

Researchers have found that acrimony, whether the parents are married or divorced, has a profound effect on many children. CRC does not hear from many young people under age 18. We usually hear from the parents, often via our websites. Sometimes, however, we do hear from children; of course, we try to help them as well. Our national office in the Washington, D.C. area, and our chapters across the country and abroad, are always ready to offer assistance to help resolve a problem. It is frustrating when we cannot do so. Sometimes we cannot help because we are called too late; that is, the situation is too out of control, positions are already polarized, and hate is rampant.

ATTITUDE AND THEN BEHAVIOR CHANGE TOWARD ABUSE

Years ago, it was acceptable in many places to engage in violence against your spouse. A husband could hit a wife (a wife hitting was less likely), either one of them could hit their child. All this has changed. A widespread educational campaign over the past several years has produced laws and policies against family violence. Laws against family violence have been strengthened at the federal and state levels, and hundreds of millions of dollars in federal and state money has been allocated to changing our attitudes and laws against family violence. Researchers have come to understand that even a single slap to a child's face is likely to be remembered years later, and be a source of sadness and hurt long after the child reaches adulthood.

Some groups contend that the family violence statistics have been overblown, and others realize that violence by women against men has been underreported, but these debates only serve to highlight the vast public resources that have been thrown into the battle to make violence against a partner or a child unacceptable. People may argue over statistics, but not over the idea that violence in family relationships is unacceptable. Whether this prohibition against violence will ever extend to nation-states (by replacing war with conflict resolution) or to capital punishment (by ending it) is another matter.

Even spanking, for generations considered to be an indispensable tool in the raising of one's child ("spare the rod and spoil the child") has fallen into disrepute. Not only is spanking considered to be an inappropriate way to discipline children, but researcher Dr. Murray Straus found that spanking actually "produces a small increase in subsequent inappropriate behavior." The spanking produces an immediate result (the child stops the unwanted behavior), but two years down the road, the behavior of such children changes for the worse, whereas children whose parents correct them by other methods see their behavior improve (Straus, 1997).

Child sexual abuse and incest have long been considered totally unacceptable behavior, and so are neglect and abandonment of children. Various forms of neglect exist, including physical, educational, and emotional. Much has been done to help children and families gain control of their lives when abuse has been involved. Between 1965–68, states started to pass legislation requiring professionals to report suspected abuse cases. All states have laws against child abuse and many professionals, such as social workers, health care workers, school personnel, daycare providers, law enforcement officials, and mental health professionals are required to report abuse cases. Child abuse and neglect are defined by both federal and state legislation. The Federal Child Abuse Prevention and Treatment Act (CAPTA) defines child abuse and neglect as "Any recent act or failure to act on the part of a parent or caretaker which results in death, serious physical or emotional harm, sexual abuse or exploitation, or an act or failure to act, which presents an imminent risk of serious harm" (National Clearinghouse on Child Abuse and Neglect, 2002). State statutes expand on definitions, including spelling out who must report abuse.[3]

The kidnapping of one's own children has also come to be unacceptable. Kidnapping presumes a sudden, secret taking of the child. All 50 states have passed laws making it a felony or a misdemeanor for the noncustodial parent to kidnap the child. In about 35 of the states, it is a crime for either parent to kidnap the child. What this means is that even if the custodial parent kidnaps the child, it is a crime. In the remaining states, it is not unlawful for the custodial parent to kidnap the child. The evolution of laws in some of the states – making it a crime for either parent to kidnap and hide the child – has grown over a period of 15 years.

In 1980, in response to protests from around the world that parents were abducting their children and taking them permanently to another country, the Hague Convention on the Civil Aspects of International Child Abduction was passed.[4] The Convention said that if a country that was a party to the Convention had already decided custody in the context of divorce or separation, a parent taking the child to another country did not authorize that "new" country to retry custody. Instead, that country had to return the child to the "country of habitual residence." A few courts even extended that practice to visitation, holding that even if the custodial parent took the child to another country, not to re-try custody (they already had custody), the parent with visitation rights could have the child returned to the country of habitual residence.

As an indication of how attitudes have changed, many people started pressing Congress to provide for criminal sanctions against the kidnapper, if he or she could be found. Congress was asked to provide for criminal penalties against the kidnapper regardless of whether the child was returned to the U.S. from a foreign country to which the abductor had gone to seek custody (despite custody having already been decided in the U.S.). How can a parent with custody be guilty of kidnapping his or her own child? Doesn't custody mean ownership? Well, the idea that children are "property," to be "owned" by a parent and moved willy-nilly without any consideration to protecting the child's relationship with the other parent or relatives is also increasingly under attack.

When he was a member of Congress, George Gekas (R-PA), invited various groups to join in the drafting of this federal legislation. The Children's Rights Council was one of the groups invited to those meetings. Congressman Gekas accepted CRC's suggestion that kidnapping in violation of an access (visitation) order be included in the legislation. As a result, it became unlawful to hide a child away from the custodial OR noncustodial parent.[5]

The U.S. Department of Justice reports about 115 kidnappings of children by strangers, and about 203,000 parental kidnappings of children, every year (9). Although many casual everyday activities that an eight- or ten-year old child used to do when I was growing up in the 1940s or 1950s (such as walking alone around the city) are inconceivable now by parents afraid of abduction of the child by strangers, it is nearly two-thousand-to-one more likely that a child will be kidnapped by a family member. Of course, if it is your child who is kidnapped, statistics do not matter. However, the fact remains that parental kidnapping is far more common than stranger kidnapping. Although this phenomenon is little understood by the general public, enough public officials understand it – in reaction to protests by affected parents – to have passed laws against it. It is possible that Congress could also pass legislation establishing parental alienation as a "crime."

APPLYING PUBLIC EFFORTS TO HELP INDIVIDUAL CASES

The Children's Rights Council offers parents suggestions that have been demonstrated as effective, based on the follow-up calls we have received from parents who have adopted these approaches. They range from ideas on how to de-escalate situations, to taking court action. The following list provides some of these suggestions:

1. Join a divorced parents support group. Discuss your situation with parents who have "been there" and know the legal and psychological road map. They can help you to develop a sensible strategy, which can help you avoid making mistakes. CRC chapters around the country are listed on the CRC website at www.gocrc.com. Hundreds of additional support groups are listed on the CRC parenting website, www.info4parents.com
2. Do not hire a lawyer until you consult with the divorced parents support groups. The strategy you develop with them may or may not include hiring a lawyer. If a lawyer is indeed necessary, they know the best lawyers. Do not hire a lawyer because he helped get you money from an insurance company three years ago, or because he drew up your will. Alienation of a child, especially if it is coupled with an abuse allegation, is a serious matter, and must be handled by experts.
3. Be prepared to spend money. Fighting alienation, especially if it is connected with an abuse allegation, takes a lot of money. But this is your life, and your children. Be prepared to spend a good deal of money, but know what you are getting. Become more of an expert with less reliance on your lawyer. Read Richard Gardner's books on parental alienation syndrome, as well as the book *Children Held Hostage* by Stanley Clawar and Brynne Rivlin (published by the American Bar Association). These and other books are available from CRC or other sources.
4. While you are waving the stick, think about the carrot. Sometimes, a parent will ease the pressure against you if you know and comply with what he or she wants. Does the parent with custody want extra money from you? Give it to him or her. It will be far cheaper than a court fight, and priceless in avoiding emotional turmoil. Parents will generally tell me that generosity will not work, because what the custodial parent wants is the parent without custody to get out of the children's lives. However, we urge them to try again.

5. Be there. Show up for your children's school, sport, and other extracurricular activities. Hope to catch a glimpse of them. Of course, this is highly frustrating, because a glimpse is not like a hug, and a hug is not equivalent to the child being part of your life. At least you know you were there for them at important events, and perhaps they also will know it, now, or later.
6. Send "care" packages. Occasionally send your child a little care package. Include photos of you and your child doing an activity that both of you enjoyed, photos of him or her as a young child. Mark their milestones, birthdays, and holidays with cards. Enclose a check. The other parent may block many of these packages, but some may get through. Perhaps someone such as a teacher or school counselor can give the package directly to your child. Because your child may not get these care packages, also mark their milestones in a journal to demonstrate your commitment and love for them and show them you can even if it must be years later. E-mail them if you can.
7. Offer to use child access centers to see your child. The CRC has established 40 centers in 13 states (NC, SC, VA, MD, NJ, NY, CT, RI, IN, NM, PA, OH, MI) and Washington, D.C., usually at church sites, where parents may peacefully transfer their children between them for the weekend. Many centers also have supervised access, where a parent may not leave the premises with the child. Children's Rights Council staff monitors these transfers and supervisions. Some children and parents are seeing each for the first time in weeks or months because of these centers. We or a parent report to the court if anything goes wrong. Other organizations, such as the Supervised Visitation Network, also operate access centers around the U.S., Canada, and elsewhere. You may not want to use an access center to see your child, but it is better than not seeing your child at all. Swallow your pride, and focus your unqualified love and acceptance on your child, who is the real victim (even if he or she is hurling insults at you). Someone has to be an adult; better that it is you than the eight-year-old.
8. When accused of a crime you committed, accept responsibility, and the consequences. Get counseling if you have the opportunity to do so, and cooperate with authorities to prevent the abuse from happening again.

EDUCATING THE PUBLIC AND THOSE WHO WORK WITH CHILDREN AND FAMILIES

Considering the fact that divorces affect about one million children per year, America needs greater recognition of problems affecting children, including PAS. For example, how does a judge in Lucas County, Ohio, come to understand PAS and apply his understanding to the cases he sees? What about the thousands of other judges in this country and around the world? As judges no longer tolerate nonpayment of financial child support and violence against children, judges must no longer tolerate alienation of children by a parent against the other parent. If you steal, there is a legal consequence. In divorce, if a parent badmouths the other parent to the child, there must be a legal consequence. Some might say: "What, I can NEVER badmouth the other parent?" Well, how often can you steal, or hit a child or adult? Isn't once too often? If you badmouth the other parent to the child, there must be legal consequences – a fine, a few hours (or a night) in jail, increased time for the child to spend with the other parent, or, in outrageous cases (in which) severe alienation occurs, a reversal of custody.

Of course, if a parent has committed some type of child abuse other than PAS, such as physical or sexual abuse, then the courts should take the appropriate action against such a perpetrator. Distinguishing between the various types of abuse is the job of the front-line worker, the social worker, the courts, the legislature, and all others who deal with children. This means that on the larger, public front, we must do more to educate lawyers, judges, social welfare agencies, and all others who work with children that such a thing as parental alienation syndrome exists, and must be dealt with. Some professionals dismiss PAS and think it does not exist. How can these individuals explain the unreasonable rejection of a parent by a child? Notice I say unreasonable – unjustified.

I once heard a young woman named Kelly Zinna, Psy.D., addressing a bar association in Prince George's County, Maryland. Zinna had been presented as an expert on PAS. She was soft-spoken, but clearly knowledgeable and articulate. She had read all the literature, and had been trained in PAS by another psychologist in Denver named Carol Marfut. I was amazed at the skillful way Zinna handled every tough question the lawyers in the audience could throw at her. I thought to myself, if the U.S. is producing experts on PAS like Zinna and Marfut, and sending them to places like Colorado and Maryland, surely more people are coming to understand this newest form of child abuse. I have encountered other experts as well, such as psychologist Barbara Steinberg in Florida. I have heard that Steinberg handles individual cases well, something I do not know about concerning Zinna and Marfut. That is, a knowledge of the literature, does not necessarily mean one knows how to handle tough cases on an individual basis. A parent must be very careful before consulting an expert.

How long will it will it take to educate these "experts" on PAS? Examples include more reading of the literature, more people becoming aware of the lingo that children use when they are parroting someone else's script, and more advocates willing to stand up for those children. We need more social activists, and social activist groups that will contact the media, their state legislators, and members of Congress. We need citizen committees to put pressure on state DCF agencies to have more training sessions about PAS. There is generally more power in numbers, but history is full of examples of determined committed individuals who effected major change.

In the joint custody field, for example, one of those individuals is James A. Cook, president of the Joint Custody Association (JCA) in Los Angeles. Actually, Jim Cook *is* the JCA. It is a one-man operation, but effective. Cook is considered the father of joint custody. After having been involved in his own custody dispute, he took what he learned and used it to lobby the California legislature. In 1979, California became the first state to pass a presumption for joint custody. In the following years, Cook visited more than 30 state legislatures, often at the request of local custody reform organizations, to promote joint custody. Armed with a discerning ability to explain the research, and a gentle manner of speaking, Cook won over many legislators. He is one reason why legal, or physical joint custody, or both, are now a presumption or preference in 37 states and Washington D.C., although in some states, both parents must agree to joint custody.[6]

Robert Fay, M.D. is another individual who made a difference. When his third grade daughter's school refused to allow him access to his daughter's report card, Dr. Fay was the first person to sue the government using the Family Educational Rights and Privacy Act. FERPA protects student rights, especially the privacy of the student and his or her school record. Yet FERPA specifically affirms that noncustodial parents have a right to look at school records (including report cards), and attend parent-teacher conferences. After the school superintendent in Fay's district said that sending report cards to him would represent an unreasonable burden on the school district. Fay, a pediatrician in Albany, New York, persisted with meetings, letters, and court actions. He finally won a U.S. District Court case upholding his right to his child's school record.[7]

Cook and Fay are but two of the many individuals and groups across the country that have made a difference for children. When more individuals and organizations work on bringing PAS to light, they will make a difference in that area as well. The result will be fewer judges who do not understand PAS, fewer social workers who bury their heads in the sand, and fewer legislators unwilling to consider alienation as a form of child abuse – because they will know the mournful dirge of alienation when they hear it.

National efforts of governmental, quasi-public, and voluntary agencies, plus legislative intervention and recognition, will serve to protect child victims of PAS – especially if more members of the public become aware that PAS behavior toward children is "unacceptable" and incurs legal consequences.

REFERENCES

Casey, (2003). Casey Foundation, Human Services Workforce Initiative.: http://www.aecf.org/initiatives.hswi. *Also see* The Unsolved Challenge of System Reform on the same site. July 22, 2003.

Child Maltreatment, (2002). What is Child Maltreatment? http://www.calib.com/nccanch/pubs/factsheets/childmal.cfm. July 24, 2003.

Gardner, R. A. (1992a). *The Parental Alienation Syndrome: A guide for mental health and legal professionals.* Cresskill, NJ: Creative Therapeutics, Inc.

Gardner, R.A., (2002). Denial of the Parental Alienation Syndrome Also Harms Women, *The American Journal of Family Therapy, 30*(3).

NCMEC, 2003. Frequently Asked Questions and Statistics. http://www.ncmec.org/missingkids/servlet/PageServlet?LanguageCountry=en_US&PageId=242. July 24, 2003.

Pearson, Jessica, Ph.D., (1996). and Thoennes, Nancy, Ph.D., Center for Policy Research, and Price, David, Ph.D., and Williams, Robert, Ph.D., Policy Studies, Inc., Denver, Colorado, in Evaluation of the Child Access Demonstration Projects, Submitted to Federal Office of Child Support Enforcement, U.S. Department of Health and Human Services, David Arnaudo, Federal Program Officer, in Report to Congress, July, 1996, p. 5.

Straus, Murray A., Ph.D, et. al. (1997). Spanking by Parents and Subsequent Antisocial Behavior of Children. Corporal Punishment, paper CP24. http://pubpages.umh.edu/~mas2. July 24, 2003.

ENDNOTES

1. CRC is located at 6200 Editors Park Drive, Suite 103, Hyattsville, MD 20782, just outside of Washington, D.C.
2. Williams, Frank S., M.D. presentation at the 5th annual conference of the Children's Rights Council (then known by the name National Council for Children's Rights), October 19–21, 1990. Williams was Director of Child Adolescent Psychiatry at Cedars-Sinai Medical Center in Los Angeles. See CRC's Speak Out for Children" newsmagazine, Fall, 1990, Vol. 5, No.4.
3. The Child Abuse Prevention and Treatment Act (CAPTA), which was originally enacted in 1974 (P.L. 93-247), has been amended several times by Congress. *See also* U.S. Code title 42, chapter 67.
4. U.S. Central Authority on the Hague Convention on the Civil Aspects of International Child Abduction is the State department Office of Children's Issues, 2401 E Street N.W., Room L127 Washington, D.C. 20037, phone: 1-888-407-4747, website: http://travel.state.gov.
5. Section 1204. International Parental Kidnapping became a U.S. Code as of January 22, 2002 and can be found at: http://www.caselaw.lp.findlaw.com/casecode/uscodes/18/parts/i/chapters/55/sections/section_12.
6. Children's Rights Council website: www.gocrc.com.
7. Fay, Robert, M.D. was highlighted in both the Fall, 1990 issue of Speak Out for Children as well as the Spring/Summer, 1991 issue.

David L. Levy thanks S. Richard Sauber, Ph.D., for his conceptual and editorial expertise in the preparation of this article, and Teresa Kaiser, J.D., for editing.

Chapter 13

FACTORS AFFECTING RECONCILIATION BETWEEN THE CHILD AND TARGET PARENT

DEIRDRE CONWAY RAND AND RANDY RAND

OVERVIEW

This chapter explores factors affecting reconciliation between the child and target parent in severe parental alienation syndrome (PAS), where the parent-child relationship has been seriously damaged or destroyed. "Severe" includes several types of scenarios: child obsessed with denigrating the target parent; child displaying chaotic, destructive and bizarre behavior in response to intense postdivorce conflict over which parent will stay and which parent will go; child abducted by the alienating parent; child involved in false allegations of sex abuse; little or no contact with the target parent for a period of several years or more.

Alienation is the process by which the child's love for the other parent is extinguished and replaced by an attitude of reflexive hostility. Reconciliation is the process of reversing alienation and becoming open to the relationship once more.

Some severely alienated children eventually seek out the target parent on their own and are able to reconcile, but little is known about how often this occurs. Gardner (2001b) conducted a follow-up study of 99 PAS children in which spontaneous reconciliation appears to have occurred in four of 77 cases, or 5 percent. Stuart-Mills-Hoch & Hoch (2003) estimated that spontaneous reconciliation occurred in 10 percent of severe PAS cases. This chapter provides numerous case examples with this type of positive outcome, as well as descriptions of failed reconciliation attempts, and worst-case scenarios.

Case reports from published sources, and from our own work over the last 30 years are used to explore the factors associated with reconciliation of the child and target parent in severe PAS. The published cases were drawn from the professional and popular literature, including books, articles in journals and magazines, and newsletters of nonprofit organizations. The vignettes designated "case known to authors" are based on the accounts of parents, children, and colleagues we have encountered over the years. They were disguised in accordance with the Publication Manual of the American Psychological Association (2001).

In the 1970s, we were fortunate enough to interface professionally with Wallerstein, Kelly, and Johnston, as their research on children of divorce was getting underway in Marin County, California. This exposure stimulated our interest in high-conflict divorce and interventions that enable children to have relationships with both parents. We learned about parental alienation in the 1980s, when Gardner began writing about PAS. In the 1990s, interventions with severe PAS families became a focal point of our work. The reunification protocol we follow involves the whole family, including the alienating parent. Children who have successfully reconciled with the target parent after participating in our brief, intensive intervention (4 days on average), typically feel that the alienating parent would benefit from the program as well. It all comes back to the idea that children of divorce, like children within intact families, need both parents.

MATURATION AND RECONCILIATION

Normal child development calls for an expanding circle of attachments as the child grows older. This facilitates emancipation from the original biological family at the end of adolescence, so the child can form a new family of their own, have offspring, and launch another generation (Kopetski, 1991). Maturation, and the drive for independence and emancipation, appear to be important factors in facilitating reconciliation in some cases.

In normal intact families, the parents provide support and encouragement for the child to emancipate in late adolescence. Children in severe PAS scenarios must cope with a complicated, problematic family situation which can make emancipation difficult. Often, the alienating parent encourages the child to remain dependent and enmeshed. The target parent has an important role to play in supporting independence and emancipation. If the target parent is perceived as the enemy, or physical access to that parent is cut off, the child is robbed of an important resource for successfully making the transition into young adulthood. In several of the cases presented here, the target parent played an active role in helping the child emancipate after graduating from high school or college. Similarly, the target parent was sometimes able to help the child overcome problems with delinquency and school failure in adolescence.

Children who remain dependent and enmeshed with the alienating parent into adulthood may be at risk for re-enacting PAS with their own children. Gordon (1998) described a case in which PAS was passed down through three generations of women who alienated their children from the father. Baker (2005a) reported on two women who were alienated from their fathers, who subsequently lost their own children to their mothers. In Baker's study, fully half the participants who had children of their own reported being alienated from their children.

TRIGGER EVENTS

Trigger events are life events that provide an impetus for the child to reconcile with the target parent, causing the child's attitude towards the target parent to change rather suddenly. Common trigger events include: serious illness or a death in the family; being rejected by the alienating parent; milestones such as graduation from high school or college, getting married or having a child. Remarriage of a parent or child can be a trigger event for reconciliation, or for alienation, depending on the circumstances (Warshak, 2000). Occasionally, reconciliation is triggered by an unforeseen, idiosyncratic event, as in the case of the 18-year-old boy who reconciled with his father after reading in the papers that his father had been exonerated in a criminal trial (Case #27, Gardner, 2001b).

RECONCILIATION IN ADULTHOOD

It appears that some children emancipate from the alienator, then reconcile with the target parent within a year or two. Once children are in their twenties, reconciliation may be more difficult. The lives of parent and child have diverged even further, and alienation may become the status quo. Rebuilding the parent-child relationship when the child is an adult requires commitment and patience. The process is fragile, and vulnerable to breaking down. The desire of parent and child to reconcile must be strong enough to work through the powerful emotions which stand in the way, such as fear, anger, and guilt.

The story Cecilie Finkelstein's reconciliation with her mother exemplifies the hard work required for the child and target parent to rebuild their relationship. Cecilie was abducted by her father at age four (Stasio, 2001). She saw her mother a few times in the years to follow, but mostly she was on the run with her father. Right before her eighteenth birthday, she got up the courage to call her mother. "I was terrified when I picked up the phone and said 'Hello, this is your daughter calling.' Neither of us was in any way prepared for how difficult it was going to be. At one point, we almost gave up" (Finkelstein, 1999a, p. 6).

Sometimes, the child seeks to reunite with the target parent, but the results are disappointing, as in the case of Kirk's relationship with his father (Wallerstein & Blakeslee, 1989). The mother was reportedly outraged by the divorce, coaching the children to say they hated their father and did not want to see him. In adolescence, Kirk tried reaching out to his father. His father responded positively, but Kirk was disappointed in what his father had to offer. As a young man in his twenties, Kirk's relationship with his father was still attenuated. Kirk was described as haunted with guilt for having driven his father away and longing for his father's forgiveness. He blamed everything that had gone wrong in his life on his mother, but remained strongly dependent on her.

The case vignettes in the section titled "Reconciliation in the Twenties and Beyond" provide examples of children who reconciled with the target parent in adulthood, anywhere from age 20 to 47. Some children were able to reconcile with the target parent after being separated for up to 40 years. According to Baker, one of the participants in her study told her that the moment he met his father for the first time in 40 years "he could feel the hole in his soul closing" Baker, in press, p. 22). These reports suggest that the parent-child bond may be quite resilient in some cases.

WORST-CASE SCENARIOS

Target parents are sometimes advised to "let go" in the hopes that the child will seek them out someday. The assumption is that the child and target parent will go on living, and that there will be enough time. However, this is not always the case. The premature death of a parent or child may foreclose the option of reconciliation and leave the alienation forever unresolved. It is painful enough when the death is caused by a fatal accident or illness. In worst-case scenarios, the death may be linked to the divorce, or to the alienation itself.

We are aware of five cases, four of them published, in which children who had been alienated from a parent committed suicide, usually in late adolescence (Baker, 2005a; Finkelstein, 2001; Smith, 1991; Villemure, 1992). Two of these adolescents wanted desperately to reunite with the lost parent but got into a row with the alienating parent and killed themselves. A young woman of 17 wrote to her therapist, "Last night, my mom and I got in a big fight and she told me Dad had committed suicide. I feel so bad. I'm to blame, because I lied [about molestation] for my mom" (Smith, 1991, p. 203). The young woman killed herself the next day. Villemure reported that a young woman was so overcome with remorse for having rejected her mother that she killed herself at 18. Finkelstein referred to a 17-year-old abducted boy who was not able to reunite with the left-behind parent. Reportedly, the young man committed suicide, saying that he just could not take it anymore. According to Baker, a woman in her study risked her life to return to the home of the alienating father in order to rescue her younger siblings from the father's violent abuse. Reportedly, she was able to escape with all but one, a young man who subsequently committed suicide.

We are aware of seven cases, several of them published, in which a parent committed suicide as a result of being alienated from their child, or forced to be physically separated (Cross, 2000; Johnston & Roseby, 1997; Smith, 1991; Warshak, 2003). The despair of these parents has been poignantly described.

> The tragic suicide of a father in one of our studies could have been prevented if the court had taken the trouble to tell him that its decision to give him once-a-month visitation with his daughter, when he was asking for joint custody, was not based on his capacity to be a loving father to his little girl but on the needs of a very vulnerable toddler to have protection from horrendous ongoing disputes that neither he nor his wife could control. This socially isolated, emotionally troubled man, whose entire identity hinged upon his fatherhood, clearly interpreted the court's judgment as a devastating indictment of his worth as a parent and a human being. (Johnston & Roseby, 1997, pp. 11–12)

In a case known to the authors, the alienated mother first attempted suicide after her ex-husband told her she would never see her children again. The father gained primary custody. The children began treating their mother more and more cruelly. The children were their mother's whole life, and she was devastated. In response to one of their hateful messages, the mother killed herself. Gardner (2001b) was profoundly moved by the depth of grief that target parents expressed to him. Their grief was ongoing and could not be resolved because the child was still alive. Life for these parents was a "living death."

We know of no completed suicides by an alienating parent who was bereft over the loss of the child. However, we are aware of several cases in which the alienating parent threatened to commit suicide if the child sought to reconcile with the target parent. A case report in Cross (2000) describes an alienating father who threatened suicide in front of the children when the mother left him. According to the mother, when her ex-husband was unsuccessful in winning her back, he alienated the children from her.

Occasionally, one hears news reports of an embittered parent who takes homicidal revenge on their estranged spouse, sometimes killing the children as well.

PROS AND CONS OF "LETTING NATURE TAKE ITS COURSE"

The experts are divided on the issue of taking a "hands-off" approach to PAS versus active interventions such as enforced visitation with the target parent, or placing the child in target parent custody. The worst-case scenarios demonstrate that dangers exist in "letting nature take its course."

Contributors such as Clawar and Rivlin (1991), Gardner (2001b), and Rand et al. (2005) tend to favor an active approach, based on their research and experience with interventions in severe cases. These experts recognize that spontaneous reconciliation occurs in a small number of severe cases. However, they have observed a greater number of cases in which alienation persisted well into adulthood, and was never resolved.

Wallerstein argues that there are great advantages in allowing natural maturation to take its course (Wallerstein et al. 2000). "We see that many children of divorce are stronger for their struggles. . . . They think of themselves as survivors who have learned to rely on their own judgment and to take responsibility for themselves and others at a young age." This may true in some cases. However, it is important to note that Wallerstein's views have been shaped by her research with children of divorce from nonlitigating, "normal" families who she has followed over the years (Wallerstein & Kelly, 1980; Wallerstein et al. 2000).

Baker interviewed adults alienated as children for their perspective (Baker, in press). The majority reported feeling bad about themselves and suffering from significant episodes of depression in their adult lives. One-third had experienced serious problems with drugs and/or alcohol at some point. One-third reported difficulties in trusting themselves and others. Two-thirds had been divorced more than once. Half of the 28 participants who were parents had been alienated from their own children. Some participants chose not to have children to avoid being rejected by them. According to Baker, all of the participants were aware that they had been manipulated by the alienating parent to turn against the other parent. This realization was the beginning of reclaiming the lost parent and the part of themselves that loved that parent. Not surprisingly, some participants harbored anger and bitterness over the lost time with the alienated parent.

Wallerstein's study of nonlitigating "normal" families led her to assert, "Not one alliance [with the alienating parent] lasted through adolescence and most crumbled within a year or two" (Wallerstein et al. 2000, p. 116). It turns out this is not quite true, however. According to Wallerstein, a young man named Larry, who had aligned with his angry father in adolescence, did not reconcile with his mother until young adulthood. Larry's story is more consistent with that of the severe PAS families who have been the focus of those contributors who are in favor of active intervention. Baker's study was made up of participants from severe scenarios, who were separated from the target parent from 7 to 47 years before reconciling (Baker, 2005).

Several of the cases in this chapter support Wallerstein's views. The majority do not. Maturation was often a factor in the child seeking out the rejected parent, but it was not the only factor. "Letting nature take its course" led to outcomes which were extremely variable. Even when the child and target parent were fully reconciled, there was a residual sadness over the loss of the missing years. As one young woman described it: "My father and I have lost so much time. Ordinarily routine moments that will never occur again. Today when I see my father we follow a pattern of behavior dictated by those lost moments. We feel awkward with one another, groveling for words and clumsy hugs. We then try to get close again" (Conigliari, 1999, p. 2).

MAINTAINING CONTACT

According to some contributors, an appropriate remedy for severe PAS may be to recommend that the target parent "let go" and end their efforts to maintain a relationship with their child (Lee & Olesen, 2001; Sullivan & Kelly, 2001). Sullivan and Kelly suggest having a "good-bye" session in which the rejected parent tells the child that they are no longer going to fight to restore the relationship, even though the parent loves the child and hopes they can be together again some day. To evaluate the efficacy of this approach, it is helpful to consider the consequences in the cases presented here in which target parents made their own decision to "let go."

Sullivan and Kelly go on to suggest that "It is advantageous for the parent to give the child the same message in writing as well as in person" (p. 313). The question is, advantageous to whom? According to Stuart-Mills-Hoch & Hoch (2003):

> The concept of the "good-bye" letter is a convenient invention of us adults who like tidy endings, and of those professionals who collapse, exhausted by these severe cases and want to see a clean ending for judicial reasons. But no matter what we, as adults, may *think* we say in a good-bye letter, no matter how many caveats we put into it, the child sees this as yet more evidence that we have abandoned him or her, just as they were usually told by the alienator. (p. 13)

A young woman who reconciled with her mother in adulthood is quoted as saying, "Mum, if you'd written me such a letter, I'd never have had the courage to pick up the phone and call you. Your consistent message was always that you loved me. . . . No matter what you'd have said in such a letter, I'd have seen it as you turning your back on me forever" (p. 13).

The alienated parents interviewed by Vassiliou and Cartwright (2001) felt it was important to send the child cards, letters and small gifts from time to time, even if the items were returned and the child complained bitterly. In our work, we have learned that adult children who reconciled often treasured these gestures, albeit secretly. Many of the participants in Baker's study described holding onto good feelings about the target parent deep inside them (Baker, in press).

The participants in Baker's study who had been alienated from their children sent cards and letters on a regular basis, and found ways of memorializing their love for their children, such as creating a photo album depicting the fun times, or creating a website for the child, in case the son might wish to contact his father at some point (Baker, 2005). Most of these rejected parents were fathers. They knew what it was like to lose a father and were determined to do whatever they could to ease the pain in their children's lives. In our experience, keeping photos, creating websites, and even writing poems for the child, have turned out to be very meaningful during the reconciliation process, providing the child with concrete evidence that the rejected parent never stopped loving them.

LITERATURE REVIEW

Professional Literature

The professional literature offers surprisingly little discussion of parent-child reconciliation. Traditionally, clinicians and divorce researchers have equated "reconciliation" with children's fantasies about their parents getting back together (Wallerstein & Kelly, 1980; Gardner, 1989; Johnston & Roseby, 1997). More information can be gleaned from the popular literature, where reconciliation accounts can be found in books, magazines, and newsletters, as well as accounts on the Web.

Gardner (2001a) sought to focus attention on reconciliation between the child and target parent by devoting a chapter to this in his book on therapeutic interventions for PAS children. Gardner observed that some children were successfully alienated in a surprisingly short period, and that reconciliation sometimes occurred in a brief time as well. He cited the case of young Elian Gonzales, whose affection for his father returned within hours of the two being reunited. It was Gardner's experience that adolescents who reconciled with the target parent typically resumed a normal level of involvement, without acknowledging the hostility and allegations that may have been expressed previously.

Baker is a developmental psychologist and professional researcher. She conducted interviews with 40 adults alienated as children in order to explore the processes by which the children came to realize that the alienating parent with whom they were aligned had been manipulating them against the other parent (Baker, 2005). Potential subjects were screened to determine whether alienation was due at least in part to the behaviors and attitudes of the aligned parent. People who reported being abandoned by a parent, and who had no reason to believe that one parent had caused the other to leave, were not included. At the time of the interviews, all of Baker's subjects had come to the realization that one parent had been manipulating the child to reject the other parent, and using the child to gratify the alienator's own needs for revenge, control, or emotional satisfaction. The adults alienated as children that Baker interviewed clearly recognized the power of the alienating parent's influence, contrary to Johnston's thesis that "both parents are to blame" (Johnston, 2003).

In analyzing the interview transcripts for each participant, Baker identified 11 different pathways by which adults alienated as children had come to the painful realization that the alienating parent had been exploiting them: (1) maturation; (2) alienating parent turned against participant; (3) participant experienced alienation from their own children; (4) target parent returned; (5) attaining a milestone; (6) therapy; (7) intervention of extended family; (8) intervention of significant other; (9) seeing the alienating parent treat others badly; (10) child caught the alienator in a significant lie; and (11) parenthood.

The experts agree on the critical need for research on what happens to the PAS child's relationship with both parents in the long-term. Gardner (2001b) responded to this need by conducting a follow-up study of 99 PAS children titled "Should Courts Order PAS Children to Visit/Reside With the Alienated Parent?" A statistically significant difference was found between two intervention groups. In one, the target parent was given custody and/or the alienator's access was reduced. In the other, the court took a "hands-off" approach and "no change" was ordered. The children in the first group maintained a relationship with the target parent and their PAS symptoms were reduced. Of the children in the second group, where "no change" was ordered, 91 percent did not have contact with the target parent at follow-up. Reading the case vignettes, it appears that there were four cases of spontaneous reconciliation involving adolescents with moderate to severe PAS (Cases #27, #28, #85, #96).

Rand et al. (2005) conducted a follow-up study of 45 PAS children from Kopetski's practice as a custody evaluator in Colorado. The study examined the efficacy of various evaluator recommendations for interrupting parental alienation toward the severe end of the spectrum. The children were divided into three outcome groups: interrupted alienation, completed alienation, and mixed outcome. The child's adjustment and relationship with both parents at evaluation and follow-up were compared.

Alienation was interrupted for 20 children who had enforced visitation with the target parent, or were placed in target parent custody. These children maintained relationships with both parents unless the alienator was too disturbed. Sometimes, interrupting alienation for one child in the family paved the way for an alienated sibling to reconcile with the target parent when they were older, illustrating the role of "bridge" relationships in facilitating reconciliation (Warshak, 2001; Baker, 2005).

Fourteen children were found to be completely alienated at follow-up. In these cases, the alienating parent had custody going into the evaluation and retained custody afterward, for one reason or another. Therapy and gradually increased visitation with the target parent were usually ordered, but the alienating parent readily sabotaged such orders and the child lost one parent in the divorce.

The mixed outcome group was comprised of 5 families with 11 children between them. These were cases in which alienation was interrupted for at least one child in the family, and for one family with an only child, who had an attenuated relationship with the target father at follow-up. Of the five children for whom alienation was interrupted, two had been placed in the custody of the target mother when they were younger. Three were older children who were supposed to have enforced visitation with the target mother, but who visited at will. Of the remaining children, three had an attenuated relationship with the target parent at follow-up. Three remained alienated into adulthood, including a man who distanced himself from both parents.

Popular Literature

Two books written by alienated mothers were found in the popular literature, *Icebound* (Nielsen & Vollers, 2001) and *Lost Children* (Cross, 2000). According to Nielsen, she made the decision to leave her children with their father when she left the marriage, rather than put them through a contentious custody battle. She took a job as the physician at the South Pole Research Station. The station was snowed in when she discovered she had breast cancer. The daring rescue mission that saved her life made national headlines. According to Nielsen, her ex-husband told reporters that she made up the story about breast cancer to get attention. Her oldest daughter was quoted as saying she that did not care about what happened to her mother.

Lost Children gives the poignant account of an alienated mother whose oldest son was reportedly living with his father when he died at 22, leaving a will that banned his mother and her relatives from coming to his funeral. The book contains the stories of eleven other mothers who were alienated from their children. This is a unique and much-needed contribution, since much of the literature on target parents has been about fathers.

Voice of the River is the autobiographical account of Marjory Stoneman Douglas (1987), who led the crusade to save the Everglades by turning them into a national park. Douglas was alienated from her father as a child. Her father reached out to her through his brother when the man she married tried to get money from her father by fraud.

Several reconciliation accounts were found in popular magazines. The story of Cecilie Finkelstein's reconciliation with her mother appeared in *Ladies Home Journal* (Stasio, 2001). *Reader's Digest* featured an article about an abducted boy who was recovered in adolescence and reconciled with his father (Ryan, 2002). *Coup de Pouce*, a French-Canadian magazine, published an award-winning article about a mother's fight to get her children back after their father abducted them (Villemure, 1992). The four children were severely alienated when they were recovered. The mother was reportedly given custody of the younger two. She took them to a battered women's shelter. At first, the children screamed hysterically if their mother touched them. Staff and residents at the shelter provided support while the mother worked with the children and, after several weeks, she was able to take the younger children home. It appears that the two older children remained alienated into adulthood.

Joe Seldner's story, "My Fight to Keep my Kids," was published in *Parents Magazine* (Seldner, 2000). The children were reportedly nine and six at the time of the divorce. Seldner describes how his daughter arrived for a visit one day, then called the police to say that he had molested her. He was thrown in jail. Seldner reported that he was eventually cleared of the charges and awarded sole custody, but his ex-wife got the venue changed to another state. Again, he was awarded custody. According to Seldner, the children were 16 and 13 when he finally got his relationship with them worked out.

Cecilie Finkelstein, who reconciled with her mother in late adolescence, founded a self-help newsletter, *The Link*, featuring personal accounts by abducted children and left-behind parents. The story of Ruth Langel is about Cecilie's father's first wife (Finkelstein, 1999b). According to the account, the father abducted the children from his first marriage, but was allowed to keep them. The article suggests that this empowered him to abduct Cecilie, the child of his second marriage.

The *ADVO Newsletter* (2001), published by "America's Looking for Its Missing Children Program," featured an article describing a brother and sister who were reunited with their father after their mother abducted them. The father's letter of gratitude to ADVO was also printed. "Thank you all so much for helping me to find my children . . . and for helping them adjust back to a regular life and reuniting them with their grandparents and others who loved and missed them so much when absent from our lives" (p. 4). This story highlights the fact that the child loses not only the target parent, but the extended family on that side. From the family's perspective, aunts, uncles and cousins miss out, as well as grandparents, who are unable to be part of their grandchildren's lives.

Maxine Berry's story was found in the *FMS Foundation Newsletter* (Berry & Berry, 2001), as was the account of a man who reconciled with his father in his thirties "One family's journey. . . ."

The story of Aric Austin was posted on the website for the National Center for Missing and Exploited Children (2005).

> In December 1981, 6-month-old Aric Austin was kidnapped by his noncustodial father. His heartbroken mother and law enforcement searched for him but with no success . . . in 2003, Special Agent Colleen Maher . . . investigated a man for falsifying government-secured student loans for his son. . . . She compared dates of birth, weights, and heights from the birth certificate with those on NCMEC'S online missing-kids database and found Aric Austin. . . . More than 20 years after Aric's abduction, he and his mother were reunited.

Aric Austin's father told him his mother was dead. When Aric learned that his mother was alive, he wanted a relationship with her.

Barbara Kurth's struggle for a relationship with her daughters, recounted in an ABC News report, resulted in heartbreak (Huang, 1998). According to the report, the girls were abducted by their father at a young age and told that their mother was dead. When the girls were located 20 years later, they learned that their mother was alive. However, they did not want anything to do with her.

Maria Conigliari's account of her estrangement from her father, and her reconciliation with him in late adolescence, was posted on a list serve for divorced fathers. According to Conigliari (1999), her parents divorced when she was six. Her father acquiesced to mother having custody. She recalls being told by her mother what a lousy father she had. According to Conigliari, he was "constantly served and arrested at work because he was unable to meet the [support] payments." She missed her father, but was not allowed to speak of it. Between 16 and 17, Conigliari underwent therapy, prompted by bouts of depression and an unending feeling of loneliness, as well a problem with drugs. The therapy helped her to grieve the lost years with her father and have a normal life, in which her father was included.

ALIENATED CHILDREN WHO CHOSE TO LIVE WITH THE TARGET PARENT IN ADOLESCENCE

Case Examples From the Literature

Two boys from different families, **Rich** and **Brian**, chose to live with the target mother in early adolescence, when the boys developed problems with delinquency and school failure (Rand et al. 2005). In both cases, the alienating father had won the custody battle, with enforced visitation for the mother. The older siblings did not comply and the mothers gave them permission not to visit. Rich moved out of state with his mother when she remarried. He was rejected by his father, but enjoyed being part of the new family with his mother and stepfather. At follow-up, he was back on track and expected to graduate from high school. Brian was working and getting his GED at follow-up. Key factors: prior orders for enforced visitation with target mother; visits gave child an opportunity to develop a good postdivorce with mother; mother's psychological functioning improved after the divorce; adolescent drive for independence.

Dave decided to move in with the target father upon learning that his father had been exonerated in a criminal trial because of the father's refusal to pay alimony while the children were alienated from him (Case #27, Gardner, 2001b). At 18, Dave had a growing awareness of the mother's programming, but the acquittal in the criminal trial served as the trigger event for reconciliation. Dave's younger sister reconciled with her father the next day (Case #28). Key factors: maturity; boy's realization that mother had been keeping him from father; trigger event/father's acquittal; father's willingness to take a stand and risk going to jail sent a powerful message that a relationship with his children was important to him.

Case Examples Known to the Authors

Steve was alienated from his father after his mother won the contentious custody battle. When he was in mid-adolescence, his mother had a psychotic break and was hospitalized. He managed to locate his father and went to live with him. Steve had difficulty feeling close to his father because of the mother's accusations against him. However, he developed warm relationships with his father's extended family. Steve emancipated, went off to college, and maintained relationships with both parents. Key factors: trigger event/alienator's psychotic episode; necessity for an adult caretaker; father available and receptive; support of father's extended family.

JoAnn's mother sought a divorce when the children were young because of domestic violence by the father, who was a relentless alienator. JoAnn was severely alienated by age 9 and went to live with her father. She moved back in with her mother in adolescence, after her father hit her during an argument. JoAnn emancipated, graduated from college and got married. Her relationship with her mother remained attenuated. However, she was close to members of the extended family on both sides. Key factors: child's realization that alienating father was motivated by revenge; alienator's abusive behavior; mother available and receptive; support of extended family.

Helen's mother had primary custody following the divorce. The father came to pick up the children one day and they were gone. The father was able to locate them within a month. He gained custody of Helen's older brothers. Helen remained living with her mother by stipulated agreement. At 17, Helen wanted to try living with her father. The father came home from work one day to find that Helen had moved back in with her mother. Helen married and had children but remained completely alienated from her father. Key factors: child remained enmeshed with alienating mother; child ambivalent about relationship with father and disliked his stricter parenting style; Helen's step towards independence was undermined by secret contact with the mother while Helen was at her father's.

Tim was young when his parents divorced. The father agreed that the mother should retain custody. The mother had been inculcating separation anxiety in her son from the time he was born, a pattern that continued into adolescence. The mother arranged a few visits with the father over the years. The father did not force visitation. At 16, Tim decided that he needed to live with his father for a year and get to know him. Tim had never spent an overnight away from his mother's home, not even at a friend's house. He was terrified and guilt-ridden over leaving his mother. However, his mother accepted her son's decision. Tim became close to his father. He emancipated and went on to pursue a distinguished career. He maintained good relationships with both parents. Key factors: maturity; father's sensitivity in not forcing visitation; less pressure for alienation from mother; adolescent drive for independence.

CHILDREN WHO EMANCIPATED AND SOUGHT TO RECONCILE SOON AFTER

Case Examples From the Literature

Larry took the side of his angry, alcoholic father in the divorce and treated his mother hatefully (Wallerstein et al. 2000). As an adolescent, he became involved in drugs and violent behavior. He harangued his mother about wanting to live with his father until she gave in. When Larry called his father to make the arrangements, his father rejected him. Larry continued blaming his mother for all his problems until he was 19, when he entered into a 12-step recovery program and made amends to her. Key factors: alienating father rejected Larry; maturation; participation in a 12-step program; mother's willingness to accept Larry's amends for his abusive treatment of her.

Cecilie Finkelstein was abducted by her father at age four. She emancipated from her father at 16, when caring adults persuaded her to leave him. Another family took her in while she finished high school. Cecilie waited until she was 18 to call her mother, in part because she was worried that her father might go to jail. According to Cecilie, letting her mother into her life was hard because it meant accepting that what her father had done was terribly wrong. Mother and daughter's efforts to rebuild their relationship were fraught with difficulty. They sought therapy individually and together. According to Cecilie, "My mom and I are really close today. She is one of the most wonderful people I have ever met, and I'm honored to be her daughter" (Finkelstein, 1999a, p. 7). Key factors: caring adults facilitated early emancipation from the alienating father; curiosity about mother; child needed mother in her life; commitment of mother and daughter to rebuilding their relationship; insight and support gained through therapy.

Irene was the older of two siblings who were severely alienated from their father (Case #96, Gardner, 2001b). As part of the custody battle, the mother abducted the children. After two years of alienation, the court ordered that the children should go into therapy. The mother successfully sabotaged this. Irene reached a point when she could no longer tolerate the conditions in her mother's home. Reportedly, the mother brought home a series of boyfriends, with episodes of domestic violence which necessitated police intervention. After living apart from her mother for a year, Irene began to realize that her mother had been indoctrinating her to hate her father. When she was 18, she called her father and they began to reconcile. Key factors: maturity; intolerable living conditions in alienating mother's home; living apart from alienator for a year; father's receptivity.

Case Examples Known to the Authors

When **Ron** reached early adolescence, he became increasingly rejecting of the target father and refused to visit. His father decided to "let go." The mother remarried. Ron did not get along with his stepfather. When he was 18, he got into an argument with his stepfather and moved out. A few months later, he reconciled with his father. The father encouraged his son to enroll in college, and to choose his direction in life. Key factors: maturity; bad relationship with alienating mother's new husband; close relationship with father growing up; father's receptivity; son needed his father, who supported his emancipation.

Vincent's mother was so antagonistic to the father having a relationship with the children that the father "let go" at the time of the divorce. In late adolescence, Vincent sought to emancipate from his mother by joining a violent, totalistic group. Soon after joining the group, Vincent contacted his father. The father was open to reestablishing a relationship with his son. Father was remarried and his current wife was supportive. Their two daughters were thrilled to discover that they had a half-brother. Father and son began reconciling. Vincent left the totalistic group after six months and moved back in with his mother. His contact with his father became sporadic, then ceased all together. Key factors: drive for independence in late adolescence; father and his current family receptive; Vincent remained enmeshed with his mother and was ambivalent about his father.

RECONCILIATION IN THE TWENTIES AND BEYOND

Case Examples From the Literature

Aric Austin was abducted as an infant by his father. His mother never stopped searching. She maintained regular contact with the caseworker at the National Center for Missing Children (NCMEC, 2005). When the authorities located Aric, NCMEC coordinated the reunion of Aric and his mother with the arrest of Aric's father for defrauding the government. NCMEC also provided an intervention specialist to facilitate the mother-son reunion. Aric's father had told him his mother was dead. Aric had not internalized the alienation and was thrilled to learn that his mother was alive. Brothers and sisters whom Aric never knew existed flew in from around the country for the reunion. Though Aric had never known his mother and siblings, the family felt immediately at home together. Key factors: trigger event/abducting father arrested; mother never stopped searching; Aric did not believe his mother was dead and wanted to find her; alienation not internalized; NCMEC's role in facilitating reunification; support of siblings and other relatives.

Pete aligned himself with his mother in the divorce and she retained custody of him (Rand et al. 2005). The younger siblings rejected the father as well, but the court placed them in his custody. The father continued to reach out to his oldest son. The young man was still living with his mother when he graduated from college and decided to reconcile with his father. The father helped his son to find an apartment and emancipate from his mother. For the first time since the divorce, Pete told his father that he loved him. Key factors: milestone/graduating from college; younger siblings had good relationship with father; father continued to reach out; son needed his father, who was able to help his son emancipate.

Marjory Stoneman Douglas (1987) was alienated from her father as a child. She was close to her mentally ill mother, and raised by her mother's family. Marjory's mother died of cancer while Marjory was in college. Marjory married a prominent newspaper editor. Her husband wrote to her father and tried to get money from him by fraud. Her father realized that Marjory's husband was engaged in illegal financial schemes. The father reached out to Marjory through his brother. Her father helped her get a divorce and she went to live with him in Florida. Marjory was at her father's bedside when he died at 84. Key factors: trigger event/husband tried to defraud father; father reached out when his daughter needed his help; father's brother provided a "bridge"; less pressure for alienation because mother was dead; alienation not internalized.

Maxine grew up in the custody of her mother, who opposed the father having contact with her (Berry & Berry, 2001). When the father expressed his desire to attend his daughter's high school graduation, the mother enrolled Maxine in therapy, ostensibly to deal with the stress of seeing her father. The therapist pressed Maxine to recover memories of sex abuse by her father. Maxine broke down under the pressure and had to be psychiatrically hospitalized. She had her tubes tied so she would not have children and repeat the cycle of abuse. With the support of her husband and primary care physician, Maxine eventually realized that her memories were false and filed a suit for malpractice. The suit brought to light the mother's manipulation of mental health professionals to convince Maxine that she had been sexually abused by her father. Eight years after her high school graduation, Maxine wrote, "I am thankful that I have had the opportunity to meet my father twice (p. 9)." Key factors: Maxine discovered mother's elaborate deception; support of Maxine's husband and primary care physician; father's receptivity.

Greg was raised by his father until the age of 15, when he wanted to try living with his mother (One family's journey . . ., 2001). For the next 18 years, Greg was alienated from his father. He made several attempts to reach out to his father, but without success. The son wrote to inform his father of his sister's fatal illness. He did not expect a response and was shocked when his father called him. They began e-mailing back and forth and talked on the phone for hours. Reconciliation was achieved in a matter of weeks. Key factors: trigger event/sister's illness; son made multiple attempts to reconcile; strong bond with father growing up; commitment of father and son to rebuilding their relationship.

Denise's mother refused to let her father visit after the parents separated when Denise was five (Gordon, 1998). By the time the court ordered joint custody, Denise had been programmed by the mother to hate her father and refused to go with him. Her father decided to "let go." In her mid-thirties, Denise sought therapy for depression, anxiety, and intimacy problems with men (Gordon, 1998). Denise came to realize how her mother had distorted her father to her. After five years of analytic treatment, Denise fell in love with a kind and reasonable man. She contacted her father, reconciled with him, and the two of them rebuilt their relationship. Key factors: Denise was having psychological problems and needed help; insight and support gained through therapy; father receptive; father and daughter committed to rebuilding their relationship.

Case Examples Known to the Authors

Liz's father maintained a secret pact with her that she would come to live him when she was 14. As a result, Liz had an attenuated relationship with her mother, even though her mother had primary custody. Liz ran away to her father's at the appointed time and he filed for a change of custody. After protracted litigation, the court ordered joint custody and increased Liz's time with her father to 50 percent. Reunification therapy for Liz and her mother was ordered, but their relationship remained badly attenuated. The father provided Liz with liquor and encouraged her use of drugs. Liz spent a year in residential treatment for substance abuse. When Liz was a senior in college, she began seeing a therapist who helped her see that she was repeating her parents' mistakes and on her way to a derailed and unsatisfying adulthood. Liz realized she could make better choices and her relationship with her mother improved. Key factors: Liz continued to have psychological problems in adulthood and needed help; insight and support gained through therapy; realization that father's constant gratifying of her impulses was for his benefit, not hers; mother continued to reach out.

Wayne was a good father until he developed bipolar disorder. His wife left him, and the children wanted nothing to do with their father. Wayne responded well to Lithium. He was able to return to work full-time. Wayne took what he had learned about having a mental illness and used it to help others, advocating for the mentally ill and founding self-help groups. The son was attending college when he called his father. The son wanted money towards his tuition. They met and Wayne gave his son $3,000. After a few brief contacts, his son disappeared. Wayne's children declined to attend the memorial service for their father when he died many years later. Key factors: alienation justified by target father's bipolar disorder; children not motivated to have a relationship with their father; son contacted father because he wanted money and felt entitled.

When **Bea's** parents divorced, Bea and her brother were articulate teens obsessed with hatred of their mother. Their father broke the law and violated court orders but the children were deemed too old and too alienated to be placed with their mother. Bea continued to live with her father into adulthood. One day they had an argument and he told her to get out. Bea went to live with a friend's family. After living apart from her father for a year, Bea called her mother to reconcile. "It was as if the 'I love my mother' switch suddenly turned on," Bea recalls. "I felt an amazing sense of relief." Bea did not resume contact with her father until she felt strong enough to deal with his anger. Key factors: maturity; father's anger; strong bond with mother growing up; mother continued to reach out; support of close friends.

Frank had a close relationship with his father until adolescence, when he aligned himself with his mother, not realizing that she was mentally ill. Frank was in his twenties when he reached out and reconciled with his father. He wrote an autobiography for his father in which he described what it was like trying to separate from his mother:

> From the time I graduated from high school, I felt very alone in the world and knew that I would have to fend for myself. The only family members I had at that time were my mother and younger siblings, who were of no help to me emotionally, spiritually, or financially. Nor were they self-sufficient. I realized that if I didn't make a change, Mom was going to continue to live off of me for the rest of my life or hers, whichever expired first. It wasn't until later in life that I learned of Mom's involvement with many of my relationship problems.

Key factors: maturity; realization that alienating mother was ruining his life; Frank's ability to be self-reliant; son reached out to father and father receptive.

Ed's children were in their twenties and thirties when they decided it was time to reconcile with their father. The children liked his new wife, who had reached out to them. Their mother, too, was about to remarry. According to Ed, the mother excluded his involvement with the children even when they were married. Following the divorce, he saw the children for a few hours at Christmas. They could not wait to leave. Ed says it is taking time to rebuild his relationship with his children. He described the first Thanksgiving they spent together in years as full of laughter and affection, the way holidays are supposed to be. Key factors: alienating mother about to remarry; pressure for alienation was less; father remarried and children liked their stepmother.

Sylvia's mother put up so much resistance to her daughter having visitation with the father that he "let go" when Sylvia was seven. Forty years later, Sylvia sought to reconcile with her father when she was diagnosed with cancer. Her father was receptive as was his current wife, who became a second mother to Sylvia. Sylvia was welcomed by her father's extended family, whom she never knew existed. She learned from her father and stepmother that she had a half-sister, whom her mother had put up for adoption. Sylvia's mother refused to give her any information that would help her find her sister. Sylvia responded well to the cancer treatment. She and her fiancé proceeded with their plans to marry. The wedding was held in her father's garden. He was proud that his daughter wanted him to give the bride away. Key factors: trigger event/child's illness; child needed emotional support; biological mother emotionally unavailable; alienation not internalized; father and stepmother were receptive; support of Sylvia's husband and father and stepmother's extended families.

DISCUSSION

Factors for Children who Reconciled in Adolescence

Factors which facilitated reconciliation in cases where the child chose to live with the target parent in adolescence included: trigger events; mental illness or physical abuse by alienating parent; child needed help from the target parent; maturity; child came to realize that the alienating parent was manipulating them against the other parent; prior orders for enforced visitation enabled child to develop a good postdivorce relationship with the target mother (Rich, Brian); desire for a relationship with the target parent. Helen's fledging effort at independence failed because she was still enmeshed with her mother and felt ambivalent about her father.

It is not easy for a severely alienated child to become independent of the alienating parent, especially in adolescence. There needs to be a strong motivation for the adolescent to cope with the burden of guilt, and to risk the alienator's anger and rejection. In the cases presented here, the motivation came from a combination of the alienating parent's bad behavior, and the strength of the adolescent's need or desire for the target parent and what that parent had to offer.

Children who Emancipated and Reconciled Soon After

The factors involved when children emancipated from the alienating parent in late adolescence and reconciled with the target parent soon after included: maturity; curiosity about the target parent; intolerable living conditions in the alienator's home; rejection by the alienating parent; living apart from the alienator for awhile; close relationship with the target parent prior to the divorce; child assumed (correctly) that the parent would be receptive; child needed target parent's support for emancipation; commitment of alienated parent and child to rebuilding their relationship; support of family and friends; insight and support gained through therapy or a 12-step program.

Emancipating from the alienating parent was a key issue for the children who reconciled with the target parent in late adolescence or young adulthood. In the case of Cecilie, caring adults who were concerned about her living situation with her father took the initiative in helping Cecilie to leave him at 16. For Irene and Ron, adverse conditions in the alienator's home provided the impetus for them to move out. Ron's father helped his son make the transition into young adulthood by providing guidance and support for going to college and choosing his direction in life. Vincent's father could have helped his son emancipate, but Vincent could not avail himself of this resource because he was still enmeshed with his mother and had not yet resolved the alienation from his father.

Larry's emancipation issues were different because the alienating father had rejected him in adolescence. Larry became involved in drugs and violent behavior, including verbal and physical abuse of his mother. At 19, he joined a 12-step recovery program, which provided the support Larry needed to turn his life around and make amends to his mother.

Children who Reconciled in Their Twenties and Beyond

A myriad of factors were found to facilitate reconciliation in adulthood, when the children were in their twenties and beyond. Factors within the child included maturity; curiosity about the target parent; trigger events such as life-threatening illness, child graduated from college; child had a close relationship with the target parent growing up; child had a sibling who had reconciled with the alienated parent; successful emancipation from the alienating parent; alienation not internalized; child worked through painful realizations about the alienating parent's motivation and the child's complicity in the alienator's agenda; child felt a strong need and/or desire for a relationship with the alienated parent; child willing to make multiple attempts at reconciliation; child had psychological problems in adulthood and needed help; therapy provided the needed insight and support.

Factors involving the alienating parent included: alienator turned on the child; child rejected by alienating parent; alienating parent emotionally unavailable when the child needed parental support; child did not get along with stepparent when alienating parent remarried; less pressure for alienation because alienator was dead or had moved on with their life.

Factors involving the target parent included: parent continued to reach out; parent's commitment to rebuilding the parent-child relationship; target parent able to provide needed support for emancipation; target parent came back into the child's life unexpectedly; parent's willingness to forgive the child for betrayal and abusive treatment; love and support of target parent's current spouse and extended family.

Potential obstacles to reconciliation in adulthood include: child's ability to withstand the alienating parent's anger; length of time child and parent were separated; child never really knew the target parent; child closer to the alienating parent prior to the divorce; child feels guilty for "betraying" the alienator by reuniting with the target parent; child's feelings of guilt and shame for having treated the target parent badly; target parent's feelings of anger and betrayal; parent or child unable or unwilling to do the emotional work which is a prerequisite for rebuilding the relationship; parent or child has psychological problems which interfere with ability to reconcile; parent or child has unrealistic expectations of what reconciliation will be like; friends, family or significant others are hostile towards reconciliation.

CONCLUSION

It is often assumed that a child's vehement expressions of hatred towards one parent means that the love bond is destroyed. The cases in this chapter suggest that this is not necessarily the case. The parent-child bond may be quite resilient in some families. Alienated children who reconcile in adulthood often say that they never stopped loving the lost parent. As one man wrote to his father, "In my heart, I've always known that we would see each other again, even if it meant waiting to see you on your deathbed."

In some cases, reconciliation was facilitated by the fact that the child had a close relationship with the target parent prior to the divorce, but not necessarily. Aric Austin was abducted by his father as an infant, and never knew his mother until they were reunited when he was 20. Sylvia reconciled with her father after

40 years of separation. In many of the cases presented here, the past relationship between the child and target parent was not as important as the mutual desire of parent and child to have a relationship in the present.

In *The Boys and Girl's Book About Divorce*, now in its 28th printing, Gardner sought to help children by speaking to them honestly and directly about some of the fears, anxieties, and sorrows that children of divorce experience, providing his young readers with down-to-earth advice for coping with specific problems. He devoted an entire chapter to *The Love of a Parent for a Child* (Gardner, 1970). Ultimately, it is the love that parents and children naturally feel for one another which makes reconciliation possible.

The message from these parents and children is, "Keep the door open and never give up hope. Remember that reconciliation is possible as long as you both are alive."

REFERENCES

ADVO Newsletter (2001). Rostykus siblings reunited with their dad. Spring, 1–4.

Baker, A. J. (2005). Parental Alienation is Emotional Abuse of Children. In A. J. Baker, *Adult children of parental alienation: The ties that bind children to emotionally abusive parents.* Manuscript submitted for publication.

Baker, A. J. (2005a). The long-term effects of parental alienation on adult children: A qualitative research study. *American Journal of Family Therapy, 33*(4), 289–302.

Baker, A. J. (in press). Patterns of parental alienation: A qualitative study of adults who were alienated from a parent as a child. *American Journal of Family Therapy.*

Baker, A. J. (2005b). The realization and reunification process. In A. J. Baker, *Adult children of parental alienation: The ties that bind children to emotionally abusive parents.* Manuscript submitted for publication.

Berry, M., & Berry, B. (2001, September/October). My story. *False Memory Syndrome Foundation Newsletter, 10*(5), 9.

Clawar, S., & Rivlin, B. (1991). *Children held hostage: Dealing with programmed and brainwashed children.* Chicago: American Bar Association.

Conigliari, M. (1999). I am a child who needs and loves you [Msg. 497]. Message posted to news://ncfc-network @egroups.com.

Cross, P. (2000). *Lost children: A guide for separating parents.* London: Velvet Glove Publishing.

Douglas, M. S. (1987). *Voice of the river: An autobiography with John Rothchild.* Sarasota, FL.: Pineapple Press.

Finkelstein, C. (1999a). (spring/summer). Reunification: My story. *The Link, 2,* 6–7.

Finkelstein, C. (1999b), (spring/summer). Ruth's story. *The Link, 2,* 3.

Finkelstein, C. (2001, spring). The heart of an abduction. *The Link, 4,* 1–2.

Gardner, R. A. (1970). *The Boys and Girls Book About Divorce.* Northvale, NJ.: Jason Aronson, Inc.

Gardner, R. A. (1989). *Family evaluation in child custody mediation, arbitration, and litigation.* Cresskill, NJ: Creative Therapeutics.

Gardner, R. A. (2001a). Recantation and reconciliation. In R. A. Gardner, *Therapeutic interventions for children with parental alienation syndrome.* Cresskill, NJ: Creative Therapeutics.

Gardner, R. A. (2001b). Should courts order PAS children to visit/reside with the alienated parent? A follow-up study. *American Journal of Forensic Psychology, 19*(3), 61–106.

Gordon, R. M. (1998). The Medea complex and the parental alienation syndrome: When mothers damage their daughters' ability to love a man. In G. Fenchel (Ed.), *The Mother-daughter relationship: Echoes through time* (pp. 207–225). Northvale, NJ.: Jason Aronson, Inc.

Huang, L. (1998). Even when there is a reunion, there may still be heartbreak. ABC News, available at http:// www.ABCNEWS.com.

Johnston, J. (2003). Parental alignments and rejection: An empirical study of alienation in children of divorce. *Journal of the American Academy of Psychiatry and the Law, 31,* 158–170.

Johnston, J., & Campbell, L. (1988). *Impasses of divorce: The dynamics and resolution of family conflict.* New York: The Free Press, A division of Macmillan, Inc.

Johnston, J., & Roseby, V. (1997). *In the name of the child: A developmental approach to understanding and helping children of conflicted and violent divorce.* New York: Free Press.

Kopetski, L. (1991). *Parental alienation syndrome: Recent research.* Paper presented at the 15th Annual Child Custody Conference, Keystone, Colorado.

Lee, M., & Olesen, N. (2001). Assessing for alienation in child custody and access evaluations. *Family Court Review, 39*(3), 282–298.

National Center for Missing and Exploited Children, (NCMEC). *Search for and recovery of Aric Austin.* Retrieved June 29, 2005, from http://www.missingkids.com/missingkids/servlet/PageServlet?LanguageCountry=en US& PageId=1660.

Nielsen, J., & Vollers, M. (2001). *Icebound: A doctor's incredible battle for survival at the South Pole.* New York: Hyperion Press.

One family's journey after 18 years of separation. (2001, November/December). *False Memory Syndrome Foundation Newsletter, 10*(6), 10–11.

Publication Manual of the American Psychological Association (Fifth ed.). (2001). Washington D.C.: American Psychological Association.

Rand, D., Rand, R., & Kopetski, L. (2005). The spectrum of parental alienation syndrome part III: The Kopetski follow-up study. *American Journal of Forensic Psychology, 23*(1), 15–43.

Ryan, M. (2002, September). Boy, interrupted. *Reader's Digest*, 119–124.

Seldner, J. (2000, April). My fight to keep my kids. *Parents*, 167–173.

Smith, J. (1991). Aftermath of a false allegation. *Issues in Child Abuse Accusations, 3*(4), 203.

Stasio, M. (2001, August). Kidnapped by my father. *Ladies' Home Journal*, 114-151.

Stuart-Mills-Hoch, P., & Hoch, R. (2003). Successful reintegration of severely alienated children and their parents. In W. Andritzky & P. Koeppel (Eds.), *The Parental Alienation Syndrome: A interdisciplinary challenge for professionals involved in divorce* (pp. 253–266). Berlin, Germany: BWV-Verlag fur Wissenshaft and Bildung.

Sullivan, M., & Kelly, J. (2001). Legal and psychological management of cases with an alienated child. *Family Court Review, 39*(3), 299–315.

Vassiliou, D., & Cartwritght, G. (2001). The lost parents' perspective on parental alienation syndrome. *American Journal of Family Therapy, 29*, 181–191.

Villemure, J. (1992, October). Femmes de coeur: Faire echec au detournement affectif des enfants [Women with heart: Overcoming the emotional kidnapping of children]. *Coup de Pouce Magazine*, 103–107.

Wallerstein, J., & Blakeslee, S. (1989). *Second chances: Men, women and children a decade after divorce.* New York: Houghton Mifflin Company.

Wallerstein, J., & Kelly, J. (1980). *Surviving the breakup: How children and parents cope with divorce.* New York: Basic Books, Inc., Publishers.

Wallerstein, J., Lewis, J., & Blakeslee, S. (2000). *The unexpected legacy of divorce: A 25 year landmark study.* New York: Hyperion Press.

Warshak, R. (2000). Remarriage as a trigger of parental alienation syndrome. *American Journal of Family Therapy, 28*, 229–241.

Warshak, R. (2001). *Divorce poison: Protecting the parent-child bond from a vindictive ex.* New York: Harper Collins Publishers.

Warshak, R. (2003). Bringing sense to parental alienation: A look at the disputes and the evidence. *Family Law Quarterly, 37*(2), 273–301.

Section II

CLINICAL CONSIDERATIONS

Chapter 14

FUTURE PREDICTIONS ON THE FATE OF PAS CHILDREN: WHAT HATH ALIENATORS WROUGHT?

RICHARD A. GARDNER

OVERVIEW

It is reasonable to view parental alienation syndrome (PAS) as a relatively new type of psychopathology. Although it was probably in existence previously, there is no question that it has become far more prevalent since the early 1980s. Accordingly, it is too early to say what will happen in the future to PAS children. In this chapter I provide my predictions regarding what will happen to them – predictions that are best viewed as extrapolations from the children we are now seeing. Predictions will be made in two categories: (1) PAS children who have not made a false sex-abuse accusation, and (2) PAS children who have made a false sex-abuse accusation.

INTRODUCTION

In this chapter, I describe what I consider to be the most likely forms of psychopathology that we will see in PAS children when they become adolescents and adults. It would be an error for the reader to conclude that these predictions are casually made or just "pulled out of the sky." They are the reasonable extrapolations from the data we have now, which are data derived from direct observations of PAS children. Most forms of adult psychopathology are not created de novo. Rather, most often, childhood foundations play an important role in determining which type of psychopathology an adolescent and adult will develop. Because both genetic and environmental factors play an important role in the creation of the childhood foundation, it is unreasonable to assume that the older person will completely switch off the track that they have been on since early childhood. The psychopathological processes of childhood become deeply embedded in the brain circuitry and persist in manifesting themselves even though the environmental factors that produced the symptoms in the first place may no longer be operative (Gardner, 1997).

With regard to the predictive process, I have divided PAS children into two categories: those who have exhibited the derivative false sex-abuse accusation and those who have not. Clearly, children who develop a false sex-abuse accusation are likely to manifest sexual problems that will probably not be seen in children who have not been programmed to believe they were sexually abused when they were not.

PAS CHILDREN IN WHOM A FALSE SEXUAL-ABUSE ACCUSATION HAS NOT BEEN INDOCTRINATED

I will use as my guideline here DSM-IV diagnoses. However, it is important for the reader to appreciate that many people do not fall neatly into DSM-IV categories, especially with regard to satisfying all the criteria necessary to warrant the diagnosis. Many people exhibit a few of the symptoms in two or more of the categories and have significant psychopathology, yet do not satisfy enough of the DSM-IV criteria to warrant their being given a particular diagnostic label. I have often said, "God forgot to read DSM-IV before he put people down on Earth." These drawbacks notwithstanding, the categories do have definite value, so reference will be made to them when there is a good "fit" between the patients I am describing and what is written in that book.

Conduct Disorder

The conduct disorder diagnosis is often applicable to the PAS child, especially in situations when the conduct disturbances are the most salient manifestation. Under such circumstances, an examiner who is not familiar with PAS may erroneously conclude that this is the only diagnosis. Such a conclusion necessitates selective inattention to the programming process, which is the hallmark of PAS. Observers often refer to PAS children as "little monsters." Although I, as a child psychiatrist, could not properly use this label, it is understandable that the epithet could reasonably come to most people's minds.

With regard to the conduct disorder diagnosis, DSM states:

A. A repetitive and persistent pattern of behavior in which the basic rights of others or major age-appropriate societal norms or rules are violated. . . .

PAS children are programmed by alienators to be insensitive to the basic rights of the alienated parent. This is seen in their guiltless disregard for the feelings of the victim parent, which is one of the primary symptoms of the PAS. Most of the criteria for the conduct disorder diagnosis can be satisfied by PAS children, especially those in the severe category. The target parent is very much scapegoated and victimized by PAS children. In severe cases they are screamed at, intimidated, and sometimes physically assaulted with objects such as bats, bottles, and knives. The child may perpetrate acts of sabotage in the home of the victim parent. Destruction of property in the alienated parent's home is common. On rare occasion, even fire setting occurs. Deceitfulness, especially fabrications facilitated and supported by the alienator is common. Stealing items, such as legal documents and important records, and bringing them to the home of the alienator is common. Running away from the home of the target parent and returning to the home of the alienator also occurs often, especially in moderate and severe cases.

PAS alienators appear to blind themselves to the fact that when they program a child to victimize a target parent the reprehensible behaviors they sanction in the child are not likely to remain confined to the target parent. Rather, the principle of ignoring the feelings of the target parent is likely to spread to other innocent victims as well. I often put it this way: If one is going to teach a child to be cruel to the butcher, but not the baker and the candlestick maker, one should not be surprised if the child then becomes cruel to the baker and the candlestick maker as well. Accordingly, children with conduct disorders are likely to become juvenile delinquents. Although this is not a DSM-IV term, most people know what a juvenile delinquent is. Juvenile delinquents are likely to become psychopathic adults.

Unfortunately, the term *psychopathy* is used in different ways, not only among laypeople but among professionals in the mental health field as well. Some use the term psychopathy to be synonymous with psychopathology, meaning psychiatric disturbance. The DSMs have tended to shy away from the use of the term psychopathy, which, I believe, is unfortunate. The original DSM (American Psychiatric Association, 1952) and DSM-II (American Psychiatric Association, 1968) preferred the term *sociopath* for such patients, and more recent editions preferred *antisocial personality disorder.* In spite of the position of the DSM, the term *psychopath* is still widely used by laypeople, the media, and even mental health professionals. Because of its ongoing and widespread utilization (the position of DSM notwithstanding), I will use it here.

Psychopathy (Antisocial Personality Disorder)

My comments here include, but are not restricted to, the DSM-IV criteria for the antisocial personality disorder. Because I view the antisocial personality disorder criteria to be somewhat restrictive, I prefer the term psychopathy because it enables me to include criteria that are not to be found in DSM-IV.

Nonconformity to the Social Order: Psychopaths exhibit an impaired obligation to comply with social standards. Those PAS children who become psychopathic have been taught to ignore social standards when it comes to the treatment of the alienated parent. Psychopaths exhibit repeated failures to conform to socially acceptable norms. Arrogance is associated with such refusal, in that psychopaths operate as if the social requirements do not apply to them. Accordingly, they can be quite rebellious – sometimes overtly, sometimes covertly, sometimes actively, sometimes obstructionistically. They exhibit an ongoing failure to respect authority, whether it be in the workplace, in the community, or in society at large. Failure to recognize the importance of social norms deprives psychopaths of any sense of pride in complying with them and "being good."

Absence of Shame and/or Guilt: Shame is the feeling of lowered self-worth that an individual experiences when one has been observed to be engaging in behaviors that are considered unacceptable by the majority of the people in that particular social group. More specifically, it is the feeling that the individual suffers at the point of being exposed and observed by others who are in agreement that the particular form of behavior is reprehensible. Most responsible parents impart to their children the dictum that children should not eat sweets before meals because sweets cause loss of appetite. When a child is caught by his or her mother, just before supper, sticking a hand in the cookie jar, he or she blushes with shame. Both the child and the mother know that this is unacceptable behavior. The child who is "caught in the act" of surreptitiously sneaking into the cookie jar before supper not only suffers a feeling of lowered self-esteem, but the anticipation of temporary loss of affection from a significant figure (in this case, the child's mother). PAS children are not taught to be ashamed of themselves when they denigrate, even publicly, the target parent.

Guilt is best understood as a feeling of low self-worth that an individual experiences after entertaining thoughts, having feelings, or perpetrating acts that he or she has learned in childhood are unacceptable to significant figures in that person's milieu. Whereas in shame the individual is exposed in the course of perpetrating the unacceptable act or saying the unacceptable thing, in guilt the process is internalized. No external authority is shaking his or her finger at the embarrassed child. Rather, it is the internal guilt-evoking mechanisms that say, "Shame on you. You have done the wrong thing." Accordingly, in the dark, dark, dark of night, hidden under the covers, the child can still feel guilt. Again, the process by which this feeling develops requires the presence of important people who care, are willing to teach the rules, and threaten withdrawal of love and affection if the child does not learn and subscribe to them. Psychopaths may not have had such individuals in their lives and so do not learn the rules and are not particularly concerned about the loss of affection or even punishment if rules are broken (Gardner, 1988a, 1988b).

Parents who induce PAS in their children often lack shame and guilt, especially over the cruelty visited upon the victimized parent. They seem to have no conscience, no internal self-blame, and no remorse over the grief they teach their children to visit upon the alienated parent. Programming parents see absolutely nothing wrong or exploitive about demanding that an excluded and vilified parent provide food, clothing, shelter, and educational expenses, and yet have no contact at all with the children. Such alienators will induce similar shameless exploitation in their programmed children. Inducers of PAS feel little guilt over the exclusionary maneuvers that deprive the target parent of opportunities for input into school activities, attendance at school recitals, participation at sports events, and the wide variety of other activities that can be such an important source of joy to parents and their children.

Absence of Empathy and/or Sympathy: Empathy is an intellectual process. It involves the ability to intellectually place oneself in the position of another person, and to see the world through that individual's eyes. *Sympathy* is the emotional concomitant of empathy. It involves the ability to somehow resonate what another individual is feeling. Psychopaths have significant impairments in this realm. This defect enables them to treat their victims quite sadistically, because they do not have the capacity to identify with the pain they are inflicting on them.

Parents who induce PAS in their children have little appreciation of the pain they are causing the target parent. The children are taught to respond similarly, without any attention being given to the grief suffered by the denigrated parent.

Impulsivity: Psychopaths can be very impulsive. They basically live for the moment, and operate on the principle: "I do what I want to do whenever I want to do it. I take whatever I want to take whenever I want to take it." They do not concern themselves much with the future consequences of their behavior. They indulge themselves in immediate pleasures. They cannot tolerate a routine, where self-restraint is required. Their frustration tolerance is at a very low level. With regard to the future consequences of their behavior, they take the position that they will deal with that when the time comes. On "the day of reckoning," they will do and say whatever may be necessary to protect themselves from the consequences of their reprehensible behavior. It matters not to them that what they say at that point may be entirely at variance with what they have said previously, or what they will say in the future.

Parents who are PAS inducers may be very impulsive. They are quick to take advantage of any opportunity that will enable them to cause grief to the victim parent – especially grief associated with the attenuation and even destruction of the bond between the alienated parent and the PAS child. They are quick to call in child protection services, no matter how frivolous the child's complaint and no matter how unlikely its validity. At such time, no input from the alienated parent is solicited. This is input that might shed doubt on the veracity of the child's abuse complaint. Similarly, the assistance of police is summoned, no matter how little the justification for their involvement. The visiting parent arrives five minutes late and the door is slammed in his or her face, with the visitation canceled for "lateness." The alienators, thereby, serve as models for similar impulsive behavior by their PAS children.

Impairment in the Ability to Form Stable Human Relationships: Typically, psychopaths are significantly deprived as children and so, when they become adults, they just do not know how to relate to other people. They have never had the experience. They go through life acting as if they are capable of involvement, but they basically are not. Stable and enduring relationships with others are generally very difficult, if not impossible, for the psychopath to form, let alone maintain.

Generally, the programming parent does not exhibit any capacity to involve himself or herself in a stable relationship with the estranged spouse. Such instability may have contributed to the breakup of the marriage. It also prevents the formation of even a semblance of the kind of cordial and cooperative relationship that more stable people are capable of forming after the divorce. When the animosity is spread to the relatives and friends of the victim parent, further instability in relationships results. The child, by identification with the PAS indoctrinator, exhibits similar instabilities with regard to the capability of forming stable human relationships. We see here yet another example of the spread of the parent's pathology from the child to others in the child's environment.

Deceitfulness: Psychopaths are typically deceitful. They are often flagrant liars and "lie with a straight face." They look another person straight in the eye – professing complete honesty – when they know at every point that they are fabricating. Those who know them recognize them to be frauds. Psychopaths not only deceive others, but they often deceive themselves. In fact, one can view deceit to others and self-deceit to be two sides of the same coin. People who lie to others generally lie to themselves.

Inducers of PAS can be extremely deceitful. Lying on the witness stand is commonplace. In fact, over the course of 35 years of involvement in child custody disputes, I have seen many examples of perjury on the witness stand by PAS inducers. Yet, not once – I repeat, not once – have I ever seen a court of law take action against such perjurers. PAS inducers know this well and predictably get away with it. If the courts were to be more stringent with regard to sanctioning the perjury of PAS inducers, fewer cases of PAS would occur. The message would get around to prospective PAS indoctrinators that courts are not going to tolerate these abuses of their children and the perjury that often accompanies it and will impose harsh sanctions upon them. Such alienators serve as models for their children becoming psychopathic liars as well.

PAS children, especially adolescents, will lie to judges in chambers, especially because they know the indoctrinating parent wants them to do so and may very well learn what they said. When they get on the witness stand (sometimes the case), they are even more likely to fabricate because the alienating parent is sitting there, right in the courtroom, looking at them directly. The children know well that the alienator wants them to lie and they fear also that if they do not do so they may suffer the rejection of the alienator.

Anger Release and Sadism: Psychopaths are generally quite cruel. The inability to feel sympathy and empathy for their victims allows for such indulgence. Absence of guilt also facilitates the wanton release of their anger. Most psychopaths have been very deprived of affection and attention in childhood and are therefore chronically angry people with a strong need for hostile release.

Targeted parents of PAS children are usually maltreated in many sadistic ways. They are the victims of an ongoing campaign of denigration by their own children – children with whom they had previously enjoyed a warm and loving relationship. They are continually vilified, maligned, and denigrated. They are treated by their children as if they had no feelings. If they do cry, their children may cruelly chant, "We like to see you cry." Programming of children into such a campaign of denigration is indeed an extremely sadistic act. The PAS target parent is often scapegoated. The indoctrinating parent programs into the children the notion that if the victim parent were to be totally destroyed all will then be well with the family and problems will cease.

Disloyalty and Betrayal: Typically, psychopaths have no sense of loyalty to anyone. This is related to the impairment in their ability to form ongoing, stable human relationships. They show absolutely no sense of gratitude for things given to them, and they are mainly "takers." Loyalty to family members may be professed but generally no follow-through is exhibited.

Parents who induce PAS in their children are betraying them. To program one's children to hate a loving parent is indeed an act of formidable betrayal. It is not only a statement of disloyalty to the spouse, the separation and divorce notwithstanding, but disloyalty to the children. It is understandable that a parent who has been betrayed by an unfaithful partner cannot be expected to feel very loyal toward the disloyal spouse. However, this does not justify betraying one's own children by brainwashing them to hate the betraying spouse. A healthy parent (the parent who genuinely and deeply loves the children) will make this important differentiation and not betray one's own children by inducing PAS in them.

Separation Anxiety Disorder

It is important for the reader to appreciate that the original diagnosis for separation anxiety disorder was school phobia. The term separation anxiety disorder is a relatively recent development emerging from the recognition that the child's fear was less that of the school per se and much more related to the fear of separation from a parent, commonly an overprotective mother (Gardner, 1985). DSM-IV recognizes this and does not necessarily require the school to be the focus of the fear; the fear is separation from the home, especially from someone on whom the child is pathologically dependent. In PAS, the pathological dependence is manifested by the child's folie à deux relationship with the indoctrinating parent. They are bound together by the common belief that they have to protect themselves from the alienated parent, who is viewed as noxious and/or dangerous.

Significant overlap between parental overprotection and the development of PAS exists. Although the two phenomena can certainly exist independently, it is clear that parents who are overprotective during the course of the marriage may incorporate the same mechanisms into the programming of their children in the course of producing PAS. Often, the overprotection serves as a foundation for subsequent superimposed PAS indoctrinations. It is almost as if the overprotection has served to give the parent "practice" for the next step: PAS indoctrinations. The overprotective parent is essentially communicating to the child this message: "The world is a dangerous place and calamity may befall you at any time. Stick ever by my side and I will protect you from these catastrophes. Separate from me, and venture forth, and you may die at any time, before you even appreciate what has happened to you (Gardner, 1985)."

In PAS, the center of the dangerous world is the target parent. However, it is unreasonable to assume that such fears will remain confined to that parent. It is highly likely that they will become generalized to others, especially those of the same gender as the target, (e.g., teachers, dates, employers, etc).

The risk for such children is that they will have trouble developing independent personalities in adolescence and even later, and become "momma's boys (girls)," fear dating, never marry, and remain living permanently in the childhood home. Inevitably, the overprotective parent dies, and at that point the dependent child may suffer serious psychiatric deterioration, or even a psychotic break.

Overprotective parents become idealized by their children. The children are taught that all other adult figures are somehow imperfect, even to the point of being unreliable, untrustworthy, and even dangerous. Such idealization contributes to the lack of ambivalence seen in PAS children. They view the alienator as having only assets with no liabilities, and they view the alienated parent as having only liabilities and no assets. Such a view of the world is likely to bring about problems in the PAS child's ultimate relationships with other people. They are likely to have trouble relating to real human beings who will inevitably exhibit both assets and liabilities. Obviously, this can create difficulties in dating and marital relationships as well as relationships with employers, friends, and others whom one may encounter in life.

Dissociative Disorders

Formidable controversy has swirled around the dissociative disorders, even with regard to whether they actually exist. It goes beyond my purposes here to discuss this controversy in detail. DSM-IV, however, describes one category of dissociative disorder about which there is general agreement, namely:

> 3. States of dissociation that occur in individuals who have been subjected to periods of prolonged and coercive persuasion (e.g., brainwashing, thought reform, or indoctrination while captive).

This category was designed for people who have been subjected to cult indoctrinations or for military prisoners subjected to brainwashing designed to convert their loyalty from their homeland to the enemy that has imprisoned them. This category of dissociative disorders is very applicable to PAS children, especially those in the severe category. Such children have been programmed to convert their loyalty from a loving parent to the brainwashing parent exclusively. Cult victims and those subjected to prisoner indoctrinations often appear to be in a trance-like state in which they profess their hatred in litany-like fashion. PAS children as well (especially those in the severe category) are often like robots or automatons in the way in which they profess the campaign of denigration. At such times, they appear to be in an altered state of consciousness. My experience has been that the vast majority of PAS children will "break out" from their altered state of consciousness soon after being transferred to the home of the alienated parent (Gardner, 2001). However, my experience also has been that those who remain with the alienator appear to permanently exhibit this dissociative symptom, with its litany-like chanting of the campaign of denigration.

Delusional Disorder

DSM-IV describes delusional disorder as:

A. *Nonbizarre delusions (i.e., involving situations that occur in real life, such as being followed, poisoned, infected, loved at a distance, or deceived by spouse or lover, or having a disease) of at least 1 month's duration.*

Of the various subtypes of delusional disorder, the one that is most applicable to PAS: **persecutory type: delusions that the person (or someone to whom the person is close) is being malevolently treated in some way**.

Often, the PAS indoctrinator may initially recognize that the complaints about the behavior of the alienated parent are conscious and deliberate fabrications. However, over time, the fabrications may become delusions, actually believed by the programming parent. The same progression may ultimately be applicable to the child. Specifically, at first the child may recognize that the professions of hatred are feigned and serve to ingratiate the child to the programmer. However, over time the child may come to actually believe what were originally conscious and deliberate fabrications. When that point is reached, the delusional disorder diagnosis is applicable to the child. Generally, this diagnosis is applicable to relentless PAS programmers who are obsessed with their hatred of the victim parent. The children of such delusional parents are likely, over time, to progress to the severe level of PAS.

When the delusional disorder diagnosis is applicable to the indoctrinating parent, one usually observes a circumscribed delusional system, confined almost exclusively to the alienated parent. However, the delusion may expand to include the friends and family network of the alienated parent. The delusional disorder diagnosis may also be applicable to the PAS child, especially the child who is in the severe category. It is unreasonable to assume that the delusion target parent is noxious and/or dangerous will remain circumscribed to that individual. Because delusional mechanisms have become embedded in the brain circuitry, it is likely to spread beyond the victim parent and may contribute to the development of more extensive paranoid symptomatology.

Narcissistic Personality Disorder

My experience has been that most PAS indoctrinators do not satisfy enough criteria (five) to warrant this diagnosis. However, many do exhibit three or four of the criteria.

Criterion 5 is especially common in PAS indoctrinators: *has a sense of entitlement, i.e., unreasonable expectations of especially favorable treatment or automatic compliance with his or her expectations.*

PAS indoctrinators often act as if court orders have absolutely nothing to do with them, even though their names may be specifically spelled out in the ruling. Unfortunately, they often violate these orders with impunity, because courts are typically lax with regard to implementing punitive measures for PAS contemners. As emphasized (Gardner, 1998; 2001, 2003), the failure of courts to take action against PAS programmers is one of the most common reasons why PAS progresses from mild, to moderate, to severe, and why the symptoms become more deeply entrenched in the children. The children, by emulation of the PAS alienator, similarly develop a sense of entitlement and have no hesitation ignoring and deliberately violating court orders. In many cases, they learn early on that the judge will do nothing to enforce their visitation.

Empowerment of children is operative in each of the eight PAS symptoms. Such empowerment is provided primarily by the alienating parent, who encourages the children to vilify the target parent in such a manner that traditional rules of good conduct and respect are ignored. The empowerment may be aided by the alienated parent if that parent is passive by personality or becomes passive because of fear of worsening the situation if he or she were to more actively attempt to constrain and/or discipline the PAS child. Often, target parents' fear is that these measures will result in the child's further alienation. They may also fear that such measures will be reported to the alienator, who will use them as justification for further programming, or even report them as abusers to law enforcement officials and child protection agencies. Furthermore, a variety of extrafamilial factors contribute significantly to the child's empowerment. The most important of these is the legal system at every level at which the family becomes involved. Child protection services, teachers, therapists, school guidance counselors, guardians ad litem, child advocates, and others who sanctimoniously profess that they are protecting children from the indignities visited upon them by the target parent all serve to empower children inordinately. These individuals may claim that they really listen to children, respect their wishes, and understand what is best for them.

On many occasions, I have heard grandparents say, "When I was a kid, if I spoke to a parent that way, I'd get a good spanking" and "When I was a child, if I ever spoke to a parent that way, they'd wash my mouth out with soap." People who implement these disciplinary measures today might find themselves the subject of investigation by child protection services and, with a high degree of likelihood, considered to be child abusers. They may be either deprived of their children permanently or only allowed to see them under supervision. Such empowerment and entitlement contributes to the development of narcissistic tendencies. Elsewhere, I have elaborated upon this important issue (Gardner, 2002).

Criterion 6: states the person *is interpersonally exploitative, i.e., takes advantage of others to achieve his or her own ends.*

This criterion is frequently satisfied by the programmer's ongoing attempts to extract ever more money from the victim parent, without allowing the target parent access to the children. The children identify with the programmer and are similarly exploitative. They feel no shame or guilt over demanding that the target parent continue to pay not only for basic necessities, but various indulgences (including an expensive private school education) and simultaneously rejecting him or her completely. Such ongoing exploitation is likely to contribute to the perpetuation of this quality in PAS children, contributing thereby to the development of narcissism.

The programmer's lack of empathy and sympathy for the victim parent is quite common and easily satisfies Criterion 7: *lacks empathy: is unwilling to recognize or identify with the feelings and needs of others.*

Via identification with and encouragement by their indoctrinating parents, PAS children take on the same qualities. PAS, by definition, is a disorder in which a programmer tries to destroy the bond between the children and a good, loving parent. In order to accomplish the goal, the alienator must have a serious deficiency in the ability to empathize with the target parent.

The following is Criterion 9: *shows arrogant, haughty behaviors or attitudes.*

This criterion is often seen in that PAS indoctrinators are often haughty and arrogant; this symptom goes along with their sense of entitlement. The children, by identification, take on these same qualities, which can ultimately contribute to the development of a narcissistic personality disorder. This defect also can contribute to the ultimate development of the narcissistic personality disorder in these children.

Gender Identity Problems

That children model themselves after their parents is a well-known phenomenon. Accordingly, if a child grows up believing that a parent is noxious and despicable, the identification process is likely to be compromised. A boy who has been programmed into a campaign of denigration against his father is going to be deprived of a healthy male role model. Although the identification process usually begins prior to the separation, the PAS indoctrinations have the capacity to overpower these earlier influences, to the point where they may ultimately be obliterated entirely. This is especially the case when the PAS is severe over a long period. Important father-son bonding will concomitantly become compromised. The impairment may spread so that the youngster is not likely to emulate other older males either. They may not reach the degree of pathology that would warrant a DSM-IV diagnosis of gender identity disorder, but certainly may reach a point at which problems in that realm will occur. This is especially the case because such a boy's primary parental identification will be his mother. The same principles hold in cases in which the father is the PAS indoctrinator, and a daughter is programmed into a campaign of denigration against her mother.

Other identity problems may also arise in PAS families. A girl's identity as a female is, in part, determined by her father's view of her as a desirable female. Feeling like she is "daddy's little girl" is an important source of ego enhancement, and lays the foundation for subsequent feelings of pride in her being a female. If she is programmed to believe that her father is noxious and despicable, then his professions of pride and joy over her femininity will fall on deaf ears. She will thereby be deprived of this important contributing factor to a healthy sense of female identification. Such a problem cannot but affect relationships when she is older, during the dating period, and during the time when she might wish to get married. Similarly, the same problems can arise in a PAS boy who has been programmed to believe that his mother is noxious and despicable. When younger, part of his identity comes from his mother saying such things as "You're a handsome young man" and "Boy, the girls are really going to fall all over you when you get older." If deprived of these important contributions to a healthy sense of male identity, he enters the dating and marriage life phases at a definite disadvantage. It is reasonable to predict, then, that gender identity problems will arise in PAS children, although not necessarily to the level at which a DSM-IV gender identity disorder will be justifiably diagnosed.

PAS CHILDREN IN WHOM A FALSE SEXUAL-ABUSE ACCUSATION HAS BEEN INDOCTRINATED

A false sex-abuse accusation is a common spin-off of a PAS. It is difficult to find reliable statistics on the frequency of this manifestation, but my own experience has been that it occurs in about 20 percent of the cases that have come my way. Most often, the sex-abuse accusation is a late development, especially after the other exclusionary maneuvers have failed. Most often, it is the father who is accused of sexual abuse. The main reason for this is that an accusation that the mother is the sexual abuser is far less credible and, statistically, far less frequent. However, PAS indoctrinating fathers do commonly accuse the mother's new male companion, or the children's stepfather, which then enhances the credibility of the accusation. PAS victim fathers who have not been accused of sexual abuse are aware of the high risk for such a development and typically take precautions, such as refraining from bathing their children or going to the bathroom with them (especially young daughters). Rather, they have their sisters, mothers, and girlfriends perform these tasks. On occasion, the sex-abuse accusation is the first exclusionary maneuver, but, in my experience, this is not the common sequence. In either case, the accusation is one of the most powerful vengeance maneuvers ever placed in the hands of an angry parent, because it can result in complete removal of the children (often instantaneously), public disgrace, and years of incarceration.

Determinants As to Whether the Child will Develop Sexual Psychopathology

Child Abuse Prevention Programs: In most schools during the last ten to fifteen years, children are subjected (I have no hesitation using this word) to the so-called child abuse prevention programs. Children are taught to differentiate between "good touches" and "bad touches" and how to protect themselves from strangers who might try to sexually abuse them. These programs inculcate into many children the notion that sex-abuse perverts are potentially lurking behind every tree in the park and playground. I have seen many cases in which the ideas introduced by these programs into these young minds have become incorporated into false sex-abuse accusations. Interrogators traditionally use "good touch/bad touch" terminology, as well as other terms borrowed from these programs (e.g., "Did he touch you any place where your bathing suit covers?") The world did quite well prior to the introduction of these programs when sex education was left to parents and others in the home. I cannot imagine our going back to those allegedly naive times, but I believe and question that more children have been harmed than helped by these programs. This is especially true in the case of children who incorporate what has been taught into false sex-abuse accusations (Krivacska, 1989).

The Home: The greater the degree of preoccupation that the programming parent has with the sexual-abuse allegation, the greater the likelihood the child will become preoccupied with sexual issues. Commonly, the PAS-indoctrinating parent will question the child repeatedly about sexual issues in the hope of eliciting a "disclosure." A common scenario is one in which the child (more often a girl) is observed to have mild inflammation of the vulva. Such reddish coloration is almost universal and has a variety of common causes (poor hygiene, sensitivity to soap, infection, allergy, tight underwear, and masturbation. The mother who wants to promulgate a sex-abuse accusation, when observing this normal phenomenon, may ask the child, "Who touched you there?" If the child denies any touching, the mother may persist with the question until the child gets the message that the mother will continue questioning until the child identifies a particular individual. The younger the child, the smaller the population of people from whom to choose as the culprit. If the child gives an answer like, "My baby brother" or "Grandma," this is not accepted, and inevitably a succeeding question will be, "Who else touched you there?" Sooner or later, the child comes up with the "right" answer: "Daddy touched me there." The next step, of course, is to call child protection – and the man's life is changed forever.

Sometimes, the same scenario will ensue after the mother observes the child to be touching his or her genitals. In order to promulgate PAS, such a mother will deny any knowledge of the well-known fact that all children, on occasion, will touch their genitals. When the mother asks the child in an accusatory way, "Who touched you there?" the child gets the message that such behavior is unacceptable, bad, or wrong. The normal, age-appropriate response is to blame someone else. In this way, the child is exonerated. I have never known a child who answered, "No one – I just like touching myself there because it feels good." Rather, it is more natural for the child to try to shift blame to another person, especially someone the child senses the mother does not like. In the context of PAS, the father is selected and immediately accepted as the perpetrator.

Child Protection Services Interrogations: These interviews are typically coercive, with leading questions, anatomical dolls, and body charts depicting naked people. The whole interview is sexualized. Any comments the child makes that do not relate to sex are usually ignored or rejected. The typical interview, the main purpose of which is to extract a sex-abuse accusation, lasts 15 to 30 minutes. The examiners are typically coercive, biased, and convinced from the outset that sex abuse took place, the only purpose of the interview is to corroborate it. Sometimes two or three people are in the room observing and even assisting. Although the interview may be conducted by a law enforcement officer, often a "specialist" from the "sex squad unit," he or she is joined by one or more people from child protection services. Although the police officer does not generally wear a uniform, the child knows quite well that this is an interrogation by law enforcement authorities, with the implication that some heinous crime has been committed. The child knows also that the sooner sex abuse is spoken about, the sooner the child will "get out of there."

Therapy: The assumption is usually made by many mental health and law enforcement officials, lawyers, and courts that any child who has had any sexual encounter – of any kind, no matter how superficial and transient – must need therapy. Under such circumstances the children are brought to a therapist, who is most often someone alleging expertise in the treatment of sexually abused children. More often than not, this expert proves to be overzealous and inclined to provide therapy for even the most "superficial" sexual contact. No consideration is given to the alternative – namely, that some unpleasant experiences are best forgotten as soon as possible, thus allowing the children involved to move on with their lives (Gardner, 1996). Accordingly, what was a transient experience is inculcated into the child's mind as a traumatic event, requiring weeks, months, and even years of discussion with some third party.

In many cases, the child has not provided a disclosure and the child is put into therapy in the hope that in the course of this treatment, a disclosure will eventually be produced. It may take weeks, months, or even years before a disclosure occurs, but the therapist knows that if one persists, "the truth" will come out. Sometimes, this approach is rationalized: "The abuse occurred when he (she) was too young to talk about it. But the memory is still there. As the child gets older, with the help of a therapist, he (she) will be able to talk about it." In the service of this uncovering type of therapy, therapists use leading questions, anatomical dolls, and body charts – presumably to help the child remember and verbalize what happened. In the course of this "treatment," when the child speaks about other issues that may be on his or her mind, they are passed over or simply ignored. The therapist is there to concentrate on sex abuse, and nothing else. While this "therapy" is going on, a simultaneous court case (sometimes criminal) is under way to determine whether the sex abuse took place. The illogicality of this does not seem to be apparent to the system's participants. Even if the court finds the alleged perpetrator "not guilty" the therapist is happy to continue with the treatment because he or she is most often certain that the sex abuse did indeed occur, regardless of the findings of the judge and jury.

The Courtroom: The younger the child, the less the likelihood that he or she will be directly involved in courtroom proceedings (Gardner, 1986). However, even such young children are generally exposed to all the commotion that surrounds them regarding the sex-abuse accusation. In the home of the parent supporting the accusation, they hear about the heinous crime that has been perpetrated. In the home of the accused, they hear about the denials and frustration in dealing with the "craziness" of the accusing parent. All this brouhaha generates in the child an ongoing preoccupation with the alleged abuse, which is added to the aforementioned sources of sexual preoccupation. Older children may be interviewed by the judge. Although the judge usually does this in chambers without a robe, the child still recognizes the importance of the interview and is still awed by the recognition that the person interviewing him or her is a judge. This, too, gets across the message that a despicable crime has been committed, and engenders a wide variety of psychopathological reactions, including anxiety, guilt, and fear – especially around sexual issues. Older children may be asked to testify in court. Even adults find courtroom testimony intimidating and very frightening. This experience also adds to the potential for sexual psychopathology.

Sexual Symptoms and Future Projections

Impaired Reality Testing: A major part of child-rearing involves helping children differentiate between fact and fantasy. Typically, children's minds are filled with misrepresentations, misperceptions, and fantasies about the world. It is the role, and even the job, of a parent to continually help correct such distortions. A parent who willfully and knowingly teaches a child the opposite of what is the truth is contributing significantly to a compromise in that child's ability to differentiate between fact and fantasy and compromise, (thereby, that child's ability to adjust in the real world). Programmed children are being taught to ignore their senses, perceptions, and memories, and believe that certain terrible events occurred that did not. Again, the continuum includes the child in whose mind the engendered fantasy will evaporate and the child in whose mind it will become a fixed delusion.

Let us take, for example, a three-year-old girl who is asked the question: "Did your daddy ever put his penis in your mouth?" The child has never had such an experience; nor has she ever thought about such an encounter. The question per se engenders in her mind a visual image of this specific kind of encounter with her father. If the child answers, "No. Yuck. That's phooey. My daddy wouldn't do such a thing," the examiner may respond with a question such as, "Are you sure?" We see here how the "no" response is not accepted by the overzealous interrogator, whose main purpose is to extract a sex-abuse accusation. In that session, the child may continue to deny the experience, or she may acquiesce and say "yes" in order to ingratiate herself to the examiner or avoid his or her rejection (which she definitely senses, even at age three). Children are suggestible and are ever ingratiating themselves to adult examiners, especially those in authority. Because of these manifestations of their cognitive immaturity, they are vulnerable to interrogators who wish to extract a false sex-abuse accusation from them (Ceci, 1995).

The child, however, may have resisted this coercive interrogation and still insisted that the father never put his penis in her mouth. Having failed in the first interview, the interrogator tries again in the next session. This time the question again evokes in the child's mind an image of her father's penis in her mouth. She does not know, however, whether the second image indicates an actual sexual encounter or is merely a repetition of the visual image engendered by the examiner in the previous interview. The mind does not have a little red light that flashes when the visual mental image is false and a little green light that flashes when the visual mental image is true. The younger the child, the greater the likelihood she will then say "yes" to this question. She does not realize, or does not remember, that this "memory" is not of a real event, but resulted from the examiner's questions during the previous interview. She might, in her confusion, say, "I think so." The use of this qualification is one of the hallmarks of the programmed child. Children who have actually been abused rarely say, "I think." They know! I am not saying that they automatically will describe their encounters to any examiner; I am only saying that they most often know that they have been abused and don't just "think so." Nor am I saying that there is no such thing as repression. What I am saying is that such repression of sexual abuse is rare, media publicity about the ubiquity of the repression phenomenon notwithstanding.

I have found the visual memory criterion to be very useful for differentiating between those children who have actually been abused and those who falsely claim sexual abuse. Specifically, those who have actually been abused will generally have some fairly good, if not very accurate, visual memories of their abuses. In contrast, programmed children, especially after a long gap between the time frame of the programming (which usually begins at the time of the "disclosure") and the time when they are asked to talk about their abuses to an examiner such as myself, may not be able to bring up any visual memory of their abuses. They may claim, however, that they were abused and that they know they were abused, but they cannot conjure up any actual memories of their experiences. The child has the delusion, the fixed belief, that the sexual abuses actually occurred, but cannot bring up any visual memory of the abuses. The falsely accusing child will easily be able to verbalize other visual memories of the perpetrator in a wide variety of settings, but cannot conjure up a particular visual memory of the abuses – no matter how hard he or she tries. Yet, although having no capacity to remember actual events, the child still believes with 100 percent certainty that the abuse occurred. It is as if the child is saying: "I do not remember having been sexually abused, and I cannot actually bring up any pictures in my mind of such abuse, but I know that it happened because so many powerful authorities around me have told me it happened. My parents, the police, the lawyers, the judge, and [in many cases] the jury have all told me that this happened, so it must have happened. He's now in jail; so he must have done it. I am only a child and they are adults. They know better than I." When such children are asked about their abuses, one may get responses like, "My mother told me," "Ask my mother; she knows," and "It's all there in those papers that you have on your desk."

Some children, however, who are falsely accusing do have some fragmentary memory of some aspect of the alleged abuse. Most often, these are children who have been in ongoing "treatment," and the inculcation process has extended over a long period, sometimes years. The delusion becomes embedded in the child's brain circuitry and becomes a fixed belief. In situations in which a group of children are from the same setting – e.g., a nursery school – the recalled fragments may be derived from the ambient scenarios. I refer to this phenomenon as the cross-fertilization process, in which, through the network of parents, therapists, and children, fragments of alleged sexual-abuse encounters become passed around and incorporated into the scenarios of the various children involved. This ambient cross-fertilization process complements those scenarios extracted from the parents and the therapists and will increase the likelihood of "memories of abuse." For example, in one nursery school case of multiple accusations in which I was involved, an ambient story included the idea that the abuses took place in a "wigwam." Nobody knew of any wigwams in the area, but the general belief (or, more accurately, a delusion) held by all the parents and children in this day care center was that such a wigwam existed. It was also a delusion shared by the many therapists who were treating these children. A few years later, a child claimed to me that she had a visual image of the wigwam and "knew" that her abuse took place in the wigwam, but had no other visual images and could give me no further information.

When such programming is completely successful, the child develops a delusion that may be lifelong. These are the children who are likely to have been subjected to the types of therapy just described. My prediction is that such children will have difficulties in other areas of reality testing, and some of them will develop paranoid delusions. The fear of strangers, the confusion between reality and unreality, the hypervigilance, and the delusional belief that they have been subjected to an abominable crime lay the foundation for the development of paranoia in the future.

Hypervigilance and Fears: Children who have been programmed to falsely believe they were sexually abused become hypervigilant. Programmed children are being continually taught that the world is a dangerous place and that calamity may befall them at any moment. They have had a unique experience; namely, they have had what they thought was a good experience with a certain person (a father, a nursery school teacher, a school bus driver) and then they learn that, without their appreciating it, they had been subjected to despicable crimes and heinous acts. This cannot but produce fears of encounters with other people who, without their knowing it, may perpetrate similar atrocities on them. Separation anxiety is likely to occur. These children appear to be operating on the principle "Stay ever close to your mother and father and you will be protected from these dangerous people."

The situation, in a sense, is more anxiety provoking than other sources of fear in which children may find themselves. Witches look like witches. "Bad guys," at least from the view of the child, are dressed in certain types of apparel. They usually have mean faces and carry guns. "Good guys" are usually clean-shaven and have nice uniforms (like police officers). People who these children thought were "good guys" may actually turn out to be "bad guys." In the family situation the father, who had always been a "good guy," suddenly turns out to be a "bad guy." When the alleged perpetrator is an outsider – e.g., a teacher, scoutmaster, or babysitter – the good guys again turn into bad guys. Under these circumstances, even the children's parents were initially deceived and naïveté thought that these people were good guys. Their parents, however, their past naiveté notwithstanding, have learned some lessons and are now considered to be the best people to be able to differentiate "safe" from "unsafe" people. One does well, then, to stick closely to them for protection because the world is indeed a dangerous place and one never knows who will turn out to be the bad guys and in what setting the abuses will be perpetrated. Even the protected setting of a school may not be safe enough. These children, then, appear to subscribe to the following dictum: "You do well to hang onto Mother's apron strings whenever possible. Do not visit with friends, do not go to day camp, and certainly do not go to sleepaway camp. These are the kinds of places where you can be least certain of protection, the seeming safety of the environment notwithstanding."

The fear of the alleged perpetrator may generalize to fears of all people of the same gender and similar appearance. Such fears may contribute to the development of dreams and nightmares. However, in the falsely accusing child these dreams and nightmares are not usually trauma specific (i.e., they do not include direct and readily recognizable elements from the trauma) (Terr, 1990). Children who have been genuinely abused are more likely to have dreams in which the perpetrator is easily identified or closely so. Programmed children have more generalized types of nightmares, which are usually not trauma specific. However, in cases in which the child's sex-abuse delusion has become deeply inculcated into the brain circuitry, the dreams may become trauma specific and the delusional perpetrator may become incorporated into them. The fears engendered in these falsely accusing children are not likely to disappear when they grow older, and this is especially the case if they are subjected to years of the aforementioned type of therapy. Fears, too, are on a continuum with paranoia. Fear includes an exaggerated reaction to danger. In fear the danger is generally identifiable, and fears are reduced when the patient feels protected. When fears develop into paranoia, protective maneuvers do not work. It is for this reason, also, that I believe that many of these falsely accusing children may ultimately become paranoid.

Antisocial and Psychopathic Behavior: Many falsely accusing children are very angry. They have been forced into situations in which they have been subjected to numerous interrogations that are often confusing and anxiety provoking. They have no choice but to acquiesce. Police and detectives may have threatened them that they will go to jail if they do not tell "the truth." They may have been told, "I am not letting you out of here until you tell me what your teacher did to you" or "Are you going to be the only kid in the class who's not going to help us put Bob in jail?" Over the past 20 years, I have viewed hundreds of hours of videotapes of such coercive interviews. Although child protection services and law enforcement officials profess that they do not use leading questions and coercive techniques, the facts are that they are still doing so, but they often do not realize or appreciate that they are. Much money is to be made and power is to be enjoyed by a whole parade of prosecutors, police investigators, sex-abuse "experts," "validators," child advocates, and others in the sex-abuse investigation and prosecution apparatus. The anger engendered in the child by these experiences may be acted out and directed toward safer targets such as peers in the neighborhood and classroom teachers. Such children may exhibit a generalized high level of tension and irritability. Under such circumstances, they have a low frustration tolerance and a "low boiling point." It does not take much to bring about outbursts of crying and rage. Such disruptive behavior may interfere with peer relationships and school functioning. Often, these children are angry at their parents. They, more than anyone else, have usually initiated the course of events that has resulted in the child's being subjected to the series of coercive inquiries. However, anger cannot be directly expressed toward them because they are viewed as the people who are most likely to protect the child from similar such abominations.

In addition, these children have been subjected to experiences that compromise development of conscience. The accusing girls at the time of the Salem witch trials clapped their hands and laughed with joy as they watched their victims being hanged (Mappan, 1980). Typically, the parents and therapists of these children encourage them to act out their anger against the alleged perpetrator. In their treatment these children are typically encouraged to hit dolls that represent the accused and to verbalize profanities. I have seen situations in which the children are brought to the courtroom to witness the sentencing. Pictures drawn of the accused in jail are hung up in the therapist's office and at home, much to the admiration of friends and relatives. Some therapists consider this healthy "working through." Any feelings of sympathy for the perpetrator (even if guilty) are not expressed. Such impairments in the development of conscience are not generally confined to the accused but tend to spread. They contribute thereby to the development of antisocial behavior and, ultimately, psychopathy.

These children exhibit a somewhat blasé attitude regarding their lying. Most children expect to be confronted with dubiety when they lie, but not these children. The most absurd and preposterous elaborations of the sex-abuse allegations are often diligently recorded and accepted as valid. Not only does this contribute to the aforementioned impairment in reality testing, but it contributes to impairments in the development of conscience. Most children when they lie are confronted by incredulous adults who routinely try to get them to separate truth from fabrication, and fact from fantasy. Not these children. Important adults around them accept the bizarre with relish and this gullibility spreads to the coterie of the alienator's supporters and enablers, both professional and nonprofessional. On those occasions when the children are confronted with the absurdity of their accusations, they will often come up with yet another lie, so programmed have they been to respond with preposterousness and even fabricated absurdity.

Programmed children are also taught scapegoatism. All of the child's undesirable behaviors that have ever existed are attributed to the alleged perpetrator. Now, according to the parents, everything falls into place. All of the child's reprehensible behaviors that could not previously be understood are now recognized as having been caused by the sexual abuse. Finding a simple cause for complicated problems is central to scapegoatism. The next step, of course, is to get rid of the scapegoat. Then all will allegedly be right with the world. This factor is especially prominent among adults who falsely accuse their parents and other elderly people of having sexually abused them in childhood. As mentioned, some of these belated accusations are true; however, many are false. It is in the false accusation category that we see the scapegoat mechanism clearly operative.

Adults who belatedly and falsely accuse their elderly parents of having sexually abused them in childhood can also be viewed as exhibiting many of the signs and symptoms of PAS. The alienator, however, is not a parent, but generally an overzealous therapist, often operating under the delusion that all of the patient's problems are the result of childhood sexual abuse (Gardner, 1992, 1995). These people are being programmed by their therapists to behave psychopathically. Those who were prepsychopathic may go down the track to grosser manifestations of psychopathy. Such accusations are often associated with a lawsuit, in part because they can pay for the years of treatment that will be necessary if the alleged victim is to "heal." Such lawsuits are generally not instituted when the elderly person has no money. If he or she has some, or any property of value, such as a house, then, with the therapist's support, the lawsuit is instituted. In such situations, we see a folie-à-deux relationship between the therapist and the patient – a relationship in which both paranoid and psychopathic elements are present. In these cases, it is the patient who is the primary victim. I have seen a few situations in which the accused parent was dying of a malignancy or other terminal disease, but this did not bring about any hesitancy on the child's part to sue him or her. A more blatant example of psychopathy would be difficult to find, even if the parent did indeed sexually abuse the child when he or she was younger.

Sexual Inhibition Problems: All of the parties involved in the investigative and therapeutic process (teachers of the sex-abuse prevention programs, the accusing parents, the law enforcement officials, the therapists, the accusing parent's lawyer, and usually the judge) inculcate into the children the view that sex is filthy and dangerous. The word "love" hardly appears in such inquiries. It is not mentioned when the accused parent (in this case, we will use the father) is discussed; rather he is viewed as noxious and dangerous, with amnesia for all loving experiences with him that preexisted the accusation. With regard to the mother's love, its main manifestation is her protection of the child from the father's reprehensible behavior. The notion that love can be combined with sex is not mentioned. Obviously, such indoctrinations can have serious effects on the child's future sex life. The aforementioned programming against the father is likely to be generalized to all men, with the result being further interference in the girl's capacity to develop a healthy sexual orientation.

The therapy of these falsely accusing children is generally interminable. The therapist is ever trying to elicit more and more details about the sexual abuses. Presumably, the more these children talk about their past sexual abuses, the more quickly they will purge themselves of the pathological memories. Although Sigmund Freud, early in his career, recognized the futility of such catharsis as a therapeutic modality, most therapists working with these children still have not learned Freud's lesson. Rather than help these children forget their traumas, this therapy entrenches into the children's brain circuitry the delusion that they have been victims of a despicable crime. The children, in order to ingratiate themselves to their therapists, continue to pour forth with a never-ending stream of abuses that soon reach the level of atrocities. Ultimately, there is no sexual abomination that is not described. I am convinced that many of these children are being programmed to become psychotic as a result of this kind of "treatment." The psychosis so engendered includes bizarre delusions in the sexual realm.

It is difficult for me to imagine that these children will grow up and view sex as a pleasurable experience. Over many years, they have been inculcated with the notion that sex is despicable, sinful, and even a criminal act. In fact, in many of these cases, the alleged perpetrator has been sent to jail, usually for many years. The children themselves were allegedly participants in this noxious act. Sexual guilt over sexual enjoyment is thereby indoctrinated.

The most likely outcome for these children will be sexual inhibition problems. These may take the form of (to use DSM-IV diagnoses) hypoactive sexual desire disorder, sexual aversion disorder, male erectile disorder, female orgasmic disorder, male orgasmic disorder, premature ejaculation, dyspareunia, and vaginismus. These basic sexual inhibition problems are likely to contribute to the development of broader interpersonal problems that are derivative of the sexual (e.g., fear of dating, perfectionistic attitudes regarding who an acceptable partner will be, fear of commitment to long-term relationships, marital difficulties, and multiple divorces). Of course, these can only be predictions, but I consider it highly likely that these problems will emerge.

Promiscuity: Common to all the inquiries described above is sexualization. These false accusers commonly claim that the children have been "deprived of their childhood innocence" or "their childhood innocence has been lost." This is true, but it was not the falsely accused party who deprived these children of their childhood innocence, but the accusers and the therapists who have made the child believe he or she has been abused when, in fact, no such abuse has occurred. Whereas some children under these circumstances are likely to develop the aforementioned sexual inhibition problems, it is highly likely that many will go in the opposite direction, by becoming sexually promiscuous. First, even before the PAS sex-abuse accusation, many have been subjected to sexualized lectures in their child sex-abuse prevention programs. Accordingly, from the earliest days of their education they were being taught that sex can be dangerous, and that predators may be lurking behind the trees in the parks, playgrounds, and their neighborhoods. Even their closest relatives cannot be trusted regarding proper differentiation between "good touches" and "bad touches." Once the PAS-derived sex-abuse accusation emerges, the children are subjected to a whole series of inquiries, each of which is primarily devoted to sex. In the course of these interrogations, they are confronted with pornographic materials (e.g., anatomical dolls and body charts). In their therapy, as well, sexual issues may be brought up in every session, consistent with the therapist's delusion that such focus is therapeutic. Accordingly, over many years sexual thoughts and feelings reverberate in their brain circuitry. Such exposures are likely to result in the injection of abnormal amounts of sexual hormones into the bloodstream of these youngsters. It should be no surprise, then, that many of them will become promiscuous.

Residua of the Sexual Abuse in Subsequent Sexual Activities: A child who has *genuinely* been sexually abused, especially in the prepubertal period, is likely to incorporate elements of the abuse into subsequent and postpubertal sexual fantasies and activities (Hindman, 1991). For example, while being sexually abused, a girl may try to distract herself from the psychological and physical pain of the experience by focusing on certain patterns on the wallpaper, lamps in the room, etc. Such elements may become deeply incorporated into her subsequent sexual fantasy life – to the point where such items may be incorporated into her masturbatory fantasies or even required for sexual excitation with lovers. A boy who was forced to submit to anal intercourse, and who cried out in pain, may compulsively use coercive techniques in subsequent heterosexual encounters even when his partner cries out in pain. An adult woman may ask her lover to reenact the scenario that reproduces exactly the behavior of her father when he would enter her room at night to molest her. Elements of the abusive sexual encounters may automatically intrude themselves into subsequent masturbatory fantasies, which deprive the individual of the full pleasure associated with the act. Although these incorporated elements are generally undesired, they may have become so deeply embedded in the mental sexual life of the individual, both in fantasy and behavior, that they cannot be obliterated. They become deeply embedded in the psychic structure; it is as if they have a life of their own (Gardner, 1997).

It is reasonable to predict that children who have *not* been sexually abused, but who have been programmed over many years to believe they were (especially by their therapists), will develop similar residual problems that will affect their future sexual lives. The principle appears to be this: It matters not whether the experience actually occurred or whether it is a delusion. In both cases it occupies "space in the brain" – often a lot of space – and develops a life of its own. Whether the belief is based on real events is by that time almost irrelevant.

The Creation of "Professional Victims": We are living in a time when being a victim enables some people to enjoy an enormous amount of prestige. Professional victims are to be seen everywhere. Practically every day, sex-abuse victims tell their stories on television or describe them in newspaper or magazine articles. Leading celebrities are now "coming out" and divulging their childhood sexual abuses. Being a victim of childhood sexual abuse is in vogue.

Children in treatment may be taught that they are victims of sexual abuse. They can become deeply indoctrinated with the notion that they have been victimized, and this cannot but affect their future psychological development. Victims of sex abuse tend to see themselves as victims in other situations. The prophecy may very well be realized, with the result that lifelong patterns of self-destructiveness may become embedded. Such an attitude engenders the notion that they are not responsible for unacceptable, painful, and even terrible things that may happen to them. Rather, they tend to view themselves as the innocent victims of persecutors, and this pattern can contribute to the development of sadomasochistic behavior as well as paranoid thinking.

It is likely that many of these falsely accusing children, especially those who have been subjected to ongoing therapy, will ultimately become "professional victims" and will entice others to support their delusion (i.e., they will expand the coterie of supporters and enablers). DSM-IV does not have a diagnostic category of "professional victim." Probably the closest diagnosis is delusional disorder, in which the patient manifests a circumscribed delusion that the alleged perpetrator sexually abused the "victim." There is no question, however, that this phenomenon exists, with all the hallmarks of psychopathology. Even people who were truly victimized generally appreciate that it is better to "try to forget about it" and go on living, rather than to wallow in self-pity and keep focusing on old injuries and traumas. Inappropriate forms of therapy may entrench these beliefs more deeply in the brain circuitry and interfere with proper "healing."

Interestingly, bona fide victims of other calamities do not go around advertising their childhood calamities, wear tee-shirts, or parade down streets. People who survived childhood physical abuse, emotional abuse, drought, starvation, profound poverty, chronic physical illness, and World War II concentration camps do not seem to feel the need to become professional victims. The sex-abuse "survivors" (both those who were really abused [and they certainly exist] and those who believe they were abused [and were not]) appear to have a special need to band together. All of this fuels group and even mass hysteria (Gardner, 1991, 1993a,1993b).

CONCLUSIONS

PAS indoctrinators are contributing to the development of new types of psychopathology. Even without the derivative sex-abuse accusation, PAS itself is a new form of psychopathology. Certainly, people in the past have been programmed. However, this is a unique kind of programming, especially because it occurs in the interfamilial situation. Certainly, PAS-type programming did exist prior to the early 1980s (when I first began to observe it en masse) but it was not as common as it is today. I am not talking here about acute psychopathology, but chronic psychopathology. One cannot subject a child to PAS programming, especially over many years, and expect that the only effect will be the exclusion of a despised former spouse. It inevitably will spread, and I have described here what I consider to be the most likely areas of the child's life into which the poison will spill over. Inculcating a false sex-abuse accusation is also a new form of psychopathology. Certainly, false sex-abuse accusers existed in the past, but there is no question that there are many more in recent years.

I have seen many PAS indoctrinators who themselves, when younger, were PAS victims. Although the indoctrinations occurred before the disorder was becoming more generally recognizable by the mental health and legal professions, it is clear from the histories provided me that they were indeed PAS children. This is not surprising, because children model themselves after their parents and modeling oneself after a PAS alienator is no exception to this principle. Accordingly, it is likely that many children who are PAS victims today will grow up to become PAS alienators themselves. This is just one example of the process by which psychopathology is transmitted through the generations. The same principle makes it reasonable to predict that the disorder will expand geometrically, because one set of parents is not likely to produce just one PAS child, but many PAS children. We see here yet another example of the aforementioned spread phenomenon so commonly seen in PAS.

We cannot know exactly the forms that these derivative psychopathologies will take, but we do know that they are developing and that they will continue to develop. The projections here seem reasonable to me on the basis of what I have seen thus far. It is my hope that bringing attention to these derivative psychopathologies will enhance the motivation of those who are attempting to bring the PAS abomination to the attention of the world and, hopefully, reduce the likelihood that the disorder will be denied.

REFERENCES

The American Psychiatric Association. (1952). *Diagnostic and Statistical Manual of Mental Disorders.* Washington, D.C.: American Psychiatric Association.

The American Psychiatric Association. (1968). *Diagnostic and Statistical Manual of Mental Disorders,* Second Edition (DSM-II). Washington, D.C.: American Psychiatric Association.

The American Psychiatric Association. (1994). *Diagnostic and Statistical Manual of Mental Disorders,* Fourth Edition (DSM-IV). Washington, D.C.: American Psychiatric Association.

Ceci, S. J. (1995). *Jeopardy in the courtroom.* Washington, D.C.: American Psychological Association.

Gardner, R. A. (1985). *Separation anxiety disorder: Psychodynamics and psychotherapy.* Cresskill, New Jersey: Creative Therapeutics, Inc.

_______ (1986). *Child custody litigation: A guide for parents and mental health professionals.* Cresskill, New Jersey: Creative Therapeutics, Inc.

_______ (1988a). *Psychotherapy with adolescents.* Cresskill, New Jersey: Creative Therapeutics, Inc.

_______ (1988b). *The girls and boys book about good and bad behavior.* Cresskill, New Jersey: Creative Therapeutics, Inc.

_______ (1991). *Sex abuse hysteria: Salem Witch Trials revisited.* Cresskill, New Jersey: Creative Therapeutics, Inc.

_______ (1992). Belated realization of child sex abuse by an adult. *Issues in Child Abuse Accusations 4*(4):177–195.

_______ (1993a). Child sex abuse and hysteria: 1890s (Austria)/1990s (U.S.). *The Bulletin of the American Society of Psychoanalytic Physicians, 81*(2), 1–20.

_______ (1993b). Sex-abuse hysteria: Diagnosis, etiology, pathogenesis, and treatment. *Academy Forum* (a publication of the American Academy of Psychoanalysis), *37*(3), 2–5.

_______ (1995). *Protocols for the sex-abuse evaluation.* Cresskill, New Jersey: Creative Therapeutics, Inc.

_______ (1996). *Psychotherapy with sex-abuse victims: True, false, and hysterical.* Cresskill, New Jersey: Creative Therapeutics, Inc.

_______ (1997). The embedment-in-the-brain-circuitry phenomenon: Implications for psychoanalytic treatment. *Journal of The American Academy of Psychoanalysis, 25*(1), 151–176.

_______ (1998). *The Parental Alienation Syndrome,* Second Edition. Cresskill, NJ: Creative Therapeutics, Inc.

_______ (2001). Should courts order PAS children to visit/reside with the alienated parent? A follow-up study. *The American Journal of Forensic Psychology, 19*(3), 61–106.

_______ (2002). The empowerment of children in the development of parental alienation syndrome. *American Journal of Forensic Psychology, 20*(2), 5–29.

_______ (2003). The judiciary's role in the etiology, symptom development, and treatment of the parental alienation syndrome (PAS). *American Journal of Forensic Psychology, 21*(1), 39–64.

Hindman, J. (1991). Sexual victim trauma assessment. *In sex offenders and their victims,* ed. Ron Langevin, pp. 151–165. Oakville, Ontario: Juniper Press.

Krivacska, J. J. (1989). *Designing child sex abuse prevention programs.* Springfield, IL: Charles C Thomas.

Mappan, M. (1980). *Witches and historians.* Malabar, FL: Robert E. Krieger Publishing Co.

Terr, L. (1990). *Too scared to cry.* New York: Basic Books, Inc.

Chapter 15

THE ROLE OF MEDICAL REPORTS IN THE DEVELOPMENT OF PARENTAL ALIENATION SYNDROME

WALTER ANDRITZKY

OVERVIEW

In the past decade, increasing divorce rates, the concept of joint custody, and an unsatisfactory legal position of unmarried fathers have led parents to attempts of alienating a child from the other parent and excluding this parent from raising or even having contact with the child. This chapter describes the behavioral patterns of alienated children and the personality structure of alienating parents as well as the "natural" and "induced" symptoms of children affected by separation of their parents. Our aim is to assist professionals and institutions of the health system in issuing appropriate medical reports and in putting a stop to the misuse of such reports in "battles for the child." Examples for unqualified reporting and of its damaging consequences for the children involved are presented. Some basic rules of good practice are then developed.

INTRODUCTION

The percentage of children who lose contact with their father or mother within the first three years of a divorce ranges, depending on the research study, from 20 to 50 percent (Brown, 1994). A considerable fraction of fathers and, increasingly, mothers, is intentionally being alienated from their children through relocation and obstruction of visitation (*see* Klenner, 1995).

In the context of the "power differential" between a custodial out-of-wedlock mother and the father of an out-of-wedlock child that has as its origin the custody laws, an analysis by Kunkel (1997) revealed that in Germany the litigation for visitation rights is much more intense than for custody rights and that children consequently suffer primarily due to conflicts over visitation. The German civil and penal code does not contain measures that effectively protect children from being torn out of their familiar environment by a parent (often in a clandestine action), and then being isolated and alienated from the other parent. Due to this fact numerous techniques which a parent could use to alienate a child from the other parent, could develop, as they did in the United States (*see* Clawar & Rivlin, 1991).

In the "war over the child," seemingly trivial excuse letters and doctor's certificates often play a fateful role in the scenario of keeping a child fully and finally isolated from the other parent. The evaluating and certificate-wielding (pediatric) doctor, psychiatrist, or psychologist, who often is not familiar with the smoldering custody and visitation fights, is not aware of the further use of such certificates. Nor does he or she have any idea of the further interpretation or evaluation of the certificates by the courts and youth welfare departments involved.

On the basis of scientifically untenable or arbitrary causal attributions, which are fabricated by the "alienating parent," these evaluations at times correspond to section 278 of the German Penal Code, "Certifying false health conditions." This section states *"doctors and other approved medical personnel, who falsely certify a health condition of a person for the use by the authorities . . . against their better judgment, will be punished with loss of freedom of up to two years or fined."*

This chapter is therefore intended to offer a frame of reference for those persons who are involved in the justice, health, and social work arenas. Differentiations are offered to clarify "natural" and "induced" separation symptoms, and personality characteristics of alienating parents, and case examples are presented. This frame of reference allows for early detection of abusive intentions regarding certification and use of physician's letters regarding the "health condition" of the child.

1. Separation Reactions: Natural Reactions and Those Strategically Induced Through Alienation

It is important for doctors, judges, and social workers to know that children develop several (psychosomatic) symptoms, depending on age and the phase of the parental separation. These appear independently of any additional stressors, and are due to a dynamic of alienation. According the alienating parent these natural reactions are due to behavior or characteristics of the other parent. Thus, a request for a doctor's certificate, which frames the child's disturbances in this light, is presented.

Especially in younger children – psychosomatic reactions (whining, diarrhea/constipation, bed-wetting, vomiting), and aggressive and resistant behaviors following the return from a visit with the other parent are attributed to that parent's negative influence and used to argue for a decrease in or termination of visitation. As a matter of fact – the child simply experiences the process of separation anew during this transition, and reacts psychosomatically. Conflicts only arise when a parent is not able to be empathetic towards the feelings elicited by the separation anxiety, or when the parent blames the symptoms on the other parent. The following section describes natural reactions due to separation, and then alienation-induced separation reactions.

1.1. Natural Reactions due to Separation

In order to differentiate between conflicts that are induced by alienating behavior and conflicts due to "natural separation reactions," the phase of the separation/divorce and the age and gender of the child must be considered.

a. Phases of the Separation and Divorce Process, Symptoms in Children: In a three-phase model (see Schmitt, 1997:22) the following are distinguished:

1. In the *ambivalence phase*, as conflict increases, the tendency to blame, attack, and hurt the other partner for the waning quality in the relationship grows steadily. For the child this phase, which can potentially span years, leads to an increasing sense of insecurity and fear of abandonment. On the other hand the child is tied into partnerships with the parents; it can become an emotional crutch, a temporary "replacement partner, a caretaker, a bearer of secrets, or messenger." (1997:25)
2. In the *separation* and *divorce phase*, which lasts up until the divorce verdict, the extent of stress is dependent on the absence or presence of a social support system. If a redefinition of the parent and partner role is not accomplished then the struggles will continue. If the child is not given an opportunity to be part of the process regarding contact with the other parent, this parent is idealized (1997:27). Potentially, alienation efforts on behalf of the other parent can easily occur, resulting in alienation symptom formation in the child.
3. In the *postdivorce*, and/or *separation phase*, disillusion occurs in regard to the anticipated relief and advantages due to the separation. Daily chores must be accomplished on one's own, substantial financial losses and losses with respect to social contacts must be accepted. Substantial burdens now exist for both parents: living arrangement and financial problems, a rift in the circle of friends, fear of being alone and loss of the child, behavioral acting-out on part of the child, management of lawyer and court communications, as well as loss of the partner's supportive behaviors (Kunkel 1997:25). Devaluation of the other parent is damaging for the child (e.g., "you are exactly like your father"), since this undermines the child's identity and sense of worth. If it now acts *"differently or perturbed . . . it is mainly the renewed consciousness of the separation that causes this behavior, since the "hello" to one parent at the same time means "goodbye" to the other."* Often the child must pass through a war zone, "build a bridge between enemy camps"; on both sides it is now at the mercy of the negative sentiments that the parents hold for one another. (1997:33)

Severity of symptoms is phase-dependent: Schmidt-Denter (1997:59) found that at the point of separation 54 percent of children exhibited "striking behavior"; fifteen months later, the number was 40 percent, and after 15 more months, it was 30 percent. The percentage of the type referred to as *highly burdened*, who display no signs of symptom alleviation, was 48 percent. The percentage of so-called *burden-managers* was 34 percent, and the *lightly burdened*, symptom-free percentage was 18 percent. The identified disturbances are related to emotional instability, fear of contact, unrealistic self-concept, inappropriate social skills and inconsistent performance behavior. The burden of symptoms proved to be the same for boys as for girls. Severity is most acute for those of preschool and elementary school age, when the children are aware of familiar strain but do not understand it, and are not able to process it. They then tend to blame themselves. Girls, more so than boys, tend to bond more with the mother during the separation period; same-sex bonds are strengthened. As the parents change their social contacts, the core family stays the same in the mind of the children. They want to see their parents "reunited." New partners therefore are only "very hesitantly accepted."

The most common *symptoms* that occur among children after a divorce that lead to appointments with doctors and child psychiatrists are, according to Figdor (1997:60): bed-wetting, restlessness, insomnia, theft, discipline problems, decline in school performance, increased dependency and/or social and emotional withdrawal stomachaches and headaches. *"In almost all children a noticeable increase in the potential for violence is apparent. This expresses itself in the form of anger and rage, which is unloaded onto one or both parents, or other children"* (1997:60). Some children exhibit these symptoms in an attempt to reunite the parents (due to their concern for the child).

b. Age- and Gender-Dependent Reactions in Regard to Separation. According to Fthenakis (1995), natural separation reactions are also age-specific:

- *From birth up to the second year of age:* "Fear of the night," problems falling asleep, nocturnal awakening with disorientation, cries for help; in cases of poor care and poor quality, also retardation in the language arena, diminished interest in toys and social contacts.
- *Second and third year:* Regression in cleanliness education, irritability, crying, general anxiety, increased aggression and resistance, increased desire for bodily contact in combination with quick turning to strangers.
- *Third to fifth years:* Aggressive-destructive behavior, diminished self-esteem, whininess, neediness, loneliness, self-blame for the breakup of the family. In boys: more intense immediate reactions. In girls: behaviors of fear and withdrawal, depression, pseudo-adult behavior, inhibited and self-righteous behavior.
- *Fifth through sixth years:* Fearfulness, restlessness, attacks of rage, overeating, dependent behavior, irritability and crying.
- *Seventh and eighth years:* Protracted grief in reaction to the separation, followed by resignation; dissolution of the family is experienced as threat of annihilation. Diminished scholastic achievements, loyalty conflicts, wish for family reunification.
- *Ninth through thirteenth years:* Psychosomatic disturbances, pseudo-maturity, intense rage towards the parent who is perceived as the initiator of the separation, identity problems, feelings of loneliness and helplessness.
- *Fourteenth through nineteenth years:* Rage, grief, pain; sense of having been abandoned and deceived, abrupt and destructive withdrawal from the home, avoidance of parental contact, doubts in regard to the ability to form a positive partner relationship.

In the study Schmidt-Denter (1997), which only focused on separations in which the father had left the family, girls experienced the relationship with the father more negatively than did boys. Systematic observations revealed that mothers were more emotionally available, more empathetic, more mentally animated, and less critical of the daughters than they were of the boys. The boys exhibited an "exchange of affect" that was more "negative." The girls were more responsive to the mothers whereas the boys behaved in a more "strained" manner. According to Schmidt-Denter (1997:58) the child of the opposite sex reminds one *"more strongly of the characteristics of the now-hated partner than the same-sex child does. . . ."* Gender specifically, the realignment following the separation with the mother is less obvious among girls. Boys experience themselves as particularly weak in relation to the more powerful mother (Figdor, 1997:64).

Children who show no reactions, but who become more *"quiet and compliant' are referred to as "children with neurotic adaptation . . . often accompanied by clear signs of prospective depressive development"* (Figdor, 1997:65). In principal, symptoms of divorce would not be regarded as neurotic, if children were allowed to freely express their rage and to accept their fears. Figdor stresses that in his investigations not one child was encountered that "only felt freed by the father's leaving, and with no increase in conflict with the mother, following the separation."

1.2 Induced Reactions to Parental Separation

How can a doctor detect the difference between a parent who has simply sought him or her out due to concern for the child's natural reactions to the separation and a parent who intends to use the stress-induced symptoms (that are a result of intentional alienation) for certification to be used for his or her purposes in the custody and visitation rights battle? The most important indicator regarding the latter is evident in the request for a doctor's certificate/attestation in itself. These are most commonly requested following a prolonged phase of a custody battle (Klenner, 1995) and subtle devaluation of the other parent. Due to the highly regarded status of doctors among courts and youth welfare departments, the "medical certification" (sometimes along with false accusations of sexual abuse) serves as an efficient method to initiate final alienation of the other parent.

With a few questions (for the child and accompanying parent) that are based on Gardner's (1998) eight characteristics of parental alienation syndrome (PAS), the pediatric doctor can detect the first signs of stress-induced symptoms in the child. These questions include the following:

- Is the nonattending parent put down by the child? Does the child demonstrate anguish/fear in response to the question of how much he or she likes visiting the other parent; or, if and how often visitation occurs?
- Does the child express rejection of the other parent paired with absurd or ludicrous rationalizations?
- Does the child demonstrate a lack of ambivalence (i.e., the accompanying parent is described as "all good," the other parent as "all bad")?
- Does the child automatically take the side of the accompanying parent?
- Does the child demonstrate lack of guilt, or sadistic/aggressive impulses directed at the other parent (e.g., ungrateful response to presents, aggressive demands)?
- Does the child repeat (often in a changed tone of voice) sentences used by the accompanying parent, the meaning of which the child does not understand when asked to explain?
- Does the child also reject the other parent's relatives, friends and acquaintances without rational reasoning?
- Does the child present borrowed scenarios?

Since doctor's certificates are mostly only requested once, these characteristics have reached a medium or high level of markedness (e.g., the child refuses visits with the other parent), and these questions will prove to be sound ones. Additional hints are gained (especially in the cases of younger children) by observing the interaction between the child and the accompanying parent. Does the child cling to the parent when questions are asked? Does he or she display anxious and questioning eye contact to be reassured that questions have been answered in "the right way"?

2. Gender Distribution and Personality Structure of the Alienating Parent

Besides knowledge of the naturally expected psychosomatic symptoms that occur in children who are victims of separation, personality and behavioral characteristics of the alienating parent offer further hints for the doctor or therapist. These hints aid in balancing the limitsetting and confrontation (that occur during the consultation) with empathy and understanding for the young patients.

2.1 Gender Relations

A survey of 50 lawyers and staff of health-related offices, all of whom had experience with PAS, revealed that 50–95 percent of mothers were estimated to be alienators (*see* Gardner, 1998:127). Turkat (1995) regards the percentage of mothers to be so high that he uses the term "malicious mother syndrome," instead of PAS.

2.2. Personality Types Among Alienating Parents

Gardner (1998:44) found that histrionic personality types (e.g., emotional outbreaks, theatrical pseudo-emoting especially in court hearings and medical consultations, sensing danger where there is none, drawing attention to oneself, presenting a scapegoat as an object of aggression) are more likely to be involved in cases of light to medium-level exhibitions of PAS. Among the more severe cases, paranoid and psychopathic styles prevailed. These are marked by thoughts such as persecution and being spied on by the other parent, low self-esteem, and the inability to admit mistakes and take responsibility for one's own part in the failure of the relationship. Projection and simplification prevail: the parent alienating blames for all suffering on the other parent. *Psychopathic elements* are evident in the lack of empathy (the ability to sympathize with the child's suffering that was created through the separation itself, and the alienating behavior; see Andritzky, 2003). Also, when the alienating parent is confronted he or she often appears to lack shame and guilt, and uses clever rhetoric, while shamelessly manipulating and lying to the alienated parent and the institutions involved. Even accusations of sexual abuse are occasionally used in a conscious and calculating manner (Gardner, 1998:71).

Upon closer observation of the phenomenologically and psychodynamically impressive patterns of experience, thinking, and behavior of the alienating parent whose children exhibit medium to high-level PAS symptoms, we see that the descriptions of self and other correspond to the nine key symptoms of the borderline personality disorder as outlined in the *Diagnostic and Statistical Manual of Mental Disorders* (DSM-IV, American Psychiatric Association, 1994):

1. Frantic efforts to avoid real or imagined abandonment.
2. A pattern of unstable and intense interpersonal relationships characterized by alternating between extremes of idealization and devaluation.
3. Identity disturbance: markedly and persistently unstable self-image or sense of self.
4. Impulsivity in at least two areas that are potentially self-damaging (e.g., spending, sex, substance abuse, reckless driving, binge eating).
5. Recurrent suicidal behavior, gestures, or threats, or self-mutilating behavior.
6. Affective instability due to a marked reactivity of mood (e.g., intense episodic dysphoria, irritability, or anxiety usually lasting a few hours and only rarely more than a few days).
7. Chronic feelings of emptiness.
8. Inappropriate, intense anger or difficulty controlling anger (e.g., frequent displays of temper, constant anger, recurrent physical fights).
9. Transient, stress-related paranoid ideation or severe dissociative symptoms.

The DSM-IV goes on to say the essential feature of Borderline Personality Disorder is a pervasive pattern of instability of interpersonal relationships, self-image, and affects, and marked impulsivity that begins by early adulthood and is present in a variety of contexts.

A self-experienced deficit in the areas of care and love, as well as a repressively authoritative style of rearing focused on appearance ("rules," "setting limits") marks the first years of development for those who later present as borderline personalities. Symptoms typical of borderline disturbance (framed psychodynamically, and in the past described as character neuroses), are identity confusion, contact and distancing disturbances, a sense of constant emptiness, insecurity, chronic anger, fear of criticism and low frustration levels, and a fragmented sense of self. These symptoms coexist with other well-functioning traits, so-called secondary ego functions, such as language, thinking, memory, and intelligence (*see* Ammon, 1979:334).

These patients present themselves as articulate and "more normal than normal." They only start feeling threatened when the child's relationship with the other parent becomes a topic, and when attention is drawn to the fact that the child has a right to contact with the other parent. Comparing results of the Minnesota Multiphasic Personality Inventory-2 between a control group and a group of 34 female "alienators," Siegel & Langford (1998) found significantly higher K values and lower L values among the "alienators." This means a drive to appear as perfect and free of emotional problems as possible. Corresponding defense mechanisms are projection, denial, and splitting. Ehrenberg and collegues (1996) also found little willingness among parents with narcissistic disturbances to cooperate with the other parent for the sake of the child. The scale values also point out a splitting mechanism of the sort that the alienating parent presents himself or herself as "all good" and the other parent as "all bad."

The PAS characteristic of *lack of ambivalence* in the child obviously is a sign that he or she is taking over this characteristic from the alienating parent. The alienators' K and L values point to a simple structural level, a tendency to deny and stretch the definitions of reality (*see* Green, 1991; Graham, 1993), and suggest proximity to the addictive personality.

When we look at alienators' individual biographies, we notice that in accordance with the compulsion to repeat experiences, they often demonstrate their own drama of parent loss and separation. This can be evidenced by verbal formulations. For example, a mother threatens the father by saying she will take their four-year-old daughter abroad, to live with her family "forever." This woman herself mentions that when she was a very young child, her parents separated. Her father left "forever" and was never mentioned by the family again.

Specialized research regarding structure and dynamics of the alienating parents' families of origin are still rare. Comparing child-abducting parents to the parents who were left behind, Johnston and Girdner (2001) found the following characteristics among the abductors:

- denial of the other parent's importance in the life of the child; only they themselves know what is "good for the child."

- the children are most often between two and three years of age, are easily taken along, do not demonstrate verbal protest, cannot communicate.
- the abductors receive support from their family, friends and cult-like groups.
- the abductors do not regard their actions as immoral, not even during court hearings.

Six additional at-risk types could be identified:

1. Parents who have already threatened abduction in a believable way; or parents who have interfered with visitation, especially when they are unemployed and have no emotional ties to where they are living, and have already withdrawn large amounts of money.
2. When one parent voices suspicions of abuse and seriously believes that the other parent is neglecting or abusing the child. The parent then attempts to "rescue" the child by interfering with visitation or by abducting him or her.
3. Paranoid ideation regarding the other parent (e.g., that he or she is brainwashing the child). There also exists a sense of having been betrayed and exploited in the past, or feelings of vengeance.
4. Existence of psychopathic tendencies, self-involvement, highly manipulative manner, and grandiosity, mostly against a background of violence in the home during one's own childhood. The child, as in (3), cannot be seen as an independent being, but is regarded as an instrument of vengeance or a trophy.
5. When, in cases of dissolution of a binational marriage, an intense connection with an extended family back home exists and is idealized.
6. Parents with no knowledge of their rights, or who might have a history of bad experiences with family courts. Members of ethnic groups that have specific rearing ideals; out-of-wedlock mothers who have little contact with the father see the child as their "exclusive property," victims of actual domestic violence inflicted by the other parent.

The characteristics in 1, 2, 5, and 6 especially add to those of the borderline personality. They can aid the doctor or therapist in forming a relatively certain assessment in regard to whether he or she is dealing with a parent who might be intending to alienate or abduct the child.

2.3. Narcissistic Abuse

As previously mentioned, the feeling of an "inner void" is typical of the borderline personality. This feeling is compensated for by the ever-present drive for recognition and narcissistic nourishment or gratification. This is why the parent clings to the child like a person who is drowning. Heyne (1993) aptly characterized the psychodynamics that the child develops as a result of "narcissistic abuse" and clearly described the patterns of behavior and self-experience:

> Hereby I understand the relational constellation between mother and child. The foreground is set by the mother's need for narcissistic satisfaction and her taking advantage of the child's dependence. Exploitative narcissistic relationships are characterized by their symbiotic nature. The child is so-to-speak a "thing" created by the mother, which she experiences as an extension of herself, which she can rule as she sees fit. She is not able to perceive the child as an independent being, recognizing its individuality. Instead, she covers the child with narcissistic meaning which relates to her. She idealizes the child and projects characteristics and mannerisms onto the child that are based solely on her expectations of what she thinks the child should be like. In such a relationship the child's duty is to repair the lack of the self the mother experiences, and to perfectly fill the void of the mother's self. The child only experiences attention when fulfilling the mother's expectations. The child's strides towards autonomy are discouraged, punished and burdened with feelings of induced guilt. Or, these strides are only allowed in so far that they can be exploited in a way that satisfies the mother's narcissistic needs. Any divergence from the mother's expectations is perceived by the mother as a hurtful or aggressive act, an expression of betrayal. Internal as well as external separation though must be avoided at any cost. Therefore, a battle for control unfolds, not only in regard to the child's behavior but also in regard to control over the child's feelings and thoughts. The mother is convinced that she herself knows the child better than the child knows her/himself. She thinks she knows so much better than the child what the child really thinks, feels, needs and wants. Therefore she knows what the child is to think, feel, want and do.

The eight characteristics of PAS can be derived from this dynamic of interaction, which can also serve as an indicator for long-term, structure-building and supportive psychotherapy. By role reversal (parentification) the child, like a "living antidepressant," fills the alienating parent's emotional void. Therefore, motivation for therapy and pressure caused by suffering only evolve on the part of the parent when the symbiotic connection with the child is loosened by the child's secured contact with the other parent, and the fear of loss can be directly experienced. Any conspiring with actions intended to alienate the other parent presents a professional error and further burdens the child with emotional caretaking.

3. Medical Letters and Physician's Certificates as Elements of the Alienation Strategy

Certificates (Andritzky, 2002) are not only requested from doctors, but also from teachers, pastors, youth leaders, neighbors, friends, family, and the police. This serves to render one's own point of view "objective" in the eyes of the court and the youth welfare department. In the case of care and custody battles, the family courts and youth welfare departments, which issue reports regarding the families, are the most important addressees for the alienating parents. Especially for judges who need to stick to presented facts, conflicts arise when they are confronted with accusations and "certifications" that are purely psychodynamic in their motivation. As already mentioned, the treating physician or psychologist is often not aware to what use the certification will be put by the alienating parent, who will read it (judges, lawyers, youth welfare workers), and what consequences it will ultimately have for the child. Following is an outline of the most important addressees for, and requests of, the alienating parents in the medical arena.

3.1. General Practitioners and Pediatricians in Clinics and Private Practice

In clinic settings, and in conversations with the doctor, the dynamic of alienation can be identified by recognizing that noncaretaking parents are kept at a distance and are devalued when they come to visit their sick child, or when they want information regarding the child's illness. At times, doctors are given negative information (e.g., the other parent "always gives the wrong medication to the child"), or scenarios of blame are suggested.

In order to comprehend the context of the complex psycho- and family dynamics during a consultation or a stay at the clinic, the doctor should insist that the other parent be included in the diagnostic and intake process. Since, in the context of the alienation strategy, the physician or psychologist is supposed to take on the "version" of the alienating parent regarding the illness, inclusion of the other parent is often rejected.

Many functionally dependent symptoms of illness can be understood as "natural" expressions due to stress caused by the separation. Within this context special attention needs to be paid to the previously mentioned differentiation between "natural" concern on part of the parent, and the tendency to want to use the symptoms to argue for alienation or visitation cessation. In cases of the latter motive, a wish for a doctor's certificate or attestation is frequently voiced. For example, one parent wants to hinder visitation by the other parent, and a medical certificate documents a child's stomachache or headache. This, in cases of court altercations, could serve to legitimize cancellation of an upcoming visitation weekend. An additional motive for obtaining a doctor's certificate or a copy of the "doctor's report" when a child shows "small bruises," "hematoma," or swelling is so these documents can potentially be used in family court, as "proof" that the other parent hit the child. Because the doctor's certificates are relayed and accompanied by the alienating parent's comments, or those of an attorney, the physician or psychologist often is not aware of what he or she is actually certifying. Following is an outline of the alienating parent's most important addressees and his or her requests/concerns in the medical arena.

3.2. Types of Physician's Letters

The child's problematic mental condition is to be attributed to the influence of or contact with the other parent, although such a causal relationship, according to scientific methodology, is known to be unreliable. The explicitly stated wish for an "evaluation" or "doctor's certificate" that recommends suspension of weekend visitation with the alienated parent, because the child thereafter appears "aggressive" or "disturbed," is typical.

Case examples from the author's archive: A doctor's certificate, of a doctor specializing in child- and adolescent psychiatry, regarding a five-year-old girl, reads: "the girl mentioned above was presented to me today during my child psychiatry appointment time. She suffers from oppressive nightmares and a severe eating disorder. This is due to a deep insecurity, which is due to the parental separation. Since the child spent disruptive, eventful and often irregular holidays with the father (from X date to X date), a respite is sorely needed. Therefore, the child should absolutely spend the next few nights in its usual/familiar environment, as well as spend a greater part of the day there. . . . Otherwise, from a child-psychiatric viewpoint, psychological decompensation is feared to occur, which will necessitate long-term interventions."

The certificate[1] reflects the mother's wishes for the termination of overnight stays and reduced contact and visitation with the father. Although in the first paragraph it is still keenly noted that what is observed is a separation reaction, the second paragraph bases its conclusions on arbitrary values (irregular holidays). The symptoms mentioned could be interpreted as the child wanting to stay with the father. The child then mirrors the conflicts elicited by the mother's alienation attempts, or merely the pressure he or she experiences due to the switch from one parent to the other.

Following a one-time consultation, a general practitioner wrote about a nine-year-old boy: "From a medical standpoint it is deemed, because of severe psychosomatic complaints, that it is currently very necessary for Peter that weekend visitations and vacations with his father be suspended." The evaluation had been written without an examination or further investigation. It was based solely on information the mother had provided. The vaguely described symptoms were most probably separation induced and a result of removal of the father, and cessation of contact with the father, with whom the child had lived for the past two years.

In the "*opinion of a specialist*," a child and youth psychiatrist writes: "Based on today's presentation of the children Michael and Susanne, as well as on the history and the actual set of problems (which the mother has described very credibly and eloquently), we conclude that both children are not only strongly burdened psychologically by the separation. The children's problems have become more severe due to the father's additional difficult life events (occurring postseparation), and the ensuing battle for custody and visitation. A clear instability on part of the children is evident in their tendency to easily fall victim to infections, expression of suicidal statements, as well as a depressive mood that was evident during today's examination. Independent of each other, both children experience the familiar constellation identically. This means that mother and grandmother are regarded as points of contact within the family system. Both children, again independently, wish to end the extremely taxing situation by wishing no immediate further visitation with the father. The mother also wishes that the children, for the immediate future, not have to visit the father. She has been experiencing increasing hardening and massive aggression on behalf of her husband. In the best interest of the children we ask that the results of our investigation be considered."

In the *Family-as-Animals-Test* (FiT) the father is not represented; only the mother, grandmother and the two children are. The depression inventory of the children reveals depressive development regarding the past situation. An interview of the father was not conducted in order to investigate the accusations. The situation suggests intentional alienation by a mother who herself is symbiotically joined with her own mother. The children orient themselves according to their wishes. The nonrepresentation of the alienated parent in the FiT (Brem-Gräser, 1992) is, according to the author, typical for children with mid to severe-level PAS.

Another type of attestation certifies for the alienating parent that they regularly attend therapy and are "psychologically sound." The cause for their decompensation is due to the other parent. For example, a medical psychologist writes: "during the whole time period Ms. Breuer appeared regularly and on time for her appointments. She appeared generally well-oriented, capable of a breadth of emotions, without extreme regression tendencies and without any evidence of harm to self or others or aggressive eruptions." "Based on these observations and my knowledge of the case history it is concluded that Mrs. B. is able to care for herself and her children."

In fact, the custodial mother suffered from bipolar affective disorder, so that contact with the father had a special compensatory meaning for the children. At a later point, due to a prolonged stay at the clinic, custody even had to be switched.

3.3. Case Example

How complex and heavily consequential apparently trivial medical evaluations can be in custody battles shall be demonstrated through use of a case example.

The 31-year-old mother of then 2.5-year-old Elena moved out, after three years of living with the father in the father's house. This was preceded by initially harmless altercations regarding different rearing philosophies and the realization that the parents did not fit together, based on their mental and social backgrounds. In the first few weeks spontaneous visits by the father occurred with no complications. Both parents were still able to communicate with each other. In the time following, the father was received in an increasingly angry manner. He was told he was "interrupting," he was invading the mother's "living space," and his visits were too frequent. After the father, following lengthy discussion, had consulted with the youth welfare department, a consensus for bimonthly

[1] Names and places for the case examples have been altered, quotes are original.

visits was reached. These visits were soon undermined by the mother, who used excuses such as children's birthday parties, kindergarten parties, visits to the grandmother, or invitations to visit other relatives on the days of visitation. Alternate dates were rejected by the mother; therefore the father did not see Elena for weeks at a time. He then filed for custody of Elena, whereupon the mother secretly made arrangements to move to a city 300 km away, close to her own mother. The father, who found out about this through Elena only two weeks beforehand, received a 14-day visitation right now by court order, which worked for about a year. He had to drive now more than 600 km twice a month to see his daughter. Yet, soon the mother's alienating tendencies manifested themselves again. The father fought these with court petitions, and police support.

Visitation had been reestablished for a few weeks, following admonishment of the mother by the police. The mother called the father and told him that the next visit would have to be canceled because Elena had a cold, and the visit could not be rescheduled. The father turned to the pediatrician, who informed him that although Elena had a slight cold she did not need to be in bed and that she could leave the house. On the day of visitation, the father also observed the mother and Elena leaving the house, in the snow, under wet and cold weather conditions, to go shopping.

During the course of investigation by the attorney general based on suspicion of child abduction (section 235 of the German Penal Code, StGB), the evaluation of a pediatrician was presented: *"The child mentioned above was examined in the medical office on xx. It was presented because of vomiting and abdominal complaints. A diet and house rest were prescribed."*

In further proceedings, the child, who was now claiming "not wanting to see the father," was to be questioned. Because the child has a right not to testify, the youth welfare department was appointed as additional caretaker in order to determine "if the right not to testify should be made use of." The youth welfare department, without questioning Elena, stated that *"the city's youth welfare department, in its capacity as additional caretaker, is relying on the right not to testify, in order not to endanger the child's well-being." The attorney general responded: "Therefore the child cannot serve as evidence. Child abduction cannot be proven any other way . . . therefore, due to process reasons, it is not possible to question the child whether child estrangement occurred based on the state of facts "deception, threat, or force." . . . In particular she [the mother] has also proven, by submitting a medical evaluation, that the child was sick on xx."*

The critical point here for escalation of the mother's months-long alienation maneuver was the consultation with the pediatrician, and his or her willingness to write a doctor's certificate, the consequences of which he could not control. Armed only with this certificate, the mother felt empowered to cancel the visitation weekend and to refer the father, as his only way of reacting, in the direction of legal proceedings, provoking the filing of a criminal complaint. A few weeks later the child was questioned by a family court judge; she stated that she did not want to see the father and that it was "nicer" at mother's. Six months later regular contact between Elena and the father was reestablished. The visits were then continued without noteworthy consequences. This happened only after several more court altercations, which also included the physician who had written the certification, and the threat of a fine for the physician. A critical evaluation of the doctor's certificate and consistent limitsetting on behalf of the family court judge in regard to the alienating parent were, in this case, able to prevent a continued disruption of connection.

4. Induced Illnesses: Munchhausen Syndrome by Proxy

In the context of divorce conflicts, requests for doctors' certificates regarding child illness should always be accompanied by consideration of the presence of *Munchhausen syndrome by proxy* (MSBP) (Yeo, 1996). This is a type of child abuse that until recently has been induced almost exclusively by women. Child illnesses are produced artificially, or symptoms are presented in a greatly exaggerated manner. This is done in order to elicit unnecessary medical and psychological interventions that can lead up to surgery. Common symptoms are diarrhea, skin rashes, falsification of lab results by adding parental blood, and giving overdoses of medication.

The mothers have a very close relationship with the children. They present themselves as ideal, *"caretaking" mothers,* appear "*completely normal* and *remarkably friendly.*" The destructive affect is split off and manipulation of the children occurs in *"a type of dissociative state. . . . The child is experienced by the mother as an extension of herself . . . used like an object,"* whose striving for autonomy elicits extreme fear (Eckhardt-Henn, 2000: 340).

In cases of MSBP, no medical explanations can be found for the illness. Yet these cases still exist despite traditionally effective medical measures. Admission into care is followed by rapid recovery; thereafter, immediate decompensation occurs at home. The father does not show up while the child is under care; the mother fosters a close relationship with the doctor and medical staff and spoils them with treats such as "cookies and tea." She is constantly at the child's bedside and is engaged in the care in an unusually intensive manner.

The psychodynamic assumption is that, through the child's induced illness, the mother receives attention from the medical and therapeutic professions, all the while binding the child to her and keeping him or her away from the other parent. In cases of marital and custodial battles, according to Rand (1997), four variations of motivation for MSBP are plausible:

1. While still married, reproaches of abuse or maltreatment are added to actual symptoms of illness in order to hurry along the divorce *(thus precipitating the divorce).*
2. The parent who feels disadvantaged wants revenge by using false accusations of abuse, or wants to maintain a symbiotic bond with the child.
3. The MSBP-inducing parent wants to obtain social support from the staff.
4. The alienation agenda is to be furthered.

The author of this chapter suggests that MSBP should also be mentioned in those cases in which children suffer stress reactions due to being ensnared in a conflict of loyalties by the alienating parent. A *case example* of the author of this chapter is used to clarify this:

Up until age two, Marco's contact with his noncustodial father worked well without court regulations, despite many altercations with and complaints made by the mother (missing child support payments, the father hadn't "cared"). Marco looked forward to the visits; no conflict existed between father and son. After the mother turned to a new partner, an old friend of the father's, the father was provoked. The mother dictated what he was to do with the child, and what places he was to avoid. The mother was not present at the time of visitation. She stated that Marco "no longer wanted to be with the father," since he had observed the father damaging the mother's car during a (provoked) fight. She stated that Marco "panicked" when the father came to pick him up. She also stated that Marco was already calling her new partner "Daddy," and that they were getting along famously. After the court had arranged for three visits, the mother stated that Marco had had a high fever the night before the first visitation date. She stated that Marco had vomited several times and upon hearing the doorbell had screamed, "He's coming to get me!" Then Marco supposedly had started to shake. By the next day, the complaints had "disappeared into thin air." For the second appointment the mother stated she had taken Marco to the doctor because he had had a fever and an earache. An ear infection had been diagnosed. Again Marco had supposedly been shaking and locked himself in his room. Right before the third visitation date the mother stated that Marco once again had a "high fever"; he "vomited several times" after asking the mother whether the father was coming the next day. The day after, Marco felt well again. The child was supposedly "completely changed," no longer wanted to play and had a "concrete will and opposes the father's visits." Besides, the new partner was "Daddy" to him. Marco had supposedly said: "I already have a great Daddy what do I still want with father?"

Examination of the mother revealed that she regarded Marco's father (as was the case with another child by a different father) merely as a "sperm donor." For rearing purposes she regarded him as "unnecessary," as he was "too permissive" with regard to the boy. At birth, she had not reported him as being the father. During the author's examination, Marco responded to the question of what his real father's name was by yelling: "He wants to steal me from my mama!" The child then freely expressed many "adopted scenarios"("no way" would he go see the father, " he did not do anything with me"). Then the child revealed: "If I see father then I have to leave mama. Then I'll live alone with father. Then I won't have a mama anymore." It was revealed that the mother had instilled in the child the fear that the father wanted to steal him and take him to his family in Spain.

The "programmed" abduction scenario and Marco's conflict of loyalties (the mother's wish to alienate the father, marked rivalry between the new partner and the father) led to an extreme state of stress and anxiety, with the resulting reported symptoms. The medical certifications were to serve as proof, in court and with the youth welfare department, of the intensity of the rejection of the father. Marco was informed, in the context of the evaluation, that he would not be abducted. He was then able to remember some of the father's positive characteristics as well as positive experiences they had had, and became open to visitations. However, the five-year-old child was not able to grasp the manipulation, but greeted the mother after the examination with the words: "Mama, you needn't be afraid of father anymore. He's not going to take me away forever."

In the sense of MSBP, the symptoms were intentionally provoked and accepted by the mother in order to alienate the child from the father. It remains to be seen whether in the context of custody and visitation battles the number of fathers with MSBP will increase (as has been the case with PAS), or whether this really is solely a "mother-specific" phenomenon.

5. Treatment of Parents with "A Wish for a Doctor's Certificate"

Knowledge of the eight characteristics of PAS (*see* section on "Induced Reactions to Parental Separation") helps the pediatrician and/or physician and/or psychologist who writes up an attestation. It aids in ascertaining whether the evaluation may be misused in the "battle for the child," especially when he or she is not familiar with the family dynamics. Because the PAS concept is not yet well known in Germany, and is often misinterpreted or denied by critics (*see* Salzgeber and Stadler, 1999; Fegert, 2001), significant educational work remains to be completed.

The problem of the misuse of physician's certificates has long been recognized. For the health professions involved, the psychoanalyst Aichhorn (1974:28) in 1932 described in exemplary fashion the "battle over the child" and the appropriate behavior on the part of the "rearing consultant":

> The consultant is often sought out for mediation when in an unhappy marriage, or in cases of divorce each parent lays claim to the child. If the consultant does not recognize that this sometimes extremely brutal and inconsiderate battle for the child only aims to hurt the other parent, then her/his interventions will be fruitless. If he grasps the situation immediately though, he will be spared fruitless efforts. Right from the beginning he establishes and informs the parents of his position as the child's advocate. These then either immediately reject him, or they comply and he can then do that which is necessary for the child.

Dolto (1996:52) came up with a fitting formula regarding demands for doctor's certificates for use in custody and visitation battles, when she wrote:

> A doctor who is supposed to write up an attestation has the best opportunity not to do this by rather talking with the child about what the symptoms are supposed to express. Or, s/he could write up a completely different type of evaluation: "Hereby I certify that the child tells me that it is very excited when it sees the father and that this causes its stomach to be upset. . . . But the child doesn't vomit because it doesn't love its father, but because it is profoundly confused when seeing him after such a long time."

The reactions are supposed to occur especially when the mother arranges for the relationship between the child and her ex-husband in a way that makes it difficult for the child to switch between parents. "This causes disturbances in the child's vegetative system. Internally it becomes confused when the mother describes the father as noncaring or even dangerous. . . ." The child would exhibit the same symptoms if it were to live with the father and rarely saw the mother, *"because this phenomenon is dependent on the situation, not the participants"* (Dolto 1996: 52).

When clinical treatment of symptoms (which are caused by the ongoing stress of alienation) of the children of separated parents are indicated, this also needs to be critically assessed.

Case Example

Following admission by a specialist, a 7-year-old girl is presented in a child and adolescent psychiatric day clinic. The mother recounts in the history that she had separated from the father, after living with him for 1.6 years, because he was "very domineering." After the initial visits the then 2-year-old Manuela "had been very conspicuous and had cried." She hadn't wanted to speak with the father about this. Following a vacation with the father and his girlfriend, Manuela had seemed "extraordinarily anxious." At night she had "come to the mother's bed over and over again, and had no longer been able to sleep through the night." The father had wanted to continue to visit the child and had shown "no understanding for the problems following the visitations." After a two-week vacation, Manuela had seemed "totally exhausted and disheveled"; the mother had packed "appropriate clothing" for her, but when Manuela rerturned, she had "only had on completely torn clothing." The father had fought with the girlfriend. He had left a week early for his apartment and had spent a week "alone with the girl." After that, Manuela had developed "noticeable fits of choking, coughing, and constipation."

Upon reproach, the father was stated to have found the vacation to be "wonderful," whereupon the mother forbid further visitation and turned to her physician. The physician was not able to find any somatic explanations. The mother then repeatedly consulted a psychiatrist. The psychiatrist "became suspicious and submitted reports that reflected this to the courts." Supposedly, Manuela (than 5 years old) had told the mother that she had been "tongue kissed" by the father. After a move by the mother to a new home there were three more visitations at the father's residence, whereupon Manuela "again seemed extremely different in her behavior." At the same time, because of the alleged kissing, the mother filed a criminal complaint against the father. Questioning by a female police officer did not uphold suspicions and proceedings were halted. A psychological evaluation recommended a reunion of Manuela and the father. Visitation was also mandated by the court, but the mother refused to comply because Manuela supposedly did not want to see her father. She had supposedly developed "distinct problems in school. . . . She often sits in class and daydreams. . . . Besides Manuela is now again wetting her bed." While in kindergarten Manuela supposedly had "marked separation anxiety."

The father is described in pathological terms as someone who "himself is under psychotherapeutic care." His mother describes him as having been "during childhood a very difficult child." The child's mother is described as being remarried a year ago. The stepfather accompanied Manuela and the mother to the clinic. In the psychological report Manuela is described as "fearful" and "internally stressed," and seemingly "suspicious."

The treatment team concluded that the child would only suffer more by further questioning and court appearances. The conclusion was based on consideration of three hypotheses regarding the causes of the problem behavior. Problematic behavior was considered to be the result of: (a) apparent refusal of the father, which can be traced back through the mother, (b) the father's "boundary-trespassing behavior" or, (c) the early separation from the mother so that now visitation with the father would be experienced as stressful. Because the child was thought to have a good relationship with the mother and stepfather, the "upholding of the already not very intense relationship with the genetic father" would not justify further attempts for reunification. It was suggested that clinic admission should only occur when and if there were no more pending court matters.

Again, in this case all the statements used were the mother's; the father was not consulted in the gathering of the evidence. The doctor's report aided the mother in legitimizing her alienation attempts. The report as well as the decision should be judged erroneous. There was a failure to recognize that (a) alienation does not occur until a few months after the separation, (b) the case of alienating the other parent while forming a "new family" is present (see Warshak, 2000), and (c) without careful evaluation (e.g., using criteria according to Gardner, 1995), false suspicions of child abuse were considered, and the child was only brought in for treatment after complete alienation of the other parent.

Inpatient treatment of stress symptoms that have been triggered by alienating behavior should be avoided, since the cause does not lie with the child but with the alienating parent. Symptoms disappear on their own as soon as the conflict of loyalties ends.

Prevention of Misuse and Quality Assurance of Doctor's Certificates

How can abuse of doctor's certificates be prevented? What basic criteria could pediatric doctors consider, in the spirit of quality assurance and misuse prevention, before they write up an attestation? From highly combative divorce and separation situations, the following steps can be deduced:

1. Inform oneself about the context within which the illness exists (e.g., divorce, separation, custody, and visitation battles).
2. Have the purpose of the desired evaluation be clearly explained.
3. If necessary, complete certifications accompanied by the words "to be presented to . . ." in order to avoid misuse in another context.
4. Also question the child by himself or herself (*see* 5).
5. Ask the eight PAS questions, observe and evaluate the child's behavior when in contact with the accompanying adult.
6. Insist on inclusion of the other parent. This is part of the obligation to exercise due care. For example, one report reads: "The inclusion of the genetic father was not necessary from a medical point of view. If he was to desire an informal discussion with the doctor he would first have to communicate with the custodial mother." From a psychodynamic perspective, as a rule, for diagnosis of the separation-induced stress symptoms, inclusion of the parents is mandatory.
7. In cases of facts that have not been personally obtained, reporting must reflect "according to the mother/father."
8. The attestation should note that drawing a causal relationship between symptoms and problematic parental conduct is not possible (as far as for a single case this cannot be proven without a doubt).

9. The attestation must state for how long and how often the child has been seen.
10. Clues as to the presence of MSPB should be investigated.
11. In the case of a first-time consultation and an accompanying request for a doctor's certificate, if the case is a transfer case, the previously treating colleague should be consulted. Alienating parents often switch doctors if he physician is familiar with the other parent and the conflict.

In my psychotherapeutic and evaluating private practice, I have often seen cases of alienating parents. From this experience comes the recommendation for an in-depth intake process of the whole family. This process should especially consider separation and custody altercations, while also thoroughly investigating the child's contact and interaction patterns with the other parent. If it becomes clear that one parent is expecting an attestation that will be presented to the youth welfare department or the court, then this should be coupled with the demand that the other parent be consulted as well, to gather and establish the facts of the case. If this request is met with refusal, then, even on the basis of the mentioned risk for penalty alone, no attestation should be written up.

By considering the aforementioned criteria, doctors' increased competence in this area can significantly contribute to reducing the negative effects of separation for the affected children, and to help them maintain contact with both parents.

REFERENCES

Aichhorn, A. (1974). *Psychoanalyse und Erziehungsberatung.* Frankfurt: Fischer.

American Psychiatric Association. (1994). *Diagnostic and statistical manual,* Fourth Edition.Washington D.C.: American Psychiatric Association.

Ammon, G. (1979). Das Borderline-Syndrom und das ichstrukurelle Arbeiten. In: Ammon, G., (Ed.), *Handbuch der Dynamische Psychiatrie* Bd.1 (pp. 295–363). München: Reinhardt.

Andritzky, W. (2002). Zur Problematik kinderärztlicher Atteste bei Umgangs- und Sorgerechtstreitigkeiten. In: *Kinder- und Jugendarzt 33*(11), 885–889.

Andritzky, W. (2003). Behavioral patterns and personality structure of PAS-indoctrinating parents: Psychosocial and diagnostic criteria for intervention: In W.v. Boch-Galhau, U. Kodjoe, W. Andritzky and P. Koeppel (Eds.) *The Parental Alienation Syndrome (PAS): An interdisciplinary challenge for professionals involved in divorce* (pp. 283–314). International Conference, Frankfurt (Main), October 18–19, 2002. Berlin: VWB.

Brem-Gräser, L. (1992). *Familie in Tieren. Die Familiensituation im Spiegel der Kindererziehung.* München: Reinhardt.

Brown, C. (1994). The impact of divorce on families. The Australian experience. In: *Family and Conciliation Review 32*(2), 149–167).

Clawar, S.S. & B.V. Rivlin (1991). *Children held hostage: Dealing with programmed and brainwashed children.* Chicago: American Bar Association.

Dolto, F. (1996). *Scheidung. Wie ein Kind sie erlebt.* Stuttgart: Klett-Cotta.

Eckhardt-Henn, A. (2000). Artifizielle Störungen und Münchhausen Syndrom. In: Kernberg, O.F., Dulz, B. & U. Sachsse, (Eds), *Handbuch der Borderline-Störungen* (pp. 340–345). Stuttgart: Schattauer.

Ehrenberg, M.E., Hunter, M.A., & M.E. Hunterman (1996). Shared parenting agreements after marital separation: The roles of empathy and narcissism. In: *Journal of Consulting and Clinical Psychology 62*(4), 808–818.

Fegert, J.M. (2001). Parental Alienation oder Parental Accusation Syndrome? Die Frage der Suggestibilität, Beeinflussung und Induktion in Umgangsrechtsgutachten. In: *KindPrax,* Januar: 3–6.

Figdor, H. (1997). '...und hab nicht mehr gewußt, wer ich eigentlich bin'. Die psychischen Folgen des Trennungstraumas am Beispiel des Scheidungskindes. In: *Familie und Recht,* Februar: 60–67.

Fthenakis, W. (1995). Kindliche Reaktionen auf Trennung und Scheidung. In: *Familiendynamik 20,* 127–154.

Gardner, R. (1995). *Protocols for the sex abuse evaluation.* New Jersey: Creative Therapeutics.

Gardner, R. (1998). *The Parental Alienation Syndrome: A guide for mental health and legal professionals.* 2nd edition. NY.: Creative Therapeutics.

Graham, J.R. (1993). *MMPI-2: Assessing personality and psychopathology.* N.Y.: Oxford University Press.

Green, R.L. (1991). *The MMPI-2/MMPI: An interpretive manual.* Boston: Allyn & Bacon.

Heyne, C. (1993). *Täterinnen- offene und versteckte Aggression von Frauen.* München: Goldmann.

Johnston, J.R. and L. K. Girdner (2001). Family abductors: Descriptive profiles and preventive interventions. In: *Juvenile Justice Bulletin* 1–7.

Klenner, W. (1995). Rituale der Umgangsvereitelung bei getrenntlebenden oder geschiedenen Eltern. In: *Fam RZ 42* (24), 1529–1535.

Kunkel, G. (1997). *Die Beziehungsdynamik im Familienrechtskonflikt. Untersuchung der Streitmuster bei strittiger elterlicher Sorge- und Umgangsregelung.* Dissertation. Eberhard-Karls-Universität. Tübingen.

Rand, D.C. (1997). The spectrum of parental alienation syndrome (part I). In: *American Journal of Forensic Psychology 15* (3).

Salzgeber, J. and M. Stadler (1999). Parental Alienation Syndrome (PAS) - alter Wein in neuen Schläuchen? In: *Familie und Recht*, April: 231–235.

Schmidt-Denter, U. (1997). Kindliche Reaktionen auf Trennung und Scheidung. In: *Familie Partnerschaft Recht*, February: 57–59.

Schmitt, M. (1997). Präventive Methoden in der Gruppenarbeit mit Kindern in Trennungs- und Scheidungssituationen. In: Krieger, W. (Ed.) *Elterliche Trennung und Scheidung im Erleben von Kindern*, (pp. 11–75). Berlin: VWB.

Siegel, J. & J.S. Langford (1998). MMPI-2 validity scales and suspected parental alienation syndrome. In: *American Journal of Forensic Psychology, 16*(4), 5–14.

Turkat, D. (1995). Divorce related malicious mother syndrome. In: *Journal of Family Violence, 10*(3), 253–264.

Warshak, R.A. (2000). Remarriage as a trigger of Parental Alienation Syndrome. In: *The American Journal of Family Therapy, 28*, 229–240.

Yeo, S.S. (1996). Munchhausen Syndrome by Proxy: Another form of child abuse. In: *Child Abuse Review, 5*(3), 170–180.

Chapter 16

THE MISDIAGNOSIS OF PAS

BARRY BRODY

"The most important thing I learned in medical school was what not to do."
Dr. Michael Ross, physician
(personal communication)

"If you are looking for truth and justice, don't go into a courtroom."
A. S. Brody, Esquire
(fatherly advice offered to his son)

"Don't do something. Stand there!"
Advice given to Dr. Richard Gardner and fellow medical students to emphasize the importance of making a diagnosis before embarking upon a treatment program.

OVERVIEW

The issue of parental alienation syndrome (PAS) is increasingly raised in court. Unfortunately, PAS is frequently misunderstood and oftentimes misdiagnosed by mental health professionals. This chapter presents the baseline data and criteria required to correctly diagnose PAS, and then focuses on potential causes for the misdiagnosis of PAS. Recommendations are included for the training of mental health professionals to correctly diagnose PAS.

INTRODUCTION

If I don't see the emperor's new clothes, what's wrong with me? If the hand is faster than the eye, then what about the mind's eye? Questions like these often careen through my mind after I have been involved in a case for which the diagnosis or misdiagnosis of PAS is at issue. By the time I testify in such a matter, I have reviewed reports by court-appointed mental health experts, law enforcement personnel, guardians ad litem, child protection team members, videotapes of interviews, transcripts of depositions of the parents and an array of motions filed by the parents' respective attorneys claiming either the existence of PAS or the nonexistence of PAS.

Having reviewed this mountain of material, I am often left wondering: Who knows what about PAS, and am I looking at the same data as these other professionals? Clearly, all the professionals behave *as if they know*. However, it is what they know, or what they think they know, or what they don't know that they don't know that interests me. How could so many professionals look at the same data and arrive at opinions that are in total opposition? Is it that we just don't see the same thing? Is it that we are looking through different lenses? Or is it that we are looking differently at the same thing?

I am oftentimes left feeling like the nameless physician from the opening scenes of Michael Crichton's movie *The Terminal Man*. The scene takes place in a large auditorium where the scientists of the future are explaining how they are going to implant a device into a man's brain to cure his violent behavior. From the back of the auditorium a doctor stands and quietly asserts that the man is obviously a paranoid schizophrenic and that to implant a device in his brain will only serve to worsen his condition. The doctor's diagnosis is ignored. The others *know* better.

One way I prefer to conceptualize the process of misdiagnosis is that what is actually being looked at is how one knows something or how one doesn't know something; in essence, how one looks at something, and what one perceives or doesn't perceive about what is being looked at. Either road can lead to error. One can perceive or know something that isn't true, or one cannot know and not perceive something that is true. Both paths lead to the creation of an illusion: one sees what isn't there, and one doesn't see what is there. It is these sleights of mind, to steal a phrase from Harold Boris (1994), that I am interested in exploring in this chapter. I believe that the misdiagnosis of PAS is based on these created illusions – these slights of mind.

This chapter begins with a presentation of the baseline data and criteria necessary to make the diagnosis of PAS, and then discusses the need to correctly diagnose PAS. The following section reviews the literature concerning the possible causes of the misdiagnosis of PAS. The subsequent section presents this author's views concerning factors that may contribute to the misdiagnosis of PAS. A final summary section offers recommendations for training professionals to correctly diagnose PAS and suggestions for future research.

Is there anything faster than the mind's eye?

BASELINE DATA AND CRITERIA NECESSARY TO DIAGNOSE PAS

Gardner (1985) introduced the term "parental alienation syndrome" in his seminal article, "Recent Trends in Divorce and Custody Litigation." The article defined PAS and enumerated its symptoms. Gardner (2001b) notes that the original definition from 1985 remains the standard for diagnosing PAS. The definition states:

> The Parental Alienation Syndrome (PAS) is a disorder that arises primarily in the context of child-custody disputes. Its primary manifestation is the child's campaign of denigration against a parent, a campaign that has no justification. It results from the *combination* of a programming (brainwashing) parent's indoctrinations and the child's own contributions to the vilification of the target parent. When true parental abuse and/or neglect is present, the child's animosity may be justified, and so the parental alienation syndrome explanation for the child's hostility is not applicable. (p. 61)

In the first edition of *The Parental Alienation Syndrome* (1992a), Gardner further delineated the concept of PAS to include three types of PAS. Table 16.1. was created by Gardner (2001b, p. 62) to assist in the differential diagnosis of PAS. The table lists the 8 primary symptomatic manifestations of PAS, additional differential diagnostic considerations, and the three types/levels of PAS. Gardner notes that in relation to Table 16.1, "the level of PAS diagnosed is based on the children's behavior and not on the degree of indoctrination to which the child may have been subjected" (Gardner, 2001b, p. 61).

This definition of PAS – including the symptomatic manifestations and different levels – is the baseline criterion necessary for the diagnosis of PAS.

Since 1985, Gardner continued to write about PAS, providing further clinical examples of the manifestation of the disorder and focusing on selected topics to assist evaluators in accurately diagnosing it. For example, in the second edition of *The Parental Alienation Syndrome* (1998b) Gardner included a new chapter to assist professionals in differentially diagnosing PAS from bona fide cases of abuse and/or neglect.

In addition to providing the criteria for the diagnosis of PAS, Gardner (1989, 1992a, 1998b) has also provided the specific protocols for evaluators to utilize in diagnosing PAS.

THE NEED TO CORRECTLY DIAGNOSE PAS

A misdiagnosis can result in either a false-positive result or a false-negative result. Both are illusions. In the misdiagnosis of PAS, a false-positive result occurs when the examiner diagnoses PAS but it is not PAS. Thus, what doesn't exist is created. The examiner creates something out of nothing, or creates PAS out of something else. A false-negative result occurs when the examiner doesn't diagnose PAS, but it is PAS. Thus, what does exist is unseen. The examiner creates nothing out of something that does exist, or creates something else out of PAS.

Gardner has repeatedly emphasized the need for the accurate diagnosis of PAS, as can be seen from the quote at the beginning of this chapter. He wrote, "I cannot emphasize strongly enough that evaluators

TABLE 16.1. Differential Diagnosis of the Three Levels of Parental Alienation Syndrome (PAS) – Children

	The Child's Symptom Level		
Factors	**Mild**	**Moderate**	**Severe**
Primary Symptomatic Manifestations			
The campaign of denigration (May or may not include a false sex-abuse accusation)	Minimal	Moderate	Formidable
Weak, frivolous, or absurd rationalizations for the deprecation	Minimal	Moderate	Multiple absurd rationalizations
Lack of ambivalence	Normal ambivalence	No ambivalence	No ambivalence
The independent-thinker phenomenon	Usually absent	Present	Present
Reflexive support of the alienating parent in the parental conflict	Minimal	Present	Present
Absence of guilt	Normal guilt	Minimal to no guilt	No guilt
Borrowed scenarios	Minimal	Present	Present
Spread of the animosity to the extended family and friends of the alienated parent	Minimal	Present	Formidable, often fanatic
Additional Differential Diagnostic Considerations			
Transitional difficulties at the time of visitation	Usually absent	Moderate	Formidable, or visit not possible
Behavior during visitation	Good	Intermittently antagonistic and provocative	No visit, or destructive and continually provocative behavior throughout visit
Bonding with the alienator	Strong, healthy	Strong, mildly to moderately pathological	Severely pathological, often paranoid bonding
Bonding with the alienated parent prior to the alienation	Strong, healthy, or minimally pathological	Strong, healthy, or minimally pathological	Strong, healthy, or minimally pathological

Note: The *diagnosis* of PAS is based on the level of symptoms in the child, not on the symptom level of the alienator.

should never lose sight of the crucial medical dictum: diagnosis before treatment"(1998b, p. 246). Gardner (1998a) also wrote: ". . . it is important that a proper diagnostic evaluation be conducted in order to ascertain specifically in which category the child's symptoms lie: mild, moderate or severe. *Each type warrants a very different approach.* Failure to make this discrimination may result in grievous results, with significant psychological trauma to all concerned parties" (p. 7).

The two major factors identified for the need to correctly, accurately, and quickly diagnose PAS are time and the effects of PAS.

Time

Concerning time, Rand (1997a) wrote: "An appropriate diagnosis of PAS, including level of severity as Gardner recommends, can make the difference between allowing a case to go beyond the point of no return or intervening effectively before it is too late." (p. 49) Ward and Harvey (1993) made a similar point to when they wrote: "By recognizing alienation in its early forms, prevention of future harm to the child and family may well be possible. Intervention, at any point along the continuum of harm is crucial to prevent further harm" (p. 17).

Niggemyer (1998) reviewed Garrity and Baris's 1994 work, *Caught In The Middle: Protecting The Children Of High Conflict Divorce.* Niggemyer wrote: "Garrity stresses the need for early recognition of parental alienation because while time is spent identifying and interrupting alienating activities, the alienation becomes more powerful and effective" (p. 584). Regarding time, Walsh and Bone (1997) wrote:

> To heal the relationship, the child requires quality time with the targeted parent and continued communication to serve as a reality check and in order to counterbalance the effect of ongoing alienation at home. The alienating parent, on the other hand, requires time to complete the brainwashing of the child without interruption. Thus manipulation of time is a prime weapon in his or her hands. (p. 95)

Dunne and Hedrick (1994) wrote the following concerning time and PAS:

> A failure to appropriately identify and intervene in the early stages of these cases may result in the alienating parent being given professional support for his/her position, reinforcing the child's need to maintain or expand complaints about the alienated parent. This has the capacity to more firmly entrench the syndrome and to enhance the severity of the dynamics. (p. 37)

Cartwright (1993) stated: "While this tends to support the old adage that time heals all wounds, such is not the case with PAS, where the passage of time worsens rather than heals the affliction" (p. 209). Cartwright then discusses how time can be utilized to counter the effects of alienation by allowing the child quality time with the alienated parent to repair that relationship, or by the alienating parent to continue and foster alienation within the child. Cartwright concludes his discussion of time: "The goal of the alienator is crystalline: deprive the lost parent, not only of the child's time, but of the time of childhood" (p. 210).

Effects of PAS

Concerning the effects of PAS, Warshak (2000) wrote the following response to some therapists who advised against treating PAS because they did not know its effects:

> My response? Parental alienation is the effect. When a child has more than a momentary hatred or fear of a parent or grandparent, when that formerly loved adult has done nothing to deserve such rejection, this is a serious problem. It seems odd to demand that we discover other effects of parental alienation before taking it seriously and trying to alleviate it. (p. 13)

In addition to the eight symptomatic manifestations of PAS delineated by Gardner, other authors have contributed to the literature on the effects of PAS. For the purposes of this chapter, the literature reviewed will be limited to the effects of PAS on children.

Cartwright (1993) expressed concern that excessive alienation might trigger mental illness in the child. He wrote: "Unfortunately, alienation can become so powerful as to trigger other forms of mental and emotional illness with resultant maladaptive behavior" (p. 212). He emphasized the need for increasing the knowledge base concerning the medium- and long-term effects of PAS. Cartwright thought that the short-term effects of PAS were "known and obvious." He described the short-term effects of PAS upon the child thusly:

> Far more serious is the effect on the child who experiences a great loss, the magnitude of which is akin to the death of a parent, two grandparents, and all the lost parent's relatives and friends, all at once! It can readily be seen that this represents a staggering loss for a child even greater than the actual death of one parent. Moreover, since the child is unable to acknowledge the loss, much less mourn it, it becomes a major tragedy of monumental proportions in the life of the child, the seriousness of which cannot be overestimated. (p. 212)

Waldron and Joanis (1996) devoted a section of their article, "Understanding and Collaboratively Treating Parental Alienation Syndrome," to the effects of PAS on the child. They wrote: "The effect of PAS on the child is never benign; it is malevolent and intense" (p. 129). These authors thought that the severity of the effects of PAS on the child would be determined by the "extent of the brainwashing," the time spent "enmeshed" with the alienating parent, the child's age, the presence of healthy support persons in the child's life, and "the degree to which the child 'believes' the delusion." Waldron and Joanis thought that these effects span all areas of the child's functioning. In the areas of identity and self-concept formation, "the child's internal psychological and emotional organization becomes centered around the rejection of the TP [target parent]." Waldron and Joanis thought that this becomes an "internalized rejection" that results in "self-loathing, fears of rejection, depression and often suicidal ideation." In addition, the child was "internalizing the rage" of the alienating parent as "part of the self-concept," and these feelings of rage oftentimes would combine with feelings of "intense guilt" concerning the harm done to the alienated parent, resulting in "chronic feeling states" (p. 129).

Waldron and Joanis also thought that the child's reality-testing abilities would be affected. This may later affect the child's interpersonal relationships with others. They thought that due to the enmeshment of the child with the alienating parent, the development of the child's social skills would be limited. Waldron and Joanis stated that, "The child also learns that hostile, obnoxious behavior is acceptable in relationships and that deceit and manipulation are a normal part of relationships" (p. 129). These authors also thought that the "dominant emotion for the child is loss" and that the effects of the loss of the parent were "pervasive" on "other aspects of adjustment." Waldron and Joanis summarized the literature on the effects upon a child of losing a parent and being raised by one parent. These effects were: "lower academic performance; increased chance of psychological disturbance; lower self-esteem; cognitive deficiencies; higher impulse control problems; school adjustment problems; higher fear and anxiety (particularly about abandonment); greater dependency, which interferes with other aspects of development; and impaired sex-role identification" (p. 129).

Ward and Harvey (1993), writing on the "harm to the child" from PAS, stated that "It is psychologically harmful to children to be deprived of a healthy relationship with one parent" (p. 2). They also stated that another effect of PAS upon the child was that it placed the child in a "severe loyalty bind," which in and of itself was damaging to the child. The authors said that if this bind resulted in the "exclusion of a parent from a child's life, the injury is irreparable" (p. 2).

Rand (1997b) devoted a section of her exhaustive series of articles on Parental Alienation Syndrome to "the child in PAS." Rand discussed children who aligned with one parent against the other in the process of a divorce. Rand stated:

> Children in these alignments came to share the views and outrage of the parent with whom the child identified, often the parent who felt abandoned and rejected in the divorce. These children rejected the parent who was perceived as deserting the family, despite a previously close, loving relationship with that parent. Children in alignments were found to be less psychologically healthy than those whose divorce adjustment allowed them to maintain the affection for both parents. (p. 41)

Rand (1997b) also reported Lampel's 1996 study where latency-age children undergoing child custody evaluations were compared on the factor of alignment. Lampel found that the aligned children tested as angrier, less well adjusted, and less able to conceptualize complex situations. They expressed greater self confidence, however, possibly reflecting the relief obtained by opting for a simplified, relatively black-and-white solution, as opposed to feeling "caught in the middle" of parental conflicts (p. 41).

Rand (1997b) also reported Johnston and Roseby's work concerning aligned children. They reserved the "PAS label" for children in their "extreme alignment" group. These children were ". . . more likely to be viewed as disturbed by parents, teachers and clinicians. These children exhibited bizarre and sometimes destructive behavior. They were more likely to display unintegrated, chaotic attitudes with few workable defenses" (p. 45). Johnston and Roseby preferred to see the etiology of these children as a "later manifestation of the failed separation-individuation process. . . ." (p. 46) Rand pointed out that children who constantly aligned with the alienating parent "may never have separated psychologically from that parent" (p. 46). Rand also stated that "Where there is a particularly enmeshed relationship between the aligned parent and the child, the child's legitimate strivings for autonomy are continually undermined" (p. 47).

Rand (1997b) also reviewed Wallerstein and Blakeslee's work on the "overburdened child." In these children, "The needs of the troubled parent override the developmental needs of the child, with the result that the child becomes psychologically depleted and their own emotional and social progress is crippled." (p. 48) Rand reports that Wallerstein is familiar with PAS, but that Wallerstein "prefers to conceptualize it from the 'overburdened child' framework" (p. 48).

Walsh and Bone (1997) discussed the potential effects of PAS upon the child. They stated that the child would be prone to becoming anxious, isolated, and depressed. If proper intervention is not forthcoming, the child develops a deep and profound sense of self-hatred and shame for condemning the other parent. These children tend to become despondent, withdrawn, and develop psychopathic manipulative characteristics that may be carried into adulthood (p. 93).

Kopetski (1998) detailed the effects of parental alienation on children in her article dealing with the identification of PAS. Kopetski considered PAS the "modern equivalent to school phobia" (p. 64), with the alienated parent replacing the school as the object of the phobia. Kopetski stated that many children affected by PAS develop symptoms of "anxious attachment or separation anxiety when they are long past the age where separation anxiety is normal" (p. 65). This results in a variety of symptoms ranging from sleep disturbance, regression in the ability to regulate bodily functions, and poor impulse control in young children, to disorganization, poor academic performance, social isolation, and moodiness in elementary school-aged children. Kopetski also reported that children affected by PAS may develop problems in the areas of reality-testing, rigidity of thought processes, and may actually come to value their symptoms as a part of their identity.

Stahl (1999) detailed the symptoms that children affected by PAS were likely to develop. These symptoms were: splittings in their relationships, difficulties in forming intimate relationships, lack of the ability to tolerate anger or hostility with other relationships, psychosomatic symptoms, sleep or eating disorders, psychological vulnerability and dependency, conflicts with authority figures, and unhealthy sense of entitlement for one's rage leading to social isolation (p. 28).

Vestal (1999) reported on studies related to the effect of PAS on children. She cited Clawar and Rivlin's 1991 study in which ". . . 40% of the children developed self-hatred and guilt because they were used as an ally in the war against the rejected parent" (p. 492).

POTENTIAL CAUSES FOR THE MISDIAGNOSIS OF PAS

Gardner (2001c) foresaw the problem of the misdiagnosis of PAS. He wrote:

> With increasing recognition of PAS, it is predictable that it will be misdiagnosed, overdiagnosed, and utilized improperly. This is true of just about any psychiatric disturbance, and as a matter of fact, of any medicine. With increasing knowledge and experience we should be able to delineate these various complications regarding correct diagnosis. In short, not all campaigns of denigration are the result of manifestations of PAS and not all campaigns of denigration are manifestations of abuse. Life is just not that simple. (p. 134)

Numerous authors have written about the potential causes for the misdiagnosis of PAS. This section reviews the work of these authors. It is organized into two major categories: *procedural variables* and *personal variables.* Procedural variables refer literally to the procedure that was utilized by the examiner during the evaluation to obtain the data on which the diagnosis was made. Personal variables refer to personal biases, assumptions and frames of mind that impact the examiner in both obtaining the data and interpreting or shaping the data on which the diagnosis was made. This division is based on Rogers' (2001) discussion of sources of diagnostic variability in mental health evaluations. Rogers wrote: "most diagnostic variability is a product of the evaluations and *not* the patients." (p. 4) Rogers divided the sources of diagnostic variability into two categories: the procedures utilized by the examiner in obtaining the data, and how the examiner interpreted the data. He reported that how the examiner interpreted the data was responsible for almost twice as much of the diagnostic variability as the procedures utilized in obtaining the data. A similar categorization of the sources of diagnostic variability is described in McGleughlin, Meyer and Baker's (1999) chapter on assessing sexual abuse allegations in divorce, custody and visitation disputes. In discussing their recommendations for clinical guidelines for these types of evaluations, they listed two types of bias: personal bias and procedural bias. Personal bias refers to "strong emotional reactions" in the evaluator that lead to diagnostic error. These authors found that "Child protective workers, mental health professionals, attorneys and judges as well, are particularly susceptible to bias when sexual abuse is alleged" (p. 370). Personal bias is synonymous with the category of personal variables utilized in this section. Procedural bias refers to bias in the procedures utilized to obtain the data during the evaluation, which lead to diagnostic error. Procedural bias is synonymous with the category of procedural variables utilized in this section. These authors note that both types of bias may lead to diagnostic errors resulting in either false-negative errors or false-positive errors.

Procedural Variables

Galatzer-Levy and Ostrov (1999) wrote, "The way in which 'facts' are collected often profoundly affects their content and significance. The information collected in custody evaluations can be profoundly shaped by the collection process." (p. 35) They also wrote that "the greatest danger occurs when the evaluator is unaware of the factors in the interview or testing situation that shape the information received" (p. 36). This section reviews how specific procedures utilized in the evaluation of PAS shape the data collected and can result in a misdiagnosis of PAS.

Context of PAS Evaluations

By definition, PAS "is a disorder that arises primarily in the context of child-custody disputes" (Gardner, 2001b, p. 61). Thus, the usual context for the diagnosis or misdiagnosis of PAS is a child custody evaluation. It is the structure of this particular type of evaluation that may actually increase the probability of misdiagnosis of PAS.

Warshak (2000) described his concerns regarding child custody evaluations thusly:

> . . . many evaluators fail to recognize the limitations of their procedures and the poor foundation for their conclusions and recommendations. They make the same errors over and over again without pausing to take stock of what they are doing. They couch personal biases in pseudo-scientific rhetoric. They pass off their tentative

> speculations as firm conclusions and truths. They shoot from the hip, often gunning down the best interests of the children and the emotional well-being of at least one parent. In the process they undermine the reputation of the entire enterprise of custody evaluations. (p. 4)

Warshak urges evaluators to "make a determined effort to separate myth from reality" (p. 4).

Concerns regarding the methodology utilized in conducting child custody evaluations – the context within which PAS is usually evaluated – have been voiced by many other forensic professionals. One focus of these concerns has been the appropriateness of utilizing traditional psychological test instruments in child-custody evaluations. Melton and colleagues (1997) cited the following statements by Grisso (1984) to highlight this problem:

> Custody cases involving divorced or divorcing parents rarely involve questions of parental fitness, but rather the choice between two parents, neither of whom [is] summarily inadequate [as a parent]. . . . Mental health professionals do not have reason to be proud of their performance in this area of forensic assessment. Too often we still evaluate the parent but not the child, a practice that makes no sense when the child's own, individual needs are the basis for the legal decision. Too often we continue to rely on the assessment instruments and methods that were designed to address *clinical* questions, questions of psychiatric diagnosis, when clinical questions bear only secondarily upon the real issues in many child custody cases. Psychiatric interviews, Rorschachs, and MMPIs might have a role to play in child custody assessments. But these tools were *not* designed to assess parents' relationships to children . . . [or their] childrearing attitudes and capacities, and *these* are often the central questions in child custody cases. (p. 484)

Schutz and colleagues (1989) reached a similar conclusion to Grisso. They wrote that after having reviewed the psychological tests available to utilize in a child custody evaluation, "We did not find a single test that met enough of the criteria to qualify as a direct measure of parenting skill" (p. 39). These authors developed a model for child custody evaluations, which utilized questionnaires, interviews and observations of all the family members.

Brodzinsky (1993) described these same problems with utilizing standard psychological tests in child custody evaluations. In his article, On the Use and Misuse of Psychological Testing in Child Custody Evaluations, Brodzinsky wrote: "Although traditional psychological testing is a legitimate means of collecting information in child custody and visitation disputes, its usefulness is more limited than most forensic evaluators recognize. The standard psychological tests used in these types of cases do not adequately address the key issues before the court" (p. 218). Brodzinsky also warned evaluators conducting child custody evaluations to "guard against the false assumption that testing inherently imbues the forensic evaluator with a scientific foundation and thus a greater degree of objectivity. There is simply no empirical evidence that this is the case" (p. 218). Finally, in discussing factors leading to the misuse and overuse of psychological tests in child custody evaluations, Brodzinsky wrote: "In most cases, the assumptions and motives of the mental health expert are the primary problem" (p. 217).

Hysjulien and colleagues (1994) reviewed assessment methods utilized in child custody evaluations and concluded that, "although psychological testing is used by nearly three-fourths of evaluators as part of child custody evaluations, the reliability as well as the construct and predictive validity of psychological tests used in child custody evaluations remains unproven" (pp. 472–473).

These authors addressed the issue of the diagnosis of PAS and discussed the usefulness of utilizing the Bricklin Perceptual Scales as a method to determine the diagnosis of PAS. Bricklin (1995) wrote the following concerning the difficulties with traditional tests: "The typical tools and tests in the mental health professional's armamentarium – procedures that are so good at measuring cognitive capacities and identifying sources of conflict and underlying personality variables – are not data-based to yield information that is maximally helpful in custody cases" (p. xii). This was one of the factors that led Bricklin to develop his ACCESS materials, which are data-based, child-custody-specific test instruments.

Melton and colleagues (1997) discussed the utilization of traditional test instruments in child custody evaluations and concluded, "It is our contention that such tests are often used inappropriately" (p. 503). These authors endorsed an assessment model for child custody evaluations, which was consistent with that proposed by Schutz et al. (1989). This model focuses on observations and interviews of the parents and children and the gathering of collateral data.

Rand (1997b) reiterated these conclusions regarding utilizing standard assessment instruments in child custody evaluations in which PAS was being considered. Rand wrote, "Psychological tests which are used for the assessment of individual patients in clinical settings cannot be considered reliable and valid for the evaluation of family systems in forensic settings" (p. 83). Rand went on to cite Stahl's opinion that, ". . . many custody evaluations are not geared to adequately diagnose the pathology of an alienating parent and the complex family interactions which produce PAS. This results in recommendations which are too shortsighted for the true level of family dysfunction" (p. 83).

In response to these concerns regarding the procedures utilized in child custody evaluations, several professional organizations designed and issued guidelines for these evaluations. The American Psychological Association, the American Academy of Child and Adolescent Psychiatry, and the Association of Family and Conciliation Courts all devised guidelines to standardize child custody evaluation procedures and to limit bias introduced into the evaluation due to both procedural variables and personal variables.

The American Psychological Association (1994) issued their "Guidelines for Child Custody Evaluations in Divorce Proceedings." These guidelines specified the focus, scope, and methodology to be utilized in child custody evaluations conducted in the context of divorce. The guidelines emphasize the use of "multiple methods of data gathering, including but not limited to, clinical interviews, observation, and/or psychological assessments" (p. 678). The guidelines also specify that the evaluator gains "specialized competence" in specific areas. Listed in the "Pertinent Literature" section are three books by Gardner – *Family Evaluation in Child Custody Mediation, Arbitration, and Litigation* (1989), *The Parental Alienation Syndrome* (1992a), and *True and False Accusations of Child Abuse* (1992b). *It should be noted that the first two books listed contain the diagnostic criteria for diagnosing PAS and the protocol for conducting an evaluation to determine the presence of PAS.*

The American Academy of Child and Adolescent Psychiatry (1997) issued their Practice Parameters for Child Custody Evaluation. The guidelines specified the scope and methodology to be utilized in conducting child custody evaluations. These guidelines emphasize an assessment model focusing on interviews and observations of all the family members. They contain a section listing common "issues in child custody disputes." Parental alienation is listed as one of these common issues.

In spite of these efforts to standardize child custody evaluations and to minimize errors caused by procedural variance, there still remain two significant factors embedded in the context of these evaluations that serve to increase the probability of a misdiagnosis of PAS.

The first factor is the continued reliance on inappropriate assessment procedures to diagnose PAS. The background and concerns regarding the misuse of assessment instruments in child custody evaluations have just been detailed. Writing about this issue, Warshak (2000) stated: "In an effort to appear more scientific, evaluators are now increasingly relying on poorly validated tests to bypass the sophisticated task of getting to know the family in enough depth to assist them, their attorneys, and the courts to make wise decisions" (p. 19). Rand (1997b) discussed Montgomery's concerns that child custody evaluators *". . . were not using the APA guidelines and that this was contributing to serious decision errors in assessment and intervention with PAS and other high conflict cases"* (p. 84).

Thus, the procedural variable of utilizing inappropriate assessment methods to diagnose PAS remains a major potential source of diagnostic error. When an evaluator utilizes inappropriate assessment methods – methods that were not designed to diagnose PAS, or methods other than the specific protocols designed to diagnose PAS – the potential for misdiagnosis is significant. Gardner (2001c) wrote that:

> . . . standard psychological testing instruments have not been designed to diagnose PAS, and most often, give little if any information regarding this diagnosis. I am not saying that such tests do not give information about a wide variety of other diagnoses; they do. I am only saying that standard psychological tests most often do not give useful information regarding the PAS diagnosis. (p. xxii)

I have frequently been involved with cases where the diagnosis of PAS was at issue, but none of the professionals involved performed an appropriate evaluation for PAS utilizing the prescribed protocols. In testifying in such cases, I have repeatedly stated to the court that since an appropriate evaluation for PAS has not been performed, the matter cannot be discussed because any such discussion will be based on the assumption that an appropriate assessment of PAS has been accomplished. This misassumption will lead to erroneous conclusions. What is required before any such discussion occurs is to perform an appropriate assessment of PAS.

Currently, there exist specific assessment protocols for the diagnosis of PAS. Gardner (1989, 1992a, 1998b) has provided these protocols, and they were specifically referenced in the American Psychological Association's guidelines for conducting child custody evaluations. Both Dunne and Hedrick (1994) and Rand (1997b) endorse the utilization of this protocol to appropriately diagnose PAS.

The second factor of procedural variables, which is embedded in the context of child custody evaluations concerning PAS, is encountered when evaluators attempt to utilize the specific protocols for the diagnosis of PAS. These protocols do not use standard psychological tests, but rely on interviews and observations. Bricklin (1995) discussed sources of bias in child custody evaluation. He wrote the following regarding interviews and observational assessment techniques: The most dangerous sources of bias are the deeply subjective forms. . . . These forms of bias more easily enter the picture when an evaluator relies on nondata-based sources of information . . . the interviewer will tend to rely on interview and observational data – data that can more readily be used to support any given subjective bias (p. 21).

Thus, in performing an evaluation utilizing the appropriate assessment protocols for diagnosing PAS, the evaluator will be more prone to the effects of subjective bias, thereby increasing the probability of misdiagnosing PAS. It should be noted that Bricklin (2000) devised the Bricklin Perceptual Scales and the Perception of Relationships Test to address this issue of interviews and observational techniques being prone to subjective bias. Bricklin utilizes these two instruments to detect signs of PAS, which are then either confirmed or disconfirmed utilizing interviews and observations. At the present time, Bricklin's assessment instruments are the only two instruments that I am familiar with that are utilized in the detection of PAS. These instruments are not a replacement for the specific interview and observational protocols utilized in conducting an assessment for PAS, but are an adjunct to them.

Thus, the two factors of procedural variables in diagnosing PAS, which are inherent to the context of child custody evaluations, are (1) utilization of inappropriate assessment methods to diagnose PAS and (2) subjective bias introduced by utilizing the appropriate assessment methods of interviews and observations.

Unintentional Evaluator Errors

This section deals with unintentional procedural errors committed by evaluators performing an assessment of PAS. These unintentional errors increase the probability of a misdiagnosis of PAS. The section focuses on two categories of unintentional errors committed by evaluators – technical errors related to the methods utilized by the evaluator, and knowledge base errors related to either a lack of knowledge concerning PAS or a misunderstanding of PAS. The term "unintentional" is used to indicate that the majority of these evaluators simply "don't know." This is not a matter of maliciousness or willful acts, but an illusion created in the mind of examiners that they know how to conduct an assessment for PAS. It is the fact that they don't know that they don't know that creates the errors.

The first unintentional technical error is the collective specific behaviors of the evaluator, which are utilized to conduct a diagnostic interview for PAS. These behaviors would include how the evaluator words questions, how the evaluator sequences questions, and the evaluator's tone of voice, facial expressions, and physical gestures. All of these evaluator behaviors can potentially shape or effect the response obtained from the interviewee. A considerable amount of research has been conducted in this area regarding allegations of sexual abuse.

Rand (1997b) reported a study that involved the analysis of 150 tape-recorded abuse interviews with children. The study was able to identify:

> . . . specific adult interviewer behaviors which influence children to alter accounts and to say things that will satisfy or please the interviewer. When the child is brought by a parent for an abuse interview, the parent's report of what occurred tends to shape the interviewer's ideas about what occurred and the questions which are asked. These interviewer expectations are communicated to the child through the adult's reactions, leading questions and other suggestive techniques. Such effects occur even among professionals trained not to use suggestive methods. (p. 62)

Hunt and Borgida (2001) studied the effect of interviewers contradicting statements made by witnesses. In discussing their results, these authors stated that "commonly used interviewing techniques can have serious, deleterious effects on children's testimony" (p. 599). The authors also stated that ". . . despite the possibility that many modifications may reflect accidental mistakes made by interviewers, they can have important effects on investigatory interviews" (p. 600).

Gardner (1992b) devoted a chapter in his book *True and False Accusations of Child Sex Abuse* to the discussion of evaluator behaviors that may result in contaminating the responses obtained. Gardner discussed the areas of "leading questions" and "leading stimuli," and introduced the term "leading gestures."

Gardner (2002b) discussed "common faulty assessment techniques" utilized by evaluators. He listed several of these faulty techniques, including suggestion, conditioning, power maneuvers, and repetitious questions. Gardner concluded that "Examiners who utilize these faulty interview techniques are likely to come to conclusions that are basically projections onto the data of their own speculations. Thus, the data are serving as projective tests for the examiner, rather than for the patient" (p. 46).

Thus, the evaluator may unintentionally create error in the assessment interview by utilizing behaviors that influence the interviewee's responses. In this case the obtained data are not allowed to speak, but instead are being unintentionally altered by the behaviors of the evaluator. To minimize this type of technical error, Gardner (2002b) has repeatedly urged evaluators to utilize the "blank-screen principle," which allows the data to be free from the contaminating effects of the evaluator. This will allow for the PAS assessment to be as accurate as possible, and will minimize the potential for misdiagnosis caused by unintentional technical error by the evaluator.

The second unintentional technical error is the evaluator's format for observing and interviewing the parents and children. Gardner (1987) specifically discussed the need for the evaluator conducting an assessment of PAS to conduct interviews with the parents and children alone and together. Gardner (1987) wrote:

> Furthermore, the data-collection process will also be compromised if the parties are seen only alone and not interviewed in various combinations. Restricting oneself to interviewing only the child alone compromises the data collection process significantly because it deprives the evaluator of obtaining data in joint interviews, which are often the most valuable part of the data collection process. (p. 26)

Niggemeyer (1998) reiterated this specific requirement for the evaluator conducting an assessment for PAS. Niggemeyer stated that in identifying parental alienation, ". . . the court should assess the relationships between and among the children, the parents, extended family, and also other parties involved in the divorce situation" (p. 583).

Bricklin (2000) wrote:

> It is essential that professionals be aware that the most commonly used observation format, each parent alone with each child, is inadequate in high conflict cases. The evaluator must be able to compare how a child behaves in the simultaneous presence of both parents, where he or she has the *choice* of which parent to approach for feelings of safety or for information, to behavior exhibited when he or she is alone with each parent. (p. 23)

In spite of these recommendations on the interview and observation format for these types of assessments, Turkat (1993) wrote, "Many custody evaluators do not specifically and systematically observe the interaction between each parent and each child involved in the custody evaluation" (p. 177).

Thus, the evaluator conducting a PAS assessment who unintentionally omits utilizing the recommended format for interviews and observations will increase the probability for a misdiagnosis of PAS. This result will be obtained because the data collected will be incomplete and compromised due to the format utilized, and the diagnosis rendered will be based on these data.

Knowledge and understanding of PAS are essential for diagnosis. Numerous authors have cited the unintentional lack of knowledge of PAS or misunderstanding of PAS as an important factor in misdiagnosis.

Walsh and Bone (1999) discussed the issue of "undiagnosed PAS." They stated that ". . . it must be understood that all mental health professionals are not aware of nor know how to treat the PAS phenomenon. In fact, when a mental health professional unfamiliar with PAS is called upon to make a recommendation about custody, access, or related issues, he or she potentially can do more harm than good" (p. 46). Walsh and Bone also state that in cases of undiagnosed PAS caused by lack of knowledge, ". . . the mental health professional expert has actually become part of the PAS, albeit unwittingly. Alarmingly, this happens often" (p. 47).

Major (1999) described a similar problem concerning "undiagnosed PAS" resulting from lack of knowledge. Major wrote:

> Therapists with master's degrees are unlikely to realize the severity and depth of the problem, because they are not trained in this level of pathology. In fact, they may unwittingly side with the alienating parent and even testify or produce evidence in court that the child is afraid of the father. This can be a serious stumbling block in getting an accurate diagnosis. Indeed, it can tip the scale into the alienating parent's agenda and do real damage. (p. 7)

Gardner (1989) emphasized this issue. He wrote:

> Examiners who evaluate families involved in custody disputes should be familiar with the etiology, pathogenesis, and manifestations of a disorder which I have referred to as the *parental alienation syndrome.* The evaluator who is not familiar with this disturbance will be compromised in conducting an adequate custody evaluation. In fact, a lack of familiarity with this disorder may result in the examiner's taking at face value the children's comments – with the result that an injudicious and even psychologically detrimental recommendation may be made. (p. 225)

The companion, knowledge-based factor of unintentional evaluator error in diagnosing PAS is the misunderstanding of PAS. In both knowledge-based factors a similar element of illusion is created. The unknowledgeable evaluator doesn't know that he or she doesn't know about PAS, but acts as if he or she knows how to perform a PAS evaluation. In the second case, the evaluator thinks that he or she knows about PAS, but doesn't know that he or she does not understand the concept.

Warshak (1999) lists seven potential diagnostic errors to consider when the diagnosis of PAS is made by an evaluator. All seven errors reflect a misunderstanding of PAS. For example, Warshak lists as a diagnostic error the evaluator who diagnoses PAS based on ". . . the child's criticism of a parent, but the child does not engage in a campaign of denigration and does not refuse to spend time with the alleged target" (p. 48). To demonstrate this diagnostic error based on misunderstanding of PAS, Warshak discusses Gardner's criticism of evaluators who ". . . confuse normal criticisms with a PAS campaign of denigration" (p. 48). Warshak then provides this quote from Gardner, "The examiner may entirely misdiagnose the children and claim that they are in the severe category even though they are happily visiting and do not even show manifestations of a mild PAS" (p. 48).

In another example of diagnostic error, Warshak describes the case where, "Although the evidence indicates that your client is trying to indoctrinate the child against the other parent, the child does not participate in the denigration and does not exhibit the other symptoms of PAS" (p. 48). The evaluator proceeds to diagnose the child with PAS. Warshak concludes that this evaluator "does not have a good understanding of the diagnosis. If the expert has endorsed Gardner as an authority on PAS, the expert can be confronted on cross examination with Gardner's statement: 'The *diagnosis* of PAS is not made on the basis of the programmer's efforts but the degree of success in each child'" (p. 49).

Williams (1990) notes that "It is unfortunate that Dr. Gardner has been misunderstood and misused by some mental health clinicians advocating for sole custody" (p. 4). Williams refers to the "misunderstanding or overstatement of the writings of Dr. Richard Gardner" (p. 4) that some mental health professionals "misuse" to support inappropriate recommendations.

Gardner (1998b) has frequently cautioned about diagnostic errors resulting from the evaluator's misunderstanding of PAS. In discussing the misunderstanding that PAS is the same as brainwashing, he (1998b) wrote:

> It has come as a surprise to me from reports in both the legal and mental health literature that the concept of the parental alienation syndrome is often misinterpreted. Specifically, there are many who use the term *parental alienation syndrome* as synonymous with parental brainwashing or programming. Those who do this have missed an extremely important point regarding the etiology, manifestations, and even the treatment of the PAS. The disorder refers to a situation in which the parental programming *is combined* with the child's own scenarios of denigration of the allegedly hated parent. (pp. 73–74)

Gardner (1998b) also discussed the misunderstanding of PAS resulting in evaluators misdiagnosing actual abuse as PAS. He wrote:

> Unfortunately, the term PAS is sometimes used to refer to the animosity that a child may harbor against a parent who has *actually* abused the child. . . . The term PAS has been used to apply to the major categories of parental abuse, namely, physical, sexual, and emotional. Such application indicates a misunderstanding of the PAS. The PAS term is applicable only when the targeted parent has not exhibited anything close to the degree of alienating behavior that might warrant the campaign of denigration exhibited by the child. Rather, in typical cases the parent would be considered by most examiners to have provided normal loving parenting or, at worst, exhibited minimal impairments in parenting capacity. It is the *exaggeration* of minor weaknesses and deficiencies that is the hallmark of the PAS. When bona fide abuse does exist, then the child's responding hostility is warranted, and the PAS diagnosis is not applicable. (p. 74)

Gardner (1998b) also discussed the misunderstanding of PAS resulting in a misdiagnosis of the level of severity of the PAS.

> I cannot emphasize strongly enough the importance of accurately defining the category of PAS (mild, moderate, or severe) *before* implementing any therapeutic or legal measures. Not to do so is likely to result in grievous errors that will predictably cause significant pathological distress and grief to all concerned parties. I have seen mental health professionals and courts who have dealt with mild or moderate cases of PAS as if they were severe, injudiciously and erroneously transferring custody to the alienated parent whose level of indoctrinations were minimal. In these cases the indoctrinations would have ceased once the programming parent was reassured that custody would remain with him (her). I have seen cases in which courts and mental health professionals have assessed PAS only on the basis of the programmer's indoctrinations, and not the degree to which the programming process has been successfully induced in the child. In such cases the children may have exhibited only mild PAS manifestations, but the programmer was treated as if the children were in the severe category and thereby was deprived of custody. Again, the *diagnosis* of PAS is not made on the basis of the programmer's efforts but the degree of "success" in each child. (p. 246)

The unintentional evaluator errors, both technical and knowledge-based, are clearly significant factors that will predispose an evaluator to misdiagnose PAS.

Personal Variables

Galatzer-Levy and Kraus (1999) wrote:

> Although corrupt individuals occasionally may act as "hired guns," testifying in favor of those who retain them for a price, a much more common and pernicious problem is the uncorrupt but inaccurate expert who presents pet theories and personal prejudices as scientific fact. In the emotionally charged arena of child custody decisions, personal needs or inadequate training may lead some individuals with professional credentials to believe and testify in a manner that is inconsistent with reasonable standards for scientific information. (p. 6)

Brodsky (1991) raised a similar concern about personal variables. He wrote: "These events constitute a far greater hazard to impartiality than the mythical bought witness. Their impact is gradual and beyond the immediate awareness of the expert. These influences are sufficiently powerful that they may be the single greatest threat to expert integrity" (p. 9).

This section reviews some of the personal variables that have been discussed in the literature pertaining to the assessment and diagnosis of PAS. Because these personal variables are unseen and unknown, they represent a significant factor that may affect the evaluator conducting a PAS assessment and result in a misdiagnosis of PAS. Because these personal variables are usually hidden from the conscious awareness of the evaluator, the illusion is created that the evaluator is basing his or her diagnosis on the data, when in fact the data may have been unknowingly shaped by these personal variables. It is the hidden influence of personal variables in shaping the data that makes them a significant factor in increasing the probability of a misdiagnosis of PAS.

Categories of Personal Variables

Ackerman (1995), Ackerman and Kane (1998), and Bricklin (1995) in their books concerning child custody evaluations reviewed the work of Arthur Williams on the major types of bias that affect evaluators, resulting in an increased probability of diagnostic error. The most relevant of these biases in the assessment of PAS are the following.

Confirmatory Bias occurs when the evaluator looks for and overvalues or emphasizes data or information that supports or confirms the evaluator's position and then tends to look away or ignore data or information that does not confirm the evaluator's position. This type of bias is descriptive of "validators." Validators will be discussed in a subsequent section.

Anchoring is considered a type of confirmatory bias in which the evaluator assigns excessive weight or importance to initial information. Bricklin (1995) views anchoring as a result of persons, including evaluators, being uncomfortable in dealing with large amounts of data and being uncertain how to structure and categorize the information. Bricklin wrote:

> The custody evaluator, in a rush to decrease anxiety, attempts to provide structure to the data, often coming to conclusions too quickly. Once this is done, he or she will tend to see other pieces of data as confirming these initial diagnostic impressions. There is also a tendency for deeply-held subjective biases to work here, since already-held biases form all-too-available categories into which incoming data can be put. (p. 22)

Anchoring will be discussed in the subsequent section concerning the view held by some professionals that PAS does not exist.

Availability refers to the phenomenon that persons, including evaluators, tend to emphasize and more easily remember data that are vivid and dramatic. Availability will be discussed later in relationship to how some evaluators become aligned with the "delusions" of a PAS child or alienating parent.

Illusionary correlation refers to an evaluator assuming that a relationship exists between events or characteristics in the absence of objective or supporting data to indicate that the relationship exists. This is a common bias seen in "validators" and persons who misinterpret PAS, resulting in a misdiagnosis.

Hindsight bias refers to the tendency of the evaluator to be influenced by prior data and information in reaching a diagnosis. For example, Gardner (2002b, p. 43) discussed this issue in relation to evaluators reviewing prior evaluations and assessments. Gardner's concern was that the prior evaluation or therapy might have been faulty, thereby contaminating the obtained data and diagnosis. If the current evaluator is not aware that the prior assessment was flawed, the evaluator might have a tendency to confirm the diagnosis of the prior assessment without actually conducting an independent assessment. This type of bias is extremely common in PAS cases because of the tendency to involve multiple professionals in these matters. I have frequently been involved in cases where four or five other professionals have already been involved, and all these professionals have rendered the same diagnosis of either the existence of PAS or that PAS is not applicable to the matter. It would be naive or arrogant to assume that one could not be affected by this prior data. Therefore, one must strive to be as thorough as possible in reviewing other professionals' data, searching for assessment errors due to procedural and/or personal variables to ensure that a misdiagnosis of PAS has not occurred.

Brodsky (1991) discussed "examiner effects" to refer to all types of personal bias. He described examiner effects as ". . . the entire range of nonobvious influences a psychological examiner has on a client" (p. 79). Brodsky discussed the problem that mental health professionals attribute variance from normal or expected behaviors to clients without realizing how much clients may vary from situation to situation, and examiner to examiner. Put another way, mental health professionals see client behaviors that, to a fair degree, may be states and interpret them as traits (p. 80). Brodsky is here referring to what I term the "co-creational" nature of the PAS assessment. The results of any assessment can be viewed as being derived from contributions of both the examiner and the client. The ideal is to minimize or eliminate any examiner contribution to the results, or else the results will be contaminated and the probability for misdiagnosis is significant. This co-creational aspect of PAS assessments will be discussed further in the last section of this chapter.

Validators

Rand (1997b) defined validators as ". . . professionals who, when presented with allegations of abuse, assume that abuse occurred. They see their role as validating the alleged abuse rather than conducting an objective investigation" (p. 62). This is an example of confirmatory bias; the evaluator is looking for confirmatory data that support the evaluator's position (that abuse occurred), and ignores or overlooks any disconfirming data.

Gardner (1994, 1995) wrote two articles about validators who start with a basic assumption and then find data to confirm this assumption. The titles of the articles are "You're Not a Paranoid Schizophrenic – You Only Have Post-Traumatic Stress Disorder" and "You're Not a Paranoid Schizophrenic – You Only Have Multiple Personality Disorder." Both articles discussed how evaluators/validators "manipulated and distorted" the symptoms of paranoid schizophrenia so that an alternate, incorrect diagnosis was confirmed.

Gardner (1996b) also discussed factors that might be operative in a validator's personality. He cited Underwager and Wakefield's (1991) work, which identified specific personality factors operative in validators. The first was cognitive dissonance. Cognitive dissonance describes discomfort a person experiences when encountering data that conflict with his or her beliefs. Gardner wrote, "People who have difficulty tolerating such dissonance are likely to selectively shut out material that conflicts with their original beliefs" (p. 338). Cognitive dissonance is very similar to the description of confirmatory bias. The second factor was intolerance of ambiguity. This factor describes persons who have difficulty dealing with contradictions, inconsistencies and ambiguous data. These persons resolve this intolerance by shaping data into mutually exclusive categories such as yes or no, and present or absent. Intolerance of ambiguity is similar to the description of anchoring.

It should be understood that this discussion of validators and confirmatory bias also applies to the assessment of PAS. Some evaluators do not believe in the existence of PAS. Such evaluators will search for data that confirms this belief, and will in many instances find it.

Gardner (2001b) wrote about other personality factors operative in mental health professionals, namely passivity and obsessive doubting. This may result in behavior opposite to what is seen in validators. Instead of shaping the data to conform to a preconceived bias, these mental health professionals have no method to sort the data, so they deal with the data by ". . . weighing the pros and cons of any particular action. The deliberative process becomes an end in itself" (p. 66). Thus, the deliberative process replaces the validator's bias as a method to deal with the data. Gardner (2001b) states that "Such people should not be working with PAS children. They will make matters worse and they will do just what the alienating parent wants them to do, mainly nothing" (p. 67). Perhaps this represents a misdiagnosis of PAS created by a failure to make any diagnosis at all.

The Nonexistence of PAS

As mentioned, some mental health professionals believe that PAS does not exist. Of course, these professionals would never diagnose PAS. Thus, if confronted with an actual case of PAS, these professionals will misdiagnose it as something else. This attitude or bias can be viewed as an example of anchoring. As was noted earlier, Bricklin viewed anchoring as a "tendency for deeply-held subjective biases" to be utilized by the evaluator to structure the data. This tendency was based on the concept that ". . . already-held biases form all-too-available categories into which incoming data can be put." In this instance the bias/category is that PAS does not exist; all data will be structured/sorted into the other-than-PAS category/bias – even data that is confirmatory of a PAS diagnosis. Some arguments offered in support of the nonexistence of PAS are the following:

PAS does not exist because it is not in the DSM-IV. Gardner(2002a) responded to this argument by pointing out that:

> From 1991 to 1993, when the DSM committees were meeting to consider the inclusion of additional disorders, there were too few articles in the literature to warrant submission of the PAS for consideration. That is no longer the case. It is my understanding that committees will begin to meet for the next edition of the DSM (probably to be called DSM-V) in 2002 or 2003. Considering the fact that there are now at least 110 articles in peer-review journals on PAS, it is highly likely that by that time there will be even more articles. (p. 101)

Gardner (2002a) also noted the following regarding noninclusion of PAS in the DSM-IV:

> It is important to note that DSM-IV does not frivolously accept every new proposal. Their requirements are very stringent with regard to the inclusion of newly described clinical entities. The committees require many years of research and numerous publications in peer-review scientific journals before considering the inclusion of a disorder, and justifiably so. Giles de La Tourette first described his syndrome in 1885. It was not until 1980, 95 years later, that the disorder found its way into the DSM. . . . Asperger first described his syndrome in 1957. It was not until 1994, 37 years later, that it was accepted into DSM-IV. . . . (p. 101)

PAS does not exist because it has not been subjected to peer review. Warshak (2001) commented on this argument by noting that:

> In addition to Gardner's work on PAS, there are currently 94 publications that focus significantly or exclusively on PAS and alienated children. Though some may question the value of peer review, or of the *Frye* test, as an index of the admissibility of syndrome research, there are no reasonable grounds for maintaining that PAS has not passed peer review. (p. 45)

PAS does not exist because it has not been recognized in court. Gardner cites 66 cases in which PAS has been recognized in court and two recent court rulings in which PAS passed the *Frye* test.

This attitude of some professionals may represent another example of confirmatory bias. All of the information to refute these arguments is contained on Gardner's website (www.rgardner.com).

Mental Health Professional's Attitudes and PAS

Walsh and Bone (1997) discussed the potential for personal bias of the mental health professional when dealing with cases of PAS. They wrote:

> Practically, it is emotionally difficult to discount such accusations because they are made with high emotional pitch, urgency, and a desperation as to a description of the incidents involved. All of the foregoing contributes to believability, especially where the minor child is relating a self-reporting trauma and a real danger to him or her. Such accounts may appear to be very convincing to the listener. Make no mistake about it, individuals with either PAS or a related malicious syndrome will and do lie! They are convincing witnesses, and their manipulative skills may influence others to follow suit. (p. 94)

In those cases where the evaluator joins with or believes the PAS child, the availability bias may be operative. This refers to the tendency to emphasize and remember data that are vivid and dramatic.

Several other authors have reported that the misdiagnosis of PAS may actually result in the mental health professional becoming part of the PAS. Rand (1997b) cited Lund's work, which found that mental health professionals can unwittingly become part of the system maintaining PAS. This is more likely to occur when the therapist takes statements by the aligned parent and child at face value, lacks knowledge about PAS, and avoids contact with the target parent (p. 60). Note that all of these factors have been discussed as either personal variables or procedural variables contributing to the misdiagnosis of PAS.

Rand (1997b) reported the results of Kopetski's (1998) study of PAS cases. Rand provided the following quote from Kopetski:

> One of the most surprising and discouraging findings in this survey was that in 15 families in which a parent was successfully alienated, the alienation was supported by a therapist on the basis that the child should not be separated from a "symbiotic relationship" (with the alienating parent), even though the "symbiosis" proceeded far beyond the time when such a parent-child relationship could even be remotely considered. It was as though the therapists had joined the delusion that the child could not survive if separated from the symbiotic parent. (p. 82)

Gardner (2002b) discussed evaluators who performed faulty assessments to shape the data to conform to projections onto the data of their own speculations. To then claim that one can use this data to make comments specifically about sex-abuse trauma vs. trauma from other sources requires the examiner to make even further journeys into his (her) fantasy-land (p. 46).

Rand (1997b) reviewed Campbell's (1992) work, which confirmed Lund's work. Campbell found that, "Therapists who are provided with incomplete, selective data are at risk for reinforcing and endorsing the idea that the child needs to be 'saved' from the alienated parent" (p. 60). Rand then cites Gardner (1992b), who observed that therapists advocating for their patients who have alleged abuse may "become so overinvolved as to exhibit what amounts to a shared paranoid disorder with the aligned parent and child" (p. 60).

Rand (1997b) discussed the influence of the mental health professional's beliefs and attitudes upon treatment of PAS cases. She stated: "The fundamental beliefs of many therapists about the etiology of psychological problems and what constitutes appropriate treatment can make the therapist an unwitting reinforcer of alienation" (p. 61). Rand cited Campbell's study that found that many therapists make ". . . significantly more negative than positive inferences about significant others in their client's lives" (p. 61). Rand went on to state that "Where the therapist's own view of the target/alienated parent is negative, even if only to mild degree, the therapist's view is likely to adversely influence the child. This provides fertile ground for the development and reinforcement of PAS" (p. 61).

Reliability of PAS

Warshak (2001) has discussed the issue of reliability of PAS in connection with the misdiagnosis of PAS. Reliability refers to ". . . the degree to which a statistical measurement, test result, or diagnosis, is consistent on repeated trials or among different observers" (p. 38). Warshak states that until a sufficiently high rate of agreement on the presence or absence of PAS is established through systematic research, the diagnosis will not attain the empirical support which is probably necessary to achieve acceptance on a par with disorders recognized in the American Psychiatric Association's official description of diagnoses (pp. 38–39).

Warshak discusses that one reason for low diagnostic agreement rates between doctors may exist because . . . the symptoms of the proposed diagnosis are too imprecise and ambiguous, or require an excessively high degree of inference on the part of the observer. . . . In such cases, the proposed syndrome should undergo further refinement. . . . (p. 38).

Warshak thinks that the symptoms of PAS "appear on the surface to be clear-cut and intelligible" (p. 38), but research studies are needed to "test the ability of clinicians to apply these symptoms to case material and agree on whether or not a particular symptom is present in a particular child" (p. 38).

Although I agree with Warshak concerning the need to study the reliability aspect of the diagnosis of PAS, I would suggest that an additional factor would need to be examined in such a study. Having reviewed in this chapter some of the procedural and personal variables that might contribute to the misdiagnosis of PAS, one would have to include these examiner effects/biases/variables as a potential source for low diagnostic agreement between clinicians. If this factor were not controlled for, it would be difficult to conclude whether the reliability data obtained were caused by a deficit in the description of PAS or by uncontrolled-for examiner effects, or a combination of the two. In other words, perhaps the reliability issue – the ability or inability for clinicians to agree on the diagnosis of PAS – has more to do with factors solely related to the clinician than with the description and definition of PAS.

In 2004, Rueda published the first inter-rater reliability study of PAS. He found that, "those who recognize PAS as a valid phenomenon closely agree in almost all aspects concerning PAS" (p. 401).

ADDITIONAL OBSERVATIONS ON THE MISDIAGNOSIS OF PAS

A variety of causes and factors that may result in the misdiagnosis of PAS have been reviewed and detailed in this chapter, along with numerous authors' views and statements concerning these causes and factors. This section is devoted to the chapter author's thoughts, views, opinions and speculations about the misdiagnosis of PAS. Hopefully some of these will lead to research that will confirm or disconfirm them. This will demonstrate whether they are valid observations or simply illusions.

Observation: "Ignorance is No Excuse Before the Law"

This was a favorite saying of my father, who seemed to repeat it on an hourly basis while I was growing up. I didn't understand it then and, now that I have experienced the court system, I think my father was mistaken. Perhaps it was an illusion of his time, or maybe things were different then. But as I look at my own field (mental health) I sometimes think I can make the same basic statement: Ignorance is no excuse for a mental health professional.

I remember a colleague of mine, who had been awarded his Ph.D. in psychology as I was completing my doctoral dissertation, counseling me that a Ph.D. in psychology should be awarded on the basis of how and who a doctoral candidate selects to sit on his doctoral committee. My colleague's concept was that if one had learned anything in psychology graduate school about the human mind and personality, it would be reflected in the ability to diagnose prospective committee members. That sounded extremely insightful to me some twenty-plus years ago, but today I think something was omitted. What was omitted was the effect of the doctoral candidate's own mental structure on his or her diagnostic acumen. None of us operate in a vacuum free from the effects of our own biases and personalities. We are all biased; perhaps it is just a matter of the type, extent and awareness of the biases that differentiates us.

The point I am trying to get to is the amount of emotion and controversy I have observed generated by the PAS concept. As Bricklin (2000) noted, a non-psychologist told him he was ". . . amazed at how 'different' the reviews of psychologists are compared to those of say, physicians or social workers. By 'different' he made it clear he meant 'nasty.' It is as if we psychologists write as though those with whom we disagree are not only wrong, but *evil*" (p. 5).

Until now, I had not seen this phenomenon in my 30-odd years in the mental health field. However, when it comes to PAS, professionals get their passions aroused – sometimes to the point of irrationality and being out of control. I have mentioned PAS at continuing education seminars and been shunned. You would think I had announced that I was infected with the plague. I have received notes from people I do not know excoriating me for being so unprofessional as to even consider PAS as worthy of scientific interest.

I think there is something to learn from all this mis-emotion and fervor. Obviously something about the PAS concept in and of itself has the ability to arouse and stimulate strong responses in mental health professionals. What is it in the mental health professional that is stimulated by PAS? This question is a major thrust of this chapter. It is the examiner effect, evaluator bias, or personal variables.

It seems, though, that we would prefer to focus on and study the first question, and ignore the second. However, if mental health professionals ignore the second, if we act as if we can erase the evaluator, then we are ignoring our own field. There does seem to be a reluctance to apply our knowledge of the human mind to ourselves. It is as if we mental health professionals at times act as if we are somehow exempt from our own field. We are somehow different from our patients and clients. We are protected from the effects of our mental structures, biases, personalities and emotions. When it comes to ourselves we are ignorant, and cannot/will not apply to ourselves the knowledge we apply to our clients and patients.

I had a supervisor who said, "Don't ask the patient to do something you wouldn't ask of yourself." I use this statement when I am asked by persons looking to enter treatment what they should look for in a therapist. My standard reply is to tell them to inquire of the therapist how much therapy he or she has had. The common response to this is shock. The lay person has been disillusioned. Most lay persons assume that we mental health professionals are required to have therapy to obtain our credentials and state licenses.

It is as if we mental health professionals assume a stance that not only are we different from our clients, but we are also immune from what affects them. We create the illusion that we can erase ourselves from the equation and we only need to study the client. So perhaps the first lesson the controversy over PAS teaches us is that we are not immune, and that because of this we need to be aware of why and how we are affected by our work. If we don't learn this, then I predict that PAS will continue to be misdiagnosed, as a result of hidden and unseen biases and personal variables.

As to what about PAS is inherently controversial and stimulative of strong emotions, perhaps the answer lies in what differentiates PAS from other diagnoses. Why is it that diagnoses such as Asperger's Syndrome, bipolar disorder or generalized anxiety disorder don't excite controversy? I think it is because these disorders and diagnoses relate to symptoms and can be conceived of as distant or separate or distinct from the medium that created them. With PAS, the symptoms cannot be separated from the medium that created them – family relationships, bonding, attachments. This medium is one we have all lived and experienced. Mental health professionals dealing with PAS matters see the process in living color, right in front of them. This is not any medium; it is the medium that has been hypothesized as creating the personality, the mental structure, the regulation of affect, and the ability to think. It is the medium that we were all in some way created from. I hypothesize that, among other factors, because PAS is so close to "home" for all of us, it has the ability to stimulate strong responses in mental health professionals.

Observation: Seeing Is Believing

This is the magician's best friend. He knows that illusions can be created, and that the hand really is faster than the eye. I recall reading about a study done by R. D. Laing. He told a psychiatric hospital ward staff that a new medication was going to be given to the patients and that it had the effect of making the patients become taller. The patients were then given placebos. Subsequent interviews with the ward staff showed that some of the staff perceived that the medication was working, and that the patients had gotten taller. Solomon Ashe's line of research showed how subjects can be influenced to see reality as something other than it is. So it seems naive of mental health professionals to believe in the illusion that our perceptions cannot be influenced into seeing what isn't there. In fact, when it comes to a PAS assessment, this is often exactly what occurs. Everyone involved is trying to get us to see it their way. The parents, the clients, the attorneys, and all the other participants are trying to capture our attention and make us *see.*

But if "seeing is believing," why can't I "judge a book by it's cover"? Why is it that "if something looks too good to be true, it probably isn't"? A good attorney knows that winning a case is all about creating illusions, capturing attention, influencing perception, and making the judge or jury see what the attorney wants them to see.

It is the mental health field that has done the majority of the research into perception and how perception can be manipulated. Knowing this, I think that we need to accept it. The evaluator of PAS is not immune from these influences on perception. In fact, I think we should view the results of an evaluation as a *co-creation.* The results are shaped by the contributions of both the persons being evaluated, and by what the evaluator contributes. This concept is accepted in clinical situations. Terms such as "countertransference" and "enactment" are used to discuss and examine this phenomenon. Clinicians accept that an interactional component exists in the consulting room. There are two of us there: the patient and the doctor. The illusion of the doctor as the neutral observer has been discarded. What occurs in the clinical setting is mutually created. I am arguing that the same process exists in the assessment setting. I call this assessment countertransference. If it is true that the data speak, then how is the PAS evaluator listening? To what is the PAS evaluator listening? Is the PAS evaluator feeling so overwhelmed by the massive amounts of data that he or she has stopped listening at all and is ignoring the data?

Perhaps the real illusion is not that seeing is believing, but that believing is seeing. You must believe before you can see. You must believe that the emperor has new clothes in order to see them. If the evaluator does not believe that PAS exists, then he or she will not see it. Of course, the argument will be made that one must believe that PAS exists before you can see it. Will this be the argument made by professionals interested in obtaining knowledge or by those who want you to believe in something other than PAS?

The questions boil down to this: If the magicians know that illusions can be created, if the psychologist knows that perception and attention can be influenced and manipulated, then why would we be so reluctant to accept that our evaluations can be tainted by our own biases and illusions? To ignore what we know about the human mind will lead to error.

Observation: "You Can't Handle the Truth"

I think this is what Jack Nicholson's character in the movie *A Few Good Men* said, and he is probably right. Most of us need our illusions. But then how do we apprehend the truth?

A PAS assessment/evaluation is, in a way, an attempt to determine the truth. Bion (1970) recommended that the analyst suspend "memory, desire, understanding" (p. 46) in order to know the truth of the analysand. Bion was describing those mental processes in the analyst that biased him or her from knowing the truth in the analysand. If the PAS assessment/evaluation is an attempt to know the truth, it would behoove the evaluator to be aware as possible of his or her own mental processes that might shape and transform the data so that the truth will not be known. It is my contention that the evaluator's own mental processes need to be studied so that misdiagnoses due to bias, personal variables, and examiner effects can be minimized. Failing this, I would expect that misdiagnosis of PAS will continue, and evaluators will believe that they have apprehended the truth when in fact they may be merely seeing the reflections of their own hidden beliefs in the data.

SUMMARY AND RECOMMENDATIONS

This chapter has presented the baseline data and criteria necessary to diagnose PAS, and the need to correctly diagnose PAS based on the effects of misdiagnosis. A review of the literature regarding the potential causes for the misdiagnosis of PAS as resulting from either procedural variables or personal variables was discussed. The final section contained the author's views of potential causes for the misdiagnosis of PAS.

Turkat (1993, p. 176) detailed the following qualifications for "the ideal evaluator" for child custody evaluations:

1. Significant training in the area of child development, with particular understanding of the stages of development and how they interact with the positive and negative attributes of each parent.
2. Significant training in psychopathology, with particular understanding of the factors that promote the development of mental disorders.
3. Special expertise in the areas of personality and personality disorder.
4. Top-notch diagnostic skill.
5. Many years of experience as a practicing clinician.
6. Able to document having accomplished a significant number of custody decisions that reflect an unbiased record.
7. Makes it clear to the court that his or her tests, interpretations, and recommendations are potentially subject to error, and gives some indication to the court regarding the range and degree of possible errors involved.

For the qualifications for "the ideal evaluator" performing a PAS assessment I would add the following:

8. Significant training in the areas of attachment theory and object relations.
9. Significant training in the area of evaluator bias, with specific focus on procedures utilized to minimize bias.
10. Significant training in the area of PAS.
11. Supervised experience in conducting PAS evaluations.
12. Personal therapy.

These 12 qualifications could be fashioned into a training module designed to teach mental health professionals the necessary tools and knowledge required to perform a PAS evaluation.

Concerning proposed areas for future research, I advocate research that would focus on identifying and remedying specific sources of evaluator bias in PAS assessments, with specific emphasis on personal variables of the evaluator that result in error. I believe/hypothesize/contend that most evaluator bias, including procedural bias, is created by personal bias in the evaluator.

REFERENCES

Ackerman, Marc J. (1995). *Clinician's guide to child custody evaluations.* New York, NY: John Wiley and Sons, Inc.

Ackerman, Marc J. and Kane, Andrew W. (1998). *Psychological experts in divorce actions,* Third Edition. New York, NY: Aspen Law and Business.

American Academy of Child and Adolescent Psychiatry (1997). Practice parameters for child custody evaluation. *Journal of the American Academy of Child and Adolescent Psychiatry, 36*(10 suppl).

Bion, Wilfred (1970). *Attention and interpretation.* Northvale, NJ: Jason Aronson, Inc.

Boris, Harold (1994). *Sleights of mind: One and multiples of one.* Northvale, NJ: Jason Aronson, Inc.

Bricklin, Barry (1995). *The custody evaluation handbook: Research-based solutions and applications.* Bristol, PA: Bruner/Mazel.

Bricklin, Barry (2000). Further reflections on the parental alienation syndrome. *The Custody Newsletter, 21*:20–23.

Brodsky, Stanley L. (1991). *Testifying in court: Guidelines and maxims for the expert witness.* Washington, D.C.: American Psychological Association.

Brodzinsky, David M. (1993). On the use and misuse of psychological testing in child custody evaluations. *Professional Psychology: Research and Practice, 24*(2), 213–219.

Campbell, T. W. (1992). Psychotherapy with children of divorce: The pitfalls of triangulated relationships. *Psychotherapy, 29*(4), 646–652.

Cartwright, Glenn F. (1993). Expanding the parameters of parental alienation syndrome. *American Journal of Family Therapy, 21*(3), 205–215.

Dunne, J. and Hedrick, M. (1994). The parental alienation syndrome: An analysis of sixteen selected cases. *Journal of Divorce and Remarriage, 21,* 21–38.

Galatzer-Levy, Robert M. and Kraus, Louis (1999). Introduction. *In the scientific basis of child custody decisions,* eds. R. M. Galatzer-Levy and Louis Kraus, pp. 1–11. New York, NY.: John Wiley & Sons, Inc.

Galatzer-Levy, Robert M. and Ostrov, Eric (1999). From empirical findings to custody decisions. *In the scientific basis of child custody decisions,* eds. R. M. Galatzer-Levy and Louis Kraus, pp. 32–57. New York, NY.: John Wiley & Sons, Inc.

Gardner, R. A. (1985). Recent trends in divorce and custody litigation. *The Academy Forum, 29*(2), 3–7.

Gardner, R. A. (1987). Judges interviewing children in custody/visitation litigation. *New Jersey Family Lawyer VII*(2):26ff.

Gardner, R. A. (1989). *Family evaluation in child custody mediation, arbitration, and litigation.* Cresskill, NJ: Creative Therapeutics, Inc.

Gardner, R. A. (1992a). *The parental alienation syndrome: A guide for mental health and legal professionals.* Cresskill, NJ: Creative Therapeutics, Inc.

Gardner, R. A. (1992b). *True and false accusations of child sex abuse.* Cresskill, NJ: Creative Therapeutics, Inc.

Gardner, R. A. (1994). You're not a paranoid schizophrenic – You only have multiple personality disorder. *The Academy Forum, 38*(3), 11–14.

Gardner, R. A. (1995). You're not a paranoid schizophrenic – You only have post-traumatic stress disorder (PTSD). *The Academy Forum, 39*(1), 12–14.

Gardner, R. A. (1996a). *Psychotherapy with children of divorce.* Northvale, NJ: Jason Aronson, Inc.

Gardner, R. A. (1996b). *Psychotherapy with sex-abuse victims: True, false, and hysterical.* Cresskill, NJ: Creative Therapeutics, Inc.

Gardner, R. A. (1998a). Recommendations for dealing with parents who induce a parental alienation syndrome in their children. *Journal of Divorce and Remarriage, 28*(3/4), 1–21.

Gardner, R. A. (1998b). *The parental alienation syndrome,* Second Edition. Cresskill, NJ: Creative Therapeutics, Inc.

Gardner, R. A. (2001a). Parental alienation syndrome (PAS): Sixteen years later. *The Academy Forum, 45*(1), 10–12.

Gardner, R. A. (2001b). Should courts order PAS children to visit/reside with the alienated parent? A follow-up study. *American Journal of Forensic Psychology, 19*(3), 61–106.

Gardner, R. A. (2001c). *Therapeutic interventions for children with parental alienation syndrome.* Cresskill, NJ: Creative Therapeutics, Inc.

Gardner, R. A. (2002a). Parental alienation syndrome vs. parental alienation: Which diagnosis should evaluators use in child-custody disputes? *The American Journal of Family Therapy, 30,* 93-115.

Gardner, R. A. (2002b). *Sex abuse trauma? Or trauma from other sources?* Cresskill, NJ: Creative Therapeutics, Inc.

Garrity, Carla B. and Baris, Mitchell A. (1994). *Caught in the middle: Protecting the children of high-conflict divorce.* San Francisco, CA: Jossey-Bass.

Grisso, Thomas. *Forensic assessment in juvenile and family cases: The state of the art 16* (keynote address to the Summer Institute on Mental Health Law, University of Nebraska-Lincoln, June 1, 1984).

Guidelines for child custody evaluations in divorce proceedings. (1994). *American Psychologist, 49*(7), 677–680.

Hunt, Jennifer S. and Borgida, Eugene. (2001). Is that what I said?: Witnesses' responses to interviewer modifications. *Law and Human Behavior, 25*(6), 583–604.

Hysjulien, Chery, Wood, Barbara and Benjamin, G. (1994). Child custody evaluations: A review of methods used in litigation and alternative dispute resolution. *Family and Conciliation Courts Review, 32*(4), 466–489.

Kopetski, Leona M. (1998). Identifying cases of parental alienation syndrome – Part I. *The Colorado Lawyer, 27*(2), 65–68.

Kopetski, Leona M. (1998). Identifying cases of parental alienation syndrome – Part II. *The Colorado Lawyer, 27*(3), 63–66.

Major, A. Jayne (1999). Parents who have successfully fought Parental Alienation Syndrome. *Aspen Family Law Journal.* (in press).

McGleughlin, Jade, Meyer, Susanne and Baker, John (1999). Assessing sexual abuse allegations in divorce, custody, and visitation disputes. In *the scientific basis of child custody decisions,* eds. R. M. Galatzer-Levy and Louis Kraus, pp. 357–388. New York, NY: John Wiley & Sons, Inc.

Melton, Gary B., Petrila, John, Poythress, Norman G. and Slobogin, Christopher (1997). *Psychological evaluations for the courts: A handbook for mental health professionals and lawyers.* New York, NY: Guilford Press.

Niggemyer, K. (1998). Parental alienation is open heart surgery: It needs more than a band-aid to fix it. *California Western Law Review, 34,* 567–589.

Rand, Deidre C. (1997a). The spectrum of parental alienation syndrome (Part 1). *American Journal of Forensic Psychology, 15*(3), 23–52

Rand, Deidre C. (1997b). The spectrum of parental alienation syndrome (Part 2). *American Journal of Forensic Psychology, 15*(4), 39–92.

Rogers, Richard (2001). *Handbook of diagnostic and structured interviewing.* New York, NY: Guilford Press.

Rueda, Carlos A. (2004). An inter-rater reliability study of Parental Alienation Syndrome. *The American Journal of Family Therapy, 32,* 391–403.

Schutz, Benjamin M., Dixon, Ellen B., Lindenberger, JoAnne C., and Ruther, Neil J. (1989). *Solomon's sword: A practical guide to conducting child custody evaluations.* San Francisco, CA: Jossey-Bass Publishers.

Stahl, Philip M. (1999). Alienation and alignment of children. *California Psychologist, 32*(3), 23–29.

Turkat, Daniel Ira (1993). Questioning the mental health expert's custody report. *American Journal of Family Law, 7,* 175–179.

Vestal, Anita. (1999). Mediation and Parental Alienation Syndrome: Considerations for an intervention model. *Family and Conciliation Courts Review, 37*(4), 487–503.

Waldron, Kenneth H. and Joanis, David E. (1996). Understanding and collaboratively treating Parental Alienation Syndrome. *American Journal of Family Law, 10,* 121-133.

Walsh, M.R. and Bone, J.M. (1997). Parental Alienation Syndrome: An age-old custody problem. *The Florida Bar Journal LXXI* (6):93–96.

Walsh, M.R. and Bone, J.M. (1999). Parental Alienation Syndrome: How to detect it and what to do about it. *The Florida Bar Journal, 73*(3), 44–48.

Ward, P. and Harvey, J. C. (1993). Family wars: The alienation of children. *The Custody Newsletter, 9.*

Warshak, Richard A. (1999). *Parental Alienation Syndrome in court.* Dallas, TX.: Clinical Psychology Associates.

Warshak, Richard A. (2000). *Obstacles and controversies in pursuit of children's best interests.* Dallas, TX: Clinical Psychology Associates.

Warshak, Richard A. (2001). Current controversies regarding Parental Alienation Syndrome. *American Journal of Forensic Psychology, 19*(3), 29–59.

Williams, Frank S. (1990). *Preventing parentectomy following divorce.* Fifth Annual Conference National Council for Children's Rights. Keynote address, Washington, D.C., October 20.

Chapter 17

FAMILY THERAPY FOR PARENTAL ALIENATION SYNDROME: UNDERSTANDING THE INTERLOCKING PATHOLOGIES

CRAIG A. EVERETT

OVERVIEW

This paper will extend Richard Gardner's work by utilizing family systems theory and the identifiable clinical phenomena present in family interaction to define the underlying dynamics and behaviors that lead to the evolution and maintenance of PAS in families. By integrating family systems theory with the specific dynamics of PAS, the clinician will be assisted in the development of specific clinical interventions.

INTRODUCTION

The process of one parent intentionally attempting to turn her or his child or children against the other parent is one of the more insidious and destructive dynamics that a family can experience. It often carries more serious and longer-lasting consequences for both the children, the parents, and the intergenerational family members than serious psychiatric pathologies and even sexual or physical abuse. It is reasonable to label this process of parental alienation syndrome as a destructive family pathology because it attributes a quality of "evil," without cause or foundation, to a parent who once nurtured and protected the same child that has now turned against her or him.

PAS does not occur in a vacuum apart from the underlying milieu and history of a family. Nor does it exist solely as a function of individual psychopathology. Rather, PAS is the culmination of powerful interactive dynamics that occur within certain family systems. It is based on a variety of clinical phenomena that occur at a singular time in the history of a family, encompassing both individual dynamics present among the family members and a unique pattern of interaction that occurs between the parents and their child or children.

Gardner (1992, 1998) defined PAS as a clinical syndrome that can be recognized and consistently diagnosed due to the predictable nature of its patterns and dynamics. He defined eight clinical dynamics or symptoms that compose the clinical syndrome and identified the manner in which these dynamics manifest themselves in certain families. The following are the eight primary symptoms of PAS (Gardner, 1992, 1998):

1. The campaign of denigration
2. Weak, frivolous, and absurd rationalizations for the deprecation
3. Lack of ambivalence
4. The "independent-thinker" phenomenon
5. Reflexive support of the alienating parent in the parental conflict
6. Absence of guilt over cruelty to and/or exploitation of the alienated parent
7. Presence of borrowed scenarios
8. Spread of the animosity to the extended family of the alienated parent

FAMILY SYSTEMS CONCEPTS THAT FACILITATE THE UNDERSTANDING OF PAS

Because PAS occurs solely and by definition within the context of a family's interactional experiences, it is important to recognize how the life of a family system can support the symptoms that are displayed as part of the syndrome. The underlying clinical questions are: What conditions would prompt one parent to turn against and attempt to alienate their children against their former partner and lover?; and what conditions in a family would support a child in not only rejecting but often vehemently hating a parent that once nurtured and protected her or him? A brief description of the following characteristics of family systems will assist in the understanding of the dynamics of PAS.

Homeostasis and Balance

In family systems, homeostasis defines the manner in which all families regulate themselves by maintaining a certain balance that ensures their survival. A common example of this is of a thermostat in a house or office that regulates the flow of heat or cooling to maintain a comfortable 72 degree temperature. Every family system has a similar built-in thermostat, or mechanism, to regulate its interaction and maintain its balance. Both healthy and dysfunctional interactions are regulated within the system. This may be understood as the system acting to create a balance to better manage its diverse components i.e., personality traits, parenting roles, children's needs, etc. Some family systems may remain "in balance" even though this very balance supports dramatic clinical symptoms such as depression, alcoholism, or violence. It is important to understand that this need for balance is a function of the life and survival of the system itself and not an indicator of health or dysfunction (Nichols & Everett, 1986).

When a family reaches the point of dissolution, it can no longer remain in a state of balance. The family system and its members are at their most vulnerable at this time, and the parents will struggle to form a new system and become single parents in new postseparation or postdivorce systems. Their goal will be to rebalance themselves and their children within a new single-parent or remarried system. Even though the marriage ends, the family continues in a reorganized state and the former spouses remain parents.

In families in which the seeds of PAS have been planted, and despite their drama and destructive nature, such a postdivorce system will typically achieve a new sense of balance that incorporates the PAS dynamics and symptoms into their identity and day-to-day functioning. Clinicians who have worked extensively with PAS family systems can recognize an inherent predictability and rhythm to such a family's behaviors. However, many clinicians may miss the presence of this balance because of their focus on the drama of the symptoms. Many nonclinical observers, particularly attorneys and judges, misread this sense of balance and predictability as evidence of the "truth" or reality of the symptomatic charges and statements against the alienated parent.

The induction of PAS requires a parent with ability i.e., power, to pull or enmesh the children into a newly formed, postseparation/divorce system, which offers a sense of safety as well as obligation to that parent. *The child's experience of a new homeostasis and balance offers a sense of safety while at the same time further empowering the alienating parent.*

Circularity and Reciprocity

Circularity refers to the manner in which certain behaviors and/or issues that are present within a family may exert a powerful interactive impact on every member of the family system. For example, a parent's depression or a child's disruptive behaviors will be experienced by each family member in a circularly connected manner. Reciprocity defines the interactive component of the circularity such that one family member's behaviors will not only have an effect on every other member in the system, but these behaviors will elicit some type of emotional or behavioral response from and among the other members. For example, the symptoms of a depressive mother in a system will evoke responses among all of the other family members in terms of how her symptoms are perceived. Reciprocally, each family member will develop her or his own response to her symptoms (e.g., anger, withdrawal, protectiveness). In some families these reciprocal responses are shared mutually and develop into an ongoing life of their own that becomes independent of the continuation or removal of the parent's symptoms. Thus, a formerly depressive parent may still be perceived as needing protection several years after the depression has subsided.

In PAS family systems, it is these powerful dynamics that both allow a parent to be targeted for the alienation and also support the "induction" of the child or children against this parent. The parent who says to their child, "I'm sorry you had to put up with your father's anger at the restaurant during your visit," identifies the "seed" of a symptomatic or pathological behavior that is now assigned to the targeted parent. Reciprocally, the father may act in an angry or agitated manner to defend himself. The child, in her or his, own reciprocal response to both parents' interactions, may then tell her or his therapist, "My father yelled at me in the restaurant . . . I was scared." These circular interactions can develop a life of their own, regardless if the father actually raised his voice in a restaurant and regardless of whether it was justified or not. Again, the alienating parent must have the power to enmesh the child into a type of coalition such that the circularity of these interactions, with and about the father, cause the desired reciprocal response on the part of the child. The response may range from fear to distrust to anger toward the other parent.

Boundaries

Boundaries are another component that define how systems function and become central to the evolution of the PAS phenomena. Boundaries are "invisible" lines that circumscribe each family system and define the system's relative territory. In other words, a system's boundaries will define who is allowed within the system and who (or what influences) is kept outside of the system. The *external boundaries* circumscribe the nuclear system of immediate parents and children. These may be *diffuse* and allow external figures, such as grandparents, to become intrusive in the system; or, they may be relatively *closed* and keep most influences out. Ideally, system boundaries should be *flexible* such that a healthy system can at times open its boundaries to allow for positive feedback and at other times close the boundaries to keep disruptive influences outside. Boundaries are also present within the nuclear system to define the existing subsystems (i.e., spousal, parent-child, and sibling).

In PAS families, the postseparation/divorce system has rebalanced itself such that the inducting and alienating system, composed of a parent and child/children, evolves as a coalition focused on creating distance from and a negative perception of the targeted parent. The inducting family system must "close" its boundaries in order to support its coalition against the other parent. Because the PAS charges against the alienated parent are fabricated or dramatized from minor events, normal feedback from this parent, other family of origin members, or other outside influences, such as a therapist, might challenge the validity of the charges and thus become a threat to the coalition. Therefore, for the coalition to evolve into a form of PAS, external corrective statements of reality must be kept out through the process of closing the boundaries.

In PAS systems, these boundaries become tightly and rigidly closed, only allowing in other family members or professionals who support the alienating system's charges against the other parent. Clinically, the process of closing these boundaries begins at the moment of induction of the child. Without the power to close and "set" these boundaries, the inducting parent would be unable to maintain and continue the fantasy of the charges against the other parent. These rigidly closed boundaries are one of the most difficult dynamics for therapists or courts to challenge in cases of PAS families.

Family Myths

All families have certain "themes" or myths that are shared as mutual beliefs within the system by all of its members. These themes may also define the collective family members' outlook on life. Themes are called myths when they identify certain behaviors or symptoms in an ongoing and pervasive manner without any basis in reality. These themes or myths are not always dysfunctional. For example, a theme may portray the sentiment that "we need to stick together as a family because no one else out there in the world will take care of us." Another theme may reinforce the value of education or of achievement for family members.

Myths can communicate more dramatic concerns and may exist at either a conscious or a preconscious level. For example, a family myth might be that "all men are untrustworthy." The theme of "we need to stick together" may evolve into a more dramatic myth that serves to isolate family members within the system's boundaries and limit their interaction with external activities. In extreme cases, this has been termed the "suicidal family myth (Gehrke & Kirschenbaum, 1967; Nichols & Everett, 1986)." Here family members are inducted into the belief that "if you leave home, or move away very far, you may not survive or the family may not survive!"

The author worked with this myth in a family where five of the six male siblings had remained in their parents' home community and had worked for their father's business. The other male member had married and tried to start a business of his own in a community several hundred miles away from his family of origin. When his business failed and his marriage had become conflicted, he reported that he "felt drawn back" to his family of origin to "feel safe" and be supported, even though his wife could not tolerate the smothering nature of his parents, nor the small town in which they resided. He told the author in his last therapy session before leaving town to return home: "I wish I could remain living here but I can't. I know I won't survive here." One other sibling in this family – a female – did not live in the same community as the parents. Apparently, all of the other family members supported and "allowed" her to live 2000 miles away because she was a Catholic nun living in a distant convent.

PAS takes on the dynamics of a typical family myth with the subsequent power to define the lives of the family's members. It is the epitome of a pathological myth, not only because it is based on fabrications, but because it defines and controls children's perceptions about their other parent. The typical PAS myth is: *"Daddy/Mommy is bad and cannot be trusted. . . . We need to stick together to protect ourselves from him (her)."*

Family Scapegoating

This is one of the most important concepts that is relevant to understanding PAS. Most family therapists recognize the process of scapegoating as common to many dysfunctional family systems. Vogel and Vogel, as early as 1960, defined this process in families whereby stress or conflict that may exist collectively within a family becomes attached to (induction) or directed toward (projection) a specific family member, primarily a child. For example, in families where the spousal relationship has been unsatisfactory or unstable, it is not uncommon that a child may be scapegoated to relieve and redirect the spousal stress. This scapegoated child often acts out the family's stress by getting in trouble in school or in the community.

Clinically, the scapegoating process illustrates the multiple levels of interlocking pathologies in family systems. Scapegoating is a powerful dynamic induced within the problematic milieu of a family system. It shapes not only the personal traits and behaviors of a scapegoated child but it also defines the child's "pathological" role in the family. These traits and symptoms may follow the scapegoated child into adulthood and influence such experiences as selection of a marital partner and future parenting roles.

In many dysfunctional families this role of a scapegoated child becomes embedded in the family members' own personal identities and their interactional experiences with the child who becomes labeled as "bad." Gradually, this negative focus on the identified child defines the makeup of the family system and characterizes the members' ongoing interactions. A family myth gradually evolves that identifies the scapegoated child's behaviors and communications as "bad" or "destructive" or "intolerable." As family therapists know, this dynamic of scapegoating also defines the energy and power (or power struggles) within a family system.

PAS takes on a form of scapegoating within the alienating family system. The difference in PAS families is that the scapegoating is directed toward the alienated parent rather than toward a child. The dynamics of the system remain the same, family members participate in the scapegoating/alienating process by collectively viewing the targeted parent as "bad" with the underlying belief that *"If we can only get rid of this dangerous person, our problems will be solved and we will be happy."* As in most dysfunctional family systems, this PAS scapegoating process is supported and reinforced by a collective and pervasive family myth, such as *"Daddy is bad because. . . ."*

Interlocking Pathologies

Many clinicians who have been trained primarily in individually oriented or psychodynamic psychotherapies, have difficulty stepping back and looking beyond the presenting symptomatology of an individual in order to see the broad and powerful underlying dynamics of an individual's family system. As early as 1956, Nathan Ackerman, one of the early pioneers of psychiatry in the then emerging family therapy field, identified the concept of interlocking pathologies to explain how multiple pathologies may not only coexist within a family system but that these pathologies may become the primary ingredients in the actual ongoing interaction and identity of the family itself. He reported:

> The stability of the family and that of its members hinges on a delicate pattern of emotional interchange. The behavior of each member is affected by every other. A shift in the emotional interaction of one pair of persons in a given family alters the interaction processes of other family pairs. Emotional illness may integrate or disintegrate a family relationship. The emotional illness of one member may complement that of another, or may have effects which are antagonistic. Some forms of emotional illness may be shared by two or more members of a family. A crisis in the life of a family may exert pervasive and far-reaching effects on the mental health of the family and its individual members. (Ackerman, 1956, p. 136)

This phenomenon suggests that multiple pathological symptoms may exist within a given family system, and that these symptoms will define and reinforce the ongoing nature, identity, functioning, and dysfunctions of the system. The nature of interlocking pathologies can be seen in other clinical family systems. For example, families with attention deficit/hyperactivity disorder (ADHD) children struggle with multiple levels of pathological dysfunctions. These include the neurobiological dynamics and associated behavioral and adjustment issues of the child's ADHD, the stress and frustration that the disorder places on the parents, the resultant potential for damage to their marriage, the vulnerability of the discouraged and frustrated parent toward depression and/or violence, and the sense of anger and alienation that the siblings may feel toward their ADHD sibling's disruption of their own and their family's life experience. For a therapist to treat only the presenting symptoms of an ADHD child would fail to recognize or address the other underlying and powerful symptoms within the family that have the potential to shape not only the self-image and emotional well-being of the identified child and the other family members, but also the future of the system itself (see Everett & Everett, 1998).

The PAS family system displays similar levels of interlocking pathologies. Gardner (1992, 1998) has suggested that the alienating parent may often display diagnosable psychiatric disorders that range from paranoia to hysteria and lesser dynamics that might include the absence of shame and/or guilt and the "absence of empathy and/or sympathy." Gardner (1992, 1998) also cited the existence of shared psychotic disorders, such as in folie à deux. The author concurs with Gardner that these psychiatric conditions, regardless of having been diagnosed, may be present in many serious cases of PAS. However, more subtle clinical patterns can also exist along with identifiable pre-existing family dynamics and patterns that may help to explain both the potential for and the evolution of PAS in certain families. (These ingredients of PAS in the family system will be discussed in the next section.) For the clinician, recognizing and understanding these interlocking pathologies aids in the definition of intervention strategies. These may range from addressing specific psychiatric disorders in a parent, to identifying underlying and historical dyadic conflicts among the parents, to treating the reactive symptoms of the inducted child.

THE CLINICAL DYNAMICS OF PAS

Gardner (1992, 1998) has identified the range of potential individual psychopathology that may be present in the role of the parent who induces a child's rejection of the other parent. In this author's experience such individual pathologies are most obvious in a parent when the PAS is dramatic and the parent is resistant to change (Gardner's levels – "moderate" and "severe"). However, in milder PAS cases, the specific pathology of the inducting parent may not be apparent or may not reach the threshold for a specific clinical diagnosis. In either case, the underlying family dynamics are identical. However, in this author's experience *the greater the potential pathology of the inducting parent, the greater will be the intensity, power, and insidiousness of the PAS.*

From a family systems perspective, it would be a mistake clinically to focus solely on the individual symptomatology or behaviors of the inducting parent, or for that matter, to focus only on the actual behaviors of the alienating child. The dynamics that support the alienation of a parent, as described, exist within the family system itself not just intrapsychically within the parent or the child. In many cases, these underlying dynamics may have been present before the parents separated or divorced. The author has been able to identify specific pre-existing patterns of PAS in about 50 percent of the cases on which he has worked.

A variety of situations or dynamics during the predivorce period may create the seeds of PAS. These might appear as subtle alliances and/or coalitions between the inducting parent and a child. Perhaps the child was historically overly dependent on the alienating parent; or the child may have been infantilized or allowed to sleep in the parent's bed. Of course, the younger a child is, the easier it is to accomplish the induction process. There are many pre-existing scenarios. For example, the marital relationship deteriorated, perhaps the child was pulled further into a coalition with one parent, either the parent who was angry and leaving, or the parent who was "abandoned" and left.

In milder PAS cases, where no clear parental pathology is diagnosable, the author has observed that it is often the circumstances surrounding the marital breakup that may provide the dynamics for PAS. Examples are situations in which extramarital affairs may have been present, in which the other parent has lost her or his job, or sudden geographical relocation has occurred. In other words, the seeds of PAS may arise from any marital or family situation that may cause hurt, insecurity, disappointment, distrust, and of course, alienation in the spouse. The evocation of these unhappy feelings in the marital relationship can also trigger formerly latent or underlying clinical psychopathologies that may exist in a spouse. Examples are a spouse who has struggled with depression or one who experiences the anger and fear associated with feelings of abandonment by the marital partner.

Certain clinical ingredients might identify the potential for PAS present in the earlier intact family system. In the author's clinical work as a custody evaluator, concerns are often raised about one parent's ability or willingness to share a child, or about a parent's use of certain personal symptoms or controlling/enmeshing behaviors that could either align a child with that parent or turn the child against the other parent. These conditions may be viewed as "pre-PAS;" however, PAS rarely occurs without the underlying interaction and personal roles that would support its induction. The author has observed that, in some cases, the alienation does not begin at the time of the separation or divorce, but evolves at a later time. In these cases, the trigger has often been the remarriage of the former spouse, which systemically creates a new imbalance, creating a target for the alienation.

In some cases, this remarriage symbolically ends the other parent's fantasy for reconciliation. In several cases, the author has observed that the PAS was triggered following the remarriage of the alienating parent (*see* Warshak, 2000). This remarriage appeared to support a need by the alienating parent to be totally enmeshed with their new partner and to pull the children into a protective environment (with resulting closed boundaries). In such cases, the new partner joins in the alienating coalition and reinforces the mythology and scapegoating of the alienated parent.

It should be clear for the clinician that by simply identifying the PAS symptoms, which in and of themselves supercede an individual's behaviors, will not help to define potential intervention strategies for work with the multiple levels of dynamics that exist within a PAS family. The typical components of PAS that the author has observed include both individual roles as well as family interactive patterns.

CLINICAL PROFILES OF ALIENATING PARENTS

The following are examples of the alienating parental roles that are often present in differing patterns of PAS.

The Vulnerable Parent with Identifiable Psychiatric Symptoms

Many alienating parents display clear psychiatric symptoms and/or disorders (*see* Gardner, 1992, 1998). Many of these parents will display, both symptomatically and historically, underlying psychiatric conditions and needs, whether they are obvious or diagnosed. These conditions render the parent vulnerable to stress, conflicts, and changes or threats in their emotional milieu. These parents depend on the marriage and/or the family structure, or explicitly on their enmeshing role with their children, for support and help to contain their psychiatric symptoms. In some clinical profiles of these parents, it is clear that their psychopathology may have been latent for some years but was triggered and/or exacerbated by the threat of a divorce. The therapist should be careful not to miss this element of personal vulnerability in these alienating parents because it is often camouflaged by anger, rage, manipulation, and denigration. These parents tend to create both the moderate and severe levels of PAS (Gardner, 1992, 1998).

The Vulnerable Parent with Primarily Dependent Needs

In less dramatic cases – typically the mild form of PAS – there may be no diagnosable psychopathology but the alienating parent may display considerable dependency needs on the family for emotional security and personal identity. These dynamics create a similar vulnerability, which would be evident in historical symptoms in their clinical profiles. Although underlying abandonment issues may be present in either of these profiles, they are often more obvious here and are clearly linked to dynamics of fear and rage. These parents are typically highly enmeshing and protective of their children. These are dynamics that are often present and identifiable prior to the threat of a divorce. Some of these parents may often hurriedly secure new partners as a way of replacing their lost sense of safety, and to find a "partner" in alienation.

For either type of alienating parent, the threat of separation and divorce may trigger a range of clinical symptoms, which in turn may trigger potential fears of abandonment. In either case two potential responses by such a parent may occur toward their children. These may occur in either of the following ways:

1. *The needy, victimized parent.* These parents may react with fear, or even terror, of being abandoned and left alone. They may even question their personal survival. They may reach out to pull the children closer to them for their own safety and protection. Their power is in their vulnerability which captures a child's loyalty and obligation to protect and rescue the parent. These parents can ensure their sense of safety indefinitely if they have the power to enmesh the children and isolate them from the other parent. This power may extend beyond the children to

the potential caretaking and rescuing dynamics of the parental family-of-origin members (e.g., the grandparents) as well as therapists and attorneys.

2. *The angry, intimidating parent.* Other parents with the same response to the threat of divorce may react with anger and rage, targeting their partner, who is leaving. Their anger colors their memories and history of their life with their partner, who is now labeled as "evil" and who is viewed as a threat to the children. These parents' power lies in the intimidating nature of their anger. Their need for revenge and retaliation captures the children's loyalties and creates a similar fear and anger in the children toward the other parent.

ASSESSING THE CLINICAL PROCESS

By definition, PAS does not exist in cases in which the "alienated" parent legitimately displayed "bad" or threatening behaviors toward the family. For example, if a parent has been abusive or violent, the children's anger and fear are based on reality. However, in PAS no empirical basis exists in present or prior behaviors for the rejection of this parent by the child. The clinical, and legal, question becomes, "How can the induction of the child occur when the alienated parent is basically 'innocent?'"

Typically, a flaw or some minor misdeed is highlighted and dramatized by the inducting parent in order to create the alienation of the other parent. The etiology of the basis for the induction is initially within the alienating parent, not within the child. It may be a recent event as simple as the angry response of a father toward a son in a restaurant, as previously mentioned. The rest of that scenario may have included that the child was playing with his food and disrupting other customers. Thus, the father's actual response was reasonable until it was interpreted and redefined by the alienating parent.

Other examples might include the alienated parent having been the primary disciplinarian in the predivorce family, or this parent having worked long hours and having rarely been home only rarely to help the children with their homework. Perhaps the parent had a brief affair, or the inducting parent may have been historically jealous in the relationship and "suspected" the other parent of having had an affair.

PAS is not based on reality (i.e., empirical evidence of misdeeds) because the superficial and circumstantial nature of the charges against the alienated parent become irrelevant and do not need to be pursued by the therapist. Their importance lies in the power of one parent to identify such an issue and to emotionally bind a child into a coalition by reframing and dramatizing the issue against the other parent. This is the systemic level of pathology. In one case, a daughter confronted her alienated mother in a therapy session, stating, "Daddy says you didn't even graduate from high school; you lied to all of us." In the next session the mother brought her actual high school diploma in a frame to show the child. The child's response was: "Anybody can have those made."

It is not necessary for a child to display psychiatric symptoms or to be at risk for behavioral or emotional difficulties in order to be inducted into PAS. The child's response to the induction is part of the powerful binding dynamics of the family system. In PAS, a perfectly normal child who had been attached to one parent as the primary caretaker can be turned against that same parent. The clinical dynamic is not typically the emotional health of the inducted child but more often issues of her or his prior role and relationship with each parent, age, and relative maturity. The older and more mature a child, the more difficult it is for one parent to have enough power to evolve and support the alienation process.

However, alienation can be successful in either of the parental typologies previously mentioned. For example, the "needy, victimized" parental model may involve a parent who was suffering from some psychiatric disorder, who may have been depressed or even suicidal, or who may have been hospitalized for a legitimate medical condition (one such mother had a hysterectomy). The power of sympathy, fear, worry, concern, and protectiveness toward a perceived vulnerable parent cannot be underestimated. Similarly, the "angry, intimidating parent" who uses rage and vindictiveness to terrorize the children (and even professionals) may be successful at alienation.

Once components just described are present, the ensuing family's dynamics that support PAS become clear and reasonably predictable. As it would occur in other family systems, *scapegoating* evolves to relieve the stress, conflict, and/or fear by directing these emotions away from one part of the system toward another part. In PAS families, this scapegoating process is directed toward the other parent. From a family system's perspective, the process of scapegoating is a broader way of identifying Gardner's use of induction. Whatever the unhappy scenario may have been that created the stress and/or dissolution of the marriage, it leads to the act of one parent focusing the source of the family's problems on some action, trait, or behavior exhibited by the offending partner. The scapegoating/induction process, initiated by a scared or angry parent, pulls the children, as well as family-of-origin members (e.g., grandparents, aunts and uncles) into an evolving *mythological* belief, no matter how irrational or unsubstantiated, that the other parent is the cause of the family's problems and breakup, and the cause of the inducting parent's sadness and/or pathology. Through the dynamics of *circularity* and *reciprocity*, the inducting parent forms a coalition with the children in the new family system. (This may exist as an identifiable subsystem before the separation and divorce occur.)

The children and other family members begin to internalize and share among themselves the anger, hurt, disappointment, and alienation felt by the alienating parent toward the other parent. These feelings take on a "life of their own," as a way of rebalancing the system in the face of potential collapse. The inducted children and the alienating parent coalesce to form a powerful system; the other parent is seen as bad, evil, untrustworthy, and the cause of the family's demise and unhappiness.

The additional family dynamic that is necessary to support scapegoating and this mythology is for the *boundaries* around this system to be essentially *closed* in order to inhibit feedback that would be contrary to the mythology. These boundaries are effectively closed by limiting outside influences and by eliciting outside individuals to support the myth and scapegoating. Reflective stories are shared by the alienating parent with their own parents and siblings, friends and neighbors, the child's teachers, parents of friends, even employers and co-workers and, of course, attorneys and caregivers to the child. Those who accept the stories as truthful are allowed into the system's boundaries, and those who respond skeptically or in a disbelieving manner are kept outside.

In PAS families, the scapegoating of the alienated parent must have sufficient power and support from the other members of the system to continue. This is why the development of the mythology is critical. Without it, the alienated parent would only be labeled in passing or in situational issues as "bad" or "at fault." However, to have the impact of separating and alienating a child from a parent, the mythology must be present and be supported by other family members. Just as in the "suicidal family myth," members of this new alienating system genuinely and collectively believe that the alienated parent displays certain characteristics that make her or him "bad" or deserving of being rejected. Family systems that support such a myth accept this blindly and collectively, despite the contrary empirical reality.

In many family interviews, when a child has been scapegoated, therapists will find that separate individual interviews with a parent or with siblings will often produce a weak, but clear, acknowledgment that their scapegoated ex-spouse or sibling "isn't so bad," or "isn't like that all of the time." However, the mythology of PAS systems is so powerful that children, extended family members, and even professionals working with these families will recite the irrational claims of misdeeds against the alienated parent. (Professionals who become advocates for the alienating system can be embarrassed when they offer court testimony having completed little clinical research beyond the story told to them by the alienating parent and the child.)

These charges and stories are offered without remorse or personal reflection, and may be stated even in the face of contrary practical reality and history. Certainly many unhappy and hurt spouses would like to exert a degree of revenge toward their former spouse by alienating children, friends, and co-workers from her or him. However, most do not have the power or the clinical circumstances to create a lasting pattern of scapegoating or to pull other family members into the belief surrounding such a family myth. For PAS to evolve, this family myth must be induced, accepted, and shared by all of the alienating family members.

For many PAS families the actual physical separation serves to reinforce the scapegoating of the other parent, who is usually the one to move out. The fact of physical separation acts to reinforce the scapegoating process and the perception that the other parent has done something wrong by "abandoning" the family. The alienated parent cannot defend against this process after leaving the home. She or he is often met with statements (or legal papers) reporting "the children do not want to see you." The additional dynamic that is necessary to support this scapegoating process is that the boundaries that define this new coalition/subsystem between the alienating parent and the children against the other parent must be essentially closed in order to maintain the often irrational nature of the beliefs and/or charges against the other parent. External feedback from therapists or attorneys who would question whether the alienated parent has really committed actual transgressions would undermine the power of the scapegoating and challenge the myth. At the same time, family members or friends who support the myth are allowed into this system. Occasionally, "experts" such as attorneys and therapists who naively support the accusations toward the alienated parent become unknowing participants in the scapegoating process; they often believe genuinely that the alienated parent is "bad," even though they typically have never met or interviewed this parent.

The author can cite many instances in which he has received letters, some quite damaging, from other community professionals or has reviewed letters written to the court by professionals who blatantly advocated for their patient, who is either the rejecting child or the alienating parent. Once again, many become so seduced into an advocacy/rescuing role that they may be manipulated into writing these documents without ever having interviewed the alienated parent or questioned the accuracy of the charges. In one dramatic case, the author had been appointed by the court to work with the alienation issues of the family of the ten-year-old child. When the author scheduled a therapeutic session that was to have included the child and her alienated parent, it was delayed for weeks while the child's therapist and the alienating parent's attorney tried to block the session. After the court gave the author the freedom to conduct the session, the ten-year-old child arrived for the meeting in the author's waiting room, carrying her parent's teddy bear and wearing her therapist's scarf. Before the session she told the author that she was taken to the therapist's office the previous night, and the therapist and her parent "made me cry because you [the author] are making me talk to my father." The child said the teddy bear and the scarf would make her "feel safe."

FAMILY THERAPY INTERVENTIONS

The provision of psychotherapy for PAS cases is best offered by seasoned therapists who have had explicit training and experience in working with complex and multiproblem families, and in working with the legal system. These therapists need to be able to conduct, manage, and control therapeutic interventions with multiple and intergenerational family members. They need to be able to remain impartial and reasonably objective, manage their own boundaries well, and be immune to intimidation. These therapists will be more successful if they are familiar with the adversarial legal process, and the role of expert witnesses, and if they can communicate effectively and authoritatively with attorneys and judges. In many highly conflicted cases, it will be crucial for the therapist to have a court order defining her or his therapeutic role and to be able to report resistances and violations directly to the judge.

Therapists working with PAS cases also need to avoid naive and/or misinformed interventions. This therapeutic role is challenging and complex, and it is also quite delicate. *A therapist working with a PAS case often has only one chance to be effective.* Thus, it is important for the therapist to avoid no-win interventions, such as the following:

1. Trying to "reason" with the rejecting child and convince her or him that the alienated parent "isn't really that bad."
2. Trying to confront the rejecting child with the "reality" that this parent has not done anything wrong.
3. Trying to directly, or inadvertently, undermine the coalition between the child and the alienating parent by questioning or challenging the charges or beliefs expressed by the alienating parent.
4. Trying to challenge the alienating parent in a direct confrontation or power struggle.

Even the most seasoned therapist armed with a court order does not have the power to change the alienation with a direct frontal approach. Although Gardner's recommendation (1992, 1998, 1999, 2001) for the use of differing forms of family therapy interventions with PAS families is certainly correct, the strategies must be thoughtful, often indirect, and well-timed. Similarly, Gardner's recommendation that a *single therapist*, rather than multiple therapists, be appointed to provide the therapy is critical. The systemic dynamics, described previously, provide the clinical focus and theoretical basis for subsequent treatment interventions. However, it is important to recognize that the resources of a family therapy approach can identify a significant range of treatment options for working with PAS families. For example, family therapy:

- Looks at the bigger clinical picture of multiple dynamics and coexisting emotional levels within a variety of family structures;
- Recognizes that interlocking pathologies may be embedded in the family's structure and interactions while at the same time being displayed symptomatically by certain individual members;
- Recognizes that these interlocking pathologies actually define the balance (homeostasis) and survival of the dysfunctional system;
- Has the resources to assemble selected members and/or groups of members representing certain subsystems, as well as the intergenerational system, and to intervene easily within the family's dysfunctional dynamics, coalitions, and interactive pathologies;

- Offers interventions to contain often dramatic and destructive internal family dynamics and conflicts; and
- Provides multiple levels of interventions simultaneously (e.g., working indirectly with individual symptomatology while at the same time working directly with family structure and dynamics).

The style and orientation of each family therapist's work may vary according to training, orientation, and personal resources. However, based on the author's clinical experience, the following are specific primary goals of family therapy for working with PAS families.

1. *Challenge the PAS family's closed boundaries immediately.* As long as the PAS system's boundaries remain closed to feedback and intervention, therapeutic efforts will fail. Recognize that the alienating system has a life of its own and it must be dealt with as a separate system before trying to arrange interactions between the child and the alienated parent. Invite the members of the alienating system to come in and tell their story, not because the therapist necessarily needs more information, but because it is important to observe and experience how the system behaves. By listening to their story, without judgment or intervention, you are allowed, even if only briefly, into this system's normally closed boundaries. Once inside the boundaries, it is important to not challenge or disrupt the system's power or mythology; if you do you will never be allowed in again.

2. *Continue to subtly challenge the system's closed boundaries by inviting-family-of origin members to a session.* The presence of grandparents, aunts, uncles, and cousins from the alienating system acts to subtly broaden further the alienating system's boundaries. The more people present for an interview, the easier it is for the therapist to "become lost" in the system and not become a target. Remember that the myth will be shared by most of these family members and they all will need to tell the therapist how bad the other parent has been. If the therapist can remain objective and neutral in this context, the perception of the therapist as a threat will at least be postponed at this early stage of therapy.

3. *Consider assembling the entire nuclear family.* This should never be the first intervention and should be used only by seasoned family therapists who believe that it is possible to successfully structure and stay in control of such a session. The value of such an intervention is that it replicates immediately the scapegoating family dynamics in the therapist's office. However, often the very process of organizing and conducting a family session with all members present may have the effect of calming the dysfunctional interactions, by placing family members in the same room with structure and some degree of safety. It should be noted that this type of intervention may carry the risk of further scapegoating or emotional explosiveness. However, it may provide the therapist with live data identifying the underlying power and interactional patterns that must be treated. It can be hard for inexperienced therapists to allow "the live history" of the family's experiences to emerge without being tempted to "jump in" and try to fix everything that is presented. Working with PAS families requires patience and caution on the part of the therapist.

4. *Use subtle interventions to block or reframe the scapegoating/alienating messages whenever possible.* A therapist who challenges the messages head-on creates a no-win confrontational situation with respect to the powerful mythology of the system. In such cases, the system's protective boundaries close immediately, and the therapist is rendered impotent against the system's power – even when aided by a court order. The therapist must use subtle or indirect interventions by asking for clarification or more information about issues, or by appearing continually surprised or incredulous about the details of the stories the alienating members of the family report.

When a therapist works with families who demonstrate the scapegoating of a child, particularly with intact families or stepfamilies, the plan is typically to include all of the nuclear members, or alternatively at times just the sibling group. The goal is to actively block the scapegoating messages from parents or siblings and, by challenging the irrational quality of the perceptions, to reinstate the scapegoated child into a more normative and functional role in the family. If this scapegoating evolved due to underlying stressors in the marriage, the focus of the therapy in more typical families would shift quickly to issues of the survival of the marriage. In these families, it is recognized clinically that when one child is removed successfully from the scapegoating role, the therapeutic interventions must focus immediately on rebalancing the system in a healthier manner. If this is not accomplished, another child may soon become a new scapegoat in the family, or the marital relationship will experience high levels of conflict.

The interventions for PAS families are similar, but the therapist has the more difficult task of dealing with a parent, instead of a child, as the target of the scapegoating. In addition, because PAS takes place primarily in separated or divorced family systems, the therapist must work with the fact that the very structure (i.e., physical separation from the alienated parent) of the system reinforces the dynamics of the alienation.

5. Divide and conquer. When the potential level of hostility in a family appears too great to risk having the nuclear family meet together, the next step would be to strategically divide the family into subsystems. The first choice typically would be to observe the siblings together and determine how strong the mythology and scapegoating has become among them. This session allows the therapist to bypass the direct scapegoating by the alienating parent that would occur if she or he were present. However, the therapist should be advised that this intervention is a more direct challenge to the control maintained by the alienating parent, as well as a potential threat to the system's mythology. Any action that removes the children from the immediate physical control of the alienating parent may be perceived as a threat, and it would not be uncommon for efforts to be made to sabotage or cancel such a meeting.

In these sessions, the therapist interacts with the siblings and looks for evidence of even minimal ambivalence with regard to the myth about the alienated parent. Often one child may not reflect the alienation as strongly as the others (this is often the youngest child in the family). The therapist needs only to find a small "crack" in the mythological armor that could potentially open the door for therapeutic change among the siblings. If the therapist is successful here, the mythology and scapegoating can be temporarily defused among the siblings. Of course, this lasts only until the siblings are reunited with the alienating parent. At that time, the siblings will revert very quickly to supporting the ongoing myth. However, the door (and the boundaries) has been opened – if only briefly – for interjecting some minimal ambivalence and interrupting the scapegoating. Of course, this intervention is not effective in families with only one child because it does not allow the therapist the opportunity to utilize creatively the interaction among siblings.

A second method of intervention would be to see the parents in joint sessions a few times. Although this may exacerbate the drama of the conflict and animosity (in some cases requiring one of the parents to sit in the therapist's office, even over the objections of their attorneys) may also serve to defuse the scapegoating process. Some parents can use this time to identify and process old hurts and wounds that may never have been voiced prior to their separation or divorce.

6. Use the resources of the intergenerational family to open the boundaries and defuse the scapegoating. Another level of intervention is to bring together family-of-origin members in a variety of possible patterns. One choice would be to schedule a three-generation session that would include the alienating parent, her or his parents, and the children. If such a session is conducted without the children present, and if the process is shared by the grandparents, the scapegoating may be much more difficult to block and control. The children's presence softens this process and gives the therapist some additional leverage.

Occasionally, this type of intergenerational session will reveal ambivalence in a grandparent, who might express some concern about the well being of their grandchild or some sadness about the grandchildren's lack of contact with the alienated parent. This may be based on a grandparent's own wisdom or experiences in her or his respective family-of-origin. An elderly grandmother once began to cry, for no apparent reason, in such a family session. She told the author, in front of her daughter (the alienating parent), "All of this is so sad. . . . My father died when I was only five and I never got over missing him. I hate to see this happen to these children." While this may be a "long shot" clinically, the author has found that in some PAS cases the grandparents can open the door to challenging the scapegoating and mythology. However, the author also has found that in some of the most difficult PAS cases the grandparents may actually be the source of the initial alienation process and may be financially funding the legal proceedings. In either situation, the inclusion of grandparents can be an important resource for the therapy process.

Two additional intergenerational interventions, with which the author has had some limited success. The first can be used to initiate a session with the alienated parent, her or his parents or even the parent's siblings (if available) and the children. Such a session will serve, indirectly, to reunite the children with the alienated family members in a potentially loving context during which the children might begin to identify and relive formerly positive times, such as holidays or birthdays spent with their grandparents. The overwhelming impact of a large and supportive group of family members can often be powerful enough to defuse the scapegoating and even temporarily suspend the children's loyalties to their alienating parent.

However, before such a session is conducted, the family-of-origin members must be "coached" or instructed to focus only on interacting and connecting with the children; they should not defend the alienated parent. If this session is somewhat successful, then visitations with this intergenerational family group (outside of therapy) should be recommended immediately. This, in effect, temporarily removes the children from the induction process and physically removes them from the closed boundaries of the alienating system. A few therapeutic sessions such as these, reinforced with several independent visits between these family members and the children, can effectively begin to change the entire PAS drama.

A second type of intergenerational session would involve both sets of grandparents. Although it is predictable that grandparents would advocate and side with their own adult child, many grandparents have a desire to retain their relationship with their grandchildren, and most have some sense of concern about the well-being of their grandchildren. These factors may serve to challenge the scapegoating and further reduce the closed boundaries that isolate the children. The author has been impressed with the ability of some grandparents, on both sides of the family, when placed in the same therapy room, to be able to communicate within their own generational language and begin to open some doors for the benefit of their grandchildren.

In one case, which was somewhat exceptional, the four grandparents, who had experienced a good mutual relationship when their adult children's marriage was still intact, cautiously reconnected and recalled a time when the grandfathers had played golf together. During this discussion the grandmother of the alienated parent began to cry and expressed her sadness about not being able to be at a recent school event in which the grandchild had participated. When the mother of the alienating parent saw the other grandmother cry, she seemed to begin a process of questioning everything that had happened. By the close of the session, she had noticeably begun to withdraw her loyalty to the alienating coalition and its mythology. Three months later, she volunteered to testify in court against her alienating son.

7. *Avoid working solely with the rejecting child and the alienated parent.* Unfortunately, working with this dyad is the most common form of intervention and the most typical format that the author has found to be ordered by courts. Attorneys and judges often have the incorrect assumption that if you put the members of the problem relationship in the same room together (much like mandatory arbitration may be ordered in business cases) the two individuals should be able to "work things out." The author has learned over the years to request specifically, as part of any court order for treatment, the therapeutic freedom to interview in whatever form or manner necessary all family members, including the parents' families of origin.

When the therapist is isolated with the rejecting child and the scapegoated parent, the child's loyalties to the alienating parent are immediately operationalized. The therapy session itself represents danger for the child; she or he is being removed from the protective boundaries of the alienating parent and is being "forced" to meet with the parent that the child has been warned to fear. The presence of the therapist offers little protection from the fears or anger within this child. (Recall the therapist who sent her scarf with the alienated child for such a session.) The therapist who tries to work solely with this dyad, except in very mild cases of PAS, simply does not have the power to challenge the child's loyalties to the alienating parent, much less to challenge or block the scapegoating process in this type of session. This is *not* the intervention of choice.

The one type of intervention that has provided some limited success in cases for which the author had no other choice but to see these alienated parent-rejecting child dyads has been the use of family photographs or videotapes. In one case, the alienated father brought to the session a video of him coaching his daughter and her soccer team. He, his daughter, and the therapist watched this video together. The rejecting and angry daughter was delighted to watch herself and her friends on the video. When the therapist asked to turn off the video after about 15 minutes, the child pleaded to continue watching. She became quite animated in her comments about former friends on the team and her relationship with her father as the coach. After a few more minutes of watching the video, she moved from across the room to sit in her father's lap. This served dramatically to reconnect the child with her father, to challenge the irrationality of the myth, and to suspend the scapegoating.

In another case, a similar intervention using home videos from a family reunion held three years previously was used successfully in a series of meetings with the paternal grandparents, the alienated father, and the alienated child. However, in another case with a 14-year-old adolescent, the child refused to even look at a videotape of himself playing baseball with his father and stepsiblings. He buried his head in his lap until the video was turned off.

8. Consider removing the child from the alienating system. In many PAS cases, particularly those described in the range of "severe" by Gardner (1992, 1998, 2001), even the best interventions and efforts to utilize the resources of the larger family system may fail. In these cases, the only reasonable prospect for therapeutic change may be to remove the child from the alienating and closed system. This intervention confronts head-on the isolating boundaries as well as the ongoing reinforcement of the scapegoating and mythology. Although this may be viewed as a traumatic intervention and, of course, one that the courts enter into reluctantly, it may be the only way to break these clinical dynamics. When this is necessary, the therapist can perform an essential role by assisting the court in defining a therapeutic structure for the removal. This involves such decisions as whether the child should be placed with family members or hospitalized, how to manage the subsequent insidiousness and intrusive power of the alienating system, how to reset boundaries for the child with the newly defined system of the alienated parent, and how to therapeutically use the resources of the family to reconcile the child with the alienated portion of the family.

In one of the author's cases, a nine-year-old child was removed from the alienating parent (mother) for six weeks during a summer. The mother had relocated away from the community two years earlier. The therapy provided work with the child individually and in family sessions with her father, paternal grandparents, and two aunts. During the first week, the alienating mother called the father's home 2 to 5 times daily to talk with the child and effectively sabotaged any progress among the family members or in therapy. These daily telephone calls expressed worry about the child's safety and ended with the mother crying on the phone. They were enough to reinforce the scapegoating process of the father and the other family members. The child remained withdrawn in her room during that week. At the request of the therapist, the court ordered only one ten-minute telephone call per week. In the week after the telephone calls were stopped, the therapist learned that the mother had sent with the child, in her suitcase, a series of letters and notes, and even packaged food for each of the 40 days that she was to be with the father. At the end of the second week the child agreed to voluntarily give the remaining unopened letters and food to one of her aunts to keep until she was to return to her mother's home.

After these two critical changes to the structure of the reconciliation plan, rather dramatic progress was made in the remaining 4 weeks. First this involved reconnecting the child with her aunts, of whom she had good early childhood memories, and who, for the child, seemed somewhat removed from her fears of her father. The comfort with her aunts was gradually broadened and they were asked to include the grandparents in their activities. After several days of success, the aunts and grandparents gently planned casual activities to reinvolve the father. By the end of the sixth week, the child had become more casually interactive with the father and even initiated some independent activities with him. The child also discussed with the therapist the possibility of remaining in the community with her father for another few weeks.

Unfortunately, the court was unable to act quickly on a request to extend the visitation and the child was allowed to return to her home with the alienating mother. Before another court hearing could be scheduled, it was learned that the mother had remarried during the time that the child was with the father; she and her new husband had moved with the child to Europe. (It was learned much later that the child knew the mother had planned to marry during the summer but had been asked to keep it a secret. She had been told that it was her father's fault that she could not attend the wedding or accompany the mother and stepfather on a trip.)

CONCLUSION

PAS cases involve difficult and complex family dynamics. Many mental health workers, along with attorneys and judges, often view these cases as "hopeless" or "involving inordinate amounts of clinical time." However, if the therapist understands the underlying family systems dynamics of the cases and the family is approached utilizing the resources of family therapy, it is possible to challenge and change many PAS dynamics.

REFERENCES

Ackerman, N.A. (1956). Interlocking pathology in family relationships. In S. Redo & G. Daniels (Eds). *Changing concepts of psychoanalytic medicine* (pp. 135–150). NY: Grune & Stratton, Inc.

Ackerman, N.A. (1958). *The psychodynamics of family life.* NY: Basic Books.

Everett, C.A. & Everett, S.V. (1998). *Family therapy for ADHD.* NY: Guilford Press.

Gardner, R.A. (1992). *The Parental Alienation Syndrome: A guide for mental health and legal professionals.* Cresskill, NJ: Creative Therapeutics, Inc.

Gardner, R.A. (1998). *The Parental Alienation Syndrome,* Second Edition. Cresskill, NJ: Creative Therapeutics, Inc.

Gardner, R.A. (1999). Family therapy of the moderate type of parental alienation syndrome.*American Journal of Family Therapy, 27,* 195–212.

Gardner, R.A. (2001). *Therapeutic interventions for children with parental alienation syndrome.* Cresskill, NJ: Creative Therapeutics, Inc.

Gehrke, S. & Kirschenbaum, M. (1967). Survival patterns in family conjoint therapy. *Family Process, 6,* 67–80.

Nichols, W.C. & Everett, C.A. (1986). *Systemic family therapy: An integrative approach.* NY: The Guilford Press.

Vogel, E. & Bell, N.W. (1960). The emotionally disturbed child as a family scapegoat. In N.W. Bell & E. Vogel (Eds.), *The family* (pp. 382–397). Glencoe, IL: The Free Press.

Warshak, R.A. (2000). Remarriage as a trigger of parental alienation syndrome. *American Journal of Family Therapy, 28,* 229-241.

Chapter 18

SEXUAL ABUSE ALLEGATIONS IN THE CONTEXT OF CHILD CUSTODY DISPUTES

William Bernet

OVERVIEW

Sexual abuse allegations sometimes occur in the context of a child custody or visitation dispute. This chapter describes the methodology a mental health professional may use in evaluating these complex cases, including the interviews of the child, the accusing parent, and the accused parent. The evaluator should consider the possible reasons that a child might allege sexual abuse, including: the sexual abuse occurred as reported by the child; the child's statements were caused by purposeful indoctrination or accidental suggestion; the possibility of parental alienation syndrome (PAS); and innocent or naive lying by the child. The credibility of the child's statements may be assessed by identifying factors that are consistent with true and false allegations of abuse.

Mental health professionals are sometimes confronted with the knotty problem of sexual abuse allegations in the context of a child custody or visitation dispute. Under several circumstances, a psychologist, social worker, or psychiatrist might face this issue. The action plan depends on the specific role that has been defined for the mental health professional. That is, a therapist engaged in clinical work and a forensic evaluator would have different interests and would proceed, to some extent, along different lines. This chapter addresses the technique or methodology of the evaluation process, the differential diagnosis to consider when allegations of sexual abuse occur in the context of parental separation and divorce, and the interpretation of the data that have been collected, especially as they relate to the question of the truthfulness of the allegations of sexual abuse.

DEFINING THE MENTAL HEALTH PROFESSIONAL'S ROLE

This type of situation – allegations of sexual abuse in the context of parental separation and divorce – may involve mental health professionals in several different roles. The most common circumstance is that a child is already in psychotherapy when his or her parents decide to separate or divorce. In this context, the child may reveal to the therapist that one or perhaps both parents have abused him or her. Of course, if the therapist has reason to suspect or know (the exact threshold depends on the jurisdiction) that the child was abused, the information should be reported to child protective services (CPS) (Kalichman, 1999). In this circumstance, the CPS staff, and not the therapist, would investigate the allegations. Although it is not the therapist's role to conduct a formal investigation, he or she should conduct a clinical evaluation that includes an assessment of the child's credibility. If the therapist has information as to whether the allegations are true or false, he or she can share that information with CPS.

Perhaps the mental health professional has been a therapist or counselor of a parent, who brings up allegations of abuse in the course of a therapy meeting. In most cases, it is best for the therapist to let the parent report his or her concerns to CPS. The therapist should not conduct an investigation, but should focus on helping the parent deal with the situation while keeping in mind that the allegations may or may not be factual.

A private practitioner or court-appointed psychologist or psychiatrist could uncover allegations of abuse during a child custody evaluation process. In fact, a formal psychiatric or psychological custody evaluation may be particularly indicated in circumstances in which one parent has accused the other of sexual abuse (raising the possibility of a true allegation of abuse) and/or it is suspected that one of the parents has tried to indoctrinate the child and alienate him from the other parent (raising the possibility of a false allegation of abuse). In an alternative situation, CPS staff could be investigating allegations of sexual abuse and learn that the parents of the child are in the middle of a hostile divorce and an ongoing dispute regarding the child's custody or visitation. Although these two forensic situations have different starting points, they both end up with the mental health professional having to evaluate allegations of abuse in the context of a child custody or visitation dispute.

Without being directly involved in specific cases, the mental health professional may address this issue by supervising front-line clinicians, providing administrative or management services, developing public policy on a state or national level, teaching graduate students, and conducting research.

REVIEW OF THE LITERATURE

This chapter highlights what the mental health professional should think and do when evaluating allegations of abuse in the context of a child custody dispute. In focusing on this topic, one should consider three sources of literature: protocols and guidelines regarding child custody and visitation evaluations; research regarding the evaluation of children who may have been sexually abused; and information regarding PAS, since false allegations of abuse are more likely to occur when PAS is present.

Child Custody and Visitation Evaluations

Although there is no uniformly accepted procedure for conducting a child custody evaluation, most practitioners would agree that a custody or visitation evaluation consists of the following: individual meetings with each parent, meetings with the child(ren), conjoint meetings of each parent and each child together, collecting information from outside sources such as therapists, and psychological testing.

Several psychiatrists (Bernet, 2002; Gardner, 1989b; Goldzband, 1988; Herman, 2002; Nurcombe & Partlett, 1994; Pruett & Pruett, 1998) and psychologists (Ackerman, 1995; Gould, 1998; Hodges, 1986; Otto, Buffington-Vollum, & Edens, 2003; Stahl, 1999; Weithorn, 1987) have published protocols and guidelines regarding child custody evaluations. A book by Galatzer-Levy & Kraus 1999 presents "the scientific basic of child custody decisions." Atkinson (2000) authored a comprehensive legal text regarding child custody. The National Interdisciplinary Colloquium on Child Custody Law (1998), an independent group of practicing and academic lawyers, mental health professionals, and judges, published a "deskbook for judges." Guidelines for performing child custody evaluations have been published by the American Academy of Child and Adolescent Psychiatry (1997a), the American Psychological Association (1994), and the Association of Family and Conciliation Courts (1994).

Sexual Abuse Evaluations

Several individuals and organizations have published protocols and recommendations regarding the clinical and forensic evaluation of children who may have been sexually abused (Benedek & Schetky, 1987a,b; Bernet, 1998; Friedrich, 2001; Gardner, 1992, 1995; Kuehnle, 1996, 2003; Ney, 1995; Nurcombe & Partlett, 1994; Quinn, 2002). The American Academy of Child and Adolescent Psychiatry (1997b) developed a practice parameter for the evaluation of children who may have been physically or sexually abused. Members of the American Professional Society on the Abuse of Children (APSAC) recently published a book on the evaluation and treatment of child abuse (Myers et al. 2002).

Sexual Abuse Allegations in the Context of Child Custody Disputes

The joining of these two issues (sexual abuse allegations and a custody dispute) results in a very complex case and unusual problems for the evaluator. The phenomenon was described in the 1980s by Benedek and Schetky (1985), Green (1986), and Gardner (1985, 1987, 1989a). A book was published on this topic by the American Bar Association (Nicholson & Bulkley, 1988). Faller (1991) and Eastman and Moran (1991) also discussed the relationship between sexual abuse allegations and divorce. More recent publications regarding the assessment of sexual abuse allegations in the context of a custody dispute include a book chapter by McGleughlin, Meyer, and Baker (1999) and an article by Gardner (1999).

Parental Alienation Syndrome

PAS is a disturbing psychological phenomenon in which a child – usually one whose parents are engaged in a hostile divorce – comes to ally himself or herself strongly with one parent and rejects a relationship with the other parent without legitimate justification. The clinical features of PAS (Gardner, 1998) include: a campaign of denigration; weak, frivolous, and absurd rationalizations for the deprecation; lack of ambivalence; independent-thinker phenomenon; reflexive support of one parent against the other; absence of guilt over exploitation of the targeted parent; presence of borrowed scenarios; and spread of the animosity to the extended family of the targeted parent. Gardner (1998) emphasized that PAS consists of two components: programming of the child by one parent to denigrate the other parent and the child's own contributions in support of the campaign of denigration. In some cases, PAS may be the basis for false allegations of sexual abuse against the alienated parent.

RECOMMENDATIONS FOR CONDUCTING THE EVALUATION

It is a difficult task to deal in a professional manner with distraught parents who are engaged in a highly adversarial custody dispute. In addition, it is a challenge to separate truth from fiction when children make allegations of sexual abuse. When one adds the possibility of PAS, the result is a road with many tight curves, narrow shoulders, steep grades, and unmarked potholes. This chapter does not discuss every aspect of evaluating children who make allegations of sexual abuse in the context of a custody dispute, but it identifies and discusses several important issues that the evaluator should keep in mind.

The purpose of the forensic evaluation in this kind of case is to address several questions at the same time. Some questions pertain more directly to the custody and visitation dispute, while others relate to the allegations of sexual abuse:

- What are the factors in this case that are consistent with true allegations of sexual abuse?
- What are the factors in this case that are consistent with false allegations of sexual abuse?
- After assessing the psychosocial strengths and weaknesses of the parents, is either parent more qualified to receive custody of the child?
- After assessing the emotional needs, attachments, and preferences of the child, does he or she have a stronger or healthier relationship with one of the parents?
- If PAS is present, what is the symptom level (mild, moderate, severe) of the child and what is the symptom level of the alienator?

Clarify Administrative Arrangements (Such as Role Definition) and Ethical Issues (Such as Confidentiality) during the Introductory Phase of the Evaluation

Regarding role definition, it is important for the parties to understand the difference between a forensic evaluation and psychotherapy. If the clinician already has a therapeutic relationship with the family, the clinician should not try to change hats and embark on a forensic evaluation. The therapist who has treated one of the parties cannot possibly claim neutrality when shifting to the role of custody evaluator. If the clinician is conducting a forensic evaluation, he or she should not try to conduct psychotherapy. That is, the forensic evaluation is not therapy, although it may be therapeutic in the general sense.

At the beginning of the evaluation, it is important to clarify ethical issues such as confidentiality. Clients need to be aware that neither clinical nor forensic evaluations provide *total* confidentiality. In both clinical and forensic work, of course, confidentiality may be breached if the client is imminently dangerous to himself or others or if child abuse is suspected. Regarding the kind of evaluation addressed in this chapter – evaluations for cases in which sexual abuse allegations have been made – the evaluator should explicitly inform the older participants (that is, adolescents and adults) that suspicions of abuse will be reported to CPS when the suspicions relate to a specific, identifiable child. If one of the participants is a pedophile who acts out his or her sexual interest in children, this warning puts the person on notice and may well reduce the amount of honest communication. However, informed consent is important because most mental health professionals would consider it unethical to trick a person into confessing to a crime.

In a forensic evaluation, the parties know the practitioner will prepare a report for court, but they may nevertheless have the idea that the clinician will keep certain information secret. For instance, one of the parents might offer the evaluator a detailed diary or a highly personal videotape. Before accepting this material, the practitioner should make sure the parent understands that the diary and the videotape may have to be given to the other side of the case if the clinician reviews it while conducting the evaluation. It is relatively easy to advise adults that the forensic evaluation is not confidential; it is more difficult to inform children because the evaluator must find a way to explain the concept in an age-appropriate manner.

When a Child Resists or Refuses Visitation with the Noncustodial Parent, Consider All the Possible Factors that Might Cause This to Happen

It is common for children to resist or avoid visitation with the noncustodial parent after the parents separate or divorce. When it happens, each parent's first reaction is often to blame the other parent. The custodial parent says the noncustodial parent was never any fun to be with or was abusive, so it is natural that the child would not want to visit. The noncustodial parent blames the custodial parent for allowing or encouraging the child to avoid visitation. The forensic evaluator, the therapist, the parents, the attorneys, and the judge should keep in mind that there are several possible explanations for a child's active rejection of visitation. PAS is an important, but not the only, reason this happens. The possibilities include the following scenarios.

Maltreated Child

Perhaps the child actually was abused, neglected, or disliked by the noncustodial parent or the current boyfriend or girlfriend of that parent. If that were the case, it is understandable that the child would not want to visit the noncustodial parent's household.

Purposeful Indoctrination

Perhaps the custodial parent has systematically and purposefully indoctrinated the child to favor him or her by emphasizing that person's affection for the child and criticizing the noncustodial parent (Clawar & Rivlin, 1991; Gardner, 1998). If that is occurring, several possible explanations exist. For example, it could simply be the custodial parent's realistic appraisal of the situation (i.e., that the noncustodial parent deserves plenty of criticism). It could be because the custodial parent has delusions about the noncustodial parent related to a serious mental illness. It could be that the purposeful indoctrination is motivated by spitefulness toward the other parent or a strongly felt need for the child's affection. Such purposeful indoctrination could result in PAS.

Accidental Indoctrination

Perhaps the custodial or primary residential parent has caused the child's alienation from the noncustodial parent, but has not done it on purpose. For example, the mother may be an overly anxious person who worries most of the day and communicates her anxiety to the child. She may start crying or be visibly upset when the child leaves for visitation, but insist that the child should go anyway. This process may cause the child to gravitate to the mother's side, both metaphorically and literally, and come to fear the father. This could result in PAS.

Parental Alienation Syndrome

Some degree of programming or indoctrination – either purposeful or accidental – is necessary but not sufficient to create PAS. In addition to parental programming, the child contributes to the process by adding his or her own scenarios to the campaign of denigration.

Worried Child

In some divorced families the child resists visitation and clearly favors the residential or custodial parent over the noncustodial parent, but neither parent did anything specific to cause the child to behave this way. For example, perhaps the child started out with a slightly better attachment to the custodial parent. The child was frightened and anxious when the parents separated. After the departure and loss of the noncustodial parent, the child became fearful that he or she was going to lose the custodial parent as well. As a result, the child experienced an attachment to the residential parent that was greatly exaggerated, and feared separation from that parent.

Stubborn Child

In this circumstance also, the locus of the problem is in the child, and not the parents. For example, perhaps the child had a good attachment to both parents and became very upset when the parents separated and divorced. The child was upset (sad, angry, resentful, worried) about the situation and did not want to participate in the process. The child expressed his or her feelings by objecting vehemently and stubbornly to the visitation, even though ordinarily he or she enjoyed being with the noncustodial parent.

Child Escaping Conflict

Cognitive dissonance is a common psychological mechanism by which the child's attitudes and affections may become extremely polarized. That is, the child's intense like of one parent and dislike of the other becomes his or her way of resolving the psychological tension that he or she experiences. For instance, if the parents have been fighting intensively with each other, the child would experience cognitive dissonance when trying to have affection for both of them at the same time. The child is unable to reconcile these two dissonant thoughts: "I love my mother" and "I love my father." The dissonance creates a tension in the child's mind, which is resolved by believing that he or she only loves one parent and refusing to visit the other.

When a Child Alleges Sexual Abuse in the Context of a Child Custody Dispute, Consider all the Possible Factors That Might Cause This to Happen

It was stated in the 1980s that "children never fabricate the kinds of explicit sexual manipulations they divulge in complaints or interrogations (Summit, 1983, p. 191)." That maxim, although mistaken, is still believed today by some forensic evaluators and even some judges. If one had to condense this complex topic to a mantra, it would be correct to say that "children are usually but not always telling the truth when they allege sexual abuse." Under several, diverse circumstances both children and adults make false allegations of sexual abuse. In general, these include: false statements that arise in the mind of a parent or other adult and are imposed on the mind of the child; false statements caused primarily by mental mechanisms in the child that are not conscious or not purposeful; and false statements caused primarily by mental mechanisms in the child that are usually considered conscious and purposeful (Bernet, 1993).

When allegations of sexual abuse are made in the context of a child custody dispute, one should consider several specific possibilities. McGleughlin and colleagues (1999) said, "Divorce can precipitate a disclosure, create the preconditions for sexual abuse to occur, or create a climate that is rife for misinterpretation or false allegations" (p. 374). The allegations could be true or false or even some combination of truth and fabrication, which can be most vexing to sort out. Following are several possible explanations for allegations of sexual abuse that arise when parents separate or divorce.

Child Previously Sexually Abused; Finally Comes Forward

This may happen in families in which one parent (usually the father) physically abused the other parent. The father also abused the children in the family, but no one said anything because they feared additional abuse. Only after the parents separated did the children feel safe enough to disclose that they had been abused. Faller (1991) described this phenomenon.

Child Sexually Abused Following Parents' Separation

Faller (1991) also pointed out that a parent (usually the father) may be more likely to sexually abuse a child after parental separation because the father and child spend an unusual amount of time together with no one else in the household. Other dynamics, such as a depressed parent who is looking for nurturing combined with a child who tries to nurture the abandoned parent, may operate.

Anxious Adult Misinterprets Child's Behavior or Physical Condition

The public now has such a high level of awareness of child sexual abuse that some adults (parents, teachers, and therapists) are apt to suspect sexual abuse based on innocent or benign circumstances.

> Julia, age 6, was in the first grade. Her class was learning about ancient Egypt and there was a good deal of discussion about mummies. The teacher asked the class to imagine what a mummy would look like if the wrapping were removed; she suggested the children draw pictures of the unwrapped mummy. Julia drew the profile of a man lying on his back. The man was nude – since he was an unwrapped mummy – and Julia included a somewhat prominent penis in her drawing. Although Julia thought she was simply following instructions, the teacher got upset and notified Julia's mother, who

got upset and consulted the child's pediatrician. The doctor suspected the child was sexually abused and contacted CPS.

Parental Delusion

An individual with paranoid schizophrenia or delusional disorder may believe that he or she was sexually molested or that his or her child was. A delusional parent who repeatedly instructs or interrogates the child may induce the child to have false beliefs and to make false allegations. If both parent and child are psychotic, this constitutes a folie à deux.

Purposeful Indoctrination

Through a variety of behaviors – ranging from blatant brainwashing and intimidation to subtle and sophisticated suggestion – a parent may purposefully cause the child to state or disclose that he or she was sexually abused by the other parent (Clawar & Rivlin, 1991; Gardner 1998). The child may react to purposeful indoctrination by simply repeating the allegations made by the indoctrinating parent, but not really believing them. On the other hand, the child may actually come to "remember" and believe the abuse occurred.

Accidental Indoctrination

An anxious and overprotective parent may have a heightened concern about sexual abuse, perhaps related to his or her own past experiences. Because of persistent worrying, the anxious parent may repeatedly question the child about whether certain people – the father, the babysitter, the gymnastics coach, etc. – touched the child in a sexual manner. If the custodial parent routinely asks these questions every time the child returns from visitation, the child may figure out that the "right answer" is to allege abusive behavior by the noncustodial parent.

Parental Alienation Syndrome

Most cases of PAS do not involve allegations of sexual abuse. In some cases of PAS, however, the campaign of denigration includes false allegations of sexual abuse. This is a powerful accusation, of course, that gets the attention of CPS, law enforcement personnel, and the court. Also, it is theoretically possible for true allegations of sexual abuse to occur in the context of PAS.

Interviewer Suggestion

A concerned parent may take a child to a psychotherapist or to CPS, where the child is interviewed for the purpose of eliciting a disclosure. If this investigative interview is not conducted properly, the interview process may cause the child to make false allegations of sexual abuse (Ceci & Bruck, 1995; Ceci, Huffman, Smith, & Loftus, 1994; White & Quinn, 1988). The most common mechanism for this process is repeatedly asking questions that are leading or suggestive. The child rapidly learns that the interviewer is looking for a particular answer. The interviewer may reward the child in some way when the child provides the desired response. Although interviewer suggestion may take place over several days or weeks, false allegations of very serious child sexual abuse may be created in a single interview (Bernet, 1997). Of course, once the child has made a false statement during a poorly conducted interview, the child is likely to repeat the false statement spontaneously in subsequent interviews.

> Freddie's father took Freddie, age 5, to see a psychiatrist because he was concerned that the boy had been sexually abused by the boy's stepfather, John. The psychiatrist asked the boy a series of suggestive questions: "Does anything ever come out of John's penis?" "You mean white like milk?" "When something comes out, does it squirt?" "So does anything like glue or anything that's sticky ever come out of John?" "Does it come out like water comes out of a hose or does it come out like something that's going squirt, squirt, squirt?" By the end of the meeting, the boy was endorsing an account of John's masturbating in front of Freddie and engaging in sexual acts with him. When CPS personnel interviewed Freddie the next day, the boy repeated these statements and embellished them further. CPS thought Freddie's statements were credible. Although Freddie did not see his mother for more than a year, the court ultimately determined the allegations were false and returned Freddie to his mother's custody.

Child's Miscommunication

When parents separate and divorce, family interactions may be tense and adults may overly scrutinize and distort the meaning of simple remarks made by children. For example:

> A young girl told her mother, "Daddy makes love to me when I'm in bed." The mother overreacted

and reported the statement to CPS. It took an elaborate investigation to establish that the girl was simply referring to her father's good-night kiss.

Child's Normal Sexual Fantasy

It is normal for young children to confuse fantasy with reality. It is also normal for children to engage in sexual behaviors such as masturbation and to fantasize about sexual encounters with other people, including adults (Rosenfeld, Nadelson, & Krieger, 1979).

> A 5-year-old girl mentioned to her teacher that her father asked her to wash his penis while the two of them were taking a shower together. Upon investigation, it was determined that the child had never in her life taken a shower with the father. It was concluded that this bright and imaginative child had fantasized this sexual activity with her father (Gardner, 2001).

Child's Innocent Lying

Young children do not like being in trouble with their parents, so they are apt to lie when they know or simply suspect they have done something wrong. This behavior is sometimes called innocent or naive, lying. That is, the child knows he or she is not speaking the truth, but does not appreciate the broader consequences (losing the parents' trust, getting another person in serious trouble, inconveniencing many people) of telling a lie. For example:

> The bus driver for a preschool had only one passenger, Hannah, age 5. The driver stopped at a convenience store and purchased a bag of candy. With the bus still parked in front of the convenience store, the driver offered Hannah some candy. However, Hannah dropped the bag and spilled the candy on the floor of the bus. The bus driver and Hannah picked up the candy and put it back in the bag. Two women in the convenience store, who saw the bus driver bobbing up and down as he picked up the candy, were suspicious and notified the police. Later that day, the police went to the preschool and interviewed Hannah, who initially said nothing unusual happened that morning on the bus. However, she sensed she was in trouble for spilling the bag of candy and she wanted to deflect blame onto the bus driver. When the investigators started asking her about sexual activities, Hannah agreed that the bus driver touched her private parts, although he had not.

Factitious Disorder by Proxy

Meadow (1993) and Schreier (1996) described cases in which a mother repeatedly stated to physicians, mental health professionals, or law enforcement personnel that her child had been sexually abused. The motivation was reportedly to obtain personal attention from the medical, mental health, or law enforcement professionals, which is the underlying reason for factitious disorder by proxy or Munchausen syndrome by proxy. When this occurs, of course, it subjects the child to numerous evaluations, interrupts the child's relationship with the other parent, and creates enormous work for CPS and court personnel. Factitious disorder by proxy is not the diagnosis when the motivation is simply to win a child custody dispute. In factitious disorder, the parent's primary goal is a perverse relationship with a powerful transferential figure, which could be a physician, a therapist, a sheriff, an attorney, or a CPS worker.

The mental health professional who is evaluating allegations of sexual abuse in the context of a child custody dispute should keep all of these possibilities in mind. A practitioner cannot identify a particular condition or make a particular diagnosis unless the person knows the condition sometimes occurs and keeps in mind the differential diagnosis. Some of these possibilities are common and some are rare. Although the exact frequencies are not known, the most common explanations for allegations of sexual abuse made during a child custody dispute are probably the following: the sexual abuse actually occurred; the child's statements are the result of parental indoctrination with or without PAS; a parent's excessive vigilance for sexual abuse combined with inept investigative interviews; and allegations initiated by the child's innocent lying.

When Evaluating a Child Who Has Made Allegations of Sexual Abuse in the Context of a Custody Dispute, it is Important to Take a Thorough History

These cases are usually complex and it is important to do much more than simply interview the child in the hopes of eliciting a disclosure or denial of sexual abuse. As in any custody evaluation, the evaluator should meet with the parents together and also individually. In the joint meeting, which usually takes place at the outset of the custody evaluation, it is possible to collect basic information about the family and explain how the evaluation will be conducted. It may be quite informative to collect some parts of the history in the joint meeting with the parents, such as tracing the evolution of the sexual abuse allegation.

The evaluator also should meet with each parent individually. He or she should understand each parent's view of the marriage, the period of separation and divorce, and the other parent. When one parent has listed allegations and grievances against the other parent, it is helpful to ask the second parent about all of these allegations. The evaluator should collect information about each parent's psychiatric history, substance abuse, and history of sexual abuse and spousal abuse. Assess the family, including information about all persons living in the household, what they do, and how they are related.

Regarding the allegations of sexual abuse, the evaluator should determine the exact circumstances of the initial statement, details of subsequent conversations and interviews regarding the alleged abuse, symptoms and behavioral changes in the child, and other traumas and stressors in the child's life. The allegations must be considered in the larger context of the child's life and development. For instance, one should consider the family's practices regarding nudity and sexuality in order to know the child's baseline knowledge and vocabulary.

Information from the detailed history may provide data that support any of the possible explanations previously mentioned, including the truthfulness of the allegations and the possibility of interviewer suggestion. If the child is engaging in innocent lying, that will only be discovered by knowing exactly who said what at the moment the allegations first arose. In order to identify parental indoctrination and PAS, it is important to have a good understanding of both parents, including their parenting attitudes, opinions about each other, personality characteristics, and clinical diagnoses.

When Interviewing the Child, Follow a Standard Protocol That Encourages the Child to Provide a Free Narrative Account of Significant Events. Avoid Common Errors, Such as Asking Repetitive, Leading, and Suggestive Questions and Rewarding the Child for Giving Certain Answers

The child interview(s) should accomplish the following tasks: completion of a clinical evaluation of the child; documentation of the child's narrative description of the alleged abuse; assessment of the child's attachment to each parent; evaluation of the child's credibility; and assessment of whether the child has been indoctrinated or influenced in some way. Since the goal is to provide a setting in which the child is able to give a reasonably spontaneous, narrative account of the alleged abuse, it is advisable to proceed in the interview from general statements ("Why did your mom bring you here today?" and "Tell me what happened next.") to more specific questions ("Did the man say anything after he touched you?"). Even the simple phrase "touched you" would be leading if introduced by the examiner; but it is not if the child first used the term and then the examiner used it to elicit further details.

Several systematic approaches, which were designed to maximize the amount of accurate information and minimize mistaken or false information elicited from the children, can be used when conducting these interviews. For example, the Cognitive Interview makes use of principles of memory and cognition in order to optimize accurate retrieval of event memories (Fisher & Geiselman, 1992). One of the techniques of the Cognitive Interview is to encourage witnesses to search their memories in various ways, such as recalling events forward and then backward. The Step-Wise Interview (Yuille, Hunter, Joffe, & Zaparniuk, 1993) and the interview protocol of Poole and Lamb (1998) emphasize the following: the "practice interview," in which the child describes a recent event and learns to report everything about the event from beginning to end; the importance of the free narrative statement regarding the abuse incident; and proceeding from open-ended questions to, if necessary, more specific questions.

In the 1980s, some mental health professionals advocated the use of anatomical dolls in evaluating children who may have been sexually abused. Some evaluators thought the character of the child's play with anatomical dolls could be used to distinguish abused from nonabused children. At this point it is clear that anatomical dolls cannot be used "to make the diagnosis" of sexual abuse (Everson & Boat, 1994).

Although Protocols and Outlines are Helpful, the Evaluator Should Also Make Use of Unstructured Time during the Interview(s) of the Child

As in any clinical or forensic interview, the child might express himself or herself through drawings (e.g., of a person or of his or her family doing something exciting), play activities, or simply conversation. Gardner (1995) suggested inviting the child to do a free drawing with the following instructions: "I'd like you to draw anything you want, anything in the whole wide world. Then, I'd like you to make up a story about what you've drawn. I'd like the story to be completely made up from your own imagination. I don't want it to be about anything you've read in books, seen on television, or anything that really happened to you or anyone you know. I want it completely made up from your own imagination" (p. 145).

Rather than directly ask the child about the alleged abuse, the evaluator may proceed in an indirect manner and see if the child brings up the subject. For example, the evaluator can make an "inventory of affects," which means asking the child to relate a time that was happy. Then he or she can ask the child to talk about a time that was sad, . . . frightening, . . . funny, . . . embarrassing, . . . anger inducing, . . . disappointing, . . . silly, . . . and so on.

Another indirect approach is for the evaluator to make a list of important adults in the child's life (such as the parents, the stepparents, and perhaps others) and ask the child what he or she likes and does not like about each person. The child's dislikes might turn out to include information about child sexual abuse. For example:

> A psychiatry trainee was conducting a child custody evaluation under supervision. The evaluator told Jimmy, age 9, that he wanted information about his parents and he wrote "Mom" and "Dad" and each person's name at the top of tablet paper. The evaluator asked Jimmy about his likes and dislikes of each parent. Jimmy had many likes and dislikes of both parents and most of them were typical, age-appropriate comments such as "I like it when Dad takes us to Chuck E. Cheese's" and "I don't like it when Mom yells." Jimmy then said he liked it when Dad let him stay up very late on weekends to watch television. Jimmy said he did not like it when Dad drank a lot late at night and started touching Jimmy's genitals. Jimmy mentioned that on the following mornings his father could not remember either the sexual touching or what was on television. The evaluator thought Jimmy was describing child sexual abuse – which started after the parents separated – that occurred during the father's alcoholic blackouts. The evaluator notified CPS.

While conducting these interviews, the evaluator should keep in mind the various possible explanations or differential diagnosis for the abuse allegations. Because of the possibility of parental indoctrination, the interviewer should explore what each parent told the child to say to the evaluator and what the parents said about each other. In considering the possibility of PAS, the evaluator should note whether the child provides an unending list of criticisms of the alleged perpetrator and makes frivolous rationalizations for the child's dislike for that parent. Through careful questioning, the evaluator can determine whether other features of PAS, such as the independent-thinker phenomenon, borrowed scenarios, and the spread of animosity to the extended family of the targeted parent, are present.

Assess the Child's Attachment to His or Her Parents. This May, in Some Cases, Include Interviewing the Alleged Perpetrator and the Child Together

In conducting custody and visitation evaluations, it is important for the mental health professional to assess the child's psychological attachment to both parents. That is something mental health professionals know how to do and it is usually outside the expertise of law enforcement personnel, attorneys, and judges. The mental health professional who is experienced in interviewing and evaluating children may find data regarding the child's attachment and bonding to the parents in various components of the evaluation. For example, the evaluator may collect important information regarding attachment through the following: observing the child and parent engaging in a task together; the child's reactions to projective stories (the baby bird story, the deserted island story, the family drawing) (Bernet, 1998); the child's lists of likes and dislikes and other parts of the semistructured interview of the child; certain psychological tests; and the parents' discussions regarding the child.

Many children have a positive relationship with both parents, which is certainly the most desirable circumstance. However, some children have a much stronger and healthier attachment to one of the parents. Kelly and Johnston (2001) described a continuum of possible relationships in divorced families that include the following positions: having a positive relationship with both parents; having an affinity for one parent over the other while still desiring contact and continuity with both parents; having an alliance with and a consistent preference for one parent, and desiring only limited contact with the other parent; estrangement from one parent because of realistic problems such as exposure to domestic disputes; and the position of the alienated child, who strongly resists contact with the other parent in the absence of realistic factors. This last position may be equivalent in many instances with PAS.

In conducting routine custody evaluations, the practitioner almost always seeks to interview both parents. If an evaluator conducts a one-sided custody evaluation – for instance, interviewing only the child and the custodial parent – it is possible to make observations about the persons interviewed but usually not appropriate to make recommendations regarding the child's custody and visitation. In evaluating allegations of sexual abuse in the context of a custody dispute, it is desirable to interview both parents. The alleged perpetrator may or may not be willing to participate in the evaluation. For example, if the allegation seems relatively minor and no criminal charges have been made or envisioned, the alleged perpetrator may be eager to participate in the evaluation in order to state his or her side of the case. On the other hand, if the parent is facing serious criminal charges, the person's attorney may advise him or her not to talk about the case to anyone, including the mental health professionals involved in the child's evaluation. Derdeyn (1994) said that including the alleged abuser in the evaluation is an "opportunity to discover additional clinical issues that may be key to evaluation of the alleged sexual abuse" (p. 281).

An important question is whether the evaluator should interview the child and the alleged perpetrator together. The answer depends on the circumstances of each case and also what has already been determined during the evaluation process. In some instances it would not be appropriate to interview the child and the alleged perpetrator together. For instance, if the evaluator has considerable reason to believe that the alleged perpetrator abused the child, the joint interview may be traumatic for the child and should not occur. Also, it should be understood that the child's behavior in the joint interview is not a way of proving or disproving the truth of the allegations. For instance, a sexually abused child may be perfectly comfortable with the perpetrator of the abuse.

There remain, however, some circumstances in which the joint interview is indicated. For example, suppose many indications suggest that the allegations are false and the child has been indoctrinated to make statements against the father. In addition, the mother has stated that the child is terrified of the father and any other male who remotely looks like him. It may be helpful to interview the father and child together in order to test the mother's claims. A second circumstance in which it is beneficial to interview the alleged perpetrator and child together is when the court is contemplating allowing the child to have supervised visitation with the alleged perpetrator. The court may find it helpful to have the observations of the mental health professional before setting up the visitation schedule. For example:

> When her parents divorced, Maggie, age 5, lived with her mother and rarely saw her father, who was a long-distance truck driver. Based on her suspicions that he had sexually abused the girl, Maggie's mother sought to deny the father access to Maggie. The mother's suspicions were derived from rather flimsy facts: Maggie drew a picture of a penis (although the family lived on a farm and the girl was apparently familiar with the anatomy of horses and cows) and Maggie supposedly drew a picture of semen (although, objectively, the picture was really just scribbles and could have been a drawing of anything or nothing). The mother's main "evidence" for sexual abuse was that Maggie was terribly frightened of her father. The mother claimed the girl had nightmares of the father and took a toy hatchet to bed with her for self-protection in case her father should enter her room at night. As part of a court-ordered custody and visitation evaluation, both parents and Maggie were interviewed. The evaluator suggested that he meet with Maggie and her father together and Maggie did not object to this plan. When the joint meeting occurred, Maggie ran to her father's arms and sat on his lap. She said, "Where have you been? Why haven't you called me?" Maggie's mother had apparently misrepresented the child's feelings about her father.

Keep Thorough and Accurate Records, Which Usually Means Electronically Recording the Interviews in Cases of Allegations of Child Sexual Abuse

When allegations of sexual abuse arise in the context of a custody dispute, it is important to keep accurate records of every aspect of the evaluation. Many times children make or exhibit subtle comments or interactions during interviews. These cannot be trusted to the interviewer's memory. Even detailed, contemporaneous notes do not fully record everything said by both the interviewer and the child.

There continues to be a debate among experts as to whether the child interviews should be recorded electronically, either by videotape or audiotape. Lanning (2002) summarized the pros (for example, knowing exactly what was said in the interview and the visual impact of a videotaped statement) and cons (such as securing and accounting for the tapes and subjecting the interview to interpretation and criticism) of electronically recording the statements of children who are being interviewed regarding sexual abuse allegations. After considering this issue, Lanning concluded, "It is my opinion that the disadvantages of taping generally outweigh the advantages" (p. 335). However, Lanning also said, "Because suggestibility is potentially a bigger problem in younger children, the assessment and evaluation phase is especially important in cases involving these young victims, and videotaping is more justified" (p. 335).

On the other hand, professional groups generally support the idea of recording these interviews. For example, research in California concluded that investigative interviews of children should be videotaped (Child Victim Witness Investigative Pilot Projects, 1994). The American Academy of Child and Adolescent Psychiatry (1997b) said, "If possible, audiotape or videotape the interview" (p. 434). Lamb, Orbach, Sternberg, Hershkowitz, and Horowitz (2000) recommended that interviews be electronically recorded. They noted that, at times, a verbatim recording is likely to help the prosecution in criminal investigations, and at other times it is likely to help the defense. Basically, the recording makes it possible for an independent person to review and assess the information collected during the interview, without its being distorted by editing that surely takes place when the interviewer tries to take notes. Given the vast opportunities for misunderstanding and misreporting what happens in these interviews, this author strongly recommends electronically recording the child interviews in cases of alleged abuse.

Collect Outside Information from Collateral Sources

It is usually important to collect information from collateral sources, such as other family members, agencies, school personnel, babysitters, therapists, and pediatricians. This can be done several ways: requesting pre-existing records, such as therapy progress notes; asking the individual to write a statement regarding the issues raised in this evaluation; and talking to these individuals either in person or by telephone. Although any of these individuals may provide useful information, the evaluator must be mindful that the informant may already be allied with one of the parents.

The evaluator should not be collecting this outside information in a random fashion, but should have in mind the various possible mechanisms (discussed previously) by which a child might refuse visitation with the noncustodial parent or make allegations of child sexual abuse. For example, the extended family members of the custodial parent may convey an intense vendetta against the noncustodial parent that is consistent with PAS, or school personnel may report that the child appears to have a comfortable, relaxed relationship with the father, although the mother says the child is terrified of the father. Or, the child's pediatrician may have the impression that one of the parents has manifested factitious disorder by proxy.

It is important to collect information – through written reports or orally – from previous and current psychotherapists of the child and the parents. Although it usually is advisable for therapists to avoid making formal recommendations regarding custody or testifying in court, it can be helpful for therapists to discuss their observations of the parties with the individual who is conducting the independent forensic evaluation (Bernet, 1983). A parent's therapist may have clinical insight into the parent's mental functioning, which is not otherwise apparent to the evaluator. For example, a parent's therapist may indicate that at times the parent was clearly paranoid. This may have a bearing on the current allegations.

Consider Using Psychological Tests

Although not required, psychological testing may be helpful in custody and visitation evaluations. Regarding the adults, personality inventories such as the Minnesota Multiphasic Personality Inventory-2 (MMPI-2) (Butcher, Graham, Dahlstrom, & Bowman, 1989) and the Personality Assessment Inventory (Morey, 1991) can be used to determine each parent's psychological adjustment and screen for unidentified psychopathology. These tests also contain scales that indicate the person's openness to providing sensitive information. Identification of a defensive parent may be particularly useful when allegations of abuse exist. The Parenting Stress Index (Abidin, 1995) can provide information about a parent's reported level of attachment to the child, perceived problem areas in the child, and the perceived helpfulness of the spouse.

Regarding the child, psychological testing may provide useful information. The Family Relations Test (Bene, 1985) is a nonthreatening means of assessing a child's feelings toward each parent and also the child's overall style of dealing with unpleasant feelings. Bricklin (1995) introduced several standardized psychological tests that are specifically intended for custody evaluations, including the Bricklin Perceptual Scales (BPS) (Bricklin, 1984) and the Perception-of-Relationships Test (PORT) (Bricklin, 1989). In administering the BPS, the evaluator asks the child 32 questions about the mother and the same 32 questions about the father, which are sequenced in such a way that the interviewer never asks the child to directly compare the merits of the mother and father. The child answers the questions verbally and also nonverbally, by punching a hole in a card with a stylus. The child's nonverbal responses can be measured and the 64 answers scored to give a composite score, which indicates which parent is the preferred parent for that child. Bricklin noticed that in some cases the child has his or her "mind made up (MMU)," so the child consistently and without hesitation gives extremely high ratings to one parent and extremely low ratings to the other parent. The MMU child of Bricklin may be equivalent in many instances with the PAS child of Gardner.

Evaluate the Child's Statements, Preferences, and Opinions regarding Custody, Visitation, and the Alleged Abuse

Every custody dispute is unique, and children express themselves in many ways. One child may enter the evaluator's office with a prepared statement of grievances and demands; a second child might discuss his or her opinions, when asked, in a reasonable and articulate manner; another child might be friendly and chatty, but refuse to express any opinion at all regarding his or her parents' divorce.

If the child does not bring up the topic of divorce and custody, the evaluator may ask the child to describe the current parenting plan or custody arrangement, where his or her parents live, the visitation schedule, and so on. The evaluator could ask whether the child would want the arrangements or the schedule changed in any way and the reasons for the proposed change. If sexual abuse has been alleged, the child's spontaneous remarks and responses to questions may help the examiner assess the credibility of the allegations. The following case vignettes illustrate different ways children may talk about sexual abuse.

True Allegation, Serious Abuse

Phyllis, age 5, was repeatedly sexually abused by her stepfather, who admitted his actions and was imprisoned. Phyllis was a timid, fearful girl who was very reluctant to talk about what happened with this man. She developed daytime enuresis that occurred when she was unusually worried, such as when her mother had to travel out of town. Although Phyllis essentially refused to say anything about the abuse that she experienced, she found it helpful to talk about how her worrying caused the enuresis and what to do about it.

True Allegation, Minimal Abuse

Nancy, age 10, was evaluated by CPS and also a private practitioner because she alleged her father touched her breasts when he was tucking her in at night, even though she told him not to. Although slightly embarrassed, Nancy related consistent accounts during the two, parallel evaluations. She missed her father and wanted to see him, as long as he clearly agreed not to touch her in an inappropriate manner.

False Allegation, PAS

Cindy, age 11, started her evaluation by saying, "Dad did bad things. Do you want me to tell them all to you?" She launched into a detailed list of criticisms of her father, in which were embedded allegations of sexual abuse. Cindy said, "He did stuff. . . . I told my preacher. . . . I don't like being at Dad's house . . . my [paternal] grandmother didn't give me anything for Christmas. . . . Dad's car was cold because it didn't have any heat. . . . Dad had two pine tree things that were supposed to be Christmas trees. . . . Dad's cat didn't have any food or water. . . . Dad pushed my brother down . . . my stepdad is very kind . . . something bad happened. . . . Dad pulled down my pants and pulled up my shirt . . . it bothers me that he is a pervert . . . he's done so much to me. . . ." Cindy was chatty and engaging while talking about the alleged abuse experiences.

Assess the Credibility of the Child by Looking at the Form of the Child's Statements

In many instances of alleged sexual abuse, there are no physical findings, no witnesses, and no confession. It may be that the most important part of the investigation is assessing the child's credibility. There is no simple or single test that can consistently distinguish factual and nonfactual statements. A number of factors – regarding the form and content of the child's statements – have been identified that may be helpful in assessing credibility, especially when they are considered cumulatively.

The factors in this section relate to the language the child uses in talking about the alleged abuse. In order to apply these criteria, it is necessary to elicit a free narrative statement from the child, which was emphasized previously. It is important to record the interviews electronically, since it may become necessary to prepare a transcript. This approach is sometimes called criterion-based content analysis (CBCA) (Raskin & Esplin, 1991, 1992). CBCA is not reliable enough by itself to distinguish truthful from nontruthful statements (Lamb, Sternberg, Esplin, Hershkowitz, & Orbach, 1997). However, some components of CBCA may be helpful in combination with other factors in assessing a child's credibility.

The following features of the child's narrative statement are **generally consistent with true allegations of abuse** (descriptors from Raskin & Esplin, 1991):

- Unstructured production with spontaneous digressions: Is the report somewhat unorganized? Are there digressions or spontaneous shifts in focus?
- A quantity of details: Are there specific descriptions of place, time, persons, and events?
- Unusual details: Are there details of persons, objects, or events that are unusual, yet meaningful in this context?
- Contextual embedding: Are events placed in spatial and temporal context? Is the action connected to other incidental events, such as routine daily occurrences?
- Spontaneous descriptions of interactions: Are there reports of actions and reactions or conversation?
- Spontaneous reproduction of conversation: Is conversation reported in its original form?
- Spontaneous corrections or additions: Were corrections offered or information added (spontaneously, not in response to questions) to material previously provided in the statement?

Assess the Credibility of the Child by Looking at the Content of the Child's Statements

The previous recommendation related to the form of the child's narrative statement, while this recommendation relates to its content. Although no criteria that absolutely distinguish true from false allegations exist, it is possible to identify features of the child's statement that may be important in making this distinction (Gardner, 1995; Kuehnle, 1996).

The following examples of content of the child's narrative statement are generally **consistent with true allegations of abuse**:

- The events related by the child are plausible.
- Advanced sexual knowledge for the child's age, especially terminology that may have been used in sexual encounters with an adult.
- Perpetrator behavior that is consistent with pedophilia, such as taking precautions against discovery, insistence on secrecy, and gradual increase in the intrusiveness of the sexual abuse.
- A grooming process that took place over a long period of time (i.e., moving gradually from noncontact to contact abuse).
- If sexual penetration is described, it constitutes a credible scenario, such as penetration done with a finger, the tongue, or the penis of the perpetrator.

The following examples of content of the child's narrative statement are generally **consistent with false allegations of abuse**:

- The events related by the child are implausible, highly dramatic, or preposterous.
- Child's use of the code term, "the truth," as the title for the sex abuse scenario.
- Adult terminology, such as "Daddy sexually abused me." Borrowed scenarios (i.e., terms, descriptors, and events the child heard from another person).
- Perpetrator behavior that is not consistent with pedophilia, such as the presence of multiple perpetrators or the perpetrator not taking ordinary steps against discovery.
- Instead of gradual grooming, the initial instances of abuse were invasive, violent, and painful.
- If sexual penetration is described, it occurred in an implausible manner, such as penetration done with a knife or a gun.

These examples are demonstrated in the following case vignette.

A 5-year-old boy whose parents were engaged in custody litigation made statements to his father that suggested sexual abuse by the mother's boyfriend. Two days later, CPS personnel interviewed the boy.

The boy made many elaborate, highly implausible allegations. For example, he said the sexual activities took place in the foyer of his mother's home. He said his siblings stood in the foyer, watched the abuse, and then held up signs indicating scores (that is, 8, 9, 10 – similar to the signs used at Olympic events). The boy also said he went with the perpetrator through the drive-through at a McDonald's restaurant. He said the perpetrator ejaculated on a hamburger in the car and then gave it to the boy to eat. The boy seemed to enjoy telling these accounts to the interviewers. The psychiatrist who consulted on this case thought this was a false allegation of sexual abuse associated with PAS.

However, the evaluator should keep in mind that implausible things sometimes happen and that children who were abused may be induced to add implausible features to their narrative account. Everson (1997) described several mental mechanisms by which fantastic or implausible elements were incorporated into truthful allegations of child abuse. For instance, Everson mentioned a case in which two young children described their father killing people and dissecting their bodies; jars of human body parts were found in the family home and the father was later convicted of murdering vagrants. In addition, a child may make use of hyperbole or fantasy as a defense against feelings of anxiety and vulnerability, and thus develop a narrative with fantastic elements.

Assess the Credibility of the Child by Assessing the Child's Emotional Reactions

Mental health professionals are trained to be sensitive to the emotional state of clients. In many cases, the child's emotional state may be hard to identify and quantify. Children who have been sexually abused may react in a variety of ways that seem contradictory. For instance, a child may be quiet and withdrawn, loud and disruptive, or fearful and anxious. The child's emotional state may be quite obvious, but the meaning of the child's emotional state might be obscure.

Despite these limitations, the following emotional reactions are generally **consistent with true allegations of abuse** (Gardner, 1995):

- Child is hesitant to divulge the abuse, especially during early interviews.
- Child feels betrayed by the perpetrator and/or the nonabusing parent.
- Child fears individuals who resemble the alleged abuser.
- Child is pessimistic about the future.

Assess the Credibility of the Child by Looking at How the Allegations of Sexual Abuse Originated

In conducting these evaluations, it is extremely important to construct an accurate chronology of the case: how and when suspicions of abuse arose; exactly what the child said and what other people said to the child; the course of psychological and behavioral symptoms; and the timing and content of interviews and physical examinations of the child. Perhaps most important are the exact circumstances and dialogue that took place the very first time the child made a statement suggesting or indicating sexual abuse. This event, which may have occurred weeks or months prior to the evaluation, can sometimes be reconstructed very accurately by interviewing the child, collecting information from adults who were present at the time, and reviewing contemporaneous notes and records.

The following features regarding the origins of the allegations are generally **consistent with true allegations of sexual abuse**:

- The allegations arose prior to the parents' separation and may have led to the separation.
- The child's initial statement was truly spontaneous (i.e., the child had not been repeatedly questioned regarding sexual abuse, either in the past or recently).

The following features regarding the origin of the allegations are generally **consistent with false allegations of sexual abuse**:

- The child's initial statement was made after repeatedly being questioned or advised regarding abuse.
- The allegations arose following the parents' separation and also following attempts by one parent to exclude the other parent from the child's life. (This feature may occur in a PAS situation.)
- The child's initial statement was made to a person who disliked the alleged perpetrator and the child knew it. (This also may occur in a PAS situation.)
- The child's initial statement was made at a time when the child thought he or she was being

blamed or criticized for some misdeed, so the child was motivated to blame another person. (This may result in innocent lying.)

In addition to understanding exactly how the initial allegation came about, it is also important to know how various adults (parents, other family members, the pediatrician, CPS interviewers, the police) reacted to the child's statements. For example, if a child were to make allegations against the noncustodial parent, the custodial parent may smother the child with attention. Likewise, some interviewers strongly praise children for coming forward with allegations, which reinforces the child's belief in true and false allegations alike (Wood & Garven, 2000). Although this attention and praise may be supportive to a child who was abused, it dangerously empowers the child who is making false allegations (Gardner, 2002). In the following case vignette, the child's allegations came about after repetitive questioning by an investigator.

Vincent, age 7, was evaluated by the county CPS because the boy made very vague comments to his mother about the father putting lotion on his bottom after the boy used the bathroom. In her report, the CPS worker said Vincent described these suspicious activities to her and she suspected he had been sexually abused. However, the transcript of the CPS interview revealed that the CPS worker had repeatedly asked the boy to tell her what he had reportedly said to the mother. Although Vincent repeatedly told the CPS worker that he did not know or did not remember what he may have said to his mother, the CPS worker asked the boy for this information 26 times. On further investigation, it was determined that the boy was talking about events that took place when he was three and four years old, when the father had helped him with toilet training.

Assess the Credibility of the Child by Looking at the Progression of the Child's Statements over Time

Witnesses, including children, are not expected to have perfect memories. It is common for a child to make small variations in a narrative statement as it is retold from day to day. Generally, the central activity in the narrative is the same, but the details may change. In addition, a child who was sexually abused may make disclosures gradually and hesitantly over several interviews. In making true allegations, the child's statements may change in small ways over time and have minor inconsistencies.

In some cases of false allegations, the child makes exactly the same statement at different parts of the same interview or in sequential interviews. These are not really "free narrative" statements; they are more like memorized accounts that are delivered verbatim. These rote statements presumably come about through parental instruction. This is demonstrated in the following case vignette.

An 8-year-old boy and his parents were interviewed during the course of a custody evaluation. The mother was extremely domineering and controlling. The father was passive and ineffective. The boy's reports of family activities sounded like a tape recording. When asked what happened over the weekend, the boy said, "Daddy was very mean to me and hit me. I went to the beach with Mommy and Aunt Betty and we had a good time." A few days later the interviewer asked the boy again what happened over the weekend. The boy said, "Daddy was very mean to me and hit me. I went to the beach with Mommy and Aunt Betty and we had a good time."

In other cases of false allegations, the opposite happens. As time goes on and in subsequent interviews, the child's statements evolve by becoming increasingly inconsistent, dramatic, or implausible. The child's statements progress from relatively innocuous behavior to increasingly intrusive, abusive, aggressive activities (Rogers, 1990). The most common mental mechanism to cause this phenomenon is that the child enjoys the attention he or she receives from making more and more dramatic and elaborate statements. This process may occur in PAS and constitutes the campaign of denigration.

Assess the Credibility of the Child by Looking at the Child's Behaviors. Distinguish Behaviors that Occurred prior to, during, and following the Time Frame of the Alleged Abuse

Children who have been abused may be preoccupied with the experience and manifest abuse-related themes in spontaneous comments, play activities, drawings, and creative writing. They may also have trauma-specific dreams. A highly specific indicator is that children who have been sexually abused manifest a wider variety of and more frequent sexual behaviors than do children who were not sexually abused. It should be kept in mind that normal, nonabused children manifest sexual behaviors, including masturbation and curiosity about the sexual parts of other people (both children and adults). Certain sexual behaviors – such as masturbating by inserting an object in the vagina, mimicking sexual intercourse, seductive behaviors, and sexual aggression against other children – are particularly indicative of sexual abuse.

One way to address the child's sexual behaviors systematically is to ask a responsible adult who is familiar with the child's day-to-day activities and behaviors to complete a sexual behavior rating scale, such as the Child Sexual Behavior Inventory (Friedrich et al. 2001). Evaluators should not routinely take parent inventories at face value. It can be very informative to review the parent's responses and inquire about those that seem unusual or inconsistent with other information. For instance, a parent who is supporting a false allegation may want to emphasize and exaggerate the multitude and intensity of the child's sexual behaviors. On the Child Sexual Behavior Inventory, the parent may give responses that greatly inflate the child's score. The examiner can identify this pattern by reviewing the responses with the parent and asking exactly what the parent observed.

When taking a detailed history of the child's emotional problems and behaviors – including symptoms of anxiety and depression, disruptive behaviors, and sexual behaviors – it is important to develop an accurate chronology. This can be done by interviewing the parents and other adults, questioning the child, and reviewing records from pediatricians and therapists. Basically, it is important to determine whether the emotional problems and behaviors took place prior to, during, or following the time frame when the abused allegedly occurred:

- If it is clear that the emotional and behavioral problems preceded the time period of the alleged sexual abuse, then some cause for the problems other than the alleged abuse must exist.
- If the emotional and behavioral problems occurred during the alleged sexual abuse and for a short time following the disclosure, the presence of emotional and behavioral problems may support the truthfulness of the allegations.
- If the emotional and behavioral problems occurred following the disclosure – and following multiple interviews, physical examinations, and other stimulating and aggravating parts of the investigatory process – it is likely that the emotional and behavioral problems were caused by the investigation, and not by any alleged sexual abuse.

Assess the Personality Traits and Credibility of the Adult Accuser

A child custody and visitation evaluation conducted by a mental health professional should include a detailed clinical interview of both parents. This assessment typically focuses on the psychosocial strengths and weaknesses of the parent. Even when no specific psychiatric diagnosis is present, it is usually possible to identify attitudes, personality traits, and styles of parenting that have a bearing on recommendations regarding custody.

When allegations of sexual abuse are made in the context of a custody and visitation dispute, the assessment of the parents takes on an additional dimension. It is necessary to assess not only each person's parenting style, but also the person's credibility regarding the allegations. If one of the parents is making allegations of abuse against another adult in the family – such as the other parent, a stepparent, or a grandparent – it is helpful to determine whether the clinical features and behaviors of the accusing parent are consistent with true or false allegations. Faller (1991, p. 90) said, "Interestingly, it appears that the interviews with accusing parents are more helpful than those with the accused in this type of case." There is, of course, no litmus test for distinguishing true and false accusers. The criteria suggested here, which are largely derived from Gardner (1995), are simply factors that should be considered along with many other pieces of information.

The following factors in the adult accuser are generally **consistent with false allegations of sexual abuse**:

- Instead of manifesting shame or embarrassment, the parent advertises the child has been abused.
- Being overly moralistic, such as seeing sexuality in circumstances that are not sexual.
- Exposing the child excessively to sex-abuse prevention materials.
- Instructing or programming the child to make statements regarding sexual abuse.
- Belief in the preposterous. (The adult accuser believes that extremely implausible sexual abuse scenarios took place.)
- Retrospective reinterpretation of past events, such that previous statements or behaviors by the child

that before disclosure were considered unrelated to sexual abuse are now reinterpreted to lend validity to the sexual abuse allegations.

- Making credible the incredible (explaining or justifying a child's preposterous statement rather than accepting that the preposterous statement was false).
- Enthusiastic commitment to collecting data regarding abuse, such as keeping diaries and notebooks of the child's statements and behaviors.
- Prompting the child's description of sexual abuse in joint interviews, such as giving the child corrections or reminders.
- Exaggerating the medical findings related to sexual abuse.
- Hysterical or paranoid personality traits, such that the person is likely to overstate or exaggerate the significance of the child's statements or behaviors.
- Duplicity or dishonesty in aspects of the evaluation not related to the sexual abuse allegations.

Assess the Personality Traits and Credibility of the Accused

When sexual abuse allegations occur in the context of a child custody dispute, the accused sexual offender is usually one of the child's parents or the love interest of one of the parents. The evaluator may be in a position to address the issues that are typical for a custody dispute (such as the psychosocial strengths and weaknesses of each parent, the relationship of each parent with the child, the relative fitness of the parents, and so on) as well as factors related to the allegations of sexual abuse (such as a psychosexual evaluation).

A psychosexual evaluation consists of a general psychological or psychiatric assessment combined with a detailed sexual history. The evaluator inquires about the person's sexual fantasies and experiences, including any history of the person being abused or offending sexually against others. Of course, the evaluator has already informed the alleged perpetrator that any suspicions of child abuse regarding a specific, identifiable child must be reported to CPS.

There is no such thing as a typical personality of a pedophile. However, Gardner (1995) has identified several clinical features and behavioral manifestations that have been frequently seen in known pedophiles and sex offenders. Some of these clinical features and behavioral manifestations are seen in both male and female offenders, although the great majority of sex offenders are male and most research and clinical information is about male offenders. The evaluator can assess whether the following characteristics are present in men and women who have been accused of sexual abuse.

- Highly dysfunctional family and a long history of emotional deprivation.
- Intellectual impairment because of retardation or psychosis.
- Childhood history of sexual abuse.
- History of very strong sexual urges or sexual deviations.
- Substance abuse.
- Unconvincing denial.
- Use of rationalizations and cognitive distortions that justify pedophilia.
- Psychopathic tendencies, especially lying.

Some clinical features and behavioral manifestations apply only to male sex offenders. These include the following.

- Impulsivity and poor judgment.
- Coercive-dominating behavior or passivity and impaired self-assertion.
- Difficulties with women, including impaired sexual interest in age-appropriate women, recent rejection by a female peer, or dysfunctional heterosexual relationship.
- Large collection of child pornographic materials.
- Career choice that brings him in contact with children.

One component of a psychosexual evaluation may be the Abel Assessment for Sexual Interest (AASI) (Abel, Huffman, Warberg, & Holland, 1998; Abel, Jordan, Hand, Holland, & Phipps, 2001). The AASI consists of two parts. The first part is a detailed questionnaire that collects information in a systematic way regarding the person's sexual experiences, victimization, and offending. In the second part of the AASI, the person is shown photographs of attractive individuals of different ages (young children, school-age children, young adolescents, older adolescents, and adults), genders, and races (Caucasian and African American). These photographs are intended to be sexually interesting, but do not include nude or pornographic images. By using the AASI, the evaluator can often determine the sexual inclinations of the alleged perpetrator.

Unless the accused makes a confession, the psychosexual history does not reveal whether the person abused a child on a particular occasion. The psychosexual history simply indicates whether an alleged sex-abuse perpetrator has pedophilic tendencies. Likewise, the AASI does not indicate whether a person molested a specific child or committed a particular crime. In a criminal trial, the AASI may be useful after a person is found guilty of a sexual offense and prior to sentencing, as the results may assist the court in deciding on the disposition of the case. The psychosexual history and the AASI may be very helpful in civil cases in which allegations of sexual abuse are made in the context of a child custody and visitation dispute.

PREPARING THE REPORT

The evaluator who follows these recommendations will collect a large amount of information, comprised of notes from the interviews of family members, information from other persons (such as teachers and therapists), records, documents, and diaries. Hopefully, the evaluator has not simply collected data in a random or exhaustive manner, but has tried to focus on specific issues and facts that relate to the questions that were posed for this evaluation or investigation. The goal for the evaluation is to address several questions, which relate to allegations of sexual abuse raised in the context of a child custody dispute, at the same time. Some issues to be addressed in the report pertain to the custody and visitation dispute, while others relate to the allegations of sexual abuse.

Describe the Evaluation Process

Forensic reports typically begin with identifying and demographic information, and the reason for and circumstances of the referral. In a custody dispute, the evaluator should cite the court order, if any, that authorized the evaluation. The evaluation process should be clear to the reader, which means listing the following: the various people interviewed; whether the parents were interviewed together; whether joint interviews of the child and parent were conducted; results of psychological testing of the parents and child; collateral sources of information, such as relatives and therapists of family members; and documents and records that were reviewed.

Summarize the Data Collected

Because the evaluator has collected a great deal of information, the challenge is to present it in a manner that is organized and adequately detailed. One way to do this is to discuss each family member individually. The sections regarding each parent should summarize: that person's statements, opinions, and concerns; the parent's psychosocial strengths and weaknesses, as perceived by the evaluator; the testing results regarding that parent; and other information regarding that parent that relates to the questions being addressed in this evaluation. The section of the report regarding each child should include: pertinent psychosocial history of the child; the history of the child's statements regarding abuse; an account of the evaluator's interviews of the child; a description of the joint interviews of the child and each parent; a description of the child's attachment to each parent; a statement regarding the child's preferences regarding custody, if any; indicators of PAS, if present; and indications of any mental disorder.

State Conclusions

Each conclusion and the factual basis for each conclusion should be stated clearly. If the statement is justified, the evaluator should preface the conclusions by saying, "The following conclusions are made with a reasonable degree of medical (or psychological) certainty."

The first conclusion might be to state the factors in this case that are consistent with true allegations of sexual abuse. Because this chapter addresses cases in which sexual abuse allegations have been made in the context of a custody dispute, it usually makes sense for the evaluator to address this issue first and summarize succinctly the data that support the allegations. The second conclusion might be to state the factors in this case that are consistent with false allegations of sexual abuse. It helps the reader if the evaluator lists and explains the factors that support both sides of this issue. Next, the evaluator may state his or her conclusion as to whether the child was sexually abused. Obviously, this opinion would follow from the factors listed in the first two conclusions.

If it is concluded that one of the parents has sexually abused the child, that finding would presumably disqualify that person from having custody of the child. If it is concluded that the sexual abuse allegations are false, explain how the allegations came about. Although the evaluator might not know about every single event and every conversation that took place in the creation and propagation of the false allegations, it should be possible to present a solid, plausible explanation based on the data that have been collected. If the false allegations came about through the process of PAS, explain how that happened. This includes identifying the PAS criteria that are present in the case and explaining how the PAS process evolved to include false allegations of sexual abuse. If PAS is present, state the symptom level (mild, moderate, or severe) of the child and the symptom level of the alienator. In the next conclusion, summarize the psychosocial strengths and weaknesses of the parents. If a parent has a psychiatric diagnosis that has a bearing on his or her parenting skills, explain that issue. If one of the parents has caused PAS to occur and promoted false allegations of sexual abuse, that is bad parenting and perhaps even psychologically abusive, because it has compromised the child's relationship with the alienated parent. Next, summarize the emotional needs, attachments, and preferences of the child. If the child has a psychiatric diagnosis that has a bearing on the issues posed in this evaluation, explain what it is. Explain whether the child has a stronger or healthier relationship with one of the parents. In PAS, the child will have a stronger attachment to the alienating parent, but not a healthier relationship. Discuss whether the child has a comfortable relationship with the parent who allegedly abused him or her.

State Recommendations

Conclusions are not the same as recommendations. Conclusions are a series of statements based on the data collected during the evaluation, as just described. Recommendations are the evaluator's statements about what should happen next. The recommendations should follow from the conclusions, of course, but also make use of the evaluator's knowledge and experience. For example, based on the conclusions already stated, make a recommendation regarding the child's custody. After reviewing the conclusions regarding the relative psychosocial strengths and weaknesses of the parents and the attachments of the child, it is usually possible to predict what the custody recommendation should be. If PAS is present and the symptom level of the alienator is severe, consider whether the custody of the child should be transferred from the alienating parent to the targeted parent. Make recommendations regarding visitation. Obviously, the underlying goal of recommendations regarding custody and visitation is that the child will have strong, healthy, positive relationships with both parents. If the evaluator has concluded that sexual abuse occurred, it may be appropriate to make recommendations regarding the child's visitation with the abusing parent. For example, the evaluator may comment on the frequency and duration of the visits and whether they should be supervised. Consider whether to recommend continuing mediation for the parents. If conflict and hostility exist between the parents, it may be helpful for them to meet on a regular basis (perhaps monthly) with a mediator. The purpose of the mediation is not to do psychotherapy, but to coordinate the visitation process and other aspects of co-parenting in order to minimize the child's exposure to conflict.

Consider whether to recommend counseling or psychotherapy for the child or the parents. If therapy for the child is recommended, it is usually a good idea to emphasize that the therapist should maintain communication with both parents.

THE ULTIMATE ISSUE

After the forensic report has been submitted, one of the parents may want the evaluator to testify in court. The evaluator should be prepared, of course, to state and explain the data that were collected, the conclusions, and the recommendations.

An important question is whether the evaluator should state opinions in court regarding the ultimate issues. For instance, should the evaluator testify, "I have concluded that so-and-so did (or did not) sexually abuse this child" or "I recommend that the mother (or the father) have custody of this child"? It is not up to the evaluator to make the final decision regarding these issues; it is up to the court. Local practice and individual judges have different expectations of expert witnesses who testify in these cases. Some judges in civil trials find it helpful to hear everything the expert witness has to say, including opinions regarding the ultimate issues under consideration in the case at trial. Judges in criminal trials are clear in that they only want to hear data and facts, and that the witness should not intrude on the turf of the jury and judge by stating in court conclusions regarding these ultimate issues.

REFERENCES

Abel, G. G., Huffman, J., Warberg, B., & Holland, C. L. (1998). Visual reaction time and plethysmography as measures of sexual interest in child molesters. *Sexual Abuse: A Journal of Research and Treatment, 10*, 81–95.

Abel, G. G., Jordan, A., Hand, C. G., Holland, L. A., & Phipps, A. (2001). Classification models of child molesters utilizing the Abel Assessment for Sexual Interest. *Child Abuse & Neglect, 25*, 703–718.

Abidin, R. R. (1995). *Parenting stress index professional manual* (3rd ed.) Odessa, FL: Psychological Assessment Resources.

Ackerman, M. J. (1995). *Clinician's guide to child custody evaluations.* New York: Wiley.

American Academy of Child and Adolescent Psychiatry (1997a). Practice parameters for child custody evaluation. *J Am Acad Child Adolesc Psychiatry, 36*(10), 57S–68S.

American Academy of Child and Adolescent Psychiatry (1997b). Practice parameters for the forensic evaluation of children and adolescents who may have been physically or sexually abused. *J Am Acad Child Adolesc Psychiatry, 36*, 423–442.

American Psychological Association (1994). Guidelines for child custody evaluations in divorce proceedings. *Am Psychol, 49*, 677–680.

Association of Family and Conciliation Courts: Model Standards of Practice for Child Custody Evaluation (1994). Available from AFCC, 329 West Wilson St., Madison, WI 53703.

Atkinson, J. (2000). *Modern child custody practice* (2nd ed.). New York: Lexis.

Bene, E. (1985). *Family relations test: Children's version.* Windsor, England: NFER-NELSON.

Benedek, E., & Schetky, D. (1985). Allegations of sexual abuse in child custody cases. In: D. Schetky & E. Benedek, (Eds.), *Emerging issues in child psychiatry and the law*, pp. 145–156. New York: Brunner/Mazel.

Benedek, E., & Schetky, D. (1987a). Problems in validating allegations of sexual abuse. Part I. Factors affecting perception and recall of events. *J Am Acad Child Adolesc Psychiatry, 26*, 912–915.

Benedek, E., & Schetky, D. (1987b). Problems in validating allegations of sexual abuse. Part II. Clinical evaluation. *J Am Acad Child Adolesc Psychiatry, 26*, 916–921.

Bernet, W. (1983). The therapist's role in child custody disputes. *J Child Psychiatry, 22*, 180–183.

Bernet, W. (1993). False statements and the differential diagnosis of abuse allegations. *J Am Acad Child Adolesc Psychiatry, 32*, 903–910.

Bernet, W. (1997). Case study: Allegations of abuse created in a single interview. *J Am Acad Child Adolesc Psychiatry, 36*, 966–970.

Bernet, W. (1998). The child and adolescent psychiatrist and the law. In: J. D. Noshpitz (Ed.), *Handbook of child and adolescent psychiatry* (pp. 438–467). New York: John Wiley & Sons.

Bernet, W. (2002). Child custody evaluations. *Child Adolesc Psychiatric Clin N Am, 11*, 781–804.

Bricklin, B. (1984). *The Bricklin Perceptual Scales: Child-perception-of-parents series.* Doylestown, PA: Village Publishing.

Bricklin, B. (1989). *The Perception-of-Relationships Test.* Doylestown, PA: Village Publishing.

Bricklin, B. (1995). *The custody evaluation handbook: Research-based solutions and applications.* New York: Brunner/Mazel.

Butcher, J. N., Graham, J. R., Dahlstrom, W. G., & Bowman, E. (1989). *Manual for Administration and Scoring: MMPI-2* (Minnesota Multiphasic Personality Inventory–2). Minneapolis: University of Minnesota Press.

Ceci, S., & Bruck, M. (1995). *Jeopardy in the courtroom: A scientific analysis of children's testimony.* Washington: American Psychological Association.

Ceci, S. J., Huffman, M. L. C., Smith, E., & Loftus, E. (1994). Repeatedly thinking about a non-event: Source misattributions among preschoolers. *Consciousness and Cognition, 3*, 388–407.

Child Victim Witness Investigative Pilot Projects (1994, July). *Research and Evaluation Final Report.* Sacramento: California Attorney General's Office.

Clawar, S. S., & Rivlin, B. V. (1991). *Children held hostage: Dealing with programmed and brainwashed children.* Chicago: American Bar Association.

Derdeyn, A. (1994). Adequate evaluation of divorce-related child sexual abuse allegations. *Bull Am Acad Psychiatry Law, 22*, 279–287.

Eastman, A. M., & Moran, T. J. (1991). Multiple perspectives: Factors related to differential diagnosis of sex abuse and divorce trauma in children under six. *Child and Youth Services, 15*, 159–175.

Everson, M. D. (1997). Understanding bizarre, improbable, and fantastic elements in children's accounts of abuse, *Child Maltreatment, 2*, 134–149.

Everson, M. D., & Boat, B. W. (1994). Putting the anatomical dolls controversy in perspective: An explanation of the major uses and criticisms of the dolls in child sexual abuse evaluations. *Child Abuse & Neglect, 18*, 113–129.

Faller, K. C. (1991). Possible explanations for child sexual abuse allegations in divorce. *Amer J Orthopsychiat, 61*, 86–91.

Fisher, R. P., & Geiselman, R. E. (1992). *Memory-enhancing techniques for investigative interviewing: The cognitive interview.* Springfield, IL: Thomas.

Friedrich, W. N. (2001). *Psychological assessment of sexually abused children and their families.* Thousand Oaks, CA.: Sage Publications.

Friedrich, W. N., Fisher, J. L., Dittner, C. A., Acton, R., Berliner, L., Butler, J., Damon, L., Davies, W. H., Gray, A., & Wright, J. (2001). Child sexual behavior inventory: Normative, psychiatric, and sexual abuse comparisons. *Child Maltreatment, 6*, 37–49.

Galatzer-Levy, R. M., & Kraus, L. (Eds.) (1999). *The scientific basis of child custody decisions.* New York: Wiley.

Gardner, R. A. (1985). Recent trends in divorce and custody litigation. *The Academy Forum 29*:3–7.

Gardner, R. A. (1987). T*he Parental Alienation Syndrome and the differentiation between fabricated and genuine child sex abuse.* Cresskill, NJ: Creative Therapeutics.

Gardner, R. A. (1989a). Differentiating between bona fide and fabricated sex abuse allegations in children. *Journal of the American Academy of Matrimonial Lawyers, 5*, 1–25.

Gardner, R. A. (1989b). *Family evaluation in child custody mediation, arbitration, and litigation.* Cresskill, NJ: Creative Therapeutics.

Gardner, R. A. (1992). *True and false accusations of child sexual abuse.* Northvale, NJ: Jason Aronson.

Gardner, R. A. (1995). *Protocols for the sex-abuse evaluation.* Cresskill, NJ: Creative Therapeutics.

Gardner, R. A. (1998). *The Parental Alienation Syndrome: A guide for mental health and legal professionals* (2nd ed.). Cresskill, NJ: Creative Therapeutics.

Gardner, R. A. (1999). Differentiating between parental alienation syndrome and bona fide abuse-neglect. *Amer J Family Therapy, 27*, 97–108.

Gardner, R. A. (2001). The normal-sexual-fantasy consideration in sex-abuse evaluations. *Amer J Family Therapy, 29*, 83–94.

Gardner, R. A. (2002). The empowerment of children in the development of parental alienation syndrome. *Am J Forensic Psychology, 20*, 5–29.

Goldzband, M. G. (1988). *Custody cases and expert witnesses: A manual for attorneys.* Clifton, NJ: Prentice-Hall.

Gould, J. W. (1998). *Conducting scientifically crafted child custody evaluations.* Thousand Oaks, CA.: Sage Publications.

Green, A. (1986). True and false allegations of sexual abuse in child custody disputes. *J Amer Acad Child Adolesc Psychiatry, 25*, 449–455.

Herman, S. (2002). Child custody evaluations. In: D. H. Schetky & E. P. Benedek (Eds.), *Principles and practice of adolescent psychiatry*, pp. 69–79. Washington, D.C.: American Psychiatric Publishing.

Hodges, W. F. (1986). *Interventions for children of divorce: Custody, access, and psychotherapy.* New York: Wiley.

Kalichman, S. C. (1999). *Mandated reporting of suspected child abuse: Ethics, law, and policy* (2nd ed.). Washington, D.C.: American Psychological Association.

Kelly, J. B., & Johnston, J. R. (2001). The alienated child: A reformulation of parental alienation syndrome. *Family Court Review, 39*, 249–267.

Kuehnle, K. (1996). *Assessing allegations of child sexual abuse.* Sarasota, FL: Professional Resource Press.

Kuehnle, K. (2003). Child sexual abuse evaluations. In: A. M. Goldstein, I. B. Weiner (Eds.), *Handbook of psychology, Volume 11, Forensic psychology*, pp. 437–460. Hoboken, NJ: John Wiley & Sons.

Lamb, M. E., Orbach, Y., Sternberg, K. J., Hershkowitz, I., & Horowitz, D. (2000). The accuracy of investigators' verbatim notes of their forensic interviews with alleged child abuse victims. *Law and Human Behavior, 24*, 699–708.

Lamb, M. E., Sternberg, K. J., Esplin, P. W., Hershkowitz, I., & Orbach, Y. (1997). Assessing the credibility of children's allegations of sexual abuse: A survey of recent research. *Learning and Individual Differences, 9*, 175–194.

Lanning, K. V. (2002). Criminal investigation of sexual victimization of children. In: J. E. B. Myers, L. Berliner, J. Briere, C. T. Hendrix, C. Jenny, & T. A. Reid (Eds.), *The APSAC handbook on child maltreatment* (2nd ed.), pp. 329–347. Thousand Oaks, CA: Sage Publications.

McGleughlin, J., Meyer, S., & Baker, J. (1999). Assessing sexual abuse allegations in divorce, custody, and visitation disputes. In: R. M. Galatzer-Levy & L. Kraus (Eds.), *The scientific basis of child custody decisions*, pp. 357–388. New York: Wiley.

Meadow, R. (1993). False allegations of abuse and Munchausen syndrome by proxy. *Archives of Disease in Children, 68*, 444–447.

Morey, L. C. (1991). *The Personality Assessment Inventory Professional Manual.* Odessa, FL: Psychological Assessment Resources.

Myers, J. E. B., Berliner, L., Briere, J., Hendrix, C. T., Jenny, C., & Reid, T. A. (Eds.) (2002). *The APSAC handbook on child maltreatment* (2nd ed.). Thousand Oaks, CA: Sage Publications.

National Interdisciplinary Colloquium on Child Custody Law (1998). *Legal and mental health perspectives on child custody law: A deskbook for judges.* Eagan, MN: West Group.

Ney, T. (Ed.) (1995). *True and false allegations of child sexual abuse: Assessment and case management.* New York: Brunner/Mazel.

Nicholson, E. B., & Bulkley, J. (Eds.) (1988). *Sexual abuse allegations in custody and visitation cases.* Washington, D.C.: American Bar Association.

Nurcombe, B., & Partlett, D. J. (1994). *Child mental health and the law.* New York: Free Press.

Otto, R. K., Buffington-Vollum, J. K., & Edens, J. F. (2003). Child custody evaluations. In: A. M. Goldstein, I. B. Weiner (Eds.), *Handbook of psychology, Volume 11, Forensic psychology*, pp. 179–208. Hoboken, NJ: John Wiley & Sons.

Poole, D. A., & Lamb, M. E. (1998). *Investigative interviews of children: A guide for helping professionals.* Washington, D.C.: American Psychological Association.

Pruett, K., & Pruett, M. K. (Eds.) (1998). Child custody. *Child Adolesc Psychiatric Clin N Am, 7*(2), 247–468.

Quinn, K. M. (2002). Interviewing children for suspected sexual abuse. In: D. H. Schetky & E. P. Benedek (Eds.), *Principles and practice of adolescent psychiatry*, pp. 149–159. Washington, DC: American Psychiatric Publishing.

Raskin, D. C., & Esplin, P. W. (1991). Assessment of children's statements of sexual abuse. In: J. Doris (Ed.), *The suggestibility of children's recollections*, pp. 153–164. Washington, DC: American Psychological Association.

Raskin, D. C., & Esplin, P. W. (1992). Statement validity assessment: Interview procedures and content analysis of children's statements of sexual abuse. *Behavioral Assessment, 13*, 265–291.

Rogers, M. L. (1990). Coping with alleged false sexual molestation: Examination and statement analysis procedures. *Issues in Child Abuse Accusations, 2*, 57–68.

Rosenfeld, A. A., Nadelson, C. C., & Krieger, M. (1979). Fantasy and reality in patients reports of incest. *J Clin Psychiatry, 40*, 159–164.

Schreier, H. A. (1996). Repeated false allegations of sexual abuse presenting to sheriffs: When is it Munchausen by proxy? *Child Abuse & Neglect, 20*, 985–991.

Stahl, P. M. (1999). *Complex issues in child custody evaluations.* Thousand Oaks, CA: Sage Publications.

Summit, R. (1983). The child sexual abuse accommodation syndrome. *Child Abuse & Neglect, 7*, 177–193.

Weithorn, L. A. (1987). *Psychology and child custody determinations.* Lincoln: University of Nebraska.

White, S., & Quinn, K. M. (1988). Investigatory independence in child sexual abuse evaluations: Conceptual considerations. *Bull Am Acad Psychiatry Law, 16*, 269–278.

Wood, J. M., & Garven, S. (2000). How sexual abuse interviews go astray: Implications for prosecutors, police, and child protection services. *Child Maltreatment, 5*, 109–118.

Yuille, J. C., Hunter, R., Joffe, R., & Zaparniuk, J. (1993). Interviewing children in sexual abuse cases. In: G. S. Goodman & B. L. Bottoms (Eds.), *Child victims, child witnesses: Understanding and improving testimony*, pp. 95–115. New York: Guilford.

Chapter 19

PSYCHOLOGICAL TEST-ASSISTED DETECTION OF PARENTAL ALIENATION SYNDROME

BARRY BRICKLIN AND GAIL ELLIOT

OVERVIEW

The research background, and clinical use of two data-based tests are described in regard to how they can red-flag and/or help corroborate the presence of PAS.

RESEARCH BACKGROUND

Forty years of research in developing tests that seek to reflect the impact various caretakers have on children in different family systems have yielded information that can be helpful in detecting Parental Alienation Syndrome (PAS) and related clinical patterns. Test-based data, as they currently exist, cannot by themselves diagnose PAS, since none that we know of systematically address the eight criteria or symptoms that define it. However, test data can help to red flag PAS, and also can be helpful in corroborating its presence. Theoretically, any psychological test that elicits a child's attitudes, opinions, behaviors, or emotional states about his or her caretakers could be used to detect signs of PAS. Examples of such tests are the Family Relation Test (Bene & Anthony, 1985), the Family Relationship Inventory (Nash, Morrison, & Taylor, 1982), and the Family Apperception Test (Sotile, Julian, Henry, & Sotile, 1991). The evaluator would have to search for signs of PAS-type inconsistency in how a child represents any particular caretaker. However, we are not aware of any research on these instruments that has generated specific and detailed clinical hypotheses about PAS detection.

Our research in this area has been done with the Perception-of-Relationships Test (PORT) (Bricklin, 1989), and the Bricklin Perceptual Scales (BPS) (Bricklin, 1984). They yield data that reveal the degree to which a particular caretaker's range of behavioral styles lead to emotionally comfortable and behaviorally competent behaviors on the part of the tested child. How these concepts were operationalized and validated will be comprehensively described. With this detailed knowledge, it will be easier for an evaluator to make practical use of the test data in applying them to clinical situations in which it may be imperative to detect PAS. Knowledge of how the tests were validated is also essential for us to be able to demonstrate the main reason the tests are useful in detecting PAS. Only when the details of how a test's data were validated are known can an evaluator (or any decision-maker, such as a courtroom judge) know for certain what the data can reveal. Our aim is to demonstrate why we believe our tests accurately reflect the degree to which a parent's behaviors lead subsequently to gut-level, motor-expressed, comfortable versus uncomfortable as well as competent versus non-competent behaviors on the part of a child. The PAS detection premise is that when a child puts forward strongly stated verbal opinions about a parent's value to him or her in creating emotionally comfortable and competent behavior, and these statements are at odds with what is reflected in the validated test data (most of which are gathered nonverbally so that the child is uncertain as to what he or she is revealing), a red flag for PAS exists. For example, a definite red flag exists if a child is claiming that his or her father is a villain, but the validated test information suggests that the child has enjoyed a comfortable and behaviorally effective relationship with that father.

THE PERCEPTION-OF-RELATIONSHIPS TEST (PORT) AND BRICKLIN PERCEPTUAL SCALES (BPS)

We will describe each test, spell out their theoretical foundations, and then tell how their data were validated. We will also present additional psychometric information considered necessary for an evaluator or decision-maker to evaluate the scientific merits of a test's data: their test-retest reliability and a description of the sample groups from which the data were gathered.

The PORT consists of seven tasks. Task I asks the child to draw each parent. Task II consists of two parts. The first presents a line drawing of a female figure and the second of a male figure. The instructions are "Here is Mom/Dad. Put yourself somewhere in the picture." Task III presents two line drawings of parent or caretaker representations to the left and right margins of the page and the child is asked to put himself or herself in the picture. Task IV is a request to draw the family. Task V is a request for the child to draw his or her family "doing something." Task VI involves a picture of a little horse between two renderings of little homes, one of which says "Mom" on it and the other of which says "Dad" on it. The instructions are: "Here's a little horsey. It's time for the horsey to go into his/her house. Please draw a line into the house where the horsey will go." Task VII consists of three separate stimulus cards. The first shows a little dog asleep in a bed and the instructions point out that the dog is having a dream about its mommy. The child is instructed to tell what that dream is. The second part has the dog dreaming of the daddy with the same instructions. The third part simply asks the child: "Which dream is nicer?"

Prior research (Bricklin & Elliot, 2002a,b) shows that each task elicits associations of the child operating within a specific family system. Tasks I through V reflect a child's: overall relationship with each parent; being actually or psychologically alone with each parent; being in the real or psychological presence of both parents; wished-for ideal, which is the child's "wishes" about what were true about the family (the child's yearnings for parental cooperation and unity are often far removed from the current reality); and view of each parent's supportiveness of family unity. Tasks VI and VII reflect a child's conscious belief systems and allow a comparison between how a child responds when he or she is aware of what is being revealed as contrasted to not being aware. The overall parent-of-choice (POC) is the POC on the greater number of tasks. Validity data have been gathered on 1,508 cases.

The BPS is scored as follows. A child responds nonverbally to 60 stimulus cards – 32 about Mom and 32 about Dad. The mother/father cards are maximally separated, so that when the child responds to a given item he or she will have less of an exactly clear memory of his or her response about the other parent in the same context. The child's attributions of value regarding each parent in 32 critical child care areas are recorded on a 0 to 60 point scale. This scale is an ordinal scale, and represents how a child differentially values the two measured caretakers in reference to each other. In spite of the fact that "points" are used to record a child's response to each BPS item (for ease of scoring and other clinical purposes), the only meaningful information in an ordinal scale is rank order. For any single BPS item, the needed data are A>B, B>A, or A=B.

The decision to use an ordinal scale to measure the assignment of the value a caretaker has for a child in some limited life area – a unique and highly personal internal attitude harbored by the child – reflects two concerns. One would be the difficulty in creating meaningful interval measurement units in regard to an entity that seeks to measure a value. Would you, for example, be able to assert how much more you value some particular food versus another by stating the difference in interval scaling units? ("I value a ham sandwich at some particular meal 38 units more than I value a chicken sandwich.") The other reason for using ordinal scales for each individual BPS item was to reduce any decision-maker's tendency to assign more significance to a parent's value to a child based on a single life area as opposed to that parent's value in many areas collectively. It was for this particular reason that we did not create even an approximate or pseudo "interval-type" scale (for example, "I would greatly value A versus B," "I would *somewhat* value A versus B," and so forth). One could, however, formulate such hypotheses from the Point Scores. However, then one would have to look for independent evidence to confirm them, as such conclusions would not be derived from a measurement scale proven to have meaningful interval measurement units. Our main point, then, is that the test-designated parent-of-choice is the parent who has greater value to the child in the *greater number of life areas*, not the magnitudes by which one parent is better than the other in limited areas. This collective number yields the Item-Difference-Score (IDS) and represents the number of categories in which one parent has greater value to the child than the other. This scale of numbers, from 0 to 32, is an interval scale, and may be used as such.

The PORT and the BPS aim to provide data-based assistance in understanding the impacts different caretakers have on a child in selected family systems (Bricklin, 1984, 1989, 1992, 1998, 1999, 2003; Bricklin & Elliot, 1997, 2001). Their theoretical bases derive from systems concepts.

As the context or system within which a child and caretaker interact changes (for example, the child alone with each parent, with both parents, within either actual or psychologically internal family groupings), the value of each parent to a child can shift, sometimes radically. For example, a parent who has little value for a child as a day-to-day manager of daily routines, may have great value in helping the child with independent decision making. A child who values alone time with a particular parent may not so much value that parent's lukewarm contribution to family unity and cooperation. A caretaker's value to a child is frequently very system-specific (Bricklin & Elliot, 2002a,b). The more one understands the implications of system concepts, the more one can grasp what the PORT and BPS seek to accomplish. A system must have two or more elements and each element must have an effect on the *whole* system. The elements (and their effects) are not only interdependent but, however subgroups form, none can have an independent effect on the system as a whole. Within this definition of a system, one cannot influence a system of which one is a part, and then not oneself be impacted by the creation of this influence (Ackoff, 1999, pp. 15–17).

Systems complexities affect both validational issues (some predictions will be true only in limited contexts) and the choice of one's measurement reference standard. A reference standard is the entity to which a measurement score is compared in order to derive relevance for a specific decision. The reference standard is a previously examined group (normative paradigm) or a previously examined individual (the single-participant paradigm), or it may be criterion-referenced (arbitrary expert opinion). What the reference standard should be is not always clear to evaluators, especially in the postdivorce world – a nightmare of shifting allegiances within a framework where an involved child may have only two main choices. To the extent that mental health professionals think of systems at all, they think of models in which stable traits interact. This is evident in the way they write about their evaluations, with sections called "Mr. Jones," "Mrs. Jones," child "Mary Jones," child "Sam Jones," as though one can assess each element in a system as a separate entity and then somehow add up the parts. In systems-based decisions, the elements of the system cannot be evaluated apart from the interactions of those elements within the system. Furthermore, as systems change, the relevant reference standard can shift. In a child custody context, the way Child 1 assigns value to his or her parents is not always meaningfully comparable to the way Child 2 or 3 would assign value either to his or her own parents or to the parents of Child 1. Knowing how a parent compares to other parents within a group reference standard yields information of a very different sort than data that reveal *the unique and specific value a specific parent has for a particular child.* To measure an individual's unique assignment of value, a single-participant reference would be used. Here we are interested in comparing the child's assignment of value to A to that of the child's own unique assignment of value to B. This is not, however, to say one cannot or should not compare measurements obtained from a given child to those derived from groups. If a decision is to be made based on the extent of the gap between how a specific child differentially assigns value to Parent A as opposed to Parent B to how children in general differentially assign value to each caretaker, the Task-Difference Scores on the PORT and the Item-Difference Scores on the BPS, interval scales, can be used for such a purpose.

Note also that systems complexities can have profound effects on the choice of validating criteria. The parent from whom a child seeks emotional closeness and/or active help can change dramatically, depending on the family subsystems in which the child-parent interactions take place (Bricklin & Elliot, 2002a,b).

Our data-based tests assess the degree to which child-parent interactions lead to emotionally comfortable and behaviorally competent behaviors on the part of the child in various family systems. The PORT generates data relevant to several systems, while the BPS is most relevant to dyadic systems. They also seek ways to understand useful cost/benefit ratios. A disorganized boy, for example, may require much more exposure to the parent who can better help him focus, prioritize, plan meaningful sequences of behavior, and so forth, even though the parent who can do this more successfully may be less emotionally warm than the other parent. This arrangement may constitute a poor cost/benefit ratio for a highly organized child who would profit more from exposure to emotional warmth than to organizational skills. Each test elicits its main information nonverbally, which eliminates both the need for a child to say anything directly negative about a parent and bias resulting from the limited expressive vocabularies of young children.

Existing and new data on 3,888 cases will be given later in this chapter, including future as well as concurrent validity numbers. The tests have previously been used only with a single-participant reference paradigm. This paradigm, as exemplified in the PORT and BPS, compares the score values a child attributes to one parent with similar score values the same child attributes to the other parent. New research (Bricklin, 2003) utilizes a group reference paradigm, in which a child's scores are compared to those established with experimental groups. A group reference allows us to see the degree to which a caretaker's parenting skills, as reflected in PORT data, compare to standards created by group norms. The research reported here allows an evaluator to detect when one or both of the parents are creating signs in a child's PORT that are characteristic of groups known to show signs of differential levels of parental attunement, ranging from adequate to inadequate.

Validating criteria focused on the degree to which child-caretaker interactions lead to a child's emotionally comfortable and behaviorally competent behavior in a wide variety of settings. How these concepts were operationalized follows. Please note the variety of sources of validating or criterion data employed, and the use of a quantified normative observation protocol with certain samples.

The original, and much of the subsequent validity research with the PORT and BPS, compared estimations derived from the tests about the particular parent with whom a child more comfortably and efficiently shared information than with the other parent to estimations derived from extensive observations, often over several years. In all instances, these observations were made by mental health professionals on the bases of criteria independent of test scores. The original observation protocol is summarized.

Emphasis was on (mainly nonverbal) ways a child demonstrated comfort and effectiveness during or immediately subsequent to interactions with each caretaker. These interactions took place in spontaneous, structured, and instructional contexts. The basic dimensions studied were a child's movements: toward (positive); against (aggressive); away from (fearful) (Bricklin & Halbert, 2003). Research interest was on what impact parental behavior had on a child – not primarily on what parents knew or did. At the outset of our research we tracked positive and negative reactions. Our research goals were adequately achieved if we counted only positive reactions. This is a practical "plus," because fewer raters are needed. The following studied categories apply when the child is speaking (initiating or responding), listening, or listening and acting:

- smooth breathing patterns;
- body movements nonhurried;
- relaxed and/or smiling facial muscles (no grimaces, contortions, etc.);
- leans toward other person;
- maintains reasonable eye contact (evaluators were taught to distinguish fearful eye contact from relaxed eye contact – the former is motivated by the child's fear of saying or doing something the parent would object to);
- moves closer to or initiates physical contact;
- willing to be hugged; and
- few signs of restlessness (even if a child is ADHD-like, one parent usually has a more calming influence than the other).

The following categories were used when the child is speaking (either initiating a communication or responding to one):

- willing to express annoyance, doubts or confusion (*not* trying to be the perfect little child);
- pauses without fear of losing caretaker's attention;
- willing to ask questions; and
- noting from whom the child most frequently and spontaneously seeks help.

The next categories were used when the child is listening or listening and acting:

- accepts limits in comfortable manner;
- muscularly comfortable with failures (no agitated moves);
- focused attention;
- facial expression animated and interested;
- no evidence of leaping to action before waiting for the entire "sent message" to be received;
- open and ready to receive information;
- willing to explore and take chances; and
- willing to try novel approaches.

Briefly, in two samples (n=60; n=37), the ages, ethnicity, and socioeconomic status were directly similar to the norms given elsewhere in this chapter (pp. 952, 953). In each sample, a child was observed with both parents present, so that he or she could make choices about with whom to interact. In a one-hour session, the distribution of positive scores ranged from 0 to 12. The mean number of positive reactions was 7.4; the standard deviation (SD) was 1.2. Six to nine positive reactions characterized 70 percent of the cases. A point difference greater than two represents a significant difference between two caretakers. These numbers may appear to be low. This is probably because each child was immersed in responding to different tasks during the observation sessions, rather than directly interacting with the parents for the entire hour. These results are *not* comparable to protocols that count the number of positive and negative interactions *initiated by parents* (Lahey, Conger, Atkeson, & Treiber, 1984; Kerig & Lindahl, 2001). Inter-rater agreement (among three raters) was high (90%), partly because the range of categories used was narrow: A>B, B>A, A=B, neither A nor B (less than two points for each parent). The actual number of positive interactions noted by each rater achieved an agreement rate of 82 percent.

Mental health professionals who offered validity designations used judgmental categories that reflect the narrow range of choices utilized by our legal system. Decisions are given in two main categories: legal custody (the right and responsibility to make key decisions for a child) and a time-share plan (or physical custody). In the former category, three choices are typically used: sole custody, shared custody, and very rarely, it is decided that neither parent should have custody. In our experience, judges currently favor shared legal custody, except when blatant reasons to exclude a parent from this role exist. As for time-share plans, few judges venture beyond two choices: sole custody or joint custody. If the former is chosen, the noncustodial parent is usually given a boilerplate arrangement according to which he or she has the child every other weekend, plus an overnight during the weeks he or she does not have the child for the weekend. When complex time-share plans are awarded, they are almost always worked out by the parents and/or their attorneys, not directly according to evaluation data or by the judge. Furthermore, complex plans are usually based on parental-convenience, not best interest, factors. Judges rarely venture beyond simplistic dispositional categories. This choice range has advantages in a research setting, decreasing hair-splitting arguments about how much better one parent is than the other. Mental health professionals can and do offer complex plans, sometimes on the bases of newly emerging research on optimal time-share plans (Kelly & Lamb, 2000). At the time this chapter was edited (2005), much controversy surrounded this research, much of which appears to "seamlessly weave together empirically-tested findings . . . with the authors' opinions" (Solomon & Biringen, 2001, p. 359). In any event, judges usually ignore complex plans unless the two sides agree on their own to implement them, although new research may change this trend.

PORT validity data collected between 1961 and 1997 consisted of 1,381 cases. The sources of independent validity designations involved the following: three observers watching each child and two parents interact from behind a one-way screen; two psychologists who had access to family therapy notes; consultations with the family therapists over a two- to-five year time span; scores derived from the BPS, and psychologists' expert opinions based on all clinical and life history data available to them, usually gathered over a multimonth period. The average validity percent of agreement between PORT suggestions for POC and those of the independent experts was 88 percent. The agreement rate between courtroom judges and the POCs selected by the PORT was 92 percent, although this is reported as information only and not as validity data, since PORT data may have influenced the judges. PORT validity data collected between 1997 and 2002 involved 127 cases. The independent validity experts were mental health professionals who had at least eight months of contact with each involved family. They were instructed to use all sources of information, including the observational format already described. Future validity was measured by comparing the PORT POCs at Time Point 1 with expert opinion carried out at Time Point 2, eight months later. Future validity was 89 percent agreement. Concurrent validity was estimated by comparing the PORT POC at Time Point 2 with the validity designations made at Time Point 2. This figure was 91 percent. BPS validation from 1964 to 1997 was available for 2,279 cases. The same validational sources were used as with the PORT – only here the family therapy data extended from two to seven years (the validity designations were never based on less than two years' worth of data). The agreement rate between the BPS and the criterion experts was 88 percent. The agreement rate for courtroom judges was 93 percent. BPS validity data collected from 1997 to 2002 on 93 cases showed a future validity score of 87 percent and a concurrent validity score of 91 percent.

Test-retest reliability will be given only from the most recent data, because the time span was longer than those previously used. Between 1997 and 2002, on 127 cases, the PORT showed a stability in POC, over an eight month span, of 97 percent. That is, 97 percent of the POCs remained the POCs over this time span. However, the test-retest reliability drops sharply as the TDS approaches 0 or 1. There is a 21 percent chance that the POC will shift over an eight month period if the TDS is 0 or 1. If the TDS is 3 or more, there is a 3 percent chance of shift. With the BPS, if the IDS is 0, 1, 2 or 3, there is a 19 percent chance the POC will shift over eight months. If the score is 4 or more, there is a 3 percent chance of shift. Three test patterns were identified that, when present, greatly suggest a future shift in POC (Bricklin & Elliot, 2002a,b).

PORT normative data gathered from 1961 to 1997 involved 797 females and 784 males. The mean age of these children was 7.76; the SD 0.17. The SES was low to high-middle. Ninety-eight percent of the children in this sample were Caucasian, and all others comprised 2 percent. Regarding data gathered between 1997 and 2002, there were 61 females and 66 males. The other numbers in the 1997 to 2002 sample are all similar, except that 8 percent of the children were non-Caucasian. For the BPS, in 2,389 cases tested between 1964 and 1997, 1,202 were female and 1,187 male. The mean age was 8.94, and the SD was 2.40. All other data were similar to the PORT. Interrater reliability of PORT scoring was obtained from two samples of seminar attendees (n=36; n=41), of which more than half of the scorers had no prior experience with the PORT. Four different percent-of-agreement scores were obtained: (1) the points scored on Task I (the most difficult to score, since additional points are used); (2) the POC on Task I; (3) the overall TDS score for all seven tasks; (4) the overall POC based on the seven tasks. The percent-of-agreement rates, respectively, were: 74, 90, 82, and 92. No interrater data for the BPS were gathered, since scoring it is mechanical and requires only the ability to read Arabic numbers and recognize when one number is larger than another. It is also assumed that an evaluator can accurately add and subtract numbers between zero and 32.

The next study is the first in which PORT data were used with a group reference (Bricklin, 2003). A consistent relationship between PORT signs and the adequacy of parenting was noted over a 40-year span. Twenty-three hypotheses about these PORT signs were developed. Following this, from the huge pool of data available, four experimental groups matched in age, income, absence of ADHD signs, and age-correct grade placement were formed. Group I (n=16) were children examined for minor reasons (most often underachievement); none involved the quality of parenting. Group II (n=34) consisted of children whose parents were involved in mild custody disputes, centered on who could provide a better school, neighborhood, or extended family, or that the child had more friends at one place rather than the other. There were no concerns about parenting by either disputant or the evaluators. All of the parents in Groups I and II met the criteria of the "good enough" parent (Schutz, Dixon, Lindenberger, & Ruther, 1989, pp. 16–24). Group III (n=40) consisted of children whose parents were involved in continual conflict, characterized by ongoing hostility – often within the courtroom – for two or more years. The involved "caught in the middle" children were used as "message carriers" to deliver scathing messages from one parent to the other or to involved mental health professionals (Bricklin & Elliot, 2000, p. 501; Doolittle & Deutsch, 1999, pp. 425–440). Parental adequacy sinks to a serious low point when parents become so engaged, and the damage to children, whether from divorced or intact families, is alarmingly high (Bricklin & Elliot, 1995, pp. 38–40; Bricklin & Elliot, 2000, pp. 501–505; Hoppe, 1993, 1997; Hoppe & Kenney, 1994, 1995, 1997). Group IV (n=40) consisted of children whose caretakers represented on the PORTs had either been threatened by the court with a possible termination of parental rights or actually had had their parental rights terminated in the past and/or were accused of substantiated abuse or neglect. In order to match the parents in this group in socioeconomic status to those in the other groups, and the children in intelligence, the majority of these cases were derived from various private practices. As one moves from the caretakers represented in the PORTs in Groups I and II toward those represented in Groups III and IV, parental attunement diminishes.

Seventeen of the 23 PORT signs yielded a probability of .05 or less that the differential occurrences of the PORT signs among the groups were random. Because the interdependencies of the signs are not known, the data were treated as a single set. Using Fisher's Exact Test the p value is .00001. Several caveats are listed to show that the manifestation of one or even several of these signs should be interpreted currently only as a red flag to launch expanded evaluations, since it is not completely clear if the signs are additive.

This last research is particularly helpful in detecting PAS. PAS cases were common in Group III, which featured high-conflict parents who typically use their children as message carriers. The specific PORT signs most common in PAS cases will be briefly noted. It would require too much space to include where the information that supports our clinical hypotheses about the psychological meanings of these signs came from. The data, information, and theoretical bases can be found elsewhere (Bricklin, 2003; www.DrBarry-Bricklin.com). Please note that these signs specifically red flag not only PAS cases, but prodromal situations that are highly likely to lead to PAS.

For example, in the PORT, the child draws two figures when only one is required to respond to the test item. For example, the child, directed to draw his mom, instead draws one figure then crosses it out and draws another. Psychologically, this reveals a parent who is confusing to the child. A close variant of this sign is one in which the child draws a single figure with two heads, one of which is grimacing and the other neutral in expression. This sign was found in the termination-of-parental rights group. It occurred in reference to substance-abusing caretakers whose behaviors were adequate when they were not under the influence of drugs, but who were poor and neglectful when they were under the influence. Our clinical hypothesis, in this case, that this sign and ones similar to it indicate confusion, came largely from having clinical information such as this at our disposal.

When a child draws something and then scribbles over it, this indicates a conflict associated with the portrayed figure. This sign applies regardless of what explanation the child gives. For example, a child drew himself and his family swimming in a pool. He drew his parents, and then, hoping to represent water, scribbled all over the drawing. The child explained that this was water. Our clinical observation is that a respondent's motor responses are always more significant than the explanations they give for them. We find this sign where there is a rather serious conflict between the respondent and the caretakers *within some specific family system.* In this case, the context was the family trying to cooperate for the sake of the boy's happiness.

Another example is the following: the child draws an "X" over any body part, (with the exception of the whole body, which is covered in another scoring category). It is often an "X" which is over the mouth. This has been found almost exclusively in alienation or intimidation cases, where the alienating or denigrating parent has literally ordered the child not to speak to him or her about the other parent. It typically shows up on Task II, when the child is asked to draw himself or herself in the psychological presence of each of the parents. If the alienating parent is, for example, the father, the "X" will be drawn on the child's mouth in reference to the father, but not the mother.

The drawing of asymmetric body parts (when one body part is much more prominent or much less prominent than others) can indicate confusion. We find this most frequently when a once-good parent has become either permanently, or at least temporarily, a poor parent, leaving the child highly perplexed. (A chronically poor parent is probably not confusing to a child – hurtful, maybe, but not confusing.)

This next sign is scored when the mouth or eyes are omitted. Our hypothesis is that this occurs when the child has been ordered (usually blatantly) either not to "see something" about a parent or to say what he or she wants to say.

In some cases, the child draws his or her self-representation on a different plane (higher) from where the caretaker is represented. These images are known as "floaters," and suggest the child's feeling that "I no longer can occupy the same space as the portrayed caretaker." The clinical meaning is: "My parents are too preoccupied to be there for me. I must be strong and rise above the situation." Those who have no faith in drawings will reject this reasoning, saying the child does not have the cognitive skills necessary to harbor a phrase such as "I must rise above the situation." Clinical, empirical and theoretical data suggest that even though the child *does not have the words*, he or she, from approximately two-and-a-half years or three years of age, *does* have the means to formulate and express such concepts (Calvin & Bickerton, 2001; Deacon, 1997).

Sometimes, the child draws himself or herself in front of a represented caretaker. The clinical meaning is similar to the one just mentioned. We find this in mature-for-their-age children who become "junior league diplomats" (Bricklin & Elliot, 2000, p. 506). They parent the parents, because the parents have "disappeared" into their battles. They put themselves in front of the parents and become leaders rather than followers. They are usually the ones who propose peaceful solutions to family problems. We also find this sign frequently in the PORTs of healthy children who have psychotic or borderline parents. Its meaning would be the same as for those children whose parents have psychologically disappeared for reasons other than psychoses.

In other cases, the child figure is drawn much bigger than the relevant stimulus (line drawings representing Mother and Father) figure. The meaning of this is similar to that of "in front of" cases; the child must parent the parents.

Sometimes the child embellishes the stick figure on Task II or III by drawing hair on the figure, putting eyes on the figure, or adding clothes to the figure. This sign is typical in high conflict cases in which a parent who was once available to a child is no longer so. The embellishment is the child's attempt to express that this parent is no longer what he or she used to be. The child is trying to "recapture" the parent as he or she used to behave.

Direct evidence of alienation occurs when a child places himself or herself closer to Parent A on Tasks I and II but represents a tie on Task III. Task I has the child draw each parent. Task II has the child in the situation of being alone with each of the parents. Task III represents the child with both parents at the same time. The hypothesis was predicted to occur mainly in PAS situations in which the child is fearful of allowing Parent B to see any kind of obvious affection manifested toward Parent A. With far less frequency, it occurs when a child indeed wants to be with Parent B but only when Parent A is there to provide protection.

In the next section, we will refer to this research as the "PORT 23 negative signs" research.

TEST-ASSISTED METHODS TO RED FLAG PAS

Our research in the field of PAS and clinically related patterns has centered on attempts to determine when what a child is representing at a verbal level to be true is in fact not based on actual interactions with the caretakers about whom the child speaks, but more likely fueled by parental bribery, intimidation, a child's attempt to save a parent he or she perceives as weak or impaired or, of course, PAS. We have summarized this research under the heading of NBOAI (Bricklin, 1995), which stands for "not based on actual interactions." Our NBOAI research is a search for situations in which what a child is verbally asserting to be true is not based on actual interactions with the persons about whom he or she is speaking, but on other (possibly psychologically malignant) influences. In describing these patterns, we will use two acronyms. One is SVP-N, which stands for "strong verbal position-negative," and SVP-P, which means "strong verbal position-positive." Because one of the critical symptoms a child must display to specifically indicate PAS is a campaign of denigration, clinical evidence that a child harbors a SVP-N toward the target parent is necessary.

In presenting the following list of test-assisted patterns, the starting point would have to be either a SVP-N (which would be necessary to red-flag the PAS) or a SVP-P, either of which is contradicted by test and/or other clinical information. To detect a NBOAI situation in general, we look for a child who is either promoting a parent as wonderful who does not appear to be this way in the validated test information, or a child who is asserting that a parent is a villain although this claim is not supported by the data. The specific PAS and NBOAI red-flags follow.

1. The PORT and BPS choose the same parent-of-choice (POC) about 83 percent of the time. Hence, in roughly 20 percent of cases they disagree. We have found that in 90 percent of the instances in which the tests disagree (that is, in 90% of the 20% group), a high probability of a PAS exists. When the tests disagree, the most common cause is that the child has used the BPS, which is easier to manipulate from a conscious position than is the PORT, to endorse the alienating parent. The PAS red flag has brought out the fact that the PORT data do not reflect that the child has had a negative relationship with the target parent. Hence, the following pattern is a strong red flag for PAS.
   a. SVP-N regarding Parent B.
   b. All BPS items are for Parent A, by wide and unusual margins.
   c. Parent B is the POC on three or more PORT tasks.
   d. When the child is asked to give *sense-based justifications* for all of the many negative responses on the BPS for Parent B and the positive ones for Parent A, the child is either unable to do so or answers with silly and frivolous reasons (for example, "Dad yelled at me when I didn't do my homework"). By sense-based justifications we mean nonconclusionary data. A conclusionary sentence would be one such as "Dad is mean." Sense-based data asks the child: "If I were present when this event you are describing was happening, what *exactly* would I see and what *exactly* would I hear?"

2. It is important to differentiate the pattern in Number 1 from the following one, which, while constituting a NBOAI scenario, features a pattern in which the critical piece that would suggest PAS is absent.
   a. No substantial SVP-N (or SVP-P) exists.
   b. The BPS items are reflexively for Parent A, by wide and unusual margins.
   c. Parent B is the POC on three or more PORT tasks.
   d. The child cannot justify the BPS responses.

In other words, these data show that the child is likely not basing the positiveness demonstrated in regard to Parent A on the BPS and the negativity shown toward Parent B on the bases of actual interactions with the two caretakers. The suggestion is that the child has more likely been the recipient of subtle bribery or intimidation, or is trying to save a parent he or she perceives as impaired. However, the special add-on piece needed for the PAS, a verbal campaign of denigration that exceeds what one would expect based solely on parental behavior, is not present.

3. The following scenario looks like PAS, but it is not. It is the test and clinical pattern found when a child is indeed campaigning for one particular parent rather than the other, but all of the test and clinical data support this choice.

a. A mild but definite SVP, often both P and N.
b. All test data support these endorsements.
c. The BPS is for the championed parent *and* the child can justify the responses.
d. The child rarely makes any blatantly negative remarks.
e. All life history and clinical data support the child's choice.

4. Another pattern exists that should not be considered PAS in spite of the fact that Parent A is an over-the-top alienator and the child is indeed alienated from Parent B. We have found this in cases where what the target parent did was so terrible in the eyes of the alienator that the alienation seems justified, at least from the alienator's perspective. Therapeutic techniques are used to reduce the alienation, but it is easy to see where the parental desire to be an alienator came from. We found this pattern in cases of wide-ranging and substantiated abuse on the part of the target parent. The test and clinical pattern are as follows.

a. SVP-N for Parent B and SVP-P for Parent A.
b. All test data support the choice for Parent A.
c. The BPS is for the alienating parent and the child (and others) can offer good sense-based justifications for these endorsements.
d. All of the clinical and life-history data support the child's choice, although therapeutic efforts are employed to stop the alienating strategies on the part of Parent A.

5. In addition to data-based tests, our research teams have also developed semiformal models (Bricklin & Elliot, 1995). The advantages of a semiformal model are:

a. They guarantee that similar data are gathered at least sometime during an evaluation from each participant. This allows meaningful comparisons, which are impossible with free-form interview data.
b. They guarantee that all of the areas deemed custody relevant by legal guidelines as well as research and expert opinion are addressed. An evaluator cannot fail to address all relevant areas, either because of a bad memory or a subjective bias.
c. Because they are fully articulated, they can be continually fine-tuned as well as challenged.

One of these tools is an interview form for children on which conclusionary statements are sought first, followed by sense-based data. This allows an evaluator to determine when a child's conclusionary statements are not supported by sense-based evidence. A further characteristic sign of a PAS child occurs when he or she recites a long series of sentences relating either to the goodness or badness of one particular parent in a tone of voice that sounds as though the child is reading from the telephone book. The affect is completely inappropriate for the content of what is said.

6. Our semi-formal model includes extensive home studies. The next sign concerns what an evaluator should consider as explanatory hypotheses when a child, being observed alone with a particular parent, exhibits wildly negative, defiant, and rude behavior. In our experience, evaluators usually conclude that this is due to a lack of parental skills in the parent who is present. Generally, children are unlikely to be obnoxious and rude unless they have been programmed to act that way. Children are rarely rude in the presence of a relative stranger (such as an evaluator) – even though they may have seen the evaluator several times. Indeed, they may *frequently* be rude and obnoxious when alone with a particular parent, but most children do not behave this way in the presence of an observer. An evaluator would be prudent to assume that rude and negative behavior in his or her presence may very well stem from sources *other than* a lack of caretaking skills in a parent. A child who acts defiantly toward a parent in front of an evaluator desires to hurt this parent. This desire may stem from some personal gripe ("I had to miss my ball game to be here for this darn evaluation") or, in many instances, PAS.

7. The child responds to either a BPS or PORT test situation with a "mini-speech" that is obviously nonresponsive to the test item. This usually takes the form of a series of sentences that sound rehearsed and are either markedly negative or markedly positive regarding one parent. In any event, the response has only a tangential relationship to the test item being administered at that moment. We consider this sign different

from those for which the child gives markedly positive or negative BPS endorsements for a parent but cannot offer sense-based evidence to back them up. Here, the child uses the test items as a way to carry out his or her own psychological agenda. This is frequent in PAS children.

8. The following is a manifestation typical of the clinical behaviors our various research teams have observed with probably only mildly alienated or NBOAI children. It reflects the fact that at some deep level the child may have more discomfort and ambivalence than is clinically suggested by his or her overt behavior. One such sign is a tendency to give responses to the test items extremely quickly, almost before the evaluator has had a chance to complete the reading of the test item. This suggests that the child is anxious to get his or her message-carrier task over with. This is an interesting counterpoint to Gardner's research, which identifies a lack of ambivalence as a defining characteristic of PAS. We have not done any data-based research to see if this sign is as true of the totally alienated child as it perhaps is of one who is somewhere in a transitional stage (e.g., at the time of testing sinking deeper and deeper into a totally alienated state, but not quite there yet). Gardner's position may well be that this quickness of response in fact reflects the very lack of ambivalence of which he speaks, rather than an anxiousness to get the "job" over with.

9. This sign is another manifestation of the phenomenon just described. The child demonstrates absolutely no contemplative pause before he or she reacts to the BPS items. As can be recalled, the BPS requires the child to punch a hole along a line on which "not so well" is represented on one end and "very well" is represented on the other. In PAS and related conditions, these responses are given quickly and without any thought. It is obvious that the child has made a conscious decision beforehand as to how he or she will respond.

10. In cases of PAS, the BPS responses will all be positive for the alienating parent and all extremely negative for the target parent. The BPS point scale ranges from 0 to 60. The child cannot see the numbers (they are on the back of the cards), but the child does know which side is a "good" endorsement and which is a "bad" endorsement. In severe alienation cases, it is typical to get all "60s" for the alienating parent and all "0's" for the target parent. In our validational and normative database of more than 2,000 cases, this is extremely atypical in non-PAS cases. Most children spread their responses out in much more thoughtful, fair, and balanced ways.

11. Another manifestation that we have seen repeatedly with children who are used as message carriers, but have not yet reached a point of harboring no ambivalence, is that they do not maintain eye contact with the evaluator. They fidget and are restless as they respond to the tests. In fact, one of the ways we teach those who use the BPS or the PORT to deal with a situation such as this is to say something such as the following to the child: "Look, John. You have made it totally obvious who you want to be with. I will be happy to write that down and report it to the judge. You can relax now and take the test honestly and spontaneously." In other words, we say to the child in a somewhat disguised way: "Look. You have succeeded admirably in your message-carrying mission. And we do get the message. You have done your duty. You can now relax and take the test in a spontaneous and honest way." This often will get a child who is being used as a message carrier to totally change the tenor of his or her test responses. Again, we are not certain if we would evoke the same behavior from a child who is totally and thoroughly alienated.

12. Along the same lines, we notice that in spite of the significant clinical skills of those who administer these tests in working with children, message-carrying, NBOAI children (*see* p. 271 in this chapter) do not progressively relax as the session moves along. In spite of the repeated contacts the evaluator has already had with these children, they are usually no more relaxed at the end of the process than they were at the beginning. This is highly atypical behavior, and indicates that at some level these children are probably uncomfortable with a message-carrying role. (However, if the evaluator gives the child the "We've-got-the-message" signal, he or she may suddenly appear *very* relaxed.)

13. This sign is related to several of the previously mentioned signs. It has been our observation that when people respond to any particular question, they allow their "gut" or whole organismic body reaction to take place first. This is often our most honest response to any stimulus. It is the same whether we try to decide on a ham versus a cheese sandwich, or seek to choose a wife or husband. Our most basic reaction is a whole organism response. Often, words are our attempts to summarize not only our most verbal and conscious cognitive belief systems but also what our bodies, so to speak, have had to say. Message-carrying children will not only respond quickly, they also hold their bodies in extremely rigid positions. They want to stamp out their more truthful gut-level reactions and replace them with quickly given verbal responses. The

conscious mind is used in an attempt to suppress the unconscious whole-organism response.

14. Several PORT patterns suggest that one should be alert for a NBOAI situation or PAS. (The BPS and the PORT help in PAS detection in different ways. Because it is much easier to control the BPS from a conscious verbal position than it is to control the PORT, the BPS results will often red flag PAS by being reflexively in favor of the alienating parent and reflexively against the target parent. The BPS is also helpful in detecting PAS when a child cannot justify his or her extreme item endorsements with meaningful, sense-based data.) Because it evokes nonverbal drawing responses (many of which present the child with tasks for which it is not clear what is being revealed), the PORT yields more complex diagnostic patterns. The first would be where the overall parent-of-choice on the PORT is the parent for whom the child has uttered a strong SVP-N.

15. The next pattern would be where the child has voted as "wonderful" with an SVP-P for that parent who is represented in a highly unfavorable way on the PORT in many of the individual test tasks.

16. The "PORT 23 negative signs" described earlier in this chapter are all negative, mildly to extensively, regarding the parents who are portrayed in the PORTs. The presence of any of these signs for a SVP-P parent would be highly suspicious. It would indicate that that parent is having a more negative effect on the child than the child is claiming to be true. It would seem from the data that the signs are additive, but this is not yet crystal clear. However, it does appear as though the more there are signs, the more negative is the effect the portrayed parent is having on the child. By the same token, PAS would be suspected if a child exhibits a strong SVP-N about the target parent but indicates no or very few of these signs in the PORT.

17. When a child draws a self-representation closer to Parent A than to Parent B, but the representation is badly distorted, it suggests that the reasons the child is seeking closeness with Parent A may not be for healthy and nurturant reasons, but rather for negative reasons that are PAS related.

THE USE OF PSYCHOLOGICAL TESTS TO RED-FLAG THE PAS

Years of research with tools that are helpful in assessing the impacts particular caretakers have on specific children suggest that the following criteria should be considered in adapting or creating a psychological test for PAS detection.

1. The test must be able to pinpoint which specific caretaker is creating positive and/or negative signs in the child-derived data.
2. The test should, in particular, elicit data that reveal how a child experiences and reacts to parental behaviors that are *custody relevant.*
3. At least some of these data should be derived using a single-participant reference standard. Group-derived reference standards cannot always help identify the psychological influence a *particular* parent is having on a child. (The PORT currently uses both standards.)
4. The test should be able to help pinpoint the specific family systems in which certain behavioral interactions are likely to occur (or *not* occur).
5. The tool should be able to detect inconsistencies between what a child verbally asserts to be true and conclusions about what is true derived from other (hopefully research-generated) test data.
6. Our data suggest that it is helpful when a test can distinguish between what a child represents to be the case when he or she is consciously aware of what is being revealed as opposed to what seems to be true when the child does not have this awareness.

REFERENCES

Ackoff, R. L. (1999). *Ackoff's best.* New York, NY: Wiley.

Bene, E., & Anthony, J. (1985). *Family relations test test manual* (Rev. ed.). Windsor, Great Britain: NFER-NELSON.

Bricklin, B. (1984). *The Bricklin perceptual scales: Child-perception-of-parents series.* Furlong, PA: Village Publishing, Inc.

Bricklin, B. (1989). *The perception-of-relationships test.* Furlong, PA: Village Publishing, Inc.

Bricklin, B. (1992). Data based tests in custody evaluations. *The American Journal of Family Therapy, 20*(3), 254–265.

Bricklin, B. (1995). *The custody evaluation handbook: Research-based solutions and applications.* New York: Brunner/Mazel.

Bricklin, B. (1998). Sequence of steps and critical assessment targets of a comprehensive custody evaluation. In G. P. Koocher & J. C. Norcross, & S. S. Hill III (Eds.), *Psychologists' desk reference* (pp. 499–502). New York, NY: Oxford University Press.

Bricklin, B. (1999). The contribution of psychological tests to custody-relevant evaluations. In R. M. Galatzer-Levy

& L. Kraus (Eds.), *The scientific basis of child custody decisions* (pp. 120–156). New York, NY: Wiley.

Bricklin, B. (2003). *The frequency of appearance of twenty-three PORT signs among four groups representing different degrees of parental competence.* Furlong, PA: Village Publishing, Inc.

Bricklin, B., & Elliot, G. (1995). *ACCESS: A comprehensive custody evaluation standard system.* Furlong, PA.: Village Publishing, Inc.

Bricklin, B., & Elliot, G. (1997). *Test manuals supplement.* Furlong, PA: Village Publishing, Inc.

Bricklin, B., & Elliot, G. (2000). Qualifications of and techniques to be used by judges, attorneys and mental health professionals who deal with children in high conflict divorce cases. *University of Arkansas At Little Rock Law Review, 122*(3), 501–528.

Bricklin, B., & Elliot, G. (2001). *Test manuals supplement.* Furlong, PA: Village Publishing, Inc.

Bricklin, B., & Elliot, G. (2002a, April). *What can empirical data on 4,500 child custody cases tell us?* Paper presented at the American College of Forensic Psychology, San Francisco, CA.

Bricklin, B., & Elliot, G. (2002b). *The Perception-of-Relationships Test (PORT) and Bricklin Perceptual Scales (BPS): Current and new empirical data on 3,880 cases, 1961–2002.* Furlong, PA: Village Publishing, Inc.

Bricklin, B., & Halbert, M. (2003). *A fully explicated evidence-to-conclusions model for two child custody tests, the PORT and BPS.* Furlong, PA: Village Publishing, Inc.

Calvin, W. H., & Bickerton, D. (2001). *Lingua ex Machina: Reconciling Darwin and Chomsky with the human brain.* Cambridge, MA: MIT Press.

Deacon, T. W. (1997). *The symbolic species: The co-evolution of language and the brain.* New York, NY: Norton.

Doolittle, D. B., & Deutsch, R. (1999). Children and high conflict divorce: Theory, research, and intervention. In R. M. Galatzer-Levy & L. Kraus (Eds.), *The scientific basis of child custody decisions* (pp. 425–440). New York, NY: Wiley.

Hoppe, C. F. (1993, August). Test characteristics of custody-visitation litigants: A data-based description of relationship disorders. In S. Podrygula (Chair), *Empirical approaches to child custody determination.* Symposium conducted at the meeting of the American Psychological Association, Toronto, Ontario, Canada.

Hoppe, C. F. (1997). Perpetually battling parents. In B. Mark and J. Incoravia (Eds.), *The handbook of infant/child and adolescent psychotherapy,* Vol. II. (pp. 485–501). Northdale, NJ: Jason Aronson.

Hoppe, C. F., & Kenney, L. (1994, August). *Characteristics of custody litigants: Data from the southern California group.* Paper presented at the meeting of the Psychological Association, Los Angeles, CA.

Hoppe, C. F., & Kenney, L. (1995, August). *MMPI-2 and Rorschach profiles of custody litigants: An intercorrelational study.* Paper presented at the meeting of the American Psychological Association, New York, NY.

Hoppe, C. F., & Kenney, L. (1997, August). *Therapeutic intervention in high conflict divorce: Countertransference and the horrible decision.* Paper presented at the meeting of the American Psychological Association, Chicago, IL.

Kelly, J.B., & Lamb, M.E. (2000). Using child development research to make appropriate custody and access decisions for young children. *Family and Conciliation Courts Review, 38*(3), 297-311.

Kerig, P. K., & Lindahl, K. M. (Eds.). (2001). *Family observational coding systems: Resources for systemic research.* Mahwah, NJ: Lawrence Erlbaum Associates.

Lahey, B. B., Conger, R. D., Atkeson, B. M., & Trieber, F. A. (1984). Parenting behavior and emotional status of physically abusive mothers. *Journal of Consulting and Clinical Psychology, 52,* 1062–1071.

Nash, L., Morrison, W. L., & Taylor, R. M. (1982). *Family relationship inventory test manual.* Thousand Oaks, CA: Psychological Publications, Inc.

Schutz, B. M., Dixon, E. B., Lindenberger, J. C., & Ruther, N. J. (1989). *Solomon's sword: A practical guide to conducting child custody evaluations.* San Francisco, CA: Jossey-Bass Publishers.

Solomon, J., & Biringen, Z. (2001). Another look at the developmental research: Commentary on Kelly and Lamb's "Using child development research to make appropriate custody and access decisions for young children." *Family and Conciliation Courts Review, 39*(4), 355-364.

Sotile, W. M., Julian, A., III, Henry, S. E., & Sotile, M. O. (1991). *Family apperception test manual.* Los Angeles, CA: Western Psychological Services.

Chapter 20

HELPING CLIENTS DEAL WITH PARENTAL ALIENATION SYNDROME

JAYNE A. MAJOR

OVERVIEW

The purpose of this chapter is to help clinicians recognize when parental alienation syndrome (PAS) is occurring in a family and to help the targeted and victimized parent be successful in containing the disturbed, alienating parent's destructive behaviors. There is an enormous need for mental health professionals who can help accurately identify PAS and then guide their clients toward those methods that have been proven to more likely lead to a positive outcome.

WHAT HAS CHANGED?

Mental health professionals are in a unique position either to help or to hurt a victimized parent who is being alienated from his or her child when PAS is occurring. Unfortunately, misguided therapists have actually helped cause the destruction of a child's relationship with the target parent, who is generally the healthier parent. The child then ends up continuing to be exposed to and cared for by the ill parent, perpetuating the alienation. Clinicians are relied upon to be healers in issues of mental health, to help their clients make better life choices, and to protect their clients from harm. Certainly clinicians' charge is to protect children from harm. However, due to a lack of understanding of or inexperience in identifying the severity of PAS, therapists can unwittingly contribute to a child's living a lifetime with psychological disorders and failed relationships.

Potential for PAS is nothing new. However, what *was* new was the astonishing proliferation of PAS in the 1980s. This proliferation was the result of sweeping social changes. A brief history will help put in context what happened. In the 1960s and through the 1970s, feminists in the United States told fathers that they must take a more active role in raising their children. Women were going to work, enrolling in college, and pursuing careers as never before. A shift began when fathers became more involved in the day-to-day care of their children than they had been in previous generations. While rigidity about parental roles began to fall away, the *"tender years doctrine"* was still in place. This doctrine presumed that, by virtue of the fact that a woman was the mother of a child, she must be the superior parent. In the early 1970s several states passed "no-fault" divorce laws, where anyone who wanted out of a marriage was free to leave. Some have called them the "no-guilt laws." As a result, an unprecedented proliferation of divorce began.

After the breakup of their families, many fathers wanted to continue to be involved in the care of their children. However, they soon discovered that they had no legal right to the custody of their children unless the mother agreed to it. Because of the lobbying efforts of James Cook, founder of the Joint Custody Association, who was confronting this problem himself, the California Legislature passed the first joint custody laws in 1980. Joint custody was viewed by many in the legal field as a better way to handle the evolving problem of sharing child custody. It was believed that joint custody would lead to fewer fights over the custody of children because it was more equal. These laws helped level the playing field for fathers. After this breakthrough in California, other states also passed joint custody laws.

The majority of divorcing mothers and fathers welcomed joint custody. Then, as with any trend, a backlash occurred. Child custody became a highly political, gender-specific issue. Thus, high-conflict disputes became more frequent in the 1980s. In most states the tender years presumption ("mother knows best") was replaced by the best-interests-of-the-child presumption of joint custody ("the best parent is both parents").

In the 1980s courts increasingly began to be more sensitive to gender in deciding child custody, which removed the automatic allocation of full custody rights to the mother. Instead, courts looked first at how the custody could be shared, and if that was not possible, judicial officers attempted to determine which parent was more interested in and better able to attend to the best interests of the child. Fathers perceived that they were at a disadvantage because of a pre-existing bias toward the mothers having custody. Thus, in the 1980s more fathers than ever started showing up at parenting classes to make sure that their skills were state of the art. It was at this time that I first became aware of PAS.

In many custody cases, parents were able to share custody of their children and work out child care issues in an amicable way. A large number of women were relieved to have the fathers share child care. This enabled more mothers to pursue their personal goals involving education and careers. However, when a friendly resolution to custody could not be reached between parents, fathers found that they had a greater opportunity to gain joint or primary custody by litigating.

WHO INDENTIFIED PAS?

In association with the burgeoning child custody litigation in the 1980s, forensic psychiatrist Dr. Richard A. Gardner first noticed a dramatic increase in the frequency of a condition rarely seen before, that of the programming or brainwashing of a child by one parent with the intent to denigrate the other parent. However, the condition associated with distinct symptoms that he was seeing was more than brainwashing or programming by a parent. It was confounded by what Gardner calls "self-created contributions by the child in support of the alienating parent's campaign of denigration against the target parent." Gardner called this cluster of symptoms *parental alienation syndrome* (PAS), a new term that included a contribution to the problem made by both the alienating parent and the child.

Gardner (1998) has defined PAS in the following way: "The parental alienation syndrome (PAS) is a disorder that arises primarily in the context of child-custody disputes. Its primary manifestation is the child's campaign of denigration against a parent, a campaign that has no justification. It results from the combination of a programming (brainwashing) parent's indoctrinations and the child's own contributions to the vilification of the target parent."

In severe cases of PAS, the child is utterly brainwashed against the alienated parent. The alienating parent can truthfully say that the child does not want to spend any time with the target parent, even though he or she has told the child that he or she has to, and that there is a court order that mandates it, and so on. The alienator typically states: "There is nothing I can do about it. I have not been telling the child that he cannot see you."

This creates a conundrum for the mental health professional. Because of the intensity of the feelings, and as the drama unfolds, it is easy to get caught up in and to believe what the alienating parent and child are saying. Having not seen the target parent, clinicians often take sides. Even when they have seen the target parent, clinicians often feel it is their duty to tell the target parent to pull back and let the alienating parent and child calm down, hoping to reintroduce the target parent and child at a later date. At this point, the mental health professional has fallen into a PAS trap. He or she does not have the full picture and may not understand that a child's graphic and hateful words and letters to the target parent are due to the child's having been taken over by the relentless programming, brainwashing, and indoctrination of the seemingly justified parent. The child's hateful words and letters in this case do not describe his or her true feelings, but are evidence of how disturbed the child has become under the circumstances in which he or she is living. Duplicity based on delusional thinking creates an environment fraught with the potential to do great harm.

In PAS there is no true parental abuse or neglect on the part of the alienated parent. If there were, the child's animosity would be justified. Also, PAS is not occurring if the child still has a positive relationship with the target parent, even if the other parent is attempting to create alienation.

Gardner notes that PAS is more than brainwashing or programming, because the child must actually participate in the denigrating of the alienated parent for PAS to occur. Gardner has identified eight ways that children who are involved in PAS act. I have added examples of behaviors that clinicians might observe that could be strong indicators that PAS is the problem – all of which should be treated as alarms to do something to alleviate the disturbance.

1. The child denigrates the alienated parent with foul language and severe oppositional behavior.

The therapist might observe the child curse or shout "I hate you!" The child might actually try to hit, bite, or kick the target parent. One nine-year-old child grabbed the glasses off of his father's face and smashed them on the floor.

2. The child offers weak, absurd, or frivolous reasons for his or her anger.
   "My mom is so fat she cannot do anything right." "He stole everything when he left. Now my mother does not have any money to live on."
3. The child is sure of himself or herself and does not demonstrate ambivalence i.e., the child does not show feelings of both love and hate for the alienated parent, but rather only hate.
   "I never want to see you again. You are evil. Leave me alone. I do not want any presents from you."
4. The child exhorts that he or she alone came up with the ideas of denigration. The "independent-thinker" phenomenon is where the child asserts that no one told him or her to do this.
   "My mother is a good person. She wouldn't do anything wrong." "My dad did not tell me to say anything bad. He is always fair."
5. The child supports and feels a need to protect the alienating parent.
   "My mother (father) never did anything to you. Leave her (him) alone. It's all your fault."
6. The child does not demonstrate guilt over cruelty towards the alienated parent.
   "You deserve to go to hell after all you have done to us."
7. The child uses borrowed scenarios or vividly describes situations that he or she could not have experienced.
   One ten-year-old child described vividly on an answering machine how her father had molested her when she was three years old. She could not have remembered any of these details from age three. The last word on the tape after her diatribe was another voice saying "Good!"
8. Animosity is generalized to include also the friends and/or the extended family of the alienated parent.
   "Grandma turned you into a mean person." "Uncle Jack shot the girl's puppy."

HOW DOES AN ALIENATING PARENT CAUSE A CHILD TO BECOME INVOLVED IN PAS?

Mild PAS

When parents first separate, they often lack restraint in making negative references to each other. For example, feeling anxiety, a mother might implicitly impart to a child that the child is not safe with his or her father. The mother might say something like, "Call me as soon as you get there to let me know you are okay. "If you get scared, you call me right away. Okay?" "I'll come get you if you want to come home," or "Do not let your father keep you out too late." A father might say, "Your mother isn't forgetting to put you to bed on time, is she?" "Remember to tell your mother that you want to spend more time with your daddy," "Who stays at the house overnight?" "I worry about you all the time," or "Call me every day and let me know that you are okay."

Generally, alienation is done by one parent to subtly make herself or himself look better than the other parent. Everyone in the family feels insecure, and it becomes difficult for some parents to control their emotions around their children. Children may overhear telephone calls that are derogatory toward the other parent or may be told directly something to the equivalent of "Dad is a jerk" or "Your mom cannot get anything right."

Usually this level of alienation dies down once the separating parents become used to the changes brought on by separation and move on with their lives. If their own alienating behavior is pointed out to them, most parents will feel badly that their child is being hurt and will have enough control to stop. Most people who commit mild alienation are unaware of what they are doing and are willing to be educated and to change. Mild PAS still has the potential to inflict serious injury on the child who hears the other parent characterized in such a bad light.

Moderate PAS

In some cases, however, the anxiety a parent feels over the family's breaking-up does not subside, but rather escalates. PAS parents are psychologically fragile. When things are going their way, they can hold themselves together. However, when they are threatened, these parents can become fiercely entrenched in preserving what they see as rightfully theirs. They may lose complete control of themselves and disregard appropriate boundaries. When matters do not go their way, they go ballistic. It does not matter to them if the child is terrified of them. When they do finally calm down, they do not want to admit that they were out of control.

Only a small percentage of parents end up with this degree of loss of control. Some of these parents can be turned around with extensive anger management instruction, therapy, and parenting education. They love their children and want to be seen as good parents. Under some circumstances they are still educable and have the strength of will to regain control of themselves. Often, parents must be ordered by the court into these helpful programs; rarely will they enter them voluntarily because they assume that someone else, usually the other parent, is to blame for their loss of control.

Severe PAS

In the severe level of PAS, alienating parents cross over from demonstrating any semblance of reason to launching an irrational, "no-holds-barred" attack on the child's other parent (or the person whom they see as most threatening to them). These parents cannot be reached by reason, because they are operating from a delusional system of thinking; they are seriously mentally ill. They are obsessed with destroying the relationship their child has with their enemy.

Unlike cases of mild or moderate levels of PAS, we do not have an effective way of treating these obsessed alienators. They will not just "get it" that what they are doing is irrational and extremely harmful. They are entrenched in their beliefs and will not listen to reason. Therefore, in these cases the disturbed parent's influence over the child must be minimized by removing the child from that parent's care. Without legal intervention the target parent is not likely to be successful at accomplishing this.

WHERE DOES PAS ORIGINATE?

One of the greatest contributions professionals can make is to help the target parent understand what is really going on with an alienating parent. Precious time can be lost while the target parent constantly tries to figure out why he or she has just been hit again with a brick in the head. Not much can be done about a problem if the problem has not been identified.

PAS does not just happen out of the blue, although that is how most target parents experience it. When the target parent finally understands what the alienating parent is doing and why, he or she realizes that many PAS characteristics were already in place when he or she met this person. PAS was a psychosocial nightmare waiting to happen. The seeds of PAS were sewn into the mental fabric of the alienating parent when he or she was a small child.

PAS needs further study as to the underlying mechanisms that cause the problem. An additional hypothesis is that personality disorders such as those in Cluster B may conceivably underlie much of PAS. Borderline personality, narcissism, histrionic, and antisocial disorders could account for exaggerated mood swings in perception of intimate relationships, when the once revered and respected person becomes an object of hatred and contempt.

It appears that PAS parents are stuck in the first stage of child development, and as a result there two characteristics of this first stage of life that are typical of PAS parents. First, just as young children need others to take care of them in order to survive, PAS parents are preoccupied with their own survival. To them, having total control over their children, whom they see literally as an extension of themselves, is a life-and-death matter. Second, like young children, PAS parents are egocentric. This may be better understood as the idea that "self is center." Young children have no sense of taking care of others; they expect to have all their needs provided to them. All they need to do is complain and someone will usually give them what they want. They have an expectation that people will do what they want them to do. They feel entitled to special treatment and expect other people to take care of them.

Unfortunately, some children grow into adulthood without ever leaving this stage. We do not think of egocentric children in the first few years of life as being selfish, but the same behavior from an adult seems selfish indeed. Adults stuck in this stage are preoccupied with their own survival. This can be seen in PAS parents. PAS parents do not understand how to please others, and any effort to do so always has strings attached. They do not know how to give; they only know how to take. Furthermore, they do not play by the rules and are not likely to obey a court order. Why?

In severe cases of PAS, the alienating parent is unable to "individuate" (to see the child as a separate human being from himself or herself). The parent is narcissistic (self-centered) and is enmeshed (overly involved) with the child. Furthermore, parents in this stage of PAS presume that they have a special entitlement to whatever they want. They think that the rules of life only apply to other people, and not to them.

Because people with these characteristics are not socially well adjusted, they are called *sociopaths*, a term used for people who have no moral conscience. This means that they are ***unable*** to have empathy or compassion for others. They are unable to see a situation from another person's point of view and especially from their child's point of view. They do not distinguish between telling the truth and lying the way rational people do. Therefore, *they do not know when they are lying.*

In spite of admonitions from judges and mental health professionals to stop alienating, they cannot. One of the most difficult aspects of PAS for the target parent is to understand that the mentally ill parent is *unable* to act differently and – when PAS reaches the severe stage – so is the child. Parent and child both are experiencing a shared psychosis, which radically affects their judgment. No one can fix them. It is also unlikely that they will ever stop trying to perpetuate the alienation, *because it is a gut-wrenching survival issue to them!*

The target parent needs to understand what has happened to what was once an affectionate and loving child, who is now unexplainably hostile. Remember Gardner's definition stated earlier. The disorder is not only brainwashing or programming by a parent, but is confounded by what Gardner calls "self-created contributions by the child in support of the alienating parent's campaign of denigration against the target parent." The problem is that children believe and trust the alienating parent. They need to try to make sense of what they are being told and create their own explanations. The PAS child increasingly shares the alienating parent's views. How does this happen?

At birth, children are totally reliant on a parent, usually the mother, for having all of their needs met. It is part of normal child development to be enmeshed with their primary caregiver, primarily because very young children do not have a separate identity from this caregiver. One of the mother's roles is to help the child develop as a separate person. Therefore, infancy and childhood become a series of tasks of learning how to become independent, such as learning to put oneself back to sleep, to eat, to use a toilet, and to care for one's hygiene. Instead of promoting this independence, the alienating parent encourages continued dependence. The parent may insist on sleeping with the child, feeding the child ("It's easier if I do it"), or taking care of these rites of passage longer than normal child development necessitates. This "spoiling" may not feel right to the child, but he or she does not have enough ego strength to do anything about it.

HOW IS TIME WITH THE TARGET PARENT COMPROMISED?

Professionals can help target parents understand that the designated time with their child is likely to be interfered with greatly. Target parents can expect interruptions of different kinds, such as frequent calls during their visits, last-minute birthday parties and other such occasions for the child to go to during their time together, or classes that the target parent is expected to take the child to and which will occupy most of their designated time together.

For example, Jenny desperately needs to control how her eight-year-old daughter, Sharon, spends time with Sharon's father, Brian. Jenny arranges several things for Sharon to do while at Brian's house. Jenny registers Sharon for ongoing lessons without consulting Brian. Jenny is very specific about who Sharon is not allowed to see, specifically the members of Brian's family, including Sharon's grandparents. Most of Brian's friends are on the list too, this includes his new girlfriend. Jenny desperately wants control over the time Sharon is not with her. Jenny's behavior is typical of PAS parents.

When asked why she so meticulously plans Sharon's time with Brian, Jenny says that when Sharon leaves with Brian, it is as though Brian is taking part of Jenny's body away from her. "It is like he is removing my right arm and taking it for the weekend. I want to know what my right arm is doing." To Jenny, it feels like she is losing a profound part of who she is. She feels fractured – pulled apart – when her daughter leaves her. PAS parents are trying to hold all the parts together so that they can be accounted for.

Here are two other examples: When Jerry picked up his sons at 9:00 a.m. on a Saturday for the weekend he found that they were very excited about spending the day at Disneyland. This idea had never crossed his mind. Mary reported that her children came to her house loaded with homework. Most of her time with her children involved helping them with this all-consuming task.

WHY IS PAS A DOUBLE-BIND FOR THE CHILD?

When Sharon spends time with Brian and enjoys it, she is put into a double-bind. Clearly, she cannot tell her mother that Dad treats her well or that they had fun together. Sharon wants a close, loving relationship with her father, but does not dare to attempt this. When she and Dad have fun together, she knows that her mother does not want to hear about the good things that happened. Furthermore, if she tells her mother, it only makes her mother worse. As a little girl, Sharon has to figure out on which side the bread is buttered (who has the power), and her own survival needs tug at her. She will tell her mother everything she did not enjoy about the time spent with Brian and may even make up things she did not enjoy, which will add to Jenny's belief that Sharon does not like to be with Brian. Sharon increasingly feels the need to protect her mother.

HOW FAMILY VOLATILITY COMPLICATES PAS FAMILIES

It is common with PAS that target parents are in a chronically defensive position. They are continuously defending themselves against one wild accusation after another. Instead of being proactive, they are most likely to become passive. In the face of overwhelming hostility from the other parent, target parents cope by trying to not rock the boat. The volatility of the disturbed parents decreases as long as they are getting their way. Therefore, one challenge of target parents is to figure out how to react appropriately. Since this is not very clear, they tend to do nothing and wait. Tension builds. Something snaps and people react. Families with PAS are volatile families.

A father may indeed have spanked a child or lashed out at the mother physically or verbally. An isolated incident can turn into a holocaust. When Rob spanked his rebellious ten-year-old, he ended up in jail on child abuse charges, followed by a six-week trial to determine his guilt. The jury returned with a "not guilty" verdict in 20 minutes. The verdict did not end the matter, however, as far as the mother was concerned. She told everyone she could, including her son, that the boy's father had been arrested for child abuse and had gone to jail. Though this was true, she refused to tell the part about his being found not guilty. Whenever she was corrected and told that he was found innocent, she would mutter, "The jury did not have all the evidence."

An alienating parent's hatred can have no bounds. The most severe form of PAS will bring out every horrible allegation known, including claims of domestic violence, stalking, and the sexual molestation of the child. Many targeted parents report that there have been repeated calls to the department of family and child services alleging child abuse and neglect on their part. In most cases the investigators found no evidence of any wrongdoing. However, the alienating parent feels that these reports are not fabrications, but are real. Regardless of the truth, in the alienating parent's mind, this abuse and/or neglect actually did happen. Most of the target parents I work with are continually befuddled by the other parent's lying. They ask, "How can she lie like that?" and "Why won't he tell what really happened?" They do not realize that the alienating parent's lies are not based on rational thinking. Alienating parents are incapable of understanding the difference between what is true and what they want to be true. A vital part of knowing how to successfully fight PAS is to understand the severity of the psychological disturbance that is the source of it.

Another complication is that PAS is intergenerational in dysfunctional families. Almost always, the alienator has people within the family who support the alienation. It might be the alienator's mother, father, or grandparent who encourages fighting. In one family I worked with the PAS supporter was the children's uncle, who controlled the family fortune. He used his financial position to tightly control all of the other family members.

PAS becomes more severe when the alienating parent uses the child as his or her therapist. In this case, the alienating parent tells the child in great detail about every miserable experience with and negative feeling toward the target parent. The child, who is already enmeshed with the alienating parent because his or her identity is still undefined, easily absorbs this parent's negativity. The child becomes aligned with the alienating parent and feels the need to be this parent's protector.

Obviously, without anyone to stop the alienation from progressing, the child will become estranged from the targeted parent. The child's relationship with this parent will eventually be severed. It is doubtful that, without psychological intervention, the child will ever understand what happened, even as he or she grows up. The child's primary role model will be the maladaptive, dysfunctional parent. Thus, the child will not have the benefit of growing up with the better-adjusted parent, nor of receiving all that this parent could have contributed to enrich the child's life. Many PAS children experience serious psychological problems that remain with them for life. They become the perfect candidates for repeating the dysfunction of their childhood as they form their own families with unsuspecting spouses.

Will children involved in PAS ever grow up and realize what happened to them? Without someone who can recognize the syndrome and counsel them about it, it is not likely that these children will ever figure it out. However, there have been exceptions where the child and the alienated parent have been successfully reunited later in life. A man named Art is one example. He wanted to see for himself what a horrible person his father was. When Art was 38 years old, he had his father traced, which was not difficult to do. He discovered that his father was anything but horrible; and knowing the truth about his mother's illness helped him understand the mysteries he had experienced in his upbringing. Nevertheless, reunification later in life is rare.

HOW CAN GOOD INTENTIONS BACKFIRE?

Those people who are on the front lines and most often called upon to handle such difficult family situations, such as police officers, social workers, attorneys, and psychologists, assume that what the distressed parent is saying is true. These things *do* happen. For example, men who are seriously disturbed, violent, out of control sexually, and stalk. Some men are rightfully feared. In these cases of PAS, the mother is very convincing in her desperation and vivid in her descriptions. The clincher is that the alienated child collaborates with the mother by saying, "Yes, I am afraid of my father." "Yes, my father did touch me down there." "Yes, he does beat me." What would you do if you were faced with having to decide how to protect a child in such a situation?

The way that well-meaning mental health professionals get hooked into siding with the alienating parent is described by Frank Williams, M.D., a psychiatrist who has written about "parentectomy," where a parent has been "cut out" of a child's life as is the case in PAS. He states:

> The alienating parent can get the potential parent victim – usually the father – to see a "friendly," "brilliant" mental health clinician or child development specialist, who will brain-drill the potential parent victim about a distorted, out-of-context version of the psychological and developmental needs of children . . . they will reiterate that children –especially young children – need the stability, constancy and consistency of one home, and that it is emotionally harmful for children to be shuttled back and forth between homes. They will reiterate that children need a primary psychological caretaker.
>
> Should the "friendly," "brilliant" mental health clinician . . . fail to convince the victim of the need for a parentectomy, the determined other parent can then enlist the aid of a "hired gun" child development expert. After a brief, superficial contact with the other parent, oftentimes without ever seeing the victim parent, or without ever seeing the children interact with the victim parent – the "hired gun" will unequivocally and with the utmost scientific certainty declare:
>
> 1. that the children mistrust and are afraid of the victim parent;
> 2. that the victim parent lacks empathy for the children;
> 3. that the victim parent emotionally abuses the children;
> 4. that the victim parent is an alcoholic or other substance abuser;
> 5. that the victim parent is impulsive and prone to potential child physical abuse; and,
> 6. worst of all, that the victim parent suffers with a serious psychiatric disorder.

Williams notes that last of all, should the methods fail, the alienating parent can allege sexual abuse of the child in an effort to promote the parentectomy. He concludes: "Attempts at parentectomy create a psychological reign of terror, for the intended parent and child victims. Those victims who survive are emotionally bloodied, bitter, war-torn, and exhausted."

When targeted parents realize that PAS is occurring, they and their attorneys will actively begin seeking out professionals who have the background to work with them in correcting the situation. The lack of trained therapists is a serious obstacle for them. We need more professionals to get the training required to recognize and work with PAS families. It is vital that the alienation be contained to the mild and moderate stages, because once PAS reaches the severe stage it is usually too late to correct it.

Our courts, social services, and mental health professions are all committed to stopping child abuse and neglect. However, in PAS situations, the tendency is that the most dramatic and loudest complaint ends up being acted upon first, before an investigation as to the accuracy of the allegation has been conducted. This allows the alienating parent more time to proceed with the campaign of alienation.

THREE KEY STEPS TO CONTAINING PAS

Step One: Going to Court

PAS can only be contained by getting a court order to limit the alienating parent's influence on the child. The target parent must appeal to a judge to do this. This is an important step for the target parent who has, for the most part, been passive in his or her approach. The goal is ultimately to convince a judge that the child is being programmed and that it is not in the child's best interests to stay in the environment of the alienating parent.

For this task, target parents need the aid of a family law attorney experienced in litigation. Especially beneficial would be an attorney who had actually been successful in turning around a PAS case to where the target parent received sole custody of the programmed child.

Together the target parent and the attorney will form a strategy for how to best approach proving that PAS exists in the family. They will document the most serious excesses and gather evidence that will hold up in court. Good record keeping is essential. Most parents keep a journal or diary of key events for evidence that the child is being alienated.

Therefore, one purpose of an order to show cause (OSC) is to get a court order for a forensic evaluation of the whole family. Judges will often order these evaluations because this is the only way that they can understand what is really happening in high-conflict families.

Step Two: The Psychological Evaluation

The psychological evaluation presents an important opportunity for the target parent. However, the result will be unsuccessful if the evaluator is not knowledgeable about PAS. Otherwise, the diagnosis will be missed and it is unlikely that the evaluator will make a proper assessment and recommendations, especially in those cases in which custodial transfer is warranted. Target parents should be very aware, however, that the forensic evaluator is not their friend or their therapist. The evaluator's role is that of an investigator. The target parent will not have a second chance to influence the evaluator after the evaluator gets to the report-writing phase.

A forensic evaluator will take a detailed history of the family, listen to him or her, and observe the parents with their child, and may require personality tests to help reveal the functioning of each parent's psychological health. The evaluator will read the declarations and other documents that have been submitted to "prove" each parent's case. Forensic evaluators can best diagnose PAS by looking for the eight characteristics of PAS identified by Gardner. They will write a report and make recommendations to the court as to what they believe should be the decision of the court regarding child custody.

Thus, the evaluation is best approached in an organized and logical way. Preparing a comprehensive parenting plan to give to the evaluator, attorney, and judge will give target parents several advantages. First, they will be able to present in writing and to articulate in person clearly what they believe to be in the best interests of their children (see *Creating a Successful Parenting Plan: A Step-by-Step Guide for the Care of Children of Divided Families* Major, 2001 for detailed guidance in this process). A thoughtful parenting plan helps to demonstrate that parents are rational and reasonable, and that they have the best interests of their children at heart.

Target parents also can prepare for the evaluation by researching today's standards for excellent parenting. What is considered to be optimal parenting has changed dramatically in recent years (*see Breakthrough Parenting: Moving Your Family from Struggle to Cooperation* Major, 2000). Parenting Education books and courses can provide abundant information on modern approaches that are psychologically healthy ways of raising children. Practicing the advanced methodologies of receptive listening, "I"-statements, discipline rather than punishment, and promoting positive self-esteem can demonstrate to evaluators a sophistication in parenting skill that can help the target parent prove himself or herself to be the better parent.

Sometimes the recommendations from the evaluator are inadequate and will not really make a difference. This may necessitate going back after six months or a year for a reevaluation. One mother I worked with took her case back to an evaluator four times to document how the father was alienating their three children. Her persistence paid off. The evaluator could see that the father had not followed any of the evaluator's recommendations to allow the children to have a healthy relationship with their mother. The mother now has full custody of all three children and the father sees them only in the presence of a monitor. However, the mother has her hands full in reversing the alienation. She has a team of therapists helping her.

Step Three: The Judge

It is rare that judges have any mental health training. They most often learn about PAS from the bench. It usually takes several trips to court to point out how badly a child is being treated before a judge is willing to act, even with a strong evaluation in the target parent's favor.

Judges are inevitably conservative in their orders. Even when the evidence is overwhelming that PAS is occurring, the court order may still end up stating that "The parents are to make joint decisions about the child's welfare," when this is impossible to do. This is further evidence that the judge does not understand the magnitude of the problem.

STRATEGIES FOR SUCCESS IN PAS CASES

The following are strategies used by parents in PAS situations who have been successful in getting primary custody of their children. Therapists can use these as guides for advising their clients.

1. These parents educated themselves about what PAS is and what it is not.
2. They were even-tempered and logical, and they kept their emotions under control while in the presence of anyone involved in the case. They never retaliated. They constantly struggled to contain the conflict, not to add to it. A person who reacts in anger is proving the alienator's point that that person is unstable.

   One father expressed it like this: "I do not know how to make it better with the mother, but I do know how to make it worse." He was one of the more successful parents I met in fighting the PAS problem because he stayed in the role of the peacekeeper.

   All of these parents went through dark nights of the soul. They became very angry and thought about taking radical action, such as kidnapping the children – or worse. However, they calmed down and worked on resolving their case through the court system.
3. They all considered giving up, but never did. No matter how awful the harassment got, they worried about leaving their children with the alienating parent. They were driven to continue trying to get the evaluator and the court to understand the seriousness of the issue and to grant primary custody to them.
4. They were willing and able to endure the financial expense of seeing it through. They became good at understanding how the courts work and understood the law as it applied to their cases. They often ended up representing themselves in court because of excessive legal expenses. Some consulted with attorneys on an hourly basis about legal questions as to the best strategy to use and then worked with a paralegal service to have the paperwork drawn up correctly.
5. A forensic evaluator concluded that PAS was occurring and made a strong statement recommending a change in the legal and primary custody to the target parent. In cases where the evaluator took a less strong stand, successful parents went back to the evaluator, usually waiting at least six months, to present new evidence to demonstrate that his or her earlier recommendations were not working and that full custody should be changed to him or her.
6. Even though they and their children were being victimized, they understood that their children were not of their own mind when they were abusive. They focused on keeping the bond that they have had with their children alive.
7. The alienated parents who got caught up in how terrible the situation was and who spent a lot of time judging it became paralyzed by the seeming hopelessness of being understood. Thus, the successful ones did not live a victim's life. They were proactive in taking constructive action. They purposely and mindfully avoided adding to the problem.
8. They always called or showed up to pick up their children at the scheduled time, even if they were sure that the children would not be there. This was often very painful, but they could then document that they had tried. Sometimes they would take a witness to prove that they were there, in case the alienator alleged that this parent had no interest in the child. It is best if parents have court orders to transfer the children at a neutral place, rather than at each other's front door. The pickup and drop-off can be at a school location or a police station.
9. They focused on making time spent with the child as nonconfrontational as possible and did not talk to the child about their legal cases. They took the high road and never talked badly about the other parent to their children. They absolutely never showed a child any court orders or other sensitive documents. They did not let the child overhear phone conversations when they were talking about their cases.

   However, they would defend themselves by saying "That is not true." "I never said (or did) that." "What you are being told is not true." "You are very bright. What do you remember?" "Your mother (father) thinks differently than I do." They avoided long justifications and clarifications of the accusations. They just did not discuss the matter with their children.
10. They had strong support groups to help them handle the turmoil they were in. The support group might have been their family, friends, house of worship, or therapist. They practiced

healthy stress management techniques-maintaining their health with regular exercise, good food, and medical checkups.

11. They did not violate court orders. They paid their child support on time and proved that they could live within the letter of the law.
12. When they did get their children back, they had carefully selected people to work with helping them with the child's deprogramming. In some cases a transition home was ordered, with limited and monitored time with the alienating parent and increasing time with the target parent. The children were helped to understand what really happened and why the judge made certain decisions. Children need to be deprogrammed from what is false and shown what is true. Procedures used in helping people leave cults are similar to what children need when they leave the environment of the alienating parent. Not just any therapist will do. Therapists have to be trained in this kind of therapy, or it is likely to be a waste of time. For information on what works in deprogramming PAS children, refer to the therapeutic interventions Gardner describes (Gardner, 2001).
13. The parents who prevailed through this terribly difficult time were truly decent, principled people. It was obvious to everyone in an official position that they loved their children and would act in their children's best interests.
14. In those cases where parents ultimately do lose their children, or where they become so marginalized that they have no parental role at all, they need considerable therapeutic support to face the magnitude of this loss. It is best if they work with mental health professionals who specialize in grieving. One of the most difficult steps for these parents is to understand that they have indeed, in spite of all their efforts and intentions, lost their children. It is very difficult to surrender to the reality of the overwhelming circumstances that they find themselves in.

CONCLUSIONS

Mental health professionals are in an unusual position to help or to harm families ravaged by PAS. Because PAS is among the most severe kinds of abuse of a child's emotions, there will be scars and lost opportunities for normal development. The child is at risk of growing up and being an alienator also, because the alienating parent has been the primary role model. Given the intensity and seriousness of the dramatic crisis – the twists and turns of events that are typical of PAS families – it is easy for therapists to mistake the underlying cause of the problem and to align themselves with the disturbed parent. Therapists who do this will do more damage than good.

More mental health professionals who can identify the disorder and can intervene in a manner that will enable the target parents to preserve their relationship with their child are needed. Without this the child victimized by PAS is likely to experience serious psychological disturbances. Often all that a therapist can do is to educate target parents as to what steps to take to overcome their overwhelming confusion and passivity. These parents are sorely in need of direction to find the legal resources that can help them turn PAS around. It is only then that target parents have a chance to rescue their children from the ravages of severe PAS.

REFERENCES

Gardner, R.A. (1998). *The Parental Alienation Syndrome*, Second Edition. Cresskill, NJ: Creative Therapeutics.

Gardner, R. A. (2001). *Therapeutic interventions for children with parental alienation syndrome.* Cresskill, New Jersey: Creative Therapeutics.

Major, Jayne A. (2000). *Breakthrough parenting: Moving your family from struggle to cooperation.* Los Angeles, CA: Breakthrough Parenting Services.

Major, Jayne A. (2002). *Creating a successful parent plan: A step-by-step guide for the care of children of divided families.* New 2002 Edition. Los Angeles, CA: Breakthrough Parenting Services.

Williams, Frank S. (1990). "Preventing Parentectomy Following Divorce," Keynote Address, Fifth Annual Conference National Council for Children's Rights, Washington, D.C., October 20, 1990.

Chapter 21

BEYOND PARENTAL ALIENATION SYNDROME: RECONCILING THE ALIENATED CHILD AND THE LOST PARENT

GLENN F. CARTWRIGHT

OVERVIEW

Little is known about the long-term effects of parental alienation syndrome (PAS), particularly the degree to which successful reconciliation between the alienated child and the lost parent can be achieved. Reconciliation is conceived as a four-stage process, the observed characteristics of which are described in this chapter. Prerequisites for good reconciliation are also outlined.

INTRODUCTION

The awful outcome of PAS is the complete separation of a child or children from a parent. Even more dreadful is that it is deliberately caused, maliciously done, and entirely preventable. This terrible form of child abuse has long-lasting and devastating effects for all concerned: the child not only loses a parent but is cheated of remembering that parent fondly, the lost parent anguishes over the loss of a child and is chronically haunted by the child's seeming rejection and hatred, and even the alienator's short-term victory is diminished by potential future guilt and possible lifelong backlash from the child (Cartwright, 1993).

Few of these sad outcomes have been sufficiently studied. It is not known, for example, how many children lose a parent in this way, how many lost parents there are, or how many alienators eventually regret their actions. Even less is known about those cases where children attempt or achieve reconciliation with their lost parent.

Many questions remain unanswered. These include: For how many PAS children is the loss of a parent permanent? What proportion of PAS children attempt reconciliation with their lost parent? How and when do they do it, under what circumstances, and how successful are they? How many unsuccessful reconciliation attempts do PAS children make before successful reconciliation? How many unsuccessful reconciliation attempts do lost parents make before giving up? What adjustments need to be made during and following reconciliation? How long do reconciliations last? Finally, how many reconciliation attempts fail due to death, absence, or unwillingness of the lost parents?

We do know that *some* children are able to reconcile with their lost parents successfully and permanently. But anecdotal evidence exists that for other PAS children reconciliation with their lost parents is neither automatic nor spontaneous. Reconciliation does not usually occur by accident; it must be nurtured, planned, and executed, and sadly is often difficult, frustrating, and unsuccessful.

RECONCILIATION VERSUS REINTEGRATION

Reconciliation is the final, happy chapter of the horrible PAS saga. Such a satisfactory resumption of a core family relationship should have a special term to describe it. The term "reconciliation" is preferred because it describes more accurately the restoration to partial familial harmony through an act of parent-child settlement or resolution. Thus, reconciliation is not synonymous with "reintegration," although some authors have used the terms interchangeably. Reconciliation is necessarily the first step in a *rapprochement* between parties, which may lead to eventual integration (had it never occurred) or reintegration (had the initial integration been subsequently interrupted, damaged, or destroyed). For this reason, integration or reintegration is seen as one stage of the overall reconciliation process as outlined in the following section.

THE RECONCILIATION PROCESS

The process of reconciliation has at least four identifiable stages: hope, reconciliation, adjustment, and integration/reintegration.

Hope

In the first stage, some hope for reconciliation must exist. In fact, it is difficult to imagine how reconciliation can occur if it is not hoped for by at least one of the parties. Even when the child and the lost parent have not seen each other for months or years, each may still miss the other and foster the hope of getting together again, re-establishing their relationship, and continuing their lives in a more normal parent-child context. From the time of the alienation, such hope is more likely to reside in the lost parent than in the child. It follows that those parents who lose hope are less likely to seek or eventually achieve satisfactory reconciliation. Conversely, those who maintain hope are more likely to achieve successful reconciliation. Fortunately, the deep love parents harbor for their children helps ensure that the hopeful are in the majority.

Among PAS children, the hope of reconciliation is usually not present immediately following the alienation, but may be rekindled later and slowly grow as children age and achieve greater independence. PAS children who do not develop some hope of reconciliation are less likely to seek it and even less likely to achieve it.

Reconciliation

Optimal reconciliation proceeds from a joint recognition by both the child and the lost parent that each wishes to play a bigger and more meaningful role in the life of the other and that they are better off together than apart. The reconciliation stage occurs after the child and lost parent have been separated (physically and/or emotionally) for a significant period of time and electively choose to come together again. The process compels a greater recognition by both and acceptance that each is not perfect. This may necessitate activation of the third stage, adjustment.

Adjustment

There are some smooth reconciliations that appear to require little or no adjustment. In these cases, the third stage of adjustment is often skipped. Such children and their lost parents often pick up during reconciliation right where they left off years earlier and carry on as if nothing untoward had happened. It is speculated that this kind of reconciliation is most likely to occur in mild cases of PAS.

Other children and parents may require some period of adjustment. They may need to rediscover each other, adjust to each other's habits, needs, tastes, and preferences, and establish an overall comfort level with one another. Those who require such adjustment are more likely to exhibit initial wariness or even lack of trust, which hopefully diminishes as adjustment proceeds and both parent and child get to know each another better.

Integration/Reintegration

Finally, the alienated child experiences a period of integration, not only with the lost parent but with the lost parent's family and friends. A similar but less significant integration occurs when the parent embraces more of the child's friends and interests. Such integration may be new (having never occurred before) or may be a re-establishment of an earlier integration (more properly called "reintegration").

Characteristics of the Reconciliation Process

In recent years, attention has been focused on defining and diagnosing the problem of PAS; relatively little has been written about reconciliation. In cases in which PAS children have successfully reconciled with their lost parents, several significant features have been observed.

Acceptance Difficulty: Having been estranged from the child for months and perhaps even years, the lost parent may have difficulty in accepting that the newly reconciled child is the same person as the alienated child. A number of reasons for this exist. First, the parent may remember the child as he or she was several years ago. Parents who lost their child when he or she was young may be surprised to find how sophisticated, grown-up, and educated the child has become as an adult or near-adult. Second, the adult son or daughter may appear quite different physically, emotionally, and behaviorally. In the parent's mind, a totally different person who is almost unrecognizable has been encountered although the parent is cognitively aware that this new adult is the same person as the lost child, emotionally and even perceptually they may perceive them to be different persons. In a superficial way, this phenomenon is similar to multiple personality disorder (MPD), except that instead of originating in the child, the dual (or possibly multiple personalities) are projected onto the child by the parent. It may seem to the parent that now two children exist where only one existed before. Although it is a strange phenomenon, it may not be altogether unpleasant. The parent may have difficulty accepting that the two personalities are really one person but at the same time may enjoy having two children (the one remembered and the one newly encountered). Similar to the resolution of MPD, in which multiple personalities eventually merge, over time these two perceived individuals will merge in the parent's mind, as realization grows that both are one and the same person. This process may occur gradually and be spread over a long period of time – months or even years – depending on the amount of interaction the parent has with the child and the amount of "relearning" the parent must do.

To a lesser extent, but in a similar fashion, the child may feel that the remembered parent is not at all like the person with whom reconciliation is sought. That the lost parent is likely to be on his or her best behavior during the reconciliation compounds the problem and contributes to this phenomenon. All being well, each successive encounter with the lost parent will progressively convince the child that the lost parent is neither the evil ogre portrayed by the alienating parent, nor the idealized angel with whom the child has imagined reconciliation. Given enough time, ogre and angel will merge in the mind of the child to produce a more balanced, imperfect, but loving parent. Again, the time this takes may vary from a period of months to years, depending on the amount of interaction between child and parent and the amount of "relearning" the child must do. This relearning facilitates the return to, or construction of, a more accurate reality for the child as he or she comes to love the lost parent, imperfections and all.

Positive Memories Aid Reconciliation: Reconciliation is more difficult, if not impossible, for children who have not maintained or recovered positive memories of the lost parent. This alone is ample reason for lost parents to do everything possible to try to keep positive memories alive during estrangement in preparation for eventual reconciliation, as well as to encourage their recall during the reconciliation process itself. This is one of the reasons lost parents should be persuaded to keep the lines of communication open during estrangement with cards, letters, gifts, and remembrances. It pays off later during reconciliation.

Repetition/Reliving of Pleasant Past Experiences: The child may indicate to the lost parent a wish to repeat pleasant experiences or revisit old haunts or vacation spots experienced as a child. Every child who has lost a parent through PAS has been cruelly cheated and deprived of one of the great joys of life: knowing and loving a parent. When given the chance the alienated child may make a conscious attempt to recover past pleasant experiences by reliving them vicariously or in reality. Thus, when reconciling with the child, the parent may find that the child wants to revisit places they had visited together, relive mutual excursions, reexperience common adventures, and retake family vacations. This may occur years later, when the child is considerably older. It is not unheard of that an alienated child who once visited Disneyland with the lost parent inexplicably wishes as an adult to return there. The lost parent should be prepared for this eventuality and encourage it where possible.

The lost parent should also understand that the child may be torn by competing child-versus-adult desires. For example, although reconciliation might trigger a wish to return to Disneyland and to experience it as the child remembered it with the lost parent, the child may not necessarily wish to go there with the lost parent. In other words, the child may wish to return to Disneyland *because* of the lost parent but not necessarily with the lost parent, and may not know why. Now closer to adulthood, the child may choose instead to go there with a companion. Again, the parent should recognize, understand, and encourage this phenomenon. That the child wishes to relive a visit previously experienced with the lost parent is in itself a great tribute.

Regression: Initially, the child may regress slightly in the presence of the lost parent, perhaps as the result of attempting to recapture aspects of the past relationship or relive joint experiences. Younger reconciling children may revert to mild "baby talk" and older children may "fool around," wrestling with and shoving the lost parent in a manner characteristic of a younger child. The need for physical contact with the lost parent may express itself in this way. The attempt to recover past experiences, real or imagined, or perhaps to recover what never was, should be understood for what it is, and should be regarded as a healthy sign.

Selective Amnesia: The child may exhibit symptoms of amnesia regarding real or imagined painful or unpleasant episodes with the lost parent. Gardner (1998) reported that in full-blown cases of PAS, the child often exhibits symptoms akin to amnesia. However, unlike generalized amnesia where most past events go unrecalled, this amnesia is selective in that only good experiences with the lost parent go unremembered while bad experiences may be magnified. This process may have helped perpetuate the alienation, much to the glee of the alienator; for the reconciling child the process is reversed. The child allows good memories to bubble into consciousness and pleasant, shared experiences to drive thoughts of reconciliation. Consequently, good experiences may now be magnified and bad memories repressed. The child may forget particular events or arguments that remain significant to the lost parent. For example, the child may forget the location of the lost parent's home or the parent's telephone number if they were originally associated with unpleasant memories.

Suppression of Negative Incidents: Both the parent and the child may be reluctant to discuss past negative incidents. Such incidents may continue to be painful or embarrassing, or conversely, may lose importance for them as reconciliation proceeds. It is best to leave these issues to resolve themselves in good time. Just as time works for the alienator and against the lost parent during the process of alienation (Cartwright, 1993), so time works to the advantage of the lost parent during reconciliation. Fostering reconciliation promotes the resolution of unresolved issues and this is yet one more reason why reconciliation is encouraged.

Alienators and/or Stepparents May Trigger Reconciliation Attempts: Fueling the reconciliation may be disagreements with the stepparent or, less likely, with the alienating parent. Warshak (2000) has suggested that remarriage can serve as a trigger of PAS. Similarly, in reverse fashion, should that subsequent marriage falter or should the child run afoul of the new stepparent, the likelihood of reconciliation with the lost parent is increased. Lost parents should also be sensitive to this possibility.

Reconciliation Aids Feelings of Completeness: Reconciled children often report "feeling complete" after reestablishing a satisfactory relationship with their lost parents. This is a positive development that contributes to their well-being and the successful undertaking of other responsibilities, such as continued schooling and/or employment and the development and maintenance of additional satisfactory relationships. Depending on the child's age, it may not be too late for the lost parent to encourage more schooling, assist with life plans, or help with career planning. Reconciling children have missed these interventions in their lives and often eagerly seek them; fortunately, lost parents enjoy advising their offspring of them and begin to feel useful and important again.

PREREQUISITES FOR GOOD RECONCILIATION

Good reconciliation does not occur in all cases. Observational data suggest it is likely that several prerequisites are necessary for satisfactory and meaningful reconciliation.

The PAS Must Not Have Been Severe

Mild cases present the best chance of reconciliation, with moderate cases being somewhat more difficult. It is not known to what degree severe cases of PAS can ever be reconciled; further research is warranted. The hope is, of course, that all alienated children can be reunited with their parents and have successful reconciliations.

Although litigation often appears as the last resort in a family dispute, it is apparent that such action discourages natural reconciliation. In fact, such court formalities may stifle the reconciliation process as the energies of the participants, particularly the lost parent, are expended on "fighting" and "winning." The lost child may be caught in the crossfire ("Be careful what you say in court!") or may take a protective role toward one of the parents to the exclusion of the other (". . . because the lawyer made Mom cry!"). Such actions weaken the probability of successful reconciliation and should be avoided where possible, especially as the child becomes more able to make independent decisions and/or approaches the age of majority.

The Diminished Role of the Alienator

Once again, reconciliation with the lost parent is easier if the alienating parent ceases to interfere. Reconciliation proceeds more smoothly without negative input from the alienator, and the likelihood of success increases as the child matures. Less interference from the alienator may be due to diminished hostility, lack of energy or enthusiasm for a "fight," or loss of control of the child (for example, when the child moves out of the alienator's home). It is also possible that the alienator has seen the error of his or her ways, forgives or partially forgives the ex-spouse, and encourages the child to make contact and work toward reconciliation.

The Presence in the Child of Pleasant Memories

Ideally, the child must have some happy memories of the lost parent on which to begin the reconciliation. These are the building blocks on which to build a new, satisfactory relationship. Again, the probability is that the child has harbored pleasant memories to enable the beginnings of reconstruction of the relationship. This, of course, is good news!

Nonlocal Reconciliation Is More Difficult

It stands to reason that parents who are living far away may be less able and therefore less likely to effect positive reconciliation. This may be through no fault of their own: it is already known how difficult it is to carry on a long-distance friendship, romance, or marriage; it is even more difficult to establish effective reconciliation at a distance. Should reconciliation take place, the long-distance maintenance of the relationship remains problematic. Although this seems simple common sense, it should give parents pause who sometimes feel the urge to move far away when alienation is at its peak. Often, alienated parents must relocate due to personal or employment reasons. However, the urge to move away simply because of anger, despair, or desperation should be suppressed. Such a move will undoubtedly make eventual reconciliation much more difficult.

Independent Thinking

One of the characteristics of PAS is the "independent-thinker" phenomenon, where the alienating parent alleges it is the child's own decision to reject the lost parent. Of course, this is seldom true; far from being an independent thinker a young child is usually just echoing the alienating parent. Strangely, at a later age, it is the independent-thinker phenomenon that nurtures attempts at reconciliation. Such independent thought often develops when the PAS child leaves the home of the alienator and begins to realize that reconciliation is not only a possibility, but a desirable possibility at that. Independent thought enables the child to compare scenarios rationally, to explore the prospects of reconciliation logically without interference from the alienator, and to make an independent decision to reunite. Overall, the development of independent thinking in the alienated child usually works to the advantage of the lost parent and to the benefit of the reconciliation process.

Availability of Lost Parents

Reconciliation depends on the availability and willingness of the lost parent to attempt to build on what has been lost with the child. Obviously the reconciliation works best when the lost parent is still alive, resides locally, and is eager to participate. However, this participation pales in comparison to the effort that must be made by the PAS child, who must sometimes make a 180-degree change in direction, swallow his or her pride, ignore the promptings of the alienator, and take the first positive step toward reconciliation. Often, this will happen only when the child leaves the alienator's home to attend school or establish an independent residence. To some degree, this is necessarily correlated with age; some children may go away to boarding school after age seven, but establishing an independent residence or attending college or university requires the child be approximately 18 years of age. Because age 18 is of great significance in many teenagers' lives, lost parents may wish to consider suspending additional legal action pending lifestyle changes for the adolescent that could facilitate reconciliation.

Parental Esteem

The reconciliation process will be helped if the lost parent is seen by the child to be held in esteem by others: family, friends, colleagues, and co-workers. Although parents should keep this in mind, they should avoid any attempt to "stage" positive situations for the benefit of the child. Children can see through phony attempts at staged positive situations, and such action may delay reconciliation. The best advice for the lost parent is "Be yourself."

Recall Shared Memories Together

Parents and children can improve the reconciliation by recalling and sharing the memories of joint experiences, and remembering and discussing trips they have taken, shows they have seen, and places they have been together. They can also share feelings by looking at family photographs and videotapes together. Most lost parents have large numbers of photographs and memorabilia of their children. Less well-known is that many alienated children who have professed indifference or even hatred for the lost parent, have secretly kept a photograph album or scrapbook of pleasant times shared with that parent. Sharing these again during the reconciliation process is both positive and healing.

The Lost Parent's New Role

In the intact family, as children grow up, the relationship between parents and children changes. The children become more independent and assertive; the parents less protective and more supportive. In normal circumstances, this is a somewhat gradual change, although it is never fast enough for teenagers! In broken families, for which PAS has wreaked havoc, relationships are often frozen in their tracks, awaiting the sudden thaw of reconciliation. In such situations, the parent must be prepared to make a more rapid transition to the supportive role without the gradual change that occurs with intact families. Thus, moving from lost parent to newly reconciled parent may require a quick shift into a new role – parent of an adult or soon-to-be adult, confidant, friend, and power source. Although many factors depend on the age of the child, in general the parent should try to minimize the past and concentrate on building the present and planning the future with the child. Be there to support the child, and make sure the child knows you are there for him or her. As the child increasingly steers the ship, the lost parent must become the gyroscope that helps keep the child on life's course. This rapid, and sometimes unexpected, role change may be the most difficult one for the lost parent to assume, but hopefully it is one that will have life-long consequences for both parent and child as they resume their relationship.

REFERENCES

Cartwright, Glenn F. (1993). Expanding the parameters of parental alienation syndrome. *The American Journal of Family Therapy, 21*, 205–215.

Gardner, R. (1998). *The Parental Alienation Syndrome* (2nd edition). Cresskill NJ: Creative Therapeutics.

Warshak, Richard A. (2000). Remarriage as a trigger parental alienation syndrome. *The American Journal of Family Therapy, 28*, 229–241.

Chapter 22

THE PSYCHOLOGICAL EFFECTS AND TREATMENT OF THE PARENTAL ALIENATION SYNDROME

Ludwig F. Lowenstein

OVERVIEW

The psychological affects and treatment of parental alienation syndrome (PAS) have been studied by pioneer Dr. Richard Gardner and others. The research establishes that children who are alienated from one of their parents by the custodial parent suffer considerably at the time of the alienation and, often, for a lifetime, unless preventative action is as soon as possible. At present, the judicial system is still reticent to provide fathers with the same rights as mothers in connection with having an influence on the rearing of children. As a result of a hostile separation or divorce, many parents subtly, or directly, attempt to turn children against one of their parents.

THE CURRENT SITUATION

What follows are attempts to present some of the problems suffered by children due to the effects of PAS. This chapter also deals with the psychological treatment of children who have suffered from PAS, as well as treating the alienator of PAS.

PAS has not been generally recognized in the author's country, the United Kingdom, but a number of court cases, many of which PAS has been a factor in, the author has attended to emphasize the PAS condition. Few psychologists in the United Kingdom have a great deal of knowledge concerning parental alienation or the syndrome associated with it. It is for this reason that this chapter is likely to be of special value to many psychologists dealing with family problems and most especially custody disputes in the United Kingdom. It should be recognized that the reaction to PAS in children is not limited to British children. It occurs worldwide in a similar manner.

Judges and Courts in the United Kingdom still have a great tendency to virtually always give the benefit of the doubt to one of the parents, usually the mother, when former partners have disputes in relation to their children. It appears to go unrecognized by the courts that the noncustodial parent frequently suffers from the fact that the custodial parent has turned the child against him or her in the process of an unhappy split in the relationship between the partners (Stamps et al. 1997; Stamps, 2002).

The current author has been virtually the only voice in the United Kingdom concerned with the process of repercussions of parental alienation as a syndrome. It is hoped as a result of further court actions that this important syndrome will be recognized and dealt with appropriately by British Courts.

PROBLEMS SUFFERED BY CHILDREN DUE TO THE EFFECTS OF PARENTAL ALIENATION SYNDROME (PAS)

The effect of PAS on children has been investigated by relatively few individuals in the United Kingdom so far. One researcher, Gardner has a great deal of work in this area. (Gardner 1992, 1998, 2001), particularly on behalf of those who find themselves in a PAS situation and need some guidance and assistance to convince others that such a phenomenon exists. PAS has both short-term and long-term effects on children. Whatever one may think, the children become victims – not of their own making, but of their parents, most especially the parent who is carrying out the alienation process.

We hear a great deal about child abuse, especially sexual abuse, but less so about emotional abuse resulting from PAS. Many would consider PAS and the process of indoctrination to be a form of child abuse, since children are being used for the purpose of animosity and even revenge. This animosity being shown toward the alienated parent can have a terrible effect on the child in question. Those children who are participating in the alienation process are often unaware of its impact. They merely feel the consequences or take on the views of the alienating parent. Such views that the other parent is "evil," "wicked," "stupid," or "dangerous," or all of these, can do untold damage to the relationship with the noncustodial alienated parent. Children may be used as "spies" or "saboteurs" in relation to the alienated parent to provide "ammunition" for the alienator or "fuel for the fire" to be used against them. In addition, the children are encouraged to treat the alienated parent with a lack of respect with the purpose of humiliating him or her. This is often taken up by the immediate family of the alienator. Some children may even be encouraged to behave in a deceitful manner toward the other parent when visiting, by lying, stealing, and causing problems with another person with whom the parent may have developed a new relationship. False accusations may also be leveled against the alienated parent on the grounds of false information supplied by the child. Eager misinterpretation of information given to the alienating parent is then grasped to denigrate the other parent with whom they may be having a custody battle. Denial of this will, of course, be made by the alienator.

Encouraging a child to betray one of the two most important members of the family produces a tendency towards psychopathic behavior within that child. Once the denigration process has started, the child, due to pressure from and the "power" of the alienator needs to carry on the process of denigration.

Children who suffer from PAS develop a concept that one parent is the loving parent who should be loved back, while the other is the hated parent who has done "wicked and nasty things," and abandoned the family. This has been consciously or unconsciously indoctrinated into the child and results in fear as well as hatred for the alienated parent. Generally, negative indoctrination is carried out by the mother, who usually retains the child in residence. Occasionally, it is the father who may have taken over the role of parenting.

Gardner (1998) lists eight cardinal symptoms of PAS:

1. The campaign of denigration.
2. Weak, frivolous, and absurd rationalizations for the denigration.
3. Lack of ambivalence.
4. The "independent-thinker" phenomenon.
5. Reflexive support of the alienating parent in the parental conflict.
6. Actions of guilt over cruelty to and/or exploitation of the alienated parent.
7. The presence of borrowed scenarios.
8. The spread of animosity to the extended family and alienated parent.

In cases of PAS in which I have been involved, I have found that the child has developed a hatred for the nonresident parent (usually the father) and the alienating parent attempts to denigrate and vilify the alienated parent. The destruction of one parent can have serious consequences. These are not immediately recognizable in the short-term, become very obvious in the long-term. One might say that the child has been robbed of the possibility of having a supportive and caring parent. All memories of a good relationship have been destroyed. In addition, the alienator often brainwashes the child in order to make the child fearful of the alienated parent. The animosity created often permeates to the extended family of the alienated parent. This means the child will not merely lose one of his or her parents but also the grandparents, and perhaps aunts and uncles, etc.

Another common reaction of children who have been programmed is to tell the alienator that they have hatred or dislike for the alienated parent, when in fact they do not feel this way, and do not demonstrate this in the presence of the alienated parent. Hence, they have practiced deception and a form of lying in order to placate the alienator, while at the same time seeking to form some kind of warm relationship with the absent parent. Such deception is unlikely to lead to an individual who will be truthful and honest in other dealings in the future.

Exploitation of the alienated parent either by the child or by the alienator can also be practiced. This is done in various ways, including seeking money, clothes, or other material objects for the children, who are being used in this scheme of manipulation. The manipulator may clothe the children in the shabbiest of clothes, hoping the alienated parent will be forced to buy new clothes for the child. This teaches children a strategy that is unlikely to endear them to others in the future and is also likely to be repeated by them. Other forms of deception can be carried out over the telephone. For example, the alienating parent may say the child is absent when the other parent calls, when in fact this is not the case. They simply are not allowed to speak to the parent who is calling. The child who is aware of the conversation learns from this that lying is acceptable. This may also cause confusion in the child and forms a further rift with the alienated parent, especially if they are not informed that the parent has called to ask about them and make an appropriate arrangement for contact.

Lying and deception can become part of the child's life, especially if he or she wishes to endear himself or herself to the alienating parent. This may be especially so if the other parent has another family or relationship. This deception will develop a power of manipulation through lies and will continue into later life and reflect on the child's own relationships in the future. In contrast, non-PAS homes do not maintain control over the child, and the custodial parent does all he or she can to promote a healthy feeling towards the other parent by being truthful and encouraging the child to love and respect that parent. It is important that parents who have been divorced or separated do all they can to enhance the feelings of the child for the parent with whom they do not reside, and vice versa.

As the child grows older in a family experiencing PAS, the position often reverses. The child realizes that he or she is in a position of strength where he or she may manipulate situations in order to get his or her way. This, in turn, reduces the capacity of the alienating parent to discipline the child. The alienated parent is dependent on the child to continue the process of alienation. The child can use this against the alienating parent and frequently becomes undisciplined as a result. Neither parent controls the child, and the child is the loser in the end.

In severe cases of PAS, the alienator can create a seriously unhappy situation for the child, who will often develop panic reactions when he or she is asked to visit the alienated parent. This, in turn, can lead to repercussions in his or her attitude toward school and his or her capacity to concentrate on education. In some cases, the child may develop psychotic delusions due to the pressure to passively submit to the alienating parent. Sometimes intensive psychological treatment is required to overcome such serious disturbances. Through therapy, the child may learn to be able to be more rational and realistic in the way he or she views the alienated parent. This is difficult to resolve in the very young as well as in the older child who may have developed a habit of hatred for the alienated parent.

The most interesting scenario is when the child who has been party to the alienation realizes what the alienating parent has done and eventually turns against him or her. This may be through a falling-out, or merely through the emotional development of the child later in life. Sometimes the child will seek the alienated parent and attempt to find out the truth. In this way the child can at least be able to see things from the alienated parent's perspective.

I have personally come across situations such as these when dealing with cases of PAS. Unfortunately, parents are often not willing to resolve these situations and the courts are not willing to uphold censures against the alienating parent. Also, severe lack of funds for treatment or mediation limit what can be done. Much of the responsibility is left to the court welfare officers, who do not have the clinical qualifications to carry out the necessary treatment for the children who are, or will be, the victims of the "warring factions." Expert testimony is sought only if the court is unsure of what direction to take in the case, or to guide the court as to the character of the alienated parent and the manner in which contact visits should continue (i.e., supervised or unsupervised). If called to assist in a case, I take it as an opportunity to spread the literature on PAS, and seek to educate the judiciary and others of the existence of PAS.

SPECIFIC PROBLEMS OF CHILDREN SUFFERING FROM THE EFFECTS OF PAS

Children who have been "brainwashed" or "programmed" against another parent often exhibit the following symptoms. The effects are both short and long-term. Not all symptoms occur in all children who are involved in PAS. There will also be some difference between the very young child and the older child whose reactions to PAS will differ. However, some symptoms will need some form of treatment to help eliminate the impact of the alienating process and the harm of psychological injury to the child:

1. *Anger.* This is a common reaction of many children. Most of the anger will be expressed at the alienated parent. The fact that the children are forced into this kind of situation causes considerable distress and frustration, and the response often is to show aggressive behavior towards the targeted parent in order to accommodate the programmer.
2. *Loss or lack of impulse control in conduct.* Children who suffer from PAS are not merely suffering

from aggression, but also often turn to delinquent behavior. Considerable evidence suggests that the presence of fathers and their influence can do much to prevent and alleviate the possibility of delinquency, especially in boys.

3. *Loss of self-confidence and self-esteem.* Losing a parent to the programming procedure can produce a lack of self-confidence and self-esteem. For example, when a boy's identification with a male figure has been curtailed, this can affect his own security.
4. *Clinging and separation anxiety.* Children (especially very young children) who have been programmed to hate or disdain one of the parents will tend to cling to the custodial parent, who generally is the programmer. Considerable anxiety may be induced in the child against the alienated parent. The alienator may tell him or her negative characteristics of that parent, including the possible use of a great deal of abusive or threatening actions against the child as well as the programming parent.
5. *Developing fears and phobias.* Many children fear being abandoned or rejected when they have been induced to feel that one of the partners in a relationship, usually the father, is less than desirable. Anxiety factors about the custodial parent may induce a school phobia, which is a child's fear of attending school due to the fear of leaving the parent. Some children suffer from hypochondriacal disorders and tend to develop psychosomatic symptoms and physical illnesses. Such children fear for the future and the safety of the custodial parent.
6. *Depression and suicidal ideation.* Children who are already unhappy about the tragic breakup of the parents' relationship are further faced with the animosity that exists between the parents. This leads to ambivalence and uncertainty, sometimes suicide attempts occur, due to the unhappiness that the child feels. In addition, children may blame themselves for the breakup.
7. *Sleep disorders.* These can also occur in a child in a PAS situation. Children frequently exhibit dreams of disturbance and often find it difficult to sleep. This is often due to their worries about the "danger" posed by the alienated parent or the guilt they may feel as a result of participating in the process of alienation.
8. *Eating disorders.* A variety of eating disorders have been noted in children who are dealing with parental alienation. These disorders include anorexia nervosa, obesity, and bulimia.
9. *Educational problems.* Children who feel pressured to reject one parent frequently suffer from academic problems. They may become disruptive or aggressive or withdraw at school and their grades begin to decline.
10. *Enuresis and Encopresis.* A number of very young children suffer from bed-wetting and soiling due to the pressure and frustrations that surround them when acrimony between the parents exists. This is the response to the psychological disturbance of losing one parent and finding one parent inimical to the rejected parent.
11. *Drug abuse and self-destructive behavior.* These frequently are present in children who have suffered from PAS. This results from a need to escape the feeling of abuse they feel they have suffered through the experience. In extreme cases such conflicts can cause self-destructive behavior, which may result in suicidal tendencies.
12. *Obsessive-compulsive behavior.* This psychological reaction is frequently present in the behavior of children who seek to find security in their environment by adopting a variety of obsessive-compulsive behavior patterns.
13. *Anxiety and panic attacks.* These are also frequently present and may be reflected through psychosomatic disorders, nightmares, and avoidant behaviors.
14. *Damaged sexual identity.* As a result of PAS, children often develop sexual identity problems, especially as they may have failed to identify with one member of the relationship. It does not matter if the alienated parent is of the same sex or opposite sex of the child.
15. *Poor peer relationships.* These may follow the PAS situation due to the fact that such children often are either very withdrawn or very aggressive in their behavior.
16. *Excessive feelings of guilt.* Guilt may be due to the deep-down knowledge that the ostracized parent has done nothing wrong to deserve the kind of treatment received. This may affect the child's later life, as he or she becomes increasingly aware of the truth and the destructive alienator's motives.

Children who are exposed to PAS suffer in a variety of general as well as specific ways from this experience. It will have both temporary and lasting effects on their lives. This was not the intention of the alienator, but it is the result of such alienation procedures and programming.

THE PSYCHOLOGICAL TREATMENT OF CHILDREN WHO HAVE SUFFERED FROM PAS

Having stated the difficulties that may arise in the behavior of children who have experienced PAS, we must consider the help that can be given. In the United Kingdom, the symptoms of PAS are rarely taught to treatment providers. This is due both to the denial of its occurrence and the lack of funding even when PAS can be proved to have happened. Less than ten percent of cases are treated. This is often due to the resistance of the alienating parent and the lack of reinforcement and cooperation by the courts. It also is difficult to overcome the continuous negative influence of the alienator, which has been brought to bear on the opinions of the children.

Before any treatment can commence, it is vital to assess or diagnose such children carefully. This is done through in-depth interviews as well as psychological personality testing. At the same time it is valuable, whenever possible, to deal with the alienating parent and make them aware of the possible damage that will be done to the child. The objective of the treatment procedure is to deprogram the child who has been turned against the target parent. Needless to say, the most effective treatment is achieved through gaining the cooperation from the family members concerned, and instructions and orders from the court process. During the treatment process, efforts should be made to reduce and eliminate, if possible, the hatred and paranoia that has been created in the child towards the alienated parent. It is important to develop independent thinking in the child so that he or she is not influenced by one party, the alienator, as has been the case in the past. The child must be helped to develop a conscience about the treatment that he or she has meted out to the alienated parent. This will assist the child in altering his or her feelings toward the alienated parent. The goal of the treatment is for the child to make contact with the alienated parent and to re-establish a positive and loving relationship with that parent.

The only instance where this would not be possible or recommended is one in which some form of emotional, physical, or sexual abuse has taken place. According to the definition of PAS, the alienated parent has done nothing to deserve the hostile treatment by the child and the alienator. The therapist must be aware that the alienator is likely to be constantly working behind the scenes against the therapist's efforts. It is essential, therefore, to have some form of support and recognition in the form of threats or orders by the court if the alienator persists in sabotaging the efforts made on behalf of the child. It is this very problem that often stops the treatment process before it starts, or causes it to be given up once it has started.

1. Dealing with the Hatred Developed

Dealing directly with the hatred and paranoia used by the alienator to encourage the child to hate or blame his or her misfortune on the alienated parent is essential. This indoctrination may have been done directly or very subtly. The therapist needs to ascertain not only the strength of the paranoia developed but also the reasons for it. He or she needs to counteract the arguments that the child has been given that have led to such antagonistic behavior towards the parent. The hatred must be demolished through rational and logical arguments from the therapist. The paranoia must be identified as a delusion and, therefore, of no substance. Children who have developed a strong hatred and paranoia are difficult to influence through logic and reason, but nevertheless, the therapist should make this effort. The real reasons for such feelings must be sought and discussed, and all other evidence must be counteracted accordingly as hearsay or the opinion of others not based on fact.

2. The Child Identifying with the Alienator

The only course for children experiencing PAS is to take the side of the alienating parent. In order for therapy to be successful, such identification with the alienator must be broken down. The alienated parent must be seen in a more realistic and favorable light, and the child needs to recognize why he or she feels as he or she does. By confronting the child with evidence from the past of positive feelings associated with the alienated parent (memories, photographs, and stories) it can be pointed out to the child that the opinions he or she held once are accurate but have been overtaken by the negative opinions of others. The child should be made aware that he or she is merely repeating the views expressed by the alienating parent. Those children who have suffered a reasonably long period of indoctrination by an alienating parent find it difficult to deal with confrontation-type therapy.

Older children who have developed freethinking are more amenable to this method than younger children.

The child experiencing PAS is a victim. The other victim, of course, is the alienated parent. Any love for the beleaguered alienated parent is destroyed, this is difficult to reverse. In the courts, many judges administering alleged fair and just decisions find it difficult to seek reversals of such powerful indoctrination against one parent they are often advised to continue with the "status quo," especially if there is resistance from the child. This is a contradiction of the evidence when alienation has obviously taken place. As a result, the judge actually enhances the difficulties of the alienated parent by providing limited or practically no contact with the child.

The child may scheme against the alienated parent and make up stories in order to avoid contact. The fact that this is a possibility should be drawn to the child's attention, and such practices should be discouraged. Even if the child has had contact with the alienated parent and has not found anything favorable in that parent, it is the role of the therapist to do all that he or she can to promote a better attitude toward that parent. In time, a relationship may grow, and having both parents willing to help a child develop positive attachments to both of them can only be to the child's advantage. Rational and logical thinking comes into play here and must overpower the emotional side of the argument. This is difficult to tackle in young children, since they have not developed the capacity for a well-developed conceptual and cognitive ability and the influence of the alienator is very strong. However, from the cognitive and attitude frame of reference, the child must be encouraged to behave properly toward the alienated parent.

Accusations made by a child against the alienated parent must be looked into thoroughly to determine the source of these impressions and why they have been expressed. For instance, the disciplinary style of one parent may be different from the other. In a case I was recently involved in, the child claimed she was "forced" to eat a certain amount of vegetables. The real explanation was that the father preferred her to try to eat different kinds of vegetables while the mother and stepfather (the custodial parents) let her eat whatever she wanted. The child obviously wanted to follow the path of least resistance and consequently exaggerated the actions of the father, knowing the mother would complain about it.

I have counseled adults who have been victims of PAS, who have been troubled in their adult lives by the guilt that they have come to feel over the alienation process. One such case involved a woman who had been teased by her father as a child about her preferred vegetarianism. She used this issue as a massive exaggeration of the father's terrible and insensitive behavior towards her when she was younger and was encouraged by the mother to do so. When she had problems later in her life with divorce and separation, she sought the help of a therapist. She realized the truth of the matter and initiated action to correct what had occurred between her and her father.

Many alienated parents are put at a disadvantage with the child by the alienator or custodial parent. A good example of this is when a father makes an arrangement to attend a soccer match with his son and the arrangement is not finalized soon enough. His plan clashes with the arrangements made by the alienating mother who then cancels the outing but also points out to the child that the father has let him or her down. Ambivalence from the child also puts the father in a no-win situation. If he offers to attend an event with the child and the child indicates to the mother that he really is not wanted, then this indicates that the father is rejected by the child, who is embarrassed by his presence. Why this is so should be carefully investigated by the therapist.

Needless to say, therapists vary in their approaches to the problem of PAS. Some will actually view the situation from the child's perspective current thinking and not attempt to alter that way of thinking in any way. This will do little to reduce PAS or eliminate it, and will in fact allow it to continue, mostly due to a lack of knowledge and understanding of the situation. The approach recommended would be to be sensitive to the indoctrination process. Logic and reason must be applied and the helpless plight of the targeted parent must be improved in order to allow a healing process, or more balanced view of the alienated parent, to take place. In extreme cases of PAS, it may be necessary to resort to "antipsychological" approaches and make the child actually feel guilty for the way he or she behaves towards the alienated parent. Such feelings of guilt can have a positive effect in removing the alienator's influences on the child. The alienator's influences may be a burden on the child, and the child may welcome the intervention of the court in the decision-making process.

A recent case illustrates this: The acrimony between the two parents had reached an absolute deadlock over access visits. The child was torn between both parents and felt compelled to support the mother and the new blended family of which she was a part. The new family was laissez-faire in their discipline of the girl, and the father was more autocratic with her and his new family members. As a result of the difference in the parenting and discipline styles of the two families toward the child, constant friction resulted. The father made physical threats toward the mother. This caused the child to feel that access visits should be terminated, which caused great distress to the father. My interview with the child revealed that the child still felt she wanted to see the father but would not accept the father's angry reactions toward the mother. My recommendations to the court were that drop-offs and pickups should be supervised and that the father attend an anger management course. Thus, the child could resume visits with the father because the court ordered it so, and the influence of the mother was less of a burden to the child, who could say, "I am only doing this because the court demands it and I want to help you avoid any trouble."

It has long been known that "broken" homes create instability in the child and can often lead to psychological problems, delinquency, and other serious difficulties. A more harmonious breakup with both partners seeking to love the child, encouraging the child to love both parents, and with both parents unified in their approach, can avoid many problems. It should always be made clear to any child involved in a marital breakup that the love for the child has not been lost and the friendship between the parents can be maintained for that reason. The child then realizes that he or she has two parents who both care for him or her even though they cannot live with each other in harmony. They may even choose partners but this does not in any way affect either parents support, love and care of the child. This is the very opposite of parental alienation, parental cooperation.

Children who turn against one parent are engaging in a process that can lead to serious consequences. Changing behavior relies on changing the attitude or cognition of the child. It is very important to change the behavior of the child towards the alienated parent. It must be remembered that both parents can practice PAS – one as the initiator and the other as the reactor – setting up a "tit-for-tat" situation, with the child often in the middle. PAS can cause children long-term suffering emotionally, educationally, and in later life relationships, which may cause them to become future alienators.

3. *Treating the Alienator*

The treatment of the alienator is the most difficult task of all. This is because the alienator feels totally justified in the programming being carried out. Alienating parents often deny that they are programming their children.

Most alienators know exactly what they are doing and are prepared to avoid any form of treatment in order to continue their alienation process. They seek to destroy or end any possible relationship between the child and the targeted parent. Normally, in order to reduce the resistance of an alienator and to get them to participate in therapy, there must be a Court Resolution and pressure by a Judge that the parental alienation must stop.

The treatment process has three objectives: (1)to prepare the alienator for the treatment itself; (2)to treat the alienator; and (3) to monitor the effects of the treatment vis-à-vis the child who has been programmed.

1. Preparation for Treatment: The therapist must be prepared for resistance from the alienator. The attitude of the alienator will reflect the following types of thinking when verbalized: "There is nothing wrong with what I am doing. I don't need any treatment"; "I am only coming along to the 'treatment,' as you call it, because the court has forced me to do so"; "There is nothing wrong with me that needs treatment, it's my former spouse who needs therapy."

With this kind of outlook, treatment involving a change in attitude seems far from simple. It is, however, important to repair step-by-step this tragically destructive interaction by a means of convincing the alienator that much will be gained by cooperating with the therapist and by accepting the irrationality of one's demeanor.

The two main reasons for this are: (1) the alienator would benefit via a better relationship with the alienated partner possibly including, greater financial help, care and support, and even friendliness from the alienated parent; and (2) the child would benefit in the short-term and long-term if contact of some kind with the alienated parent were established.

2. The Treatment: The treatment initially will have to be spontaneous. It is vital to win the confidence of the alienator. It is important to listen carefully and sensitively to the grievances of the alienator and to sympathize with their feelings of hurt, anger, and in some cases, betrayal.

The treatment must not only be concerned with the past, it must consider the future hope of the alienator. Hatred and resentment toward the alienated parent have permeated the life of the alienator. It is vital to seek to establish a new relationship and possibly a new direction in life by developing new pursuits that have a positive aspect and can eliminate or counteract those negative feelings that tend to originate totally within the person. Alienation often becomes an obsessive, compulsive and habit-forming process.

Promoting and guiding the alienator to develop hope for the future does much to reduce or remove the often pathological animosity towards the targeted parent, which has become the centre of the alienator's 'modus vivendi.' This negative way of life can only be counteracted by optimism. The alienating parent needs to put behind them the acts of evil and betrayal they perceive to have happened to them.

The therapeutic intention is to simultaneously change the attitude and behavior of the alienating individual. This involves cognitive and behavioral treatment. The success of the therapeutic approach can only be ascertained via two interacting factors: (1) changing the hostility of the programmer towards the targeted parent; and (2) the child being encouraged to have contact with the alienated parent and by actually spending positive time with that parent. This obviously means requiring the child be involved in treatment, once the alienating parent has proven he or she is cooperating with the efforts of the therapist.

4. Monitoring the Effects of the Treatment Against PAS

In order to prepare fertile ground for therapeutic success, the therapist must be involved in a positive reintroduction of the child to the targeted parent. This can only be achieved with the full agreement of the alienating parent. In turn, the alienated parent must also be prepared to deal with the initial likely difficulties of having contact with the child, who has hitherto been adversely programmed against him or her. If possible, the therapist should establish ways whereby some communication takes place between the alienator and the targeted parent. A form of mediation should take place between the two adults with the help of the therapist. In this way an agreement can be developed that can then lead to some kind of ongoing cooperation. This should be sought initially on an individual basis, with the parents showing sufficient signs of agreement regarding the two of them meeting.

The therapist must consider, with great care each step of the way, how much further he can go, or what can be further achieved to advance the process of harmonizing a former acrimonious relationship. Success in reducing acrimony can only be measured in degree. It depends on the skill of the therapist and the sincere willingness, voluntarily, or ordered by the court, of the alienator to cooperate in the healing process. It also depends on the continuous support of the court, which must maintain pressure on the alienator to comply with its request for reconciliation for the sake of the child.

5. Outcome of PAS Treatment When Ordered by the Court

In Great Britain, very few courts would endorse establishing pressure on the alienator to be involved in treatment to counteract PAS. This is because judges generally consider it counterproductive, they find it unlikely that any form of treatment will be successful. Judges, therefore, rarely order an alleged perpetrator of PAS to participate in therapy. The outcome of therapy, in the few cases where it is ordered, may be surprising. Table 22.1. illustrates the outcomes of therapeutic intervention used by the author in severe or recalcitrant cases.

TABLE 22.1. Result of Treatment for PAS

Outcome	Relationship Between Targeted and Former PAS Parent	Relationship with Child
Has led to effective harmony being developed	7	6
Some positive contact established	3	5
No effective change	1	0

DISCUSSION OF RESULTS

The results of this rather small sample indicate what can be achieved through a form of mediation and therapy with those individuals involved intensively in programming a child against another parent. Parental alienation is a process that occurs over time, and it occurs more often than is realized. It not only occurs in acrimonious separations and divorces, it also may be manifested in unhappy marital relationships in which one partner's motivation is to seek almost total control over a child at the expense of the other partner.

In a happy, loving relationship, these attempts at alienation are much less likely to occur, as each partner will consider the other in making decisions concerning the children. They will adopt a unified approach to the rearing of the children and especially to the application of discipline. PAS-practicing parents are just the opposite, they often feel and express a great deal of antagonism, hatred, and hostility toward the other, estranged partner, and will do anything they can to cause damage to that partner. In extreme cases, alienation becomes pathological meaning the individual virtually thrives on antagonism and animosity towards the other party. Unfortunately, the real victim is the child.

Judges are reluctant to force the recalcitrant programming parent into therapy, realizing that treatment against their will is likely to fail. This, however, is not always the case, and Table 22.1. illustrates that when the court upholds the desire to resolve the alienation process, much can be done by mental health professionals. They can help to deal with the alienation, reduce its extent, or even eliminate it.

The judiciary must realize their responsibility and adopt a firmer approach to confront those who practice PAS. Judges, therefore, should develop a plan of action to include punishment for the lack of cooperation with a court order. Both parents should have a responsibility for the rearing of their children if they so desire. Mediation at an earlier stage of the proceedings should be made available, with a set timetable for reaching the necessary decisions. In order for successful and long-lasting rulings to be made, judges must have the "teeth" to do this. This would place strong pressure on the participant who is the alienator, to seek to benefit from the treatment being carried out. It can also eventually lead to better relationships eventually between the alienator and the former targeted parent. There is much to be gained, but the course of action is not easy and relies heavily on the commitment and strength of the judicial system supporting the therapeutic process. It also relies greatly upon the wisdom, sensitivity, and skill of the therapist.

RECENT CHANGES IN THE PAS APPROACH BY THE JUDICIARY IN THE UNITED KINGDOM

PAS is slowly becoming recognized in Great Britain. Attention has been drawn by barristers such as Willbourne and Cull (1997) and by this author (1998a,b; 1999a,b,c,d). Tony Coe has even developed a political party, the Equal Parenting Party. Another organization that has become involved is the Association for Shared Parenting. Rand (1997) produced her series of articles, "The Spectrum of Parental Alienation Syndrome," published in the *American Journal of Forensic Psychology*. Despite the small number of studies already mentioned, the recognition of parental alienation syndrome in Great Britain is still quite limited, but one particular article appearing in the *Sunday Times* (Dobson, May 22, 2000), titled "Children with Fathers in Family Have Head Start in Life," points to the importance of both parents playing a role in the rearing of children.

There have recently been some remarkable cases that have highlighted the importance of judging parental alienation in the courts. Judges are becoming bolder in insisting that, all things being equal, both parents have the right to have contact with their children. The exceptions, of course, are when one or both parents have proclivities towards violence or pedophilia, to name but two negative features that must be considered.

The case of *Cox v. Cox* (1990) discussed in *Family Law*, was one of the first to approve the sentencing and imprisonment of parents who refused access to fathers for contact with the child. This was done by a highly courageous Judge, who truly believed in "justice for all," even though there was considerable embarrassment in having to put a mother in prison. This was also done despite the likelihood of being castigated by the press. What is often not mentioned are the efforts made beforehand to gain the assent of the alienating parent for contact between the child and target parent by threatening less stringent means than imprisonment. Most cases of lack of cooperation involve the mothers refusing the fathers. Sometimes, following an acrimonious separation or divorce, the mother will claim to know of a serious cause for concern about the father, such as his being excessively punitive or permissive, a substance abuser, or even a pedophile. In many of these cases, such allegations are shown to be unfounded. Unfortunately, it is often the fathers who are considered guilty by allegation alone and need to prove their innocence, rather than the alienator having to prove the guiltiness of the alienated father!

Judges are naturally averse to imprisoning mothers for failing to honor contact arrangements with fathers. This is because mothers usually are responsible for the day-to-day care of the children. Judges are also aware of the likely adverse publicity that would follow such a judgment. The alternatives, however, often fail to achieve what is desired – that is, to comply with offers of mediation such as recommended by one psychologist

(Lowenstein, 1999a,b,c,d). However, threatening punishment, including the possibility of imprisonment, might lead some to the "negotiating table." Those who alienate children, much as anyone else, must stand before the law as either innocent or guilty of such an offense. Failing to adhere to the judgment of a court must be considered as breaking the law, with threatened punishment following.

Parents who thus fail to observe their legal responsibility to cooperate are likely to develop increasingly severe and often unfounded hostility towards the other parent. Such hostility can, and often does, reach pathological proportions. Only two possible solutions exist: (1) in extreme cases, imprisonment until the parent is willing to cooperate with the law must be threatened; and (2) the alienating parent must accept some form of mediation and treatment by a qualified psychologist over a prescribed period, normally two weeks to a month or longer, in order to resolve the "impasse." Failure by the alienating parent to cooperate must lead to punishment, including imprisonment as a final alternative only. It could also result in the alienated parent being given custody of the children temporarily or permanently.

Most alienating parents would and should learn to cooperate under such strictures and resolve the matter of PAS. It is hoped that future legal procedures will make it easier to deal with such cases and follow the courageous footsteps of earlier pioneering judges. These judges were not deflected from doing the just and right thing, despite criticism from individuals and the mass media.

REFERENCES

Dobson, R. (2000, May 21). Children with fathers in the family have a head start in life. *Sunday Times*, 11.

Gardner, R. A. (1992). *True and false accusations of child sex abuse*. Cresskill, NJ: Creative Therapeutics.

Gardner, R. A. (1998). *The Parent Alienation Syndrome – A guide for mental health and legal professionals*. Second Edition, Cresskill, NJ: Creative Therapeutics.

Gardner, R. A. (2001). *Therapeutic interventions for children with parental alienation syndrome*. Cresskill, NJ: Creative Therapeutics.

Lowenstein, L. F. (1998a). Parent alienation syndrome, (Chapter 20). In L. F. Lowenstein, *Paedophilia* (pp. 257–277). Hertfordshire,UK: Able Publishers.

Lowenstein, L. F. (1998b). Parent alienation syndrome: A two-step approach toward a solution. *Contemporary Family Therapy, 20*(4), 505–520.

Lowenstein, L.F. (1999a). Mediation in the legal profession. *Justice of the Peace, 163*, 709–710.

Lowenstein, L. F. (1999b). Parent alienation and the judiciary. *Medico-Legal Journal, 67*(3), 121–123.

Lowenstein, L. F. (1999c). Parent alienation syndrome (PAS). *Justice of the Peace, 163*(3), 47–50.

Lowenstein, L. F. (1999d). Parent alienation syndrome: What the legal profession should know. *Medico-Legal Journal, 66*(4), 151–161.

Rand, D. C. (1997). The spectrum of parental alienation syndrome (Part II). *The American Journal of Forensic Psychology, 15*(4), 1–13.

Stamps, L. E., Kunen, S., and Rock-Faucheux, A. (1997). Judges' beliefs dealing with child custody decisions. *Journal of Divorce and Remarriage, 28*(1/2), 3–16.

Stamps, L. E. (2002). Maternal preference in child custody decisions. *Journal of Divorce and Remarriage, 37*(1/2), 1–11.

Willbourne, C., and Cull, L. (1997). The emerging problem of parental alienation. *Family Law*, 807–808.

Chapter 23

WHAT MOTIVATES PARENTS TO INDOCTRINATE THEIR CHILDREN WITH PARENTAL ALIENATION SYNDROME? A PERSPECTIVE FROM THE CZECH REPUBLIC

EDUARD BAKALÁŘ

OVERVIEW

Parents generally want their children to "follow in their footsteps" – regarding values, religion, attitudes, lifestyles, and stories – to perpetuate the family name and the parent's legacy. The child's identity is intertwined with the personalities and convictions of the mother and father in their respective roles (the apple did not fall far from the tree). Competition and narcissism may play a part in the rivalry between some parents who consciously or unconsciously wish that their children will look like, act like, and think like they do. Mothers typically guard their unique position of power as the primary caregiver to their children. Typically from the mother's perspective, children witness and interpret their fathers' actions and other family discourse, including conflicts within the family. Parents during marital separation often assert "my child's needs are primary." Neurotic egotistical projection on the part of at least one parent can cause the child to favor a point of view and take sides when the child observes parental conflict and separation of the household. Thus, the stage is set with the cast of characters to act out the PAS scenario, often with the motive of revenge against the target parent couched as "protection" of the child.

INTRODUCTION

The commitment towards parenthood is probably one of the most widespread in the world. It is particularly rich, varied and long-lasting in human beings. People develop and enforce it from the moment they discover that they are to become parents. A parental role – especially the educational and nurturing side of it – lasts for approximately twenty years (in "unhealthy" cases, until the end of the parents' lives). Within the framework of parental care, people would like their children – if possible – to carry on the same family and national traditions as they do. Using a poetic term, one could say that parents want their children to "follow in their footsteps," or that they want to be "the architects of their children's souls." Yet another way of putting it would be that we – humans – want to pass down to the future not only our genes but also, if possible, a certain part of our inner world – a certain part of our unique self – even if in a modified form.

What, particularly, do we want to pass down? As previously mentioned, this includes our basic attitudes, habits, skills, ways of acting, values, and lifestyle. In concrete terms, this could be religious tendency vs. atheism (within the framework of Christian religion it could be Protestantism vs. Catholicism); political orientation – right wing vs. left wing, radicalism vs. conservatism; attitudes towards people; approach to work, to obligations, to career, etc. We also want to pass down family stories, traditions (i.e., of our original family, region, or nation) family myths, secrets, etc. It could also be some unique experience, such as an escape from certain death, fulfillment of a strange prediction, or personal decoration by an emperor or a president. Almost certainly it will be our version of some important family conflict. Certainly, it will not be information such as this computer can do "this and that" or that the number of inhabitants of Saudi Arabia is 18,860,000.

It is far more important for parents in their formative role to pass down their attitudes, interests, and values than facts and skills. We yearn either unknowingly or in some cases deliberately for our children to imitate our lifestyle, so that they become "like us" and give our ego a narcissistic illusion of "survival." However, we also desire them to do so for other reasons.

It is unlikely that anyone would deny humans' tendency to inculcate upon a child important attitudes, values, lifestyles, etc. The following generally known facts illustrate this concept:

- In most cases, people want to raise and are raising their children without being instructed, trained, or forced to do so.
- Childless couples adopt children, dedicate themselves to them, and raise them even though they are not their biological children.
- Teachers like to teach, and other educators like to educate (despite low salaries).
- National folklore is actually one of the forms of passing down national, regional, district, and family traditions. It is examined in a scientific discipline called ethnography.
- Believers, whatever their beliefs may be, like to gain new souls.
- Even homosexuals fight for their "right" to have and raise children.
- Literature contains many examples of biographies, and sagas of dynasties, and organizations.

Parent's tendency to inculcate children with important attitudes, values, and lifestyles is also evidenced by other phenomena and activities, e.g.:

- Fathers' pass down their trades to sons.
- Parents, especially fathers, teach their children sports in gyms, playgrounds, etc.
- Parents are sensitive to criticism that they have not raised their children well.

Sometimes a comment about the parent's formative tendency appears in the work of a philosopher who might have been working on a different subject, as happened in the case of Bertrand Russell who once opined that the fundamental mistake of fathers is that they expect their children to honor them.

The child's identity also plays an important role. If we ask children "who they are," they will think of information about themselves, and choose the most important aspects. If the children are very young, they might be able to tell you only their names, but even that places them into one's family, as they have the same family name. Parents want to be the authors of these important memory anagrams. Adoptive parents who devote themselves to somebody else's child hope that the child would answer such questions with information about them and not about the biological parents. The fact that the "real" identity of the child suffers and is "overwritten" by their desire to form the child according their own vision is, unfortunately, not important to the adoptive parents. They are often preoccupied with creating their own memorial within the child. It may be that such an upbringing will seriously harm the child and one day a psychiatrist might hear from him that he has an oppressive feeling that he is not himself.

We know very little about the intensity of this formative tendency to raise children to follow in one's footsteps; we have not measured it, as it is very difficult to measure methodically. In the normal conditions of a traditional family, biological parents solve this situation "as it comes." Somehow they manage; maybe one of them tactically gives way to the other so that next time he/she could veto. Theoretically, parents have the right to influence their child's psyche by a 50:50 ratio. It is acceptable if a father influences his son a bit more than 50 percent; the same is true of a mother and her daughter.

Imagine an analogy of a company with two co-workers. One of them is mainly producing and the other is mainly acquiring material and selling products. If both of them put in an equal amount of work, it is easy to imagine they would share the profit 50:50. The company should run without any problems providing that the personalities of both co-owners are emotionally and psychologically mature. By maturity, we mean the overcoming of childhood developmental stages filled with egoism, sibling rivalry, and jealousy, and also feelings of injustice, hurt, and aggression. If the co-owners have not grown out of these emotional models, they will bring them into the work place. Under these conditions, the company will be unproductive, experience problems, go bankrupt and, as is often the case, end up in court.

THE MARRIAGE

If a marriage is harmonious, even if some inherent obstacle exists, the impact on the child's soul is not too significant. By obstacle, we mean a difficulty in comparing the contributions of both parents in the shared "business" – the child. In addition, an inner voice "tells" each parent that they deserve more credit for the child's existence, for the child doing well, etc.

The inner voice tells the mother: "You carried the child in you, and gave birth to him; he is a part of you. You had to get up for him a thousand times at night. You fed him, changed his diapers. You could not continue your career or go out for a chat with your friends. You want your child to know how much you always thought of him and you want him to take on all the tender emotions and love you have for him. . . . You have the greater right to him!"

The inner voice tells the father: "You turned the questionable suitor away – with whom your wife would probably have had some defective child. You arranged an apartment or house; you borrowed money for it from relatives. You are earning money, you are protecting, and you are taking care of the family. You are trying to encourage the child, to make him happy. The job you are doing is killing you; you have to lower yourself in front of your boss. If you did not have a family, you would go somewhere else – maybe for less money, but you would really enjoy the job. You have every right to say "no" to the peculiar educational methods of your mother-in-law and say that the upbringing of your child will have firm rules."

Yes, parents are under pressure from these or similar voices. The father is usually in a disadvantageous, vulnerable position, as he spends less time with the child and his professional capability, used to be admired by children in the past (e.g., in the families of craftsmen or farmers) has disappeared in the unheard-of world of offices and research institutes. Furthermore, his skills in convincing and influencing but also dramatizing and emotional blackmailing are weaker and, in the case where a father demands order, discipline, and fulfillment of tasks, the mother can corrupt the child by forgiving duties and tolerating misbehavior. However, as noted earlier, in harmonious marriages the fight for control of the child is not that significant.

The human psychological need to pass down one's attitudes, values, lifestyle, and the traditions of one's original family currently does not have any accurate description. It usually is mentioned only indirectly in statements such as "He is the spitting image of his father; he took over his construction company," "The apple didn't fall far from the tree; she helps charity organizations like her mother does," etc.

Records of legal divorce proceedings give countless examples of the narcissistic delight in raising and molding a child. Very rarely, this need surfaces in conjunction with other phenomenon. Elisabeth Badinter, a leading French family sociologist, stated in her research:

> Within the framework of two investigations in the 80s, it was found that in cases where fathers gave their children more attention without being encouraged to do so by their wives: 60–80 percent of the wives did not welcome it. To explain their reluctant attitude, many of these women pointed out that their husbands' incompetence created more work for them than it saved. But the truth is that they see their privileged position of a mother as a position of power, which they do not like to share even at the cost of total mental and physical exhaustion.
>
> The conclusions of Diane Ehrensaft's ample research shows that mothers are often jealous of the relationship between the father and the child. They feel excluded and complain that the relationship between themselves and their husbands is not as close and intimate as the one between the father and the child. From this Ehrensaft comes to the conclusion that if the mother loses her position of power, she must come to terms with the idea that her child is not an extension of herself. The child belongs to someone else as well and identifies himself/herself with him. 'This feeling is even more painful if the child is a boy.' (1995, pp. 11–12)

Robert Bly (1999) also deals with the same subject:

> C. G. Jung came up with an alarming idea which sheds some light as to the source of this burning uncertainty. According to Jung, a son is introduced to the emotional sphere mainly by his mother; the son learns about women's attitude to masculinity and gains women's ideas about his father and his own masculinity. Therefore he sees his father through his mother's eyes. As father and mother compete for their son's affection, we cannot expect to get a reliable picture of the father from the mother or of the mother from the father. Some mothers inculcate in their children the idea that civilization, culture, emotions and personal relationships are values shared between mother and daughter or a sensitive son, while the father represents and at the same time personifies coldness or even heartlessness, violence, blindness, rationality, obsession with money and the inability to be sympathetic. 'This is the way your father is.' Because of this upbringing, sons often grow up with a distorted image of their father which is not based on their father's acts or words but more likely on their mother's interpretation of those acts and words. (pp. 35–36)

How large a part of a child's psyche are we talking about? After all, some of the child's qualities are inherited, and therefore fixed, and so it is almost impossible to influence them. David Buss stated: "Individual differences in personal characteristics between people emerge from a variety of genetic dispositions and the varied influences of the environment. The conclusions of behavior-genetic studies of personality show clearly that both sources are important. Personal characteristics usually show a slight influence of inheritance, usually in a range of 30–50 percent. At the same time these studies show that the strongest source of variance is the influence of the environment, range 50–70 percent" (1999, p. 395).

"FOOTSTEPS FOR THE CHILD" AND DEVELOPMENTAL NEEDS DURING PARENTAL SEPARATION

When a couple considers separation, thoughts inevitably turn to whose side the child will be inclined to take, whose version of the conflict the child will accept, and whom he or she will believe. To the parent whose side the child takes, this is very satisfying; to the other parent, it is not. He or she feels the child was manipulated, corrupted – deceit and lies have won. However, if a more serious conflict appears, the parents may fight to influence the child's psyche by different means. For example, parents might do this by:

- Surreptitiously or even openly setting the child against the other parent.
- Limiting access of the other parent to the child; or in some cases eliminating the other parent from the scene altogether (driving them from the home or, if that is not possible, by moving away).

Naturally, fighting parents do not view their situation in an objective way and the fact that they do not even realize the true cause of their behavior makes them sound even more convincing. The truth would sound too selfish and ruthless, and that is why they hide it even from themselves. Therefore, we often hear arguments that sound very rational, but are more likely to be just a facade of rationalizations. For example:

- My child needs a calm environment for normal healthy development.
- I do not want my child to live with stress; he (or she) should have the basics readily available.
- I do not want my child to live with conflicts; his (or her) head full of crazy ideas.

They usually say about the other parent:

- He (or she) was an unbearable person.
- He (or she) had a low level of social intelligence.
- He (or she) had no interest in the family, in the child.
- The child did not want him (or her), they had nothing to talk about, and the child was afraid of him (or her).

When the child is brainwashed, we hear:

- I was trying but there was no interest from the other side.
- The child can see for himself (or herself) who loves him (or her) and I do not want to interfere in his (or her) choice.

In these circumstances, it could be said that parents are stealing these areas from each other as if there was some special form of ownership; it is not a fight for money, a house or an apartment but for the "child's soul." However, the fight has the same intensity and various methods – including very dishonest ones – being used to secure victory. The detrimental ones are naturally also the influential ones. This point of view might help us to understand a whole range of important phenomena, which would otherwise remain hidden. People steal all kinds of items from each other, not only material goods but also intangible items of all kinds, such as discoveries, inventions, authorship, modern technology, and various other properties. That is why we should not be too surprised that in their efforts to grab a larger share of the quest for transcendence (i.e., overstepping the defined boundaries of their own existence), some parents attempt to continue their personality through their children. We will return to this topic later.

I now concentrate on the actions of the parent who, for egoistic reasons, decides to usurp as large a part as possible of the child's psyche, whatever the cost. The only lawful rival is the other parent, provided, of course, that he or she is a biological parent. He or she can be a strong, mature, determined personality with considerable influence. Such a personality is the biggest obstacle for our egoist and that is why such a clash usually ends in rejection, separation, divorce, and in stopping the relationship with the child after the divorce. If the other parent is of a weak, submissive personality, he or she might be tolerated as a helping member of the family but have almost no rights to make decisions or authority. Another example of when a parent might be tolerated is if the parent's opinions are so ridiculous that even the child recognizes this and chooses not to share them.

Another possibility is that one parent does not realize that the other wants to have the child formed only in his or her image and he or she leaves this matter fully to the other parent, with the euphemistic explanation "His mother knows best what to do with children; she knows very well how to explain things to them" (the mother here is used as the more knowledgeable, active, as she is in this position far more often than the father).

Parents who have problems with their children's upbringing visit the children's educational institutions. It is often the case that parents have different attitudes towards the methods of upbringing. The child is then in a no-win situation (you cannot serve two masters at the same time), so, he or she often finds himself or herself in a so-called conflict of loyalty. This commonly results in the child's problem behavior. This is only a fraction of the case, probably about 50 percent. The rest could be children who are hyperactive, of below average intelligence, or have psychiatric disorders.

We regularly find the strongest form of this fight in guardianship and in divorce courts in disputes over the child's upbringing after divorce and also in disputes over contact between the child and the noncustodial parent after divorce. The total number of marriages ending in divorce in 2000 in the Czech Republic was 29,704; of which 19,068 of them involved at least one child. A total of 28,201 children were affected by divorce. The courts had to decide the destiny of each one of these children. In 7.7 percent of the cases, custody was given to the fathers (a total of 2,171 children). As we can see, the courts traditionally entrust children to mothers. This is especially so if the child is young.

The Czech Republic records basic statistics about divorce involving children. We know how many marriages end up in divorce, how many children are affected, and to whom the children are entrusted. However, other facts such as the following are missing:

- We do not know how many mothers requested custody of their children but we suspect that the percentage is high, about 98 to 99 percent.
- We do not know what percentage of fathers consider raising their children but are dissuaded by their colleagues, relatives, and even attorneys.
- We do not know what percentage of fathers request custody of their children only to be denied by the courts.

As has already been mentioned we do know the percentage of fathers who are given custody of their children. In the past few years, this percentage has been in the order of 7 to 8 percent of all cases. (This percentage also includes fathers who originally did not request custody of their child but the court had no option, as the mother had died, disappeared, or was completely incapable of taking care of her child.)

We also do not have information about the atmosphere in which these proceedings take place. We do not know whether the atmosphere is mainly conflictual, whether the extent of the conflict corresponds roughly to the normal curve, or whether conflicts are rare but usually highly visible, so that we subconsciously think of this as a "run-of-the-mill" version of the guardianship/divorce conflict.

The number of children about which the courts decided in 2000 (regarding their upbringing and their educational needs) was 127,088; the number of cases in which the rights of children about were decided was 216,825. Obviously, this number also includes children about whom the court decided in previous years but whose needs changed and so required new decisions. We can assume that a large number of these decisions are begun over disagreements or arguments between the parents, not only about the amount of child support paid but also about the fight for influence over the child's soul.

Some parents who win these court cases cut off all contact between the child and the other parent immediately after the divorce by using a simple trick: They fabricate an image of the other parent so character-flawed or even dangerous that the child cannot possibly meet with him or her. The "winning" parent makes this obvious to the child, who is fully dependent on their view.

Even in cases where the winning parent is not so difficult, immediately following the court's decision, this parent may gradually start to try to win over the child, and the frequency of meetings with the other parent drops. In the Czech Republic, no statistics are kept about contact with the other parent after divorce.

We do have statistics from neighboring Austria at our disposal, from which we can see a remarkable decrease in after-divorce contact. Very often the child simply loses the other parent. This is often due to the influence of the winning parent, but not always.

According to ÖSTAT (Central Statistics Office of Austria) data, there were 16,296 divorces in 1992; the number of children affected was 17,028. By age, they were:

- under 3 years: 12 percent
- from 3 to 6 years: 17.7 percent
- from 6 to 10 years: 20.3 percent
- from 10 to 14 years: 15.5 percent
- from 14 to 19 years: 14.9 percent
- grown-up children: 19.3 percent

Respectively the children in the first five groups met their biological father as follows:

- 14 percent of the children daily
- 17 percent of the children at least once a week
- 21 percent at least once a month
- 12 percent at least once a year
- 31 percent even less or not at all

From these results, we can generalize that roughly two-thirds of the children, in fact, "lose" their fathers after divorce.

It seems that divorce statistics in European countries confirm the described preferential trend: If there is a higher standard of living and less binding family law, more and more parents (usually mothers, because they instigate the divorce in 75–80% of cases) choose exclusive care of a child. Take for example, the situation in the United Kingdom: According to the Office for National Statistics, one-quarter of all households with children are single-parent families, one-third of all births are out of wedlock, and (an estimated) 40 percent of marriages begun in 1994 will end in a divorce. Many publications indicate that this problem has a visible impact on the functioning of society.

Naturally, in fights over a child's psyche/soul and in fights over his or her future, postdivorce upbringing, a wide range of motives for both parents can be seen. They have already appeared in the literature (Bakalář, Novák, Nováková, 1996). Here we borrow from this source – the chapter "Setting children against the other parent." "Setting against" is defined here as any kind of influence over a child, directly or indirectly, with intent to decrease a parent's value in the child's eyes. In a broader sense, we also include in the term "setting against" making someone angry; someone cross with someone else, making someone lose trust, causing him or her to be scared of someone, to have a bad opinion of him or her, to hate him or her, to wish to do him or her harm, or to make him or her not want to meet the other person, to push him or her out of his emotional life, etc. As we can see from the definition, setting someone against someone else is a very effective method to thwart the influence of the other parent on the child's psyche.

MOTIVES FOR PAS

Revenge

People have used revenge since the beginning of time. Targeted fathers often claim alienating mothers are seeking revenge. This motive is the most obvious one; it is more difficult to detect the other motives. They are more hidden and parents do not know how to correctly describe them. Why should people take revenge on their ex-partners? Several reasons are possible. They are mostly irrational ones, except in cases where the flow of material goods is interrupted.

Protection or 'Protection' of the Child

During the escalation of conflict between a couple, the disappointed and angry partner fundamentally changes his or her original evaluation of the other. For example, the gentle, sensitive, noble knight becomes a thoughtless egoist, bore, brute, etc. (How could I have not seen it before?!) In this case, the professional competence of the rejected husband is affected very little by this change, but his nature, morals, and character change 100 percent (such a change in evaluation is in the expert literature called Brunhilde's complex). The ex does not believe in anything positive about the father, but she is absolutely sure of the negative qualities. The motive for protection of the child can then be formulated as follows: "I surely cannot allow my child to meet such a person who would negatively influence him (or her). It is my duty to raise the child well! I would be a bad mother if I didn't protect him (or her)!"

Security

The father worries, quite realistically, that his ex-wife could get some important information about him from the child which she could use in one way or another against him later on. It could be basically anything (fights with his new partner, bribes, not-quite-legal business, tax evasion etc.).

Power

The existence of an outside enemy (i.e., the ex-husband) makes it easier for the mother to manipulate the child and to have a certain supremacy over the other members of the family and possibly also over her new partner. Out of all the family "left" on the wife's side (her parents, brothers and sisters, and, of course, her children) it is she who holds the status of the most knowledgeable evaluator of what the "enemy" (the ex-husband) intends to do and what precautionary measures should be taken, etc.

The Preventively Practical Motive

If the parent is trying to establish a new relationship with a new partner, he or she can procure this person more easily (and strongly) if he or she shows that the previous relationship is definitely over, is irreconcilable and, of course, will involve as little contact as possible. In the opposite case (a nonproblematic course of contact with a child, peaceful dealings with the ex-spouse about important matters concerning the child, or even more frequent contact between the parent and the child than was agreed to in court) the new partner could have doubts such as: "But she is showing him that she is open for discussion." "What if his ex-wife wants reconciliation?! After all, my partner is quite a nice person. . . ." etc.

Worries About Losing the Child Completely

Older children can enforce their emotional preferences. The day they legally become adults they do not have to ask their mothers' permission to live somewhere else. Some older children manage to have their own way even if they are still a long way from legal adulthood.

To the six motives for setting a child against his other parent and preventing contact with the other parent just mentioned, we will now add the motive of parents wanting children to "follow in their footsteps." The motives, then, are as follows:

1. The motive of revenge.
2. The motive of protection or "protection" of the child.
3. The motive of security.
4. The motive of power.
5. The preventively practical motive.
6. The motive of worries about losing the child completely.
7. The motive of forming a child's psyche.

How can we find out which one of the motives is the strongest, the most long lasting? Direct research is methodologically difficult because people often do not realize their negative motives and if they do, they hate to admit them. Let's think, then, of the indirect indicators of what people really want to achieve, or what is mainly on their minds. The wishes of dying people could be one such indisputable indicator. We will mention one such discovery, from the work of a leading thanatologist, Elisabeth Kübler-Ross:

> What kind of hope do dying patients express when they have reached the state of acceptance, inner calm? Their hope is often connected with the closest people whom they are leaving, patients express hope that after their lives have finished some memory will be left in the world, some trace of them, hope that they have managed to raise their children so that they would be able to provide for themselves, hope that God will accept them to his garden. (1993, page 138)

The inscriptions on gravestones express a positive relationship with the deceased and put in concrete terms something they would wish. Regularly we meet with an assurance that the deceased are remembered and that they are not forgotten. One inscription expresses this: "The one who lives in memories has not died."

An Unexpected (but Probably True) Title

It seems that the "formative" motive is the strongest one, at least from the long-term perspective.

Two of the motives mentioned, namely motive No. 2 (protection or protection of the child) and No. 6 (worries about losing the child completely later on) are very close in their content to motive No. 7 "forming the child's psyche." This issue deserves serious research. If research continues to support our sense of these motives, then the way we look at custody/divorce fights over a child and the after-divorce contact with a child will certainly change.

It seems that with the exception of cases of real pathology, the intention to appropriate the moldable psyche of the child for oneself plays an important role – to steal the other parents' "half." The human tendency to steal was described earlier. We are especially tempted to steal if (1) a high value is involved, (2) we are unlikely to be a suspect, and (3) even if the theft were discovered we would not be punished. This kind of theft is not indictable. A parent forming a child's soul can unknowingly feel extremely powerful. The title of Erich Fromm's work *You will be like Gods* (1993) springs to mind. As if the string of human desire to survive was stretched to its magic limit.

THE MORAL LESSON

What lesson does this offer? In principle just one thing: If you hear one parent saying very convincingly that married life was terrible and how he or she had to (1) return to his or her parents, (2) move to his or her new partner's place, (3) leave for the asylum, (4) or rent a new apartment, then it might be the truth. However, it might not be. Ask the control question: "Isn't the child missing something if contact with the other parent has decreased so dramatically?" You may hear practically nothing. Then everything becomes clear, because at that moment you know that the forming of the child's soul was already "taken care of." It was already marked out. The child's tears have already dried and the trauma will be forgotten. But why then is an excellent psychological study on early childhood trauma called *Soul Murder* (Shengold, 1995)?

REFERENCES

Badinter, Elisabeth (1995). Die Revolution der Väter. In *Denkanstösse. Ein Lesebuch aus Philosophie, Natur- und Humanwissenschaften.* München: Piper.

Bakalář, E., Novák, D., Nováková, M. (1996). *Divorce guide.* Prague: Lidové Noviny.

Blackmore, Susan (1999). *The Meme Machine.* New York: Oxford University Press.

Blankenhorn, David (1996). *Fatherless America: Confronting our most urgent social problem.* New York: Harper Perennial.

Bly, Robert (1999). *Iron John.* Prague: Argo.

Buss, David (1999). *Evolutionary psychology: The new science of the mind.* Needham Heights, MA: Allyn & Bacon.

Conway, David (1998). *The free-market feminism.* London: IEA Health and Welfare Unit.

Corneau, Guy (1993). *Abwesende Väter – Verlorene Söhne. Die Suche nach der männlichen Identität.* Solothurn und Düsseldorf: Walter – Verlag AG.

Dennis, Norman, Erdos, George (1993). *Families without fatherhood.* London: IEA Health and Welfare Unit.

Fromm, Erich (1993). *You will be like Gods.* Prague: Nakladatelství Lidové Noviny.

Gardner, R.A. (1998). *The Parental Alienation Syndrome: A guide for mental health and legal professionals.* Second Edition. Cresskill, New Jersey: Creative Therapeutics.

K.C. (2000). *Where's daddy? The mythologies behind custody-access-support.* Richmond, VA: Harbinger Press.

Kübler-Ross, Elisabeth (1993). *Questions and answers about death and dying.* Turnov: Arica.

Shengold, Leonard (1995). *Soul murder. (Seelenmord - die Anwirkungen von Missbrauch und Vernachlässigung in der Kindheit.)* Franktfurt am Main: Brandes & Apsel Verlag.

Vogt, G.M., Sirridge, S.T. (1993). *Söhne ohne Väter. Wom Fehlen des männlichen Vorbildes.* Franktfurt am Main: Fischer Verlag.

Chapter 24

PSYCHOLOGICAL CONSEQUENCES OF PAS INDOCTRINATION FOR ADULT CHILDREN OF DIVORCE AND THE EFFECTS OF ALIENATION ON PARENTS

WILFRID VON BOCH-GALHAU AND URSULA KODJOE
(TRANSLATED FROM GERMAN BY CHRISTIAN T. DUM)

OVERVIEW

From the viewpoint of psychiatry and psychotherapy, PAS, according to the symptoms described by Dr. Richard Gardner, is to be seen as a special subcategory of parental alienation in separation/divorce conflicts, with an accompanying disorder in the child due to severe manipulative (indoctrinating) parental misconduct. The induction of PAS in the child must be considered a form of psychological/emotional abuse. It can be connected with traumatizing long-term effects in the child that endure into adulthood. It is difficult to understand that this phenomenon – despite corresponding clinical findings and despite relevant results of recent traumatology and victimology research – is still trivialized, denied, or even opposed by many experts. Science is dealing extensively with the consequences for children and young adults of the loss of parent-child contact. However, there is far less research and literature about the consequences for fathers and mothers who permanently lose contact with their children due to institutional intervention and family dynamic reasons. This loss of contact greatly impairs life organization and quality of life.

PSYCHIATRIC AND PSYCHOSOMATIC CONSEQUENCES OF PAS INDOCTRINATION FOR ADULT CHILDREN OF DIVORCE

Parental alienation syndrome (PAS) is not merely obstruction of visitation by a parent, or any kind of contact refusal by a child with the nonresident parent – as many believe – but a psychiatrically relevant disorder of the child (Gardner, 1998, 2002, 2003; Warshak, 2003; Camps, 2003). In contrast to other, psychodynamic explanations of children's refusal of contact, PAS is usually connected with massive visitation interference or obstruction and manipulation or indoctrination.

Active manipulation is carried out – consciously or not – by the parent raising the child and/or any other person the child is dependent upon. The child's negative attitude in PAS cases is not based upon actual negative experience with the rejected parent (*otherwise one cannot speak of PAS*). Important factors in the development of PAS are denigration, reality-distorting images of the other parent, disruption of contact (Klenner, 1995), goal-oriented disinformation, or confusing double-bind-messages (Clawar and Rivlin, 1991). The child's loyalty conflict is exacerbated. Of paramount significance in the emergence of the child's symptoms are fear, dependence, and identification with the alienator. Related psychodynamics can be found, for example, in the Stockholm syndrome, after kidnappings, or in cults.

The induction of PAS must be perceived as emotional or narcissistic child abuse (Gardner, 1998, 2001a; van Gyseghem, 1999; Jopt, 1998; Heyne, 1996; Dulz and Schneider, 1999; Eckhardt-Henn, 2000). ICD 10 (1994) contains "psychological abuse" under diagnose number T 74.3 (Deutsches Institut für medizinische Dokumentation und Information [DIMDI], 1994). From a legal point of view, PAS is to be classified as psychological harm to the child's welfare by abusive exercise of parental custody, in the sense of Section 1666 of the German civil code (c.f. Kodjoe and

Koeppel, 1998a,b, and also OLG [Oberlandesgericht = Appellate Court] Frankfurt/M. 6WF168/00 of October 26, 2000, in FamRZ 48 (10) 2001, p. 638). This fact, unfortunately, is often played down or even denied by the numerous critics of the PAS concept (recently e.g., Bruch, 2001, 2002 and others, thus reducing the problem to parental conflict or loyalty conflict connected with separation or divorce (e.g., Salzgeber & Stadler, 1998; Salzgeber et al. 1999; Stadler & Salzgeber, 1999; Lehmkuhl and Lehmkuhl, 1999; Fegert, 2001; Dettenborn, 2001). As a result, the necessary decisive psychological or legal interventions are frequently neglected or dragged out. In severe PAS cases frequently a long-term, or a permanent rupture of the relation and contact between the child and the once-loved parent results. Rupture of the relation sometimes happens also between siblings.

The severe traumatization of the PAS child, the left-behind parent, and other close relatives (e.g., grandparents) is rarely taken into adequate consideration (van der Kolk et al. 1996, 2000; Kodjoe, 2000; Suren, 2001). Such traumatized people can frequently later be found in psychiatric or psychotherapeutic practices and clinics with considerable psychological, psychosomatic, and psychiatric problems (Napp-Peters, 1995; Franz et al. 1999; Franz et al. 2000; Bron et al. 1991; Paris, 2000; Kernberg et al. 2000).

PAS causes a systematic confusion of the child's awareness and self-awareness, and deep-seated self-alienation. The PAS child has lost the ability to trust his or her own feelings and cognition. The child is completely and utterly dependent upon the programming parent, having lost his or her sense of reality and his or her own self-concept. The child's identity becomes undermined, faded and cracked. Negative self-assessment, a lack of self-esteem, and deep-seated insecurity are the consequences (Finkelstein, 2003).

Subjected to strong pressures for adaptation and loyalty to the alienating parent, the child learns to adjust to the expectations of others. A clear individuality and autonomy cannot develop under these circumstances. Severe, often hardly curable personality disorders can develop – the phenomenon of the "false self" (Winnicott, 1990). We find this phenomenon, for example, in eating disorders, addictions, and other psychosomatic disorders. "Who am I?" "What do I think?" "What do I really feel?" These questions are for those affected often with lifelong, tormenting sources of uncertainty.

The affected child's self and core is even more harmed by the heteronomous active rejection, denial, and negative casting of an originally loved parent than by the actual loss itself (as, for example, by death). Both, considerable guilt feelings and the parental contribution to one's own personality traits, have to be strongly suppressed or dissociated, "amputated," metaphorically speaking. This hampers or even prevents the child from detaching himself or herself in puberty from the idealized custodial parent as well as from the denigrated parent. As a consequence, further long-term developmental problems may result.

Unresolved pathological symbiotic complexes, as present in PAS, are at the core of so-called "ego illnesses," which range from psychiatric illnesses to borderline personality disorder, depression, anxiety disorders, sexual disorders and deviations, to addiction and psychosomatic illness. Less severe cases may be without obvious pathological findings, yet they still considerably impair the quality of the affected person's life (von Uexküll, 1996; Mentzos, 1998; Dulz and Schneider, 1999; Kernberg et al. 2000; Bäuerle and Moll-Strobel, 2001; von Boch-Galhau et al. 2003).

PAS children learn a pattern of extremes, either subjugation or total control in relationships (bow to superiors or kick underlings). Because – in their experience – love and attachment can be abused to control and manipulate others, subsequent intimacy and affection are accepted with difficulty in many instances, due to fear of renewed identity-destroying manipulation. The repercussions include difficulties in forming appropriate closeness and distance in relationships.

Emotional or narcissistic abuse is frequently very difficult to identify, because it is often not done with the intention to harm, but appears under the guise of love. Yet, considering its disastrous and lasting psychopathological effects, it should not be any more tolerated than other forms of abuse. Children must be protected from it (Gardner, 1998, 2001a,b, 2002, 2003; Clawar and Rivlin, 1991; Fischer and Riedesser, 1998; Andritzky, 2002).

When assessing the child's supposed will, it must be carefully observed whether what is said pertains to the child's actual will or whether it arises from manipulation, and also whether certain measures, for example, preventing contact, are actually necessary and beneficial for the child or whether they are detrimental. In general, maintaining or restoring the child's developed attachment to his or her mother and father is a central aspect of the child's well-being, and tolerating these bonds should be a fundamental criterion for awarding custody.

CONSEQUENCES OF ALIENATION AND LOSS OF CONTACT FOR AFFECTED PARENTS

The short-term and long-term effects of loss of contact with one parent on personality development of children have been researched for a long time. However, very little research, literature, or discussion concerning the effects on parents exists. This section deals with the effects of loss of contact with one's own child on parents' personality development, their satisfaction in life, and quality of life. These matters are closely connected to the entire complex of relationships in the family system after separation and divorce.

With the transition to parenthood, the life cycle of a couple enters a phase which for both of them, as well as for their child, poses a specific developmental task: the mutual development of attachment and relationship (Schneewind, 1985; Levinson, 1978; Lamb, 1986). With this attachment to the child the assumption of the roles of mother and fathers – in the diverse forms of primary love objects, caretakers, protectors, educators, providers, and role models – the mother and father identity and personality develop in conjunction with the personality development of the child.

Society does not question the development of a mother identity or the close relationship of mother and child and their mutual love. The development of the father, his identification with the role of father and his affiliation with and love for the child, is different. After a separation the parental qualities of fathers are frequently questioned or devalued.

With the birth of the first child, awareness can develop in the "new father" about what his own father meant to him and taught him about life, what he missed as a child, what he had wished for, and what he had needed. From this experience with his own father an extended self-concept – his own father ideal – develops, which he wants to fulfill. The care and responsibility for the family stabilize his total identity and secure his external social recognition.

According to existing evidence from research, the loss of togetherness of father and child, along with an insecure visitation arrangement, is connected with massive deterioration of the father's identity, self-concept, and self-esteem (Napp-Peters, 1987, 1995). The loss is clearly far more severe in the case of total severance of contact. Only with difficulty can one come to terms, in a kind of mourning process, with the loss of a still living, yet (through family dynamical internal processes and external judicial and institutional intervention) unreachable child, and overcome and accept this loss. Understanding and empathy exist in the social environment only in a limited manner for men in general and fathers in particular in cases of separation, compared to that which exists for women and mothers with whom the children still live. In interdisciplinary research one frequently finds in fathers without contact with their children psychological and physical destabilization, a collapse of the self-concept, identity crises, and various psychosomatic illnesses, as well as an increased rate of accidents and suicides (Hetherington et al. 1982). Analogous data for alienated mothers do not exist.

Some fathers are so incapacited, they do not attend work, they do attend work; some become workaholics. Both reactions have multiple psychosomatic effects. Studies of separated families (Hetherington et al. 1982; Hess and Camara, 1979; Keshet and Rosenthal, 1978; Napp-Peters, 1987, 1995; Wallerstein and Kelly, 1980) clearly show that in addition to these effects, the adjustment of fathers, their coming to terms with the separation event, and their psychological and physical states a few years after divorce is connected with the maintenance of a close relationship with their children.

The loss of the external and internal role as a father can cause an irreparable destruction of the entire identity. This can lead to deep sorrow, from which the father recovers only with difficulty or never at all. Even many years after the loss of contact, the psychological tenor can still be governed by feelings of guilt and shame about the betrayal of one's father ideals (Petri, 1999). Feelings of powerlessness and helplessness and lack of self-worth frequently lead to being stuck in a passive role of victim and to the unloading of responsibility for other aspects of one's life. For these reasons, one can appropriately speak of a "rupture in the biography" of parents who, despite all efforts, have lost all contact with their children, can no longer contribute to the children's development and cannot even take part in the children's lives (Kodjoe and Wiestler, 1994).

Mothers are increasingly experiencing this fate. The forced rupture of mother-child contact has comparable consequences. Differences arise from the different socialization of men and women, the psychophysiological structure of women versus that of men, and the biologically-based development of the mother-child attachment during pregnancy and birth and in the first few months of life. A close emotional attachment exists between mother and child due to her being the primary person of reference. For some time, the children often are also the primary sources of identification for caretaking mothers.

A social environment that is attached to an almost mystic mother ideal responds with prejudice toward and distrust of mothers who, after a separation, lose contact with their children. In these cases mothers frequently experience, in a painful manner, additional rejection, even from their families of origin, at a time when they most need understanding and support. They react, out of fear of further traumatization, with withdrawal and depression, rather than with an active confrontation of the problem. This kind of powerless paralysis, which frequently afflicts mothers facing separation from their own children, shows symptoms of "acquired helplessness" (Seligman, 1992). This can further the development of psychosomatic illnesses.

An intact, active parent-child relationship is only one factor for general satisfaction in the lives of fathers and mothers. This factor, however, affects all other aspects of life and deeply influences the quality, the plans and the course of one's own life.

The following taped interviews illustrate the issues just discussed.

INTERVIEW ONE

S, 20 years old, student

Five years without contact with her father, lives now with her father, but, as a result, separated from her mother and two alienated siblings:

UK: May I present to you S. It is best if she, herself, tells you how it came about that she now lives with her father.

S: My name is S. My story began when I was 11 years old. At that time my mother told me and my siblings that she is getting a divorce. My father was abroad at the time. She gave us a choice – either we can come along with her or we can stay where we are. If we are not joining her, we would also not see her again. As we were alone with her at the time, we had no choice but to go with her. From this time on we practically had no contact with our father, only in court, or at the youth welfare authority, but no other contacts.

UK: How old were your siblings then?

S: My sister was almost 14; my brother was 8.

UK: You lived with your mother in K. Didn't you see your father, or weren't you allowed to see him? How did you feel about it? What happened?

S: When we talked about him, my mother denigrated him, as if he would harm us. She presented him to us as if he were a monster. She induced real feelings of fear in us, so badly that we had nightmares. In this way we really had problems to recall the happy times when we still did things with our father. When we referred to these times, she only responded: "If you go join your father then you will never see me again." We constantly heard this threat.

UK: Could you talk about it between you and your siblings?

S: Yes, at the beginning, but later on we didn't, because we saw no more sense in it.

UK: What do you think – what kind of support would you have needed then?

S: I think I would have needed more support from the youth welfare authority. The case workers – whenever they were newly assigned – visited and talked to us. They, however, were not especially understanding, they simply spooled off their list; that was it. They should have paid more attention to us and related to us in a more personal manner. As to the judge, we had also wished for someone who would be friendlier, in a more personal manner, with children. Also, he only posed his questions; it did not matter to him how we felt about it. He just carried out his program, whether we shed tears or not.

UK: Was there anybody at all at this point in time by whom you felt understood, with whom you could talk about how you felt?

S: Nobody, from the authorities – nobody.

UK: And within your family – except for your mother – with the grandparents perhaps?

S: My mother has completely isolated us; we even had then no more contact with her own family. My mother, my siblings, and I were totally isolated. There was no way to establish contacts.

UK: How has the situation then changed for you?

S: At about age 15 or16 I felt somehow a deep inner conflict. On the one hand, there was my mother, but I also knew that there was my father. My memories returned. Somehow I wanted to know the truth. Thus, I began to build a contact by letter with my father, although this turned out to be very difficult, because my mother was strongly against it. Because of it, I had lots of trouble with her. I had to insist on my way and this was very difficult for me.

UK: Did your siblings undertake similar activities?

S: At the beginning my sister also tried to write letters to him. She made the mistake, however, to show the letters to my mother. My mother interpreted every sentence to the effect that my father would attack her personally for it. My sister believed this and consequently terminated the contact.

UK: How did things continue in your case?

S: I forbade my mother from the beginning to read the letters. I told her "You cannot touch them." I called my father and then found out that he was no monster at all, the way my mother always pictured him. I noticed that he really was the father that I remembered – in a happy memory. What always came back were these happy memories. As the situation became more and more difficult, because my mother was strictly against these contacts and I could not endure it anymore, I asked my father to get me out of there.

UK: Did I understand you correctly: The situation at home became more and more unbearable, because you refused to have this contact with your father taken away from you?

S: I was hit and was berated – almost daily. I simply could not endure it anymore.

UK: Was there solidarity, a kind of coalition between mother and siblings against you?

S: I also heard from them that I should not leave for my father. My siblings made it clear to me: "Either we all maintain contacts with daddy or nobody." Thus, I should not do it either.

UK: But you still did? How do you recall the time when you made this decision? When you left – how did you feel about it?

S: At the beginning I was doing badly, but I also felt relieved. I was somehow happy to finally have escaped from this critical situation, to have succeeded, finally finding out who and how my father really was, and to not have to endure all these lies.

UK: How was the start with your father?

S: At first we had a very distant relationship, because we were missing five years without intensive contact. These contacts had to be rebuilt step by step.

UK: How long did this take?

S: I now have lived with my father for three years.

UK: What kind of relation do you have now with your siblings and your mother?

S: I met my mother twice after I had left. I had to endure admonishments from her as to the effect that I am unfeeling, that I abandoned her, and that, as a result, I have caused her financial difficulties. As to my brother: I was at first not allowed to talk to him on the phone, thus I could not develop any contacts with him. My mother had told him that I had left just out of a mood. She did not tell the truth. When I told him the truth, he did not believe me. With my sister I only had fights over it. She also terminated the contacts with me.

UK: How do you feel now about it – about this rupture of contacts?

S: It is damned difficult. I love my siblings and I wish that I could reestablish the contacts with them.

UK: Do you have an idea how this could be accomplished?

S: I cannot do anything about my sister, because she has already reached legal maturity. However, with respect to my brother – he is 16 – it may be possible that I can get my legal rights granted to have contact with him and that I then can enlighten him about the situation, about what really happened. Perhaps in this manner we can rebuild a relationship.

UK: This is what you decided?

S: Yes!

v. B-G: May I ask you an additional question? In this conference we intensively thought about measures that could be taken when a child absolutely does not want to see or visit his or her separated parent. What would you have wished for at the time – that the youth welfare authority or the family court interferes more strongly? For example, that you would have been forced in some manner to see your father? This was a very difficult question in the entire discussion we had.

S: I think that this would have been a good solution, because then we would not have had this kind of bad conscience with respect to my mother. We simply could have said: "We are forced; there is nothing we can do about it," and she would have had to accept it.

UK: Thank you very much!

INTERVIEW TWO

D, 42 years old, press officer
Mother affected by alienation from children.

v. B-G: You are Mrs. D. We have met about a year ago. Would you like to tell us a bit about your experience with your children, how it developed in the past few years and how you feel about it today?

D: Perhaps I should start at the point where the separation occurred. This was three years ago, in a dramatic action at dead of night. I freed myself from a 23-year verbally, and also physically abusive marriage. It was not possible for me in this night to also take my children along; who at that time were 13 and 16 years old. My husband was already – for health reasons – in early retirement. I worked. After that night, in which I had left the house, I was more or less without financial means. We agreed afterwards that the children should for the time being stay with my ex-husband in their familiar environment, also because he was taking care of the household, not being employed. This agreement worked for one year – more or less.

It was already foreseeable that tendencies of alienation were developing insidiously. However, this term was not familiar to me at the time. I had a lawyer and also a therapist. However, neither the lawyer nor the therapist knew anything or told me anything about PAS when I began to talk about the problems and told them: "This or that had happened" or "I cannot reach my children" or "Something is wrong." By accident – while searching with the entry "borderline" – I found about three-fourth years later an internet page with the keyword PAS. It was like an "aha" experience for me – to learn that what I experience has a name. In the meantime, however, almost a year had passed and this was, of course, valuable time lost. My daughter still visited me regularly – my son too – but it was made more and more difficult.

v. B-G: How old are your children?

D: The children are now 19 (son) and 16 (daughter). I have not seen them for two years now, with one exception: In April a meeting took place about which I will tell more later on. My chief problem was the following: When I began, with the help of my lawyer, who represented me out of court, to become active, it was only a beginning, until I had a lawyer who had tried to familiarize himself with the PAS problem. When, finally, the youth welfare authority was ready to hear my daughter, the alienation was already present, i.e., the contact with my children was already severed.

v. B-G: How did your children react?

D: There is one very grave example which shows what happened. It was made more and more difficult for my daughter to visit me on weekends. When I called her, I could only extract a "yes" or "no" from her. This was an indication for me and I knew then that her father was nearby. When she was on the phone without her father present, she was totally relaxed. She then was able to interact with me in a totally normal manner, talk to me and tell me what she was doing. On weekends, it was very difficult. She was not allowed to tell her father when I had met members of my own family. Then the following happened: My son – he had already distanced himself – relayed through my daughter: "If you don't return to the side of your husband then you will never see me again." He carried out this threat. What happened then was that my husband gave my daughter the choice: "You either join your mother, then you will never see us again; or you stay with us, then you will not see your mother anymore."

v. B-G: Who said that?

D: My ex-husband as well as my son. My daughter could not be subjugated during this night. She said: "I will join my mother then." They packed – against her will – all of her clothes into a suitcase. The school bag, also the Rollerblades, was placed during the night at my doorstep. My daughter was totally beside herself, had cried all night in desperation. The result was that she and I withdrew for five days. Then my husband called and told our daughter: "You can – if you want – return and see Mom whenever you want to." I asked her to stay, but because of her living environment, school and friends, and also because of her brother, she wanted to return.

v. B-G: What did you undertake then?

D: I heavyheartedly drove her back, corresponding to her wish. This really was the beginning of the end. From this moment on, the influence of my son and my husband took place on another level. They influenced her in another way: On December 23 they left this choice to her: "Either you stay here on Christmas Eve or you never see us again."

v. B-G: How did you conclude that she was influenced?

D: From what my husband had decided with the children and from how my husband talked about me (my son, for example, talked about the "ex-mother").

v. B-G: Thus, a massive denigration.

D: An extremely massive denigration.

v. B-G: You talked about letters which you had received.

D: Perhaps I should first tell you about the meeting in which I saw my children. The last time I saw my children (this was in April), after I had sued for sole custody, with the help of Ms. Kodjoe, my son – not my ex-husband – had arranged a meeting with my lawyer, sent faxes there and called me in the evening, very briefly, asking for a meeting between my daughter, him, and me. I agreed and the next day he arrived. He rang my cell phone and told me that he is downstairs, I should come down. I went downstairs; but could not see them at first. The car of my ex-husband was parked nearby and in it were my son and my daughter. My son had driven. He beckoned to me that I should enter the car, indicating the backseat with his finger.

v. B-G: Thus, a complete reversal of who is here – the adult – and who is here – child or adolescent.

D: Yes, completely, he also assumed his role in this manner.

v. B-G: An extremely empowered adolescent.

D: Yes. I opened the door and said "Good day." I said "Why don't you come out?" "No," he said I should get in. "We are leaving." Then I said "Let us walk around here." "No," he said he cannot find a parking spot here. "Get in." We drove away. I saw a free parking spot. "Let us walk here, if you want." He said "For a royal meeting a royal place." We continued and I said to him "If it is a talk, this is O.K." My son said "Are you afraid that we are going to kill you? The cemetery is in the other direction."

v. B-G: You told me that you informed the youth welfare authority and that it was considered to call criminal police, in order to set limits to his behavior.

D: In parallel there were massive threats by my husband against me. Therefore – this was the reasoning of the youth welfare authority, as well as of my lawyer – one cannot intervene. The youth welfare office told me that custody should be taken away immediately from this man, but because of the threatening situation they saw no possibility for it. They suggested to the court in three lines, without the supporting arguments that would be required, that a guardian ad litem should be appointed. This, of course, was immediately criticized by the other side: How could the court appoint a guardian ad litem, without supporting arguments by the youth welfare authority? From the viewpoint of the youth welfare authority and lawyer the situation seemed simply too dangerous.

v. B-G: Was a psychiatrist involved?

D: No, there was absolute noncooperation. There was a meeting arranged at a psychologist between my husband and me. He constantly terminated the conversation – just as at the youth welfare office. He did not last for three-fourths of an hour in the discussions with me. He got up, interrupted the meeting, and left. There was also a meeting between the youth welfare authority and my daughter. She blocked any conversation with "No comment" as soon as it turned to me. Otherwise, it was a very pleasant conversation.

v. B-G: Exclusion and alienation are an experience which is frequently connected with men. How is this experience for you now, as a woman? Did you meet other women with whom you could exchange your experience?

D: Both ways. I met, of course, in the course of time, similarly affected women. There are more and more affected women. This is becoming apparent. To deal with it is infinitely painful and difficult. It is not only that one has lost the children, also the time is irretrievable. When I then hear about the studies of Professor Jopt, that often nothing will change, it is difficult to carry on. One also has one's feelings as a mother which are amputated from one day to the next, i. e., it is not possible to carry on. Where to put the emotions, the mothering in which one was just engulfed? Not only that. Everything is severed: the life plan, the plans for the family – everything is gone. Everything is put into question and gone. A purpose is searched, the meaninglessness becomes evident. One has to reflect anew on what should happen.

v. B-G: You terminated the proceedings at a certain point.

D: After the guardian ad litem was appointed, my husband has appealed again and again and constantly came up with new arguments and stories. The guardian ad litem could not do his job, as long as there were appeals. It was said, as long as there is an appeal, the guardian ad litem cannot be mandated. For these reasons, I said to myself, "Now it is enough," and withdrew my request for sole custody. We have joint custody, which, however, I cannot exercise, not in any way. I cannot fulfill my duties nor exercise my rights. For these reasons I withdrew my request. I told myself: It cannot be in my interest to force my daughter (it does not concern my son anymore) to my side by legal action. Only if she wants to come voluntarily does it make sense. I am ready at any time; I also maintain contacts in that I still write to her, send parcels – only that everything is returned. I still send e-mail, even when only what I write into the reference line cannot be erased. This, I still do. Everything is still returned to me.

v. B-G: At what point along the road do you think intervention of the involved institutions would have been helpful?

D: It would have been helpful if my attorney had known anything about PAS. Just as important it would have been if my therapist had known anything about it. The proceedings at the youth welfare office were relatively prompt, judging from what I hear from others – for me, they took much too long. And I felt, as much effort the youth welfare authority may have made – they even had extra supervision – they felt unable to deal with the situation. I had the feeling they were at the end of their options, they no longer had means to really intervene, and they also shied away from the necessary decision. This decision would necessarily have been: We remove the child from there. One was, of course, terribly afraid of the possible consequences.

v. B-G: Has the behavior of your son shown aggressiveness only against you, or also against other persons or in school, for example?

D: My son has, according to what I just heard, completed high school with great success. My daughter is top ranked in her grade (I have contact with her teacher). Thus, the social environment seems intact. However, they have no contact whatsoever with my family of origin. Even the contact to the family of my ex-husband has been completely severed, also with anybody who in any way has contact with me. These patterns are all very prominent.

v. B-G: I thank you for your openness!

INTERVIEW THREE

B, 39 years old, civil service employee

Father of a nine-year-old daughter and 11- and 13-year-old sons.

The children suffered from severe PAS. For three years now they have lived with their father, who was awarded sole custody by the court because of unmanageable, severe manipulation by the mother.

UK: When we met, your three children lived with their mother. Today they live with you. Would you, please, briefly describe how this happened?

B: The trigger for this transfer of the children, who after the return of their mother to her hometown had vehemently and totally irrationally rejected me, was the compulsory hospitalization of my former wife in a psychiatric ward. The youth welfare office in charge, which at first had opposed the transfer, now considered it appropriate that the children be transferred to me. Because of unmanageable, severe manipulation of the children by the mother, the family court considered it necessary to withdraw custody rights from the mother and transfer custody and residence rights to me. I believe also in my case it was considered at first, if it would not be better to place the children in a shelter or foster home. I have strongly intervened against such plans – thank God, with success.

The mother was granted extensive visitation rights. Because – due to her illness – she continued her efforts to indoctrinate the children against me, her visitation rights were suspended a few months ago. The children at present, however, regularly call their mother and also have letter and e-mail contacts.

The extremely difficult, but persistent effort of the guardian ad litem whom we had at the time was very helpful in this very complicated situation. Based upon the experience with this guardian ad litem, I consider the institution of guardian ad litem as very helpful in high-conflict custody cases, although certainly dependent upon the personality and competence of the appointee.

After what I experienced with three strongly manipulated children, I would like to suggest that more courageous custody – and visitation rights decisions are issued in the case of PAS children. Our children suffered, according to the clinical classification by Professor Gardner, from PAS of the severe degree, with a totally entrenched, radical, and unjustified attitude of rejection against me as well as against the entire paternal environment [e.g., grandmother, with whom they previously had a loving and warm relationship].

I showed you a drawing which my son – encouraged by his mother – made in the office of two guardians ad litem: "Everybody is very decent; only my daddy is an ass." My children were completely indoctrinated against me.

UK: What happened during the transfer of the children to you?

B: After the court-ordered transfer of the children to me, their belligerent attitude of rejection eased within hours. In case of the older children it took about three hours until they gave up their resistance. The daughter, at that time only 5, at first cried along, but after about 10–15 minutes started playing with the toys which had been readied for her. In the evening of that day a relaxed atmosphere reigned, with all the children caressing me. Yet, true coping of the older children with the situation started only after about one and a half years.

I have in the discussions of the last two days heard from various experts' concerns that children would again be traumatized by removal from the influence of the programming parent, transfer of custody and residence to the alienating parent, and reduction of visitation with the irrationally manipulative parent.

I consider this to be wrong. Let me elaborate: When my children, after my leaving the home, called me names and hit me, I began to inform myself. This was in 1999. I heard for the first time about the PAS phenomenon in a lecture by Professor Jopt. For the first time I understood then what had occurred in our desperately messed-up family situation. It had been an intense strain on me to barely be able to understand and categorize the sudden onset of a hostile campaign by the children in rejection of me and the entire paternal environment. In due course I underwent psychological counseling in order to gain a better understanding of the situation, also for assessing my own contributions to the situation and to develop appropriate strategies, rather than to simply withdraw from the children. The extreme strain on me was constituted, among other things, by the fact that the youth welfare office did not recognize the then already existing mental illness of my former wife and repeatedly advised me that I should withdraw and let peace enter. As time showed, this was very bad advice! It required the compulsory hospitalization of my former wife before the responsible people could no longer ignore the possible harm to the children.

The worst moment of my life came when the official in charge at the youth welfare authority told me that I should undergo psychotherapy in order to understand why my children reject me.

UK: How have the children now adjusted to life with you and how do you cope with the situation as a single parent?

B: It finally happened – as I already told you – that the children, despite their vehement, but superficial objection, were transferred to me. The children, as a supportive measure, are since seeing psychologists. Over a longer period I was also included in every second therapy session. About January of this year (after about 1½ years) my younger son suddenly began to open up. Until then he always said: "Oh, this does not matter to me that I now live with you; I am a boy and I take this easy." Such phrases he had repeatedly professed in a stereotypical manner. In January of this year he suddenly began to tell the psychologist about the time when he was living with his mother. At this time he was only 9 years old. The boy told similar things to what we just heard in the first interview. He told, for example, about a party his mother had organized after I had left the home. The children had wanted to cry, but instead they were supposed to celebrate. A year after I had left they had to have another anniversary celebration, "that this asshole isn't here anymore." I believe that, with the help of the created reality after the change of residence in which the children found out that in truth I am not a monster (as they had been indoctrinated) and with the help of psychotherapy, the children could slowly begin to understand what the actual situation is like and how much they had been manipulated – as a result of the mother's mental illness.

My younger son intensively begs me now that nothing is said about his now critical views on the experience with his mother. He reports that the mother even today still asks on the phone again and again: "Did the asshole hit you again?" He tells me afterwards: "I again said 'Yes.' Mommy is so strong. I don't want to say

'Yes,' but I also don't want to say 'No.' When I say 'No,' I lose Mommy." He had carefully observed that everybody who opposes his mother's views is eliminated in some manner, that they are evil in her view, and that they are banned from her life. For these reasons he panics with fear to say "No" to his mother.

UK: Do the children have contact with their mother?

B: With the help of the court, youth welfare authority, and guardian ad litem, it was tried to establish a generous visitation arrangement with the mother. After the transfer of the children to me, visitation had been suspended by the court for about half a year. I visited, however, the mother about every four weeks with the children in the psychiatric ward.

As a rule, a walk of the mother with the children in the (locked) clinic garden took place during which I stayed in the background. After about six months (and the release from the ward) my former wife had three hours of supervised visitation every two weeks.

Then, reasonable visitation arrangements worked for about twenty months, which had been suspended once, after the mother's relapse. This arrangement included half of the vacation and every second weekend with the mother. I personally accepted and supported this arrangement, because the children wanted to see their mother, although the oldest, at 15 now, spends almost every weekend with friends.

After the last Easter vacation in which the children had spent two weeks with their mother, I suddenly learned from my lawyer that a charge for sexual child abuse has been brought against me by the mother. Then I also learned that my wife refuses to return the children.

My former wife then, without the help of a lawyer – she already had changed lawyers five times – made a request for sole custody. She refused to return the children, claiming that she had to protect them from me. She then barricaded herself with my daughter at her parents' home. The younger son was at her home, with her new partner. The oldest child had not been with her at all. He had been with his school on a skiing vacation.

The judge, who after years of experience was familiar in detail with our family situation, immediately convened a hearing. He issued a very strict decision in that he refused the transfer of custody and ordered the immediate return of the children – if necessary, also by forcible police measures. It was carried out in this manner.

Because of the critical and certainly unusual situation, I want to describe the transfer in some detail. Both children had been, during this vacation, for two weeks with the mother – separated from me. My daughter, because her mother did not want to return her, was taken by the police from the apartment of my former wife's parents and brought to the police station to which I was asked to come and to wait there. It took quite a long time until my daughter was handed over to me. As they wanted to turn her over, she yelled at me: "I hate you. I will kill myself (She is 9 years old!), if I have to return." She continued hysterically: "He hits me, he strangulates me, he has – ouch, ouch, my bottom hurts so much – kicked me." These allegations she continued for some time while the police officers stood next to her, completely helpless. But after she was in my arms it took exactly one minute until she calmed down, stopped yelling and crying, and cuddled with me. In response to my question she said: "Daddy, I love you" and a little later she even confirmed my remark that only a few weeks ago she had said: "You are the most wonderful daddy in the whole world." The child continued to sob and asked: "When do I see Mommy again?" This I considered to be a lot more realistic. There were four or five police officers standing there, gazing with open mouth. They obviously could not believe that a child could change to such a different opinion and behavior within minutes. Later on my daughter told me that she had believed everything and that her mother had told her to behave in this manner. The psychologist raised concerns that the child later on could develop severe psychological problems. The behavior of my daughter – when she was with her mother – she termed "folie à deux."

Now, I am again, for the last six months, together with my children at my place of residence. The visitation with the mother was temporarily suspended but should, as soon as possible, slowly be re-established, with accompanying psychological support, depending on how the mother's behavior presents itself. The children still have psychotherapy twice a week. Their behavior – also in school – is without outward symptoms. They do even very well in school, average to above average in all reports.

They can increasingly well appreciate that the behavior of their mother is so very problematic not because she is "evil," but because she is sick. They constantly ask me if Mommy can get well again. The theme "mother" is constantly present.

It is important for me to tell you about my experience, because I know about other cases in which youth welfare authority, psychological experts and courts intervene in a much less decisive manner and are leaning towards accepting the superficial will of the manipulated children, such that superficial "peace" returns. The children are often, through resignation, left with the alienating parent, even when the behavior of this parent is very conspicuous and also when in this manner the long-term or even permanent rupture of contact to the alienated parent is a likely outcome.

UK: Many thanks!

We would like to thank the young woman, S., who had the courage and openness to speak about the experience she has gone through. We also thank the father, B., and the mother, D., who agreed to talk with us about how they experienced (and experience) the loss of contact with their children. Their motivation was to make it clear to parents what harm they cause their children when, after separation, they stop them from having contacts with the other parent.

CONCLUSIONS

Based on the reported sorrowful experience and the traumatizing long-term psychological effects on parents and children affected by PAS, induction of the syndrome can no longer be considered a private matter. It is necessary to early on take preventive or, as the case may be, counteractive interdisciplinary measures against this impairment of mental health and quality of life. All members of the involved professions should resolutely and consistently intervene for the protection of the child, if one or both parents use the child against the other parent, endangering thus the development of the child and his or her relationship with the other parent.

Experts in the field are probably aware of the lack of support for PAS-affected parents and children and of how necessary cooperation of all persons involved is. The primary goal of this chapter is to state the importance of making the needs of each individual child, and also of mothers and fathers, the center of attention and for employing all the necessary professional and social skills and empathy in dealing with these needs.

REFERENCES

Andritzky, W. (2002). Verhaltensmuster und Persönlichkeitsstruktur entfremdender Eltern: Psychosoziale Diagnostik und Orientierungskriterien für Interventionen. *Psychotherapie in Psychiatrie, Psychotherapeutischer Medizin und Klinischer Psychologie, 7*(2), 166–182.

Bäuerle, S. and Moll-Strobel, H. (2001). *Eltern sägen ihr Kind entzwei, Trennungserfahrungen und Entfremdung von einem Elternteil*. Donauwörth: Auer.

Bron, B., Strack, M. & Rudolph, G. (1991).Childhood experiences of loss and suicide attempts: Significance in depressive states of major depressed and dysthymic or adjustment disordered patients. *Journal of Affective Disorders, 23*, 165–172.

Bruch, Carol S. (2001). Parental Alienation Syndrome: Getting it wrong in child custody cases. *Family Law Quarterly, 35*(3), 527–552.

Bruch, Carol S. (2002). Parental Alienation Syndrome and Parental Alienation: Wie man sich in Sorgerechtsfällen irren kann. *Zeitschrift für das gesamte Familienrecht [FamRZ] 49*(19), 1304–1315.

Camps, Astrid (2003). Psychiatrische und psychosomatische Konsequenzen für PAS-Kinder. In: von Boch-Galhau, W., Kodjoe, U., Andritzky, W., and Koeppel, P. (Eds.): *Psychiatric and psychosomatic consequences for PAS Children.* ibd., pp. 143–155.

Clawar, S. S. & Rivlin, B. V. (1991).*Children held hostage: Dealing with programmed and brainwashed children.* Chicago: American Bar Association, Division of Family Law.

Dettenborn, H. (2001). *Kindeswohl und Kindeswille: Psychologische und rechtliche Aspekte.* München: Ernst Reinhardt.

Deutsches Institut für medizinische Dokumentation und Information (DIMDI) (1994). ICD 10–*Internationale statistische Klassifikation der Krankheiten und verwandter Gesundheitsprobleme*, 10th Revision, Bern: Huber.

Dulz, B. and Schneider, A. (1999). *Borderline-Störungen, Theorie und therapie, 2.* Auflage, Stuttgart: Schattauer.

Eckhardt-Henn, A.(2000). Artifizielle Störungen und Münchhausen-Syndrom. In: Kernberg, O. F., Dulz, B., and Sachsse, U. (Eds.), *Handbuch der Borderline-Störungen* (pp. 331–345) Stuttgart: Schattauer.

Fegert, J. M. (2001). Parental Alienation oder Parental Accusation Syndrome? Die Frage der Suggestibilität, Beeinflussung und Induktion in Umgangsrechtsgutachten. *Kindschaftsrechtliche Praxis [Kind-Prax], 4*(1), 3–7.

Finkelstein, C. (2003).The Heart of an Abducted and Alienated Child/ Sarah or Cecilie – The Identity Issue; In: von Boch-Galhau, W., Kodjoe, U., Andritzky, W., and Koeppel, P. (Eds.) ibd., pp. 175–185.

Fischer, G., and Riedesser, P. (1998). *Lehrbuch der Psychotraumatologie.* München, Basel: Ernst Reinhardt.

Franz, M, Lieberz, K., Schmitz, N., and Schepank, H. (1999). Wenn der Vater fehlt. Epidemiologische Befunde zur Bedeutung früher Abwesenheit des Vaters für die psychische Gesundheit im späteren Leben. *Zsch. Psychosom. Med. 45,* 260–278.

Franz, M., Häfner, S., Lieberz, K., Reister, G., and Tress, W. (2000). Der Spontanverlauf psychogener Beeinträchtigung in einer Bevölkerungsstichprobe über 11 Jahre. *Psychotherapeut, 45,* 99–107.

Gardner, R. A. (1998). *The Parental Alienation Syndrome,* Second Edition. Cresskill, NJ: Creative Therapeutics.

Gardner, R. A. (2001a). *Therapeutic interventions for children with parental alienation syndrome.* Cresskill, NJ: Creative Therapeutics.

Gardner, R. A. (2001b). Should courts order PAS-children to visit/reside with the alienated parent? A Follow-up Study. *American Journal Forensic Psychology, 19*(3), 61–106.

Gardner, R. A. (2002). *Das elterliche Entfremdungssyndrom, Anregungen für gerichtliche Sorge - und Umgangsregelungen.* Berlin, Wissenschaft und Bildung (VWB).

Gardner, R. A. (2003). The Parental Alienation Syndrome – Past, present and future. In von Boch-Galhau, W., Kodjoe, U., Andritzky, W., and Koeppel, P. (Eds.): ibd., pp. 89–124.

Hess, A., and Camara, K. (1979). Postdivorce family relationships. *Journal of Social Issues, 35,* 79–96.

Hetherington, E., Hetherington, G., Cox, R., and Cox, M. (1982). Effects of divorce on parents and children. In Lamb, M. (Ed.), *Nontraditional families. Parenting and child development.* Hillsdale, NJ.: Erlbaum Associates.

Heyne, C. (1996). Die sanfte Gewalt: Narzisstischer Missbrauch. In: Heyne, C. (Ed.): *Täterinnen – offene und versteckte Aggression von Frauen* (pp. 337–356). München: Knaur.

Jopt, U. J. (1998). Wir müssen den seelischen Missbrauch von Kindern verhindern. In: Schmidt A. (Ed.), *Mehr Vater fürs Kind – auch nach Trennung und Scheidung, Wege aus der vaterlosen Gesellschaft* (pp. 224–232). Weinheim: Beltz.

Kernberg, O.F., Dulz, B., and Sachsse, U. (Eds.) (2000). *Handbuch der Borderlinestörungen.* Stuttgart: Schattauer.

Keshet, H. and Rosenthal, K.(1978). Fathering after marital separation. *Social Work, 23,* 11–18.

Klenner, W. (1995). Rituale der Umgangsvereitelung bei getrenntlebenden oder geschiedenen Eltern. *FamRZ, 42*(24), 1529–1535.

Kodjoe, U. (2000). Auswirkungen des Vater-Kind-Kontaktverlustes: der immaterielle Schaden aus psychologischer Sicht - Anmerkungen zur Elsholz-Entscheidung des Europäischen. Gerichtshofes für Menschenrechte. *Der Amtsvormund, 73*(8), 641–643.

Kodjoe, U. & Koeppel, P. (1998a). The Parental Alienation Syndrome (PAS). *Der Amtsvormund, Sonderdruck, 71*(1), 9–26, 135–140.

Kodjoe, U. & Koeppel, P. (1998b). Früherkennung von PAS – Möglichkeiten psychologischer und rechtlicher Interventionen. *Kindschaftsrechtliche Praxis [Kind-Prax]1,* 138–144.

Kodjoe, U., and Wiestler, S. (1994). Unveröffentlichte (unpublished) Diplomarbeit: Die psychosoziale Situation nichtsorgeberechtigter Väter. Universität Freiburg.

Lamb, M. (1986). *The father's role.* New York: John Wiley & Sons.

Lehmkuhl, U., and Lehmkuhl, G. (1999). Wie ernst nehmen wir den Kindeswillen? *Kindschaftsrechtliche Praxis [Kind-Prax], 2*(5), 159–161.

Levinson, D. L. (1978). *The seasons of a man's life.* New York: Knopf.

Mentzos, S. (1998). *Neurotische Konfliktverarbeitung.* Frankfurt: Fischer.

Napp-Peters, A. (1987). Sozialisation durch den Vater – Rollenwandel oder Diversifikation familialer Lebensformen? *Neue Praxis, 17*(5), 413–422.

Napp-Peters, A. (1995). *Familien nach der Scheidung.* München: Kunstmann.

Paris, J. (2000). Kindheitstrauma und Boderline-/Persönlichkeitsstörung. In: Kernberg, O.F., Dulz, B., and Sachsse, U., *Handbuch der Borderlinestörungen* (pp. 159–166). Stuttgart: Schattauer.

Petri, H. (1999). *Das Drama der Vaterentbehrung.* Freiburg: Herder.

Salzgeber, J. and Stadler, M. (1998). Beziehung kontra Erziehung. Kritische Anmerkungen zur aktuellen Rezeption von PAS. *Kindschaftsrechtliche Praxis [KindPrax], 1*(6), 167–171.

Salzgeber, J., Stadler, M., Schmidt, S. M., and Partale, C. (1999). Umgangsprobleme – Ursachen des Kontaktabbruchs durch das Kind jenseits des Parental Alienation Syndrome. 2(4) *Kindschaftsrechtliche Praxis [Kind-Prax] 1*(6), 107–111.

Schneewind, K.-A. (1985). *Der Familienlebenszyklus: Herausforderung für die Psychologische Forschung.* Universität München, Report, October 1985.

Seligman, M. E. (1992). *Erlernte Hilflosigkeit.* Weinheim: Beltz.

Stadler, M., and Salzgeber, J. (1999). Parental Alienation Syndrom (PAS) - alter Wein in neuen Schläuchen? *Familie, Partnerschaft und Recht [FPR], 99*(4), 231–235.

Suren, A. (2001). *Das Parental Alienation Syndrom (PAS) – Belastungsreaktionen und Bewältigungsstrategien betroffener Mütter* (Diplomarbeit an der Fakultät für Psychologie und Sportwissenschaften, Abteilung für Psychologie der Universität), Bielefeld.

van Gyseghem, H. (1999). *Us et Abus de la mise en mots en matière d'abus sexuel.* Montréal: Méridien.

van der Kolk, B. A., McFarlane, A. C., and Weisaeth, L. (Eds.) (1996). *Traumatic stress – The effects of overwhelming experience on mind, body and society.* New York: Guilford Press.

van der Kolk, B. A, McFarlane, A. C., and Weisaeth, L. (Eds.) (2000). *Traumatic Stress, Grundlagen und Behandlungsansätze – Theorie, Praxis und Forschung zu posttraumatischem Stress sowie Traumatherapie.* Paderborn: Junfermann.

von Boch-Galhau, W., Kodjoe, U., Andritzky, W., and Koeppel, P. (Eds.) (2003). Das Parental Alienation Syndrom - Eine interdisziplinäre Herausforderung für scheidungsbegleitende Berufe (The Parental Alienation Syndrome [PAS] – An Interdisciplinary Challenge for Professionals Involved in Divorce). Berlin: Wissenschaft und Bildung (VWB).

von Uexküll, Th. (1996). *Psychosomatische Medizin, 5.* Auflage, München-Wien-Baltimore: Urban & Schwarzenberg.

Wallerstein, J., and Kelly, J. (1980). *Surviving the breakup: How children and parents cope with divorce.* New York: Basic Books.

Warshak, R. A. (2003). *Current controversies regarding the Parental Alienation Syndrome.* In: Boch-Galhau, W. von/Kodjoe, U., Andritzky, W., Koeppel, P. (Ed.s): ibd., pp. 207–233.

Winnicott, D. W. (1990). *Reifungsprozesse und fördernde Umwelt.* Frankfurt: Fischer.

Chapter 25

RELUCTANCE TO VERIFY PAS AS A LEGITIMATE SYNDROME

JANELLE BURRILL

OVERVIEW

A healthy parent – a parent who truly loves his or her child – appreciates the importance of the other parent in the life of the child and, with the exception of the genuinely abusive parent, facilitates meaningful contact between the child and the other parent. Each parent naturally attempts to induce the child's loyalty towards him or her in the majority of custody disputes. When this turns into indoctrinations or "programming," PAS symptoms may develop in the child. Richard Gardner believed that the stronger the programming, the greater the likelihood the child will contribute to the PAS. A diagnosis of parental alienation syndrome is then justified. This is not parental alienation ("PA"), which is a broad definition including many causes with many variations. Rather, PAS is a syndrome that is defined by specific signs and symptoms, based upon a frequent occurrence that suggests a common underlying pathogenesis, course, familial pattern, or treatment selection. The syndrome identified by Gardner seeks to understand the process of a child aligning with one parent against the other parent in a legal context.

DEVIATIONS FROM DEVELOPMENTAL NORMS

Children resistant to visitation deviate from usual developmental trends. Johnston and Roseby (1997) believe children who form consistent alignments with an alienating parent may not have separated psychologically from that parent. Contributing factors for children forming stronger than normal parent-child alignments before the "highest risk period of nine to twelve years of age" include: (1) failed separation-individuation process between the parent and child; (2) intense parental pressure; and (3) a child who is more sensitive and vulnerable to parental conflict (Johnston and Roseby, 1997). However, some children become aligned with one parent with little overt conflict between the parents (Johnston, 1993). Even mild and subtle forms of parental influence can have significant effects (Clawar and Rivlin, 1991).

However, Johnston and Roseby (1997) have failed to explain the wide variety of symptoms that may result from or be associated with PA. The syndrome identified by Gardner (1985, 2002) seeks to understand the process of a child aligning with one parent against the other parent in a legal context. Families are best served when the more specific term "parental alienation syndrome" is used, rather than the more general term "parental alienation."

PARENTAL ALIENATION

PA is a wide variety of symptoms resulting from or associated with a child's alienation from a parent. Children may become alienated from a parent because of physical abuse (Burrill, 2001). Children's alienation also may be the result of parental emotional abuse, which may be displayed as overt verbal abuse, or more covert abuse such as neglect of physical and/or emotional care of the child. PAS is a form of emotional abuse, which is also a form of parental alienation. Children may become alienated as a result of parental abandonment or ongoing parental acrimony, especially if associated with domestic violence. They may become alienated from a parent because of that parent's own behavior, which would be alienating to most people, such as alcoholism or substance abuse, antisocial behavior, or behavior due to mental health issues. Impaired parenting capacity, particularly physical or emotional capacity, may result in a child's alienation of a parent. Parents frequently are critical of one another in front of the children and may even demean one another in front of the children. This, too, may cause alienation. However, if these denunciations escalate, the foundation for PAS may be laid, leading to the exclusion of a parent. "These and many other parental behaviors can produce children's alienation, but none of them can justifiably be considered PAS" (Gardner, 2002, p. 2).

PARENTAL ALIENATION SYNDROME

The norm for children of divorce is to continue to love and long for both parents despite the passage of time subsequent to separation or divorce. In 1985, Gardner introduced the PAS concept. Gardner's PAS refers to the child's denigrating and rejecting a previously loved parent in the context of divorce or custody disputes. During child custody evaluations, Gardner observed that children were preoccupied with denigrating one parent, even to the point of expressing hatred toward him or her.

Legal, psychological, and psychiatric communities still "cringe" when PAS is suggested outright in court or as part of a court report. The psychology community denounces PAS as not being a valid syndrome (Sullivan, 2000; Johnston and Roseby, 1997). The psychology community suggests only the medical community should be able to define a "syndrome." However, this researcher's professional experience supports Gardner's observation of PAS. In addition, descriptive statistics were used to describe the findings of a study using 30 court-referred cases referred for evaluation, therapy, or mediation (Burrill, 2001). Nonparametric statistics analyzed the differences between the children's groups and parents' groups in the study. The data from this study support Gardner's clinical observations of PAS since 1985. The children in the severe PAS group were more disturbed than children in the moderate or mild PAS group. Gardner's specific PAS criteria were used for the children and for the parent groups. Identification of the symptoms allowed for the appropriate placement of the parents and children into each category within the groups. The study supports the seriousness of PAS, particularly the moderate and severe types. An appropriate diagnosis, including the level of severity, is essential to stop the progression of the syndrome. The findings of the study's 30 cases with 59 children support the existence of PAS. According to these results, the criticism and denial of PAS by practitioners and the legal community is unjustified.

PAS is a disorder that arises almost exclusively in the context of child custody disputes. It includes a cluster of symptoms that typically appear together – a cluster that warrants the designation syndrome. These symptoms include the alienating parent's denigration of the alienated parent and the programming of the child, and the child's own scenarios. These appear together to form the syndrome. The phenomenon of PAS occurs in the context of a highly conflicted family system that is composed of a child, an alienating parent, and an alienated parent, who is victimized by this process. Actually, the child is the real victim. The child frequently becomes estranged from the alienated parent by the alienating parent. This family system has a number of identifiable signs, symptoms, and behaviors. The characteristics and behaviors of the alienating parents, the alienated parents, the children, and specific criteria for determining PAS lend themselves very well to be identified as a "syndrome." In contrast to PAS, PA is a very general term and is not a syndrome.

The alienating parent's programming of the child's brain circuitry of ideas and attitudes about the other parent are at variance with the child's previous experiences. Frequently, PAS children contribute their own scenarios to the alienating parent's denigration, which are recognized by the child as complementary contributions desired by the alienating parent. The child's contributions are always welcomed and reinforced by the programming parent, resulting in even further contributions by the child (Gardner, 2002). The PAS diagnosis is based on the symptoms of the child, but the problem is always a familial problem in that in each case one parent is programming the child, one parent is alienated against, and the children exhibit certain behaviors. PAS is not animosity that a child harbors against a parent who has actually abused him or her. It is never considered if the alienated parent is found neglectful and/or abusive. Rather, in typical cases, the alienated parent would be considered by most practitioners to have been a normal, loving parent or, at worst, to have exhibited minimal impairments in parenting capacity.

PARENTAL ALIENATION SYNDROME IS NOT THE EQUIVALENT OF PARENTAL ALIENATION

Parental alienation syndrome and parental alienation are not interchangeable although some courts, evaluators, and mental health providers treat them as such. This is an error. "Parental alienation" is a more general term, whereas "parental alienation syndrome" is a very specific subtype of parental alienation (Gardner, 2002). "To equate the parental alienation syndrome with parental alienation cannot but produce confusion in that the former is a subtype of the latter" (p. 7). To even consider proper therapeutic and legal remedies, one must first define specifically the client's particular type of disorder before one can properly consider the various treatment options. Failure to make the differentiation between PA and PAS will result in inappropriate therapeutic treatment and/or legal remedies.

"A parent who inculcates a PAS in a child is indeed perpetrating a form of child abuse" (Gardner, 2002, p. 5). Specifically, it is a form of emotional abuse that can produce a child's lifelong alienation from a loving parent and lifelong psychiatric disturbance in the child. The alienating parent exhibits complete disregard for the alienated parent's role in the child's upbringing. The alienating parent causes an attenuation and even total destruction of a psychological bond that could, in most cases, prove of great value to the child, particularly since the parents are separated or divorced. Alienating parents exhibit a serious parenting deficit – a deficit that should be given serious consideration by courts when deciding primary custodial status.

RELUCTANCE TO VERIFY PAS AS A TRUE SYNDROME

Professional groups, particularly the psychological community and the medical community of psychiatrists have differences of opinion regarding PAS. Some groups prefer the term parental alienation, Johnston and Roseby, (1997); M. Sullivan, (2000). They believe that PAS is not really a syndrome. This position can be seen in the courts of law in the context of child custody disputes. It also be seen in the child custody evaluators' reports to the courts. A syndrome by any definition, including a medical definition, is described as "a grouping of signs and symptoms, based upon their frequent occurrence that may suggest a common underlying pathogenesis, course, familial pattern, or treatment selection" (DSM IV; American Psychiatric Association 1994, 2000). The syndrome identified by Gardner seeks to understand and identify the process of a child aligning with one parent against the other parent in a legal context of a custody dispute, not a general alienation of a parent by a child due to many causes. Based upon the specific criteria of PAS, early recognition and intervention will minimize the effects of PAS and improve parent-child relations.

WHAT IS PA IN CHILDREN?

Johnston and Roseby (1997) indicate that PA is a result of children becoming vigilant and highly attuned to the alienating parent. To disappoint or abandon the depressed, emotionally volatile, or raging parent could result in punishment, rejection, or neglect. The child acts as though the alienating parent's survival depends on his or her caretaking. To betray that parent is "going over to the other side" (Johnston and Roseby, p. 198, 1997).

These PA children usually find themselves alone and isolated (Kelly, 1996). These children may be caring for a disorganized, depressed, dependent, enraged, or mentally or physically ill parent (Rand, 1997). Wallerstein and Blakeslee (1989) use the term "overburdened child" to describe these problems. Roseby and Kelly (1997) have encountered PAS, but prefer to conceptualize PAS-like cases from the "overburdened" child framework rather than PAS. An "overburdened" child does not describe the cause, the effect, or the treatment for this family constellation. PAS does. If PAS criteria are applied, the diagnosis, cause, treatment, and legal remedies can be delineated for evaluators and for the courts. PAS demands the identification of the programmer. PA does not. The parent-child relation is lost. PAS demands to know the cause of the children's alienations. PA does not demand to know anything about the alienation or who is programming the child. PAS has very specific criteria so that very important questions for the evaluators and court can be answered. The programming parent can be identified and very specific treatment for the family, including judicial remedies can be fashioned.

SYNDROME

The symptoms observed in a syndrome, such as PAS, occur together and characterize the disorder. In either medical or psychological communities, syndromes are symptoms, occurring together, that identify a specific disease or disorder. The DSM has for many years identified mental illness, and various disorders, including personality disorders and syndromes such as Tourette's syndrome. Most of the DSM illnesses and disorders were first labeled syndromes. The term "syndrome" is very specific. It allows for appropriate identification because of a common etiology or basic underlying cause. Gardner (2002, p. 3) indicated that a syndrome is more specific than a disease because a "disease is usually a more general term because there can be many causes of a particular disease." For example, pneumonia is a disease, but there are many types of pneumonia; for example, pneumococcal pneumonia and bronchopneumonia each have specific symptoms, and each could be reasonably considered a syndrome. The same can be applied to PAS, whether it is a mild, moderate, or severe case. The parents and the child can be identified by specific symptoms and behaviors within a specific context (legal) and in varying degrees on the PAS spectrum.

The PAS syndrome has the same purity of the term "syndrome" because most of the symptoms and behaviors in the mild, moderate, and severe groups predictably manifest themselves together as a group and become easily recognizable. It is the same etiology; although the symptoms appear to be unrelated, but they are. This allows PAS to be recognized as a syndrome. The same applies for Down syndrome, which includes a number of disparate symptoms. These include mental retardation, with specific facial characteristics such as drooping lips, slanting eyes, and short fifth finger, and atypical creases in the palms of the hands (Gardner, 2002). Most people with Down syndrome look very much alike, and most typically exhibit all these symptoms. A genetic factor – a specific chromosomal abnormality – links these disparate symptoms. There is a primary basic cause of Down syndrome. The same is true for PAS. Moderate and severe PAS children exhibit a cluster of symptoms which appear together and include: (1) a campaign of denigration; (2) lack of ambivalence; (3) the "independent thinker" phenomenon; (4) absence of guilt over the cruelty exhibited towards the alienated parent; (5) creation of their own scenarios to legitimize their hostility towards the alienated parent; (6) spread of the animosity to others including family, teachers, and friends; and (7) weak, frivolous, and absurd rationalizations for the deprecations and reflexive support of the alienating parent in the parental conflict (Gardner, 2002; Burrill, 2001).

Typically, children who suffer with PAS will exhibit most of these symptoms. Furthermore, when mild cases of PAS progress to moderate and severe types, all of the PAS symptoms are present. However, usually children with PA do not suffer from a cluster of symptoms, except perhaps for those with severe PAS, which is acknowledged as similar to Gardner's PAS (Johnston and Roseby, 1997). Still, the etiology of PA, even in its most severe form, cannot be recognized by identifiable causes or any specific criteria.

DIAGNOSING PAS IN CHILD CUSTODY DISPUTES

Accurate recognition, diagnosis, and proper treatment of PAS may prevent further deterioration and rupture of the alienated parent-child relationship. In order to move forward, support from the courts, judges, lawyers, evaluators, and mental health community, it is important that the existence and validity of PAS as a syndrome is acknowledged. Delays in diagnosis and treatment can compromise the best interests of the children.

One study addressed the relationship between findings of the study and Gardner's criteria for PAS based on the children's' symptoms (Burrill, 2001). The data from the study indicate a relationship between the alienating parents' behaviors and their children's' negative behaviors towards the alienated parent. One should anticipate that a mildly alienated child should have a mildly alienating parent with mild symptoms, a moderately alienated child should have a moderately alienating parent, and a severely alienated child should have a severely alienating parent.

In the study, the differences in the number of negative behaviors towards the alienated parent among the three groups of children were compared. The childrens' symptoms and behaviors, based upon Gardner's children's criteria for mild, moderate, or severe PAS, determined the child's group. ANOVA (one-way analysis of variance) was used to compare these three groups. The children in the severe group exhibited more negative behaviors. Therefore, the parents in the mild category had children with mild symptoms. Their parent-child relations with the alienated parent were more positive, with fewer negative behaviors. However, the children whose parents were in the severe category had more negative behaviors. In addition, the children of these parents were identified as having more parent-child problems and resistance to visitation with the alienated parent. The study provided data that support Gardner's clinical observations of PAS as a syndrome. It is believed by this researcher that an appropriate diagnosis of PAS can make the difference between intervening effectively before it is too late to maintain the emotional stability of children and save the parent-child relationship or allowing cases to go beyond the point of no return.

PAS IS EASILY IDENTIFIED

PAS remains distinctive to intractable conflict in custody disputes in which the child becomes aligned with one parent and preoccupied with unjustified and/or exaggerated denigration of the other parent. PAS is very easy to clinically identify. PAS exists, but the lack of appropriate clinical recognition continues to delay treatments and legal remedies to restore the children's relationships alienated parents. Factions of various professional groups within the mental health community and, to a lesser degree, the legal community, have continued to delay its acceptance. Certainly, Gardner's 1985 clinical observations of PAS in custody disputes have not halted the continuing harm to parent-child relations. This is largely because the mental health and legal communities have been unwilling to work together to halt the destruction of parent-child relations and avoid the mental disturbance that results in children experiencing PAS.

Gardner (2002, pp. 14–15) noted that supporters of PAS and PA do agree that in severe cases, the only hope for the victimized children is significant restriction of the programmer's access to the children including reversal of custody in some cases. Warshak (1999) also addressed the conflict between those who use the term PAS and those who use PA. He concluded that the arguments for the utilization for PAS clearly outweigh any arguments for the utilization of PA. The use of the term syndrome in the PAS diagnosis is appropriate because it identifies the cause of the children's alienation. Not only are the terms PAS and PA very different in their meaning, but their differences have significant implications that are exploited in the courtroom, thereby causing significant grief for PAS families. The identifying criteria of PAS will prove useful to mental health and legal professionals who deal with PAS families in courts of law. PAS clarifies the criteria for the evaluator and the court. Most important, PAS identifies the problem of the child and offers remedies for the parent-child relation.

JUDICIAL UNDERSTANDING OF PAS

Courts must deal every day with high conflict custody disputes. Judges must decide whether allegations are frivolous or reliable. When cases of alienation come before the court, the court must ask about the following important questions: (1) Is the child alienated, and (2) What interventions are recommended or indicated?

The real question is: What is the cause of the child's alienation? PA does not tell the court very much. PAS tells the court that the alienation is caused by the mother or father's programming of the child, and the court must remedy the situation to protect the child from the programming. This is the central issue for the court in PAS. It is important to give the courts a framework to assist judges in making their decisions. This can be accomplished using the PAS diagnosis. The same is not true for PA, a very general term.

The difference of opinion about the use of the terms "PA" or "PAS" have significant implications for the families that ultimately appear before the court. It is here where these are often ultimately important and are exaggerated thereby causing significant grief and continuing emotional disturbance for PAS families. PAS is an identifiable children's disorder with a specific cause, which has caused controversy in the mental health and legal communities. It is essential that PAS be more universally recognized for the full syndrome and disorder that it is within the context of custody disputes. Once the appropriate recognition replaces the quagmire of fear and anger that has accompanied its diagnosis, then clinical treatment and legal remedies can be fashioned.

CONCLUDING COMMENTS

Programming of children by one parent to cause alienation from the other parent is increasingly prevalent in the context of child custody disputes. The identity of the programmer of the child is not gender specific; men induce PAS in their children "to the point where the ratio is now approximately a 50:50 ratio" (Gardner, 2002, p. 9). The programming of the child serves to strengthen the position of the programming parent with their child and in the court of law. While some evaluators use the term "parental alienation syndrome" to refer to this disorder of children, others use the term "parental alienation." The genesis of the controversy between the terms is primarily within the mental health community, as the legal community becomes more involved in the context of hearings, trials, expert testimony, and evaluations. Some of the sources of this controversy can be traced to a lack of understanding, and fear of reprisal from parents, courts, the mental health community, and the attorneys.

Gardner's observations of a "cluster of symptoms" that typically appear together in the context of child custody disputes continues to warrant the designation syndrome. PAS was introduced to encompass the combination of a parent's programming of the child to denigrate the other parent along with the child's self-created vilifying contributions to support the alienating parent's campaign of denigration against the alienated parent. Gardner defined PAS:

> as a childhood disorder that arises almost exclusively in the context of child custody disputes. Its primary manifestation is the child's campaign of denigration against a parent, a campaign that has no justification. It results from the combination of a programming parent's indoctrinations and the child's own contributions to the vilification of the alienated parent. When true parental abuse and/or neglect is present, the child's animosity may be justified and so the parental alienation syndrome explanation for the child's hostility is not applicable. (Gardner 2002, p. 2)

PAS continues to exist as when it was first identified by Gardner in 1985, with the identical symptoms exhibited in the alienating parent, the child, and the alienated parent. Gardner's syndrome has a purity that warrants recognition which could end the unnecessary emotional abuse of children in the context of child custody disputes.

BIBLIOGRAPHY

American Psychiatric Association. (1994; 2000). *Diagnostic and statistical manual of mental disorders*, (4th ed.) Washington, D.C.: Author.

Anastasi, A, Urbina, S. (1997). *Psychological testing*, 7th Ed. Prentice Hall: Upper River Saddle, New Jersey: Prentice Hall.

Bee, H. (1985). *The developing child.* New York: Harper & Row.

Berk, L. (1997). *Child development*, 4th Ed. Boston: Allyn & Bacon.

Blush, G., Ross, K (1987). Sexual allegation in divorce: The SAID syndrome. *Conciliation Courts Review, 25*(1), 1–11.

Burrill, J. (2001). *Parental alienation syndrome in court referred custody cases.* Dissertation.com: USA.

Calabrese, R., Miller, J., Dooley, B. (1987). The identification of alienated parents and children: Implications for school psychologists. *Psychology in the Schools, 24*(2), 145–150.

Campbell, K., (1982). The psychotherapy relationship for borderline personality disorders. *Psychotherapy: Research and Practice, 19*(2), 166–186.

Caplan, F., Caplan, T. (1980). *The second twelve months of life: Your baby's growth month by month.* New York: Bantam.

Cartwright, G. (1993). Expanding the parameters of parental alienation syndrome. *American Journal of Family Therapy, 21*(3), 205–215.

Clawar, S., Rivlin, (1991). *Children held hostage: Dealing with programmed and brainwashed children.* Chicago, Illinois: American Bar Association.

Craig, R. (1997). *Clinical and diagnostic interviewing.* Northvale, NJ.: Jason Aronson.

Doherty, W., Kouneski, E., & Erickson, M. *Responsible fathering: An overview and conceptual framework.* University of Minnesota, September 1997.

Donaldson-Pressman, S. & Pressman, R. (1994). *The narcissistic family: Diagnosis and treatment.* New York: Lexington.

Dunne, J., Hedrick, M. (1994). The parental alienation syndrome: Analysis of sixteen selected cases. *Journal of Divorce & Remarriage, 21*(3–4), 21–38.

Evergreen Consultants in Human Behavior (1997). *What is attachment disorder?* Colorado: Axces.

F. Turner (1988). *Child psychopathology: A social work perspective.* New York: The Free Press.

Faller, K. (1998). The parental alienation syndrome: What is it and what data support it? *Child Maltreatment: Journal of the American Professional Society on the Abuse of Children 3*(2):100–115.

Folberg, J. (1991). *Joint custody and shared parenting.* New York: Guilford Press.

Folberg, J., Milne, A. (1988). *Divorce mediation.* New York: Guilford Press.

Gardner, R. (1984). *Recommendations for dealing with parents who induce a parental alienation syndrome in their children: A guide for mental health and legal professionals.* Cresskill, NJ: Creative Therapeutics.

Gardner, R. (1986a). *Child custody litigation.* Cresskill, NJ: Creative Therapeutics.

Gardner, R. (1986b). *Family evaluation and child custody mediation, arbitration, and litigation.* Cresskill, NJ: Creative Therapeutics.

Gardner, R. (1986c). *The psychotherapeutic techniques of Richard A. Gardner.* Rev. ed., Cresskill, NJ: Creative Therapeutics.

Gardner, R. (1987). *The parental alienation syndrome and the differentiation between fabricated and genuine child sex abuse.* Cresskill, NJ: Creative Therapeutics.

Gardner, R. (1991). *Sex abuse hysteria.* Cresskill, NJ: Creative Therapeutics.

Gardner, R. (1992a). *The parental alienation syndrome.* Cresskill, NJ.: Creative Therapeutics.

Gardner. R. (1992b). *The parents' book about divorce* (Rev. ed.) New York: Bantam.

Gardner, R. (1998a). Recommendations for dealing with parents who induce a parental alienation syndrome in their children. *Journal of Divorce and Remarriage, 28*(3–4), 1–28.

Gardner, R. (1998b). The parental alienation syndrome: What is it and what data support it? *Child Maltreatment: Journal of the American Professional Society on the Abuse of Children, 3*(4), 309–312.

Gardner, R. (1999). Family therapy of the moderate type of parental alienation syndrome. *American Journal of Family Therapy, 27*(3), 195–212.

Gardner, R. (1999a). Differentiating between parental alienation syndrome and bona fide abuse-neglect. *American Journal of Family Therapy, 27*(2), 97–107.

Gardner, R. (2002). Parental alienation syndrome vs. parental alienation: Which diagnosis should evaluators use in child-custody cases? *The American Journal of Family Therapy, 30*(2), 93–115.

Geffner, R. (1992). Guidelines for using mediation with abusive couples. *Psychotherapy in Private Practice, 10*(1–2), 77–92.

Greenspan, S. (1990). *The development of the ego.* Madison, CT.: International Universities Press, Inc.

Heinz, M., Grisso, T. (1996). Review of instruments assessing parenting competencies used in child custody evaluations. *Behavioral Sciences and the Law, 14*(3), 293–313.

Hilsenroth, M., Hibbard, S., Nash, M., Handler, L., (1993). A research study of narcissism, defense, and aggression in borderline, narcissistic and Cluster C personality disorders. *Journal of Personality Assessment, 60*, 346–361.

Huntington, D., S., (1986). The forgotten figures in divorce. In *Divorce and fatherhood: The struggle for parental identity.* Edited by Jacobs, J., W., Washington D.C.: American Psychiatric Association Press.

Hysjulien, C., Wood, B., Benjamin, G., Andrew, H. (1994). Child custody evaluations: A review of methods used in litigation and alternative dispute resolution. *Family & Conciliation Courts Review, 32*(4), 466–489.

Johnston, J., & Campbell, L. (1988). *Impasses of divorce.* New York: The Free Press.

Johnston, J., R., (1993). Children of divorce who refuse visitation. In *Nonresidential parenting: New vistas in family living.* Edited by Depner, C. E., and Bray J.H. London: Sage Publications.

Johnston, J., V. Roseby. (1997). *In the name of the child: A developmental approach to understanding and helping children of conflicted and violent divorce.* New York: The Free Press.

Kelley, J. (1996). *Divorce related distortions in parent-child relationships: Parental alignment and alienation.* Unpublished manuscript.

Kernberg, O. (1986). *Severe personality disorders.* New Haven, CT: Yale University Press.

Kopetski, L. (1991). "Parental alienation syndrome: Recent research." Presented at the 15th Annual Child Custody Conference, Keystone, CO.

Kreisman, J., Straus. H. (1989). *I hate you – Don't leave me.* Los Angeles, CA.: The Body Press.

Lampel, A. (1999). Use of the Million clinical multiaxial inventory-III in evaluating child custody litigants. *American Journal of Forensic Psychology, 17*(4), 19–31.

Livesley, W. (1995). *DSM-IV personality disorders.* New York: Gilford Press.

Lowenstein, L. (1998). Parental alienation syndrome: A two-step approach toward a solution. *Contemporary Family Therapy: An International Journal, 20*(4), 505–520.

Lund, M. (1995). A therapist's view of parental alienation syndrome. *Family and Conciliation Courts Review, 33*(3), 308–316.

M. Ehrenber, Hunter, M., Elterman, M. (1996). Shared parenting agreements after marital separation: The roles of empathy and narcissism. *Journal of Consulting and Clinical Psychology, 64*(4), 808–818.

Maccoby, E., Buchanan, C., Mnookin, R., Dornbusch, S., (1993). Post divorce roles of mothers and fathers in the lives of their children. *Journal of Family Psychology, 7*(1), 24–38.

Manfield, P. (1992). *Split self/Split object.* Northvale, NJ.: Jason Aronson, Inc.

Millon, T. (1981). *Disorders of personality DSM-III: Axis II.* New York: John Wiley & Sons.

National Center on Child Abuse and Neglect, Executive Summary (1988). *Study of national incidence and prevalence of child abuse and neglect.* Washington, D.C.: Department of Health and Human Services, Contract 105-85-1702.

National Council on Children's Rights (1996–97), CAPTA revised to provide relief for false allegations. *Speak Out for Children*, Fall/Winter.

Nicholas, L. (1995). *Parental alienation: Assessing and treating coercion of children during divorce and custody disputes.* Unpublished manuscript, Sacramento, CA.

Nicholas, L. (1997). *Does parental alienation exist? A preliminary empirical study of the phenomenon in custody and visitation disputes?* Unpublished manuscript, Sacramento, CA.

Nurcombe, B., Partlett, D. (1994). *Child mental health and the law.* New York: The Free Press.

Othmer, E., & Othmer, S. (1994). *The clinical interview using DSM-IV, Volume I: Fundamentals.* Washington, D.C.: American Psychiatric Press.

Palmer, N. (1988). Legal recognition of the parental alienation syndrome. *American Journal of Family Therapy, 16*(4), 361–363.

Pett, M., Wampold, B., Turner, C., Vaughan-Cole, B. (1999). Paths of influence of divorce on preschool children's psychosocial adjustment. *Journal of Family Psychology, 13*(2), 145–164.

Rand, D. (1997). The spectrum of parental alienation syndrome (part II). *American Journal of Forensic Psychology, 15*(4), 39–92.

Rosen, K., Rothbaum, F. (1993). Quality of parental caregiving and security of attachment. *Developmental Psychology, 29*(2), 358–367.

Siegel, J. (1996). Traditional MMPI-2 validity indicators and initial presentation in custody evaluation. *American Journal of Forensic Psychology, 14*(3), 55–63.

Siegel, J., Langford, J. (1998). MMPI-2 validity scales and suspected parental alienation syndrome. *American Journal of Forensic Psychology, 16*(4), 5–14.

Simon, L. (1995). A therapeutic jurisprudence approach to the legal processing of domestic violence cases. *Psychology, Public Policy and Law, 1*(1), 43–79.

Singer, D. (1993). *Playing for their lives.* New York: The Free Press.

Stahl, P. (1994). *Conducting child custody evaluations.* Thousand Oaks, CA: Sage Press.

Stahl, P. (1999) Alienation and alignment of children. *California Psychologist*, March 1999.

Stahl, P. (1999). *Complex issues in child custody evaluations.* Thousand Oaks, CA: Sage.

Sullivan, M. (2000). The alienated child. Unpublished paper, presentation.

Turner, F. (1988). *Child psychopathology: A social work perspective.* New York: The Free Press.

Turkat, I. (1994). Child visitation interference in divorce. *Clinical Psychology Review, 8,* 737–742.

Vestal, A. (1999). Mediation and parental alienation syndrome. *Family & Conciliation Courts Review, 37*(4), 487–503.

Wallerstein J., S., Blakeslee, S. (1989). *Second chances.* New York: Tricknor & Fields.

Wallerstein, J., & J. Kelly. (1980). *Surviving the breakup.* New York: Basic Books.

Warshak, R. (1992). *The custody revolution.* New York: Poseidon Press.

Warshak, R. (1999). Psychological syndromes: Parental alienation syndrome. *Expert Witness Manual.* Dallas, TX: State Bar of Texas, Family Law Section.

Section III

LEGAL ISSUES

Chapter 26

PARENTAL ALIENATION SYNDROME IN AMERICAN LAW

Demosthenes Lorandos

OVERVIEW

This article describes the history of parental alienation syndrome [PAS] in American case law. Fifteen years of cases from 1987 through 2003 are described with illustrations from the public record. Special attention is given to the use and abuse of expert testimony from behavioral sciences professionals. Material cited by trial or appellate courts that was produced by PAS "detractors" is cited as a cross reference to the chapter, Parental Alienation Syndrome: Detractors and the Junk Science Vacuum, of this work, which analyzes three specific examples of articles written by these detractors.

I wish either my father or my mother, or indeed both of them,
as they were in duty both equally bound to it, had minded
what they were about when they begot me.
Laurence Sterne, *Tristram Shandy*

There is no doubt that in the difficult context of child custody battles, parents occasionally resort to outrageous acts of interpersonal sabotage. Every experienced family court judge and child custody practitioner can testify to examples of parental manipulation. Parental campaigns to distance children from another parent have been reported in the literature of psychology and law for decades.[1] The most common heuristic in this regard is *PAS*, first reported by psychiatrist Richard Gardner in 1985.[2]

Cases describing PAS can be found in 15 years of American jurisprudence.[3] Reported decisions describing the quagmire of polarized child custody and parental alienation processes run the gamut from the sublime to the ridiculous. This review focuses on exemplary cases from 1987 through 2003. The material has been gleaned from the public record.

FIFTEEN YEARS OF PAS IN AMERICAN COURTS

A Failure Of Proof

In *Coursey v. Superior Court* (1987), a trial judge in the foothills of the California mountains found Loretta Coursey in contempt of court when Gene and Loretta Coursey's 14-year-old daughter refused to visit her dad following a divorce. After a hearing, the trial court found Loretta in contempt for willfully violating the terms of a stipulated order. The trial court fined Loretta $500 and committed her to five days in jail. The trial court concluded:

> "In summary, Loretta Coursey was aware of the order. She had agreed to the order, otherwise there would not have been an order on October 31. She complied with the order on two occasions prior to November 9th. Then her attorney advised Gene Coursey's attorney that there would be no visitation on November 9th. There were no other explanations provided that I'm aware of. Specifically, there was no indication that there was physical in-

capacity as far as [the child] was concerned. The only indication was mental or emotional disinclination."[4]

When Loretta Coursey appealed the decision, the California Court of Appeals for the Third District concluded that:

> "No evidence of Loretta's ability to compel her daughter's visitation was adduced at the hearing. As noted, Loretta's guilt was established on the testimony of Gene and Loretta's attorney. However, neither witness addressed the issue of Loretta's ability to control her daughter. . . . In these circumstances, absent additional evidence, it cannot be fairly inferred that the failure of visitation was caused by the mother's willful violation of the visitation order."[5]

In this first reported PAS case, the proofs failed when the alienated parent could not prove the acts or intent of the alienating parent.

A Constitutional Right to Be Nasty

In 1988, the Florida Court of Appeals described what seemed to be Laurel Schutz's argument that she had a constitutional right to be nasty.[6] Writing for the Appeals Court, Judge Schwartz described Laurel Schutz's

> "assiduous and unfortunately largely successful efforts both to secrete physically the parties' two daughters from their father and to poison their hearts and minds against him. . . . On ample evidence, the trial court found: '. . . having observed the demeanor of the witnesses, having listened to the nuances of the testimony, having examined the exhibits and the pleadings, the Court has no doubt – not a reasonable one, not even an unreasonable one, or even a scintilla, shadow or peradventure of doubt – that the cause of the blind, brainwashed, bigoted belligerence of the children toward the Father grew from the soil nurtured, watered and tilled by the Mother. The Court is thoroughly convinced that the Mother breached every duty she owed as the custodial parent to the noncustodial parent of instilling love, respect and feeling in the children for their Father. Worse, she slowly dripped poison into the minds of these children, maybe even beyond the power of the Court to find the antidote. But the Court will try."[7]

The trial court ordered Ms. Schutz to "do everything in her power to create in the minds of [the children] a loving, caring feeling toward the Father."[8] Ms. Schutz appealed, citing an impingement on her rights to free speech.[9] Citing to Gardner and a variety of cases from around the country, the Court of Appeals labeled Ms. Schutz's argument of a constitutional right to her invective "baseless." Not to be deterred in her mission, Ms. Schutz appealed to the Florida Supreme Court.[10] After the expenditure of thousands of dollars, the Florida Supreme Court affirmed the appeals and trial courts, holding that in view of the circumstances "any burden on the mother's first amendment rights is merely 'incidental.'"[11]

A Resolution In Counseling

In the next reported case addressing PAS, Gardner was appointed an independent and impartial examiner for "A.R." and "S.E." in New York. Gardner reported a mild degree of *parental alienation* but recommended the children stay with their mother.[12] A number of post evaluation difficulties arose, and the plaintiff called numerous fathers' rights advocates to testify. Following a great deal of psychiatric and psychological testimony, the trial court refused to transfer custody and ordered both parents to counseling. The court ordered "the therapist to immediately communicate with the Court if the therapist is of the opinion that any of the participants is not fully cooperating with the therapeutic treatment plan."[13]

The Case Of The Murder's Mom

When Violetta B. was four months old, her parents murdered her four-year-old sister.[14] Placed in foster care, Violetta flourished. When she was two years old, her paternal grandmother sought physical custody. The trial court appointed a family therapist to supervise visits and make a report. He testified that the child seemed to enjoy the visits with her grandmother, but was very happy and anxious to return to her foster mother. He further testified he was directing all of his efforts toward placing the child with the grandmother.[15] The trial court then made the grandmother the child's private guardian and custodian. Through her guardian ad litem, the child requested a "bonding assessment," and the court appointed a psychologist.[16] Proofs at a hearing demonstrated that after the family therapist recommended that the grandmother tell the child that she wanted her to stay with her, separation from the foster mother became increasingly stressful.[17] At a follow-up hearing, a psychologist stated that the child and the foster mother had a very strong primary bond. She described the primary bond as a relationship the child used to determine both her security and also a sense of what is right. The psychologist also testified that disruption of the child's primary relationship dramatically affected the child's ability to trust. She opined that the child would be unlikely to form deep sustaining relationships with others because the risk of losing such a relationship was too painful. She went on to characterize PAS by offering that as the transitions between the two homes were becoming more difficult, the child became depressed, combative and aggressive.[18]

Although the appellate court mischaracterized the psychologist's credentials several times,[19] it relied heavily on her testimony:

> The primary basis for [the psychologist's] opinion, however, was her belief that given the strong primary bond between [the child] and [the foster mother], a transfer of custody would be extremely deleterious to [the child] psychologically and would cause her to suffer severe and irreparable trauma. [The psychologist] testified that, in her opinion, counseling would not serve to alleviate the trauma.[20]

The appellate court's reliance on its reevaluation of the record found the trial court's order of custody with the grandmother reversed on the great weight of the evidence.[21]

Medea's Selfish Goal

In a decision as eloquent as trial judge Richard Yale Feder's in *Schutz v. Schutz*,[22] New York family court judge David F. Jung got it all right in *Karen B. v. Clyde M.*[23] This case involved spurious allegations of child sexual abuse and the trial judge's extensive efforts to find the facts.

In September of 1990, a four-year-old girl allegedly told her mother that she had been sexually abused by her father. Mom told a friend of hers, and this friend interviewed the girl at home.[24] When the friend called the Department of Social Services "hotline," a social worker investigated the complaint. In now her third interview with a concerned adult, the little girl recounted a story about her father and sexual abuse.[25] Following her story, the DSS social worker referred the girl to a local validator.[26] This particular validator was a master's level psychologist, under contract with the DSS. According to her testimony, she "interviewed approximately two hundred children concerning allegations of sexual abuse and has validated seventy-five percent of them."[27]

In a statement that was unusual for a validator,[28] she testified that the mother seemed to be repeating the story by rote. When asked what she meant by the term "rote," she testified that the mother had to start from the beginning and repeat the whole story each time. She could not respond to questions without starting from the beginning and completing the entire story.[29] In her interviews with the child, the validator used some of the most ill-advised and suggestible techniques imaginable.[30] Still, she noted that no "sex-play" occurred during her interviews and the child repeatedly told her she was "making believe."[31] She went on to testify that, in her judgment, the mother had a "vested interest in the outcome of the case."[32] Judge Jung then took the testimony of the child's pediatrician, who had examined *and* interviewed the child.[33] The pediatrician testified that the mother brought the young girl to him for an examination, and that his physical examination of the child revealed nothing. He specifically testified that the child denied to him that anything had happened.[34] After collating all of this data, the Department of Social Services concluded that the mother's allegation was unfounded.[35]

Not to be denied, the mother waited five months, and started the whole process up again.[36] This time, another worker was assigned; this person also interviewed the little girl. By the time she was interviewed by the *sixth* concerned adult, she had developed a story about an "electric dinkie."[37] Mom found a polygrapher, who was the next person in line to interact with her and her daughter. Despite the fact that the polygrapher admitted he had never attempted a validation process with a young child, the "electric dinkie" story seemed to have an impact on him, as he testified that he thought the girl had been abused.[38] On cross-examination, the polygrapher stated that he was familiar with the *Sexual Allegations in Divorce (SAID) Syndrome* which describes increased numbers of false allegations when the factors he admitted to are present.[39]

The trial judge took the testimony of the girl's preschool teacher, a probation officer, and a certified social worker in the mental health clinic, none of whom observed any fear of the father by the child.[40] Following a review of a lengthy law guardian report, the trial judge made the following findings:

1. The trained validator conducted numerous interviews with the child and "concluded no abuse had taken place";[41]
2. When reading the polygrapher's report, the validator testified that the statements the child reportedly made to the polygrapher were "an almost exact verbatim statement to her" from the mother;[42]
3. The polygrapher who got the "electric dinkie" story "only had one interview with the child which occurred many months after the alleged incident or incidents;"[43]
4. "When asked to provide details, the youngster is either unable to do so or creates a scenario

for the purposes of the interview. However, in subsequent interviews a different scenario may be presented."[44]

5. The child's "descriptions of sexual activity between herself and her father vary considerably depending upon whether she was talking to" this adult interviewer or that adult interviewer.[45]
6. "There was no credible testimony to suggest that the child was afraid of her father and in fact the testimony suggested a relaxed and warm relationship."[46]
7. "There was no testimony to suggest that [the girl] had any awareness of her sexuality or had become involved in any sexual activity."[47]
8. "None of the adults to whom [the girl] made disclosures could conclude with ***any*** certainty that [she] was describing one or more than one experience."[48]
9. "[The] Court had the unique opportunity of observing the demeanor of all witnesses who appeared before it and concludes that the testimony of the father is more credible than that of the mother."[49]
10. The court agreed with the validator and the child's law guardian "that it is likely that the mother programmed her daughter to accuse the father of sexually abusing the child so that she could obtain sole custody and control or even preclude any contact that the father might have with his daughter."[50]

Rather eloquently, Judge Jung concluded: "In the opinion of this Court, any parent that would denigrate the other by casting the false aspersion of child sex abuse and involving the child as an instrument to achieve his or her selfish purpose is not fit to continue in the role of a parent. . . . Like Medea, she is ready to sacrifice her child to accomplish her selfish goal."[51]

"Toto" Annihilation

In *Toto v. Toto*,[52] the parties really taxed the Ohio Court of Appeals' demonstrated orientation to boilerplate.[53] As the court noted, post decree litigation began in 1984 with the first of 132 motions. Dad filed 75 motions and Mom filed 57 motions. Additional motions were filed by three different guardians ad litem.[54] It seems the annihilation process began because, although the parties entered an agreement whereby they were to consult on all major decisions affecting the children's welfare, and any disputes were to be resolved by mediation, the father was granted veto power over any mediation decisions. In effect, he was given authority to impose his own solutions at will.[55]

Over the course of six years of litigation, the trial court appointed three guardian ad litems, two at the father's request and one on its own motion. Each guardian ad litem stressed the importance of re-establishing visitation between the dad and his children, but found that the visitation and companionship problems were the fault of the father, not the mother or children. During an interview with the children, the trial court learned that they loved their father, but could not cope with his erratic behavior toward them.

According to the GALs and the trial court, the dad had repeatedly terminated visitation, at will. The court concluded that there was no evidence in the record to support the father's claim that the mother was brainwashing the children. The appellate record indicates that seven psychologists evaluated the parties and their children. They determined that the father loved his children and they loved their father, but that the protracted litigation had a detrimental effect on everyone. The psychologists found that the children suffered from PAS, which was further compounded by the parties' inability to communicate.

Ultimately, the trial court entered orders, assessing well over $100,000 in attorney fees and restricting visitation. Everyone appealed. The county Court of Appeals rubber-stamped the trial court with page after page of boilerplate and concluded: "All of the psychologists and guardians ad litem gave credible testimony which stressed the need for visitation. However, as a result of Appellant's "erratic" behavior in exercising his visitation, and the resulting psychological problems of the children, it is both just and reasonable for the trial court to limit visitation to a specific schedule."[56]

The Tree Climbers

In *Wiederholt v. Fischer*,[57] the father petitioned a Wisconsin trial court for a change in custody of his children. He alleged that their mother was fomenting PAS. The trial court noted that when the dad attempted visitation with his three girls, they "would run away and climb trees when he came to pick them up."[58] Numerous motions were filed dealing with "accusations involving what the parties told the children, whether photographs could be taken of the children, problems with the pick-up and drop-off time and locations, problems with telephone contact, and issues over the children's clothes and toys."[59] Finally, the father petitioned the trial court to change custody.

At a three-day hearing, the trial court took the testimony of a local psychologist. The court noted that he was well respected and that the court respected his opinions.[60] He testified that: "Parental Alienation Syndrome' can be one of four types: (1) one parent actively brainwashing or manipulating the feelings of a child concerning the other parent, (2) one parent unconsciously rewarding a child for turning his or her affections away from the other parent, (3) a child alienating himself or herself on the basis of fear of loss of love, and (4) a child alienating himself or herself because of certain situational factors."[61] The psychologist then testified that the children were suffering from the severe form of the syndrome and that it was "one of the worst cases I've ever seen in doing this kind of work."[62] His testimony indicated that the proposed cure was controversial, and that research data to support the success of transferring the children to the "hated" parent was limited. The court concluded that the evidence was not strong enough that the alienation would be cured by placing the children with their father.[63] The court left things as they were, out on a limb.

The appellate court opined *inter alia*: "Based on the weighing of all the evidence, the court found that the cure proposed by [the father] was not better than the current primary placement with [the mother]. The court found that the psychological impact on the children is risky and uncertain. These findings are not clearly erroneous."[64]

Parental Alienation As A Defense: Bite Marks In Nevada

Three young children were placed with the dad following a divorce. According to the record, the parties fought over custody of the kids for years.[65] When the mom petitioned to change custody, she asked for a *court-appointed special advocate* (CASA) to investigate allegations of physical abuse.

In a hearing during which three experts testified, the CASA reported that the children claimed they were being left unsupervised with their dad's daughter from a previous marriage. This was determined to be a clear violation of a prior court order. Each child also claimed that this daughter was physically abusive on several occasions. The father brought an expert who testified that the children suffered from PAS, developed by the children's mother. The dad further claimed that because of this PAS, the CASA "was duped by the three children, and thus, the CASA's testimony was skewed" in favor of the mother.[66]

The mother enlisted the aid of an expert, who agreed with the CASA. Both the mother's expert and the CASA recommended a change of custody to her. According to the appellate court, the scales were tipped "by the severe bite mark inflicted on the litigants' son" while in the dad's care.[67]

The Doctors' Case

In *In re Marriage of Rosenfeld*,[68] an Iowa trial and appellate court took exactly the action the Wisconsin trial court refused in *Wiederholt v. Fischer*[69] two years before. In *Rosenfeld*, the couple, both doctors of osteopathy, were divorced in December, 1990. Physical care of the children was awarded to the father. As a part of its findings in making the physical care determination, the trial court noted that the mother suffered migraine headaches and was addicted to her medication, and had attempted to alienate the children from her ex-husband. Two years later, the mother moved the court to change custody. During an eighteen-day hearing, she brought an expert who testified extensively about PAS. The trial court found that the father had attempted to alienate the children from his ex-wife and that her "drug addiction" was traced to a food allergy; that she had overcome this and succeeded in establishing a successful medical practice. The trial court granted the mother physical care. The father appealed.

According to the trial court:

> Two material changes in circumstances have occurred since the decree. At that time, [the mother] had a warm and loving reciprocated relationship with her children then ages nine and three. The relationship now cannot be expressed as mutual. [She] continues trying to be their mother and is devoted to them, but the conduct of the children toward their mother is appalling. . . . These children have been turned against [their mother] and it has happened by conduct from [the father's} household. The only way this most unfortunate situation can be corrected is to place the children in the primary physical care of [the mother].[70]

The trial court found that this was a case of PAS involving both children, and that it was severe.[71] By way of illustration, the court cited to two incidents, both of which involved the father's new wife.

> The first involved the prior fourth of July weekend. [Mother] asked to trade holidays because she had to work a sixty-hour weekend. [Father] refused to change the holiday schedule and, although he knew [Mother] was working, he got [the four-year-old son] up to get ready for his mother's visitation and let him sit for two hours with his bag by the window watching for his

mother who did not come. When she did not come on Monday, the same scene was reenacted. . . . The second was an attempt to charge [Mother] or someone who cared for [the four-year-old son] under [her] direction with sexually molesting or abusing him. [The new wife] took [the four-year-old] to doctors four times on two separate occasions with her complaints. All medical opinions refuted [her] claims but [she] told others about them, including their Rabbi, and she made her complaints in front of [the four-year-old son].[72]

In reaching its conclusions, the trial court noted considerable animosity between the father's new wife, and his ex-wife. The appellate panel specifically found, as did the trial court, that his new wife "contributed substantially to the discord."[73]

On appeal, the father attacked the validity of PAS and the testimony of his ex-wife's expert. The appellate panel side stepped the issue, and re-focused on the parties' behavior:

> We do not pass upon the issue of whether parental alienation syndrome is a reliable theory. Rather, we look at the evidence induced and draw our own conclusion. . . . Our major concern focuses on [the new wife]. . . . She has been manipulative, forbidding [the four-year-old son] to talk to his mother at school and church functions. The trial court in its findings noted the fact [she] had alienated her three children from a prior marriage from their father after she divorced him.[74]

Angry and Violent PAS in Indiana

In 1993, an Indiana woman filed a divorce petition against her husband and asked for sole custody of their two minor children. Before the trial court heard the case, she filed objections to the psychologist her husband wanted to use "and instead requested that the parties utilize the services of a specific person."[75] When the trial court took testimony the following year, witnesses testified that the mother was hostile and violent and had, on at least one occasion, kicked her minor son.[76] When the clinical psychologist she had insisted upon took the stand, he testified that:

> it would be in the best interests of the children for the trial court to award sole custody of the children to [father] because [mother] was engaging in a pattern of behavior known as parental alienation syndrome, a series of actions and 'maneuvers' by which she would attempt to exclude [father] and to denigrate him in the eyes of the children. [The psychologist] also stated that [she] displayed excessive anger and hostility toward [father].[77]

The mother responded by asserting that she had to put the ten-year-old boy on the stand to rebut the expert and the witnesses who testified they saw her kick the boy. The trial court refused to subject the child to the process and the Court of Appeals affirmed.[78]

Insults and Obsessions in Florida

After a Florida couple was divorced, the husband's visitation with the children became vexatious.[79] When he petitioned to change custody due to PAS, the trial court undertook a six-day trial. The trial court first noted that there were "allegations that the parents insulted each other and displayed ill-will toward each other in front of the children"[80]

In a basic litigator's sense of what PAS is, the appellate court noted the following:

> During the six-day trial, the court heard testimony from lay and expert witnesses, including a psychiatrist and two psychologists, examined exhibits, and observed the behavior of the parties. . . . There was testimony that the former wife would create a scene when the former husband tried to exercise visitation, and that when the children were with the former husband she would telephone them constantly and cry. . . . The former wife . . . intentionally or inadvertently communicated to the children her intense dislike of the former husband to the extent that it affected their emotional well-being and their relationship with the former husband. There was also evidence that the former wife was obsessed with making shared parenting as difficult as possible for the former husband, that she made questionable parenting decisions, and that her behavior was damaging to the children.[81]

As the *Rosenfeld*[82] court did in Iowa, the Florida trial and appellate courts dealt with a serious PAS case by changing custody to the alienated parent.

It is important to note that the PAS is not gender specific. In another Florida PAS case of insults and obsessions the same year, the court in *Williams v. Williams*[83] took custody from an alienating father and vested it in the alienated mother.

The "Big Time Trouble" Case

In *Hanson v. Spolnik*[84] a special judge found a mother in contempt of a restraining order, awarded sole custody to the father, restricted the mother's visitation rights, and awarded attorney fees to the father.[85]

In this matter, the mother and father's marriage was dissolved in 1995. Pursuant to the parties' dissolution agreement, the trial court awarded them joint legal and physical custody of their four-year-old daughter. Under the terms of the agreement, the father retained custody of the child for three days per week and the mother had custody for four days per week. In addition, all major decisions regarding the child's care – including education, extracurricular activities and medical treatment – were to be made by both parents.

Later that year the mother started taking the child to a child psychologist because she believed the child "was anxious and confused about the divorce and the visitation schedule."[86] During the sessions with the psychologist the mother repeatedly indicated that she desired a modification in the child custody arrangement, stating that she suspected the father of sexually abusing the child. The mother went on to offer that the father "had a long history of 'psych' treatment."[87] After interviewing the little girl, the psychologist determined that she was not unduly upset by the visitation schedule and that a modification in the custody arrangement was not necessary at that time.

The trial court noted that tensions between the parties continued to grow. The court found that in the presence of the four-year-old girl, the mother accused the father of disrupting her class and making her cry. The mother then told him to go to hell, indicated that he was going to get AIDS, and informed the child that she would have to be decontaminated after her father placed his hat on her head. The court went on to note that according to the father, the child also heard her mother repeatedly call him "Satan" and accuse him of being a homosexual.[88]

Soon thereafter, the father filed a petition for a mutual restraining order, claiming that his ex-wife had made numerous harassing telephone calls to him with regard to the modification proceedings and requesting that the parties' communication with each other be restricted to visitation issues. The trial court granted the petition for the restraining order the next day.

In early 1996, the father hired a private investigator to accompany him as a witness when he exchanged the child at the mother's residence because he believed the mother "would attempt to fabricate allegations against him."[89] After the father and the investigator arrived to pick-up the little girl, the mother followed them to a local truck stop where the investigator had left his car. The mother then proceeded to photograph the investigator and obtain his license plate number. Later that evening, said the court, she left the following message on the father's answering machine: "You can play this for the Judge because I would gladly be in contempt with you. You know what, buddy? You've got big-time problems. You are traumatizing that little girl, and you're going to court this week, and you'll see what's going to happen to you. And I hope you play this for the father's attorney and all your other goons, because ***you are in big-time trouble.***"[90]

The court found the mother in contempt and ordered her to complete eight hours of community service, apologize to her ex-husband and pay his attorney's fees.

Three months later, the father filed an emergency petition for modification of custody and supervised visitation. At the hearing, the father presented the testimony of a child psychologist,[91] who, after reviewing records and reports from Child Protective Services, the psychologist, and several other counselors, indicated that the mother had not taken appropriate action in resolving a sexual incident between the child and the mother's older daughter from a previous relationship.[92] He also indicated that the mother's comments and allegations against the father were directed at alienating his four-year-old daughter from the father and that the mother's behavior endangered the child's emotional and psychological development.

Following the hearing, the trial court entered findings of fact and conclusions of law, determining that there had been a substantial change in circumstances that justified a modification in custody. Specifically, the court determined that the mother had engaged in a concerted effort to destroy the child's relationship with the father since the divorce. As a result, the court awarded sole physical and legal custody of the child to the father. In addition, the court denied the mother visitation for a period of 60 days, followed by two hours of supervised visitation with the child every two weeks for three months. Further, the mother was ordered to pay the father's attorney's fees.[93] The mother appealed.

The appellate court reasoned that the evidence presented at the modification hearing revealed that immediately after the father and the mother were awarded joint custody of the child, numerous disputes arose. Specifically, the appellate court noted that the mother made repeated allegations of sexual abuse against the father, none of which were substantiated. In addition, the evidence, as set forth in the trial court's findings of fact, indicated that the mother made numerous disparaging comments about, and allegations against, the father in front of the child and others, including the comment that the child would have to be decontaminated after wearing the dad's hat and that the father had hired a hit man. The appellate panel noted that despite the fact that the trial court attempted to minimize the hostility by restricting the parties' interaction and communication to visitation issues, the animosity escalated to the point that a private investigator and the police were involved in simple exchanges.

The appellate panel ruled that: "Based on this evidence, the trial court could have reasonably concluded that [the child's] mental and physical welfare was in jeopardy and, as a result, a modification in the joint custody arrangement was necessary."[94]

New York Gets It Right – Again

In *J.F. v. L.F.*[95] Judge Sandra B. Edlitz of the family court in Westchester County demonstrates that family court judge David F. Jung's decision in *Karen B. v. Clyde M.*,[96] was not a fluke. They *can* get it right in New York.

In this case, the mom and dad were divorced in 1993, with sole custody of the parties' two children given to the mom. A consent order was entered the following year specifying joint custody, with the mother retaining primary custody. A visitation schedule was included in the 1995 order. Three years later, by order to show cause against the children's mother, the father applied for an order transferring custody to him. Annexed to the order to show cause was an affidavit of the psychiatrist previously involved in the case. In his affidavit, he recommended a change of custody to the father. Also included in the request for a change of custody was an affidavit of the father, along with an extensive exhibit. This affidavit and exhibit provided a summary of the mother's interference with visitation and examples of ways in which the mother allegedly alienated the children from their father during the years 1996, 1997 and 1998.[97]

The court conducted a continued hearing over the course of 15 days. The trial judge conducted in camera interviews of both children, and withheld her decision until school was out for the summer.

During the fifteen-day hearing, the mother bitterly contested the concept of PAS. The court's position was that: "Generally the New York Courts, in the context of a custody/visitation case, rather than discussing the acceptability of PAS as a theory, have discussed the issue in terms of whether the child has been programmed to disfavor the noncustodial parent, thus warranting a change in custody."[98]

The trial judge noted that two expert witnesses testified that the PAS existed in this case. The psychologist who evaluated the children and provided a written report to the court found that PAS was "clear" and "definite" with both children. She quoted a New York criminal case and wrote that: "Parental Alienation Syndrome occurs when 'one parent uses his/her influence with his/her child to undermine the relationship between the child and the other parent. . . . It typically arises when the parents are engaged in divorce proceedings or a custody dispute."[99] Judge Edlitz explained that she had an opportunity to observe the children closely during the extensive in camera interviews. She was so taken by the children's behavior, she reported her in camera sessions extensively:

> Yet, particularly when discussing their father and his family, they present themselves at times in a surreal way with a pseudo-maturity which is unnatural and, even, strange. They seem like 'little adults.' This Court finds that they live a somewhat sheltered, cloistered existence with their mother, emotionally and socially. They do not have friends to their home on a regular basis, and they do not go to other children's homes with any frequency. They do not have friends in their mother's neighborhood. The loving way in which the children perceive their mother, and the way in which they uncritically describe her as being perfect, stands in stark contrast to their descriptions of their father. Their opinions about their father are unrealistic, misshapen and cruel. They speak about and to him in a way which seems, at times, to be malicious in its quality. Nothing in the father's behavior warranted that treatment. The psychiatrists testified that the children are aligned in an unhealthy manner with the mother and her family. This is evidenced not only in the testimony of the father but also in the in camera interview. They repeatedly refer to the mother's family as 'my family,' but they do not refer to the father or his family that way. Both children used identical language in dismissing the happy times they spent with their father as evidenced in the videotape and picture album as 'Kodak moments.' They deny anything positive in their relationship with their father to an unnatural extreme.[100]

The judge went on to note that the predictions of the mental health evaluators "have unfortunately come true. All three of the experts agree that the children have been alienated from their father by their mother."[101] She summarized that a Board-certified psychiatrist served as the independent court psychiatrist in the case in 1994, again in 1995, and for the current proceeding. In 1994 and 1995 he recommended a change in custody to the father.[102] She continued that a clinical psychologist concluded in his reports that the PAS was "clear" and "definite" with both children.[103] She went on to summarize the work of the psychiatrist whose affidavit was annexed to the petition to change custody to the father.[104] The court offered that he had a subspecialty in child and adolescent psychiatry, and he submitted a report which in part offered:

> As predicted in my lengthy testimony in 1994, the alienation from the father has become more severe, probably the most severe case of alienation I have personally witnessed in my 33 years of doing child psychiatry. All of the classic signs of Alienation Syndrome are there and have been in place at least since 1991. If the children are allowed to remain with their mother, their paranoia will harden into pathological personality traits as so clearly seen in their mother and her extended family. If the children are placed in their father's custody at this time, emotional upset and some possible turmoil in the short term may occur. This will require competent professional intervention.[105]

The trial court found that in this case, the subject children were alienated from their father by their mother. The court opined that the children's "negative view of their father is out of all proportion to reality. . . . The children do not want to visit with their father. With the passage of time, these children have become 'staunch corroborators' of their mother's ill opinion of the father. They call their father names, they make fun of his personal appearance, they treat him as though he were incompetent, and they speak of and treat his wife similarly."[106]

Judge Edlitz went on to point out that "after a review of all of the evidence, and being in the unique position to observe the demeanor and credibility of the witnesses" she could not countenance the mother's behavior or influence over the children. She reasoned that, "The father has continued to keep fighting to have access to his children over the years, despite the clear attempts on the part of the mother to undermine his relationship with them."[107]

Judge Edlitz's conclusion was that:

> The animosity that the mother, the physical "custodial" parent has long harbored for the father has not lessened with time. As predicted by the mental health professionals at the inception of these matters, the mother has succeeded in causing parental alienation of the children from their father, such that they wish no longer to have frequent and regular visitation or anything much else to do with him. Ultimately, with much deliberation, this Court has determined that the long-term emotional best interests of these children mandate a change of custody to the father.[108]

From the Sublime in New York to the Ridiculous in Ohio

Just a few months after Judge Edlitz' detailed work in *In the Matter of J.F. v. L.F* for the Westchester County family court, the folks in Dayton, Ohio demonstrated that they may never get it right. *Pathan v. Pathan*[109] illustrates classic PAS behaviors by an American woman against her Pakistani husband and child. The court-appointed psychologist committed numerous egregious errors, in this author's opinion, and the trial judge did not do a good job. True to form, the appellate court lathered on the boilerplate, and did little else.

In *this case*, Dr. Pathan, a native of Pakistan, and his wife were married in Dayton, Ohio on November 2, 1985. During the marriage, the parties resided in California. One child, "S," was born to the parties in 1989. The couple obtained dissolution of their marriage in Los Angeles, California in 1993. During the separation, the wife returned to Dayton, Ohio, with "S," where she was employed as a music teacher.[110]

In 1993, Dr. Pathan entered into an arranged marriage to his first cousin, a native of Pakistan. She came to the United States in 1994, after the marriage. Problems began when, in mid-1994, the ex-wife learned of Dr. Pathan's marriage to his cousin. The problems were serious enough to necessitate court intervention for compliance with the visitation schedule because the ex-wife began interfering in Dr. Pathan's phone conversations with his young daughter.

At the hearings on Dr. Pathan's attempts to change custody, the ex-wife tried to show that the child was frightened by her father. She produced a videotape taken at her home showing the little girl lying on the ground in a state of distress, pleading not to attend visitation with Dr. Pathan. However, another video was admitted into evidence. This depicted the visitation exchange just hours later, showing the child hugging Dr. Pathan and happily getting into his car for the visit.[111]

According to the appellate court, there was evidence in the record indicating that the mother actively tried to cause the little girl to think less of her father. She told the child that Dr. Pathan was not present at her birth and also told her that Dr. Pathan had had a preference for a son.[112]

The record also reveals that knowing that Dr. Pathan was a devout Muslim; the mother enrolled the girl in a Christian academy. At the school, the mother completed the information form and placed a large "N/A" in the location for information about the child's father. In the blank that requested information as to with whom the child resided, she placed the words "Mother only" and underlined "only" three times. She also failed to provide any other information about Dr. Pathan on the form. The magistrate and the trial court also noted that the mother subjected the child to unnecessary drug testing at a children's medical center both before and after a weekend visit with Dr. Pathan.[113]

The magistrate and the trial court found that the mother's sister showed the child a movie called "Not Without My Daughter" (1991). According to the appellate court:

> The movie is a true story of an American woman married to a physician who was Iranian, but who practiced in Michigan. The characters in the story have one child, a young daughter. The physician asks the wife to accompany him to Iran for a family vacation, and while there, it becomes clear to the wife that he intends to remain there. In the film, the father beats and imprisons the mother. The film graphically depicts the cultural differences between Iran and the United States, particularly in the differences in the treatment of women and children. The general feeling from the movie is hatred and great trepidation toward the culture and the physician.[114]

The appellate court went on to opine: "The story is remarkably similar to [the child's] situation with her physician father from a similar national origin, and a mother and child with whom [the child] could identify."[115]

The court-appointed psychologist had demonstrated significant bias in her work with Dr. Pathan. First, she used standardized testing measures wholly inappropriate for Pakistanis.[116] She merely stated that she "took his ethnicity into account."[117] Next, she determined that Dr. Pathan was depressed and had a "paranoid predisposition" and based these diagnoses on Dr. Pathan's beliefs that his ex-wife had interfered with his telephone contact with his daughter, was on a "rage of vindictiveness" to block visitation, and had enrolled the child in a Christian school to spite him.[118] Finally, she required Dr. Pathan to participate in an unethical, dual relationship. With the trial court's blessing, the psychologist conducted a course of "family counseling sessions." These were serious breaches of professional ethics in this author's opinion.[119]

Dr. Pathan asked for an independent evaluation and named a local psychologist. On the suggestion of his ex-wife's counsel, Dr. Richard Gardner was appointed for the limited purpose of determining if the child suffered from PAS. Although he did not render an opinion as to custody, Dr. Gardner found that the ex-wife had induced a moderate amount of alienation in the parties' daughter, based upon her course of conduct in discouraging all forms of contact with Dr. Pathan. Gardner cited her exclusion of Dr. Pathan from the child's school enrollment forms and attempts to gather negative information about Dr. Pathan. In addition, Dr. Gardner stated in his report that he believed that the mother was a "child abuser."

The hearing officer noted that evidence existed that the mother had participated in psychologically abusing the little girl. This magistrate also noted that she had engaged in conduct involving psychological abuse and active interference with visitation and telephone contact. Nevertheless, the magistrate felt that it would be too traumatic to relocate the child.

Everyone objected and the case went to the trial court. The trial judge opined that the mother had been the primary offender in continuously and willfully denying and impeding Dr. Pathan's visitation with the child since Dr. Pathan's remarriage. The trial court found that the mother had unreasonably limited telephone visitation and had generally discouraged Dr. Pathan's relationship with his daughter. The trial court noted that even the girl's first-grade teacher was aware that the mother did not want the child visiting with Dr. Pathan. According to the reviewing court, the record is abundant with evidence of Merry discouraging and interfering with Dr. Pathan's visitation, both in person and by telephone. As the trial court noted, the problems ranged from intentionally leaving home when Dr. Pathan called during scheduled hours to not placing the little girl on the telephone and offering him a weak excuse for her not speaking, to the ex-wife hanging up on Dr. Pathan when he did call.

With five full years of this history, the Ohio court merely opined that if the mother did not mend her ways, "it might, in the future, be in [the child's] best interest for the court to grant the father's request for a change in custody."[120] The reviewing court provided six pages of boilerplate and little else.

Ample Evidence of PAS in Michigan

In the Matter of Spencley v. Spencley[121] found the Michigan appeals court dealing with the complaints of two parents against the state for its abuse and neglect determination. The family came to the attention of the court when the wife made several unsubstantiated allegations of child sexual abuse against the husband. The Michigan version of the Department of Social Services[122] came to the family court during the divorce proceedings and asserted that the three children were being emotionally abused by the parents. The court took evidence and found that the mother's latest complaint of child sexual abuse was unfounded but that the manner in which the couple handled their divorce and the parenting of the children amounted to abuse.

One of the psychologists who had worked with the family members testified at trial that the parents' behavior amounted to PAS. This psychologist testified that evidence showed that the mother was, during the course of the divorce, attempting to alienate the children from their father. On appeal, the mother challenged the concept of PAS, but the appellate court ruled that ample evidence of emotional injury to the children existed, and the psychologist merely used the concept of PAS as an explanatory tool: "The family court's factual findings are amply supported by the evidence presented at trial and, indeed, there was overwhelming evidence that the children were suffering from 'severe emotional problems.'"[123]

Debbie Does It in Arkansas

In *Chambers v. Chambers*,[124] the chancery court in Bradley County, Arkansas was faced with a completely successful campaign of *parental alienation.* Indeed, the record reveals that the mother's campaign spanned many years and totally destroyed the father's relationship with his children.

The parties were married in 1984. They had five children. During their divorce process in 1994, the father's difficulties with visitation caused the chancery court to appoint a psychiatrist to provide family therapy. The psychiatrist eventually concluded that the relationship between the appellant and his children had deteriorated to such an extent that visitation with the minor children posed the risk of emotional harm.[125] The father was so incensed at the psychiatrist's efforts, he filed suit against him for malpractice, and he withdrew.

The chancery court appointed another doctor in 1995, but it took until early 1996 to get the family members to participate in treatment. Two years after the process of court-ordered family treatment began, the doctor issued a report which *inter alia* noted that the process of alienation had been so successful, he was "concerned about the children's emotional state" and "recommending the court not force the minor children to visit" their father.[126] The chancery judge then denied the father's request for immediate required visitation and recused himself.[127]

A new chancery judge was assigned, and the father finally got a hearing *two years later.*[128] At the hearing, he relied on the expertise of an adolescent and child psychiatrist, in arguing that a material change of circumstances had occurred. Based upon his review of the medical records, court filings, and deposition transcripts and videotapes in this case, this psychiatrist testified that PAS was so severe that the children were "hopelessly estranged from him."[129] Indeed, he described the mother's efforts at PAS as so successful that " alienation was so complete that therapy would have no chance, under those circumstances."

In many ways, this psychiatrist agreed with the court-appointed therapist that the prospects for the mother's help in visitation were "hopeless." The appellate court put a good deal of stock in these opinions and quoted his testimony extensively:

> I don't think therapy would do anything, other than further prolong the agony. The court would have to be willing to order visitation with the expressed intent that if visitation is interfered with in any way it would have to consider seriously reversing the custody of [the youngest child] which would no doubt cause a lot of wailing and gnashing of teeth. I'm just suggesting that if visitation is awarded, I would suggest as an expert, that the court would have to anticipate that that is going to be interfered with. This child is going to protest. There will be no support of it. It will put her in a bind.[130]

In the face of the severe (and successful) *parental alienation*, the psychiatrist went on to testify: "I'm recommending visitation with the understanding that the court should be able to enforce it if there is any disruption or anyone trying to disrupt with that visitation. The child is going to refuse to go for visitation. That would be my guess. I feel that the court should force the visitation. It is kinda like after children get their first shot they don't want to go get a second one but you have to force them."[131]

Relying on the total success of her campaign of *parental alienation*, the mother moved for a directed verdict – to deny her ex-husband's motion for forced reintegration with his children.

The chancery judge explained *inter alia*: "I don't know y'all. . . . All . . . I know . . . there's been a war between the two of you for years. . . . But we've got to deal with what the situation is today. [The psychiatrist] . . . I believe . . . quoting [the court-appointed therapist] . . . said 'The relationship is over. It's gone, and I agree.' So that's the situation I'm dealing with today."[132]

Whereupon, the judge granted the mother's request for a directed verdict and ordered that the father had to keep sending her money.

Fortunately, the Arkansas appellate court did not follow the state of Ohio's habit of pasting in page after page of boilerplate. The appellate panel merely reasoned that because the mother had been at it for so long, "what the record abundantly shows [is what] has become an extremely hostile and unfortunate family situation resulting in a relationship that even [the psychiatrist] deemed 'hopeless." Therefore, reasoned the appellate panel, the father failed to show the statutory requisite "change of circumstances" warranting the court's intervention.[133]

Indiana Gets It Wrong – Then Right – Then Wrong

Just as chancery Judges Jerry Mazzanti and Robert Garrett of Arkansas participated in the *Chambers v. Chambers*[134] mess for five years, Lake County, Indiana Special Judge Mary Beth Bonaventura participated in a five-year battle for the daughter involved in *Kirk v. Kirk*. Unlike Arkansas or Ohio, the Court of Appeals in Indiana put a stop to it.[135] Unfortunately, it appears, behind the scenes machinations found the Indiana Supreme Court intervening with what seems a disregard for the record.[136]

The child was six years old when the mother began making spurious child sexual abuse claims. The little girl was twelve years old when Special Judge Bonaventura made a final decision.[137] During the intervening six years, the record reflects that the couple's marriage was dissolved in 1992. The mother was awarded legal and physical custody of their daughter, who was born in 1989. At first, the father exercised unsupervised visitation with the child every other weekend. Until mid-1995, he continued visitation in this fashion. In September 1995, the mother accused him of sexually molesting the child and refused to allow further visitation.[138]

Over the next five years, the trial court appointed expert after expert but consistently failed to make a final decision. The court appointed a total of seven experts and two GALs, received two more petitions from the father, and held the mother in contempt three times (with little or no real penalties). All experts and GALs who filed reports with the court expressed concern over the mother's and the child's mental health and recommended that the court consider a change in custody because the mother would not cooperate with attempts at reunification. It is important to note that none of the experts felt that there was *any* credible evidence that the alleged molestation had actually taken place. No criminal charges were ever filed. Finally, in 2001, the court ruled on all issues, denying the father's petition for change of custody and ordering more family counseling. The father appealed.[139]

The appellate panel noted that in November 1996, a clinical psychologist recommended that the court order professionally directed reunification efforts and that if such reunification could not reasonably occur within four months, "an alternate residential setting *that would promote* [the child's] *health* . . . be considered."[140] This recommendation was seconded one month later in a report by the GAL, who stated that reunification efforts utilizing professional guidance by a qualified therapist should commence immediately and that if reunification "cannot reasonably occur within four months, an alternate residential setting for [the child] shall be determined by the court *to promote* [the child's] health."[141] Four months later, the GAL reported that there had been no progress since her earlier report.

She opined that the child's belief in the allegations of molestation was directly related and substantially caused by the pathology between the mother and the child. In July 1997, the GAL filed an additional report with the court. She noted the emotional distancing between the child and the father, stating, "Every indication suggests that the mother has continuously and persuasively supported and orchestrated this distancing. . . . The mother has systematically refused to cooperate with a *therapeutic reuniting of child with father.*"[142] She again recommended that the court oversee the therapeutic reunification of the father and the child.

Six months later, a clinical psychologist reported to the court that reunification

> between [the father] and [the child] will be extremely difficult due to the *dysfunctional, highly symbiotic, codependency which exists between* [the mother and the child] . . . [Mother's] noninclusion of [father] and total desire for her daughter to deny and disown her father's existence and presence in her life is extremely emotionally unhealthy. It is my opinion that this psychopathology relates to [mother's] dysfunctional nature with respect to wanting to maintain almost total control of her daughter's life.[143]

The psychologist recommended therapeutic reunification efforts and "that serious consideration be given to removing [the child] to a neutral residential placement which would allow her the opportunity to develop her sense of identity, autonomy, and to effect a more positive relationship with her father."[144]

In April 1998, he diagnosed the child with PAS and again recommended "that the court consider removing [the child] to a more neutral setting so that she can have the opportunity to form her own, independent views of her father without any potential interference or alienation."[145]

In July 1998, another clinical psychologist submitted his report to the court. He noted that "[d]ata generated in this evaluation is strikingly similar to the previous professional reports" and that: "[t]he recommendations offered by [an earlier psychologist] in her report are extremely accurate, concise and should be given the strongest consideration." As to the mother, he wrote: "she should not be allowed to continue in the role of custodial parent."[146] Concerning the mother's participation in any reunification plan, he went on to write about mother's refusal to cooperate in reunification sessions and advised that "[i]f this lack of cooperation is substantiated, it . . . indicates a strong need for judicial intervention as soon as possible to resolve this impasse. I believe that continued obstruction of the healing process by any of the parties involved is *detrimental to the well-being of the minor child in this case*, and must be dealt with directly."[147]

In March 1998, an ACSW/LCSW, appointed by the court to begin therapeutic reunification sessions, reported the mother's total lack of cooperation. She summarized the previous professional evaluations and recommendations and noted her agreement with the expressed concerns, beginning with the original psychologist's fears first expressed in 1996 regarding the welfare of the child. She advised the court:

> The help that each of us; [psychologists, GAL] the court and I attempted to provide this little girl, [the child], has long been thwarted by [mother]. . . . I respectfully submit to this court that too many years have passed without this child getting the limits and boundaries set to protect her. . . . I believe the time has come to place [the child] in a residential environment away from her mother's full-time influence. [The child] *is a victim in a severe case of parental alienation syndrome*. . . . This is, indeed, a drastic level of intervention, however, this situation has become in need of drastic solutions or history will repeat itself.[148]

A few days following this report, one of the psychologists, appointed by the court as the therapy coordinator, advised the court of the mother's failure to cooperate, supported the recommendations, and stated: "[G]iven the history of this case and data available to me, I expect that [mother's] efforts to sabotage reunification will exceed her cooperation, continuing a *destructive influence on* [the child's] *psychological well-being and development*."[149] In August 1998, the same person reported that he still was not receiving cooperation from the mother and "that an intervention by the court *will be necessary*."[150]

In August 1999, the social worker informed the court that "[w]e appear to be at a crisis point in efforts toward reunification" and that neither the child "[n]or her mother understand the seriousness of the process."[151] She recommended that the mother be found in contempt unless she took immediate steps to bring herself into compliance. A few weeks later the social worker made her final report to the court, recommending that the child be removed from the mother's home and stating that the mother "has proved once again that she will not change."[152] She also noted that there was evidence that the child had told many of her classmates and teachers that her father had sexually molested her.[153]

In October 1999, a different social worker wrote to the court, "I feel I underestimated the dangerousness and level of pathology of [mother]. I feel she is extremely destructive. She will go to great lengths to sabotage reunification efforts between [the child] and [father]."[154] She insisted that she had to withdraw from the case because, as she put it: "I cannot submit myself to false allegations of abuse and place my license and reputation on the line. I feel [mother] will continue to fabricate false accusations against anyone who is attempting to aide [*sic*] in the reunification process."[155]

One year later, yet another court-appointed custody evaluator recommended that legal custody of the child be given to the father. He also recommended that the father move to the child's neighborhood and that he assume physical custody. In the face of this overwhelming evidence, Special Judge Bonaventura denied the father's petition to modify custody.[156]

The Court of Appeals did what needed to be done. The panel concluded unanimously that: "The trial court abused its discretion in allowing Mother to retain legal and physical custody of the child despite ***overwhelming evidence*** that their relationship was harmful to the child's mental health."[157] Their reasoning was simple: "The voluminous evidence leads unerringly to but one conclusion: that there has been a substantial negative change in the child's mental health since the last custody determination and that a change of custody is not only in her best interests but also is ***imperative and long overdue***."[158] The appellate court reversed, with an immediate remand for a change of custody. The truly unfortunate part of this case involves the action taken by the Indiana Supreme Court in June 2002.[159] In their review, the Court actually commended the judge. It seems the members of the Supreme Court had no appreciation whatsoever for her multiyear indecision. Unfortunately, the current members of the Indiana Supreme Court did not pay adequate attention to what the appellate panel clearly saw as the child's deepening pathology during the process of indecision. Indeed, if the judge had been a behavioral scientist, a board of review may very well have described the deepening pathology in the child as iatrogenic. Had the judge been a behavioral scientist, she very well may have been sued for incompetence and subjected to licensure revocation. It would be difficult to envision a judicial officer less able to grasp what the numerous competent behavioral sciences professionals were telling her.

While the problems for the family worsened as the judge watched the child's pathology deepen, the action of the Indiana Supreme Court in lowering the standard to that of Ohio and its rubber-stamp appellate processes will likely harm many more children and families. In their rush to overturn what the appellate panel worked so hard to explain, the current members of Indiana's Supreme Court underscored the importance of new research describing most judicial officers as inadequate regarding understanding science in general and the behavioral sciences in particular.[160] For in their brief published opinion, the current members of the Indiana Supreme Court completely neglected the spurious nature of the original claim of sexual abuse and the reports and testimony of seven competent behavioral sciences professionals, and characterized the five-year trauma as simply "a situation that centers on the personalities of two parents battling for control of a child."[161] What's more, the current members of Indiana's highest court described the child as now thoroughly believing the spurious claims of sexual assault[162] but were unable to connect the dots concerning the development of a false memory. And this despite seven experts doing everything they could to make that clear.

CONCLUSION

Certainly other PAS cases can be found in fifteen years of American jurisprudence. Several more boilerplate redundancies and interesting criminal cases exist. However, these cases provide a representative sample of the court's developing approach to PAS. One more bears mention. On January 17, 2002 after a hearing, the trial court in DuPage County, Illinois, ruled: "The Parental Alienation Syndrome is generally accepted in the mental health community and has met the requirements of the *Frye* test."[163]

ENDNOTES

1. *See e.g.*: Emery, Robert E. (1982). Interparental Conflict and the Children of Discord and Divorce, 92 *Psychological Bulletin. 310*; Hetherington, E. Mavis et al. (1982). Effects of Divorce on Parents and Children, in *Non-Traditional Families 233* (Michael E. Lamb ed.); Hetherington, E. Mavis (1989). Coping with Family Transitions: Winners, Losers, and Survivors, 60 *Child Development. 1*; Johnston, Janet R. et al., (1989). Ongoing Postdivorce Conflict: Effects on Children of Joint Custody and Frequent Access, 59 *American Journal of Orthopsychiatry 576*; Walsh, P.E. & Stolberg, A.L. (1989). Parental and Environmental Determinants of Children's Behavioral, Affective and Cognitive Adjustment to Divorce, 12 *Journal of Divorce 265*; Tschann, Jeane M. et al. (1990). Conflict, Loss. Change and Parent-Child Relationships: Predicting Children's Adjustment During Divorce, 13 *Journal of Divorce 1*; Amato, Paul R. & Keith, Bruce (1991). Parental Divorce and the Well-Being of Children: A Meta-Analysis, 110 *Psychological Bulletin. 26*; Hodges , William F. et al. (1991). Infant and Toddlers and Postdivorce Parental Access: An Initial Exploration, 16 *Journal of Divorce & Remarriage 239*; Brown, Joseph H. et al. (1991). Family Functioning Factors Associated with the Adjustment of Children of Divorce, 17 *Journal of Divorce & Remarriage 81.*
2. Gardner, Richard A. (1985). Recent trends in divorce and custody litigation. 29 *The Academy Forum (2)*3–7. New York: The American Academy of Psychoanalysis. Gardner's original anecdotal rendering of this phenomena described purposely contrived false allegations of child sexual abuse in custody litigation. Since that time, Gardner continually updated and rediscussed his sense of this phenomena, *e.g.*: Gardner, Richard A. (1992). *The Parental Alienation Syndrome.* Cresskill, NJ, Creative Therapeutics, Inc. Gardner, Richard A. (1998). *The Parental Alienation Syndrome,* Second Edition. Cresskill, NJ, Creative Therapeutics, Inc. and a wealth of peer reviewed, scientific journal articles. For a listing, please see: http://www.rgardner.com/refs/pas_peerreviewarticles.html. Dr. Gardner defines PAS:

   > The parental alienation syndrome (PAS) is a childhood disorder that arises almost exclusively in the context of child-custody disputes. Its primary manifestation is the child's campaign of denigration against a parent, a campaign that has no justification. It results from the combination of a programming (brainwashing) parent's indoctrinations and the child's own contributions to the vilification of the target parent. When true parental abuse and/or neglect is present, the child's animosity may be justified and so the parental alienation syndrome explanation for the child's hostility is not applicable. [http://www.rgardner.com/refs/pas_intro.html]

3. *Coursey v. Superior Court* 194 Cal App 3d 147; 239 Cal Rptr 365 (1987) through *Bates v. Bates* Docket No. 99 D 958 – Eighteenth Judicial Circuit Court, Illinois (January 17th, 2002).
4. *Coursey v. Superior Court* 194 Cal App 3d 147, 152; 239 Cal Rptr 365, 368 (1987).
5. *Id.* at 194 Cal App 3d 155-156; 239 Cal Rptr 370.
6. *Schutz v. Schutz,* 522 So. 2d 874 (Florida App. 1988).
7. *Schutz* , 522 So. 2d at 875.
8. *Id.*
9. *Id.* at 874.

10. *Schutz v. Schutz*, 581 So. 2d 1290 (1991).
11. *Id.* at 1292.
12. *A.R. v. S.E.*, *New York Law Journal*, December 11, 1990 pg 27–28, at 27.
13. *Id.* at pg 28.
14. *In re Violetta B.*, 210 Ill. App 3d 521,524; 568 N.E.2d 1345 (1991).
15. *Id.* at 525.
16. *Id.* at 528.
17. *Id.*
18. *Id.* at 530.
19. The court referred to her having completed an "American *Psychiatric* Association approved internship in clinical psychology." 210 Ill. App. 3d at 529, *emphasis added*, and then characterized her as: "a *psychiatrist* who testified as an expert witness in the area of child development and *psychology*." 210 Ill. App. 3d at 535, *emphasis added*.
20. *Id.* at 210 Ill. App. 3d 535.
21. *Id.* at 210 Ill. App. 3d 536.
22. Supra, at notes 7 through 12.
23. *Karen B. v. Clyde M.*, 151 Misc. 2d 794; 574 N.Y.S. 2d 267 (1991).
24. *Id.* at pg 795. In child sexual abuse allegations, the difficulty with children's suggestibility makes it critical to document the number and quality of interviews with the child. *See* e.g.: Lorandos, D. & Campbell, T. (1995). Myths and Realities of Sexual Abuse Evaluation and Diagnosis: A Call for Judicial Guidelines. 7 *Issues in Child Abuse Accusations, 1*; *See also*: Wakefield, H., & Underwager, R. (1991). Sexual allegations in divorce and custody disputes 9 *Behavioral Sciences and the Law, 451.* Wakefield and Underwager suggest understanding the "natural history" of an allegation, paying close attention to the origin, nature, and timing of the allegation.
25. *Karen B. v. Clyde M.*, 151 Misc. 2d 794 at 795–796.
26. A "validator" in the context of allegations of child sexual abuse is distinct from an "examiner" or an "evaluator." Validators tend to reason from preconceived notions which may lead to errors of "causism" and "hyperclaiming". *See* e.g.: Lorandos, D. (1995). Finding the right expert, in *Expert Witnesses: Beyond Junk Science and Daubert.* Institute of Continuing Legal Education, Ann Arbor, Mich. for a description of causism and hyperclaiming; *See also*: Gardner, R. A. (1991). The "validators" and other examiners. 2 *Issues in Child Abuse Accusations, 38.*
27. *Karen B. v. Clyde M.*, 151 Misc. 2d 794 at 796. This 75% "validation" rate is of course, astoundingly higher than the national average of substantiated cases of child sexual abuse. For this time period, *see* e.g.: Daro, D., & Mitchel, L. (1990). Current trends in child abuse reporting and fatalities: The results of the 1989 annual 50 states survey. Washington, DC: National Commission for the Prevention of Child Abuse. Daro and Mitchel indicate that the 1989 annual 50 state survey found a 63% unsubstantiated rate. *See also*: Flango, V. E. (1991). Can central registries improve substantiation rates in child abuse and neglect cases? 15 *Child Abuse & Neglect 403.* Flango surveyed New York state and found that 61% of sexual abuse allegations for a period of one year (1985). could not be substantiated.
28. Many experienced litigators refer to validators as "never hearing an allegation they didn't like" Personal communication, California criminal defense attorney Patrick Clancy. http://www.accused.com.
29. *Karen B. v. Clyde M.*, 151 Misc.2d 794 at 796.
30. *Karen B. v. Clyde M.*, 151 Misc.2d 794 at 796 : "The witness observed no sexual play with the anatomically correct doll." Anatomically detailed (breasts, genitalia, public hair etc.) dolls are widely considered extremely suggestive and leading, in child sexual abuse investigations. *See* e.g.: White, S., Strom, G., Santilli, G., & Haplin, B. (1986). Interviewing young sexual abuse victims with anatomically correct dolls. 10 *Child Abuse & Neglect 519*; Glaser, D., & Collins, C. (1989). The response of young, nonsexually abused children to anatomically correct dolls. 30 *Journal of Child Psychology & Psychiatry 547*; Levy, R. J. (1989). Using "Scientific" Testimony to Prove Child Sexual Abuse: The Dorsey & Whitney Professorship Lecture. 23 *Family Law Quarterly 383*; Realmuto, G. M., Jensen, J. B., & Wescoe, S. (1990). Specificity and sensitivity of sexually anatomically correct dolls in substantiating abuse: A pilot study. 29 *Journal of the American Academy of Child & Adolescent Psychiatry 743*; Gardner, R. A. (1992). Leading stimuli, leading gestures and leading questions. 4 *Issues in Child Abuse Accusations 144*; Skinner, L. J,. & Berry, K. K. (1993). Anatomically detailed dolls and the evaluation of child sexual abuse allegations. 17 *Law and Human Behavior 399*; Wolfner, G., Faust, D., & Dawes, R.M. (1993). The use of anatomically detailed dolls in sexual abuse evaluations: The state of the science. 2 *Applied and Preventative Psychology 1*; DeLoache, J. S. (1995). The use of dolls in interviewing young children. In M. S. Zaragosa, J. R. Graham, G. C. N. Hall, R. Hirschman, Y. S. Ben-Porath (Eds.), *Memory and Testimony in the Child Witness* (pp. 160–178). Thousand Oaks, CA: Sage Publications; Lorandos, D. & Campbell, T. (1995). Myths and Realities of Sexual Abuse Evaluation and Diagnosis: A Call for Judicial Guidelines. 7 *Issues in Child Abuse Accusations, 1.*
31. *Karen B. v. Clyde M.*, 151 Misc.2d 794 at 797.
32. *Id.*
33. *Id.* By reckoning from the appellate opinion, this was the *fifth* concerned adult to interview the little girl.
34. *Karen B. v. Clyde M.*, 151 Misc.2d 794 at 797.
35. *Id.*
36. *Karen B. v. Clyde M.*, 151 Misc.2d 794 at 797 & 798.
37. *Id.* at 798.
38. *Id.* at 798. The record is silent on what attempts were made to determine the reliability of a polygraph with a child less than $4^1/_2$ years old *or* what, if any, attempts were made to describe it's utility in child sexual abuse evaluations.

39. *Id. See also:* Blush, G. L., & Ross, K. L. (1987). Sexual allegations in divorce: The SAID syndrome. 25 *Conciliation Courts Review 45.*
40. *Karen B. v. Clyde M.*, 151 Misc.2d 794 at 798 & 799.
41. *Id.* at 799.
42. *Id.*
43. *Id.*
44. *Id.* at 800.
45. *Id.*
46. *Id.*
47. *Id.*
48. *Karen B. v. Clyde M.*, 151 Misc.2d 794 at 801 *emphasis added.*
49. *Id.*
50. *Id.*
51. *Karen B. v. Clyde M.*, 151 Misc.2d 794 at 801.
52. *Zigmont fka Toto v. Toto*, 1992 WL 6034 (Ohio App. 8th District) Docket No. 62149.
53. A review of Ohio appellate decisions involving PAS cases, and indeed family law cases in general, finds a dramatic proclivity to rubber-stamp their trial courts and simply rewrite the same conclusory citations to statutory law. *See* e.g.: *Zigmont fka Toto v. Toto*, 1992 WL 6034; *Hornsby (Sims) v. Hornsby*, 1992 WL 193682; *Renz (Conner) v. Renz*, 1995 WL 23365; *Pisaini v. Pisaini*, 1998 WL 655484; *Bates v. Bates*, 2001 WL 1560916.
54. *Zigmont fka Toto v. Toto*, 1992 WL 6034 (Ohio App. 8th District) Docket No. 62149. Westlaw page *2.
55. *Id.* at Westlaw pages *1 & *2.
56. *Zigmont fka Toto v. Toto*, 1992 WL 6034 (Ohio App. 8th District) Docket No. 62149. Westlaw page *8.
57. *Wiederholt v. Fischer*, 169 Wis 2d 524; 485 NW 2d 442 (1992).
58. 169 Wis 2d at 529.
59. *Id.*
60. 169 Wis 2d at 531.
61. *Id.*
62. *Id.*
63. 169 Wis 2d at 532.
64. 169 Wis 2d at 533.
65. *Truax v. Truax*, 110 Nev 437; 874 P 2d 10 (1994).
66. *Id.* at 439.
67. *Id.*
68. In *re Marriage of Rosenfeld*, 524 NW 2d 212 (Iowa App, 1994).
69. *Wiederholt v. Fischer*, 169 Wis 2d 524; 485 NW 2d 442 (1992).
70. In *re Marriage of Rosenfeld*, 524 NW 2d 212, 214 (Iowa App, 1994).
71. *Id.*
72. *Id.* at 214 & 215. Please note that it is a convention of this author, *not* to mention the name of children referred to in cited cases, even though they may be found in the cited text.
73. *Id.* at 215.
74. *Id.*
75. *White v. White*, 655 NE 2d 523, 526 n 2 (Indiana App, 1995).
76. *Id.* 655 NE 2d at 526 & 527.
77. *Id.* at 526.
78. *Id.* at 532.
79. *Tucker fka Greenberg v. Greenberg*, 674 So 2d 807, 808 (Florida App, 1996).
80. *Id.*
81. *Id.* at 674 So 2d 808 & 809.
82. In *re Marriage of Rosenfeld*, 524 NW 2d 212 (Iowa App, 1994).
83. *Williams v. Williams*, 676 So 2d 493 (Florida App, 1996).
84. *Hanson v. Spolnik*, 685 NE 2d 71 (Indiana App, 1997).
85. *Id.*
86. *Id.* 685 NE 2d at 74.
87. *Id.*
88. *Id.*
89. *Id.*
90. *Id. emphasis added.*
91. *Id.* at 76. This was the same psychologist who testified in *White v. White*, 655 NE 2d 523 (Indiana App, 1995). Both cases took place in Indianapolis, Indiana.
92. *Id.* at 77. The trial court also took testimony from a clinical psychologist who interviewed the older girl and the four-year-old, who specifically stated that "there was inappropriate sex play between the two children."
93. *Id.* at 76.
94. *Id.* at 79.
95. In *the Matter of J.F. v. L.F.*,181 Misc.2d 722; 694 N.Y.S.2d 592 (1999).
96. *Karen B. v. Clyde M.*, 151 Misc.2d 794; 574 N.Y.S.2d 267 (1991).
97. *Id.* 181 Misc.2d at 724.
98. *Id.* at 723.
99. *Id.* at 723, quoting *People v. Loomis*, 172 Misc. 2d 265, 267; 658 N.Y.S.2d 787 (New York App, 1997).
100. *Id.* at 725.
101. *Id.* at 726.
102. *Id.* at 726–727. In connection with this proceeding, and pursuant to order of the court, the psychiatrist conducted evaluations of the parents and children and submitted reports. He found *inter alia* that the mother continued to have a DSM-IV psychiatric diagnosis of "moderate-to-severe Personality Disorder, NOS, with Borderline, Obsessive, and Passive-Aggressive features." He testified that: "Father is painted in a highly derogatory and negative fashion, way out of proportion to any possible deficiencies that he may have. This is clearly a borderline mental device within the mother's psychology which has been clearly duplicated in the children."
103. *Id.* at 727.
104. *Id.* This psychiatrist was a diplomate in psychiatry and neurology, a member of the American Academy of Psychiatry and the Law, and a diplomate of the American College of Forensic Examiners.

105. *Id.*
106. *Id.*
107. *Id.* at 731.
108. *Id.* at 723.
109. *Pathan v. Pathan*, 2000 WL 43711 (Ohio App. 2 Dist).
110. *Id.* Westlaw page *1
111. *Id.*, page *2.
112. *Id.*
113. *Id.*
114. *Id.*
115. *Id.* Although the mother alleged she just happened to get some tapes from her sister, it was discovered that the "Not Without My Daughter" movie was specifically chosen for the child's viewing.
116. *Id.* Westlaw page *3. She acknowledged that none of the tests had been adjusted to account for Dr. Pathan's Pakistani ethnicity, and in fact there had been no statistical attempts to standardize the MMPI-II for individuals with Dr. Pathan's ethnicity at all. *Please see*: American Psychological Association (1992). Ethical principles of psychologists and code of conduct. 47 *American Psychologist 1597.*

   Standard 2.02 (a) of the American Psychological Association's ethical code – addressing issues of "Competence and Appropriate Use of Assessments and Interventions" states:

   > "Psychologists who develop, administer, score, interpret, or use psychological assessment techniques, interviews, tests, or instruments do so in a manner and for purposes that are appropriate in light of the research on or evidence of the usefulness and proper application of the techniques."

   Standard 2.02 (a) therefore obligates psychologists to use assessment procedures for which there is validation evidence supporting those assessment procedures. *For example*: In *In re Cheryl H.*, 200 Cal. Rptr. 789 (Ct. App 1984), the court disallowed the use of psychological testing to establish a "profile" characteristic of fathers who commit sexual abuse. According to the expert witness, 85 percent of fathers who commit sexual abuse have personality traits of high passive-dependency and highly guarded and defensive tendencies. The court pointed out that the statistical evidence was not persuasive.

   The court in *Gier v. The Educational Service Unit No. 16*, 845 F. Supp. 1342 (D. Neb. 1994)., applied the analysis prescribed by the United States Supreme Court in *Daubert v. Merrell Dow Pharmaceutical, Inc.*, 113 S. Ct. 2786 (1993)., to disallow testing which had been offered for the proof of child molestation. The witnesses' conclusions were based in part on the use of Child Behavior Check Lists. The trial judge felt that the reliability of the methodologies used by plaintiff's witnesses had not been sufficiently established; no records or tapes were made of the interviews and thus it could not be determined whether the interviewer either inappropriately suggested an answer or incorrectly interpreted a response.

   It is also necessary to consider Standard 2.03 of the Ethical Code of the American Psychological Association. This Standard states:

   > "Psychologists who develop and conduct research with tests and other assessment techniques use scientific procedures and current professional knowledge for test design, standardization, validation, reduction or elimination of bias, and recommendations for use." *Id.*

   As a result of the potential for arbitrarily undermining the civil rights of those evaluated, Standard 2.03 obligates psychologists who do psychological testing to support their conclusions with properly conducted validity studies. *For example*: The court in *Argen v. New York State Bd. of Law Examiners*, 860 F. Supp. 84 (W.D.N.Y. 1994), rejected the testimony of psychologists who purported to establish that plaintiff had a learning disability that entitled him to reasonable accommodation in taking the bar examination. The first witness relied on tests not generally accepted in this scientific community as a reliable basis to establish a learning disability. Another witness, who reported on his interpretation of the tests, was unable to explain how he used the test to arrive at his conclusions.

   And see: American Educational Research Association, American Psychological Association, National Council on Measurement in Education (1999). *Standards for educational and psychological testing.* Washington, DC: American Educational Research Association. These 1999 Standards are also relevant to the testimony of psychologists in legal proceedings. In particular, consider the following Testing standards:

   > Standard 11.1:
   > "Prior to the adoption and use of a published test, the test user should study and evaluate the materials provided by the test developer. Of particular importance are those that summarize the test's purposes, specify the procedures for test administration, define the intended populations of test takers, and discuss the score interpretations for which validity and reliability data are available."
   >
   > Standard 11.2:
   > "When a test is to be used for a purpose for which little or no documentation is available, the user is responsible for obtaining evidence of the test's validity and reliability for this purpose."
   >
   > Standard 12.13:
   > "Those who select tests and draw inferences from test scores should be familiar with the relevant evidence of validity and reliability for tests and inventories used and should be prepared to articulate a logical analysis that supports all facets of the assessment and the inferences made from the assessment."

   In August 1999, the Council of Representatives of the American Psychological Association approved the 1999 Standards for Educational and Psychological Testing [American Psychological Association (2000).

Proceedings of the American Psychological Association, Incorporated, for the legislative year 1999: Minutes of the annual meeting of the Council of Representatives. 55 *American Psychologist 837*, p. 885).] The American Psychological Association, therefore, formally recognizes the 1999 Standards and their applicability to the professional work of psychologists.

117. *Id.* The magistrate determined that: "[The doctor's] clinical impressions were 'distorted' by the test data and her apparent dislike of Dr. Pathan's style during the evaluation process." At Westlaw page *11.
118. *Id.* Both the magistrate and the trial court found Dr. Pathan's beliefs to be justified.
119. *See* e.g.: Campbell, T.W. (1992). Psychotherapy with children of divorce: The pitfalls of triangulated relationships. 29 *Psychotherapy, 646*, 651. Discussing the common problem of evaluators in custody circumstances falling into the dual role of counselor or therapist. *See also*: Campbell, T.W. and Lorandos, D. (2001). *Cross Examining Experts in the Behavioral Sciences.* Minneapolis, MN. West Group two volumes. Specifically, Chapter Two provides a detailed discussion of the literature of science, ethics, and law on impermissible dual relationships.

Also see:

American Psychological Association (1992). Ethical principles of psychologists and code of conduct. 47 *American Psychologist 1597*, p. 1601. The ethical code for psychologists also prohibits dual relationships. Standard 1.17 (a–c) of the code of ethics for the American Psychological Association – addressing "Multiple Relationships" – states:

"(a) In many communities and situations, it may not be feasible or reasonable for psychologists to avoid social or other nonprofessional contacts with persons such as patients, clients, students, supervisees, or research participants. Psychologists must always be sensitive to the potential harmful effects of other contacts on their work and on those persons with whom they deal. A psychologist refrains from entering into or promising another personal, scientific, professional, financial, or other relationship with such persons if it appears likely that such a relationship reasonably might impair the psychologist's objectivity or otherwise interfere with the psychologist's effectively performing his or her functions as a psychologist, or might harm or exploit the other party.

(b) Likewise, whenever feasible, a psychologist refrains from taking on professional or scientific obligations when preexisting relationships would create a risk of such harm.

(c) If a psychologist finds that due to unforeseen factors, a potentially harmful multiple relationship has arisen, the psychologist attempts to resolve it with due regard for the best interests of the affected person and maximal compliance with the Ethics Codes."

Additionally, the ethical standards regarding the "Forensic Activities" of psychologists – specifically Standard 7.03 addressing "Clarification of Role" –states:

"In most circumstances, psychologists avoid performing multiple and potentially conflicting roles in forensic matters. When psychologists may be called on to serve in more than one role in a legal proceeding – for example, as consultant or expert for one party or for the court and as a fact witness – they clarify the role expectations and the extent of confidentiality in advance to the extent feasible, and thereafter as changes occur, in order to avoid compromising their professional judgment and objectivity and in order to avoid misleading others regarding their role."

And, *also see*: Committee on Ethical Guidelines for Forensic Psychologists (1991). Specialty guidelines for forensic psychologists. 15 *Law and Human Behavior 655.* The Specialty Guidelines for Forensic Psychologists indicate the following:

"Forensic psychologists avoid providing professional services to parties in a legal proceeding with whom they have personal or professional relationships that are inconsistent with the anticipated relationship.
When it is necessary to provide both evaluation and treatment services to a party in a legal proceeding (as may be the case in small forensic hospital settings or small communities), the forensic psychologist takes reasonable steps to minimize the potential negative effects of these circumstances on the rights of the party, confidentiality, and the process of treatment and evaluation."

120. *Id.*,Westlaw page *4. On a positive note: The case returned to Magistrate Jeffrey Taylor for further hearings. On January 15th, 2000 the magistrate and the assigned judge Hon. Charles A. Lowman III ordered that custody of the child be changed to the alienated father. The child is reported to be doing well. Personal communication to Dr. Gardner from the father, May, 2002.
121. *Spencley v. Spencley*, 2000 WL 33519710 (Mich App).
122. Renamed the *Family Independence Agency* when the new Republican governor slashed state welfare payments and completely eliminated "general assistance" payments to indigents.
123. *Spencley v. Spencley*, 2000 WL 33519710 (Mich App) at Westlaw page *4.
124. *Chambers v. Chambers*, 2000 WL 795278 (Arkansas App).
125. *Id.* at WL *1.
126. *Id.*
127. *Id.* Chancery judge Jerry Mazzanti entered his order denying the father's motion on December 4th and recused himself on December 11th, 1996.
128. *Id.* The new judge took over January 13th, 1997. The hearing on the father's request for visitation was held January 29th, 1999.
129. *Id.*, Westlaw page *3.

130. *Id. emphasis in original.*
131. *Id.*
132. *Id.*, Westlaw page *4.
133. *Id.*, Westlaw pages *4 & *5.
134. *Id.*
135. *Kirk v. Kirk*, 759 N. E.2d 265 (Indiana App, December, 2001).
136. *Kirk v. Kirk*, 770 N.E.2d 304 (June 21, 2002).
137. *Id.* 759 N. E.2d at 266.
138. *Id.*
139. *Id.*
140. *Id.* at 267.
141. *Id.* at 268, *emphasis added.*
142. *Id.* at 268, *emphasis added.*
143. *Id.* at 268, *emphasis added.*
144. *Id.* at 268, *emphasis added.*
145. *Id.* at 268, *emphasis added.*
146. *Id.*
147. *Id.* at 268, *emphasis added.*
148. *Id.* at 268–269, *emphasis added.*
149. *Id.* at 269, *emphasis added.*
150. *Id.* at 269, *emphasis added.*
151. *Id.* at 269.
152. *Id.*
153. *Id.*
154. *Id.* at 269.
155. *Id.* at 270.
156. *Id.* at 266.
157. *Id.* at 270, *emphasis added.*
158. *Id.* at 270, *emphasis added.*
159. *Kirk v. Kirk*, 770 N.E.2d 304 (June 21, 2002).
160. *See* e.g.: Kovera, M.B. and McAuliff, B.D. (2000). The Effects of Peer Review and Evidence Quality on Judge Evaluations of Psychological Science: Are Judges Effective Gatekeepers? 85 *Journal of Applied Psychology 574*; Gatowski, S. I.; Dobbin, S.A.; Richardson, J.T.; Ginsburg, G.P.; Merlino, M.L. & Dahir, V. (2001). Asking the Gatekeepers: A National Survey of Judges on Judging Expert Evidence in a Post – *Daubert* World. 24 *Law and Human Behavior 433. See also*: Lorandos, D. & Campbell, T.W. (2005), *Benchbook in the Behavioral Sciences – Psychiatry – Psychology – Social Work.* Durham, NC: Carolina Academic Press. Chapter Two describes research into attorneys' and judges' inabilities to meet the requirements of the *Daubert* tests for validity and reliability.
161. *Kirk v. Kirk*, 770 N.E.2d 304 (June 21, 2002).
162. *Id.* at 306, footnote one.
163. *Bates v. Bates*, Circuit Court for DuPage County, Illinois. Docket No. 99-D 958, January 17th, 2002.

Chapter 27

SOCIAL SCIENCE AND PARENTAL ALIENATION: EXAMINING THE DISPUTES AND THE EVIDENCE

RICHARD A. WARSHAK

OVERVIEW

This chapter examines a continuum of opinions about parental alienation with reference to relevant scientific literature. Professionals agree that children can become irrationally alienated from a parent but disagree about what to call this problem and about how to conceptualize it. A conceptualization that emphasizes the influence of the favored parent, such as parental alienation syndrome (PAS), has intellectual and scientific roots in developmental and cognitive psychology, particularly research on children's suggestibility. A conceptualization that emphasizes the role of multiple interrelated factors enjoys support in family systems theory that regards children's problematic behavior as an expression of family-wide dysfunction. The available research supports the prevailing opinion among mental health professionals that the court's authority is a key element in successful remedies of severe alienation.

INTRODUCTION

A growing number of child custody decisions refer to children who irrationally reject one parent as a result primarily of the negative influence of the other parent. Critics of such decisions form a continuum from those who deny the possibility that any child could develop an irrational alienation from a parent, to those who acknowledge the existence of irrational alienation but doubt that it is abnormal, to those who believe that alignment with one parent against the other parent is an unfortunate but natural by-product of divorce or a developmentally expected reaction, to those who believe that irrational alienation exists but is never a product mainly of the favored parent's influence, to those who agree that some parents succeed in undermining their children's relationship with the other parent but object to specific terms that courts and mental health professionals have used to designate the phenomenon (such as brainwashing, parental alienation syndrome [PAS], and parental alienation), to those who disagree only about how courts should respond to children's irrational alienation.

This chapter draws on a wide body of scientific literature to examine disputes about the existence, conceptualization, and treatment of parental alienation. The intent is to illuminate the nature of the major disputes and to provide information to assist attorneys and judges in evaluating the utility of alternative perspectives.

I. CAN CHILDREN BECOME PATHOLOGICALLY ALIENATED FROM A PARENT?

A. Can Alienation From a Parent Ever Be Irrational?

No one disputes the existence of children who become alienated (in the dictionary sense of being estranged) from a parent. At issue is whether such alienation can ever be unreasonable and, if so, whether it can be considered abnormal.

Mental health and legal professionals generally agree that some children whose parents live apart develop extreme animosity toward or fear of one parent that is not reasonable or consistent with the prior history of the child's relationship with the rejected parent. Some parents, though, claim that any child's rejection of a parent is *prima facie* evidence of severe mistreatment by the rejected parent.[1] The position that irrational alienation does not exist essentially means that all rejected parents deserve what they get. They are not victims. They are perpetrators of some type of behavior that warrants their children's fear, hatred, or both. Those who subscribe to this position believe that courts regularly place children in the custody of abusive parents who have fooled the courts into believing that the children's negative attitudes are the result of the favored parent's influence over the child rather than the rejected parent's mistreatment.[2]

In the early years following the recognition by health care professionals of the prevalence and destructiveness of the physical and sexual abuse of children and the tendency for people to deny the extent of the problem,[3] some psychotherapists and child advocates subscribed to the view that "children never lie" about parental mistreatment and that "where there's smoke, there's fire." Such views were (and still are) expressed in reports and testimony.[4] More common are the predispositions to believe children's allegations of mistreatment (as opposed to the automatic acceptance of the truth of all such allegations) and to deny the possibility of false accusations. A corollary to these predispositions is concern that scholars who emphasize children's suggestibility and the possibility of inaccurate memories overstate their case and make unwarranted generalizations from empirical research that, by necessity, cannot duplicate the experience of an abused child.[5]

A central problem for those who deny the possibility of irrational alienation is the wealth of highly respected research that has demonstrated that young children are easily manipulated and suggestible and that it is a mistake for examiners and courts, particularly in the context of a contentious divorce, to assume that allegations of abuse and mistreatment are always likely to be true.[6]

Another problem for those who dispute the existence of irrational alienation is that very often children who reject a formerly loved parent offer trivial reasons for their change of heart.[7] In some cases, favored parents accept trivial complaints as sufficient explanation for the child's alienation either because they do not think objectively about their ex-spouse or because they welcome their child's negative attitudes toward the ex-spouse. In other cases, a parent or examiner assumes that trivial complaints mask severe mistreatment that the child is too scared, inhibited, or immature to articulate. In some cases this assumption may be warranted, but it does not account for children who, in the absence of any direct contact, develop an aversion to relatives with whom they previously had a loving relationship. Nor does this assumption accord with observations made by custody evaluators and clinicians that some children who refuse contact with a parent are very relaxed and affectionate with that parent as soon as they are outside the presence of the favored parent. In addition, research has shown that some alienated children, when they become adults, acknowledge that their rejection of a parent was unreasonable.[8]

B. Is Irrational Alienation Abnormal?

Despite agreement among professionals that some children whose parents divorce develop an irrational extreme animosity toward or anxiety about one parent, not everyone agrees that such alienation should be regarded as pathological, abnormal, or something requiring correction. One author argued that we have no basis for regarding parental alienation as abnormal because we lack normative data from intact and low-conflict divorced families, i.e., we lack research on the prevalence of this phenomenon.[9] In this view, irrational alienation from a parent could be considered a normal part of growing up. Bruch argued – citing a telephone conversation with Wallerstein regarding a noncontrolled study of a nonrepresentative sample of 60 families in Marin County, California who responded to an offer for free counseling in the early 1970s – that alignment with one parent and alienation from the other is natural for older children whose parents divorce. In this view irrational alienation is no cause for concern because every case of alienation in that study resolved itself before the children reached age 18, most within one or two years.[10] The position that it might be normal for children to be alienated from their parents is inconsistent with the scientific literature. It overlooks research on children's adjustment in divorced families and on healthy parent-child relations in intact families.

The scientific literature on the effects of parent conflict on children documents the harm to children who are caught in the middle of the conflict, as in situations where they are encouraged to side with one parent against the other.[11] Studies of children's attitudes about their parents' divorces consistently reveal that most children long for more time with each parent and wish their parents would reunite.[12] Another study found that three out of four college students who grew up in divorced families thought that the best parenting plans were those that gave children equal time in each parent's home.[13] The desire to be with a divorced parent is normative; the desire to avoid a parent is not.

The research is clear that the type of denigration, hatred, and fear characteristic of irrational alienation is foreign to most intact families and would be considered a symptom worthy of treatment.[14] Even in clinical samples with children who are enmeshed with one parent, usually the mother, the children still tolerate their fathers. I am unaware of any reports in the literature, or any therapeutic programs, in which a parent in an intact family who is not guilty of child abuse or gross mistreatment is advised to cut off contact with the children in response to overtly conflicted parent-child relationships. Instead, articles and books on treatment suggest strategies for helping the family understand and heal damaged parent-child.[15]

The view that irrational alienation requires no intervention because it resolves itself by age 18 also is difficult to defend. To begin with, the Marin County study reported that children between the ages of nine and 12 were most likely to align themselves with one parent against the other. This means that some of these cases could have lasted as long as six to nine years. The study reported no measure of the quality of the child's relationship with each parent after the alienation abated, nor of the mental anguish suffered by the alienated parents during the period of estrangement, and the regret, guilt, and remorse suffered by the children when they confronted the irreplaceable lost years of childhood spent with one parent instead of two (and often one extended family instead of two).[16] Gardner reported 33 cases in which alienation persisted for more than two years,[17] and this accords with the many reports the present author has received of families in which a child's irrational alienation persisted for more than two years, often far beyond the age of 18.[18]

Despite Bruch's citation of a telephone conversation with Wallerstein in support of the idea that parental alienation is a short-lived phenomenon, some of Wallerstein's published work conveys a vastly different impression. Introducing the term "Medea syndrome" to refer to parents who use their children to exact revenge on their former spouse, Wallerstein and Blakeslee wrote, "They exact it by destroying the relationship between the other parent and the child. In so doing, they severely damage and sometimes destroy the child's psyche as well. . . . I have seen a great deal of evidence that Medea-like anger severely injures children at every age."[19] Note the reference to the *destruction*, rather than the temporary *interruption*, of the parent-child relationship. Underscoring this point, they added, "When one or both parents act the Medea role, children are affected for years to come. Some grow up with warped consciences, having learned how to manipulate people as the result of their parents' behavior. Some grow up with enormous rage, having understood that they were used as weapons. Some grow up guilty, with low self-esteem and recurrent depression."[20]

When viewed in a wider context, the idea that children can develop pathological hatred and fear of a parent seems not at all controversial. It is well-known that children can be, and are, taught to hate and fear other people for no good reason, often based on racial or cultural differences. In addition, it has long been recognized that some children develop irrational aversions to objects and situations; such disturbances are codified in several different diagnoses of anxiety and phobia.[21] There is no reason to assume that parents are exempt from becoming the target of such irrational feelings.

If a child begins to develop racial hatred, many reasonable people would consider this a problem worthy of attention. When children suffer from irrational anxieties that interfere with functioning, we do not ignore the suffering with the hope that eventually the fears will be overcome. We try to alleviate the fears in order to improve the child's current quality of life. Pathologically alienated children cannot experience or share affectionate feelings toward a parent. It would seem that this disturbance warrants at least as much concern as other irrational aversions.

II. CONCEPTUALIZING PATHOLOGICAL PARENTAL ALIENATION

Despite the opposition of some advocacy groups, and a few attorneys, and mental health professionals, discussions in learned treatises for child custody evaluators are testament to the widespread acceptance among therapists and courts that irrational alienation exists and that it should be considered a severe disturbance of normal functioning.[22] Controversy continues, though, regarding the issues of how to conceptualize the problem, what to call it, how to treat it, and why it has received such widespread acceptance.[23]

The central controversy about the conceptualization of this disturbance concerns the role attributed to one parent in fostering, encouraging, supporting, and accepting the child's irrational aversion toward the other parent. Wallerstein's description of the Medea syndrome echoes earlier accounts by Reich and Despert that attribute to the behavior of the favored parent primary responsibility for some cases of alienation.[24] Wallerstein and Kelly also emphasized the pernicious contributions of a vindictive parent in their description of children who:

> were particularly vulnerable to being swept up into the anger of one parent against the other. They were faithful and valuable battle allies in efforts to hurt the other parent. Not infrequently, they turned on the parent they had loved and been very close to prior to the marital separation.
>
> The most extreme identification with the parent's cause we have called an "alignment" – a divorce-specific relationship that occurs when a parent and one or more children join in a vigorous attack on the other parent. *It is the embattled parent, often the one who opposes the divorce in the first place, who initiates and fuels the alignment.*[25]

The idea captured in the preceding quotes that the attack on one parent results from the children joining with the other parent is central to Richard Gardner's formulation of the problem.[26] His formulation, termed "parental alienation syndrome" (PAS), has garnered the most attention and dominates the literature on the problem. It was the first to systematically describe in detail common behaviors of alienated children and the underlying psychological factors in parents and children that contribute to the problem. As a result, PAS became the model to which others responded, either with supporting observations, refinements, or criticisms, often with misunderstanding and misrepresentation.[27]

A. PAS

Parental alienation syndrome refers to a disturbance whose primary manifestation is a child's unreasonable campaign of denigration against, or rejection of, one parent, due to the influence of the other parent combined with the child's own contributions.[28] Note three essential elements in this definition: (1) rejection or denigration of a parent that reaches the level of a campaign, i.e., it is persistent and not merely an occasional episode; (2) the rejection is irrational, i.e., the alienation is not a reasonable response to the alienated parent's behavior; and (3) it is a partial result of the nonalienated parent's influence. If any of these three elements is absent, the term "PAS" is not applicable. Properly understood, a clinician using the term "PAS" does not automatically assume that the favored parent has influenced a child's alienation from the other parent. Rather, PAS is used only when evidence for all three elements exists.

Some critics of PAS mistakenly equate it with only the first element – the child's negative attitudes and behavior toward a parent – and fear that the term obscures the difference between children who are reasonably and unreasonably alienated. With this confused understanding of PAS, these critics attack a straw man by pointing out the obvious fact that children develop conflicted relationships with parents for a variety of reasons and that alienation is not always irrational.[29] When Gardner introduced the term "PAS," he had already written extensively about other sources of parent-child conflicts and he used the new term to differentiate one type of alienation from all others – alienation that is unwarranted by the rejected parent's behavior and is influenced by the favored parent. Those who use the term "PAS" believe that this phenomenon is different enough from other types of parent-child disturbances to warrant a separate designation.

Those who oppose the use of the term "PAS" either deny the existence of children who, under the influence of one parent, turn against the other parent, or believe that such a disturbance does not warrant a diagnosis, or believe that all forms of irrational alienation should be grouped in one category and designated with a single term, rather than reserve a term for cases in which the alienation is traced to the influence of the favored parent.[30] The latter position reflects a belief that the literature on PAS overemphasizes the contributions of the favored parent and underemphasizes the importance of multiple contributing factors.

B. The Scope of Mental Health Diagnoses

Some disputes about PAS can be traced to different ideas about what exactly a diagnosis entails. A few critics have dismissed PAS as invalid based on their disagreement with Gardner's ideas about the etiology, treatment, prognosis, and incidence of PAS.[31] The implication is that a diagnosis logically entails only one view on such issues (in this case the view of the person who originally described and named it). In this vein, Kelly and Johnston criticized PAS because it "sheds no light on cause, prognosis, and treatment." They argued that in high-conflict divorces, "many parents engage in indoctrinating behaviors, but only a small proportion of children become alienated."[32] Because the favored parent's behavior alone is insufficient to account for alienation, and Gardner's definition of PAS does not include the multiple factors that contribute to a child developing this disturbance, these authors reject the term "PAS."

The assumption that a proposed diagnostic term must include a well-established, comprehensive body of knowledge regarding the causes, prognosis, and treatment of the condition is a novel standard that is inconsistent with the way medicine, including psychiatry, generally regards diagnoses and syndromes. The American Psychiatric Association defines a syndrome as "a grouping of signs and symptoms, based on their frequent co-occurrence, that may suggest a common underlying pathogenesis, course, familial pattern, or treatment selection."[33] There is no requirement that a syndrome include definitive statements about causes, prognosis, incidence, or treatment. Professionals disagree about the causes and appropriate treatment of many, if not most, of the diagnoses listed by the American Psychiatric Association. Diagnostic terms are independent of the discovery or proposal of new treatments. Many syndromes in physical medicine have no currently known effective treatment. The professional community ordinarily regards the presentation of a new diagnostic term based on clinical observations as just the beginning of work in the area. It is assumed that the original formulation, sometimes even the definition, will undergo revision as more is learned about the condition. New information may result in more precise descriptions of what the diagnosis includes as well as what it excludes. Gardner acknowledged his expectation that others will refine and expand on his contributions, and such revisions are evident in several articles on PAS.[34]

PAS fits a basic pattern of many psychiatric syndromes. Such syndromes denote conditions in which people who are exposed to a designated stimulus develop a certain cluster of symptoms. "Posttraumatic stress disorder" (PTSD) refers to a particular cluster of symptoms developed in the aftermath of a traumatic event. "Specific phobia" refers to a cluster of symptoms that develops in the presence of a circumscribed object or situation. "Adjustment disorder" refers to symptoms that develop in reaction to psychosocial stress. These diagnoses carry no implication that everyone exposed to the same stimulus develops the condition, nor that similar symptoms never develop in the absence of the designated stimulus. For instance, a full understanding of why some women develop PTSD in the aftermath of a rape and others do not would require an understanding of multiple factors, including knowledge of the individual in question and the circumstances of the trauma. Similarly, some, but not all, children develop PAS when exposed to a parent's negative influence. Other factors beyond the stimulus of an alienating parent can help elucidate the etiology for any particular child. However, such explanatory factors are not part of the definition of the condition. For instance, one hypothesis is that only children who have suffered a certain type of disturbance in their early psychological development are susceptible to developing PAS.[35] If this generalization is valid it would not change the diagnosis of PAS, it would merely refine our understanding of it. With all diagnoses it is assumed that further knowledge will continue to reveal more dimensions of the disturbance, its causes, and its effective treatment.

When a proposed syndrome, such as PAS, is properly understood as referring to a cluster of observed symptoms rather than to a set of ideas about etiology, incidence, prognosis, and treatment, it becomes clear why it is a mistake to refer to PAS as a "theory," as some critics have done.[36] PAS, similar to other diagnoses, describes observations. The term "PAS" is used to label the condition of children who develop an irrational alienation of affection for one parent when exposed to the other parent's negative influence. There is nothing theoretical about the existence of such children. Conjectures about the best way to treat PAS are theoretical, but the diagnosis itself is not. (Technically, such conjectures are more properly termed "hypotheses," although in colloquial usage the terms "theory" and "hypothesis" have become synonymous.)

An example of a newly proposed syndrome in physical medicine illustrates the distinction between the acceptance of a term to describe a condition and conjectures about etiology and treatment. The *Harvard Health Letter* published an article about a condition known as Red Wine Headache Syndrome.[37] This syndrome describes a familiar condition in which a person gets a headache shortly after ingesting a small amount of red wine (not to be confused with the headache that arrives hours after a full evening of drinking, i.e., a hangover). There are competing hypotheses about what substance in red wines causes the syndrome, and why some people, but not others, develop this reaction, but there is no generally accepted causal explanation or treatment. Nevertheless, disputes about causal mechanisms do not undermine the recognition that the syndrome exists.

C. Validity and Reliability of PAS

For any newly proposed diagnosis to be accepted, it should accurately, adequately, and usefully describe a recognizable disturbance that is not better accounted for by other diagnostic or explanatory terms. Psychologists generally refer to these issues as related to the validity of a construct. With regard to PAS, a central issue is whether it is useful to think in terms of a category of alienated children who are influenced by one parent to turn against the other, or is it preferable to think only in terms of a wider category of children who have significant conflicts with a parent?

Prior to the introduction of the term "PAS," the literature on child development and on divorce contained only passing references to the phenomenon of pathologically alienated children. Clearly, the professional community has found the concept of PAS valuable as evidenced by a recent survey of child custody evaluators[38] and by the large volume of articles published in refereed (peer-review) journals on the appropriate identification and treatment of children suffering with this problem.[39] In an effort to supplement clinical analyses with more extensive data organized and analyzed in some systematic fashion, Kopetski published two reports on severe PAS in a sample of 413 court-ordered custody evaluations conducted by the Family and Children's Evaluation Team in Colorado.[40] Prior to learning of Gardner's work, the team identified 84 cases of severe alienation that led them "independently to conclusions that were remarkably similar to Gardner's conclusions regarding the characteristics of the syndrome."[41] Independent identification of the same cluster of symptoms would generally be considered strong support for the validity of a newly proposed syndrome. Dunne and Hedrick found Gardner's criteria useful in differentiating 16 cases of severe PAS from cases with other postdivorce disturbances.[42] As is typical in clinical research, though, neither Kopetski nor Dunne and Hedrick conducted statistical analyses, and details were not provided about the methods used to analyze clinical case material.

A survey of custody evaluators that did include some statistical analyses found significant correlations between symptoms of alienation and behaviors on the part of the alienating parent, but few links between the child's alienation and the target parent's behavior. This lends support to the position that the core problem in pathological alienation is between the alienating parent and the child. However, this study was merely exploratory and has a number of methodological limitations including a small sample of 21 completed surveys.[43]

The American Psychological Association's document, *Guidelines for Child Custody Evaluations in Divorce Proceedings*, provides another index of the value of the PAS concept to child custody evaluators.[44] The guidelines conclude with a highly selective reference section titled "Pertinent Literature." Three of the 39 references are books by Gardner; one is titled *The Parental Alienation Syndrome* (1992) and the other two include discussions about PAS.

Taken together, the frequency of reports in the clinical literature, the close similarity of reported cases to Gardner's descriptions, and the reference section of the APA guidelines, lend support to the validity of PAS in terms of its utility to a sizeable group of experienced practitioners in the field.[45] Nevertheless, clinical observations must be corroborated by systematic empirical investigations with larger samples of subjects, standardized and systematic measures, and appropriate scientific controls to test hypotheses drawn from the clinical literature.

A 12-year study of 700 families, published by the American Bar Association Section of Family Law, is the one large-scale study that delineated the phenomenon in which divorced and divorcing parents manipulate and program their children to turn against the other parent.[46] This study provides some empirical support for the validity of PAS. As an early study in the field, it is heavily descriptive, and the description of procedures does not make clear exactly how the data were analyzed and what procedures were used to ensure the reliability of the results. Nevertheless, because of the wealth of experience reflected in the large number of families studied, and the detailed and sophisticated analysis of the problem, this study's observations and conclusions merit significant weight. According to Gold-Bikin "This treatise is based on years of experience counseling families in divorce and evaluating children during custody litigation. It should provide guidance to the bar, bench, and mental health professionals in ascertaining whether a child has been intentionally brainwashed or alienated from one parent by the other parent."[47]

The conclusions of the ABA-published study support the PAS conceptualization of pathological alienation as a child's response to the negative influence of the favored parent. The strongest scientific support for this conceptualization is found in studies that were first published in academic (as opposed to clinical) journals that meet the most rigorous standards of scientific methodology, have very high rejection rates for submitted manuscripts, and thus enjoy reputations of the highest stature. Such research documents and elucidates the ways in which beliefs, attitudes, and memories can be altered under the influence of authority figures.

Studies on memory, suggestibility, stereotype induction, social influence, and coercive influence demonstrate that children are susceptible to accepting, and repeating as if true, suggestions implanted by adult interviewers that innocent adults did harmful or illegal things.[48] Tactics such as leading and suggestive interviews, selective attention, skewed information, repetition, and intimidation can corrupt a child's view of reality to the point where children will incorporate misinformation into their memories and manufacture and report elaborate details of events that never occurred. These research findings help to explain how one parent could exert enough influence over a child to cause that child to lose affection and respect for the other parent and the rejected parent's relatives.[49] Studies on persuasion and attitude change explain how a child's predominantly negative opinion of a parent is liable to become deeply entrenched and highly resistant to modification even in the face of information that directly contradicts misconceptions, particularly if the opinion is expressed publicly.[50] For this reason caution should be exercised before giving children forums in which to publicly take a stand in custody disputes.[51]

The academic research cited above forms a scientific foundation for understanding and testifying about how children can be manipulated by adults in general to develop negative attitudes about other people as well as false memories of harmful events.[52] That parents can be the agents of such manipulation and teach their children to hate people of a different race or culture is hardly controversial. Two methodologically rigorous studies have extended prior research by demonstrating that coaching and misinformation provided specifically by parents (as opposed to research interviewers) can corrupt their children's eyewitness reports.[53] What is needed to provide further evidence of the validity of PAS and to strengthen its scientific legitimacy is research that focuses more directly and specifically on children in high conflict families who are manipulated by a parent (as opposed to another adult such as a research interviewer) to develop negative attitudes and distorted views of the other parent (as opposed to another race or culture or research confederate). Future studies should attempt to clarify the number and combination of factors that most effectively discriminate among the different types of alienation (e.g., reasonable versus unreasonable in light of the history of the parent-child relationship, or influenced by the favored parent versus arrived at independently by the child in response to the circumstances of the family conflict). This type of research will help clinicians classify children more precisely and reduce the possibility of misidentification of pathological alienation, regardless of what terminology and conceptualization of the problem is preferred.[54] In turn, such research may help resolve controversy about how to conceptualize pathological alienation.

D. Reliability of PAS

Part of the effort to identify the most accurate diagnostic approach must include research on reliability. For social scientists this means something different from legal reliability. For scientists, reliability refers to the degree to which a statistical measurement, test result, or diagnosis is consistent on repeated trials or among different observers. A proposed syndrome, such as PAS, has high reliability if different clinicians examining the same children can reach a high rate of agreement on which children do or do not have the syndrome. As with other diagnoses, it is unrealistic to expect 100 percent agreement among all clinicians in all cases; this is why the medical profession recommends that patients seek second opinions prior to undergoing costly or dangerous procedures. Discrepancies in diagnostic impressions will be most prevalent in complex cases and cases whose features suggest more than one possible diagnosis. If the symptoms of a proposed diagnosis are too imprecise and ambiguous, though, or require an excessively high degree of inference on the part of the observer, the rates of disagreement may be unacceptably high and reliability will not be achieved.

Gardner lists eight symptoms of PAS.[55] Kelly and Johnston, who offer an alternative framework for classifying alienated children, list nearly the identical symptoms as features of what they call "the alienated child."[56] Both lists appear on the surface to be clear-cut, but neither has verification from empirical research regarding the ability of clinicians to apply the list of symptoms to case material and agree on whether a particular symptom is present in a particular child. For example, Gardner's list includes "weak, absurd, or frivolous rationalizations for the deprecation" of a parent; Kelly and Johnston's list includes "trivial or false reasons used to justify hatred." Research needs to determine whether or not different observers can agree on what constitutes frivolous or trivial justifications.

To date, one study in a peer-review journal has directly measured the reliability of the symptoms of PAS as well as the reliability of the diagnosis itself.[57] Among doctoral level mental health professionals with extensive experience in child custody matters, the study found a high rate of agreement regarding the presence or absence of PAS symptoms. This finding suggests that the description of PAS symptoms is clear and precise enough to achieve high reliability. Also, the study found a high rate of agreement regarding the type of alienation present in each case, i.e., whether or not it was classified as PAS. This supports the reliability of PAS as a diagnosis. In addition, the study found high rates of consistency when experts rated the same case material on two different occasions. This provides a measure of what social scientists term test-retest, or rater-rerater, reliability. This study is the beginning of research on the reliability of different formulations of pathological alienation. Additional studies that replicate this study's conclusions will strengthen confidence in the reliability of PAS.[58] The absence of such studies does not mean that PAS lacks reliability, any more than it meant that the diagnosis of AIDS lacked reliability prior to the publication of empirical research on the syndrome.

E. Arguments Ad Hominem

Normally, arguments ad hominem merit no response in academic works. New ideas should be judged on their own merits rather than on who originates or espouses them. In the case of PAS, though, personal attacks have been used not just to challenge the validity of the concept, but to dismiss the significance of the widespread acceptance of PAS. Bruch acknowledged that PAS "has entered into public usage" and is referred to often, but asserted that PAS is accepted not for its own value as an explanatory construct, but because legal and mental health professionals (not cited or named) "do not know how to evaluate new psychological theories"[59] and have been duped by an "aura of expertise"[60] that accompanies Gardner's work. Presumably these intellectual deficiencies extend not only to the many clinicians, attorneys, and parents who have found the concept helpful, but to the authors of the more than 125 articles on PAS published in refereed journals and the panels of reviewers, chosen for their expertise in the field, who recommended publication of all these articles.

Ultimately, the assault on Gardner and on others who write about PAS is unsuccessful, not just because of mischaracterizations, but because it patently offers personal attacks in place of reasonable arguments and scholarship.[61] As with most ad hominem arguments, the more those who rely on such tactics the more it suggests that the attempt to change the focus from the idea to the person is an attempt to distract attention from the paucity of substance underlying their opinions about PAS. The evidence does not support the view that the widespread acceptance of PAS is because judges, lawyers, and mental health professionals naively labor under a misconception about Gardner's credentials.[62] Indeed, the attempt on the part of some critics to alienate the legal and mental health professional community from Gardner's work and any ideas associated with him is reminiscent of the dynamics and tactics used by one parent to demonize the other parent. Nevertheless, we should be clear that the positive or negative reputation of the person who initially formulates a diagnosis should be irrelevant in judging the value of the diagnosis.

F. Is Pathological Alienation a Syndrome?

Despite the widespread recognition of the phenomenon of pathologically alienated children, the use of the term "syndrome" in reference to such children has sparked heated debate. Some clinicians prefer the term "parental alienation." Others limit themselves to behavioral descriptions and avoid the term "syndrome" when testifying about irrationally alienated children in order to avoid challenges to the admissibility of syndrome testimony. One concern is that the designation "syndrome" conveys to the court an established stature and legitimacy that may be more appropriate following the type of rigorous empirical research called for earlier in this chapter. In court, the term "syndrome" may strengthen confidence in the scientific basis of the witness's testimony and, by implication, in the value and reliability of that testimony.

An additional concern about syndrome evidence is that expert witnesses sometimes offer a collection of symptoms as a test to prove the existence of one particular causal agent, even in the absence of independent verification of the cause. In the case of PAS this would mean that, after determining that a child has the behaviors characteristic of alienated children, the expert assumes that the existence of alienation supports a claim that the favored parent must have fostered the alienation. This is a misuse of PAS; by definition, the negative influence of the favored parent must be identified in order to diagnose PAS. Perhaps future studies will identify a particular constellation of symptoms that effectively discriminates between children who have and those who have not been exposed to alienating influences. Until such time, though, the alienating influence of the favored parent cannot be inferred merely from the presence of alienation symptoms.

Mosteller has proposed that the purpose for which syndrome evidence is used should govern its admissibility.[63] When an expert proffers syndrome evidence as a test of whether certain conduct has occurred, such as child sexual abuse, "the science must be of the highest quality and should satisfy the standards set out in *Daubert v. Merrell Dow Pharmaceuticals, Inc.*"[64] Mosteller argues that less exacting scientific standards should apply when the expert relies on syndrome evidence "to correct human misunderstandings of the apparently unusual and therefore suspicious reactions of a trial participant."[65] Although PAS testimony should not be used as a test of whether the aligned parent promulgated the child's alienation, it can provide the court with an alternative explanation of a child's negative or fearful conduct and attitudes. Also, PAS testimony can assist the court in evaluating a child's ability to perceive, recollect, or communicate. When PAS has been misdiagnosed, as in the case of children who are not alienated, or whose alienation is justified by the rejected parent's behavior, expert testimony on the reasons why testimony regarding PAS was irrelevant may be proffered in rebuttal.[66]

Despite the widespread acceptance of the term "PAS," experts testifying about alienated children do not have to accept the term "syndrome" or use it during their testimony. What is important is that they provide descriptions of the behavior and statements of the child and each parent. Regardless of whether the term "PAS" is used, experts can educate the court about the scientific literature that demonstrates how children are susceptible to manipulation by adults to develop negative attitudes and false memories about other adults. This information can be used to elucidate the significance of the specific facts in the case.

The validity of PAS is often challenged on the grounds that it does not appear in the *Diagnostic and Statistical Manual of Mental Disorders* (Fourth Edition) (DSM-IV) of the American Psychiatric Association. This is one of the weaker criticisms of the use of PAS in court. The DSM is not a test of whether a disorder exists. For example, Tourette's syndrome was first described 95 years before it was included in the DSM and Asperger's syndrome took 37 years before being included. Preparations for the DSM-IV began in 1990, just five years after the publication of the first article on PAS and prior to the burgeoning of the PAS literature. Furthermore, the process that leads to the inclusion of a proposed diagnosis is not purely scientific; it is driven by politics, economics, tradition, and compromises.[67] Inclusion in DSM does not necessarily end debate on the validity of a diagnosis.[68] Most important, the DSM-IV specifically cautions about its use in forensic settings. In short, inclusion in DSM-IV is not necessarily an appropriate test for court purposes.[69]

G. The Alienated Child Formulation

Alternative conceptualizations of PAS, such as Wallerstein's Medea syndrome, have not generated anything approaching the volume of literature on PAS. One recent formulation, though, has stimulated more interest than the others. Responding to concerns about the misdiagnosis and misuse of PAS in court, a Northern California group has recommended replacing the term "PAS" with the term "the alienated child," and using this term to describe all children who express persistent and unreasonable negative feelings and beliefs about a parent.[70] This formulation emphasizes the importance of multiple contributing factors, sees no need for a separate term to designate a subcategory of children whose alienation is primarily influenced by the favored parent, and does not find it useful to label this phenomenon as a "syndrome."

Apart from rejecting the concept of the favored parent being the primary cause of alienation, most aspects of this formulation are nearly identical to or consistent with the PAS literature. The aspects of similarity include the foundation in clinical experience as opposed to systematic empirical research, the distinction between alienated children and children whose rejection is rooted in mistreatment by the alienated parent (a phenomenon this formulation labels "estrangement"), the list of characteristics of irrationally alienated children, the description of the psychological factors operative in cases of alienation, the view that parent-child relationships exist on a continuum, and the view that the majority of children from divorced homes have positive relationships with both parents. Both regard irrational alienation as pathological and advocate the importance of making attempts to remedy the problem. Both recommend interventions with all members of the family; both believe that the court must intervene in order for such interventions to be successful; both advocate enforcing contact between alienated children and their rejected parents (although the authors of the alienated child model do not advocate custodial transfers as strongly as does Gardner); and both have been criticized for their advocacy of coercive judicial interventions.[71] It is too early to tell whether or not the alienated child formulation will generate a substantial literature on par with PAS.[72]

H. New Labels for Established Concepts?

The term "PAS" has served a valuable purpose in facilitating professional communication about pathological parental alienation and drawing attention to this phenomenon. The term has also been misused, misunderstood, misrepresented, politicized, and closely associated with specific positions on the incidence, treatment, and course of the condition.[73] It is possible that the climate of controversy and misperception of the meaning of PAS will spread and eventually detract sufficiently from its value that another term will gain acceptance in its place. This would be unfortunate because the introduction of any new term carries the risk of impeding the integration of professional work in the field and confusing consumers of mental health services. Nevertheless, a term such as *pathological alienation* might serve as a suitable substitute, particularly if it was defined in a manner that accommodated alternative formulations and helped circumvent unproductive debates. One possible definition is: a disturbance in which children, usually in the context of sharing a parent's negative attitudes, suffer unreasonable aversion to a person or persons with whom they formerly enjoyed normal relations or with whom they would normally develop affectionate relations.

The term "pathological alienation" has certain advantages:

1. Including the word "pathological" in the term reduces the likelihood that it will be mistaken for cases in which a child has good reasons for feeling alienated. This avoids an issue that has been a key concern of critics who fear that PAS lends itself to misapplication to cases of reasonable alienation.
2. A clear discrimination between pathological and rational alienation is made without the term "syndrome," which can generate much controversy in legal settings.
3. The term accommodates the observation that children can become estranged from other people in addition to their parents.
4. Something along the lines of the suggested definition offers a compromise between those who believe that a specific term is needed to delineate children whose alienation can be traced in part to the influence of the favored parent and those who believe that such children should be subsumed in a more general category of pathologically alienated children, including children in whom the favored parent's negative influence is neither a necessary nor a sufficient etiological factor. The definition acknowledges the reality that frequently the pathologically alienated child acts in the shadow of the favored parent, while leaving open the question of the exact role that such a parent's attitudes have in shaping the child's perceptions and feelings.

A drawback of the term "pathological alienation" is that among social scientists it has traditionally meant something very different from parental alienation. Alienation has been used to refer to people who are either self-alienated, i.e., significantly out of touch with their feelings, or alienated from the dominant values of their surrounding culture, e.g., adolescents who perceive themselves as "outsiders." In fact, Harvard researchers used the term "alienation syndrome" to identify the cluster of attitudes that corresponded to the latter type of alienation.[74] This drawback is to some extent alleviated by the context of discussion which should make clear the type of alienation being referenced. Finally, it should be noted that any term that replaces PAS, such as *alienated child, Medea syndrome,* or *pathological alienation* is just as susceptible to distortion and misdiagnosis as is PAS or any other diagnosis.

III. TREATING PATHOLOGICAL PARENTAL ALIENATION

The literature regarding the proper response to pathological parental alienation has generated much dispute. Different conceptualizations of alienation lead to different treatment approaches. Naturally, those who deny the existence of irrational alienation and those who believe that irrational alienation is normal see no need for treating the child's condition and instead recommend acquiescing to a child's refusal to relate to a parent. Despite disagreements in conceptual frameworks, those who recognize the phenomenon of pathological alienation agree that intervention is warranted for children who persistently and unreasonably refuse to spend time with one parent and who hold polarized unrealistic views of both parents. The most controversial aspects of the treatments for these children proposed by Gardner, Kelly and Johnston, and other clinicians are the coercive elements. These clinicians recommend court-mandated treatment, some enforced contact between the children and the rejected parent, and sanctions for failure to comply with such orders.

With severe alienation Gardner recommends transfer of custody to the alienated parent, the use of transition sites to facilitate the reconciliation between the alienated child and parent, and court-imposed sanctions on the favored parent and perhaps the child for failure to obey court orders. Other clinicians accept the value of reducing the alienated child's dependence on the favored parent and requiring the child to spend time with the rejected parent, but are more cautious about recommending transfer of legal custody.[75] A challenge for court-mandated treatment is the need for periodic adjustments in the structure and schedule of contact between the child and each parent depending on the progress of treatment. Rather than require the parents to return to court each time they disagree about proposed changes, some clinicians recommend that the court delegate some decision-making authority to therapists, or specially appointed "parenting coordinators," or "special masters." The use of professionals in such quasi-judicial roles has been criticized, as have court-enforced attempts to assist children who profess hatred toward formerly loved parents, grandparents, and entire extended families. Bruch cites opinions by Wallerstein and by Johnston to support a laissez-faire approach to children who refuse contact with a parent, although she acknowledges that Johnston now supports a more active role for the court.[76]

Based on a sample of approximately 26 children whom they described as "aligned" with one parent, Wallerstein and colleagues concluded that, "There is great advantage in allowing natural maturation to take its course and to avoid overzealous intervention to break these alliances, which are usually strengthened by efforts to separate the allies."[77] However, Clawar and Rivlin, in an ABA-published study of 700 children, reached the opposite conclusion: "One of the most powerful tools the courts have is the threat and implementation of environmental modification. Of the approximately four hundred cases we have seen where the courts have increased the contact with the target parent (and in half of these, over the objection of the children), there has been positive change in 90 percent of the relationships between the child and the target parent, including the elimination or reduction of many social-psychological, educational, and physical problems that the child presented prior to the modification."[78]

Gardner's follow-up study of 99 children diagnosed with PAS found a strong association between environmental modification and reduction in PAS symptoms.[79] In 22 instances, the alienated child's contact with the rejected parent was increased and contact with the alienating parent was decreased. In all 22 cases, PAS symptoms were reduced or eliminated. By contrast, only nine percent of the children (7 out of 77) whose contact with the rejected parent was not increased by the court showed a reduction in PAS symptoms. This study also provides a beginning understanding of the factors that lead alienated children to initiate their own reconciliation with the rejected parent. Further study along these lines may assist decision makers in determining which children might not require environmental changes in order to heal their alienated relationships.[80] The large sample and the statistical test of significance allowed by this size sample make this an important study. Nevertheless, its limitations must be noted, chiefly that the children were not interviewed, the only informant for the follow-up was the rejected parent, and the interviews were conducted by a clinician who had formulated the hypothesis being tested.[81]

Treatment approaches to severe PAS other than environmental changes have been reported in the clinical literature, but in general such approaches have met with failure. A follow-up study of 45 children with PAS concluded that structural interventions involving custody and time share were the key components in the successful interruption and prevention of alienation. Psychotherapy as the primary intervention either was ineffective or made situations worse.[82] Dunne and Hedrick published a clinical study of 16 severe PAS cases.[83] The court ordered a custody change and/or strict limitation of contact between the alienating parent and the children in only three of these cases. In all three cases PAS was eliminated. The other 13 cases were treated with various, less restrictive interventions, ranging from individual or conjoint therapy for the parents, therapy for the children with either the alienating parent or target parent, or the assignment of a guardian ad litem. In none of these cases was PAS eliminated. Two cases showed "some" or "minimal" improvement, nine showed no improvement, and two were worse after the interventions. This study has significant limitations. The sample size is small. Details are not provided about the methods used to analyze clinical case material. As is typical in clinical research with small samples, no statistical analyses were conducted to document that the findings were not due to chance. Nevertheless, the 100% correspondence between elimination of severe PAS and strict environmental modification does provide some evidence in support of this intervention.

Lampel analyzed clinical case studies on 18 families, out of which seven children were described as rejecting a father who had no objectively noted parental dysfunction.[84] The therapists conceptualized the children's rejection of the father as a phobia with hysterical features and tried two different approaches commonly used to treat phobias. The first approach, used with six children, included individual therapy sessions with the child followed by gradually increasing times with the father both in and out of the therapist's office. Sessions were also held for the mother, both individually and jointly with the child, for the father, and for both parents and child jointly. This approach is similar to Gardner's recommended treatment for moderate PAS cases. The second approach, used with one child, is similar to Gardner's recommendation for severe PAS. The child was placed with the father for six to eight weeks while the therapist provided individual therapy sessions for the child and parents, and joint sessions with the child and father. This child was the only one of the seven children whose symptoms reduced markedly. The children whose treatment did not include placement with the rejected father experienced results varying from minor improvement to deterioration. In three cases the treatment was regarded as a clear failure. Lampel attributed the failures to the mothers' "collusive involvement" with their children. Again, although this is a very small sample, the results support the effectiveness of placing the child with the alienated parent.

Treatment approaches to pathologically alienated children should benefit from more and higher quality long-term outcome studies on the effectiveness of different interventions. Until such scientific evidence is available, controversy will probably continue concerning the proper treatment of alienated children and their parents. Given the limitations in the available studies, some might dismiss the current professional literature as too inadequate to serve as an authoritative guide to decisions for alienated children. However, no study is free of limitations. The issue is whether the limitations render the study useless. The peer review process, though no guarantee of a study's lasting value, is designed to weed out studies whose flaws outweigh their contributions.

Courts and clinicians face decisions about alienated children on a daily basis. These decisions can draw on the best available information, while duly noting its limitations, and thereby benefit from the experience of the families reflected in the published reports. Or the decisions can ignore this information. At this point in time, the published findings on treatment outcomes support the effectiveness of enforcing contact between the child and alienated parent and only Wallerstein's observations oppose this policy.[85] Although the circumstances of any single case may dictate an alternative treatment approach, an emerging consensus among mental health professionals supports the idea that "court orders for continued contact are the cornerstone for treatment" of PAS cases.[86] Similarly, Stahl refers to "general agreement" that recommendations should include "forced consistent time between the child and the alienated parent."[87]

Apart from the issue of what structures of treatment are most effective in healing alienated child-parent relationships, Bruch raises important questions about the proper role of the state in regard to families where parents live apart from each other, and further questions about the amount and quality of research necessary to justify a court's response to families with alienated children.[88] Her criticism of the treatment recommendations of the group of professionals who formulated the alienated child model states: "They ask courts to order parties who are neither abusive nor neglectful to employ and cooperate with intrusive, costly teams of professionals, even when there is no assurance that improvement will be achieved before the family's resources are exhausted or that the results will be appreciably better than what is likely to occur without intervention."[89]

Bruch also believes that appointment of a special master over a parent's objections and court-ordered waivers of therapist-parent confidentiality constitute "an impermissible delegation of judicial authority,"[90] that would require that "judges violate their statutory duties,"[91] and would allow mental health professionals to assume "quasi-judicial roles that will authorize them to prescribe the details of life for many parents and children . . . in a framework that lacks due process protections such as a record, evidentiary privileges, and full access to the courts."[92] More generally, Bruch questions the best-interests-of-the-child standard and "enhanced roles for noncustodial parents," and concludes "Although parental separation may, of course, cause or exacerbate intra-familial difficulties, the degree to which these difficulties justify public intervention is a question of policy and law. Some difficulties, although extremely unfortunate, are appropriately left to families and individuals to address as a private matter, if at all."[93]

Bruch's arguments should stimulate greater elaboration and refinement of the best-interests-of-the-child standard in order to clarify the basis for state intervention, and the extent to which the court may delegate its authority to intervene in disputes between parents who both want to participate in child-rearing while living apart from each other.[94] One issue is how to reconcile court-imposed child access schedules that are readily accepted as within the province of the court with a policy that would preclude any means of enforcing such schedules if one parent supports a child's refusal to see the other parent. The only alternative to judicial intervention seems to be a public policy that takes away the court's role in deciding such matters other than by designating one parent or the child as the final authority regarding the child's contacts with the other parent.

Apart from fundamental questions about the proper role of the court when two divorced parents are in dispute about the allocation of financial resources or child-rearing authority and responsibilities, opinions about the proper reach of the court in intervening with pathologically alienated children and their parents may depend in part on how the problem is construed. Some mental health professionals, including Clawar and Rivlin, Gardner, and Kelly and Johnston, regard it as a form of emotional abuse when a vindictive parent systematically attempts to poison children's affections for the other parent, exploit the children by using them to express hostility toward the other parent, or prevent contact with the other parent (even to the point of abducting the child). In essence, the parent is inculcating fears and hatred in the children that induce a loss of the greatest magnitude – the loss of a parent and often an entire extended family.[95] In this view, when such harmful parental behavior is identified, the court is justified in intervening to protect the children, just as when children are subjected to other forms of abuse at the hands of their parents.[96] On the other hand, those who construe such a hostile environment merely as an unfortunate by-product of growing up in a troubled family may believe that the state is overreaching its legitimate role by intruding into private family affairs. Bruch raises a valuable line of inquiry directing attention to a difficult policy issue with no simple answers.

IV. CONCLUSION

Ample evidence exists, and has received widespread acceptance among mental health professionals, that some children develop an irrational alienation from their parents that is not warranted by the history of the parent-child relationship and that should be considered a deviation from normal functioning. Denials of the existence of pathological alienation are reminiscent of past generations' denial of the existence, prevalence, and destructiveness of physical and sexual child abuse. Furthermore, it is clear that some cases of pathological alienation arise when children are exposed to behavior on the part of the favored parent that either discourages or fails to encourage an amicable relationship between the children and the alienated parent. What remains controversial is whether the behavior of the favored parent is primarily responsible for the alienation, or whether it is more accurate to conceptualize the problem as due to multiple factors, with the favored parent's behavior being neither necessary nor sufficient nor primarily responsible for the development of pathological alienation.

A conceptualization, such as PAS, that regards the influence of the favored parent as a primary causal factor has intellectual and scientific roots in developmental and cognitive psychology. Developmental psychology research has shown how children's attitudes are shaped by the socialization practices of adults. Cognitive psychology research has shown that children's memory and reports can be molded by suggestions implanted by adults. The PAS type of explanation for alienation is consistent with the way social scientists view the propagation of racial hatred in children. No fair-minded person blames such hatred on the targets themselves. Research on the interpersonal dynamics of power imbalances helps to explain why some children will identify with an angry parent just as some hostages bond with their captors (in what is known as the Stockholm syndrome) and some battered spouses bond with their abusive spouses.

A conceptualization, such as the alienated child formulation, that deemphasizes the role of the favored parent and emphasizes the role of multiple interrelated factors also enjoys support in a well-established literature. Its intellectual roots rest on principles of family systems theory that regard children's problematic behavior as an expression of familywide dysfunction.

A possible resolution of the controversy regarding conceptualization may be found in the recognition that each explanation may fit some alienated children but not others. Some children's negative attitudes may be best understood as a product of cognitive and affective manipulation. Other children's negative attitudes may be best understood as the end result of a complex interplay of factors, such as the circumstances of the ruptured relationship between the parents and the behavior of the child, the alienated parent, the aligned parent, new partners, other family members, and therapists.

Other controversies concern the appropriateness of using the term "PAS" in court and whether this term, more than other formal diagnoses, lends itself to misuse by abusive parents who have actually earned their children's enmity and choose to blame the situation on the other parent rather than acknowledge the children's alienation as reasonable. It remains an empirical question whether conceptualizing pathological alienation in a broader sense, without delineating a subgroup of children whose alienation is primarily the result of the favored parent's influence, will contribute to a reduction in the incidence of misdiagnosis and misunderstanding, or whether all that is needed is continued clarification about what PAS is and what it is not. Finally, prevailing opinion among mental health professionals regards the court's authority as a key element in successful remedies of severe alienation unless parents are able to agree on a course of action. However, this consensus is rooted in clinical experience without extensive support in large-scale, well-controlled outcome studies, and it does not extend to agreement on the exact manner and extent of judicial intervention.

Future empirical research should help resolve some of the controversies by providing data on the reliability and validity of PAS, the effectiveness of various interventions, and the long-term course of pathological alienation.[97] The results of such studies should help refine and enhance our understanding of how best to help families with alienated children. When it comes to such families, legal and mental health professionals who work in the trenches of consultation rooms and courtrooms know that there are plenty of tales of misery to go around – misery from parents who worry that their children are being forced to spend time with a physically or sexually abusive parent, misery from children who are required to spend time with a parent they profess to hate or fear, misery from desperate parents who are cut off from contact with the children they raised and love, and misery from grandparents who fear that even if their grandchildren eventually recover their desire to visit, it will be too late. We can best serve this constituency by reducing inflammatory rhetoric and ad hominem attacks, appreciating the limits of our knowledge, continuing to pursue new knowledge, and applying what we have learned to safeguard the best interests of children.

ENDNOTES

 This chapter incorporates material first published in Warshak, R. A. (2003). Bringing Sense to Parental Alienation: A Look at the Disputes and the Evidence, 37 *Family Law Quarterly*, 273.

1. This attitude was exemplified by one woman who sought my services. She described herself as a former leading advocate against PAS – she had hosted an anti-PAS Web site and had lobbied the state legislature – because she had believed that when children reject a parent, they always have good reasons. She changed her stand when her children suddenly and unreasonably refused all contact with her.
2. *See e.g.*, Heim, S., Grieco, H., Di Paola, S. and Allen, R. (2002). *NOW Family Court Report*, available from California National Organization for Women, 926 J St. Suite 424, Sacramento CA. 95814. http://www.canow.org; Mothers of Lost Children, *Sample of California Family Law Cases: Children Taken Away from Safe Parents, Forced to Live With Abusive Parents* (2000). available from Mothers of Lost Children, P.O. Box 1803, Davis, CA. 95617.
3. Kempe, C. H., Silverman, F. N., Steele, B. F., Droegmuller, W. and Silver, H. K. (1962). The Battered-Child Syndrome, 181 *Journal of the American Medical Association*, 105.
4. Mantell wrote, "[A]n article of faith seems to have arisen which holds that 'children never lie about something like this.'" Mantell, D. M. (1988). Clarifying Erroneous Child Sexual Abuse Allegations, 58 *American Journal of Orthopsychiatry* 618. *Also see*, Horner, T. M. and Guyer, M. (1991) Prediction, Prevention, and Clinical Expertise in Child Custody Cases in Which Allegations of Child Sexual Abuse Have Been Made: I. Predictable Rates of Diagnostic Error in Relation to Various Clinical Decision Making Strategies, 25 *Family Law Quarterly* 217; Horner, T. M. and Guyer, M. and Kalter, N. M. (1992). Prediction, Prevention, and Clinical Expertise in Child Custody Cases in Which Allegations of Child Sexual Abuse Have Been Made: III. Studies of Expert Opinion Formation, 26 *Family Law Quarterly* 141; Mason, M.A. (1998). Expert Testimony Regarding the Characteristics of Sexually Abused Children: A Controversy on Both Sides of the Bench. In S. J. Ceci and H. Hembrooke (Eds.), *Expert Witnesses in Child Abuse Cases*; Milchman, S. (1992). Professional Controversies in Child Sexual Abuse Assessment, (Spring) *Journal of Psychiatry & the Law* 49.
5. Differing views on the prevalence of false memories are presented in (1998). 4 *Psychology, Public Policy, & the Law* 931. *Also see*, Myers, J. (1995). New Era of Skepticism Regarding Children's Credibility, 1 *Psychology, Public Policy, & the Law* 387.
6. For an excellent, award-winning, overview of this literature see Ceci, S. J. and Bruck, M. (1995). *Jeopardy in the Courtroom: A Scientific Analysis of Children's Testimony*, Washington, D.C.: American Psychological Association Press.
7. Darnall, D. (1999). Parental Alienation: Not in the Best Interest of the Children. 75(2) *North Dakota Law Review*, 323; Gardner, R. A. (1998). *The Parental Alienation Syndrome*. Second Edition. Cresskill, NJ: Creative Therapeutics; Kelly, J. B. and Johnston, J. R. (2001). The

Alienated Child: A Reformulation of Parental Alienation Syndrome, 39 Family Court Review 249; Warshak, R. A. (2002). *Divorce Poison: Protecting the Parent-Child Bond From a Vindictive Ex.* NY: Regan Books.

8. Baker, A. J. L. (2005). The Long-term Effects of Parental Alienation on Adult Children: A Qualitative Research Study, 33 *American Journal of Family Therapy* 289.
9. Roseby, V. (1997). Symposium on Child Custody Evaluations, *Association of Family & Conciliation Courts.* For an attorney's argument that PAS symptoms are common and normal, *see "But I've Seen PAS!" No, You Haven't.* http://www.gate.net/~liz/liz/parental alienation syndrome.html (last visited January 29, 2003).
10. Bruch, C. S. (2001). Parental Alienation Syndrome and Parental Alienation: Getting It Wrong in Child Custody Cases, 35 *Family Law Quarterly* 533 (FN20) citing a telephone conversation with Judith Wallerstein.
11. Kelly, J. B. (2000). Children's Adjustment in Conflicted Marriage and Divorce: A Decade Review of Research, 39(8) *Journal of Child & Adolescent Psychiatry* 963.
12. Wallerstein, J. and Kelly, J. B. (1980). *Surviving the Breakup.* NY.: Basic Books; Richard A. Warshak, R. A. and Santrock, J. W. (1983). The Impact of Divorce in Father-Custody and Mother-Custody Homes: The Child's Perspective. In L. A. Kurdek (Ed.), *Children and Divorce* (pp. 29–46). San Francisco: Jossey-Bass; Fabricius, W. V. and Hall, J. A. (2000). Young Adults' Perspectives on Divorce: Living Arrangements, 38 *Family & Conciliation Courts Review* 446; Rosen, R. (1979). Some Crucial Issues Concerning Children of Divorce. 3 *Journal of Divorce* 19.
13. Fabricius & Hall, *supra* note 12.
14. *See* Offer, D. Ostrov, Howard, E. K., and Atkinson, R. (1988). *The Teenage World: Adolescents' Self-image in Ten Countries* for a study of 6000 teenagers in 10 countries that found that most liked their parents. Also, Gallup Organization (1988). *America's Youth 1977–1988* found that only five percent of U.S. adolescents reported not getting along with their parents at all.
15. *See e.g.*, Greene, R. W. (2001). *The Explosive Child.* New York: Harper Paperbacks; Lewis J. M., Beavers, W. R., Gosett J. T., and Phillips, V. A. (1976). *No Single Thread: Psychological Health In Family Systems.* New York: Brunner/Mazel; Patterson, G. R. (1977). *Living with Children: New Methods for Parents and Teachers.* Champaign, IL: Research Press.
16. My email folder is filled with hundreds of pleas from bereaved parents – about 60% from mothers – whose anguish at being shut out of their children's lives is heartbreaking. The distribution between mothers and fathers is not necessarily representative of the entire population of alienated parents. One bereaved man attributed his wife's suicide to her reactive depression to the hatred her formerly loving children, allegedly under their father's influence, heaped on her. July 3, 2002 posting from "John" to: http://www.custodyevaluation.com/parentalalienation / disc103/0000004d.htm (last visited January 29, 2003). Two bereaved sisters wrote to me about the suicide of their brother that they attribute to the rejection of his children allegedly under their mother's influence. As with anecdotal reports of children damaged by court decisions, such emotionally compelling accounts dictate serious attention and caution but should not serve as a basis for blanket policies without further investigation. For an exploratory study on cases involving suicide of an alienated parent, *see* Rand, D.C. and Rand, R. *Alienated Children and Target Parents: Factors Affecting Reconciliation in PAS Families*, this volume. For an exploratory study of the general impact of alienation on a small sample of alienated parents, *see* Vassiliou, D. and Cartwright, G. (2001). The Lost Parent's Perspective on Parental Alienation Syndrome. 29(3) *American Journal of Family Therapy* 181.
17. Gardner, R. A. (2001). Should Courts Order PAS Children to Visit/Reside with the Alienated Parent? A Follow-up Study. 19(3) *American Journal of Forensic Psychology* 61.
18. *Also see*, Hoch, P. and Hoch, R. (2003). Successful Reintegration of Severely Alienated Children and Their Parents. In W. von Boch-Galhau, U. Kodjoe, W. Andritzky & P. Koeppel, (Eds.) *The Parental Alienation Syndrome: An Interdisciplinary Challenge for Professionals Involved in Divorce* (pp. 353–365), labeling as a "troubling fallacy" the belief that alienated children, as adults, will reunite with their rejected parents: "In the hundreds of families I have followed through the years, there is no shred of evidence that this will happen, especially when we are talking about children alienated at a young age (under eleven) . . . . This does sometimes happen, but in my experience, this is the exception, not the rule. For every one case where child and parent successfully rebuilt a relationship in adulthood, I can bring ten cases where they did not."
19. Wallerstein, J. S. and Blakeslee, S. (1989). *Second Chances: Men, Women, and Children a Decade After Divorce.* (p. 196). New York: Ticknor & Fields.
20. *Id.* p. 196.
21. American Psychiatric Association (1994). *Diagnostic and Statistical Manual of Mental Disorders* Fourth Edition: DSM IV. Washington, D.C.: American Psychiatric Association.
22. Ackerman, M. J. and Kane, A. (1993). *Psychological Experts in Divorce, Personal Injury, and Other Civil Actions* (2nd ed.). New York: Aspen Law & Business; Gould, J. W. (1998). *Conducting Scientifically Crafted Child Custody Evaluations.* Thousand Oaks, CA.: Sage Publications; Stahl, P. M. (1994). *Conducting Child Custody Evaluations.* Thousand Oaks, CA.: Sage Publications. *Also see* Ellis, E. M. (2000). *Divorce Wars: Interventions with Families in Conflict.* Washington, D.C.: American Psychological Association Press.
23. Warshak, R. A. (2001). Current Controversies Regarding Parental Alienation Syndrome, 19 *American Journal of Forensic Psychology* 29.

24. Wallerstein & Blakeslee, *supra* note 19; Reich, W. (1949). *Character Analysis.* New York, Farrar, Straus and Giroux, referring to parents who seek "revenge on the partner through robbing him or her of the pleasure in the child" (p. 265); Despert, J. L. (1953/1962). *Children of Divorce.* Garden City, NY: Dolphin Books, referring to the temptation for one parent "to break down" their child's love for the other parent (p. 52).
25. Wallerstein and Kelly, *supra* note 12 page 77.
26. Gardner, *supra* note 7; Gardner, R. A. (2000). Addendum to The Parental Alienation Syndrome (2nd ed.) (2000). http://www.rgardner.com/refs/addendum2..html (last visited January 29, 2003).
27. For reviews of this literature *see* Rand D. C. (1997). The Spectrum of Parental Alienation Syndrome (part I). 15 *American Journal of Forensic Psychology 23*; Rand D. C. (1997). The Spectrum of Parental Alienation Syndrome (part II). 15 *American Journal of Forensic Psychology 39*; Warshak, R. A. (1999). Psychological Syndromes: Parental Alienation Syndrome. In R. A. Orsinger (Ed.), *Expert Witness Manual.* Austin, TX: State Bar of Texas. A slightly different version of this chapter is available separately as *Parental Alienation Syndrome in Court* through http://www.warshak.com.
28. Gardner, *supra* note 7.
29. In a response to an article by Kelly and Johnston, Gardner made perfectly clear that alienated children do not necessary have a programming parent, that there are many causes for a child's alienation, and that PAS is only one particular type of alienation. He wrote: "There are a wide variety of causes of children becoming alienated from their parents, e.g., abuse (physical, verbal, emotional, and sexual), neglect, parental abandonment, and adolescent rebellion (Garber, 1996; Lund, 1995; Warshak, 2002a, 2002b). All these are sources of *parental alienation.* PAS is one specific *subtype* of parental alienation, the subtype that is primarily caused (or at least initiated by) a programming parent." Gardner, R. A. (2004). Commentary on Kelly and Johnston's "The Alienated Child: A Reformulation of Parental Alienation Syndrome," 42 *Family Court Review* 611. Johnston and Kelly wrote a rejoinder to Gardner's rebuttal, thereby acknowledging that they read this article. Yet in a later article, Johnston and Kelly, citing the article in which Gardner clarifies this point, continue to characterize his view incorrectly and then criticize their incorrect version. They write that Gardner's "proposition as to the causes of PAS is rendered tautological by the following kind of circular reasoning: an alienated child (who is supposedly distinct from an abused child) has by definition a brainwashing parent; hence if a child is alienated, then a brainwashing parent exists and is the sole cause." Johnston, J. R. and Kelly, J. B. (2005). Commentary on Walker, Brantley, and Rigsbee's (2004). "A Critical Analysis of Parental Alienation Syndrome & Its Admissibility in the Family Court," 1 *Journal of Child Custody* 77.
30. Kelly and Johnston, *supra* note 7. Johnston and Kelly, *ibid.*, refer to PAS as a "unidimensional model" despite Gardner's clarification that although he regards the programming parent to be primarily responsible for the alienation, he recognizes multiple factors that contribute to the alienation: "I view the programming parent to be primarily responsible for the creation of the disorder in the child and that if the programming did not take place, the disorder would not have arisen (for a similar view see Clawar & Rivlin, 1991). This does not mean that some children are not more susceptible and some less susceptible. Nor does it mean that other factors may not be operative in the child such as anger over the divorce being directed toward one parent or adolescent rebellion fueling the anger. Of course, *I fully recognize that these sources of parental alienation can exist independently, and alongside, of the PAS.* However, I still hold that these additional factors are contributory and that the primary cause of the disorder is the programming parent who hopes to gain leverage in court by indoctrinating a campaign of denigration into the child against a good, loving parent" [emphasis added]. Gardner *ibid.*
31. *See e.g.*, Bruch, *supra* note 10, pp. 530–534, in which three of the five deficiencies she posits about PAS concern Gardner's ideas about incidence, prognosis, and treatment. The other two "flaws" that Bruch mentions are concerns about the misidentification of PAS and a gross misstatement about Gardner's views on the relation between alienation and psychosis.
32. Kelly and Johnston, *supra* note 7, pp. 249–250.
33. American Psychiatric Association, *supra* note 21 p. 771.
34. *See e.g.*, Cartwright, G. F. (1993). Expanding the Parameters of Parental Alienation Syndrome, 21 *American Journal of Family Therapy* 205 and Warshak, R. A. (2000). Remarriage as a Trigger of Parental Alienation Syndrome, 28 *American Journal of Family Therapy* 229 describing situations other than child custody litigation that can accompany PAS. *Also see* Garber, B. D. (March 1996). Alternatives to Parental Alienation: Acknowledging the Broader Scope of Children's Emotional Difficulties During Parental Separation and Divorce, *New Hampshire Bar Journal* 51; Lund, M. (1995). A Therapist's View of Parental Alienation Syndrome, 33 *Family & Conciliation Courts Review* 308; Waldron, K. H. & Joanis, D. E. (1996). Understanding and Collaboratively Treating Parental Alienation Syndrome, 10 *American Journal of Family Law* 121; and Warshak, R. A. (2002). Misdiagnosis of Parental Alienation Syndrome, 20 *American Journal of Forensic Psychology* 31. These authors accept the term PAS while delineating types of parent-child conflicts that should be excluded from PAS and factors in addition to the influence of the favored parent that contribute to the development of PAS.
35. Johnston, J. R. and Roseby, V. (1997). *In the Name of the Child: A Developmental Approach to Understanding and Helping Children of Conflicted and Violent Divorce.* New York: Free Press, p. 202.

36. Bruch, *supra* note 10.
37. Red Wine Headaches, *Harvard Health Letter*, June 2002.
38. Bow, J. N., Quinell, F. A., Zaroff, M. & Assemony, A. (2002). Assessment of Sexual Abuse Allegations in Child Custody Cases, 23(6) *Professional Psychology: Research and Practice* 566.
39. Rand *supra* note 27. Dr. Gardner's website, http://www.rgardner.com, lists three groups of articles: 18 articles on PAS authored by Gardner that have appeared in peer-review journals, 66 articles by other authors specifically on PAS, and 51 articles that focus significantly on the phenomenon of pathological alienation. (These articles are also listed on www.warshak.com.) Bruch, *supra* note 11 at 536 (fn 33) claimed that Gardner identifies as PAS articles that are either negative toward PAS or discuss "entirely distinct phenomena (such as alignments)." A review of Gardner's list reveals that only some of articles in the third group are by authors who use or prefer a different term or different conceptualization of the problem of pathologically alienated children, and all 84 articles in the first two groups specifically elucidate various aspects of the identification, clarification, and treatment of PAS. Many of these articles can be found at: http://www.fact.on.ca/Info/pas/. Clinicians who have found the PAS concept useful in organizing their impressions of alienated children include: Cartwright *supra* note 34; Lund, *supra* note 34; Price, J. L. & Pioske, K. S. (1994). Parental Alienation Syndrome: A Developmental Analysis of a Vulnerable Population. 32 *Journal of Psychosocial Nursing* 9; Rand, *supra* note 27; Rogers, M. (1992). Delusional Disorder and the Evolution of Mistaken Sexual Allegations in Child Custody Cases, 10 *American Journal of Forensic Psychology* 47; Waldron & Joanis, *supra* note 34; Warshak, *supra* note 34.
40. Kopetski, L. M. (1998). Identifying Cases of Parental Alienation Syndrome – Part I, 29 (2). *The Colorado Lawyer* 65; Kopetski, L. M. (1998). Identifying Cases of Parental Alienation Syndrome – Part II, 29 (3). *The Colorado Lawyer* 63 http://www.fact.on.ca/Info/pas/kopet98b.htm (last visited July 13, 2005).
41. *Id.* Part I p. 65.
42. Dunne, J. & Hedrick, M. (1994). The Parental Alienation Syndrome: An Analysis of Sixteen Selected Cases, 21(3/4) *Journal of Divorce and Remarriage* 21.
43. Nicholas, L. (1997). *Does Parental Alienation Exist? Preliminary Empirical Study of the Phenomenon in Custody and Visitation Disputes*, presented at the 13th Annual Symposium in Forensic Psychology of the American College of Forensic Psychology, Vancouver, British Columbia; Nicholas, L. (2000). Parental Alienation Syndrome, in G. Thisdelle (Ed.) *Fathers, Children, Family & Community: A Programming Manual for Counsellors* (Canadian spelling), *Parent Educators, and Family Advocates*, pp. 12–14.
44. American Psychological Association (1994). Guidelines for Child Custody Evaluations in Divorce Proceedings. 49(7) *American Psychologist* 677.
45. Cf Slobogin, C. (1999). The Admissibility of Behavioral Science Information in Criminal Trials: from Primitivism to Daubert to Voice. 5 *Psychology, Public Policy, and the Law* 113. With respect to syndrome testimony in criminal trials, Slobogin argues for a formulation of the *Frye* test that would admit testimony "that a sizeable group of professionals find plausible, based on their specialized knowledge."
46. Clawar, S. S. & Rivlin, B. V. (1991). *Children Held Hostage: Dealing with Programmed and Brainwashed Children.* Chicago: American Bar Association. In a significant oversight, Bruch, *supra* note 11, failed to cite this study which is the largest study of alienated children and provides data and reaches conclusions diametrically opposite to many of Bruch's opinions.
47. Gold-Biken, L. Z. Foreword to *Id.* at ix.
48. *See* e.g., Ceci, S. J. & Bruck, M. (1993). The Suggestibility of the Child Witness: A Historical Review and Synthesis, 113 *Psychological Bulletin* 403–439 (1993). This article received two prestigious awards; it was named one of the 20 outstanding articles in *Child Psychiatry and Child Development* and was awarded a prize by the American Psychological Association for the best article dealing with child abuse. Reviews and citations to these studies also can be found in Ceci & Bruck, *supra* note 6.
49. It bears emphasis that such influence is only one possible source of a child's alienation.
50. Festinger, L. & Carlsmith, J. M. (1959). Cognitive Consequences of Forced Compliance. 58 *Journal of Abnormal and Social Psychology* 203; Jelalian, E. & Miller, A. G. (1984). The Perseverance of Beliefs: Conceptual Perspectives and Research Developments, 2 *Journal of Social and Clinical Psychology* 25; Ross, L., Lepper, M. R. & Hubbard, M. (1975). Perseverance in Self-perception and Social Perception: Biased Attribution Processes in the Debriefing Paradigm. 32 *Journal of Personality and Social Psychology* 880; Schauss, S. L., Chase, P. N. & Hawkins, R.P. (1977). Environment-behavior Relations, Behavior Therapy, and the Process of Persuasion and Attitude Change, 28 *Journal of Behavior Therapy and Experimental Psychiatry* 31.
51. *See* Warshak, R. A. (2003). Payoffs and Pitfalls of Listening to Children. 54 (4) *Family Relations* 373.
52. For a discussion of PAS and *Daubert* standards, see Warshak, *supra* note 23. In a text for child custody evaluators, Gould, *supra* note 22 at 67, suggests the following application of the research on children's suggestibility: "If parent-child verbal exchanges in alienating families can be construed as a form of suggestive interviewing, then the evaluator may attempt to identify how the parent has used specific suggestive interview techniques to alter the child's perception of his or her father or mother." *Also see* Zervopoulos, J. A. (2001). Robinson/Daubert and Mental Health Testimony: The Sky Is Not Falling, 64 *Texas Bar Journal* 350 for a discussion of two guides to use in assessing the reliability of syndrome testimony.

53. Poole, D. A. & Lindsay, D. S. (1995). Interviewing Preschoolers: Effects of Nonsuggestive Techniques, Parental Coaching, and Leading Questions on Reports of Nonexperienced Events, 60 *Journal of Experimental Child Psychology* 129; Poole, D. A. & Lindsay, D. S. (2001). Children's Eyewitness Reports After Exposure to Misinformation From Parents, 7 *Journal of Experimental Psychology: Applied* 27.
54. Kelly & Johnston, *supra* note 7; Warshak, *Misdiagnosis of Parental Alienation Syndrome*, *supra* note 34.
55. Gardner, *supra* note 7.
56. Kelly & Johnston, *supra* note 7.
57. Rueda, C. A. (2004). An Inter-rater Reliability Study of Parental Alienation Syndrome, *American Journal of Family Therapy* 391.
58. In all inter-rater reliability research, the degree of concordance in recognizing symptoms and classifying cases is heavily dependent on the details and complexity of the case material presented to experts.
59. Bruch, *supra* note 10, at 541.
60. *Id.* at 535.
61. For Gardner's response to Bruch, see Gardner, R. A. (2001). *Comments on Carol S. Bruch's Article "Parental Alienation Syndrome and Parental Alienation: Getting it Wrong in Child Custody Cases,"* http://www.rgardner.com/refs /ar17.html (last visited October 8, 2003).
62. Bruch, *supra* note 10, at 535 (fn 26) went to the extreme of denigrating Gardner's status at Columbia University by labeling his faculty position, Clinical Professor of Medicine, as a "courtesy" title provided to doctors who allow students to observe their practice. For Gardner's response to this attack see Gardner, *Ibid.*
63. Mosteller, R. P. (1996). Syndromes and Politics in Criminal Trials and Evidence Law 46 *Duke Law Journal* 461.
64. *Id.* at 468. *See also* Daniel Shuman, D. (2002). What Role Should Mental Health Experts Play, 36 *Family Law Quarterly* 135.
65. *Id.* at 467.
66. *See* Warshak, Misdiagnosis of Parental Alienation Syndrome, *supra* note 31.
67. Cf, Regarding the DSM, "Many forces besides science shape it, including politics, fashion and tradition." Cloud, J. How We Get Labeled, *Time*, January 20, 2003 at 104.
68. *See* Grove, W. M. & Barden, R. C. (1999). Protecting the Integrity of the Legal System: The Admissibility of Testimony From Mental Health Experts Under *Daubert/Kumho* Analyses 5 *Psychology, Public Policy & Law* 224 arguing that common testimony about PTSD and Dissociative Identity Disorder does not meet *Daubert* criteria for admissibility.
69. Regarding its diagnostic criteria and classifications, the DSM-IV states, "They do not encompass, however, all the conditions for which people may be treated or that may be appropriate topics for research efforts." Also, "The clinical and scientific considerations involved in categorization of these conditions as mental disorders may not be wholly relevant to legal judgments. . . ." American Psychiatric Association, *supra* note 22, at xxvii. *Also see* Greenberg, S. A., Shuman, D. W., and Meyer, R. G. (2004). Unmasking Forensic Diagnosis, 27 *International Journal of Law and Psychiatry* 1, arguing that "The use of the DSM risks obfuscating the presentation of psychological and psychiatric testimony."
70. Kelly & Johnston, *supra* note 7. For a comparison of the alienated child model with PAS, *see* Warshak, *supra* note 23.
71. Bruch, *supra* note 10.
72. *See* Johnston, J.R. (2003). Parental Alignments and Rejection: An Empirical Study of Alienation in Children of Divorce, 31 *Journal of the American Academy of Psychiatry & Law* 158, for "a preliminary correlational study" that sought to elucidate the various contributing factors to alienation. The study relied on subjective clinical ratings (some of which were derived from a projective test) made 10–20 years earlier of a nonrepresentative sample that had received counseling and mediation services. The author acknowledged several significant drawbacks that limit the extent to which the results can be relied upon. Nevertheless, early studies such as this can serve a valuable function by stimulating subsequent research with more current and representative samples, more objective measures, and a design that sheds light on causal mechanisms rather then correlations. Johnston and her colleagues have issued additional articles based on this sample and on a newer sample. *See* e.g., Johnston and Kelly *supra* note 29. But the recent work suffers from many of the same limitations as the work based on the older sample. For instance, Johnston and her colleagues try to support their conceptualization that pathological alienation is best understood as the end result of multiple factors, with no one factor identified as the primary contributor, by citing correlations between the behavior of alienated parents and the behavior of their alienated children. As they recognize, though, this finding is as compatible with a PAS view as it is support for the view that alienated parents make a significant contribution to their children's pathological alienation. The fact that alienated children who cruelly mistreat and reject a parent evoke certain responses from the rejected parent is hardly evidence that the children's cruel mistreatment is caused by the rejected parent's behavior.
73. An example of the strong feelings aroused by PAS as well as gross misunderstanding about it is found in the work of certain groups and Websites that claim to advocate on behalf of women's issues and mistakenly believe that a charge of fostering PAS is only raised in court by men against women. *See e.g.*, "CA NOW'S research into these syndromes indicates that they have been invented for the sole purpose of targeting women in custody disputes, and that they are never used against men under reversed conditions." Heim, S., Grieco, H., Di Paola, S. & Allen, R. (June 26, 2002) CA NOW *Family Court Report*, p. 5, http://www.canow.org. This statement

was removed from the CA Now Family Court Report when a revised version was issued on September 26, 2002. Included in the revision are the following statements: "PAS is founded on sexist and perverted premises. . . . PAS is a 'syndrome' created to affect custody decisions, to pathologize women, to discredit children who speak out about abuse, and to portray fathers vying for custody as the victims of a mother's revenge." (p. 8).

This author has been involved in several cases in which alienated mothers accused their ex-husbands of turning the children against them. Also, to the author's knowledge currently there are two established foundations and one being formed that deal with some aspect of pathological alienation and all three were founded by alienated mothers. Many of the women involved in such organizations, and those who participate in on-line discussion groups, view PAS as a lifeline offering understanding and hope for their own distressing situations. *See* e.g., http://www.helpstoppas.com. For the perspective of an adult who, as a child, was alienated by her father against her mother, *see* Finkelstein, C. S. (2003). PAS Perspectives: An Adult Parentally Abducted and Alienated as a Child, Reflects on Current PAS Treatment Modules. In von Boch-Galhau, Kodjoe, Andritzky & Koeppel, (Eds.) *supra* note 18, pp. 367–371: "The PAS concept so well describes what happened to me as a child. Tragically, at one point I convinced myself that I had never even had a mother. . . . PAS is real, very real."

An analysis of unreported judgments in Australia over a five-year period reported approximately equal numbers of male and female alienators. Berns, S. (2001). Parents Behaving Badly: Parental Alienation Syndrome in The Family Cour – Magic Bullet or Poisoned Chalice, 15 (3) *Australian Journal of Family Law* 191–214. In Kopetski's sample, about one-third of the alienating parents were men. Kopetski, L. M. and Rand, D. C. *Descriptive Statistics on Incidence, Gender, and Abuse Allegations in PAS*, this volume.

74. Keniston, K. (1968). *Young Radicals: Notes on Committed Youth.* New York: Harcourt, Brace & World, p. 327.
75. Kelly and Johnston, *supra* note 7; Stahl, P. M. (1999). *Complex Issues in Child Custody Evaluations.* Thousand Oaks, CA: Sage Publications. Cf, Warshak, *supra* note 7 at 275: "If efforts to reduce divorce poison are unsuccessful, the alienating parent will continue to do a poor job of supporting the children's relationship with the target. In other respects, though, the alienating parent may be better situated to manage the children. For example, a mother who influences her children to turn against their father may be more available during the school week to supervise the children. Or the father may have limited skills in dealing with the routines of the school week and easily lose his patience. Ultimately the custody decision must rest on a careful consideration of all the factors that influence children's welfare and of each parent's capacity to provide a healthy growth-promoting environment."
76. Bruch, *supra* note 10, at 548.
77. Wallerstein, J. S., Lewis, J. M. & Blakeslee, S. (2000). *The Unexpected Legacy of Divorce: A 25 Year Landmark Study.* New York: Hyperion, page 116.
78. Clawar and Rivlin, *supra* note 46, at 150.
79. Gardner, *supra* note 17.
80. For an exploratory study *see* Rand and Rand, *supra* note 16.
81. Bruch, *supra* note 10, at 535 (FN28), dismissed this study because there was a lack of homogeneity of the legal context in which the family was involved (criminal, family law, and personal injury cases) and factors such as the children's ages and presence or absence of abuse allegations were not included in the data analysis. Although it would be helpful to assess the impact of such factors on the effectiveness of environmental modification, the type of legal case in which the irrationally alienated child's parents are involved seems less relevant for understanding the role of environmental changes in helping to heal alienated child-parent relationships.
82. Rand, D., Rand, R., & Kopetski, L. (2005). The Spectrum of Parental Alienation Syndrome (part III), 23 *American Journal of Forensic Psychology* 15.
83. Dunne & Hedrick, *supra* note 42.
84. Lampel, A. K. (1986). Post-Divorce Therapy with Highly Conflicted Families, 6 *The Independent Practitioner* 22. http:www.fact.on.ca/Info/pas/lampel01.htm (last visited January 28, 2003).
85. Bruch, *supra* note 10, at 550 (FN 83) cites a reporter's investigation and a phone conversation with a psychologist to support speculations regarding the pernicious effect of treatments that enforce a child's contact with an alienated parent. To date I know of no mental health professional who has documented any such cases in a peer-reviewed article appearing in the professional literature. As with the outcome studies documenting the positive effects of environmental modification, it is important that observations of the negative effects of such treatment be documented in refereed publications. Such clinical data may make valuable contributions toward a more differentiated approach to treating alienated children.
86. Lund, *supra* note 34, at 309.
87. Stahl, *supra* note 75, at 6.
88. Bruch, *supra* note 10.
89. *Id.* at 546.
90. *Id.* at 544.
91. *Id.* at 544 (FN 62).
92. *Id.* at 546. *See* Warshak, *supra* note 7, at 264, for a similar concern about due process when the therapist's opinions shape recommendations and testimony made in court by third parties, but the therapist is shielded from the litigation.
93. Bruch, *supra* note 10, at 546.

94. For an excellent analysis and an interesting proposal of a "reasonable child" standard to help courts define the best interests of the child, *see* Chambers, D. L. (1984). Rethinking the Substantive Rules for Custody Disputes in Divorce, 83 *Michigan Law Review* 477.
95. Clawar & Rivlin, *supra* note 46, at 172: "The legal system in most states is not currently adequate to protect children from this form of abuse." Accord, Gardner, *supra* note 7 at xxi; Kelly & Johnston, *supra* note 7 at 257: "Whether such parents are aware of the negative impact on the child, these behaviors of the aligned parent (and his or her supporters) constitute emotional abuse of the child."
96. A problem for those who espouse this position is that, usually when a parent is engaged in such behavior, reports are not made to the local authorities to investigate abuse concerns as is done in cases of suspected physical or sexual abuse. This relates to the difficulties in defining the boundaries of emotional abuse, a topic that is outside the scope of this article. Cf, Clawar & Rivlin, *supra* note 46, at 172: "Mental-health professionals who discover that the programming/brainwashing process is taking place with subsequent damage to various aspects of the child's life should operate on the ethic that they have an obligation to intervene on behalf of the child. This may mean contacting attorneys, the courts, or others on behalf of the child (similar to the social/legal ethic in abuse cases)."
97. For a qualitative retrospective study on the long-term impact of pathological alienation, *see* Baker, A. J. L. *supra* note 8.

Chapter 28

CRITICISM OF PAS IN COURTS OF LAW: HOW TO DEAL WITH IT AND WHY IT OCCURS

BARRY BRODY

OVERVIEW

In courts of law, in the U.S. and abroad, controversy swirls around PAS. We are not dealing here with simple differences of opinion, calmly and objectively discussed. Rather, the debate is often quite heated and emotional. PAS has become politicized and genderized. Ad hominem attacks are not uncommon, especially against those who testify about PAS in courts of law. A better understanding of some of the underlying factors operative in the PAS controversy can be useful for those who deal with PAS in the legal arena.

PAS IN COURTS OF LAW

PAS Literature and Research, Forensic Protocols, Ethics and Laws

Dr. Barry Bricklin, the editor of the *Custody Newsletter*, once noted: "Many professionals with lots of experience do not fully understand Dr. Gardner's work. This is probably because they have never really taken the time to read his books" (2000, p. 5).

By definition, "The Parental Alienation Syndrome (PAS) is a disorder that arises primarily in the context of child-custody disputes" (Gardner, 2001a, p. 61). Because PAS is embedded in the legal context, most mental health professionals will be dealing with PAS in the role of a mental health expert.

A forensic mental health expert is qualified by "knowledge, skill, experience, training or education. . . ." (Florida Statute 90–702). A forensic mental health expert is allowed to testify "if scientific, technical, or other specialized knowledge will assist the trier of fact in understanding the evidence or in determining a fact in issue" (Fla. Stat. 90–702). This point is reiterated in the American Psychological Association's *Specialty Guidelines for Forensic Psychologists*, which state, "Forensic psychologists provide services only in areas of psychology in which they have specialized knowledge, skill, experience, and education" (1991, p. 658).

Thus, the mental health professional dealing with PAS is already pre-positioned to possess "specialized knowledge" by the law's definition of what constitutes an expert. This specialized knowledge of PAS is contained in the literature and research. It is crucial to know this literature and research, including that which is critical of PAS.

How crucial is it? Woody (2000) lists "The Six Harbingers of Doom," which lead to ethical and legal complaints against mental health professionals. Number four is "when the mental health practitioner blindly wanders into child custody cases without adequate specialized or advanced training" (p. 90). In addition, because PAS by definition occurs "primarily in the context of child-custody disputes," one must be familiar with the standards for conducting child custody evaluations, and specifically the appropriate protocols for diagnosing PAS and the relevant ethical guidelines and laws governing forensic mental health professional's work.

In my experience, a majority of the criticisms of PAS are based on a misunderstanding of what PAS is and/or an inappropriate evaluation protocol to determine the presence or absence of PAS. The criticisms then made regarding PAS are based on misconceptions of PAS and assessment techniques that do not allow one to render a valid or accurate opinion regarding PAS. The result is confusion. To counteract this confusion one must be ready to provide the court with the correct information regarding what PAS is and how it is assessed. As Bricklin (1995) wrote, "the only thing an expert should bring to a court is information" (p. 8).

Some Dynamics in the Courtroom

Although knowledge of the PAS literature and the associated forensic protocols is essential, in my experience it isn't enough. Obviously, the mental health expert must understand PAS, be able to apply the concepts of PAS, and have the ability to communicate this understanding of PAS to the court. True understanding of a concept is demonstrated by the ability to apply that concept. Without understanding PAS, the expert will appear to be simply parroting information that they do not truly understand. Therefore, it is crucial when testifying about PAS that the expert understands the subject and can apply this understanding to the case. In addition, the mental health expert should know and understand the dynamics of the courtroom, or one risks being prevented from presenting the data and information that will be useful to the court.

Polarized Preconceptions – The Mental Health Expert vs. the Legal Professional

I recently was waiting to testify in court and observed two attorneys bickering over an issue of supervised visitation. Afterward, it struck me how comfortable they were in arguing, and how they appeared to relish this form of communication. In fact, it appeared to me that they were enjoying the bickering more than the actual facts of the case.

This point was made by Gould and colleagues (2004):

> As a general rule, MHPs [mental health professionals] have much to learn from our legal colleagues about the capacity to accept critical feedback about our forensic work. It is not uncommon for attorneys, zealously advocating for their clients, to challenge each other and offer stinging and sometimes harsh criticisms of their colleagues' opinions and competence. Such criticism is often seen in written correspondence and heard in open court. Appellate reviews can provide strong rebukes of a lower court's reasoning and decision-making. By and large, attorneys and judges have learned not to take such criticisms personally and to see these criticisms as an integral part of the legal process. (p. 40)

This difference in training and approaches to knowing is a major dynamic in the legal setting in which PAS is embedded. In the arena/playing field of the courtroom, life is simple. Complex issues are reduced to merely two opposing positions. The preconception of the legal system is that knowing is obtained from an adversarial proceeding during which two opposing sides are presented and one will be judged as the truth/right. This is a system that frames matters as dichotomies and polarities. Issues are either black or white, right or wrong. The preconception of the mental health field is that knowing is obtained from the application of scientific principles and from understanding the data. This is a system that eschews bias and applies scientific principles to observe what does exist. It is not interested in right or wrong, but in understanding what is observed. Dichotomies, polarities, and opposing views are both valued and considered valid. The emphasis is on understanding both sides and how they interact, not on judging which one is correct.

These two different approaches/preconceptions collide in the courtroom. For example, here according to Gardner (2001b), "In short, not all campaigns of denigration are the result of manifestations of PAS and not all campaigns of denigration are manifestations of abuse. Life is just not that simple" (p. 134).

Positioning, or "It's the Data, Dummy!"

The conflict between these two preconceptions – mental health versus legal, is magnified and intensified in cases involving allegations of PAS.

The reason for this is partly due to the fact that PAS involves the same type of preconception/thinking as does the legal approach. Both view matters as dichotomous and polarized. Life is simple. The alienated parent is seen as all bad. The alienating parent is seen as all good. In fact, the symptoms of the alienated child used to diagnose PAS include lack of ambivalence, reflexive support of the alienating parent, and absence of guilt. These are all hallmarks of polarized thought.

The result is that PAS cases place significant stresses or "pulls" upon the mental health expert that must be recognized and resolved. Brodsky (1991) described this as the "pull to affiliate." Brodsky stated: "The affiliation process is rarely deliberate or conscious. Instead the pull, and sometimes the reality, is to shape one's opinion in small ways to conform to what is seen as the right side" (p. 8).

Brodsky (1991) described the impact of the pull to affiliate upon the mental health expert "These events constitute a far greater hazard to impartiality than the mythical bought witness. Their impact is gradual and beyond immediate awareness of the expert. These influences are sufficiently powerful that they may be the single greatest threat to expert integrity" (p. 9).

In PAS cases, it is critical that this dilemma of competing approaches be resolved. Some mental health experts resolve this dilemma by adopting the legal approach. They trade their professional identity for the professional identity of an attorney. They begin to think and act like attorneys. They choose a side and advocate for that party. The pressures to do this are significant in the legal arena. Although this solves the dilemma, it is not accomplished without a price. For in order for the mental health expert to do this, they must abandon their own knowledge, skill, and training in the mental health field – the very traits that made them experts to begin with. An additional price paid is usually the expert's credibility in the courtroom. In fact, Woody (2000) lists "any form of legal advocacy" by the mental health expert as his fifth "Harbinger of Doom." He writes: "Stated bluntly, the mental health practitioner must allow no bias or discrimination, regardless of reason to contaminate objectivity and impartiality" (p. 90).

My solution/resolution to the dilemma is to remind myself that "It's the data, dummy!" No matter who the client is, no matter who is paying for my services, my affiliation is to the data and the science – my knowledge of PAS and how to assess it. I position myself as aligned with my training and education. This positioning will frustrate attorneys, alienating parents, and alienated children – who all want me to take their side. In reality, there are no sides to take, unless I give up my mental health preconception and begin thinking like an attorney or an alienating parent or an alienated child.

As Bricklin (1995) wrote: "An expert witness is neutral regarding "sides," and is there solely to offer information to the trier of fact. It is good preparation to rid your mind of any notions of being a defender-of-the-truth, no matter how appealing or righteous such a position seems to be. You are there to present information, not "truths," which are really something different" (p. 228).

This positioning is consistent with the American Psychological Association's *Guidelines for Child Custody Evaluations in Divorce Proceedings* (1994), which state:

> The psychologist does not act as a judge, who makes the ultimate decision applying the law to all relevant evidence. Neither does the psychologist act as an advocating attorney, who strives to present his or her client's best possible case. The psychologist, in a balanced, impartial manner, informs and advises the court and the prospective custodians of the child of the relevant psychological factors pertaining to the custody issue. The psychologist should be impartial regardless of whether he or she is retained by the court or by a party to the proceedings. If either the psychologist or client cannot accept this neutral role, the psychologist should consider withdrawing from the case. (p. 678)

I recently reviewed an evaluation report. In the report the examiner stated that he was retained by the attorneys of one of the parties to conduct the evaluation. Unfortunately for the examiner, he was actually court-appointed to perform an independent, neutral, and unbiased examination. As attorneys like to say, the document speaks for itself. I heard echoes of Freud and Brodsky when I read it.

To Be the Object of Envy: The Role of the Expert

The mental health expert in the courtroom becomes the object of envy due to his or her "specialized knowledge." This is what sets the expert apart from everyone else in the courtroom – the judge, the attorneys, the parties. The mental health expert, by definition, knows what the others don't. However, being the object of envy is not always an enviable position to find oneself in.

And so the neophyte mental health expert strides confidently into the courtroom, totally forgetting about envy. Instead, the neophyte expects and assumes that all the others present in the courtroom will not only want to hear, but also value and appreciate, the specialized knowledge the expert is about to impart. This expectation is rarely met. Instead, this expectation is quickly dispelled and the neophyte leaves the courtroom feeling devalued, attacked, unappreciated, and mystified.

What happened? What happened was that the mental health expert forgot his or her own training and expertise – his or her "specialized knowledge," the knowledge of how the human mind works and how this is manifested in human behavior and interactions. Instead, as often happens, the mental health professional accepted the perception/illusion that the courtroom operates on principles different from the rest of the world. Although it is true that the courtroom does have a different set of rules and regulations, what is more true is that the common denominator in the courtroom is the human mind. Everyone there has one. If you can remember this, it may assist you in demystifying the courtroom process and dynamics.

This brings me back to envy. Envy usually travels with spite, revenge, greed, devaluing, and spoiling. Coincidentally, this is similar to what is often found in PAS cases. The antidote to envy is appreciation and gratitude. Envy demarks that which is valued, and is manifested by the "wish . . . to own or replace the source" (Boris, 1994, p.viii). In the courtroom, the expert is by definition the source, the person distinguishable by his or her "specialized knowledge." This brings the dynamics of envy into play.

The attorneys and the parties want to "own" the expert's knowledge. They want the expert to take their side. If the expert does this, then the expert will be valued and appreciated. However, if the parties can't own the expert's knowledge, if the expert won't take their side, then the expert's knowledge must be replaced. Attorneys employ a variety of tactics to accomplish this. Most of these tactics attempt to devalue the expert or the expert's specialized knowledge, resulting in the expert being replaced as a credible source of information for the court. When these tactics are employed, the expert will feel devalued, attacked, and unappreciated – which is exactly the point.

SOURCES OF THE CONTROVERSY OVER PAS (OR, THE PRICE TO BE PAID TO HEAR THE DONKEY BRAYING)

Gardner (2002) addressed the issue of the sources of the controversy surrounding PAS. He observed that the major causal factor of the controversy is that "PAS is very much a product of the adversary system" (p. 12). Gardner described the following aspects of the legal system as contributing to the creation of this controversy: attorneys taking adversarial stances to prevail, attorneys' dilemma to vigorously defend their clients versus the attorney's view of the client, financial greed of attorneys, and PAS being identified with Gardner, who has been openly critical of both attorneys and mental health professionals. I agree that all of these factors play a role in creating the controversy surrounding PAS in the legal and mental health arena, but I also believe that additional factors are at play here.

In rethinking this issue, I am consistently struck by the extreme emotionality that PAS stirs in some professionals. Many mental health professionals claim that this is purely a matter of science for them, but their emotionality overshadows their arguments and makes me believe that this is something else masquerading as science. It is this "something else" that I am attempting to illuminate.

For example, I have been put on notice by some professionals that if I were to "dare" to present PAS in court as a valid scientific phenomenon, I would be exposed as unscientific, not credible, and a boob. Now what's all this fuss about? Why does PAS so significantly impact some professionals that they would resort to threatening me? It is as if PAS is perceived as a *threat* to some professionals. But a threat to what, or threat of what?

Perhaps the threat is related to what Turkat (1993) described when he wrote the following:

> The problem is well illustrated when a mental health expert who has an excellent courtroom presentation style is actually incompetent. The Court, relying on someone believed to be an expert, actually receives poor advice that the Court does not have the expertise to evaluate.
>
> Unfortunately, . . . many individuals engaged in the business of providing custody recommendations probably have no business doing so. (p. 175)

Turkat is describing an illusion here created by the professional. This is the illusion of professional competency created by a good presentation in the courtroom – *the appearance of illusion.* It is the threat of the exposure of this illusion of appearance, this illusion of knowledge and competency, that I believe is responsible for generating much of the controversy surrounding PAS. This is the "something else" I am referring to.

Make no mistake and don't be fooled by the appearance of some professionals. This is not a matter of science, theoretical orientation, or constructs. It is a matter of mental structure and personality. These professionals have become overidentified with the role they play. They have been seduced into believing that they are experts, not professionals. They have become wedded to their professional identity of "expert" – the one who knows. No longer are they messengers merely delivering the message; they have become the message. They present themselves in court, not the data. They have become the data. In fact, their view of the data has supplanted the data itself. The basis of science – observation – becomes replaced with "I know." There is no room for space between themselves and the data. That space utilized to observe the data has been collapsed and replaced with the identity of the expert. There is no space or room for different views or opinions. There is only one view – "My way or the highway; I'm right therefore you're wrong." They have an intolerance for differences and an aversion to space, gaps, and separation. Others and other viewpoints are experienced as threats to their identity as the all-knowing, the one in the know, the know-it-all.

Gaps in knowledge are quickly filled with their views. If the data do not fit, they are shaped to fit their preconceptions of how matters should be. For these professionals there is nothing to learn from the data, because they know it all. They, not the data are the focus, and what is to be reported is their view, not what the data say. It is the substitution of arrogance for self-confidence. It is the substitution of dogma for an appreciation of different views.

It is easy to believe that these professionals are scientists. However, this presupposes that they actually see the data and operate from a basis of theory and constructs. These professionals only see themselves. They will utilize any theory at hand to reinforce their identity as the expert. They have replaced theory and observation with themselves. They have the appearance of being scientific, but their "knowledge" doesn't fit the data, let alone any theory. It was this "appearance of knowledge," this "illusion of knowing," that I believe PAS threatened to unmask.

I remember overhearing a conversation in court where a well-known mental health expert stated, "My job is to protect the judge's ass." I later had the opportunity to observe this expert critiquing my PAS evaluation in court. The expert testified that because I had not administered a thematic apperception test to the minor child, my evaluation was unacceptable and therefore my conclusions were irrelevant concerning PAS. The court accepted the expert's opinion. I was shocked and discussed this testimony with an attorney who, while admitting the scientific errors in the expert's testimony, advised me to admire the expert's ability to think on her feet and her strong presence in the courtroom.

Of course, the courtroom is a good place to go hunting for the appearance of illusions, as they are plentiful there. We all like to believe that the court system is fair and just, that judges are as wise as Solomon, that attorneys seek the truth and the best interests of the children, and that experts are competent, can discern the truth, and are all-knowing. However, the professionals who work in the courts all know that it is the appearance of illusion that is rewarded and reinforced in the courtroom. Because attorneys attempt to "unmask" these illusions of appearance, the expert is pressured to keep these illusions of appearance intact and untarnished.

In 1985, when for the first time Gardner put his clinical observations in writing, he was sharing a view of a "psychological disturbance" that could be brought about by child custody litigation. Due to the "increasing frequency" of this observed phenomenon, Gardner gave it a special name, "parental alienation syndrome." Before that time, PAS was unseen and unobserved. It was unknown. Perhaps some professional jealousy/envy that Gardner had observed what others missed existed, but I believe that this "something else" that Gardner couldn't have foreseen occurred.

PAS was a new point of view. It was a different point of view. PAS represented another perspective from which to see the data. There is nothing wrong with this. I can conceive that this is a basis of all scientific endeavors – observation – and that one dynamic that characterizes science is a process of observation and discovery, followed by disillusionment about the initial view, eventually leading to greater, more realistic sight and more discoveries. Therefore, a scientific perspective has space for multiple views, even conflicting perspectives.

However, this did not apply to PAS for some professionals. For these professionals there was only one point of view – theirs – and the introduction of PAS represented the throwing down of the gauntlet. "Who are you going to believe? Gardner or me? I'm the expert. I'm the professional. I tell you what the data says and means. **I know** how things are. I know." This was the unforeseen "something else."

So instead of PAS becoming part of a scientific dialogue, an exchange of views, it became embroiled in a scientific diatribe where the stakes were high for some professionals. The reason that the stakes were so high for some professionals and the emotional fervor so intense regarding PAS was that these professionals had come to believe that they were the experts, the ones who knew. If PAS was accepted, it would mean that not only had these professionals committed serious mistakes that would have significant negative consequences for many families, but, more importantly, these experts were wrong – they didn't really know. If they were wrong, they would have to deal with the disillusionment that their identification as the expert was merely an illusion, an appearance, a pseudo-identity that was not based on data, observation, science, and theory, but was based on personal variables.

I am reminded of a famous Sufi teaching story of Idries Shah (1983). It goes like this:

Nasrudin's neighbor came over and asked to borrow his donkey.
Nasrudin said the donkey was not there.
At that moment the donkey brayed.
The man said, "The donkey is here; I just heard him bray."
To which Nasrudin replied, "Who are you going to believe? Me or a donkey?"

Disillusioning people is a risky business. Most of us intensely dislike being disillusioned, or fooled, even though illusions are a necessary part of the mental structure. We prefer to believe that the magician can create magic with his or her special powers. Many of my patients have told me that it was easier when they did not know what they had eventually come to learn about themselves in treatment. Knowledge and awareness come with a price – the death of our illusions. Ignorance is bliss. We prefer to believe Nasrudin, and ignore our own senses. When the data does not fit our illusions, it is sometimes easier for all of us to reshape the data and leave our illusions intact.

When we finally become aware of the fact that we have been disillusioned, we usually react with strong emotions. When, for example, a mother fools us with a story that her children were kidnapped, but has actually killed them herself, we react strongly and emotionally. When we learn that a crematorium operator fools us with what he actually did with the remains of our loved ones, we are outraged. And when we learn that our nation is not secure from attack, that we are not as safe and secure as we had thought, that our leaders cannot protect us from all types of heinous acts, we are shocked into the realization that it was all an illusion.

What makes PAS dangerous and a threat to some professionals is that it inadvertently illuminates the appearance of illusion. It threatens to demonstrate that some professionals are not competent, scientific, or interested in the best interests of children, that their views and opinions sometimes do not fit the data. They are merely "experts" and professionals whose status in the court system relies solely on their reputations, and nothing more. Such a threat will be met with great emotionality and resistance. Most of us dislike having to confront our illusions, let alone having someone else point them out to us. This is what I believe is a major driving force in the fervor surrounding PAS. This is the "something else."

Or perhaps that wasn't a donkey I heard braying.

REFERENCES

Boris, Harold (1994). *Envy.* Northvale, NJ: Jason Aronson, Inc.

Bricklin, Barry (1995). *The custody evaluation handbook, Research-based solutions and applications.* Bristol, PA: Bruner/Mazel.

Bricklin, Barry (2000). *21 The Custody Newsletter, 5.*

Brodsky, Stanley L. (1991). *Testifying in court: Guidelines and maxims for the expert witness.* Washington, D.C.: American Psychological Association.

Gardner, R. A. (1985). Recent trends in divorce and custody litigation. *The Academy Forum, 29*(2), 3–7.

Gardner, R. A. (2001a). Should courts order PAS children to visit/reside with the alienated parent? A follow-up study. *American Journal of Forensic Psychology, 19*(3), 61–106.

Gardner, R. A. (2001b). *Therapeutic interventions for children with parental alienation syndrome.* Cresskill, NJ: Creative Therapeutics, Inc.

Gardner, R. A. (2002). *Sex abuse trauma? Or trauma from other sources?* Cresskill, NJ: Creative Therapeutics, Inc.

Gould, Jonathan W., Kirkpatrick, H. D., Austin, William G. & Martindale, David A. (2004). Critiquing a colleague's forensic advisory report: A suggested protocol for application to child custody evaluations. *Journal of Child Custody, 1*(3), 37–64.

Guidelines for child custody evaluations in divorce proceedings (1994). *American Psychologist, 49*(7), 677–680.

Shah, Idries. (1983). *The pleasantries of the incredible Mulla Nasrudin.* London, England: Octagon Press.

Specialty Guidelines for Forensic Psychologists (1991). *Law and Human Behavior, 15*(6), 655–665.

Turkat, Daniel Ira (1993). Questioning the mental health expert's custody report. *American Journal of Family Law, 7,* 175–179.

Woody, R. H. (2000). *Child custody practice standards, ethical issues, and legal safeguards for mental health professionals.* Sarasota, Florida: Professional Resource Press.

Chapter 29

COMMENTARY: PARENTAL ALIENATION SYNDROME

LEONA M. KOPETSKI

OVERVIEW

In July 2001, Family Court Review published a special issue on parental alienation syndrome (PAS) or "the alienated child," as it is renamed in the journal (Schepard [Ed.], 2001). Kopetski draws on her experience of 23 years performing over 600 hundred custody evaluations as part of an interdisciplinary team in Colorado. Kopetski also draws upon her research, presentations and review of others research to lend an evaluator's perspective to the theory and research on PAS.

Like the authors in the journal, I have considerable clinical experience working with divorced families, and I am pleased that the serious problem of children of divorce who lose one parent unnecessarily is finally being acknowledged by leaders in the field. The authors note that there has been some resistance to the observations first named and published by Gardner regarding PAS (Gardner, 1985, 1987), and since elaborated upon by others, including myself (Clawar & Rivlin, 1991; Dunne & Hedrick, 1994; Rand, 1997a,b; Kopetski, 1998a,b; Warshak, 2001; Rand et al. 2005). However, I was disappointed to see that the journal authors repeat and leave unchallenged personal attacks on Gardner, and those of us who share his concern for children caught up in this destructive syndrome. The repeated references to Gardner and his ideas as "coercive," "punitive," and "simplisitic" detract from the substance of the material offered. As Schepard notes in his editorial comments, an alienated child who is not the victim of real abuse or neglect by the parent targeted for alienation is the victim of profound and real emotional cruelty by the alienating parent.

According to the introduction, the articles represent the collaborative work of a self-appointed task force of mental health professionals and are intended as a "complementary set" (p. 246). The authors argue that PAS as Gardner conceived it needs to be reformulated. The rationale they provide appears to come down to two main points. Gardner put too much emphasis on the alienating parent as the cause of the child's alienation and his recommendation for change of custody in severe cases is ill advised. There are two articles written from a legal perspective, which argue that PAS testimony should not be admissible in court. The reformulation offered by the mental health experts is used to bolster the legal argument against PAS.

The journal provides a number of clinical descriptions which are similar to my experience, and to the observations of other contributors published over the past 20 years. These dynamic descriptions confirm that we are talking about the same kinds of cases, although I was disappointed to find no new information. Kelly and Johnston (2001) acknowledge that their observations of the behaviors and emotional responses of alienated children are similar to those reported by Gardner and others (p. 262). Their description of "common behaviors and organizing beliefs of the aligned parent" are also similar (pp. 257–258).

According to Kelly and Johnston, Gardner's emphasis on the alienating parent as the primary cause of PAS is "simplistic." In their view, alienation is caused by a series of complex factors, and the target parent's contributions should be taken into account. The reformulation they offer proposes to focus on the child, rather than on parental alienation. They suggest replacing PAS with "a new formulation," which they call the "alienated child."

> An alienated child is defined as one who expresses, freely and persistently, unreasonable negative feelings and beliefs (such as anger, hatred, rejection, and/or fear) toward a parent that are significantly disproportionate to the child's actual experience with that parent. From this viewpoint, the pernicious behaviors of a "programming parent" are no longer the starting point. Rather, the problem of the alienated child begins with a primary focus on the child, his or her observable behaviors, and parent-child relationships. (Kelly & Johnston, p. 251)

It is helpful to review Gardner's reasons for introducing the term PAS, and how he defined it. According to Gardner, the notion that the child is merely "brainwashed" is too narrow. Factors arising within the child, independent of parental contributions, also play an important role in the development of the syndrome. It was the *combination* of parental programming and the child's own contributions which prompted him to come up with a new term which encompassed both contributory factors. According to Gardner "The *parental alienation syndrome* (PAS) is a disorder that arises primarily in the context of child-custody disputes. Its primary manifestation is the child's campaign of denigration against a parent, a campaign that has no justification. It results from a *combination* of a programming (brainwashing) parent's indoctrinations and the child's own contributions to the vilification of the target parent" (Gardner, 1998, p. xx). Gardner stated that situational factors such as the remarriage of a parent, or the litigation process itself may also contribute, becoming entwined with the internal psychological processes of the parents and the child.

The definition of "alienated child" appears to be quite similar to Gardner's definition of PAS. There is a difference of emphasis on the role of the alienating parent and the kinds of interventions which should be applied. Contributors to the journal are disturbed by Gardner's recommendation for change of custody in severe cases, which comprise five to ten percent of PAS cases in his estimate. According to Johnston et al. Gardner's approach is "coercive and punitive" (p. 316).

In many important ways, the journal contributors have made inferences and generalizations which do not follow from the clinical data given. In all but the most serious cases, they recommend leaving the child in the custody of the alienating parent while a program of therapy and intensive case management by a team of legal and mental health professionals is put in place (Sullivan & Kelly, 2001). In the most severe and entrenched cases, Lee and Olesen suggest that it may be appropriate for the evaluator to recommend that the rejected parent "let go," or that custody be removed from both parents. This ambivalence about protecting the child's relationship with the target parent is found in the chapter on therapy, as well. According to Johnston et al., "reunification with the rejected parent is not the primary goal of the intervention" (p. 316). This ambivalence about reuniting the child and target parent illustrates one reason why traditional therapy is not effective in reversing alienation. There is a growing body of research which shows that therapy is not an effective remedy for PAS, and may actually make things worse (Clawar & Rivlin, 1991; Kopetski, 1991; Dunne & Hedrick, 1994; Gardner 2001; Rand et al. 2005).

My commentary is divided into five sections, beginning with a description of the professional context in which my views on PAS were forged. This is followed with sections on the name PAS, the issue of gender bias, criticisms of Gardner, the scientific basis of PAS, and the problem of interventions.

AN EXPERIENTIAL CONTEXT

In my 23 years as an evaluator, I conducted more than 600 custody and visitation evaluations, all either court ordered or performed by agreement of both parents and the guardian ad litem, if there was one, as there usually was in cases evaluated from the early 1990s on. I have never worked as a hired gun. As those who know me will attest, I have spoken militantly and passionately against the practice. I have annoyed people with my strident views on the subject. I strongly object to the suggestion that those of us who are concerned about PAS commonly engage in this practice. Frankly, I have observed that the practice of evaluating only one parent and perhaps the child, then making conclusions about the parent not seen, is more common among those who are assessing allegations of abuse by one parent which, if true, might justify the exclusion of the accused parent from a child's life. I note that Sullivan and Kelly make a similar observation, "It is not unusual that children's therapists fuel the alienating through involvement with only the aligned parent, through inappropriate advocacy to the court, or by reinforcing negative distortions in the child" (p. 301).

I firmly believe that every serious allegation in custody or visitation disputes should be thoroughly evaluated and that competent evaluation of such claims involves individual evaluation of the child and both parents, as well as observing the interaction between the child and each parent. This is the protocol I followed in all the evaluations I conducted. If a parent refused to allow the child to be observed with the other parent, I declined to do the evaluation.

As part of my evaluation protocol, children received psychological testing appropriate to their ages. Testing of parents and stepparents became standard from 1985 on. Grandparents and significant others were also evaluated when relevant. In addition to direct observation, collateral information was obtained from pediatricians, schools, therapists, and any social or law enforcement agency who had contact with the family. In cases where physical illness of a parent or child might be relevant, medical providers were contacted directly. My focus in writing reports was to provide detailed descriptions of observations of behavior, with inferences and conclusions which could be checked against the data by anyone reading them. I did not use labels and clinical jargon as these were often injurious to parents reading them and could be readily misused in legal proceedings.

When I first began encountering the alienation cases in the 1970s, I thought of these families simply as disturbed. It would be another decade before Gardner introduced the term PAS. I became concerned that children in these scenarios usually lost one parent in the divorce, often the parent with whom a healthier relationship was possible. As a clinical social worker, I was all too aware of what it means to a child to lose a parent, whether by death, abandonment or any other cause. The divorce research coming out at that time indicated that children who maintained relationships with both parents tended to be better adjusted both socially and psychologically (Levitin [ed.], 1979). This strengthened my conviction that children of divorce, like children in intact families, need both parents. I wondered what I could do as an evaluator to prevent the unnecessary loss of a parent in alienation scenarios. Children should be spared the loss of a parent if possible, and have to deal only with a restructuring of their relationships with each parent (Ahrons and Rodgers, 1987).

I knew that my recommendations for custody, visitation and therapy could make the difference between protecting the child's access to both parents or the loss of the parent to be alienated. I made it a practice to review completed cases to learn more about the distinctive characteristics of the PAS families, in which the child formed an exclusive alliance with one parent and rejected the other. Based on my experience, I found that recommendations for therapy and gradually increased visitation with the rejected parent were ineffective for interrupting alienation. I began making custody recommendations based on an assessment of which parent was more likely to support the child's relationship with the other parent. Appropriately applied, I found that this remedy interrupted alienation and could even be used to prevent it. Enforced visitation with the target parent helped interrupt alienation in some cases. The study by Rand et al. (2005) examines the efficacy of these interventions, and effects of these interventions based on children's adjustment and relationship with both parents at follow-up.

After learning of Gardner's work in 1987, I began using the term PAS in the context of communicating with other professionals. In keeping with my policy, I did not use the PAS label in my evaluation reports but gave detailed descriptions of behavior, from which the diagnosis could be inferred. The data from my cases led me to disagree with Gardner on some issues, such as his reliance on primary parent theory to explain why the mother was so often the alienating parent (Kopetski, 1991). On balance, his work was extremely helpful to me as it confirmed my independently derived observations of the characteristics of PAS families (Kopetski, 1998a,b).

In 1991, I presented a paper on PAS at the 15th Annual Child Custody Conference in Keystone, Colorado (Kopetski, 1991). For this presentation, I reviewed all the evaluations I had conducted from 1975 to 1990, and determined that 84 of the 413 cases evaluated were distinctive for PAS. The evaluation issues in the remaining cases included healthy divorcing parents who wanted a professional opinion about the best arrangement for their children, high conflict cases in which both parents were contributing significantly to the hostilities, and scenarios involving bona fide child abuse and neglect, spousal abuse, or mental illness of a parent.

Among the 84 PAS cases, I identified 19 different justifications used by alienating parents of both genders to rationalize restricting the target parent's access, including allegations of child abuse. There appeared to be a significant shift in the kinds of accusations which occurred over the years, as different social causes became the focus of attention. Thirty years ago, mothers seeking to restrict the father's access were more likely to assert that the child had separation anxiety from the mother or was not emotionally attached to the father. The increased recognition of problems such as child abuse, rape and domestic violence were readily exploited by alienating parents, especially mothers, who found they could use such allegations to their advantage (Kopetski et al., in press).

My commentary on the special issue of Family Court Review is written from my perspective as a clinician and custody evaluator in Colorado. My goal was to help children of divorce, and especially PAS children, to maintain relationships with both parents. The contributors to the journal each have their own goals and perspective. Some are clinicians, like myself, who have devoted their careers to providing mental health services to children of divorce and their families. Williams and Zirogiannis argue from a legal perspective that PAS testimony should be admissible in court. These articles seem out of place.

WHAT'S IN A NAME?

It is not at all that there are sound reasons for changing the name from "parental alienation syndrome" to "alienated child." The journal alleges that the term PAS is misused in court, but no evidence is offered to support this claim. Schepard's description of PAS as a "nuclear weapon" is not consistent with my experience. According to Schepard, "If a *Parental Alienation Syndrome* (PAS) label could be attached to a parent's behavior, the rejected parent potentially won a great victory, a shift of custody to him or her" (p. 243). In the jurisdictions in which I worked, I did not encounter any judge who automatically accepted the diagnosis of PAS without question. The only "nuclear bomb" I encountered was an allegation of sexual abuse. That allegation almost always led to automatic and immediate disruption of the child's relationship with the accused parent. In some cases, it took years before adequate evaluation determined whether the allegation was founded or not. The feminists and child advocates claim that alienated parents accused of abuse use PAS to exonerate themselves and blame the mother for the child's rejection. Zigoriannis articulates this view in his argument that PAS testimony should be inadmissible in court. In this view, judges' ready acceptance of PAS causes them to strip protective mothers of custody and place children in the custody of their abusers.

In my opinion, the name "alienated child" is too general and too mild for the pathology described. The definition given applies primarily to older children whose contemptuous and angry behavior is clearly not normal and often causes social difficulties. The definition specifically eliminates the role of the alienating parent's influence on the child. According to Kelly and Johnston, the child's behavior should be treated as originating solely from the child. In the cases I evaluated, there was often clear and convincing evidence of what the alienating parent was doing. Why they feel the need to be protective of alienating parents is not clear.

Taken out of the context of the relationship with both parents, the behavior of these children is not *alienated.* It is *alienating.* The child is an actor, not just the acted upon. Of course, in a scenario where the child has internalized the alienating parent's pathology and is expressing shared beliefs about the target parent as their own, the argument could be made that the feelings expressed originate solely in the child. This is what the alienating parent would have others believe.

The "alienated child" has just as much potential for misuse as PAS. If there is a question of PAS, the alienating parent can invoke the "alienated child" and argue that the child may be alienated, but it is not the parent's fault. The distinction Kelly and Johnston make between the "alienated child" and "realistic estrangement" (p. 253) is likely to be misused as well. The claim can be made that the child's rejection of the target parent is not PAS but "realistic estrangement," due to the rejected parent's history of violence, abuse or neglect, whether the behavior was directed at the child, or at another family member, witnessed by the child.

As an evaluator, I did not use the PAS label in my reports, but found it was extremely important to clearly identify the alienating parent's behavior as a problem and make recommendations accordingly. Many of my colleagues were influenced by Johnston's views on high conflict divorce, and took the approach that "both parents are to blame." In my experience, the failure of the evaluator to identify PAS as a problem increased the likelihood that the alienation would progress. Thus, alienation might be completed by the time interveners were willing to acknowledge that the alienating parent had successfully alienated the child.

Generally speaking, when children treat friends, relatives, teachers and other authority figures the way severely alienated children treat the hated parent, they are expected to change. Most clinicians agree that children need appropriate limits on their behavior and that it is the duty of parents and other adult authority figures to provide such limits and structure. In PAS, one often finds that the alienating parent is encouraging the child's unruly, disrespectful behavior, and exploiting it in the service of the alienation agenda.

As Johnston and Roseby (1997) point out, some children align with and try to comfort the parent who seems more hurt and psychologically vulnerable in the divorce. In any other setting, such a role reversal would lead to interventions designed to help the parent find more appropriate resources for managing their emotions and meeting their needs. Every effort would be made to help the child feel less guilty and responsible. For years, we have asked parents not to use their children in this way. Why should the divorce context be different? Johnston, et al. suggest that good parenting should be a condition of the alienating parent maintaining custody. I heartily agree.

Unfortunately, our adversarial legal system is such that words and labels which reflect negatively on the other parent are frequently misused. We need good descriptions of the phenomenon, and the features which differentiate it from other problems, so that evaluators and judges can make accurate determinations when faced with cross allegations of PAS.

THE QUESTION OF GENDER BIAS

Schepard states that gender issues have fueled much of the resistance to recognizing the existence of PAS. Father's groups see it as an antidote to an epidemic of false allegations of violence and abuse against men, while women's groups view it as "a political plot" to roll back the protections for victims of child abuse and domestic violence. According to Schepard, "PAS focused us on what custody rules were good for fathers or mothers, globally, rather than the best interests of children" (p. 243). In my view, the problem is that those who associate PAS with gender bias see only two possible positions, bias against mothers or bias against fathers. Schepard takes the position that PAS is biased against mothers. He believes judges have succumbed to the influence of discredited mental health experts and are too ready to accept PAS. Like the feminist and child protection advocates, Schepard seems to think that fathers are frequently awarded custody based questionable findings that PAS by the mother is the cause of the child's rejection, not the alienated parent's abusive behavior.

At the end of his introductory notes, Schepard indicates that it was his suggestion to include "a note" by one of his students on evidentiary issues in PAS. The article by Zigoriannis argues that PAS testimony should not be admissible in court. Zigoriannis uses two well-known legal cases to illustrate his contention that courts improperly use PAS as the justification for changing custody to the father in scenarios where the mother has accused the father of sexual abuse. When PAS emerged as a growing social problem in the 1980s, Gardner reported that the mother was the alienating parent in the majority of cases. He came under strong attack from some feminists, though similar findings were reported by other contributors, including Clawar and Rivlin (1991), with a sample of 700 divorce families, and Kelly, who is the co-author of two articles in the journal (Wallerstein & Kelly, 1980; Kelly & Johnston, 2001; Sullivan & Kelly, 2001).

As time passed, Gardner and others reported a change in the ratio of alienating mothers to fathers, with a significant increase in the proportion of alienating fathers. The personal attacks against Gardner have continued, however, spearheaded for the most part by feminist and child protection advocates like Faller (1998) and Bruch (2001), who mistakenly equate Gardner's Sex Abuse Legitimacy Scale with his criteria for PAS. Zirogiannis makes this mistake as well.

According to Schepard, PAS has fueled a gender war. I disagree. The gender war exists independently of PAS, or any other diagnostic syndrome, though the politics of gender have entered the courtroom through the merging of feminist and child advocacy agendas. It was a feminist lawyer who said to me that, "PAS is just one more way for hostile men to attack already beleaguered women." There are indeed father's rights advocates, but they have not been nearly as successful in pushing their agendas in court as feminist advocates.

In my work, I found that PAS is not a gender-determined disorder. The characteristics I used to identify alienating parents were not specific to mothers or fathers. They included behaviors such as obsession with denigrating the target parent, sharing a distorted, essentially negative perception of the target parent with the child, and relentless efforts to terminate the target parent's access. I note that Kelly and Johnston do not differentiate between mothers and fathers when they report that "a range of alienating behaviors on the part of the aligned parent have long been recognized as contributing to the child's alienated stance (Clawar & Rivlin, 1991; Gardner, 1987; Wallerstein & Kelly, 1980)" (p. 257). However, there seems to be an element of mother bias in the objections journal contributors express about change of custody.

I believe that the primary reason that more mothers have been found to be alienating is that more social causes are available to them. I am old enough to have done custody evaluations when divorce was granted only in cases where the other spouse had committed adultery, or had serious problems such as alcoholism or mental illness. A father who wanted custody had to persuade the court that the mother was unfit. A neglectful mother then caused moral outrage just as a sexually abusing father does now. Then, as now, an accusation was an effective weapon, regardless of whether it was true, false, or based on transitory circumstances which were amenable to help or likely to change.

The evaluations I conducted were "sex blind," especially after 1980, when the basis of my recommendations for custody changed. Like most other evaluators, I had been making custody recommendations based on primary parent theory. Custody was usually recommended to the mother, with therapy and gradually increased visits for the father. Alienating mothers found they could readily sabotage such recommendations and the child lost their relationship with the father. When I realized what was happening, I developed a paradigm for custody evaluations which would protect the child's access to both parents and began making custody recommendations based on which parent was most likely to support the child's relationship with the other parent. This criterion put fathers and mothers on equal footing.

In one particularly contentious alienation case, I recommended custody to the target father, while a second opinion evaluation by a feminist evaluator recommended custody to the mother. The feminist evaluator accused me of being biased towards fathers. I reviewed all the cases I had evaluated and found that I had recommended custody to mothers and fathers about equally. By my calculations, the feminist evaluator had recommended custody to the mother in 90 percent of the cases she evaluated. Another source of gender bias was the parents themselves. Women were more likely to choose an evaluator with a reputation for mother bias, while men looked for an evaluator who gave fathers equal consideration. A reputation for bias, whether true or not, affects the type of cases one is asked to evaluate.

ON THE CRITICISMS OF GARDNER

Though the special issue gives token credit to Gardner, as is ethically required, criticisms intended to discredit his ideas are left standing as though they still have some credibility. The journal suggests that if Gardner had published in more peer-reviewed journals, he would be more credible and his ideas would have more scientific validity. Like other Gardner critics, contributors to the journal conveniently overlook the fact that Gardner had more than 130 articles published in peer-reviewed journals. Another frequently repeated criticism is that Gardner's books were self-published. Gardner's best selling book, *The Boys and Girls Book About Divorce*, was published by Jason Aaronson (Gardner, 1976). Sequels to this popular book, such as *The Boys and Girls Book About Step-Families*, were published by Bantam (Gardner, 1982). It is instructive to read Gardner's reasons for establishing Creative Therapeutics, the company which published his later books. "It is important to take risks, and provide people with the information they need – information that others might find too controversial, or would find no profitability in publishing. My primary objective is to provide the best information I have at the time it is needed. And my greatest gratification is in having the freedom, with Creative Therapeutics, to do this (Gardner, 2003)."

There are problems with judging ideas according to their general acceptance in the scientific community. If the professional journals of clinicians were committed to science there might be better reason to trust what appears to be the common opinion. But they are not. Many journals have either a preferred theoretical approach, or a commitment to advocate for a social cause and use the trappings of science to advance that position or cause. The goal of this advocacy based approach to science is not to test the validity of the idea, but to "prove" that the cause is right. There is a certain elitism and cliquishness which serves to exclude those whose ideas and opinions may differ.

Science by consensus does not necessarily arrive at the truth of anything, as is clear to anyone who has knowledge of the history of scientific thought. Galileo, for example, failed the peer review test, and we now know that his ideas presented an accurate picture of reality. More recently, in 1961, Dr. Judah Folkman made an important discovery in the field of cancer research. His discovery was treated with profound disrespect by his peers, who could not conceive that his ideas were plausible, because they were not traditional. In 1998, some 47 years after his discovery, The National Institute of Health finally began to fund the study of his ideas. Today, his clinical observations and inferences are accepted, and the process of clinical trials for treatment of humans based on his ideas have finally begun (Cooke, 2001).

A good example of the problems with science by consensus can be found in the lead article of the journal. Kelly and Johnston state that "indiscriminate use of PAS terminology has led to widespread confusion and misunderstanding in judicial, legal, and psychological circles (p. 250). However, the substance of those misunderstandings is not discussed. For "a more extensive review of the support for, and rejection of,

PAS" (p. 250), the reader is referred to Faller (1998), among others. Faller is not an expert in divorce or PAS. Her specialty is sex abuse. Faller takes the child advocate position that allegations of sex abuse are almost always true, even in divorce. Faller is a harsh critic of Gardner, primarily for his views on sex abuse. Gardner opined that sex abuse allegations may be true or false and that it is vitally important to make accurate determinations one way or the other. Faller strongly disagreed with Gardner's view that false allegations of abuse were more frequent in divorce than in other contexts. In her critique of PAS, Faller describes allegations of sex abuse as Gardner's criteria for PAS, which is incorrect. Kelly and Johnston are apparently unaware that Faller's critique of PAS is based on a misunderstanding of Gardner's work.

Gardner's "sin" was not his observations of PAS, but his temerity in questioning the automatic acceptance that all sex abuse allegations are true. Gardner was one of very few people who had the courage to challenge the child advocates and sexual abuse experts who asserted that "children never lie about abuse." In my view, we should be grateful to Gardner for his willingness to stand up to the feminist and child protection advocates. Many clinicians in my community complained privately about how sex abuse allegations were handled. However, they were reluctant to state their views publicly, as doing so would result in harsh criticisms by colleagues and the media, threats to sue, and, in my case, death threats. There is a beginning public awareness that the sexual abuse movement has caused harm to some parents and children, but it has taken years, and a lot of people have been harmed in the meantime.

Kelly and Johnston are critical of Gardner's "overly simplistic focus on the brainwashing parent as the primary etiological agent" (p. 246). Schepard echoes this sentiment when he expresses his views about change of custody, which he describes as "a crude one-size-fits-all remedy of shifting custody from the alienating to the rejecting (sic) parent" (p. 244). Words such as "coercive" and "punitive" are used to describe Gardner's recommendation for change of custody. The use of such derogatory statements to discredit Gardner's work is unscientific and unprofessional. The American Psychological Association prohibits the use of biased, value laden language for that reason (Publication Manual, 2003).

Schepard is mistaken when he asserts that Gardner recommended a "one-size-fits-all" remedy for PAS. Gardner recognized that PAS could be mild, moderate, or severe and recommended a specific treatment approach for each category. In mild to moderate PAS, he recommended that the mother retain custody, along with case management and PAS specific therapy. It was in the small minority of severe cases that he recommended placing the child in the custody of the rejected parent. The alienating parents in those cases were seriously disturbed and had a pathological relationship with the child. I believe that any responsible custody evaluator would have made the same recommendation, regardless of their views on PAS. Sullivan and Kelly report that "changing custody has [sometimes] resulted in an adverse outcome for children because the new custodial parent had limited abilities to parent" (p. 312). In some of the severe PAS cases I evaluated, I considered recommending a change of custody, but decided against it, based on my negative assessment of the target parent's parenting capacity. There were two or three cases in which subsequent events proved that my assessment had been wrong. In my experience, recognizing mistakes and analyzing what had been done wrong led to new and improved ideas for how to approach things.

There has been a great deal of controversy over Gardner's ideas about custody and court ordered contact between the child and target parent. Much of the debate has centered on "who is right and who is wrong." Gardner focused on the substance. When it became apparent that research-based information was needed to move the debate along, he conducted a study designed to answer the question: Should courts order PAS children to visit/reside with the alienated parent? (Gardner, 2001)

THE SCIENTIFIC BASIS OF PAS

According to Kelly and Johnston, there is "no scientific basis to PAS other than Gardner's clinical experience" and that of "other proponents" (p. 250). By this standard, there is no scientific basis to their "alienated child" formulation, either. According to Johnston and Kelly, the views and ideas expressed in the journal are "based largely on clinical insights and practical experience in working with a broad array of high-conflict divorcing families, a subgroup of whom comprise alienated children as we have defined them" (p. 247). I note that the same could be said of my background, or Gardner's, for that matter. Gardner's credentials are every bit as impressive as those of the the journal contributors, if not more so.

Zigoriannis argues that PAS is not a scientific concept because it is not grounded in traditional methods and procedures of science, such as laboratory experiments, random sampling, control groups, and statistical analysis of data. Zigoriannis acknowledges that these methods are not often feasible or ethical for social science researchers. This is especially true when it comes to high conflict divorce and PAS. He believes that social science concepts can still be considered as "scientific evidence," as long as they are "derived through the recognition and formulation of a problem, the collection of data through experimentation, the formulation of a hypothesis, and the testing and confirmation of the hypothesis formulated" (p. 336). As I understand it, this is very much how Gardner's work on PAS evolved.

Science refers to a systematic process for investigating reality in a way which is as clear, comprehensive and undistorted as possible. The fact that the observations of PAS described by different contributors over the past 20 years have been remarkably consistent is scientifically significant, indicating that PAS is a valid concept which can be reliably identified. According to Johnston (1993), she was able to reliably distinguish between "strong and mild alignments," referring to children's alignments with the alienating parent. The fact that the clinical descriptions in the journal are similar to what Gardner reported only verifies Gardner's observations.

The journal presents the "alienated child" formulation as something "new." According to Johnston and Kelly, the "alienated child" is an improvement over PAS because it distinguishes between alienated children who are aligned with one parent (PAS), and children who are realistically estranged because of bona fide abuse. In fact, Gardner dealt with this issue in his definition of PAS. "When true parental abuse and/or neglect is present the child's animosity may be justified, and so the parental alienation syndrome explanation for the child's hostility is not applicable" (Gardner, 1992, p. xx). Johnston and Kelly overlook this important point.

There is one important difference between PAS and the "alienated child," and that is the emphasis on the role of the alienating parent. Kelly and Johnston believe that Gardner's focus on the brainwashing parent as the primary cause of PAS is "overly simplistic" (p. 250). In making this judgment, they miss a fundamental component of Gardner's definition of PAS, which he defines as a *combination* (emphasis added) of the alienating parent's influence and *the child's own contributions* (emphasis added). As I read the material presented in the journal, it seemed that parts of the critique were based on a selective portrayal of Gardner's work.

Kelly and Johnston view their reformulation of PAS as superior for its focus on the problem of the alienated child, rather than the "pernicious behaviors" of a brainwashing parent. In their formulation, alienation is a complex phenomenon with many contributing factors, including normal developmental processes, the child's need to take care of the alienating parent, and the parenting style of the rejected parent. In my experience, recognition of these factors is not new. I took them into consideration in the custody evaluations I conducted. Gardner did, too, judging from the detailed instructions he gives for conducting custody evaluations in his books (Gardner, 1982, 1989). Kelly and Johnston describe the alienating parent as "brainwashing," but fail to recognize the importance of "exclusionary maneuvers," Gardner's term for visitation interference and other efforts to physically disrupt the child's contact with the target parent.

In support of their view that the alienating parent plays a minimal role, Kelly and Johnston cite to Johnston's clinical research with high-conflict families, a subgroup of whom were PAS families. They point out that many high-conflict parents engage in indoctrinating behaviors, but only a small proportion of children become alienated (Johnston, 1993). The flaw with this argument is that they generalize from high-conflict families to families with PAS dynamics. Clawar and Rivlin (1991) found strong evidence that the alienating parent played a primary role in PAS but reported that the alienating parent's influence was mitigated in cases where the child's time with the target parent was increased. Warshak (2002) identified four protective factors that help children in PAS scenarios to resist the influence of the alienating parent: specific characteristics of the child; context in which denigration of the target parent occurs; quality of the child's predivorce relationship with the denigrated parent; and the target parent's response to the other parent's efforts to alienate.

Citing again to Johnston (1993), Kelly and Johnston assert that some children, especially adolescents, develop unjustified animosity towards a parent in the absence of alienating behaviors by the rejected parent. Warshak (2002) refers to this as "child-driven alienation," a phenomenon that mimics PAS and is quite rare. Warshak's 2002 article on misdiagnosis of PAS was intended to address the allegation by Kelly and Johnston that the term PAS is indiscriminately applied in custody litigation to any child who is rejecting a parent, regardless of the type of rejection or the reasons for it. Kelly and Johnston interpret the existence of child-driven alienation as support for their conclusion that "alienating behavior by a parent is neither a sufficient nor a necessary condition for a child to become alienated" (p. 249). Warshak offers a different interpretation. In his view, child-driven alienation does not meet Gardner's criteria for PAS and therefore should not be labeled PAS.

The idea that PAS can be misdiagnosed has bearing on Kelly and Johnston's assertion that Gardner's hypothesized theory of the role of the alienating parent in causing PAS does not meet the test of "falsification," an important principle for differentiating science from pseudoscience (Popper, 1988). The falsification test does not refer to corroboration of the theory or hypothesis but to the survival of attempts to prove that the theory is false. If there is no conceivable way to prove an idea false, then the idea is not scientifically valid. In practical terms, it means that if you cannot rule something out, you cannot rule it in.

According to Kelly and Johnston's argument, Gardner's theory of PAS is unfalsifiable because "its hypothesized etiological agents (i.e., an alienating parent and a receptive child) . . . [are] true by definition" (p. 249). The problem with Kelly and Johnston's falsification argument is that it confuses Gardner's definition of PAS in general, which is a theoretical construct based on his observations of a social phenomenon, with his criteria for making a diagnosis of PAS in a particular case. Gardner was very clear on the fact that one could not simply assume that the child's rejection of one parent was the result of an alienating parent's influence. He insisted that a diagnosis of PAS did not apply if the child's rejection of the target parent was justified because of bone fide abuse. If one accepts the idea that PAS can be ruled out in cases where there has been bone fide abuse by the rejected parent, then the role of the alienating parent in causing PAS can be ruled out, or falsified, in the particular case. In the custody evaluations I conducted, I considered all the possibilities that might be contributing to a child's rejection of a parent before determining which one was supported by the data. Applying theoretical generalizations without evaluating the individual case is akin to applying the law without hearing the evidence.

THE PROBLEM OF INTERVENTIONS

The journal faults PAS as an adversarial formulation of the problem of a child's alienation. However, all parents now have the options of negotiation and mediation as well as formal adversarial court proceedings. The alienating parents I encountered preferred the adversarial system and would litigate for years, if necessary, to have the target parent's access terminated. I agree that target parents may have their own problems, although some were excellent parents, in my experience. I found that target parents were usually more inclined to mediate and compromise, a quality which has led to the characterization of target parents as overly passive.

The adversarial system was created to decide disputes which were not otherwise amenable to resolution. Parties involved in severe, entrenched PAS are more likely to end up in court than families who are less disturbed. Legal proceedings provide an ideal setting for parents to "prove" wrongdoing by the other parent which can be used to justify alienation. It is not the PAS theorists who advocate for adversarial proceedings. Most of us have tried very hard but unsuccessfully to encourage parents to use mediation and negotiation rather than adversarial proceedings. Some of my PAS cases had three or more unsuccessful attempts at court-ordered mediation. If the journal contributors have been successful in getting the more severe alienating parents to mediate, they should publish both some cases and their protocols. We would be more than pleased to have them.

Contributors to the journal are evidently concerned that the litigation process may result in the alienating parent being "punished" by loss of custody. The contributors assume that the alienating parent is the custodial parent, and therefore refer to placing the child with the rejected parent as a "change of custody." This characterization is misleading. As Sullivan and Kelly point out, the initial custody arrangements when a petition for dissolution is filed are considered temporary until there is a permanent decision, either by stipulated agreement between the parents or by order of the court. In some of the cases I evaluated, the target parent had custody going into the evaluation, or the alienating parent only had temporary custody. If custody was awarded to the target parent following the evaluation, it was usually the final determination. Final orders are usually made after substantial time from the inception of the case, and the alienating dynamics have become clear to anyone who is alert to the signs.

Lee and Olesen (2001) emphasize the importance of a comprehensive custody evaluation to aid the court in its decision. I could not agree more. Gardner has written two excellent books on family evaluation in child custody disputes (Gardner, 1982, 1989). Lee and Olesen present a model they describe as "complete and preferred" p. 282. "Preferred" by whom is not specified. They provide a list of issues to be addressed in the evaluator's recommendations, but do not mention custody, only visitation. Another problem is that the article focuses primarily on the assessment process itself, with no discussion of the criteria for making custody and visitations recommendations. In most states, legislation on joint custody emphasizes that consideration must be given to the ability of each parent to support the child's relationship with the other parent. The model presented by Lee and Olesen does not deal with this issue.

The authors are critical of courts, but recognize that without court orders, therapeutic interventions with these families often do not work. That has been my experience, also. In many of the PAS cases I evaluated, I strongly recommended that the court monitor and review the case at least yearly to insure compliance with court orders and to see what progress had been made toward establishing age-appropriate contact with the alienated parent and resolving the alienation. A reevaluation of the effectiveness of the therapy and/or mediation by an independent clinician was very helpful in such reviews. Court-ordered therapy without clear expectations by the court does not usually work in terms of resolving alienation. The court should make sure that the therapist has the same goal as the court. In my experience, cases in which the court did not clearly define the goals sometimes resulted in therapy going on for five or ten years, with no significant improvement in individual functioning or family relationships.

As Johnston et al. (2001) state, therapy with PAS families is fraught with difficulty. They indicate that therapy should be combined with legal constraints and case management to be effective. Gardner makes this point as well. Where they differ is on the goal of therapy. Gardner views therapy as a means for normalizing the child's relationship with the target parent and reversing alienation. According to Johnston et al., reunification with the rejected parent is not the primary goal of intervention. They note that reunification with the target parent is usually viewed as the most desirable result. They go on to state that, in reality, therapeutic work with alienated children and their families can end in many different ways, with varying degrees of resolution, or lack thereof. Johnston et al. argue that the therapeutic approach they recommend is superior, but acknowledge that "The long-term outcomes are a matter of conjecture and currently unknown" (p. 329).

According to the journal, it takes a team of legal and mental health professionals to successfully manage and treat these cases. Sullivan and Kelly (2001) give a rationale for their intensive case management approach which is compelling, but acknowledge that there is no research support for its efficacy. Their model calls for a special master or parenting coordinator to manage the case on a day-to-day basis. However, the expense of this approach is out of the reach of most divorced parents. In the community where I practiced, judges sometimes took it upon themselves to monitor these cases until things settled down and the problems were resolved. This was very helpful.

Ultimately, it is the court's responsibility to structure the time and responsibilities of each parent with respect to the child. Judges have the authority to make and modify orders for custody and visitation as needed, provide incentives for compliance, and levy sanctions if necessary. Sullivan and Kelly make a good point when they explain that permitting the violation of court orders emboldens alienating parents in their efforts to disrupt the child's relationship with the other parent. They point out that traditional sanctions often take too long to levy. They suggest using alternative consequences which are more related to the infraction, such as having the parent transport the child more than the agreement requires as a consequence for violations involving transitions. Another suggestion is to provide additional make-up time as a consequence for obstructing scheduled visitation. These measures are very mild. They seem more in line with the interventions of a special master or parenting coordinator working with high conflict families in which the child goes back and forth between homes despite the parental hostilities. The consequences Sullivan and Kelly suggest are too lightweight for PAS families in which the child is aligned with the alienating parent.

Sullivan and Kelly assert that traditional sanctions are often too heavy-handed, but provide no support for their view. In my experience, the exact opposite was true. For example, the alienating mother in one of my cases perjured herself. Perjury in that jurisdiction carried a mandatory sentence of jail time. The judge did not want to put the mother in jail, so he found that she had only *attempted* perjury. He then awarded her sole custody, despite my recommendation for custody to the father. After the hearing, the mother disappeared with the children and established residency in another state. When the father eventually located her, he discovered that the mother had obtained orders putting severe restrictions on his visitation. The children would not have lost their father if the judge had sanctioned the mother for perjury instead of rewarding her with custody.

In one of my cases, the judge's willingness to levy sanctions was the key to turning the alienation around.

The mother adamantly refused to comply with the visitation orders. The judge sanctioned her with jail time and ordered an evaluation. After being incarcerated, the mother was able to cooperate and participated meaningfully in the structured mediation ordered by the court. When the family was re-evaluated a year later, the parents were communicating amicably and the child was going back and forth between homes without difficulty.

I believe that consequences other than traditional sanctions can be effective in modifying the alienating parent's behavior. However, the kinds of consequences I would recommend would be more meaningful to an alienating parent, and more akin to sanctions. I have had several cases in which the custodial alienating parent refused to comply with court-ordered visitation until threatened to change custody. Johnston et al. appear to view this as a viable option, suggesting that it may be appropriate to make facilitating normal visitation a condition of the alienating parent maintaining custody. Some alienating parents engage in endless litigation and make constant demands for increased support. An effective consequence is for the court to signal that it will no longer put up with this behavior by firmly denying the alienating parent's financial motion and ordering the alienating parent pay out large sums of money, not just for the other parent's attorneys fees, but for other large expense items as well.

The contributors to the journal would have us believe that they have strong differences of opinion with Gardner over interventions. Kelly and Johnston (2001) assert that Gardner's recommendation for change of custody in severe cases is "punitive" (p. 250). According to Johnston et al., the therapeutic approach they recommend for alienated children and their families "stands in marked contrast to others that are largely coercive and punitive in nature" (p. 316). Sullivan and Kelly express the view that "sanctions that involve . . . custody . . . are rarely based on the best interests of the child" (p. 309). Lee and Olesen add their voice by cautioning evaluators against recommending "a simplistic intervention" (p. 295) such as change of custody.

These criticisms are inconsistent with recommendations the contributors make elsewhere in the journal. For example, Lee and Olesen concede "In the most severe and entrenched cases, the evaluator may be making recommendations . . . for a change of custody" (p. 296). Johnston et al. refer the reader to the article by Sullivan and Kelly as providing "the criteria for termination of treatment or change of custody in cases of unsuccessful treatment" (p. 332). In my view, the differences the contributors have with Gardner are more about who is recommending the intervention than with the intervention itself.

The references to Gardner's methods as "coercive" and "punitive" appear to reflect an underlying difference of opinion about whether an intervention which distresses the child, even temporarily, is justifiable. Should the child's preference be the paramount consideration in making custody and visitation decisions? Should the child be placed in the custody of the parent they prefer or the parent who is most likely to facilitate the child's relationship with the other parent? Under what circumstances is it appropriate to cause the child distress by insisting that the child do something the child does not want to do? Does distressing a child cause permanent psychological damage? Are children capable of adjusting to changes which may be distressing at first but better for them in the long run? The answers to these kinds of questions may have more to do with a professional's theoretical orientation and belief system than with empirical data and scientific research.

The contributors to the journal favor leaving children in the custody of the alienating parent, except in the most extreme cases where the alienating is so disturbed that a change of custody is needed. They seem to assume that therapy for the alienating parent will be ordered and that the alienating parent is treatable. It is generally agreed that severe alienating parents with narcissistic or paranoid personality disorders do not benefit from therapy. Their way of coping in the world is to externalize problems and project blame. They cannot, or will not, tolerate being questioned and have no awareness that they have a problem.

The therapeutic approach described by Johnston et al. is more appropriate for less disturbed alienating parents who have the capacity for empathy and can form a therapeutic alliance with the therapist. In such cases, it makes sense to educate the alienating parent about the impact their behavior has on the child and to teach better parenting skills. Alienating parents in the mild category may be more motivated to change because they are more capable of empathizing with the child's needs and experience. The same cannot be said of alienating parents in the severe category, or some in the moderate category, for that matter.

Johnston et al. state that rejected parents are more motivated to engage in therapy. This was my experience as well. In their view, the reason that target parents are more motivated is because they see themselves as victims in the custody war and are seeking allies. The tone of this statement is in marked contrast to the importance the authors place on being empathic to the alienating parent's concerns. In my experience, target parents often sought therapy on their own and often benefited from it. They utilized therapy to deal with problems such as adjusting to the divorce, moving on with their lives, and improving their parenting skills. According to Johnston et al., rejected parents can have an array of problems with their parenting but are usually educable. They advise that therapists should be careful not to "inadvertently confirm the rejected parent's often-distorted, simplistic view of the situation, especially their tendency to blame the problem entirely on the other parent" (p. 321). The authors do not acknowledge that the target parent may have good reason to blame the other parent, as in cases where the alienating parent uses child abduction or false allegations of abuse to disrupt the target parent's relationship with the child. In my experience, parents who were falsely accused were often traumatized by the experience, and sometimes developed symptoms of post-traumatic stress disorder, which required treatment. Johnston et al. also do not mention helping the target parent with grief, though the loss of a child is one of the most painful things that a parent can experience.

Johnston et al. make some good points in their discussion of therapy with the child. They note that the child may have more worries about the alienating parent, despite their stated concerns about the target parent, who is reflexively described as the source of all their problems. The authors suggest that the therapist should help the child develop better skills for reality testing. Alienated children have distorted perceptions when it comes to the target parent and anything having to do with the alienation. Their need to cling to these distortions causes them to reject new information which is contradictory. Too often, therapists see their role as validating the child's views, even if they are distorted. What these children need is a trusted adult who can question the distortions and help the child absorb new information which is more in line with reality.

The topic of grief is missing from the discussion of therapeutic interventions with alienated children. Divorce by its very nature entails loss for children. The child needs to be able to grieve in order to move on with life and adjust to their new circumstances. Alienated children have difficulty with grief and other tender emotions. They are much more comfortable with anger. Alienating parents, too, have problems with tender feelings, and discourage grieving as disloyal. The alienating parent may become enraged at the idea that the child has anything to grieve about. As a child psychiatrist, Gardner was concerned about helping children with grief, whatever the source. In his view, if a child was old enough to appreciate what the divorce meant but did not react with grief, there was a psychiatric problem which needed to be treated. "Although the child of divorce does not actually lose a parent, he may never again live with the departed parent and is likely to react grievously to the separation. . . . The failure on the parents' part to appreciate and encourage grieving at this crucial time may cause the child to suppress and repress his reactions to the separation and this may contribute to his developing . . . untoward reactions" (Gardner, 1982, p. 108).

FINAL COMMENTS

There is much to do with respect to helping families with parental alienation syndrome. We have a beginning agreement that the problem is a serious one. Contributors to the journal make a call for more science. I have offered specific suggestions of questions I believe need to be researched. It is a mistake for clinicians to demur and leave the responsibility for research up to career scientists. Clinicians who work with divorced families also have obligations to science. To fulfill those obligations, they need to use clinical experience to pose precise, specific questions, framed in such a way that they can be answered by means of scientific methods and procedures. The contributors criticize PAS for not being research based and scientific. Their reformulation, the "alienated child," is more speculative and has no scientific basis at all. There was no evidence of the self-questioning modesty to which Bronowski (1956) refers.

We need to respect the contributions of colleagues, not by agreeing with them all the time, but by describing the data which forms the basis for differing opinions, and the rationale for the inferences drawn from the data. All data should be placed in context. Generalizations from one or a few cases are seldom valid. The sources of data and the procedures used to collect it need to be clearly identified. Theoretical assumptions should be separated from the facts and observations on which they are based. Enough information needs to be provided so that others can check inferences and conclusions given. We need to refrain from personal attacks on intentions and motivations. The moralistic attitudes that characterize the mental health field need to go. If we cannot cooperate and resolve our disagreements by reasonable inferences and systematic investigation, how can we expect the divorced families we serve to deal with their problems in a rational and civilized manner?

REFERENCES

Ahrons, C. R., & Rodgers, R. (1987). *Divorced families: Meeting the challenge of divorce and remarriage.* New York: W. W. Norton and Company.

Bronowski, J. (1956). *Science and human values.* New York: Harper and Row.

Bruch, C. S. (2001). Parental alienation syndrome and parental alienation: Getting it wrong in child custody cases. *Family Law Quarterly, 35*(3), 527–552.

Clawar, S., & Rivlin, B. (1991). *Children held hostage: Dealing with programmed and brainwashed children.* Chicago: American Bar Association.

Cooke, R. (2001). *Dr. Folkman's war.* New York: Random House.

Dunne, J., & Hedrick, M. (1994). The parental alienation syndrome: An analysis of sixteen selected cases, *Journal of Divorce and Remarriage, 21*(3/4), 21–38.

Faller, K. C. (1998). The parental alienation syndrome: What is it and what data support it? *Child Maltreatment, 3*(2), 100–115.

Gardner, R. A. (1976). *The boys and girls book about divorce.* New York: Jason Aaronson, Inc.

Gardner, R. A. (1982). *Family evaluation in child custody litigation.* Cresskill, NJ: Creative Therapeutics, Inc.

Gardner, R. A. (1982). *Psychotherapy with children of divorce.* New York: Jason Aronson, Inc.

Gardner, R. A. (1982). *The boys and girls book about step-families.* New York: Bantam Books.

Gardner, R. A. (1985). Recent trends in divorce and custody litigation. *Academy Forum, 29*(2), 3–7.

Gardner, R. A. (1987). T*he Parental Alienation Syndrome and the differentiation between fabricated and genuine child sex abuse.* Cresskill, NJ: Creative Therapeutics, Inc.

Gardner, R. A. (1989). *Family evaluation in child custody mediation, arbitration, and litigation.* Cresskill, NJ: Creative Therapeutics, Inc.

Gardner, R. A. (2001). Should courts order PAS children to visit/reside with the alienated parent? A follow-up study. *American Journal of Forensic Psychology, l9*(3), 61–106.

Gardner, R. A. (June, 2003). What is Creative Therapeutics? Downloaded from Creative Therapeutics website.

Johnston, J. R. (1993). Children of divorce who refuse visitation. In C. Depner & J. H. Bray (Eds.), *Non-residential parenting: New vistas in family living* (pp. 109–135). Newbury Park, CA: Sage Publications.

Johnston, J. R., & Kelly, J. B. (2001). Guest editorial notes. *Family Court Review, 39*(3), 246–248.

Johnston, J. R., & Roseby, V. (1997). *In the name of the child: A developmental approach to children in high conflict and violent divorce.* New York: Free Press.

Johnston, J. R., Walters, M. J., & Friedlander, S. (2001). Therapeutic work with alienated children and their families. *Family Court Review, 39*(3), 316–333.

Kelly, J. B., & Johnston, J. R. (2001). The alienated child: A reformulation of parental alienation syndrome. *Family Court Review, 39*(3), 249–266.

Kopetski, L. M. (1991). *Parental alienation syndrome: Recent research.* Paper presented at the 15th Annual Child Custody Conference, Keystone, Colorado.

Kopetski, L. M. (1998a). Identifying cases of parent alienation syndrome, Part I. *The Colorado Lawyer, 27*(2), 65–68.

Kopetski, L. M. (1998b). Identifying cases of parent alienation syndrome, Part II. *The Colorado Lawyer, 27*(3), 61–84.

Kopetski, L. M., Rand, D. C., & Rand, R. (2005 in press). Incidence, gender and false allegations of child abuse: Descriptive statistics on 84 parental alienation syndrome cases.

Lee, M., & Olesen, N. (2001). Assessing for alienation in child custody and access evaluations. *Family Court Review, 39*(3), 282–298.

Levitin, T. E. (Ed.). (1979). Children of divorce [Special Issue]. *The Journal of Social Issues, 35*(4).

Popper, K. (1988). Science, conjectures and refutations. In *Introductory readings in the philosophy of science,* Revised Edition, E. D. Klemke, R. Hollinger and A. D. Kline (Eds.). Buffalo, NY.: Prometheus Books.

Publication Manual of the American Psychological Association (Fifth ed.). (2001). Washington, D.C.: American Psychological Association.

Rand, D., Rand, R., & Kopetski, L. M. (2005). The spectrum of parental alienation syndrome part III: The Kopetski follow-up study. *American Journal of Forensic Psychology, 23*(1), 15–43.

Schepard, A. (Ed.). (2001). Special issue: Alienated children in divorce. *Family Court Review, 39*(3).

Sullivan, M., & Kelly, J. B. (2001). Legal and psychological management of cases with an alienated child. *Family Court Review, 39*(3), 299–315.

Wallerstein, J., & Kelly, J. B. (1980). *Surviving the breakup: How children and parents cope with divorce.* New York: Basic Books, Inc., Publishers.

Warshak, R. (2001). Divorce poison: *Protecting the parent-child bond from a vindictive ex.* New York: Harper Collins.

Warshak, R. A. (2002). Misdiagnosis of parental alienation syndrome. *American College of Forensic Psychology 20*(2), 31–52.

Williams, J. J. (2001). Should judges close the gate on PAS and PA? *Family Court Review, 39*(3), 267–281.

Zirogiannis, L. (2001). Student note: Evidentiary issues with parental alienation syndrome. *Family Court Review, 39*(3), 334–343.

Chapter 30

THE PARENTAL ALIENATION SYNDROME AND GENDER BIAS IN THE COURTS

JEFFERY M. LEVING

OVERVIEW

In this chapter a prominent child custody attorney reveals how the interplay between traditional gender bias in the courts and parental alienation syndrome (PAS) often undermines legislative enactments requiring gender neutrality in custody, support, and visitation disputes. The author analyzes a number of reported appellate cases, and finds that the same gender bias that affects custody disputes also inhibits the acceptance by some courts of PAS as a scientifically recognized diagnostic tool, unnecessarily impeding the admissibility of crucial expert testimony and analysis on this issue. Drawing on his personal experience as an attorney involved in the celebrated international custody case of Elian Gonzalez, the author observes that many of the hallmarks of PAS may have been present in that case. The author concludes that the judicial response to the PAS reflects a systematic gender bias on the part of the judiciary that can only be overcome by competent, zealous and passionate representation of men by lawyers experienced in PAS and gender bias. Only such lawyers can reverse the current prevailing trends in matrimonial jurisprudence that denigrate the rights of men and ignore significant advances in the application of forensic psychology and psychiatry to family law.

INTRODUCTION

Dr. Richard A. Gardner's groundbreaking scholarship brought diagnostic coherence to a phenomenon well-known to many custody lawyers: parental alienation syndrome (PAS). Gardner identified the dynamic inherent in this concept as having three players: (1) the programming parent (usually custodial), (2) the target parent (usually noncustodial), and (3) the child (Gardner, 1998).

In my view, the law has failed to craft adequate remedies to address this destructive and destabilizing behavior. In this chapter, I will advance a sociolegal critique of the judicial response to this social phenomenon, a critique which is informed by both critical gender theory and my opinions derived from more than two decades of advocacy on behalf of the cause of fathers' rights.

GENDER BIAS IN FAMILY LAW

Most states have enacted legislation concerning gender neutrality in custody, support, and visitation disputes. However, a review of the case law in this area throughout the United States often demonstrates that outdated cultural stereotype and social presumption can overwhelm consistent application of the law. Whatever statutory equality in family law has been granted to men has often been undermined by gender-biased application of those laws to custody, support, and visitation disputes. For example, the Colorado Supreme Court Task Force on Gender Bias examined hundreds of family court rulings and found "a clear preference for the mother." In fact, this study team wrote, a mother had to be "nearly dysfunctional" not to win custody of her children (Leving, 1997, p. 27).

This gender bias appears to derive from outmoded notions of gender roles that were defined when American society was patriarchal. The Industrial Revolution, which followed this patriarchal period, exacerbated this tendency because an efficient division of labor made the home the maternal domain, while the breadwinner (almost always the father) toiled away from home and family: "By the end of the nineteenth century, society had imposed gender-based identities and expectations. . . . Parental roles and responsibilities were considered to be mutually exclusive" (Leving, 1997, pp. 27–28). What resulted from this was a stereotypification of parental roles that was rooted in the notion that women were "biologically programmed" to nurture their offspring (Leving, 1997, p. 28).

These notions found juridical expression in the "tender years" doctrine (Leving, 1997, p. 28). Under this doctrine, mothers were presumptively awarded custody of a child age five or under (Leving, 1997, p. 28). The tender years doctrine yielded over time to the "best interest of the child" standard. Unfortunately, this later standard allows for wide latitude in judicial application because it is discretionary, and therefore enables the judiciary to interpret and apply this doctrine in such a way as to enforce those outmoded gender stereotypes that this very change in the law should have eliminated.

In my book *Fathers' Rights*, I catalog some examples of this:

1. There is the story of Tony, whose wife deserted him. After six years, during which she never visited the children, she nevertheless successfully petitioned for custody.
2. I also relate the story of Alex, who lost custody of his son, Jon, even though a psychologist testified that Alex would provide a better home for Jon than his mother. The judge agreed, but ruled that Jon would stay with his mother even though there would be risk of emotional damage to Jon.
3. Darla was a pathological liar with a histrionic personality disorder who verbally abused with profanity her seven-year-old daughter in front of others. In spite of her numerous psychological problems, she was awarded custody of the daughter she abused. Moreover, the court generously awarded Darla maintenance, attorney's fees and marital property. Darla's husband was also forced to pay for Darla's therapy and her debts.
4. Mike lost custody of his children to Lila, even though Lila's boyfriend sexually abused one of Mike's children (Leving, 1997, pp. 25–37).

PARENTAL ALIENATION SYNDROME

In my view, an interplay exists between gender bias in the award of custody to a woman and the epidemic of PAS: "(T)he daily access inherent in sole custody allows a mother to control, manipulate, and if she wishes, destroy the father-child relationship.

Largely because of pro-mother bias, legal protection against these offenses is expensive and ineffective" (Leving 1997, p. 43).

According to Gardner's publications on PAS in the time frame from 1985 to 1995, he generally found that custodial mothers were the programmers in 90 percent of the cases. This was largely because, for the most part, women had been awarded residential custody (Gardner, 2001, 2002). Vengeful, angry mothers acted as the programming parent; the objective was the total destruction of their children's relationship with the target parent (Leving, 1997, pp. 43–44). In the late 1990s, however, Gardner found a gender shift, which others have seen as well (Gardner, 2001, 2002). Specifically, Gardner referenced that fathers, now having more access and more familiarity with PAS, frequently program children into a PAS campaign of denigration (Gardner, 2001, 2002). His own experience in the past few years was that the ratio is about fifty-fifty (Gardner, 2002). Furthermore, Gardner concluded that a gender bias was still operative because when the mother is the indoctrinator she is not likely to lose her children, but when the father is the indoctrinator, he *is* likely to lose the children. Anti-father gender bias in custody rulings continually encourages behavior underlying PAS.

1. Parental Alienation Syndrome and the Law

PAS becomes relevant and material in custody disputes; the question presents itself as to whether expert testimony on PAS encounters the same gender bias as custody rulings. A review of the case law leads to the conclusion that this is, in fact, the primary trend of the law.

Judicial Hostility to Parental Alienation Syndrome

In *In the Interest of TMW*,[1] a man was divorced from his wife, who kept custody of TMW and their two younger children (Florida App. Ct. 1st Dist., 1989). She remarried and her new husband petitioned to adopt these children. The biological father had no contact with TMW and the adoptive parent argued that the biological father had abandoned his daughter. As a defense to the charge of abandonment, the biological father asserted the defense of PAS, arguing that his lack of contact resulted from the fact that TMW was alienated from him by persistent programming. A psychologist testified that PAS might be present and recommended examination by a qualified expert of TMW, for the purposes of exploring the presence of PAS. The trial court entered an order granting the request for a psychological examination, finding that expert guidance and assistance was essential in order to resolve the issues presented in the case, and that it would be "foolish" not to use the services of the psychologist, because of his familiarity with the case resulting from his previous contact with the father (*In the Interest of TMW*, p. 261).

In ruling on review of the trial court's order granting the motion to compel the psychological examination, the appellate court tripped over itself in eviscerating the biological father's position. First, the court held that whether PAS was a defense to abandonment was not the issue at hand. Having done so, the court then launched a vigorous attack on the concept of PAS as a diagnostic tool and further criticized the general use of the term "syndrome." Having trashed a diagnosis that it determined to be immaterial in the first instance, the court reversed the order of the lower court permitting a psychological examination of TMW on narrow procedural grounds.

Another case that demonstrates a possible gender-driven judicial bias against the admissibility of PAS is *Weiderholt v. Fischer*[2] (Wisconsin App. Ct., 1992). In *Weiderholt*, the father petitioned for a change of custody of his three children. At the hearing on his petition, he produced a qualified expert who testified that at least two of the three children not only "severely" suffered from PAS, but that they had one of the worst cases that he had ever seen in his career. His expert opinion forcefully stated that the mother of the children was the cause of the children's alienation. Although the trial court acknowledged that the expert was credentialed, it nevertheless ruled against the father on custody in spite of the uncontradicted expert opinion that such a change of custody was necessary, given the gravity and extent of PAS. In reviewing the trial court's decision, the appellate court held that the trial court was not obliged to accept the uncontradicted expert testimony, and held that the trial court's refusal to accept the uncontradicted expert testimony and opinion was not, error.

In *Chambers v. Chambers*,[3] the appellate court affirmed a trial court's determination that it would not order visitation between a father and his daughter (Arkansas App. Ct., 2000). In that case, an expert witness testified on the father's behalf that PAS existed, and was attributable to the mother's hostility to the father, which affected the way the father was viewed by his daughter. The expert's opinion was that the only way to have successful visitation would be if the court were to order visitation, even though such court-ordered visitation would be traumatic and painful to the daughter. The expert witness further testified that prior evaluators had failed to make the diagnosis of PAS, and that the current diagnosis made by the expert was a material change in circumstances, which warranted further judicial intervention. In spite of this analysis, both the trial court and the appellate court held that visitation would not be ordered by the court, and instead the trial court made the following statement, which was approved by the appellate court: "Now, I'm not ordering her to visit. If she wants to visit, ma'am [mother], I'd hope you encourage her to" (*Chambers v. Chambers*, p. 13).

Judicial Reluctance to Recognize Parental Alienation Syndrome in Cases Where the Evidence Is Overwhelming

In cases where overwhelming evidence of the PAS existed, appellate courts have been reluctant to give judicial recognition to PAS. Instead, they have upheld custody determinations on narrow, factual grounds that are designed to be of no precedential value.

In *C. J. L. v. M. W. B.*,[4] the trial court granted a father's petition for modification of custody and changed residential custody of the parties' three children from mother to father based on the mother's concerted campaign to alienate the children from their father (Alabama App. Ct., 2003). The trial court had relied in part on testimony from a psychologist, who was appointed by the court to conduct a custody evaluation. At trial the custody evaluator was questioned at length about his understanding of and reliance on the PAS. The psychologist testified that although the term "PAS" was coined by Gardner, the concept of parental alienation had been researched by other professionals for more than 20 years. The psychologist testified that he considered PAS, or the behaviors that form what has been labeled PAS, to be a form of parenting style that has been considered to have long-term detrimental effects on the children of divorce. The court-appointed psychologist concluded that he had found evidence indicating that the children were alienated, and had concluded that alternatives other than a change in custody were not viable, when they were seen in the light of the mother's persistent false charges of sexual abuse of one of the children.

The mother's retained expert witness testified at trial in order to refute the general acceptance of PAS in the scientific community. However, the mother's expert conceded that patterns of behaviors that might be referred to as PAS, such as bitter fighting between the divorced parents and accusations concerning the other parent, occur in postdivorce setting. The mother's expert further testified that the custody evaluator's evaluation was hasty and could easily be biased.

On appeal, the mother attacked the trial court's order changing custody by arguing that the court-appointed evaluator's use of a PAS analysis did not meet the applicable test for admissibility of scientific evidence; the mother alleged that PAS is not generally accepted in the scientific community. The mother concluded that the trial court's custody decision should be reversed because the court-appointed psychologist's custody evaluation was based on a diagnosis of PAS.

The appellate court affirmed the trial court's custody decision, stating that the trial court was presented with myriad evidence that the mother desired to end all contact between her children and their father, even to the point of expressing a desire for termination of the father's parental rights. This evidence was sufficient to overcome the mother's legal arguments relative to the admissibility of the PAS analysis, which the appellate court indicated it was inclined to favor, if "faced squarely with the question whether evidence concerning an actual diagnosis was admissible" (*C.J. L. v. M. W. B*, pp. 22–23).

In other words, the appellate court found that the evidence of parental alienation in this case was so overwhelming that it supported a remedial change of custody, even though the court opined that it might not recognize a specific diagnosis of PAS, because such a diagnosis would not be admissible if the appellate court were faced "squarely" with a challenge to such a diagnosis. This result was reached because, in general, appellate review of the evidence that is admitted and actually considered by the trial court, as opposed to legal rulings on the admissibility of scientific techniques, diagnoses, or theories, is highly deferential. Appellate courts are reluctant to engage in re-weighing of evidence and to pass on issues of witness credibility, which are left to the discretion of the trial courts. However, an appellate court's decision that is based solely on the particular facts of a case has generally very limited precedential application to future cases.

A similar result was reached in the case of in re the *Marriage of Ovando*[5] (California App. Ct., 2002). That case involved a protracted custody battle over the parties' daughter, which soon centered around a barrage of allegations of sexual abuse against the father. The charges of sexual abuse were determined by the trial court to be unfounded. Persistent attempts by the mother to alienate the daughter from the father and the trial court's determination that there was a significant risk that the mother would abduct the child led the trial court to award temporary custody of the daughter to the father, pending further order of court. The court-appointed psychologist issued reports that stated that from the beginning the mother had attempted to interfere with the daughter's relationship with her father and placed great pressure on her daughter to say something about her father sexually abusing her. The court-appointed psychologist stated that it would be in the child's best interest if she were to be removed from the overwhelming burden of her mother's needs, and this could only be accomplished if the father had primary physical custody.

Other court-appointed mental health professionals, including a psychiatrist and the child's therapist, buttressed these conclusions. The trial court found that the daughter was doing materially better in her father's custody, except when her mother engaged in alienating or other inappropriate conduct.

At the conclusion of the final hearing, the trial court found that the mother had made repeated reports of sexual abuse that she knew were false when she made them. In addition to awarding the father sole legal and physical custody, with the mother having contact with the daughter only during the course of their conjoint therapy, the trial court ordered the mother to pay the father $258,297.08 in attorney's fees and costs as sanctions for frustrating the policy of the law to promote settlement of litigation.

On appeal, the mother and the California National Organization for Women (CA NOW), who had filed a friend of the court brief, attacked the decision of the trial court, primarily because they stated that the decision was based on a diagnosis of PAS. Indeed the mother contended that she was "deprived of due process, equal protection and her statutory rights by the court's application of the unscientific, unaccepted and sexist 'parental alienation syndrome'" (In re *Marriage of Ovando*, p. 51). Similarly, CA NOW argued that "Parental Alienation Syndrome – or 'alienation' as it was referred to by the trial judge herein – is so illogical and nonsensical that its application denied due process of law to appellant" (In re *Marriage of Ovando*, p. 51).

In an unpublished opinion of limited precedential value, the appellate court side-stepped these arguments by finding that the trial court's custody determination was made on the basis of the evidence and facts presented, and not in reliance on the existence of PAS: "The trial court's references to the existence of the [mother's] efforts to alienate [daughter] from [father] were based on specific evidence with which the court was presented, not on the existence or application of a so-called syndrome" (In re *Marriage of Ovando*, p. 53).

Admissibility of Scientific Evidence in the State Courts

These cases serve to underscore the importance that the application of uniform, objective guidelines with respect to the admissibility of scientific evidence should have in the family courts of the United States. However, the reality of practice in the family courts is often different from the ideal.

Although the United States Supreme Court forged new ground for the admissibility of scientific evidence in federal courts in the 1993 case of *Daubert v. Merrell Dow Pharmaceuticals, Inc.*,[6] the majority of states continue to employ a standard for admissibility of scientific evidence set forth in the 1923 case of *Frye v. United States.*[7] This is because the *Daubert* test interpreted Federal Rule of Evidence 702, which governs admission of scientific evidence, while the state courts that interpreted state rules and decisions continue to rely on the earlier *Frye* test (Miltenberg, 2001), (Walsh, 1999). Under the *Frye* analysis, it must be shown that novel scientific evidence is "sufficiently established to have gained acceptance in the particular field in which it belongs" (*Frye*, p. 1014).

The *Frye* test is subjective and discretionary. This practice means that a trial or appellate court that is hostile to PAS as a diagnostic tool is free to shut the gate on this evidence, under the guise of conforming to a legal analysis that PAS has failed to gain widespread acceptability in the scientific community.

Judicial Refusal to Create Remedies for Victims of Parental Alienation Syndrome

Not only does a review of the case law demonstrate a general judicial resistance to consideration of evidence of PAS in custody disputes, but also a refusal to craft remedies for fathers who are victims of programming mothers. For instance, in *Bartanus v. Lis*,[8] the court held that no separate cause of action was available to a parent for alienation of their child's affection (Pennsylvania Superior Ct., 1984).

A Minority of Courts Have Recognized Parental Alienation Syndrome

However, in a small minority of cases, the court has recognized PAS and acted accordingly. For example, the Supreme Court of Alaska found that although the parental alienation syndrome may not be "universally accepted," the trial court was free to consider conflicting expert testimony on this issue in reaching its custody determination (*Pearson v. Pearson*,[9] Alaska Sup. Ct., 2000). In the case of *Kirk v. Kirk*, the Indiana Appellate Court reversed and remanded the trial court's decision to have the mother maintain legal and physical custody in spite of uncontradicted evidence of the existence of PAS and the detrimental effect on the child of maintaining custody with the mother (*Kirk v. Kirk*,[10] Indiana App. Ct., 2001). However, the relief afforded by the Appellate Court of Indiana was short-lived, as the Indiana Supreme Court later overruled the decision of the Appellate Court, and reinstated the trial court's determination, based on the mandate required of reviewing courts to grant great deference to the trial courts under the abuse of discretion standard (*Kirk v. Kirk*,[11] Indiana Sup. Ct., 2002).

In *In The Matter of S.G.*,[12] the Court of Appeals of Ohio reversed a trial court's decision to keep custody with the mother (Ohio App. Ct., 2003). In the *S.G.* case the appellate court found that it was an error for the trial court to ignore evidence, including expert testimony from a court-appointed psychologist, of a pattern of behavior on the part of the mother and her father that indicated the existence of PAS (*In the Matter of S.G.*, Ohio App. Ct., 2003).

In *Barton v. Hirshberg*,[13] the Appellate Court of Maryland upheld a trial court's reliance on the court-appointed custody evaluator's diagnosis of PAS in reaching its custody determination (App. Ct. Maryland, 2001).

For the sake of balance, a review of additional cases that recognize PAS on http://www.rgardner.com/refs is recommended by this author.

AN INTERNATIONAL EXAMPLE

A particularly interesting example of a subtype of possible alienation in which the biological parents were not the adverse parties was the Elian Gonzalez case. I helped to reunite this young Cuban boy with his father. Elian, a five-year-old child, became the center of a stormy international incident after his mother, with Elian in tow, attempted to escape from Communist Cuba to Florida. However, before she could complete her journey, the boat transporting her, Elian, and other refugees sank, drowning her and several others. Elian survived and was taken ashore to Florida.

Once he arrived in Florida, some of his American relatives attempted to take custody, and an application for political asylum was filed on his behalf. This was done even though, I believed, his relatives could show no actual persecution of Elian or that he had a credible fear of persecution if returned to Castro's Cuba. Indeed, at the tender age of five, I felt that Elian could never have been in any way political except as a symbol, or as some more acerbic critics have suggested, a political pawn of the anti-Castro community in South Florida.

Those who may have sought to use Elian as a propaganda tool may have ignored the fact that this young boy was a human being with a family. Although he had lost his mother at sea, his father survived in Cuba and was entitled to have his son back regardless of the larger political issues.

Against this background, I was retained to litigate in the middle of this international political controversy. Although some may believe that this case was not an example of either PAS or gender bias, it did present an example of a disregard for Fathers' Rights because, as I see it, that dispute demonstrated an interesting subtype of PAS. In the Elian Gonzalez case, Elian was not in the custody of a vindictive parent, but rather he was in the custody of relatives whose anger presumably was not directed at Elian's father, but rather at Cuban communism.

Nevertheless, by taking control of Elian and advancing a generally un-meritorious claim in Immigration Court, relatives of Elian appeared to me to be disparaging Elian's father's right to have his son returned to him and his home in Cuba. As stated to me by Gardner, a dramatic example of the PAS was evident from the videotape in which Elian was seen waving an American Flag and denouncing Cuba and his father.

Through my legal efforts and those of others, Elian was returned home to his father, and Elian's relationship with his father was not sacrificed on the altar of political propaganda. Although I admire everyone who fights for freedom and against any totalitarian regime, the emotional well-being of children and the sanctity of the family must never be sacrificed as collateral damage in a propaganda war.

CONCLUSION

The judicial response to PAS reflects systematic gender bias on the part of the judiciary because: (1) The Courts have rejected expert testimony by qualified mental health professionals about this issue; (2) The Courts have refused to consider this issue in custody determinations; and (3) Courts have refused to craft fair remedies to address this problem.

The foregoing underlies the importance of competent, zealous, and even passionate representation of men by lawyers experienced in PAS and gender bias. Only lawyers who can strategize around the problem of judicial bias toward fathers can reverse the prevailing trend in the case law that marginalizes both the rights of men and important advances in the application of forensic psychology and psychiatry to family law.

ENDNOTES

1. *In the Interest of T.M.W.* 553 So2d 260 (Fla. App. 1st Dist. 1989).
2. *Wiederholt v. Fischer* 485 N.W. 2d 442 (Wis. App. 1992).
3. *Chambers v. Chambers* CA99-688, 2000 Ark. App. Lexis 476 (Ark. App. 2nd Div. 2000).
4. *C.J. L. v. W. M. B.* 201073, 2003 Ala. Civ. App. Lexis 100 (Ala. App. 2003).
5. *In re the Marriage of Ovando* B146948, 2002 Cal. App. Unpub. Lexis 7275 (Cal. App. 2002).
6. *Daubert v. Merrell Dow Pharmaceuticals, Inc.* 526 U.S. 137 (1999).
7. *Frye v. United States* 293 F. 103 (D.C. Cir. 1923).
8. *Bartanus v. Lis* 480 A2d 1178 (Pa. Super. 1984).
9. *Pearson v. Pearson* 5 P. 3d 239, 2000 Alas. Lexis 69 (Alaska S. Ct. 2000).
10. *Kirk v. Kirk* 759 N.E. 2d 265, 2001 Ind. App. Lexis 2067 (Ind. App. 3rd Dist. 2001).
11. *Kirk v. Kirk* 770 N.E. 2d 304, 2002 Ind. Lexis 518 (Ind. S. Ct. 2002).
12. *In the Matter of S. G.* 2003 Ohio 161, 2003 Ohio Lexis 109 (Ohio App. Ct. 8th Dist. 2003).
13. *Barton v. Hirshberg* 767 A. 2d 874, 137 Md. App. 1, 2001 Md. App. Lexis 27 (Md. App. 2001).

REFERENCES

Gardner, R. A. (1998). *The Parental Alienation Syndrome: A guide for mental health and legal professionals.* (Second Ed.) Cresskill, NJ.: Creative Therapeutics, Inc.

Gardner, R.A. (2001). The recent shift in PAS indoctrinators. *News for Women in Psychiatry, 19*(4), 11–13.

Gardner, R. A. (2002). Denial of the Parental Alienation Syndrome also harms women. *The American Journal of Family Therapy, 30*(3), 191-202.

Leving, J.M. (1997). *Fathers' rights.* New York: Basic Books.

Miltenberg, N. (2001, March). Out of the fire and into the Fryeing pan of back to the future. *Trial.*

Walsh, J.T. (1999). Keeping the gate: The evolving role of the judiciary in admitting scientific evidence. *Judicature, 83*(3), 140–143.

Chapter 31

PARENTAL ALIENATION SYNDROME: DETRACTORS AND THE JUNK SCIENCE VACUUM

DEMOSTHENES LORANDOS

Justice cannot fulfill its ends
when deprived of its own proper excellence.
Plato, *The Republic*, Book One

OVERVIEW

This article describes the work of three parental alienation syndrome "detractors," Wood, Faller, and Bruch. Their work and their grasp of scientific concepts are described. This analysis is set against the current research that finds judges and court personnel needing new tools to better make science-based judgments. The vacuum created by court personnel uninformed about scientific analysis finds "junk science" from detractors creeping into important family law adjudications. An overview of the scientific method is provided, along with recommendations for the education of judge and court personnel.

PART ONE: THE JUNK SCIENCE VACUUM

Since its first formulation, *Parental Alienation Syndrome* (PAS) has been a valuable means for describing a particular type of polarized child custody process, but it is not without its detractors. In recent years, a number of commentators have begun an ad hominem campaign against Dr. Richard Gardner, and worked to denigrate his descriptive syndrome. The mendacity of some commentators is not uncommon in the social sciences. If the personal attacks and the debate concerning the value of PAS, were confined to academe, perhaps they could be shrugged off. Unfortunately for our busy family court practitioners, some of the misinformation has begun to stick. One reason for this is that legal professionals[1] have great difficulty understanding behavioral science.

This lack of scientific understanding creates a vacuum in which the PAS detractors, and the purveyors of advocacy disguised as science, do their mischief. Furthermore, the lack of scientific understanding is troublesome because testimony from the behavioral sciences is growing at an exponential rate.[2] Facing the junk science vacuum squarely,[3] the United States Supreme Court held that "the trial judge must ensure that any and all scientific testimony or evidence admitted is not only relevant, but reliable."[4]

The Supreme Court reasoned that compared to lay witnesses, experts purport to offer testimony that is scientific. Justice Blackmun indicated that by using the term "scientific," the witness implies "grounding in the methods and procedures of science."[5] The word "knowledge," the Court instructed, "connotes more than subjective belief or unsupported speculation."[6] The Court made it clear that "in order to qualify as 'scientific knowledge,' an inference or assertion must be derived by the scientific method. Proposed testimony must be supported by appropriate validation – i.e., 'good grounds,' based on what is known."[7]

Basing its rule as to admissibility on reasoning and methodology, the Court quoted from a learned treatise and offered: "Scientific methodology today is based on generating hypotheses and testing them to see if they can be falsified; indeed, this methodology is what distinguishes science from other fields of human inquiry."[8] The Court instructed that there is now a "key question" that must be answered, and that is "whether a theory or technique is scientific knowledge that will assist the trier of fact will be whether it can be (and has been) tested."[9]

The Court's instruction to the trial courts was that when "expert," "scientific" testimony is offered, "the trial judge must determine at the outset, pursuant to Rule 104 (a), whether the expert is proposing to testify to (1) scientific knowledge that (2) will assist the trier of fact to understand or determine a fact in issue. This entails a preliminary assessment of whether the reasoning or methodology underlying the testimony is scientifically valid and of whether that reasoning or methodology properly can be applied to the facts in issue."[10]

Because experts are permitted wide latitude in their opinions and are not required to base their pronouncements on firsthand knowledge, the Court required that "the expert's opinion must have a reliable basis in the knowledge and experience of his discipline."[11] In this analysis, courts are required to excuse proposed experts who do not have a grasp of the "knowledge and experience of [their] discipline."

Emphasizing that the "focus . . . must be solely on principles and methodology,"[12] the Court's analysis cites to *United States v. Smith*,[13] and informs that "error rate" in the predictions and techniques espoused in the opinions of the experts must be considered.[14] Grounding its admissibility analysis in the principles and methodology of science, the Court notes "that scientists typically distinguish between "validity" (does the principle support what it purports to show?) and "reliability" (does application of the principle produce consistent results?). . . . Our reference here is to evidentiary reliability – that is, trustworthiness. . . . In a case involving scientific evidence, evidentiary reliability will be based upon scientific validity."[15]

Four years later, in *General Electric Co. v. Joiner*,[16] the Court broadened the scope of the judicial gatekeeping. Three years later, in a decision widely hailed as the "tombstone" for "junk science" in the courtroom, *Kumho Tire*[17] simply held: "*Daubert* . . . applies to all expert testimony."[18] At this writing, more than half the states are *Daubert* or *Daubert*-leaning jurisdictions.[19]

Unfortunately for litigants, research demonstrates that our courts are not prepared for gatekeeping in this important area of expert evidence.[20] For example, Lehman and colleagues demonstrated that laypersons often fail to recognize problems associated with confounds or missing control groups in scientific studies.[21] Looking at court personnel, these researchers demonstrated that judges were not found to be more skilled in the evaluation of science than laypeople. In fact, Lehman and colleagues demonstrated that legal education does not improve either methodological or statistical reasoning abilities.[22] Cooper and colleagues found that even highly motivated triers of fact may be unable to attend to argument quality, if they lack the requisite knowledge to understand the communication.[23]

Cognizant of these problems, the Federal Judicial Center put out a reference manual to aid judges and staff in separating "junk" from "science." However, in a study surveying all of the trial court-level judges in the state of Florida, Kovera and McAuliff discovered that "Very few of the judges reported being familiar with the Federal Judicial Center's reference manual."[24] Indeed, in this study, 96 percent of the judges surveyed reported being unfamiliar with this important post-*Daubert* reference.[25]

In this important research, Kovera and McAuliff examined the essential variable of study validity. They found that judges' decisions about whether to admit a psychological study into evidence was unaffected by the validity of the study.[26] Kovera and McAuliff concluded:

> In sum, synthesis of the research literatures on methodological reasoning and persuasion suggests that decision makers who lack the reasoning abilities needed to make sense of scientific evidence might rely on peripheral cues or heuristics when reasoning about psychological science. For example, judges may use simple heuristics (e.g., a published study is better than an unpublished study) to evaluate the reliability of experimental psychological research. This approach also suggests that if judges lack the ability to reason systematically about the expert evidence, they will be insensitive to the methodological quality of the evidence (e.g., the importance of an appropriate control group).[27]

With respect to behavioral science concepts such as PAS, Kovera and McAuliff concluded that the scientific training judges received was inadequate to help them differentiate between good and flawed psychological data.[28] Following their survey research, this team concluded: "Our research suggests that high quality psychological science may be frequently excluded from evidence."[29] This certainly seems to be what has happened in the past with cogent testimony about PAS.

In October 2001, Gatowski and colleagues published the results of their detailed study of 9,715 state trial court judges from all 50 states and the District of Columbia.[30] More than half the judges surveyed were from *Daubert* States.[31] Half of the 9,715 trial judges had been on the bench for more than ten years.[32] They tested their survey on focus groups of judges attending classes at the National Judicial College,[33] and conducted 400 telephone surveys of approximately an hour each that focused on six major *Daubert* topics.[34] They reported that follow-up questions were developed for structured interviews to allow the researchers to infer how well the judge actually understood the scientific meaning of the criterion about which they were being questioned.[35]

These researchers report that: "Judges who gave an ambiguous response were probed by the interviewer to elicit further discussion with the aim of getting the judge to talk through his or her unarticulated understanding. Yet, despite these efforts, the majority of judges were unable to provide an answer that clearly demonstrated their understanding of the concepts,"[36] and "[an] overwhelming 91% of the 400 judges surveyed (N = 364) believed that the role of 'gatekeeper' was an appropriate one for a judge, irrespective of the admissibility standard followed in their state."[37]

According to Gatowski and colleagues "Fifty-two percent (N = 209) of the judges felt that they had been adequately prepared to deal with the range of scientific evidence proffered in their courtrooms"[38] and "[The] majority of the judges surveyed (88%, N = 352) . . . believed falsifiability to be a useful guideline for determining the merits of proffered scientific evidence."[39] Gatowski and colleagues go on to report that from the answers that were provided, the researchers could only infer a true understanding of the scientific meaning of the concept of falsifiability in six percent of the judges' responses.[40] Furthermore, the vast majority of judges surveyed indicated that a consideration of the concept of error rate was useful when determining the merits of proffered scientific evidence, with just over half stating that it was "very useful." Unfortunately, the responses revealed a general lack of understanding of the scientific meaning of the concept of error rate.[41] The researchers explained that "Judges had the most difficulty operationalizing falsifiability and error rate, with only five percent of the respondents demonstrating a clear understanding of falsifiability and only four percent demonstrating a clear understanding of error rate."[42]

In their discussion of this far-reaching survey and interview research, Gatowski and colleagues insist that while the surveyed judges confidently and overwhelmingly responded that the *Daubert* criteria were useful decision-making guides, the majority did not seem to recognize or acknowledge their lack of understanding about how to apply some of the guidelines as part of the admissibility decision-making process.[43]

They continue: "Although judges surveyed reported that they found *Daubert* criteria useful for determining the admissibility of proffered expert evidence, the extent to which judges understand and can properly apply the criteria when assessing the validity and reliability of proffered scientific evidence was questionable at best. The survey findings strongly suggest that judges have difficulty operationalizing the *Daubert* criteria and applying them, especially with respect to falsifiability and error rate.[44]

The authors conclude: "Judges' lack of sophistication regarding the scientific meaning of the *Daubert* criteria should cause concern about whether judges are making accurate and reliable assessments of proffered scientific evidence using the *Daubert* criteria."[45]

Clearly, the lack of scientific reasoning know-how creates a vacuum in which the mudslingers and junk science practitioners can do their mischief. Fortunately, research on methodological reasoning suggests that training in the scientific method can improve individuals' reasoning abilities. For example, Lehman and colleagues demonstrated that graduate students in disciplines emphasizing methodological reasoning were more likely to apply these reasoning skills to everyday problems than were graduate students in other disciplines.[46] Researchers Fong, Krantz, and Nisbett demonstrated that research subjects given brief training in methodological reasoning provided more scientifically sophisticated answers to a series of real-world problems.[47]

A review of this research recommends training for family law practitioners in behavioral science principles and methods. With even moderate training, the impact of advocacy-based "junk science," and the purveyors of misinformation could be significantly diminished.

PART TWO: CONFUSION AND MISREPRESENTATION IN THE DATUM OF LAW

We look for what we believe; we find what we look for.
Goethe

The articles by law student Cheri L. Wood,[48] social workers Kathleen Faller and Ellen DeVoe,[49,50,51] and law professor Carol Bruch,[52] are rife with the kind of flawed scholarship and outright misrepresentation that are the hallmark of much of today's anti-PAS rhetoric.

Taken together, the writings of these detractors reveal that debate over PAS is not so much about science as the politics of science, and the influence of ideology. On one side of the debate are Gardner and others who believe that PAS is a valuable concept that should be further investigated, so that children of divorce do not lose one parent unnecessarily (perhaps adherents to this school of thought should be termed "family advocates"). The opposing view, promulgated by Wood, Faller, and Bruch, is that of the so-called "child advocates," who hold the fundamental belief that children never lie about abuse. In their view, PAS is a concept that harms children, because they believe it is used to invalidate allegations of sex abuse and justify placing children in the custody of an abusive parent.

PAS detractors such as Wood, Faller, and Bruch mistakenly equate PAS with allegations of sex abuse, despite the fact that the majority of PAS cases do not involve such accusations. They assert, incorrectly, that it is the presence of sex abuse allegations which forms the criteria for what they refer to as "Gardner's PAS." The Reality is that Gardner defined PAS as a psychological disturbance in the child with eight characteristic symptoms such as a campaign of denigration against the parent targeted for alienation and rationalizations for the deprecation that are often weak, frivolous, and absurd, etc. It should be noted that the eight manifestations of PAS that Gardner identified do not include allegations of sex abuse.

The arguments put forth by the PAS detractors should be considered suspect for the simple fact that they reflect a misunderstanding of Gardner's work, and make no effort to understand his point of view.

Review: The Parental Alienation Syndrome: A Dangerous Aura Of Reliability

In her note arguing her views on PAS, law student Cheri L. Wood described the unfortunate case of little "Mandi," who reportedly came home one day from a visitation and told her mother "in explicit detail, how her father had sexually molested her."[53] Wood went on to offer: "The judge determined that since the four year-old's story was not always consistent; her mother must have "programmed" her to say such things about her father. Consequently, the court not only gave custody of the child to the accused father, but also denied the child all contact with her mother. The court's leap of reasoning was based on a theory known as the Parental Alienation Syndrome."[54]

This portrayal completely mischaracterized the extensive work done by Judge David F. Jung of the Family Court, Fulton County, New York,[55] as well as the review of a five-judge panel of the Supreme Court, Appellate Division, Third Department, New York.[56]

Even more to the point is Wood's thesis that PAS should not be admissible in court because, according to Wood, "Gardner's theories about PAS" are used to "invalidate child sex abuse charges."[57] Wood mistakenly asserted that Gardener's criteria to determine whether PAS is present are based on his "Sex Abuse Legitimacy Scale (SAL)."[58] Wood places heavy emphasis on criticizing Gardner's SAL, which posits that allegations of sex abuse are sometimes fabricated, an idea which goes against the child advocate position that there is no such thing as a false allegation because "children never lie about abuse." Wood misrepresents the foundation of PAS as Gardner and others have conceived it, which focused on the child's obsession with denigrating a once-loved parent, brought on by an "unholy alliance" with the alienating parent.

Having argued that Gardner used PAS as a ploy to invalidate charges of sex abuse, Wood then makes the misleading claim that "Dr. Gardner espouses these theories in his self-published books"[59] referring to his company, Creative Therapeutics, and that "the inherent problem with such self-published work is the lack of peer review."[60] Significantly, Wood failed to mention that Dr. Gardner's books have also been published by the likes of Bantam, Putnam, and Jason Aronson, and that Gardner authored 130 articles published in peer-reviewed journals.

Wood also mischaracterized the scientific literature: "Ironically, while PAS has been admitted in courts, it has not been accepted by experts in the field: psychologists, child abuse evidentiary experts, or child advocates."[61]

The implication is that PAS is not accepted by the greater professional community, as if this were a single, like-minded body. In reality, the professional community is made up of diverse individuals with diverse points of view. The "experts" Wood is referring to are the child advocates, who make up but one segment of the larger professional community. For support, Wood cites Dr. Jon Conte, one of the "children never lie" social workers, and his group of students.[62] "In a recent submission to a psychiatric journal, a multidisciplinary group of experts noted that an 'overwhelming majority of professionals' do not agree with Dr. Gardner's interviewing methods."[63]

Note that in this quote, Wood switches from the assertion that "PAS is not accepted in the professional community" to the idea that "many experts disagree with Dr. Gardner's interviewing methods." However, Woods fails to state which of his interview methods she is referring to – those involved in the administration of the controversial SAL, or those described in Dr. Gardner's books on family evaluation and psychotherapy with children of divorce,[64] which continue to be widely used and accepted to this day, even among those who disagree with the concept of PAS.

Returning to her discussion of "Mandi," Wood mischaracterized the testimony of a witness whose comments did not support the mother's allegations of sex abuse: "[Witness] concluded that because 'Mandi's' mother had a vested interest in the outcome of the case – that is, she wanted full custody – and because [witness] had observed no outward signs of emotion when 'Mandi's' mother spoke, there was no information that would indicate that 'Mandi' had been sexually abused by her father."[65] Wood went on to mischaracterize Judge Jung's conclusions: "Relying on Dr. Richard Gardner's Parental Alienation Syndrome theory, the court determined that 'Mandi's' allegations were consistent with those that Dr. Gardner would describe as the type made by a fabricator. Thus, the court concluded that because 'Mandi's' mother must have 'programmed' her daughter to accuse her father of sexually abusing her, she was not fit to continue in the role of 'Mandi's' parent."[66] "The court further ordered that, because it had no assurance that Mandi's mother would not continue to 'brainwash' or 'program' Mandi, Mandi's mother would be allowed no visitation or contact with her daughter."[67]

Having finished with "Mandi," Wood took on another high-profile case involving PAS, *Schultz v. Schultz*, once again skewing the facts to support her thesis.[68] In an effort to further refute Gardner's view that the sex abuse claims in custody litigation are often contrived, Wood turned her attention to another of the notable PAS/Gardner critics: Dr. Kathleen Coulborn Faller of the University of Michigan School of Social Work. Wood neglects to tell the reader that Faller escalated her efforts to discredit Gardner and PAS after Gardner was subpoenaed to testify against Faller in a million-dollar civil lawsuit.[69]

Citing to Faller (1991), Wood reported: "Research indicates that false allegations made in the context of divorce are . . . by no means the majority."[70] However, Wood failed to mention any studies which indicate that false allegations of abuse occur more frequently than one would like to think. For example, Daro and Mitchel in a 1989 survey of 50 states found a 63 percent unsubstantiated rate.[71] Flango surveyed New York State and found that 61 percent of sexual abuse allegations for a period of one year could not be substantiated.[72] It should be noted that these researchers were not even looking specifically at child abuse allegations in the highly charged context of divorce. On issues of base rate alone, Gardner is clearly correct. Wood's characterization of this issue demonstrates how easy it is for the uninitiated to misconstrue scientific concepts such as "frequency" and "base rate."

Wood then returns to "Mandi." Setting the stage for her treatment of the differences between the *Frye* standard and the then-emerging *Daubert* rules: "Recall 'Mandi's' fate in *Karen B. v. Clyde M.* Clearly, the decision to admit psychological testimony in child custody cases carries with it serious ramifications. The *Karen B.* court, basing its decision on the PAS to not only take Mandi away from her mother, but to limit all contact with her. . . ."[73]

Ironically, Ms. Wood's discussion of the dangers of admitting psychological testimony in child custody disputes demonstrates most of the common errors nonscientists commit when analyzing behavioral sciences data.[74]

As described in Part One, it is challenging for judges, attorneys, and court personnel to master the datum of the behavioral sciences.[75] This difficulty is compounded when one considers that judges, attorneys, and court personnel tend to rely on published papers and treatises in the law, and the representations in and about such treatises. Unfortunately, once published in a law review, a student paper like that of Ms. Wood tends to be cited without critical analysis.[76] In this way, both law an behavioral science are undercut.

Review: Child Maltreatment and Endangerment In The Context Of Divorce

Adherence to a valid and reliable methodology separates "junk" from "science."[77] With the changes in the expert evidence rules, judges are now required to be "gatekeepers."[78] In this gatekeeping role, courts must now qualify only proposed experts who are grounded in the principles and methodology of science.[79] These gatekeepers must also determine the validity, reliability and trustworthiness of proposed evidence.[80]

In 1995, Faller and student social worker Ellen DeVoe set out to refute Gardner's proposition that many of the sex abuse allegations encountered in divorce litigation are fabricated.[81] Not only has Faller's work been found to be methodologically flawed, the gap between what she *says* she and her colleagues do, and what they actually do, is enormous. Utilizing a sample of 174 children from their clinic, Faller and DeVoe sought to validate their idea that sex abuse allegations on divorce are – more often then not – true. They reported that sex abuse was substantiated for 72.5 percent of the children. They acknowledged that this was "a higher substantiation rate than other studies,"[82] and sought to explain this finding by citing their superior clinical acumen in substantiating abuse.

Unfortunately, "unaided clinical judgment" is not a reliable method for making abuse determinations. The researchers and professionals who make this claim typically ask questions and interpret answers in a way that confirms their *a priori* hypotheses. The result is a problem called "confirmatory bias." Nowhere is this methodology more devastating, or prevalent, than in the area of child sexual abuse investigations.[83]

It was the potentially horrific consequences for innocent parents accused of abuse, and for children who become involved in false allegations, which prompted Gardner to title his first book on PAS *The Parental Alienation Syndrome and the Differentiation Between Fabricated and Genuine Child Sex Abuse*, published in 1987.[84] Gardner expressed the view that sex abuse allegations may very well be one manifestation of PAS and that abuse allegations that occur in conjunction with severe PAS symptoms in the child may very well be fabricated. However, he did not include false allegations of abuse in his criteria for PAS, and believed that false allegations of sex abuse occurred in only a minority of PAS cases.

According to Faller, however, PAS as conceived by Gardner almost always involves allegations of sex abuse.[85] What Gardner actually opined was that a significant proportion of sex abuse allegations in divorce (and by extension in PAS) were probably fabricated, but that PAS with false allegations of sex abuse occurred in only a minority of cases.

It was Gardner's outspoken criticism of professionals who act as "validators" for abuse which seems to have touched a nerve for Faller, who accurately portrayed Gardner's view: "These people are poorly educated and poorly trained. Their incompetence and use of flawed techniques lead hundreds of children to falsely claim or affirm sexual victimization."[86] Gardner's indictment was aimed directly at professionals who used leading, suggestive, and coercive interview techniques to validate or confirm their preconceived ideas about the abuse. A review of three high-profile Michigan cases demonstrated that these were precisely the techniques that Faller and her group were using.[87]

Rarely do courts have the benefit of a thorough and objective analysis of the work of a proposed expert. In the case of Dr. Faller, three objective analyses of what she and her Faller Group actually do (as opposed to what she says they do), were accomplished in the Michigan cases.

In *Bielaska v. Orley*, a specialty panel of the Michigan Court of Appeals was assembled to review the work of Faller and her group in a case involving allegations of child sexual abuse and PAS. The court began a 49-page opinion by explaining that they had undertaken a "painstaking review of the entire record."[88] The panel "watched the [videotaped] interviews in their entirety."[89] In addition, the Court reviewed the testimony of several highly qualified experts who critiqued the interviews.

First, the court's special panel noted numerous "inaccuracies" and deficiencies in the Faller Group's work, including misstatements of fact, failure to review any other court records or psychological evaluations, and relaying on information from one party only – the mother – who was accusing the child's father of sex abuse.

Second, the court noted with approval the deposition of Dr. Elizabeth Benedek, who was then president of the American Psychiatric Association. Dr. Benedek testified, after having reviewed a videotaped interview done by Dr. Faller of a child, that she did not believe the interview met the standards for unbiased interview regarding the question whether sexual abuse occurred. Dr. Benedek opined Dr. Faller's interview was replete with leading questions, and that Dr. Faller engaged in repeated questioning while giving the child rare opportunity to tell her story."[90]

Third, the court adopted the findings of two doctors with regards to the taped child interviews by the Faller Group.[91] The first doctor made several observations of note:

- The younger child was being coached, rehearsed and prepared to tell what the interviewer and defendant [mother] . . . want her to say."[92]
- [The children] were set up verbally several times about [what] they were going to have to testify to.[93]
- The interviewer *undressed the male doll and fumbled with the penis* while [the older child] *was asked leading "penis-related questions* which provided visual as well as auditor[y] 'markers.'"[94]
- The interviewer . . . showed the child both visually and auditorially what she should say.[95]

The second doctor opined:

- The interviewers asked slanted one-sided questions that were designed to obtain only information that was consistent with the hypothesis the children had been sexually abused.[96]
- The interviewers did not ask questions that could obtain information that disconfirmed their expectations [re the alleged abuse].[97]
- The interviewers' questions create imagery in the child's mind, and can result in the problem that the questions create the child's imagination. Over time, what the child imagines and what the child remembers may become confused . . . the method of interviewing he saw on the videotapes was "very, very conducive to that outcome."[98]

Finally, the Court came to the independent conclusion that the interview methods of Faller and the Faller Group were "suggestive," "coercive," and "untrustworthy."[99]

In *Champney v. Champney*, Michigan judge Chad Schmucker discounted the Faller Group's Findings about abuse after reading the Faller Group report and watching the videotapes of their interviews.[100] In the damages case that followed, Judge Donald Shelton appointed his own expert to conduct an objective evaluation of the little girl and the manner in which the Faller Group had interviewed her. The court's expert opined the Faller Group's process involved a "nonstandard approach to child interviewing,"[101] with "a strong preconception of what had happened to the child."[102]

In *Recchia v. Recchia*, the court made a specific request of its own court clinic to conduct an objective assessment of the Faller Group's methodology. A psychologist who was a senior clinician at the court's clinic, conducted the assessment.[103] According to the psychologist: "These interviewing techniques embraced by Dr. Faller . . . represent those techniques which are said to produce tainted and unreliable responses in children."[104]

She was particularly perturbed by Dr. Faller's statement, "I tried to redirect her [the child] to the penis."[105] The psychologist opined: "This statement about 'redirecting the child to the penis' is another example of the use of leading questions and is the antithesis of the open-ended questioning procedure advocated by most researchers."[106] Finally, the psychologist criticized the Faller Group for not taking into account neurological deficits of the child, which may have impacted the child's ability to understand the questions put to her.[107]

It should be noted that Gardner was among the experts who testified against Faller in *Champney v. Faller et al.*[108] It was after his testimony that Faller escalated her efforts to discredit Gardner and PAS.

In her article titled "Child Maltreatment and Endangerment in the Context of Divorce," Faller (2000) cited herself in support of the proposition that there is "no empirical evidence to support" mental health experts who utilize Gardner's formulation.[109] Curiously, in the article immediately following Faller's 2000 effort, psychologist Barry Bricklin and Gail Elliot provide citation to a great deal of empirical evidence an research studies in support of Gardner's core hypothesis about PAS.[110]

Review: Parental Alienation Syndrome and Parental Alienation: Getting It Wrong In Child Custody Cases

Like Wood and Faller, law professor Carol Bruch[111] begins her critique of Gardner's work by misstating his central hypothesis. "Child psychiatrist Richard Gardner coined the term Parental Alienation Syndrome in 1985 in order to describe his clinical impressions of cases he believed involved false allegations of child sexual abuse."[112] What Gardner actually wrote when he introduced the term PAS in 1985 was: "I have introduced this term [parental alienation syndrome] to refer to a disturbance in which children are obsessed with deprecation and criticism of a parent – denigration that is unjustified and/or exaggerated."[113]

Gardner devoted the entire first half of his 1985 paper to describing what he observed to be eight manifestations of PAS in the child, the pathogenesis of the disorder, and common behaviors of the alienating that appeared to be largely responsible for it. He devoted only three paragraphs, in the middle of the article, to the implications of rising interest in sex abuse allegation, which he identified as its own phenomenon, different from PAS. According to Gardner:

> We are now observing *another* phenomenon that is contributing to the development of the parental alienation syndrome: the widespread attention being given to the sexual abuse of children by parents. Heretofore, the general consensus among those who worked with sexually-abused children was that it was extremely rare for a child to fabricate abuse. This is no longer the case. The child's accusation of a parent's sexual abuse can now be a powerful weapon in the alienation campaign.[114]

Gardner was careful to qualify his position: "I am not claiming that bona fide sex abuse does not take place in families in which there is a custody conflict; I am only stating that the possibility of fabrication is increased in this situation."[115]

Bruch then accuses Gardner of exaggerating the prevalence of PAS, and of false allegations of sex abuse: "Gardner first stated that PAS was present in approximately ninety percent of the children whose families were involved in custody litigation . . . his initial estimates appear to have been dramatically overstated . . . particularly as to the frequency of false sexua abuse allegations."[116]

As to the prevalence of PAS, Bruch fails to mention a study of 700 divorce families, sponsored by the American Bar Association, which found 80 percent of cases involved alienation processes, a figure close to Gardner's estimate.[117]

As for false allegations of sex abuse, Bruch argues the child advocate position that false allegations are rare, even in high-conflict divorce, because "children never lie about abuse." She cites to Thoennes and Tjaden (1990) for support: "Less than two percent of the approximately 9,000 families with *custody and visitation disputes* served by eight domestic relations courts included in this study involved an allegation of sexual abuse."[118]

This characterization is misleading in two respects. Thoennes and Tjaden concluded that the rate of sex abuse reporting among families involved in custody disputes was six times greater than that observed in a 1988 National Incidence Study conducted by the National Center on Child Abuse and Neglect. In addition, they reported that in 50 percent of custody cases, the allegations were deemed unfounded or unsubstantiated.[119]

Bruch then cites to Faller to rebut Gardner's view that a "significant proportion" of sex abuse allegations in divorce are probably false.[120] Ceci and Bruck, in a book published by the American Psychological Association, sought to determine whether the rate of false allegations was unusually high in custody disputes, reviewing a number of studies, including by Thoennes and Tjaden (1990), Faller (1991), and Faller and Devoe (1995).[121] According to Ceci and Bruck, the data suggested that, on average, about 50 percent of sex abuse reports in divorce appeared to be valid, while the remaining 50 percent, in which abuse was not substantiated, were due to a variety of factors, such as adult-initiated allegations that were deliberately fabricated, and child reports reflecting the influence of repeated and suggestive questioning by adults in positions of authority, including parents.

Next, Bruch turns to "The Setting in Which PAS Is Said to Occur," referring to high-conflict families. Bruch cites to a study of mandatory mediation cases to support her claim that domestic violence and child abuse are common among high-conflict families involved in custody and visitation disputes:

> In statewide study of most [mandated] custody mediation sessions conducted by court personnel in a single day, serious issues of child abuse, family violence and substance abuse were raised by the parties in 42 percent of all mediating families, with an additional 24 percent raising one of these issues alone. . . . Nearly half of the access denial cases at every site involve allegations of the child's imperiled safety. Most allegations are made by the residential parent, regardless of sex, against the nonresidential parent and other people in his of her household."[122]

Bruch takes this to mean that there is such a high rate (66 percent) of family violence, and problems such as substance abuse, that the safety of children in high-conflict custody disputes is often endangered. This, in her view explains why so many custodial mothers seek to deny access. However, as research by Thoennes and Tjaden demonstrates, there is a difference between the percentage of cases in which issues of abuse are raised (i.e., alleged) and the percentage of cases in which it is determined that abuse occurred.

Next, Bruch provides a five-part analysis of what she terms "The Flaws in PAS Theory."[123] Her insistence on calling PAS a "theory" is in itself misleading. When Gardner coined the term "PAS," he was not referring to a theory, but to his empirical observations of an emerging psychological disturbance among children of divorce, who displayed a distinctive set of observable behaviors, of the "eight manifestations of PAS in the child" as Gardner called them.

First, Bruch takes issue with Gardner's views on the relationship between PAS and a psychiatric disorder known as folie à duex:

> Gardner confounds a child's developmentally related reaction to divorce and high parental conflict (including violence) with psychosis. In doing so, he fails to recognize parents' and children's angry, often inappropriate, and totally predictable behavior following separation. This error leads him to claim that PAS constitutes a frequent example of *folie à deux* or *folie à trios*, Shared Psychotic Disorders that the American Psychiatric Association and scholarly studies report occur only rarely.[124]

According to Bruch, the renowned child psychiatrist was unable to distinguish between children displaying normal reaction to divorce and children with serious psychiatric disturbances, such as psychosis. However, she offers no citation in support of this seeming confusion in the board-certified psychiatrist's thinking.

Gardner believed, based on his experience, that folie à duex was more prevalent among *severe* PAS indoctrinators than in general population,[125] and that severe PAS was itself relatively rare, constituting 5 percent to 10 percent of all PAS cases.[126] In Bruch's view, this is inconsistent with the Diagnostic and Statistical Manual of Mental Disorders (DSM-IV), which describes shared delusional relationships as relatively rare. However, the DSM-IV also states that there is little systematic information about the prevalence of folie à deux and that an unknown number of cases go unrecognized.[127]

The key features of folie à deux, for the purposes of understanding its relationship to PAS, include:

> 1. An individual in a subordinate position (e.g., a child) comes to share the delusion of a person who is dominant in the relationship (e.g., a parent). 2. Individuals who come to share delusional beliefs are often related and may have lived together for a long time, sometimes in social isolation. 3. The shared beliefs, and the closeness they engender, are firmly maintained despite clear evidence to the contrary. 4. The shared delusions and paranoia are often limited to the denigrated spouse at first, and may not interfere with functioning in other areas. 5. In the course of ongoing litigation, the paranoid delusional system may become increasingly illogical and expand to include all those seen as supporting the target parent.[128]

The second "PAS theory" is a reiteration of Bruch's objections to Gardner's views on prevalence of false allegations: "Taken together [Gardner's] assertions have the practical effect of impugning all abuse allegations, allegations which Gardner asserts are usually false in the divorce context. Here, too, Gardner cites no evidence in support of his personal view, and the relevant literature reports the contrary – that such allegations are usually well founded."[129]

Bruch's implication that Gardner automatically assumed that sex abuse allegations in divorce were false is absurd. A distinguishing feature of Gardner's work was the importance he placed on differentiating between allegations which were likely true, and which were likely false, on a case-by-case basis.[130] The fact that Gardner did not cite to the robust literature that supports his views on the prevalence of false allegations in divorce does not invalidate his views.[131] The "relevant literature" Bruch cites to, by Faller, Myer, and Wood,[132] is pale by comparison.

Bruch describes the third flaw of PAS: "In this fashion, PAS shifts attention away from the perhaps dangerous behavior of the parent seeking custody to that of the custodial parent. . . . For Gardner, the concerned custodial parent's steps to obtain professional assistance in diagnosing, treating and protecting the child constitute evidence of false allegations."[133]

Bruch asserts that courts readily assume that allegations of abuse are false when PAS is offered as the explanation, focusing on "the accuser as the abuser," citing to a 1993 news report as her only support.[134] On the contrary, allegations of sex abuse made in a custody dispute are the "lethal weapon," resulting in immediate restrictions on access, as courts prefer to err on the side of caution when the possibility of sex abuse is raised.

Nor is there any evidence to support Bruch's claim that Gardner automatically assumes it is evidence of a false allegation when a custodial parent alleging abuse seeks professional assistance to help protect the child. Gardner opined that there was no such thing as a typical personality pattern of a parent who initiates an promulgates false allegations of sex abuse.[135] He identified 30 indicators that could be helpful in assessing whether a parent was likely making a false allegation. Obsessive efforts to "prove" abuse was one criterion, but no conclusion could be drawn from a single indicator. According to Gardner, the greater the number and quality of indicators, the more likely the parent was making a false allegation.

What Bruch describes as the fourth flaw in "PAS theory" is the most grave so far: "Gardner believes that, particularly in serious cases, the relationship of an alienated child with the rejected parent will be irreparably damaged . . . unless immediate, drastic measures (custody transfer, isolation from the loved parent, and deprogramming) are taken."[136]

Bruch cites to Dr. Janet Johnston as support, but confounds Johnston's research on a "less troubled population"[137] with Gardner's observations of "serious cases." According to Johnston: "In that less-troubled population [children whose parents had been recently divorced] 20 percent of the children were in alignments (most of them in the 9-to-12 year group), but every case resolved itself before the child reached 18."[138]

Johnston's research on a sample of more troubled children, who had been involved in protracted custody litigation, is more germane:

> A follow-up of the first sample of [less troubled] children, 2 or 3 years later, suggests that these alliances [between child and alienating parent] typically last several years into mid adolescence. . . . Under the best of circumstances, this greater objectivity allows them to use their cognitive skills to withdraw strategically from the parental fights. Unfortunately, it appears that a significant proportion of children are not able to do this, and the remaining caught up in the parental fights is associated with their having more emotional and behavioral difficulties.[139]

In addition, the work of Dr. Judith Wallerstein documents the damage suffered by children in high-conflict families who are used as pawns, to get revenge against the other parent: "Modern Medeas want revenge on their former wives or husbands – and they exact it by destroying the relationship between the other parent and the child. In so doing, they severely damage and sometimes destroy the child's psyche as well. . . . I have seen a great deal of evidence that Medea-like anger severely injures children at every age."[140]

Bruch is quite simply mistaken when she claims that there is no support in the wider scientific literature for Gardner's views about the damage to children in cases of severe PAS.[141]

Bruch then argues that the "drastic measures" Gardner recommends in the five percent to 10 percent of severe PAS cases, such as placing the child in the hated parent's custody and restricting the alienator's access, are unwarranted, citing again Johnston for support: "It has been our experience that forcibly removing these children from the aligned parent and placing them in the custody of the rejected parent, as recommended by Gardner (1987), is a misguided resolution. . . . Rather, the process needs to be one of effecting a gradual separation in a supportive, therapeutic environment."[142]

Johnston provides few details about her negative experiences with alienated children who were placed in the custody of the rejected parent. The approach Johnston recommends involves therapeutic interventions with each member of the family, although she provides no case examples of successful treatment of severe PAS using this approach. What studies there are suggest that structural interventions, such as the orders for custody and access, are the key to successful intervention in severe PAS, while therapy as the primary intervention is ineffective, and often makes things worse.[143]

Despite her reservations about forcibly removing the alienated child from the aligned parent, Johnston acknowledges that this may be necessary in cases where the alienating parent is severely disturbed and inducing a folie à deux. "When the child is caught in a folie à deux relationship with an extremely disturbed psychotic parent, the separation [of parent and child] may need to be undertaken within the protective confines of an inpatient psychiatric unit or in a residential school for emotionally disturbed children."[144]

Bruch disagrees with Johnston on this issue: "Specifically disapproved is Gardner's recommendation that children, even those who are supposedly engaged in a folie à deux with their custodial parent, be removed immediately and cut off from all contact with that parent pending reverse brain-washing or deprogramming."[145]

Bruch's reference to "reverse brainwashing" reflects a fundamental misunderstanding of Gardner's approach. Gardner believed the best antidote to the brainwashing by the alienating parent was "to provide the children with living experiences that the targeted parent is not the terribly dangerous person he (she) has been portrayed to be by the alienator."[146]

Bruch describes the fifth flaw of "PAS theory" as the worst of all – children being transferred to the custody of an abusive parent: "To the extent that PAS results in placing children with a parent who is, in fact, abusive, the youngsters will be bereft of contact with the parent who might help them. . . . Parent groups and investigative reporting describe, for example, numerous cases in which trial courts have transferred children's custody to known or likely abusers and custodial parents have been denied contact with the children they have been trying to protect."[147]

In support of this assertion, Bruch cites to a newspaper article in the Pasadena Star and to a study by Karen Winner, commissioned by the California Protective Parents Association.[148] The group appears to be part of a nationwide network made up of parents, particularly mothers, who feel they were deprived of custody by a corrupt legal system that gives preference to fathers. Some of these parents have fought back by taking their cases to the media, where their experiences at the hands of the family law system have been well publicized.

Ms. Winner is described as an "investigative reporter." She is also the author of a book titled "Divorced from Justice: The Abuse of Women and Children by Divorce Lawyers and Judges."[149] An Internet search conducted in 2002 led to her Web-site, The Justice Seekers Inc., which advertised:

> Need an expert to debunk the fraudulent diagnosis, "Parental Alienation Syndrome?" Need an expert to evaluate whether your divorce lawyer has engaged in business practices that put his or her financial interests above the client's welfare? This small but growing list is a free public service to help litigants in divorce and custody cases find the experts they need. Check back periodically to see new additions. Courtesy of The Justice Seekers, Inc.[150]

PART THREE: THE SCIENTIFIC METHOD AND THE EVOLUTION OF SCIENCE

When Wood, Faller, and Bruch claim "lack of empirical support" for Gardner's formulation of the PAS,[151] they display a naive misconception of what science is and the way that scientific understanding evolves.[152] The most common misconception is that "science" refers to carefully designed laboratory studies where the impact of different variables on some outcome of interest is quantitatively measured and statistically analyzed. This type of scientific inquiry is called quantitative research. The so-called "hard sciences" (e.g., astronomy, chemistry, and biology) are particularly well-suited for this approach.

PAS is a behavioral science concept. As it happens, the most meaningful insights into psychology and the social and behavioral sciences often have less to do with laboratories, experiments, and statistics and more to do with behavioral observation, which is the focus of a different scientific strategy, called qualitative research.[153] Qualitative researchers study things in their natural settings. According to Professor Kazdin of Yale University: "*Qualitative research* is an approach to the subject matter of human experience and focuses on narrative accounts, description, interpretation, context, and meaning. The goal is to describe, interpret, and understand the phenomena of interest."[154]

Qualitative research yields data and information not likely to emerge from quantitative studies. Qualitative process studies and quantitative hypothesis testing have complementary roles. Each has its characteristic strengths and weaknesses.[155]

Science Is a Way of Thinking

The scientific method is neither quantitative nor qualitative, but a way of thinking and approaching problems. Knowledge gained from scientific inquiry is something that tends to progress over long periods of time, and often unfolds in "messy" and unpredictable ways. The scientific method dictates that researchers engage in a process known as "proof by disproof," or "falsification."[156] The process begins with a theory, or hypothesis, which is then tested by attempting to prove alternative explanations for the phenomenon. This is similar to the process physicians use to reach their diagnostic conclusions, which involves developing a theory as to what might be wrong with the patient, and ruling out alternative explanations for the condition before a diagnosis is reached. When all the alternative possibilities have been investigated and ruled out, the theory is granted provisional acceptance. Thus, the scientific method is designed to test alternative explanations in an effort to disprove the theory or hypothesis.

A theory is intended to highlight and explain something that one would otherwise not see, or would find puzzling. Often, it is an answer to the question "Why?"[157] "The role of theory is precisely to make things that were hidden visible, to define some patterns and give some meanings to the sorts of observations that social researchers continually make when investigating society."[158]

In the early 1980s, Gardner began asking "Why?" about a type of divorce-specific psychopathology in children that he was seeing with such increasing frequency that he decided it deserved a special name. He called it "parental alienation syndrome."[159] The disorder had several puzzling features. For example: The child was obsessed with hatred and deprecation of a once-loved parent; the child's complaints about the hated parent were characteristically unjustified and/or exaggerated; the intensity of the anger expressed by the PAS child was not normal even for children who have been severely abused by a parent; the child's animosity towards the hated parent spread to include the family and friends of that parent; and it appeared that the child made his or her own contributions to the campaign of denigration, and did not simply mirror the alienating parent's views.

Based on clinical observation, and his training and experience as a child psychiatrist, Gardner identified three key factors which appeared to explain, or contribute to, the pathogenesis of the disorder: "brainwashing" by the alienating parent; situational factors, such as undue physical separation from the target parent; and the child's own contributions.

Critics such as Johnston argue that PAS theory automatically, and unfairly, blames the aligned parent for the child's rejection of the target parent and is not "falsifiable": "Gardner has formulated a definition of PAS that includes its hypothesized etiological agents (i.e., an alienating parent and a receptive child). This renders his theory of the cause of PAS unfalsifiable because it is tautological (i.e., true by definition)."[160]

This portrayal reflects a misunderstanding of Gardner's views, taking his generic observations about common characteristics of the PAS phenomenon (i.e., PAS symptoms in the child often associated with alienating behaviors of aligned parent) and equating these observations with a case-specific diagnosis of PAS, based on a comprehensive family evaluation in which a causal connection between the alienator's behavior and the child's symptoms was found. In other words, the idea that a particular parent, in a particular case, may be inducing PAS is a falsifiable hypothesis, assuming that alternative explanations were considered as part of the family evaluation process, and disproved before the PAS diagnosis was reached.

Gardner differentiated between three levels of PAS – mild, moderate, and severe – and outlined specific interventions for each one.[161] He recommended that the court consider changing custody in severe cases, which accounted for only five percent to ten percent of all PAS cases, by his estimate.[162] Critics, such as Johnston, often take the position that changing custody is a misguided solution, though Johnston acknowledges that changing custody may be necessary in very rare cases, where the alienating parent is flagrantly psychotic or unremittingly sociopathic.[163]

By its very nature, science entertains different theories, and does not work toward a single, "right" point of view. Theory is like the lens of a kaleidoscope. Different theories bring different aspects of the world into view. "Seeing the world in different ways is the essential and fundamental role of social research and the ability to see these differences and to make sense of different points of view that a researcher can take is the basic contribution that theory makes to the research process."[164]

The Role of Case Studies in the Evolution of Science

Qualitative information drawn from case studies plays an important role in both quantitative and qualitative research. "Case studies are crucial in the early stages of science, in the newer sciences, and in mature sciences when new phenomena arise."[165]

Case studies are an important method of "falsification" in qualitative research and the social sciences. The temptation is to just stick with cases that fit the original theory.[166] "Falsification" utilizing case studies means always looking at the "awkward cases," searching for new insights by analyzing what is controversial and what may have gone wrong and why. As a behavioral science concept, in the "early stages of science," PAS lends itself well to this approach.

Gardner's efforts to understand the pattern of "awkward cases" he was seeing in the early 1980s gave rise to his description and analysis of the PAS phenomenon.[167] A decade later, he noted the emergence of another new phenomenon, the "false parental alienation syndrome," which he attributed to the increasing popularity and acceptance of PAS.[168] Gardner sought to preserve the purity of the original PAS concept, and emphasized the importance of differentiating between bona fide and fraudulent PAS: "Truly neutral and unbiased examiners recognize the phenomenon of false PAS diagnoses, do a proper examination, determine whether a PAS is present, and, if so, which of the parents is attempting to program the children into a campaign of denigration."[169]

Putting Gardner's Work on PAS in Perspective

To put Gardner's formulation of PAS in the proper perspective, it helps to remember that, long before there were laboratories, Timothy Bright (1551–1615), an English physician, published the first treatise on mental illness, presaging the present-day understanding of endogenous and exogenous depression.[170] Another Englishman, Robert Burton (1577–1640), authored the most famous book on psychiatry in the seventeenth century,[171] while Swiss physician Felix Plater (1536–1614), created a classification of diseases based on symptoms, causes, and treatments.[172]

In Scotland, William Cullen (1710–1790) became the first physician to use the terms "neurosis" and "neurotic" to describe mental diseases.[173] In France, Philippe Pinel (1745–1826) classified mental illness and established humane treatments for inmates of insane asylums.[174] In the newly established United States, Benjamin Rush (1745–1813), a signer of the Declaration of Independence, authored the first general book on psychiatry in America and became known as the father of American psychiatry.[175]

The 1800s saw a dramatic upturn in the development of psychiatry. In 1814, Joseph Adams (1756–1818) authored the first book on the hereditary properties of diseases.[176] In 1818, Johann Christian Heinroth (1773–1843) wrote the first systematic textbook of psychiatry and attempted to formulate an actual clinical system of psychotherapy.[177] In 1835, James Cowles Prichard (1786–1848) authored a standard textbook of psychiatry covering all the literature on all known diseases of the time. Prichard was the first to describe "moral insanity," which later came to be called psychopathic personality.[178] In 1838, Jean Etienne Dominique Esquirol (1782–1840) coined the term "hallucination."[179] That same year, Issac Ray (1807–1881) founded American forensic psychiatry, with his text *Treatise on Medical Jurisprudence of Insanity*.[180]

The early 1900s produced careful studies of the natural course of mental illness by German psychiatrist Emil Kraepelin (1856–1926), who developed a comprehensive classification of mental illness that is quite similar to the system used today, and hypothesized that the bulk of psychiatric illness may have a genetic or physical basis.[181] A member of Kraepelin's staff, Alois Alzheimer (1864–1915), described the anatomical changes in the brain in a common form of dementia that still bears his name.[182]

All of these early works were based on the careful observation of phenomena. This is called qualitative research. They contributed to our understanding of mental illness over a period of 400 years. They are no less important for not being laboratory based.

Gardner's process of careful observation carries on this tradition. Gardner worked to codify his observations of a phenomenon that all family law practitioners have observed. Others who wrote about the phenomenon sometimes used different terminology, such as "parental alienation," "Medea syndrome," " divorce-related mother syndrome," and "alienated child."[183]

Is this science? Certainly it is. Gardner's process over the years has been qualitative research,[184] whereby he has systematically and cumulatively described a type of divorce-specific, familial interaction, which he properly labeled a syndrome. As a qualitative researcher, Gardner's goal was to understand and elaborate the phenomena of interest, rather than to reduce and simplify them to laboratory variables. To augment this work, he decided toward the end of his life to try his hand at quantitative research, producing a follow-up study of 99 PAS children (which was the first of its kind) designed to address the question "Should courts order PAS children to visit/reside with the alienated parent?"[185]

PART FOUR: IMPORTANCE OF SPECIALTY TRAINING IN SCIENTIFIC CONCEPTS

Part Two of this analysis illustrates how efforts like that of Wood, Faller. and Bruch tend to confuse, rather than elucidate, understanding of behavioral science concepts such as PAS. Research has shown that courts, too, have difficulty with behavioral science concepts.[186] Perhaps the difficult decisions in *Toto, Wiederholt, Pathan, Chambers* and *Kirk*[187] could have been avoided with a better-educated judiciary. The decisions in *Daubert* and *Kumho*[188] demonstrate that our judiciary can do better.

In this important endeavor, we cannot rely on cross-examination or opposing experts. Indeed, courts and attorneys overestimate the value of a typical cross-examination to educate jurors about what constitutes flawed science.[189] Furthermore, research indicates that courts and attorneys typically overestimate the value of an opposing expert's examination to educate jurors "junk science."[190] Current research explains that "the general lack of scientific literacy among the state trial judiciary, and the increasingly complex nature of the science that comes before the court, the research presented herein clearly demonstrates the need for more science-based judicial education.[191]

Indeed, the research of the National Judicial College recommends:

> Judges . . . need to be trained to be critical consumers of the science that comes before them . . . to become critical consumers of proffered expert evidence. Judges need to know what critical questions to ask, they need to know what methodological and statistical issues scientific experts, and other purveyors of science, should address and comment on when proffering science for use in the court. Judges need to know what to listen and look for when expert evidence is presented and what they should be asking about when the information is not forthcoming.[192]

Fortunately for this endeavor, research on methodological reasoning illustrates that specialty training in the scientific method can improve reasoning skills. For example, Lehman and colleagues demonstrated that graduate students in disciplines emphasizing methodological reasoning were more likely to apply these reasoning skills to everyday problems than were graduate students in other disciplines.[193] Fong, Krantz, and Nisbett demonstrated that research subjects given brief training in methodological reasoning provided more scientifically sophisticated answers to a series of real-world problems.[194]

As the team affiliated with the National Judicial College recommend, with specialty training, judges can become "critical consumers of the science that comes before them."[195]

ENDNOTES

1. Legal professionals, for the purposes of this article, include attorneys, GAL's, judges, and judicial officers.
2. Approximately 86 percent of civil trials contain expert testimony in some form. Gross, S.R. & Syverud, K.D. (1991). Getting to no: A study of settlement negotiations and the selection of cases for trial. *Michigan Law Review,* 90, 319. *And see:* Gross, S.R. (1991). Expert evidence. *Wisconsin Law Review* 1113, 1119, finding that experts testified in 80 percent of civil trials studied for the article. *See also:* Imwinkelried, E.J. (1994). The next step after *Daubert:* Developing a similarly epistemological approach to ensuring the reliability of nonscientific

expert testimony, 15 *Cardozo Law Review* 2271, 2273; *and see* McClellan, E. (1997). Comment, sharpening the focus on *Daubert's* distinction between scientific and nonscientific expert testimony. 34 *San Diego Law Review* 1719, 1721, asserting that the use of expert testimony has increased proportionately with the increase in technology in society.

3. *Daubert v. Merrell Dow Pharmaceuticals Inc.*, 509 U.S. 579, 113 S.Ct. 2786, (1993).
4. *Id.* at 113 S.Ct. at 2795.
5. *Id.*
6. *Id.*
7. *Id.*
8. *Id.* 509 U.S. 579, 113 S.Ct. at 2796.
9. *Id.*
10. *Id.* emphasis added.
11. *Id.*
12. *Id.* at 509 U.S. 579, 113 S.Ct. at 2797.
13. 869 F2d 348, 353-354 (7th Cir. 1989).
14. *Daubert* at *Id.* 509 U.S. 579, S.Ct. at 2797; 125 L Ed 2d at 483.
15. *Daubert* 509 U.S. 579, 113 S Ct at 2795 n. 9, *emphasis in original.*
16. 522 U.S. 136; 118 S.Ct. 512 (1997).
17. *Kumho Tire Company, Ltd. v. Carmichael*, 526 U.S. 137; 119 S.Ct. 1167 (1999).
18. *Id.* at 119 S.Ct. 1167 at 1174.
19. *See e.g.*: Lorandos, D. and Campbell, T.W. (2005). *Benchbook in the behavioral sciences – psychiatry –psychology – social work.* Durham, NC: Carolina Academic Press. Chapter One provides a detailed description of jurisdictional *Daubert* tests.
20. *See e.g.*: Kovera, M.B. and McAuliff, B.D. (2000). The effects of peer review and evidence quality on judge evaluations of psychological science: Are judges effective gatekeepers? 85 *Journal of Applied Psychology* 574. *And see:* Gatowski, S.I.; Dobbin, S.A.; Richardson, J.T.; Ginsburg, G.P.; Merlino, M.L. and Dahir, V. (2001). Asking the gatekeepers: A national survey of judges on judging expert evidence in a post-*Daubert* world. 24 *Law and Human Behavior* 433.
21. Lehman, D.R., Lempert, R.O. and Nisbett, R.E. (1988). The effects of graduate training on reasoning: Formal discipline and thinking about everyday life events. 43 *American Psychologist*, 431.
22. *Id.*
23. Cooper, J., Bennett, E.A. and Sukel, H.L. (1996). Complex scientific testimony: How do jurors make decisions? 20 *Law and Human Behavior*, 379.
24. Kovera, M.B. and McAuliff, B.D. (2000). The effects of peer review and evidence quality on judge evaluations of psychological science: Are judges effective gatekeepers? 85 *Journal of Applied Psychology* 574.
25. *Id.*
26. *Id.*
27. *Id.* at 575.
28. *Id.* at 583.
29. *Id.* at 582.
30. Gatowski, S.I.; Dobbin, S.A.; Richardson, J.T.; Ginsburg, G.P.; Merlino, M.L. and Dahir, V. (2001). Asking the gatekeepers: A national survey of judges on judging expert evidence in a post-*Daubert* world. 24 *Law and Human Behavior* 433.
31. *Id.* at 442.
32. *Id.*
33. *Id.* at 439.
34. *Id.* at 439–440.
35. *Id.* at 444.
36. *Id.* at 452.
37. *Id.* at 443 *emphasis in original.*
38. *Id.* at 442.
39. *Id.* at 444.
40. *Id.*
41. *Id.* at 444–445.
42. *Id.* at 433.
43. *Id.* at 452.
44. *Id.*
45. *Id.* at 453.
46. Lehman, D.R., Lempert, R.O. and Nisbett, R.E. (1988). The effects of graduate training on reasoning: Formal discipline and thinking about everyday life events. *42, American Psychologist,* 431.
47. Fong, G.T., Krantz, D.H. and Nisbett, R.E. (1986). The effects of statistical training on thinking about everyday problems. *18, Cognitive Psychology,* 253–292.
48. Wood, C. (1994). The Parental Alienation Syndrome: A dangerous aura of reliability. *27, Loyola of Los Angeles Law Review,* 1367.
49. Faller, K. and DeVoe, E. (1995). Allegations of sexual abuse in divorce. *4, Journal of Child Sexual Abuse, 5.*
50. Faller, K.C. (1998). The Parental Alienation Syndrome: What is it and what data supports it? *27, Child Maltreatment,* 261.
51. Faller, K.C. (2000). Child maltreatment and endangerment in the context of divorce. *22, University of Arkansas Little Rock, Law Review,* 429.
52. Bruch, C (2001). Parental Alienation Syndrome and Parental Alienation: Getting it wrong in child custody cases. *35, Family Law Quarterly,* 527.
53. Wood, C. (1994). The Parental Alienation Syndrome: A dangerous aura of reliability *27, Loyola of Los Angeles Law Review,* 1367.
54. *Id.*
55. *In the Matter of Karen B., Petitioner v.Clyde M., Respondent.*, 151 Misc.2d 794; 574 N.Y.S. 2d 267 (1991). Judge Jung heard testimony from eleven different expert witnesses, including two PhDs, the child's pediatrician, preschool teacher, interviewers trained in child sex abuse, and others, all of whom seemed to believe the girl's description of sexual activity between herself and her father varied considerably depending upon [whom] . . . she was talking to." The Court observed that "there was no credible testimony to suggest that the child was afraid of her father and in fact the testimony

suggested a relaxed and warm relationship" *Id.* at 801. The Court also observed that it "had the unique opportunity of observing the demeanor of all witnesses who appeared before it" and the Court concluded "that the testimony of the father is more credible than that of the mother." *Id.* at 801. Finally, the Court wrote: "In the opinion of this Court, any parent that would denigrate the other by casting the false aspersion of child sex abuse and involving the child as an instrument to achieve his or her selfish purpose is not fit to continue in the role of a parent." *Id.* at 801. Judge Jung did not "rely on PAS theory" as Wood claims, but used Gardner's PAS heuristic as a means of describing the case specific evidence that he had heard.

56. *In the Matter of Karen "PP", Appellant, v. Clyde "QQ",1 Respondent.*, 197 A.D.2d 753; 602 N.Y.S.2d 709 (1993).
57. *Loyola of Los Angeles Law Review, 27,* 1367 at 1368. Curiously, the thesis that PAS should not be admissible in court resurfaced in another law student essay in 2001. Zirogiannis L. (2001). Evidentiary issues with parental alienation syndrome. *Family Court Review, 39,* 334 at 339. Zirogiannis reiterated the false claim that Gardner's work was not peer reviewed. He also misportrayed PAS as "a predictive syndrome," rather than as a "descriptive syndrome." Zirogiannis's advocacy agenda is revealed in his statement that, "One mental health syndrome, which will pass the *Frye* general-acceptance standard and qualify as social science expert testimony, is the Child Sexual Abuse Accommodation Syndrome (CSAAS)" p. 338. This, despite the fact that there is absolutely no scientific support whatsoever for the CSAAS.
58. *Id.* at 1374–1375.
59. *Id.* at 1368.
60. *Id.* at 1368, footnote 7.
61. *Id.* At 1368.
62. *27, Loyola of Los Angeles Law Review,* 1367 at 1375 note 64. Citing to: Conte et al. (1991). Evaluating children's reports of sexual abuse: Results from a survey of professionals. *American Journal of Orthopsychiatry, 61,* 428, 434. For this particular article, Dr. Conte and his students mailed out questionnaires to other social workers who appear to have been friendly to their position that "children never lie about abuse," without including any independent authorities from psychiatry and psychology.
63. *Id.* at 1375.
64. *See e.g.,* Gardner, R. (1979). *Psychotherapy with Children of Divorce.* NY.: Jason Aronson; Gardner, R. (1982). *Family Evaluation in Child Custody Litigation,* Cresskill, NJ: Creative Therapeutics; Gardner, R. (1986). *The Psychotherapeutic Techniques of Richard A. Gardner.* Cresskill, NJ.: Creative Therapeutics; Gardner, R. (1989). *Family Evaluation in Child Custody, Mediation, Arbitration and Litigation.* Creskill, NJ: Creative Therapeutics.
65. *Loyola of Los Angeles Law Review, 27,* 1367 at 1379. This abbreviated sense of what one of the witnesses testified to served Ms. Wood's purpose well. Wood neglected to inform the reader that his honor, Judge Jung heard testimony from numerous expert witnesses, (two Ph.D's, two trained child sex abuse interviewers, the child's pediatrician, preschool teacher and others). The Court observed that the child dealt with at least eleven different professionals all of whom seemed to believe "Mandi's descriptions of sexual activity between herself and her father varied considerably depending upon" (whom) ". . . she was talking too. . . ." The Court observed that ". . . there was no credible testimony to suggest that the child was afraid of her father and in fact the testimony suggested a relaxed and warm relationship" *Id.* at 801. The Court also observed that it ". . . had the unique opportunity of observing the demeanor of all witnesses who appeared before it. . . ." and the Court concluded ". . . that the testimony of the father is more credible than that of the mother" *Id.* at 801. Finally, the Court specifically wrote: "In the opinion of this Court, any parent that would denigrate the other by casting the false aspersion of child sex abuse and involving the child as an instrument to achieve his or her selfish purpose is not fit to continue in the role of a parent." After hearing extensive evidence, the Court concluded that this psychiatrically dysfunctional mother was: "Like Medea, she is ready to sacrifice her child to accomplish her selfish goal" *Id.* at 801 *In the Matter of Karen B., Petitioner v. Clyde M., Respondent,* 151 Misc.2d 794; 574 N.Y.S. 2d 267 (1991).
66. *27, Loyola of Los Angeles Law Review,* 1367 at 1382. Again, in a serious disservice to readers, this cavalier sense of the truth, neglected to inform the reader that his honor, Judge Jung listened to scores of expert witnesses and used Gardner's P.A.S. heuristic as a method of describing the evidence that he'd heard. The Court used Gardner's template as a background to his own finding that the child's story had mother's syntactic characteristics; that the story varied with each of eleven different adults to whom it was recounted; that not even anatomically detailed dolls in the hands of one examiner led to a sense of abuse in this child and that: "*None* of the adults to whom Mandi made disclosures could conclude with *any* certainty that Mandi was describing one or more than one experience" *Id.* at 801 *emphasis added.* More to the point, when the psychiatrically dysfunctional mother was not present, the interviewing adults found the child and her father to have a "relaxed and warm relationship" *Id.* at 800. *In the Matter of Karen B., Petitioner v. Clyde M., Respondent,* 151 Misc.2d 794; 574 N.Y.S. 2d 267 (1991).
67. *27, Loyola of Los Angeles Law Review,* 1367 at 1382. Here, Ms. Wood specifically left out the many, many reasons the child's mother was chastised and that his honor immediately ordered his probation department to supervise the mother and reintegrate the child and mother as soon as therapeutically viable! And Wood knew she was leaving this important part out. As his

honor put it: "The Probation Department . . . is directed to formulate a program including, if necessary, psychological or psychiatric consultation and treatment for all members of the family. The Probation Department shall advise the Court in writing within thirty (30) days from the date of this Order. . ." *Id.* at 802. *In the Matter of Karen B., Petitioner v. Clyde M., Respondent,* 151 Misc.2d 794; 574 N.Y.S. 2d 267 (1991).

68. *Schutz v. Schutz,* 581 So.2d 1290 (Florida 1991).

69. Answering to a subpoena, Dr. Gardner watched videotape of Faller and her group coercing a three-year-old child with repeated leading questions and sexually explicit pictures and dolls. Gardner testified that the process Faller and her group carried out was among the worst he'd ever seen. Soon after this testimony, Faller began to attack Dr. Gardner in the social work literature. Faller and her "Faller Group" of child abuse validators have been sued numerous times. Each time she and her group are sued, her university employer spends thousands of dollars claiming that Faller and her group should not be sued no matter what they do to children. The claim is always: No matter *what* they do, they're "*immune*" from suit! According to the *Detroit Free Press,* the lawsuit in which Gardner testified, found Faller's university employer spending well over one and a half million dollars in defense costs to avoid a plaintiff who would have settled for one-tenth that amount. (*Champney v. Faller et al.* Washtenaw County [Ann Arbor] Michigan Case No. 95-4760CK) *See: Detroit Free Press* November 3rd & 4th, 1997 "Expert and her methods on trial" – http://www.freep.com/news/childrenfirst/qfaller3.htm *and* follow-up articles detailing the *Free Press's Freedom of Information Act* suit to discover the taxpayer dollars spend on Faller's defense.

See also: Michigan Daily November 4th, 1997 – "U Prof. faces trial on charges of improperly interviewing a child" http://www.pub.umich.edu/daily/1997/nov/11-04-97/news/news5.html. Faller's vitriol should not be underestimated: The journalism student who wrote this article dissolved into tears in the plaintiff's lawyer's office sobbing that Faller had telephoned and threatened her graduation from the University. In this case, the Court's own independent expert viewed the Faller Group in action and read transcripts of their interviews. This independent examiner described Faller and her group as engaging in "nonstandard approach to child interviewing" where they had a ". . . a strong preconception of what had happened. . ." and ". . . went about trying to elicit it with no orientation to alternatives: interviewer bias." Report: 11-3-97 p. 20. Faller's first hatchet job on Dr. Gardner was published in the stellar professional journal: *Child Maltreatment* edited by her "believe the children" and "children never lie" colleagues in A.P.S.A.C.: Faller, K.C. (1998). The Parental Alienation Syndrome, What Is It and What Data Support It? *Child Maltreatment, 3,* 100.

70. *27, Loyola of Los Angeles Law Review,* 1367 at note 54 & subsequently citing: Faller, K. (1991). Possible Explanations for Child Sexual Abuse Allegations in Divorce, 61 *Am. J. Orthopsychiatry* 86. *Please also see infra* concerning Faller's research acumen and typical practice methodology.

71. Daro, D., & Mitchel, L. (1990). Current trends in child abuse reporting and fatalities: The results of the 1989 annual 50 states survey. Washington, D.C.: National Commission for the Prevention of Child Abuse.

72. Flango, V. E. (1991). Can central registries improve substantiation rates in child abuse and neglect cases? *Child Abuse & Neglect, 15,* 403.

73. *27, Loyola of Los Angeles Law Review,* 1367 at 1402–1403. Again, Wood completely misrepresented what the Honorable David F. Jung of the Family Court actually did. Judge Jung immediately ordered his probation department to supervise the mother and reintegrate the child and mother as soon as therapeutically viable. As clearly written in the published opinion: "The Probation Department . . . is directed to formulate a program including, if necessary, psychological or psychiatric consultation and treatment for all members of the family. The Probation Department shall advise the Court in writing within thirty (30) days from the date of this Order. . ." *Id.* at 802. *In the Matter of Karen B., Petitioner v. Clyde M., Respondent,* 151 Misc.2d 794; 574 N.Y.S. 2d 267 (1991).

74. *Please see* introductory comments, *supra.* A fuller discussion of the complexities of behavioral sciences in the *Daubert* era can be found in Campbell, T.W. and Lorandos, D. (2001). *Cross Examining Experts In The Behavioral Sciences.* Eagan, Minnesota, West Group, Two Volumes; *also see:* Lorandos, D. and Campbell, T.W. *Benchbook In The Behavioral Sciences: Psychiatry – Psychology – Social Work.* Durham, North Carolina: Carolina Academic Press.

75. *Please see* introductory comments, *supra* citing to: Kovera, M.B. and McAuliff, B.D. (2000). The Effects of Peer Review and Evidence Quality on Judge Evaluations of Psychological Science: Are Judges Effective Gatekeepers? 85 *Journal of Applied Psychology* 574; and Gatowski, S. I.; Dobbin, S.A.; Richardson, J.T.; Ginsburg, G.P.; Merlino, M.L. & Dahir, V. (2001). Asking the Gatekeepers: A National Survey of Judges on Judging Expert Evidence in a Post-*Daubert* World. 24, *Law and Human Behavior* 433.

76. A review of cases and law reviews finds Ms. Wood's student paper cited *without* any critical analysis in *Hanson v. Spolnik,* 605 NE 2d 71 (Indiana App 1997); *J.F. v. L.F.,* 181 Misc. 2d 722; 694 NYS2d 592 (1999) and *People v. Fortin,* 184 Misc. 2d 10; 706 NYS2d 611 (2000). *and* in Levit, N. (1994). Annotated Torts Bibliography 12 *Journal of the American Academy of Matrimonial Lawyers* 415; Feinberg, J. M. (1994). Custody And Visitation Interference: Alternative Remedies, 12 *Journal of the American Academy of Matrimonial Lawyers* 271;

Behnke, J. (1995). *Comment* Pawns Or People? Protecting The Best Interests Of Children In Interstate Custody Disputes, *28, Loyola of Los Angeles Law Review* 699; Lazo, J. (1995). *Comment* True Or False: Expert Testimony On Repressed Memory, *28, Loyola of Los Angeles Law Review* 1345; Scott, E. S. (1995). Parents As Fiduciaries *81, Virginia Law Review* 2401; Becker, S. (1996). Child Sexual Abuse Allegations Against A Lesbian Or Gay Parent In A Custody Or Visitation Dispute: Battling The Overt And Insidious Bias Of Experts And Judges *74, Denver University Law Review*; Elrod, L. (1996). Annual Survey Of Periodical Literature, 29 *Family Law Quarterly* 877; West's Legal News (1996). "Parental Alienation Syndrome" Alleged In Texas Custody Case, 2–2–96 WLN 595; Borris, E. (1997). Interference With Parental Rights Of Noncustodial Parent As Grounds For Modification Of Child Custody, 8 No. 1 *Divorce Litigation 1*; Walsh, M. & Bone, J.M. (1997). *Column* Parental Alienation Syndrome: An Age-Old Custody Problem, 71-JUN *Forida Bar Journal* 93; Smith, R. (1997). Fairness And Accuracy In Evaluations Of Domestic Violence And Child Abuse In Custody Determinations 36 No. 4 *Judges' Journal 38*; McKeon; M. (1998). The Impact Of Domestic Violence On Child Custody Determination In California: Who Will Understand? 19, *Whittier Law Review* 459; Niggemyer, K. (1998). *Comment* Parental Alienation Is Open Heart Surgery: It Needs More Than A Band-Aid To Fix It, 34, *California Western Law Review* 567; McGlynn, L. (2001). *Comment* Parent And Child – Custody And Control Of Child: Parental Alienation: Trash Talking The Non-Custodial Parent Is Not Okay *Hendrickson V. Hendrickson*, 77, *North Dakota Law Review* 525; Elrod, L. (2001). Reforming The System To Protect Children In High Conflict Custody Cases, 28, *William M. Mitchell Law Review* 495; Salinger, P. (2001). True Or False Accusations?: Protecting Victims Of Child Sexual Abuse During Custody Disputes, 32 *McGeorge Law Review* 693; Bruch, C. (2001). Parental Alienation Syndrome and Parental Alienation: Getting it Wrong in Child Custody Cases, 35, *Family Law Quarterly* 527. *Please see* the following pages, for a discussion of this most recent effort.

77. Huber, P. (1993). *Galileo's Revenge: Junk Science in the Courtroom*, New York: Basic Books. *And see:* Begley, S. (1993). *The Meaning of Junk Science, Newsweek*, Mar. 22, 1993, at 64. – Faigman, D. L. (1989). *To Have and Have Not: Assessing the Value of Social Science to the Law as Science and Policy, 38, Emory Law Journal* 1005. – Lorandos, D. (1995). Finding the Right Expert, In: *Expert Witnesses: Beyond Junk Science and Daubert.* Institute of Continuing Legal Education, Ann Arbor, Michigan; Campbell T.W. & Lorandos, D. (2001). *Cross Examining Experts in the Behavioral Sciences.* Egan, Minnesota, West Group – Two volumes.
78. *Daubert v. Merrell Dow Pharmaceuticals Inc.*, 509 U.S. 579, 113 S.Ct. 2786, 125 L Ed 2d 469, (1993).: *Trial Court* must be the gatekeeper who must make a preliminary assessment as to whether the reasoning and methodology proffered are scientifically valid. 509 U.S. 579, 113 S.Ct. at 2796, 125 L Ed 2d at 482.
79. According to the *Daubert* Court, the Trial Court must ensure that proffered testimony is relevant and reliable with a focus solely on principles and methodology. 509 U.S. 579, 113 S.Ct. at 2797. – Evidentiary Admissibility shall be based upon reliability determined by the degree of scientific validity. 509 U.S. 579, 113 S.Ct. at 2795. – Experts must be grounded in the methods and procedures of science. 509 U.S. 579, 113 S.Ct. at 2795.
80. The *Daubert* Court explicitly instructed that "*This entails a preliminary assessment* of whether the reasoning or methodology underlying the testimony is *scientifically valid* and of whether that reasoning or methodology properly can be applied to the facts in issue" *Id.* 509 U.S. 579, 113 S.Ct. at 2796. Grounding its admissibility analysis in the principles and methodology of science, the Court noted: "that scientists typically distinguish between 'validity' (does the principle support what it purports to show?) and 'reliability' (does application of the principle produce consistent results?) . . . our reference here is to *evidentiary* reliability – that is, trustworthiness. . . . In a case involving scientific evidence, *evidentiary reliability* will be based upon *scientific validity*." *Daubert* 509 U.S. 579, 113 S.Ct. at 2795 n. 9, *emphasis in original.*
81. As discussed above, as most allegations of child sexual abuse cannot be substantiated, considerations of *base rate* alone find Gardner's position to be clearly correct. When one considers the highly charged atmosphere found among parents *post*filing of petitions for exclusive parenting, it is merely silly to suggest that somehow allegations during this difficult time are more accurate. *Base rate* in the behavioral sciences refers to essentially the *prevalence* of a phenomena in a population. For more information on this concept and its impact upon the reliability and validity of assessments in the behavioral sciences, *please see*: Dawes, R. (1988). *Rational Choice in an Uncertain World*, New York: Harcourt Brace; Dawes, R. (1992). The importance of alternative hypothesis and hypothetical counterfactuals in general social science. *2 General Psychologist*; Lorandos, D. & Campbell, T. (1995). Myths & Realities of Sexual Abuse Evaluation, and Diagnosis: A Call for Judicial Guidelines, 4 *Issues in Child Abuse Accusations* 1; Lorandos, D. (1995). Finding the Right Expert, In: *Expert Witnesses: Beyond Junk Science and Daubert.* Institute of Continuing Legal Education, Ann Arbor, Michigan. Campbell T.W. & Lorandos, D. (2001). *Cross Examining Experts in the Behavioral Sciences.* Egan, Minnesota, West Group Two volumes.
82. Faller, K. and DeVoe, E. (1995). Allegations of sexual abuse in divorce. 4 *Journal of Child Sexual Abuse* 5, p. 21.
83. *See e.g.*: Poole, D. & White, L. (1991). Effects of questions repetition on the eyewitness testimony of children

and adults. 27 *Developmental Psychology* 975; Goodman, G. S., & Clarke-Stewart, A. (1991). Suggestibility in children's testimony: Implications for child sexual abuse investigations. In J. L. Doris (Eds.), *The suggestibility of children's recollections*. pp. 92–105. Washington DC: American Psychological Association; Wakefield, H., & Underwager, R. (1991). Sexual allegations in divorce and custody disputes, 9, *Behavioral Sciences and the Law* 451; Dawes, R. (1992). The importance of alternative hypothesis and hypothetical counterfactuals in general social science. *General Psychologist.* 2; Ceci, S. J., Loftus, E. F., Leichtman, M., & Bruck, M. (1994). The role of source misattributions in the creation of false beliefs among preschoolers. 62 *International Journal of Clinical and Experimental Hypnosis*, 62, 304; Lepore, S. J., & Sesco, B. (1994). Distorting children's reports and interpretations of events through suggestion. 79 *Applied Psychology* 108; Lorandos, D. & Campbell, T. (1995). Myths and Realities of Sexual Abuse Evaluation and Diagnosis: A Call for Judicial Guidelines 7 *Issues in Child Abuse Accusations* 1; Poole, D & Lindsay, D. (1995). Interviewing preschoolers: Effect of nonsuggestive techniques, parental coaching, and leading questions on reports of nonexperienced events. 60 *Journal of Experimental Child Psychology* 129; Ceci, S. J., Leichtman, M., & White, T. (2001). Interviewing preschoolers: Remembrance of things planted. In D. P. Peters (Ed.), *The child witness in context: Cognitive, social, and legal perspectives.* The Netherlands: Kluwer. *And see:* Ceci, S. & Bruck, M. (1995). *Jeopardy in the Courtroom: A Scientific Analysis of Children's Testimony.* Washington, D.C. American Psychological Press; Ceci, S. & Hembrooke, H. (Eds.) (1998). *Expert Witnesses in Child Abuse Cases.* Washington, D.C.: American Psychological Press; Campbell, T. W., (1998). *Smoke and Mirrors: The Devastating Effect of False Sexual Abuse Claims.* New York: Plenum Press; Poole, D. & Lamb, M. (1999). *Investigative Interviews of Children: A Guide for Helping Professionals.* Washington, D.C.: American Psychological Press.

84. Gardner, R. (1987). *The Parental Alienation Syndrome and the Differentiation Between Fabricated and Genuine Child Sex Abuse.* Cresskill, NJ.: Creative Threapeutics.
85. Faller, K. (2000). Child Maltreatment and Endangerment in the Context of Divorce, 22, *University of Arkansas at Little Rock Law Review* 429, 432.
86. *Id.* at 269.
87. *Bielaska v. Orley*, Michigan Court of Appeals Docket Nos. 173666; 174949; 175287 and 175388; *Champney v. Champney* Jackson County, Michigan Case No. 92-062071-DM; *Recchia v. Recchia* Macomb County, Michigan Case No. 89-5210-DM. The author represented the father in each of these cases.
88. *Bielaska v. Orley*, Michigan Court of Appeals Docket Nos. 173666; 174949; 175287 and 175388 at 31. Slip Opinion July 19th, 1996. Former Chief Justice Thomas G. Kavanagh; Court of Appeals Judge Helene White and Oakland County, Michigan, trial court Judge Stephen N. Andrews. Available online from the Michigan Court of Appeals. http://courtofappeals.mijud.net/documents/OPINIONS/FINAL/COA/19960719_C173666(0065)_173666.OPN.PDF. Hereinafter referred to as *Bielaska.*
89. *Id.* at 37.
90. *Id.* at 22 *emphasis added.*
91. Patricia Wallace, Ph.D. was the trial court's hand-picked independent evaluator. She is a licensed clinical psychologist, a certified forensic psychologist and the former chief psychologist of the Detroit Recorder's Court forensic services. Terence Campbell, Ph.D. is a licensed clinical psychologist, former chief psychologist of the Macomb County Circuit Court's *Psycho-Diagnostic Clinic*, the author of numerous studies in this field and literally, the author of the standard of care in these matters: *Fletcher v. Fletcher*, 447 Mich 871, 901 note 4; 526 NW2d 998 (1994).
92. *Id.* at 22 *emphasis added.*
93. *Id.* at 23.
94. *Id.* at 24 *emphasis added.*
95. *Id.* at 25.
96. *Id.* at 25 *emphasis added.*
97. *Id.*
98. *Id. emphasis added.*
99. *Id.* at 34 *emphasis added.*
100. *Champney v. Champney* Jackson County, Michigan Case No. 92-062071-DM.
101. *Champney v. Faller et al.* Washtenaw County (Ann Arbor), Michigan Case No. 95-4760CK, Report of Court's Expert, November 3, 1997, p. 20.
102. *Id.*
103. *Recchia v. Recchia* Macomb County, Michigan Case No. 89-5210-DM. The doctor is a psychologist and law school graduate. She has lectured widely on the proper methodology for custody, PAS and sexual abuse evaluations. *See e.g.*: Blush, G.L., and Ross, K.L. (1987). Sexual allegations in divorce: The SAID syndrome. 25 *Conciliation Courts Review* 45.
104. *Id.*
105. *Recchia v Recchia* Macomb County, Michigan Case No. 89-5210-DM. Exhibit: Kathleen C. Faller 11-21-95 Psychosocial Evaluation p. 3.
106. *Recchia v. Recchia* Macomb County, Michigan Case No. 89-5210-DM. Psychodiagnostic Clinic Report p. 26.
107. *Id.* at 31.
108. *Champney v. Faller et al.* Washtenaw County (Ann Arbor), Michigan Case No. 95-4760CK, Report of Court's Expert, November 3, 1997.
109. Faller, K.C. (2000). Child maltreatment and endangerment in the context of divorce, 22, *University of Arkansas Little Rock, Law Review* 429.
110. Bricklin, B. and Elliot, G. (2000). Qualifications of and techniques to be used by judges, attorneys, and mental health professionals who deal with children in high-conflict divorce cases. 22, *University of Arkansas Little*

Rock Law Review 501. Drs. Bricklin and Elliot cite to many research papers providing empirical support for the concepts inculcated by Gardner. In fact, they opine: "Since manipulation and/or parental alienation patterns are so frequently encountered in high-conflict cases, it is imperative that professionals be aware of some of the diagnostic tools and procedures without which these patterns may escape detection. . . . We are especially concerned about recent articles and "shop-talk" among professionals which are dismissive of Gardner's contributions. *Try as we might, we cannot understand this negative commentary*" (p. 517 *emphasis added*).

111. Following Bruch's 2001 article, *Family Law Quarterly* featured a rebuttal by Warshak, R. (2003). Bringing sense to parental alienation: A look at the disputes and the evidence. 37, *Family Law Quarterly* 273. A modified version of Warshak's critique can be found in this handbook.
112. Bruch, C. (2001). Parental Alienation Syndrome and Parental Alienation: Getting it wrong in child custody cases. 35, *Family Law Quarterly* 527, pp. 527–528.
113. Gardner, R. (1985). Recent trends in divorce and custody litigation. 29 *Academy Forum* 3.
114. *Id.* at 5, *emphasis added.*
115. *Id.*
116. Bruch (2001). p. 528.
117. Clawar, S. and Rivlin, B. (1991). *Children Held Hostage: Dealing with Programmed and Brainwashed Children.* Chicago: American Bar Association.
118. Bruch (2001). p. 528, footnote 3.
119. Ceci, S. and Bruck, M. (1995). *Jeopardy in the Courtroom: A Scientific Analysis of Children's Testimony.* Washington, D.C.: American Psychological Press, p. 32.
120. Bruch (2001). p. 528, footnote 3.
121. Ceci, S. and Bruck, M. (1995). *Jeopardy in the Courtroom: A Scientific Analysis of Children's Testimony.* Washington, D.C.: American Psychological Press, pp. 30–34.
122. Bruch (2001). pp. 529–530, footnote 9.
123. *Id.* p. 530.
124. *Id.*
125. Gardner, R. (1998). *The Parental Alienation Syndrome Second Edition.* Cresskill, NJ.: Creative Therapeutics, p. 309.
126. *Id.* p. 355.
127. *Diagnostic and Statistical Manual of Mental Disorders, Fourth Edition (DSM-IV)* (1994). Washington, D.C.: American Psychiatric Association. In the DSM-IV, *folie à deux* is referred to as Shared Psychotic Disorder, while earlier editions of the manual used names such as Shared Delusional Disorder or Shared Paranoid Disorder. The different names given to *folie à deux* have created confusion about what it actually means. When described as "shared psychotic disorder," people tend to assume that *folie à deux* must involve bizarre behavior and hallucinations. When *folie à deux* is referred to as "Shared Delusional Disorder," it is often assumed that the false fixed beliefs which two people share must be psychotic or bizarre in order to qualify as "delusions." The psychiatric glossary defines "delusions" simply as false beliefs based on an incorrect inference about external reality which are firmly sustained despite clear evidence to the contrary. Thus, it is the fixed nature of the false beliefs which make them delusions, not their bizarreness. Similarly, the defining feature of psychosis is the gross impairment in reality testing, which may take the form of bizarre *or* nonbizarre delusions.
128. Gardner, R. (1998). *The Parental Alienation Syndrome, Second Edition.* Cresskill, NJ.: Creative Therapeutics, Inc., p. 309.
129. Bruch (2001). p. 531.
130. Gardner, R. (1987). *The Parental Alienation Syndrome and the Differentiation Between Fabricated and Genuine Child Sex Abuse.* Cresskill, NJ: Creative Therapeutics; Gardner, R. (1992). *True and False Accusations of Sex Abuse.* Cresskill, NJ.: Creative Therapeutics.
131. The studies reviewed by Ceci and Bruck (1995). represent only a small portion of the literature on false allegations of abuse. Literature on child custody cases in the mid 1980s indicated that false allegations of sex abuse were becoming a serious problem. *See e.g.* Benedek, E.P. and Schetky, D.H. (1985). Allegations of sexual abuse in child custody and visitation disputes. In D.H. Schetky and E.P. Benedek (Eds.), *Emerging issues in child psychiatry and the law* (pp. 145–156). New York: Brunner/Mazel; Green, A.H. (1986). True and false allegations of sexual abuse in child custody disputes. 25 *Journal of the American Academy of Child & Adolescent Psychiatry*, 449; Blush, G.L., and Ross, K.L. (1987). Sexual allegations in divorce: The SAID syndrome. 25 *Conciliation Courts Review*, 45, etc. The literature on false allegations continued to burgeon in the 1990s. *See e.g.*, Wakefield, H. and Underwager, R. (1990). Personality characteristics of parents making false accusations of sexual abuse in custody disputes. 2 *Issues in Child Abuse Accusations* 121; Elterman, M.F., and Ehrenberg, M.F. (1991). Sexual abuse allegations in child custody disputes. 14 *International Journal of Law & Psychiatry*, 269; Campbell, T.W. (1992). False allegations of sexual abuse and their apparent credibility. 10 *American Journal of Forensic Psychology* 21; Horner, T., Guyer, M., and Kalter, N. (1993). Clinical expertise and the assessment of child sexual abuse 32 *Journal of American Academy of Child and Adolescent Psychiatry*, 925; Loftus, E. and Ketcham, E. (1994). *The Myth of Repressed Memory: False Memories and Allegations of Child Sexual Abuse.* New York: St. Martin's Press.
132. Bruch (2001). p. 531.
133. *Id.* p. 532.
134. *Id.* p. 532, note 17.
135. Gardner, R. (1992). *True and False Accusations of Sex Abuse.* Cresskill, NJ.: Creative Therapeutics, p. 136.
136. Bruch (2001). pp. 532–533, *emphasis added.*

137. Johnston, J. (1993). Children who refuse visitation non-residential parenting: New vistas in family living. In Charlene Depner and James Bray, eds., Newbury Park, California: Sage Publications.
138. Bruch (2001) p. 533, footnote 20, "less troubled population" *emphasis added*, "every case" *emphasis in original*.
139. Johnston, J. (1993). Children who refuse visitation. Nonresidential Parenting: New vistas in family living. In Charlene Depner and James Bray, eds., Newbury Park, CA: Sage Publications, pp.123–124, *emphasis added.*
140. Wallerstein, J. and Blakeslee, S. (1989). *Second Chances: Men, Women and Children a Decade After Divorce.* Boston: Houghton Mifflin Company, pp. 195–196, *emphasis added.*
141. Gardner's concerns about the effects on children of PAS and the unnecessary loss of a parent are supported by years of scholarship into family dysfunction and divorce, only a small portion of which are listed here: Rutter, M. (1971). Parent-child separation: Psychological effects on the children. 12 *Journal of Child Psychology and Psychiatry*, 233; Sorosky, A. (1977). The psychological effects of divorce on adolescents. 12 *Adolescence*, 123; Santrock, J. and Warshak, R. (1979). Father custody and social development in boys and girls. 35 *Journal of Social Issues*, 112 ; Nelson, G. (1981). Moderators of women's and children's adjustment following parental divorce. 4 *Journal of Divorce*, 71; Hetherington, E.M. et al. (1982). Effects of divorce on parents and children, in Non-Traditional Families. 233, Michael E. Lamb (ed.); Pett, M. (1982). Correlates of children's social adjustment following divorce. 5 *Journal of Divorce*, 25; Stolberg, A. and Anker, J. (1983). Cognitive and behavioral changes in children resulting from parental divorce and consequent environmental changes. 6 *Journal of Divorce* 23; Stolberg A.L. and Bush J.P. (1985). A path analysis of factors predicting children's divorce adjustment. 14 *Journal of Clinical Child Psychology* 49; Warshak, R.A. (1986). Father custody and child development: A review and analysis of the psychological research. 4 *Behavioral Sciences and the Law* 185; Felner, R. and Terre, L. (1987). Child custody dispositions and children's adaptation following divorce. In L. Weithorn (ed.), *Psychology and child custody determinations: Knowledge, roles, and expertise.* Lincoln, NE.: University of Nebraska Press; Walsh, P.E. &. Stolberg, A.L (1989). Parental and environmental determinants of children's behavioral, affective and cognitive adjustment to divorce. 12 *Journal of Divorce* 265; Fauber, Robert et al. (1990). A mediational model of the impact of marital conflict on adolescent adjustment in intact and divorced families: The role of disrupted parenting. 61 *Child Development*, 1112; Tschann, J.M. et al. (1990). Conflict, loss, change and parent-child relationships: Predicting children's adjustment during divorce. 13 *Journal of Divorce*, 1; Borrine, Lisa et al. (1991). Family conflict and adolescent adjustment in intact, divorced, and blended families. 59 *Journal of Consulting and Clinical Psychology* 753; Brown, Joseph H. et al. (1991). Family functioning factors associated with the adjustment of children of divorce. 17 *Journal of Divorce and Remarriage* 81; Shaw, Daniel S. et al. (1993). Parental functioning and children's adjustment in families of divorce: A prospective study, 21 *Journal of Abnormal Child Psychology*, 119; Ward, P. and Harvey, J. (1993). Family wars: The alienation of children. 34 *The New Hampshire Bar Journal* 30; Dunne, J. and Hedrick, M. (1994). The Parental Alienation Syndrome: An analysis of sixteen selected cases. 21 *Journal of Divorce and Remarriage* 21; Lampel, A. (1996). Children's alignment with parents in highly conflicted custody cases. 34 *Family & Conciliation Courts Review* 229; Hetherington, E.M., Bridges, M., and Insabella, G.M. (1998). What matters? What does not?: Five perspectives on the association between marital transitions and children's adjustment. 53 *American Psychologist* 167.
142. Bruch (2001). p. 548.
143. A review of studies relating to interventions in severe PAS can be found in Rand, D., Rand, R., and Kopetski, L. (2005). The Spectrum of Parental Alienation Syndrome Part III: The Kopetski Follow-Up Study. 23 *American Journal of Forensic Psychology* 15.
144. Johnston, J. (1993). Children who refuse visitation. In *Nonresidential Parenting: New Vistas in Family Living.* Charlene Depner and James Bray (eds.), Newbury Park, CA: Sage Publications, p. 132.
145. Bruch (2001). p. 543.
146. Gardner, R. (1998). *The Parental Alienation Syndrome, Second Edition.* Cresskill, NJ: Creative Therapeutics, p. 357, *emphasis in the original.*
147. Bruch (2001). p. 533.
148. Bruch (2001). p. 533, footnote 22. Keating, G. (2000, April 23). Disputed theory used in custody cases: Children often victims in Parental Alienation Syndrome strategy. *Pasadena Star - News*; Winner, K. (2000). Placing Children at Risk: Questionnable Psychologists and Therapists in the Sacramento Family Court and Surrounding Counties. *Study Commissioned by California Protective Parents Association.*
149. Winner, K. (1996). *Divorced from Justice: The Abuse of Women and Children by Divorce Lawyers and Judges.* New York: Regan Books.
150. From: http://www.divorcedfromjustice.com/home.html. May 31, 2002.
151. Wood, Faller, and Bruch do not define what is meant by "empirical" when they assert "no empirical evidence" supports Gardner's formulation, or what is meant by "science" and the "scientific method" when they claim that Gardner's work "lacks scientific foundation and scientific rigor."
152. Empiricism describes a search for knowledge based on what can be observed or perceived. *See e.g.*: Lorandos, D. and Campbell, T.W. (2005). *Benchbook in the Behavioral Sciences – Psychiatry – Psychology – Social Work.*

Durham, NC: Carolina Academic Press. Chapter Three provides a detailed history of the principles and methodology of the behavioral sciences.

153. Denzin, N.H. and Lincoln, Y.S. (eds.) (2000). *Handbook of qualitative research* (2nd ed.). Thousand Oaks, CA: Sage; Berg, B.L. (2001). *Qualitative Research Methods for theSsocial Sciences* (4th ed.). Needham Heights, MA.: Allyn & Bacon; Shadish, W.K., Cook, T.D., and Campbell, D.T. (2002). *Experimental and Quasi-Experimental Designs for Generalized Causal Inference.* Boston: Houghton Mifflin; and Kazdin, A.E. (2003). *Research Design in Clinical Psychology, 4th Edition.* Boston: Allyn & Bacon.
154. Kazdin, A.E. (2003). *Research Design in Clinical Psychology, 4th Edition,* Boston: Allyn & Bacon.
155. Light, R. and Pillemer, D. (1984). *Summing Up: The Science of Reviewing Research.* Cambridge, MA: Harvard University Press.
156. Schuck, P.H. (1993). Multi-culturalism redux: Science, law and politics. 11 *Yale Law & Policy Review* 1, 16.
157. Gilbert, N. (1993). Research, theory and method. Gilbert, N. (ed.), In *Researching Social Life,* London: Sage Publications, p. 21.
158. O'Brien, M. (1993). Social Research and Sociology. Gilbert, N. (ed.), In *Researching Social Life,* London: Sage Publications, p. 11.
159. Gardner, R. (1985). Recent trends in divorce and custody litigation. 29 *Academy Forum* 3.
160. Kelly, J. and Johnston, J. (2001). The alienated child: A reformulation of parental alienation syndrome. 39 *Family Court Review: An Interdisciplinary Journal,* p. 249.
161. Gardner, R. (1989). *Family Evaluation in Child Custody, Mediation, Arbitration and Litigation,* Cresskill, NJ: Creative Therapeutics.
162. Gardner, R. (1998). *The Parental Alienation Syndrome, Second Edition.* Cresskill, NJ: Creative Therapeutics, p. 355.
163. Johnston, J. and Roseby, V. (1997). *In the Name of the Child.* New York: The Free Press, p. 198. It is interesting to note that these authors utilize what they term "qualitative data," p. 28.
164. Gilbert, N. (1993). Research, Theory and Method. Gilbert, N. (ed.). In *Researching Social Life.* London: Sage Publications, p. 11, *emphasis added.*
165. Light, R. and Pillemer, D. (1984). *Summing Up: The Science of Reviewing Research.* Cambridge, MA.: Harvard University Press, p. 115, *emphasis added.*
166. Gilbert, N. (1993). Research, Theory and Method. Gilbert, N. (Ed.). In *Researching Social Life.* London: Sage Publications, p. 24.
167. Gardner, R. (1985). Recent trends in divorce and custody litigation. 29 *Academy Forum* 3.
168. Gardner, R. (1998). *The Parental Alienation Syndrome, Second Edition.* Cresskill, NJ: Creative Therapeutics.
169. *Id.* at p. xxix.
170. Bright, Timothy (1586). *A Treatise of Melancholia.* England.
171. Burton, Robert (1621). *The Anatomy of Melancholy.* England.
172. Plater, F. (1602–1614). *Practice of Medicine, Observations of Diseases Injurious to Body and Mind.* Switzerland.
173. Cullen, William (1710–1790). *Nosology or a Systematic Arrangement of Diseases.* (1800). Scotland.
174. Pinel, Philippe (1801). *A treatise on insanity, in which are contained the principles of a new and more practical nosology of mental disorders,* Pinel's treatment was termed "the moral treatment of insanity."
175. Rush, Benjamin (1812). *Medical Inquiries and Observations upon the Diseases of the Mind.* United States.
176. Adams, Joseph (1814). *A Treatise on the supposed hereditary properties of diseases particularly in madness and scrofula.* England.
177. Heinroth, Johann Christian (1818). *Disturbances of the Mind.* Germany.
178. Prichard, James Cowles (1835). *A Treatise on Insanity and Other Disorders Affecting the Mind.* England.
179. Esquirol, Jean Etienne Dominique (1838). *Des maladies mentales considerees souls les rapports medicals hygieniques et medicolegals.* France.
180. Ray, Issac (1838). *Treatise on Medical Jurisprudence of Insanity.* United States.
181. Kraepelin, Emil (1927). *Textbook of Psychiatry* (9th ed.) Barth Verlag, Leipzig.
182. Alzheimer, Alois (1882). Ueber einen Fall von spinaler progressiver Muskelatrophie mit hinzutretender Erkrankung bulbärer Kerne in der Rinde. *Sonder-Abdruck aus dem Archiv für Psychiatrie.* Bd. XXIII. Heft 2.
183. Warshak, R. (2001). Current controversies regarding parental alienation syndrome. 19 *American College of Forensic Psychology* 29; Gardner, R. (2002). Parental Alienation Syndrome vs. Parental Alienation: Which diagnosis should evaluators use in child custody litigation? 30 *American College of Forensic Psychology* 101.
184. *See e.g.*: Lorandos, D. and Campbell, T.W. (2005). *Benchbook in the Behavioral Sciences – Psychiatry – Psychology – Social Work.* Durham, NC.: Carolina Academic Press. Chapter Three provides a detailed history of the principles and methodology of the behavioral sciences.
185. Gardner, R. (2001). Should courts order PAS children to visit/reside with the alienated parent? A follow-up study. 19 *American Journal of Forensic Psychology* 61.
186. Kovera, M.B. and McAuliff, B.D. (2000). The effects of peer review and evidence quality on judge evaluations of psychological science: Are judges effective gatekeepers? 85 *Journal of Applied Psychology* 574; Gatowski, S., Dobbin, S., Richardson, J., Ginsburg, G., Merlino, M. and Dahir, V. (2001). Asking the gatekeepers: A national survey of judges on judging expert evidence in a post-*Daubert* world. 24, *Law and Human Behavior* 433.
187. *Zigmont fka Toto v. Toto, 1992 WL 6034 (Ohio App. 8th District)* Docket No. 62149; *Kirk v. Kirk,* 759 N E 2d 265 (Indiana App, December, 2001) and 770 N.E. 2d 304 (June 21, 2002); and Lorandos, D. (2005). The Parental Alienation Syndrome in American Law, in this handbook.

188. *Daubert v. Merrell Dow Pharmaceuticals Inc.*, 509 U.S. 579, 113 S.Ct. 2786, at 2797 (1993).; *Kumho Tire Company, Ltd. v. Carmichael*, 526 U.S. 137; 119 S.Ct. 1167 (1999).
189. Kovera, M.B., Levy, R.J., Borgida, E. and Penrod, S.D. (1994). Expert testimony in child sexual abuse cases: Effects of expert evidence type and cross-examination. 18, *Law and Human Behavior* 653.
190. Cutler, B.L. and Penrod, S.D. (1995). *Mistaken identification: The Eyewitness, Psychology, and the Law.* New York: Cambridge University Press.
191. Gatowski, S.I.; Dobbin, S.A.; Richardson, J.T.; Ginsburg, G.P.; Merlino, M.L. and Dahir, V. (2001). Asking the gatekeepers: A national survey of judges on judging expert evidence in a post-*Daubert* world. 24, *Law and Human Behavior* 433, at pp. 454–455.
192. *Id.* p. 455. *See, also:* Richardson, J.T.; Ginsburg, G.P.; Gatowski, S.I. and Dobbin, S.A. (1995). The problem of applying *Daubert* to psychological syndrome evidence. 79 *Judicature* 10; Saks, M.J. (2000). The aftermath of *Daubert*: An evolving jurisprudence of expert evidence. 40 *Jurimetrics*, 229.
193. Lehman, D.R., Lempert, R.O. and Nisbett, R.E. (1988). The effects of graduate training on reasoning: Formal discipline and thinking about everyday life events. 43 *American Psychologist*, 431.
194. Fong, G.T., Krantz, D.H. and Nisbett, R.E. (1986). The effects of statistical training on thinking about everyday problems. 18 *Cognitive Psychology* 253.
195. Gatowski, S.I.; Dobbin, S.A.; Richardson, J.T.; Ginsburg, G.P.; Merlino, M.L. and Dahir, V. (2001). Asking the gatekeepers: A national survey of judges on judging expert evidence in a post-*Daubert* World. 24 *Law and Human Behavior* 433.

Chapter 32

PROTECTING THE FUNDAMENTAL RIGHTS OF CHILDREN AND FAMILIES: PARENTAL ALIENATION SYNDROME AND FAMILY LAW REFORM

R. CHRISTOPHER BARDEN

OVERVIEW

The legal, mental health and scientific communities share a sacred obligation to prevent children from becoming pawns in custody litigation. Protecting fundamental parental rights while aggressively preventing, investigating, and punishing child abuse are essential goals for family law. Efforts to attain such goals must be based in fact rather than prejudice, science rather than hysteria, and reason rather than political ideology. Multidisciplinary analyses of parental alienation processes – including parental alienation syndrome (PAS) – demonstrate why the family law system so often fails to protect the fundamental rights of children and families. Parental influence on children is not a novel nor controversial concept. Decades of research in psychology, psychiatry, and related fields have documented the powerful ability of adults to shape the ideas, beliefs, statements, and even memories of children. Improper legal incentives and substandard legal practices often generate and maintain alienation processes resulting in severe injuries to families. Parental alienation is also exacerbated when courts accept junk science "expert" testimony.

Science (not clinical) experts are a mandatory component of competent and effective family law litigation teams. Reforming the family law system would greatly reduce the tragedy of PAS and related processes.

PARENTAL ALIENATION IS A SERIOUS PROBLEM IN THE FAMILY LAW SYSTEM

Civilization has struggled for centuries to create just, cost-effective and rational procedures in civil, business, and criminal law. In contrast, much of current divorce and child custody law has been hastily created over recent decades and remains in a young and often confused stage of development. As a result of defective and confused standards of care for family law legal professionals and widespread, unreliable "expert" testimony in child custody cases, the family law system often produces improper incentives with tragic results (Grove & Barden, 2000; Hagen, 1997; Dawes, 1997).

Protecting the fundamental rights of parents and children to unfettered family relationships should be the primary responsibility and essential goal of the family law system. Preventing the mistreatment of children is another primary responsibility and essential goal of the family law system. Family law professionals should strive to reduce the incidence of child abuse, assist victims of abuse, and punish those who harm children. Efforts to reach and balance these critical goals must be based in fact rather than prejudice, science rather than hysteria, and reason rather than political ideology. Children must be vigorously protected from all forms of abuse including physical abuse and neglect, sexual abuse, and emotional abuse – including mistreatment and harm caused by alienating parents, science-illiterate attorneys, poorly trained evaluators, and negligent physicians and psychotherapists (Barden, 1994; Barden, 2001a; Hagen, 1997; Dawes, 1997; Lilienfeld et al. 2003).

Legal processes that fail to properly balance the essential goals of family law may create or exacerbate familial problems – including the parental alienation syndrome (PAS) and related processes. PAS has generally been described as a process in which children's attitudes, beliefs, and memories are manipulated by a parent until such children actively dishonor, dislike, and/or fear a once-loved parent or other relative. In such cases, the parent and manipulated child engage in a campaign of denigration towards the targeted parent (American Psychological Association, 1994; Gardner, 1998; Gardner, 1985; Gardner, 1986; Gardner, 2003; Vassiliou & Cartwright, 2001; Warshak, 2001a; Wallerstein & Kelly, 1980, Cartwright, 1993). Surveys of high conflict families in custody proceedings indicate that PAS and related processes are distressingly common in high conflict custody cases (Clavar & Rivlin, 1991; Bone & Walsh, 1999).

In a larger sense, parental alienation behaviors go far beyond manipulating the attitudes of children. Analyses of PAS-related processes should also include all unethical attempts to harm, distress and/or imprison the targeted parent – even if such acts do not include efforts to manipulate the child's beliefs, attitudes, and memories. In addition, as the following analysis explains in detail, PAS and related processes often involve much more than the troubled behaviors of a single parent. Ignorance, misconduct, and negligence by local family law and affiliated professionals can be primary causes of the serious harms that result from PAS and related processes.

In practice, PAS and related alienation processes are often readily discernible to properly trained experts and judges. Such cases typically involve a series of quite predictable attempts to manipulate or control the legal process – and damage the targeted parent – by filing false criminal allegations of abuse, repeatedly failing to honor court orders regarding visitation, repeatedly failing to honor settlement agreements, attempting to manipulate witnesses (including and especially children), contaminating teachers' perceptions with biasing misinformation, hiring incompetent "therapists" to "validate" abuse claims, and/or other unethical actions. Such abusive acts are limited only by the creativity of the offending parent and the parent's advisors.

PAS and related alienation processes are best viewed as forms of emotional abuse (Gardner, 1998; Vassiliou & Cartwright, 2001; Warshak, 2001a; Wallerstein & Kelly, 1980). Unless halted by judicial action, PAS and related processes may pose a significant risk of psychological, social and financial injury to children and families. Failure to properly evaluate and deal with PAS and alienating behaviors often produces years of unnecessary litigation, oppressive expense and – far too often – the tragic destruction of once cherished family relationships.

PARENTAL ALIENATION SYNDROME AND RELATED PROCESSES: NOT NOVEL CONCEPTS

There is a good deal of confusion in some segments of the legal community regarding the term "parental alienation syndrome." PAS and related concepts have, in fact, been in widespread use for many years. Clearly, these are not new nor novel concepts (Gardner, 1986; American Psychological Association, 1994). More importantly, the basic, psychological processes underlying PAS have been well documented in the peer-reviewed professional literature over many decades. Reliable research on the processes underlying PAS has been published in the highest quality peer-reviewed journals. In sum, the theoretical foundations of PAS are, in fact, built upon some of the most reliable and best documented of all psychological processes – parental influences on children.

Academic and clinical researchers in the fields of developmental (child) psychology, social psychology, anthropology, clinical psychology and psychiatry have spent decades documenting the ways in which childrens' (and adults') memories, emotions, and attitudes can be changed by the influence of powerful others – especially authority figures (Ceci & Bruck, 1996; Ofshe & Watters, 1996; Cialdini, 1993; Mazzoni & Memon, 2003; Loftus, 1997; Bruck & Ceci, 1995; etc.). Currently, it is incontestable in the relevant scientific communities that parental influence processes are well understood and widely documented. The successful transmission of culture itself depends upon the ability of parents to instill beliefs, emotions, and memories in children.

There can be no credible controversy about the power of parents to influence children. It is unfortunate that in reviewing PAS-type issues, courts have often stumbled over the meaning of technical terms such as "syndrome," the inclusion of specific labels in official diagnostic manuals, and other largely irrelevant minutiae – thus missing the critical obligation to carefully review the influence of parents, therapists or other adults on the attitudes, beliefs and memories of children (Bruck & Ceci, 1995).

Although the underlying psychological mechanisms – parental influence processes – that cause and sustain PAS are well understood and documented, rigorous longitudinal research on the long-term consequences of PAS has not yet been completed. Fully understanding how to prevent and treat the long-term consequences of PAS and related processes will require rigorous scientific investigation by clinical, social science, and legal professionals. This research should be done at major university medical centers, university psychological programs, and similar settings by professional researchers. Such research should be published in the official journals of the leading professional associations in psychiatry, psychology, and related fields (the American Psychological Society, American Medical Association, American Psychological Association, and American Psychiatric Association) – not "trauma," "abuse," "therapy," or other politicized journals published by 'specialty clique' associations. Researchers in this field should guard themselves against the social, professional, and economic pressures and even personal attacks that may accompany such politically-charged research issues. The focus of this research should be on determining the ways in which parents may improve or harm parent-child relationships with ex-spouses and the long-term consequences of such actions. Given this information, courts will be better able to create behavioral contingencies to encourage and enforce kinder, more supportive, and more honorable interactions between ex-spouses.

Although academic psychologists are just now beginning to study the specific, long-term effects of PAS, the obvious harmful impacts of PAS and related processes on children and families have long been noted by observant judges and attorneys. In many jurisdictions, there is a long-standing tradition of awarding a change of custody where the custodial parent has improperly interfered with the fundamental parental rights of an ex-spouse (Borris, 1997).

Despite the strong scientific foundation documenting the underlying mechanisms of PAS and related alienation processes (e.g., parental influence processes), the almost total lack of basic scientific training among attorneys and mental health clinicians has resulted in some courts losing the forest (the well documented effects of parental influence on children) for the trees (details of defining a medical "syndrome" and other often irrelevant minutiae). Given the decades of reliable, hard science research documenting parental influences on children, courts need not wait for more specific research on PAS to act decisively when faced with evidence of willful and manipulative efforts to harm parent-child relationships. Legal and scientific communities share a sacred obligation to prevent children from becoming pawns in custody litigation.

In short, although much scientific work will be required to fully understand the long-term consequences of specific syndromes such as PAS, powerful parental alienation processes have been well documented over several decades by scientists and professionals in a number of relevant fields (American Psychological Association, 1994; Gardner, 1998; Gardner, 1985; Gardner, 1986; Gardner, 2003; Vassiliou & Cartwright, 2001; Warshak, 2001b; Wallerstein & Kelly, 1980, Cartwright, 1993; Clavar & Rivlin, 1991; Bone & Walsh, 1999).

DANGERS POSED BY IMPROPER, SUBSTANDARD AND INADEQUATE LEGAL PRACTICES

An important step towards preventing and/or terminating PAS and related processes is for family law professionals to cease and desist from practices that create or exacerbate unnecessary familial conflict. Such practices include failing to consistently and promptly sanction alienating parents for unethical behaviors such as: filing false abuse charges, perjury, coercing children into making false statements, submitting false information to evaluators, surreptitiously taking children to "therapists" known to "validate" abuse claims, and other hostile, alienating acts. When courts fail to appropriately sanction such serious misconduct it sends a clear message to the alienator that they may take "free shots" at the targeted parent without consequence. Often, such judicial indifference results in years of unproductive legal hearings that may: (1) bankrupt the family (while unjustly enriching the local family law system); (2) result in months of worthless "therapy" for nonexistent "emotional problems" (thus unjustly enriching family law affiliated mental health professionals); and (3) result in numerous unnecessary custody evaluations, often including junk science assessment methodology (thus unjustly enriching these affiliated "experts").

In contrast, courts could, in many cases, aggressively enforce simple rules of appropriate conduct (e.g., obeying visitation rulings, complying with previous settlement agreements, not filing false allegations, audiotaping all phone calls between parents) and thus save families much emotional trauma, years of "he said versus she said" unproductive litigation, and tens (or hundreds) of thousands of dollars in unnecessary family law, "expert" and "therapist" fees.

Why do family law systems permit – even encourage – such long, drawn-out litigation battles in which targeted parents must repeatedly defend themselves against alleged, unsupported personal attacks? What are the major impediments to reforming a family law system that permits and even encourages such runaway litigation? The greatest current impediment to reforming the family law system is the permeating influence of the economic incentives to increase litigation. Such incentives permit legal professionals, affiliated experts, and affiliated psychotherapists to financially feast on family conflicts as extended and heightened levels of conflict mean more hearings, more evaluations, more "therapy," and greater fees for the attorneys and affiliated professionals.

Such high conflict custody battles and PAS processes often involve a predictable pattern of joint misconduct by the alienator and local family law professionals, including:

1. false allegations by a parent against an ex-spouse (often based upon misinformation from an "expert," "therapist," or attorney),
2. improper or substandard interviewing and assessment techniques by a local family law-affiliated "expert,"
3. failure of local family lawyers to consult a competent social science expert leading to an abject failure to properly cross-examine or expose junk science diagnostic and interviewing methods,
4. science illiterate legal professionals (including virtually all of even the best and most talented JD-only attorneys) naively accepting improper assessments and erroneous diagnoses of mental illness in children and parents often leading to vague, unsupported requests for "therapy" or "counseling," and
5. incompetent and negligent psychotherapy by family law affiliated mental health professionals (including failures to obtain informed consent, failures to use scientifically validated treatments, failures to use scientifically validated measures of patient improvement and other indicators of malpractice (Chambless & Hollon, 1998; Weisz & Jensen, 1999; Pushak, 2002; Lilienfeld et al. 2003).

Such serious errors frequently go uncovered because all too often local therapists and family attorneys "work together" on so many cases that family lawyers operate under profound (and undisclosed) conflicts of interest that preclude them from effectively exposing even the most egregious misconduct of custody evaluators and "therapists" closely affiliated with local family law systems (Barden, 2001a; Hagen, 1997).

Under this system of conflicted interests even the most serious and harmful errors of evaluators and therapists are rarely exposed in open court. As these errors compound throughout the case, negligent misdiagnoses (coupled with incompetent cross-examinations) often lead to vague and unwarranted orders for "testing" or "therapy" and then on to more improper "evaluations" to assess the results of "therapy." A common error is a vague, subjective request for "supervised visitation." Such requests are often starkly contradicted by objective test results (e.g., on the Child Behavior Checklist), school records, and other reliable data sources. Such contradictions are rarely exposed by science illiterate (JD-only) legal professionals.

This spiral of misconduct often continues on to more contested hearings, more motions, more briefs, more arguments, and – of course – more money for the family law and affiliated divorce industry professionals. Given the powerful and ubiquitous economic incentives rewarding family law professionals for increases in family conflict, extra-professional authority including but not limited to investigations by national litigation experts, malpractice litigation, licensing board complaints, criminal investigations, and ultimately legislative action, may well be necessary to reign in the worst of the widespread abuses of the current family law system (Hays, 2003; Newman, 2003).

To further explicate the nature of these problems, brief case examples are instructive. In one case, a father spent hundreds of thousands of dollars escaping from an order for "supervised visitation" even though the case included no reliable evidence of mental illness, criminal history, or child abuse. Years of investigation documented a highly improper, ongoing personal relationship between the ex-wife and the judge handling the case. The judge later resigned from the bench.

Another case involved a mother losing custody of her child after a error-ridden "evaluation" by a court-appointed psychiatrist that included improper testing, numerous violations of the standard of care, and even fabricated psychological test data. Several local judges had inexplicably delayed basic discovery of the expert's raw data files and original records. Months of expensive investigation revealed a series of improper meetings between the expert and the judges as well as undisclosed gifts from the expert to the judges. Upon exposure of this information, these judges recused themselves (one by one), a national science-litigation expert exposed the expert's misconduct in a detailed court hearing, and the court-appointed "expert" closed her forensic practice.

In another example, hundreds of thousands of dollars were spent litigating a custody dispute in which none of the parties or children had any history of mental illness or abuse. Even so, local therapists and evaluators – in direct contradiction to medical and school records – offered subjective opinions of a need for "counseling' and "supervised visitation." This situation went on for many months until a national science-law consultant became involved. The consultant exposed the fact that the psychological recommendations were based upon unethical and improper psychological testing and misreported test data. Further, the national science-law expert exposed subtly fabricated test settings that skewed the results against one of the parents. Such errors by local "experts" –though common – are rarely exposed by science-illiterate (JD-only) legal professionals. After exposure of these errors, the main local expert "withdrew" from the case and others were openly criticized by the newly educated court. The court ended supervised visitation, made immediate changes in custody, and the expensive parade (and charade) of litigation ended.

A final notable example involves one of the few family law systems in America to be extensively investigated by prosecutors. In a detailed sting operation lasting months, prosecutors in New York have reportedly obtained evidence of fraud, corruption, and bribery in local family law courts. As *The New York Times* reported, "A State Supreme Court judge in Brooklyn and five other men, including his former court clerk, a court officer, and a divorce lawyer who frequently appeared before him, were arraigned yesterday on charges that they ran a bribery scheme to rig the outcome of divorce and child custody cases. . . . Prosecutors said it was part of a culture of corruption in the matrimonial section of State Supreme Court in Brooklyn. . . . Prosecutors said that beginning in 2001, [the conspirators] would find people looking for an advantage in their divorce cases and help arrange payoffs to the people who could provide it: "court personnel who would break rules to direct cases to . . . court-appointed psychologists whose testimony could sway a custody hearing, and to the judge himself." (Hays, 2003; Newman, 2003a; 2003b).

Dozens of additional examples of corruption and institutionalized incompetence of various kinds in the family law system could be provided from jurisdictions across the U.S. Such cases clearly demonstrate: (a) the need for significant, systemic reforms in the family law system, and (b) the need for science-litigation trained professionals in the courtroom. This last point cannot be overemphasized. Traditionally educated JD-only attorneys – due to a lack of sophisticated scientific training – are virtually never capable of conducting even minimal science-intensive litigation procedures. Such methodologically-focused procedures are necessary to rein in and reform widespread misconduct in the family law system.

The medical world long ago replaced the lone "horse and buggy" physician of the early 1900s with a complex multidisciplinary team approach to medical care. Too many litigators (and virtually all family lawyers) remain in the early 1900s, "Lone Ranger" JD-only approach to litigation – thus depriving clients of the in-court, real-time science consultation so critical to success in complex family law cases. Such consultants are often available in the psychology and medical schools of major universities across the U.S. The lack of an in-court, real-time science consultant leaves families vulnerable to endless litigation, bogus assessments, junk science testimony, and enormous amounts of wasted legal, "therapist" and "expert witness" fees.

FACTORS LEADING TO PARENTAL ALIENATION PROCESSES

Detailed questions regarding causation and motivation in PAS cases are often neglected. Why do alienators begin a process that so often leads to devastating emotional and financial injuries to ex-spouses, children, and even themselves? Experience indicates that a small percentage of alienators are indeed suffering from mental illness (e.g., paranoid disorders), while others simply refuse to control negative traits such as selfishness, and angry hostility. Many, however, seem to be individuals who led reasonably normal lives prior to divorce. Such individuals, under the stresses of family breakup, rely upon erroneous information provided by local "therapists," lawyers, "evaluators," or even political activist "support persons." Alienators are sometimes motivated by advice from counsel that filing an abuse allegation is the best way to secure custody. Other alienators have been told distressing, yet false, psychological information about "indicators" or "symptoms" of abuse in children. For example, they may have been instructed that if their child has nightmares or trouble sleeping at night (or has gained weight, or is depressed, or has an eating disorder, etc.) that they "must have been abused." Such junk science misinformation is distressingly widespread in family law-affiliated psychotherapy circles (Pope, 1997; Poole & Lamb, 1998; Hagen, 1997; Dawes, 1997; Pushak, 2002). Parents who gullibly act on such misinformation often target an ex-spouse as the source of the predicted "abuse." Often, a misguided, incompetent or unethical therapist will "validate" the suspicions of the alienator with misinformation, poor logic, and negligent assessment methods, thus reinforcing an expanding series of acts of poor judgment. This is yet another example, where a highly-trained science consultant is an essential component of any family law litigation team. Such a consultant could draft devastating cross-examination questions, submit the necessary licensing complaints, and provide peer-reviewed journal articles for Frye/Daubert hearings to exclude junk science "expert" testimony (Kumho Tire, 1999; Barden, 2001a; Grove & Barden, 2000). JD-only attorneys often wildly overestimate their ability to perform such essential tasks. Such overconfidence often produces disastrous results – leading to the glut of junk science experts freely roaming the family law system (Hagen, 1997; Dawes, 1997; Pope, 1997; Barden, 2001a; Grove & Barden, 2000).

In sum, PAS and related cases often result from a series of negligent acts by local family law affiliated professionals. Such acts may include:

1. "experts" improperly using bogus assessment instruments (e.g., "drawing tests," "ink blots," or other tests not validated by peer-reviewed published research studies) (Grove & Barden, 2000; Grove et al. 2002);
2. "experts" claiming a need for "therapy" when more reliable sources of information (e.g., school records) show the children to be functioning quite well;
3. local family lawyers failing to competently cross-examine local "experts" and "therapists" because they often hire the very same experts in other cases while such egregious conflicts of interest are rarely disclosed to clients;
4. local family lawyers failing to file motions to exclude junk science evaluations via Frye/Daubert junk science hearings (Kumho Tire, 1999);
5. courts ordering children and adults into negligent "therapies" that are not validated by peer-reviewed treatment outcome studies (Bickman, 1999); and
6. courts repeatedly failing to enforce basic laws and standards of behavior – permitting even multiple false allegations, willful violations of visitation agreements, and other harmful acts to go unpunished, thus providing powerful incentives for more attacks by the alienator on the targeted parent. Such misconduct often results in months or even years of unnecessary litigation, producing emotional and other damages to the family and unjust enrichment for the local family law and affiliated professionals. The widespread use of science litigation consultants could eliminate much of this misconduct and harm.

HOW LEGAL PROFESSIONALS COULD REDUCE OR ELIMINATE PARENTAL ALIENATION AND RELATED PROCESSES

Legal professionals contribute to PAS problems by (1) setting up inappropriate behavioral contingencies, (2) failing to enforce minimal standards for appropriate, responsible parental behavior, (3) admitting junk science "expert" testimony, (4) failing to competently cross-examine bogus expert witness testimony, and (5) failing to create the necessary multi-disciplinary legal/science teams to deal with complex legal/science cases.

On the other hand, legal professionals may prevent, reduce or eliminate PAS and related problems with simple acts of reason and educated good judgment. The most important change must be the essential realization that JD-only attorneys simply lack the scientific knowledge and training to competently select or cross-examine therapists, evaluators, and "experts" in complex family law cases. Acquiring a competent science consultant in such cases (from local university faculty or national experts) must be a minimal standard of care for family attorneys in the twenty-first century. Failure to comply with this simple rule often ends in years of unnecessary, expensive litigation without clear results. The presence of a competent science-intensive litigation consultant greatly decreases the dangers of junk science "evaluations," injurious unvalidated "therapies" and other common errors.

Judges can reduce or eliminate PAS and related processes by enforcing order in the process. For example, an expectation of clear, forceful, serious sanctions for misconduct would deter most parents from even beginning the process of alienation with their children. As one commentator noted: "If parents who engage in PAS know that aware judges may give custody to the innocent parent, and perhaps apply sanctions against parents who use a child to prevent the other parent's access to the child, the PAS, which is itself a form of child abuse, may suffer a fatal and well-deserved setback" (Levy, 1992).

Currently, too many courts fail to enforce their own rulings or even provide for follow-up procedures, thus reducing the power and majesty of the legal system to a kind of ineffectual psychotherapist – complete with endless talking and negotiating without any meaningful enforcement of agreements. In fact, the lack of a swift, clear sanction is often perceived by the alienator as a green light to proceed with additional alienating, manipulative, unethical misconduct. Inaction or late action by courts is often devastating to the family involved as the alienator's bad behavior is reinforced, the targeted parent's nightmarish persecution continues, the children are injured emotionally (and financially) by the expensive, contentious custody war that ensues. Many parents simply walk away and lose years of contact with their children rather than deal with the dysfunctional family law system. Inaction or late action by courts – though ultimately financially enriching to the local family law and affiliated professionals – is best viewed as enabling the abuse of children via PAS and related processes.

In reforming the family law system, it is important to note that perhaps the most essential – and often neglected – role of family courts in the U.S. is the protection of fundamental parental rights. It is surprising how few family law professionals seem familiar in detail with a series of cases in which the U.S. Supreme Court has consistently held – in the absence of reliable, objective, and persuasive proof (not psychotherapist musings) of harm to the individual children involved – that natural parents have a fundamental right to unfettered relationships with their children free from judicial or governmental interference or restraint (e.g., *Lehr v. Robertson*, 463 U.S. 248 (1983).; *Santosky v. Kramer*, 455 U.S. 745 (1982); *Caban v. Mohammed*, 441 U.S. 380 (1979).; *Pierce v. Society of Sisters*, 268 U.S. 510 (1925).; *Michael H. et al v. Gerald D*, 491 U.S. 110 (1989); *May v. Anderson*, 345 U.S. 528, 533, 97 L. Ed. 1221, 73 S.Ct. 840, 843 (1952).; *Lassiter v. Department of Social Services*, 452 U.S. 18, 27, 68 L. Ed. 2d 640, 102 S.Ct. 2153, 2159–60 (1981).; *Stanley v. Illinois*, 405 U.S. 645, 651, 31 L. Ed 2d 551, 92 S.Ct. 1208 (1972).; *Franz v. United States*, 707 F.2d 582, 594–602 and 712 F.2d 1428 (D.C. Cir. 1983).; *Smith v. City of Fontana*, 818 F.2d 1411 (9th Cir. 1987).; *Kelson v. Springfield*, 767 F.2d 651, (9th Cir. 1985).; *Bell v. City of Milwaukee*, 746 F.2d 1205, 1242–45 (7th Cir. 1985). It is rare indeed to hear these hallmark Supreme Court decisions cited in family court arguments or briefs. An analysis of this absence should focus on the role of powerful economic incentives in the ongoing neglect of the U.S. Constitutional rights of parents in family law courtrooms. If followed, such Supreme Court case law would largely eviscerate the "chronic tinkering" with parental rights (e.g., "supervised visitation" based on "therapist" recommendations or vague orders for "counseling") so commonly seen in local family law systems.

WHAT LAWYERS AND JUDGES NEED TO KNOW ABOUT IMPROPER EXPERT WITNESS TESTIMONY

As a result of the twentieth century legal trend to freely admit experts, cross-examining attorneys bore an increasingly difficult burden of exposing inappropriate "junk science" testimony. Unfortunately, the legal educational system has traditionally offered little in the way of science, statistical and methodological training. As a result, JD-only attorneys (those lacking formal multidisciplinary training) have been and continue to be uniformly unable to expose even the most striking methodological errors of "expert" witnesses. Millions of children and families have been damaged by this glaring, ongoing deficiency of the legal profession. Examples of the types of bogus testimony routinely admitted in family law cases include the use of so-called "projective testing" (e.g., the Draw-A-Person and related "tests"), the misuse and/or misreporting of objective personality tests, the flagrant misreporting of research findings, the failure to produce or even cite peer-reviewed journal articles to support "expert" opinions, reliance upon junk journals published by political/professional cliques (e.g., "trauma," "dissociation," non-APA, non-APS, and non-AMA journals), and reliance on the long-discredited "clinical judgment" methods of mental health professionals, etc. (Lilienfeld, et al. 2003; Hagen, 1997; Grove, et al. 2002 ; Garb, 1998).

With increasing awareness of the harm done by improper "expert" testimony the legal system of the United States has taken powerful, affirmative steps to limit the damage caused by junk science in the courtroom. See, *Daubert v. Merrell Dow Pharmaceuticals, Inc.*, 113 SCt 2786 (1993). *General Electric Co. v. Joiner*, 118 5. Ct. 512(1997). and *Kumho Tire Co., Ltd. v. Carmichael*, 119 S.Ct. 1167 (1999). cf. *Frye v. U.S.*, 293 Fed. 1013 (DCir. 1923). In the pre-Daubert world, legal professionals were rarely required to obtain even a cursory comprehension of the methodologies of science. A profound ignorance of scientific methodology is still endemic within the legal profession and will require many years – perhaps a full generation – to properly correct. Family law – far more contaminated with junk science than civil, business or, criminal law – rarely uses the powerful tools of Daubert/Kumho or even Frye to evict junk science "expert" testimony.

Given this widespread lack of scientific knowledge and the severe harm often caused by bogus expert testimony in family law cases, even the most skilled and experienced family attorneys should always rely upon science-litigation-clinical consultants or co-counsel to prepare cross-examinations of "experts." Working in harmony and building upon each other's specialized skills, attorneys and law-science-clinical experts can conduct highly effective science-intensive litigation that will protect the rights of families and the integrity of the legal process. The small costs of such multidisciplinary efforts tend to save years and tens (in some cases hundreds) of thousands of dollars of unnecessary litigation expenses. This kind of multidisciplinary process is essential in preventing the serious damage to children and families so tragically common in the family courts of today.

A brief summary of quotations from well-known peer-reviewed journal articles in this field demonstrate the kind of essential information that is so often lacking in local family law courtrooms:

> The present system of mental health regulation primarily relying on educational training, experience, and examinations in general psychology, social work or medicine, has not been found to bear any significant relationship to competence, particularly in forensic mental health services. (Bolocofsky, 1989)

> recent research provides evidence that biased thinking is prevalent among both novices and experienced [mental health] practitioners. (Arnoult, & Anderson, 1988)

> Mental health experts often justify diagnostic and predictive judgments on the basis of "years of experience" with a particular type of person. . . . However, research shows that the validity of clinical judgment and amount of clinical experience are unrelated. (Dawes, 1989)

> [research studies] generally fail to support the value of on-the-job experience in mental health fields. (Garb, 1989)

> clinicians may have considerable difficulties distinguishing valid and invalid variables. They further discuss factors that make it difficult for clinicians to appraise their own level of judgmental accuracy objectively, and which promote a sense of overconfidence. (Dawes, Faust & Meehl, 1989)

> the most comprehensive study to date found no significant relationship between the amount of [psychotherapy] treatment children received and outcomes. . . . After concluding a review of the literature, Bickman (1999). concluded that there is no evidence that any of our current quality-assurance mechanisms (e.g., degree programs, licensing, clinical supervision, etc.) exert any positive impact on clinical treatment outcomes . . . many or most community psychotherapists do not even read scientific journals . . . communities are squandering a substantial amount of money on untested [therapy] programs or programs that have been shown to be ineffective. (Pushak, 2002; Weisz & Jensen, 1999; Lilienfeld, Lohr & Lynn, 2003).

JD-only family law professionals who rely upon junk science "testing," recommendations for unspecified "therapy," or the "clinical judgment" of local therapists and evaluators are clearly violating minimal standards of reason and care. Children and families deserve better (multidisciplinary) care and higher standards of conduct.

Clear signs of incompetent and unethical therapists, evaluators and "experts" are often seen in local family courtrooms. These signs appear to be largely invisible to JD-only attorneys yet quite obvious to competent science-law consultants. Such signs include:

- the use of bogus assessment tests (e.g., "ink blots," "drawing tests," unvalidated personality measures, etc.) (Grove & Barden, 2000; Grove et al. 2002);
- misrepresentations of assessment tests (e.g., using stale MMPI-2 data, using tests known to overpathologize normal individuals). (Barden, 1997; Barden, 2001a; Hagen, 1997);
- unethical manipulation of psychological test data (e.g., using computer scored personality tests but mislabeling the scoring settings thus producing overly pathological results in a targeted parent);
- inaccurate and unsupported diagnoses of "mental illness" or "trauma" when more reliable indices (e.g., school records) document that the children are doing very well and are, in fact, quite normal (Barden, 1997; Dawes, 1997);
- failing to inform the court of serious limitations of methodology (e.g., offering bogus "diagnoses" that do not conform to professional standards of care or the use of unreliable DSM-IV diagnostic categories, etc. (Grove & Barden, 2000; Barden, 2001a);
- recommendations for "therapy" or "counseling" without specific reference to what kind (of the hundreds of types) of "therapy" the patient should receive. Failure to bring peer-reviewed journal evidence that the recommended "therapy" has been validated by peer-reviewed scientific research. Ethical expert witnesses should inform the court that the majority of "therapies" involved in family law cases appear to nonvalidated, junk science procedures (Chambless & Hollon, 1998; Weisz & Jensen, 1999; Pushak, 2002; Lilienfeld et al. 2003). Mental health professionals who bill families for unproven treatments should be referred to law enforcement for prosecution of health care fraud;
- violations of basic ethics codes of the relevant professions (e.g., therapists trying to offer expert testimony in custody cases are engaging in a dual

role violation) (e.g., Texas State Board of Psychology, 2003; Barden, 1997);

- failing to disclose important conflicts of interest to the clients and/or court (e.g., a testifying or even court-appointed expert or therapist is currently working on other cases with the opposing parent's lawyers, thus precluding aggressive cross-examination).

Courts and attorneys have a firm (and widely ignored) obligation to report such misconduct to the local licensing boards for disciplinary action. Guardian ad litem's (GAL) have a firm (and universally ignored) duty to inform children and/or guardians of misconduct by family lawyers, experts and therapists. Courts, attorneys and GAL's have a firm (and universally ignored) obligation to acquire competent expert assistance from science experts (not clinicians) to prevent these all-too-common ethical violations from harming children and families.

SCIENCE-INTENSIVE LITIGATION METHODS ARE UNIQUELY SUCCESSFUL IN PREVENTING MISCONDUCT

As every litigator knows, each case is different and no guarantees or absolute predictions are possible in litigation. However, science-intensive litigation (SIL) methods (JD-only attorneys working in teams with Ph.D., J.D. or other scientifically trained litigation experts to eliminate junk science testimony and methodologies from the courtroom), when properly applied, have produced striking success. Three of the initial cases using these new SIL procedures yielded world-record verdicts ($2.51 Million and $2.54 Million) in psychotherapy negligence trials and a world record settlement ($10.6 Million) in a very complex psychotherapy negligence suit (Barden, 2001a; Gustafson, 1997; Gustafson, 1996; Belluck, 1997). Similarly, historic results have been obtained in criminal cases using SIL methods including a month-long Daubert hearing generally credited with ending criminal prosecutions throughout the U.S. based upon an alleged "victims" so-called "repressed memory" testimony (Barden, 2001a; Mooney, 1999).

Most relevant to the present discussion, a number of volatile family law custody battles that lasted for years in standard litigation were successfully ended within weeks using science-intensive litigation methods. In addition, the practices of incompetent, unethical experts and family lawyers have been severely curtailed or ended when improper behaviors were exposed by science-intensive litigation methods.

In civil, criminal and family law cases, SIL methods have been proven time and again to constitute a dramatic improvement over traditional legal procedures. National legal associations and local bar associations are now offering training in science-intensive litigation methods (Barden, 1997; 2001a).

QUALIFICATIONS FOR SCIENCE-INTENSIVE LITIGATION EXPERTS

The rules of ethical conduct for mental health professionals (psychiatrists, psychologists, social workers, therapists, etc.) typically require them to testify honestly. For example, experts must "describe fairly the bases for their testimony and/or conclusions" and/or "acknowledge the limits of their data or conclusions" or related rules (e.g., American Psychological Association, 1992). In family courts, such rules are uniformly violated. These violations – even the most egregious – are almost never exposed by JD-only litigators. In order to force family law "experts" to comply with these simple yet powerful ethical guidelines, the examining attorneys must have a detailed and highly technical knowledge base in the relevant field of science. This knowledge base is clearly impossible for JD-only lawyers to obtain without on-the-spot, real-time expert assistance from highly-trained scientists (not clinicians). The examining attorney must have minute-to-minute access during cross-examinations to someone with an extensive, detailed, and highly technical knowledge of the history of the relevant scientific disciplines, the methods for determining reliability and validity in that profession, the most recent advances in the relevant discipline, the clinical applications of the relevant science, and ethical rules governing expert testimony, etc. Such experts should be national of local science figures who will not be compromised by ties to the improper economic incentives and inbred political intrigue of local family law systems.

Examples of important types of information SIL experts should know for such cases include the history and reliability of so-called "projective test" scoring systems, proper and improper use of MMPI-2 personality test settings for computer scoring, results of research demonstrating the unreliability of "clinical judgment," Kappa coefficients of recent field trials for various Diagnostic and Statistical Manual classifications, the appropriate use and misuse of statistics, the appropriate use and misuse of philosophy of science issues, the names and backgrounds of the opposing expert witness's advisors and mentors, the severe limitations on controversial diagnostic labels such as "Post Traumatic Stress Syndrome," "Multiple Personality Disorder" and "Borderline Personality Disorder," and the methodological strengths and weaknesses of research presented to the court (Grove & Barden, 2000). In sum, having a legal-science-clinical consultant in the courtroom at all times is essential in efforts to maintain control of improper "junk science" expert testimony.

Attorneys seeking science-literate information should carefully consider the qualifications of experts. Minimal qualifications to consider include: (1) a Ph.D. or M.D. in a relevant field from a nationally ranked, top university program fully accredited by one of more of the four major national associations (e.g., American Psychological Society (APS), American Psychological Association (APA – Ph.D.), American Psychiatric Association (APA – M.D.), American Medical Association (AMA) – e.g., not from a so-called "professional school of psychology"; (2) First author on original research published in two or more prestigious journals in relevant fields (journals published by one of the four major national associations; (3) Served in an editorial or reviewer capacity for several major peer-reviewed journals (journals published by one of the four major national associations); (4) Service on government or professional association ethics/licensing boards; (5) Principal investigator on peer-reviewed research grants totaling more than U.S. $100,000 (National Institutes of Health, National Science Foundation, or leading private funding sources); (6) Tenure or tenure track faculty experience at a highly ranked university or universities (psychology, medicine, and/or law); (7) Licensed clinical health care provider in the relevant field if they are to assist with standard of care, psychotherapy, assessment issues, or other clinical issues; and (8) Any qualified expert should be very familiar with the relevant research fields, including limitations on "clinical judgment" and the hazards of using inappropriate psychological tests (Grove & Barden, 2000; Grove, et al. 2002; Hagen, 1997). The family law system's reliance on local "clinicians" (who are rarely if ever scientists) for "expert" testimony has been one of the greatest failings of the system and has flooded the family law courts with egregious examples of junk science based upon unreliable methodology and the fads and frauds of the psychotherapy industry (Hagen, 1997; Dawes, 1997; Ceci and Bruck, 1996; Dineen, 1996).

MULTIDISCIPLINARY EFFORTS ARE REQUIRED TO REFORM THE FAMILY LAW SYSTEM

Long-term solutions to the problems of PAS and related parental alienation processes are unlikely until outside judicial, academic-science, and public-policy-legislative professionals become involved in reforming the family law system. Multidisciplinary efforts to reduce the number of children abused in custody battles by indoctrinating, manipulative parents and incompetent family law professionals should closely follow the example set by successful reform movements in other complex systems. For example, in the early 1990s the U.S. emergency medical system was shockingly inadequate for many types of pediatric emergencies. The systems were largely designed for adult injuries. Many hospital emergency room and ambulance systems lacked basic equipment and training to handle pediatric emergencies. As a result, thousands of U.S. children were dying needlessly (Barden, et al. 1993).

To reform this very entrenched and financially powerful system a consortium of medical, psychological, legal, economic, and other experts drafted legislation to correct these complex problems (Barden, et al. 1993). Detailed reforms, enacted into law against the opposition of powerful industry forces with competing financial incentives, required updated pediatric equipment and advanced pediatric emergency training for ER professionals. With public support from a current and former U.S. Surgeon General (e.g., Novello, 1992) and positive national media coverage, this law was first enacted in New Jersey, then in many other states, thus saving an estimated 4,000 children per year in the United States. Similar, far-reaching reforms are needed and possible in the family law system (Barden, et al. 1993).

Another instructive historical example involves psychotherapy reforms dating from 1994, a time when the U.S. mental health system was inundated with "repressed and recovered memory" cases of "abuse." Tens of thousands of families per year were reporting losing members to dangerous junk science practices known as "recovered memory therapy." Despite decades of research debunking the notion of "repressed memories," many poorly educated therapists were using coercive interviewing and hypnosis techniques on highly suggestible patients with predictable results. Suddenly, thousands of mental patients were claiming "recovered repressed memories" of abuse by parents, teachers, international cults, and even aliens from outer space in UFO's (Ofshe & Watters, 1996; Loftus & Ketcham, 1994).

Despite the almost total lack of reliable evidence for the theory of "repressed memories" by the early 1990s an enormous, politically correct, "trauma" treatment industry had sprouted tentacles into many hospitals, clinics, and even some medical schools (McNally, 2003; Pope, et al. 1999; Brandon, et al. 1998). Thousands of poorly trained psychiatrists, psychologists, social workers and unlicensed "healers" participated in this dangerous, yet lucrative industry (Ofshe & Watters, 1996).

Despite the political power, massive size, and financial clout of the "recovered memory" therapy industry, it was massively and coercively reformed or destroyed within five years by a national wave of science-intensive malpractice lawsuits. This was accomplished by the dedicated efforts of private foundations, prominent scientists, science-literate media analysts, and litigators with advanced degrees in science. These dangerous and negligent practices would likely have lasted decades but for the very successful prosecution of hundreds of lawsuits against the practitioners of "recovered memory therapy." Most of these successful psychotherapy negligence lawsuits involved the use of science-intensive litigation methods (Barden, 1997; 2001a; Gustafson, 1995; Gustafson, 1996; Belluck, 1997; Acocella, 1998).

The multidisciplinary model for correcting complex social problems that brought successful reforms to the emergency medical and psychotherapy systems should now be employed to reduce the rising numbers of children who are injured by failures in the current family law system – including PAS and related processes. "Experts" who contribute to PAS conflicts by failing to report alternative hypotheses, offering opinions based upon "clinical judgment," overpathologizing families with unreliable assessment methods, and other such misconduct should be subject to legal liability for fraud and reported to licensing agencies. Family lawyers who fail to obtain the minimal information or scientific assistance required for competent cross-examinations of "experts" should be faced with malpractice litigation and reported to attorney licensing boards for disciplinary action. Guardian ad litems must begin to meet minimal methodological and legal standards of care by competently cross-examining bogus "experts" and advising children of their valuable rights to sue incompetent psychotherapists who promulgate and/or exacerbate familial conflicts via unvalidated "therapies" that maximize anger, contention and blame. Press releases, media exposes and informational Internet sites are needed to raise national awareness of the economic misincentives and other hazards of the current family law system.

In addition to massive reforms of the family law system, extensive scientific research is also needed on the parameters, nature, etiologies and long-term implications of Parental Alienation Syndrome and related processes. A number of significant questions need immediate attention including:

1. What is the incidence and prevalence of the PAS problem? (Clavar and Rivlin, 1991);
2. Is parental alienation best described as a syndrome, a process, a crime of abuse, etc.? (Gardner, 1998);
3. What is the diagnostic reliability and validity of PAS and related processes?;
4. What, if any, treatments might be possible for PAS including efforts to reintegrate families and prevent alienating acts?

These and other research questions should be addressed by professional scientists at universities and medical schools. The results of these research articles should be published in respected, mainstream scientific journals (e.g., Psychological Science, Child Development, Journal of Personality and Social Psychology, Developmental Psychology, Journal of Abnormal Psychology) and not in lower level, poor quality journals (e.g., family therapy, trauma, abuse, clinical, or psychotherapy journals). Reliable scientific information and essential reforms in the family law system will help to protect children from the abuses of PAS and related processes.

CONCLUSIONS

Despite the hard work of many well-meaning professionals, the serious problems of PAS and related processes in child custody cases are often the product of improper incentives and misinformation produced by science-illiterate family law systems and affiliated professions. The reforms necessary to protect children from such abusive alienation processes (including prolonged and abusive litigation processes) are simple yet difficult to implement, given the powerful economic misincentives that reward many family law and affiliated professionals for generating unnecessary anger, blame, conflict, and expense.

Multidisciplinary efforts are required to protect children from the dangers of the current family law system. Only with significant reforms in the operation of family law can we expect protection of the universal and fundamental rights of families to relationships free from unreasonable government restraint. Without multidisciplinary reform efforts, too many children will continue to face the dangers of a family law system that is rife with junk science "experts," pseudoscience "therapists" and science-illiterate attorneys. Families and children deserve greater respect and better care.

Proper exclusion of junk science "evaluations," junk science "therapies," bogus psychological "testing," "custody recommendations" based upon unreliable "clinical judgment" and other improper methodologies are essential steps to improving the integrity of the family law process. Frye and or Daubert/Kumho hearings to exclude junk science – conducted by experts in science-intensive litigation – should set the necessary precedents to exclude the kinds of improper and misleading testimony that is so very common in the family courts of today (Kumho, 1999; Grove & Barden, 2000; Hagen, 1997).

Courts that clearly investigate and punish unethical behavior, false allegations, violations of court orders, efforts to impede fair visitation processes, and actions to violate the constitutional rights of parents will rarely see prolonged parental alienation battles. Courts that give an alienating parent "free shots" at the liberty, property, and parental rights of others are likely to generate the kind of prolonged, harmful litigation currently seen in many family courts.

Given the decades of research on parental influences, courts need not wait for research on the specifics of PAS – or long overdue reforms in the family law system – to move aggressively to control parents, "experts," "therapists" and attorneys who injure children and families with unethical and incompetent acts and omissions. The legal and scientific communities must share the responsibility and sacred obligation to prevent children from becoming pawns in custody litigation. Children deserve competent protection and nothing less.

REFERENCES

Acocella, J. The Politics of Hysteria, *The New Yorker*, April 6, 1998, pp. 64–79.

American Psychological Association. (1992). Ethical principles of psychologists and code of conduct, *American Psychologist, 47*, 1597–1611.

American Psychological Association Guidelines for Child Custody Evaluations in Divorce Proceedings (1994). Washington, D.C.: American Psychological Association Pres, at p. 11.

Arnoult, L.H. & Anderson, C.A. (1988). Identifying and reducing causal reasoning biases in clinical practice, in D.C. Turk and P. Salovey (Eds.), *Reasoning, inference, & judgment in clinical psychology*. New York: The Free Press (pp. 209–232).

Barden, R. C. (1994). Letter to the Congress of the United States of America regarding reform of the mental health system. (With signatories Paul E. Meehl, Terence W. Campbell, Richard Ofshe, Richard A. Gardner, Margaret Singer, William Grove, Michael D. Yapko, Robyn Dawes, Richard Flyer, Robert Kinscherff, Mel Guyer, Francis Fincham, Thom Moore, Henry E. Adams, E. Mark Cummings, Lewis P. Lipsitt, Donald M. Kaplan, Robert R. Holt, Richard M. McFall, Hans H. Strupp, Stephen J. Lepore, Lee Sechrest, Paul Ekman, Hans J. Eysenck, Jerome Kagan, George Stricker, Debra Ann Poole, Mark L. Howe, J. Don Read, Howard Shevrin.) Reprinted in Dineen, Tana. 1996 *Manufacturing victims.* and Montreal: Robert Davies Publishing.

Barden, R. C. (2001a). "Protecting the Integrity of the Legal System: Eliminating Junk science "expert" Testimony with Science-intensive Litigation Methods," American Bar Association Litigation Section National Meetings, Phoenix, Arizona, May 11.

Barden, R. C. (2001b). Informed consent in psychotherapy: A multidisciplinary perspective. *The Journal of the American Academy of Psychiatry and the Law, Vol 29*, No. 2, pp. 160–166, 2001.

Barden, R.C. (2003). "Building multi-disciplinary legal-scientific teams in Parental Alienation Syndrome cases," In Boch-Galhau, W., Kodjoe, U., Andritzky, W. and Koeppel, P. (Eds) *Parental Alienation Syndrome (PAS): A challenge for professionals involved in family law.* VWB – Verlag fur Wissenschaft und Bildung. Frankfurt, Germany.

Barden, R. C., Kinscherff, R., George, W., Flyer, R., Seidel, J., & Henderson, D. (1993). Emergency medical care and injury prevention systems for children: An economic-medical-legal-psychological analysis and legislative proposals, *Harvard Journal on Legislation, Vol. 30*, No. 2, pp. 461–497.

Barden, R.C. (1997). Science and the Legal System: Science-intensive Litigation. Professional training seminar presented at Washington D.C. Bar Association/National Practice Institute, CLE Seminars, Washington, D.C., November 21.

Bell v. City of Milwaukee, 746 F.2d 1205, 1242-45 (7th Cir. 1985).

Belluck, P. Memory therapy leads to a lawsuit and $10.6 million settlement, *The New York Times*, Page 1, Column 1, Nov. 6, 1997.

Bickman, L. (1999). Practice makes perfect and other myths about mental health services. *American Psychologist, 54*, 965–978.

Bolocofsky, D.N. (1989). Use and abuse of mental health experts in child custody determinations. *Behavioral Sciences & the Law, 7*, 197–213.

Bone, J. Michael & Walsh, Michael R., (March 1999). Parental Alienation Syndrome: How to detect it and what to do about it. *The Florida Bar Journal, Vol. 73*, No. 3, pp. 44–48.

Borris, Edward, Interference with parental rights of noncustodial parent as grounds for modification of child custody (1997). *Divorce Litigation 8*, No. 1, pp. 88–98.

Brandon, S., J. Boakes, D.Glaser, R. Green (1998). Recovered memories of childhood sexual abuse: Implications for clinical practice. *British Journal of Psychiatry, 172*:296–3

Bruck, M. and Ceci, S., Amicus Brief for the case of *State of New Jersey v. Michaels* presented by Committee of Concerned Social Scientists. [Docket Number 36,633, *State of New Jersey, Appellant vs. Margaret Kelly Michaels, Respondent.*] *Psychology, Public Policy, and Law* (1995). Vol. 1, No. 2, 272–322.

Caban v. Mohammed, 441 U.S. 380 (1979).

Cartwright, G. F. (1993). Expanding the parameters of Parental Alienation Syndrome. *American Journal of Family Therapy, 21*(3), 205–215.

Ceci, S. and Bruck, M. *Jeopardy in the courtroom: A scientific analysis of children's testimony.* Washington, D.C.: American Psychological Association Press, 1996.

Chambless, D and Hollon, S. Defining empirically supported therapies. *Journal of Consulting and Clinical Psychology*, 1998, Vol. 66, No. 1, 7–18.

Cialdini, R. B. (1993). *Influence: Science and practice.* New York: Harper Collins Press.

Clavar and Rivlin. *Children held hostage: Dealing with programmed and brainwashed children.* Chicago: American Bar Association Press (1991).

Dawes, R.M. (1989). Experience and validity of clinical judgment: The illusory correlation. *Behavioral Sciences & the Law, 7*, 457–467.

Dawes, R.M. (1997). *House of cards: Psychology and psychotherapy built on myth.* New York: Free Press.

Dawes, R.M., Faust, D., and Meehl, P.E. (1989). Clinical versus actuarial judgment. *Science, 243*, 1668–1674.

Dineen, Tana. (1996). *Manufacturing victims.* Montreal: Robert Davies Publishing.

Franz v. United States, 707 F.2d 582, 594-602 and 712 F.2d 1428 (D.C. Cir. 1983).

Garb H.N. (1989). Clinical judgment, clinical training, and professional experience. *Psychological Bulletin, 105*, 387–396.

Garb, Howard. (1998). *Studying the clinician: Judgment research and psychological assessment.* Washington D.C.:American Psychological Association Press.

Gardner, R. (1985). Recent trends in divorce and custody litigation. *Academy Forum, 29*(2): 3–7.

Gardner, R. (1998). *The parental alienation syndrome: A guide for mental health and legal professionals.* 2nd Ed. Cresskill, N.J.: Creative Therapeutics.

Gardner, R. (2003). List of references on PAS at http://www.rgardner.com/refs/

Gardner, Richard (1986). Child custody. In Noshpitz (Ed) *Basic handbook of child psychiatry*, Vol. 5, pp. 637–646, New York: Basic Books.

Gardner, Richard A. M.D. (2002). The judiciary's role in the etiology, symptom development, and treatment of the Parental Alienation Syndrome (PAS). *American Journal of Forensic Psychology, 21*(1):39–64.

Grove, W. M. and Barden, R.C. (2000). Protecting the integrity of the legal system: The admissibility of testimony from mental health experts under Daubert/Kumho analyses. *Psychology, Public Policy and Law, Vol 5*, No. 1, 234–242.

Grove, W., Barden R. C., Garb, H. & Lilienfeld, S. (2002). Failure of Rorschach-Comprehensive-System-based testimony to be admissible under the Daubert-Joiner-Kumho standard. *Psychology, Public Policy, and Law, 8*, 216–234.

Gustafson, Paul. Jury awards patient $2.6 million: Verdict finds therapist Humenansky liable in repressed-memory trial, *The Minneapolis-St. Paul Tribune*, 1995. West Law Document 3673222, August 1, 1995.

Gustafson, Paul. Jury awards $2.5 million in lawsuit against psychiatrist: "Memories" were induced. *The Minneapolis-St. Paul Tribune*, 1996 WL 6898881, January 25, 1996.

Hagen, M. (1997). *Whores of the court: The fraud of psychiatric testimony and the rape of American justice.* New York: Harper Collins Press.

Hays, Tom (2003). New York judge faces corruption charges, *Associated Press National Newswire*, April 24.

Kelson v. Springfield, 767 F.2d 651, (9th Cir. 1985).

Kumho Tire Co., Ltd. v. Carmichael, 119 S.Ct. 1167 (1999).

Lassiter v. Department of Social Services, 452 U.S. 18, 27, 68 L. Ed. 2d 640, 102 S.Ct. 2153, 2159-60 (1981).

Lehr v. Robertson, 463 U.S. 248 (1983).

Levy, D. (1992). Review of Parental Alienation Syndrome: A guide for mental health and legal professionals. *American Journal of Family Therapy, 20*(3), 276–277.

Lilienfeld, Scott, Lohr, Jeffrey & Lynn, Steven (2003). *Science and pseudoscience in clinical psychology.* New York: Guilford Press.

Loftus, E. F. Creating false memories. *Scientific American*, Sept. 1997 at pp. 71–75.

Loftus, E., & Ketcham, K. (1994). *The myth of repressed memory: False allegations of sexual abuse.* New York: St. Martin's Press.

May v. Anderson, 345 U.S. 528, 533, 97 L. Ed. 1221, 73 S.Ct. 840, 843 (1952).

Mazzoni, G. and Memon, A. Imagination can create false autobiographical memories. *Psychological Science, Vol. 14*, No. 2, March, 2003 pp. 186–193.

McNally, Richard (2003). *Remembering trauma.* Cambridge, Mass.: Harvard University Press.

Michael H, et al. v. Gerald D, 491 U.S. 110 (1989)

Mooney, Tom. Recovered Memory Rejected: Judge rules out key element in landmark case. *The Providence Rhode Island Journal.* April 28, 1999.

Newman, Andy. "Brooklyn Judge Faces Charges of Corruption: The judge is to be arraigned on charges that he took gifts from lawyers in return for favoritism toward their clients in divorce cases. *The New York Times*, April, 24, 2003a.

Newman, Andy. Investigation of Judge Touched Off Wider Inquiry. *The New York Times*, April 25, 2003b.

Novello, Antonio C. M.D., M.P.H., Former Surgeon General of the United States of America, personal letter to the Legislature of the State of New Jersey, dated Sept. 9, 1992.

Ofshe, R. and Watters, E. (1996). *Making monsters: False memories, psychotherapy, and sexual hysteria.* 2nd Edition. University of California.

Palmer, N. (1988). Legal recognition of the parental alienation syndrome. *American Journal of Family Therapy, 16(*4), pp. 360–363.

Pierce v. Society of Sisters, 268 U.S. 510 (1925).

Poole, D. A. and Lamb, M. E. (1998). *Investigative interviews of children.* Washington D.C.: American Psychological Association Press.

Pope, H.G. Jr. (1997). *Psychology astray: Fallacies in studies of "repressed memory" and childhood trauma.* Boca Raton, FL: Social Issues Resources Series.

Pope, H.G., Oliva, P.S. and Hudson, J. I. (1999). The scientific status of research on repressed memories. In Faigman, D.L., Kaye, D.H., Saks, M.J., and Sanders, J. (Eds) *Modern scientific evidence: The law and science of expert testimony*, Vol I, 1999 Pocket Part, West Publishing, pp. 115–155.

Pushak, Robert E., (2002). The dearth of empirically supported mental health services for children. *The Scientific Review of Mental Health Practice, Vol. 1*, No. 2, Fall/Wtr.

Santosky v. Kramer, 455 U.S. 745 (1982).

Smith v. City of Fontana, 818 F.2d 1411 (9th Cir. 1987).

Stanley v. Illinois, 405 U.S. 645, 651, 31 L. Ed 2d 551, 92 S. Ct. 1208 (1972).

Texas State Board of Examiners of Psychologists Newsletter, (2003). Texas Board Rule 465.18 pertaining to forensic services. "Therapist and Expert: Prohibited dual roles." Vol. 16, Issue 1, Winter.

Vassiliou, D. and Cartwright, G. (2001). The lost parent's perspective on Parental Alienation Syndrome. *The American Journal of Family Therapy 29*, pp. 181–191.

Wallerstein, J. S. & Kelly, J.B. (1980). *Surviving the breakup.* New York: Basic Books.

Warshak, R.A. (2001). *Divorce poison: Protecting the parent-child bond from a vindictive ex.* New York: Regan Books.

Warshak, Richard, (2001). Current controversies regarding Parental Alienation Syndrome. *American Jour. of Forensic Psychology, 19*(3), pp. 29–59.

Weisz, J. & Jensen, P. (1999). Efficacy and effectiveness of child and adolescent psychotherapy and pharmacotherapy. *Mental Health Services Research 1*(3), pp. 125-157.

The author is grateful for research and training support from a Foundation for Child Development Young Scholar Award and a W.T. Grant Foundation Faculty Scholar Award in Psychology as well as funding from Harvard Law School.

Chapter 33

PARENTAL ALIENATION SYNDROME AND INTERNATIONAL CHILD ABDUCTION: A MULTIGENERATIONAL SYNDROME

BARBARA BEVANDO SOBAL

OVERVIEW

The purpose of this Chapter is to bring awareness to the fact that parental alienation syndrome (PAS) is a multigenerational syndrome. The group studied is composed of children who were abducted internationally before the Hague Convention was adopted on October 25, 1980, and ratified by the United States on July 1, 1988, since it is that group of children who have produced a new generation of children who exhibit the same PAS symptoms as their parents toward their grandparents. In accordance with Clawar and Rivlin[1] these groups of internationally abducted children were "programmed by their parents to the point of no return." This means that intervention was not found to be effective in deprogramming these children. They were emotionally and physically lost to the targeted parent. These are the children that the late Dr. Richard Gardner describes as victims of parental alienation syndrome. Unless successful deprogramming by trained professionals – who are closely supervised, whose credentials are verified and who are specifically licensed in this field – is accomplished, there will be no end to the generations of PAS victims. Great caution should be taken to eliminate those programs who claim to deprogram, but who do more harm than the alienating/abducting parent has done.

INTRODUCTION

. . . Your children are not your children.
They are the sons and daughters of Life's longing for itself . . .[2]

This is so with the internationally abducted child who is also a victim of PAS.

PAS is nothing new. In fact, it dates back to biblical times[3] and to the Ancient Greeks.[4] Moreover, PAS has become multigenerational with the internationally abducted PAS child, just as with a child who is emotionally abducted. It starts with the alienating parent, who passes the behavior on to the child, who in turn becomes an alienator, and passes it on to his or her own child.

These children are not the sons and daughters of Life. Rather, their "life" involves "living" in the world of the alienating parent. They are robbed of their childhoods by the alienating parent. For the internationally abducted child, their language and customs are also stolen away from them. They belong to the alienating parent and to that parent's country.

They are not loved in the true sense by the alienating parent. Rather, the alienating parent uses the child as a vessel to pass on their hatred for the alienated parent, and disguises it as "love – to the extent that the child never really knows what love is.

They do not develop their own thoughts. Rather, they are programmed. According to Gardner, "Programming refers, to the implantation of information that may be directly at variance with what the PAS child has previously believed about and experienced with the alienated parent."[5]

In PAS, the alienating parent programs into the child's brain circuitry ideas and attitudes that are directly at variance with the child's previous experiences. In mild cases the child is taught to disrespect, disagree with, and even act out antagonistically against the targeted parent. As the disorder progresses from mild to moderate to severe, this antagonism becomes converted and expanded into a campaign of denigration. PAS children respond to the programming in such a way that it appears that they have become completely amnesiac for any and all positive and loving experiences they may have had previously with the targeted parent.[6]

. . . PAS children have been programmed, and they need to be deprogrammed. They have been taught to hate, so they must be reeducated in such a way that the suppressed loving feelings can once again emerge. Attempts must be made to replace the unhealthy material in the child's brain circuitry with healthy material.[7]

[The] child's pathological PAS material [is] superimposed on and suppressive of healthy thoughts and feelings about the victimized parent that are still very much in the child's brain circuitry. It is like a black cloud that covers the brain circuitry but has not obliterated the healthy, loving thoughts and feelings that are still there. The more prolonged the period of indoctrination, the more deeply embedded the pathological material becomes and the more difficult it will be to remove it. The goal of the deprogramming process is to remove this superimposed PAS material in order to allow the expression, once again, of healthier material that lies beneath it. The treatment is analogous to the detoxification process in which poisons are removed from the body so that healthy functioning can resume. It is a process by which the automatic routinized thinking of the child is removed, allowing thereby the expression of the child's own earlier judgments and critical thinking.[8]

PAS children are deprived of their own souls. Their souls are selfishly possessed by the alienating parent. The PAS child has no identity of his/her own. The child's identity is enmeshed with the alienator. For the PAS child, life is always going backward. They are frozen in time at the point of the abduction and/or alienation. The bow from which the internationally abducted PAS child is set forth is unstable, because the alienating parent is unstable.

The International abduction and/or PAS can begin before, after, or during the divorce process. This is a process that children, especially the very young, are completely helpless to combat. The obsessed parent is angry, bitter, or feels betrayed by the other parent. The initial reasons for the bitterness may be justified. They could have been verbally and physically abused, betrayed by an affair, or financially cheated. Or, there could be cultural differences that cannot be resolved. The problems occur when the feelings don't heal but, instead, become more intense due to the necessary continued relationship with the person they despise because of their common parenthood. Just having to see or talk to the other parent is a reminder of the past, and this can trigger the hate. Although, Clawar and Rivlin did not specifically discuss the obsessed alienator in their book, they found that five percent of the children in their study were programmed by similar parents "to the point of no return," meaning that no interventions were found to be effective in deprogramming these children. These children were emotionally and physically lost to the targeted parent.[9] These are the children that Gardner described as a victim of PAS.

PARENTAL ALIENATION SYNDROME

PAS is a disorder that arises primarily in the context of child custody and International Child Abduction disputes. Its primary manifestation is the child's campaign of denigration against one parent – a campaign that has no justification.[10] It results from the *combination* of the programming (brainwashing) parent's indoctrinations and the child's own contributions to the vilification of the target parent. When true parental abuse and/or neglect is present, the child's animosity may be justified, and so the PAS explanation for the child hostility is not applicable.

Symptoms of Parental Alienation Syndrome[11]

The eight cardinal symptoms of PAS are:

- A campaign of denigration.
- Weak, frivolous, and absurd rationalizations for the depreciation.
- Lack of ambivalence.
- The "independent-thinker" phenomenon.
- Reflexive support of the alienating parent in the parental conflict.
- Absence of guilt over cruelty to and/or exploitation of the alienated parent.
- Presence of borrowed scenarios.
- Spread of the animosity to the extended family and friends of the alienated parent.

The Campaign of Denigration[12]

Typically, the child is obsessed with "hatred of a parent." These children speak of the alienated parent with every vilification and profanity in their vocabulary – without embarrassment or guilt. The denigration of the vilified parent often has the quality of a litany. After only minimal prompting by a lawyer, judge, probation officer, mental health professional, or other person involved in the litigation, the brain recording will be turned on, and a command performance is provided in which the targeted parent's defects are listed at length.

Weak, Frivolous, and Absurd Rationalizations for the Depreciation[13]

Typically, PAS children provide irrational and often ludicrous justifications for their alienation from the targeted parent. The child may justify the alienation with memories of minor altercations experienced in the relationship with the estranged parent, even years after they have taken place. These are usually trivial experiences that most children quickly forget. When PAS children are asked to give more compelling reasons for their rejection, they are unable to provide them. Typically, the alienating parent will agree with the child that these professed reasons justify the ongoing animosity.

Lack of Ambivalence[14]

Another symptom of PAS is complete lack of ambivalence. All human relationships are ambivalent, and parent-child relationships are no exception. However, the concept of mixed feelings has no place in PAS children's lives. The victimized parent is all bad, and the indoctrinating parent is all good. Most children ("normal" ones, as well as those with a wide variety of psychiatric problems), when asked to list both good and bad things about each parent, will generally be able to do so. When PAS children are asked to provide the same list, they will typically recite a long list of criticisms of the targeted parent, but will not be able to think of one positive or redeeming personality trait. In contrast, they will provide only positive and endearing qualities for the alienating parent and claim to be unable to think of even one trait they dislike. The vilified parent may have been deeply dedicated to the child's upbringing, and a strong bond may have been created over many years. Yet, it seems to evaporate, almost overnight, at the time of the onset of PAS. In contrast, the alienating parent, toward whom the child was previously ambivalent, becomes idealized and "can do no wrong."

The "Independent-Thinker" Phenomenon[15]

Many PAS children profoundly profess that their decision to reject the targeted parent is their own. They deny any contribution from the programming parent, who supports this "independence" vociferously. In fact, alienators will typically proclaim that they want the child to visit and profess recognition of the importance of such involvement. Yet, the indoctrinator's every act indicates otherwise.

Reflexive Support of the Alienating Parent in the Parental Conflict[16]

In family conferences, in which the children are seen together with both the alienating and alienated parent, the children reflexive take the position of the indoctrinating parent – sometimes even before the victimized parent has had the opportunity to present his or her side of the argument. Even the alienating parent may not present the argument as forcefully as the supporting child. Thus, PAS children may even refuse to accept evidence that is obvious proof of the vilified parent's position.

Absence of Guilt over Cruelty to and/or Exploitation of the Alienated Parent[17]

The child may exhibit a guiltless disregard for the feelings of the victimized parent. He or she will show a complete absence of gratitude for gifts, support payments, and other manifestations of the vilified parent's continued involvement and affection.

Presence of Borrowed Scenarios[18]

The presence of borrowed scenarios should clue examiners into the high probability that they are dealing with the PAS. Not only is there a rehearsed quality to PAS children's litanies, but one often hears phraseology that is not commonly used by children of that age. Many expressions are identical to those used by the indoctrinating parent. The parental terms and phrases become scripted into the children's litanies of denigration. Frequently, the children attribute a particular statement to the programming parent, thereby "letting the cat out of the bag" and confirming that the particular phrase has been programmed.

Spread of the Animosity to the Extended Family and Friends of the Alienated Parent[19]

The hatred of the alienated parent often extends to include that parent's complete extended family. Cousins, aunts, uncles, and grandparents – with whom the child previously may have had loving relationships – are now viewed as similarly obnoxious. Grandparents, who previously had a loving and tender relationship with the child, now find themselves suddenly and inexplicably rejected. The child has no guilt over such rejection, nor does the alienator. Greeting cards are not reciprocated. Presents sent to the child are refused, remain unopened, or even are destroyed (generally in the presence of the programming parent). When the denigrated parent's relatives call on the telephone, the child will respond with angry vilifications or quickly hang up on the caller. (These responses are more likely to occur if the alienating parent is within hearing distance of the conversation.) With regard to the denigration of the relatives, the child is even less capable of providing justification for the animosity. The rage of these children is often so great that they become completely oblivious to the privations they are causing themselves. Again, the indoctrinating parent is typically unconcerned with the untoward psychological effects on the child of this rejection of the network of relatives who previously provided important psychological gratifications.

HAGUE CONVENTION

The Hague Convention on the Civil Aspects of International Child Abduction was adopted on October 25, 1980.[20] The Hague Convention was adopted by the signatory nations and addressed the increasing problem of international child abduction in the context of international law while respecting rights of custody and visitation under national law.

According to the preamble, "the Convention aims 'to protect children' internationally from the harmful effects of their wrongful removal or retention and to establish procedures to ensure their prompt return to the State of their habitual residence."

The United States ratified the Hague Convention on July 1, 1988. In the United States, the enabling legislation is codified by the International Child Abduction Remedies Act (hereinafter referred to as ICARA).

Because the language of the Convention is somewhat conclusory, United States courts look to two sources of official commentary for guidance: (1) The Explanatory Report by Elisa Perez-Vera, the official Hague Conference reporter (the "Perez-Vera Report"); and (2) The Legal Analysis of the Hague Convention on the Civil Aspects of International Child Abduction ("Legal Analysis").

As noted in the Legal Analysis notes in pertinent part "Access rights" correspond to "visitation rights." The Perez-Vera Explanatory Report is "recognized by the Conference as the official history and commentary on the Convention and is a source of background on the meaning of the provisions of the Convention available to all States becoming parties to it."

Case Analysis

The following are cases that are unpublished because they existed before PAS and/or International Child Abduction were known. In fact, the Hague Convention did not exist. Therefore, the parties' names are not used. Instead, the cases will be referred to by the countries in which they occurred.

All of these cases involve PAS, two of the cases are multigenerational and involve the spouses and the children of the abducted child.

Iran/United States

I once interviewed an American mother who was married to an Iranian. They had a successful son, who was in his thirties and married with two children. The mother divorced the father when their son was one year old. The father abducted the son from the United States and brought him to Tehran. When the mother tried to get her son back, she was told that she would be shot in the streets, and that acid would be thrown in her face.

The mother did not see her son again until he was forced to come to the United States during the Iranian Revolution, when her son was in his late teens. Once he was back in the United States, she was not invited to his lavish wedding. Her son accuses her of abandoning him and of being a sinner by not following the Muslim religion. He is verbally abusive, to the point that he sounds just like his father. Her son's wife is verbally abusive to her and makes statements such as, "How can a mother abandon her child?" Her two grandchildren (a boy, 4, and a girl, 6) mimic their father, mother, and their grandfather by also being abusive to her.

To date, Iran has not ratified the Hague Convention Treaty.

Japan/United States

I interviewed a beautiful 32-year-old Japanese woman with a flawless porcelain face. She told me that she had a Japanese-born father and a Japanese-American mother. She was abducted from the United States to Japan by her father when she was five years old. As a result of the abduction, she no longer spoke English. She spoke through the aid of a translator, her Japanese ex-husband.

After years of being denied access and visitation, her mother was finally able to make contact with her when the woman was a young adult. At that point, the woman tried to kill herself by slitting her wrists. She was very abusive toward her mother, as her father once was, and told her mother that she would "rather kill herself and wanted nothing to do with the American woman who 'abandoned' her as a young child," that she only identified with her father and that she would not betray her father.

She had married a Japanese man against her Japanese family's wishes and refused to invite her mother to the wedding. One year later, she was forced by her Japanese family to divorce her husband because of the Japanese tradition of being the first-born child of a prominent family. According to tradition, as a first-born child, her husband had to take on her family name. However, the husband was also a first-born child of a prominent family. Only if the husband were a second-born son, could he carry his wife's family name. The fact that she loved her husband made no difference. She again tried to commit suicide after the divorce by slitting her wrists.

Japan is still considered to be an "abduction-friendly" country. It is the only member of the "Group of Seven" industrialized countries that has not ratified the Hague Convention.

United States/Lebanon

I once interviewed an American mother, who was a doctor, she had divorced a Lebanese-born doctor. They had one daughter. She was a fair, blond, blue-eyed girl who looked like her American mother. When the child was two, the couple divorced over cultural differences because the father was an alcoholic, drug abuser, and wife batterer. The father abducted the child and took her to Lebanon. The child was also taken back and forth to Syria.

Despite numerous unsuccessful legal efforts, the mother did not see her daughter again until the daughter was in her twenties. No matter how hard the mother tried to establish a relationship with her daughter, the mother was constantly told that she abandoned her daughter; that she was an enemy of Allah, because she ate pork and had an occasional drink; that she was an infidel and that the daughter wanted nothing to do with her mother or nothing to do with being American.

The daughter is now married, with three children. She refused to invite her mother to her wedding. The daughter's husband is also abusive to the mother. Although the mother was able to see her first grandchild, a boy, age four, on only a few occasions, her daughter will not allow her to see, or, know, her second and third grandchildren, a boy, age 2 and a new-born girl. The mother has only recently seen a picture of the 2-year-old boy, given to her by a sympathetic relative.

To date, Lebanon has not ratified the Hague Convention.

Unites States/Egypt

I interviewed an American-born father who was married to an Egyptian-born woman. Once they were divorced, the mother abducted their four-year-old daughter and took her to Egypt. At the age of nine, the daughter was vaginally mutilated in accordance with the custom in her mother's town. The daughter also no longer spoke English.

The father did not see his daughter until she was in her late twenties. At that time, through a translator, the daughter blamed the father for abandoning her, denied being abducted, spewed obscenities at him in the same way and tone that the mother did, and told him that she never wanted to see him again.

To date, Egypt has not ratified the Hague Convention.

CONCLUSION

Programs who claim to deprogram that are not closely supervised or run by professionals who are specifically licensed in this field, do more harm than the alienating abducting parent has done, creating endless generations of PAS victims.

ENDNOTES

1. Stanley S. Clawar & Brynne V. Rivlin, Children Held Hostage Dealing With Programmed And Brain-Washed Children. (1991). American Bar Association, Chicago, Illinois, p. 142.
2. Kahlil, Gibran, *The Prophet* (1994). New York: Random House, Inc., pp. 18–19.
3. Ephesians, 6:4, NT (King James) Version.
4. Euripedes, *Medea* (431 B.C.). Available at http://classics.mit.edu/Euripides/medea.html.
5. Richard A. Gardner (2000). *Therapeutic interventions for children with Parental Alienation Syndrome.* Cresskill NJ: Creative Therapeutics. x-xi-xiv-xv.

6. *Ibid*, xxv.
7. *Ibid*.
8. *Ibid*, xxvi.
9. Stanley S. Clawar and Byrnne V. Rivlin (1991). Children Held Hostage: Dealing With Programmed And Brainwashed Children. American Bar Association, Chicago, Illinois, p. 142.
10. Richard A. Gardner (1998). *The Parental Alienation Syndrome*, Second Edition, Creskill NJ: Creative Therapeutics pp. 76–109. xxi-xxii; *see also* http://www.rgardner.com.
11. *Ibid*, pp. 76–109.
12. *Ibid*, pp. 77–86.
13. *Ibid*, pp. 86–94.
14. *Ibid*, pp. 94–96.
15. *Ibid*, pp. 96–99.
16. *Ibid*, pp. 99–100.
17. *Ibid*, pp. 100–101.
18. *Ibid*, pp. 101–107.
19. *Ibid*, pp. 107–109.
20. Hague Convention Preamble, T.I.A.S. No. 11, 670, p. 40.

Chapter 34

LEGAL REQUIREMENTS OF EXPERTS GIVING EVIDENCE TO COURTS IN THE UNITED KINGDOM: PAS AND THE EXPERTS' FAILURE TO COMPLY

TONY HOBBS

OVERVIEW

In this chapter, the legal requirements of expert witnesses' evidence to United Kingdom courts is summarized. The various tests applied to new scientific evidence in the United States and Canada's jurisdictions are reviewed with regard to their recently acknowledged acceptability in United Kingdom courts. The crucial United Kingdom "Experts" Court Report' by Sturge and Glaser (2000), which dismissed the existence of PAS, is reviewed in light of these requirements.

REQUIREMENTS OF EXPERT WITNESSES IN UNITED KINGDOM COURTS

Where new scientific knowledge is relevant to a case in court, judges rely heavily on the provision of accurate evidence from appropriately competent court-appointed experts. Lord Justice Wall (Wall and Hamilton, 2000) observed: "Expert evidence is often of critical importance in a difficult child case. Sometimes it is determinative of a child's future. The court therefore places substantial reliance on the professional integrity of the experts who advise it" (p. 1).

In the same volume, the President of the High Court Family Division, Dame Elizabeth Butler-Sloss, stressed that: "The reliance of the court upon the medical expert places a considerable burden upon him/her to provide an impartial and objective assessment of the situation with recommendations based upon the welfare of the child concerned" (p. v).

Wall and Hamilton further underscore the fundamental *sine qua non* legal requirement that United Kingdom courts' appointed experts must be thoroughly impartial and objective in their evidence to the court by citing verbatim an extract from the judgment of Mr. Justice Cazalet in Re R (A minor) (Expert Evidence) [1991] 1 FLR 291:

(2) Such experts must express only opinions which they genuinely hold and which are not biased in favor of one particular party. Opinions can, of course, differ and indeed quite frequently experts who have expressed their objective and honest opinion will differ, but such differences are usually within a legitimate area of disagreement.
(3) Experts should not mislead by omissions. They should consider all the material facts in reaching their conclusions and must not omit to consider the material facts which would detract from their concluded opinion.
(4) If experts look for and report on factors which tend to support a particular proposition or case, their report should still;
    (a) provide a straightforward and not a misleading opinion;
    (b) be objective and not omit factors which do not support their opinion; and
    (c) be properly researched.
(5) If the expert's opinion is not properly researched because he or she considers that insufficient data is available, then the expert must say so and indicate that the opinion is no more than a provisional one.
(6) . . . if, contrary to the appropriate practice, an expert does provide a report which is other than

wholly objective – that is one which seeks to promote a particular case – the report must make this clear. However, such an approach should be avoided because it would (a) be an abuse of the position of the expert's proper function and privilege and (b) render the report an argument, not an opinion. (Wall and Hamilton, p. 14)

Application of these fundamental principles to the UK family courts' current denial of the existence of PAS provides a source of considerable concern. The relevant UK case law precedent appears to be that of the Court of Appeal conjoined cases of *Re L (Contact: Domestic Violence); Re V (Contact: Domestic Violence); Re M (Contact: Domestic Violence); Re H (Contact: Domestic Violence)* [2000] 2 FLR 334. In Chapter 9, I noted that Sturge and Glaser "sought to promote" (to use Cazalet's phraseology) the denial of the existence of PAS in their "Experts' Court Report," which had been specially commissioned for this Court of Appeal case (and was later published [2000]). In dismissing the existence of PAS, these experts made reference to just one article written about PAS, that by Kathleen Faller (1998). In their report they omitted even to mention to the court the existence of the large PAS theoretical and research literature, or the many judicial decisions successfully based on it in other countries. This means that Sturge and Glaser omitted to mention to the court the several books written specifically on PAS, the 160-plus research articles published in peer-reviewed journals on PAS, and the more than 70 cases in different jurisdictions that have addressed PAS (*see* www.rgardner.com/refs/). These two experts not only failed to inform the court of all of this key evidence, but even in referring to Faller's article they failed to mention the crucial fact that Faller's article had already been significantly discredited in the same journal in which it had earlier been published (Gardner, 1998).

The proportionate significance and nationwide impact of this specially commissioned report were predictable, if the report were to be accepted by the Court of Appeal in such a high-profile case. The court did subsequently accept, almost in its entirety, Sturge and Glaser's report on issues in contact and domestic violence as a fundamental and definitive statement of basic principle, and accepted their expert evidence that PAS does not exist. Their report was also accepted in its entirety into the 2001 consultation paper for *Making Contact Work* (see Section 2, Part 1); and it was again accepted in its entirety in the resultant February 2002 *Making Contact Work* Report to the Lord Chancellor (see the Report's Recommendation 1, p. 113); and again by the government's own subsequent acceptance of *Making Contact Work's* Recommendation (see the Government's Response to the Children Act Subcommittee Report *Making Contact Work,* August 2002, p. 4). Whereas Sturge and Glaser's report is impeccable with regard to its key focus area, that of contact and domestic violence, their report's denial of the existence of PAS based on gross omissions and one flawed article has meant that the Family Division of the Court of Appeal, the Lord Chancellor's Children Act Sub-Committee of his Advisory Board on Family Law, and the government itself via the Lord Chancellor were not made aware of the increasing global scientific and judicial acceptance of PAS, and have therefore not considered its existence.

Our family court system is currently unable to recognize or appropriately manage PAS cases, which, due to the nature of the PAS process and the adversarial nature of our family court system, will continue directly to target the courts' power unabated. The courts' impotence is a direct result of their bona fide appointed and trusted experts' failure to meet the legal requirements of them in their capacity as experts by providing the comprehensive and impartial review required of them with regard to PAS.

Considering the possibility that PAS may be a factor in 90 percent of unresolved conflicted cases before the courts (Johnston, 1993), the enormous ramifications of this failure and the terrible nationwide impact on thousands of children and parents begin to become apparent. What the Court of Appeal should have been able to rely on from their appointed experts is nothing less than a rigorously comprehensive, professionally objective, and strictly impartial review of all relevant knowledge. In short, this experts' report was required to be of impeccable objectivity, impartiality, and professional integrity *throughout,* but was not.

It is likely that their report's influence will not be limited only to within the United Kingdom. The potential international impact of the Sturge and Glaser report has been acknowledged and applauded by Bruch (2002). Unfortunately, Bruch herself fails to adequately clarify to her readers the fact that the Sturge and Glaser report was fundamentally focused on contact issues in domestic violence cases. It was not and did not make claims to be an exhaustive treatise solely on PAS. Nevertheless, Bruch focuses almost exclusively on the report's dismissal of PAS. She proclaims the report's wide acceptance by the UK courts and government:

[Their] report has already proved important in England and will undoubtedly have a favorable impact elsewhere as it becomes more widely known. Because it accurately reflects leading research and scholarship in the field, it stands in contrast to the literature that seeks to advance the acceptance of PAS. There, too often the scientific literature and the case-law are omitted from discussion or, if discussed, either misunderstood or mis-stated. (p. 392)

Bruch's claim that Sturge and Glaser's report "accurately reflects leading research and scholarship in the field" when it drew on just one, already discredited article is a most remarkable claim on its own. That Bruch then criticizes the PAS literature with "too often the scientific literature and the case-law are omitted from discussion" when Sturge and Glaser themselves did precisely and exactly that is an almost unbelievably hypocritical, subjective, and grossly partisan statement.

Bruch's article is, in fact, a version of two earlier articles, "revised to address the English authorities" (Bruch 2001a; 2001b). Bruch's original article also drew heavily on Faller's article, and was itself also comprehensively criticized for its remarkably biased unprofessionalism (*see* Gardner's rebuttal at www.rgardner.com/refs/ar17.html; Lorandos's rebuttal at www.rgardner.com/refs/lor_b.pdf). Gardner was refused a right of reply by the original publishing journal. However, the original article was subsequently published in a German journal and German law states that if a published article contains factual errors, the publishers must publish corrections addressing those factual errors. This the German publishers duly did (see FamRz, 2002, Vol. 24, pp. 1689–1690).

SOCIO-POLITICAL INFLUENCE ON JUDICIAL AND OTHER SYSTEMS

From a UK standpoint, it is evident that in America PAS has become the focus of considerable hostility from extreme feminist groups, as it is seen as impugning mothers and is erroneously perceived to be another form of paternalistic oppression. In America at least, political pressure from such a lobby has considerable effect; indeed, Kutchins and Kirk have noted that even those compiling the DSM have been unduly influenced by these pressure groups (Kutchins and Kirk, 1997).

Furthermore, it appears Bruch may be linked with the Californian political pressure group National Organization for Women (CA NOW). This organization, in its 2002 *Family Court Report* (online at http://canow.org/famlaw_report/famlawreport.html) cites in full, Bruch's original article on PAS. The CA NOW report includes a section specifically devoted to criticism and denial of the existence of PAS. The NOW Position Paper on PAS states:

Unless "parental alienation syndrome" is revealed for what it truly is – a theory that is not only totally unsubstantiated by any evidence, but inherently biased against women and carefully arranged to be used against mothers in custody battles – its use in the court as a weapon against women will continue.
(http://canow.org/famlaw_report/NOW_position.pdf)

It is deeply saddening to read such needlessly and counterproductively defensive material. Such a statement is factually inaccurate in its presumption of gender bias in PAS. It also apparently seeks to deny that women could themselves behave in such a manner. This appears to replicate further various feminist groups' similar erroneous denials that women could ever possibly be the instigators of violence against or oppression of their partners, either male or female (*see* Grady, 1997, 2002).

The NOW report further recommends, in the section titled "Conclusions & Solutions": "The use of false syndromes (such as PAS) should be made illegal under the Family Code." California NOW is recommending here that legislatures pass laws that make it a crime to use the term "PAS." It follows that such legislation would include the relevant punishments for those who break this law (e.g., fines or imprisonment). The Report's "Judicial Solutions" further recommend: "Along with damages suit, sue for declaratory relief, making Parental Alienation Syndrome, mandatory joint custody, mandatory psychological evaluations and mandatory mediation unconstitutional."

Yet it is through these same legal procedures that all men who love their children and seek to be evolved, involved and effective parents themselves are legally sanctioned to share their children's parenting time with their former spouses. California NOW would apparently outlaw these procedures by making them unconstitutional. Those who make a PAS diagnosis or mandate the listed procedures would be breaking the law and subject to punishment, and could also be sued for damages and declaratory relief.

Aided by inaccurate articles such as Bruch's, this California group seems to be entirely missing the point that PAS is no longer a simple gender issue. Men now are just as likely as women to induce PAS in their children, and women are now just as likely as men to end up being the target; alienated parent who suffers the grief of being victimized by a spouse's PAS indoctrinations and rejected and despised by their children.

Further evidence of the extreme gender-based political sexism prevalent among those opposed to recognition of PAS in the US comes from Texas. In 2003, the Texas legislature heard a proposed Bill to prevent any courtroom testimony about PAS until and unless it is included in the *Diagnostic and Statistical Manual* of the American Psychiatric Association (H.B. No. 1903, heard March 20, 2003, online at http://www.capitol.state.tx.us/tlo/78R/billtext/HB01903I.HTM). Because DSM-V committees will not start meeting until 2006 and the DSM-V will not be published until 2010 at the earliest, the successful passage of this bill would have precluded PAS testimony in Texas courts for the next 8 years. The bill's proposers clearly believe that PAS is a gender issue and that it discriminates against women. Unfortunately, their response is to attempt to oppress children and one of their parents, in a manner comparable to that so often used in past decades by men during their deplorable oppression of women. Two wrongs can never make a right, and they certainly do not do so in this instance. As a species, we need to evolve in our sociopolitical ability to relate to one another, and not simply repeat others' earlier acknowledged and regretted errors.

It has to be questioned why PAS so often arouses such a strong and deeply felt response as this – one that results in supposedly normal, rational, and even professionally highly competent people denying its existence, apparently failing to see the evidence that is before their own eyes. I readily acknowledge that it is highly probable that Bruch may indeed generally produce academic work of unbiased objectivity; this author is simply not acquainted with her other work. Yet, as so strongly demonstrated in the comprehensive rebuttals by Gardner and by Lorandos, Bruch's original article dismissing PAS is flawed and biased in the extreme. California NOW seems to angrily seek to defend all mothers by denying that PAS could possibly be inculcated by a woman, yet their own membership comprises many mothers, and they and their own children are now just as likely to become victims of PAS as are the fathers whose claims for fathers' rights NOW ridicules and decries.

In the United Kingdom, Sturge and Glaser are appropriately respected psychiatrists who produced a professional and comprehensive report of high quality in all other respects on contact in domestic violence cases, yet they signally failed to report to the Court of Appeal with the required competence, impartiality, and objective comprehensiveness about PAS. Much rational research has been carried out on PAS (as evidenced by the lengthy list on Gardner's website) and it has been rationally adjudicated upon in many courts. Our most senior family judges frequently describe PAS children in their judgments, yet, as described in this volume in Chapter 9, they to date will not openly question the validity of the seriously flawed section of their experts' report.

As a properly functioning democratic society we crucially rely on our judges' ability to rise above the political hoodwinking of such militant pressure groups, but it begins to seem likely that even they may not yet comprehend the apparent significant sociopolitical bias inherent in their own experts' report.

The fundamental notion of PAS (of a parent "harming" his or her own offspring) is so unpalatable that many normal human beings are instinctively repulsed by the prospect. Most sections of the feminist movement have been a force for tremendously positive developments in other settings, so it is sad to see the influence of a radical wing that is so affronted by the prospect that any mother could do anything as harmful to a child as inculcate PAS that it, blindly and quite irrationally, recoils from any objective acknowledgement of the evidence, and seeks to obstruct children and parents enjoying each other. The unpalatability of PAS is in reality doubtlessly due to a combination of factors, but it is indisputable that it provokes deeply ingrained emotional responses. Those in the UK, as elsewhere, who are to work with others in this emotive area may well benefit from training to help identify and manage their own inherent personal attitudes, in order for them to be effective in assisting PAS-afflicted families.

Certainly Gardner, who first identified PAS, has remained a controversial figure, apparently despised by some feminist groups since he first demonstrated that some allegations of sexual abuse of their own children made against fathers were false. His work in that arena attracted a similar degree of unsubstantiated vitriol, as has his work on PAS. However, the passage of time has shown that Canadian Senator Cools' description of false accusations of child abuse as the new "weapon of choice" during child custody proceedings has all too accurately portrayed reality (Cools, 2000). The recently established and incontrovertible judicial fact is that Gardner's sex abuse protocols successfully passed the stringent *Daubert* test in the US Territorial Court in the Virgin Islands in November 2002, in the case of the *Government of the Virgin Islands v. Glenn Elskoe* (Territorial Court of the Virgin Islands, Division of St. Thomas and St. John, CRIM. NO. F249/2001, Violation of 14 V.I.C. § 1708). Such a seriously misplaced rejection of these protocols in the US holds uncanny echoes of Sturge and Glaser's strong denial of PAS to the UK Court of Appeal only months before it was subjected to and successfully passed the *Frye* test in Florida and Illinois, and the *Mohan* test in Ontario.

JUDICIAL ASSESSMENT OF NEW SCIENTIFIC EVIDENCE

How does new scientific knowledge such as PAS generally achieve judicial acceptance in the UK? A recent case commentary by Barsby and Ormerod (2001) on the case of *R v. Gilfoyle* [2001] 2 Cr App R 5 observed that: "unfortunately the criteria for assessing reliability are not clearly explained in English case-law, even where a novel scientific technique is in issue" (p. 313).

Subsequent developments more recently established in UK case-law are discussed in the following sections. However, it is first relevant to briefly examine procedures in other jurisdictions and to link these with the objective criteria available from research on PAS.

The Frye Test

In *Gilfoyle* [2001] the court acknowledged with approval the U.S. *Frye* test criteria, stating that "evidence based on a developing new brand of science or medicine is not admissible until accepted by the scientific community as being able to provide accurate and reliable opinion" (para 25).

Van Orsdel J in giving the judgment in *Frye v. United States* (293 F.10113 [1923], available online at http://www.daubertontheweb.com/frye_opinion.htm) stated:

> Just when a scientific principle or discovery crosses the line between the experimental and demonstrable stages is difficult to define. Somewhere in this twilight zone the evidential force of the principle must be recognized, and while courts will go a long way in admitting expert testimony deduced from a well-recognized scientific principle or discovery, the thing from which the deduction is made must be sufficiently established to have gained general acceptance in the particular field in which it belongs. (p. 1014)

Application of this test requires no decision by the judge about scientific validity. PAS has been successfully subjected to the *Frye* test in November 2000 in *Kilgore v. Boyd* (Circuit Court of the 13th Judicial Circuit of the State of Florida, Hillsborough County, Family Law Division. Case no. 94-7573, Div. D) Nov 22, 2000), and in January 2002 in *Bates v. Bates* (18th Judicial Circuit, Dupage County, IL Case No. 99D958, Jan 17, 2002).

Konetski J, in *Bates v. Bates* observed: "With respect to the balance of the test as to whether it is sufficiently established to have gained general acceptance, I would take note that general acceptance does not require the absence of adverse opinion – does not require a unanimous opinion." Excerpts from the Kilgore and Bates judgments are available online at: http://www.rgardner. com/refs/pas_legalcites.html.

The Daubert Test

In the United States, subsequent to the introduction of Federal Rules of Evidence in 1975, the *Frye* test has been replaced at a federal level by the test applied in *Daubert v Merrell Dow Pharmaceuticals, Inc.* ([1993] 113 S Ct 2786; available online at http://www.publichealthlaw.net/Reader/docs/Daubert.pdf). The rules govern the introduction of evidence in proceedings, both civil and criminal, but only in federal courts. Although they do not apply to suits in state courts, most of which still use the *Frye* test, the rules of many states have been closely modeled on these rules. In *Daubert*, the court was called upon to determine the standard for admitting expert scientific testimony in a federal trial. In summary, a new scientific theory must:

1. be of demonstrable scientific validity, and therefore testable and falsifiable;
2. be relevant to the case before the court;
3. have been scrutinized by the scientific community (as demonstrated by publications in learned peer-reviewed journals);
4. have an error rate determined by scientific studies.

The judge must determine whether the theory is scientifically valid. This may present a significant problem, because judges are not trained as scientists. It is also worth noting here that most DSM-IV diagnoses and many psychological tests do not satisfy item 4 (and nor would PAS), yet they are admissible in state courts that use the *Daubert* test. PAS has not been subjected to the *Daubert* test.

In *Daubert*, Blackmun J observed that:

> Given the [Federal] Rules' permissive backdrop and their inclusion of a specific rule on expert testimony that does not mention "general acceptance," the assertion that the Rules somehow assimilated *Frye* is unconvincing. *Frye* made "general acceptance" the exclusive test for admitting expert scientific testimony. That austere standard, absent from and incompatible with the Federal Rules of Evidence, should not be applied in federal trials. . . . That the *Frye* test was displaced by the Rules of Evidence does not mean, however, that the Rules themselves place no limits on the admissibility of purportedly scientific evidence. . . . Of course, it would be unreasonable to conclude that the subject of scientific testimony must be "known" to a certainty; arguably, there are no certainties in science. But, in order to qualify as "scientific knowledge," an inference or assertion must be derived by the scientific method. Proposed testimony must be supported

by appropriate validation – i.e., "good grounds," based on what is known. In short, the requirement that an expert's testimony pertain to "scientific knowledge" establishes a standard of evidentiary reliability.

Having reviewed the various relevant rules, Blackmun J. summarized the Federal standard for admitting expert scientific testimony:

> Faced with a proffer of expert scientific testimony, then, the trial judge must determine at the outset, . . . whether the expert is proposing to testify to (1) scientific knowledge that (2) will assist the trier of fact to understand or determine a fact in issue. . . . This entails a preliminary assessment of whether the reasoning or methodology underlying the testimony is scientifically valid and of whether that reasoning or methodology properly can be applied to the facts in issue. We are confident that federal judges possess the capacity to undertake this review. Many factors will bear on the inquiry, and we do not presume to set out a definitive checklist or test. But some general observations are appropriate.
>
> Ordinarily, a key question to be answered in determining whether a theory or technique is scientific knowledge that will assist the trier of fact will be whether it can be (and has been) tested. . . . Another pertinent consideration is whether the theory or technique has been subjected to peer review and publication. . . . Submission to the scrutiny of the scientific community is a component of "good science," in part because it increases the likelihood that substantive flaws in methodology will be detected. The fact of publication (or lack thereof) in a peer-reviewed journal thus will be a relevant, though not dispositive, consideration in assessing the scientific validity of a particular technique or methodology on which an opinion is premised.
>
> Additionally, in the case of a particular scientific technique, the court ordinarily should consider the known or potential rate of error. . . and the existence and maintenance of standards controlling the technique's operation. . . . Finally, "general acceptance" can yet have a bearing on the inquiry.

Blackmun also gives a caveat on the relative importance of judicial versus scientific accuracy in the application of new scientific knowledge:

> It is true that open debate is an essential part of both legal and scientific analyses. Yet there are important differences between the quest for truth in the courtroom and the quest for truth in the laboratory. Scientific conclusions are subject to perpetual revision. Law, on the other hand, must resolve disputes finally and quickly. The scientific project is advanced by broad and wide-ranging consideration of a multitude of hypotheses, for those that are incorrect will eventually be shown to be so, and that in itself is an advance. Conjectures that are probably wrong are of little use, however, in the project of reaching a quick, final, and binding legal judgment – often of great consequence – about a particular set of events in the past. We recognize that in practice, a gatekeeping role for the judge, no matter how flexible, inevitably on occasion will prevent the jury from learning of authentic insights and innovations. That, nevertheless, is the balance that is struck by Rules of Evidence designed not for the exhaustive search for cosmic understanding but for the particularized resolution of legal disputes.

This valid "gatekeeping role" of the judge surely applies in any jurisdiction and, as exercised currently with regard to PAS by our most senior judges sitting in the UK Court of Appeal, it keeps PAS out of formal judicial recognition and therefore beyond judicial management. The "gate" kept by these UK judges rests on the "gateposts" of the flawed "experts'" report, which is now demonstrably outdated. It is indeed a gate that continues to be "of great consequence" for many children and their parents.

Partially dissenting from the judgment in *Daubert*, Rehnquist CJ quotes Cardozo (1921): "The work of a judge is in one sense enduring and in another ephemeral. . . . In the endless process of testing and retesting, there is a constant rejection of the dross and a constant retention of whatever is pure and sound and fine" (p. 179). For this to be applicable in reality, however, the quality of expert advice received by the court has to be of an adequate standard.

Federal Rule 702, 'Testimony of Experts,' was amended in December 2000 subsequent to the *Daubert* case law. It now reads:

> If scientific, technical, or other specialized knowledge will assist the trier of fact to understand the evidence or to determine a fact in issue, a witness qualified as an expert by knowledge, skill, experience, training, or education, may testify thereto in the form of an opinion or otherwise, if
> (1) the testimony is based upon sufficient facts or data,
> (2) the testimony is the product of reliable principles and methods, and
> (3) the witness has applied the principles and methods reliably to the facts of the case.

This means that what Blackmun in Daubert described as "that austere standard" of 'general acceptance' is not required by the Federal Rule, whereas most individual States do continue to require that new scientific evidence meets this criterion also.

The Mohan Test

In Canada, the relevant test is that applied in *R v. Mohan* ([1994] 2 SCR 9, online at www.canlii.org/ca/cas/scc/1994/1994scc34.html). This test is more stringent than the US *Frye* test. Sopinka J reviewed the rules relating to expert and character evidence. In an extensive and detailed review, he stated that admission of expert evidence depends on the application of the following criteria: (a) relevance; (b) necessity in assisting the trier of fact; (c) the absence of any exclusionary rule; and (d) a properly qualified expert.

- Relevance is a threshold requirement for the admission of expert evidence as with all other evidence. Relevance is a matter to be decided by a judge as question of law. . . .
- Necessity in Assisting the Trier of Fact: . . . This pre-condition is often expressed in terms as to whether the evidence would be helpful to the trier of fact. The word "helpful" is not quite appropriate and sets too low a standard. However, I would not judge necessity by too strict a standard. What is required is that the opinion be necessary in the sense that it provide information "which is likely to be outside the experience and knowledge of a judge or jury" as quoted by Dickson J. in R. v. Abbey, [1982] 2 S.C.R. 24: . . . the evidence must be necessary to enable the trier of fact to appreciate the matters in issue due to their technical nature.
- The Absence of any Exclusionary Rule: Compliance with criteria (a), (b), and (d) will not ensure the admissibility of expert evidence if it falls afoul of an exclusionary rule of evidence separate and apart from the opinion rule itself. . . .
- A Properly Qualified Expert: Finally the evidence must be given by a witness who is shown to have acquired special or peculiar knowledge through study or experience in respect of the matters on which he or she undertakes to testify.

In summary, therefore, it appears from the foregoing that expert evidence which advances a novel scientific theory or technique is subjected to special scrutiny to determine whether it meets a basic threshold of reliability and whether it is essential in the sense that the trier of fact will be unable to come to a satisfactory conclusion without the assistance of the expert. The closer the evidence approaches an opinion on an ultimate issue, the stricter the application of this principle.

PAS was subjected to and successfully passed the *Mohan* Test in August 2002 in the Canadian case of *Her Majesty the Queen v. K.C.* (Superior Court of Justice, Ontario, County of Durham, Central-East Region, Court File No. 9520/01. August 9, 2002). This case was in the criminal courts, and so was subject to criminal standards of proof.

ADMITTING NEW SCIENTIFIC EVIDENCE IN COURTS IN THE UNITED KINGDOM

It will be highly relevant to the practice of family law in the United Kingdom that PAS was successfully subjected to the *Frye* test in November 2000 in *Kilgore v. Boyd* and in January 2002 in *Bates v. Bates*, and to the Mohan test in August 2002. Our own UK family courts must soon take into account these formal judicial acceptances of PAS, and they must begin to address PAS accordingly, or face being adjudged to have breached its citizen's human rights in the European Court of Human Rights. The necessity of their taking this new scientific knowledge into account is established by European case-law (*see Elsholz v. Germany* [2000] 2 FLR 486; *Sahin v. Germany; Sommerfeld v. Germany; Hoffmann v. Germany* [2002] 1 FLR 119). If our courts do not act in accordance with these European precedents, they will also be adjudged by the population they serve to have failed the nation's children in this particular regard. Considerable public unrest is already being expressed, as many responsible individuals have begun to exercise their democratic right by demonstrating on the streets of the UK.

In the UK, however, the current and relatively undeveloped position appears to be that a judicial weighting is applied to new evidence presented. The justification for instructing an expert lies in the Civil Evidence Act 1972. Section 3 reads:

> (1) Subject to any rules of court made in pursuance of Part 1 of the Civil Evidence Act 1968 or this Act, where a person is called as a witness in any civil proceedings, his opinion on any relevant matter on which he is qualified to give expert evidence shall be admissible in evidence.
> (2) It is hereby declared that where any person is called as a witness in any civil proceedings, a statement of opinion by him on any relevant matter on which he is not qualified to give expert evidence, if made as a way of conveying relevant facts personally perceived by him, is admissible as evidence of what he perceived.
> (3) in this section "relevant matter" includes an issue in the proceedings in question.

Civil Evidence Act 1972, Section 5(3) reads:

> (3) Nothing in this Act shall prejudice –
> (a) any power of a court, in any civil proceedings, to exclude evidence (whether by preventing questions from being put or otherwise) at its discretion.

Butler-Sloss (then Lady Justice, now former President of the High Court Family Division) highlighted the central points of the 1972 Act in *Re M and R (Child Abuse: Evidence)* [1996] 4 All ER 239:

> So the passing of the Act should not operate to force the court to, in Wigmore's words "waste its time in listening to superfluous and cumbersome testimony" provided that the judge never loses sight of the central truths: namely that the ultimate decision is for him, and that all questions of relevance and weight are for him. If the expert's opinion is clearly irrelevant, he will say so. But if arguably relevant but in his view ultimately unhelpful, he can generally prevent its reception by indicating that the expert's answer to the question would carry little weight with him. The modern view is to regulate such matters by way of weight rather than admissibility.
>
> But when the judge is of the opinion that the witness's expertise is still required to assist him to answer the ultimate questions (including, where appropriate, credibility) then the judge can gratefully rely upon such evidence, while never losing sight of the fact that the final decision is for him. (pp. 254j–255b)

In April 1999, the coming into force in the UK of the Civil Procedure Rules replaced the Rules of the Supreme Court 1965 and County Court Rules 1981. Their aim is to streamline the civil justice process (see CPR 1.1) and to resolve as many cases as possible without resorting to court proceedings by introducing new "protocols" for some forms of litigation (for example, the use of one jointly instructed expert [CPR 35.7] presenting a written report on which questions can be asked [CPR 35.5i]). Part 35 of the Civil Procedure Rules covers the use of experts:

> 35.1 Expert evidence shall be restricted to that which is reasonably required to resolve the proceedings.
> 35.2 A reference to an "expert" in this Part is a reference to an expert who has been instructed to give or prepare evidence for the purpose of court proceedings.

These Part 35 rules should be read in conjunction with Practice Direction 35:

> 1.1 It is the duty of an expert to help the court on matters within his own expertise: rule 35.3(1). This duty is paramount and overrides any obligation to the person from whom the expert has received instructions or by whom he is paid: rule 35.3(2).
> 1.2 Expert evidence should be the independent product of the expert uninfluenced by the pressures of litigation.
> 1.3 An expert should assist the court by providing objective, unbiased opinion on matters within his expertise, and should not assume the role of an advocate.
> 1.4 An expert should consider all material facts, including those which might detract from his opinion.
> 1.5 An expert should make it clear: (a) when a question or issue falls outside his expertise; and (b) when he is not able to reach a definite opinion, for example because he has insufficient information.
> 1.6 If, after producing a report, an expert changes his view on any material matter, such change of view should be communicated to all the parties without delay, and when appropriate to the court.

By way of example, in *R v. Gilfoyle* [2001] the Court of Appeal addressed the question of whether the new procedure of "psychological autopsy" was admissible. Professor Canter, a most distinguished forensic psychologist, acknowledged that this was a procedure that had "taken off and been used before it has reached the maturity needed to be allowed safely out of the careful confines of its professional birthplace" (para 25).

In that respect this specific procedure differs considerably from PAS, which has substantial theoretical and research literature behind it, plus crucial judicial decisions recognizing it. However, the court briefly reviewed the role of expert evidence in introducing new scientific knowledge. With regard to when expert evidence would be required, Lawton LJ's comment was cited from Turner ([1974] 60 Cr App R 80):

> An expert's opinion is admissible to furnish the court with scientific information which is likely to be outside the experience and knowledge of a judge or jury. If on the proven facts a judge or jury can form their own conclusions without help, then the opinion of an expert is unnecessary. . . . The fact that an expert witness has impressive scientific qualifications does not by that fact alone make his opinion on matters of human nature and behavior within the limits of normality any more helpful than that of the jurors themselves; there is a danger that they think it does. . . . Jurors do not need psychiatrists to tell them how ordinary folk who are not suffering from any mental illness are likely to react to the stresses and strains of life. (p. 24)

The court in *Gilfoyle* made reference to Farquharson LJ's summary of the relevant question in *Strudwick & Merry* (1993) 99 Cr App R 326: "The question for the judge was whether the response of the second appellant to her child's suffering was something that could be understood and evaluated by a jury or whether they would need expert assistance in such a task" (p. 332).

Having approved of the U.S. use of the *Frye* Test, the court confirmed that previous case law still applied:

> Expert witnesses must furnish the court "with the necessary scientific criteria for testing the accuracy of their conclusions, so as to enable the judge or jury to form their own independent judgment by the application of these criteria to the facts proved in evidence." (para 24)

Professor Canter's evidence on "psychological autopsy" was dismissed, as he could give the court no criteria by which the court could test the quality of his professional opinion, no relevant database existed, and there was "no substantial body of academic writing approving his methodology" (para 25). In comparison, PAS would qualify for admissibility on each of these criteria.

Within the UK criminal courts, strong approval has been given of the *Frye* and *Daubert* tests, and even of U.S. Federal Rule 702. The development of the current position on expert evidence can be traced through criminal case-law via *R v. Dallagher* [2003] 1 Cr App R 12; Case comment on *R v. Dallagher* CLR [2002] 821-823; *R v. Pendleton* [2002] 1 Cr App R 34; *R v. Gilfoyle* [2001] Cr App R 5; *R v. Steven Jones* [1997] 1 Cr App R 86; *R v. D* [1996] 1 All E.R. 881; *R v. Parks* [1961] 3 All E.R. 633.

In the recent case of *R v. Dallagher* [2003], there was extensive discussion on the weight to be given to earprint evidence, which was arguably not regarded as "generally accepted in the scientific community," had "very few people working in the field, and . . . the comparison work was in its infancy" (paras 11 & 14). The court briefly reviewed the *Frye* and *Daubert* tests and confirmed that Federal Rule 702 was analogous to the leading English case law established in *R v Clarke* [1995] 2 Cr App R 425, which stated that "the probative value of such evidence depends on the reliability of the scientific technique (and that is a matter of fact), and it is one fit for debate and for exploration in evidence" (p. 431).

The court in *Dallagher* also cited the leading handbook, *Cross & Tapper on Evidence* (1999), which, after a reference to *Frye* states, "The better, and now more widely accepted, view is that so long as the field is sufficiently well-established to pass the ordinary tests of relevance and reliability, then no enhanced test of admissibility should be applied, but the weight of the evidence should be established by the same adversarial forensic techniques applicable elsewhere" (p. 523).

Recently, in the House of Lords in *R v. Pendleton* [2002] 1 Cr App R 34, Bingham L set out the principle that the Court of Appeal should adopt in relation to new scientific evidence. Although this was a criminal case, its *ratio decidendi* applies to civil cases. "It will usually be wise for the Court of Appeal, in a case of any difficulty, to test their own provisional view by asking whether the evidence, if given at the trial, might reasonably have affected the decision of the trial jury to convict. If it might, the conviction must be thought to be unsafe" (para 19).

APPLICATION OF THESE PRINCIPLES TO PAS IN THE UNITED KINGDOM

Application of these principles yields the following statement. "The diagnosis and management of PAS is relatively new scientific knowledge. PAS is accepted by an increasing proportion of the scientific community, as evidenced by the substantial and growing peer-reviewed research literature. In addition, PAS has been successfully tested in the courts of various jurisdictions around the world, including via the *Frye* and *Mohan* tests. PAS is an observable psychological dysfunction (alienation of the child from the target parent) in a child subjected to an identifiable cause (pressure from the alienating parent) which is relatively easy to diagnose with reliability (although in certain instances there may need to be a prior judicial finding of fact if allegations of abuse have been made), and PAS has a predictable outcome that can be ameliorated by appropriate intervention. PAS is a syndrome by appropriate medical definition, and its consideration for inclusion in the next editions of the two international psychiatric diagnostic manuals will be relevant."

With regard to PAS, the application of some of the earlier discussed principles can be traced in regard to expert evidence on PAS in the leading case of *Re L, V, M, H (Contact: Domestic Violence)* [2000], most particularly that of variable judicial weight being accorded to expert evidence. In the appeal of Re M in this conjoined case, Butler-Sloss P initially draws on the evidence from the two experts commissioned to review these matters by the Official Solicitor, as then titled. Their evidence, although flawed, was accorded very substantial weight; "In the psychiatric report of Dr. Sturge and Dr. Glaser, they indicated that parental alienation syndrome was not recognised in either the American classification of mental disorders or the international classification of disorders. It is not generally recognised in psychiatric or allied child mental health specialities" (pp. 282–283).

As a relatively new diagnosis, the degree to which PAS is recognized within the UK is indeed debatable. However, if a global view is taken of PAS recognition within psychiatric and psychological practice, rather than the comparatively parochial view taken by Sturge and Glaser, there is considerable recognition of PAS by relevant scientific and judicial bodies. The hard fact remains that just six months after the UK Court of Appeal used these experts' report to set the law in this area, PAS successfully had the *Frye* test applied in America, and the *Mohan* test was applied successfully in Canada only seven months after that. Therefore, our Court of Appeal was clearly and demonstrably ill-advised with regard to PAS by its two experts. The current Civil Procedure Rules Practice Direction 35, had it been applied at the time of the experts' report, would show the experts' significant failure with regard to informing the court properly about PAS in what, I repeat, was an otherwise exemplary report. This Practice Direction at 1.3 requires an expert to provide "objective, unbiased opinion." At 1.4 it requires the expert to "consider all material facts, including those which might detract from his opinion." At 1.5 it requires the expert to make it clear when the matter is beyond the expert's knowledge or expertise.

In *Re L, V, M, H* Butler-Sloss P accorded psychologist Dr. Lowenstein's evidence minimal weight, and dismissed his submission on PAS:

> It would be fair to say that Dr Lowenstein is at one end of a broad spectrum of mental health practitioners and that the existence of parental alienation syndrome is not universally accepted. There is, of course, no doubt that some parents, particularly mothers, are responsible for alienating their children from their fathers without good reason and thereby creating this sometimes insoluble problem. That unhappy state of affairs, well known in the family courts, is a long way from a recognised syndrome requiring mental health professionals to play an expert role. (p. 351g-h)

The quotations from the *Frye* and *Daubert* tests provided earlier demonstrate that there is no requirement in either of these tests, which are both accepted in UK courts as valid yardsticks, for anything approaching "universal acceptance," however, figuratively Butler-Sloss may have used this phrase. That PAS is a recognizable 'syndrome' is demonstrated by other jurisdictions' satisfaction that PAS passes the *Frye* and *Mohan* tests, the PAS literature, and by a simple comparison of the recognized symptoms of PAS with the criteria for a bona-fide medical "syndrome." Furthermore, it is already well recognized that PAS is not an "insoluble problem," as it responds well and generally quickly to appropriate management. This is necessary management that can only be applied once the problem facing the court is accurately recognized and appreciated for what it is, i.e., PAS.

Butler-Sloss P continued:

> The judge, in my view, was entitled to reject the report and the oral evidence of Dr Lowenstein, even though the psychologist was jointly instructed. Lord Goff of Chieveley said in *Re F (Mental Patient: Sterilisation)* [1990] 2 AC 1, 80 that experts were to be listened to with respect but their opinions must be weighed and judged by the court. The judge [at first instance] said: "I cannot accept the effect of what Dr Lowenstein has told me, namely that PAS [parent alienation syndrome] is such a serious state that the child involved and the parent should be subjected to treatment by way of therapy with direct threats to the mother in the event of non-cooperation. It appears from the literature that some schools of PAS thought advocate the immediate removal of the child from the alienating parent and thereafter no contact with the alienating parent for a period. It also appears that 'long-term psychoanalytically informed therapy in the order of years rather than months' is the treatment of choice." (p. 352a-d)

Sadly, if Lowenstein did claim that long-term therapy, of any sort, was the treatment of choice, he, too, misled the court on this specific point.

Currently, in the UK, in addition to the relevance of admitting novel scientific evidence into a case, the position is further clarified where one party disagrees with the professional quality of expert evidence submitted to the court, even where the expert was jointly instructed. These issues were discussed in the pre-Human Rights Act case of D *(A Child) v. Walker* [2000] 1 WLR 1382. Here, Lord Woolf M.R. stated, "Where the parties have sensibly agreed to instruct an expert, it is obviously preferable that the form of instructions should be agreed if possible. Failing agreement, it is perfectly proper for either separate instructions to be given by one of the parties or for supplementary instructions to be given by one of the parties" (p. 3).

Lord Woolf continued:

> If, having agreed to a joint expert's report a party subsequently wishes to call evidence, and it would be unjust having regard to the overriding objective of the CPR not to allow that party to call that evidence, they must be allowed to call it.
>
> In civil jurisdictions the position is different. Expert issues are frequently determined on the basis of a court expert and the parties have to put up with it in the majority of situations. They have an opportunity to question the expert but that was going to be allowed by the judge here in any event. No-one suggests that the way matters are conducted in civil jurisdictions could contravene Article 6 in the normal manner, nor could the proper use of the CPR. . . . It would be highly undesirable if the consideration of those issues was made more complex by the injection into them of Article 6-style arguments. I hope that judges will be robust in resisting any attempt to introduce those arguments.
>
> . . . Where a party sensibly agrees to a joint report and the report is obtained as a result of joint instructions in the manner which I have indicated, the fact that a party has agreed to adopt that course does not prevent that party being allowed facilities to obtain a report from another expert, or, if appropriate, to rely on the evidence of another expert.

In a substantial case such as this, the correct approach is to regard the instruction of an expert jointly by the parties as the first step in obtaining expert evidence on a particular issue. It is to be hoped that in the majority of cases it will not only be the first step but the last step. If, having obtained a joint expert's report, a party, for reasons which are not fanciful, wishes to obtain further information before making a decision as to whether or not there is a particular part (or indeed the whole) of the expert's report which he or she may wish to challenge, then they should, subject to the discretion of the court, be permitted to obtain that evidence. In the majority of cases, the sensible approach will not be to ask the court straight away to allow the dissatisfied party to call a second expert. In many cases it would be wrong to make a decision until one is in a position to consider the position in the round. You cannot make generalisations, but in a case where there is a modest sum involved a court may take a more rigorous approach. It may be said in a case where there is a modest amount involved that it would be disproportionate to obtain a second report in any circumstances. At most what should be allowed is merely to put a question to the expert who has already prepared a report. However, in this case a substantial sum of money depended on the issue as to whether full-time or part-time care was required. In those circumstances it was perfectly reasonable for the defendant, if the matter had been properly explained, to say that he would like to have the claimant examined by [the defendant's selected expert]. (pp. 7–8)

This principle supports the argument that where the evidence of the state's own appointed experts is used in a family case to dismiss the potential of the case involving PAS (i.e., by reference to the Sturge and Glaser report), the other party has the right to appoint his or her own expert with regard to PAS, particularly as the human "costs" of not doing so are so high.

CONCLUSION

It can therefore be argued, with reference to the facts and principles outlined, that in the interests of justice the UK Court of Appeal's current stance with respect to PAS, if it rests on *Re L, V, M, H (Contact: Domestic Violence)* [2000] rather than on *Re C (Children) (Prohibition on Further Applications)* [2002] needs to be formally reviewed. This has to take place either within our UK Court of Appeal, the House of Lords, or the European Court of Human Rights. In light of the recent developments in recognition of PAS in other jurisdictions and the necessity of taking these into account as already recognized by the European Court of Human Rights in recent cases, a strong argument is that our judges are misdirecting themselves should they continue to dismiss the existence and relevance of PAS through a continued reliance on their own commissioned "experts'" flawed report.

REFERENCES

Barsby, C. and Ormerod, D.C., (2001). Evidence: Murder – Whether "psychological autopsy" of a victim admissable, to show likelihood of suicide. *Crim LR*, 312–314.

Bruch, C.S. (2001a). Parental Alienation Syndrome and Parental Alienation: Getting it wrong in child custody cases. *Family Law Quarterly, 35*, 527.

Bruch, C.S. (2001b). Parental Alienation Syndrome: Junk science in child custody determinations. *E.J.L.R. 3*, 383.

Bruch, C.S. (2002). Parental Alienation Syndrome and alienated children – Getting it wrong in child custody cases. *CFLQ 14*, 381.

Cardozo, B. (1921). *The nature of the judicial process.* New Haven: Yale University Press.

Cools, Hon. Anne C. (2000). Lawyers conniving in false allegations during divorce proceedings. Canadian Senate Debate, 17 February. (Verbatim transcript on website at http://www.fact.on.ca/politics/cools/s09deb1.htm)

Faller, K. (1998). The Parental Alienation Syndrome: What is it and what data support it? *Child Maltreatment, 3*(2), 100–115.

Gardner, R. A. (1998). Rebuttal to K. Faller's Article. *Child Maltreatment, 3*(4), 309–312.

Gardner, R.A (2001). Rebuttal to Carol S. Bruch's Article. (Published online at http://www.rgardner.com/refs/ar17.html).

Gardner, R.A. – 'Erratum' (2002a) 24 FamRz 1689 (An English translation is available online at http://www.rgardner.com/refs/famrz.html).

Gardner, R.A. (2002b). Rebuttal to C. Sturge and D. Glaser's Article: "Contact and Domestic Violence – The Experts' Court Report." *Family Law*, September, 2000, pp. 615–629. (Published online at http://www.rgardner.com/refs/ar19.html).

Grady, A. (1997). Genuine victimisation theory: Acknowledging the male domestic violence victim. *Holdsworth Law Review, 18*, 166.

Grady, A. (2002). Female-on-male domestic abuse: Uncommon or ignored? In (eds) Young, R. and Hoyle, C. (2002), *New visions of crime victims.* Oxford: Hart Publishing.

Johnston, J. R. (1993). Children of divorce who refuse visitation in (ed) Depner, C. E. *Non-residential parenting: New vistas in family living.* London: Sage.

Kutchins, H. and Kirk, S.A. (1999). *Making us crazy, DSM: The psychiatric bible and the creation of mental disorders.* London: Constable.

Lorandos, D. (2002). A rebuttal to Bruch's article: "Parental alienation syndrome and parental alienation: Getting it wrong in child custody cases. (Published online at http://www.rgardner.com/refs/lor_b.pdf).

Lord Chancellor's Advisory Board on Family Law: Children Act Sub-committee. "Making Contact Work: The Facilitation of Arrangements for Contact between Children and their Non-Residential Parents and the Enforcement of Court Orders for Contact. Consultation Paper." March, 2001.

Lord Chancellor's Advisory Board on Family Law: Children Act Sub-committee. "Making Contact Work: A Report to the Lord Chancellor on the Facilitation of Arrangements for Contact between Children and their Non-Residential Parents and the Enforcement of Court Orders for Contact." February, 2002.

The Lord Chancellor's Dept. "The Government's Response to the Report of the Children Act Sub-Committee of the Lord Chancellor's Advisory Board on Family Law Report "Making Contact Work," Family Policy Division 2, August, 2002.

Sturge, C. and Glaser, D. (2000). Contact and domestic violence: The experts' court report. *Family Law, 30*, 615–629.

Tapper, C. (1999). *Cross & Tapper on Evidence.* (Ninth Edition) London: Butterworths.

Wall, N. and Hamilton, I. (2000). *A handbook for expert witnesses in children act cases.* Bristol: Jordan Publishing Ltd.

INDEX

D